Lerwick•

Kirkwall•

Wick•

erland

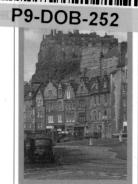

GLASGOW
Pages 644–659

EDINBURGH
Pages 582–609

LANCASHIRE AND THE LAKES
Pages 404–437

YORKSHIRE AND HUMBERSIDE
Pages 438–479

NORTHUMBRIA
Pages 480–503

NTRY

Kingston
upon Hull
ds

ffield

E MIDLANDS

Nottingham
y

eicester
ntry

Cambridge
Northampton

Ipswich

Luton

ford **LONDON**

SOUTHEAST ENGLAND
Dover

hampton Brighton
Portsmouth

LONDON
Pages 74–149

THE HEART OF ENGLAND
Pages 340–371

EAST MIDLANDS
Pages 372–393

THE DOWNS AND CHANNEL COAST
Pages 158–191

THAMES VALLEY
Pages 226–255

EAST ANGLIA
Pages 192–225

0 kilometres   100

0 miles   50

PORTRAIT OF
BRITAIN

PORTRAIT OF BRITAIN

Main contributor: MICHAEL LEAPMAN

DORLING KINDERSLEY
LONDON • NEW YORK • SYDNEY
www.dk.com

A DORLING KINDERSLEY BOOK

www.dk.com

ART EDITOR Stephen Bere
PROJECT EDITOR Marian Broderick
EDITORS Carey Combe, Sara Harper, Elaine Harries, Kim Inglis,
Esther Labi, Ella Milroy, Andrew Szudek, Nia Williams
DESIGNERS Jill Andrews, Susan Blackburn, Gail Jones,
Elly King, Tony Limerick, Rebecca Milner,
Colin Loughrey, Andy Wilkinson
MAP CO-ORDINATORS Michael Ellis, David Pugh
RESEARCHER Pippa Leahy

MANAGING EDITORS Louise B Lang, Georgina Matthews
SENIOR ART EDITOR Sally Ann Hibbard
MANAGING ART EDITOR Jane Ewart
ART DIRECTION Gillian Allan, Gaye Allen
EDITORIAL DIRECTOR Vivien Crump
PUBLISHER Douglas Amrine

PRODUCTION Marie Ingledew
PICTURE RESEARCH Brigitte Arora, Ellen Root
DTP DESIGNERS Samantha Borland, Ingrid Vienings

MAIN CONTRIBUTORS
Josie Barnard, Christopher Catling, Juliet Clough,
Lindsay Hunt, Polly Phillimore, Martin Symington, Roger Thomas

MAPS
Jane Hanson, Phil Rose, Jennifer Skelley (Lovell Johns Ltd)
Gary Bowes (Era-Maptec Ltd)

PHOTOGRAPHERS
Joe Cornish, Paul Harris, Rob Reichenfeld, Kim Sayer

ILLUSTRATORS
Richard Draper, Jared Gilby (Kevin Jones Assocs), Paul Guest,
Roger Hutchins, Chris Orr & Assocs, Maltings Partnership,
Ann Winterbotham, John Woodcock

Film output by Quadrant Typesetters (London)
Reproduced by Colourscan (Singapore)
Printed and bound by Graphicom (Italy)

First published in Great Britain in 1999
by Dorling Kindersley Limited
9 Henrietta Street, London WC2E 8PS

A CIP CATALOGUE RECORD IS AVAILABLE FROM THE BRITISH LIBRARY.

ISBN 0 7513 0808 0

CONTENTS

HOW TO USE
THIS GUIDE 6

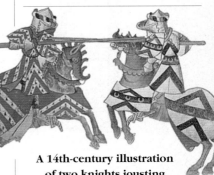

A 14th-century illustration
of two knights jousting

INTRODUCING GREAT BRITAIN

PUTTING GREAT
BRITAIN ON THE MAP 10

A PORTRAIT OF
GREAT BRITAIN 16

THE HISTORY OF
GREAT BRITAIN 42

GREAT BRITAIN
THROUGH THE YEAR 66

Beefeater at the Tower of London

LONDON

INTRODUCING LONDON
76

WEST END AND
WESTMINSTER 82

SOUTH KENSINGTON
AND HYDE PARK 100

Eilean Donan Castle on Loch Duich in the Scottish Highlands

REGENT'S PARK AND
BLOOMSBURY *108*

THE CITY AND
SOUTHWARK *114*

FURTHER
AFIELD *132*

STREET FINDER *144*

SOUTHEAST ENGLAND

INTRODUCING SOUTH-
EAST ENGLAND *152*

THE DOWNS AND
CHANNEL COAST *158*

EAST ANGLIA *192*

THAMES VALLEY *226*

THE WEST COUNTRY

INTRODUCING THE
WEST COUNTRY *258*

WESSEX *264*

DEVON AND CORNWALL
298

THE MIDLANDS

INTRODUCING THE
MIDLANDS *332*

THE HEART OF
ENGLAND *340*

EAST MIDLANDS *372*

Jacobean "Old House" in Hereford

THE NORTH COUNTRY

INTRODUCING THE
NORTH COUNTRY *396*

LANCASHIRE AND
THE LAKES *404*

YORKSHIRE AND
HUMBERSIDE *438*

NORTHUMBRIA *480*

WALES

INTRODUCING WALES
506

NORTH WALES *514*

SOUTH AND MID-WALES
538

SCOTLAND

INTRODUCING
SCOTLAND *568*

EDINBURGH *582*

THE LOWLANDS *610*

GLASGOW *644*

THE HIGHLANDS AND
ISLANDS *660*

The 7th-century Kingston Brooch in Liverpool Museum

GENERAL INDEX *702*

MILLENNIUM PROJECTS *721*

View of the Usk Valley and the Brecon Beacons, Wales

HOW TO USE THIS GUIDE

THIS GUIDE helps you to get the most from your holidays in Great Britain. It provides both detailed practical information and expert recommendations. *Introducing Great Britain* maps the country and sets it in its historical and cultural context. The regional chapters, plus the chapter on *London,* describe the most important sights, using informative maps, pictures and illustrations. There is also a feature in every region that highlights aspects of British life. The features cover topics from thatched houses and famous gardens to sport and great Scottish battles.

LONDON

The centre of London has been divided into four sightseeing areas. Each has its own chapter, which opens with a list of the sights described. The last section, *Further Afield,* covers the most attractive suburbs. All sights are numbered and plotted on an area map. The information for each sight follows the map's numerical order, making sights easy to locate within the chapter.

Sights at a Glance lists the chapter's sights by category: Historic Streets and Buildings; Museums and Galleries; Churches and Cathedrals; Shops; Parks and Gardens.

All pages relating to London have red thumb tabs.

A locator map shows where you are in relation to other areas of the city centre.

1 Area Map
For easy reference, the sights are numbered and located on a map. Sights in the city centre are also marked on the Street Finder *on pages 141–9.*

2 Street-by-Street Map
This gives a bird's-eye view of the key areas in each chapter.

Stars indicate the sights that no visitor should miss.

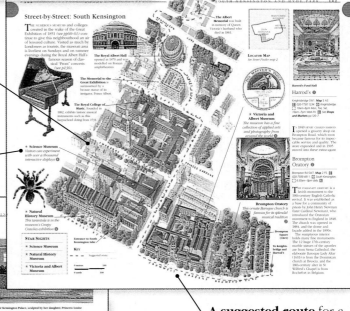

A suggested route for a walk is shown in red.

3 Detailed information
The sights in London are described individually. Addresses, telephone numbers, opening hours, admission charges, tours, photography and wheelchair access are also provided, as well as public transport links.

1 Introduction
The landscape, history and character of each region is outlined here, showing how the area has developed over the centuries and what it has to offer the visitor today.

GREAT BRITAIN AREA BY AREA
Apart from London, Great Britain has been divided into 14 regions, each of which has a separate chapter. The most interesting towns and places to visit have been numbered on a *Pictorial Map*.

Each area of Great Britain can be identified quickly by its colour coding, shown on the inside front cover.

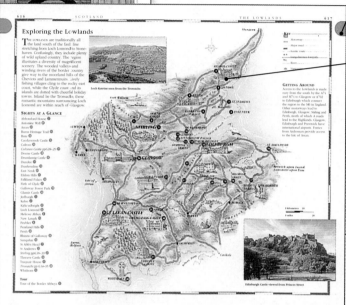

2 Pictorial Map
This shows the main road network and gives an illustrated overview of the whole region. All entries are numbered and there are also useful tips on getting around the region by car, train and other forms of transport.

3 Detailed information
All the important sights, towns and other places to visit are described individually. They are listed in order, following the numbering on the Pictorial Map. Within each entry, there is detailed information on important buildings and other sights.

Story boxes explore related topics.

For all the top sights, a Visitors' Checklist provides the practical information you need to plan your visit.

4 The top sights
These are given one or more full pages. Three-dimensional illustrations reveal the interiors of historic buildings. Interesting town and city centres are given street-by-street maps, featuring individual sights.

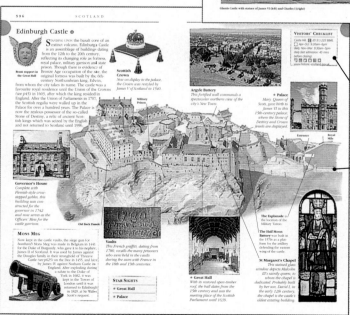

INTRODUCING GREAT BRITAIN

PUTTING GREAT BRITAIN ON THE MAP 10-15

A PORTRAIT OF GREAT BRITAIN 16-41

THE HISTORY OF GREAT BRITAIN 42-65

GREAT BRITAIN THROUGH THE YEAR 66-73

Putting Great Britain on the Map

LYING IN NORTHWESTERN EUROPE, Great Britain is bounded by the Atlantic Ocean, the North Sea and the English Channel. The island's landscape and climate are varied, and it is this variety that even today affects the pattern of settlement. The remote shores of the West Country peninsula and the inhospitable mountains of Scotland and Wales are less populated than the relatively flat and fertile Midlands and Southeast, where the vast majority of the country's 58 million people live. Due to this population density, the south is today the most built-up part of the country.

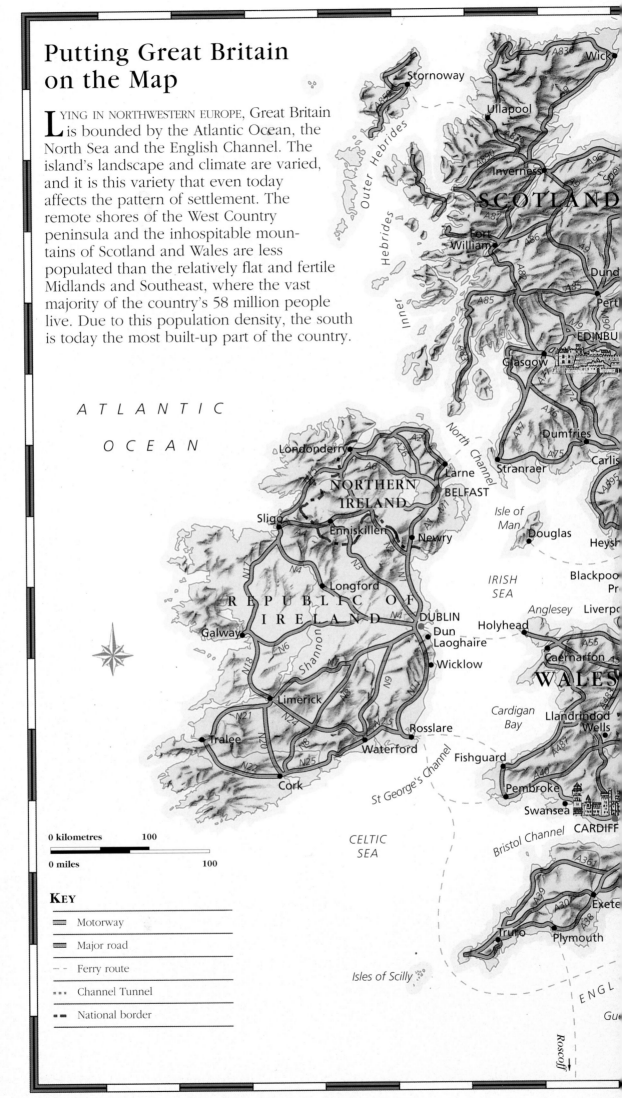

ATLANTIC

OCEAN

KEY

━━ Motorway

━━ Major road

- - - Ferry route

▪▪▪ Channel Tunnel

▪━ National border

0 kilometres   100

0 miles   100

◁ **Salisbury Cathedral: from the meadows** by John Constable (1776–1837)

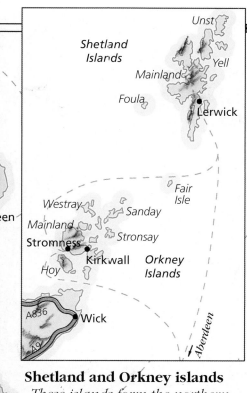

Europe

Great Britain is situated in the northwest corner of Europe. Its nearest neighbours are Ireland to the west, and the Netherlands, Belgium and France across the Channel. Denmark, Norway and Sweden are also easily accessible.

Shetland and Orkney islands

These islands form the northernmost part of Great Britain, with the Shetlands lying six degrees south of the Arctic Circle. There are transport links to the mainland.

Shetland Islands

Unst
Yell
Mainland
Foula
Lerwick

Orkney Islands

Fair Isle
Westray
Sanday
Mainland
Stronsay
Stromness
Kirkwall
Hoy

A836
Wick
A9
Aberdeen

deen

EUROPE

NORWAY
SWEDEN
FINLAND
ESTONIA
RUSSIAN FED.
LATVIA
LITHUANIA
RUSSIAN FED.
DENMARK
BELORUSSIA
NETHERLANDS
POLAND
London
GERMANY
BELGIUM
UKRAINE
LUXEMBOURG
CZECH REPUBLIC
SLOVAKIA
FRANCE
AUSTRIA
HUNGARY
SWITZERLAND
SLOVENIA
ROMANIA
ITALY
CROATIA
YUGOSLAVIA
BOSNIA AND HERZEGOVINA
BULGARIA
SPAIN
ALBANIA
PORTUGAL
GREECE
ALGERIA
TUNISIA

NORTH

SEA

Göteborg
Esbjerg
Hamburg

ENGLAND

n Tyne
Sunderland
Swale
York
A165
A1(M)
Kingston upon Hull
ford Leeds
M62
Huddersfield
M180
Grimsby
Manchester
A16
Sheffield
oke-
n-Trent
Derby
Nottingham
A47
Norwich
Peterborough
A11
A1
A12
mingham
A14
wick
Northampton
A1(M)
Cambridge
M40
M11
Ipswich
Stratford-upon-Avon
Harlow
Felixstowe
A446
Gloucester
A12
Harwich
Oxford
ol
Windsor
LONDON
M2
Ramsgate
Canterbury
M3
Dover
Salisbury
M25
M23
Folkestone
A36
Brighton
Strait of Dover
ampton
Portsmouth
Newhaven
nemouth
Isle of Wight

NETHERLANDS

Groningen
A7
A31
A7
A28
N37
AMSTERDAM
A6
Zwolle
A4
A1
The Hague
Utrecht
A50
Arnhem
A15
A12
A31
Rotterdam
A59
A57
A3
Duisburg
A58
A467
Essen
Eindhoven
A61
Zeebrugge
A1
A2
Cologne
Ostend
N9
A14
Antwerp
Dunkirk
BRUSSELS
A2
A3
Aachen
Calais
A10
A4
BELGIUM
A14
A16
Liege
Boulogne
A25
Lille
A3
A1
GERMANY
A26
A2
A15
A4

CHANNEL

Dieppe
N1
Amiens
GERMANY
Le Havre
N15
N27
D901
A28
A26
LUXEMBOURG
A4
Cherbourg
N13
Rouen
FRANCE
N51
LUXEMBOURG
St Malo
N175
Caen
A13
N138
N1
A1
A4
Reims
Metz
N158
A13
N14
A4
A31
PARIS

Regional Great Britain: London, the South, the Midlands and Wales

GREAT BRITAIN has airline connections with most cities in the world. London is the main transport hub with two major international airports, including Heathrow, the world's busiest. Southern England, Britain's most populous area, is divided, within this book, into four regions – Southeast England, the West Country, Wales and the Midlands – with a separate chapter for London. Road and rail links to the North and Scotland (*see pp14–15*) are plentiful, as are links between all main towns.

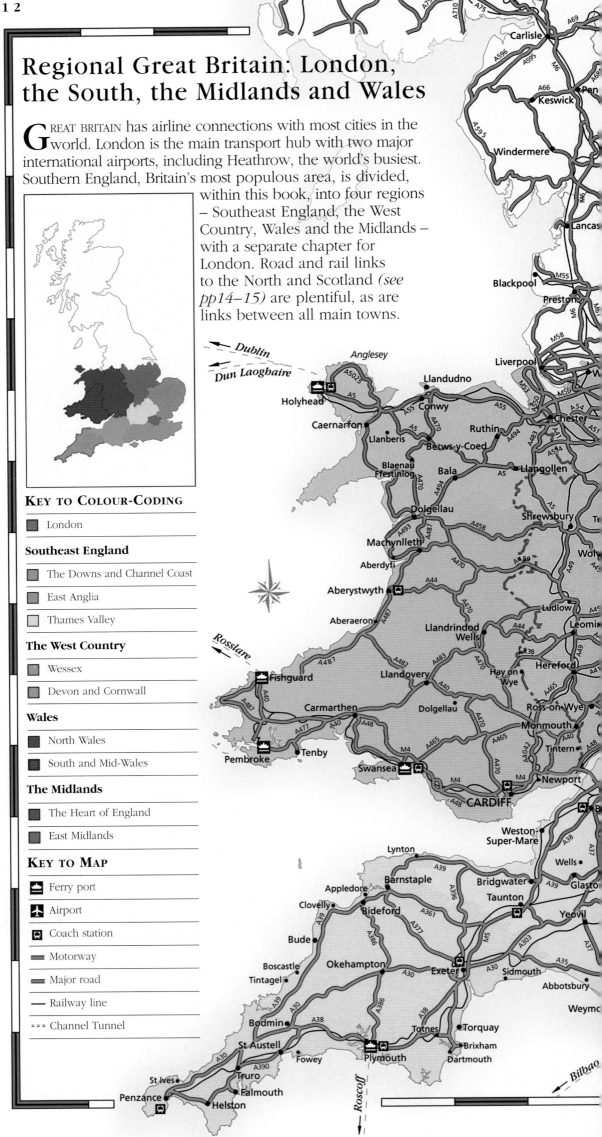

KEY TO COLOUR-CODING

London

Southeast England

The Downs and Channel Coast

East Anglia

Thames Valley

The West Country

Wessex

Devon and Cornwall

Wales

North Wales

South and Mid-Wales

The Midlands

The Heart of England

East Midlands

KEY TO MAP

Ferry port

Airport

Coach station

Motorway

Major road

Railway line

Channel Tunnel

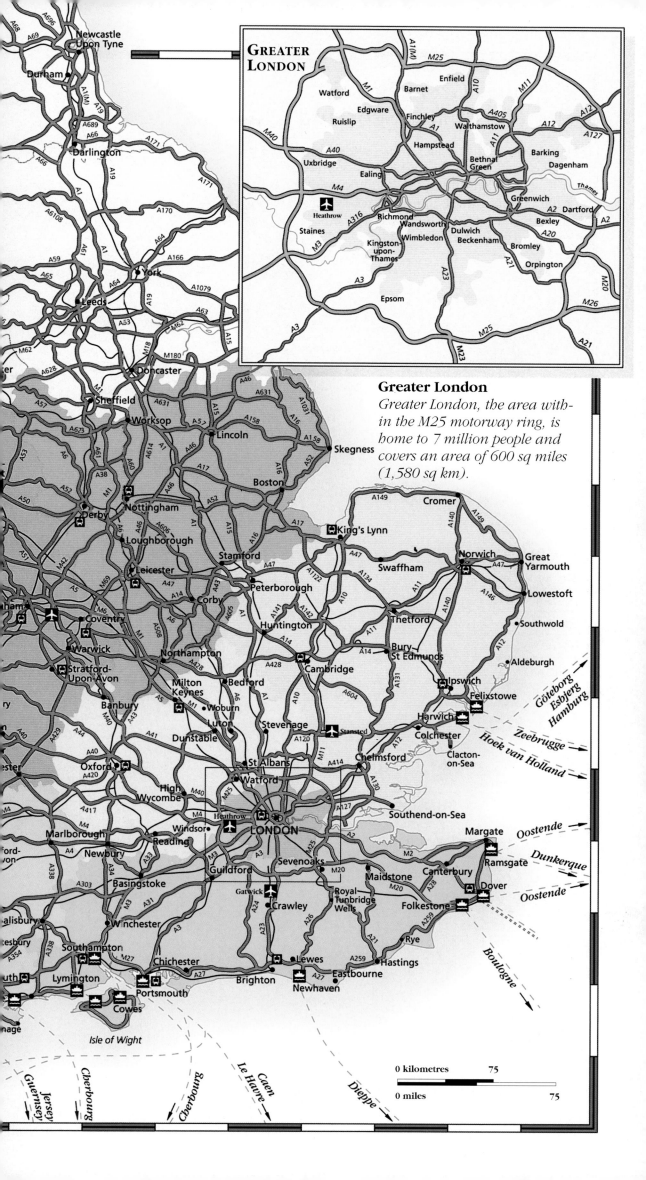

Greater London

Greater London, the area within the M25 motorway ring, is home to 7 million people and covers an area of 600 sq miles (1,580 sq km).

GREATER LONDON (inset map)

Watford, Edgware, Ruislip, Barnet, Enfield, Finchley, Walthamstow, Hampstead, Bethnal Green, Barking, Dagenham, Uxbridge, Ealing, Greenwich, Dartford, Heathrow, Richmond, Wandsworth, Bexley, Staines, Wimbledon, Dulwich, Beckenham, Bromley, Kingston-upon-Thames, Orpington, Epsom

M1, M25, M11, A1(M), A10, A405, A12, A127, A1, A11, A40, A2, A20, A316, A316, M40, M4, M3, A3, A23, A21, M26, M23, M20, A21

Main map place names

Newcastle Upon Tyne, Durham, Darlington, York, Leeds, Doncaster, Sheffield, Worksop, Lincoln, Skegness, Boston, Derby, Nottingham, Loughborough, Stamford, King's Lynn, Cromer, Leicester, Peterborough, Swaffham, Norwich, Great Yarmouth, Corby, Huntington, Thetford, Lowestoft, Northampton, Cambridge, Bury St Edmunds, Southwold, Warwick, Coventry, Bedford, Aldeburgh, Stratford-Upon-Avon, Milton Keynes, Woburn, Stevenage, Ipswich, Banbury, Luton, Felixstowe, Dunstable, St Albans, Harwich, Oxford, Watford, Chelmsford, Colchester, Clacton-on-Sea, High Wycombe, London, Southend-on-Sea, Marlborough, Windsor, Heathrow, Margate, Newbury, Reading, Sevenoaks, Ramsgate, Guildford, Maidstone, Canterbury, Dover, Basingstoke, Gatwick, Royal Tunbridge Wells, Folkestone, Crawley, Winchester, Rye, Southampton, Chichester, Lewes, Hastings, Lymington, Brighton, Eastbourne, Portsmouth, Newhaven, Cowes

Isle of Wight

Ferry destinations

Göteborg, Esbjerg, Hamburg, Zeebrugge, Hoek van Holland, Oostende, Dunkerque, Oostende, Boulogne, Cherbourg, Le Havre, Caen, Dieppe, Jersey, Guernsey

0 kilometres 75
0 miles 75

Regional Great Britain: The North and Scotland

THIS PART OF GREAT BRITAIN is divided into two sections in this book. Although it is far less populated than the southern sector of the country, there are good road and rail connections, and ferry services link the islands with the mainland.

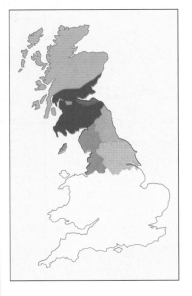

KEY TO COLOUR-CODING

The North Country

- Lancashire and the Lakes
- Yorkshire and Humberside
- Northumbria

Scotland

- Edinburgh
- The Lowlands
- Glasgow
- The Highlands and Islands

Isle of Lewis

Stornoway

Tarbert

Ullapool

Lochmaddy

Uig

Isle of Skye

Kyle of Lochalsh

Lochboisdale

Castlebay

Mallaig

Fort Willia

Arinagour

Tobermory

Scarinish

Craignure

Oban

Crainlarich

Scalasaig · Jura

Greenock

Kennacraig

Islay

Pa

Port Ellen

Ardrossa

Brodick

Irvine

Campbeltown

Isle of Arran

Larne

Cairnryan

Belfast

Stranraer

Isle of Man

Douglas

Holyhead

MILEAGE CHART

LONDON										
111 / 179	BIRMINGHAM									
150 / 241	102 / 164	CARDIFF								
74 / 119	185 / 298	228 / 367	DOVER							
372 / 599	290 / 466	373 / 600	442 / 711	EDINBURGH						
389 / 626	292 / 470	374 / 602	466 / 750	45 / 72	GLASGOW					
529 / 851	448 / 721	530 / 853	600 / 966	158 / 254	167 / 269	INVERNESS				
184 / 296	81 / 130	173 / 278	257 / 414	213 / 343	214 / 344	371 / 597	MANCHESTER			
274 / 441	204 / 328	301 / 484	343 / 552	107 / 172	145 / 233	265 / 426	131 / 211	NEWCASTLE		
112 / 180	161 / 259	235 / 378	167 / 269	360 / 579	383 / 616	517 / 832	185 / 298	260 / 418	NORWICH	
212 / 341	206 / 332	152 / 261	287 / 462	427 / 784	426 / 785	545 / 1038	250 / 451	427 / 655	324 / 521	PLYMOUTH

10 = Distance in miles
10 = Distance in kilometres

0 kilometres · 100

0 miles 100

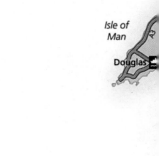

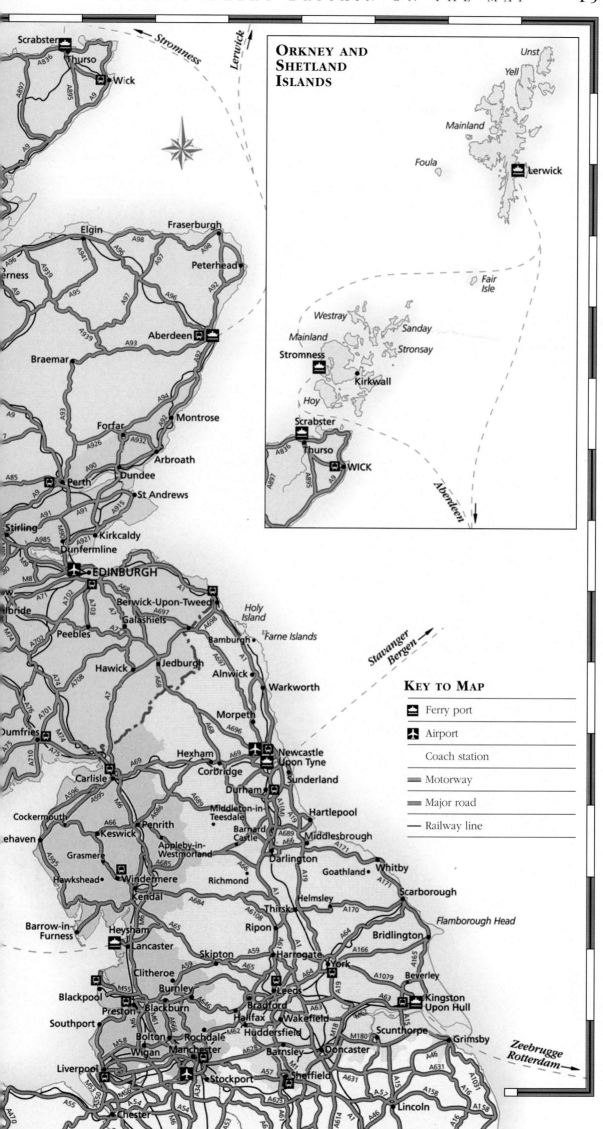

ORKNEY AND SHETLAND ISLANDS

Unst

Yell

Mainland

Foula

Lerwick

Fair Isle

Westray

Mainland

Sanday

Stromness

Stronsay

Kirkwall

Hoy

Scrabster

Thurso

WICK

Aberdeen

Scrabster

Thurso

Wick

Stromness

Lerwick

Elgin

Fraserburgh

Peterhead

Aberdeen

Braemar

Forfar

Montrose

Arbroath

Perth

Dundee

St Andrews

Stirling

Kirkcaldy

Dunfermline

EDINBURGH

Berwick-Upon-Tweed

Galashiels

Holy Island

Peebles

Bamburgh

Farne Islands

Hawick

Jedburgh

Alnwick

Warkworth

Dumfries

Morpeth

Stavanger Bergen

KEY TO MAP

Ferry port

Airport

Coach station

Motorway

Major road

Railway line

Hexham

Newcastle Upon Tyne

Corbridge

Sunderland

Carlisle

Durham

Cockermouth

Middleton-in-Teesdale

Hartlepool

Penrith

Barnard Castle

Middlesbrough

Keswick

Grasmere

Appleby-in-Westmorland

Darlington

Goathland

Whitby

Hawkshead

Windermere

Richmond

Scarborough

Kendal

Helmsley

Thirsk

Flamborough Head

Barrow-in-Furness

Heysham

Ripon

Bridlington

Lancaster

Harrogate

York

Beverley

Skipton

Clitheroe

Leeds

Kingston Upon Hull

Blackpool

Burnley

Bradford

Preston

Blackburn

Halifax

Wakefield

Scunthorpe

Southport

Huddersfield

Grimsby

Bolton

Rochdale

Wigan

Manchester

Barnsley

Doncaster

Zeebrugge Rotterdam

Liverpool

Stockport

Sheffield

Chester

Lincoln

A PORTRAIT OF GREAT BRITAIN

RITAIN ENTERS THE *21st century confident that it is developing a fresh role in the community of nations. Similar optimism prevailed as the 20th century dawned, only to be dashed by war and social turbulence. Recovery has taken time, but the country is now rebuilding its confidence once more.*

One hundred years ago, Britain was a prosperous industrial nation boasting a far-reaching global empire. Today, with a shrunken manufacturing base, it looks mainly towards Europe for economic links and development. As an island not successfully invaded since 1066, Britain has been able to stand aloof from aspects of the mainland not to its taste. It has developed distinctive traditions that set it apart from the rest of the continent, even in superficial ways such as driving on the left-hand side of the road rather than the right. (Britons delight in such nonconformity.) Some people still see Europe as "abroad", a place to go on holiday rather than as a community of which they feel a part.

Tudor rose

The British have been assiduous in preserving their heritage. All over the country there are ancient castles, cathedrals and stately homes with formal gardens and classical parklands. Age-old customs are renewed year after year, from royal ceremonies to local well dressing festivals. These displays are not staged simply for the benefit of visitors (although thousands do flock to them); they are an expression of the people's pride in their unique roots.

For a small island, Britain encompasses a surprising variety of regions, and the inhabitants of each of these

Walking along the east bank of the River Avon, Bath

◁ **Punting, a popular pastime on the River Cam, Cambridge**

Widecombe-in-the-Moor, a Devon village clustered round a church and set in hills

areas have maintained strong regional identities. Scotland and Wales, although ultimately governed from London, are separate from England in many respects, with newly created national assemblies to exercise autonomy on local issues. These countries have different customs and, in the case of Scotland, different legal and educational systems. Their Celtic languages, spoken on a day-to-day basis by relatively few people, are sustained by local radio and television programmes. The English counties, too, have retained their distinctive characteristics, including a rich variety of accents. There are also enduring traditions of regional architecture, arts, crafts, culture and food. Yet despite these differences,

Scottish coat of arms at Edinburgh Castle

there remain qualities that can be defined as essentially British, such as a certain stoicism and a marked reluctance to indulge in flamboyant displays of emotion. Some people have said, not entirely as a joke, that the archetypal British institution is the queue, where people wait in an orderly line for a shop to open or a bus to arrive, respectful of the rights of fellow citizens who arrived earlier.

Some regional distinctions can be accounted for by geography. Britain's landscape is varied, from craggy mountains in Scotland, Wales and the north of England, through the flat expanses of the Midlands and the east to the soft, rolling hills and chalk cliffs of the south and west. The broad beaches of East Anglia contrast sharply with the rocky inlets along the west coast. Furthermore, the imposing red-brick Victorian factories and warehouses of northern urban areas such as Manchester are worlds apart from the quaint half-timbered cottages in villages further south.

British food used to be derided for a lack of imagination. Traditional cuisine relied on a limited range of good quality ingredients, plainly prepared.

Lake and gardens at Petworth House, Sussex

However, international influences have brought changes in recent years, with an increased range of ingredients and more adventurous techniques. Typical British food can still be found, but it is increasingly being replaced by a modern international cuisine that draws particularly on Oriental and southern European styles.

Crowds at Petticoat Lane market in London's East End

BIRTH OF A NATION

A central theme in the story of Britain is the island's relationship with the rest of Europe. The Roman invaders came and went within 350 years and, unlike in France and southern Europe, left comparatively little of their culture behind. The Catholic Church, too unbending to make accommodations with Henry VIII over his divorce, lost its primacy in the 16th century. It was replaced by a less dogmatic established church (headed by the monarch) that could coexist with a broad range of

Priest in the Close at Winchester Cathedral

Protestant denominations. Since then, pragmatism has become a British characteristic, taking precedence over rigid dogma. Accordingly, there has been no nationwide civil conflict since the 1640s. While the Russians, Americans and French were undergoing revolution and civil war, radical social and political change came to Britain relatively peacefully. Clement Attlee, leader of the reforming Labour Government from 1945 to 1951, said: "The British have the distinction above all other nations of being able to put new wine into old bottles without bursting them".

Bosses in Norwich Cathedral cloisters

In the 19th and early 20th centuries, trade with the other countries of the British Empire – fuelled by abundant coal supplies and the technological innovations of the Industrial Revolution – created a labour-intensive manufacturing industry that produced the wealth and confidence of the Victorian and Edwardian eras. As a result, thousands of people moved from the countryside to the towns and cities that were near the mines, mills and factories. By 1900, Britain was the world's strongest industrial nation. Yet in the second half of the 20th century, many of these manufacturing centres have declined and are searching for new economic roles. Although manufacturing today employs only 20 per cent of the labour force, 66 per cent work in the growing service sector. These service industries are found mainly in the southeast, but businesses using the new technology have sprung up all round the country.

SOCIETY AND POLITICS

Modern British cities are home to people from different parts of the country and from overseas. Ireland has always been a major source of immigrants, and since the 1950s hundreds of thousands of people have come from former colonies that are now part of the Commonwealth, especially the Caribbean and the Indian sub-continent. Although legislation from the 1960s onwards has curbed immigration, nearly five per cent of Britain's 58 million inhabitants are from non-white ethnic groups. About half of these were born in Britain.

Afternoon tea on the back lawn at the Thornbury Castle Hotel, Avon

These immigrants have brought much to the nation, transforming it into a multi-cultural society that boasts a wide range of art, music, food and religions. Ethnic restaurants proliferate and appeal to all racial groups. And although prejudice and racial tension do sometimes surface, the British are generally a tolerant people.

Britain's class structure intrigues and bewilders many visitors, based as it is on a subtle mixture of heredity and wealth. Some members of the aristocracy and of the old land-owning families – the traditional upper class – still live on their estates, many of which are now open to the public. However, class divisions are less visible these days. Many point to Britain's private education system as the mainstay of the country's class structure. But today, the products of private (confusingly called "public") schools, such as Eton and Harrow, are less in evidence in government and business.

An expansion of the universities since the 1980s has added impetus to this change by improving educational opportunities for everyone.

Many hold that Britain's devotion to tradition hinders its progress in the modern world. Some parts of industry have been slow to adapt to technological innovation, in part because of the ingrained social structure that highlights the divisions between owners, managers and labourers. However,

Schoolboys at Eton, th famous public schoo

one of the recent positive forces for change is the increasingly widespread use of modern management techniques, largely introduced by overseas companies with bases in Britain.

Today's Britain resents inherited privilege. The Government wants to abolish the archaic right of hereditary peers to vote in the House of Lords (the second chamber of Parliament), which since 1997 has occasionally thwarted legislation proposed by the Labour-dominated Commons. Furthermore, the position of the monarchy brings into focus the dilemma of a people seeking to preserve its most potent

The House of Lords, in Parliament

symbol of national unity, while simultaneously wanting to dismantle the hierarchical social system that gave rise to it. Without real political influence, the Queen and her family are reduced to little more than celebrities, their private

Reading the newspaper in Kensington Gardens

lives being put under the microscope by an increasingly intrusive mass media. However, in 1997 the death of Princess Diana in a Paris car accident provoked unprecedented demonstrations of grief. She had won widespread sympathy because her openness and compassion struck a chord with ordinary people.

The royal family perhaps owes its survival to the pragmatism at the core of the British character: with the

Naomi Campbell, a British supermodel

stark exception of the 17th-century Civil War (which ended with the execution of the king), power has generally passed gradually and by consensus from the Crown to the people's representatives. This is partly because the ruling class has, since that damaging conflict, been prepared to concede just enough power to appease the reformers. A series of Reform Acts between 1832 and 1884 gave votes to all male citizens, although women had to wait until 1928 before receiving the same right. The first Socialist was elected to Parliament in 1891, and the first Labour Government came to power in 1924.

Between World War II and 1979, the Conservative (right wing) and Labour (left wing) parties spent about equal periods in office and mostly pursued policies that developed partnerships between management and labour and

between the private and public sectors of industry. Extremist parties such as the Communists and the neo-fascist National Front never attracted a wide following. In 1945, a reforming Labour government was swept into office on a national wave of egalitarianism inspired by the men and women who had fought in the war and had become aware of the shortcomings of the so-called "officer class". The new government made several radical reforms, including bringing many large industries into public ownership and instituting well-funded State health and welfare services.

In 1979, the Conservatives began 18 years of uninterrupted power, first led by Margaret Thatcher – Britain's first woman prime

Whitby harbour, with St Mary's Church, Yorkshire

minister – and then by John Major. Under Mrs Thatcher, the Conservative Party changed. The "enlightened" wing that supported the liberal consensus was eclipsed by a more radical intake of Conservatives, many from the entrepreneurial rather than the aristocratic class. This government implemented a series of measures that pleased the Right, including returning most of the large nationalized industries to private ownership, and introducing laws that curbed the power of the trade unions to call strikes, which had seriously hindered economic progress in the 1970s.

During its long period in opposition, Labour initially moved sharply to the Left, but eventually recognized that the nation had lost its appetite for socialism. Rebranded as the more moderate "New Labour", the party returned to office under Tony Blair in a landslide victory in 1997. The new government did not try to unpick the policies of its predecessor: there was no re-nationalization of industry, no attempt to redistribute income through higher taxation and no move to return trade unions to their

Kensington Palace after the death of Princess Diana

Punch and Judy show, Brighton

former position of strength. This shows that the differences between the two main parties have narrowed considerably, with both moving closer to the position of the third party, the centrist Liberal Democrats.

The question of Ireland has been an intractable political issue since the 17th century. The predominantly Catholic southern counties became independent from Britain in 1921, but the mainly Protestant north remained, by choice, part of the United Kingdom. Since the 1970s, Catholic terrorists advocating Irish unity, and their Protestant counterparts who want the north to stay in the United Kingdom, have bombed and murdered for their respective causes. The Good Friday Peace Agreement of 1998 put an end to much of the violence, but there are still some serious obstacles to its full implementation.

TOWN AND COUNTRY

Despite the rapid spread of towns and cities over the last two centuries, rural Britain still flourishes: nearly three quarters of the nation's land is used for agriculture. The main commercial crops grown in Britain are wheat, barley, sugar beet and potatoes, though most eye-catching are the early-summer fields carpeted with bright yellow oilseed rape or slate-blue flax.

Anglers and surfers at Porthcothan Bay, Cornwall, with Trevose Head and lighthouse in the distance

Mount Snowdon and Capel Curig, Snowdonia National Park, North Wales

British farms are often grouped around charming villages, which feature picturesque cottages and lovingly tended gardens. The typical village is centred on an ancient church – although church attendance continues to wane – and a small, friendly pub. To drink a pint of ale in a cosy, half-timbered village inn and relax before a blazing fire is an age-old and unique pleasure.

However, the apparently idyllic rural landscape conceals tensions and some difficult compromises. To remain economic in a competitive food market, farmers make use not only of ever more sophisticated machinery and techniques, but also of fertilizers, pesticides and herbicides. Many people believe that these modern farming methods do irreversible harm to the environment, threaten wildlife and can create serious health problems for humans. There is also tension over rights of access for walkers on to privately owned land, and opposition to traditional country blood sports (such as fox hunting) on compassionate grounds.

Part of the
Avebury
Stone Circle

CULTURE AND THE ARTS

Britain has a famous theatrical tradition stretching back to before the time of William Shakespeare. However, it is Shakespeare's plays that have survived best: they have been performed almost continuously since he wrote them in the 16th century. The faithful replica of the Globe Theatre in Southwark, where some of his plays were first performed, allows theatregoers to see Shakespeare's works in the arena for which they were written.

Twentieth-century British playwrights – among them Alan Bennett and Harold Pinter – draw on the Shakespearean tradition with their vivid language and use of comedy to illuminate serious themes. British actors such as Judi Dench and Ralph Fiennes have an international reputation.

Crofter (owner of a small farm) stacking peat to dry, Outer Hebrides, Scotland

While London is the focal point of British performing arts, these still thrive in many other parts of the country. In August, the Edinburgh Festival and its Fringe are a high point of the cultural calendar. Festivals of classical and popular music are held across the country, chiefly in summer. Glyndebourne in Sussex is a renowned venue for opera, while the Promenade Concerts in London's Albert Hall have become a national institution. The Aldeburgh Festival in Suffolk was established by the composer Benjamin Britten and remains an annual showcase for his work. Rock festivals – the largest at Glastonbury – and a lively club scene in the big cities have produced internationally known groups, such as Oasis.

Timber-framed Tudor cottages built late in the 15th century, Lavenham, Suffolk

Britain's rich literary tradition – created by the likes of Jane Austen and Charles Dickens – is carried forward by a number of contemporary writers. Poetry has had an enthusiastic following since Geoffrey Chaucer wrote *The Canterbury Tales* in the 14th century. More recent popular poets include WH Auden and Ted Hughes. There are annual festivals of literature at Cheltenham and Hay-on-Wye, a town on the England-Wales border famous for its second-hand bookshops.

Steam trains, north Yorkshire

In the visual arts, Britain has long excelled in portraiture (Thomas Gainsborough), caricature (William Hogarth) and landscape (John Constable and JMW Turner). This century, David Hockney and Francis Bacon, and the sculptors Henry Moore and Barbara Hepworth, have enjoyed worldwide recognition. Architects such as Christopher Wren and Robert Adam created styles that still define many British cities, while Richard Rogers, Terry Farrell and Norman Foster (architect of the Dome at Greenwich) carry the standard for post-modernism.

Technological developments over the last 50 years have revolutionized Britain's cultural and artistic life. Since the 1960s, watching television has been the nation's most popular leisure activity. The most successful televized soap operas regularly attract audiences of more than 15 million – a quarter of the population. British television and radio are admired the world over for the quality of their programmes. The publicly funded British Broadcasting Corporation (BBC) was the nation's only radio and television broadcaster until 1955, when the first commercial television channels were licensed. Because it has traditionally been under less commercial pressure

Shakespearean Globe Theatre, Southwark, London

than the other channels, the BBC has been able to experiment and has led the way in making "quality" television.

The people of Britain are avid newspaper readers. There are ten national newspapers published from London on weekdays: the standard of the broadsheets is very high and papers such as *The Times* are

Horsey Mill, Norfolk Broads

read all over the globe because of their reputation for strong international reporting. Most popular, however, are the tabloids, which are packed with gossip and sport. These papers account for 80 per cent of total newspaper sales.

In recent years, the media have made a powerful impact on professional sport, providing new audiences and increased revenue. Football, the most popular spectator sport, has shed its cloth cap image with the introduction of all-seat stadiums and high ticket prices. Many of the biggest clubs are now public companies and the best players are paid superstar salaries, moving from club to club for transfer fees of many millions of pounds. In summer, cricket is the national game, and most international matches attract sellout crowds. Other sports, such as rugby, are also trying to market themselves more professionally, though so far with less success. Horse racing has been a British enthusiasm for more than 300 years.

The indigenous film industry, which flourished in the mid-20th century with a string of light comedies, has been squeezed almost into insignificance by the almighty Hollywood. However, in the 1990s Britain produced some smash hit comedies, including *Four Weddings and a Funeral* and *The Full Monty*.

In general, the popularity of American films and television has increased the influence of transatlantic culture. American expressions continue to enter the language, shopping malls proliferate, American fast foods are widely available and jeans have become standard leisurewear for millions. So, as they have done for many centuries, the British are accommodating their own traditions to influences from other cultures, while leaving the essential elements of their national life and character intact.

Sculpture on the British Library, London

The Dome at dawn, Greenwich, London

Gardens Through the Ages

S TYLES OF GARDENING in Britain have expanded alongside architecture and other evolving fashions. The Elizabethan knot
garden became more elaborate and formal in Jacobean times,
when the range of plants greatly increased. The 18th century
brought a taste for large-scale "natural" landscapes with lakes,
woods and pastures, creating the most distinctively English
style to have emerged. In the 19th century, fierce debate raged
between supporters of natural and formal gardens,
developing into the eclecticism
of the 20th century when
"garden rooms" in differing
styles became popular.

Capability Brown (1715–83)
*was Britain's most influential
garden designer, favouring the
move away from formal gardens
to man-made pastoral settings.*

Blackthorn

Classical temples were a
much appreciated feature in
18th-century gardens and
were often exact replicas of
buildings that the designers
had seen in Greece.

**Monumental
column**

A grotto and cascade
brought romance
and mystery.

Elaborate parterres *were a feature of
aristocratic gardens of the 17th century, when
the fashion spread from Europe. This is the
Privy Garden at Hampton Court Palace, restored in 1995 to its design under William III.*

IDEAL LANDSCAPE GARDEN

Classical Greece and Rome
inspired the grand gardens of
the early 18th century, such
as Stourhead and Stowe. Informal clumps of trees played
a critical part in the serene,
manicured landscapes.

Maple

Winding paths
were carefully
planned to allow
changing vistas to
open out as
visitors strolled
around the garden.

DESIGN AND FORMALITY

A flower garden is a work of
artifice, an attempt to tame nature
rather than to copy it. Growing
plants in rows or regular patterns,
interspersed with statues and
ornaments, imposes a sense of
order. Designs change to reflect
the fashion of the time and the
introduction of new plants.

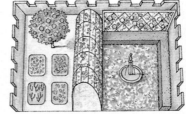

Medieval gardens usually had a
herber (a turfed sitting area) and a
vine arbour. A good reconstruction is
Queen Eleanor's Garden, Winchester.

Tudor gardens featured edged
borders and sometimes mazes. The
Tudor House Garden, Southampton
also has beehives and heraldic statue

Herbaceous borders, full of lush plants, are the glory of the summer garden. Gertrude Jekyll (1843–1932), was high priestess of the mixed border, with her eye for seductive colour combinations.

Cedar of Lebanon

Yew

Rhododendron

The Palladian bridge was a favourite feature, often decorative rather than practical.

Knot Gardens were in vogue in the 1500s. Intersecting lines of lavender or box were filled with flowers, herbs or vegetables, as in this restoration at Pitmedden in Scotland.

DEVELOPMENT OF THE MODERN PANSY

All garden plants derive from wild flowers, bred over the years to produce qualities that appeal to gardeners. The story of the pansy, one of our most popular flowers, is typical.

The wild pansy (Viola tricolor) native to Britain is commonly known as heartsease. It is a small-flowered annual which can vary considerably in colour.

The mountain pansy (Viola lutea) is a perennial. The first cultivated varieties resulted from crossing it with heartsease in the early 19th century.

The Show Pansy was bred by florists after the blotch appeared as a chance seedling in 1840. It was round in form with a small, symmetrical blotch.

The Fancy Pansy, developed in the 1860s, was much larger. The blotch covered all three lower petals save for a thin margin of colour.

Modern hybrids of pansies, violas and violettas, developed by selective breeding, are varied and versatile in a wide range of vibrant new colours.

17th-century gardening was more elaborate. Water gardens like those at Blenheim were often combined with parterres of exotic foreign plants.

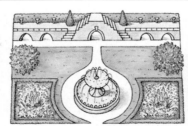

Victorian gardens, their formal beds a mass of colour, were a reaction to the landscapes of Capability Brown. Alton Towers has a good example.

20th-century gardens mix historic and modern styles, as at Hidcote Manor, Gloucestershire. Growing wild flowers is becoming a popular choice.

Stately Homes

THE GRAND COUNTRY HOUSE reached its zenith in the 18th and 19th centuries, when the old landed families and the new captains of industry enjoyed their wealth, looked after by a retinue of servants. The earliest stately homes date from the 14th century, when defence was paramount. By the 16th century, when the opulent taste of the European Renaissance spread to England, houses became centres of pleasure and showplaces for fine art *(see pp336–7)*. The Georgians favoured chaste Classical architecture with rich interiors, the Victorians flamboyant Gothic. Due to 20th-century social change many stately homes have been opened to the public, some administered by the National Trust.

Adam sketch (c.1760) for ornate panel

The saloon, a domed rotunda based on the Pantheon in Rome, was designed to display the Scarsdale family's Classical sculpture collection to 18th-century society.

The Drawing Room, *the main room for entertaining, contains the most important pictures and some exquisite plasterwork.*

The Family Wing is a self-contained "pavilion" of private living quarters; the servants lived in rooms above the kitchen. The Scarsdale family still live here.

The Music Room is decorated with musical themes. Music was the main entertainment on social occasions.

TIMELINE OF ARCHITECTS

1650				1750

Colen Campbell (1676–1729) designed Burlington House *(see p87)*

William Kent (1685–1748) built Holkham Hall *(see p205)* in the Palladian style

Robert Adam (1728–92), who often worked with his brother James (1730–94) was as famous for decorative details as for buildings

Henry Holland (1745–1806) designed the Neo-Classical south range of Woburn Abbey *(see p248)*

Sir John Vanbrugh *(see p462)* was helped by **Nicholas Hawksmoor** (1661–1736) on Blenheim Palace *(see pp246–7)*

John Carr (1723–1807) designed the Palladian Harewood House *(see p476)*

Castle Howard (1702) by Sir John Vanbrugh

Adam fireplace, Kedleston Hall, adorned with Classical motifs

NATIONAL TRUST

At the end of the 19th century, there were real fears that burgeoning factories, mines, roads and houses would obliterate much of Britain's historic landscape and finest buildings. In 1895 a group that included the social reformer Octavia Hill formed the National Trust, to preserve the nation's valuable heritage.

National Trust logo with oak leaf design

The first building acquired was the medieval Clergy House at Alfriston in Sussex, in 1896 *(see p180)*. Today the National Trust is a charity that runs many historic houses and gardens, and vast stretches of countryside and coastline. It is supported by two million members.

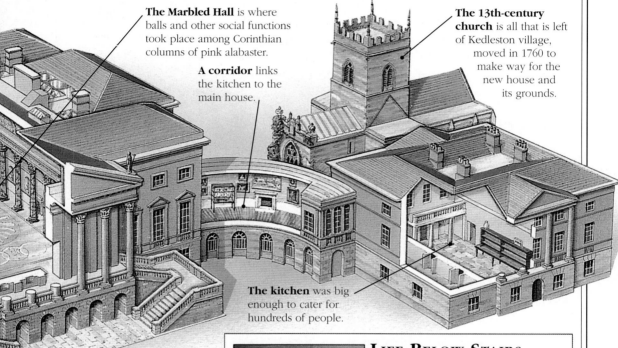

The Marbled Hall is where balls and other social functions took place among Corinthian columns of pink alabaster.

A corridor links the kitchen to the main house.

The 13th-century church is all that is left of Kedleston village, moved in 1760 to make way for the new house and its grounds.

The kitchen was big enough to cater for hundreds of people.

KEDLESTON HALL

This Derbyshire mansion *(see p386)* is an early work of the influential Georgian architect Robert Adam, who was a pioneer of the Neo-Classical style derived from ancient Greece and Rome. It was built for Lord Scarsdale in the 1760s.

Life Below Stairs by Charles Hunt (c.1890)

LIFE BELOW STAIRS

A large community of resident staff was essential to run a country house smoothly. The butler was in overall charge, ensuring that meals were served on time. The housekeeper supervised uniformed maids who made sure the place was clean. The cook ran the kitchen, using fresh produce from the estate. Ladies' maids and valets acted as personal servants.

1800	1850

Philip Webb (1831–1915) was a leading architect of the influential Arts and Crafts movement, whose buildings favoured the simpler forms of an "Old English" style, instead of flamboyant Victorian Gothic

Sir Edwin Lutyens (1869–1944) designed the elaborate Castle Drogo in Devon *(see p329)*, one of the last grand country houses

Dining Room, Cragside, Northumberland

Norman Shaw (1831–1912) was an exponent of Victorian Gothic, as in Cragside (above), and a pioneer of the Arts and Crafts movement

Standen, West Sussex (1891–94) by Philip Webb

Heraldry and the Aristocracy

Order of the Garter medal

THE BRITISH ARISTOCRACY has evolved over 900 years from the feudal obligations of noblemen to the Norman kings, who conferred privileges of rank and land in return for armed support. Subsequent monarchs bestowed titles and property on their supporters, establishing new aristocratic dynasties. The title of "earl" dates from the 11th century; that of "duke" from the 14th century. Soon the nobility began to choose their own symbols, partly to identify a knight concealed by his armour: these were often painted on the knight's coat (hence the term "coat of arms") and also copied onto his shield.

The College of Arms, London: housing records of all coats of arms and devising new ones

ROYAL COAT OF ARMS

The most familiar British coat of arms is the sovereign's. It appears on the royal standard, or flag, as well as on official documents and on shops that enjoy royal patronage. Over nearly 900 years, various monarchs have made modifications. The quartered shield in the middle displays the arms of England (twice), Scotland and Ireland. Surrounding it are other traditional images including the lion and unicorn, topped by the crown and the royal helm (helmet).

Edward III (1327–77) was the founder of the chivalric Order of the Garter. The garter, bearing the motto, Honi soit qui mal y pense (evil be to him who thinks of evil), goes round the central shield.

The lion is the most common beast in heraldry.

The red lion is the symbol of Scotland.

The unicorn is a mythical beast, generally regarded as a Scottish royal beast in heraldry.

Henry II (1154–89) formalized his coat of arms to include three lions. This was developed by his son Richard I to become the "Gules three lions passant guardant or" seen on today's arms.

The royal helm with gold protective bars was introduced to the arms by Elizabeth I (1558–1603).

Dieu et mon droit (God and my right) has been the royal motto since the reign of Henry V (1413–22).

Henry VII (1485–1509) devised the Tudor rose, joining the white and red roses of York and Lancaster.

ADMIRAL LORD NELSON

When people are ennobled they may choose their own coat of arms if they do not already have one. Britain's naval hero (1758–1805) was made Baron Nelson of the Nile in 1798 and a viscount in 1801. His arms relate to his life and career at sea; but some symbols were added after his death.

A seaman supports the shield.

The motto means "Let him wear the palm (or laurel) who deserves it".

A tropical scene shows the Battle of the Nile (1798).

The San Joseph was a Spanish man o'war that Nelson daringly captured.

TRACING YOUR ANCESTRY

Records of births, deaths and marriages in England and Wales since 1837 are at the **General Register Office**, St Catherine's House, London (0151-471 4200), and in Scotland at **New Register House**, Edinburgh (0131 334 0380). For help in tracing your family history, consult the **Society of Genealogists**, 14 Charterhouse Buildings, London (020-7251 8799).

Inherited titles usually pass to the eldest son or the closest male relative, but some titles may go to women if there is no male heir.

The Duke of Edinburgh (born 1921), husband of the Queen, is one of several dukes who are members of the Royal Family.

Earl Mountbatten of Burma (1900–79) was ennobled in 1947 for diplomatic and military services.

The Marquess of Salisbury (1830–1903), Prime Minister three times between 1885 and 1902, was descended from the Elizabethan statesman Robert Cecil.

Viscount Montgomery (1887–1976) was raised to the peerage for his military leadership in World War II.

Lord Byron (1788–1824), the Romantic poet, was the 6th Baron Byron: the 1st Baron was an MP ennobled by Charles I in 1625.

PEERS OF THE REALM

There are nearly 1,200 peers of the realm. In 1999 the process began to abolish the hereditary system in favour of life peerages which expire on the death of the recipient *(see left and below)*. All peers are entitled to sit in the House of Lords, including the Lords Spiritual – archbishops and senior bishops of the Church of England – and the Law Lords. In 1958 the Queen expanded the list of life peerages to honour people who had performed notable public service. From 1999 the system of "peoples peerages" began to replace inherited honours.

KEY TO THE PEERS

☐	25 dukes
☐	35 marquesses
☐	175 earls and countesses
☐	100 viscounts
☐	800+ barons and baronesses

THE QUEEN'S HONOURS LIST

Twice a year several hundred men and women nominated by the Prime Minister and political leaders for outstanding public service receive honours from the Queen. Some are made dames or knights, a few receive the prestigious OM (Order of Merit), but far more receive lesser honours such as OBEs or MBEs (Orders or Members of the British Empire).

Mother Theresa *received the OM in 1983 for her work in India.*

Terence Conran, *founder of Habitat, was knighted for services to industry.*

The Beatles *were given MBEs in 1965. Paul McCartney was knighted in 1997.*

Rural Architecture

OR MANY, THE ESSENCE OF BRITISH LIFE is found in
villages. Their scale and serenity nurture a way of
life envied by those who live in towns and cities. The
pattern of British villages dates back some 1,500 years,
when the Saxons cleared forests and established settlements, usually centred around a green or pond. Most
of today's English villages existed at the time of the
Domesday Book in 1086, though few actual buildings
survive from then. The settlements evolved organically
around a church or manor; the cottages and gardens
were created from local materials. Today, a typical
village will contain structures of various dates,
from the Middle Ages onward. The church is
usually the oldest, followed perhaps by a
tithe barn, manor house and cottages.

**Abbotsbury, in Dorset – a typical
village built up around a church**

A steep-pitched roof
covers the whole house.

Timbers are of
Wealden oak.

Eaves are supported
by curved braces.

*Wealden Hall House in Sussex is
a medieval timber-framed house,
of a type found in southeast
England. It has a tall central open
hall flanked by bays of two storeys
and the upper floor is "jettied",
overhanging the lower storey.*

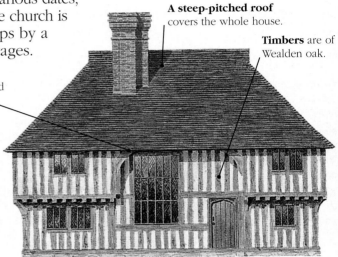

A tiled roof keeps
the grain dry.

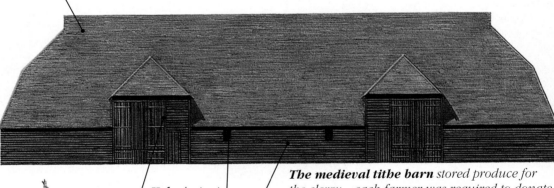

The entrance
is big enough
for ox-wagons.

Holes let in air
– and birds.

Walls and doors
are weatherboarded.

*The medieval tithe barn stored produce for
the clergy – each farmer was required to donate
one tenth (tithe) of his annual harvest. The
enormous roofs may be supported by crucks,
large curved timbers extending from the low walls.*

THE PARISH CHURCH

The church is the focal point of the village
and, traditionally, of village life. Its tall spire
could be seen – and its bells heard – by
travellers from a distance. The church is
also a chronicle of local history: a large
church in a tiny village indicates
a once-prosperous settlement. A
typical church contains architectural
features from many centuries,
occasionally as far back as Saxon times.
These may include medieval brasses,
wall paintings, misericords *(see p391)*,
and Tudor and Stuart carvings. Many
sell informative guide books inside.

**Slender spire from
the Georgian era**

West elevation

Pinnacled towers
dating from the
15th century are
situated at the
west end.

Bells summon
the congregation.

Buttresses
support
old walls.

**Norman
arches** are
rounded.

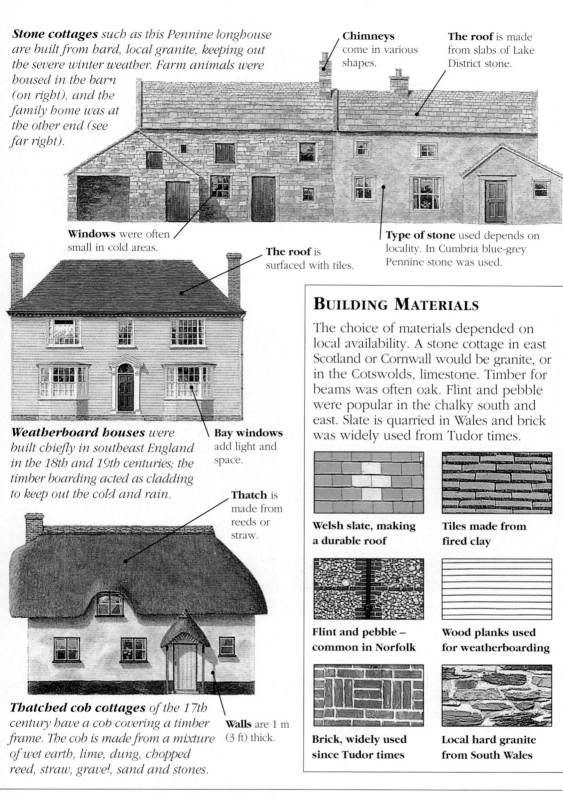

Stone cottages such as this Pennine longhouse are built from hard, local granite, keeping out the severe winter weather. Farm animals were housed in the barn (on right), and the family home was at the other end (see far right).

Chimneys come in various shapes.

The roof is made from slabs of Lake District stone.

Windows were often small in cold areas.

The roof is surfaced with tiles.

Type of stone used depends on locality. In Cumbria blue-grey Pennine stone was used.

Weatherboard houses were built chiefly in southeast England in the 18th and 19th centuries; the timber boarding acted as cladding to keep out the cold and rain.

Bay windows add light and space.

Thatch is made from reeds or straw.

Thatched cob cottages of the 17th century have a cob covering a timber frame. The cob is made from a mixture of wet earth, lime, dung, chopped reed, straw, gravel, sand and stones.

Walls are 1 m (3 ft) thick.

BUILDING MATERIALS

The choice of materials depended on local availability. A stone cottage in east Scotland or Cornwall would be granite, or in the Cotswolds, limestone. Timber for beams was often oak. Flint and pebble were popular in the chalky south and east. Slate is quarried in Wales and brick was widely used from Tudor times.

Welsh slate, making a durable roof

Tiles made from fired clay

Flint and pebble – common in Norfolk

Wood planks used for weatherboarding

Brick, widely used since Tudor times

Local hard granite from South Wales

South elevation

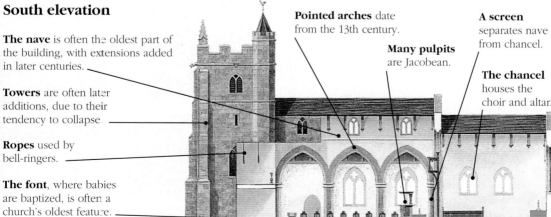

The nave is often the oldest part of the building, with extensions added in later centuries.

Towers are often later additions, due to their tendency to collapse.

Ropes used by bell-ringers.

The font, where babies are baptized, is often a church's oldest feature.

Pointed arches date from the 13th century.

Many pulpits are Jacobean.

A screen separates nave from chancel.

The chancel houses the choir and altar.

The Countryside

Common Blue butterfly

FOR ITS SIZE, Britain contains an unusual variety of geological and climatic conditions that have shaped diverse landscapes, from treeless windswept moorland to boggy marshes and small hedged cattle pastures. Each terrain nurtures its typical wildlife and displays its own charm through the seasons. With the reduction in farming and the creation of footpaths and nature reserves, the countryside is becoming more of a leisure resource.

INDIGENOUS ANIMALS AND BIRDS

There are no large or dangerous wild animals in Britain but a wealth of small mammals, rodents and insects inhabit the countryside, and the rivers and streams are home to many varieties of fish. For bird-watchers there is a great range of songbirds, birds of prey and seabirds.

Livestock graze on low pastures.

Trees provide shelter and protection for wildlife.

Higher land is uncultivated.

Bushes and trees grow between rocks.

Streams flow over a stony bed from mountain springs.

The highest ground is often covered in snow until spring.

WOODED DOWNLAND

Chalk downland, seen here at Ditchling Beacon on the Downs *(see p181)*, has soil of low fertility and is grazed by sheep. However crops are sometimes grown on the lower slopes. Distinctive wild flowers and butterflies thrive here, while beech and yew predominate in the woods.

WILD HILLSIDE

Large tracts of Britain's uplands remain wild terrain, unsuitable for crops, forestry or even grazing sheep. Purple heather is tough enough to survive in moorland, the haunt of deer and game birds. The highest craggy uplands, such as the Cairngorms *(see p682–3)* in Scotland, pictured here, are the habitat of numerous birds of prey.

Spear thistle has pink heads in summer that attract several species of butterfly.

The dog rose is one of Britain's best-loved wild flowers; its pink single flower is widely seen in hedgerows.

Ling, a low-growing heather with tiny pink bell-flowers, adds splashes of colour to peaty moors and uplands.

Hogweed *has robust stems and leaves with large clusters of white flowers.*

Meadow cranes-bill is a wild geranium with distinctive purple flowers.

Tormentil resembles wild strawberry plants with its small yellow flowers. It is found near water on heaths and moors in summer

***Swallows**, swifts and house martins are all summer visitors.*

***Kestrels** are small falcons that prey on mammals such as voles.*

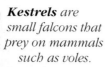

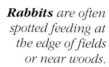

***Rabbits** are often spotted feeding at the edge of fields or near woods.*

***Robins**, common in gardens and hedgerows, have distinctive red breast feathers.*

***Foxes**, little bigger than domestic cats, live in hideaways in woods, near farmland.*

Cereal crops ripen in small fields.

Hedgerows provide refuge for wildlife.

Small mixed woods break up the field pattern.

Sheep graze on salty marshes.

Culverts drain water from the field.

Reed beds edge the water.

TRADITIONAL FIELDS

The patchwork fields here in the Cotswolds *(see p338)* reflect generations of small-scale farming. A typical farm would produce silage, hay and cereal crops, and keep a few dairy cows and sheep in enclosed pastures. The tree-dotted hedgerows mark boundaries that may be centuries old.

MARSHLAND

Flat and low-lying wetlands, criss-crossed with dykes and drainage canals, provide the scenery of Romney Marsh *(see also p183)* as well as much of East Anglia. Some areas have rich, peaty soil for crops, or salty marshland for sheep, but there are extensive uncultivated sections, where reed beds shelter wildlife.

***Sea lavender** is a saltmarsh plant that is tolerant of saline soils. It flowers in late summer.*

***The oxeye daisy** is a larger relative of the common white daisy, found in grassland from spring to late summer.*

***Orchids** are among the rarer wild flowers. This species is the Common Spotted Orchid.*

***Cowslips** belong to the primrose family. In spring they are often found in the grass on open meadowlands.*

***Poppies** glow brilliant red in cornfields.*

***Buttercups** are among the most common wild flowers. They brighten meadows in summer.*

Walkers' Britain

WALKERS OF ALL LEVELS of ability and enthusiasm are well served in Britain. There is an unrivalled network of long-distance paths through some spectacular scenery, which can be tackled in stages with overnight stays en route, or dipped into for a single day's walking. For shorter walks, Britain is dotted with signposts showing public footpaths across common or private land. You will find books of walk routes in local shops and a large map will keep you on track. Choose river routes for easy walking or take to the hills for a greater challenge.

Walker resting on Scafell Pike, Lake District

The West Highland Way is an arduous 95 mile (153 km) route from Milngavie, near Glasgow, to north of Fort William, across mountainous terrain with fine lochs and moorland scenery *(see p634).*

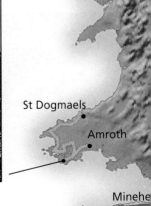

The Pennine Way was Britain's first designated long-distance path. The 256 mile (412 km) route from Edale in Derbyshire to Kirk Yetholm on the Scottish border is a challenging upland hike, with long, lonely stretches of moorland. It is only for experienced hill walkers.

Offa's Dyke Footpath follows the boundary between Wales and England. The 168 mile (270 km) path goes through the beautiful Wye Valley (see p549) in the Welsh borders.

Dales Way runs from Ilkley in West Yorkshire to Bowness-on-Windermere in the Lake District, 81 miles (130 km) of delightful flat riverside walking and valley scenery.

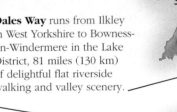

Pembrokeshire Coastal path is 186 miles (229 km) of rugged cliff-top walking from Amroth on Carmarthen Bay to the west tip of Wales at Cardigan.

ORDNANCE SURVEY MAPS

The best maps for walkers are published by the Ordnance Survey, the official mapping agency. Out of a wide range of maps the most useful are the green-covered *Pathfinder* series, on a scale of 1:25,000, and the *Landranger* series at 1:50;000. The *Outdoor Leisure and Explorer* series are maps of the more popular regions and cover a larger area.

The Southwest Coastal Path offers varied scenery from Minehead on the north Somerset coast to Poole in Dorset, via Devon and Cornwall – in all a marathon 600 mile (965 km) round trip.

Fort William

Glasgow

St Bees Head

Win

Prest

St Dogmaels

Amroth

Minehe

SIGNPOSTS

Long-distance paths are well signposted, some of them with an acorn symbol (or with a thistle in Scotland). Many shorter routes are marked with coloured arrows by local authorities or hiking groups. Local councils generally mark public footpaths with yellow arrows. Public bridleways, marked by blue arrows, are paths that can be used by both walkers and horse riders – remember, horses churn up mud. Signs appear on posts, trees and stiles.

TIPS FOR WALKERS

Be prepared: *The weather can change very quickly: dress for the worst. Always take a compass, a proper walking map and get local advice before undertaking any ambitious walking. Pack some food and drink if the map does not show a pub en route.*

On the walk: *Always keep to the footpath and close gates behind you. Never feed or upset farm animals, leave litter, pick flowers or damage plants.*

Where to stay: *The International Youth Hostel Federation has a network of hostels which cater particularly for walkers. Bed-and-breakfast accommodation is also available near most routes.*

Further information: *The Ramblers' Association (tel: 0171-582 6878) is a national organiza-tion for walkers, with a magazine and a guide to accommodation.*

__The Coast to Coast Walk__ crosses the Lake District, Yorkshire Dales and North York Moors, on a 190 mile (306 km) route. This demanding walk covers a spectacular range of North Country landscapes. All cross-country routes are best walked from west to east to take advantage of the prevailing wind.

__The Ridgeway__ is a fairly easy path that follows an ancient track once used by cattle drovers. Start-ing near Avebury (see p289) it covers 85 miles (137 km) to Ivinghoe Beacon.

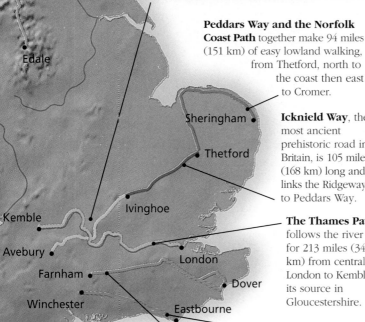

Ilkley

Robin
Hood's
Bay

Edale

Peddars Way and the Norfolk Coast Path together make 94 miles (151 km) of easy lowland walking, from Thetford, north to the coast then east to Cromer.

Sheringham

Icknield Way, the most ancient prehistoric road in Britain, is 105 miles (168 km) long and links the Ridgeway to Peddars Way.

Thetford

Ivinghoe

Kemble

The Thames Path follows the river for 213 miles (341 km) from central London to Kemble, its source in Gloucestershire.

Avebury

London

Farnham

Dover

Winchester

Eastbourne

arbour

The Isle of Wight Coastal Path circles the entire island on an easy 65 mile (105 km) footpath.

The North Downs Way is an ancient route through 141 miles (227 km) of low-lying hills from Farnham in Surrey to Dover or Folkestone in Kent.

__The South Downs Way__ is a varied 106 mile (171 km) walk from Eastbourne on the south coast to Winchester (see p170-71). It can be completed in a week.

The Traditional British Pub

Beer label c.1900

EVERY COUNTRY HAS ITS BARS, but Britain is famous for its pubs or "public houses". Ale was brewed in England in Roman times – mostly at home – and by the Middle Ages there were inns and taverns which brewed their own. The 18th century was the heyday of the coaching inn as stage coaches brought more custom. In the 19th century came railway taverns for travellers and "gin palaces" for the new industrial workers. Today, pubs come in all styles and sizes and many cater to families, serving food as well as drink.

Early 19th-century coaching inn – also a social centre and post office

THE VICTORIAN PUB

A century ago, many pubs in towns and cities had smart interiors, to contrast with the poor housing of their clients.

Elaborately etched glass is a feature of many Victorian interiors.

Pub games, *such as cribbage, bar billiards, pool and dominoes are part of British pub culture. Here some regular customers are competing against a rival pub's darts team.*

Pint glasses (containing just over half a litre) are used for beer.

The Red Lion pub name is derived from Scottish heraldry *(see p30)*.

Beer gardens *outside pubs are a favourite venue for family summer treats.*

Old-fashioned cash register contributes to the period atmosphere of the bar.

Pewter tankards, seldom used by drinkers today, add a traditional touch.

WHAT TO DRINK

Draught bitter is the most traditional British beer. Brewed from malted barley, hops, yeast and water, and usually matured in a wooden cask, it varies from region to region. In the north of England the sweeter mild ale is popular, and lagers served in bottles or on tap are also widely drunk. Stout, made from black malt, is another variation.

Beer pump

Draught bitter is drunk at room temperature.

Draught lager is a light-coloured, carbonated beer.

Guinness is a thick, creamy Irish stout.

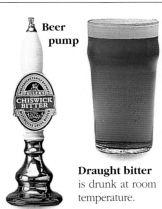

Pavement tables, crowded with city drinkers during the summer months

A village pub, offering a waterside view and serving drinks in the garden

Bottles of spirits, as well as the popular port and sherry, are ranged behind the bar.

Glass lamps imitate the Victorian style.

Wine, once rarely found in pubs, is now increasingly popular.

A deep-toned mahogany bar forms part of the traditional setting.

Draught beer, served from pumps or taps, comes from national and local brewers.

Optics dispense spirits in precise measures.

Mild may be served by the pint or in a half-pint tankard (as above).

Top cocktails are gin-and-tonic (right) and Pimm's.

PUB SIGNS

Early medieval inns used vines or evergreens as signs – the symbol of Bacchus, the Roman god of wine. Soon pubs acquired names that signalled support for monarchs or noblemen, or celebrated victories in battle. As many customers could not read, pub signs had vivid images.

The George *may derive from one of the six English kings of that name, or, as here, from England's patron saint.*

The Bat and Ball *celebrates cricket, and may be sited near a village green where the game can be played.*

The Green Man *is a woodland spirit from pagan mythology, possibly the basis for the legend of Robin Hood (see p386).*

The Magna Carta *sign commemorates and illustrates the "great charter" signed by King John in 1215 (see p52).*

The Bird in Hand *refers to the ancient country sport of falconry, traditionally practised by noblemen.*

A Flavour of British Food

BRITAIN'S UNIQUE contributions to gastronomy include its cooked breakfasts, afternoon teas and satisfying puddings. Fast food and takeaways were pioneered here with fish and chips, the sandwich and the Cornish pasty. Modern British cuisine is innovative and varied, but it is also worth seeking out traditional dishes which use first-rate ingredients: beef, lamb and game figure prominently. As an island, Britain has historically been a fish-eating nation, although shellfish, once cheap, has become pricier.

Fish and chips *are made from white sea fish (such as cod), batter-coated and fried in oil, with chipped potatoes, salt and vinegar.*

A full English breakfast *can include fried bacon and egg, mushrooms, sausage, tomatoes, fried bread and black pudding.*

Cockles and whelks *remain cheap compared with larger shellfish. They are sold from small stalls outside pubs, and can be awkward to eat.*

Laverbread *is a Welsh speciality made from dark-coloured seaweed. It is served cold with seafood, or, as here, hot with bacon, toast and tomato.*

Cornish pasties *are filled with meat and vegetables baked in a pastry crust. They originated as a handy way for farm labourers to take their lunch to work.*

TEA TIME

Afternoon tea, taken at around 4pm, is a British tradition enacted daily in homes, tea-shops and grand hotels. The tea is usually from India or Sri Lanka, served with optional milk and sugar; but it could be scented China or herbal tea served with or without lemon. Small, delicately cut sandwiches are eaten first: fish paste and cucumber are traditional fillings. These may be followed by scones, jam and cream, especially in the west of England *(see p317).* Other options include buttered toast or crumpets, but leave room for a slice of fruit cake or jam sponge, a chocolate éclair or a regional speciality such as Scottish shortbread.

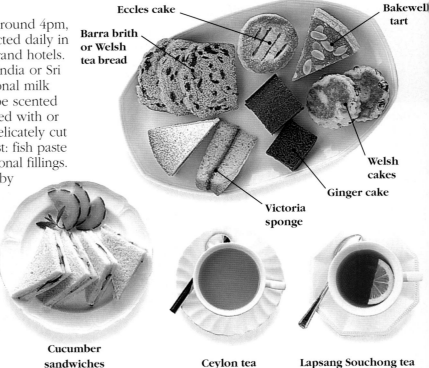

Eccles cake

Barra brith or Welsh tea bread

Bakewell tart

Welsh cakes

Ginger cake

Victoria sponge

Cucumber sandwiches

Ceylon tea

Lapsang Souchong tea

Ploughman's lunch *is served in many pubs. It consists of bread, cheese (often Cheddar), and pickles, garnished with salad. Ham or pâté may be substituted for cheese.*

Horseradish sauce

Gravy

Roast beef

Yorkshire pudding

Broccoli

Roast potatoes

Shepherd's pie *is made from minced lamb baked with a topping of mashed potato. If minced beef is used instead, the dish will be called cottage pie.*

Roast beef *is Britain's traditional Sunday lunch. It usually comes with Yorkshire pudding (savoury batter baked with the meat), roast potatoes and seasonal vegetables. A rich gravy enhances the flavour, and horseradish sauce is a favourite relish.*

Dover sole *is Britain's most prized flat fish. Served on the bone or filleted, it is firm fleshed and delicately flavoured.*

Cumberland sausage*, a regional speciality, is in a coil. Sausages and mashed potatoes are called "bangers and mash".*

Steak and kidney pie *is beef and kidney in thick gravy baked in pastry or in a suet crust, when it is known as a pudding.*

Strawberries and cream *are the delight of early summer, associated with outdoor social occasions of all types. Later, raspberries come into season. Both fruits make excellent jam.*

Cheese *is often served to finish lunch and dinner. Mature Cheddar is one of the most popular regional varieties. Blue-veined cheeses such as Stilton are an acquired taste.*

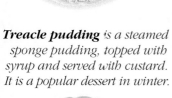

Stilton

Cheddar

Treacle pudding *is a steamed sponge pudding, topped with syrup and served with custard. It is a popular dessert in winter.*

Cornish Yarg

Sage Derby

Sherry trifle *was originally sponge cake soaked in sweet sherry and served with custard. Modern versions may include sponge fingers covered with fruit, jelly and a layer of cream, and decorated with angelica and cherries.*

Cheshire

Red Leicester

THE HISTORY OF GREAT BRITAIN

BRITAIN BEGAN TO assume a cohesive character as early as the 7th century, with the Anglo-Saxon tribes absorbing Celtic and Roman influences and finally achieving supremacy. They suffered repeated Viking incursions and were overcome by the Normans at the Battle of Hastings in 1066. Over centuries, the disparate cultures of the Normans and Anglo-Saxons combined to form the English nation, a process nurtured by Britain's position as an island. The next 400 years saw English kings involved in military expeditions to Europe, but their control over these areas was gradually wrested from them. As a result they extended their domain over Scotland and Wales. The Tudor monarchs consolidated this control and laid the foundations for Britain's future commercial success. Henry VIII recognized the vital importance of sea power and under his daughter, Elizabeth I, English sailors ranged far across the world, often coming into

Medieval knights, masters of the arts of war

conflict with the Spanish. The total defeat of the Spanish Armada in 1588 confirmed Britain's position as a major maritime power. The Stuart period saw a number of internal struggles, most importantly the Civil War in 1641. But by the time of the Act of the Union in 1707 the whole island was united and the foundations for representative government had been laid. The combination of this internal security with continuing maritime strength allowed Britain to seek wealth overseas. By the end of the Napoleonic Wars in 1815, Britain was the leading trading nation in the world. The opportunities offered by industrialization were seized, and by the late 19th century, a colossal empire had been established across the globe. Challenged by Europe and the rise of the US, and drained by its leading role in two world wars, Britain's influence waned after 1945. By the 1970s almost all the colonies had become independent Commonwealth nations.

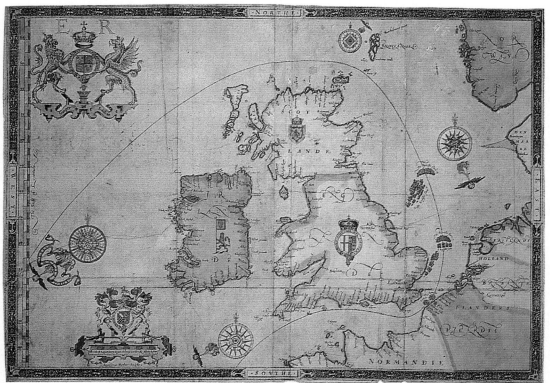

Contemporary map showing the defeat of the Armada (1588), making Britain into a world power

◁ **Henry VIII, founder of the British navy, seen here with his children Edward and Mary**

Kings and Queens

ALL ENGLISH MONARCHS since the Norman Conquest in 1066 have been descendants of William the Conqueror. Scottish rulers, until James VI and the Union of Crowns in 1603 *(see pp574–5)*, have been more diverse. When the Crown passes to someone other than the monarch's eldest son, the name of the ruling family usually changes. The rules of succession have been precisely laid down and strongly favour men over women, but Britain has still had six queens since 1553. In Norman times the monarchy enjoyed absolute power, but today the position is largely symbolic.

1413–22 Henry V

1509–47 Henry VIII

1399–1413 Henry IV

1485–1509 Henry VII

1066–87 William the Conqueror

1087–1100 William II

1100–35 Henry I

1135–54 Stephen

1327–77 Edward III

1483–5 Richard III

1050	1100	1150	1200	1250	1300	1350	1400	1450	150
NORMAN		PLANTAGENET					LANCASTER	YORK	TUD
1050	1100	1150	1200	1250	1300	1350	1400	1450	150

1307–27 Edward II

1154–89 Henry II

1272–1307 Edward I

1422–61 and 1470–1 Henry VI

1189–99 Richard I

1199–1216 John

1216–72 Henry III

1461–70 and 1471–83 Edward IV

1377–99 Richard II

Matthew Paris's 13th-century chronicle showing clockwise from top left, Richard I, Henry II, John and Henry III

1483 Edward V

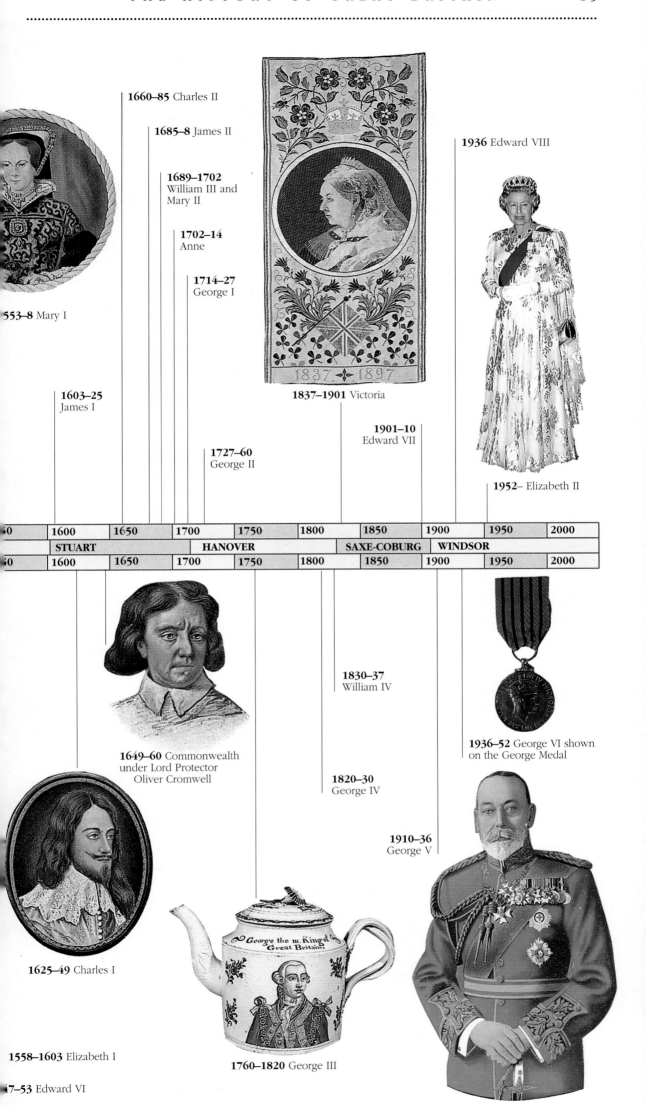

1660–85 Charles II

1685–8 James II

1689–1702
William III and
Mary II

1702–14
Anne

1714–27
George I

1936 Edward VIII

553–8 Mary I

1603–25
James I

1837–1901 Victoria

1901–10
Edward VII

1727–60
George II

1952– Elizabeth II

	1600	1650	1700	1750	1800	1850	1900	1950	2000
	STUART		HANOVER			SAXE-COBURG	WINDSOR		
	1600	1650	1700	1750	1800	1850	1900	1950	2000

1830–37
William IV

1936–52 George VI shown
on the George Medal

1649–60 Commonwealth
under Lord Protector
Oliver Cromwell

1820–30
George IV

1910–36
George V

1625–49 Charles I

1558–1603 Elizabeth I

1760–1820 George III

47–53 Edward VI

Prehistoric Britain

BRITAIN WAS PART of the European landmass until the end of the last Ice Age, around 6000 BC, when the English Channel was formed by melting ice. The earliest inhabitants lived in limestone caves: settlements and farming skills developed gradually through the Stone Age. The magnificent wooden and stone henges and circles are masterworks from around 3000 BC, but their significance is a mystery. Flint mines and ancient pathways are evidence of early trading and many burial mounds (barrows) survive from the Stone and Bronze Ages.

Axe Heads
Stone axes, like this one found at Stonehenge, were used by Neolithic men.

Cup and ring marks were carved on standing stones, such as this one at Ballymeanoch.

MAPPING THE PAST

Monuments from the Neolithic (New Stone), Bronze and Iron Ages, together with artefacts found from these periods, provide a wealth of information about Britain's early settlers, before written history began with the Romans.

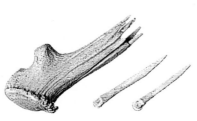

Neolithic Tools
Antlers and bones were made into Neolithic leather-working tools. These were found at Avebury (see p289).

Pottery Beaker
The Beaker People, who came from Europe in the early Bronze Age, take their name from these drinking cups often found in their graves.

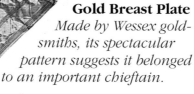

Gold Breast Plate
Made by Wessex goldsmiths, its spectacular pattern suggests it belonged to an important chieftain.

Pentre Ifan, an impressive Neolithic burial chamber in south Wales, was once covered with a huge earth mound.

Mold Cape
Gold was mined in Wales and Cornwall in the Bronze Age. This intricately worked warrior's cape was buried in a grave at Mold, Clwyd.

This gold cup, found in a Cornish barrow, is evidence of the wealth of Bronze Age tribes.

TIMELINE

6000–5000 As the Ice Age comes to an end, sea levels rise, submerging the landlink between Britain and the Continent

Neolithic flint axes

6000 BC	5500 BC	5000 BC	4500 BC	4000 BC

A gold pendant and button (1700 BC), found in Bronze Age graves

3500 Neolithic Age begins. Long barrows and stone circles built around Britain

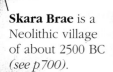

Skara Brae is a Neolithic village of about 2500 BC *(see p700).*

Maiden Castle

An impressive Iron Age hill fort in Dorset, its concentric lines of ramparts and ditches follow the contours of the hill top (see p295).

Iron Age Brochs, round towers with thick stone walls, are found only in Scotland.

Iron Age Axe

The technique of smelting iron came to Britain around 700 BC, brought from Europe by the Celts.

Castlerigg Stone Circle is one of Britain's earliest Neolithic monuments *(see p417).*

WHERE TO SEE PREHISTORIC BRITAIN

Wiltshire, with Stonehenge *(p288)* and Avebury *(p289),* has the best group of Neolithic monuments, and the Uffington White Horse is nearby *(p237).* The Scottish islands have many early sites and the British Museum *(pp112–13)* houses a huge collection of artefacts.

*A **circular bank** with over 180 stones encloses the Neolithic site at Avebury (see p289).*

Uffington White Horse

Thought to be 3,000 years old, the shape has to be "scoured" to keep grass at bay (see p237).

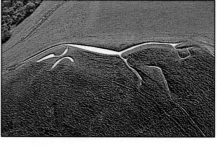

A chalk figure, thought to be a fertility goddess, was found at Grimes Graves *(see p202).*

This bronze Celtic helmet (50 BC) was found in the River Thames, London.

Snettisham Torc

A torc was a neck ring worn by Celtic men. This one, found in Norfolk, dates from 50 BC and is made from silver and gold.

Stonehenge was begun around 3,500 years ago *(see pp288–9).*

2500 Temples, or henges, are built of wood or stone	**1650–1200** Wessex is at the hub of trading routes between Europe and the mines of Cornwall, Wales and Ireland		**1000** First farmsteads are settled	**550–350** Migration of Celtic people from southern Europe	**500** Iron Age begins. Hill forts are built	

0 BC	2500 BC	2000 BC	1500 BC	1000 BC	500 BC

	2100–1650 The Bronze Age reaches Britain. Immigration of the Beaker People, who make bronze implements and build ritual temples	*Chieftain's bronze sceptre (1700 BC)* **1200** Small, self-sufficient villages start to appear		**150** Tribes from Gaul begin to migrate to Britain	

Roman Britain

THROUGHOUT the 350-year Roman occupation, Britain was ruled as a colony. After the defeat of rebellious local tribes, such as Boadicea's Iceni, the Romans remained an unassimilated occupying power. Their legacy is in military and civil construction: forts, walls, towns and public buildings. Their long, straight roads, built for easy movement of troops, are still a feature of the landscape.

Roman jasper seal

Cavalry Sports Helmet
Found in Lancashire, it was used in tournaments by horsemen. Cavalry races and other sports were held in amphitheatres near towns.

Silver Jug
This 3rd-century jug, the earliest known silver item with Christian symbols, was excavated near Peterborough.

Exercise corridor

Main baths

Fishbourne Palace was built at the site of a natural harbour and ships could moor here.

Entrance hall

Hadrian's Wall
Started in 120 as a defence against the Scots; it marked the northern frontier of the Roman Empire and was guarded by 17 forts housing over 18,500 foot-soldiers and cavalry.

Mithras
This head of the god Mithras was found on the London site of a temple devoted to the cult of Mithraism. The sect demanded of its Roman followers loyalty and discipline.

TIMELINE

54 BC Julius Caesar lands in Britain but withdraws

Julius Caesar (c.102–44 BC)

AD 61 Boadicea rebels against Romans and burns their towns, including St Albans and Colchester, but is defeated *(see p203)*

AD 70 Romans conquer Wales and the North

Boadicea (1st century), Queen of the Iceni

140–143 Romans occupy southern Scotland and build Antonine Wall to mark the frontier

55 BC	AD 1	AD 50		150

AD 43 Claudius invades; Britain becomes part of the Roman Empire

AD 78–84 Agricola advances into Scotland, then retreats

120 Emperor Hadrian builds a wall on the border with Scotland

Flavian Mosaic

Roman floors of the 1st century used patterns in black and white stone. More mosaics survive at Fishbourne than at any other British site.

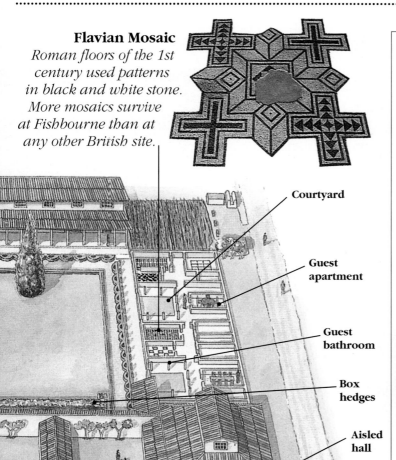

Courtyard

Guest apartment

Guest bathroom

Box hedges

Aisled hall

WHERE TO SEE ROMAN BRITAIN

Many of Britain's main towns and cities were established by the Romans and have Roman remains, including York *(see pp470–71)*, Chester *(see pp350–51)*, St Albans *(see p250)*, Colchester *(see p213)*, Bath *(see pp282–3)*, Lincoln *(see pp390–91)* and London *(see pp74–125)*. Several Roman villas were built in southern England, favoured for its mild climate and proximity to Europe.

The Roman baths in Bath
(see pp284–5), *known as Aquae Sulis, were built between the 1st and 4th centuries around a natural hot spring.*

FISHBOURNE PALACE

Built during the 1st century for Cogidubnus, a pro-Roman governor, the palace (here reconstructed) had sophisticated functions such as under-floor heating and indoor plumbing for baths *(see p171)*.

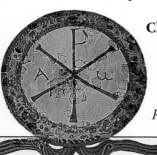

Chi-Rho Symbol

This early Christian symbol is from a 3rd-century fresco at Lullingstone Roman villa in Kent.

Battersea Shield

Found in the Thames near Battersea, the shield bears Celtic symbols and was probably made at about the time of the first Roman invasion. Archaeologists suspect it may have been lost by a warrior while crossing the river, or offered as a sacrifice to one of the many river gods. It is now at the British Museum (see pp112–13).

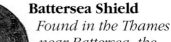

---

206 Tribes from northern Scotland attack Hadrian's Wall

254 St Alban is beheaded, and becomes Britain's first Christian martyr

Aberlemno Pictish stone in Scotland

410 Romans withdraw from Britain

| 200 | 250 | 300 | 350 | 400 |

306 Roman troops in York declare Constantine emperor

350–69 Border raids by Picts and Scots

440–450 Invasions of Angles, Saxons and Jutes

209 Septimius Severus arrives from Rome with reinforcements

Anglo-Saxon Kingdoms

**King Canute
(1016–35)**

BY THE MID-5TH CENTURY, Angles and Saxons from Germany had started to raid the eastern shores of Britain. Increasingly they decided to settle, and within 100 years Saxon kingdoms, including Wessex, Mercia and Northumbria, were established over the entire country. Viking raids throughout the 8th and 9th centuries were largely contained, but in 1066, the last invasion of England saw William the Conqueror from Normandy defeat the Anglo-Saxon King Harold at the Battle of Hastings. William then went on to assume control of the whole country.

Viking Axe
The principal weapons of the Viking warriors were spear, axe and sword. They were skilled metal-workers with an eye for decoration, as seen in this axe-head from a Copenhagen museum.

Vikings on a Raiding Expedition
Scandinavian boat-building skills were in advance of anything known in Britain. People were terrified by these large, fast boats with their intimidating figureheads, which sailed up the Thames and along the coasts.

ANGLO-SAXON CALENDAR

These scenes from a chronicle of seasons, made just before the Norman invasion, show life in late Anglo-Saxon Britain. At first people lived in small farming communities, but by the 7th century towns began to spring up and trade increased. Saxon kings were supported by nobles but most of the population were free peasants.

TIMELINE

c.470–495 Saxons and Angles settle in Essex, Sussex and East Anglia	**c.556** Saxons move across Britain and set up seven kingdoms		*St Augustine (d.604)*	**730–821** Supremacy of Mercia, whose king, Offa (d.796), builds a dyke along the Mercia–Wales border
			635 St Aidan establishes a monastery on Lindisfarne	

450	500	550	600	650	700	75(

450 Saxons first settle in Kent	**563** St Columba lands on Iona		**617–85** Supremacy of Northumbrian kingdom	
		597 St Augustine sent by Rome to convert English to Christianity	*Mercian coin which bears the name of King Offa*	

Ox-drawn plough for tilling

Minstrels entertaining at a feast

Hawks, used to kill game

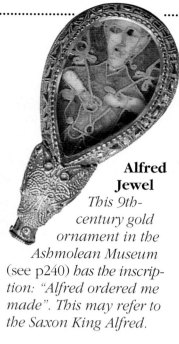

Alfred Jewel

This 9th-century gold ornament in the Ashmolean Museum (see p240) has the inscription: "Alfred ordered me made". This may refer to the Saxon King Alfred.

Edward the Confessor

In 1042, Edward – known as "the Confessor" because of his piety – became king. He died in 1066 and William of Normandy claimed the throne.

Harold's Death

This 14th-century illustration depicts the victorious William of Normandy after King Harold was killed with an arrow in his eye. The Battle of Hastings (see p181) was the last invasion of Britain.

WHERE TO SEE ANGLO-SAXON BRITAIN

The best collection of Saxon artefacts is from a burial ship unearthed at Sutton Hoo in Suffolk in 1938 and now on display at the British Museum *(see pp112–13)*. There are fine Saxon churches at Bradwell in Essex and Bosham in Sussex *(see p171)*. In York the Viking town of Jorvik has been excavated *(see pp470–71)* and actual relics are shown alongside models of people and dwellings.

The Saxon church *of St Laurence (see p279) was built in the late 8th century.*

Legend of King Arthur

Arthur is thought to have been a chieftain who fought the Saxons in the early 6th century. Legends of his knights' exploits appeared in 1155 (see p315).

800	850	900	950	1000	1050	1100

802–839 After the death of Cenwulf (821), Wessex gains control over most of England

867 Northumbria falls to the Vikings

An invading Norman ship

1016 Danish King Canute *(see p171)* seizes English crown

878 King Alfred defeats Vikings but allows them to settle in eastern England

843 Kenneth McAlpin becomes king of all Scotland

926 Eastern England, the Danelaw, is reconquered by the Saxons

1042 The Anglo-Saxon Edward the Confessor becomes king (d.1066)

1066 William of Normandy claims the throne, and defeats Harold at the Battle of Hastings. He is crowned at Westminster

c.793 Lindisfarne sacked by Viking invaders; first Viking raid on Scotland about a year later

The Middle Ages

Noblemen stag hunting

REMAINS OF Norman castles on English hill tops bear testimony to the military might used by the invaders to sustain their conquest – although Wales and Scotland resisted for centuries. The Normans operated a feudal system, creating an aristocracy that treated native Anglo-Saxons as serfs. The ruling class spoke French until the 13th century, when it mixed with the Old English used by the peasants. The medieval church's power is shown in the cathedrals that grace British cities today.

Magna Carta
To protect themselves and the church from arbitrary taxation, the powerful English barons compelled King John to sign a "great charter" in 1215 (see p253). This laid the foundations for an independent legal system.

Craft Skills
An illustration from a 14th-century manuscript depicts a weaver and a copper-beater – two of the trades that created a wealthy class of artisans.

Becket is received into heaven.

Henry II's knights
murder Becket in Canterbury Cathedral.

MURDER OF THOMAS À BECKET
The struggle between church and king for ultimate control of the country was brought to a head by the murder of Becket, the Archbishop of Canterbury. After Becket's canonization in 1173, Canterbury became a major centre of pilgrimage.

Ecclesiastical Art
Nearly all medieval art had religious themes, such as this window at Canterbury Cathedral (see pp188–9) depicting Jeroboam.

Black Death
A plague swept Britain and Europe several times in the 14th century, killing millions of people. This illustration, in a religious tract, produced around 100 years later, represents death taking its heavy toll.

TIMELINE

1071 Hereward the Wake, leader of the Anglo-Saxon resistance, defeated at Ely

1154 Henry II, the first Plantagenet king, demolishes castles, and exacts money from barons instead of military service

1170 Archbishop of Canterbury, Thomas à Becket, is murdered by four knights after quarrelling with Henry II

1100	1150	1200	1250

1086 The *Domesday Book*, a survey of every manor in England, is compiled for tax purposes

Domesday Book

1215 Barons compel King John to sign the *Magna Carta*

1256 Fi
Parliament
inclu
ordina
citize

Battle of Agincourt

In 1415, Henry V took an army to France to claim its throne. This 15th-century chronicle depicts Henry beating the French army at Agincourt.

The university cities of Oxford *(pp238–9)* and Cambridge *(pp220–21)* contain the largest concentrations of Gothic buildings. Magnificent medieval cathedrals rise high above many historic cities, among them Lincoln *(p390)* and York *(pp470–73)*. Both cities still retain at least part of their ancient street pattern. Military architecture is best seen in Wales *(pp512–13)* with the formidable border castles of Edward I.

All Souls College *in Oxford (see p242), which only takes graduates, is a superb blend of medieval and later architecture.*

This casket (1190), in a private collection, is said to have contained Becket's remains.

Becket takes his place in Heaven after his canonization.

Two clergymen look on in horror at Becket's murder.

Richard III

Richard, shown in this 16th-century painting, became king during the Wars of the Roses: a bitter struggle for power between two factions of the royal family – the houses of York and Lancaster.

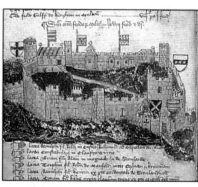

Castle Life

Every section of a castle was allotted to a baron whose soldiers helped defend it. This 14th-century illustration shows the coats of arms (see p30) of the barons for each area.

John Wycliffe *(1329–84)*

This painting by Ford Madox Brown (1821–93) shows Wycliffe with the Bible he translated into English to make it accessible to everyone.

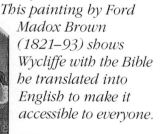

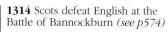

1282–3 Edward I conquers Wales

1314 Scots defeat English at the Battle of Bannockburn *(see p574)*

1348 Europe's population halved by Black Death

1387 Chaucer starts writing the *Canterbury Tales (see p188)*

Geoffrey Chaucer (c.1345–1400)

1485 Battle of Bosworth ends Wars of the Roses

| 1300 | 1350 | 1400 | 1450 |

1296 Edward I invades Scotland but Scots resist stoutly

Edward I (1239–1307)

1381 Peasants' revolt after the imposition of a poll tax on everyone in the country over 14

1415 English victory at Agincourt

1453 End of Hundred Years' War against France

Tudor Renaissance

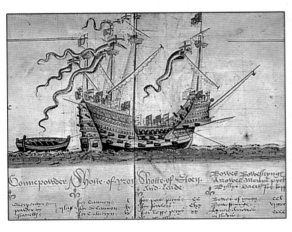

Hawking, a popular pastime

AFTER YEARS OF DEBILITATING civil war, the Tudor monarchs established peace and national self-confidence, reflected in the split from the church of Rome – due to Henry VIII's divorce from Catherine of Aragon – and the consequent closure of the monasteries. Henry's daughter, Mary I, tried to re-establish Catholicism but under her half-sister, Elizabeth I, the Protestant church secured its position. Overseas exploration began, provoking clashes with other European powers seeking to exploit the New World. The Renaissance in arts and learning spread from Europe to Britain, with playwright William Shakespeare adding his own unique contribution.

Curtains behind the queen are open to reveal scenes of the great English victory over the Spanish Armada in 1588.

Sea Power
Henry VIII laid the foundations of the powerful English navy. In 1545, his flagship, the Mary Rose *(see p169), sank before his eyes in Portsmouth harbour on its way to do battle with the French.*

Theatre
Some of Shakespeare's plays were first seen in purpose-built theatres such as the Globe (see p123) in south London.

The globe signifies that the queen reigns supreme far and wide.

Monasteries
With Henry VIII's split from Rome, England's religious houses, like Fountains Abbey (see pp454–5), were dissolved. Henry stole their riches and used them to finance his foreign policy.

TIMELINE

1497 John Colet denounces the corruption of the clergy, supported by Erasmus and Sir Thomas More

1533–4 Henry VIII divorces Catherine of Aragon and is excommunicated by the Pope. He forms the Church of England

1542–1567 Mary, Queen of Scots rules Scotland

1490 — **1510** — **1530**

1497 John Cabot *(see p280)* becomes the first European to reach Newfoundland

1513 English defeat Scots at Flodden *(see p574)*

Henry VIII (1491–1547)

1535 Act of Union with Wales

1536–40 Dissolution of the Monasteries

1549 First Book of Common Prayer introduced

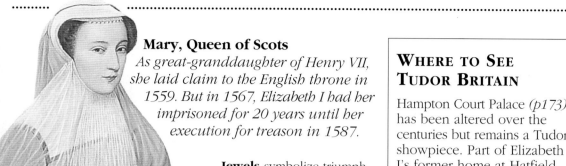

Mary, Queen of Scots
As great-granddaughter of Henry VII, she laid claim to the English throne in 1559. But in 1567, Elizabeth I had her imprisoned for 20 years until her execution for treason in 1587.

Jewels symbolize triumph.

WHERE TO SEE TUDOR BRITAIN

Hampton Court Palace *(p173)* has been altered over the centuries but remains a Tudor showpiece. Part of Elizabeth I's former home at Hatfield *(p249)* still survives. In Kent, Leeds Castle, Knole *(pp190–91)* and Hever Castle *(p191)* all have connections with Tudor royalty. Burghley House *(pp392–3)* and Hardwick Hall *(p336)*, both Midlands mansions, retain their 16th-century character.

This astronomical clock *at Hampton Court (see p173), with its intriguing zodiac symbols, was installed in 1540 by Henry VIII.*

DEFEAT OF THE ARMADA
Spain was England's main rival for supremacy on the seas, and in 1588 Philip II sent 100 powerfully armed galleons towards England, bent on invasion. The English fleet – under Lord Howard, Francis Drake, John Hawkins and Martin Frobisher – sailed from Plymouth and destroyed the Spanish navy in a famous victory. This commemorative portrait of Elizabeth I by George Gower (d.1596) celebrates the triumph.

Protestant Martyrs
Catholic Mary I reigned from 1553 to 1558. Protestants who opposed her rule were burned, such as these six churchmen at Canterbury in 1555.

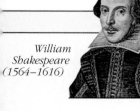

William Shakespeare (1564–1616)

1570 Sir Francis Drake's first voyage to the West Indies

1584 Sir Walter Raleigh tries to colonize Virginia after Drake's first unsuccessful attempt

1591 First play by Shakespeare performed

1600 East India Company founded, beginning British involvement on the Indian continent

| 1570 | 1590 |

1553 Death of Edward VI; throne passes to the Catholic Mary I

1559 Mary, Queen of Scots lays claim to English throne

1558 Elizabeth I ascends the throne

1587 Execution of Mary, Queen of Scots on the orders of Elizabeth I

1588 Defeat of the Spanish Armada

Sir Walter Raleigh (1552–1618)

1603 Union of Crowns. James VI of Scotland becomes James I of England

Stuart Britain

THE END of Elizabeth I's reign signalled the start of internal turmoil. The throne passed to James I, whose belief that kings ruled by divine right provoked clashes with Parliament. Under his son, Charles I, the conflict escalated into Civil War that ended with his execution. In 1660 Charles II regained the throne, but after his death James II was ousted for Catholic leanings. Protestantism was reaffirmed with the reign of William and Mary, who suppressed the Catholic Jacobites *(see p575).*

A 17th-century barber's bowl

Science
Sir Isaac Newton (1642–1727) invented this reflecting telescope, laying the foundation for a greater understanding of the universe, including the law of gravity.

Charles I stayed silent at his trial.

Oliver Cromwell
A strict Protestant and a passionate champion of the rights of Parliament, he led the victorious Parliamentary forces in the Civil War. He became Lord Protector of the Commonwealth from 1653 to 1658.

On the way to his death, the king wore two shirts for warmth, so onlookers should not think he was shivering with fright.

Theatre
After the Restoration in 1660, when Parliament restored the monarchy, theatre thrived. Plays were performed on temporary outdoor stages.

EXECUTION OF CHARLES I
Cromwell was convinced there would be no peace until the king was dead. At his trial for treason, Charles refused to recognize the authority of the court and offered no defence. He faced his death with dignity on 30 January 1649, the only English king to be executed. His death was followed by a republic known as the Commonwealth.

TIMELINE

1605 "Gunpowder Plot" to blow up Parliament thwarted

1614 "Addled Parliament" refuses to vote money for James I

1620 Pilgrim Fathers sail in the *Mayflower* to New England

1642 Civil War breaks out

1653–8 Cromwell rules as Lord Protector

| 1625 | 1650 |

James I (1566–1625)

1611 New translation of Bible published, known as King James Version

1638 Scots sign National Covenant, opposing Charles I's Catholic leanings

1649 Charles I executed outside Banqueting House and Commonwealth declared by Parliament

1660 Restoration of the monarchy under Charles II

Restoration of the Monarchy

This silk embroidery celebrates the fact that Charles II escaped his father's fate by hiding in an oak tree. There was joy at his return from exile in France.

The headless body kneels by the block.

The axeman holds the severed head of Charles I.

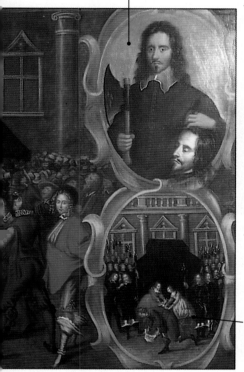

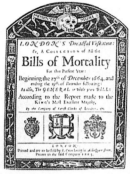

Plague

Bills of mortality showed the weekly deaths as bubonic plague swept London in 1665. Up to 100,000 Londoners died.

Hatfield House (p249) *is a splendid Jacobean mansion.*

Onlookers soaked up the king's blood with their handkerchiefs to have a memento.

Anatomy

By dissecting corpses, physicians began to gain an understanding of the working of the human body – a crucial step towards modern surgery and medicine.

Pilgrim Fathers

In 1620 a group of Puritans sailed to America. They forged good relations with the native Indians; here they are shown being visited by the chief of the Pokanokets.

1665–6 Great Plague

The Great Fire of London

1707 Act of Union with Scotland

1666 Great Fire of London

1688 The Glorious Revolution: Catholic James II deposed by Parliament

1675

1700

1690 Battle of the Boyne: William's English/Dutch army defeats James II's Irish/French army

1692 Glencoe Massacre of Jacobites (Stuart supporters) by William III's forces

William III (1689–1702)

Georgian Britain

THE 18TH CENTURY saw Britain, now recovered from the trauma of its Civil War, develop as a commercial and industrial powerhouse. London became a centre of banking, and a mercantile and professional class grew up. Continuing supremacy at sea laid the foundations of an empire; steam engines, canals and railways heralded the Industrial Revolution. Growing confidence was reflected in stately architecture and elegant fashions but, as cities became more crowded, conditions for the underclass grew worse.

Actress Sarah Siddons (1785), Gainsborough

Slate became the preferred tile for Georgian buildings. Roofs became less steep to achieve an Italian look.

A row of sash windows is one of the most characteristic features of a Georgian house.

Battle of Bunker Hill
In 1775 American colonists rebelled against British rule. The British won this early battle in Massachusetts, but in 1783 Britain recognized the United States of America.

Oak was used in the best dwellings for doors and stairs, but pine was standard in most houses.

The saloon was covered in wallpaper, a cheaper alternative to hanging walls with tapestries or fabrics.

The drawing room was richly ornamented and used for entertaining visitors.

The dining room was used for all family meals.

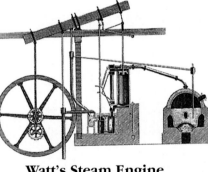

Watt's Steam Engine
The Scottish engineer James Watt (1736–1819) patented his engine in 1769 and then developed it for locomotion.

Lord Horatio Nelson
Nelson (see p31) became a hero after his death at the Battle of Trafalgar fighting the French.

Steps led to the servants' entrance in the basement.

TIMELINE

1720 "South Sea Bubble" bursts: many speculators ruined in securities fraud

1746 Bonnie Prince Charlie *(see p695)*, Jacobite claimant to throne, defeated at the Battle of Culloden

1715	1730	1745	1760

1714 George, Elector of Hanover, succeeds Queen Anne, ending the Stuart dynasty and giving Britain a German-speaking monarch

1721 Robert Walpole (1646–1745) becomes the first Prime Minister

George I (1660–1727)

The Dutch Bubblers

Satirical engraving about the South Sea Bubble, 1720

1757 Britain's first canal completed

Canal Barge *(1827)*
Canals were a cheap way to carry the new industrial goods but were gradually superseded by railways during the 19th century.

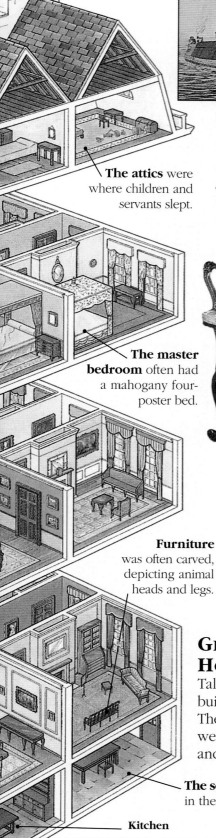

The attics were where children and servants slept.

The master bedroom often had a mahogany four-poster bed.

Furniture was often carved, depicting animal heads and legs.

Chippendale Armchair *(1760)*
Thomas Chippendale (1718–79) designed elegant furniture in a style still popular today.

WHERE TO SEE GEORGIAN BRITAIN

Bath *(see pp282–5)* and Edinburgh *(see pp582–605)* are two of Britain's best-preserved Georgian towns. The Building of Bath Museum in Bath *(see p285)* has a real Georgian flavour and Brighton's Royal Pavilion *(see pp178–9)* is a Regency extravaganza by John Nash.

Charlotte Square *in Edinburgh has fine examples of Georgian architecture.*

Hogarth's Gin Lane
Conditions in London's slums shocked William Hogarth (1694–1764), who made prints like this to urge social reform.

GEORGIAN TOWN HOUSE

Tall, terraced dwellings were built to house wealthy families. The main architects of the time were Robert Adam *(see p28)* and John Nash *(see p111).*

The servants lived and worked in the basement during the day.

Kitchen

	1788 First convict ships are sent to Australia	**1811–17** Riots against growing unemployment	**1815** Duke of Wellington beats Napoleon at Waterloo	*Caricature of Wellington (1769–1852)*
1776 American Declaration of Independence	**1805** The British, led by Lord Nelson, beat Napoleon's French fleet at Battle of Trafalgar			

775	1790	1805	1820	
	1783 Steam-powered cotton mill invented by Sir Richard Arkwright (1732–92)	**1807** Abolition of slave trade	**1811** Prince of Wales made Regent during George III's madness	**1825** Stockton to Darlington railway opens
				1829 Catholic Emancipation Act passed

Silver tureen, 1774

Victorian Britain

WHEN VICTORIA BECAME QUEEN in 1837, she was only 18. Britain was in the throes of its transformation from an agricultural country to the world's most powerful industrial nation. The growth of the Empire fuelled the country's confidence and opened up markets for Britain's manufactured goods. The accelerating growth of cities created problems of health and housing and a powerful Labour movement began to emerge. But by the end of Victoria's long and popular reign in 1901, conditions had begun to improve as more people got the vote and universal education was introduced.

Victoria and Disraeli, 1887

Florence Nightingale *(1820–1910) Known as the Lady with the Lamp, she nursed soldiers in the Crimean War and pioneered many improvements in army medical care.*

Glass walls and ceiling

Prefabricated girders

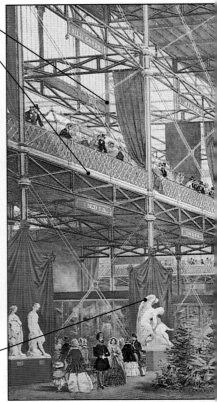

Newcastle Slum *(1880) Rows of cheap houses were built for an influx of workers to the major industrial cities. The awful conditions spread disease and social discontent.*

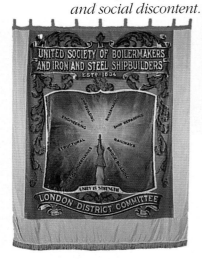

UNITED SOCIETY OF BOILERMAKERS AND IRON AND STEEL SHIPBUILDERS
ESTP 1834

LONDON DISTRICT COMMITTEE

As well as silk textiles exhibits included carriages, engines, jewels, glass, plants, cutlery and sculptures.

Union Banner *Trade unions were set up to protect industrial workers against unscrupulous employers.*

Ophelia by Sir John Everett Millais *(1829–96) The Pre-Raphaelite painters chose Romantic themes, reflecting a desire to escape industrial Britain.*

TIMELINE

1832 Great Reform Bill extends the vote to all male property owners

1841 London to Brighton railway makes resort accessible

Vase made for the Great Exhibition

1851 Great Exhibition

1867 Second Reform Act gives the vote to all male householders in town

1830	1840	1850	1860

1834 Tolpuddle Martyrs transported to Australia for forming a union

1833 Factory Act forbids employment of children for more than 48 hours per week

1854–6 Britain victorious against Russia in Crimean War

1863 Opening of the London Underground

Triumph of Steam and Electricity

This picture from the Illustrated London News *(1897) sums up the feeling of optimism engendered by industrial advances.*

Elm trees were incorporated into the building along with sparrows, and sparrow hawks to control them.

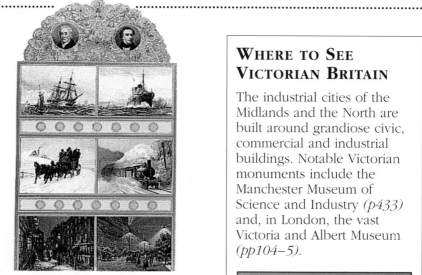

WHERE TO SEE VICTORIAN BRITAIN

The industrial cities of the Midlands and the North are built around grandiose civic, commercial and industrial buildings. Notable Victorian monuments include the Manchester Museum of Science and Industry *(p433)* and, in London, the vast Victoria and Albert Museum *(pp104–5).*

The Rotunda, Manchester *is a stately Victorian building.*

Cycling Craze
The bicycle, invented in 1865, became immensely popular with young people, as illustrated by this photograph of 1898.

GREAT EXHIBITION OF 1851

The brainchild of Prince Albert, Victoria's consort, the exhibition celebrated industry, technology and the expanding British Empire. It was the biggest of its kind held up till then. Between May and October, six million people visited Joseph Paxton's lavish crystal palace, in London's Hyde Park. Nearly 14,000 exhibitors brought 100,000 exhibits from all over the world. In 1852 it was moved to south London where it burned down in 1936.

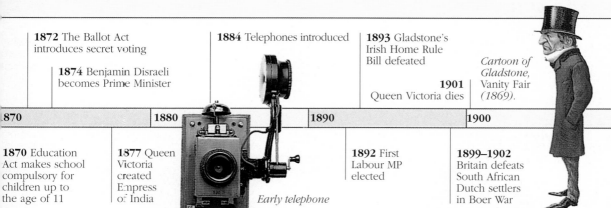

1872 The Ballot Act introduces secret voting

1874 Benjamin Disraeli becomes Prime Minister

1884 Telephones introduced

1893 Gladstone's Irish Home Rule Bill defeated

Cartoon of Gladstone, Vanity Fair *(1869).*

1901 Queen Victoria dies

1870   1880   1890   1900

1870 Education Act makes school compulsory for children up to the age of 11

1877 Queen Victoria created Empress of India

Early telephone

1892 First Labour MP elected

1899–1902 Britain defeats South African Dutch settlers in Boer War

Britain from 1900 to 1950

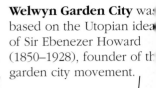

WHEN QUEEN VICTORIA'S REIGN ended in 1901, British society threw off many of its 19th-century inhibitions, and an era of gaiety and excitement began. This was interrupted by World War I. The economic troubles that ensued, which culminated in the Depression of the 1930s, brought misery to millions. In 1939 the ambitions of Germany provoked World War II. After emerging victorious from this conflict, Britain embarked on an ambitious programme of social, educational and health reform.

Playwright Noel Coward

Welwyn Garden City wa: based on the Utopian idea of Sir Ebenezer Howard (1850–1928), founder of th garden city movement.

Suffragettes
Women marched and chained themselves to railings in their effort to get the vote; many went to prison. Women over 30 won the vote in 1919.

The Roaring Twenties
Young flappers discarded the rigid social codes of their parents and instead dis-covered jazz, cocktails and the Charleston.

NEW TOWNS

A string of new towns was created on the outskirts of London, planned to give residents greenery and fresh air. Welwyn Garden City was originally founded in 1919 as a self-contained community, but fast rail links turned it into a base for London commuters.

World War I
British troops in Europe dug into deep trenches protected by barbed wire and machine guns, only metres from the enemy, in a war of attrition that cost the lives of 17 million.

Wireless
Invented by Guglielmo Marconi, radios brought news and entertainment into homes for the first time

---

TIMELINE

1903 Suffragette movement founded

1911 MPs are given a salary for the first time, allowing working men to be elected

1914–18 World War I

1924 F: Labc governme

Henry Asquith (1852–1928), Prime Minister

1905	1910	1915	1920

1908 Asquith's Liberal government introduces old age pensions

1919 Vote given to all women over 30

1922 First national radi service begin

Marching for Jobs

These men were among thousands who marched for their jobs after being put out of work in the 1920s. The stock market crash of 1929 and the ensuing Depression caused even more unemployment.

Garden cities
ll had trees,
onds and
pen spaces.

World War II

German night-time air raids targeted transport, military and industrial sites and cities, such as Sheffield, in what was known as the "Blitz".

Family Motoring

By the middle of the century, more families could afford to buy mass-produced automobiles, like the 1950s Hillman Minx pictured in this advertisement.

Modern Homes

Labour-saving devices, such as the vacuum cleaner, invented by William Hoover in 1908, were very popular. This was due to the virtual disappearance of domestic servants, as women took jobs outside the home.

Cheap housing and the promise of a cleaner environment attracted many people to these new cities.

1926 General Strike		**1936** Abdication of Edward VIII	**1944** Education Act: school leaving age raised to 15; grants provided for university students	**1948** National Health Service introduced
Edward VIII (1894–1972) and Wallis Simpson (1896–1986)				**1947** Independence for India and Pakistan
1930	**1935**		**1940**	**1945**
1929 Stock market crashes	**1936** First scheduled television service begins	**1939–45** Winston Churchill leads Britain to victory in World War II		**1945** Majority Labour government; nationalization of railways, road haulage, civil aviation, Bank of England, gas, electricity and steel
1928 Votes for all men and women over 21		*Food ration book*		

Britain Today

WITH THE DEPRIVATIONS of war receding, Britain entered the Swinging Sixties, an explosion of youth culture characterized by the mini-skirt and the emergence of pop groups. The Age of Empire came to an end as most colonies gained independence by the 1970s – although Britain went to war again in 1982 when Argentina sought to annexe the tiny Falkland Islands.

People were on the move; immigration from the former colonies enriched British culture – though it also gave rise to social problems – and increasing prosperity allowed millions of people to travel abroad. Britain joined the European Community in 1973, and forged a more tangible link when the Channel Tunnel opened in 1994.

Designer Vivienne Westwood and Naomi Campbell

1960s The mini-skirt takes British fashion to new heights of daring – and Flower Power arrives from California

1951 Winston Churchill comes back as Prime Minister as Conservatives win general election

1958 Campaign for Nuclear Disarmament launched, reflecting young people's fear of global annihilation

1965 Death penalty is abolished

1950	1955	1960	1965	1970
1950	1955	1960	1965	1970

1953 Elizabeth II crowned in first televised Coronation

1963 The Beatles pop group from Liverpool captures the spirit of the age with numerous chart-topping hits

1959 First motorway, the M1, built from London to the Midlands

1951 Festival of Britain lifts postwar spirits

1957 First immigrants arrive from the Caribbean by boat

VOTE!

...GET BRITAIN OUT

1973 After years of negotiation, Britain joins the European Community

1970s The outlandish clothes, hair and make-up of Punk Rockers shock the country

1990 Mrs Thatcher forced to resign by Conservative MPs; replaced by John Major

1991 Britain's tallest building, Canada Tower *(see p135)*, erected as part of the huge Docklands development – London's new financial centre

1982 British troops set sail to drive the Argentinians from the British-owned Falkland Islands

1992 Conservative Government elected for fourth term – a record for this century

1997 New Labour ends 18 years of Conservative government

1976 Supersonic Concorde makes first commercial flight

1984 Year-long miners' strike fails to stop pit closures and heralds decline in trade union power

5	1980	1985	1990	1995	2000

5	1980	1985	1990	1995	2000

1981 Charles, Prince of Wales, marries Lady Diana Spencer in "fairytale" wedding at St Paul's Cathedral

1999 Formation of Scottish Parliament and Welsh Assembly

1997 Funeral of Princess Diana

5 Drilling ns for h Sea oil

1979 The "Iron Lady" Margaret Thatcher becomes Britain's first woman Prime Minister; her right-wing Conservative Government privatizes several state-owned industries

1985 Concern for famine in Africa gives rise to giant Live Aid pop concert to raise money for the starving

1994 Channel Tunnel opens to give direct rail link between Britain and Continental Europe

GREAT BRITAIN THROUGH THE YEAR

Film festival sign

EVERY BRITISH SEASON has its particular charms. Most major sights are open all year round, but many secondary attractions may be closed in winter. The weather is changeable in all seasons and the visitor is as likely to experience a crisp, sunny February day as to be caught in a cold, heavy shower in July. Long periods of adverse weather and extremes of temperature are rare. Spring is characterized by daffodils and bluebells, summer by roses and autumn by the vivid colours of changing leaves. In wintertime, country vistas are visible through the bare branches of the trees. Annual events and ceremonies, many stemming from age-old traditions, reflect the attributes of the seasons.

Bluebells in spring in Angrove woodland, Wiltshire

SPRING

As THE DAYS get longer and warmer, the countryside starts to come alive. At Easter many stately homes and gardens open their gates to visitors for the first time, and during the week before Whit Sunday, or Whitsun (the seventh Sunday after Easter), the Chelsea Flower Show takes place. This is the focal point of the gardening year and spurs on the nation's gardeners to prepare their summer displays. Outside the capital, many music and arts festivals mark the middle months of the year.

MARCH

Ideal Home Exhibition *(second week)*, Earl's Court, London. New products and ideas for the home.
Crufts Dog Show *(second week)*, National Exhibition Centre, Birmingham.
International Book Fair *(third week)*, Olympia, London.
St Patrick's Day *(17 March)*. Musical events in major cities celebrate the feast day of Ireland's patron saint.

APRIL

Maundy Thursday (Thursday before Easter), the Queen gives money to pensioners.
St George's Day *(23 April)*, English patron saint's day.
British International Antiques Fair *(last week)*, National Exhibition Centre, Birmingham.

Water garden exhibited at the Chelsea Flower Show

MAY

Furry Dancing Festival *(8 May)*, Helston, Cornwall. Spring celebration *(see p312)*.
Well-dressing festivals *(Ascension Day)*, Tissington, Derbyshire *(see p387)*.
Chelsea Flower Show *(mid-May)*, Royal Hospital, London.
Brighton Festival *(last three weeks)*. Performing arts.
Glyndebourne Festival Opera Season *(mid-May–end Aug)*, near Lewes, East Sussex. Opera productions.
International Highland Games *(last weekend)*, Blair Atholl, Scotland.

Yeomen of the Guard conducting the Maundy money ceremony

SUMMER

LIFE MOVES OUTDOORS in the summer months. Cafés and restaurants place tables on the pavements and pub customers take their drinks outside. The Queen holds garden parties for privileged guests at Buckingham Palace while, more modestly, village fêtes – a combination of a carnival and street party – are organized. Beaches and swimming pools become crowded and office workers picnic in city parks at lunch. The rose, England's national flower, bursts into bloom in millions of gardens. Cultural treats include open-air theatre per-formances, outdoor concerts, the Proms in London, the National Eisteddfod in Wales, Glyndebourne's opera festival, and Edin-burgh's festival of the performing arts.

Glastonbury music festival, a major event attracting thousands of people

Deck chair at Brighton

JUNE

Royal Academy Summer Exhibitions *(Jun–Aug)*. Large and varied London show of new work by many artists.
Bath International Festival *(19 May–4 Jun)*, various venues. Arts events.
Beaumaris Festival *(27 May–4 Jun)*, varicus venues. Concerts, craft fairs plus fringe activities.
Trooping the Colour *(Sat closest to 10 Jun)*, Whitehall,

London. The Queen's official birthday parade.
Glastonbury Festival *(23–25 June)*, Somerset.
Aldeburgh Festival *(second and third weeks)*, Suffolk. Arts festival with concerts and opera.
Royal Highland Show *(third week)*, Ingliston, near Edin-burgh. Scotland's agricultural show.
Leeds Castle *(last week)*. Open-air concerts.
Glasgow International Jazz Festival *(last weekend)*. Various venues.

JULY

Royal Show *(first week)*, near Kenilworth, Warwickshire. National agricultural show.
International Eisteddfod *(first week)*, Llangollen, North Wales. International music and dance competition *(see p530)*.
Hampton Court Flower Show *(early July)*, Hampton Court Palace, Surrey.
Summer Music Festival *(third weekend)*, Stourhead, Wiltshire.
Royal Tournament *(third and fourth weeks)*, Earl's Court, London. Displays by the armed forces.
Cambridge Folk Festival *(last weekend)*. Music festival with top international artists.
Royal Welsh Show *(last weekend)*, Builth Wells, Wales. Agricultural show.
International Festival of Folk Arts *(late Jul–early Aug)*, Sidmouth, Devon *(see p323)*.

AUGUST

Royal National Eisteddfod *(early in month)*. Traditional arts competitions, in Welsh *(see p509)*. Various locations.

Assessment of sheep at the Royal Welsh Show, Builth Wells

Reveller in bright costume at the Notting Hill Carnival

Henry Wood Promenade Concerts *(mid-Jul–mid-Sep)*, Royal Albert Hall, London. Famous concert series popu-larly known as the Proms.
Edinburgh International Festival *(mid-Aug–mid-Sep)*. The largest festival of theatre, dance and music in the world *(see p590–91)*.
Edinburgh Festival Fringe. Alongside the festival, there are 400 shows a day.
Brecon Jazz *(mid-Aug)*, jazz festival in Brecon, Wales.
Beatles Festival *(last week-end)*, Liverpool. Music and entertainment related to the Fab Four *(see p435)*.
Notting Hill Carnival *(last weekend)*, London. West Indian street carnival with floats, bands and stalls.

Boxes of apples from the autumn harvest

AUTUMN

AFTER THE HEADY escapism of summer, the start of the new season is marked by the various party political conferences held in October and the royal opening of Parliament. All over the country on 5 November, bonfires are lit and fireworks let off to celebrate the foiling of an attempt to blow up the Houses of Parliament by Guy Fawkes and his co-conspirators in 1605. Cornfields become golden, trees turn fiery yellow through to russet and orchards

Shot putting at Braemar

are heavy with apples and other autumn fruits. In churches throughout the country, thanksgiving festivals mark the harvest. The shops stock up for the run-up to Christmas, their busiest time of the year.

SEPTEMBER

Blackpool Illuminations *(beg Sep–end Oct)*. A 5 mile (8 km) spectacle of lighting along Blackpool's seafront.
Royal Highland Gathering *(first Sat)*, Braemar, Scotland. Kilted clansmen from all over the country toss cabers, shot putt, dance and play the bagpipes. The royal family usually attends.
International Sheepdog Trials *(14–16 Sep)*, all over Britain, with venues changing from year to year.
Great Autumn Flower Show *(third weekend)*, Harrogate, N Yorks. Displays by nurserymen and national flower organizations.
Horse of the Year Show *(last weekend)*, Wembley, London *(see p71)*.
Oyster Festival *(Sat at beginning of oyster season)*, Colchester. Lunch hosted by the mayor to celebrate the start of the oyster season.

OCTOBER

Harvest Festivals *(whole month)*, all over Britain especially in farming areas.
Nottingham Goose Fair *(second weekend)*. One of Britain's oldest traditional fairs now has a funfair.
Canterbury Festival *(second and third weeks)*. Music, drama and the arts.
Aldeburgh Britten Festival *(third weekend)*. Concerts with music by Britten *(see p211)* and other composers.
Hallowe'en *(31 Oct)*, "trick or treat" games countrywide.

Procession leading to the state opening of Parliament

NOVEMBER

Opening of Parliament *(Oct or Nov)*. The Queen goes from Buckingham Palace to Westminster in a state coach, to open the new parliamentary session.
Lord Mayor's Procession and Show *(second Sat)*. Parade in the City, London.
Remembrance Day *(second Sun)*. Services and parades at the Cenotaph in Whitehall, London, and all over Britain.
RAC London to Brighton Veteran Car Rally *(first Sun)*. A 7am start from Hyde Park, London to Brighton, East Sussex.
Guy Fawkes Night *(5 Nov)*, fireworks and bonfires all over the country.
London Film Festival *(first two weeks)*. Forum for new films, various venues.
Regent Street Christmas Lights *(mid-Nov)*, London.

Fireworks over Edinburgh on Guy Fawkes Night

Winter landscape in the Scottish Highlands, near Glen Coe

WINTER

BRIGHTLY COLOURED fairy lights and Christmas trees decorate Britain's principal shopping streets as shoppers rush to buy their seasonal gifts. Carol services are held in churches across the country, and pantomime, a traditional entertainment for children deriving from the Victorian music hall, fills theatres in major towns.

Brightly lit Christmas tree at the centre of Trafalgar Square

Many offices close between Christmas and the New Year. Shops reopen for the January sales on 27 December – a paradise for bargain-hunters.

DECEMBER

Christmas Tree *(first Thu)*, Trafalgar Square, London. The tree is donated by the people of Norway and is lit by the Mayor of Oslo; this is followed by carol singing.
Carol concerts *(whole month)*, all over Britain.
Grand Christmas Parade *(beg Dec)*, London. Parade with floats to celebrate myth of Santa Claus.
Midnight Mass *(24 Dec)*, in churches everywhere around Britain.
Allendale Baal Festival *(31 Dec)*, Northumberland. Parade by villagers with burning tar barrels on their heads to celebrate the New Year.

Sprig of holly

JANUARY

Hogmanay *(1 Jan)*, Scottish New Year celebrations.
Burns Night *(25 Jan)*. Scots everywhere celebrate poet Robert Burns' birth with poetry, feasting and drinking.

FEBRUARY

Chinese New Year *(late Jan or early Feb)*. Lion dances, firecrackers and processions in Chinatown, London.

PUBLIC HOLIDAYS

New Year's Day (1 Jan).
2 Jan (Scotland only).
Easter weekend (March or April). In England it begins on **Good Friday** and ends on **Easter Monday**; in Scotland there is no Easter Monday holiday.
May Day (usually first Mon in May).
Late Spring Bank Holiday (last Mon in May).
Bank Holiday (first Mon in August, Scotland only).
August Bank Holiday (last Mon in August, except Scotland).
Christmas and Boxing Day (25–26 December).

Morris dancing on May Day in Midhurst, Sussex

The Sporting Year

MANY OF THE WORLD's major competitive sports, including soccer, cricket and tennis, were invented in Britain. Originally devised as recreation for the wealthy, they have since entered the arena of mass entertainment. Some, however, such as the Royal Ascot race meeting and Wimbledon tennis tournament, are still valued as much for their social prestige as for the sport itself. Other delightful sporting events in Britain take place at a local level: village cricket, point-to-point racing and the Highland Games are all popular amateur events.

Ewan Thomas

Royal Ascot is the four day social highlight of the horse racing year. The high class of the thoroughbreds is matched by the high style of the fashions, with royalty attending.

Oxford and Cambridge Boat Race, first held in 1829 at Henley, has become a national event, with the two university eights now battling it out between Putney and Mortlake on the Thames.

FA Cup Final *at Wembley is the apex of the football season.*

Derby Day horse races, Epsom

January	February	March	April	May	June

Cheltenham Gold Cup steeplechase *(see p370)*

Grand National steeple- chase, Aintree *(see p434),* **Liverpool**

Rugby League Cup Final, Wembley

Embassy World Snooker Championships, Sheffield

Wimbledon Lawn Tennis Tournament is the world's most prestigious lawn tennis championship.

Six Nations Rugby Union is an annual contest between England (right), France, Ireland, Scotland, Italy and Wales (left). This league-based competition runs through the winter months, ending in March.

London Marathon attracts thousands of long-distance runners, from the world's best to fancy-dressed fund raisers.

Henley Royal Regatta (see p253) is an international rowing event that takes place on the River Thames. It is also a glamorous social occasion.

British Grand Prix, held at Silverstone, is Britain's round of the Formula One World Championship.

TICKETS AND TOUTS

For many big sporting events, the only official source of tickets is the club concerned. Booking agencies may offer hard-to-get tickets – though often at high prices. Unauthorized touts may lurk at popular events but their expensive tickets are not always valid. Check carefully.

Tickets for the Grand Prix

British Open Golf Championship, a major golf event, is held at one of several British courses. Here, Nick Faldo putts.

NatWest Trophy. This is the final, held over one or two days, of a season of competition to find the year's county cricket champions. It takes place at Lord's (see p131).

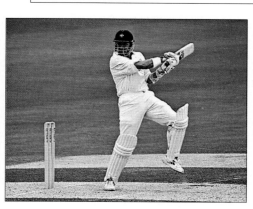

Cowes week (see p168), a yachting festival, covers all classes of racing.

Horse of the Year Show brings together top show-jumpers to compete on a tough indoor course (see p68).

Oxford versus Cambridge rugby union, Twickenham

August	September	October	November	December

European Showjumping Championships at Hickstead

Gold Cup Humber powerboat race, Hull

Braemar Highland Games (see p68)

British Figure Skating and Ice Dance Championships are a feast of elegance on ice (various venues).

Winmau World Masters Darts Championships

Cartier International Polo, at the Guards Club, Windsor (see p253), is one of the main events for this peculiarly British game, played mainly by royalty and army officers.

Steven Cousins

KEY TO SPORT SEASONS

- Cricket
- River fishing
- Football
- Hunting and shooting
- Rugby (union and league)
- Flat racing
- Jump racing
- Athletics – track and field
- Road running and cross-country
- Polo

The Climate of Great Britain

BRITAIN HAS A TEMPERATE CLIMATE. No region is far from the sea, which exerts a moderating influence on temperatures. Seldom are winter nights colder than -15° C, even in the far north, or summer days warmer than 30° C in the south and west: a much narrower range than in most European countries. Despite Britain's reputation, the average annual rainfall is quite low – less than 100 cm (40 inches) – and heavy rain is rare. The Atlantic coast is warmed by the Gulf Stream, making the west slightly warmer, though wetter, than the east.

Wick

Inverness

The Highlands and Islands

EDINBURGH

Glasgow

The Lowlands

Lan the

Liverpool

North Wales
Caernarfon

South and Mid-Wales

CARDIFF

Devon and Cornwall
Exeter

LANCASHIRE AND THE LAKES

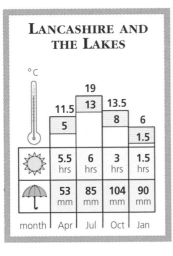

°C

	Apr	Jul	Oct	Jan
max	11.5	19	13.5	6
		13		
min	5		8	1.5
sun	5.5 hrs	6 hrs	3 hrs	1.5 hrs
rain	53 mm	85 mm	104 mm	90 mm

month | Apr | Jul | Oct | Jan

THE HEART OF ENGLAND

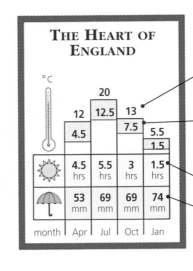

°C

	Apr	Jul	Oct	Jan
max	12	20	13	5.5
		12.5		
min	4.5		7.5	1.5
sun	4.5 hrs	5.5 hrs	3 hrs	1.5 hrs
rain	53 mm	69 mm	69 mm	74 mm

month | Apr | Jul | Oct | Jan

Average monthly maximum temperature

Average monthly minimum temperature

Average daily hours of sunshine

Average monthly rainfall

SOUTH AND MID-WALES

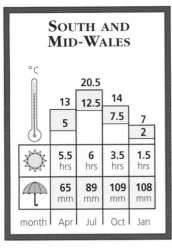

°C

	Apr	Jul	Oct	Jan
max	13	20.5	14	7
		12.5		
min	5		7.5	2
sun	5.5 hrs	6 hrs	3.5 hrs	1.5 hrs
rain	65 mm	89 mm	109 mm	108 mm

month | Apr | Jul | Oct | Jan

NORTH WALES

°C

	Apr	Jul	Oct	Jan
max	11	17	13.5	6
		11		
min	4.5		8	1
sun	3 hrs	3.5 hrs	2.5 hrs	1.5 hrs
rain	144 mm	206 mm	261 mm	252 mm

month | Apr | Jul | Oct | Jan

DEVON AND CORNWALL

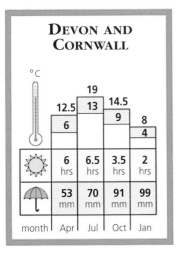

°C

	Apr	Jul	Oct	Jan
max	12.5	19	14.5	8
		13	9	
min	6			4
sun	6 hrs	6.5 hrs	3.5 hrs	2 hrs
rain	53 mm	70 mm	91 mm	99 mm

month | Apr | Jul | Oct | Jan

WEST COUNTRY

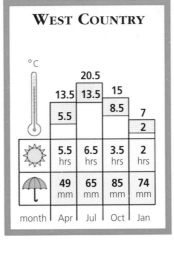

°C

	Apr	Jul	Oct	Jan
max	13.5	20.5	15	7
		13.5	8.5	
min	5.5			2
sun	5.5 hrs	6.5 hrs	3.5 hrs	2 hrs
rain	49 mm	65 mm	85 mm	74 mm

month | Apr | Jul | Oct | Jan

THAMES VALLEY

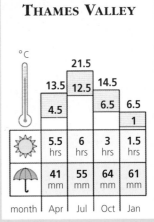

°C

	Apr	Jul	Oct	Jan
max	13.5	21.5	14.5	6.5
		12.5	6.5	
min	4.5			1
sun	5.5 hrs	6 hrs	3 hrs	1.5 hrs
rain	41 mm	55 mm	64 mm	61 mm

month | Apr | Jul | Oct | Jan

THE HIGHLANDS AND ISLANDS

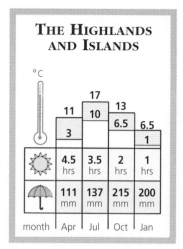

°C				
	11	17 10	13 6.5	6.5
	3			1
☀	4.5 hrs	3.5 hrs	2 hrs	1 hrs
☂	111 mm	137 mm	215 mm	200 mm
month	Apr	Jul	Oct	Jan

THE LOWLANDS

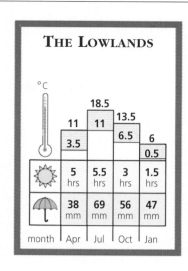

°C				
	11	18.5 11	13.5 6.5	6
	3.5			0.5
☀	5 hrs	5.5 hrs	3 hrs	1.5 hrs
☂	38 mm	69 mm	56 mm	47 mm
month	Apr	Jul	Oct	Jan

NORTHUMBRIA

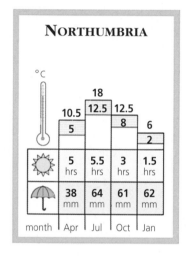

°C				
	10.5	18 12.5	12.5 8	6
	5			2
☀	5 hrs	5.5 hrs	3 hrs	1.5 hrs
☂	38 mm	64 mm	61 mm	62 mm
month	Apr	Jul	Oct	Jan

YORKSHIRE AND HUMBERSIDE

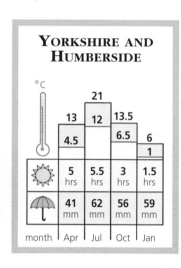

°C				
	13	21 12	13.5 6.5	6
	4.5			1
☀	5 hrs	5.5 hrs	3 hrs	1.5 hrs
☂	41 mm	62 mm	56 mm	59 mm
month	Apr	Jul	Oct	Jan

EAST MIDLANDS

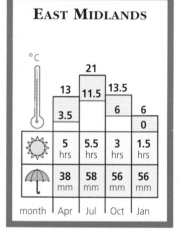

°C				
	13	21 11.5	13.5 6	6
	3.5			0
☀	5 hrs	5.5 hrs	3 hrs	1.5 hrs
☂	38 mm	58 mm	56 mm	56 mm
month	Apr	Jul	Oct	Jan

THE DOWNS AND CHANNEL COAST

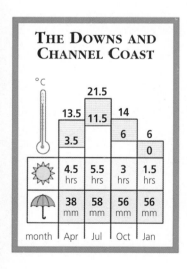

°C				
	13.5	21.5 11.5	14 6	6
	3.5			0
☀	4.5 hrs	5.5 hrs	3 hrs	1.5 hrs
☂	38 mm	58 mm	56 mm	56 mm
month	Apr	Jul	Oct	Jan

LONDON

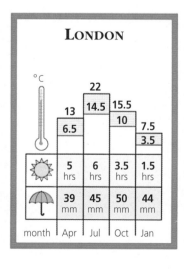

°C				
	13	22 14.5	15.5 10	7.5
	6.5			3.5
☀	5 hrs	6 hrs	3.5 hrs	1.5 hrs
☂	39 mm	45 mm	50 mm	44 mm
month	Apr	Jul	Oct	Jan

EAST ANGLIA

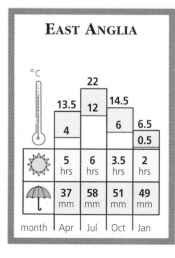

°C				
	13.5	22 12	14.5 6	6.5
	4			0.5
☀	5 hrs	6 hrs	3.5 hrs	2 hrs
☂	37 mm	58 mm	51 mm	49 mm
month	Apr	Jul	Oct	Jan

Northumbria
Newcastle
upon Tyne
Yorkshire and
Humberside
York
Manchester
East Midlands
Birmingham
Norwich
Heart of
England
Cambridge
East Anglia
Thames Valley
Oxford
London
Downs and Channel
Coast
Dover
Portsmouth

LONDON

INTRODUCING LONDON 76–81
WEST END AND WESTMINSTER 82–99
SOUTH KENSINGTON AND HYDE PARK 100–107
REGENT'S PARK AND BLOOMSBURY 108–113
THE CITY AND SOUTHWARK 114–125
SHOPS AND MARKETS 126–127
ENTERTAINMENT IN LONDON 128–131
FURTHER AFIELD 132–140
STREET FINDER 141–149

London at a Glance

THE LARGEST CITY IN EUROPE, London is home to about seven million people and covers 625 sq miles (1,600 sq km). The capital was founded by the Romans in the first century AD as a convenient administrative and communications centre and a port for trade with Continental Europe. For a thousand years it has been the principal residence of British monarchs as well as the centre of business and government, and it is rich in historic buildings and treasures from all periods. In addition to its diverse range of museums, galleries and churches, London is an exciting contemporary city, packed with a vast array of entertainments and shops. The attractions on offer are virtually endless but this map highlights the most important of those described in detail on the following pages.

Buckingham Palace (pp92–3) *is London home and office to the monarchy. The Changing of the Guard takes place on the palace forecourt.*

REGENT'S PARK AND BLOOMSBURY
(see pp108–113)

WEST EN
AND
WESTMINS
(see pp82–

SOUTH KENSINGTON AND HYDE PARK
(see pp100–7)

Hyde Park (p81), *the largest central London park, boasts numerous sports facilities, restaurants, an art gallery and Speakers' Corner. The highlight is the Serpentine Lake.*

0 kilometres   1

0 miles   0.5

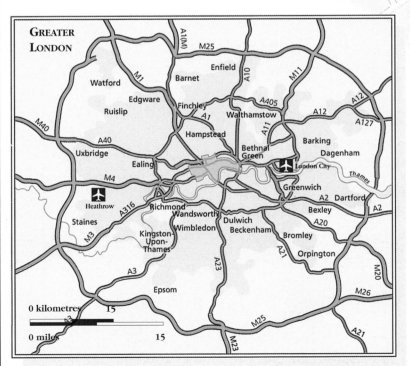

GREATER LONDON

A10(M)
M25
Enfield
Watford
Barnet
M1
A10
M11
Edgware
Finchley
A405
A12
Ruislip
A1
Walthamstow
A12
A127
M40
Hampstead
A11
A40
Barking
Uxbridge
Bethnal Green
Dagenham
Ealing
London City
Thames
M4
Greenwich
Heathrow
A2   Dartford
A316
Richmond
Bexley
A2
Staines
Wandsworth
A20
Wimbledon
Dulwich
Beckenham
Bromley
M3
Kingston-Upon-Thames
A23
A21
Orpington
M20
A3
Epsom
M26
M25
A21
M23

0 kilometres   15

0 miles   15

The Victoria and Albert Museum (pp104–5) *is the world's largest museum of decorative arts. This German cup is 15th century.*

KEY

☐ Main sightseeing area

The British Museum's (pp112–3) *vast collection of antiquities from all over the world includes this Portland Vase from the 1st century BC.*

The National Gallery's (pp88–9) *world-famous collection of paintings includes works such as Christ Mocked (c.1495) by Hieronymus Bosch.*

THAMES

THE CITY AND SOUTHWARK *(see pp114–125)*

St Paul's (pp120–21) *huge dome is the cathedral's most distinctive feature. Three galleries around the dome give spectacular views of London.*

Westminster Abbey (pp98–9) *has glorious medieval architecture and is crammed with impressive tombs and monuments to some of Britain's greatest public figures.*

The Tate Gallery (p97) *has two outstanding collections: British art dating from 1550 and 20th-century international modern art. This explosive image, Whaam! (1963), is by Roy Lichtenstein.*

The Tower of London (pp124–5) *is most famous as the prison where enemies of the Crown were executed. The Tower houses the Crown Jewels, including the Imperial State Crown.*

A River View of London

THE RIVER THAMES was the artery for much of the country's commerce from Roman times until the 1950s. Today the river is one of London's foremost leisure amenities, with wharves and warehouses converted into riverside marinas, bars and restaurants. One of the most enjoyable ways to see the capital is by boat, and the most popular river trips travel downstream from the Houses of Parliament to Tower Bridge. This 30-minute cruise gives a different perspective on some of London's historic buildings and sights.

St Paul's Cathedral (pp120–21), *Wren's masterpiece, dominates the north bank of the river.*

Shell Mex House *was built in 1931 on the site of the vast Cecil Hotel.*

Temple and the Inns of Court (p116) *have been the offices of lawyers and barristers for over 500 years.*

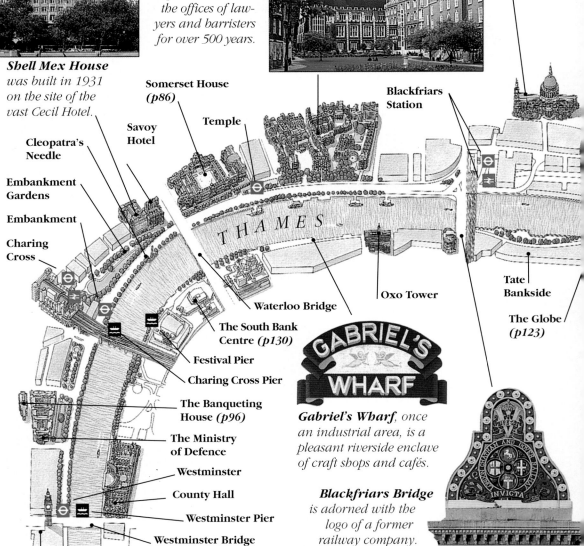

Somerset House (p86)

Blackfriars Station

Temple

Savoy Hotel

Cleopatra's Needle

Embankment Gardens

Embankment

Charing Cross

THAMES

Tate Bankside

Oxo Tower

The Globe (p123)

Waterloo Bridge

The South Bank Centre (p130)

Festival Pier

Charing Cross Pier

The Banqueting House (p96)

The Ministry of Defence

Westminster

County Hall

Westminster Pier

Westminster Bridge

Gabriel's Wharf, once an industrial area, is a pleasant riverside enclave of craft shops and cafés.

Blackfriars Bridge is adorned with the logo of a former railway company.

The Houses of Parliament (p96) *were designed by Charles Barry after a fire burnt down the 14th-century Palace of Westminster in 1834. The tall tower housing Big Ben dominates the skyline.*

BOAT TOUR OPERATORS

The most popular boat trips run through central London round the year, with reduced schedules in winter. In the summer months there are trips downriver to Greenwich *(see p135)* and upriver to Hampton Court *(see p173).*

East End & Docklands

Rotherhithe Tunnel

Blackwall Tunnel

ISLE OF DOGS

Greenwich Foot Tunnel

Greenwich

KEY

▢	City centre area
▣	River boat stop
⊖	Underground station
⇌	Railway station

Chiswick

Hammersmith

Chelsea

Battersea

Kew

Richmond

Hampton Court

Putney

River boats from Westminster Pier

Map 6 F2. ⊖ *Westminster.*
to Tower Pier (*020-7515 1415;*
to Greenwich (*020-7930 4097;*
to Thames Barrier (*020-7930 3373;*
to Kew, Richmond & Hampton Court
(*020-7930 4721.*

Lunchtime & Supper Cruises
(*020-7839 3572.*
Evening Cruises (*020-7930 2062.*

River boats from Charing Cross Pier

Map 6 F1. ⊖ *Embankment.*
to Tower Pier & Greenwich (*020-7839 3572.*

River boats from Tower Pier

Map 8 E4. ⊖ *Tower Hill.*
to Greenwich (*020-7839 3572.*
Evening Cruises (*020-7839 3572.*

Cannon Street

Swan Lane Pier

Fishmongers' Hall

Monument

London Bridge

Old Billingsgate

Custom House

Tower Pier

Tower of London
(pp124–5) *has an eerie
Traitors' Gate, where
prisoners entered the
Tower by boat.*

St Katharine's Dock

Southwark Bridge

London Bridge

St Olave's House

London City Pier

Hay's Galleria

Victorian warehouses

Design Museum *(p122)*

HMS Belfast
*is a World
War II cruiser
built in 1939.
It opened as
a naval mus-
eum in 1971.*

Southwark Cathedral
(p123) *is one of London's
finest Gothic buildings.
Among the many monu-
ments is a memorial to
William Shakespeare.*

Tower Bridge (p122)
*was built in 1886–94
and is an easily recog-
nized landmark. It still
opens to allow tall ships
to pass underneath.*

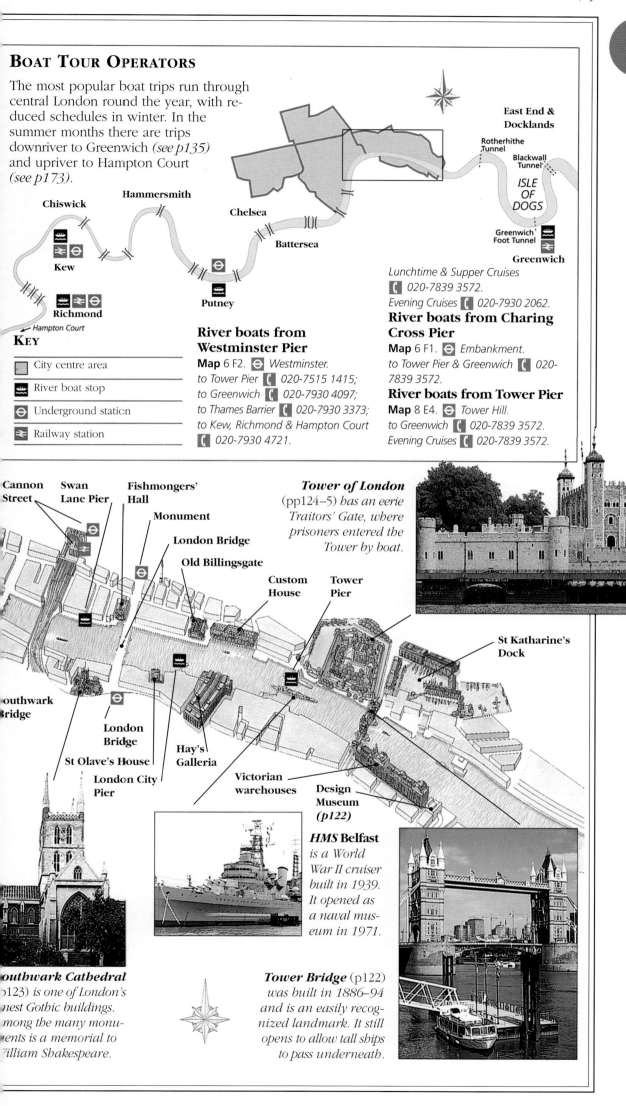

London's Parks and Gardens

Camilla japonica

L ONDON HAS ONE OF THE WORLD'S greenest city centres, full of tree-filled squares and large expanses of grass, some of which have been public lands since medieval times. From the elegant terraces of Regent's Park to the botanic gardens of Kew, every London park and garden has its own charm and character. Some are ancient crown or public lands, while others were created from the grounds of private houses or disused land. Londoners make the most of these open spaces: for exercise, listening to music, or simply escaping the bustle of the city.

Holland Park (see pp132–3) *offers acres of peaceful woodland, an open-air theatre* (see p129) *and a café.*

Kew Gardens (see p140) *are the world's premiere botanic gardens. An amazing variety of plants from all over the world is complemented by an array of temples, monuments and a landscaped lake.*

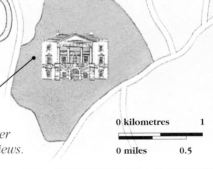

Richmond Park (see p140), *London's largest royal park, remains unspoiled with roaming deer and magnificent river views.*

0 kilometres   1

0 miles   0.5

SEASONAL BEST

As winter draws to a close, spectacular drifts of crocuses, daffodils and tulips are to be found peeping above the ground in Green Park and Kew. Easter weekend marks the start of outdoor events with funfairs on many commons and parks. During the summer months the parks are packed with picnickers and sunbathers and you can often catch a free open-air concert in St James's or Regent's parks. The energetic can play tennis in most

Winter in Kensington Gardens, adjoining Hyde Park

parks, swim in Hyde Park's Serpentine or the ponds on Hampstead Heath, or take rowing boats out on the lakes in Regent's and Battersea parks. Autumn brings a different atmosphere, and on 5 November firework displays and bonfires celebrate Guy Fawkes Night *(see p68).* Winter is a good time to visit the tropical glasshouses and the colourful outdoor winter garden at Kew. If the weather gets really cold, the Round Pond in Kensington Gardens may be fit for ice-skating.

Hampstead Heath *(see p134)* is a breezy open space embracing a variety of landscapes.

Regent's Park (see p109) *has a large boating lake, an open-air theatre (see p129) and London Zoo. Surrounded by Nash's graceful buildings, it is one of London's most civilized retreats.*

St James's Park, *in the heart of the city, is a popular escape for office workers. It is also a reserve for wildfowl.*

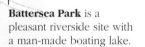

Green Park, *with its shady trees and benches, offers a cool, restful spot in the heart of London.*

Battersea Park is a pleasant riverside site with a man-made boating lake.

Greenwich Park (see p135) *is dominated by the National Maritime Museum. There are fine views from the Old Royal Observatory on the hill top.*

Hyde Park and Kensington Gardens (see p107) *are both popular London retreats. There are sporting facilities, a lake and art gallery in Hyde Park. This plaque is from the ornate Italian Garden in Kensington Gardens.*

HISTORIC CEMETERIES

In the late 1830s, a ring of private cemeteries was established around London to ease the pressure on the monstrously overcrowded and unhealthy burial grounds of the inner city. Today the cemeteries, notably **Highgate** *(see p134)* and **Kensal Green,** are well worth visiting for their flamboyant Victorian monuments.

Kensal Green cemetery on the Harrow Road

WEST END AND WESTMINSTER

THE WEST END is the city's social and cultural centre and the London home of the royal family. Stretching from the edge of Hyde Park to Covent Garden, the district bustles all day and late into the night. Whether you're looking for art, history, street- or café-life, it is the most rewarding area in which to begin an exploration of the city.

Horse Guard on Whitehall

Westminster has been at the centre of political and religious power for a thousand years. In the 11th century, King Canute founded Westminster Palace and Edward the Confessor built Westminster Abbey, where all English monarchs have been crowned since 1066. As modern government developed, the great offices of state were established in the area.

SIGHTS AT A GLANCE

Historic Streets and Buildings
Banqueting House 17
Buckingham Palace pp92–3 12
Cabinet War Rooms 15
Downing Street 16
Houses of Parliament pp96–7 18
Piccadilly Circus 7
Ritz Hotel 9
Royal Mews 14
The Mall 11
The Piazza and Central Market 1

Museums and Galleries
Courtauld Gallery and Somerset House 4
London Transport Museum 2
National Gallery pp88–9 6
National Portrait Gallery 5
Queen's Gallery 13
Royal Academy 8

Tate Gallery 20
Theatre Museum 3

Churches
Queen's Chapel 10
Westminster Abbey pp98–9 19

KEY

Street-by-Street map pp84–5

Street-by-Street map pp90–91

Street-by-Street map pp94–5

Underground station

Railway station

P Parking

River boat boarding point

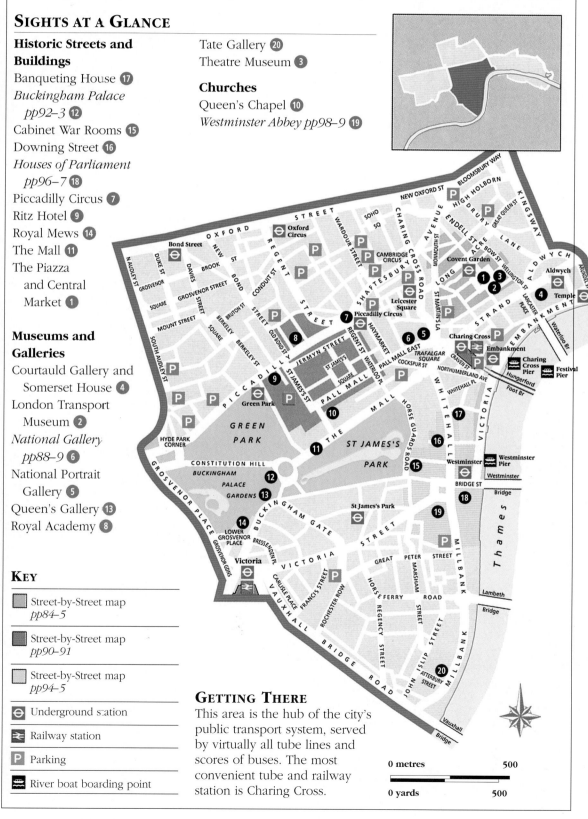

GETTING THERE

This area is the hub of the city's public transport system, served by virtually all tube lines and scores of buses. The most convenient tube and railway station is Charing Cross.

0 metres 500

0 yards 500

◁ **Westminster Bridge, Big Ben and the Houses of Parliament viewed from the South Bank**

Street-by-Street: Covent Garden

UNTIL 1973, COVENT GARDEN was an area of decaying streets and warehouses, which only came alive after dark when the fruit and vegetable market traders packed up for the day. Since then the Victorian market and elegant buildings nearby have been converted into stylish shops, restaurants, bars and cafés, creating an animated district which attracts a lively young crowd, night and day.

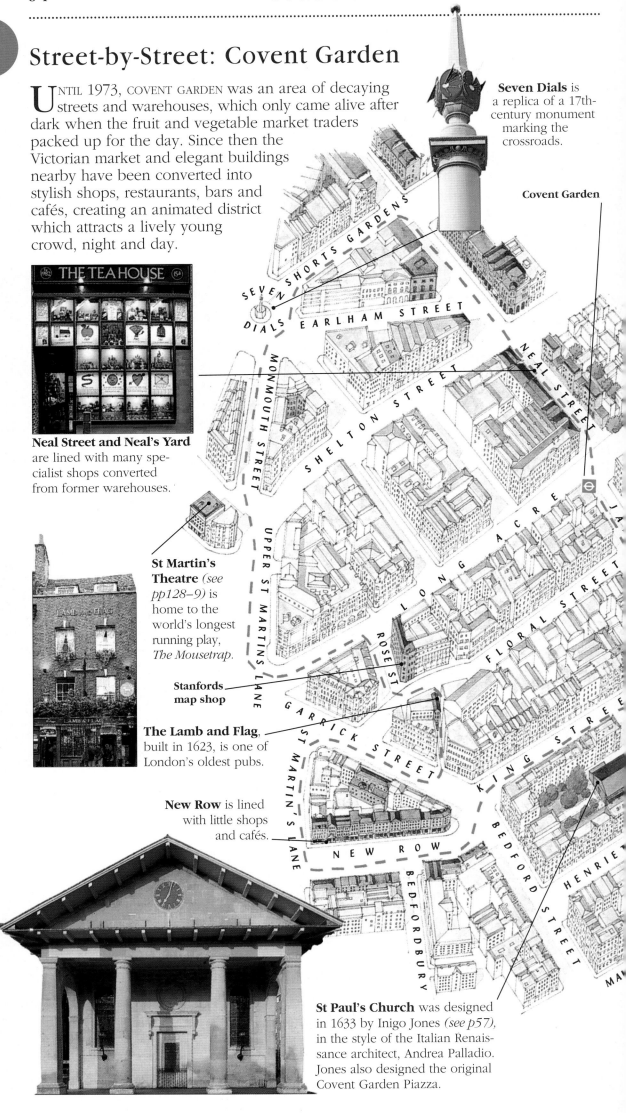

Seven Dials is a replica of a 17th-century monument marking the crossroads.

Covent Garden

Neal Street and Neal's Yard are lined with many specialist shops converted from former warehouses.

St Martin's Theatre (*see pp128–9*) is home to the world's longest running play, *The Mousetrap*.

Stanfords map shop

The Lamb and Flag, built in 1623, is one of London's oldest pubs.

New Row is lined with little shops and cafés.

St Paul's Church was designed in 1633 by Inigo Jones (*see p57*), in the style of the Italian Renaissance architect, Andrea Palladio. Jones also designed the original Covent Garden Piazza.

Theatre Museum
This houses a collection of theatrical memorabilia ❸

The Royal Opera House
(see p130) is where many of the greatest opera singers and ballet dancers have performed.

LOCATOR MAP
See Street Finder map 4

KEY

– – – Suggested route

0 metres	100
0 yards	100

London Transport Museum
This museum's intriguing collection brings to life the history of the city's tubes, buses and trains. It also displays examples of 20th-century commercial art ❷

Jubilee Market

★ **Piazza and Central Market**
Street performers entertain passers-by in the square ❶

STAR SIGHTS

★ **Piazza and Central Market**

The Piazza and Central Market ❶

Covent Garden WC2. **Map** 4 F5.
🚇 *Covent Garden.* ♿ *cobbled streets.* **Street performers in Piazza:** *10am–dusk daily.*

T HE 17TH-CENTURY ARCHITECT Inigo Jones *(see p57)* planned the Piazza in Covent Garden as an elegant residential square, modelled on the piazza in the Tuscan town of Livorno, which he had seen under construction during his travels in Italy. For a brief period, the Piazza became one of the most fashionable addresses in London, but it was superseded by the even grander St James's Square *(see pp90–91)* which lies to the southwest.

Decline accelerated when a fruit and vegetable market developed. By the mid-18th century, the Piazza had become a haunt of prostitutes and most of its houses had turned into seedy lodgings, gambling dens, brothels and taverns.

A mid-18th-century view of Covent Garden's Piazza

Meanwhile the wholesale produce market became the largest in the country and in 1828 a market hall was erected to ease congestion. The market, however, soon outgrew its new home and despite the construction of new buildings, such as Floral and Jubilee halls, the congestion grew worse. In 1973 the market moved to a new site in south London, and over the last two decades Covent Garden has been redeveloped. Today only St Paul's remains of Inigo Jones's buildings, and Covent Garden, with its many small shops, cafés, restaurants, market stalls and street entertainers, is one of central London's liveliest districts.

London Transport Museum ❷

The Piazza, Covent Garden WC2.
Map 4 F5. 📞 020-7379 6344.
⊖ Covent Garden. ◯ 10am–6pm
Sat–Thu; 11am–6pm Fri (last adm
5:15pm). ● 24–26 Dec. 🖐 ♿
🗞 phone in advance. 📷 🛍

Tʜɪs ᴄᴏʟʟᴇᴄᴛɪᴏɴ of buses, trams and underground trains ranges from the earliest horse-drawn omnibuses to a present-day Hoppa bus. Housed in the iron, glass and brick Victorian Flower Market of Covent Garden, which was built in 1872, the museum is particularly good for children, who can put themselves in the driver's seat of a bus or an underground train, operate signals and chat to one of the actors playing the part of a 19th-century tube-tunnel miner.

London's bus and train companies have long been prolific patrons of artists, and the museum holds a fine collection of 19th- and 20th-century commercial art. Copies of some of the best posters and works by artists such as Graham Sutherland and Paul Nash – are on sale at the museum shop.

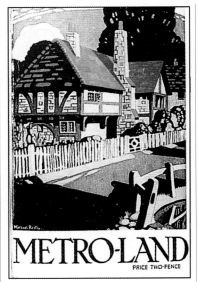

Poster by Michael Reilly (1929), London Transport Museum

Theatre Museum ❸

7 Russell St WC2. **Map** 4 F5. 📞 020-7836 7891. ⊖ Covent Garden.
◯ 10am–6pm Tue–Sun. ● public hols. 🖐 ♿

A ʟᴀʀɢᴇ ɢᴏʟᴅ sᴛᴀᴛᴜᴇ of the Spirit of Gaiety lures you down into the subterranean galleries of this museum. Children can be made up with gruesome wounds and find out how Cyrano de Bergerac's nose was created for the film. An exhibition reveals how a theatre production is mounted, from cast readings of the author's original script, through videoed rehearsals and back-stage procedures, to the first staged performance.

More conventionally, the intriguing history of show business is traced through a collection of memorabilia – playbills, programmes, props and costumes, such as a slinky silver jumpsuit worn by the rock singer Mick Jagger.

Courtauld Gallery and Somerset House ❹

Courtauld Institute of Art, Somerset House, Strand WC2. **Map** 4 F5.
📞 020-7873 2526. ⊖ Temple, Embankment. ◯ 10am–6pm Mon–Sat, 2–6pm Sun. ● 24–26 Dec, 1 Jan, Good Fri. 🖐 ♿ 🖥

Dᴇsɪɢɴᴇᴅ ɪɴ 1770 by William Chambers, Somerset House was the first purpose-built office block in London. Much of the building is still used by civil servants, but the

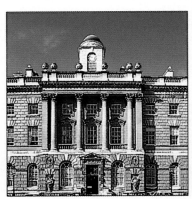

Somerset House: Strand façade

north block (the original home of the Royal Academy) now houses a spectacular display of paintings. The collection is based on the magnate Samuel Courtauld's Impressionist and Post-Impressionist works which includes Manet's *Bar at the Folies-Bergère* (1882), a version of *Le Déjeuner sur l'Herbe* (c.1863) and Van Gogh's *Self-Portrait with Bandaged Ear* (1889). There are also earlier works by Giovanni Bellini, Botticelli and Brueghel, and paintings by 20th-century British artists, such as *Painting 1937* by Ben Nicholson (see p309).

Sᴏʜᴏ ᴀɴᴅ Cʜɪɴᴀᴛᴏᴡɴ

Soho has been renowned for pleasures of the table, the flesh and the intellect ever since it was first developed in the late 17th century. At first a fashionable residential area, it declined when high society shifted west to Mayfair and immigrants from Europe moved into its narrow streets. Furniture-makers and tailors set up shop here and were joined in the late 19th century by pubs, nightclubs, restaurants and brothels. In the 1960s, Hong Kong Chinese moved into the area around Gerrard and Lisle streets and they created an aromatic Chinatown, packed with many restaurants and food shops. Soho's raffish reputation has long attracted artists and writers, ranging from the 18th-century essayist Thomas de Quincey to poet Dylan Thomas and painter Francis Bacon. Although strip joints and peep shows remain, Soho has enjoyed something of a renaissance, and today is full of stylish and lively bars and restaurants.

Lion dancer in February's Chinese New Year celebrations

The opulent Palm Court of the Ritz Hotel

National Portrait Gallery ⑤

2 St Martin's Place WC2. **Map** 6 E1.
📞 020-7306 0055. ⊖ Leicester Sq.
◯ 10am–6pm Mon–Sat, noon–6pm
Sun. ◑ 24–25 Dec, ¹ Jan, Good Fri,
May Day. ♿ 🎞 Aug. ▭ 🗂

THIS MUSEUM CELEBRATES Britain's history through portraits, photographs and sculptures; subjects range from Elizabeth I and Shakespeare to the Beatles and Margaret Thatcher. Early works include a sketch of Henry VIII by Hans Holbein and aristocratic portraits by Gainsborough, Van Dyck and Reynolds. The most popular part of the gallery, however, is the 20th-century section, with paintings and photographs of the royal family, politicians, rock stars, designers, artists and writers.

National Gallery ⑥

See pp88–9.

Piccadilly Circus ⑦

W1. **Map** 6 D1. ⊖ Piccadilly Circus.

DOMINATED BY garish neon advertising hoardings, Piccadilly Circus is a hectic traffic junction surrounded by shopping malls and fast food outlets. It began as an early 19th-century crossroads between Piccadilly and John Nash's (see p111) Regent Street.

It was briefly an elegant space, edged by curving stucco façades, but by 1910 the first electric advertisements had been installed. The Circus marks the beginning of London's entertainment district, and for years people have congregated at its centre, beneath the delicately poised figure of Eros, the Greek god of love. Erected in 1892, the figure was originally intended to be an angel of Christian mercy.

The Statue of Eros

Royal Academy ⑧

Burlington House, Piccadilly W1.
Map 6 D1. 📞 020-7300 8000.
⊖ Piccadilly Circus, Green Park.
◯ 10am–6pm daily. ◑ 24–26 Dec,
Good Fri. 🎟 ♿ 🎞 Tue–Fri.

FOUNDED IN 1768, the Royal Academy is best known for its summer exhibition, which has been an annual

Vivien Leigh by Angus McBean
(1952), National Portrait Gallery

event for over 200 years and comprises a rewarding mix of around 1,200 new works by established and unknown painters, sculptors and architects. During the rest of the year the gallery shows prestigious touring exhibitions from around the world.

Quite apart from its aesthetic delights, the Royal Academy can provide the weary traveller with a little lacuna of tranquillity. Its interior decoration inspires calm, and seems to be in some way cut off from the stresses of modern city life.

Ritz Hotel ⑨

Piccadilly W1. **Map** 5 C1.
📞 020-7493 8181. ⊖ Green Park.
♿

CESAR RITZ, the Swiss hotelier who inspired the word "ritzy", had virtually settled down to a quiet, modest retirement by 1906 when this hotel was built and named after him. The colonnaded front of the dominant, château-style building was erected in 1906 to suggest just the merest whiff of Paris, where the grandest hotels were to be found at the turn of the century. It still manages to maintain its Edwardian air of *fin de siècle* opulence and sophisticated grandeur and is a popular venue, with those suitably attired of course, for an extravagant yet genteel afternoon tea. The refined atmosphere of chic suavity is enhanced by the tea dances and fashion parades which are held in the Palm Court; a touch of *soigné* danger may also be found within the casino, where it is probably not the wisest of moves to gamble with the professionals who dart like sharks through the murky waters of high-risk wagers, looking for small-fry to toy with. If you want to taste the zenith of ritzian *savoir-vivre*, the Louis XVI dining room, with its view over Green Park, connects you with all the splendour you could ever need.

National Gallery ⑥

THE NATIONAL GALLERY is London's leading art museum, with over 2,200 paintings, most on permanent display. It has flourished since 1824 when George IV persuaded a reluctant government to purchase 38 major paintings. These became the core of a national collection of European art that now ranges from Giotto in the 13th century to 19-century Impressionists. The gallery's particular strengths are in Dutch, Italian Renaissance and 17th-century Spanish painting. In 1991 the Sainsbury Wing was added to the main Neo-Classical building (1834–8) to hold the Early Renaissance collection.

The Adoration of the Kings *(1564)*
This realisitic work is by Flemish artist Pieter Brueghel the Elder (1520–1569).

★ **The Leonardo Cartoon** *(c.1510)*
The genius of Leonardo da Vinci glows through this chalk drawing of the Virgin and Child, St Anne and John the Baptist.

Orange Street entrance ♿

Stairs to lower floor

KEY TO FLOORPLAN

- ☐ Painting 1260–1510
- ☐ Painting 1510–1600
- ☐ Painting 1600–1700
- ☐ Painting 1700–1900
- ☐ Special exhibitions
- ☐ Non-exhibition space

Link to main building

Stairs to lower floors

Arnolfini Portrait
Jan van Eyck (1389–1441), one of the pioneers of oil painting, shows his mastery of colour, texture, and minute detail in this portrait of 1434.

Main entrance to Sainsbury Wing ♿

The Annunciation
This refined work of 1448, by Fra Filippo Lippi, forms part of the gallery's exceptional Italian Renaissance collection.

★ **Rokeby Venus**
This is Velazquez's only surviving female nude (1649).

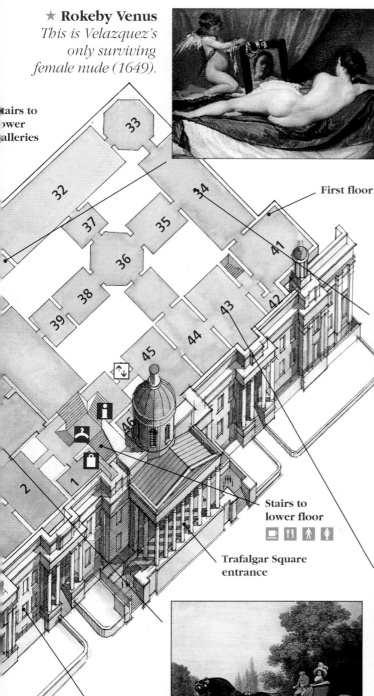

Stairs to lower galleries

33

32

37

35

36

34

First floor

38

41

39

43

42

44

45

46

2

1

Stairs to lower floor

Trafalgar Square entrance

The Neo-Classical façade is made of Portland stone.

VISITORS' CHECKLIST

Trafalgar Sq WC2. **Map** 6 E1.
020-7747 2885. Charing Cross, Leicester Sq, Piccadilly Circus. 3, 6, 9, 11, 12, 13, 15, X15 23, 24, 29, 53, X53, 77A, 88, 91, 94, 109, 139, 159, 176. Charing Cross.
10am–6pm daily (8pm Wed).
24–26 Dec, 1 Jan, Good Fri, May Day. via Sainsbury Wing entrance.

★ **The Haywain** *(1821)*
The great age of 19th-century landscape painting is represented by Constable and Turner (see p97). This picture shows how Constable caught changing light and shadow.

GALLERY GUIDE
Most of the collection is housed on the first floor, divided into four wings. The paintings hang chronologically, with the earliest works, notably the Italian Renaissance collection (1260–1510), in the Sainsbury Wing. Lesser paintings of all periods are displayed on the lower floor of the main building. The better of the two restaurants is on the first floor in the Sainsbury Wing.

A Lady and a Gentleman in a Carriage *(1787)*
George Stubbs was celebrated for his portraits of horses, often shown with their owners. This work displays his versatility.

STAR PAINTINGS

★ **Cartoon by Leonardo da Vinci**

★ **Rokeby Venus by Diego Velazquez**

★ **The Haywain by John Constable**

Umbrellas *(1881–6)*
Renoir was one of the greatest painters to be influenced by the Impressionist movement. In this painting he used the free, flickering touch of Impressionism that captures the fleeting moment.

Street-by-Street: Piccadilly and St James's

AS SOON AS HENRY VIII built St James's Palace in the 1530s, the surrounding area became the centre of fashionable court life. Today Piccadilly forms a contrast between the bustling commercial district full of shopping arcades, eateries and cinemas, with St James's, to the south, which is still the domain of the wealthy and the influential.

St James's Church was designed by Sir Christopher Wren in 1684.

★ Royal Academy
The permanent art collection here includes this Michelangelo relief of the Madonna and Child (1505) **8**

Fortnum and Mason
(see p126) was founded in 1707.

The Ritz
César Ritz founded one of London's most famous hotels in 1906 **9**

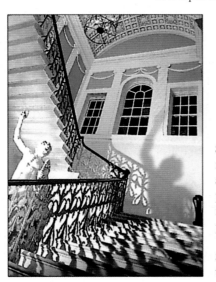

Burlington Arcade, an opulent covered walk, has fine shops and beadles on patrol.

St James's Palace
was built on the site of a leper hospital.

To the Mall and Buckingham Palace *(see pp92–3)*

Spencer House, recently restored to its 18th-century splendour, contains fine period furniture and paintings. This Palladian palace was completed in 1766 for the 1st Earl Spencer, an ancestor of the late Princess of Wales.

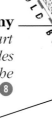

STAR SIGHTS

★ Piccadilly Circus

★ Royal Academy

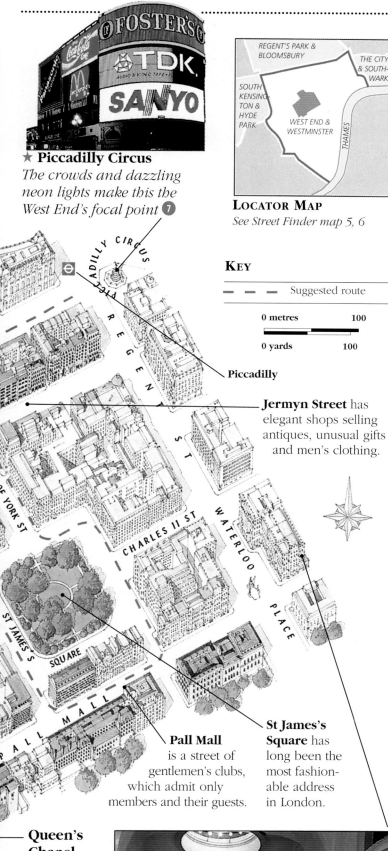

★ **Piccadilly Circus**
The crowds and dazzling neon lights make this the West End's focal point **7**

LOCATOR MAP
See Street Finder map 5, 6

REGENT'S PARK & BLOOMSBURY

THE CITY & SOUTHWARK

SOUTH KENSINGTON & HYDE PARK

WEST END & WESTMINSTER

THAMES

KEY

– – – – Suggested route

0 metres   100

0 yards   100

Piccadilly

Jermyn Street has elegant shops selling antiques, unusual gifts and men's clothing.

Pall Mall
is a street of gentlemen's clubs, which admit only members and their guests.

St James's Square has long been the most fashionable address in London.

Queen's Chapel
This was the first Classical church in England **10**

Royal Opera Arcade is lined with quality shops. Designed by John Nash, it was completed in 1818.

Queen's Chapel **10**

Marlborough Rd SW1. **Map** 6 D1.
☎ 020-7930 4832. ⊖ *Green Park.*
◯ *to the public Sun services only (Easter–end Jul).* ♿

THE SUMPTUOUS Queen's Chapel was designed by Inigo Jones for the Infanta of Spain, the intended bride of Charles I (*see p56–7*). Work started in 1623 but ceased when the marriage negotiations were shelved. The chapel was finally completed in 1627 for Charles's eventual queen, Henrietta Maria. It was the first church in England to be built in a Classical style, with a coffered ceiling based on a reconstruction by Palladio of an ancient Roman temple.

Interior of Queen's Chapel

The Mall **11**

SW1. **Map** 6 D2. ⊖ *Charing Cross, Green Park.*

THIS BROAD TRIUMPHAL approach from Trafalgar Square to Buckingham Palace was created by Aston Webb when he redesigned the front of the palace and the Victoria Monument in 1911. The spacious tree-lined avenue follows the course of an old path at the edge of St James's Park. The path was laid out in the reign of Charles II, when it became London's most fashionable and cosmopolitan promenade. The Mall is used for royal processions on special occasions. Flagpoles down both sides fly the national flags of foreign heads of state during official visits. The Mall is closed to traffic on Sundays.

Buckingham Palace ⑫

Queen Elizabeth II

Opened to visitors for the first time in 1993 to raise money for repairing fire damage to Windsor Castle *(see pp254–5)*, The Queen's official London home and office is an extremely popular attraction in August and September. John Nash *(see p111)* began converting the 18th-century Buckingham House into a palace for George IV in 1826 but was taken off the job in 1830 for overspending his budget. The first monarch to occupy the palace was Queen Victoria, just after she came to the throne in 1837. The tour takes visitors up the grand staircase and through the splendour of the state rooms, but not into the royal family's private apartments.

Music Room
State guests are presented and royal babies christened in this room.

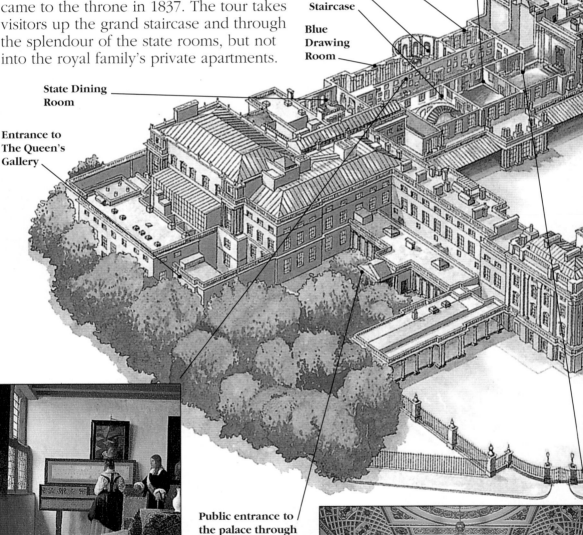

White Drawing Room

Green Drawing Room

Grand Staircase

Blue Drawing Room

State Dining Room

Entrance to The Queen's Gallery

Public entrance to the palace through Ambassador's Court

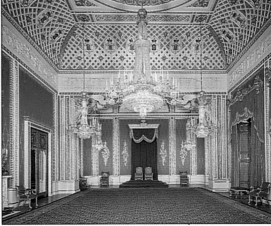

Picture Gallery
The valuable collection on display includes this painting by Dutch master Johannes Vermeer: The Music Lesson (c.1660).

Throne Room
The Queen carries out many formal ceremonial duties here, under the richly gilded ceiling.

View over the Mall
On special occasions The Royal Family wave to crowds from the balcony.

The Royal Standard flies while The Queen is in residence.

The East Wing façade was added by Aston Webb in 1913.

The Changing of the Guard takes place on the palace forecourt.

THE CHANGING OF THE GUARD

Dressed in brilliant scarlet tunics and tall furry hats called bearskins, the palace guards stand in sentry boxes outside the Palace. Crowds gather in front of the railings to watch the colourful and musical military ceremony as the guards march down the Mall from St James's Palace, parading for half an hour while the palace keys are handed by the old guards to the new.

Queen's Gallery 13

Buckingham Palace Rd SW1. **Map** 5 C2. 020-7839 1377. St James's Park, Victoria. for refurbishment until 2002.

THE QUEEN'S ART COLLECTION is one of the finest and most valuable in the world. A selection of works is displayed here in themed exhibitions that change once or twice a year. This small building at the side of Buckingham Palace was used as a conservatory until 1962; part of it is a private chapel screened from the public. A large and interesting shop sells a selection of royal merchandise.

Detail: The Gold State Coach (1762), Royal Mews

Royal Mews 14

Buckingham Palace Rd SW1. **Map** 5 C3. 020-7839 1377. Victoria. noon–4pm Tue–Thu (last adm 3:30pm). 25, 26 Dec, 1 Jan.

LOVERS OF HORSES and royal pomp should try to fit in with the restricted opening hours of this working stable and coach house. Designed by John Nash in 1825, it accommodates the horses and state coaches used on official occasions. Among them are the Rolls-Royce limousines with transparent tops that allow their royal occupants to be seen, and the glass coach used for royal weddings and foreign ambassadors. The star exhibit is the ornate gold state coach, built for George III in 1762, with panels painted by Giovanni Cipriani.

Street-by-Street: Whitehall and Westminster

THE BROAD AVENUES of Whitehall and Westminster are lined with imposing buildings that serve the historic seat of both government and the established church. On weekdays the streets are crowded with civil servants whose work is based here, while at weekends the area takes on a different atmosphere with a steady flow of tourists.

Downing Street
Sir Robert Walpole was the first Prime Minister to live here in 1732 16

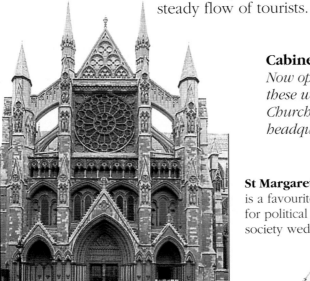

★ **Westminster Abbey**
The abbey is London's oldest and most important church 19

Central Hall (1911) is a florid example of the Beaux Arts style.

Richard I's Statue is an 1860 depiction of the king, killed in battle in 1199.

Cabinet War Rooms
Now open to the public, these were Winston Churchill's World War II headquarters 15

St Margaret's Church is a favourite venue for political and society weddings.

KING CHARLES STREET

STOREY'S GATE

GREAT GEORGE STREET

PARLIA

BRID

BROAD   SANCTUARY

PARLIAMENT SQUARE

ST MARGARET STREET

GREAT COLLEGE STREET

ABINGDON STREET

Dean's Yard is a secluded grassy square surrounded by picturesque buildings from different periods, many used by Westminster School.

The Burghers of Calais is a cast of Auguste Rodin's 1886 original in France.

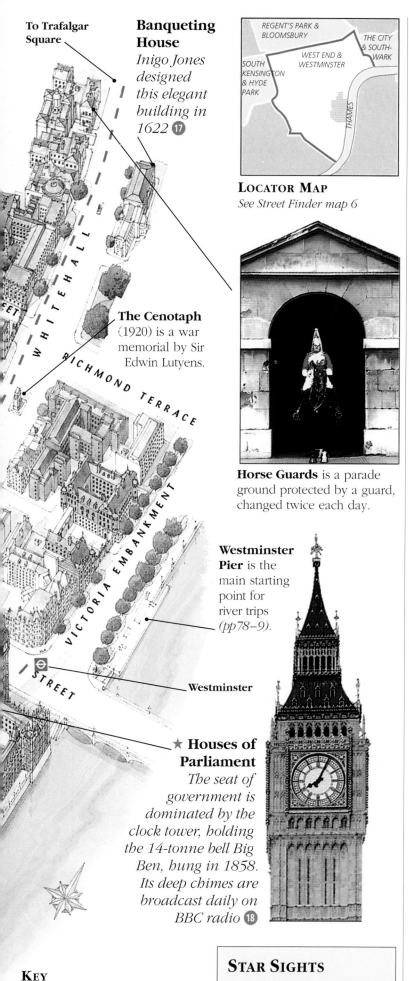

To Trafalgar Square

Banqueting House
Inigo Jones designed this elegant building in 1622 ⓱

LOCATOR MAP
See Street Finder map 6

REGENT'S PARK & BLOOMSBURY

THE CITY & SOUTH-WARK

WEST END & WESTMINSTER

SOUTH KENSINGTON & HYDE PARK

THAMES

The Cenotaph
(1920) is a war memorial by Sir Edwin Lutyens.

WHITEHALL

RICHMOND TERRACE

VICTORIA EMBANKMENT

STREET

Horse Guards is a parade ground protected by a guard, changed twice each day.

Westminster Pier is the main starting point for river trips *(pp78–9)*.

Westminster

★ **Houses of Parliament**
The seat of government is dominated by the clock tower, holding the 14-tonne bell Big Ben, hung in 1858. Its deep chimes are broadcast daily on BBC radio ⓲

KEY

- - - Suggested route

0 metres 100

0 yards 100

STAR SIGHTS

★ **Westminster Abbey**

★ **Houses of Parliament**

Cabinet War Rooms ⓯

Clive Steps, King Charles St SW1. **Map** 6 E2. ☏ 020-7930 6961. ⊖ *Westminster.* ○ *Apr–Sep: 9:30am–6pm; Oct–Mar: 10am–6pm.* ● *24–26 Dec.*

THIS WARREN OF CELLARS below a government office building is where the War Cabinet – first under Neville Chamberlain, then Winston Churchill from 1940 – met during World War II when German bombs were falling on London. The rooms include living quarters for ministers and military leaders and a sound-proofed Cabinet Room, where strategic decisions were taken. All rooms are protected by a concrete layer about a metre (3 ft) thick and are laid out as they were when the war ended, complete with Churchill's desk, communications equipment, and maps with markers for plotting battles and strategies.

Telephones in the Map Room, Cabinet War Rooms

Downing Street ⓰

SW1. **Map** 6 E2. ⊖ *Westminster.* ● *to the public.*

NUMBER 10 Downing Street has been the official residence of the British Prime Minister since 1732. It contains a Cabinet Room in which government policy is decided, an impressive State Dining Room and a private apartment; outside is a well-protected garden.

Next door at No. 11 is the official residence of the Chancellor of the Exchequer, who is in charge of the nation's financial affairs. In 1989, iron gates were erected at the Whitehall end of Downing Street for security purposes.

Banqueting House ⑰

Whitehall SW1. **Map** 6 E1. 📞 020-7839 8919. 🚇 *Charing Cross.* ⬤ *10am–5pm Mon–Sat.* ⬤ *public hols & for functions.* 🖎 📷 ♿

COMPLETED BY INIGO JONES *(see p57)* in 1622, this was the first building in central London to embody the classical Palladian style of Renaissance Italy. In 1629 Charles I commissioned Rubens to paint the ceiling with scenes exalting the reign of his father, James I. They symbolize a belief in the divine nature of kingship, despised by the Parliamentarians, who executed Charles I outside the building in 1649 *(see pp56–7).*

Panels from the Rubens ceiling (1629–34), Banqueting House

Houses of Parliament ⑱

SW1. **Map** 6 E2. 📞 020-7219 3000. 🚇 *Westminster.* **Visitors' Galleries** ⬤ *2:30–10pm Mon, Tue, Thu, 9:30am–10pm Wed, 9:30am–3pm Fri. Question Time (2:30–3:30pm Mon–Thu): apply in advance to your MP or embassy.* ⬤ *Easter, late Jul–mid-Oct (summer recess), 3 wks over Christmas, public hols.* ♿ 🛍 🖎 *by appt.*

THERE HAS BEEN a Palace of Westminster here since the 11th century, though only Westminster Hall remains from that time. The present Neo-Gothic structure, designed by Sir Charles Barry, was built after the old palace was destroyed by fire in 1834. Since the 16th century it has been the seat of the two Houses of Parliament, the Lords and the Commons. The House of Commons is made up of elected Members of Parliament (MPs) of different parties. The party with most MPs forms the Government, and its leader becomes Prime Minister. The House of Lords is made up of peers *(see p31)*, law lords, bishops and archbishops. Legislation must be debated in both houses before becoming law.

Westminster Abbey ⑲

See pp98–9.

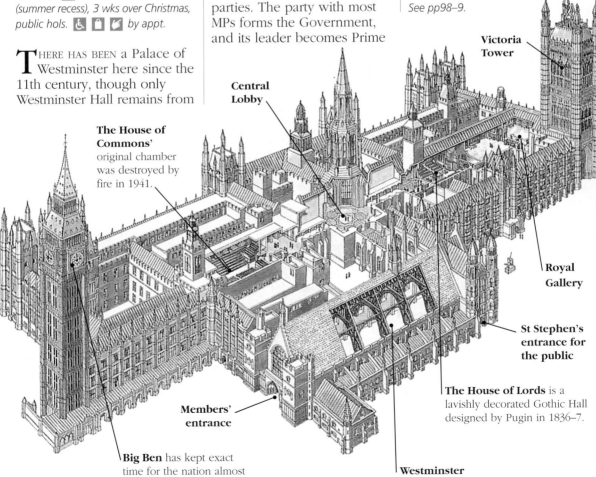

Victoria Tower

Central Lobby

The House of Commons' original chamber was destroyed by fire in 1941.

Royal Gallery

St Stephen's entrance for the public

Members' entrance

The House of Lords is a lavishly decorated Gothic Hall designed by Pugin in 1836–7.

Big Ben has kept exact time for the nation almost continuously since 1859.

Westminster Hall

Portico of the Tate Gallery

Tate Gallery 🔟

Millbank SW1. **Map** 6 E4. ☎ 020-7887 8000. 🚇 *Pimlico.* 🕐 *10am–5:50pm daily.* 🔴 *24–26 Dec, Good Fri, May Day.* 🎫 *for major exhibitions.* 📷 ♿ 🛍

F OUNDED IN 1897, the Tate Gallery is best known for its magnificent Turner Bequest and its international collection of late 19th- and 20th-century art, but it also has an extensive range of earlier British works.

Until 2000 this stately gallery housed all of the collections. Now most of the modern works have moved to a stunning new gallery, housed in a transformed power station at Bankside (see p123), and the Millbank site focuses primarily on British art. With the transfer of the modern collection, the Tate has taken the opportunity of upgrading and expanding its facilities. A £32 million programme of improvements will enable the galleries to house the world's largest display of British art, ranging from Tudor times to the present day. This change means that the gallery is

Mr and Mrs Clark and Percy (1971) by Hockney

reverting to the purpose that Sir Henry Tate intended when he endowed it and presented it with his own collection.

British art was dominated by formal portraiture through the 16th and 17th centuries. One of the most exquisite early works is a portrait of a bejewelled Elizabeth I (c.1575), by Nicholas Hilliard. In the 17th century, the influence of the Flemish artist Sir Anthony Van Dyck, inspired a grand and elegant style of portrait painting. Van Dyck's *Lady of the Spencer Family* (1633–8) – depicting one of Princess Diana's ancestors – and William Dobson's *Endymion Porter* (1642–5) are both superb examples. Van Dyck's continuing influence on English portrait artists can be seen in works by the late 18th-century artist Thomas Gainsborough.

The Three Dancers image:
The Three Dancers (1925) by Picasso

The Tate holds a large number of works by the 19th-century visionary poet and artist William Blake, which contrast with the reassuring landscapes painted by his contemporary John Constable (see pp212–3), and the vibrant images created in the mid-19th century by Pre-Raphaelites such as Millais and Rossetti.

Many of the Tate gallery's best Impressionist and Post-Impressionist paintings were transferred to the National Gallery in 1954 (see pp88–9), but it retains works by major figures such as Renoir, Gauguin, Degas, Toulouse-Lautrec and Van Gogh.

Displays change frequently to highlight different aspects of the collection, and not all of the works are on display at ony one time. Exhibits may also move between sites, and some modern British works of international importance will be on view at the new Tate Gallery of Modern Art on Bankside.

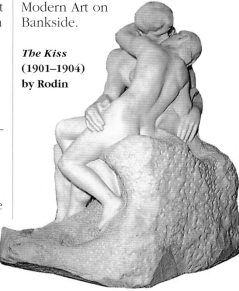
The Kiss (1901–1904) by Rodin

THE TURNER BEQUEST

The landscape artist JMW Turner (1775–1851) left his works to the nation, on the condition that they were kept together. It was not until 1987 with the opening of the Clore Gallery, an extension of the Tate, that this became possible. There are early watercolours, Turner's first exhibited oil-painting, *Fishermen at Sea* (1796), and later works in an Impressionistic style which Constable described as appearing to be painted with "tinted steam".

A City on a River at Sunset (1832)

Westminster Abbey ⑲

W ESTMINSTER ABBEY has been the burial place of
Britain's monarchs since the 13th century and
the setting for many coronations and royal weddings. It
is one of the most beautiful buildings in London, with
an exceptionally diverse array of architectural styles,
ranging from the austere French Gothic of the nave to
the astonishing complexity of Henry VII's chapel. Half
national church, half national museum, the abbey aisles
and transepts are crammed with an extraordinary collection of tombs and monuments honouring some of Britain's
greatest public figures, ranging from politicians to poets.

Main Entrance
*The mock-medieval
stonework is
Victorian.*

**Statesmen's
Aisle**

Flying buttresses help
re-distribute the great
weight of the roof.

★ Nave
*At a height of 31 m
(102 ft), the nave is
the highest in England.
The ratio of height to
width is 3:1.*

CORONATION

The coronation ceremony
is over 1,000 years old
and since 1066, with the
crowning of William the
Conqueror on Christmas
Day, the abbey has been
its sumptuous setting.
The coronation of Queen
Elizabeth II, in 1953, was
the first to be televised.

Cloisters
*Tombs here include those
of several medieval knights.*

STAR FEATURES

★ **Nave**

★ **Henry VII Chapel**

★ **Chapter House**

★ Henry VII Chapel

The chapel, built in 1503–12, has superb late Perpendicular vaultings and choir stalls dating from 1512.

The Sanctuary, built by Henry III, has been the scene of 38 coronations.

WILLIAM SHAKESPEARE 1564 - 1616
BURIED AT STRATFORD-ON-AVON

Poets' Corner

A host of great poets are honoured here, including Shakespeare, Chaucer and TS Eliot.

VISITORS' CHECKLIST

Broad Sanctuary SW1. **Map** 6 E2.
☎ 020-7222 5152. ⊖ *St James's Park, Westminster.* 🚌 *3, 11, 12, 24, 29, 53, 70, 77, 77a, 88, 109, 159, 170.* 🚆 *Victoria, Waterloo.* 🚢 *Westminster Pier.*
Cloisters ◯ *8am–6pm daily.*
Chapter House, Museum & Pyx Chamber ◯ *10:30am–4pm daily.* **Royal Chapels, Poets' Corner, Choir, Statesmen's Aisle & Nave**
◯ *9am–3:45pm Mon–Fri, 9am–1:45pm Sat.* 🎟 *for Royal Chapels, Poets' Corner, Chapter House Choir, Statesmen's Aisle, Pyx Chamber, Museum & Nave.*
✝ *Evensong: 5pm Mon–Fri, 3pm Sat & Sun.* ♿ *limited.*
🎦 *for all visitors.*

The Pyx Chamber is where the coinage was tested in medieval times.

The Museum has many of the abbey's treasures including wood, plaster and wax effigies of monarchs.

★ Chapter House

A beautiful octagonal room, remarkable for its 13th-century tile floor. It is lit by six huge stained glass windows showing scenes from the abbey's history.

St Edward's Chapel

The Coronation Chair is housed here, along with the tombs of many medieval monarchs.

HISTORICAL PLAN OF THE ABBEY

The first abbey church was established as early as the 10th century, but the present French-influenced Gothic structure was begun in 1245 at the behest of Henry III. Because of its unique role as the coronation church, the abbey escaped Henry VIII's mid-16th-century onslaught on Britain's monastic buildings *(see pp54–5).*

KEY

- ▨ Built before 1400
- ▨ Added in 15th century
- ▨ Built in 1503–19
- ▨ Completed by 1745
- ▨ Completed after 1850

SOUTH KENSINGTON AND HYDE PARK

THIS EXCLUSIVE district embraces one of London's largest parks and some of its finest museums, shops, restaurants and hotels. Until the mid-19th century it was a genteel, semi-rural backwater of large houses and private schools lying to the south of Kensington Palace. In 1851, the Great Exhibition, until then the largest arts and science event ever staged *(see p60–61)*, was held in Hyde Park, transforming the area into a celebration of Victorian learning and self-confidence.

Peter Pan statue in Kensington Gardens

The brainchild of Queen Victoria's husband, Prince Albert, the exhibition was a massive success and the profits were used to buy 35 ha (87 acres) of land in South Kensington. Here, Prince Albert encouraged the construction of a concert hall, museums and colleges devoted to the applied arts and sciences; most of them survive. The neighbourhood soon became modish, full of flamboyant red-brick mansion blocks, garden squares and the elite shops still to be found in Knightsbridge.

SIGHTS AT A GLANCE

Historic Buildings
Kensington Palace 7

Churches
Brompton Oratory 2

Shops
Harrod's 1

Parks and Gardens
Hyde Park and Kensington Gardens 6

Museums and Galleries
Natural History Museum 5
Science Museum 4
Victoria and Albert Museum pp104–5 3

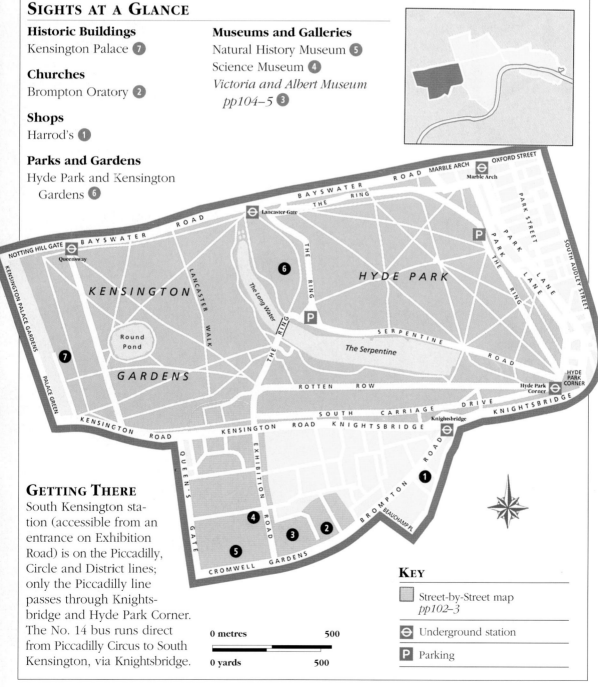

KEY

Street-by-Street map
pp102–3

Underground station

Parking

GETTING THERE
South Kensington station (accessible from an entrance on Exhibition Road) is on the Piccadilly, Circle and District lines; only the Piccadilly line passes through Knightsbridge and Hyde Park Corner. The No. 14 bus runs direct from Piccadilly Circus to South Kensington, via Knightsbridge.

0 metres 500

0 yards 500

◁ **Ennismore Mews in South Kensington, built 1843–6**

Street-by-Street: South Kensington

THE NUMEROUS MUSEUMS and colleges created in the wake of the Great Exhibition of 1851 *(see pp60–61)* continue to give this neighbourhood an air of leisured culture. Visited as much by Londoners as tourists, the museum area is liveliest on Sundays and on summer evenings during the Royal Albert Hall's famous season of classical "Prom" concerts *(see p130)*.

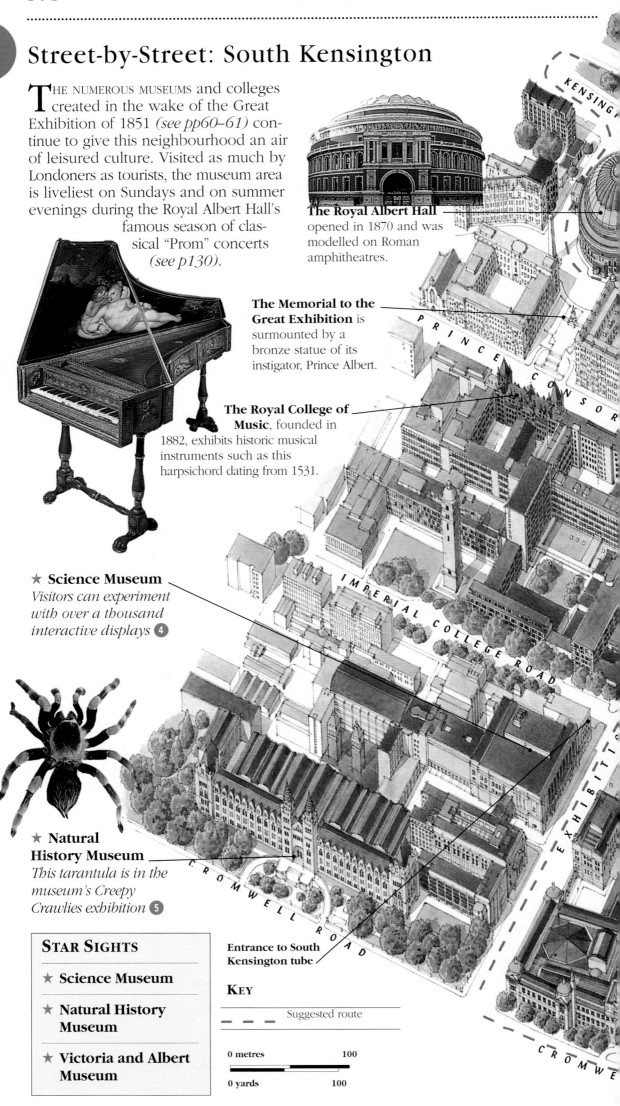

The Royal Albert Hall opened in 1870 and was modelled on Roman amphitheatres.

The Memorial to the Great Exhibition is surmounted by a bronze statue of its instigator, Prince Albert.

The Royal College of Music, founded in 1882, exhibits historic musical instruments such as this harpsichord dating from 1531.

★ **Science Museum**
Visitors can experiment with over a thousand interactive displays ❹

★ **Natural History Museum**
This tarantula is in the museum's Creepy Crawlies exhibition ❺

Entrance to South Kensington tube

STAR SIGHTS

★ **Science Museum**

★ **Natural History Museum**

★ **Victoria and Albert Museum**

KEY

— — — Suggested route

0 metres	100
0 yards	100

The Albert Memorial was built in memory of Queen Victoria's husband who died in 1861.

REGENT'S PARK & BLOOMSBURY

WEST END & WESTMINSTER

SOUTH KENSINGTON & HYDE PARK

LOCATOR MAP
See Street Finder map 2

★ **Victoria and Albert Museum**
The museum has a fine collection of applied arts and photography from around the world ③

Brompton Oratory
This ornate Baroque church is famous for its splendid musical tradition
②

Brompton Square (1821)

To Knightsbridge and Harrod's

ALBERT COURT

ROAD

PRINCES GARDENS

GARDENS

BROMPTON ROAD

Harrod's Food Hall

Harrod's ①

Knightsbridge SW1. **Map** 5 A3. 020-7730 1234. Knightsbridge. 10am–6pm Mon, Tue, Sat, 10am–7pm Wed–Fri. See **Shops and Markets** pp126–7.

IN 1849 HENRY CHARLES HARROD opened a grocery shop on Brompton Road, which soon became famous for its impeccable service and quality. The store expanded and in 1905 moved into these extravagant premises in Knightsbridge.

Brompton Oratory ②

Brompton Rd SW7. **Map** 2 F5. 020-7589 4811. South Kensington. 6:30am–8pm daily.

THE ITALIANATE ORATORY is a lavish monument to the 19th-century English Catholic revival. It was established as a base for a community of priests by John Henry Newman (later Cardinal Newman), who introduced the Oratorian movement to England in 1848. The church was opened in 1884, and the dome and façade added in the 1890s.

The sumptuous interior holds many fine monuments. The 12 huge 17th-century marble statues of the apostles are from Siena Cathedral, the elaborate Baroque Lady Altar (1693) is from the Dominican church at Brescia, and the 18th-century alter in St Wilfred's Chapel is from Rochefort in Belgium.

Victoria and Albert Museum ❸

DESCRIBED AS an "extremely capacious handbag" by its former director Sir Roy Strong, the V&A contains one of the world's richest collections of fine and applied arts from all periods and cultures. So broad is the range that it embraces Doc Marten boots, paintings by Constable, Islamic ceramics and the greatest collection of Indian art outside India. Since 1909 the museum has been housed in a building designed by Sir Aston Webb. A stunning extension – "The Spiral" by Daniel Libeskind – will see the museum into the 21st century.

Main entrance

Textiles

94
81 87
82 88
69
68
67
66
65
220
209
202
203
70a
70
71
72
73
74a
74b
74c
40a
52
53
113
54
5

★ 20th-Century Gallery
This shows modern design such as Daniel Weil's Radio in a Bag *(1983).*

Musical instruments

Stairs to Levels C and D

British Art and Design 1500–1750
The elaborate Great Bed of Ware (c.1590) is the V&A's most celebrated piece of furniture.

Exhibition Road entrance

GALLERY GUIDE

The V&A consists of 7 miles (11 km) of galleries occupying four main floor levels. The galleries are divided between those devoted to art and design, and those concentrating on materials and techniques. In the former, a wide variety of artefacts are assembled to illustrate the art and design of a particular period or civilization – such as Europe 1600–1800. These galleries occupy most of Level A and Lower A, with British arts on Levels B and C. The materials and techniques galleries contain collections of particular forms of craft, for example, porcelain, tapestries, metalwork, jewellery and glass. Many are situated on Levels C and D. The six-storey Henry Cole Wing, on the northwest side of the main building, holds the museum's collection of paintings, drawings, prints and photographs. There is also a gallery devoted to American architect Frank Lloyd Wright (1867–1959).

Henry Cole Wing
Highlights here include 200 paintings by John Constable and this graceful portrait, A Young Man Among Roses *(1588), by court miniaturist Nicholas Hilliard.*

KEY TO FLOORPLAN

☐ Lower A

☐ Level A

☐ Lower B

☐ Level B

☐ Henry Cole Wing

STAR EXHIBITS

★ **20th-Century Gallery**

★ **Morris, Gamble and Poynter Rooms**

★ **Medieval Treasury**

★ **Nehru Gallery of Indian Art**

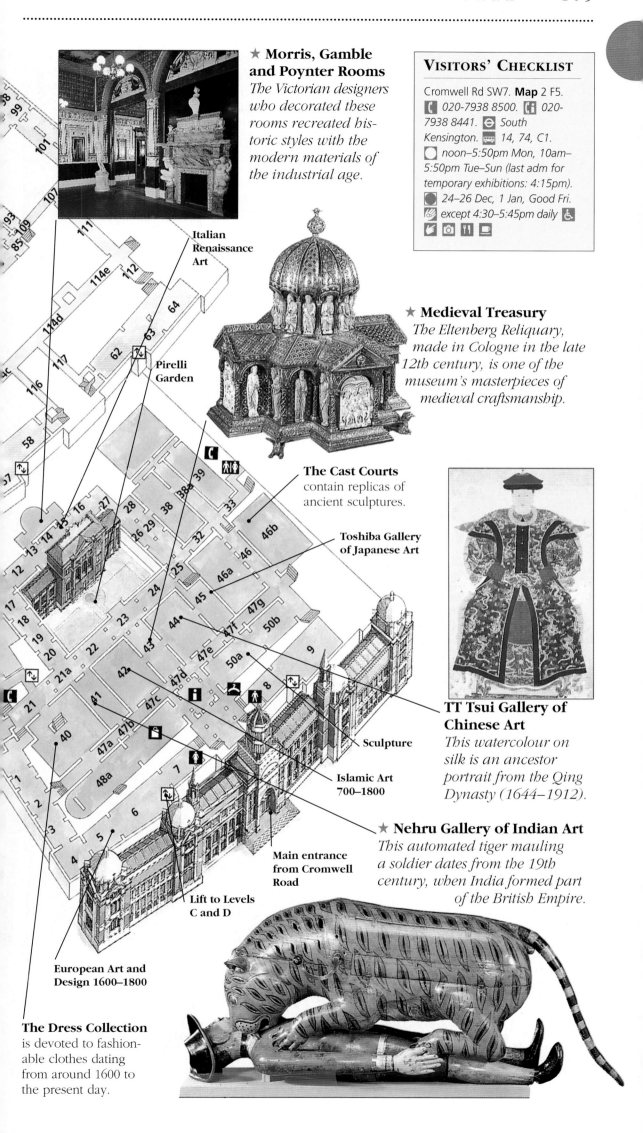

★ Morris, Gamble and Poynter Rooms

The Victorian designers who decorated these rooms recreated historic styles with the modern materials of the industrial age.

Italian Renaissance Art

Pirelli Garden

★ Medieval Treasury

The Eltenberg Reliquary, made in Cologne in the late 12th century, is one of the museum's masterpieces of medieval craftsmanship.

The Cast Courts contain replicas of ancient sculptures.

Toshiba Gallery of Japanese Art

TT Tsui Gallery of Chinese Art

This watercolour on silk is an ancestor portrait from the Qing Dynasty (1644–1912).

Sculpture

Islamic Art 700–1800

Main entrance from Cromwell Road

Lift to Levels C and D

★ Nehru Gallery of Indian Art

This automated tiger mauling a soldier dates from the 19th century, when India formed part of the British Empire.

European Art and Design 1600–1800

The Dress Collection is devoted to fashionable clothes dating from around 1600 to the present day.

Science Museum ④

Exhibition Rd SW7. **Map** 2 E5.
020-7938 8000. South
Kensington. 10am–6pm daily.
24–26 Dec.

CENTURIES OF continuing scientific and technological development lie at the heart of the Science Museum, ranging from Ancient Greek and Roman medicine to space exploration and nuclear fission. The massive and impressive collection brings entertainment to the process of learning, with many interactive displays that you do not need

Newcomen's Steam Engine (1712), Science Museum

a science degree to understand. Others are aimed at children, with staff on hand to give further explanations. Of equal importance is the social context of science: what discoveries and inventions mean for day-to-day life, and the process of discovery itself.

The best of the displays are Flight, which gives a chance to experiment with aeronautical principles, and Launch Pad, designed to give 7- to 13-year-olds a knowledge of basic scientific principles. The Exploration of Space displays the scarred Apollo 10 spacecraft which carried three astronauts to the moon and back in May 1969. There is also a video of the Apollo 11 moon landing which took place a few weeks later. More down-to-earth, but just as absorbing, is Food for Thought, which reveals the impact of science and technology

on every aspect of food. You can play shops with a laser scanner cash register, learn about additives, with a computer programme, and see how eating habits have changed by peering into a series of larders from 1900 to 1970. Other popular sections include: Power and Land Transport, which displays working steam engines, vintage trains, cars and motorbikes; and Optics, which has holograms, lasers and colourmixing experiments.

The Wellcome Wing of The History of Medicine has been expanded for the new millennium, and charts medical practices from ancient times through to the present day. Exhibits range from a replica of an Etruscan dental bridge to the latest leading edge biotechnological advances.

Natural History Museum ⑤

Cromwell Rd SW7. **Map** 2 E5.
020-7938 9123. South
Kensington. 10am–5:50pm
Mon–Sat, 11am–5:50pm Sun & public
hols. 23–26 Dec.

THIS VAST CATHEDRAL-LIKE building is the most architecturally flamboyant of the South Kensington museums. Its richly sculpted stonework conceals an iron and steel frame; this building technique was revolutionary when the museum opened in 1881. The imaginative displays tackle fundamental issues such as the ecology and evolution of the planet, the origin of species and the development of human beings – all explained through a dynamic

Relief from a decorative panel in the Natural History Museum

combination of the latest technology, interactive techniques and traditional displays.

The museum is divided into the Life and Earth Galleries. In the former, the Ecology exhibition begins its exploration of the complex web of the natural world, and man's role in it, through a convincing replica of a moonlit rainforest buzzing with the sounds of insects. The most popular exhibits here are in the Dinosaur section which has a moving, roaring tableau of three life-sized, animatronic beasts devouring a dead Tenonotosaurus. The Earth Galleries explore the history of Earth and its wealth of natural resources, and offer the opportunity to experience the rumblings of an earthquake.

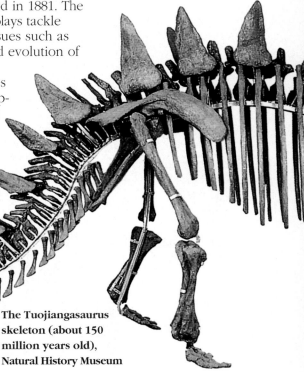
The Tuojiangasaurus skeleton (about 150 million years old), Natural History Museum

Statue of the young Queen Victoria outside Kensington Palace, sculpted by her daughter, Princess Louise

Hyde Park and Kensington Gardens ⑥

W2. **Map** 2 F2. 020-7298 2100.
Hyde Park ⊖ Hyde Park Corner,
Knightsbridge, Lancaster Gate, Marble
Arch. ○ dawn–midnight daily. ♿
Kensington Gardens ⊖ Queensway,
Lancaster Gate. ○ dawn–dusk daily.
♿ See **Parks and Gardens** pp80–81.

THE ANCIENT MANOR of Hyde was part of the lands of Westminster Abbey seized by Henry VIII at the Dissolution of the Monasteries in 1536 (see pp54–5). James I opened the park to the public in the early 17th century, and it was soon one of the city's most fashionable public spaces. Unfortunately it also became popular with duellists and highwaymen, and consequently William III had 300 lights hung along Rotten Row, the first street in England to be lit up at night.

In 1730, the Westbourne River was dammed by Queen Caroline in order to create the Serpentine, an artificial lake where Britain's victory over the French at Trafalgar was celebrated in 1814 with a re-enactment of the battle to the strains of the National Anthem. Today the Serpentine is used for boating and swimming, and Rotten Row for horse riding. The park is also a rallying point for political demonstrations, while at Speaker's Corner, in the northeast, anyone has had the right to address the public since 1872. Sundays are particularly lively, with many budding orators and a number of eccentrics revealing their plans for the betterment of mankind.

Adjoining Hyde Park is Kensington Gardens, the former grounds of Kensington Palace which were opened to the public in 1841. Two great attractions for children are the bronze statue of JM Barrie's fictional Peter Pan (1912), by George Frampton, and the Round Pond where people sail model boats. Also worth seeing is the dignified Orangery (1704), once used by Queen Anne as a "summer supper house" and now used as a summer café.

Detail of the Coalbrookdale Gate, Kensington Gardens

Kensington Palace ⑦

Kensington Palace Gdns W8.
Map 2 D3. 020-7937 9561.
⊖ High St Kensington, Queensway.
○ summer: 10am–6pm daily; winter:
10am–5pm Wed–Sun. ● 24–26 Dec,
1 Jan, Good Fri. ♿ ground floor.

KENSINGTON PALACE was the principal residence of the royal family from the 1690s until 1760, when George III moved to Buckingham Palace. Over the years it has seen a number of important royal events. In 1714 Queen Anne died here from a fit of apoplexy brought on by over-eating and, in June 1837, Princess Victoria of Kent was woken to be told that her uncle William IV had died and she was now queen – the beginning of her 64-year reign. Half of the palace still holds royal apartments, but the other half is open to the public. Among the highlights are the 18th-century state rooms with ceilings and murals by William Kent (see p28). In the days following the death of Princess Diana in 1997, the palace became a focal point for mourners who gathered in their thousands at its gates and turned the surrounding area into a field of bouquets.

REGENT'S PARK AND BLOOMSBURY

CREAM STUCCOED terraces built by John Nash *(see p111)* fringe the southern edge of Regent's Park in London's highest concentration of quality Georgian housing. The park, named for the Prince Regent, was also designed by Nash, as the culmination of a triumphal route from the Prince's house in St James *(see pp90–91)*. Today it is the busiest of the royal parks and boasts a zoo, an open air theatre, boating lake, rose garden, cafés and London's largest mosque. To the northeast is Camden Town *(see p134)* with its popular market, shops and cafés, reached by walking, or taking a boat, along the picturesque Regent's Canal.

Ancient Greek vase, British Museum

Bloomsbury, an enclave of attractive garden squares and Georgian brick terraces, was one of the most fashionable areas of the city until the mid-19th century, when the arrival of large hospitals and railway stations persuaded many of the wealthier residents to move west to Mayfair, Knightsbridge and Kensington. Home to the British Museum since 1753 and the University of London since 1828, Bloomsbury has long been the domain of artists, writers and intellectuals, including the Bloomsbury Group *(see p157)*, George Bernard Shaw, Charles Dickens and Karl Marx. Traditionally a centre for the book trade, it remains a good place for literary browsing.

SIGHTS AT A GLANCE

Historic Streets
Bloomsbury ❺

Museums and Galleries
British Museum pp112–13 ❹

Madame Tussaud's and
  the Planetarium ❶
Sherlock Holmes
  Museum ❷
Wallace Collection ❸

KEY

🚇 Underground station

🅿 Parking

0 metres   500
0 yards   500

GETTING THERE

For most of Regent's Park, the nearest tube stations are Regent's Park, Great Portland Street and Baker Street. Buses 13, 139 and 159 run from Trafalgar Square to near Baker Street. The closest station to the zoo is Camden Town. Russell Square tube station is in the heart of Bloomsbury.

◁ **St Andrew's Place, Regent's Park**

Madame Tussaud's and the Planetarium ❶

Marylebone Rd NW1. **Map** 3 B3.
☎ 020-7935 6861. ⊖ Baker St.
◯ 10am–5:30pm Mon–Fri, 9:30am–
5:30pm Sat, Sun. ◑ 25 Dec. 🎟 📷
♿

Wax figure of Elizabeth II

MADAME TUSSAUD began her wax-modelling career making death masks of victims of the French Revolution. She moved to England and in 1835 set up an exhibition of her work in Baker Street, near the present site. Traditional techniques are still used to create figures of royalty, politicians, actors, pop stars, and sporting heroes. The main sections of the exhibition are: the Garden Party, where visitors mingle with life-like models of celebrities; Super Stars, devoted to the giants of the entertainment world; and the Grand Hall, a collection of various royalty, statesmen, world leaders, writers and artists, from Lenin and Martin Luther King to Shakespeare and Picasso.

The Chamber of Horrors is the most renowned part of Madame Tussaud's. Alongside some of the original French Revolution death masks are recreations of murders and

Wax model of Luciano Pavarotti (1990), Madame Tussaud's

Conan Doyle's fictional detective Sherlock Holmes

executions. The Spirit of London finale allows visitors travel in stylized taxi-cabs through the city's history, to "witness" events, from the Great Fire of 1666 to the Swinging 1960s. Next door, the Planetarium, built in 1958, has spectacularly exciting star and laser shows.

Sherlock Holmes Museum ❷

221b Baker St NW1. **Map** 3 A3.
☎ 020-7935 8866. ⊖ Baker St. ◯
9:30am–6pm daily. ◑ 25 Dec. 🎟 📷

SIR ARTHUR CONAN DOYLE'S fictional detective was supposed to live at 221B Baker Street, which did not exist. The museum, labelled 221B, actually stands between Nos. 237 and 239, and is the only surviving Victorian lodging house in the street. There is a reconstruction of Holmes' front room, and memorabilia from the stories decorate the walls. Visitors can buy plaques, Holmes hats, Toby jugs and meerschaum pipes.

Wallace Collection ❸

Hertford House, Manchester Sq W1.
Map 3 B4. ☎ 020-7935 0687.
⊖ Bond St. ◯ 10am–5pm Mon–
Sat, 2–5pm Sun. ◑ 24–26 Dec, 1 Jan,
Good Fri, May Day. ♿ phone first. 📷

ONE OF THE WORLD'S finest private collections of art, it has remained intact since 1897. The product of passionate

collecting by four generations of the Seymour-Conway family who were Marquesses of Hertford, it was bequeathed to the state on the condition that it would go on permanent public display with nothing added or taken away. The 25 beautiful galleries are a must for anyone with even a passing interest in European art.

The 3rd Marquess (1777–1842), a flamboyant London figure, used his Italian wife's fortune to build on the rich collection of family portraits he had inherited, buying works by Titian and Canaletto, along with numerous 17th-century Dutch paintings including works by Van Dyck. The collection's particular strength, however, is in 18th-century French painting, sculpture, and decorative arts, acquired in France by the 4th Marquess (1800–70) and his natural son, Sir Richard Wallace (1818–90). The Marquess had a taste for lush romanticism rather than realism, a distinct advantage in post-Revolution

A 16th-century Italian majolica dish from the Wallace Collection

France, where most collectors had little time for the dreamy canvasses painted for Louis XV and his court. Notable among these are Watteau's *Champs Elysées* (1716–17), Fragonard's *The Swing* (1766) and Boucher's *The Rising and Setting of the Sun* (1753).

Other highlights include Rembrandt's *Titus, the Artist's Son* (1650s), Titian's *Perseus and Andromeda* (1554–6) and Franz Hals's famous *Laughing Cavalier* (1624). There is also an important collection of Renaissance armour, and superb examples of Sèvres porcelain and Italian majolica.

John Nash's Regency London

JOHN NASH, the son of a Lambeth millwright, was designing houses from the 1780s. However, it was not until the 1820s that he also became known as an inspired town planner, when his "royal route" was completed. This took George IV from his Pall Mall palace, through Piccadilly Circus and up the elegant sweep of Regent Street to Regent's Park, which Nash bordered with rows of

Statue of John Nash (1752–1835)

beautiful Neo-Classical villas, such as Park Crescent and Cumberland Terrace. Though many of his plans were never completed, this map of 1851, which unusually places the south at the top, shows Nash's overall architectural impact on London. His other work included the revamping of Buckingham Palace *(see pp92–3)*, and the building of several theatres and churches.

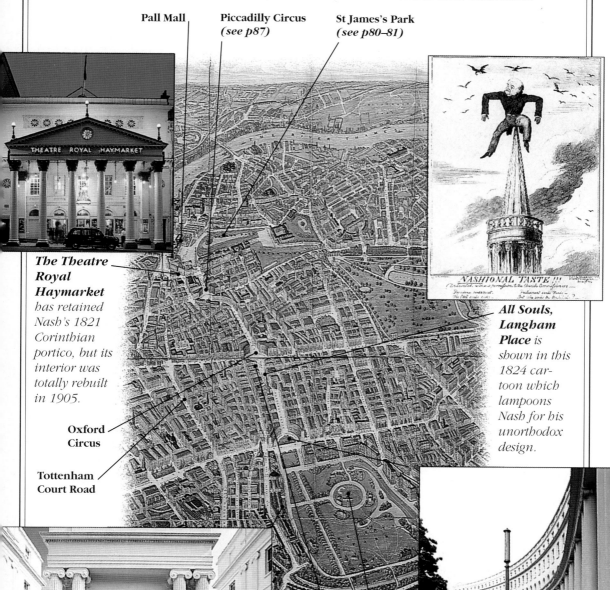

Pall Mall

Piccadilly Circus *(see p87)*

St James's Park *(see p80–81)*

NASHIONAL TASTE !!!

The Theatre Royal Haymarket *has retained Nash's 1821 Corinthian portico, but its interior was totally rebuilt in 1905.*

Oxford Circus

Tottenham Court Road

All Souls, Langham Place *is shown in this 1824 cartoon which lampoons Nash for his unorthodox design.*

Regent Street

Regent's Park *(see p109)*

Cumberland Terrace, *the longest and most ornate of the stuccoed terraces surrounding Regent's Park, was intended to face a royal palace, which was never built.*

Park Crescent *was designed by Nash to be the southern half of a circle, but the northern half was never built. The interiors were refurbished in the 1960s but the dramatic façade was kept intact.*

British Museum ❹

Helmet from Sutton Hoo ship burial

THE OLDEST PUBLIC MUSEUM in the world, the British Museum was established in 1753 to house the extensive collections of the physician Sir Hans Sloane (1660–1753). The main part of the building (1823–50) is by architect Robert Smirke. Sloane's collection has been added to by gifts and purchases from all over the world, and the museum now contains artefacts spanning thousands of years of world culture. The British Library, which used to be in the museum's east wing, moved to Euston in 1997.

★ **Egyptian Mummies**
Animals such as this cat (30 BC) were preserved alongside humans by the ancient Egyptians.

North stairs

West stairs

Entrance from Montague Place

Mexican Gallery

Bronze Figure Shiva Nataraja
This statue of the Hindu God Shiva Nataraja (c.1100) from South India forms part of the fine collection of Oriental art.

North stairs

North American Gallery
illustrates the diverse richness of the development of the most culturally influential part of the world.

West stairs

GALLERY GUIDE
The museum's 94 galleries cover 2.5 miles (4 km). Greek, Roman, Egyptian and Western Asiatic exhibits are on the west side of the ground floor; the Oriental collection is on the north side, and the new Mexican Gallery on the east gives way to a walk-though area which leads to Great Court exhibits. Collections are continued on the first floor and in the basement. Temporary exhibitions are held throughout the museum and near the entrance in rooms 27 and 28.

★ **Elgin Marbles**
These 5th-century BC reliefs from the Parthenon in Athens were brought to London by Lord Elgin around 1802 and are the museum's most famous treasure.

Stairs to basement

KEY TO FLOORPLAN

☐ Early British collections	☐ Egyptian collections
☐ Coins, medals and drawings	☐ Greek and Roman collections
☐ Medieval, Renaissance and Modern collections	☐ Oriental collections
☐ Western Asiatic archaeological collections	☐ Former British Library
	☐ Non-exhibition space
☐ Mexican Gallery	☐ Temporary exhibitions

STAR EXHIBITS

★ **Egyptian Mummies**

★ **Elgin Marbles**

★ **Lindow Man**

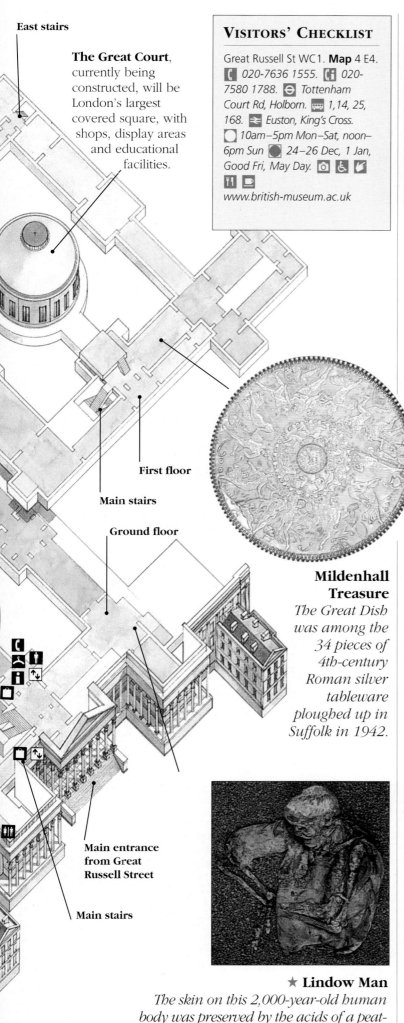

East stairs

The Great Court, currently being constructed, will be London's largest covered square, with shops, display areas and educational facilities.

First floor

Main stairs

Ground floor

Main entrance from Great Russell Street

Main stairs

VISITORS' CHECKLIST

Great Russell St WC1. **Map** 4 E4. 020-7636 1555. 020-7580 1788. Tottenham Court Rd, Holborn. 1,14, 25, 168. Euston, King's Cross. 10am–5pm Mon–Sat, noon–6pm Sun 24–26 Dec, 1 Jan, Good Fri, May Day.

www.british-museum.ac.uk

Mildenhall Treasure
The Great Dish was among the 34 pieces of 4th-century Roman silver tableware ploughed up in Suffolk in 1942.

Private gardens of Bedford Square

Bloomsbury ⑤

WC1. **Map** 4 F4. *Russell Sq, Tottenham Court Rd.* **Dickens House Museum** *48 Doughty St WC1.* 020-7405 2127. *9:45am–5:30pm Mon–Fri, 10am–5pm Sat.*

HOME TO NUMEROUS WRITERS and artists, Bloomsbury is a traditional centre of the book trade. It is dominated by the British Museum and the University of London and characterized by a number of fine Georgian squares. These include **Russell Square**, where the poet TS Eliot (1888–1965) worked for a publisher for 40 years; **Queen Square** which contains a statue of Queen Charlotte, wife of George III; and **Bloomsbury Square**, laid out in 1661. A plaque here commemorates members of the literary and artistic Bloomsbury Group *(see p157)*. One of London's best-preserved 18th-century oases is **Bedford Square**. Charles Dickens *(see p191)* lived at 48 Doughty Street during a brief but critical stage in his career, and it was here that he wrote *Oliver Twist* and *Nicholas Nickleby*, both completed in 1839.

Queen Charlotte (1744–1818)

His former home has become the **Dickens House Museum**, which has rooms laid out as they were in Dickens' time, with miscellaneous objects taken from his other London homes and first editions of many of his works.

★ **Lindow Man**
The skin on this 2,000-year-old human body was preserved by the acids of a peat-bog in Cheshire. He was probably killed in an elaborate ritual.

THE CITY AND SOUTHWARK

DOMINATED TODAY BY glossy office blocks, the City is the oldest part of the capital. The Great Fire of 1666 obliterated four-fifths of its buildings. Sir Christopher Wren rebuilt much of it and many of his churches survived World War II *(see pp62–3)*. Commerce has always been its lifeblood, and the power of its merchants and bankers secured it a degree of autonomy from state control. Even today the monarch cannot cross its boundaries without permission from the Lord Mayor. Humming with activity in business hours, the City empties at night.

Old bank sign on Lombard Street

In the Middle Ages Southwark, on the south bank of the Thames, was a refuge for pleasure-seekers, prostitutes, gamblers and criminals. Even after 1550, when the area fell under the jurisdiction of the City, its brothels and taverns thrived. There were also several bear-baiting arenas in which plays were staged until the building of theatres such as the Globe (1598), where many of Shakespeare's works were first performed. Relics of old Southwark are mostly on the waterfront, which has been imaginatively redeveloped and provided with a pleasant walkway.

SIGHTS AT A GLANCE

Historic Sights and Buildings
Lloyd's Building **7**
The Old Operating Theatre **11**
Temple **1**
Tower Bridge **9**
Tower of London pp124–25 **8**

Museums and Galleries
Design Museum **10**
Museum of London **4**
Shakespeare's Globe **14**
Sir John Soane's Museum **2**
Tate Gallery of Modern Art at Bankside **13**

Churches and Cathedrals
St Bartholomew-the-Great **3**
St Paul's Cathedral pp116–17 **5**
St Stephen Walbrook **6**
Southwark Cathedral **12**

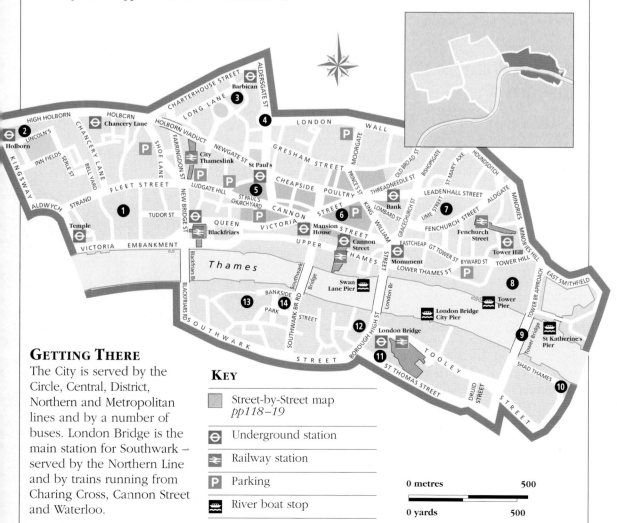

GETTING THERE

The City is served by the Circle, Central, District, Northern and Metropolitan lines and by a number of buses. London Bridge is the main station for Southwark – served by the Northern Line and by trains running from Charing Cross, Cannon Street and Waterloo.

KEY

	Street-by-Street map *pp118–19*
⊖	Underground station
⇌	Railway station
P	Parking
⛴	River boat stop

0 metres   500
0 yards   500

◁ **St Paul's Cathedral in the heart of the City, with the NatWest Tower (1980) to the left**

Wigged and robed barristers, Lincoln's Inn

Temple ①

Middle Temple Lane EC4. **Map** 7 A3.
🚇 *Temple.* **Middle Temple Hall**
📞 *020-7427 4800.* ◻ *10am–noon & 3–4pm Mon–Fri.* ⬤ *academic hols, phone first.* ♿ *phone first.*

A CLUSTER of atmospheric squares form the Inner and Middle Temples, two of London's four Inns of Court, where law students are trained (Lincoln's Inn and Gray's Inn

are the other two). The four Inns fulfil identical functions but each remains conscious of its separate traditions. According to an age-old custom anyone in Britain training to be a barrister has to join one of the Inns and must dine there 24 times – as well as passing exams – before being officially qualified.

The name Temple derives from the medieval Knights Templar, a religious order founded here in 1118 to protect pilgrims going to the Holy Land. The Templars owned this area until 1312 when the order was suppressed on charges of immorality and heresy. But the real reason was that they had become very wealthy, and their power was seen as a threat to the throne. Marble effigies of knights lie on the floor of the circular Temple church, part of which dates from the 12th century.

The finest of the Temple's other ancient buildings is the opulent Middle Temple Hall, which retains a wonderful Elizabethan hammer-beamed roof that was restored after bomb damage in World War II. It is thought that Shakespeare took part in a performance of *Twelfth Night* here in 1601.

St Bartholomew-the-Great ③

West Smithfield EC1. **Map** 7 B2.
📞 *020-7606 5171.* 🚇 *Barbican, St Paul's.* ◻ *8:30am–5pm Mon–Fri (mid-Nov–mid-Feb: 8:30am–4pm), 9am–1pm Sat.* ⬤ *25, 26 Dec, 1 Jan.*
📷 ♿ 🎦

THE HISTORIC AREA of Smithfield has witnessed a number of bloody events over the years, among them the execution of rebel peasant leader Wat Tyler in 1381, and, in the reign of Mary I (1553–58), the burning of scores of Protestant martyrs.

Hidden in a quiet corner behind Smithfield meat market (central London's only surviving wholesale food market),

Sir John Soane's Museum ②

13 Lincoln's Inn Fields WC2. **Map** 4 F4. 📞 *020-7430 0175.* 🚇 *Holborn.* ◻ *10am–5pm Tue–Sat, 6–9pm 1st Tue of month.* ⬤ *public hols, 24 Dec.* 📷

ONE OF THE MOST eccentric museums in London, this house was left to the nation by Sir John Soane in 1837, with a stipulation that nothing should be changed. The son of a bricklayer, Soane became one of Britain's leading late Georgian architects developing a restrained Neo-Classical style of his own. After marrying the niece of a wealthy builder, whose fortune he inherited, he bought and reconstructed No. 12 Lincoln's Inn Fields. In 1813 he and his wife moved into No. 13 and in 1824 he rebuilt No. 14, adding a picture gallery and the mock medieval Monk's Parlour. Today, true to Soane's

wishes, the collections are much as he left them – an eclectic gathering of beautiful, instructional and often simply peculiar artefacts. There are casts, bronzes, vases, antique fragments, paintings and a selection of bizarre trivia which ranges from a giant fungus from Sumatra to a scold-bridle, a device designed to silence nagging wives. Highlights include the sarcophagus of Seti I, Soanes's own designs, including those for the Bank of England, models by leading Neo-Classical sculptors such as Banks and Flaxman and the *Rake's Progress* series of paintings (1734), by William Hogarth, which Mrs Soane bought for £520.

The building itself is full of architectural surprises and illusions. In the main ground floor room, cunningly placed mirrors play tricks with light and space, while an atrium stretching from the basement to the glass-domed roof allows light onto every floor.

A glass dome lets light on to all the floors.

A vast sarcophagus (1300 BC) stands on the floor of the crypt.

St Bartholomew-the-Great is one of London's oldest churches. It once formed part of a priory founded in 1123 by a monk named Rahere, whose tomb is inside. Rahere was Henry I's court jester until he dreamed that St Bartholomew had saved him from a winged monster. As prior, he would sometimes revert to his former role, entertaining crowds with juggling tricks at the annual Bartholomew Fair.

The 13th-century arch, now topped by a Tudor gatehouse, used to be the entrance to the church until the old nave was pulled down during the Dissolution of the Monasteries (*see pp54–5*).

St Bartholomew's gatehouse

Delft plate made in London 1602, Museum of London

Museum of London ④

London Wall EC2. **Map** 7 C2.
📞 020-7600 3699. 🚇 Barbican, St Paul's. 🕐 10am–5:50pm Mon–Sat & public hols, noon–5:50pm Sun.
⬤ 24–26 Dec, 1 Jan. 🖼 📷 ♿

THIS MUSEUM traces life in London from prehistoric times to the 20th century. Displays of archaeological finds and original domestic objects alternate with reconstructed street scenes and interiors, culminating in a 1932 broadcasting studio and a shop counter from Woolworth's.

Objects from Roman London include a brightly coloured 2nd-century fresco which came from a Southwark bath house, while from the Tudor city come a Delft plate and costumes, including leather clothes found on a rubbish tip. The 17th-century section holds the shirt Charles I wore on the scaffold (*see pp56–7*), and an audio-visual display recreating the Great Fire of 1666.

One of the most popular exhibits is the lavishly gilded Lord Mayor's State Coach, built in 1757 and still used for the colourful Lord Mayor's Show in November (*see pp68–9*).

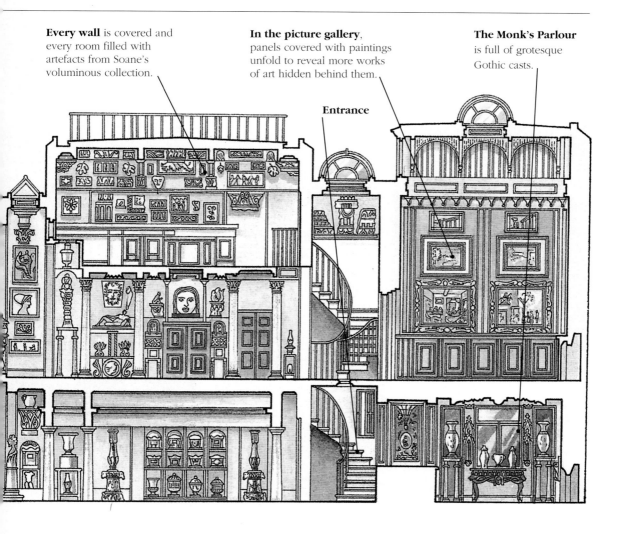

Every wall is covered and every room filled with artefacts from Soane's voluminous collection.

In the picture gallery, panels covered with paintings unfold to reveal more works of art hidden behind them.

The Monk's Parlour is full of grotesque Gothic casts.

Entrance

Street-by-Street: The City

Detail: St Paul's Cathedral

THIS IS THE FINANCIAL HEART of London and has been ever since the Romans set up a trading post here 2,000 years ago. For years it was London's main residential area but today very few people live here. The City was severely bombed in World War II and the main clues to its past are streets named after vanished inns and markets. Its numerous churches, many built after the Great Fire of 1666 by the architect Sir Christopher Wren (see p120), are now dwarfed by lavish banks and post-modern developments.

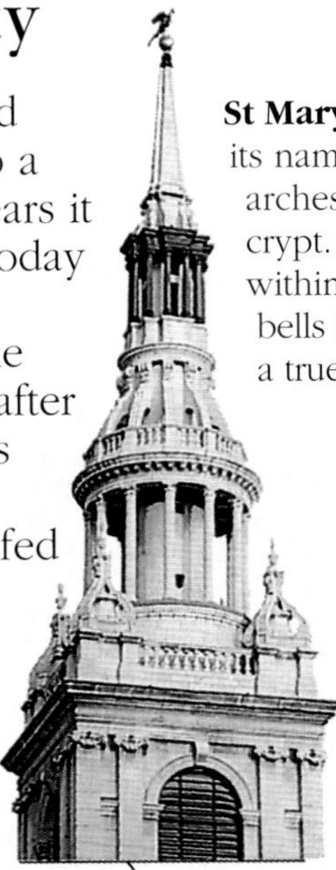

St Mary-le-Bow takes its name from the bow arches in the Norman crypt. Anyone born within earshot of its bells is said to be a true Cockney.

The Temple of Mithras is an important Roman relic (see p49).

New Change replaces Old Change, a 13th-century street destroyed in World War II.

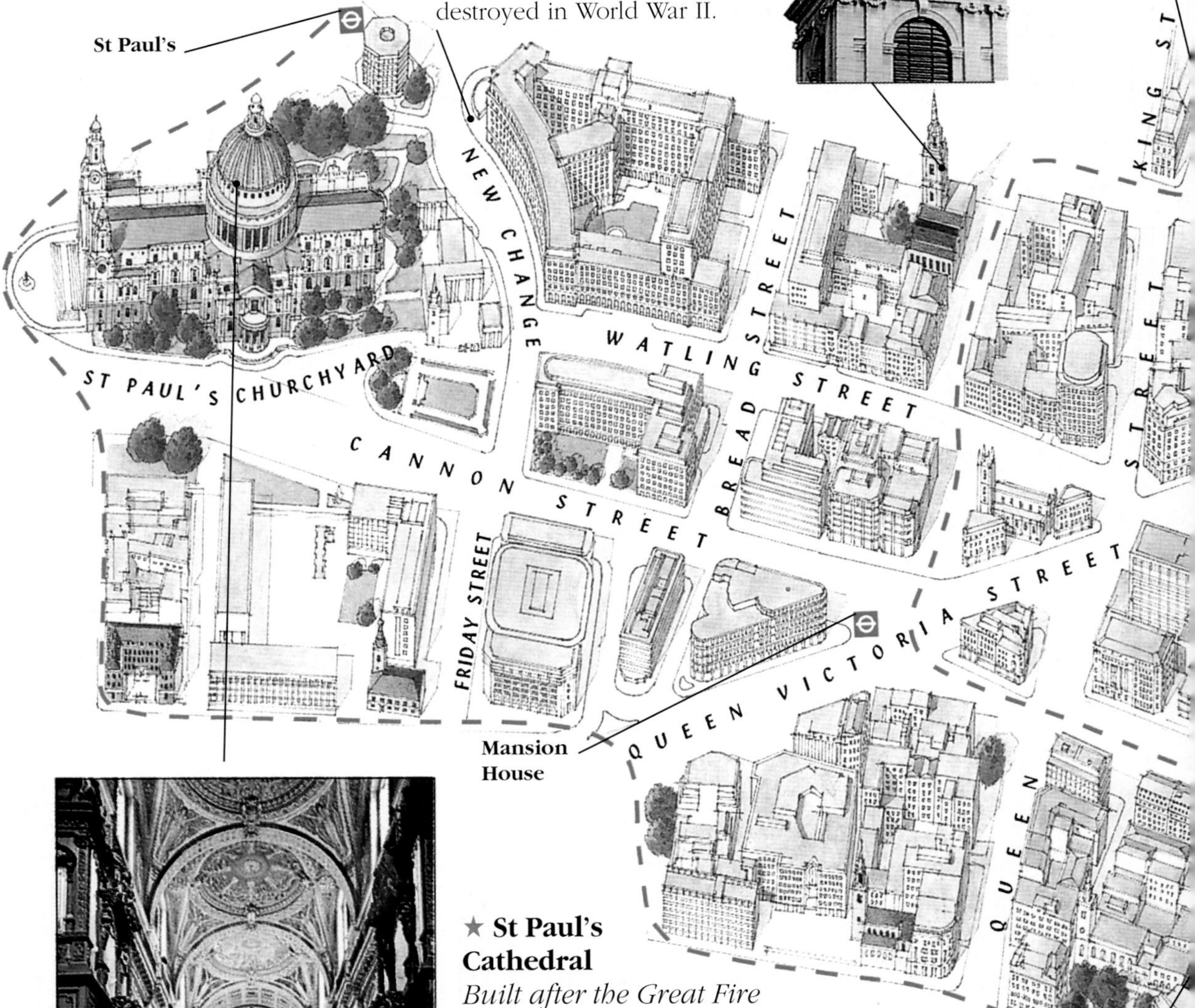

St Paul's

NEW CHANGE

WATLING STREET

BREAD STREET

KING ST

ST PAUL'S CHURCHYARD

CANNON STREET

FRIDAY STREET

QUEEN VICTORIA STREET

STREET

QUEEN

Mansion House

★ **St Paul's Cathedral**
Built after the Great Fire of 1666, Wren's master-piece was funded by a tax on coal ⑤

STAR SIGHTS

★ **St Paul's Cathedral**

★ **St Stephen Walbrook**

KEY

- - - - - Suggested route

0 metres   100

0 yards   100

Skinners' Hall is an 18th-century Italianate building constructed for the ancient guild that controlled trade in fur and leather.

Lombard Street, named after bankers who came from Lombardy in the 13th century, retains its traditional banking signs.

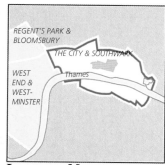

REGENT'S PARK & BLOOMSBURY

THE CITY & SOUTHWARK

WEST END & WEST-MINSTER

Thames

LOCATOR MAP
See Street Finder map 7 , 8

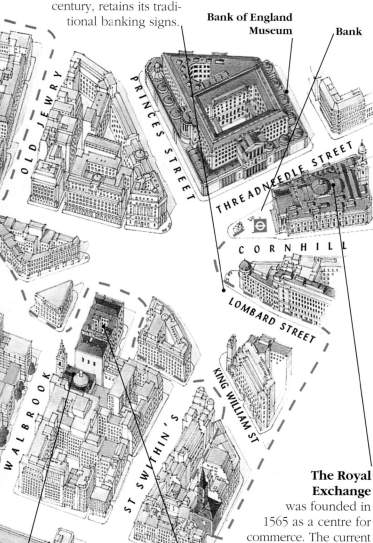

Bank of England Museum

Bank

OLD JEWRY

PRINCES STREET

THREADNEEDLE STREET

CORNHILL

LOMBARD STREET

WALBROOK

ST SWITHIN'S

KING WILLIAM ST

★ **St Stephen Walbrook**
The Walbrook is a tributary of the Thames, now underground ⑥

The Royal Exchange was founded in 1565 as a centre for commerce. The current building dates from 1844.

Mansion House (1753), designed by George Dance the Elder, is the official home of the Lord Mayor. One of the most spectacular rooms is the Egyptian Hall.

St Paul's ⑤

See pp120–21.

St Stephen Walbrook ⑥

39 Walbrook EC4. **Map** 8 D3.
020-7283 4444. Bank, Cannon St. 10am–4pm Mon–Thu, 10am–3pm Fri. public hols.

THE LORD MAYOR's parish church was built by Sir Christopher Wren in the 1670s and is among the finest of all his City churches. The bright, airy interior is flooded with light by a huge dome that appears to float above the eight columns and arches that support it. Original fittings, such as the ornate font and rich pulpit, contrast with the stark simplicity of Henry Moore's massive white stone altar (1987). The best way to see the church is during one of its free organ recitals or lunchtime concerts.

Original 17th-century font

Lloyd's Building ⑦

1 Lime St EC3. **Map** 8 E2. 020-7327 1000. Monument, Bank, Aldgate. to the public.

THIS BUILDING, designed by Richard Rogers in 1986 for the world's largest insurance marketplace, echoes his famous Pompidou Centre.

One of London's most interesting modern buildings, it is a vast glass construction, with its functional elements, such as stainless steel pipes, high-tech ducts and lifts, on the exterior.

Tower of London ⑧

See pp124–5.

St Paul's Cathedral ⑤

★ Dome
At 113 m (360 ft), the elaborate dome is one of the highest in the world.

THE GREAT FIRE OF LONDON in 1666 left the medieval cathedral of St Paul's in ruins. Wren was commissioned to rebuild it, but his design for a church on a Greek Cross plan (where all four arms are equal) met with considerable resistance. The authorities insisted on a conventional Latin cross, with a long nave and short transepts, which was believed to focus the congregation's attention on the altar. Despite the compromises, Wren created a magnificent Baroque cathedral, which was built between 1675 and 1710 and has since formed the lavish setting for many state ceremonies.

The balustrade
along the top was added in 1718 against Wren's wishes.

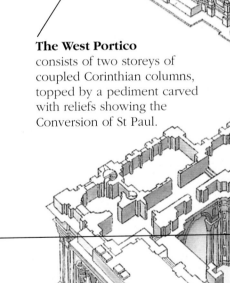

★ West Front and Towers
Inspired by the Italian Baroque architect, Borromini, the towers were added by Wren in 1707.

The West Portico
consists of two storeys of coupled Corinthian columns, topped by a pediment carved with reliefs showing the Conversion of St Paul.

The Nave
An imposing succession of massive arches and saucer domes open out into the vast space below the cathedral's main dome.

CHRISTOPHER WREN

Trained as a scientist, Sir Christopher Wren (1632–1723) began his impressive architectural career at the age of 31. He became a leading figure in the rebuilding of London after the Great Fire of 1666, building a total of 52 new churches. Although Wren never visited Italy, his work was influenced by Roman, Baroque and Renaissance architecture, as is apparent in his masterpiece, St Paul's Cathedral.

West Porch

Main entrance
approached from Ludgate Hill

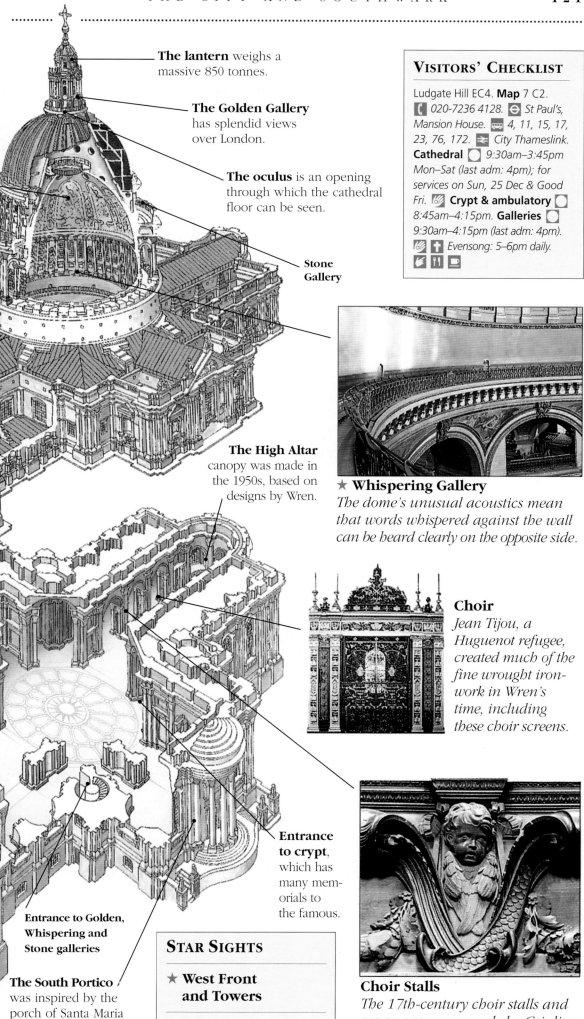

The lantern weighs a massive 850 tonnes.

The Golden Gallery has splendid views over London.

The oculus is an opening through which the cathedral floor can be seen.

Stone Gallery

The High Altar canopy was made in the 1950s, based on designs by Wren.

VISITORS' CHECKLIST

Ludgate Hill EC4. **Map** 7 C2.
020-7236 4128. St Paul's, Mansion House. 4, 11, 15, 17, 23, 76, 172. City Thameslink.
Cathedral 9:30am–3:45pm Mon–Sat (last adm: 4pm); for services on Sun, 25 Dec & Good Fri. **Crypt & ambulatory** 8:45am–4:15pm. **Galleries** 9:30am–4:15pm (last adm: 4pm). Evensong: 5–6pm daily.

★ Whispering Gallery
The dome's unusual acoustics mean that words whispered against the wall can be heard clearly on the opposite side.

Choir
Jean Tijou, a Huguenot refugee, created much of the fine wrought ironwork in Wren's time, including these choir screens.

Entrance to crypt, which has many memorials to the famous.

Entrance to Golden, Whispering and Stone galleries

The South Portico was inspired by the porch of Santa Maria della Pace in Rome. Wren absorbed the detail by studying a friend's collection of architectural engravings.

STAR SIGHTS

★ **West Front and Towers**

★ **Dome**

★ **Whispering Gallery**

Choir Stalls
The 17th-century choir stalls and organ case were made by Grinling Gibbons (1648–1721), a woodcarver from Rotterdam. He and his team of craftsmen worked on these intricate carvings for two years.

Tower Bridge ⑨

SE1. **Map** 16 D3. 📞 *020-7378 1928.*
🚇 *Tower Hill.* **The Tower Bridge Experience** ◯ *Apr–Oct: 10am–6.30pm daily; Nov–Mar: 9.30am–6pm daily (last adm: 75 mins before closing).* ⬤ *24–26 Dec.* **Adm charge.** 📷 ♿ 🔒 *Video.*

T HIS FLAMBOYANT piece of Victorian engineering, designed by Sir Horace Jones, was completed in 1894 and soon became a symbol of London. Its two Gothic towers contain the mechanism for raising the roadway to permit large ships to pass through. The towers are made of a supporting steel framework clad in stone, and are linked by two high level walkways which were closed between 1909 and 1982 due to their popularity with suicides and prostitutes. The bridge now houses The Tower Bridge Experience, with interactive displays bringing the bridge's history to life. There are fine river views from the walkways, and a look at the steam engine room that powered the lifting machinery until 1976, when the system was electrified.

Walkways, open to the public, give panoramic views over the Thames and London.

The roadway, when raised creates a space 40 m (135 ft) high and 60 m (200 ft) wide, big enough for large cargo ships.

Engine room

South Bank

Lifts and 300 steps lead to the top of the towers.

The Victorian winding machinery was originally powered by steam.

Entrance

North Bank

Design Museum ⑩

Butlers Wharf, Shad Thames SE1.
Map 8 F4. 📞 *020-7378 6055.*
🚇 *Tower Hill, London Bridge.*
◯ *11:30am–6pm daily.* ⬤ *24–26 Dec.* ♿ ✏️ 🍴 🖥 🔒

T HIS MUSEUM was the first in the world to be devoted solely to the design of mass-produced everyday objects.

Sculpture by Paolozzi (1986) outside the Design Museum

The permanent collection charts technical innovation, changes in taste and commercial success or failure through an eclectic range of furniture, office equipment, cars, radios, TV sets and household utensils. Elite design classics such as chairs by GT Rietveld and a kettle by Philippe Starck are on show alongside Pyrex dishes, Tupperware cups and a Kodak Instamatic camera. Also worth seeing are prototypes that disappeared without trace, such as a television designed so that people could watch it lying down.

Temporary exhibitions of international design held in the Review and Collections galleries give a taste of what may become familiar in the future, and a chance to catch up on various new trends.

The Old Operating Theatre ⑪

9A St Thomas St SE1. **Map** 8 D4.
📞 *020-7955 47691.* 🚇 *London Bridge.* ◯ *10am–4:30pm daily.*
⬤ *20 Dec–2 Jan.* ♿ 📷 🔒

M OST OF the old St Thomas's hospital was demolished in 1862 to make room for a railway. The women's operating theatre (1821) survived in a garret over the hospital church, where it lay forgotten until the 1950s. It has since been restored and fitted out exactly as it would have been in the 19th century, before the discovery of anaesthetics. Displays show pre-operative care: patients were blindfolded, gagged and bound to the operating table.

Spectacular downstream view of the Tate's Bankside Gallery, from Blackfriars

Southwark Cathedral ⑫

Montague Close SE1. **Map** 8 D4.
📞 *020-7407 2939.* 🚇 *London Bridge.* ⏰ *9am–6pm daily.*

ALTHOUGH SOME PARTS OF this building date back to the 12th century, it was not until 1905 that it became a cathedral. Many original medieval features remain, notably the superb Gothic choir, and the tomb of John Gower (c.1325–1408), Chaucer's *(see p188)* contemporary and fellow poet.

There is a monument to Shakespeare *(see pp312–13),* carved in 1912 and a memorial window above, installed in 1954. A chapel commemorates John Harvard, the founder of Harvard University, who was born in Southwark and baptized here in 1607.

Shakespeare's *Henry IV*
(performed at the Globe Theatre

Tate Gallery of Modern Art at Bankside ⑬

48 Hopton St SE1. **Map** 7 C3. 📞 *020-7401 7302.* 🚇 *Blackfriars, Waterloo.* ⏰ *10am–5:50pm daily.* 🔴 *24–26 Dec.* 🎟 *major exhibitions only.* ♿ 🍴 🖥 📷

ONE OF THE WORLD'S most important collections of 20th-century art now has a home worthy of its importance in this classic former power station of 1947. Its vast, cathedral-like spaces are the perfect settings for works by giants of modern art such as Picasso, Dali, Warhol, Moore, Hockney and Bacon.

Shakespeare's Globe ⑭

New Globe Walk SE1. **Map** 7 C3.
📞 *020-7902 1500.* 🚇 *London Bridge, Mansion House.* ⏰ *mid-May–Sep: 9:15am–12:15pm daily; Oct–mid-May: 10am–5pm daily.* **Performances** *mid-May–Sep.* 🎟 🎫 *every 30 mins.* 📷

A DETAILED REPRODUCTION of an Elizabethan theatre has been built on the riverside a few hundred metres from the site of the original Globe, Shakespeare's "wooden O" where many of his plays were first performed. Open to the elements (although the seats

are protected) the theatre operates only in the summer, and seeing a play here can be a lively experience, with the "groundlings" standing just in front of the stage encouraged to cheer or jeer.

When there is no performance, visitors are taken on an informative tour of the theatre by resting actors who talk of the struggle of the late Sam Wanamaker to get his dream project completed against enormous odds. Sadly, he did not live to see its first performance, but the fact that the theatre now exists is a tribute to his vision. An exhibition and video tell the story of Shakespeare and other Elizabethan dramatists, and of the Globe itself, as well its contemporaries such as the Rose, which is buried under offices nearby.

Shakespeare window (1954),
Southwark Cathedral

Tower of London ⑧

Beauchamp Tower
Many high-ranking prisoners were held here, often with their own retinues of servants. The tower was built by Edward I around 1281.

Soon after he became king in 1066, William the Conqueror built a fortress here to guard the entrance to London from the Thames Estuary. In 1097 the White Tower, standing today at the centre of the complex, was completed in sturdy stone; other fine buildings have been added over the centuries. The Tower has served as a royal residence, armoury, treasury and most famously as a prison for enemies of the crown. Many were tortured and among those who met their death there were the "princes in the tower", the sons and heirs of Edward IV. Today the tower is a popular attraction, housing the Crown Jewels and other exhibits. Its most celebrated residents are seven ravens whose presence is protected by the legend that the kingdom will fall if they desert the tower.

"Beefeaters"
Forty Yeoman Warders guard the Tower and live there. Their uniforms hark back to Tudor times.

Two 13th-century curtain walls protect the tower.

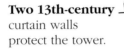

Tower Green was the execution site for favoured prisoners, away from crowds on Tower Hill, where many had to submit to public execution. Seven people died here, including two of Henry VIII's eight wives, Anne Boleyn and Catherine Howard.

Queen's House
This Tudor building is the sovereign's official residence at the Tower.

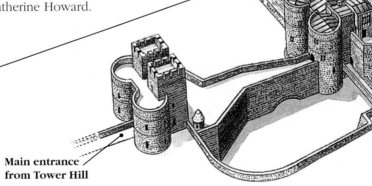

Main entrance from Tower Hill

THE CROWN JEWELS

The world's best-known collection of precious objects, now displayed in a splendid exhibition room, includes the gorgeous regalia of crowns, sceptres, orbs and swords used at coronations and other state occasions. Most date from 1661, when Charles II commissioned replacements for regalia destroyed by Parliament after the execution of Charles I *(see pp56–7)*. Only a few older pieces survived, hidden by royalist clergymen until the Restoration – notably, Edward the Confessor's sapphire ring, now incorporated into the Imperial State Crown *(see p77)*. The crown was made for Queen Victoria in 1837 and has been used at every coronation since.

The Sovereign's Ring (1831)

The Sovereign's Orb (1661), a hollow gold sphere encrusted with jewels

★ **Jewel House**
Among the magnificent Crown Jewels is the Sceptre with the Cross (1660), which now contains the world's biggest diamond.

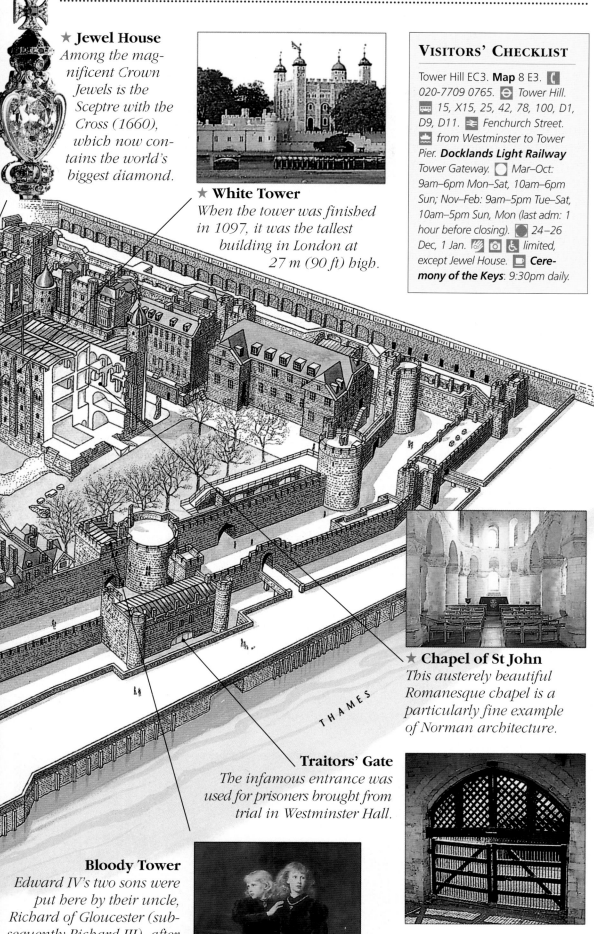

★ **White Tower**
When the tower was finished in 1097, it was the tallest building in London at 27 m (90 ft) high.

VISITORS' CHECKLIST

Tower Hill EC3. **Map** 8 E3. ☎ 020-7709 0765. ⊖ Tower Hill. 🚌 15, X15, 25, 42, 78, 100, D1, D9, D11. 🚉 Fenchurch Street. ⛴ from Westminster to Tower Pier. **Docklands Light Railway** Tower Gateway. ◯ Mar–Oct: 9am–6pm Mon–Sat, 10am–6pm Sun; Nov–Feb: 9am–5pm Tue–Sat, 10am–5pm Sun, Mon (last adm: 1 hour before closing). ◯ 24–26 Dec, 1 Jan. limited, except Jewel House. **Ceremony of the Keys**: 9:30pm daily.

★ **Chapel of St John**
This austerely beautiful Romanesque chapel is a particularly fine example of Norman architecture.

THAMES

Traitors' Gate
The infamous entrance was used for prisoners brought from trial in Westminster Hall.

Bloody Tower
Edward IV's two sons were put here by their uncle, Richard of Gloucester (subsequently Richard III), after their father died in 1483. The princes, depicted here by John Millais (1829–96), disappeared mysteriously and Richard was crowned later that year. In 1674 the skeletons of two children were found nearby.

STAR SIGHTS

★ **Jewel House**

★ **White Tower**

★ **Chapel of St John**

SHOPS AND MARKETS

LONDON is one of the great shopping cities of Europe, with bustling, lively street markets, world-famous department stores, and a wide variety of eclectic shops selling clothes, crafts and antiques. The best shopping areas range from elegant, upmarket districts such as Knightsbridge, which sells expensive clothes, porcelain and jew-

Bags from two famous West End shops

ellery, to the busy, chaotic stretch of Oxford Street, and the colourful, noisy markets of Covent Garden *(see p85)*, Berwick Street and Brick Lane. The city is best known however, for its inexhaustible range of clothes shops selling everything from traditional tweeds to the latest zany designs of an ever changing high-street fashion.

CHAIN AND DEPARTMENT STORES

Façade of Liberty (1925)

THE MOST FAMOUS of London's many department stores is **Harrod's**, with some 300 departments, 4,000 staff, and a spectacular Edwardian food hall. Nearby **Harvey Nichols** stocks high fashion and boasts the city's most stylish food hall. Gourmets should make a pilgrimage to **Fortnum and Mason** which has stocked high quality food for nearly 300 years. Traditional teas are available in the top floor café.

Selfridge's sells virtually everything from fine cashmeres to household gadgets, while **John Lewis** and its Chelsea partner **Peter Jones** specialize in fabrics, china, glass and household items. **Liberty**, the West End's last privately owned department store, still sells the hand-blocked silks and Oriental goods for which it was famous when it first opened in 1875. **Marks and Spencer**, long known for its good quality own-label clothes,

began as a market stall in Leeds in 1882, and now has some 700 branches worldwide.

The best chain store record shops are **Virgin Megastore**, **Tower Records** and **HMV**.

CLOTHES AND SHOES

BRITISH DESIGNERS range from elegant **Jasper Conran** to **Vivienne Westwood**, doyenne of the punkish avant-garde. Somewhere between are **Katharine Hamnett** and **Paul Smith**, while an ever-changing host of adventurous young designers produce outrageous clothes for trendy clubbers. You can find these in shops such as **Hype DF**, while the creations of more established international designers are stocked at places such as **Browns**.

Traditional English clothing – waxed Barbour jackets and Burberry trench coats – are

found in outlets such as **The Scotch House, Burberry** and **Gieves & Hawkes**, while **Laura Ashley** is renowned for its floral print dresses.

Shoes range from Oxfords and traditional brogues from **Church's Shoes** and hand-made footwear from **John Lobb**, to the stylish, more affordable designs at **Hobbs** and **Pied à Terre**.

MARKETS

LONDON'S MARKETS sell everything from street fashion and vintage clothes to canned food past its sell-by date and cheap household goods. The fashionable markets are **Camden Lock, Greenwich, Portobello Road** and **Covent Garden** where you can find an assortment of handmade crafts, old clothes and antiques. For those more serious about antique collecting, go early

Harrod's at night, illuminated by 11,500 lights

on a Friday to **Bermondsey Market** in South London.

The most famous London market is **Petticoat Lane**, worth a visit for the sheer volume of leather goods and the noisy, cheerful atmosphere created by the many Cockney stallholders. **Brick Lane** is another authentic East End market where dubious characters hustle gold watches and jewellery, and sheds are piled high with tatty furniture and bric-a-brac. For a glimpse of spirited costermongers in central London head for **Berwick Street**, which is lined with fruit and vegetables, fabrics and household goods.

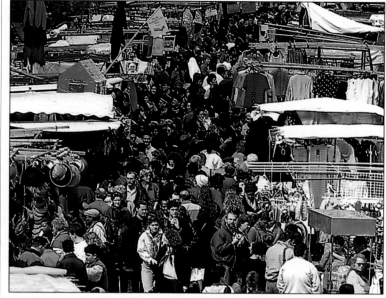

Bustling Petticoat Lane market, officially known as Middlesex Street

---

DIRECTORY

CHAIN AND DEPARTMENT STORES

Fortnum and Mason
181 Piccadilly W1.
Map 6 D1.
☎ 020-7734 8040.

Harrod's
87–135 Brompton Rd SW1.
Map 5 A3.
☎ 020-7730 1234.

Harvey Nichols
109–125 Knightsbridge SW1.
Map 5 B2.
☎ 020-7235 5000.

HMV
150 Oxford St W1.
Map 4 D4.
☎ 020-7631 3423.

John Lewis
278–306 Oxford St W1.
Map 3 C5.
☎ 020-7629 7711.

Liberty
210–20 Regent St W1.
Map 3 C5.
☎ 020-7734 1234.

Marks & Spencer
173 & 458 Oxford St W1.
Map 3 C5/3 B5.
☎ 020-7935 7954.
Two of many branches.

Peter Jones
Sloane Square SW1.
Map 5 A4.
☎ 020-7730 3434.

Selfridge's
400 Oxford St W1.
Map 3 B5.
☎ 020-7629 1234.

Tower Records
1 Piccadilly Circus W1.
Map 6 D1.
☎ 020-7439 2500.

Virgin Megastore
14–16 Oxford St W1.
Map 4 E4.
☎ 020-7631 1234.

CLOTHES AND SHOES

Browns
23–27 South Molton St W1.
Map 3 B5.
☎ 020-7514 0000.
One of several branches.

Burberry
18–22 Haymarket SW1.
Map 6 D1.
☎ 020-7930 3343.
One of two branches.

Church's Shoes
163 New Bond St W1.
Map 3 C5.
☎ 020-7499 9449.
One of several branches.

Gieves & Hawkes
1 Savile Row W1.
Map 3 C5.
☎ 020-7434 2001.

Hobbs
47 South Molton St W1.
Map 3 C5.
☎ 020-7629 0750.
One of several branches.

Hype D F
48–52 Kensington High St W8. **Map** 1 C4.
☎ 020-7938 3801.

Jasper Conran
6 Burnsall St SW3.
☎ 020-7352 3572.

John Lobb
9 St James's St SW1.
Map 6 D1.
☎ 020-7930 3664.

Katharine Hamnett
20 Sloane St SW1.
Map 5 A3.
☎ 020-7823 1002.

Laura Ashley
256–258 Regent St W1.
Map 4 D5.
☎ 020-7437 9760.
One of several branches.

Paul Smith
40–44 Floral St WC2.
Map 4 E5.
☎ 020-7379 7133.

Pied à Terre
19 South Molton St W1
Map 3 B5.
☎ 020-7493 3637.
One of several branches.

The Scotch House
2 Brompton Rd SW1.
Map 5 A2.
☎ 020-7581 2151.
One of several branches.

Vivienne Westwood
6 Davies St W1.
Map 3 B5.
☎ 020-7629 3757.

MARKETS

Bermondsey
Long Lane & Bermondsey St SE1.
Map 8 E5.
◻ *5am–2pm Fri.*

Berwick Street
Berwick St W1.
Map 4 D5.
◻ *9am–6pm Mon–Sat.*

Brick Lane
Brick Lane E1.
⊖ *Shoreditch, Liverpool St, Aldgate East.*
◻ *dawn–1pm Sun.*

Camden Lock
Chalk Farm Rd NW1.
⊖ *Camden Town, Chalk Farm.* ◻ *9:30am–5:30pm daily.*

Covent Garden
The Piazza WC2.
Map 4 F5. ◻ *9am–5pm daily (antiques: Mon).*

Petticoat Lane
Middlesex St E1.
⊖ *Liverpool St, Aldgate, Aldgate East.*
◻ *9am–2pm Sun.*

Portobello Road
Portobello Rd W10.
⊖ *Notting Hill Gate, Ladbroke Grove.*
◻ *7am–5:30pm Sat (general market: 9am–5pm Fri–Wed, 9am–1pm Thu).*

Greenwich
College Approach SE10.
⇌ *Greenwich.*
◻ *9am–6pm Sat, Sun.*

ENTERTAINMENT IN LONDON

LONDON HAS THE ENORMOUS variety of entertainment that only the great cities of the world can provide. The historical backdrop and the lively bustling atmosphere add to the excitement. Whether dancing the night away at a famous disco or making the most of London's varied arts scene, the visitor has a bewildering choice. A trip to London is not complete without a visit to the theatre which ranges from glamorous West End musicals to experimental Fringe plays. There is world-class ballet and opera in fabled venues such as Sadler's Wells and the Royal Opera House. The musical menu covers everything from classical, jazz and rock to rhythm and

Many London cafés have free live music

blues performed in atmospheric basement clubs, old converted cinemas and outdoor venues such as Wembley. Movie buffs can choose from hundreds of films each night. Sports fans can watch cricket at Lord's or participate in a host of activities from water sports to ice skating.

Time Out, published every Wednesday, is the most comprehensive guide to what's on in London, with detailed weekly listings and reviews. *The Evening Standard*, *The Guardian* (Saturday) and *The Independent* also have reviews and information on events. If you buy tickets from booking agencies rather than direct from box offices, do compare prices – and only buy from ticket touts if you're desperate.

WEST END AND NATIONAL THEATRES

Palace Theatre poster (1898)

THE GLAMOROUS, glittering world of West End theatreland, emblazoned with the names of world-famous performers, offers an extraordinary range of entertainment.

West End theatres (see Directory for individual theatres) survive on their profits and rely on an army of financial backers, known as "angels". Consequently, they tend to stage commercial productions with mass appeal:

musicals, classics, comedies and plays by bankable contemporary playwrights which can, if successful, run for years.

The state-subsidized Royal National Theatre is based in the riverside **South Bank Centre** *(see p130)*. Its three auditoriums – the large, open-staged Olivier, the proscenium-arched Lyttleton, and the small but flexible studio space of the Cottesloe – make a diversity of productions possible.

The Royal Shakespeare Company regularly stages plays by Shakespeare, but its large repertoire includes ancient Greek tragedies, Restoration comedies and modern works. Its main base is at Stratford-upon-Avon *(see pp368–9)* but its major productions also come to its London headquarters at the **Barbican** *(see p130)*, where it performs in the magnificent Barbican Theatre and in the Pit, a more intimate stage in the same complex.

Theatre tickets cost from £5 to £30 and can be bought direct from box offices, by telephone or by post. Many venues sell unclaimed tickets just before a performance. A ticket booth in Leicester Square, open 2:30–6:30pm (from noon for matinées) Monday to Saturday, sells cheap tickets on the day (cash only) for a wide range of shows.

OFF-WEST END AND FRINGE THEATRES

OFF-WEST END THEATRE is a middle category bridging the gap between West End and Fringe theatre. It includes venues that, regardless of location, have a permanent management team and often provide the opportunity for established directors and actors to turn their hands to more adventurous works in a smaller, more intimate, environment. Fringe theatres, on the other hand, are normally venues hired out to visiting companies. Both offer a vast array of innovative productions, serving as an outlet for new, often experimental writing, and for plays by gay, feminist and ethnic minority writers.

The Old Vic, the first home of the National Theatre from 1963

Open-air theatre at Regent's Park

Venues (too numerous to list – see newspaper listings), range from tiny theatres or rooms above pubs such as the Gate, which has a reputation for high quality productions of neglected European classics, to centrally based theatres such as the Donmar Warehouse, which regularly attracts major directors and actors.

OPEN-AIR THEATRE

IN SUMMER, a performance of one of Shakespeare's airier creations such as *Comedy of Errors, A Midsummer Night's Dream* or *As You Like It,* takes on an atmosphere of pure enchantment and magic among the green vistas of Regent's Park or Holland Park. Be sure to take a rug or blanket.

CINEMAS

THE WEST END abounds with multiplex cinema chains (MGM, Odeon, UCI) which show big budget Hollywood films, usually in advance of the rest of the country, although release dates tend to lag well behind the US and many other European countries.

The Odeon Marble Arch has the largest commercial screen in Europe, while the Odeon Leicester Square boasts London's biggest auditorium with almost 2,000 seats.

Londoners are well-informed cinema-goers and even the larger cinema chains include some low-budget and foreign films in their repertoire. The majority of foreign films are subtitled, rather than dubbed. A number of independent cinemas, such as the Metro, Renoir and Prince Charles in central London, and the Curzon in Mayfair, show foreign-language and slightly more offbeat art films.

The largest concentration of cinemas is in and around Leicester Square although there are local cinemas in most areas. Just off Leicester Square, the Prince Charles is the West End's cheapest cinema. Elsewhere in the area you can expect to pay between £6 and £9 for an evening performance – almost twice the price of the local cinemas. Monday and afternoon performances in the West End are often cheaper.

The National Film Theatre (NFT), on the South Bank, is London's flagship repertory cinema. Subsidized by the British Film Institute, it screens a wide range of films, old and new, from all around the world. Just next door is the fun and innovative Museum of the Moving Image (MOMI), which is an absolute must for movie enthusiasts.

Life-sized models at the Museum of the Moving Image

DIRECTORY			
WEST END THEATRES	**Dominion** Tottenham Court Rd. **Map** 4 E4. ℂ *020-7416 6060.*	**Lyric** Shaftesbury Ave. **Map** 4 D5. ℂ *020-7494 5045.*	**Savoy** Strand. **Map** 4 F5. ℂ *020-7836 8888.*
Adelphi Strand. **Map** 4 F5. ℂ *020-7344 0055.*	**Duchess** Catherine St. **Map** 4 F5. ℂ *020-7494 5075.*	**New London** Drury Lane. **Map** 4 E5. ℂ *020-7405 0072.*	**Shaftesbury** Shaftesbury Ave. **Map** 4 E4. ℂ *020-7379 5399.*
Albery St Martin's Lane. **Map** 4 E5. ℂ *020-7369 1730.*	**Duke of York's** St Martin's Lane. **Map** 4 E5. ℂ *020-7836 5122.*	**Palace** Shaftesbury Ave. **Map** 4 E5. ℂ *020-7434 0909.*	**Strand** Aldwych. **Map** 4 F5. ℂ *020-7930 8800.*
Aldwych Aldwych. **Map** 4 F5. ℂ *020-7416 6003.*	**Fortune** Russell St. **Map** 4 F5. ℂ *020-7836 2238.*	**Phoenix** Charing Cross Rd. **Map** 4 E5. ℂ *020-7369 1733.*	**St Martin's** West St. **Map** 4 E5. ℂ *020-7836 1443.*
Apollo Shaftesbury Ave. **Map** 4 E5. ℂ *020-7494 5070.*	**Garrick** Charing Cross Rd. **Map** 4 E5. ℂ *020-7494 5085.*	**Piccadilly** Denman St. **Map** 4 D5. ℂ *020-7369 1734.*	**Theatre Royal:** **–Drury Lane** Catherine St. **Map** 4 F5. ℂ *020-7494 5062.*
Cambridge Earlham St. **Map** 4 E5. ℂ *020-7494 5054.*	**Gielgud** Shaftesbury Ave. **Map** 4 D5. ℂ *020-7494 5065.*	**Prince Edward** Old Compton St. **Map** 4 D5. ℂ *020-7447 5400.*	**–Haymarket** Haymarket. **Map** 6 E1. ℂ *020-7930 8800.*
Comedy Panton St. **Map** 6 E1. ℂ *020-7369 1731.*	**Her Majesty's** Haymarket. **Map** 6 E1. ℂ *020-7494 5400.*	**Prince of Wales** Coventry St. **Map** 4 D5. ℂ *020-7839 5972.*	**Vaudeville** Strand. **Map** 4 F5. ℂ *020-7836 9987.*
Criterion Piccadilly Circus. **Map** 4 D5. ℂ *020-7369 1747.*	**London Palladium** Argyll St. **Map** 3 C5. ℂ *020-7494 5020.*	**Queen's** Shaftesbury Ave. **Map** 4 E5. ℂ *020-7494 5040.*	**Wyndham's** Charing Cross Rd. **Map** 4 E5. ℂ *020-7369 1736.*

Royal Festival Hall, South Bank Centre

CLASSICAL MUSIC, OPERA AND DANCE

L ONDON IS ONE of the world's great centres for classical music, with five symphony orchestras, internationally renowned chamber groups such as the Academy of St-Martin-in-the-Fields and the English Chamber Orchestra, as well as a number of contemporary groups. There are performances virtually every week by major international orchestras and artists, reaching a peak during the summer proms season at the **Royal Albert Hall** *(see pp66–7)*. The newly restored **Wigmore Hall** has excellent acoustics and is a fine setting for chamber music, as is the converted Baroque church (1728) of **St John's, Smith Square**.

Although televised and outdoor performances by major stars have greatly increased the popularity of opera, prices at the **Royal Opera House** are still aimed at corporate entertainment and many of the tickets never go on general sale. The building (closed for modernization until 2000) is elaborate and productions are often extremely lavish. English National Opera, based at the **London Coliseum**, has more adventurous productions, appealing to a younger audience (nearly all operas are sung in English). Tickets range from £5 to £200 and it is advisable to book well in advance.

The Royal Opera House is also home to the Royal Ballet, and the London Coliseum to the English National Ballet, the two leading classical ballet companies in Britain. Visiting ballets also perform in both. There are numerous young contemporary dance companies that have their own

distinctive style, notably the London Contemporary Dance Theatre, based at **The Place Theatre**. Other major dance venues are **Sadler's Wells**, the **ICA**, the **Royalty Theatre** and the **Chisenhale Dance Space**.

The **Barbican** and **South Bank Centre** (comprising the Royal Festival Hall, Queen Elizabeth Hall and Purcell Room) host an impressive variety of events ranging from touring opera performances to free foyer concerts.

Elsewhere in London many outdoor musical events take place in summer *(see p66–7)* at venues such as **Kenwood House**. Events to look out for are: the London Opera Festival (June) with singers from all over the world; the City of London Festival (July) which hosts a range of varied musical events; and contemporary dance festivals Spring Loaded (February–April) and Dance Umbrella (October) – see *Time Out* and newspaper listings.

Kenwood House on Hampstead Heath *(see p134)*

DIRECTORY

CLASSICAL MUSIC, OPERA AND DANCE

Barbican
Silk St EC2. **Map** 7 C1.
📞 020-7638 8891.

Chisenhale Dance Space
64–84 Chisenhale Rd E3.
🚇 Bethnal Green, Mile End. 📞 020-8981 6617.

ICA
The Mall SW1. **Map** 6 E1.
📞 020-7930 3647.

Kenwood House
Hampstead Lane NW3.

🚇 Archway. 📞 020-8348 1286.

London Coliseum
St Martin's Lane WC2. **Map** 4 E5. 📞 020-7632 8300.

Royal Albert Hall
Kensington Gore SW7. **Map** 2 E4. 📞 020-7589 8212.

Royal Opera House
Floral St WC2. **Map** 4 F5. 📞 020-7304 4000.

Royalty Theatre
Portugal St WC2. **Map** 4 F5. 📞 020-7494 5090.

Sadler's Wells
Rosebery Ave EC1. 🚇 Angel. 📞 020-7278 8916.

St John's, Smith Square
Smith Sq SW1. **Map** 6 E3. 📞 020-7222 1061.

South Bank Centre
Belvedere Rd SE1. **Map** 6 F1. 📞 020-7452 3000.

The Place Theatre
17 Duke's Road WC1. **Map** 4 E2. 📞 020-7380 1268.

Wigmore Hall
Wigmore St W1. **Map** 3 B4. 📞 020-7935 2141.

ROCK, POP, JAZZ AND CLUBS

100 Club
100 Oxford St W1. **Map** 4 D5. 📞 020-7636 0933.

Brixton Academy
211 Stockwell Rd SW9.
🚇 Brixton. 📞 020-7924 9999.

Fridge
Town Hall Parade, Brixton Hill SW2. 🚇 Brixton. 📞 020-7326 5100.

Forum
9–17 Highgate Rd NW5.
🚇 Kentish Town. 📞 020-7284 1001.

Gossips
69 Dean St W1. **Map** 4 D4. 📞 020-7434 4480.

Heaven
Underneath the Arches, Villiers St WC2. **Map** 6 E1. 📞 020-7930 2020.

The Hippodrome, Leicester Square

ROCK, POP, JAZZ AND CLUBS

AN ORDINARY WEEKNIGHT in London features scores of concerts, ranging from rock and pop, to jazz, Latin, world, folk and reggae. Artists guaranteed to fill thousands of seats play large venues such as **Wembley Stadium, Wembley Arena**, or the **Royal Albert Hall**. However, many major bands prefer to play the **Brixton Academy** and the **Forum**, both former cinemas.

The number of jazz venues has increased over the last few years. Best of the old crop is **Ronnie Scott's**, while of the newcomers the **100 Club**, **Jazz Café** and **Pizza on the Park** have good reputations.

London's club scene is one of the most innovative in Europe, particularly since 1990, when all-night clubbing (though not drinking) was legalized. It is dominated by big-name DJs, who host different nights in different clubs and some of the best clubs are one-nighters (see *Time Out* and newspaper listings). The world-famous mainstream discos **Stringfellows** and the **Hippodrome** are glitzy, expensive and very much part of the tourist circuit, as is the **Limelight** nearby. In contrast the young and trendy **Wag Club**, New York-style **Ministry of Sound**, the camp cabaret of **Madame Jojo's** and a host of other venues ensure that you will never be short of choice. Alternatives are the excellent laser and light shows at **Heaven**, or the fun 1970s

Ticket agency, Shaftesbury Avenue

atmosphere at **Le Scandale** on Saturdays, or the ska, classic soul and R'n'B at **Gossips** on Thursdays. **Heaven** and the **Fridge** are among the most popular of London's gay clubs.

Opening times are usually 10pm–3am, but on weekends many clubs open until 6am.

SPORTS

AN IMPRESSIVE variety of public sports facilities are to be found in London and they are generally inexpensive to use. Swimming pools, squash courts, gyms and sports centres, with an assortment of keep-fit classes, can be found in most districts, and tennis courts are hired by the hour in most parks. Water sports, ice skating and golf are among the variety of activities on offer. Spectator sports range from football and rugby at **Wembley Stadium** to cricket at **Lord's** or the **Oval**, and tennis at the **All England Lawn Tennis Club**, Wimbledon. Tickets for the most popular of these matches can often be difficult to come by *(see p71)*. More traditional sports include polo at **Guards**, croquet at **Hurlingham** and medieval tennis at **Queen's Club Real Tennis**.

Hippodrome
Leicester Square WC2.
Map 4 E5.
020-7437 4311.

Jazz Café
3-5 Parkway NW1.
Camden Town.
020-7916 6060.

Le Scandale
53–54 Berwick St W1.
Map 4 D5.
020-7 437 6830.

Limelight
136 Shaftesbury Ave, W1.
Map 4 E5.
020-7 434 0572.

Madame Jojo's
8–10 Brewer St W1.
Map 4 D5.
020-7734 2473.

Ministry of Sound
103 Gaunt St SE1.
Map 7 C5.
020-7378 6528.

Pizza on the Park
11 Knightsbridge SW1.
Map 5 B2.
020-7235 5550.

Ronnie Scott's
47 Frith St W1.
Map 4 D5.
020-7439 0747.

Stringfellows
16–19 Upper St Martin's Lane WC2. **Map** 4 E5.
020-7240 5534.

Wag Club
35 Wardour St W1. **Map** 4 D5. 020-7437 5534.

Wembley Stadium and Arena
Empire Way, Wembley, Middlesex. Wembley Park. 020-8900 1234.

SPORTS

General Sports Information Line
020-7222 8000.

All England Lawn Tennis Club
Church Rd, Wimbledon SW19. Southfields.
020-8946 2244.

Guards Polo Club
Windsor Great Park, Englefield Green, Egham, Surrey. Egham.
01784 434212.

Hurlingham Club
Ranelagh Gdns SW6.
Map 5 B5.
020-7736 8411.

Lord's Cricket Ground
St John's Wood NW8.
St John's Wood.
020-7289 1611.

Oval Cricket Ground
The Oval, Kennington SE11.
Oval.
020-7582 6660.

Queen's Club Real Tennis
Palliser Rd W14.
Barons Court.
020-7385 3421.

FURTHER AFIELD

OVER THE CENTURIES London has steadily expanded to embrace the scores of villages that surrounded it, leaving the City as a reminder of London's original boundaries. Although now linked in an almost unbroken urban sprawl, many of these areas, have maintained their old village atmosphere and character. Hampstead and Highgate are still distinct enclaves, as are artistic Chelsea and literary Islington. Greenwich, Chiswick and Richmond have retained features that hark back to the days when the Thames was an important artery for transport and commerce, while just to the east of the City the wide expanses of the former docks have, in the last 20 years, been imaginatively rebuilt as new commercial and residential areas.

SIGHTS AT A GLANCE

Camden and Islington ⑦
Chelsea ①
Chiswick ⑪
East End and Docklands ⑧

Greenwich ⑨
Hampstead ④
Hampstead Heath ⑤
Highgate ⑥

Holland Park ②
The Dome ⑩
Notting Hill and Portobello Rd ③
Richmond and Kew ⑫

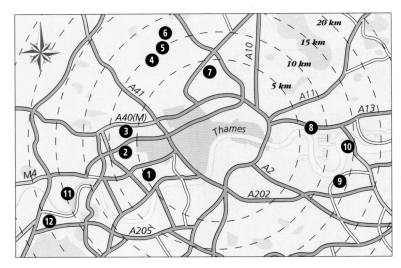

KEY

▨	Main sightseeing areas
☐	Greater London
▨	Parks
▬	Motorway
═	Major road
═	Minor road

10 miles = 15 km

Chelsea ①

SW3. ⊖ *Sloane Square.*

RIVERSIDE CHELSEA has been fashionable since Tudor times when Sir Thomas More, Henry VIII's Lord Chancellor

**Statue of Sir Thomas More
(1478–1535), Cheyne Walk**

(*see p54*), lived here. The river views attracted artists and the arrival of the historian Thomas Carlyle and essayist Leigh Hunt in the 1830s began a literary connection. Blue plaques on the houses of **Cheyne Walk** celebrate former residents such as the painter JMW Turner (*see p97*) and writers George Eliot, Henry James and TS Eliot.

Chelsea's artistic tradition is maintained by its galleries and antique shops, many of them scattered among the clothes boutiques on **King's Road**. This begins at **Sloane Square**, named after the physician Sir Hans Sloane, who bought the manor of Chelsea in 1712. Sloane expanded the **Chelsea Physic Garden** (1673) along Swan Walk to cultivate plants and herbs.

Wren's **Royal Hospital**, on Royal Hospital Road was built in 1692 as a retirement home for old soldiers and still houses 400 Chelsea Pensioners.

Arab Hall, Leighton House (1866)

Holland Park ②

W8, W14. ⊖ *Holland Park.*

THIS SMALL but delightful park is more intimate than the large royal parks such as Hyde Park (*see p107*). It was opened in 1952 on the grounds of **Holland House**, a centre of social and political intrigue in its 19th-century heyday.

Around the park are some magnificent late Victorian

houses. **Linley Sambourne House** was built about 1870 and has hardly changed since Sambourne furnished it in the cluttered Victorian manner, with china ornaments and heavy velvet drapes. He was a political cartoonist for the satirical magazine *Punch,* and drawings, including a number of his own, cram the walls.

Leighton House, built for the Neo-Classical painter Lord Leighton in 1866, has been preserved as an extraordinary monument to the Victorian Aesthetic movement. The highlight is the Arab Hall, which was added in 1879 to house Leighton's stupendous collection of 13th- to 17th-century Islamic tiles. The best paintings include some by Leighton himself and by his contemporaries Edward Burne-Jones and John Millais.

Georgian house, Hampstead

🏛 **Linley Sambourne House**
18 Stafford Terrace W8. 📞 020-8994 1019. ⊖ High St Kensington. ◯ Mar–Oct: Wed, Sun. 📷
🏛 **Leighton House**
12 Holland Park Rd W14.
📞 020-7602 3316. ⊖ High St Kensington. ◯ Mon–Sat.
⬤ public hols.

Notting Hill and Portobello Road ❸

W11. ⊖ Notting Hill Gate.

IN THE 1950S AND '60S, Notting Hill became a centre for the Caribbean community and today it is a vibrant cosmopolitan part of London. It is also home to Europe's largest street carnival *(see p62–3)* which began in 1966 and takes over the entire area on the August bank holiday weekend, when costumed parades flood through the crowded streets.

Nearby, Portobello Road market *(see p122–3)* has a bustling atmosphere with hundreds of stalls and shops selling a variety of collectables.

Hampstead ❹

NW3, N6. ⊖ Hampstead. ⊠ Hampstead Heath.

POSITIONED ON A high ridge north of the metropolis, Hampstead has always remained aloof from London. Essentially a Georgian village with many perfectly maintained mansions and houses, it is one of London's most desirable residential areas, home to a community of artists and writers since Georgian times.

Situated in a quiet Hampstead street, **Keats House** (1816), is an evocative and memorable tribute to the life and work of the poet John Keats (1795–1821). Keats lived here for two years before his tragic death from consumption at the age of 25, and it was under a plum tree in the garden that he wrote his celebrated *Ode to a Nightingale.*

Original manuscripts and books are among the mementoes of Keats and of Fanny Brawne, the neighbour to whom he was engaged.

The **Freud Museum**, which opened in 1986, is dedicated to the dramatic life of Sigmund Freud (1856–1939), the founder of psychoanalysis. At the age of 82, Freud fled from Nazi persecution in Vienna to this Hampstead house where he lived and worked for the last year of his life. His daughter Anna, pioneer of child psychoanalysis, continued to live here until her death in 1982. Inside, Freud's rich Viennese-style consulting rooms remain unaltered, and 1930s home movies show moments of Freud's life, including scenes of the Nazi attack on his home in Vienna.

🏛 **Keats House**
Keats Grove NW3. 📞 020-7435 2062. ⊖ Hampstead, Belsize Park. ⬤ for restoration, please phone for details.
🏛 **Freud Museum**
20 Maresfield Gdns NW3.
📞 020-7435 2002. ⊖ Finchley Rd. ◯ Wed–Sun. ♿ limited.

Antique shop on Portobello Road

Views east across Hampstead Heath to Highgate

Hampstead Heath ⑤

N6. ⊖ *Hampstead, Highgate.* ⇄ *Hampstead Heath.*

Separating the hill-top villages of Hampstead and Highgate, the open spaces of Hampstead Heath are a precious retreat from the city. There are meadows, lakes and ponds for bathing and fishing, and fine views over the capital from **Parliament Hill**, to the east.

Situated in landscaped grounds high on the edge of the Heath is the magnificent **Kenwood House**, where classical concerts *(see p130)* are held by the lake in summer. The house was remodelled by Robert Adam *(see p28)* in 1764 and most of his interiors have survived, the highlight of which is the library. The mansion is filled with Old Master paintings, including works by Van Dyck, Vermeer, Turner *(see p97)* and Romney. The star attraction of this collection is Rembrandt's self-portrait, painted in 1663.

🏛 **Kenwood House**
Hampstead Lane NW3. ▌ *020-8348 1286.* ◯ *daily.* ⬤ *24–25 Dec.* ♿

Handmade crafts and antiques, Camden Lock indoor market

Highgate ⑥

N6. ⊖ *Highgate, Archway.*

A settlement since the Middle Ages, Highgate, like Hampstead, became a fashionable aristocratic retreat in the 16th century. Today, it still has an exclusive rural feel, aloof from the urban sprawl below, with a Georgian high street and many expensive houses.

Highgate Cemetery *(see p81)*, with its marvellous monuments and hidden overgrown corners, has an extraordinary, magical atmosphere. Tour guides (daily in summer, weekends in winter) tell of the many tales of intrigue, mystery and vandalism connected with the cemetery since it opened in 1839. In the newer eastern section is the tomb of Victorian novelist George Eliot (1819–80) and of the cemetery's most famous incumbent, Karl Marx (1818–83).

🏛 **Highgate Cemetery**
Swains Lane N6. ▌ *020-8340 1834.* ⊖ *Archway, Highgate.* ◯ *daily.* ⬤ *25–26 Dec.* 🅿

Camden and Islington ⑦

N1, NW1. ⊖ *Angel, Highbury & Islington.*

Camden is a lively area packed with restaurants, shops and a busy **market** *(see p126–7)*. Thousands of people come here each weekend to browse among the wide variety of stalls or simply to soak up the atmosphere of the lively cobbled area around the canal, which is enhanced by the buskers and street performers.

Neighbouring Islington was once a highly fashionable spa but the rich moved out in the late 18th century and the area deteriorated rapidly. In the 20th century, writers such as Evelyn Waugh, George Orwell and Joe Orton lived here. In recent decades, Islington has been rediscovered and is once again fashionable as one of the first areas in London to become "gentrified", with many professionals buying and refurbishing the old houses.

East End and Docklands ⑧

E1, E2, E14. ⊖ *Aldgate East, Bethnal Green.* **Docklands Light Railway**: *Canary Wharf.*

IN THE MIDDLE AGES the East End was full of craftsmen practising noxious trades such as brewing, bleaching and vinegar-making, which were banned within the City. The area has also been home to numerous immigrant communities since the 17th century, when French Huguenots, escaping religious persecution moved into Spitalfields, and made it a silk-weaving centre. Even after the decline of the silk industry, textiles and clothing continued to dominate, with Jewish tailors and furriers setting up workshops in the 1880s, and Bengali machinists sewing in cramped premises from the 1950s.

A good way to get a taste of the East End is to explore its Sunday street markets (*see pp126–7*), and sample freshly baked bagels and spicy Indian food. By way of contrast, anyone interested in contemporary architecture should visit the **Docklands**, an ambitious re-development of disused docks, dominated by the Canada Tower; at 250 m (800 ft) it is London's tallest building. Other attractions include the **Bethnal Green Museum of Childhood,** a toy museum with a good display of dolls' houses and **Dennis Severs' House**, in which Dennis Severs takes you on a historic journey from the 17th to the 19th centuries.

Royal Naval College framing the Queen's House, Greenwich

🏛 Dennis Severs' House
18 Folgate St E1. 📞 *020-7247 4013.* ◯ *eve performances 1st Mon of month (by appt).* 🎟

🏛 Bethnal Green Museum of Childhood
Cambridge Heath Rd E2. 📞 *020-8980 5200.* ◯ *Sat–Thu.* ● *24 Dec, 25 Dec, 1 Jan, May Day.*

Greenwich ⑨

SE10. ⇌ *Greenwich, Maze Hill.*

THE WORLD'S TIME has been measured from the **Old Royal Observatory** (now housing a museum) since 1884. Greenwich was therefore the obvious setting for the Millennium Dome (*see pp136–9*), built to celebrate Britain for the year 2000. The Greenwich area is full of maritime and royal history, with Neo-Classical mansions, a park, many antique and book shops and various markets (*see pp126–7*). The **Queen's House**, designed by Inigo Jones for the wife of James I, was completed in 1637 for Henrietta Maria, Charles I's

Canada Tower, Canary Wharf

queen. It has been restored to its original state. Highlights include the perfectly cubic main hall and the unusual spiral "tulip staircase".

The adjoining **National Maritime Museum** has exhibits ranging from primitive canoes, through Elizabethan galleons, to modern ships. Anyone interested in naval history should visit the **Royal Naval College** nearby, which

An 18th-century compass, National Maritime Museum

was designed by Christopher Wren (*see p120*) in two halves so that the Queen's House would not be deprived of its river view. The building began life as a royal palace. It became a hospital in 1692, and was taken over by the Royal Naval College in 1873. The Rococo chapel and the 18th-century *trompe l'oeil* Painted Hall, are both open to the public.

🏛 Old Royal Observatory
Greenwich Park SE10. 📞 *020-8858 4422.* ◯ *daily.* ● *23–26 Dec.* 🎟

🏛 Queen's House and National Maritime Museum
Romney Rd SE10. 📞 *020-8858 4422.* ◯ *daily.* ● *24–26 Dec.* 🎟 ♿ *limited.*

🏛 Royal Naval College
King William Walk, Greenwich SE10. 📞 *020-8858 2154.* ◯ *daily (pm).* ● *public hols.*

The Dome 🔟

THE DOME is the focal point for Great Britain's celebration of the year 2000. From its spectacular opening ceremony on 31 December 1999 its vast interior is home to a year-long exhibition that welcomes and examines the choices facing humanity in the 21st century and beyond. Offering fourteen unique zones to explore, the Dome is above all an experience to be enjoyed, with elements to astonish, inspire and enlighten.

Self Portrait is a celebration of Britishness in all its aspects. The Andscape brings together symbols of Britain selected by hundreds of thousands of people from all over the country.

Talk explores the ways in which we communicate, from smoke signals to the mobile phone.

Cables and Masts
Over 70 km (43 miles) of steel cable form the netting that supports the canopy. Abseilers spent three months rigging it to the twelve 100-m (328-ft) masts.

Faith is a zone designed to encourage personal reflection on belief and the spirit, and the common values that underpin the religions of the world.

Mind is an imagination-expanding experience including works of art from some of Britain's best known artists.

Rest offers visitors time to switch off and relax in a quiet place at the heart of the zone.

Money and the way we use it faces huge changes in the 21st century. Visitors can find out just how easy it is to spend £1 million.

Blackwall Tunnel vent

Work explores the changing world of work. A vast kinetic machine links it to the Learning Life zone, symbolizing the interdependence of education and work.

Learning Life contains a magical film experience, showing visitors the way into the future of learning.

Dome Statistics
The base of the Dome is ten times that of St Paul's Cathedral. Nelson's Column could stand beneath its roof and the Eiffel Tower could lie on its side within. The roof could take the weight of a jumbo jet.

Roof Panels
The 72 panels that form the canopy are made of Teflon-coated glass-fibre cloth. More than 100,000 sq m (109,000 sq yards) of fabric was needed to cover the Dome.

VISITORS' CHECKLIST

North Greenwich SE10.
📞 0870-606 2000. 🚇 North Greenwich/The Dome (Jubilee Line). 🚌 108. **Open** Jan–Dec 1999: daily (times vary). Allow 5–6 hours for your visit. **Adm charge**. Tickets must be purchased in advance. On sale by phone, website, from many National Lottery retailers, and travel outlets and operators. **SkyScape open** daily for movies, concerts and other live events. **Millennium Show** up to six shows daily.
📷 ♿ 🍴 💻 🚻
www.dome2000.co.uk

Home Planet includes a journey through some of the most extreme environments on the Earth.

Living Island explores our relationship to the environment through a reconstruction of a seaside town. The slot machines and games are used to convey ecological messages.

Journey examines the future of travel and transport, using a thrilling virtual reality journey.

One of 24 hoppers for recycling water

Shared ground contains seven fantasy rooms showing people in their private space, and constructed of recycled cardboard. Visitors can also walk down a city street and become part of a wider community.

Millennium Show
A spectacular multi-media show plays up to six times a day to 12,000 spectators at the centre of the Dome. Many young people have been specially trained in acrobatic skills for this event.

Entrance

Body is centred on the astonishing **Giant Body Sculpture**, through which visitors move to find out about just how amazing and complex the "human machine" really is.

Play combines the age-old traditions of fun and games with the breathtaking advances of the digital playground. Absorbing, entertaining, interactive and personally challenging games make this a hard zone to leave behind, at any age.

STAR ATTRACTIONS

Giant Body Sculpture

Millennium Show

Mind zone

Chiswick ⑪

W4. ⊖ *Chiswick.*

CHISWICK IS A PLEASANT suburb of London, with
pubs, cottages and a
variety of birdlife,
such as herons,
along the pictur-
esque riverside.
One of the main
reasons for a visit is
Chiswick House, a
magnificent country villa
inspired by the Renaissance
architecture of Andrea Palladio.
It was designed in the early
18th century by the 3rd Earl
of Burlington as an annexe
to his larger house (demolished in 1758), so that he
could display his collection of
art and entertain friends. The
gardens, with their Classical
temples and statues, are now
restored to their former glory.

Heron

🏛 **Chiswick House**
Burlington Lane W4. 📞 020-8995
0508. ◯ Apr–Oct: daily; Nov–Mar:
Wed–Sun. ● 24, 25 Dec. 🖼

Richmond and Kew ⑫

SW15. ⊖ ⇄ *Richmond.*

THE ATTRACTIVE village of
Richmond took its name
from a palace built by Henry
VII (the former Earl of Richmond in Yorkshire) in 1500,
the remains of which can be
seen off the green. Nearby is
the expansive **Richmond
Park** *(see p80)*, which was
once Charles I's royal hunting

ground. In summer, boats
sail down the Thames from
Westminster Pier, making a
pleasant day's excursion from
central London *(see pp78–9)*.
The nobility continued to
favour Richmond after royalty
had left, and some of their
mansions have survived. The
Palladian villa, **Marble Hill
House**, was built in 1729
for the mistress of
George II and has
been restored to its
elegant original
appearance.
On the opposite side of
the Thames, the brooding
Ham House, built in
1610, had its heyday
later that century when
it became the home of the
Lauderdales. The Countess of
Lauderdale inherited the
house from her father, who
had been Charles I's "whip-
ping boy" – meaning that he
was punished whenever the
future king misbehaved. He
was rewarded as an adult by
being given a peerage and
the lease of Ham estate.
A little further north along
the Thames, **Syon House** has
been inhabited by the Dukes
and Earls of Northumberland
for over 400 years. Numerous
attractions here include a butterfly house, a museum of
historic cars and a spectacular
conservatory built in 1830.
The lavish Neo-Classical interiors of the house, created by
Robert Adam in the 1760s *(see
pp28–9)*, remain the highlight.

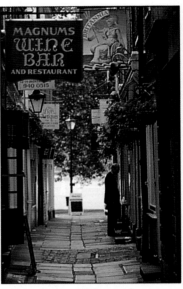

Brewers Lane, Richmond

On the riverbank to the south,
Kew Gardens *(see p80)*, the
most complete botanic gardens
in the world, are flawlessly
maintained, with examples of
nearly every plant that can be
grown in Britain. There are
also conservatories where
thousands of exotic tropical
blooms are on display.

🏛 **Marble Hill House**
Richmond Rd, Twickenham. 📞 020-
8892 5115. ◯ daily (Nov–Mar:
Wed–Sun). ● 24–26 Dec. ♿ limited.

🏛 **Ham House**
Ham St, Richmond. 📞 020-8940
1950. ◯ Apr–Oct: Sat–Wed.
🖼 ♿

🏛 **Syon House**
London Rd, Brentford. 📞 020-8560
0881. **House** ◯ mid-Mar–Oct: Wed,
Thu, Sun. **Gardens** ◯ daily.
● Nov–mid-Mar. 🖼
♿ gardens only.

🌿 **Kew Gardens**
Kew Rd, Richmond. 📞 020-8940
1171. ◯ daily. ● 25 Dec, 1 Jan.
🖼 ♿

**Chiswick
House**

◁ **The Thames Barrier at night**

STREET FINDER

THE MAP REFERENCES given with the sights, hotels, restaurants, shops and entertainment venues based in central London refer to the following four maps. All the main places of interest within the central area are marked on the maps in addition to useful practical information, such as tube, railway and coach stations. The key map below shows the area of London that is covered by the *Street Finder*. The four main city-centre areas (colour-coded in pink) are shown in more detail on the inside back cover.

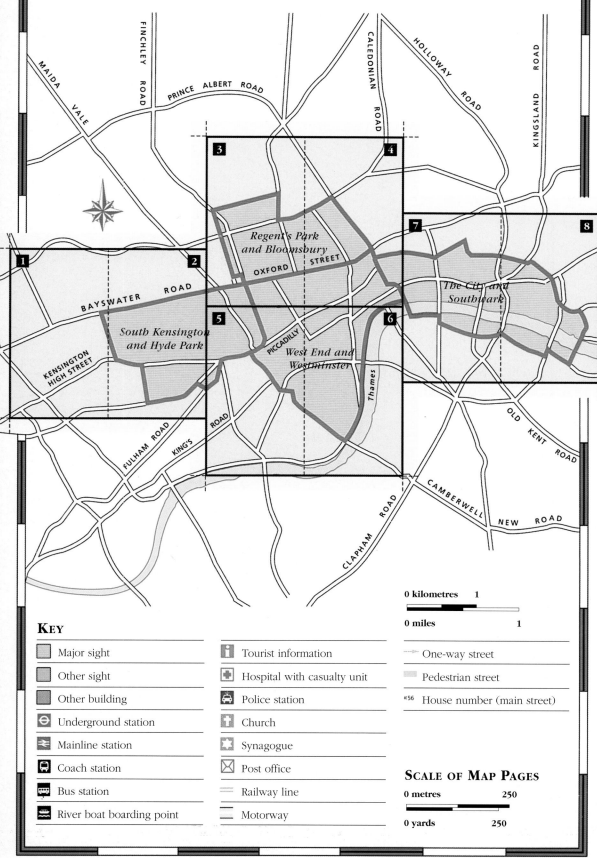

3 **4**

Regent's Park and Bloomsbury

OXFORD STREET

7 **8**

The City and Southwark

1 **2**

BAYSWATER ROAD

5 **6**

South Kensington and Hyde Park

PICCADILLY

West End and Westminster

Thames

0 kilometres 1

0 miles 1

KEY

⬜ Major sight	ℹ Tourist information	→ One-way street
⬜ Other sight	✚ Hospital with casualty unit	▨ Pedestrian street
⬛ Other building	🚓 Police station	⁴⁵⁶ House number (main street)
⊖ Underground station	⛪ Church	
🚉 Mainline station	✡ Synagogue	
🚌 Coach station	⊠ Post office	**SCALE OF MAP PAGES**
🚍 Bus station	═ Railway line	0 metres 250
🛥 River boat boarding point	▬ Motorway	0 yards 250

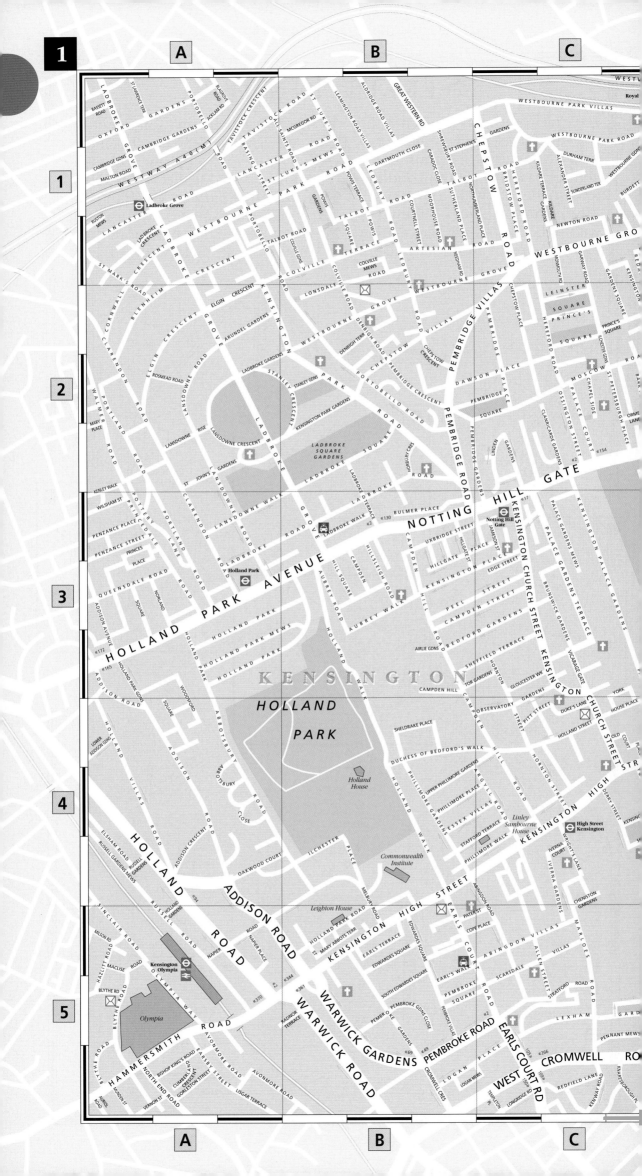

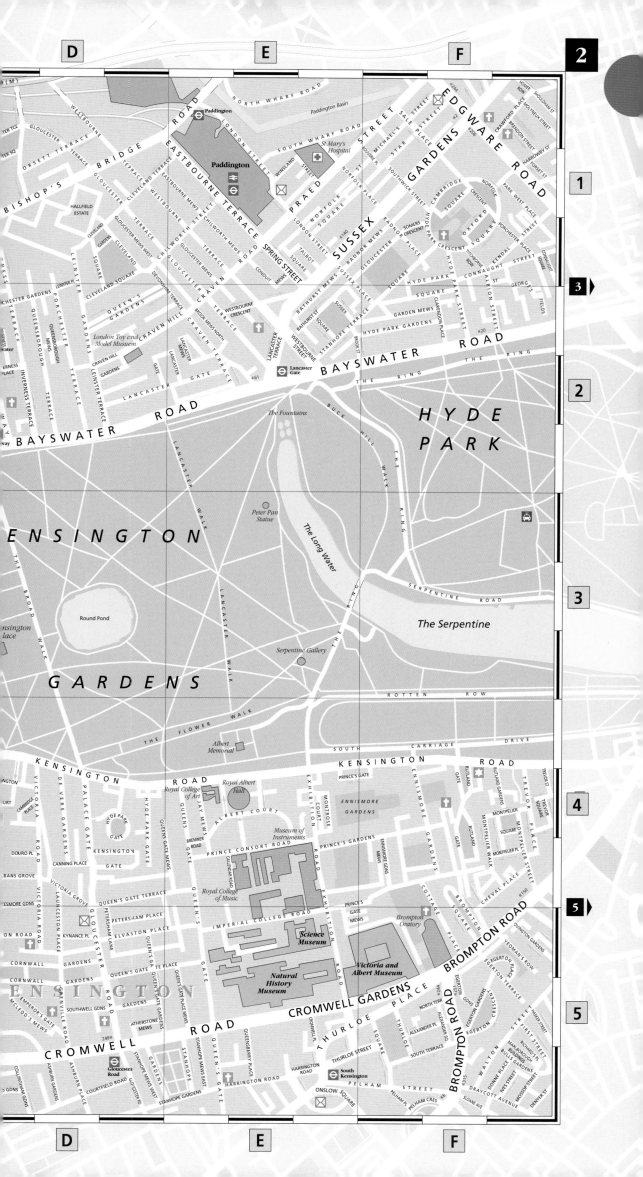

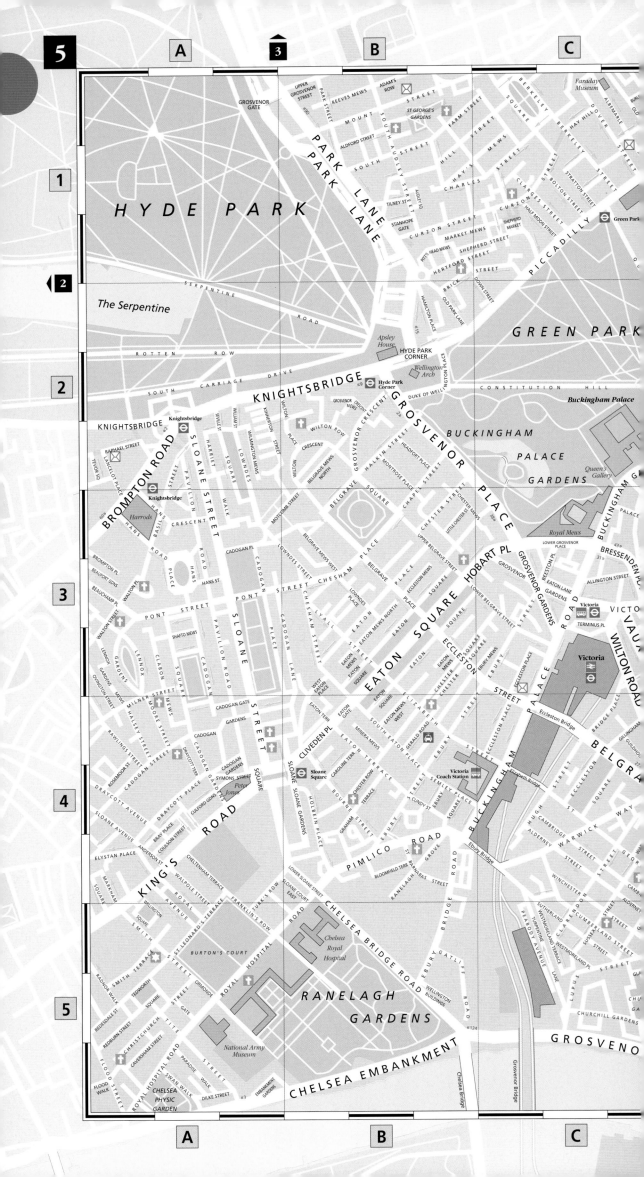

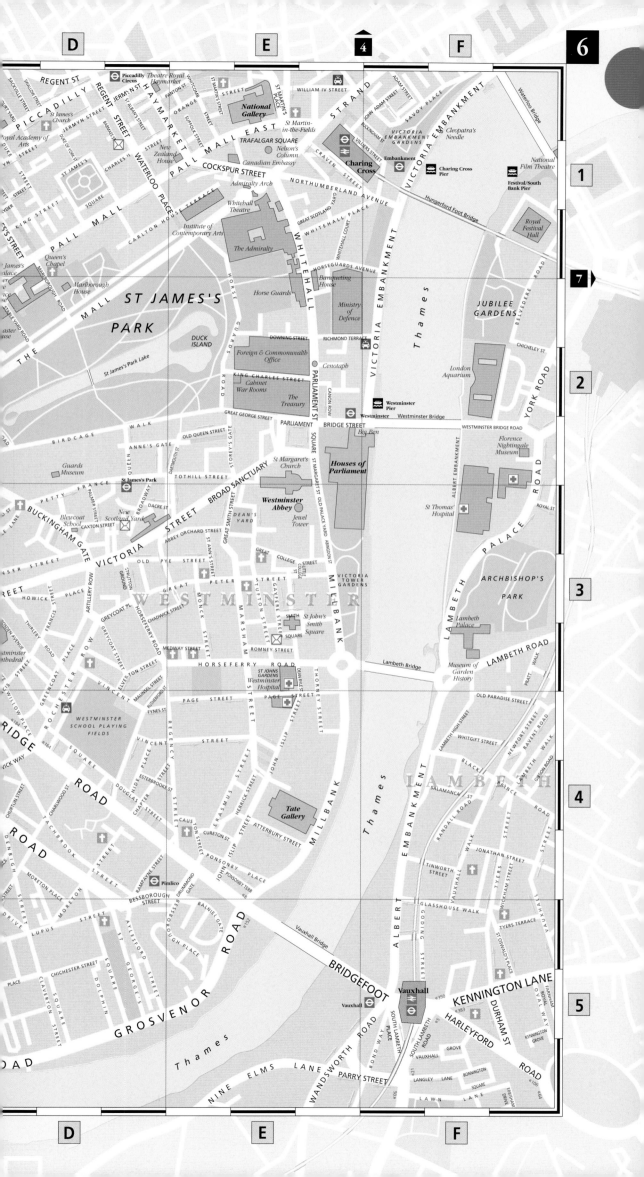

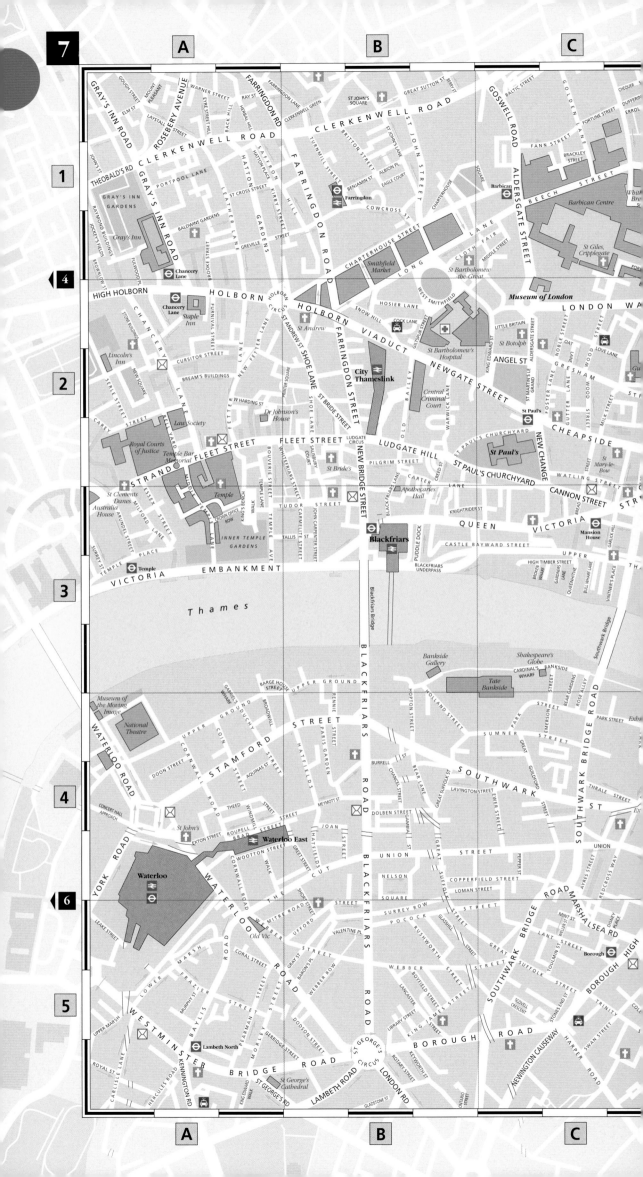

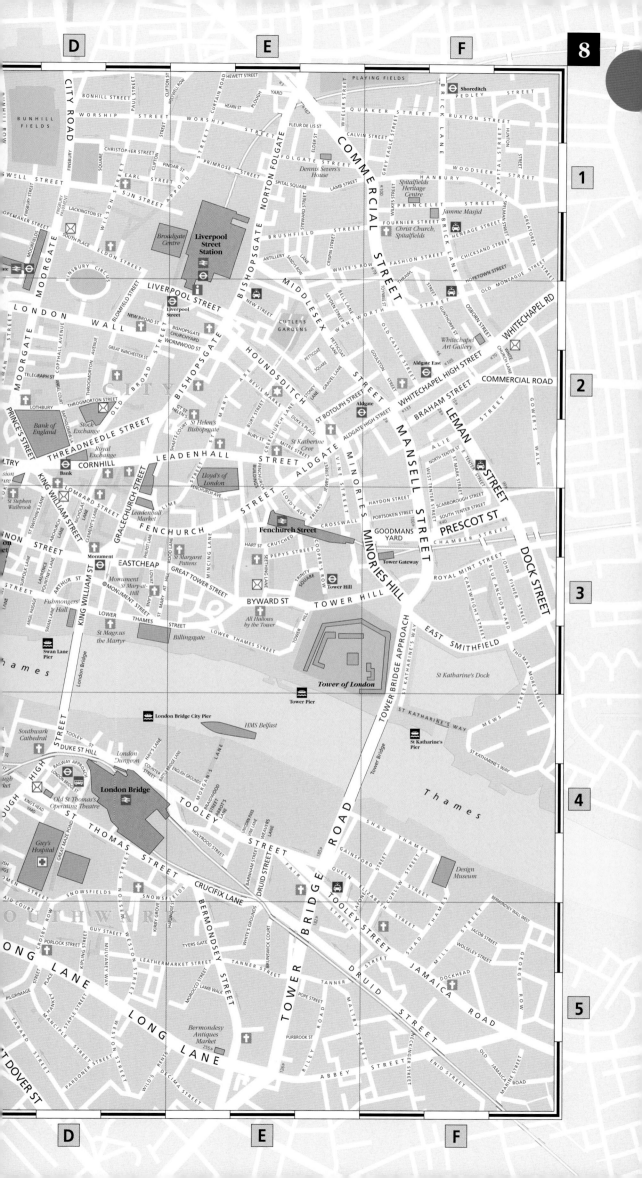

SOUTHEAST
ENGLAND

INTRODUCING SOUTHEAST ENGLAND 152-157
THE DOWNS AND CHANNEL COAST 158-191
EAST ANGLIA 192-225
THAMES VALLEY 226-255

Southeast England at a Glance

THE OLD SAXON KINGDOMS covered the
areas surrounding London, and today,
while their accessibility to the capital
makes them a magnet for commuters, each
region retains a character and history of its
own. The attractions include England's
oldest universities, royal palaces, castles,
stately homes and cathedrals, many
of which played critical roles in the
nation's early history. The landscape
is soft, with the green and rounded
hills of the south country levelling
out to the flat fertile plains and fens of East
Anglia, fringed by broad, sandy beaches.

Blenheim Palace (see pp246–
7) *is a Baroque masterpiece.
The Mermaid Fountain
(1892) is part of the
spectacular
gardens.*

Oxford University's *buildings (see pp238–43)
amount to a textbook of English architecture
from the Middle Ages to the present. Christ Church
College (1525) is the largest in the university.*

Bedfordshire

Hertford

Buckinghamshire

THAMES VALLEY
(see pp226–55)

Oxfordshire

Surrey

Hampshire

West Sussex

Windsor Castle (see pp254–5) *is
Britain's oldest royal residence. The
Round Tower was built in the 11th
century when the palace guarded the
western approaches to London.*

Winchester Cathedral (see pp170–71)
*was begun in 1097 on the ruins of a Saxon
church. The city has been an important
centre of Christianity since the 7th century.
The cathedral's northwest door is built
in a characteristic medieval style.*

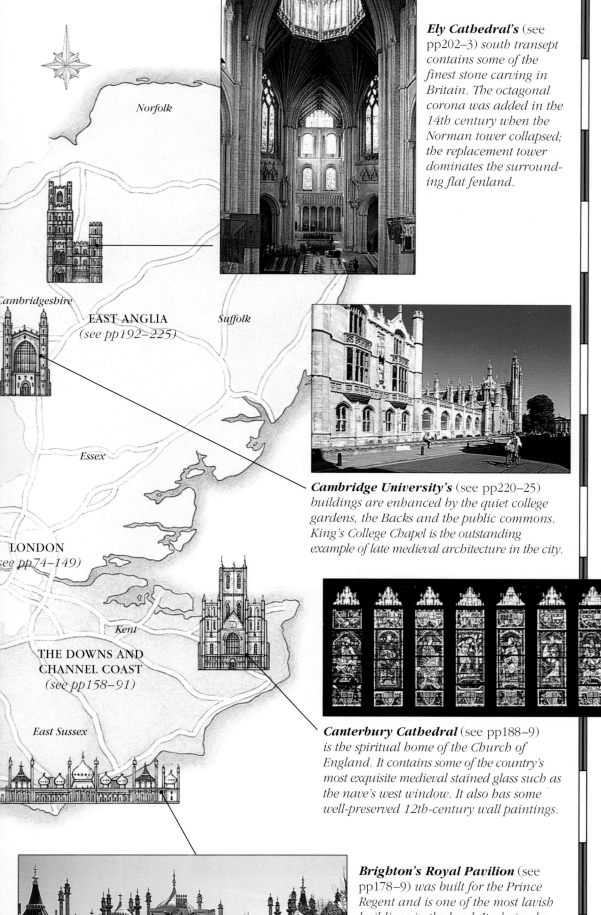

Ely Cathedral's (see pp202–3) *south transept contains some of the finest stone carving in Britain. The octagonal corona was added in the 14th century when the Norman tower collapsed; the replacement tower dominates the surrounding flat fenland.*

Norfolk

Cambridgeshire

EAST ANGLIA
(see pp192–225)

Suffolk

Essex

LONDON
(see pp74–149)

Kent

THE DOWNS AND
CHANNEL COAST
(see pp158–91)

East Sussex

Cambridge University's (see pp220–25) *buildings are enhanced by the quiet college gardens, the Backs and the public commons. King's College Chapel is the outstanding example of late medieval architecture in the city.*

Canterbury Cathedral (see pp188–9) *is the spiritual home of the Church of England. It contains some of the country's most exquisite medieval stained glass such as the nave's west window. It also has some well-preserved 12th-century wall paintings.*

Brighton's Royal Pavilion (see pp178–9) *was built for the Prince Regent and is one of the most lavish buildings in the land. Its design by John Nash (see p111) is based on Oriental themes and it has recently been restored to its original splendour.*

| 0 kilometres | 25 |
| 0 miles | 25 |

The Garden of England

HOPS AND HOPPING

Hop-picking, a family affair

WITH ITS FERTILE SOIL, mild climate and regular rainfall, the Kentish countryside has flourished as a fruit-growing region ever since its first orchards were planted by the Romans. There has been a recent boom in wine-making, as the vine-covered hillsides around Lamberhurst show, and several vineyards may be visited. The orchards are dazzling in the blossom season, and in the autumn the branches sag with ripening fruit – a familiar sight which inspired William Cobbett (1762–1835) to describe the area as "the very finest as to fertility and diminutive beauty in the whole world". Near Faversham, the fruit research station of Brogdale is open to the public, offering orchard walks, tastings and informative displays.

White wine from the southeast

Oast houses, topped with distinctive angled cowls, are a common feature of the Kentish landscape, and many have now been turned into houses. They were originally

SEASONAL FRUIT

This timeline shows the major crops in each month of the farming year. The first blossoms may appear when the fields are still dusted with snow. As the petals fall, fruit appears among the leaves. After ripening in the summer sun, the fruit is harvested in the autumn.

Raspberries are a luscious soft fruit. Many growers allow you to pick your own from the fields, and then pay by weight

Peach blossom *is usually to be found on south-facing walls, as its fruit requires warm conditions.*

Orchards *are used to grow plums, pears and apples. The latter (blossoming above) remain Kent's most important orchard crop.*

MARCH	APRIL	MAY	JUNE	JULY

Srawberries *are Britain's favourite and earliest soft fruit. New strains allow them to be picked all summer.*

Sour cherry blossom *is the earliest flower. Its fruit is used for cooking.*

Pear blossom *has creamy white flowers which appear two or three weeks before apple blossom.*

Cherry plum blossom *is one of the most beautiful blossoms; the plum is grown more for its flowers than its fruit.*

Gooseberries *are not always sweet enough to eat raw, though all types are superb in pies and other desserts.*

OAST HOUSE

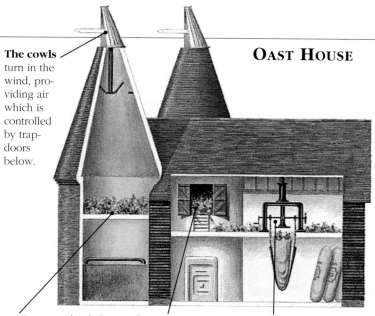

uilt to dry hops, an ingredient brewing beer *(see pp38–9).* any are still used for that, for though imports have reduced omestic hop-growing. more an four million tonnes are roduced in Britain annually, ostly in Kent.

In summer, the fruiting plants n be seen climbing the rect-ngular wire frames in fields by e roadside. Until the middle of e 20th century thousands of milies from London's East End ould move to the Kentish hop elds every autumn for working olidays harvesting the crop and mping in barns. That tradition is faded, because now the ops are picked by machine.

The cowls turn in the wind, pro-viding air which is controlled by trap-doors below.

Hops are dried above a fan which blows hot air from the underlying radiators.

After drying, the hops are cooled and stored.

A press packs the hops into bags, ready for the breweries.

Cherries *are the sweetest of Kent's fruit: two popular varieties are Stella (top) and Duke.*

Plums *are often served stewed, in pies, or dried into prunes. The Victoria plum (left) is the classic English dessert plum and is eatern raw. The Purple plum is also popular.*

Greengages *are green plums. They have a distinctive taste and can be made into jam.*

Bramley Seedling *is one of the best cooking apples, but it is not sweet enough to eat raw.*

Pears, *such as the William (left), should be eaten at the height of ripe-ness. The Conference keeps better.*

AUGUST	SEPTEMBER	OCTOBER	NOVEMBER

urrants *are mong the most assertively avoured fruit and are sed in desserts and jams.*

Peaches, *grown in China 4,000 years ago, came to England in the 19th century.*

Dessert apples, *such as Cox's Orange Pippin (right), are some of England's best-loved fruits. The newer Discovery is easier to grow.*

The Kentish cob, *a variety of hazelnut, is undergoing a revival, having been eclipsed by European imports. Unlike many nuts, it is best picked fresh from the tree.*

Vineyards *are now a familiar sight in Kent (as well as Sussex and Hampshire). Most of the wine produced, such as Lamberhurst, is white.*

Houses of Historical Figures

V ISITING THE HOMES OF ARTISTS, writers, politicians and royalty is a rewarding way of gaining an insight into their private lives. Southeast England, near London, boasts many historic houses that have been preserved as they were when their illustrious occupants were alive. All these houses, from large mansions such as Lord Mountbatten's Broadlands to the more modest dwellings, like Jane Austen's House, contain exhibits relating to the life of the famous people who lived there.

Florence Nightingale *(1820–1910), the "Lady with the Lamp", was a nurse during the Crimean War* (see p60). *She stayed at Claydon with her sister, Lady Verney.*

Nancy Astor *(1879–1964) was the first woman to sit in Parliament in 1919. She lived at Cliveden until her death and made it famous for political hospitality.*

Claydon House, Winslow, nr Milton Keynes

THAMES VALLEY *(see pp226–55)*

The Duke of Wellington *(1769–1852) was given this house by the nation in 1817, in gratitude for leading the British to victory at Waterloo* (see p59).

Cliveden House, nr Maidenhead

Stratfield Saye, Basingstoke, nr Windsor

Jane Austen *(1775–1817) wrote three of her novels, including* Emma, *and revised the others at this house where she lived for eight years until shortly before her death (see p172).*

Jane Austen's House, Chawton, nr Winchester

Broadlands, Southampton

Lord Mountbatten (1900–79), a British naval commander and statesman, was the last Viceroy of India in 1947. He lived here all his married life and remodelled the original house considerably.

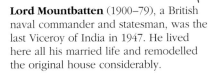

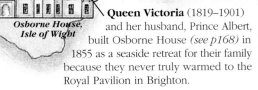

Osborne House, Isle of Wight

Queen Victoria (1819–1901) and her husband, Prince Albert, built Osborne House *(see p168)* in 1855 as a seaside retreat for their family because they never truly warmed to the Royal Pavilion in Brighton.

BLOOMSBURY GROUP

A circle of avant-garde artists, designers and writers, many of them friends as students, began to meet at a house in Bloomsbury, London, in 1904 and soon gained a reputation for their Bohemian lifestyle. When Duncan Grant and Vanessa Bell moved to Charleston in 1916, it became a Sussex outpost of the celebrated group. Many of the prominent figures associated with the circle, such as Virginia Woolf, EM Forster, Vita Sackville-West and JM Keynes paid visits here. The Bloomsbury Group was also known for the Omega Workshops, which made innovative ceramics, furniture and textiles.

Vanessa Bell at Charleston **by Duncan Grant (1885–1978)**

Gainsborough's House, Sudbury, nr Ipswich

EAST ANGLIA
(see pp192–225)

Thomas Gainsborough *(1727–88), one of Britain's greatest painters, was born in this house* (see p216). *He was best known for his portraits, such as this one of* Mr and Mrs Andrews.

Charles Darwin *(1809–82), who developed the theory that man and apes have a common ancestor, wrote his most famous book,* On the Origin of Species, *at the house where he lived.*

Down House, Downe, nr Sevenoaks

THE DOWNS AND CHANNEL COAST
(see pp158–91)

Bleak House, Broadstairs, nr Margate

Charles Dickens (1812–70), the prolific and popular Victorian novelist *(see p191)*, had many connections with Kent. He took holidays at Bleak House, later named after his famous novel.

Chartwell, Westerham, nr Sevenoaks

Batemans, Burwash, nr Hastings

Winston Churchill (1874–1965), Britain's inspirational Prime Minister in World War II *(see p191)*, lived here for 40 years until his death. He relaxed by rebuilding parts of the house.

Charleston, Lewes

Vanessa Bell (1879–1961), artist and member of the Bloomsbury Group, lived here until her death in 1961. The 18th-century farmhouse reflects her unusual decorative ideas and is filled with murals, paintings and painted furniture.

Rudyard Kipling *(1865–1936), the poet and novelist, was born in India, but lived here for 34 years until his death. His most famous works include* Kim, *the two* Jungle Books *and the* Just So Stories.

Sunset over the Needles, a group of rocks on the west coast of the Isle of Wight ▷

THE DOWNS
AND CHANNEL
COAST

THE DOWNS AND CHANNEL COAST

WHEN SETTLERS and invaders came to Britain from Europe, the southeast coast was their first landfall. The wooded chalk ridges and lower-lying Weald beyond them made an ideal base for settlement and proved to be productive farmland.

The Romans made their first landing at Richborough (near Dover) and built a triumphal arch, the foundations of which survive today. They were the first to construct major fortifications along the Channel Coast to discourage potential attackers, and there are Roman remains from Reculver in the east to Southampton in the west. Dover and Portchester Castles are both large defensive buildings enlarged over the years from their Roman foundations, while Fishbourne Palace is one of the most magnificent Roman dwellings ever discovered in Britain. This palace, which is near the market town of Chichester, was built in the 1st century.

Because the Normans had used this coast for their invasion in 1066, it was natural that the area should become an important medieval power base. Ports in Kent and Sussex grew prosperous through trade with the Continent, as did the hundreds of smugglers who operated from these harbours. The magnificent cathedrals at Canterbury and Winchester bear witness to their central role in the medieval Christian Church, which in those days was nearly as powerful as the State. After the murder of Thomas à Becket in 1170, Canterbury became a magnet for pilgrimages, such as the one documented by the poet Geoffrey Chaucer. Much of the travellers' route from London can still be followed along a series of roads and footpaths called the Pilgrims' Way.

From Tudor times on, monarchs, noblemen and courtiers (who all appreciated the area's moderate climate and proximity to the capital) acquired estates in the verdant countryside and built great houses, some of which still stand. Today, the southeast corner of

Aerial view of the medieval and moated Leeds Castle

◁ **A lush covering of bluebells in the deciduous woodlands of Kent**

Buttercups in spring bloom on a section of the South Downs Way walk, near East Dean, East Sussex

England is the country's most prosperous and heavily populated region. It has an excellent network of transport links to the capital, which makes the area prime commuter country. The parts of Surrey and Kent within about 38 miles (60 km) of the capital are known as the Stockbroker Belt. High earners in the money-related businesses

Farm buildings, including an oast house, in Kent

of the City – who tend to live in large, luxurious villas – are drawn to these areas by the same virtues that attracted the Tudor gentry. Their houses were mostly built in the early 20th century, some on the scenic slopes of the North Downs, others on lower ground. Much of the farmland that used to surround these buildings has been converted into golf courses, catering to a favourite leisure pursuit of the rich. Some of the country's greatest and most-visited private gardens, including those at Sissinghurst, were established here in the 19th and 20th centuries.

The region as a whole played a vital role in Britain's survival in World War II. In 1940, hundreds of small boats set sail from the coastal ports to rescue over 300,000 members of the British Expeditionary Force, who were fleeing from occupied France. That same year, the fighter planes that defended London against German bombers in the Battle of Britain took off from airfields in Kent. In 1944, the south coast beaches were used to launch the D-Day invasion of France that led to the final victory. Some wartime coastal fortifications may still be seen.

Kent, with a mild climate that encourages plant growth, has long been known as "The Garden of England". Despite the incursion of bricks and mortar, it is still a leading area for producing fruit, and is conveniently located for easy access to the vast metropolitan market of London. Hop fields and oast houses are common sights, and flourishing breweries produce their distinctive beers and ales. Sussex is still an agricultural county, famous for its Southdown sheep. The small amount of heavy industry once present in the region, including iron working in Sussex and coal mining in Kent, has now been abandoned.

Pebble beach and cliffs at Alum Bay, Isle of Wight

The opening of the Channel Tunnel to France in 1994 brought new prosperity to the areas around Folkestone and Dover, providing hundreds of jobs and transporting many thousands of tourists between England and Europe. Ashford, in Kent, the first stop in England on the trains from Europe, has especially benefited. Despite the Tunnel's popularity, the ferries and hovercraft services that once enjoyed domination of cross-channel transport have so far competed successfully. They tend to be favoured by those who like to stand on deck as the craft approaches the English coast, waiting for the legendary white cliffs of Dover to come into view. A high-speed rail link between London and the Tunnel is being constructed, but has been delayed by objections from people who live near the proposed route.

Channel Tunnel Terminal, Folkestone, Kent

The North and South Downs are popular with walkers. Long-distance footpaths follow the line of both ranges, and there are also fine walks along the chalk cliffs at the sea's edge (although some suffer badly from erosion). Between the North and South Downs are the fields and cool woodlands of the fertile Weald. Visitors will find

Cottage in the New Forest, Hampshire

scores of delightful ancient churches with "Sussex cap" spires in picturesque villages, some of which were already established by the time of the Domesday survey of 1086. For a much more boisterous atmosphere, Brighton, Southsea, Bognor Regis and other such seaside resorts provide raucous amusement arcades and fairground entertainments. A common feature of such holiday settlements is Victorian iron piers that jut into the sea, the Palace Pier at Brighton (built in 1899) being particularly famous. Although these resorts reached their peak of popularity in the first half of the 20th century, echoes of their glory days remain.

Boats moored beside the fortified town of Rye, East Sussex

Exploring the Downs and Channel Coast

The NORTH AND SOUTH DOWNS, separated by the lower-lying Weald are ideal walking country as well as being the site of many stately homes. From Tudor times, wealthy, London-based merchants and courtiers built their country residences in Kent, a day's ride from the capital, and many are open to the public. On the coast are the remains of sturdy castles put up to deter invaders from across the Channel. Today, though, the seashore is largely devoted to pleasure. Some of Britain's earliest beach resorts were developed along this coast, and sea bathing is said to have been invented in Brighton.

View of Brighton's Palace Pier from the promenade

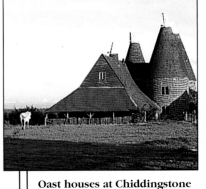

Oast houses at Chiddingstone near Royal Tunbridge Wells

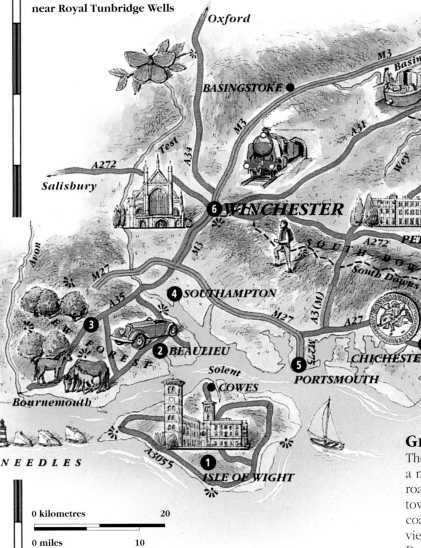

GETTING AROUND

The area is well served, with a network of motorways and A roads from London to the major towns. The A259 is a scenic coast road which offers fine views over the English Channel. Bus and rail transport is also good, with a number of coach companies providing regular tours to the major sites. An InterCity train service runs to all the major towns.

0 kilometres 20

0 miles 10

SIGHTS AT A GLANCE

Arundel **8**
Beaulieu **2**
Bodiam Castle **18**
Brighton pp175–9 **13**
Canterbury pp188–9 **23**
Chichester **7**
Dover **21**
The Downs **16**
Eastbourne **15**
Guildford **10**
Hampton Court p173 **11**
Hastings **17**
Hever Castle **27**
Isle of Wight **1**

Knole **26**
Leeds Castle **24**
Lewes **14**
Margate **22**
Rochester **25**
New Forest **3**
Petworth House **9**
Portsmouth **5**
Romney Marsh **20**
Royal Tunbridge Wells **28**
Rye pp186–7 **19**
Southampton **4**
Steyning **12**
Winchester pp170–71 **6**

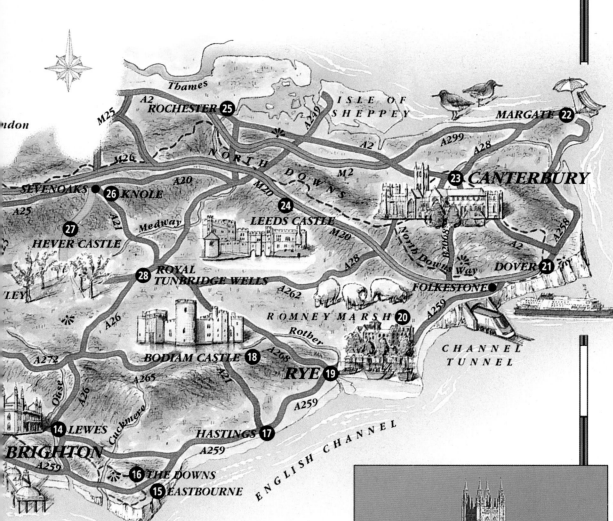

KEY

▰	Motorway
▰	Major road
▰	Minor road
▰	Scenic route
●▬	Scenic path
▰	River
☀	Viewpoint

Canterbury Cathedral's spire, dominating the skyline

The Pilgrim's Way

Stained glass detail from Cantebury Cathedral, c.1220

THE ROUTE FROM WINCHESTER to Canterbury was once taken by Christian pilgrims to visit Canterbury cathedral and pay homage at the tomb of Thomas à Becket *(see pp52–3)*. The pilgrimages continued until the Protestant Reformation under King Henry VIII in 1532. The many towns and villages along the way are littered with fascinating cultural details originating from before and after the heyday of the pilgrimage.

The North Downs (near Wrotham) is ideal walking country

THE CANTERBURY TALES

This llustration shows pilgrims on their journey from the Prologue to Chaucer's *Canterbury Tales*. Written in the 14th century in Middle English verse, the *Tales*, and especially the Prologue, provide a detailed and colourful impression of the pilgrims travelling the road to Canterbury. Chaucer himself died in 1400, and was buried in Westminster Abbey *(see p99)*, in a part of the building now known as Poet's Corner.

Alresford Station, from which steam trains still run, is one of the many attractions which today line the pilgrim route.

Guildford High Street in 1850 was as popular with visitors as it is now. The High Street was once described by Charles Dickens as the most beautiful in England.

The chalkhill blue butterfly can be seen in considerable numbers in spring and summer on the south facing slopes of the chalky downs, which line part of the route.

Hop-growing was for centuries a common activity in the region along the Pilgrim's Way. But today, with increased mechanization and competition from other countries, the industry has almost disappeared.

THE ROYAL CONNECTION

The cities of Winchester and Canterbury have been important centres for the monarchy and for the Church for many centuries. King Alfred (849–901) – perhaps best known for burning the cakes – made Winchester his capital in the 9th century. Canterbury, an important town for the Romans, became the centre of St Augustine's Church in England in the 6th century.

King Alfred lets the cakes burn while hiding from the Danes

The medieval city walls were built about 1,000 years after the original Roman walls were erected.

Leeds Castle, *with its distinctive lake, is perhaps one of the most impressive sights on the Pilgrim's Way. The construction of this medieval castle was started in 1119, and it became a royal residence in the 13th century.*

Only wealthy pilgrims were affluent enough to be able to travel the Pilrgim's Way by horse. Most made the arduous and often dangerous journey on foot.

The steps leading to Trinity Chapel, *in Canterbury Cathedral have been worn down by the numberless pilgrims who have approached it on their knees over the centuries. Thomas à Becket's tomb was housed here until 1538, when it was destroyed.*

The Victorian Osborne House, Isle of Wight

Isle of Wight ❶

Isle of Wight. 👥 *135,000.* 🚢 *from Lymington, Southampton, Portsmouth.* ℹ️ *Westridge Centre, Brading Road, Westridge (01983 813800).*

A VISIT TO **Osborne House**, the favoured seaside retreat of Queen Victoria and Prince Albert *(see p156)*, is alone worth the ferry ride from the mainland. Furnished much as they left it, the house provides a marvellous insight into royal life and is dotted with family mementoes.

The **Swiss Cottage** was built for the royal children to play in. It is now a museum attached to Osborne House. Adjacent to it you can see the bathing machine used by the queen to preserve her modesty while taking her to the edge of the sea *(see p461)*.

The other main sight on the island is **Carisbrooke Castle**, built in the 11th century. A walk on its outer wall and the climb to the top of its keep provides spectacular views. It was here that Charles I *(see pp56–7)* was held prisoner in 1647; an attempt to escape was foiled when he got stuck between the bars of a window.

The island is a base for ocean sailing, especially during Cowes Week *(see p71)*. The scenic highlight is the **Needles** – three towers of rock jutting out of the sea at the island's western end. This is only a short walk from

Alum Bay, famous for its multi-coloured cliffs and sand.

🏛 **Osborne House**
East Cowes. 📞 *01983 200022.* ⬜ *Apr–Oct: daily. Nov–mid-Dec & Feb–Mar: daily, by* 🎫 *only, phone to arrange.* ⬤ *late Dec–Jan.* 🏴 ♿ *limited.* 📷
🏰 **Carisbrooke Castle**
Newport. 📞 *01983 522107.* ⬜ *daily.* ⬤ *24–26 Dec.* 🏴 ♿ *limited.* 📷 📷 🖥 📷

Beaulieu ❷

Brockenhurst, Hampshire. 📞 *01590 612345.* 🚉 *Brockenhurst then taxi.* ⬜ *daily.* ⬤ *25 Dec.* 🏴 ♿ 🎫 *by arrangement.* 📷 🖥 📷

P ALACE HOUSE, once the gate-house of Beaulieu Abbey, has been the home of Lord Montagu's family since 1538. It now contains the finest collection of cars in the country. The **National Motor Museum** has over 250 vintage cars ranging from the 1890s to the present.

There is also an exhibition of monastic life in the ruined ancient **abbey**, founded in

1204 by King John *(see p52)* for Cistercian monks. The original abbey church now serves as the parish church.

ENVIRONS: Just south is the maritime museum at **Buckler's Hard**, telling the story of ship-building in the 18th century. The yard employed 4,000 people at its peak but declined when steel began to be used for shipbuilding.

🏛 **Buckler's Hard**
Beaulieu. 📞 *01590 616203.* ⬜ *daily.* ⬤ *25 Dec.* 🏴 ♿ *limited.*

New Forest ❸

Hampshire. 🚉 *Brockenhurst.* 🚌 *Lymington then bus.* ℹ️ *main car park, Lyndhurst (023 8028 2269).*

T HIS UNIQUE EXPANSE of heath and woodland is, at 145 sq miles (375 sq km), the lar-gest area of unenclosed land in southern Britain.

William the Conqueror's "new" forest, despite its name, is one of the few primeval oak woods in England. It was the popular hunting ground of Norman kings, and in 1100 William II was fatally wounded here in a hunting accident.

Today it is enjoyed by up to seven million visitors a year who share it with the shaggy New Forest ponies – unique to the area – and over 1,500 fal-low deer which graze here.

Southampton ❹

Hampshire. 👥 *200,000.* ✈️ 🚉 🚌 🚢 ℹ️ *9 Civic Centre (023 8022 1106).* 🛍 *Wed–Sat.*

F OR CENTURIES this has been a flourishing port. The *Mayflower* sailed from here to America in 1620 with the

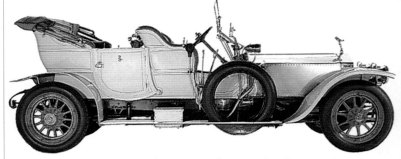

A 1909 Rolls-Royce Silver Ghost at Beaulieu's National Motor Museum

Pilgrim Fathers, as did the supposedly unsinkable *Titanic* at the start of its maiden and ultimately tragic voyage in 1912, when it went down after hitting an iceberg.

The **Maritime Museum** has exhibits about both these ships, along with displays on the huge romantic liners that sailed from the port in the first half of the 20th century, the heyday of ocean travel.

There is a walk around the remains of the medieval city wall. At the head of the High Street stands the old city gate, **Bargate**, the most elaborate gate to survive in England.

Illustration of the luxurious liner the *Titanic* which sank in 1912

It still has its 13th-century drum towers and is decorated with intricate, 17th-century armorial carvings.

The **Tudor House Museum** has exhibits on Victorian and Edwardian domestic life.

🏛 **Maritime Museum**
Town Quay Rd. 📞 *023 8063 5904.*
◯ *Tue–Sun.* ● *25, 26 Dec, 1 Jan & public hols.* ♿ *limited.* ⬚

🏛 **Tudor House Museum**
St Michael's Sq. 📞 *023 8063 5904.*
◯ *Tue–Sun.* ● *25, 26 Dec, 1 Jan & public hols.* ♿ *limited.* ⬚

Portsmouth ⑤

Hampshire. 👥 *190,000.* ⇌ 🚌
ℹ *The Hard (023 9282 6722).*
🛒 *Thu–Sat.*

O NCE A VITAL naval port, with all the nightlife that entails, Portsmouth is today a much quieter town but fascinating for those interested in English naval history.

Under the banner of **Portsmouth Historic Ships**, the city's ancient dockyard is the hub of Portsmouth's most important sights. Among these is the hull of the **Mary Rose**, Henry VIII's flagship *(see p54)*, which capsized on its maiden voyage as it left to fight the French in 1545. It was recovered from the sea bed in 1982 along with thousands of 16th-century objects now on display nearby, giving an absorbing insight into life at sea 450 years ago.

Alongside it is HMS **Victory**, the English flagship on which Admiral Nelson was killed at Trafalgar *(see p31)* and now restored to its former glory. You can also visit the **Royal Naval Museum** which deals with naval history from the 16th century to the Falklands War, and the 19th-century ironclad HMS **Warrior**.

Portsmouth's other military memorial is the **D-Day Museum**. This is centred on the *Overlord Embroidery*, a masterpiece of needlework which was commissioned in 1968 from the Royal School of Needlework and took five years to complete. At 83 m (272 ft), its 34 panels are 12 m

The figurehead on the bow of HMS *Victory* at Portsmouth

(41 ft) longer than the *Bayeux Tapestry*, held in France, and it depicts the events surrounding the World War II Allied landing in Normandy in 1944.

Portchester Castle, on the north edge of the harbour, was fortified in the third century and is the best example of Roman sea defences in northern Europe. The Normans later used the Roman walls to enclose a castle – only the keep survives – and a church. Henry V used the castle as a garrison to assemble his army before the Battle of Agincourt *(see p53)*. In the 18th and 19th centuries the castle was a prisoner-of-war camp and you can still see where the prisoners carved their names, and dates on the walls.

Among less warlike attractions is the **Charles Dickens Museum** *(see p191)*. The house where the author was born in 1812 – his father was a Navy clerk – is furnished in the style of that time.

🏛 **Portsmouth Historic Ships**
The Hard. 📞 *023 9286 1512.*
◯ *daily.* ● *25 Dec.* 📷 ♿ ⬚

🏛 **D-Day Museum**
Clarence Esplanade. 📞 *023 9282 7261.* ◯ *daily.* ● *24–26, 31 Dec & 1 Jan.* 📷 ♿ 📷 🖥 ⬚

🏰 **Portchester Castle**
Castle St, Porchester. 📞 *023 9237 8291.* ◯ *daily.* ● *24–26, 31 Dec & 1 Jan.* 📷 📷 *by arrangement.*

🏛 **Charles Dickens Museum**
393 Old Commercial Rd. 📞 *023 9282 7261.* ◯ *Apr–Oct, 1–21 Dec: daily.* 📷

A wild pony and her foal roaming freely in the New Forest

Winchester ❻

Hampshire. 🚶 34,000. 🚆 🚌
ℹ️ Guildhall, The Broadway (01962 840500). 🏛️ Mon, Wed, Fri, Sat.

Capital of the ancient kingdom of Wessex, the city of Winchester was also the headquarters of the Anglo-Saxon kings until the Norman Conquest (see p51).

William the Conqueror built one of his first English castles here. The only surviving part of the castle is the **Great Hall**, erected in 1235 to replace the original. It is now home to

the legendary Round Table. The story behind the table is a mix of history and myth. King Arthur (see p315) had it shaped so no knight could claim precedence. It was said to have been built by the wizard Merlin but was actually made in the 13th century.

The **Westgate Museum** is one of the four surviving 12th-century gatehouses in the city wall. The room (once a prison) above the gate has a 16th-century painted ceiling. It was moved here from Winchester College, England's oldest fee-paying, or "public school", founded in 1382 by William of Wykeham – known as the father of the public school.

The 13th-century Round Table, Great Hall, Winchester

Winchester has been an ecclesiastical centre for many centuries. **Wolvesey Castle** (first built around 1110) was the magnificent home to the **cathedral's** bishops before the Conquest but is now in ruins.

STUDY TO BE QUIET

Author Izaac Walton (1593–1683) is depicted in the stained glass Anglers' Window made in 1914.

These magnificent choir-stalls (c.1308) are England's oldest.

The Lady Chapel was rebuilt by Elizabeth of York (c.1500) after her son was baptized in the cathedral.

The Perpendicular nave is the highlight of the building.

Jane Austen's grave

Main entrance

WINCHESTER CATHEDRAL

The Close. 📞 01962 853137.
⬜ daily. 🔵 during services. ♿
Donation 🎫 groups: book in advance.

The first church was built here in 648 but the present building was begun in 1079. Originally a Benedictine monastery, much of the Norman architecture remains despite continual modifications until the early 16th century.

The 12th-century black Tournai marble fo

The **Hospital of St Cross** is an old almshouse built in 1446. Weary strangers may claim the "Wayfarer's Dole", a horn (cup) of ale and bread, given out since medieval times.

Great Hall
Castle Ave. (01962 846476.
☐ daily. ● 25, 26 Dec. &
Westgate Museum
High St. (01962 869864.
☐ Feb, Mar, Oct: Tue–Sun;
Apr–Sep: Mon–Sun.
Hospital of St Cross
St Cross Rd. (01962 851375. ☐
Mon–Sat. ● 25 Dec, Good Fri.

The Library has over 4,000 books. This "B" from Psalm 1 is found in the Winchester Bible, an exquisite work of 12th-century illumination.

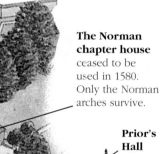

The Norman chapter house ceased to be used in 1580. Only the Norman arches survive.

Prior's Hall

The Close originally contained the domestic buildings for the monks of the Priory of St Swithun's – the name before it became Winchester Cathedral. Most of the buildings, such as the refectory and cloisters, were destroyed during the Dissolution of the Monasteries (see p54)

Chichester ⑦

West Sussex. 🚶 26,000. ≥ 🚌
ℹ 29A South St (01243 775888).
🏛 Wed, Sat.

THIS WONDERFULLY preserved market town, with an elaborate early 16th-century market cross at its centre, is dominated by its **cathedral**, consecrated in 1108. The exterior is a lovely mix of greenish limestone and Caen stone and its graceful spire, said to be the only English cathedral spire visible from the sea, dominates the town. Although vandalized in the Civil War (see p56), the cathedral still contains much of interest, including a unique detached bell tower (1436).

There are two sculpted stone panels in the choir, dating from 1140. Modern works include paintings by Graham Sutherland (1903–80), and a stained glass window by Marc Chagall (1889–1985).

ENVIRONS: Just west at Bosham is the Saxon **Holy Trinity Church,** known to have been used by King Canute (see p50). Myth has it that this was where Canute failed to stop the incoming tide and so proved to his courtiers that his powers had limits. The church appears in the *Bayeux Tapestry,* held in France, because Harold heard mass here in 1064 before he was shipwrecked off Normandy and then rescued by William the Conqueror (see p51).

Fishbourne Palace (see pp48–9), further west, is the largest Roman villa in Britain. It covers 3 ha (7 acres) and was discovered in 1960 by a workman digging for drains.

Chagall's stained glass window (1978), Chichester Cathedral

Constructed from AD 75, it had over 100 rooms, but was destroyed by fire in 285. The north wing has some of the finest mosaics discovered in Britain, including one with Cupid riding a dolphin.

To the north is the 18th-century **Goodwood House**. Its magnificent art collection features works by Canaletto (1697–1768) and Stubbs (1724–1806). This impressive house, home to the Earl of March, has a racecourse on the Downs.

Chichester Cathedral
West St. (01243 782595.
☐ daily. ● during services. &
Fishbourne Palace
Fishbourne. (01243 785859. ☐
mid-Feb–mid-Dec: daily; mid-Dec–mid-Feb: Sat, Sun.
Goodwood House
Goodwood. (01243 755048.
🅵 01243 755040. ☐ Easter–Sep:
Sun, Mon; Aug: Sun–Thu (pm).
● special events.

WILLIAM WALKER

At the beginning of the 20th century, the cathedral's east end seemed certain to collapse unless its foundations were underpinned. But because the water table lies only just below the surface, the work had to be done under water. From 1906 to 1911, Walker, a deep-sea diver, worked six hours a day laying sacks of cement beneath the unsteady walls, until the building was safe.

William Walker in his diving suit

The dominating position of Arundel Castle, West Sussex

Arundel Castle ⑧

Arundel, West Sussex. 📞 01903
883136. 🚊 Arundel. ◯ Apr–Oct:
Sun–Fri. ◉ Good Fri; Nov–Mar. ♿
🎞 🖥 🍴 🛍

Dominating the small riverside town below, this vast,
grey hill-top castle, surrounded
by castellated walls, was first
built by the Normans.

During the 16th century it
was acquired by the powerful
Dukes of Norfolk, the country's
senior Roman Catholic family,
who still live here. They rebuilt
it after the original was virtually
destroyed by Parliamentarians
in 1643 (see p56), and restored
it again in the 19th century.

In the castle grounds is the
parish church of **St Nicholas**.
Its most unusual feature is the
small Catholic Fitzalan chapel
(c.1380) built into its east end
by the castle's first owners,
the Fitzalans. Separated from
the church by a superb 14th-
century iron grille, it can only
be entered from the grounds.

Petworth House ⑨

(**NT**) Petworth, West Sussex.
📞 01798 342207. 🚊 Pulborough
then bus. **House** ◯ Apr–Oct: Sat–
Wed & Good Fri. **Park** ◯ daily. ♿
♿ limited. 🍴 🛍

This late 17th-century house
was immortalized in a
series of famous views by the
painter JMW Turner (see p97).
Some of his best paintings are
on display here and are part
of Petworth's outstanding art
collection which also includes

works by Titian (1488–1576),
Van Dyck (1599–1641) and
Gainsborough (see p157). Also
extremely well represented is
ancient Roman and Greek
sculpture, such as the 4th-
century BC *Leconfield
Aphrodite,* widely thought to
be by Praxiteles.

One of the main attractions
is the Carved Room, decorated with intricately carved
wood panels of birds, flowers
and musical instruments, by
Grinling Gibbons (1648–1721).

The large deer park includes
some of the earliest work of
Capability Brown (see p27).

**The Restoration clock on the
Tudor Guildhall, Guildford**

Guildford ⑩

Surrey. 🏙 63,000. 🚊 🚌 🛈 14
Tunsgate (01483 444333). 🏪 Fri, Sat.

The county town of Surrey,
settled since Saxon times,
incorporates the remains of a
small Norman **castle**. The
attractive High Street is lined

with buildings of the Tudor
period, such as the impressive
Guildhall. But it is the huge
modern red-brick cathedral,
completed in 1954, that
dominates the town's skyline.

Environs: Guildford stands on
the end of the North Downs,
a range of chalk hills which
are popular for walking (see
p37). The area also has two
famous beauty spots: **Leith
Hill** – the highest point in
southeast England – and **Box
Hill**. The view from the latter
is well worth the short, gentle
climb from West Humble.

Just to the south of the town
is the perfect red brickwork
of **Clandon Park**. This 18th-
century house has a sump-
tuous interior, especially the
Marble Hall – one of the
grandest English interiors of
the period. It has an intricate
Baroque ceiling, and the hall's
side lamps are supported by
black ivory forearms jutting
from the wall, which represent
the Park's West Indian servants.

Southwest is Chawton,
where **Jane Austen's House**
(see p156) is located. This
small red-brick house is where
she wrote most of her gentle,
witty comedies of middle-class
manners in Georgian England,
such as *Pride and Prejudice.*

🏛 **Clandon Park**
West Clandon, Surrey. 📞 01483
222482. ◯ Apr–Oct: Tue–Thu, Sun;
Good Fri & public hols. ◉ Nov–Mar.
♿ ♿ limited. 🛍
🏛 **Jane Austen's House**
Alton, Hants. 📞 01420 83262.
◯ Jan–Feb: Sat, Sun; Mar–Dec: daily.
◉ 25, 26 Dec. ♿ ♿ limited. 🛍

Hampton Court ⑪

East Molesey, Surrey. 📞 *020-8781-9500.* 🚂 *Hampton Court.* ⭕ *daily.* ⬤ *24–26 Dec.* ♿🅿️🎫📷🍴🛍️

THE POWERFUL chief minister and Archbishop of York to Henry VIII *(see p55)*, Cardinal Wolsey, leased Hampton Court in 1514 as his riverside country residence. In 1528, in the hope of retaining royal favour, Wolsey gave it to the king. After the royal takeover, Hampton Court was extended twice, first by Henry himself and then in the 1690s by William and Mary, who used Christopher Wren *(see p120)* as the architect. From the outside the palace is a harmonious blend of Tudor and English Baroque, inside there is a striking contrast between Wren's Classical royal rooms, which include the King's Apartments, and

Ceiling decoration, Hampton Court

Tudor architecture, such as the Great Hall. Many of the state apartments are decorated with furniture, paintings and tapestries taken from the Royal Collection *(see p255)*. Also from this period are the restored Baroque gardens with their radiating avenues of majestic limes, collections of rare and exotic plants and formal plant beds.

The Baroque maze is one of the garden's most famous features; visitors often become lost in it.

The Queen's Apartments, including the Presence Chamber and Bedchamber, are arranged around the the north and east sides of Fountain Court.

Fountain Court

The Fountain Garden still has a few of the original yews planted by William and Mary *(see p57).* Only one fountain remains out of the original 13 built.

Great Hall

Main entrance

Anne Boleyn's Gateway is at the entrance to Clock Court.

River Thames

The Mantegna Gallery houses Andrea Mantegna's nine canvasses depicting *The Triumph of Julius Caesar* (1490).

Long Water

Broad Walk

The pond garden, a sunken water garden, was part of Henry VIII's elaborate redesigns. The small pond in the middle contains a single-jet fountain.

The Tudor Chapel Royal was completed by Henry VIII. But the superb woodwork, including the massive reredos by Grinling Gibbons, all date from a major refurbishment by Queen Anne (c.1711).

Steyning ⑫

West Sussex. 🚶 *5,000* 🚌 ℹ️ *9 The Causeway, Horsham (01403 211661).*

THIS LOVELY little town in the lee of the Downs is packed with timber-framed houses from the Tudor period and earlier, with some built of flint and others in sandstone.

In Saxon times, Steyning was an important port and ship-building centre on the River Adur: King Ethelwulf, father of King Alfred *(see p50)*, was buried here in 858; his body was later moved to Winchester. The *Domesday Book (see p52)* records that Steyning had 123 houses, making it one of the largest towns in the south. The 12th-century church is spacious and splendid, evidence of the area's ancient prosperity: the tower, of chequered stone and flint, was added around 1600.

In the 14th century the river silted up and changed course away from the town, putting an end to its days as a port. Later it became an important coaching stop on the south coast road: the **Chequer Inn** recalls this prosperous period, with its unusual 18th-century flint and stone façade.

ENVIRONS: The remains of a **Norman castle** can be visited at Bramber, west of Steyning. This small, pretty village also contains the timber-framed **St Mary's House** (1470). It has fine panelled rooms, including the Elizabethan Painted Room, and one of the oldest trees in the country, a Ginkgo biloba. **Chanctonbury Ring** and **Cissbury Ring**, on the hills west of Steyning, were Iron Age forts and the latter has the remains of a Neolithic flint mine. Worthing is the resort where Oscar Wilde (1854–1900) wrote *The Importance of Being Earnest*.

🏛️ **St Mary's House**
Bramber. 📞 *01903 816205.*
◻️ *Easter–Sep: Sun, Thu (pm) & public hols.* 🅿️ 🎫

Street-by-Street: Brighton ⑬

A stick of Brighton rock

AS THE NEAREST south coast resort to London, Brighton is perennially popular, but has always been more refined than its boisterous rivals further east, such as Margate *(see p183)* and Southend. The spirit of the Prince Regent *(see p179)* lives on, not only in the magnificence of his Royal Pavilion, but in the town's raffish reputation as a venue for adulterous weekends in small, discreet hotels. Brighton has always attracted actors and variety artists – Laurence Olivier made his final home here.

Old Ship Hotel
Built in 1559, it was later bought by Nicholas Tettersells, with the money given to him by Charles II as a reward for taking him to France during the Civil War (see p56).

★ **Palace Pier**
Built in 1899, this typical late-Victorian pier now caters for today's visitors with amusement arcades.

KEY

– – – Suggested route

STAR SIGHTS

★ **Palace Pier**

★ **Royal Pavilion**

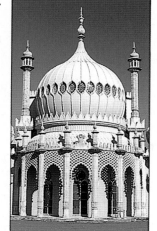

★ **Royal Pavilion**

The Prince Regent's fantastic Oriental palace helped turn Brighton into a fashionable resort, and is today its principal attraction.

VISITORS' CHECKLIST

East Sussex. 🚶 154,000. 🚆 Brighton Central. 🚌 Pool Valley. ℹ 10 Bartholomew Sq (01273 292599). 🚪 Mon–Sat. 🎭 International Arts Festival: May.

Many new plays are first staged in the charming Theatre Royal, established in 1807, before they move to the West End of London.

The Dome, an Indian-style building opposite the Royal Pavilion and once George IV's stables, is now used for orchestral and pop concerts.

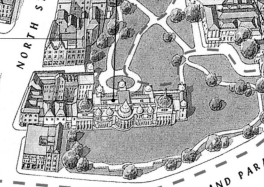

Art Deco
This 1920s Art Deco bronze lamp is on display at the Brighton Museum and Art Gallery.

THE LANES

0 metres 100

0 yards 100

Sea Life Centre
Built in 1872 as a menagerie, it became an aquarium in 1929. Don't miss the sharks and other British marine life.

Eastbourne

The Lanes
Today an engrossing maze of antique shops, the Lanes were the original streets of the village of Brighthelmstone.

Brighton: Royal Pavilion

A S SEA BATHING became fashionable in the mid-18th century, Brighton was transformed into England's first seaside resort. Its gaiety soon appealed to the rakish Prince of Wales, who became George IV in 1820 *(see p59)*. When, in 1785, he secretly married Mrs Fitzherbert, it was here that they conducted their liaison. He moved to a farmhouse near the shore and had it enlarged by Henry Holland *(see p28)*. As his parties grew more lavish, George needed a suitably extravagant setting for them, and in 1815 he employed John Nash *(see p111)* to transform the house into a lavish Oriental palace. Completed in 1822, the exterior has remained largely unaltered. Queen Victoria sold the Pavilion to the town of Brighton in 1850.

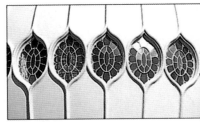

Central Dome
Nash adopted what he called the Hindu Style, as in this delicate tracery on one of the imposing turban domes.

★ **Banqueting Room**
Fiery dragons feature in many of the interior schemes. This colourful one dominates the centre of the Banqueting Room's extraordinary ceiling, and has a huge crystal chandelier suspended from it.

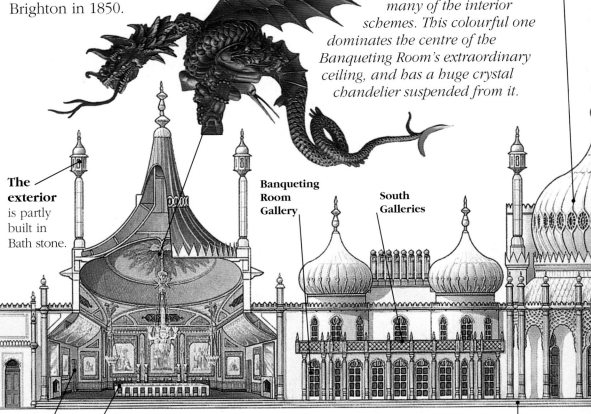

The exterior is partly built in Bath stone.

Banqueting Room Gallery

South Galleries

The banqueting table, which seats 24 people, is laid as for a splendid feast.

The eastern façade of the Pavilion

Standard Lamps
More dragons, along with dolphins and lotus flowers, figure on the Banqueting Room's eight original standard lamps, made of porcelain, ormolu and gilded wood.

STAR SIGHTS

★ **Banqueting Room**

★ **Great Kitchen**

★ **Great Kitchen**
The Prince's epic banquets required a kitchen of huge proportions. The vast ranges and long shelves of gleaming copper pans were used by famous chefs of the day.

◁ **Front façade of George IV's extravagant Royal Pavilion, Brighton**

Saloon

The gilded wall decorations were designed on Indian themes, but the Chinese wallpaper harks back to an earlier decorative scheme. The long couch mimics an Egyptian river boat.

Long Gallery

Mandarin figures, which can nod their heads, line the pink and blue walls of this 49 m (162 ft) gallery.

Queen Victoria's Bedroom

This reproduction four-poster is on display in the upper floor apartments that were used by Queen Victoria (see p60).

The Music Room, with its crimson and gold murals, was where a 70-piece orchestra played to the Prince's guests.

The domes are made of cast iron.

Music Room Gallery

Bow Rooms

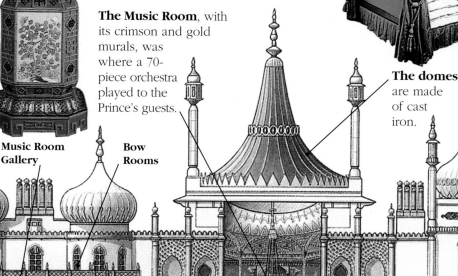

PLAN OF THE ROYAL PAVILION

Exit   Entrance   Stairs to upper floor   King's Apartments

Octagon Hall

...hop
...d café

...reat
...itchen

Banqueting Room
...kers
...m
Banqueting Room Gallery
Saloon
Long Gallery
Music Room Gallery
Music Room

Both Holland and Nash made additions and changes to the original farmhouse. The upper floor contains bedrooms, such as the Bow Rooms, which George's brothers used. The shaded areas represent the artwork above.

PRINCE OF WALES AND MRS FITZHERBERT

The Prince of Wales was only 23 when he fell in love with Maria Fitzherbert, a 29-year-old Catholic widow, and secretly married her. They lived in the farmhouse together and were the toast of Brighton society until George's official marriage took place to Caroline of Brunswick in 1795. Mrs Fitzherbert moved into a small house nearby.

Upstairs interior of Anne of Cleves House, Lewes

Lewes ⑭

East Sussex. 🚶 *16,000.* 🚆 **i** *187 High St (01273 483448).* 🛒 *Tue.*

THE ANCIENT COUNTY TOWN of Sussex was a vital strategic site for the Saxons, because from its high vantage point you can look out over a long stretch of coastline.

William the Conqueror built a wooden castle here in 1067 but this was soon replaced by a large stone structure whose remains can be visited today.

In 1264 it was the site of a critical battle in which Simon de Montfort and his barons defeated Henry III, enabling them to establish the first English Parliament.

The Tudor **Anne of Cleves House** is a museum of local history, although Anne of Cleves, Henry VIII's fourth wife, never actually lived here.

On Bonfire Night *(see p68)* lighted tar barrels are rolled to the river and effigies of the pope are burned instead of the customary Guy Fawkes. This commemorates the town's 17 Protestant martyrs burnt at the stake by Mary I *(see p56).*

ENVIRONS: Nearby is the 16th-century **Glynde Place**, a handsome courtyard house. It has an extensive display of early 18th-century needle-work and Derby china.

🏛 **Anne of Cleves House**
Lewes. **(** *01273 474610.*
◯ *mid-Feb–9 Nov: daily; 10 Nov–23 Dec: Tue–Sun; 28 Dec–mid-Feb: Tues, Thu, Sat.* 🗓
🎟 *by arrangement.* 📷
🏚 **Glynde Place**
Lewes. **i** *01273 858224.* ◯ *May: Sun; Jun, Sep: Wed, Sun; Jul, Aug: Wed, Thu, Sun.* 🗓 💻 📷

Eastbourne ⑮

East Sussex. 🚶 *86,000.* 🚆 🚌 **i** *Cornfield Rd (01323 411400).* 🛒 *Wed, Sat.*

THIS VICTORIAN SEASIDE resort is a popular place for retirement, as well as a first-rate centre for touring the Downs. The South Downs Way *(see p37)* begins at **Beachy Head**, the spectacular 163 m (536 ft) chalk cliff just on the outskirts of the town. From here it is a bracing walk to the cliff top at Birling Gap, with views to the **Seven Sisters**, the chalk hills that end abruptly as they meet the sea.

ENVIRONS: To the west of Eastbourne is **Seven Sisters Country Park**, a 285 ha (700 acre) area of chalk cliffs and Downland marsh. The **Park Visitor's Centre** contains *The Living World* – a display of local wildlife and geology.

Just north is the pretty village of **Alfriston**, with an ancient market cross and a 15th-century inn, **The Star**, in its quaint main street. Near the church is the 14th-century **Clergy House** that, in 1896, became the first National Trust property *(see p29)*. To the east is the huge prehistoric chalk carving, the **Long Man of Wilmington** *(see p237)*.

i **Park Visitor's Centre**
Exceat, Seaford. **(** *01323 870280.*
◯ *Apr–Oct: daily; Nov–Mar: Sat, Sun.*
● *25 Dec.* ♿
🏚 **Clergy House**
(NT) Alfriston. **(** *01323 870001.*
◯ *Apr–Oct: Sat–Mon, Wed, Thur & Good Fri.* 🗓 📷

The lighthouse (1902) at the foot of Beachy Head, Eastbourne

The meandering River Cuckmere flowing through the South Downs to the beach at Cuckmere Haven

The Downs 16

East Sussex. ⚉ 🚌 *Eastbourne.*
ℹ *Cornfield Rd, Eastbourne (01323 411400).*

THE NORTH and South Downs are parallel chalk ridges that run from east to west all the way across Kent, Sussex and Surrey, separated by the lower-lying and fertile Kent and Sussex Weald.

The smooth Downland hills are covered with springy turf, kept short by grazing sheep, making an ideal surface for walkers. The hill above the precipitous **Devil's Dyke**, just north of Brighton, offers spectacular views for miles across the Downs. The legend is that the Devil cut the gorge to let in the sea and flood the countryside, but was foiled by divine intervention. The River Cuckmere runs through one of the most picturesque parts of the South Downs.

Located at the highest point of the Downs is **Uppark House**. This neat square building has been meticulously restored to its mid-18th-century appearance after a fire in 1989.

🏛 Uppark House
(NT) Petersfield, West Sussex.
📞 *01730 825857.* ⏰ *Apr–Oct: Sun–Thu.* ♿ &

Hastings 17

East Sussex. 👥 *83,000.* ⚉ 🚌
ℹ *Queens Square , Priory Meadow (01424 781111).*

THIS FASCINATING seaside town was one of the first Cinque Ports *(see p182)* and is still a thriving fishing port. The town is characterized by the unique tall wooden "net shops" on the beach, where for hundreds of years fishermen have stored their nets. In the 19th century, the area to

the west of the Old Town was built up as a seaside resort, which left the narrow, characterful streets of the old fishermen's quarter intact.

The wooden net shops, on Hastings' shingle beach

Other attractions include two cliff railways and smugglers' caves with a display of this once vital part of the town's economy *(see p312)*.

ENVIRONS: Seven miles (11 km) from Hastings is Battle. The centre square of this small town is dominated by the gatehouse of **Battle Abbey**. This was built by William the Conqueror on the site of his great victory – he reputedly placed the high altar on the spot where Harold fell. But the abbey was destroyed in the Dissolution *(see p54)*. There is an evocative walk around the actual battlefield.

🏛 Battle Abbey
High St, Battle. 📞 *01424 773792.*
⏰ *daily.* ⬤ *24–26, 31 Dec, 1 Jan.*
♿ & 📷

BATTLE OF HASTINGS

In 1066, William the Conqueror's *(see p51)* invading army from Normandy landed on the south coast, aiming to take Winchester and London. Hearing that King Harold and his army were camped just inland from Hastings, William confronted them. He won the battle after Harold was mortally wounded by an arrow in his eye. This last successful invasion of England is depicted on the *Bayeux Tapestry* in Normandy, France.

King Harold's death, *Bayeux Tapestry*

The fairy-tale 14th-century Bodiam Castle surrounded by its moat

Bodiam Castle ⑱

(NT) Nr Robertsbridge, East Sussex.
☎ *01580 830436.* ⮂ *Robertsbridge then taxi.* ◯ *mid-Feb–Oct: daily; Nov–Dec: Tue–Sun.* ● *24–26 Dec.* 🅰
♿ *limited.* ▯ 🏠

SURROUNDED BY its wide, glistening moat, this late 14th-century castle is one of the most romantic in England.

It was originally built as a defence against an anticipated invasion by the French. The attack never came but the castle saw action during the Civil War *(see pp56–7)* when it was damaged in an assault by Parliamentary soldiers. They removed the roof to reduce its use as a base for Charles I.

It has been uninhabited since, but its grey stone has proved indestructible. With the exception of the roof, it was restored in 1919 by the statesman Lord Curzon who gave it to the nation. The round towers offer fine views of the surrounding countryside.

ENVIRONS: To the east is **Great Dixter**, a 15th-century manor house restored by Sir Edwin Lutyens *(see pp28–9)* in 1910 for the Lloyd family. The writer Christopher Lloyd created a magnificent garden with an Edwardian blend of terraces and borders *(see pp26–7)*.

🏛 **Great Dixter**
Northiam, Rye. ☎ *01797 252878.* ◯ *Apr–Oct: Tue–Sun & public hols.* 🅰

Rye ⑲

See pp186–7.

Romney Marsh ⑳

Kent. ⮂ *Ashford.* 🚌 *Ashford, Hythe.* ℹ *Civic centre (01233 637311).*

UNTIL ROMAN TIMES Romney Marsh and its southern neighbour Walland Marsh were entirely covered by the sea at high tide. The Romans drained the Romney section, and Walland Marsh was gradually reclaimed during the Middle Ages. Together they formed a large area of fertile land for arable crops and grazing – particularly suitable for the bulky Romney Marsh sheep bred for the quality and quantity of their wool.

Dungeness, a desolate and lonely spot at the southeastern tip of the area, is dominated by a lighthouse and two nuclear power stations that

---

COASTAL DEFENCE AND THE CINQUE PORTS

Before the Norman Conquest *(see pp50–51)*, national government was weak and, with threats from Europe, it was important for Saxon kings to keep on good terms with the Channel ports. So, in return for keeping the royal fleet supplied with ships and men, five ports – Hastings, Romney, Hythe, Sandwich and Dover – were granted the right to levy taxes; others were added later. "Cinque" came from the old French word for five. The privileges were revoked during the 17th century. In 1803, in response to the growing threat from France, 74 fixed defences were built along the coast. Only 24 of these Martello towers still exist.

The cliff-top position of Dover Castle

A Martello tower, built as part of the Channel's defences

break up the skyline. It is also the southern terminus of the popular **Romney, Hythe and Dymchurch Light Railway** which was opened in 1927. During the summer this takes passengers 14 miles (23 km) up the coast to Hythe on trains a third the conventional size.

The northern edge of the marsh is crossed by the Royal Military Canal, built to serve both as a defence and supply line in 1804, when it was feared Napoleon was planning an invasion *(see p59)*.

Dover ㉑

Kent. 🏃 41,000. ⇌ 🚌 ⚓
ℹ️ Townwall St (01304 205108).
🏛 Sat.

ITS PROXIMITY to the European mainland makes Dover, with its neighbour Folkestone, now the terminal for the Channel Tunnel, the leading port for cross-Channel travel. Its famous white cliffs exert a strong pull on returning travellers.

Dover's strategic position and large natural harbour mean the town has always had an important role to play in the nation's defences.

Built on the original site of an ancient Saxon fortification, **Dover Castle**, superbly positioned on top of the high cliffs, has helped defend the town from 1198, when Henry II first built the keep, right up to World War II, when it was used as the command post for the Dunkirk evacuation. Exhibits in the castle and in the labyrinth of tunnels beneath made by prisoners in the Napoleonic Wars *(see p59)* cover all these periods.

ENVIRONS: One of the most significant sites in England's early history is the ruin of **Richborough Fort**. This extensive, grassy site, now two miles (3 km) inland, was where, in AD 43, Claudius's Roman invaders *(see p48)* made their first landing. For hundreds of years afterwards, Rutupiae, as it was known, was one of the most important ports of entry and military encampments in the country.

⚓ **Dover Castle**
Castle Hill. ☏ 01304 211067.
○ daily. ● 1 Jan, 25–26 Dec. 🎦 ♿
🏰 **Richborough Fort**
Richborough. ☏ 01304 612013.
○ Oct–Mar: Sat–Sun; Apr–Nov: daily.
● 24–26 Dec.

Margate ㉒

Kent. 🏃 39,000. ⇌ 🚌
ℹ️ 22 High St (01843 220241).

TRADITIONALLY the most boisterous of the three seaside resorts on the Isle of Thanet (the other two are Ramsgate and Broadstairs), Margate has for a long time been a popular destination for day trippers from London, travelling in Victorian times by steam boat and later by train. The town has theme parks and fairground rides.

ENVIRONS: Just south is a 19th-century gentleman's residence, **Quex House,** which has two unusual towers in its grounds. The adjoining museum has a fine collection of African and Oriental art, as well as unique dioramas of tropical wildlife.

Visitors relaxing on Margate's popular sandy beach

To the west is a Saxon church, built within the remains of the bleak Roman coastal fort of **Reculver**. Dramatic twin towers, known as the Two Sisters, were added to the church in the 12th century – these were luckily saved from destruction in 1809 because they were a useful navigational aid for shipping. The church now stands at the centre of a very pleasant, if rather windy, 37 ha (91 acre) country park.

🏯 **Quex House**
Birchington. ☏ 01843 842168.
○ Apr–Oct: Tue–Thu, Sun & public holidays (Museum only: Nov–Dec, Mar: Sun). 🎦 ♿ 🎫 for groups. 🍴
🏰 **Reculver Fort**
Reculver. ☏ 01227 361911 (Herne Bay Tourist Information). ○ daily.

A drainage dyke running through the fertile plains of Romney Marsh

Street-by-Street: Rye ⑲

The Mermaid Inn sign

THIS ANCIENT and delightful fortified town was added to the original Cinque ports *(see p182)* in the 11th century. A huge storm in 1287 diverted the River Rother so that it met the sea at Rye, and for more than 300 years it was one of the most important channel ports. However, in the 16th century the harbour began to silt up and the town is now 2 miles (3 km) inland. Rye was frequently attacked by the French, culminating in 1377 when it was burnt to the ground.

★ **Mermaid Street**
This delightful cobbled street, its huddled houses jutting out at unlikely angles, has hardly altered since it was rebuilt in the 14th century.

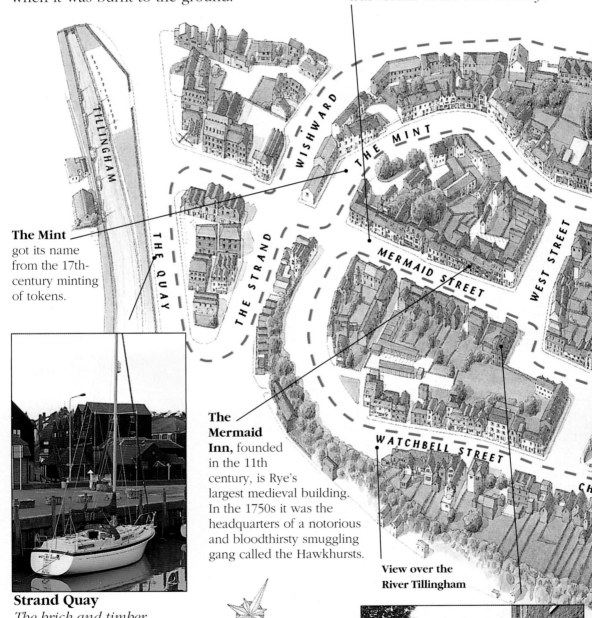

The Mint
got its name from the 17th-century minting of tokens.

The Mermaid Inn, founded in the 11th century, is Rye's largest medieval building. In the 1750s it was the headquarters of a notorious and bloodthirsty smuggling gang called the Hawkhursts.

View over the River Tillingham

Strand Quay
The brick and timber warehouses survive from the prosperous days when Rye was a thriving port.

STAR SIGHTS

★ **Mermaid Street**

★ **Ypres Tower**

Lamb House
This fine Georgian house was built in 1722. George I stayed here when stranded in a storm, and author Henry James (1843–1916) lived here.

◁ **Hot-air balloons over Leeds Castle, near Maidstone, Kent**

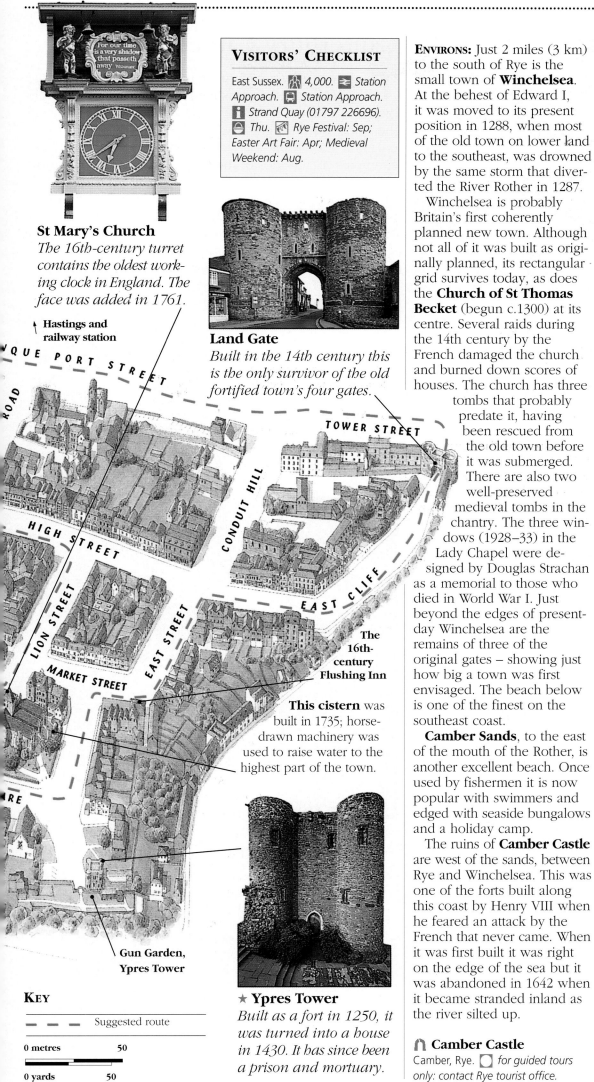

St Mary's Church
The 16th-century turret contains the oldest working clock in England. The face was added in 1761.

↑ **Hastings and railway station**

Land Gate
Built in the 14th century this is the only survivor of the old fortified town's four gates.

This cistern was built in 1735; horse-drawn machinery was used to raise water to the highest part of the town.

The 16th-century Flushing Inn

Gun Garden, Ypres Tower

KEY

– – – Suggested route

0 metres   50

0 yards   50

★ **Ypres Tower**
Built as a fort in 1250, it was turned into a house in 1430. It has since been a prison and mortuary.

ENVIRONS: Just 2 miles (3 km) to the south of Rye is the small town of **Winchelsea**. At the behest of Edward I, it was moved to its present position in 1288, when most of the old town on lower land to the southeast, was drowned by the same storm that diverted the River Rother in 1287.

Winchelsea is probably Britain's first coherently planned new town. Although not all of it was built as originally planned, its rectangular grid survives today, as does the **Church of St Thomas Becket** (begun c.1300) at its centre. Several raids during the 14th century by the French damaged the church and burned down scores of houses. The church has three tombs that probably predate it, having been rescued from the old town before it was submerged. There are also two well-preserved medieval tombs in the chantry. The three windows (1928–33) in the Lady Chapel were designed by Douglas Strachan as a memorial to those who died in World War I. Just beyond the edges of present-day Winchelsea are the remains of three of the original gates – showing just how big a town was first envisaged. The beach below is one of the finest on the southeast coast.

Camber Sands, to the east of the mouth of the Rother, is another excellent beach. Once used by fishermen it is now popular with swimmers and edged with seaside bungalows and a holiday camp.

The ruins of **Camber Castle** are west of the sands, between Rye and Winchelsea. This was one of the forts built along this coast by Henry VIII when he feared an attack by the French that never came. When it was first built it was right on the edge of the sea but it was abandoned in 1642 when it became stranded inland as the river silted up.

🏛 **Camber Castle**
Camber, Rye. ⬜ *for guided tours only: contact Rye tourist office.*

Jesus on Christ Church Gate, Canterbury Cathedral

Canterbury ㉓

Kent. 🏛 *50,000.* ⇄ 🚌 ℹ️ *34 St Margaret's St (01227 766567).* 🛒 *Wed, Fri.*

I TS POSITION on the London to Dover route meant Canterbury was an important Roman town even before the arrival of St Augustine in 597, sent by the pope to convert the Anglo-Saxons to Christianity. The town rose in importance, soon becoming the centre of the Christian Church in England.

With the building of the **cathedral** and the martyrdom of Thomas Becket *(see p52),* Canterbury's future as a religious centre was assured.

Adjacent to the ruins of **St Augustine's Abbey**, destroyed in the Dissolution *(see p54),* is **St Martin's Church**, one of the oldest in England. This was where St Augustine first worshipped and it has impressive Norman and Saxon work.

West Gate Museum, with its round towers, is an imposing medieval gatehouse. It was built in 1381 and contains a display of arms and armoury.

The Poor Priests' Hospital, founded in the 12th century, now houses the **Canterbury Heritage Museum**.

🏛 **West Gate Museum**
St Peter's St. 📞 *01227 452747.* ⬜ *Mon–Sat.* ⬤ *23–27 Dec, Good Fri.* ♿ 📷

🏛 **Canterbury Heritage Museum**
Stour St. 📞 *01227 452747.* ⬜ *Jun–Oct: daily; Nov–May: Mon–Sat.* ⬤ *Christmas wk, Good Fri.* ♿ 📷

Canterbury Cathedral

T O MATCH CANTERBURY'S growing ecclesiastical rank as a major centre of Christianity, the first Norman archbishop, Lanfranc, ordered a new cathedral to be built on the ruins of the Anglo-Saxon cathedral in 1070. It was enlarged and rebuilt many times and as a result embraces examples of all styles of medieval architecture. The most poignant moment in its history came in 1170 when Thomas Becket was murdered here *(see p52).* Four years after his death a fire devastated the cathedral and Trinity Chapel was built to house Becket's remains. The shrine quickly became an important religious site and until the Dissolution *(see p54)* the cathedral was one of Christendom's chief places of pilgrimage *(see pp166–7).*

The nave at 100 m (328 ft) makes Canterbury Europe's longest medieval church.

The South West Porch (1426) may have been built to commemorate the victory at Agincourt *(see p53).*

Main entrance

★ **Medieval Stained Glass**
This depiction of the 1,000-year-old Methuselah is a detail from the southwest transept window.

GEOFFREY CHAUCER

Considered to be the first great English poet, Geoffrey Chaucer (c.1345–1400), a customs official by profession, wrote a rumbustious and witty account of a group of pilgrims travelling from London to Becket's shrine in 1387 in the *Canterbury Tales.* The pilgrims represent a cross-section of 14th-century English society and the tales remain one of the greatest and most entertaining works of early English literature.

Wife of Bath, *Canterbury Tales*

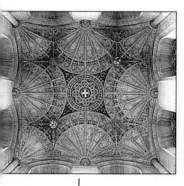

Bell Harry Tower

The central tower, dominating the skyline, was built in 1496 to house a bell donated by Henry of Eastry 100 years before. The fan tracery is a superb example of the late Perpendicular style.

VISITORS' CHECKLIST

Christ Church Gate, Canterbury.
📞 01227 762862. ⬤ Easter–Sep: 9am–5pm Mon–Fri; 12:30–2:30pm & 4:30–5:30pm Sun; times often change phone first.
⬤ during services & concerts; 25 Dec. 🎟 ✝ 8am daily; 11am Sun; 3:15pm Sat, Sun; 5:30pm Mon–Fri. 📷 ♿ ✍

★ Site of the Shrine of St Thomas Becket

This Victorian illustration (anon) portrays Becket's canonization. The Trinity Chapel was built to house his tomb which stood here until it was destroyed in 1538 (see p54). The spot is now marked by a lighted candle.

Great Cloister

Chapter House

★ Black Prince's Tomb

This copper effigy is on the tomb of Edward III's son, who died in 1376.

The Great South Window has four stained glass panels (1958) by Erwin Bossanyi.

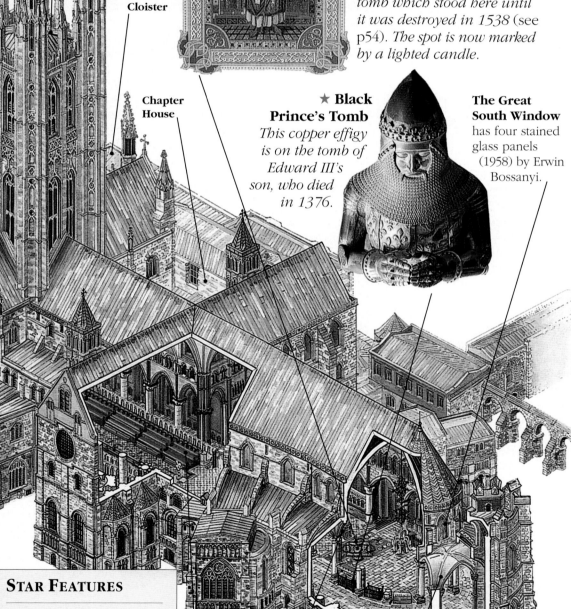

St Augustine's Chair

The quire, completed in 1184, is one of the longest in England.

Trinity Chapel

The circular Corona Chapel

STAR FEATURES

★ **Medieval Stained Glass**

★ **Site of the Shrine of St Thomas Becket**

★ **Black Prince's Tomb**

The keep of Rochester Castle, dominating Rochester and the Medway Valley

Leeds Castle ㉔

Maidstone, Kent. 01622 765400.
Maidstone then bus. daily.
for concerts & 25 Dec.

SURROUNDED BY A LAKE that
reflects the warm buff
stone of its crenellated turrets,
Leeds is often considered to
be the most beautiful castle in
England. Begun in the early
12th century, it has been continuously inhabited and its
present appearance is a result
of centuries of rebuilding and
extensions, most recently in
the 1930s. Leeds has royal connections going back to 1278,
when it was given to Edward I
by a courtier seeking favour.

Henry VIII loved the castle
and visited it often, escaping
from the plague in London.
It contains a life-sized bust of
Henry from the late 16th century. Leeds passed out of royal
ownership when Edward VI
gave it to Sir Anthony St Leger
in 1552 as a reward for helping to pacify the Irish. The
garden, designed by Capability
Brown *(see p27),* has a maze.

Rochester ㉕

Kent. 145,000.
95 High Street (01634 843666).

CLUSTERED AT THE MOUTH of
the River Medway are the
towns of Rochester, Chatham
and Gillingham, all rich in
naval history, but none more

so than Rochester, which
occupied a strategic site on
the London to Dover road.

England's tallest Norman
keep is at **Rochester Castle,**
worth climbing for the views
over the Medway. The town's
medieval history is still visible,
with the original city walls –
which followed the lines of the
Roman fortifications – on view
in the High Street, and some
well-preserved wall paintings
in the **cathedral**, built in 1088.

ENVIRONS: In Chatham, the
Historic Dockyard is now a
museum of shipbuilding and
nautical crafts. **Fort Amherst**
nearby was built in 1756 to
protect the dockyard and river
entrance from attack, and has
1,800 m (5,570 ft) of tunnels
to explore that were hewn by
Napoleonic prisoners of war.

⚓ Rochester Castle
The Esplanade. 01634 402276.
daily. 24–26 Dec.
limited

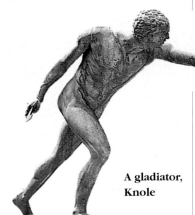

**A gladiator,
Knole**

🏛 Historic Dockyard
Dock Rd, Chatham. 01634
823800. April–Oct: daily; Nov,
Feb–Mar: Wed, Sat, Sun.
🏰 Fort Amherst
Dock Rd, Chatham. 01634
847747. daily. 24, 25 Dec,
1 Jan.

Knole ㉖

(NT) Sevenoaks, Kent. 01732
462100. Sevenoaks then taxi.
House Apr–Oct: Wed–Sat (pm),
Good Fri & public hols. **Park**
daily. limited. by
arrangement.

WITH A DISTINGUISHED royal
history, this huge Tudor
mansion is also one of the
finest houses in the country.
Built in the late 15th century,
it was seized by Henry VIII
from the Archbishop of
Canterbury, Thomas Cranmer,
at the time of the Dissolution
(see p54). In 1566 Queen
Elizabeth I gave it to her
cousin Thomas Sackville. His
descendants have lived
here ever since,
including the writer
Vita Sackville-West,
(1892–1962) who
set her novel, *The Edwardians*
(1930) here. Apart from its
splendid decorative detail and
the valuable collection of
paintings, the house is best
known for its beautiful 17th-
century furniture, such as the
elaborate state bed made for
James II, and a rare silver

table with candlesticks and mirror. The 405 ha (1,000 acre) park and gardens have some lovely walks.

ENVIRONS: A small, square manor house, **Ightham Mote**, situated just east of Knole, is one of the finest examples of medieval architecture in England. Its 14th-century timber-and-stone building encloses a central court and is encircled by a moat.

⊞ Ightham Mote
(NT) Ivy Hatch, Sevenoaks. 〖 *01732 810378.* ◯ *Apr–end-Oct: Wed–Fri, Sun, Mon & public hols.* ⌂ ⌂

Hever Castle ㉗

Edenbridge, Kent. 〖 *01732 865224.* ⇌ *Edenbridge.* ◯ *Mar–Nov: daily.* ⌂ ⌂ ⌂ ⌂

THIS SMALL, MOATED CASTLE is famous as the 16th-century home of Anne Boleyn, the doomed wife of Henry VIII, executed for adultery. She

CHARLES DICKENS

Charles Dickens (1812–70), a popular writer in his own time, is still widely read today. He was born in Portsmouth but moved to Chatham aged five. As an adult, Dickens lived in London but kept up his Kent connections, taking holidays in Broadstairs, just south of Margate – where he wrote *David Copperfield* – and spending his last years at Gad's Hill, near Rochester. The town celebrates the famous connection with an annual Dickens festival.

The façade of Chartwell, Winston Churchill's home

lived here as a young woman and the king often visited her while staying at Leeds Castle. In 1903 Hever was bought by William Waldorf Astor, who undertook a restoration programme, building a Neo-Tudor village alongside it to accommodate guests and servants. The moat and gatehouse remain from when they were first built, around 1270.

ENVIRONS: To the northwest of Hever is **Chartwell**, the home of World War II leader Sir Winston Churchill *(see p63).* It remains furnished as it was when he lived here. To relax, he used to rebuild parts of the house. A few of his paintings are on display.

⊞ Chartwell
(NT) Westerham, Kent. 〖 *01732 866368.* ◯ *Apr–Jun, Sep, Oct: Wed–Sun & public hols; Jul–Aug: Tue–Sun & public hols.* ⌂ ⌂ ⌂ ⌂

Royal Tunbridge Wells ㉘

Kent. 🚶 *51,000.* ⇌ 🚌 ⓘ *The Old Fish Market, The Pantiles (01892 515675).* 🛒 *Wed.*

HELPED BY ROYAL patronage, the town became a popular spa in the 17th and 18th centuries after mineral springs were discovered in the town in 1606. The Pantiles – the historic colonnaded and paved promenade, named after the original square tiles – was laid out in the 1700s.

ENVIRONS: Nearby is a superb example of a medieval manor house, **Penshurst Place**. Built in the 1340s, it has an 18 m (60 ft) high Great Hall.

⊞ Penshurst Place
Royal Tunbridge Wells, Kent. 〖 *01892 870307.* ◯ *Apr–Oct: daily; Mar: Sat, Sun.* ⌂ ⌂ *limited.* ⌂

An early 18th-century astrolabe to measure the stars, Hever Castle garden

Wild poppies mingled with linseed, a familiar sight in southern England ▷

EAST ANGLIA

EAST ANGLIA

THE STRETCH OF LAND *between the Thames Estuary and the Wash, flat but far from featureless, sits aside from the main north-south axis through Britain, and for that reason it has succeeded in maintaining and preserving its distinctive architecture, traditions and rural character in both cities and countryside.*

East Anglia's name derives from the Angles, people from northern Germany who settled here during the 5th and 6th centuries. However, they were by no means the earliest inhabitants: the extensive flint mines at Grimes Graves, near Thetford in Norfolk, date from before 2000 BC. In AD 43, the Romans invaded and established important bases at Peterborough, Cambridge and England's oldest recorded town, Colchester. It was here that they defeated a spirited revolt led by Queen Boadicea, leader of the Iceni tribe. After the Romans left, the poorly protected coast suffered badly from invasions by the Vikings, who in 870 killed the East Anglian king, St Edmund, at Bury St Edmunds. A century later, another local leader, Byrhtnoth, was slain by Vikings during the battle of Maldon, at the mouth of the Blackwater River.

East Anglia is swept by icy east winds that blow off the North Sea in winter, and the region has long harboured a breed of practical, plain-spoken and independent people. It is no accident that the two most prominent East Anglians in English history – Queen Boadicea and Oliver Cromwell – were renowned for their stubbornness and for refusing to bow to constituted authority. Nor is it coincidence that during the Civil War, East Anglia proved Cromwell's most reliable source of support. The hardy, determined people who made a difficult living hunting and fishing in the swampy fens were called the Fen Tigers.

Lavender fields in full bloom in July, Heacham, Norfolk

◁ **Willy Lott's Cottage, East Bergholt, Suffolk**

Picture-perfect Flatford Mill, in the village of East Bergholt, Suffolk

The Fens were drained in the 17th century, and the peaty soil proved ideal for arable farming. Today, East Anglia grows about one third of Britain's vegetables and is a leading producer of root crops, especially sugar beet. The rotation of crops, which heralded the beginning of Britain's agricultural revolution, was perfected in Norfolk during the 18th century. Inland, large flocks of sheep were kept, and towns such as Lavenham, Bury St Edmunds and Sudbury became wealthy and important centres for the wool trade. In such towns, some of the half-timbered medieval buildings – found alongside the more humble pink-washed cottages that are typical of the region – stand as evidence of former prosperity.

Little Hall, Lavenham

The rich grasslands of East Anglia gave rise to another industry: breeding racehorses. Newmarket is the headquarters of British horse racing. It is home to two racecourses and several stables and stud farms, which are characterized by paddocks with white-railed fences.

Colourful awnings at Norwich Market

Horse racing inspired one of Britain's most prominent 20th-century painters, Sir Alfred Munnings, who lived near the Essex village of Dedham. This settlement was made famous 100 years earlier by another painter: John Constable. The 18th-century artist Thomas Gainsborough was born in Sudbury, where his former house is now a museum.

The thriving agricultural economy of the region provided finance for distinctive features such as the cathedrals at Ely and Norwich (which has retained its medieval street pattern), and the country's second oldest university: Cambridge. This university is a compendium of medieval and later architecture, perhaps best showcased by King's College chapel, probably Britain's most splendid building from the late 15th century.

The sea also plays a prominent role in East Anglian life. Coastal settlements near Lowestoft and Great Yarmouth support communities of fishermen. These people work the North Sea, which was formerly rich in herring but is now better known for flat fish, such as plaice. West Mersea, near Colchester, and Butley, near Woodbridge, were once famous for their oysters, and the towns of Harwich and Felixstowe are important commercial and passenger ports.

The area has recently become a centre for recreational boating, and cabin cruisers are ever popular among those wanting to explore the Norfolk Broads – an extensive inland waterway system – at a leisurely pace. Occasionally you will see a sturdy old Thames barge, with traditional slate-red sails, making its dignified progress through the water. These are sometimes crewed by keen trainee sailors. The sandy north-facing beaches of Norfolk are popular with holidaymakers, while coves, marshes and offshore islets provide important refuges for birds and marine life. On the Suffolk coast, Southwold is a picturesque Georgian resort with a museum and a 15th-century church, as well as excellent bathing and sailing. To the south, Aldeburgh and Snape are associated with the annual music festival established by the famous English composer Sir

Thames barges moored at Maldon, Essex

Benjamin Britten. Moot Hall, a Tudor building that is now a museum, can be found in the town of Aldeburgh.

The part of Essex that borders London is commuter country. Historic towns such as Romford and Barking expanded greatly after World War II, when many families from London's East End (their homes destroyed by bombing or in slum clearance schemes) moved to new houses and flats provided by the State. As a result, the traditional Cockney accent of east London was transplanted to Essex in a modified form now known as "Estuary English". Due to the rapid growth in population in London and Essex, the historic Epping Forest (which was once a hunting ground for the Tudor monarchs) has become

Mound of harvested sugar beets, Norfolk

increasingly important as a recreational facility for east Londoners. A point of interest in the forest is Queen Elizabeth's Hunting Lodge, which was built in the 16th century.

Early spring frost in the Fens, near Whittlesey, Cambridgeshire

Exploring East Anglia

As you move away from London, you soon reach the countryside immortalized by the painter Constable *(see p212)* and in many ways unchanged since his day, scattered with churches, windmills and medieval agricultural barns. Nature lovers will find it fruitful territory, especially North Norfolk with its bird reserves and seal colonies. Boating enthusiasts, too, are well catered for in this, Britain's driest and sunniest region. The local architecture ranges from a mix of medieval to modern. The distinctive pink-washed cottages in Suffolk, flint cottages in Norfolk and thatched roofs everywhere, are also much in evidence.

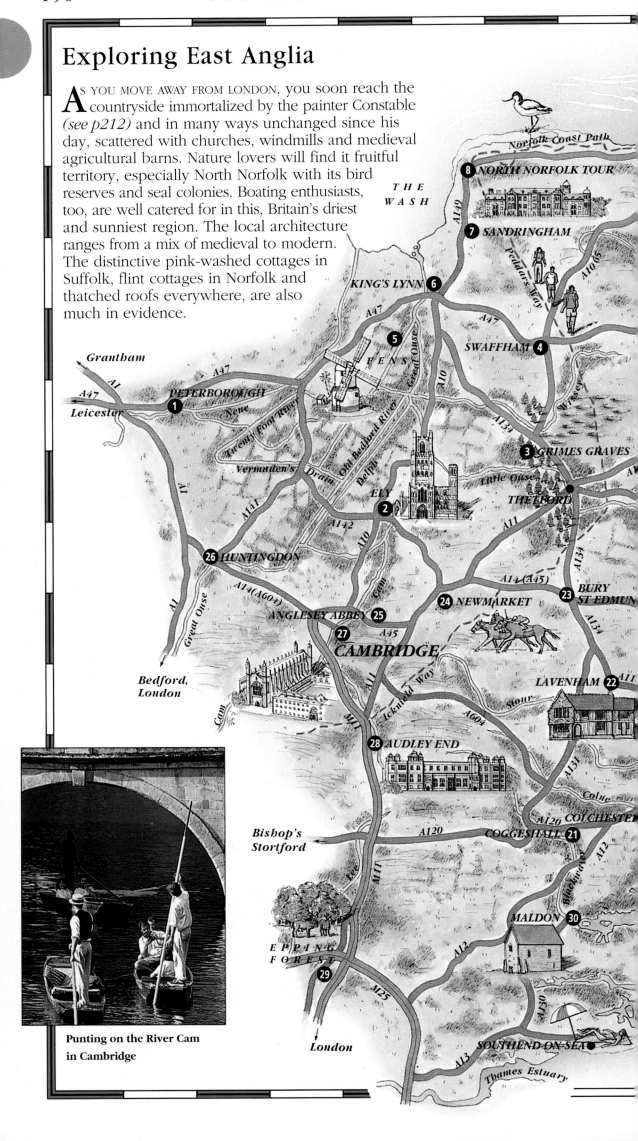

Punting on the River Cam
in Cambridge

KEY

▤	Motorway
▭	Major road
▬	Minor road
▭	Scenic route
▬▬	Scenic path
≋	River
✳	Viewpoint

GETTING AROUND

The region's more isolated sights can be very difficult to reach by public transport and, for a few people, car rental may be a cheaper and more efficient method of travelling around. The M11 motorway runs from London to Cambridge. The coast road from Aldeburgh to King's Lynn takes you through some of the best countryside in the area. There are frequent InterCity trains to Norwich, Ipswich and Cambridge although the local trains are more sporadic. There is an international and domestic airport at Norwich.

Beach huts on Wells-next-the-Sea beach, north Norfolk

SIGHTS AT A GLANCE

Aldeburgh ⑯
Anglesey Abbey ㉕
Audley End ㉘
Blickling Hall ⑨
Broads ⑪
Bury St Edmunds ㉓
Cambridge pp220–25 ㉗
Coggeshall ㉑
Colchester ⑳
Dunwich ⑮
Ely ②
Epping Forest ㉙
Fens ⑤
Framlingham Castle ⑰
Great Yarmouth ⑫
Grimes Graves ③

Huntingdon ㉖
Ipswich ⑱
King's Lynn ⑥
Lavenham ㉒
Lowestoft ⑬
Maldon ㉚
Newmarket ㉔
Norwich ⑩
Peterborough ①
Sandringham ⑦
Southwold ⑭
Swaffham ④

Walks and Tours
Constable Walk ⑲
North Norfolk Tour ⑧

0 kilometres 10

0 miles 10

The Fens

THE MARSHES AND BROADS that comprise the fens were originally a shallow bay of the North Sea that became partially silted up. The Romans and then the Normans introduced drainage channels and sea barriers to the area in their efforts to reclaim the land for farming and for settlement. Progress was made in the 17th century when Dutch engineers brought their experience of land reclamation in the Netherlands to East Anglia. They constructed dykes and erected more than 700 windmills to pump away the unwanted water. The resulting farmland was extremely fertile.

A group of reed-cutters coming home from the marshes, 1887

ENJOYING THE FENS

These flat, fertile lands are interwoven by a network of man-made waterways, many of which were created when peat cutting was a common activity. Although much of the land has been claimed for agriculture and residential development, the fens still offer a varied and interesting environment for people to enjoy all year round, from boating and walking to bird-watching.

The fens are the last remaining haunt of the European swallowtail butterfly in the British Isles.

The green-winged orchid is a rare and unusual wild flower found in the area. Its purple side petals have a slight green tinge.

Windmills by the dozen still litter the fens. Few are working mills and many have been converted into homes.

The shy bittern is an increasingly rare member of the heron family and can be quite difficult to see among the reeds.

The Norfolk Hawker is a large dragonfly commonly found in the Norfolk fens. The female has a bright blue body.

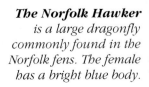

BOATING ON THE BROADS

Many of the traditional industries of the Norfolk Broads have now disappeared, but in recent decades its network of waterways has become very popular with tourists. The main activity here is pleasure cruising, and a variety of vessels are used. Boats range in size from canoes to the traditional narrow boats, with many others in between. Waterways are particularly crowded during holiday periods, and rules, including a strict speed limit, are enforced to prevent degradation of the environment. One of the prime boating areas is at Horning Water, a man-made lake near Norwich.

Boating on the Norfolk Broads

Noctule bats can often be seen in large numbers flying over the waters of the fens. This is due to the fact that they start looking for food, consisting largely of mosquitoes and midges, well before the sun sets.

Under the ground there is often a thick layer of peat, which in past centuries was valuable as a household fuel.

The stems from dense reed beds are still harvested for making thatch.

The impressive marsh harrier patrols the reed beds at low altitude, searching for prey. In adulthood, this bird of prey can grow up to 22 in (55 cm) long.

Wicken Fen, northeast of Cambridge, has been preserved in its natural undrained state, providing a vital habitat for wildlife. To maintain the environment, however, the reeds are harvested annually.

Peterborough ❶

Cambridgeshire. 👥 *152,000.* 🚊 🚌
ℹ️ *45 Bridge St (01733 452336).*
🛒 *Tue–Sat.*

ALTHOUGH ONE OF the oldest
settlements in Britain,
Peterborough was designated
a New Town in 1967 – part of
a scheme to shift people from
the larger cities – and is now
a mix of ancient and modern.

The city centre is dominated
by the 12th-century **St Peter's
Cathedral** which gave the city
its name. The interior of this
classic Norman building, with
its vast yet simple nave, was
badly damaged by Cromwell's
troops *(see p56),* but its unique
painted wooden ceiling (1220)
has survived intact. Catherine
of Aragon, the first wife of

**Peterborough's coat of arms with
a Latin inscription: Upon this Rock**

Henry VIII, is buried here,
although Cromwell's troops
also destroyed her tomb.

ENVIRONS: The oldest wheel in
Britain (10,000 BC) was found
preserved in peat at **Flag Fen
Bronze Age Excavations**.
The site provides a fascinating
glimpse into prehistory.

🏛 **Flag Fen Bronze Age
Excavations**
Fourth Drive, Fengate, Peterborough.
📞 *01733 313414.* ⭕ *daily.*
⬤ *Christmas week.* 🎫 ♿ 📷

Grimes Graves ❸

Brandon, Norfolk. 📞 *01842 810656.*
🚊 *Brandon then taxi.* ⭕ *Easter–Oct:
daily; Nov–Easter: Wed–Sun.*
⬤ *24–27 Dec.* 🎫 📷 🏛

ONE OF THE MOST important
Neolithic sites in England,
this was once an extensive
complex of flint mines – 366
shafts have been located –
dating from before 2000 BC.

Using antlers as pickaxes,
Stone Age miners hacked
through the soft chalk to
extract the hard flint below to
make axes, weapons and tools.
The flint was transported long
distances around England on
the prehistoric network of
paths. You can descend 9 m
(30 ft) by ladder into one of
the shafts and see the galleries

Ely ❷

Cambridgeshire. 👥 *14,000.* 🚊
ℹ️ *29 St Mary's St (01353 662062).*
🛒 *Thu, Sat (craft & antiques).*

BUILT ON A chalk hill, this
small city is thought to be
named after the eels in the
nearby River Ouse.

The hill was once a strategic
and inaccessible island in the
middle of the then marshy and
treacherous Fens *(see p204)*.
It was also the last stronghold
of Anglo-Saxon resistance,
under the "Last Englishman",
Hereward the Wake *(see p50)*,
who hid in the cathedral until
the conquering Normans
crossed the Fens in 1071.

Today this small prosperous
city, totally dominated by the
huge **cathedral**, is the
market centre for the rich
agricultural area surrounding it.

The lantern's glass
windows admit light
into the dome.

Octagon

*This painted
wooden angel is
one of hundreds of
bosses that were
carved all over the
south and north
transepts in the 13th
and 14th centuries.*

**Stained glass
museum**

The tomb is that of
Alan de Walsingham,
designer of the
unique Octagon.

*The Octagon,
made of wood, was built
in 1322 when the Norman
tower collapsed. Its roof,
the lantern, took an extra
24 years to build and
weighs 200 tonnes.*

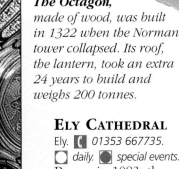

Area of cutaway

ELY CATHEDRAL
Ely. 📞 *01353 667735.*
⭕ *daily.* ⬤ *special events.* 🎫 ♿ 🍴 🖥 🏛
Begun in 1083, the cathedral took 268 years to
complete. It survived the Dissolution *(see p54)*
but was closed for 17 years by Cromwell *(see
p56)* who lived in Ely for a time.

where the flint was mined. During excavations, unusual chalk models of a fertility goddess *(see p47)* and a phallus were discovered.

ENVIRONS: Nearby, at the centre of the once fertile plain known as the Breckland, is the small market town of **Thetford**.

Once a prosperous trading town, its fortunes dipped in the 16th century, when its priory was destroyed *(see p55)* and the surrounding land deteriorated due to excessive sheep grazing. The area was later planted with pine trees. A mound in the city marks the site of a pre-Norman castle.

The revolutionary writer and philosopher Tom Paine, author of *The Rights of Man*, was born here in 1737.

The huge cathedral spire *dominates the flat Fens countryside surrounding Ely.*

Painted ceiling, 19th century

The Prior's Door (c.1150)

The south aisle has 12 classic Norman arches at its foot, with pointed Early English windows above.

Oxburgh Hall surrounded by its medieval moat

Swaffham ➍

Norfolk. 🏘 *6,500.* 🚌 ℹ️ *Market Place (01760 722255).* 🛒 *Sat.*

THE BEST-PRESERVED Georgian town in East Anglia and a fashionable resort during the Regency period, Swaffham is at its liveliest on Saturdays when a market is held in the square around the elegant and unusual market cross of 1783. In the centre of the town is the 15th-century **Church of St Peter and St Paul**, with a small spire added to the tower in the 19th century. It has a magnificent Tudor north aisle, said to have been paid for by John Chapman, the Pedlar of Swaffham. He is depicted on the unusual two-sided town sign found in the market place. Myth has it that he went to London and met a stranger who told him of hidden treasure at Swaffham. He returned, dug it up and embellished the church on the proceeds. He is shown in a window.

ENVIRONS: Castle Acre, north of the town, has the remains of a massive Cluniac **priory**. Founded in 1090, its stunning Norman front still stands.

A short drive south is **Oxburgh Hall**, built by Sir Edmund Bedingfeld in 1482. The core of the hall, entered through a huge 24 m (80 ft) fortified gatehouse, is a good example of a house built for comfort as well as defence. The velvet Oxburgh Hangings, embroidered by Mary, Queen of Scots *(see p55)*, are on display.

Swaffham town sign

🏛 **Castle Acre Priory**
Castle Acre. 📞 *01760 755394.* 🕐 *Apr–Oct: daily; Nov–Mar: Wed– Sun.* 🕐 *24-26 Dec, Jan 1.* 🏷 ♿ *limited.*

🏛 **Oxburgh Hall**
Oxborough. 📞 *01366 328258.* 🕐 *Apr–Oct: Sat–Wed.* 🏷 ♿ *limited.*

BOADICEA AND THE ICENI

When the Romans invaded Britain, the Iceni, the main tribe in East Anglia, joined forces with them to defeat the Catuvellauni, a rival tribe. But the Romans then turned on the Iceni, torturing Queen Boadicea (or Boudicca). In AD 61, she led a revolt against Roman rule: her followers burned down London, Colchester and St Albans. The rebellion was put down and the queen took poison rather than submit. At Cockley Cley, near Swaffham, an Iceni camp has been excavated.

Illustration of Queen Boadicea leading her Iceni followers

A windmill on Wicken Fen

The Fens ⑤

Cambridgeshire/Norfolk. ⌦ Ely. ℹ
29 St Mary's St, Ely (01353 662062).

THIS IS THE OPEN, flat, fertile expanse that lies between Lincoln, Cambridge, Bedford and King's Lynn. Up until the 17th century it was a swamp, and settlement was possible only on "islands", such as Ely (see p202), raised above their low-lying surroundings.

During the 17th century, the fen lands were drained so that the peaty soil could be used for farmland (see pp200-201). However, as the peat dried it contracted, and so the fens have slowly been sinking. Originally pumped by windmills, the area now needs powerful electric pumps to keep it drained.

Nine miles (14 km) from Ely is Wicken Fen, 243 ha (600 acres) of undrained fen providing a habitat for an abundance of indigenous water life, wildfowl and wild flowers.

King's Lynn ⑥

Norfolk. 👥 42,000. ⌦ 🚌
ℹ Saturday Market Place (01553 763044). ⌂ Tue, Fri, Sat.

FORMERLY BISHOP'S LYNN, its name was changed at the Reformation (see p55) to reflect the changing political reality. In the Middle Ages it was one of England's most prosperous ports, shipping grain and wool from the surrounding countryside to Europe. There are still a few warehouses and merchants' houses by the River Ouse surviving from this period. At the north end of the town is **True's Yard**, a relic of the old fishermen's quarter.

Trinity Guildhall, King's Lynn

North Norfolk Coastal Tour ⑧

THIS TOUR TAKES YOU THROUGH some of the most beautiful areas of East Anglia; nearly all of the north Norfolk coast has been designated an Area of Outstanding Natural Beauty. The sea has dictated the character of the area. With continuing deposits of silt, once busy ports are now far inland and the shingle and sand banks that have been built up are home to a huge variety of wildlife. Along the coast the sea has taken a different toll and eroded great tracts of land, creating spectacular cliffs.

TIPS FOR DRIVERS

Tour length: 28 miles (45 km).
Stopping-off points: The impressive Holkham Hall makes a pleasant stop for a picnic lunch. There are some good pubs in Wells-next-the-Sea.

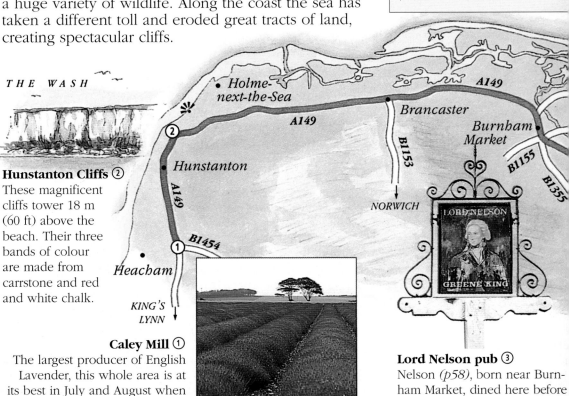

THE WASH

Hunstanton Cliffs ②
These magnificent cliffs tower 18 m (60 ft) above the beach. Their three bands of colour are made from carrstone and red and white chalk.

Holme-next-the-Sea

A149

Hunstanton

A149

B1454

Heacham

KING'S LYNN

Caley Mill ①
The largest producer of English Lavender, this whole area is at its best in July and August when the fields are a blaze of purple.

Brancaster

Burnham Market

B1153

B1155

B1355

NORWICH

LORD NELSON

GREENE KING

Lord Nelson pub ③
Nelson (p58), born near Burnham Market, dined here before he went to sea for the last time.

The **Trinity Guildhall** was built in the 1420s, and among the town regalia on display inside is an early 13th-century sword thought to have been a gift to the town from King John *(see p52)*, who visited the town several times. The last occasion was in 1216. He dined here on his way to the north of England to flee rebellious barons. The next day, while crossing the sea, he lost all his treasure – people have been dredging and diving to try and find it ever since.

On the Market Place is **St Margaret's Church** with work from the 13th-century onwards, including a fine Elizabethan screen.

🏛 **Trinity Guildhall**
Saturday Market Place. 📞 *01553 763044.* ◯ *Easter–Oct: daily; Nov–Easter: Fri–Tue.* ⬤ *24–26 Dec.* 🖼 ♿

Sandringham House, where the Royal Family spend every Christmas

Sandringham ⑦

Norfolk. 📞 *01553 772675.* 🚌 *from King's Lynn.* ◯ *Easter–Sep: daily.* ⬤ *three wks Jul–Aug.* 🖼 ♿ 🍴

THIS SIZEABLE NORFOLK estate has been in royal hands since 1862 when it was bought by the Prince of Wales, who later became Edward VII. The 18th-century house was elaborately embellished and refurbished by the Prince and now retains an appropriately Edwardian atmosphere.

The large stables are now a museum and contain several hundred trophies that relate to hunting, shooting and horse racing – all favourite royal activities. A popular feature is an intriguing display of royal motor cars spanning nearly a century. In the country park there are scenic nature trails.

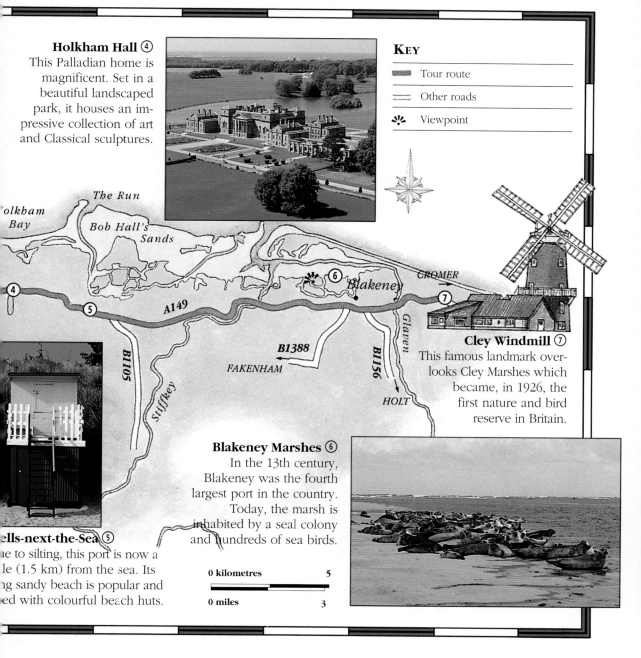

Holkham Hall ④
This Palladian home is magnificent. Set in a beautiful landscaped park, it houses an impressive collection of art and Classical sculptures.

KEY

▬ Tour route
═ Other roads
☀ Viewpoint

The Run

Holkham Bay

Bob Hall's Sands

CROMER

④

⑤

A149

⑥ *Blakeney*

⑦

Glaven

Cley Windmill ⑦
This famous landmark overlooks Cley Marshes which became, in 1926, the first nature and bird reserve in Britain.

B1388

B1105

Stiffkey

FAKENHAM

B1156

HOLT

Blakeney Marshes ⑥
In the 13th century, Blakeney was the fourth largest port in the country. Today, the marsh is inhabited by a seal colony and hundreds of sea birds.

ells-next-the-Sea ⑤
...e to silting, this port is now a ...le (1.5 km) from the sea. Its ...g sandy beach is popular and ...ed with colourful beach huts.

0 kilometres   5

0 miles   3

The symmetrical red-brick façade of the 16th-century Blickling Hall

Blickling Hall ⑨

(NT) Aylsham, Norfolk. 📞 *01263 738030.* 🚌 *from Norwich (summer).* **House** ⬭ *Apr–Oct: Wed–Sun & public hols (pm).* **Park** ⬭ *Apr–Oct: daily; Nov–Mar: Sat–Sun.* 🏷️ ♿ 🍽️

APPROACHED FROM the east, its symmetrical Jacobean front framed by trees and flanked by two yew hedges, Blickling Hall offers one of the most impressive vistas of any country house in the area.

Anne Boleyn, Henry VIII's tragic second queen, spent her childhood here, but very little of the original house remains. Most of the present structure dates from 1628, when it was home to James I's Chief Justice Sir Henry Hobart. Later in 1767 the 2nd Earl of Buckinghamshire, John Hobart, celebrated the Boleyn connection with reliefs in the Great Hall depicting Anne and her daughter, Elizabeth I.

The Long Gallery is the most spectacular room to survive from the 1620s. Its ceiling depicts symbolic representations of learning mingled with the Hobart coat of arms.

The Peter the Great Room marks the 2nd earl's service as ambassador to Russia and was built to display a huge spectacular tapestry (1764) of the Russian tsar on horseback, a gift from the empress, Catherine the Great. It also has portraits (1760) of the ambassador and his wife by Gainsborough *(see p157).*

Norwich ⑩

See pp208–9.

The Broads ⑪

Norfolk. 🚆 *Hoveton, Wroxham.* 🚌 *Norwich, then bus.* ℹ️ *Station Rd, Hoveton (01603 782281).*

THESE SHALLOW LAKES and waterways south and northeast of Norwich, joined by six rivers – the Bure, Thurne, Ant, Yare, Waveney and Chet –

were once thought to have been naturally formed, but in actual fact they are medieval peat diggings which flooded when the water level rose in the 13th century.

During summer the 125 miles (200 km) of open waterways, uninterrupted by locks, teem with thousands of boating enthusiasts, from devotees of pure sail to those who prefer motorboats. You can either hire a boat yourself or take one of the many trips on offer to view the plants and wildlife of the area. Look out for Britain's largest butterfly, the swallowtail. Wroxham, the unofficial capital of the Broads, is the starting point for many of these excursions.

The waterways support substantial clumps of strong and durable reeds, much in demand for thatching *(see p33).* They are cut in winter and carried to shore in the distinctive Broads punts – also used for hunting wildfowl.

For a more detailed look at the origins of the Broads and their varied wildlife, visit the **Broadland Conservation Centre** – a large thatched floating information centre on Ranworth Broad, with displays on all aspects of the area, and a bird-watching gallery.

In the centre of Ranworth is **St Helen's Church** which has a painted medieval screen, a well-preserved 14th-century illuminated manuscript and spectacular views over the entire area from its tower.

🦋 **Broadland Conservation Centre**
Ranworth. 📞 *01603 270479.* ⬭ *Apr–Oct: daily.* ♿

Sailing boat, Wroxham Broad, Norfolk

Great Yarmouth 12

Norfolk. 82,000.
Town Hall (01493 846345).
Wed, Fri (in summer), Sat.

HERRING FISHING was once the major industry of this port, with 1,000 boats engaged in it just before World War I. Over-fishing led to a depletion of stocks and, for the port to survive without the herring, it started to earn its living from servicing container ships and the North Sea oil rigs.

It is also the most popular seaside resort on the Norfolk coast and has been since the 19th century, when Dickens (*see p191*) gave it useful publicity by setting part of his novel *David Copperfield* here.

The **Elizabethan House Museum** has a large, eclectic display which illustrates the social history of the area.

In the old part of the town, around South Quay, are a number of charming houses including the 17th-century **Old Merchant's House**. It retains its original patterned plaster ceilings as well as examples of old ironwork and architectural fittings from

Fishing trawlers at Lowestoft's quays

nearby houses, which were destroyed during World War II. The guided tour of the house includes a visit to the adjoining cloister of a 13th-century friary.

🏛 **Elizabethan House Museum**
4 South Quay. 01493 855746.
Jun–Sep: Sun–Fri: 2 wks over Easter. Good Fri.
🏚 **Old Merchant's House**
South Quay. 01493 857900.
Apr–Oct: daily.

WINDMILLS ON THE FENS AND BROADS

The flat, open countryside and the stiff breezes from the North Sea made windmills an obvious power source for East Anglia well into the 20th century, and today they are an evocative and recurring feature of the landscape. On the Broads and Fens, some were used for drainage, while others, such as that at Saxtead Green, ground corn. On the boggy fens they were not built on hard foundations, so few survived, but elsewhere, especially on the Broads, many have been restored to working order. The seven-storey Berney Arms Windmill is the tallest on the Broads. Thurne Dyke Drainage Mill is the site of an exhibition about the occasionally idiosyncratic mills and their more unusual mechanisms.

Corn mill at Saxtead Green, near Framlingham

Herringfleet Smock Mill, near Lowestoft

Lowestoft 13

Suffolk. 55,000.
East Point Pavilion, Royal Plain (01502 523000). Tue, Sat.

THE MOST EASTERLY TOWN in Britain was long a rival to Great Yarmouth, both as a holiday resort and a fishing port. Its fishing industry has survived better than that of its neighbour as it has turned to flat fish, like plaice, to replace the disappearing herring.

The coming of the railway in the 1840s gave the town an advantage over other resorts, and the solid Victorian and Edwardian boarding houses are evidence of its popularity.

Lowestoft Museum, in a 17th-century house, has a good display of the fine porcelain made here in the 18th century, as well as exhibits on local archaeology and domestic life.

ENVIRONS: To the northwest is **Somerleyton Hall**, built in a Victorian mock-Tudor style on the foundations of a smaller Elizabethan mansion, parts of which survive. Its gardens are a real delight, and there is a genuinely baffling maze.

🏛 **Lowestoft Museum**
Oulton Broad. 01502 572811.
Easter fortnight, 24 May–3 Oct: daily.
limited. by arrangement.
🏚 **Somerleyton Hall**
On B1074. 01502 730224.
Apr–Sep: Thu, Sun & public hols (Jul–Aug: Tue–Thu, Sun).
by arrangement.

Norwich ⑩

IN THE HEART of the fertile East Anglian countryside, Norwich, one of the best-preserved cities in Britain, is steeped in a relaxed provincial atmosphere. The town was first fortified by the Saxons in the 9th century and still has the irregular street plan of that time. With the arrival of Flemish settlers in the early 12th century and the establishment of a textile industry, the town soon became a prosperous market and was the second city of England until the Industrial Revolution in the 19th century *(see pp60–61)*.

The cobbled street, Elm Hill

Exploring Norwich

The oldest parts of the city are Elm Hill, one of the finest medieval streets in England, and Tombland, the old Saxon market place by the cathedral. Both have well-preserved medieval buildings, which are now incorporated into pleasant areas of small shops.

With a trading history spanning hundreds of years, the colourful market in the city centre is well worth a visit. A good walk meanders around the surviving sections of the 14th-century flint city wall.

🔒 Norwich Cathedral

The Close. 📞 *01603 764385.*
◯ *daily.* **Donations**. ♿ 📷 🍴 🛒
This magnificent building was founded in 1096 by Bishop Losinga who had the unusual white stone shipped in from Normandy in France.

The precinct originally included a monastery, and the surviving cloister is the most extensive in England. The thin cathedral spire was added in the 15th century, making it, at 96 m (315 ft), the second tallest in England after Salisbury's *(see pp290–91)*. In the majestic nave, soaring Norman pillars

and arches support a 15th-century vaulted roof whose stone bosses, many of which illustrate well-known Bible stories, have recently been beautifully restored.

Easier to appreciate at close hand is the elaborate wood carving in the choir – the canopies over the stalls and the misericords beneath the seats, one showing a small boy being smacked. Not to be missed is the 14th-century Despenser Reredos in St Luke's Chapel. It was hidden for years under a carpenter's table to prevent its destruction by Puritans.

Two gates to the cathedral close survive: **St Ethelbert's**, a 13th-century flint arch, and

One of over a thousand carved bosses in the cathedral cloisters

the **Erpingham Gate** at the west end, built by Sir Thomas Erpingham, who led the triumphant English archers at the Battle of Agincourt in 1415 *(see p53)*.

Beneath the east outer wall is the grave of Edith Cavell, the Norwich-born nurse who was captured and executed in 1915 by the Germans for helping Allied soldiers escape from occupied Belgium.

🏛 Castle Museum

Castle Meadow. 📞 *01603 223624.*
🔘 *for renovation until 2001.*
The brooding keep of this 12th-century castle, refaced in Bath stone in 1834, has been a museum since 1894, when it ended 650 years of service as a prison. The most important Norman feature is a carved door that used to be the main entrance.

Exhibits include medieval armour, pottery, porcelain and the largest collection of ceramic teapots in the world.

A view of Norwich Cathedral's spire and tower from the southeast

COLMAN'S MUSTARD

It was said of the Colmans that they made their fortune from what diners left on their plate. In 1814 Jeremiah Colman started milling mustard at Norwich because it was at the centre of a fertile plain where mustard was grown. Today at Bridewell Alley a shop sells mustard and related items, while a small museum illustrates the history of the company.

A 1950s advertisement for Colman's Mustard

🏛 **Strangers' Hall**
Charing Cross. 📞 *01603 667229.*
⬤ *for renovation until 2002.*
This 14th-century merchant's house gives a glimpse into English domestic life through the ages. The costume display features a unique collection of underwear. The house was lived in by immigrant weavers – the "strangers". It has a fine 15th-century Great Hall.

The art gallery is dominated by works from the Norwich School of painters. This group of early 19th century landscape artists painted directly from nature, getting away from the stylized studio landscapes that had been fashionable up to then. Chief among the group were John Crome (1768–1821), whom many compare with Constable *(see p212)*, and John Sell Cotman (1782–1842), known for his watercolours.

🏛 **Church of St Peter Mancroft**
Market Place. 📞 *01603 610443.*
⬤ *Mon–Fri; Sat (summer only); Sun (services only).* **Donations.** ♿ 📷
This imposing Perpendicular church, built around 1455, so dominates the city centre that many visitors assume it is the cathedral. John Wesley *(see p311)* wrote of it, "I scarcely ever remember to have seen a more beautiful parish church".

The large windows make the church very light, and the dramatic east window still has most of its 15th-century glass. The roof is unusual in having wooden fan tracery – it is normally in stone – covering the hammerbeam construction. The famous peal of 13 bells rang out in 1588 to celebrate the defeat of the Spanish Armada *(see p55)* and is still heard every Sunday.

Its name derives from the Latin *magna crofta* (great meadow) which described the area before the Normans built an earlier church here.

🏛 **Bridewell Museum**
Bridewell Alley. 📞 *01603 667228.*
⬤ *Apr–Sep: Tue–Sat.*
⬤ *Oct–Mar.* 📷 📷 🛍
One of the oldest houses in Norwich, this 14th-century flint-faced building was for years used as a jail. It now houses an exhibition on local industries, with displays of old machines, advertisements and reconstructed shops.

🏛 **Guildhall**
Gaol Hill. 📞 *01603 666071.*
⬤ *Mon–Fri (pm).* ⬤ *public hols.* ♿
Above the city's 900-year-old market place is the imposing 15th-century flint and stone Guildhall with its gable of checkered flushwork. A display of civic regalia includes a flamboyant sword presented to Norwich by Nelson *(see p58)*, who captured it from a Spanish admiral in 1797.

🏛 **The Sainsbury Centre for Visual Arts**
University of East Anglia (on B1108).
📞 *01603 593199.* ⬤ *Tue–Sun.*
⬤ *24 Dec–1 Jan.* 📷 ♿ 🛍 *by arrangement.* 📷 📷
This important art gallery was built in 1978 to house the collection of Robert and Lisa Sainsbury given to the University of East Anglia in 1973.

The collection's strength is in its modern European paintings, including works by Modigliani, Picasso and Bacon, and in its scupltures by Giacometti and Moore. There are also displays of ethnographic art from Africa, the Pacific and the Americas.

The centre, designed by Sir Norman Foster, one of Britain's leading and most innovative architects, was among the first to display its steel structure openly. This style was to be imitated around the world.

***Back of the New Mills* (1814) by John Crome of the Norwich School**

Purple heather in flower on Dunwich Heath

Southwold ⑭

Suffolk. 🏛 *1,400.* 🚌 ℹ️ *Market Place (01502 724729).* 🛒 *Mon, Thu.*

THIS PICTURE-POSTCARD seaside resort, with its charming whitewashed villas clustered around grassy slopes, has, largely by historical accident, remained unspoiled. The railway line which connected it with London was closed in 1929, which effectively isolated this Georgian town from an influx of day-trippers.

That this was also once a large port can be judged from the size of the 15th-century **St Edmund King and Martyr Church**, worth a visit for the 16th-century painted screens. On its tower is a small figure dressed in the uniform of a 15th-century soldier and known as Jack o'the Clock. **Southwold Museum** tells the story of the bloody Battle of Sole Bay, which was fought offshore between the English and Dutch navies in 1672.

Jack o'the Clock, Southwold

ENVIRONS: The rail closure in Southwold also cut the link with the pretty village of **Walberswick**, across the creek. By road it is a long detour and the only alternative is a rowing-boat ferry across the harbour. Just inland at Blythburgh, the 15th-century **Holy Trinity Church** dominates the surrounding land. Cromwell's troops *(see p56)* used it as a stable and you can see the iron rings outside where they tied their horses.

In 1944 a US bomber blew up over the church, killing Joseph Kennedy Jr, brother of the future American president.

🏛 **Southwold Museum**
9–11 Victoria St. 📞 *01502 722437.* ○ *Easter–Oct: daily.* ♿

Dunwich ⑮

Suffolk. 🏛 *1,400.*

THIS TINY VILLAGE with a few cottages and the odd fishing boat, is all that remains of a "lost city" consigned to the sea by erosion.

In the 7th century Dunwich was the seat of the powerful East Anglian kings. In the 13th century it was still the biggest port in Suffolk and some 12 churches were constructed during its time of prosperity. But the land was being eroded at about a metre (3 ft) a year, and the last of the original churches collapsed into the sea in 1919.

Dunwich Heath, just to the south, runs down to a sandy beach and is now an important nature reserve. **Minsmere Reserve** has observation hides for watching a huge variety of water dependent birds .

🦅 **Minsmere Reserve**
Westleton. 📞 *01728 648281.* ○ *Wed–Mon.* ● *25, 26 Dec.*

Aldeburgh ⑯

Suffolk. 🏛 *2,500.* 🚌 ℹ️ *High St (01728 453637).*

BEST KNOWN TODAY for the music festivals at Snape Maltings just up the River Alde, Aldeburgh has been a

Intricate carving on the exterior of the Tudor Moot Hall, Aldeburgh

port since Roman times, although the Roman end of the town is now under the sea.

Erosion has resulted in the fine Tudor **Moot Hall**, once far inland, now being close to the beach and promenade. Its ground floor, originally the market, is now a museum. The large timbered court room above can only be reached by the original outside staircase.

The **church**, also Tudor, contains a large stained glass window placed in 1979 as a memorial to Benjamin Britten.

Moot Hall
Market Cross Pl. 01728 452730. Jun–Sep: daily; Apr–May, Oct: Sat, Sun.

Framlingham Castle ⓱

Framlingham, Suffolk. 01728 724189. Wickham Market then taxi. daily. 24–26 Dec.

PERCHED ON A HILL, the small village of Framlingham has long been an important strategic site, even before the present castle was built in 1190 by the Earl of Norfolk.

Little of the castle from that period survives except the powerful curtain wall and its turrets; walk round the top of it for fine views of the town.

Mary Tudor, daughter of Henry VIII, was staying here in 1553 when she heard she was to become queen.

ENVIRONS: To the southeast, on the coast, is the 27 m (90 ft) keep of **Orford Castle**, built for Henry II as a coastal defence at around the same time as Framlingham. It is the earliest known example of an English castle with a five-sided keep; earlier they were square and later round. A short climb to the top of the castle gives fantastic views of the surrounding land.

Orford Castle
Orford. 01394 450472. Mar–Oct: daily; Nov–Feb: Wed–Sun. 25–26 Dec, 1 Jan.

ALDEBURGH MUSIC FESTIVAL

Composer Benjamin Britten (1913–76), born in Lowestoft, Suffolk, moved to Snape in 1937. In 1945 his opera *Peter Grimes* – inspired by the poet George Crabbe (1754–1832), once a curate at Aldeburgh – was performed in Snape. Since then the area has become the centre of musical activity. In 1948, Britten began the Aldeburgh Music Festival, held every June *(see p67)*. He acquired the Maltings at Snape and converted it into a music venue opened by the Queen in 1967. It has since become the focus of an annual series of East Anglian musical events in churches and halls throughout the entire region.

Benjamin Britten in Aldeburgh

Ipswich ⓲

Suffolk. 102,000. St Stephen's Lane (01473 258070). Tue, Fri, Sat.

SUFFOLK'S COUNTY TOWN has a largely modern centre but several buildings remain from earlier times. It rose to prominence after the 13th century as a port for the rich Suffolk wool trade *(see p217)*. Later, with the Industrial Revolution, it began to export coal.

The **Ancient House** in Buttermarket has a superb example of pargeting – the ancient craft of ornamental façade plastering. The town's museum and art gallery, **Christchurch Mansion**, is a Tudor house from 1548, where Elizabeth I stayed in 1561. It also boasts the best collection of Constable's paintings out of London *(see p212)*, including four marvellous Suffolk landscapes, as well as pictures by the Suffolk-born painter Gainsborough *(see p157)*.

Ipswich Museum contains replicas of the locally excavated Mildenhall and Sutton Hoo treasures, the originals of which are held in the British Museum *(see pp112–13)*.

In the centre of the town is **St Margaret's**, a lavish 15th-century church built in flint and stone with a double hammerbeam roof and some beautiful 17th-century painted ceiling panels. A Tudor gateway of 1527 provides a link with Ipswich's most famous son, Cardinal Wolsey *(see p54)*. He started to build an ecclesiastical college in the town, but fell from royal favour before it was completed.

Christchurch Mansion
Soane St. 01473 253246. Tue–Sun & public hols. 24–26 Dec, 1 Jan, Good Fri. limited. by arrangement.

Ipswich Museum
High St. 01473 213761. Tue–Sat. 24–26 Dec, 1 Jan, Good Fri.

Pargeting on the Ancient House in Ipswich

Constable Walk ⑲

THIS WALK in Constable country follows one of the most picturesque sections of the River Stour. The path followed would have been familiar to the landscape painter John Constable (1776–1837). Constable's father was a wealthy merchant who owned Flatford Mill; the scenery of at least ten of the artist's most important paintings was within view of this much-loved mill. Constable claimed to know and love "every stile and stump, and every lane" around East Bergholt, and the walk encompasses his favourite areas.

The River Stour, used as a backdrop for Constable's *Boatbuilding* **(1814)**

Tips for Walkers

Starting point: Car park off Flatford Lane, East Bergholt.
ℹ **(NT)** Bridge Cottage Information Centre (01206 298260).
Getting there: A12 to Ipswich, then B1070 to East Bergholt, follow signs to Flatford Mill.
Stopping-off point: Dedham.
Length: 3 miles (5 km).
Difficulty: Flat trail along riverside footpath with stiles.

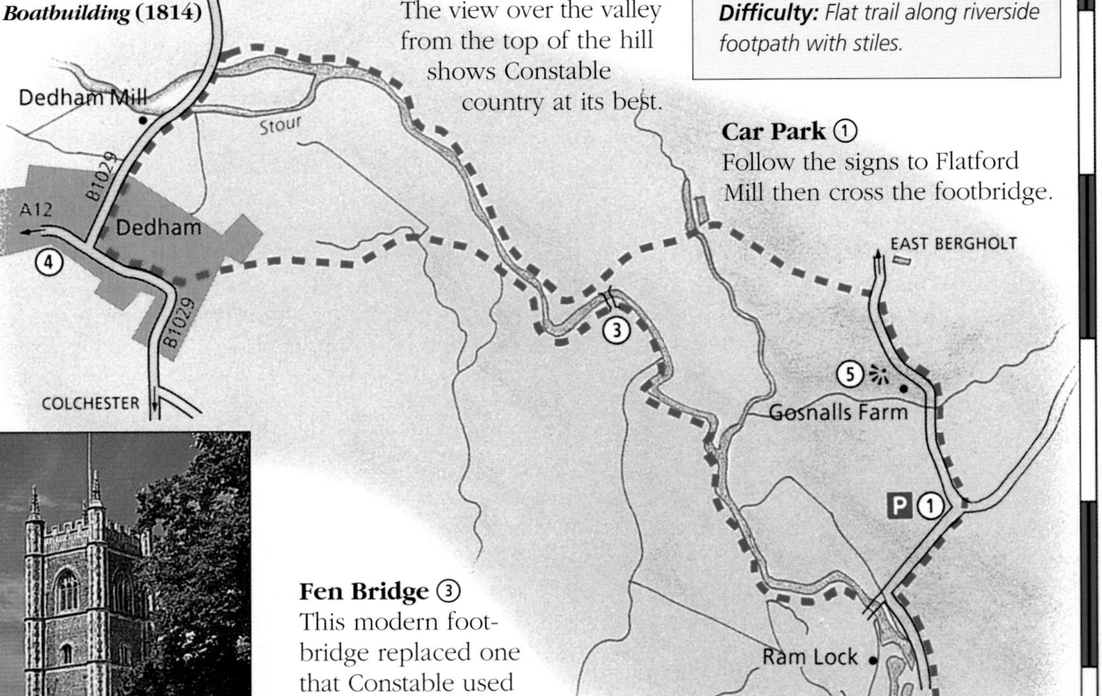

Viewpoint ⑤
The view over the valley from the top of the hill shows Constable country at its best.

Car Park ①
Follow the signs to Flatford Mill then cross the footbridge.

Dedham Mill

Stour

B1029

A12

Dedham

④

B1029

COLCHESTER

EAST BERGHOLT

③

⑤ 🌿
Gosnalls Farm

P ①

Fen Bridge ③
This modern foot-bridge replaced one that Constable used as a focus for many of his paintings.

Ram Lock

Flatford Mill

②

Dedham Church ④
The tall church tower appears in many of Constable's pictures including the *View on the Stour near Dedham* (1822).

KEY

▬ ▬	Route
▬▬	B road
▭▭	Minor road
🌿	Viewpoint
P	Parking

0 metres   500

0 yards   500

Willy Lott's Cottage ②
This cottage remains much the same as it did when featured in Constable's painting *The Haywain* (see p89).

Colchester ⑳

Essex. 👥 150,000. 🚄 🚌 🛈 Queen St (01206 282920). 🛒 Fri, Sat.

THE OLDEST recorded town in Britain, Colchester was the effective capital of south-east England when the Romans invaded in AD 43, and it was here that the first permanent Roman colony was established.

After Boadicea (see p203) burnt the town in AD 60, a 2 mile (3 km) defensive wall was built, 3 m (10 ft) thick and 9 m (30 ft) high, to deter any future attackers. You can still see these walls and the surviving Roman town gate, which is the largest in Britain.

During the Middle Ages Colchester developed into an important weaving centre. In the 16th century, a number of immigrant Flemish weavers settled in an area west of the castle, known as the **Dutch Quarter**, which still retains the original tall houses and steep, narrow streets.

Colchester was besieged for 11 weeks during the Civil War (see p56) before being captured by Cromwell's troops.

🏛 **Tymperleys**
Trinity St. 📞 01206 282943.
◯ Apr–Oct: Tue–Sat. ♿ ⑃
Clock-making was an important craft in Colchester, and it is celebrated in this restored half-timbered, 15th-century mansion, also worth visiting for its formal Tudor garden.

🏛 **Hollytrees Museum**
Castle Park. 📞 01206 282939.
◯ Tue–Sat. ● public hols.
This elegant Georgian town-house, on the edge of Castle Park, was built in 1719. Now a charming museum of social history, it houses interesting displays of toys and dolls, costumes and ceramics dating back to the 18th century.

🏛 **Castle Museum**
High St. 📞 01206 282932. ◯
Mar–Nov: daily; Dec–Feb: Mon–Sat.
● 24–27 Dec. ♿ ⑃ ⑃
This is the oldest and largest Norman keep still standing in England. Twice the size of the White Tower at the Tower of London (see pp124–5), it was built in 1076 on the platform

The Norman keep of the Castle Museum, Colchester

of a Roman temple dedicated to Claudius I (see p48), using stones and tiles from other Roman buildings. Today, the museum is packed full of exhibits relating the story of the town from prehistoric times to the Civil War. You can also visit the medieval prison.

🏛 **Layer Marney Tower**
Off B1022. 📞 01206 330784. ◯
Apr–Sep: Sun–Fri (pm). ♿ ⑃ limited.
⑃ by arrangement. 📷 🖥 ⑃
This remarkable Tudor gatehouse is the tallest in Britain: its pair of six-sided, eight-storey turrets reach to 24 m (80 ft). It was intended to be part of a larger complex but the designer, Sir Henry Marney, died before it was completed. The brickwork and terracotta ornamentation around the roof and windows are models of Tudor craftsmanship. There are fine views of the gardens and deer park from the top.

🍁 **Beth Chatto Garden**
Elmstead Market. 📞 01206 822007.
◯ Mar–Oct: Mon–Sat; Nov–Feb: Mon–Fri. ● 24 Dec–6 Jan, public hols.
♿
One of Britain's most eminent gardening writers began this experiment in the 1960s to test her belief that it is possible to create a garden in the most adverse conditions. The large garden consists of dry and windy slopes, boggy patches, gravel beds and wooded areas, all of which support an array of plants best suited to that particular environment.

Coggeshall ㉑

Essex. 👥 4,000. 🛒 Thu.

THIS SMALL TOWN has two of the most important and best-preserved medieval and Tudor buildings in the country. Dating from 1140, **Coggeshall Grange Barn** is the oldest surviving timber-framed barn in Europe. Inside is a display of historic farm wagons. The half-timbered merchant's house, **Paycocke's**, was built around 1500 and has a beautifully panelled interior. There is a display of Coggeshall lace.

🏛 **Coggeshall Grange Barn**
(NT) Grange Hill. 📞 01376 562226.
◯ Apr–Oct: Tue, Thu, Sun & public hols (pm). ● Good Fri. ♿ ⑃
🏛 **Paycocke's**
(NT) West St. 📞 01376 561305.
◯ Apr–Oct: Tue, Thu, Sun & public hols (pm). ● Good Fri. ♿ ♿

Beth Chatto Garden, Colchester, in full summer bloom

Lavenham ②

Suffolk. 🏠 *1,700.* ℹ️ *Lady St (01787 248207).*

OFTEN CONSIDERED the most perfect of all English small towns, Lavenham is a treasure trove of black and white timber-framed houses ranged along streets whose pattern is virtually unchanged from medieval times. For 150 years, between the 14th and 16th centuries, Lavenham was the prosperous centre of the Suffolk wool trade. It still has many outstanding and well-preserved buildings; indeed no less than 300 of the town's buildings are listed, including the magnificent **Little Hall**.

ENVIRONS: Gainsborough's House, Sudbury, is a museum on this painter (*see p157*).

🏛 **Little Hall**
Market Place. ☎ *01787 247179.*
◯ *Apr–Oct: Wed, Thu, Sat, Sun & public hols pm only.* 📷
🏛 **Gainsborough's House**
Sudbury. ☎ *01787 372958.* ◯ *Tue–Sun.* ● *public hols, Christmas.* 📷

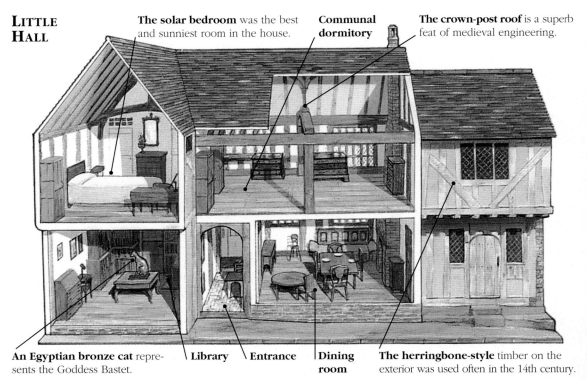

LITTLE HALL

The solar bedroom was the best and sunniest room in the house.

Communal dormitory

The crown-post roof is a superb feat of medieval engineering.

An Egyptian bronze cat represents the Goddess Bastet.

Library   **Entrance**   **Dining room**

The herringbone-style timber on the exterior was used often in the 14th century.

Bury St Edmunds ㉓

Suffolk. 🏠 *33,000.* 🚆 🚌 ℹ️ *Angel Hill (01284 764667).* 🛒 *Wed, Sat.*

ST EDMUND was the last Saxon king of East Anglia, decapitated by Danish raiders in 870. Legend has it that a wolf picked up the severed head – an image that appears in a number of medieval carvings. Edmund was canonized in 900 and buried in Bury, where in 1014 King Canute (*see p171*) built an **abbey** in his honour, the wealthiest in the country, until razed by fire in 1347. The abbey ruins now lie in a garden in the town centre.

Nearby are two large 15th-century churches, built when the wool trade made the town wealthy. **St James's** was designated a cathedral in 1914. The best features of **St Mary's** are the north porch and the hammer-beam roof over the nave. A stone slab in the north-east corner of the church marks the tomb of Mary Tudor (*see p54*).

Just below the **market cross** in Cornhill – remodelled by Robert Adam (*see p28*) in 1714 – stands the large 12th-century **Moyse's Hall**, a merchant's house that serves as the town museum. It has Iron Age exhibits, excavated from West Stowe to the north.

Illustration of St Edmund

ENVIRONS: Three miles (5 km) southwest of Bury is the late 18th-century **Ickworth House**. This eccentric Neo-Classical mansion features an unusual rotunda with a

The 18th-century rotunda of Ickworth House, Bury St Edmunds

◁ **Windmill in the village of Cley-next-the-Sea, Norfolk**

domed roof flanked by two huge wings. The art collection includes works by Reynolds and Titian. There are also fine displays of silver, porcelain and sculpture, for example, John Flaxman's (1755–1826) moving *The Fury of Athamas*. The house is set in a large park.

🏛 **Moyse's Hall**
Cornhill. 📞 *01284 757489.* ⭘ *daily.* ⬤ *24–26 Dec, Good Fri.* ♿ *limited.*
🏛 **Ickworth House**
Horringer. 📞 *01284 735270.* ⭘ *Apr–Oct: Tue, Wed, Fri–Sun; public hols (pm).* 📷♿🍴📷

Newmarket 24

Suffolk. 👥 *1,700.* 🚆 🚌 ℹ️ *Palace House, Palace St (01638 667200).* 📆 *Tue, Sat.*

A WALK DOWN the short main street tells you all you need to know about this busy and wealthy little town. The shops sell horse feed and all manner of riding accessories; the clothes on sale are tweeds, jodhpurs and the soft brown hats rarely worn by anyone except racehorse trainers.

Newmarket has been the headquarters of British horse racing since James I decided that its open heaths were ideal for testing the mettle of his fastest steeds against those of his friends. The first ever

The stallion unit at the National Stud, Newmarket

recorded horse race was held here in 1622. Charles II shared his grandfather's enthusiasm and after the Restoration *(see p57)* would move the whole court to Newmarket, every spring and summer, for the sport – he is the only British king to have ridden a winner.

A horse being exercised on Newmarket Heath

The modern racing industry began to take shape here in the late 18th century. There are now over 2,500 horses in training in and around the town, and two racecourses staging regular race meetings from around April to October *(see p70)*. Training stables are

occasionally open to the public but you can view the horses being exercised on the heath surrounding the town in the early morning.

The **National Stud** can also be visited. You will see the seven or eight stallions on stud, mares in foal and if you are lucky a newborn foal – most likely in April or May. Tattersall's, the auction house for thoroughbreds, is also here.

The **National Horseracing Museum** tells the history of the sport and contains many offbeat exhibits such as the skeleton of Eclipse, one of the greatest horses ever, unbeaten in 18 races in 1769 and 1770, and the ancestor of many of today's fastest performers. It also has an interesting and large display of sporting art.

🕹 **National Stud**
Newmarket. 📞 *01638 663464.* ⭘ *Mar–Sep: daily.* 📷♿📷📷
🏛 **National Horseracing Museum**
99 High St, Newmarket. 📞 *01638 667333.* ⭘ *Apr–Oct: Tue–Sun.* 📷 ♿📷 *by arrangement.* 💻📷

THE RISE AND FALL OF THE WOOL TRADE

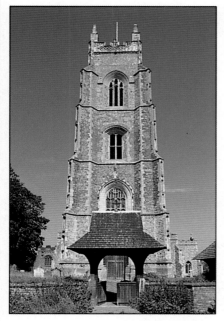
St Mary's Church, Stoke-by-Nayland, southeast of Bury St Edmunds

Wool was a major English product from the 13th century and by 1310 some ten million fleeces were exported every year. The Black Death *(see p52)*, which swept Britain in 1348, perversely provided a boost for the industry: with labour in short supply, land could not be cultivated and was grassed over for sheep. Around 1350 Edward III decided it was time to establish a home-based cloth industry and encouraged Flemish weavers to come to Britain. Many settled in East Anglia, particularly Suffolk, and their skills helped establish a flourishing trade. This time of prosperity saw the construction of the sumptuous churches, such as the one at Stoke-by-Nayland, that we see today – East Anglia has more than 2,000 churches. The cloth trade here began to decline in the late 16th century with the development of water-powered looms. These were not suited to the area, which never regained its former wealth. Today's visitors are the beneficiaries of this decline, because the wool towns such as Lavenham and Bury St Edmunds never became rich enough to destroy their magnificent Tudor halls and houses and construct new buildings.

The façade of Anglesey Abbey

Anglesey Abbey 25

(NT) Lode, Cambridgeshire. 📞 01223 811200. 🚃 Cambridge then bus. **House** and **Gardens.** ⭕ Apr–Oct: Wed–Sun; (Jun–mid-Sep Gardens open daily). ♿ limited. 🍴 🛍

THE ORIGINAL ABBEY was built in 1135 for an Augustinian order. But only the crypt – also known as the monks' parlour – with its vaulted ceiling on marble and stone pillars, survived the Dissolution (see p54).

This was later incorporated into a manor house whose treasures include furniture from many periods and a rare seascape by Gainsborough (see p216). The superb garden was created in the 1930s by Lord Fairhaven as an ambitious, Classical landscape of trees, sculptures and borders.

Huntingdon 26

Cambridgeshire. 🏃 18,000. 🚃 🚌 🛈 Princes St (01480 388588). 🛒 Wed, Sat.

MORE THAN 300 YEARS after his death, Oliver Cromwell (see p56) still dominates this small town. Born here in 1599, a record of his baptism can be seen in **All Saints' and St John's Church**, off Market Square. You can see his name and traces of ancient graffiti scrawled all over it which says "England's plague for five years". **Cromwell Museum**, his former school, traces his life with pictures and mementoes, including his death mask.

Cromwell remains one of the most disputed figures in British history. An MP before he was 30, he quickly became embroiled in the disputes between Charles I and Parliament over taxes and religion. In the Civil War (see p56) he proved an inspired general and – after refusing the title of king – was made Lord Protector in 1653, four years after the King was beheaded. But just two years after his death the monarchy was restored by popular demand, and his body was taken out of Westminster Abbey (see pp98–9) to hang on gallows.

There is a 13th-century bridge across the River Ouse which links Huntingdon with Godmanchester, the site of a Roman settlement on the road between London and York.

🏛 **Cromwell Museum**
Grammar School Walk. 📞 01480 375830. ⭕ Tue–Sun (pm). ⬤ 24 Dec & public hols. ♿ limited.

Cambridge 27

See pp220–25.

Audley End 28

Saffron Walden, Essex. 📞 01799 522842. 🚃 Audley End then taxi. ⭕ Apr–Sep: Wed–Sun & public hols; Oct: tours only. ♿ limited. 🎧 by arrangement. 🍴 ☕ 🛍

THIS WAS THE largest house in England when built in 1614 for Thomas Howard, Lord Treasurer and 1st Earl of Suffolk. James I joked that Howard's house was too big for a king but not for a Lord Treasurer. Charles II, his grandson, disagreed and bought it in 1667 as an extra palace; but he and his successors seldom went there and in 1701 it was given back to the Howards, who demolished two thirds of it to make it more manageable.

What remains is a Jacobean mansion, retaining its original hall and many fine plaster ceilings. Robert Adam (see p28) remodelled most of the interior in the 1760s and many rooms have been restored to his original designs. At the same time, Capability Brown (see p27) landscaped the magnificent 18th-century park.

The Chapel was completed in 1772 to a Gothic design. The furniture was made to complement the wooden pillars and vaulting which are painted to imitate stone.

The painted window, built in 1768, represents the Last Supper.

Main entrance

The Great Hall, hung with family portraits, is the highlight of the house, with the massive oak screen and elaborate hammerbeam roof surviving in their Jacobean form.

Epping Forest ㉙

Essex. ⇌ *Chingford.* ⊖ *Theydon Bois.* ℹ *High Beach, Loughton (020-8508 0028).*

As one of the large open spaces near London, the 2,400 ha (6,000 acre) forest is popular with walkers, just as, centuries ago, it was a favourite hunting ground for kings and courtiers – the word forest denoted an area for hunting.

Epping Forest contains oaks and beeches up to 400 years old

A depiction of the Battle of Maldon (991) on the *Maldon Embroidery*

Henry VIII had a lodge built in 1543 on the edge of the forest. His daughter Elizabeth I, also a keen hunter, often used the lodge and it soon became known as **Queen Elizabeth's Hunting Lodge**.

This three-storey timbered building has been fully renovated and now houses an exhibition explaining the lodge's history and other aspects of the forest's life.

The tracts of open land and woods interspersed with a number of lakes, make an ideal habitat for a variety of plant, bird and animal life: deer roam the northern part, many of a special dark strain introduced by James I. The Corporation of London bought the forest in the early 19th century to ensure it remained open to the public.

🏛 **Queen Elizabeth's Hunting Lodge**
Rangers Rd, Chingford. 📞 *020-8529 6681.* ⬜ *Wed–Sun (pm).* ⬤ *24–26 Dec, 1 Jan.* 🚫 ♿ *limited.* 🎬 📷

Maldon ㉚

Essex. 🏘 *15,000* ⇌ *Chelmsford then bus.* ℹ *Coach Lane (01621 856503).* 🔺 *Thu, Sat.*

This delightful old town on the River Blackwater, its High Street lined with shops and inns from the 16th century on, was once an important harbour and is still popular with weekend sailors. One of its main industries is the production of Maldon sea salt, panned in the traditional way.

A fierce battle here in 991, when Viking invaders defeated the Saxon defenders, is told in *The Battle of Maldon,* one of the earliest known Saxon poems. The battle is also celebrated in the *Maldon Embroidery* on display in the **Maeldune Centre**. This 13 m (42 ft) long embroidery, made by locals, depicts the history of Maldon from 991 to 1991.

Environs: East of Maldon at Bradwell-on-Sea is the sturdy Saxon church of **St Peter's-on-the-Wall**, a simple stone box of a building that stands quite isolated on the shore. It was built in 654, from the stones of a former Roman fort, by St Cedd, who used it as his cathedral. It was fully restored in the 1920s.

🏛 **Maeldune Centre**
High St. 📞 *01621 851628.* ⬜ *Oct–Mar: Thu–Sat; Apr–Sep: Mon–Sat.* ⬤ *24–26 Dec, 1 Jan.* 🎬

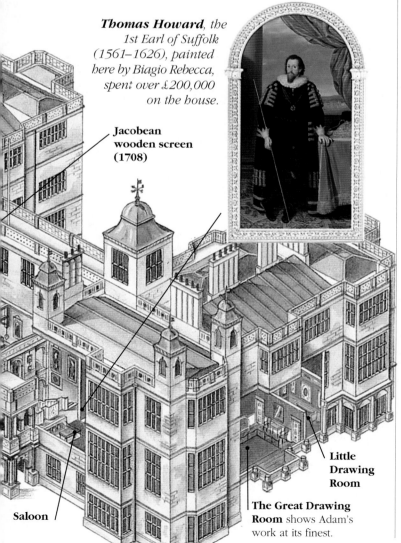

***Thomas Howard**, the 1st Earl of Suffolk (1561–1626), painted here by Biagio Rebecca, spent over £200,000 on the house.*

Jacobean wooden screen (1708)

Saloon

The Great Drawing Room shows Adam's work at its finest.

Little Drawing Room

Street-by-Street: Cambridge 27

Carving, King's College Chapel

CAMBRIDGE HAS BEEN an important town since Roman times as it is sited at the first navigable point on the River Cam. In the 11th century religious orders began to be established in the town and, in 1209, a group of religious scholars broke away from Oxford University *(see pp238–43)* after academic and religious disputes and came here. Student life dominates the city but it is also a thriving market centre serving a rich agricultural region.

Cyclists in Cambridge

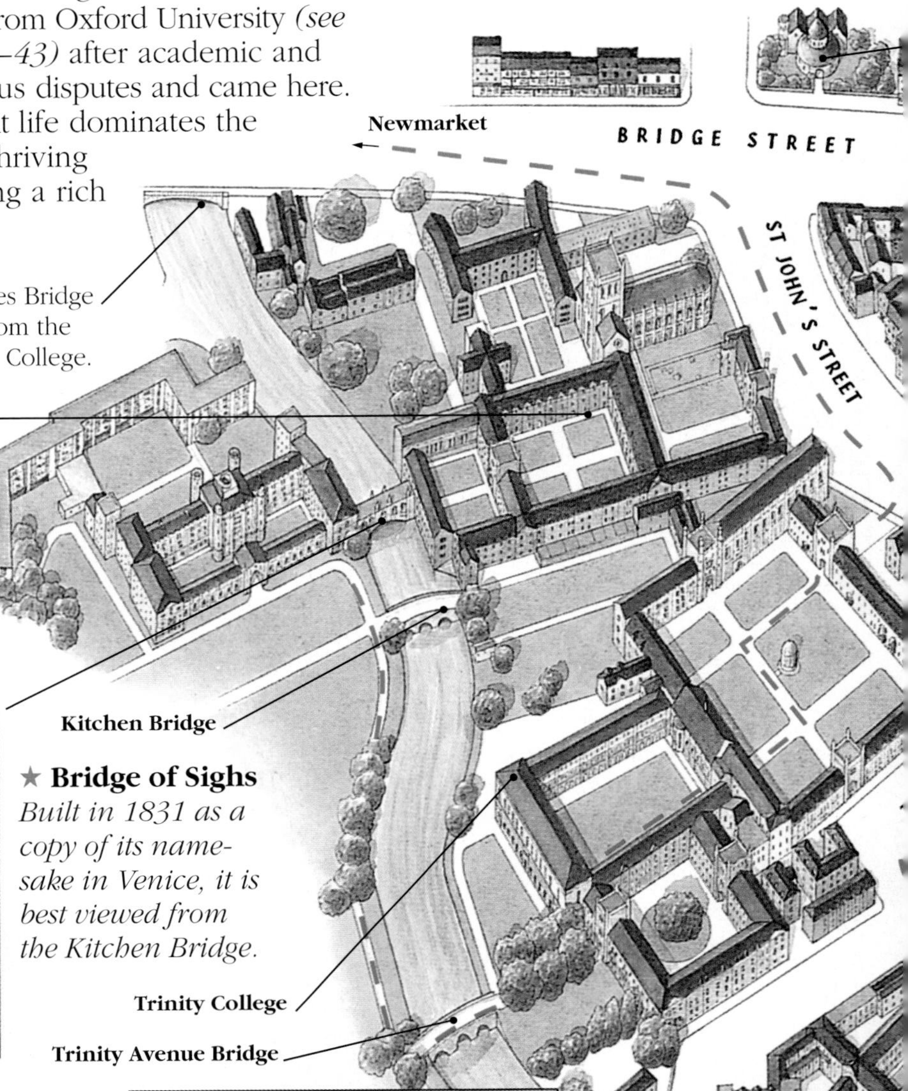

Newmarket ←

BRIDGE STREET

ST JOHN'S STREET

Magdalene Bridge carries Bridge Street across the Cam from the city centre to Magdalene College.

St John's College has superb Tudor and Jacobean architecture.

Kitchen Bridge

★ **Bridge of Sighs**
Built in 1831 as a copy of its name-sake in Venice, it is best viewed from the Kitchen Bridge.

Trinity College

Trinity Avenue Bridge

The Backs
This is the name given to the grassy strip lying between the backs of the big colleges and the banks of the Cam – a good spot to enjoy this classic view of King's College Chapel.

KEY

– – – Suggested route

STAR SIGHTS

★ **Bridge of Sighs**

★ **King's College Chapel**

Clare College

Clare Bridge

Grantchester →

0 metres 75

0 yards 75

St Mary's Church
This clock is over the west door of the university's official church. Its tower offers fine views.

VISITORS' CHECKLIST

Cambridgeshire. 100,000.
Stansted. Cambridge.
Station Rd. Drummer St.
Wheeler St (01223 322640).
Mon–Sat. Folk Festival:
July; Cambridge Festival: June;
Strawberry Festival: June.

Round Church
The 12th-century Church of the Holy Sepulchre has one of the few round naves in the country. Its design is based on the Holy Sepulchre in Jerusalem.

Gonville and Caius
(pronounced "keys"), founded in 1348, is one of the oldest colleges.

★ King's College Chapel
This late medieval masterpiece took 70 years to build (see pp222–3).

Market square

Coach station →

King's College
Henry VIII, king when the chapel was completed in 1515, is commemorated in this statue near the main gate.

Queens' College
Its Tudor courts are among the university's finest. This 17th-century sundial is over the old chapel – now a reading room.

Corpus Christi College

To London and railway station

Mathematical Bridge
Linking the two parts of Queens' College across the Cam, the bridge was first built without nuts or bolts.

🏛 Fitzwilliam Museum

Trumpington St. 📞 *01223 332900.*
⏰ *Tue–Sun; public hols.* ⬤ *24 Dec–*
1 Jan. Good Fri, May Day. **Donation.**
♿ *limited.* 📷 *Sun pm.* 📱 📷

One of Britain's oldest public museums, this massive Classical building has works of exceptional quality and rarity, especially antiquities, ceramics, paintings and manuscripts.

The core of the collection was bequeathed in 1816 by the 7th Viscount Fitzwilliam. Other gifts have since greatly added to the exhibits.

Works by Titian (1488–1576) and the 17th-century Dutch masters, including Hals, Cuyp and Hobbema's *Wooded Landscape* (1866), stand out among the paintings. French Impressionist gems include Monet's *Le Printemps* (1866) and Renoir's *La Place Clichy* (1880), while Picasso's *Still Life* (1923) is notable among the modern works. Most of the important British artists are represented, from Hogarth in the 18th century through Constable in the 19th to Ben Nicholson in the 20th.

The miniatures include the earliest surviving depiction of Henry VIII. In the same gallery are some dazzling illuminated manuscripts, notably the 15th-century *Metz Pontifical*, a sumptuous French liturgical work produced for a bishop.

The impressive Glaisher collection of European earthenware and stoneware includes a unique display of English delftware from the 16th and 17th centuries.

Handel's bookcase contains folios of his work, and nearby is Keats's original manuscript for *Ode to a Nightingale* (1819).

**Portrait of Richard James
(c.1740s) by William Hogarth**

Cambridge: King's College

**King's College
Chapel Coat of Arms**

HENRY VI FOUNDED this college in 1441. Work on the chapel – one of the most important examples of late medieval English architecture – began five years later, and took 70 years to complete. Henry himself decided that it should dominate the city and gave specific instructions about its dimensions: 88 m (289 ft) long, 12 m (40 ft) wide and 29 m (94 ft) high. The detailed design is thought to have been by master stonemason Reginald Ely, although it was altered in later years.

★ Fan Vaulted Ceiling
This awe-inspiring ceiling, supported by 22 buttresses, was built by master stonemason John Wastell in 1515.

The Fellows' Building was designed in 1724 by James Gibbs, as part of an uncompleted design for a Great Court.

**Entrance to the
Fellows' Building**

Henry VI's statue
This bronze statue of the college's founder was erected in 1879.

KING'S COLLEGE CHOIR

When he founded the chapel, Henry VI stipulated that a choir of six lay clerks and 16 boy choristers – educated at the College school – should sing daily at services. This still happens in term time but today the choir also gives concerts all over the world. Its televised service of carols has become a much-loved Christmas tradition.

Choristers singing in King's Chapel

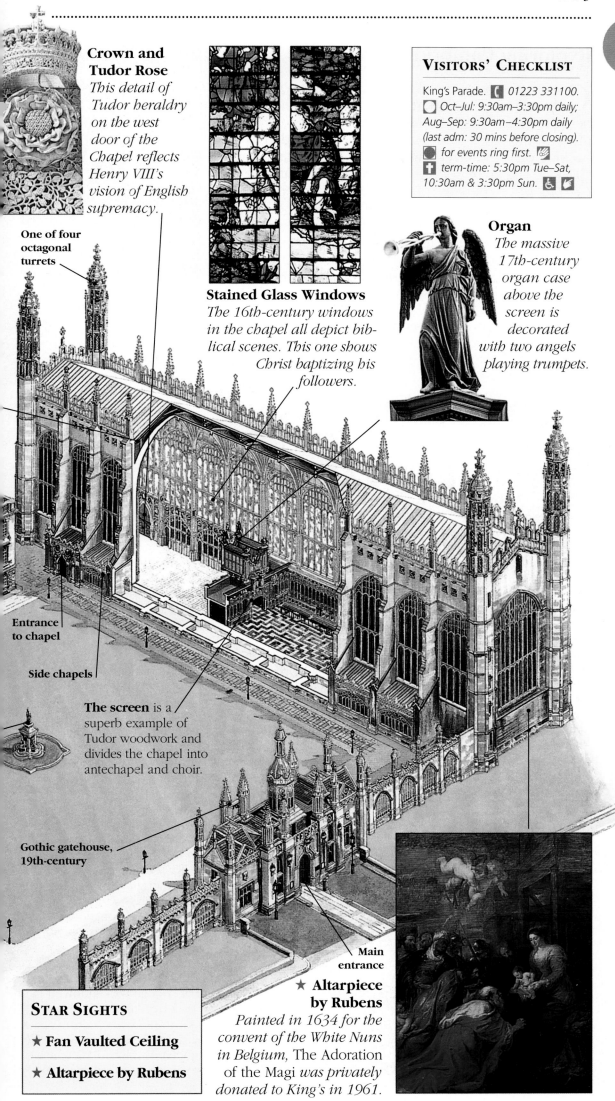

Crown and Tudor Rose
This detail of Tudor heraldry on the west door of the Chapel reflects Henry VIII's vision of English supremacy.

Stained Glass Windows
The 16th-century windows in the chapel all depict biblical scenes. This one shows Christ baptizing his followers.

VISITORS' CHECKLIST

King's Parade. 01223 331100.
Oct–Jul: 9:30am–3:30pm daily;
Aug–Sep: 9:30am–4:30pm daily
(last adm: 30 mins before closing).
for events ring first.
term-time: 5:30pm Tue–Sat,
10:30am & 3:30pm Sun.

Organ
The massive 17th-century organ case above the screen is decorated with two angels playing trumpets.

One of four octagonal turrets

Entrance to chapel

Side chapels

The screen is a superb example of Tudor woodwork and divides the chapel into antechapel and choir.

Gothic gatehouse, 19th-century

Main entrance

STAR SIGHTS

★ **Fan Vaulted Ceiling**

★ **Altarpiece by Rubens**

★ **Altarpiece by Rubens**
Painted in 1634 for the convent of the White Nuns in Belgium, The Adoration of the Magi *was privately donated to King's in 1961.*

Exploring Cambridge University

CAMBRIDGE UNIVERSITY HAS 31 COLLEGES *(see pp220–21)*, the oldest being Peterhouse (1284) and the newest being Robinson (1979). Clustered around the city centre, many of the older colleges have peaceful gardens backing onto the River Cam, which are known as the "Backs". The layout of the older colleges, as at Oxford *(see pp242–3)*, derives from their early connections with religious institutions, although few escaped heavy-handed modification in the Victorian era. The college buildings are generally grouped around squares called courts and offer an unrivalled mix of over 600 years of architecture from the late medieval period through Wren's masterpieces and up to the present day.

The nave of the Wren Chapel at Pembroke College

The imposing façade of Emmanuel College

Emmanuel College
Built in 1677 on St Andrew's Street, Sir Christopher Wren's *(see p120)* chapel is the high-light of the college. Some of the intricate interior details, particularly the plaster ceiling and Amigoni's altar rails (1734), are superb. Founded in 1584, the college has a Puritan tradi-tion. One notable graduate was the clergyman John Harvard, who emigrated to America in 1636 and left all his money to the Massachusetts college that now bears his name.

Senate House
King's Parade is the site of this Palladian building, which is used primarily for university ceremonies. It was designed by James Gibbs in 1722 as part of a grand square of university buildings – which was never completed.

Corpus Christi College
Just down from Senate House, this was founded in 1352 by the local trade guilds, anxious to ensure that education was not the sole prerogative of

church and nobility. Its Old Court is remarkably well preserved and looks today much as it would have done when built in the 14th century.

The college is connected by a 15th-century gallery of red brick to St Bene't's Church (short for St Benedict's), whose large Saxon tower is the oldest structure in Cambridge.

King's College
See pp222–3.

Pembroke College
The college chapel was the first building completed by Wren *(see p120)*. A formal classical design, it replaced a 14th-century chapel that was turned into a library. The college, just off Trumpington Street, also has fine gardens.

Jesus College
Although founded in 1497, some of its buildings on Jesus Lane are older, as the college took over St Radegond's nun-nery, built in the 12th century. There are traces of Norman columns, windows and a well-preserved hammerbeam roof in the college dining hall.

The chapel keeps the core of the original church but the stained glass windows are modern and contain work by William Morris *(see pp236–7)*.

Queens' College
Built in 1446 on Queens' Land, the college was endowed in 1448 by Margaret of Anjou, queen of Henry VI, and again in 1465 by Elizabeth Woodville, queen of Edward IV, which explains the position of the apostrophe. Queens' has a

PUNTING ON THE CAM

Punting captures the essence of carefree college days: a student leaning on a long pole, lazily guiding the flat-bottomed river craft along, while others stretch out and relax. Punting is still popular both with students and visitors, who can hire punts from boat-yards along the river – with a chauffeur if required. Punts do sometimes capsize, and novices should prepare for a dip.

Punting by the King's College "Backs"

marvellous collection of Tudor buildings, notably the half-timbered President's Gallery, built in the mid-16th century on top of the brick arches in the charming Cloister Court. The Principal Court is 15th century, as is Erasmus's Tower, named after the Dutch scholar.

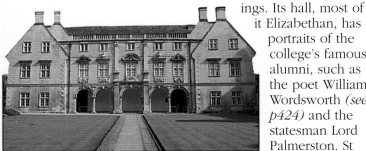

Pepys Library in Magdalene College

The college has buildings on both sides of the Cam, linked by the bizarre Mathematical Bridge, built in 1749 to hold together without the use of nuts and bolts – although they have had to be used in subsequent repairs.

Magdalene College
Pronounced "maudlin" – as is the Oxford college (see p242) – the college, on Bridge Street, was established in 1482. The diarist Samuel Pepys (1633–1703) was a student here and left his large library to the college on his death. The 12 red-oak bookcases have over 3,000 books. Magdalene was the last all-male Cambridge college and it admitted women students only in 1987.

St John's College
Sited on St John's Street, the imposing turreted brick and stone gatehouse of 1514, with its colourful heraldic symbols, provides a fitting entrance to the second largest Cambridge college and its rich store of 16th- and 17th-century buildings. Its hall, most of it Elizabethan, has portraits of the college's famous alumni, such as the poet William Wordsworth (see p424) and the statesman Lord Palmerston. St John's spans the Cam and boasts two bridges, one built in 1712 and the other, the Bridge of Sighs, in 1831, based on its Venetian namesake.

Peterhouse
The first Cambridge college, on Trumpington Street, is also one of the smallest. The hall still has original features from 1286 but its best details are later – a Tudor fireplace which is backed with 19th-century tiles by William Morris (see pp236–7). A gallery connects the college to the 12th-century church of St Mary the Less, which used to be called St Peter's Church – hence the college's name.

William Morris tiles, Peterhouse

> ## VISITORS' CHECKLIST
>
> **Cambridge Colleges** can usually be visited from 2–5pm daily, but there are no set opening hours. See noticeboards at each college for daily opening times. Some colleges charge admission.

Trinity College
The largest college, situated on Trinity Street, was founded by Henry VIII in 1547 and has a massive court and hall. The entrance gate, with statues of Henry and James I (added later), was built in 1529 for King's Hall, an earlier college incorporated into Trinity. The Great Court features a late Elizabethan fountain – at one time the main water supply. The chapel, built in 1567, has life-size statues of college members, notably Roubiliac's statue of the scientist Isaac Newton (1755).

University Botanic Garden
A delightful place for a leisurely stroll, just off Trumpington Street, as well as an important academic resource, the garden has been on this site since 1846. It has a superb collection of trees and a sensational water garden. The winter garden is one of the finest in the country.

The Bridge of Sighs over the River Cam, linking the buildings of St John's College

The River Thames at Henley, host to the annual Royal Regatta ▷

THAMES VALLEY

THAMES VALLEY

THE MIGHTY TIDAL RIVER *on which Britain's capital city was founded has modest origins, meandering from its source in the hills of Gloucestershire through the lush countryside towards London. Almost entirely agricultural land in the 19th century, the Thames Valley maintains its pastoral beauty despite the incursion of modern industry.*

Several towns in the Thames Valley grew up as staging posts on the trunk routes between London and the west. One such settlement is Burford, which is among England's most picturesque small towns and has scarcely altered since the 18th century. With the introduction of fast commuter transport in the early 20th century, much of the area became an extension of suburbia and saw some experiments in Utopian town planning. Welwyn and Letchworth were "garden cities" generously provided with trees and lawns, in keeping with the ideas of the social reformer Sir Ebenezer Howard. William Penn – an early Quaker and founder of Pennsylvania, USA – is buried in the village of Jordans, which is near Beaconsfield. A Quaker community settlement has been erected around Jordans' green. After World War II, Stevenage and later Milton Keynes were two of the new towns built in formerly rural areas to ease population pressure on the capital. They are showcases of the planning ideas that were prevalent at the time.

Oxford, the principal city of the Thames Valley, owes its importance to the foundation of Britain's first university in 1167. Many of Oxford's colleges and halls are gems of medieval architecture. Apart from the university, Oxford has many sites of historic interest, including the Ashmolean Museum, which opened in the 17th century, and the 14th-century Carfax Tower. The city is also the site of one of the few heavy industries in

Punting on the River Cherwell, Oxford

◁ **Medieval staircase in Christchurch College, Oxford**

this region: the Rover car factory, located in the suburb of Cowley. (Other industries in the Thames Valley – including furniture making in High Wycombe, and carpet weaving in Witney – have emerged from a local tradition of rural crafts.) In the 17th century, a number of battles in the Civil War were fought around Oxford. The city was, for a time, the headquarters of King Charles I, who retained the support of most of the students. When the Royalists finally fled Oxford, Cromwell made himself chancellor of the university to prevent it becoming a focus for resistance to his new Commonwealth.

There are other ancient royal connections with the area. Windsor Castle has been a residence of kings and queens for more than 900 years. It played a critical role in history in 1215, when King John set out from here to sign the Magna Carta at Runnymede on the Thames. Close by is a secondary royal residence, Frogmore. This is home to a mausoleum that contains the remains of Queen Victoria and Prince Albert and a cemetery where King Edward VIII and his wife, the Duchess of Windsor, are buried. Further north, Queen Anne had the lavish Blenheim Palace constructed for her military commander, the 1st Duke of Marlborough, John Churchill. Descendants of the duke still live at the palace, which was the birthplace of the wartime Prime Minister Winston Churchill. The palace, gardens and surrounding park are today all open to the public. Elizabeth I spent her childhood in the Tudor palace at

Signpost on the Ridgeway walk

Georgian shops in the town of Windsor

Hatfield, part of which still stands alongside the magnificent Jacobean mansion (Hatfield House), which was built for the influential Cecil family.

The twin attractions of a soft rural landscape and of living close to people of power persuaded other aristocrats to build homes in the vicinity. Today, many of these establishments welcome visitors. The Duke of Bedford was one of the first to open his house, Woburn Abbey, to the public, recognizing that this was the only way he could afford to continue living there. Stowe, now a public school, has kept its huge 18th-century landscaped garden, complete with classical temples and statuary. At Rousham, near Oxford, is a rare garden designed by William Kent. Luton Hoo, Cliveden, Knebworth House and Hughenden Manor (home of 19th-century Prime Minister Benjamin Disraeli) are other houses and gardens well worth visiting. Kelmscott House, by the Thames east of Oxford, was the long-time residence of the Victorian painter, designer, poet and early socialist William Morris.

In the eastern part of the region, St Albans contains the Roman city of

Sculptured concrete cows in a field near Milton Keynes, Buckinghamshire

Milton's Cottage, a museum dedicated to poet John Milton, Chalfont St Giles, Buckinghamshire

Verulamium, which boasts some of the best-preserved Roman remains in the Home Counties. The Roman theatre here is one of only six built in Britain, and the Verulamium Museum, within the walls of the ancient city, displays some marvellous mosaics. The cathedral, in the centre of the present town, contains wonderful examples of medieval architecture and extraordinary wall paintings. The Gardens of the Rose, the headquarters of the Royal National Rose Society, are on the outskirts of the city. Visiting the gardens in summer is a real treat, with over 1,500 rose varieties on display.

Many outdoor leisure activities can be pursued in this region. Long-distance walkers can choose between the Thames Path, which sticks to the flat ground close to the river bank, and the more strenuous Ridgeway. This ancient track offers spectacular views from the top of the ridge that runs from Wiltshire to Ivinghoe Beacon, which is in the Chiltern Hills near Tring. Stretches of the Thames are used for rowing, and the annual Royal Regatta at Henley-on-Thames (in July) is a highlight of the summer social season. This regatta has made Henley famous, and every year hundreds of enthusiastic spectators line the river banks. Amateur boating enthusiasts enjoy negotiating the picturesque canals and locks up to the river's navigable limit, which is at Lechlade, in Gloucestershire. Messing about in boats on the Thames was the subject of Jerome K Jerome's comic

Flock of ewes at tupping time on Ivinghoe Beacon in the Chiltern Hills, Buckinghamshire

classic *Three Men in a Boat* and of *The Wind in the Willows*, the ever-popular children's story by Kenneth Grahame, who lived by the river at Pangbourne.

Radcot Bridge – which was built using the local Taynton stone – near Kelmscott, Oxfordshire

Exploring the Thames Valley

THE PLEASANT COUNTRYSIDE of the Chiltern Hills and of the Thames Valley itself appealed to aristocrats who built stately homes close to London. Many of these are among the grandest in the country, including Hatfield House and Blenheim. Around these great houses grew picturesque villages, with half-timbered buildings and, as you move towards the Cotswolds, houses built in attractive buff-coloured stone. That the area has been inhabited for thousands of years is shown by the number of prehistoric remains, including the most remarkable chalk hillside figure, the White Horse of Uffington.

SIGHTS AT A GLANCE

Blenheim Palace pp246–7 **6**
Burford **2**
Gardens of the Rose **14**
Great Tew **1**
Hatfield House **12**
Hughendon Manor **15**
Kelmscott **3**
Knebworth House **11**
Luton Hoo **10**
Oxford pp238–43 **5**
St Albans **13**
Stowe **7**
Vale of the White Horse **4**
Whipsnade Wild Animal Park **9**
Windsor pp252–5 **17**
Woburn Abbey **8**

Walks and Tours
Touring the Thames **16**

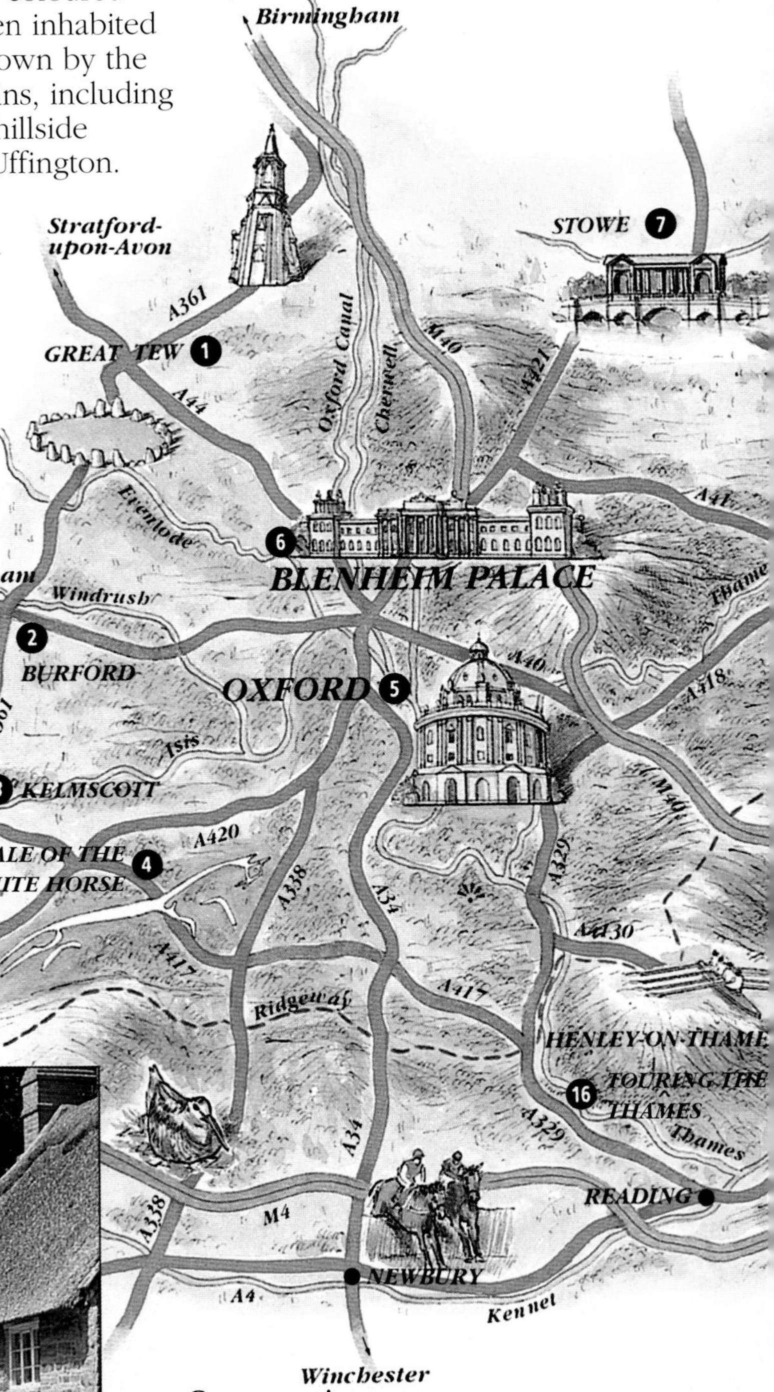

A thatched cottage, Upper Swarford, Banbury

GETTING AROUND

As an important commuter belt, the Thames Valley is well served by public transport, as well as a good network of motorways and major roads into London. InterCity trains travel to all the major towns and there are many coach services that run from London to the major sights and attractions.

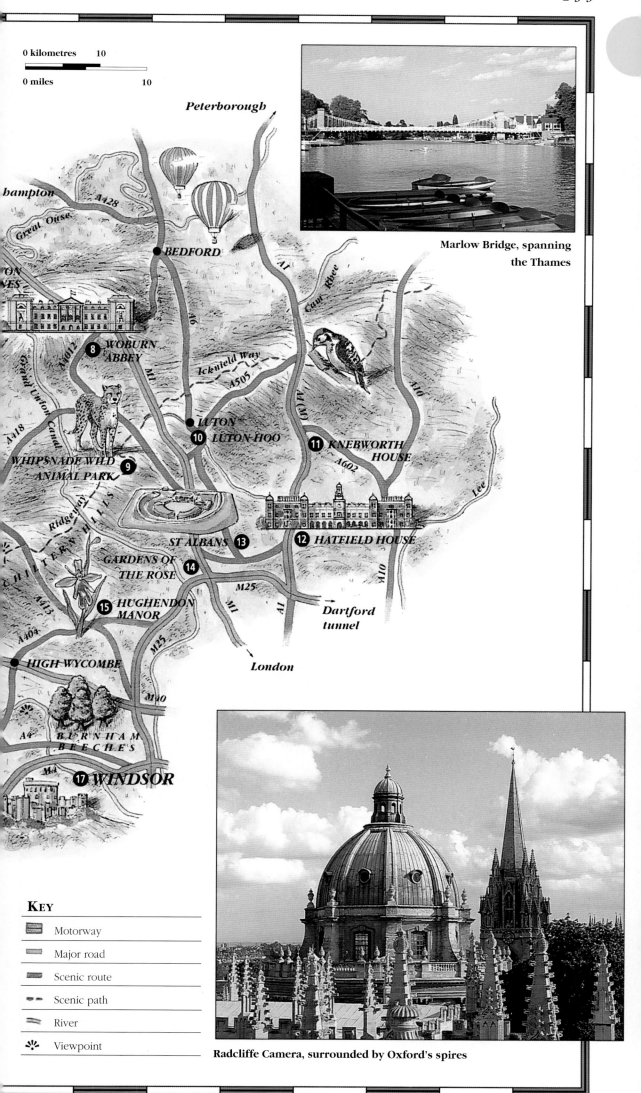

0 kilometres   10

0 miles   10

Peterborough

hampton

A428

Great Ouse

BEDFORD

A1

Caut River

A6

M1

**Marlow Bridge, spanning
the Thames**

8 *WOBURN
ABBEY*

A5012

Icknield Way

A505

A10

M1 (M)

Luton Canal

A418

LUTON

10 *LUTON HOO*

11 *KNEBWORTH
HOUSE*

A602

*WHIPSNADE WILD
ANIMAL PARK*

9

Lee

Ridgeway

CHILTERN HILLS

ST ALBANS **13**

12 *HATFIELD HOUSE*

*GARDENS OF
THE ROSE* **14**

A10

M25

A413

15 *HUGHENDON
MANOR*

M1

A1

*Dartford
tunnel*

A404

M25

HIGH WYCOMBE

London

M40

*BURNHAM
BEECHES*

A4

M4

17 *WINDSOR*

Radcliffe Camera, surrounded by Oxford's spires

KEY

▬	Motorway
▬	Major road
▬	Scenic route
▬	Scenic path
▬	River
☀	Viewpoint

Rowing and Regattas

THE BANKS OF THE RIVER THAMES are a hive of activity on most weekend mornings, as more than 70 rowing clubs turn out their boats, and rowers train on some of the best waters in Britain. To see this activity at its most concentrated, take a Sunday morning walk along the river at Putney, in London, where more than 10 clubs have their boathouses. This training is for a purpose – there are more than 270 regattas around the country, with some 80 races held on the River Thames throughout the year, from the University Boat Race in March to the Fours Head of the River Race in November.

The University Boat Race pits two of Britain's leading universities, Oxford and Cambridge, against each other. The two crews have eight oarsmen each.

THE HENLEY ROYAL REGATTA

This five-day event is one of the key dates in the British social calendar *(see p70)*. First held in 1939, it has taken place annually ever since, except during World War II. As the Regatta was instituted before any national or international rowing federation was established, it occupies a unique slot in the world of rowing, and attracts more than 500 crews from all over the world.

The hundreds of boats that compete at Henley are kept in large boat tents. The tents are also used by the athletes to get away from the hubbub of the regatta.

Picnicking on the banks of the most beautiful stretch of the Thames at the Henley Regatta is a truly British summer experience.

The River and Rowing Museum at Henley explores the history of the Thames and its influence on riverside towns and wildlife. It also covers, of course, all aspects of rowing.

The first women's full regatta event *of the whole course at Henley was in 1993, when a new event for women's single sculls was introduced.*

The Head of the River Race course runs for 4¼ miles (6.8 km) from Mortlake to Putney, London.

The course at Henley is 1 mile 550 yds (2,113 m) long and always lined with spectators.

The Great River Race is held in September over a 22-mile (35.5-km) course from Richmond to Greenwich Pier in London. More than 150 traditional boats take part and the impressive flotilla includes skiffs, gigs, dragon boats, canoes and curraghs.

THAMES ROWING YEAR

SPRING

Head of the River (Mar)
Kingston Head (Mar)
Veterans Head (Mar)
Women's Head of
    the River (Mar)
University Boat Race
    (Mar/Apr)
Sculler's Head (Apr)
Veteran Sculler's Head (Apr)
Chiswick Regatta (May)
Marlow Spring Regatta (May)
Putney Amateur Regatta (May)
Putney Town Regatta (May)

SUMMER

Barnes and Mortlake
    Regatta (Jun)
Henley Women's Regatta (Jun)
London Docklands
    Regatta (Jun)
Marlow Regatta (Jun)
Reading Regatta (Jun)
Richmond Regatta (Jun)
Henley Royal Regatta (Jun/Jul)
Henley Town Regatta (Jul)
Henley Veteran's Regatta (Jul)
Kingston Regatta (Jul)
Staines Regatta (Jul)
Hammersmith Summer
    Regatta (Aug)

AUTUMN

Great River Race (Sep)
Henley Sculler's Head (Oct)
Marlow Long Distance
    Sculls (Oct)
Pairs Head (Oct)
Reading Small Boats
    Head (Oct)
Upper Thames Four and
    Small Boats Head (Oct)
Weybridge Silver Sculls (Oct)
Head of the River Fours (Nov)
Kingston Small Boats
    Head (Nov)
Marlow Fours and Pairs
    Head (Nov)

WINTER

Tideway Small Boats
    Head (Dec)
Walton Small Boats
    Head (Dec)
Hampton Head (Jan)
Henley Fours Head (Feb)

Great Tew ❶

Oxfordshire. 🏘 *250.* 🚉 *Oxford then taxi.* ℹ *8 Horsefair, Banbury (01295 259855).*

THIS SECLUDED village of ironstone was founded in the 1630s by Lord Falkland for estate workers. It was heavily restored between 1809 and 1811 in the Gothic style then fashionable. Thatched cottages stand in gardens with clipped box hedges, and in the centre of the village is the 17th-century pub, the **Falkland Arms**, which retains its original period atmosphere.

ENVIRONS: Five miles (8 km) west are the **Rollright Stones**, three Bronze Age monuments. They comprise a stone circle of 77 stones, about 30 m (100 ft) in diameter, known as the King's Men; the remains of a burial chamber called the Whispering Knights; and the solitary King Stone.
  Further north is **Banbury**, well known for its spicy flat cakes and its market cross, immortalized in the nursery rhyme, *Ride a Cock-horse to*

The 19th-century Banbury Cross

Banbury Cross. The original medieval cross was destroyed but it was replaced in 1859.

🍴 **Falkland Arms**
Great Tew. ☎ *01608 683653.* ◯ *daily.* ⬤ *25 Dec.* 🍴

Burford ❷

Oxfordshire. 🏘 *1,000.* ℹ *Sheep St (01993 823558).*

A CHARMING SMALL town, Burford has hardly changed from Georgian times, when it was an important coach stop between Oxford and the West Country. Cotswold stone houses, inns and shops, many built in the 16th century, line its main street. **Tolsey Hall** is a Tudor house with an open ground floor where stalls are still set up. The house is located on the corner of Sheep Street, itself a reminder of the importance of the medieval wool trade *(see p217).*

ENVIRONS: Just east of Burford is **Swinbrook**, whose church contains the Fettiplace Monuments, six carved figures from the Tudor and Stuart periods.

Two miles (3 km) beyond are the ruins of **Minster Lovell Hall**, a 15th-century manor house whose unusual dovecote survives intact.
  Witney, further west, has a town hall dating from 1730. On its outskirts **Cogges Manor Farm**, founded in the 13th-century, has been restored to its Victorian state and is now a museum of farm life.

🏛 **Minster Lovell Hall**
Minster Lovell. ☎ *01732 778027.* ◯ *daily.*
🏛 **Cogges Manor Farm**
Witney. ☎ *01993 772602.* ◯ *Apr–Oct: Tue–Sun & public hols.* ♿

Kelmscott ❸

Oxfordshire. 🏘 *100.* ℹ *Faringdon (01367 242191).*

THE IMAGINATIVE designer and writer William Morris lived in this pretty Thameside village from 1871 until his death in 1896. He shared his house, the classic Elizabethan **Kelmscott Manor**, with fellow painter Dante Gabriel Rossetti (1828–82), who left after an affair with Morris's wife Jane – the model for many pre-Raphaelite paintings.
  Morris and his followers in the Arts and Crafts movement *(see p29)* were attracted by

Cotswold stone houses, Burford, Oxfordshire

The formal entrance of the Elizabethan Kelmscott Manor

the medieval feel of the village and several cottages were later built in Morris's memory.

Today Kelmscott Manor has works of art by members of the movement – including some William de Morgan tiles. Morris is buried in the village churchyard, with a tomb designed by Philip Webb.

Two miles (3 km) to the east is **Radcot Bridge**, the oldest bridge still standing over the Thames. Built in 1160 from the local Taynton stone, it was a strategic river crossing, and in 1387 was damaged in a battle between Richard II and his barons. In the 17th and 18th centuries, Taynton stone was shipped from here to London in the building boom.

🏛 Kelmscott Manor

Kelmscott. 📞 01367 252486. ⬜ Apr–Sep: Wed, one Sat in each month. 📷 ♿ limited.

Vale of the White Horse 4

Oxfordshire. 🚆 Didcot. 🅸 25 Bridge St, Abingdon (01235 522711).

THIS LOVELY VALLEY gets its name from the huge chalk horse, 100 m (350 ft) from nose to tail, carved into the hillside above Uffington. It is believed to be Britain's oldest hillside carving and has sparked many legends: some say it was cut by the Saxon leader Hengist (whose name means stallion in German), while others believe it has more to do with Alfred the Great (see p51), thought to have been born nearby.

It is, however, a great deal older than either of these stories suggest, having been dated at around 3000 BC.

Nearby is the Celtic earth ramparts of the Iron Age hill fort, **Uffington Castle**. A mile (1.5 km) west along the Ridgeway, an ancient trade route,

(see p37), is an even older monument, a large Stone Age burial mound which is known as **Wayland's Smithy**. This is immersed in legends that Sir Walter Scott (see p622) used in his novel *Kenilworth*.

The best view of the horse is to be had from Uffington village which is also worth visiting for the **Tom Brown's School Museum**. This 17th-century school house contains exhibits devoted to the author Thomas Hughes (1822–96). Hughes set the early chapters of his Victorian novel, *Tom Brown's Schooldays*, here. The museum also contains material about excavations on White Horse Hill.

🏛 Tom Brown's School Museum

Broad St, Uffington. 🅸 01367 820259. ⬜ Easter–Oct: Sat, Sun & public hols (pm). 📷 ♿ limited.

HILLSIDE CHALK FIGURES

It was the Celts who first saw the potential for creating large-scale artworks on the chalk hills of southern England. Horses – held in high regard by both the Celts and later the Saxons, and the objects of cult worship – were often a favourite subject, but people were also depicted, notably Cerne Abbas, Dorset (see p295) and the Long Man of Wilmington (see p180). The figures may have served as religious symbols or as landmarks by which tribes identified their territory. Many chalk figures have been obliterated, because without any attention they are quickly overrun by grass. Uffington is "scoured", to prevent encroachment by grass, a tradition once accompanied by a fair and other festivities. There was a second flush of hillside carving in the 18th century, especially in Wiltshire. In some cases – for instance at Bratton Castle near Westbury – an 18th-century carving has been superimposed on an ancient one.

Britain's oldest hillside carving, the White Horse of Uffington

Street-by-Street: Oxford ⑤

OXFORD HAS LONG BEEN a strategic point on the western routes into London – its name describes its position as a convenient spot for crossing the river (a ford for oxen). The city's first scholars, who founded the university, came from France in 1167. The development of England's first university created the spectacular skyline of tall towers and "dreaming spires".

Old Ashmolean
Now the Museum of the History of Science, this resplendent building was designed in 1683 to show Elias Ashmole's collection of curiosities. The displays were moved in 1845.

The Ashmolean Museum
displays one of Britain's foremost collections of fine art and antiquities.

St John's College

Balliol College

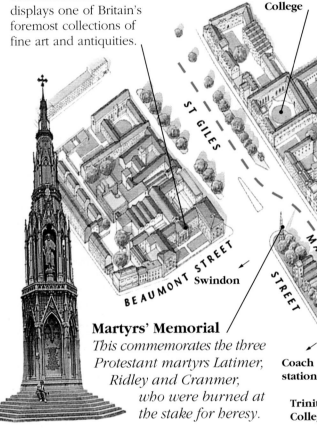

ST GILES

BEAUMONT STREET   *Swindon*

MAGDALEN STREET

BROAD STREET

TURL

BRAS

Martyrs' Memorial
This commemorates the three Protestant martyrs Latimer, Ridley and Cranmer, who were burned at the stake for heresy.

Coach station

Trinity College

CORNMARKET STREET

MARKET STREET

STR

0 metres	100
0 yards	100

KEY

– – – Suggested route

Oxford Story

Jesus College

Lincoln College

Covered market

Railway station

All Saints Church

ST ALD

ℹ

Museum of Oxford

PERCY BYSSHE SHELLEY

Shelley (1792–1822), one of the Romantic poets *(see p424),* attended University College, Oxford, but was expelled after writing the revolutionary pamphlet *The Necessity of Atheism.* Despite that disgrace, the college has put up a marble memorial to him.

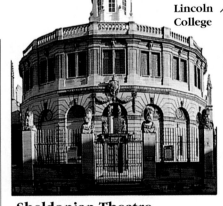

Sheldonian Theatre
The first building designed by Wren (see p120) is the scene of Oxford University's traditional degree-giving ceremonies.

STAR SIGHTS

★ **Radcliffe Camera**

★ **Christ Church**

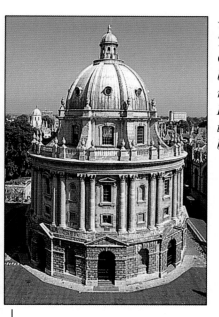

★ Radcliffe Camera
This Classical rotunda is Oxford's most distinctive building and is now a reading room of the Bodleian. It was one of the library's original buildings (see p243).

VISITORS' CHECKLIST

Oxfordshire. 130,000. Botley Rd. Gloucester Green. Gloucester Green (01865 726871). Wed, Thu (flea market). St Giles Fair: Sep.

Bridge of Sighs
A copy of the steeply arched bridge in Venice, this picturesque landmark, built in 1914, joins the old and new buildings of Hertford College.

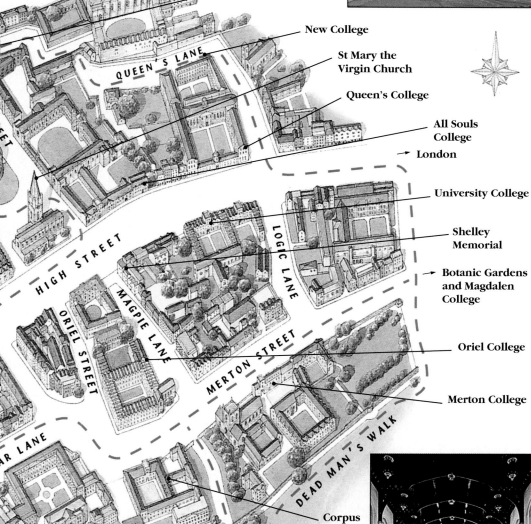

New College

St Mary the Virgin Church

Queen's College

All Souls College

→ London

University College

Shelley Memorial

→ Botanic Gardens and Magdalen College

Oriel College

Merton College

Corpus Christi College

★ Christ Church
Students still eat at long tables in all the college halls. Fellows (professors) sit at the high table and grace is always said in Latin.

Exploring Oxford

OXFORD IS MORE than just a university city; it has one of Britain's most important car factories in the suburb of Cowley. Despite this, Oxford is dominated by institutions related to its huge academic community: like Blackwell's bookshop which has over 20,000 titles in stock. The two rivers, the Cherwell and the Isis (the name given to the Thames as it flows through the city), provide lovely riverside walks, or you can hire a punt and spend an afternoon on the Cherwell.

A bust on the Sheldonian Theatre

🏛 Ashmolean Museum

Beaumont St. ☎ 01865 278000. ⭘ Tue–Sun & public hols. ● 25–28 Dec, 1 Jan, Good Fri. ♿ ✔ Tues, Fri, Sat. ▱ ▯

One of the best museums in Britain outside London, the Ashmolean – the first purpose-built museum in England – was opened in 1683, based on a display known internationally as "The Ark" collected by the two John Tradescants, father and son.

On their many voyages to the Orient and the Americas they collected stuffed animals and tribal artefacts, the like of which had never before been displayed in England. The collection was acquired on their death by the antiquarian Elias Ashmole, who donated it to the university and had a building made for the exhibits on Broad Street – the Old Ashmolean, now the Museum of the History of Science.

During the 19th century part of the Tradescant collection was moved to the University Galleries, a magnificent Neo-Classical building of 1845. This greatly expanded museum is now known as the Ashmolean.

However, what is left of the original curio collection is overshadowed by the other exhibits in the museum, in particular the paintings and drawings. These include Bellini's *St Jerome Reading in a Landscape* (late 15th century); Raphael's *Heads of Two Apostles* (1519); Turner's *Venice: The Grand Canal* (1840); Rembrandt's *Saskia Asleep* (1635); Michelangelo's *Crucifixion* (1557), Picasso's *Blue Roofs* (1901) and a large group of Pre-Raphaelites, including Rossetti, Millais and Holman Hunt. There are also fine Greek and Roman carvings and a collection of stringed musical instruments. Items of more local interest include a Rowlandson watercolour of Radcliffe Square in about 1790 and the Oxford Crown. This silver coin was minted here during the Civil War in 1644 *(see p56)* when Charles I was based in Oxford, and forms part of the second largest coin collection in Britain. Perhaps the single most important item is the gold enamelled ring known as the Alfred Jewel *(see p51)*, which is over 1,000 years old.

The entrance to the Ashmolean Museum

🌿 Botanic Gardens

Rose Lane. ☎ 01865 276920. ⭘ daily. ● 25 Dec, Good Fri. 🎫 Jun–Aug. ♿ 📷

Britain's oldest botanic garden was founded in 1621 – one ancient yew tree survives from that period. The ornate entrance gates were designed by Nicholas Stone in 1633 and paid for, like the garden itself, by the Earl of Danby. His statue adorns the gate, along with those of Charles I and Charles II. Though small, the garden is a delightful spot for a stroll, with well-labelled flower beds in the original walled garden and a newer section with a herbaceous border and a rock garden.

The 17th-century Botanic Gardens

🗼 Carfax Tower

Carfax Sq. ☎ 01865 792653. ⭘ daily. ● 24–26 Dec, 1 Jan, Good Fri. 🎫 📷 ▯

The tower is all that remains of the 14th-century Church of St Martin, demolished in 1896 so that the adjoining road could be widened. Be there to watch the clock strike the quarter hours, and climb to the top for a panoramic view of the city. Carfax was the crossing point of the original north-to-south and east-to-west routes through Oxford and the word comes from the French *quatre voies,* or "four ways".

🎵 Holywell Music Room

Holywell St. ⭘ concerts only. 🎫 ♿

This was the first building in Europe designed, in 1752, specifically for public musical performances. Previously, concerts had been held in private houses for invited guests only. Its two splendid chandeliers originally adorned Westminster Hall at the coronation of George IV in 1820, and were given by the king to Wadham College, of which the music room technically forms a part. The room is regularly used for contemporary and classical concerts.

🏛 Museum of Oxford

St Aldate. 01865 815559. Tue–Sun. 25, 26 Dec, 1 Jan.

A well-organized display in the Victorian town hall illustrates the long history of Oxford and its university. Exhibits include a Roman pottery kiln and a town seal from 1191.

The main features are a series of well-reconstructed rooms, including one from an Elizabethan inn and an 18th-century student's room.

🏛 Martyrs' Memorial

This commemorates the three Protestants burned at the stake on Broad Street – Bishops Latimer and Ridley in 1555, and Archbishop Cranmer in 1556. On the accession of Queen Mary in 1553 (see p55), they were committed to the Tower of London, then sent to Oxford to defend their views before the doctors of divinity who, after the hearing, condemned them as heretics.

The memorial was designed in 1843 by George Gilbert Scott and based on the Eleanor crosses erected in 12 English towns by Edward I (1239–1307) to honour his queen.

🏛 Oxford Story

6 Broad St. 01865 728822. daily. 25 Dec.

This audio-visual account of the city's history has a train ride through exhibits which are brought to life with animated, life-size models of major historical characters.

🏛 St Mary the Virgin Church

High St. 01865 279111. daily.

This, the official church of the university, is said to be the most visited parish church in England. The oldest parts date from the early 14th century and include the tower, from the top of which you can enjoy a fine view. Its Congregation House, of the same date, served as the university's first library until the Bodleian was founded in 1488 (see p243). The church is where the three Oxford Martyrs were pronounced heretics in 1555. The architectural highlight of the church is the Baroque south porch, constructed in 1637.

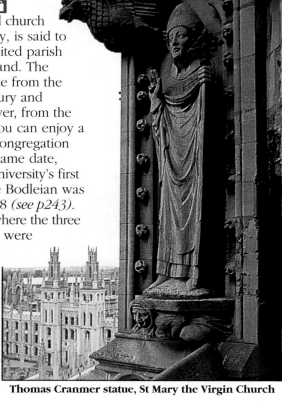

Thomas Cranmer statue, St Mary the Virgin Church

🏛 University Museum and Pitt Rivers Museum

Parks Rd. 01865 272950. daily (pm). 24–26 Dec, Easter Thu–Sat. limited.

Two of Oxford's most interesting museums adjoin each other. The first is a museum of natural history containing relics of dinosaurs as well as a stuffed dodo. This flightless bird has been extinct since the 17th century, but was immortalized by Lewis Carroll (an Oxford mathematics lecturer whose real name was Charles Dodgson) in his book *Alice in Wonderland (see p467)*. The exhibits are housed in a large Victorian building with cast-iron columns which support a glass roof leading to a cavernous interior. This leads into the Pitt Rivers Museum,

which has one of the world's most extensive ethnographic collections – masks and tribal totems from Africa and the Far East – and archaeological displays, including exhibits collected by the explorer Captain Cook. An annexe on Banbury Road has an unusual collection of musical instruments, with audio equipment so you can hear them playing.

🏛 Sheldonian Theatre

Broad St. 01865 277299. Mon–Sat. 23 Dec–4 Jan, Easter & public hols.

Completed in 1669, this was the first building designed by Christopher Wren (see p120). It was paid for by Gilbert Sheldon, the Archbishop of Canterbury, as a place to hold university degree ceremonies. The Classical design of the oval building is based on the Theatre of Marcellus in Rome. The octagonal cupola – larger than the original – was built in 1838 and there is a very famous view from its huge Lantern. In the theatre the beautifully painted ceiling depicts the triumph of religion, art and science over envy, hatred and malice.

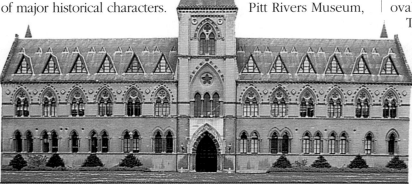

The impressive frontage of the University Museum and Pitt Rivers Museum

Exploring Oxford University

MANY OF THE 36 COLLEGES which go to make up the university were founded between the 13th and 16th centuries and cluster around the city centre. As scholarship was then the exclusive preserve of the church, the colleges were designed along the lines of monastic buildings but were often surrounded by beautiful gardens. Although most colleges have been altered over the years, many still incorporate a lot of their original features.

The spectacular view of All Souls College from St Mary's Church

All Souls College
Founded in 1438 on the High Street by Henry VI, the chapel on the college's north side has a classic hammerbeam roof, unusual misericords *(see p391)* on the choir stalls and 15th-century stained glass.

Christ Church College
The best way to view this, the largest of the Oxford colleges, is to approach through the meadows from St Aldate's. Christ Church dates from 1525 when Cardinal Wolsey founded it as an ecclesiastical college to train cardinals. The upper part of the tower in Tom Quad – a rectangular courtyard – was built by Wren *(see p120)* in 1682 and is the largest in the city. When its bell, Great Tom, was hung in 1648, the college had 101 students, which is why the bell is rung 101 times at 9:05pm, to mark the curfew for students (which has not been enforced since 1963). The odd timing is because night falls here five minutes later than at Greenwich *(see p135)*. Christ Church has produced 16 British prime ministers in the last 200 years. Beside the main quad is the 12th-century Christ Church Cathedral, one of the smallest in England.

Lincoln College
One of the best-preserved of the medieval colleges, it was founded in 1427 on Turl Street, and the front quad and façade are 15th century. The hall still has its original roof, including the gap where smoke used to escape. The Jacobean chapel is notable for its stained glass. John Wesley *(see p311)* was at college here and his rooms, now a chapel, can be visited.

Magdalen College
At the end of the High Street is perhaps the most typical and beautiful Oxford college. Its 15th-century quads in contrasting styles are set in a park by the Cherwell, crossed by Magdalen Bridge. Every May Day at 6am, the college choir sings from the top of Magdalen's bell tower (1508) – a 16th-century custom to mark the start of summer.

New College
One of the grandest colleges, it was founded by William of Wykeham *(see p170)* in 1379 to educate clergy to replace those killed by the Black Death of 1348 *(see p53)*.

Magdalen Bridge spanning the River Cherwell

Its magnificent chapel on New College Lane, restored in the 19th century, has vigorous 14th-century misericords and El Greco's (1541–1614) famous painting of *St James*.

Queen's College
Most of the college buildings date from the 18th century and represent some of the finest work from that period in Oxford. Its superb library was built in 1695 by Henry Aldrich (1647–1710) The front screen with its bell-topped gatehouse is a feature of the High Street.

STUDENT LIFE

Students belong to individual colleges and usually live in them for the duration of their course. The university gives lectures, sets exams and awards degrees but much of the students' tuition and social life is based around their college. Many university traditions date back hundreds of years, like the graduation ceremonies at the Sheldonian which are still held in Latin.

Graduation at the Sheldonian *(see p240)*

Merton College seen from Christ Church Meadows

St John's College

The impressive frontage on St Giles dates from 1437, when it was founded for Cistercian scholars. The old library has lovely 17th-century bookcases and stained glass, while the Baylie Chapel has a display of 15th-century vestments.

Trinity College

The oldest part of the college on Broad Street, Durham Quad, is named after the earlier college of 1296 which was incorporated into Trinity in 1555. The late 17th-century chapel has a magnificent reredos and wooden screen.

Corpus Christi College

The whole of the charming front quad on Merton Street dates from 1517, when the college was founded. The quad's sundial, topped by a pelican – the college symbol – bears an early 17th-century calendar. The chapel has a rare 16th-century eagle lectern.

Merton College

Off Merton Street, this is the oldest college (1264) in Oxford. Much of its hall dates from then, including a sturdy decorated door. The chapel choir contains allegorical reliefs representing music, arithmetic, rhetoric and grammar. Merton's Mob Quad served as a model for the later colleges.

BODLEIAN LIBRARY

Founded in 1320, the library was expanded in 1426 by Humphrey, Duke of Gloucester (1391–1447) and brother of Henry VI, when his collection of manuscripts would not fit into the old library. It was refounded in 1602 by Thomas Bodley, a wealthy scholar, who insisted on strict rules: the keeper was forbidden to marry. The library is one of the six copyright deposit libraries in the country – it is entitled to receive a copy of every book published in Britain.

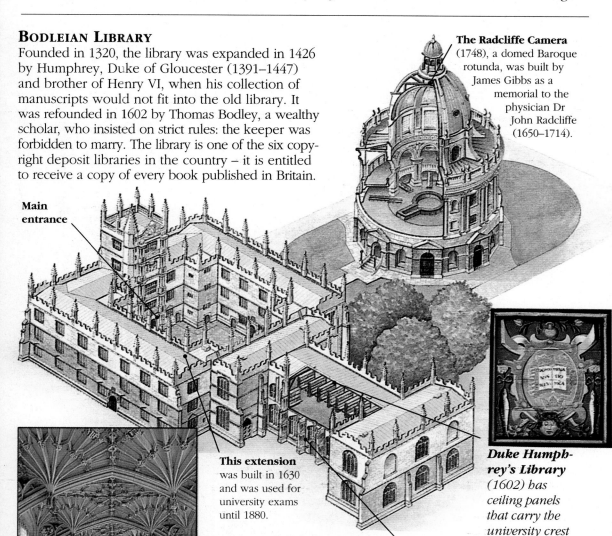

The Radcliffe Camera (1748), a domed Baroque rotunda, was built by James Gibbs as a memorial to the physician Dr John Radcliffe (1650–1714).

Main entrance

This extension was built in 1630 and was used for university exams until 1880.

The Divinity School *(1488) has a unique vaulted ceiling with 455 carved bosses representing biblical scenes and both mythical and real beasts – one of the country's finest Gothic interiors.*

Duke Humphrey's Library *(1602) has ceiling panels that carry the university crest and Latin motto* Dominus Illuminatio Mea – *the Lord, my Light.*

Blenheim Palace ❻

AFTER JOHN CHURCHILL, the 1st Duke of Marlborough, defeated the French at the Battle of Blenheim in 1704, Queen Anne gave him the Manor of Woodstock and had this palatial house built for him in gratitude. Designed by both Nicholas Hawksmoor and Sir John Vanbrugh *(see p462)*, it is a Baroque masterpiece. It was also the birthplace of Britain's World War II leader, Winston Churchill, in 1874.

Winston Churchill and his wife, Clementine

★ **Long Library**
This 55 m (183 ft) room was designed by Vanbrugh as a picture gallery. The portraits include one of Queen Anne by Sir Godfrey Kneller (1646–1723). The stucco on the ceiling is by Isaac Mansfield (1725).

The Grand Bridge was built in 1708. It has a 31 m (101 ft) main span and contains rooms within its structure.

Chapel
The marble monument to the 1st Duke of Marlborough and his family was sculpted by Michael Rysbrack in 1733.

Water Terrace Gardens
These magnificent gardens were laid out in the 1920s by French architect Achille Duchêne in 17th-century style, with detailed patterned beds and fountains.

STAR SIGHTS

★ **Long Library**

★ **Saloon**

★ **Park and Gardens**

◁ **Burnham Beeches forest, Buckinghamshire, in autumn**

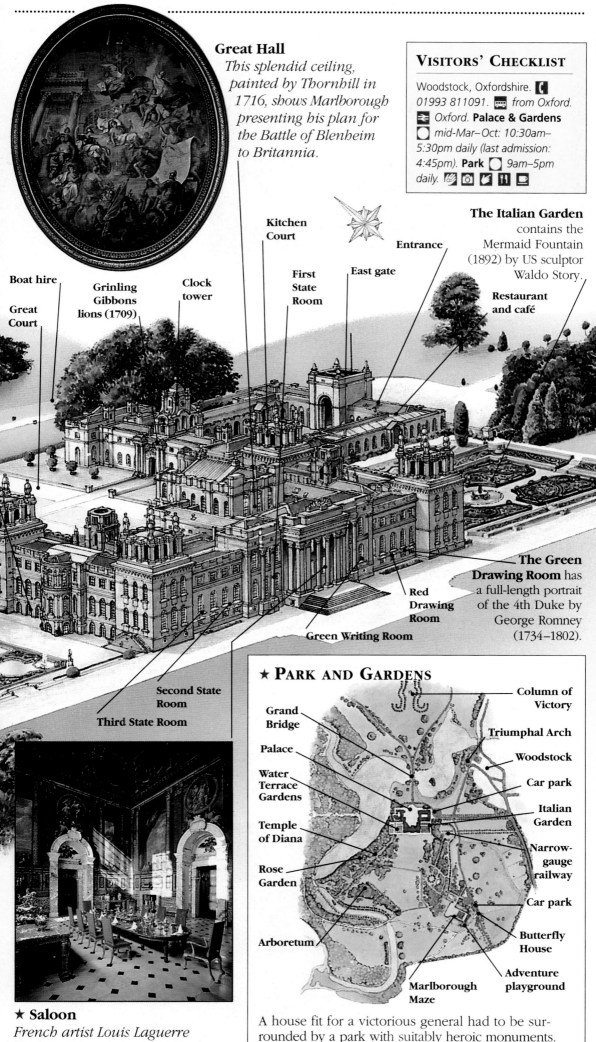

Great Hall
This splendid ceiling, painted by Thornhill in 1716, shows Marlborough presenting his plan for the Battle of Blenheim to Britannia.

VISITORS' CHECKLIST

Woodstock, Oxfordshire. 01993 811091. from Oxford. Oxford. **Palace & Gardens** mid-Mar–Oct: 10:30am–5:30pm daily (last admission: 4:45pm). **Park** 9am–5pm daily.

The Italian Garden
contains the Mermaid Fountain (1892) by US sculptor Waldo Story.

Kitchen Court

Entrance

East gate

First State Room

Restaurant and café

Boat hire

Grinling Gibbons lions (1709)

Clock tower

Great Court

The Green Drawing Room has a full-length portrait of the 4th Duke by George Romney (1734–1802).

Red Drawing Room

Green Writing Room

Second State Room

Third State Room

★ **PARK AND GARDENS**

Grand Bridge

Palace

Water Terrace Gardens

Temple of Diana

Rose Garden

Arboretum

Column of Victory

Triumphal Arch

Woodstock

Car park

Italian Garden

Narrow-gauge railway

Car park

Butterfly House

Adventure playground

Marlborough Maze

★ **Saloon**
French artist Louis Laguerre (1663–1721) painted the detailed scenes on the walls and ceiling of the state dining room.

A house fit for a victorious general had to be surrounded by a park with suitably heroic monuments. They were kept when Capability Brown *(see p27)* re-landscaped the park in 1764 and created the lake.

Canaletto's *Entrance to the Arsenal* (1730) hangs at Woburn Abbey

Stowe ⑦

(NT) Buckingham, Buckinghamshire.
📞 01280 822850. 🚉 Milton Keynes
then bus. ◑ school hols: daily;
termtime: Mon, Wed, Fri, & Sun.
● 1 Nov–10 Dec, 24 Dec–20 Mar.
🎫 ♿ limited. 🖥 🏠

THIS IS THE MOST ambitious
and important landscaped
garden in Britain as well as
also being one of the finest
examples of the 18th-century
passion for trying to shape and
improve on nature to make it
conform to fashionable
notions of taste (see pp26–7).

In the space of nearly 100
years the original garden, first
laid out around 1680, was
enlarged and transformed by
the addition of monuments,
Greek and Gothic temples,
grottoes, statues, ornamental
bridges, artificial lakes and
"natural" tree plantings.

Most of the leading designers
and architects of the period
contributed to the design,
including Sir John Vanbrugh,
James Gibbs and Capability
Brown (see pp26–7) who was
head gardener at Stowe for 10
years, at the start of his career.

From 1593 to 1921 the huge
property was owned outright
by the Temple and Grenville
families – later the Dukes of
Buckingham – until the large
Palladian house at its centre
was sold and converted into
an elite boys' public school.

The family were soldiers
and politicians in the liberal
tradition, and many of the
buildings and sculptures in
the garden symbolize Utopian
ideals of democracy and free-
dom. There are temples of
British Worthies, of Ancient
Virtue, of Concord and Victory,
the Fane (temple) of Pastoral
Poetry and the Elysian fields.
Some of these features deteriorated in the 19th century and
many statues were sold. But a
comprehensive restoration
programme has meant that
statues have been bought back
and copies made of others.

Woburn Abbey ⑧

Woburn, Bedfordshire. 📞 01525
290666. 🚉 Bletchley then taxi.
◑ Mar–Sep: daily; Jan, Feb, Oct: Sat,
Sun. ● Nov–Dec. 🎫 ♿ ring first.
📷 by arrangement. 🏠

THE DUKES OF BEDFORD have
lived here for over 350
years and were among the first
owners of an English stately
home to open their house to
the public some 40 years ago.

The abbey was built in the
mid-18th century on the foundations of a large 12th-century
Cistercian monastery. Its mix
of styles range from Henry
Flitcroft and Henry Holland
(see p28). It's is also popular
for its 142 ha (350 acre) safari
park and attractive deer park

with nine species including the
Milu, originally the imperial
herd of China.

Its magnificent state apartments house an important
private art collection with
works by Reynolds (1723–92)
and Canaletto (1697–1768).

Whipsnade Wild Animal Park ⑨

Nr Dunstable, Bedfordshire.
📞 01582 872171. 🚃 Whipsnade.
(Victoria Station, London: May–Oct.)
◑ daily. ● 25 Dec. 🎫 ♿ 📷 🖥

THE RURAL BRANCH of London
Zoo, this was one of the
first zoos to minimise the use
of cages and devise areas
where wild animals could be
confined safely but without
too much constriction.

At 240 ha (600 acres), it is
Europe's largest conservation
park, with more than 3,000
species. You can drive through
some areas, or try the steam
train that travels around the
park. Also popular are the
adventure playground and
sea lions' underwater display.

Luton Hoo ⑩

Luton, Bedfordshire. 📞 01582
722955. ● closed to the public.

SINCE ROBERT ADAM designed
it in 1767, the house has
undergone a transformation.
In 1903 Sir Julius Wernher,
who made a fortune from
South African diamond mines,
rebuilt it in a French classical
style, using the same architects
as the Ritz Hotel (see p87).

The 17th-century Palladian bridge over the Octagon Lake in Stowe Park

Hatfield House, one of the largest Jacobean mansions in the country

There is also a pleasant park landscaped by Capability Brown *(see pp26–7)*.

Until 1997 it was the home of the Wernher family. Lady Zia Wernher, a descendant of the czars, inherited items from the royal Russian treasures, including some exquisite Fabergé jewellery.

The Wernher art collection, which includes paintings by Sargent (1856–1925) and Titian (1488–1576) along with rare medieval ivories, is now in the hands of Somerset House *(see p86)*. Plans are being made to turn Luton Hoo itself into an up-market hotel.

Knebworth House ⑪

Knebworth, Hertfordshire.
☎ 01438 812661. ☒ Stevenage then taxi. ◯ 27 Mar–11 Apr: daily; 17 Apr–23 May: Sat, Sun & public hols; 29 May–5 Sep: daily; 11 Sep– 26 Sep: Sat, Sun & public hols. 🖼️ 🔖 limited. 🗓️ 🏠

A NOTABLE TUDOR mansion, with a beautiful Jacobean banqueting hall, Knebworth was overlain with a 19th-century Gothic exterior by Lord Lytton, the head of one of the most colourful families in Victorian England.

His eldest son, the 1st Earl of Lytton, was Viceroy of India, and several exhibits illustrate the Delhi Durbar of 1877, when Queen Victoria became Empress of India. Constance Lytton was a leading member of the suffragette movement during the 1920s *(see p62)*.

Hatfield House ⑫

Hatfield, Hertfordshire. ☎ 01707 262823. ☒ Hatfield. ◯ Apr–Sep: Tue–Thu, Sat, Sun & public hols. 🖼️ 🔖 🍴 🏠

O NE OF ENGLAND's finest Jacobean houses, it was built mainly between 1607 and 1611 for the powerful statesman Robert Cecil.

Its chief historical interest, though, lies in the surviving wing of the original Tudor Hatfield Palace, where Queen Elizabeth I *(see pp50–51)* spent much of her childhood. She held her first Council of State here when she was crowned in 1558. The palace, which was partly demolished in 1607 to make way for the new house, contains mementoes of her life, including the *Rainbow* portrait painted around 1600 by Isaac Oliver. Visitors can also attend medieval banquets held in its Great Hall.

The house has one of the few 17th-century gardens to survive, laid out by Robert Cecil with help from John Tradescant *(see p240)*.

FAMOUS PURITANS

18th-century engraving of John Bunyan

Three major figures connected with the 17th-century Puritan movement are celebrated in the Thames area. John Bunyan (1628–88), who wrote the allegorical tale *The Pilgrim's Progress*, was born at Elstow, near Bedford. A passionate Puritan orator, he was jailed for his beliefs for 17 years. The Bunyan Museum in Bedford is a former site of Puritan worship. William Penn (1644–1718), founder of Pennsylvania in the USA, lived, worshipped and is buried at Jordans, near Beaconsfield. A bit further north at Chalfont St Giles is the cottage where the poet John Milton (1608–74) stayed to escape London's plague. There he completed his greatest work, *Paradise Lost*. The house is now a museum based on his life and works.

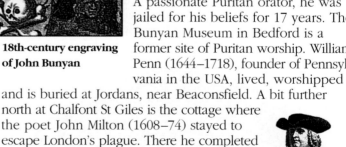

William Penn, founder of Pennsylvania

John Milton painted by Pieter van der Plas

St Albans ⑬

Today a thriving market town and a base for London commuters, St Albans was for centuries at the heart of some of the most stirring events in English history. A regional capital of ancient Britain, it became a major Roman settlement and then a key ecclesiastical centre – so important that during the Wars of the Roses *(see p53)*, two battles were fought for it. In 1455 the Yorkists drove King Henry VI from the town and six years later the Lancastrians retook it.

The martyr St Alban

Exploring St Albans

Part of the appeal of this ancient and fascinating town, little more than an hour's drive from London, is that its 2,000-year history can be traced vividly by visiting a few sites within easy walking distance of one another. There is a large car park within the walls of the Roman city of Verulamium, between the museum and St Michael's Church and across the road from the excavated theatre. From there it is a pleasant lakeside walk across the park, passing more Roman sites, Ye Olde Fighting Cocks inn, the massive cathedral and the historic High Street. Marking the centre of the town, the High Street is lined with several Tudor buildings and a clock tower dating from 1412, from which the curfew bell used to ring at 4am in the morning and 8:30pm at night.

⋔ Verulamium

Just outside the city centre are the walls of Verulamium, one of the first British cities the Romans established after their invasion of Britain in AD 43. Boadicea *(see p203)* razed it to the ground during her unsuccessful rebellion against the Romans in AD 62, but its position on Watling Street, an important trading route, meant that it was quickly rebuilt on an even larger scale and the city flourished until 410.

🏛 Verulamium Museum

St Michael's. ☎ *01727 866100.* ◯ *daily.* ● *25, 26 Dec.* 🚫 ♿
This excellent museum tells the story of the city, but its main attraction is its splendid collection of well-preserved Roman artefacts, notably some breathtaking mosaic floors, including one depicting the head of a sea god, and another of a scallop shell with intricate three-dimensional shading. Other finds included burial urns and lead coffins.

On the basis of excavated plaster fragments, a Roman room has been painstakingly recreated, its walls painted in startlingly bright colours and geometric patterns.

Between here and St Albans Cathedral are a bath house with more mosaics, remnants of the ancient city wall and one of the original gates.

One of the oldest surviving pubs in England

🛖 Ye Olde Fighting Cocks

Abbey Mill Lane. ☎ *01727 865830.* ◯ *daily.* ● *25 Dec.* ♿
Believed to be England's oldest surviving pub, Ye Olde Fighting Cocks is certainly, with its octagonal shape, one of the most unusual. It originated as the medieval dovecote of the old abbey and moved here after the Dissolution *(see p54)*.

⋔ Roman Theatre

St Michael's. ☎ *01727 835035.* ◯ *daily.* ● *25, 26 Dec.* 🚫 ♿
Just across the road from the museum are the foundations of the open-air theatre, first built around 160 but enlarged several times. It is one of only six known to have been built throughout Roman Britain.

Alongside it are traces of a row of Roman shops and a house, from which many of the museum's treasures – such as a bronze statuette of Venus – were excavated in the 1930s.

🏛 St Michael's Church

St Michael's. ☎ *01727 835037.* ◯ *Apr–Sep: daily.* ♿
This church was first founded during the Saxon reign and is built partly with bricks taken from Verulamium, which by then was in decline. Numerous additions have been made since then, including a truly splendid Jacobean pulpit.

The church contains an early 17th-century monument to the Elizabethan statesman and writer Sir Francis Bacon; his father owned nearby Gorhambury, a large Tudor house, now in ruins.

A scallop shell, one of the mosaic floors at the Verulamium Museum

🔒 St Albans Cathedral

Sumpter Yard. 📞 *01727 860780.*
⭕ *daily.* ♿ 📷 *by arrangement.*
This outstanding example of
medieval architecture has
some classic features such as
the 13th- and 14th-century wall
paintings on the Norman piers.

It was begun in 793, when
King Offa of Mercia founded
the abbey in honour of St
Alban, Britain's first Christian
martyr, put to death by the
Romans in the third century
for sheltering a priest. The
oldest parts, which still stand,

**The imposing west side of
St Albans Cathedral**

were first built in 1077 and
are easily recognizable as
Norman by the round-headed
arches and windows. They
form part of the 84 m (276 ft)
nave – the longest in England.

The pointed arches further
east are Early English (13th
century), while the decorated
work of the 14th century was
added when some of the
Norman arches collapsed.

East of the crossing is
what remains of St Alban's
shrine – a marble pedestal
made up of more than
2,000 tiny fragments. Next to
it is the tomb of Humphrey,
Duke of Gloucester *(see p243).*

A copy of the *Magna Carta
(see p52)* is displayed on the
wall. It was here that the
English barons drafted this
document, which King John
was then forced to sign.

The splendour of the Gardens of the Rose in June

Gardens of the Rose ⑭

Chiswell Green, Hertfordshire. 📞
01727 850461. 🚆 *St Albans then bus.*
⭕ *4 Apr–31 May: Sun & public hols;*
5 Jun–26 Sep: daily. 📷 ♿ 🖥️ 🏠

AS WELL AS BEING England's
national symbol, the rose
is the most popular flower
with British gardeners.

The 5 ha (12 acre) garden
of the Royal National Rose
Society, with over 30,000
plants and 1,700 varieties, is
at its peak in late June. The
gardens trace the history of
the flower as far back as the
white rose of York, the red
rose of Lancaster *(see p53)*
and the Rosa Mundi – named
by Henry II for his mistress
Fair Rosamond after she was
poisoned by Queen Eleanor
in 1177. But the nuns who
buried Rosamond implied in
verse on her tomb that,
despite her name, her reputation did not smell of roses.

Hughenden Manor ⑮

High Wycombe, Buckinghamshire.
📞 *01494 755573.* 🚆 *High Wycombe*
then bus. ⭕ *Mar: Sat, Sun; Apr–Oct:*
Wed–Sun & public hols. ⚫ *Good Fri.*
📷 ♿ *limited.* 🖥️ 🏠

THE VICTORIAN STATESMAN and
novelist Benjamin Disraeli,
Prime Minister from 1874 to
1880, lived here for 33 years
until his death. Originally a
Georgian villa, Disraeli adapted
it in 1862 to the Gothic style.
Furnished as it was in his day,
the house gives an idea of
the life of a wealthy Victorian
gentleman and shows some
portraits of his contemporaries.

GEORGE BERNARD SHAW

Although a controversial playwright and known
as a mischievous character, the Irish-born
George Bernard Shaw (1856–1950) was a man
of settled habits. He lived near St Albans in a
house at Ayot St Lawrence, now called Shaw's
Corner, for the last 44 years of his life,
working until his last weeks in a
summer-house at the bottom of
his large garden. His plays,
combining wit with a powerful
political and social message, still
seem fresh today. One of the most
enduring is *Pygmalion* (1913),
on which the musical *My Fair
Lady* is based. The house and
garden are now a museum
of his life and works.

Touring the Thames ⑯

THE THAMES between Pangbourne and Eton is leafy and romantic and best seen by boat. But if time is short, the road keeps close to its bank for much of the way. Swans glide gracefully below ancient bridges, voles dive into the water for cover, and elegant herons stand impassive at the river's edge. Huge beech trees overhang the banks which are lined with fine houses, their gardens sloping to the water. The tranquil scene has inspired painters and writers through the ages as well as operating, until recently, as an important transport link.

Hambledon Mill ⑥
The white weather-boarded mill, which was operational until 1955, is one of the largest on the Thames as well as one of the oldest in origin. There are traces of the original 16th-century mill.

Beale Park ①
The philanthropist Gilbert Beale (1868–1967) created a 10 ha (25 acre) park to preserve this beautiful stretch of river intact and breed endangered birds like owls, ornamental water fowl, pheasants and peacocks.

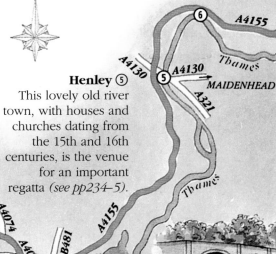

Henley ⑤
This lovely old river town, with houses and churches dating from the 15th and 16th centuries, is the venue for an important regatta (see pp234–5).

Pangbourne ②
Kenneth Grahame (1859–1932), author of *The Wind in the Willows*, lived here until his death. Pangbourne was used as the setting by artist Ernest Shepard (1879–1976) to illustrate the book.

Sonning Bridge ④
The 18th-century bridge is made up of 11 brick arches of varying width.

TIPS FOR DRIVERS

Tour length: 50 miles (75 km).
Stopping-off points: The picturesque town of Henley has a large number of riverside pubs; most of these serve food and make excellent places to stop for lunch. If you are boating you can often moor your boat alongside the river bank.

Whitchurch Mill ③
This charming village, linked to Pangbourne by a Victorian toll bridge, has a picturesque church and one of the many disused watermills that once harnessed the power of this stretch of river.

Cookham ⑦
This is famous as the home of Stanley Spencer (1891–1959), one of Britain's leading 20th-century artists. His old studio is now a museum containing some of his paintings and equipment, including a sign that warned visitors to leave him alone when he was working. This work, entitled *Swan Upping* (1914–19), recalls a Thames custom.

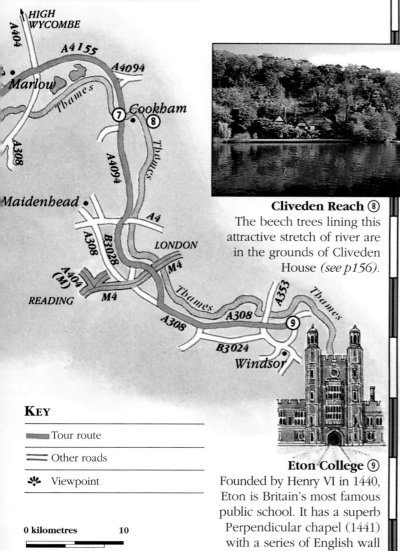

Cliveden Reach ⑧
The beech trees lining this attractive stretch of river are in the grounds of Cliveden House (*see p156*).

Eton College ⑨
Founded by Henry VI in 1440, Eton is Britain's most famous public school. It has a superb Perpendicular chapel (1441) with a series of English wall paintings (1479–88).

KEY
- Tour route
- Other roads
- ※ Viewpoint

0 kilometres 10

0 miles 5

BOATING TOURS

In summer, scheduled river services run between Henley, Windsor, Runnymede and Marlow. Several companies operate from towns along the route. You can hire boats by the hour or the day or, for a longer tour, you can rent cabin cruisers and sleep on board. Ring Salter Bros on 01753 865 832 for more information.

Salter Bros hire boats, moored at Henley

Windsor ⑰

Berkshire. 30,000. ⤢ HighSt (01753 743900). Sat.

THE TOWN of Windsor is dwarfed by the enormous **castle** (*see p254–5*) on the hill above – appropriately enough because its original purpose was to serve the castle's needs. The town is full of quaint Georgian shops, houses and inns. The most prominent building on the High Street is the **Guildhall** completed by Wren (*see p120*) in 1689. The **Household Cavalry Museum** has an extensive collection of arms and uniforms.

The huge 809 ha (2,000 acre) **Windsor Great Park** stretches straight from the castle three miles (5 km) to Snow Hill, where there is a statue of George III.

ENVIRONS: Four miles (7 km) to the southeast is the level grassy meadow known as **Runnymede**. This is one of England's most historic sights, where in 1215 King John was forced by his rebellious barons to sign the *Magna Carta* (*see p52*), thereby limiting his royal powers. The dainty memorial pavilion at the top of the meadow was erected in 1957.

🏛 Household Cavalry Museum
Leonard's Rd. 01753 755203. Mon–Fri. public hols. **Donation.**

King John signing the *Magna Carta*, Runnymede

Windsor Castle

Henry II rebuilt the castle

T HE OLDEST CONTINUOUSLY inhabited royal residence in Britain, the castle, originally made of wood, was built by William the Conqueror in 1070 to guard the western approaches to London. He chose the site because it was on high ground and just a day's journey from his base in the Tower of London. Successive monarchs have made alterations that render it a remarkable monument to royalty's changing tastes. King George V's affection for it was shown when he chose Windsor for his family surname in 1917. The castle is the primary residence of the Queen and her family who stay here many weekends.

Albert Memorial Chapel
First built in 1240, it was rebuilt in 1485 and finally converted into a memorial for Prince Albert in 1863.

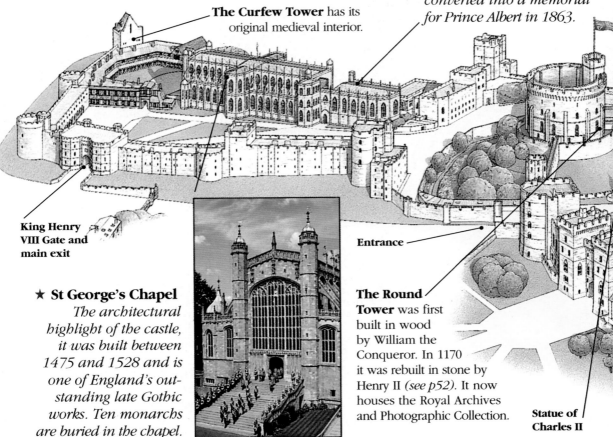

The Curfew Tower has its original medieval interior.

King Henry VIII Gate and main exit

★ **St George's Chapel**
The architectural highlight of the castle, it was built between 1475 and 1528 and is one of England's outstanding late Gothic works. Ten monarchs are buried in the chapel.

Entrance

The Round Tower was first built in wood by William the Conqueror. In 1170 it was rebuilt in stone by Henry II (*see p52*). It now houses the Royal Archives and Photographic Collection.

Statue of Charles II

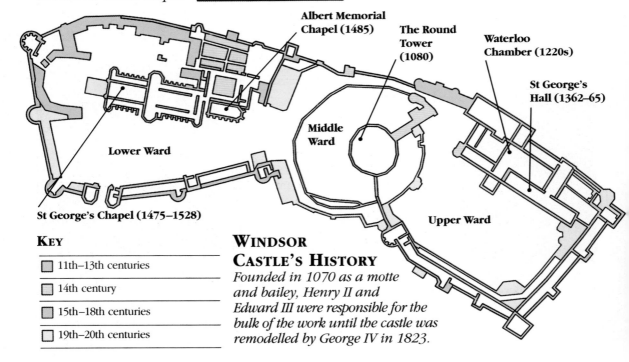

Albert Memorial Chapel (1485)

The Round Tower (1080)

Waterloo Chamber (1220s)

St George's Hall (1362–65)

Middle Ward

Lower Ward

St George's Chapel (1475–1528)

Upper Ward

KEY

☐ 11th–13th centuries

☐ 14th century

☐ 15th–18th centuries

☐ 19th–20th centuries

WINDSOR CASTLE'S HISTORY
Founded in 1070 as a motte and bailey, Henry II and Edward III were responsible for the bulk of the work until the castle was remodelled by George IV in 1823.

Royal Collection
This chalk etching of Christ by Michelangelo is part of the Resurrection Series. *The great size of this collection means that the exhibition is always changing and works are often loaned to other museums.*

The Audience Chamber is where the Queen greets her guests.

The Queen's Ballroom

Queen Mary's Dolls' House was designed by Sir Edwin Lutyens in 1924. Every item was built on a 1:12 ratio. The wine cellar contains genuine vintage wine.

Waterloo Chamber
The walls of this banqueting hall, first built in the 13th century, are lined with portraits of the leaders who played a part in Napoleon's defeat (see p59).

Brunswick Tower

The East Terrace Garden was created by Sir Jeffry Wyatville for King George IV in the 1820s.

★ **State Apartments**
These rooms contain many treasures, including this late 18th-century state bed in the King's State Bedchamber, made for the visit in 1855 of Napoleon III.

STAR SIGHTS

★ **St George's Chapel**

★ **State Apartments**

The Fire of 1992
A devastating blaze began during maintenance work on the State Apartments. St George's Hall was destroyed but has been rebuilt.

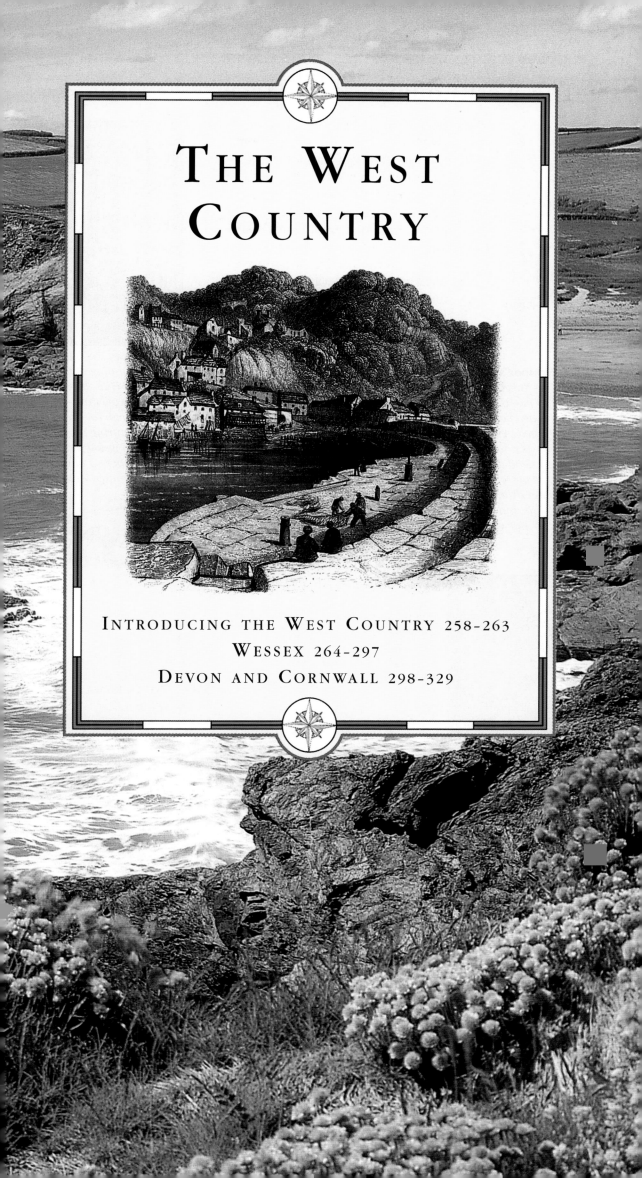

THE WEST
COUNTRY

INTRODUCING THE WEST COUNTRY 258-263
WESSEX 264-297
DEVON AND CORNWALL 298-329

The West Country at a Glance

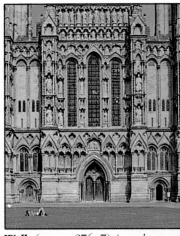

THE WEST COUNTRY forms a long peninsula bounded by the Atlantic to the north and the English Channel to the south, tapering down to Land's End, mainland Britain's westernmost point. Whether exploring the great cities and cathedrals, experiencing the awesome solitude of the moors and their prehistoric monuments, or simply enjoying the miles of coastline and mild climate, this region has an enduring appeal for holiday-makers.

Exmoor's *(see pp274–5) heather-clad moors and wooded valleys, grazed by wild ponies and red deer, lead down to some of Devon's most dramatic cliffs and seaside coves.*

Wells *(see pp276–7) is a charming town nestling at the foot of the Mendip Hills. It is famous for its exquisite three-towered cathedral with an ornate west façade, featuring an array of statues. Alongside stand the moated Bishop's Palace and the 15th-century Vicar's Close.*

St Ives *(see p309) has a branch of the Tate Gallery that shows modern works by artists associated with the area. Patrick Heron's bold coloured glass (1993) is on permanent display.*

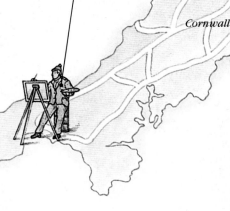

Devon

DEVON AND CORNWALL
(see pp298–329)

Cornwall

Dartmoor *(see pp328–9) is a wilderness of great natural beauty covering an area of 365 sq miles (945 sq km). Stone clapper bridges, picturesque villages and weathered granite tors punctuate the landscape.*

◁ **Stunning views of the Lizard Peninsula**

Bath (see pp282–5) is named after the Roman baths that stand at the heart of the old city next to the splendid medieval abbey. It is one of Britain's liveliest and most rewarding cities, full of elegant Georgian terraces, built in local honey-coloured limestone by the two John Woods (Elder and Younger).

Stonehenge (see pp288–9), the world-famous prehistoric monument, was built in several stages from 3000 BC. Moving and erecting its massive stones was an extraordinary feat for its time. It is likely that this magical stone circle was a place of worship to the sun.

WESSEX
(see pp264–97)

Wiltshire

Somerset

Dorset

Salisbury's (see pp290–91) cathedral with its soaring spire, was the inspiration for one of John Constable's best-loved paintings. The picturesque Cathedral Close has a number of fine medieval buildings.

0 kilometres   25

0 miles   25

Stourhead garden (see pp292–3) was inspired by the paintings of Claude and Poussin. Created in the 18th century, the garden is itself a work of art. Contrived vistas, light and shade and a mixture of landscape and gracious buildings, such as the Neo-Classical Pantheon at its centre, are vital to the overall effect.

Coastal Wildlife

THE LONG AND VARIED West Country coastline, ranging from the stark, granite cliffs of Land's End to the pebble-strewn stretch of Chesil Bank, is matched with an equally diverse range of wildlife. Beaches are scattered with colourful shells, while rock pools form miniature marine habitats teeming with life. Caves are used by larger creatures, such as grey seals, and cliffs provide nest sites for birds. In the spring and early summer, an astonishing range of plants grow on the foreshore and cliffs which can be seen at their best from the Southwest Coastal Path *(see p36)*. The plants in turn attract numerous moths and butterflies.

Cliff-tops of Land's End with safe ledges for nesting birds

Chesil Bank is an unusual ridge of pebbles (see p294) *stretching 18 miles (29 km) along the Dorset coast. The bank was created by storms and the pebbles increase in size from northwest to southeast due to varying strengths of coastal currents. The bank encloses a lagoon called the Fleet, habitat of the Abbotsbury swans, as well as a large number of wildfowl.*

The Painted Lady, *often seen on cliff-top coastal plants, migrates to Britain in the spring.*

High tides wash up driftwood and shells.

Cliff-top turf contains many species of wild flowers.

Thrift, in hummocks of honey-scented flowers, is a familiar sight on cliff ledges in spring.

Yellowhammers *are to be seen perched on cliff-top bushes.*

Marram grass roots help hold back sand against wind erosion.

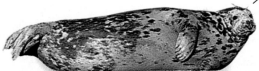

Grey seals come on land to give birth to their young. They can be spotted on remote beaches.

A BEACHCOMBER'S GUIDE

The best time to observe the natural life of the sea shore is when the tide begins to roll back, before the scavenging seagulls pick up the stranded crabs, fish and sandhoppers, and the seaweed dries up. Much plant and marine life can be found in the secure habitat provided by rock pools.

COLLECTING SHELLS

Most of the edible molluscs, such as scallops and cockles, are known as bivalves; others, such as whelks and limpets, are known as gastropods.

Great scallop

Common cockle

Common whelk

Common limpet

Durdle Door was formed by waves continually eroding the weaker chalk layers of this cliff (see p296) in Dorset, leaving the stronger oolite to create a striking arch, known in geology as an eyelet.

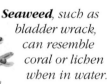

Seaweed, such as bladder wrack, can resemble coral or lichen when in water.

Rocks are colonized by clusters of barnacles, mussels and limpets.

Oystercatchers have a distinctive orange beak. They hunt along the shore, feeding on all kinds of shellfish.

Starfish can be aggressive predators on shellfish. The light-sensitive tips of their tentacles help them to "see" the way.

Mussels are widespread and can be harvested for food.

Rock pools teem with crabs, mussels, shrimps and plant life.

The Velvet Crab, often found hiding in seaweed, is covered with fine downy hair all over its shell.

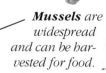

Grey mullet, when newly hatched, can often be seen in rock pools.

West Country Gardens

G ARDENERS HAVE LONG BEEN ATTRACTED to the West Country. Its mild climate is perfect for growing tender and exotic plants, many of which were brought from Asia in the 19th century. As a result, the region has some of England's finest and most varied gardens, covering the whole sweep of garden styles and history *(see pp26–7)*, from the clipped formality of Elizabethan Montacute, to the colourful and crowded cottage-garden style of East Lambrook Manor.

Lanbydrock's (p314) *clipped yews and low box hedges frame a blaze of colourful annuals.*

Trewithen (p313) *is renowned for its rare camellias, rhododendrons and magnolias, grown from seed collected in Asia. The huge garden is at its most impressive in March and June.*

Cotehele *(p325)* has a lovely lush valley garden.

DEVON AND CORNWALL *(see pp298–329*

Trelissick *(p313)* has memorable views over the Fal Estuary through shrub-filled woodland.

Glendurgan *(p313)* is a plant-lover's paradise set in a steep, sheltered valley.

Mount Edgcumbe *(p324)* preserves its 18th-century French, Italian and English gardens.

Trengwainton (p308) *has a fine stream garden, whose banks are crowded with moisture-loving plants, beneath a lush canopy of New Zealand tree ferns.*

Overbecks (near Salcombe) *enjoys a spectacular site overlooking the Salcombe Estuary. There are secret gardens, terraces and rocky dells.*

CREATIVE GARDENING

Gardens are not simply collections of plants; they rely for much of their appeal on man-made features. Whimsical topiary, ornate architecture, fanciful statuary and mazes help to create an atmosphere of adventure or pure escapism. The many gardens dotted around the West Country offer engaging examples of the vivid imagination of designers.

Mazes were created in medieval monasteries to teach patience and persistence. This laurel maze at Glendurgan was planted in 1833.

Fountains and flamboyant statuary have adorned gardens since Roman times. Such eye-catching embellishments add poetic and Classical touches to the design of formal gardens, such as Mount Edgcumbe.

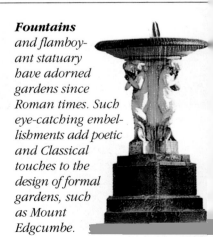

Knightshayes Court (p321) *is designed as a series of formal garden "rooms", planted for scent, colour or seasonal effect.*

WESSEX
(see pp264–97)

East Lambrook Manor (near South Petherton) is a riot of colours, as old-fashioned cottage plants grow without restraint.

Stourhead (see pp292–3) is a magnificent example of 18th-century landscape gardening.

Athelhampton's (p295) gardens make use of fountains, statues, pavilions and columnar yews.

Montacute House (p294) has pavilions and a centuries-old yew hedge, and is renowned for its collection of old roses.

0 kilometres   25

0 miles   25

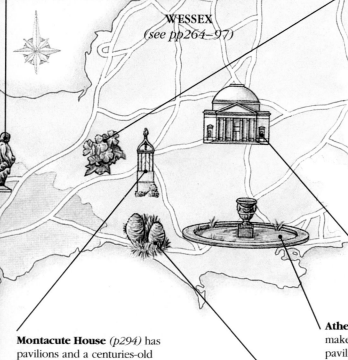

Parnham (near Beaminster), like many West Country gardens, has several parts devoted to different themes. Here conical yews comple-ment the formality of the stone balustrade; elsewhere there are woodland, kitchen, shade and Mediterranean gardens.

Many garden buildings are linked by an element of fantasy; while country houses had to conform to everyday practicalities, the design of many smaller buildings gave more scope for imagination. This fanciful Elizabethan pavilion on the forecourt at Montacute House was first and foremost decora-tive, but sometimes served as a lodging house.

Topiary can be traced back to the Greeks. Since that time the sculpting of trees into unusual, often eccentric shapes has been de-veloped over the centuries. The yew topiary of 1920s Knightshayes features a fox being chased by a pack of hounds. The figures form a delightful conceit and come into their own in winter when little else is in leaf.

Three-arched bridge and cottages made of Cotswold stone, Castle Combe, Wiltshire ▷

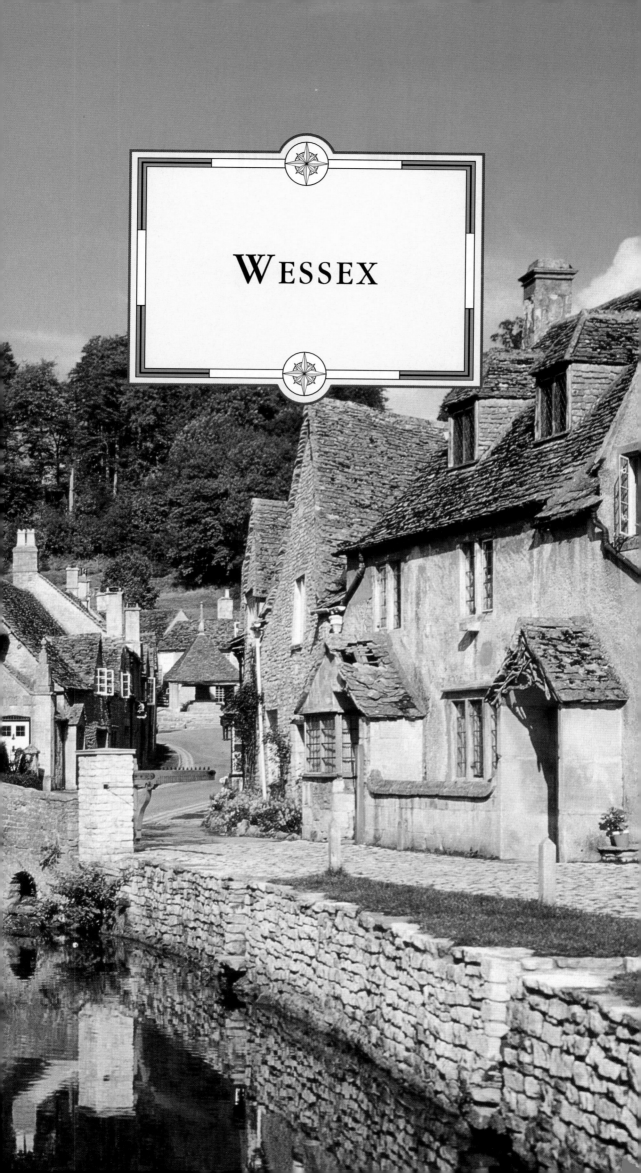

WESSEX

WESSEX

THE NATURAL BEAUTY *of this mostly rural region includes features as diverse as bare, windswept downlands and lush river valleys. The area is enriched by a wealth of historical and architectural attractions, ranging from the prehistoric stone circle of Stonehenge to the Roman baths and Georgian townscape of Bath.*

Between the northwestern coast of Wessex and the spectacular Channel coastline in the south, you are likely to encounter rolling hills, green valleys, reclaimed marshlands, sweeping chalk downlands and isolated remnants of the once-common heaths and moors. Picturesque villages with characterful churches and streets lined with thatched cottages can be found throughout the region. Wessex also features two of the most famous buildings in England: Salisbury Cathedral, the soaring spire of which is the tallest in Britain; and the vast, imposing Wells Cathedral. Pervading almost every scene in Wessex is a brooding, almost tangible sense of the ancient past.

Adding further to the historic atmosphere of the region is the common belief that the semi-mythical Dark Age leaders, Arthur and Alfred, lived in Wessex. It was King Arthur who is thought to have led British resistance to the Saxon invasion in the 6th century. The Saxons finally emerged the victors and one of them, King Alfred, first united the West Country into one political unit, called the Kingdom of Wessex (the "land of the West Saxons"). This ancient kingdom of Wessex ceased to exist with the coming of the Normans in 1066 yet, over nine centuries later, the name still persists as a universally recognized and much-loved region of Britain.

Long before it was named, Wessex was first populated by Stone Age people.

Two visitors enjoying the Elizabethan gardens of Montacute House, Somerset

◁ **Eighteenth-century cottages lining Gold Hill, Shaftesbury**

White Horse, possibly originally cut in the 9th century, on a hill above the town of Westbury, Wiltshire

The early settlers in the region were attracted to the great plateau of Salisbury Plain, the elevated, dry chalklands (much of which is used by today's army for training) proving particularly suitable for habitation. It was these Stone Age people who constructed the mysterious megalithic monuments that are scattered around the area. The most celebrated of these is Stonehenge, probably the most famous prehistoric site in Europe. South of Stonehenge are the remains of a 1st-century hill fort, Old Sarum.

Although Stonehenge is the best-known ancient monument in Wessex,

Glastonbury Tor, Somerset

the whole region is rich in archaeological interest, particularly around Avebury. The Avebury Stone Circle itself is a strange and fascinating site, and nearby is the mound of Silbury Hill. Also close by are the striking chambered tombs of West Kennet Long Barrow.

In the northwest corner of Wessex, at the mouth of the River Severn, is Bristol. This city has a maritime history that stretches back to the 15th century and includes the launching of John Cabot's historic voyage to North America. It was through this bustling port that the New World was opened up, and the centuries of ocean-going endeavour that followed are perhaps best symbolized by Brunel's restored passenger ship, *s.s. Great Britain*, which can be found near the Maritime Heritage Centre in Bristol.

The River Avon winds inland from Bristol between encircling hills towards the elegant spa city of Bath. The city was initially a Roman settlement, as shown by the remarkably well-preserved Roman baths. Later, Bath become the height of Georgian fashion and style, the famous Royal Crescent and impressive Pulteney Bridge being excellent examples of that period's architecture. The city also

Flooded flatlands of Tealham Moor, Somerset

has a superb medieval abbey. Further eastwards along the Avon is the pretty former mill town of Bradford-on-Avon, which is home to a medieval bridge and converted mill buildings.

The limestone Mendip Hills, south of Bristol, are a surprisingly wild area of deep, wooded valleys known as "coombes" with open, heather-covered heathland

Pulpit Rock, on the Isle of Portland, Dorset

above. The showplaces of this region are the deep gorges, such as Cheddar, where caves – once inhabited by prehistoric man, and previously used to store the cheese for which the area is famous – can be visited.

South of the Mendips, the great willow-dotted expanse of the Somerset Levels stretch down to Ilminster and Taunton, which is a good place to sample the famous Somerset cider. Taunton also features a 12th-century castle, now home to the Somerset County Museum. Perhaps the most visited township in this area is Glastonbury, where the symbolic site of King Arthur's Avalon (marked by the tower-topped tor) and the ruins of Glastonbury Abbey (built in around AD 700) can be visited. To the west are the heather-covered sandstone heights of Exmoor, one of Britain's smallest and most intimate National Parks.

On the Channel Coast, west from the resort of Bournemouth, are the great chalk and limestone headlands of Studland Bay and the Isle of Purbeck, which mark the start of the Dorset Coast. Among the geological showplaces are the perfect scallop-shaped bay of Lulworth Cove and the great natural arch of Durdle Door. Inland from the Isle of Purbeck are the romantic ruins of 11th-century Corfe Castle.

Centred around the market town of Dorchester is the area known as "Thomas Hardy Country". Hardy, a Victorian novelist, is the man almost single-handedly responsible for the survival of the area's ancient name of Wessex into today's world. It was Hardy who glamorized the English rural idyll in novels such as *Tess of the D'Urbervilles*. Near Dorchester, his birthplace (Hardy's Cottage) can be visited, as can his burial site in Stinsford. Also in this region is Maiden Castle, one of the most impressive hill forts in Britain. Dorchester itself contains the Dorset County Museum and a Roman amphitheatre. South of Dorchester is the seaside resort of Weymouth, beyond which is the great pebble expanse of Chesil Beach. Further west, on the other side of Lyme Bay, are the spectacular fossil cliffs of Lyme Regis.

Circular entrenchments of Maiden Castle, and the western portion of the town of Dorchester

Exploring Wessex

FROM THE ROLLING CHALK PLAINS around Stonehenge to the rocky cliffs of Cheddar Gorge and the heather-covered uplands of Exmoor, Wessex is a scenically varied microcosm of England. Reflecting the underlying geology, each part of Wessex contributes its own distinctive architecture, with the Neo-Classically inspired buildings of Bath giving way to the mellow brick and timber of Salisbury and the thatched flint-and-chalk cottages of the Dorset landscape.

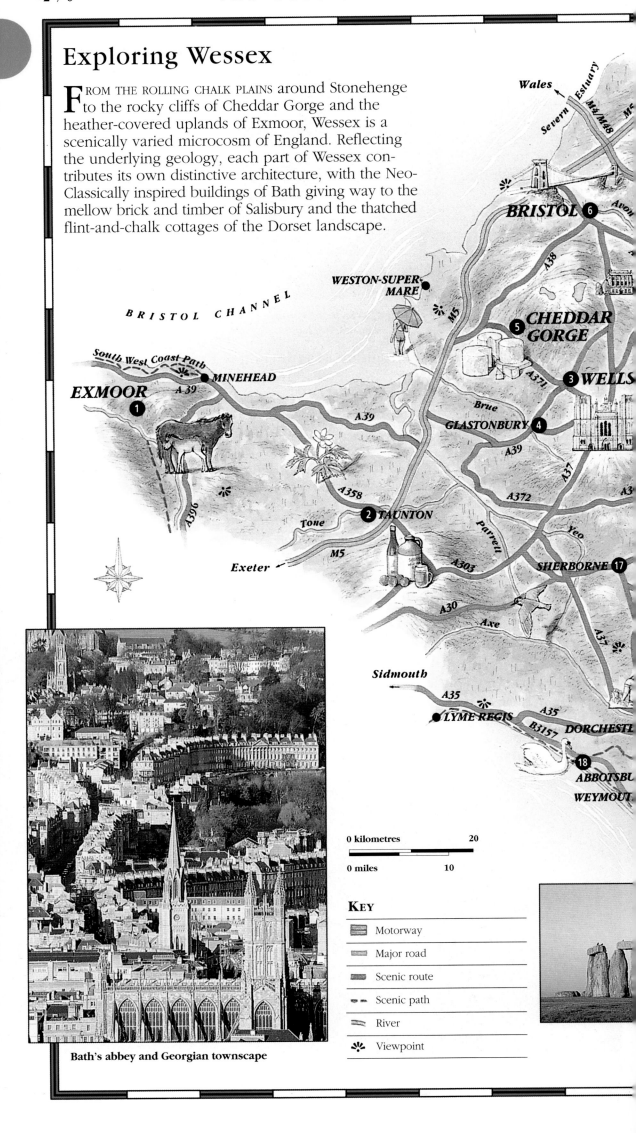

Wales

Severn Estuary

M4/M48

BRISTOL **6**

Avon

A38

WESTON-SUPER-MARE

BRISTOL CHANNEL

CHEDDAR **5** GORGE

A371

3 WELLS

South West Coast Path

MINEHEAD

A39

EXMOOR **1**

A39

Brue

GLASTONBURY **4**

A39

A37

A3

A372

A372

A358

Tone

2 TAUNTON

Parrett

Yeo

M5

A303

SHERBORNE **17**

Exeter

A30

A396

Axe

A37

Sidmouth

A35

LYME REGIS

A35

B3157

DORCHESTE

18

ABBOTSBU

WEYMOUT

| 0 kilometres | 20 |
| 0 miles | 10 |

KEY

	Motorway
	Major road
	Scenic route
	Scenic path
	River
	Viewpoint

Bath's abbey and Georgian townscape

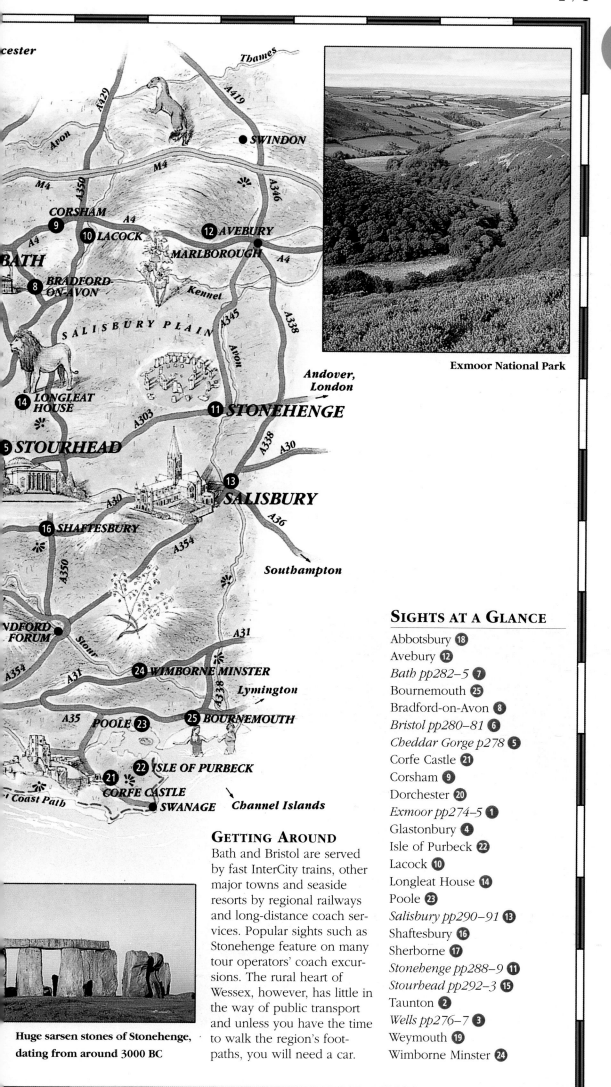

Exmoor National Park

Huge sarsen stones of Stonehenge, dating from around 3000 BC

GETTING AROUND

Bath and Bristol are served by fast InterCity trains, other major towns and seaside resorts by regional railways and long-distance coach services. Popular sights such as Stonehenge feature on many tour operators' coach excursions. The rural heart of Wessex, however, has little in the way of public transport and unless you have the time to walk the region's footpaths, you will need a car.

SIGHTS AT A GLANCE

Abbotsbury **18**
Avebury **12**
Bath pp282–5 **7**
Bournemouth **25**
Bradford-on-Avon **8**
Bristol pp280–81 **6**
Cheddar Gorge p278 **5**
Corfe Castle **21**
Corsham **9**
Dorchester **20**
Exmoor pp274–5 **1**
Glastonbury **4**
Isle of Purbeck **22**
Lacock **10**
Longleat House **14**
Poole **23**
Salisbury pp290–91 **13**
Shaftesbury **16**
Sherborne **17**
Stonehenge pp288–9 **11**
Stourhead pp292–3 **15**
Taunton **2**
Wells pp276–7 **3**
Weymouth **19**
Wimborne Minster **24**

Ancient Sites of Wessex

Bronze Age cup

WESSEX CONTAINS ONE OF the greatest concentrations of ancient sites in Great Britain. Between a quarter and a third of all henge monuments are in Wessex and surrounding areas: Dorset has about 1,800 burial mounds (barrows) and Wiltshire has around 2,200. Ceremonial sites dating from the Neolithic Age (c.3500 BC) to the Bronze Age (c.2100 BC) proliferate in the area, including causewayed enclosures, cursus earthworks and magnificent henge monuments and stone circles.

Gold breastplate

Flint arrowheads

WINDMILL HILL, WILTSHIRE

SITUATED 2 MILES (3.2 KM) north of Avebury, Windmill Hill is the largest known causewayed enclosure in Great Britain. The enclosure is roughly circular in shape with three rings of ditches surrounding it. There are gaps in the ditches over which paths, or causeways, would have led to the enclosure entrances. It is thought that such enclosures were trading and religious centres where scattered farming communities would meet to perform rituals or to celebrate with feasting. Several Bronze Age barrows (burial mounds) are also located at Windmill Hill.

Windmill Hill covers about 21 acres (8.5 ha)

Thickthorn long barrows on the Dorset Cursus

DORSET CURSUS

CURSUSES ARE LINEAR earthworks flanked by parallel banks and ditches, and were probably used for ritual processions. Barrows are often situated near or adjoining them, providing further evidence of their sacred nature. Dorset Cursus runs from Bokerley Down to Thickthorn Down and, at around 6 miles (9.6 km) long, is one of the longest examples of its type in Great Britain. Ancient sites near Dorset Cursus include the barrows at Thickthorn, Knowlton henge monuments and the Bronze Age cemetery of Oakley Down, which consists of 25 barrows.

STANTON DREW STONE CIRCLE

ONE OF THE MOST evocative types of ancient site is the stone circle. Located 6 miles (9.6 km) south of Bristol, Stanton Drew features the second largest stone circle after Avebury (see p289). This Bronze Age site comprises three circles – with 8, 10 and 27 surviving stones respectively – as well as two stone avenues. There are also three standing stones collectively called the Cove. According to local folklore, the three stones are a bride, groom and priest, who were turned to stone after dancing to the Devil's music at the wedding night celebrations.

The megaliths at Stanton Drew

WHERE TO SEE ANCIENT ARTEFACTS

Beaker pot

Polished axehead

Artefacts from excavations in the southern part of Wessex can be found in the Salisbury and South Wiltshire Museum *(see p291)*, including items from Stonehenge *(see pp288–9)* and surrounding sites. Artefacts from excavations in the northern part of Wessex, including the Avebury sites *(see pp289)*, are housed in the Alexander Keiller Museum, Avebury, and the Devizes Museum, Devizes. Domestic items and tools help to provide insight into the everyday lives of the people who once inhabited and used the ancient sites. Many less functional artefacts, such as gold breastplates and bone-decorated sceptres, have also been found, revealing the artistic skills of the ancient Britons.

Polished sceptre

DEVIL'S DEN, WILTSHIRE

THOUSANDS OF SARSEN STONES are scattered across Fyfield Down, about 3 miles (4.8 km) southeast of Avebury. Various theories about the origins of single standing stones and groups of megaliths have been put forward, but none is certain. Some, like Devil's Den, are probably the remains of Neolithic chambered tombs (long barrows) that would originally have been covered with an earth mound. Like many other pagan sites, the Devil's Den megaliths came to be associated with Satan after the spread of Christianity.

Devil's Den, a chambered tomb on Fyfield Down

Cadbury Castle is to the southeast of Glastonbury

CADBURY CASTLE

CADBURY CASTLE IS AN oval enclosure at the top of a 120 m- (400 ft-) high hill surrounded by four rings of ditches and banks. Built on the site of a Neolithic farming community, the hillfort was fortified during the Iron Age with massive 6-m (20-ft) ramparts. Despite such defences, hillforts were community settlements, rather than military sites. Excavations have revealed that the fort was occupied by Romanized Britons during the time of King Arthur, and it is widely believed that Cadbury Castle could be the site of the fortress of Camelot.

GLASTONBURY TOR, SOMERSET

GLASTONBURY TOR is a distinctive hill, 150 m (500 ft) high and conical in shape. Originally, it was almost completely surrounded by water, and is believed by many to have been the Isle of Avalon, where the dying King Arthur was taken by barge to begin his journey into the afterlife. It was also at Glastonbury that Joseph of Arimathea reputedly hid the Holy Grail – the cup used by Christ at the Last Supper – for which Arthur and the Knights of the Round Table searched in vain. The ruins of a medieval church can be visited at the hill's summit.

Glastonbury Tor, Somerset

Exmoor National Park ●

THE MAJESTIC CLIFFS plunging into the Atlantic along Exmoor's northern coast are interrupted by lush, wooded valleys carrying rivers from the high moorland down to sheltered fishing coves. Inland, wild rolling hills are grazed by sturdy Exmoor ponies, horned sheep and the wild red deer **Curlew** that were introduced in the 12th century, when Exmoor was a royal hunting reserve. Curlews and buzzards are a common sight wheeling over the bracken-clad terrain looking for prey. For walkers, Exmoor offers 620 miles (1,000 km) of footpaths and varied, dramatic scenery, while the tamer perimeters of the park have everything from traditional seaside entertainments to picturesque villages and ancient churches.

View east along the Southwest Coastal Path

Combe Martin is a pretty setting for the Pack of Cards Inn *(see p320)*.

Parracombe church has a Georgian interior with a complete set of wooden furnishings.

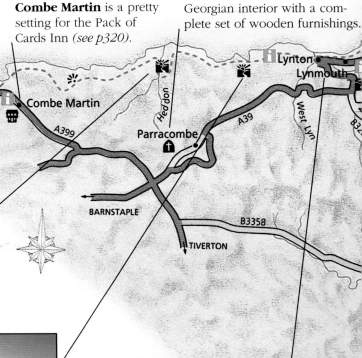

Heddon's Mouth
The River Heddon passes through woodland and meadows down to this attractive point on the coast.

Valley of the Rocks
Gritstone outcrops, eroded into fantastical shapes, characterize this natural gorge.

KEY

🛈	Tourist information
▬	A road
▬	B road
▬	Minor road
- -	Coastal path
☀	Viewpoint

Lynmouth
Above the charming fishing village of Lynmouth stands hill-top Lynton. The two villages are connected by a cliff railway (see p320).

Watersmeet

The East Lyn and Hoar Oak Water join together in a tumbling cascade at this spot in the middle of a beautifully wooded valley. There is also a tearoom with a pretty garden.

Culbone church, a mere 10.6 m (35 ft) in length, claims to be Britain's smallest parish church.

VISITORS' CHECKLIST

Somerset/Devon. 🚂 🚌 *Tiverton then bus.* ℹ️ *Fore St, Dulverton (01398 323841).*
Natural History Centre, Malmsmead. 📞 *01643 707624.* ⊙ *mid-May–Jun: Wed, Thu; Jul–Sep: Tue–Thu (pm).* ♿
Dunster Castle (NT), Dunster. 📞 *01643 821314.* ⊙ *Apr–Oct: Sat–Wed.* ♿

Malmsmead has a Natural History Centre illustrating local wildlife.

Oare's church commemorates the writer RD Blackmore, whose romantic novel *Lorna Doone* (1869) is set in the area.

Porlock

The flower-filled village of Porlock has retained its charm, with steep winding streets, thatched houses and a 13th-century church.

Selworthy is a picturesque estate village built in 1810.

Minehead is a major resort built around a pretty quay. A steam railway runs all the way from here to Bishop's Lydeard.

Dunster has a 13th-century castle and an unusual octagonal Yarn Market (1609) where local cloth was once sold.

imonsbath is a ood starting point r walkers. The onies found loc-ly are thought to escend from Iron ge ancestors.

xford has been a entre for stag-hunting ince Norman times.

Tarr Steps is an ancient "clapper" bridge built of stone slabs for pack-horses carrying wool to Dunster market.

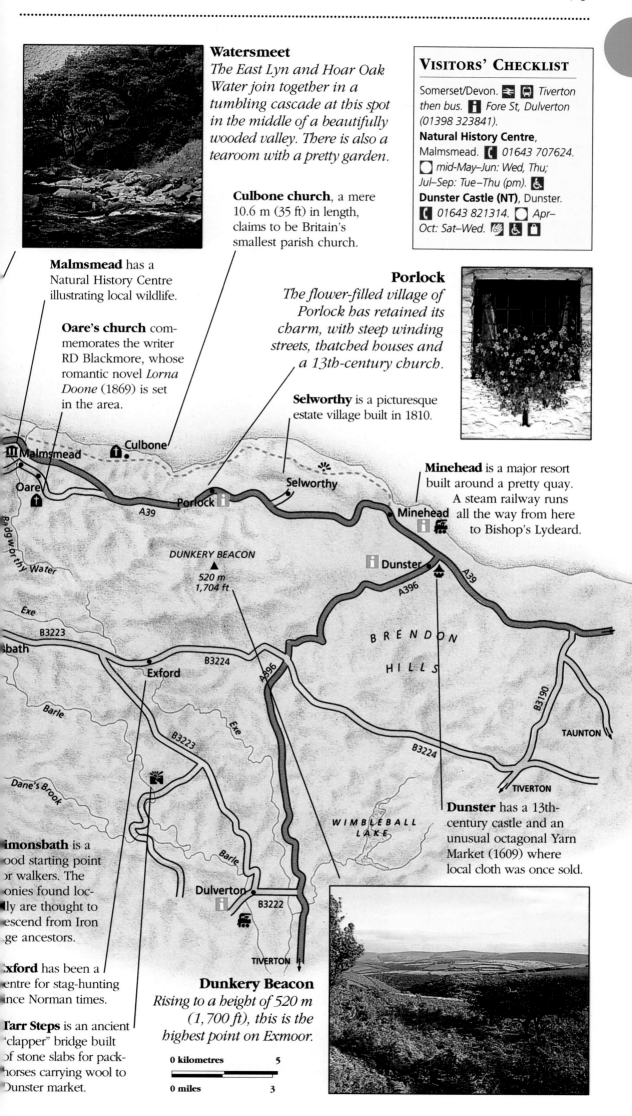

Dunkery Beacon
Rising to a height of 520 m (1,700 ft), this is the highest point on Exmoor.

0 kilometres 5

0 miles 3

Taunton ❷

Somerset. 🏘 77,000. ✈ 🚆 🚌
i *Paul St (01823 336 344).*
🛒 *Tue (livestock), Sat.*

TAUNTON LIES at the heart of a fertile region famous for its apples and cider, but it was the prosperous wool industry that financed the massive church of **St Mary Magdalene** (1488–1514) with its glorious tower. Taunton's **castle** was the setting for the notorious Bloody Assizes of 1685 when "Hanging" Judge Jeffreys dispensed harsh retribution on the Duke of Monmouth and his followers for an uprising against King James II *(see pp56–7)*. The 12th-century building now houses the **Somerset County Museum**, covering local history. A star exhibit is the Roman mosaic from a villa at Low Ham, Somerset, showing the love story of Dido and Aeneas.

ENVIRONS: Created in 1903–8, **Hestercombe Garden** is one of Sir Edwin Lutyens' *(see p29)* and Gertrude Jekyll's *(see p27)* greatest surviving masterpieces.

🏛 **Somerset County Museum**
Castle Green. **(** *01823 355504.* ◯
Tue–Sat & public hols. ● *25, 26 Dec, 1 Jan, Good Fri.* 💷 ♿ *ground floor.*
🌿 **Hestercombe Garden**
Cheddon Fitzpaine. **(** *01823 413923.* ◯ *daily.* 💷 🖥 🎁

SOMERSET CIDER

Somerset is one of the few English counties where real farmhouse cider, known as "scrumpy", is still made using the traditional methods. Cider once formed part of the farm labourer's wages and local folklore has it that various unsavoury additives, such as iron nails, were added to give strength. Cider-making can be seen at **Sheppy's** farm, on the A38 near Taunton.

Scrumpy cider

Wells ❸

Somerset. 🏘 10,000. 🚌 **i** *Market Place (01749 672552).* 🛒 *Wed, Sat.*

WELLS IS NAMED after St Andrew's Well, the sacred spring that bubbles up from the ground near the 14th-century **Bishop's Palace**, residence of the Bishop of Bath and Wells. A tranquil market town, Wells is famous for its magnificent cathedral which was begun in the late 1100s. Pennyless Porch, where beggars once received alms, leads from the bustling market place to the calm of the cathedral close. **Wells Museum** has prehistoric finds from nearby Wookey Hole caves.

Cathedral clock (1386–92)

ENVIRONS: To the northeast of Wells lies the impressive cave complex of **Wookey Hole**, which has an extensive range of popular amusements.

🏛 **Wells Museum**
8 Cathedral Green. **(** *01749 673477.* ◯ *Easter–Oct: daily; Nov–Easter: Wed–Mon.* ● *24–25 Dec.* 💷 📷
🦇 **Wookey Hole**
Off A371. **(** *01749 672243.* ◯ *daily.* ● *17–25 Dec.* 💷 🎥 🍴

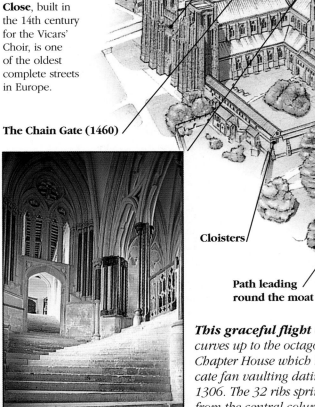

The West Front features 365 fine medieval statues of kings, knights and saints – many of them life-size.

The Vicars' Close, built in the 14th century for the Vicars' Choir, is one of the oldest complete streets in Europe.

The Chain Gate (1460)

Cloisters

Path leading round the moat

This graceful flight of steps curves up to the octagonal Chapter House which has delicate fan vaulting dating from 1306. The 32 ribs springing from the central column create a beautiful palm-tree effect.

Glastonbury Abbey, left in ruins in 1539 after the Dissolution

Glastonbury ④

Somerset. 👥 *9,000.* 🚌 ℹ️ *Tribunal, High St (01458 832954).* 🚌 *Tue.*

SHROUDED in Arthurian myth and rich in mystical association, the town of Glastonbury was once one of the most important destinations for pilgrims in England. Now thousands flock here for the annual rock festival *(see p67)* and for the summer solstice on Midsummer's Day (21 June).

Over the years history and legend have become intertwined, and the monks who founded **Glastonbury Abbey,** around 700, found it profitable to encourage the association between Glastonbury and the mythical "Blessed Isle" known as Avalon – alleged to be the last resting place of King Arthur and the Holy Grail *(see p315).*

The great abbey was left in ruins after the Dissolution of the Monasteries *(see pp54–5).* Even so, some magnificent relics survive, including parts of the vast Norman abbey church, the unusual Abbot's Kitchen, with its octagonal roof, and the wonderful abbey barn, now the **Somerset Rural Life Museum**.

Growing in the abbey grounds is a cutting from the famous Glastonbury thorn which is said to have miraculously grown from the staff of St Joseph of Arimathea. According to myth, he was sent around AD 60 to convert England to Christianity. The English hawthorn still astonishes everyone by flowering at Christmas as well as in May.

The **Lake Village Museum** has some interesting finds from the Iron Age lake settlements that once fringed the marshlands around **Glastonbury Tor**. A landmark seen for miles around, the Tor is a natural hill, crowned by the remains of a 14th-century church.

🏛 **Somerset Rural Life Museum**
Chilkwell St. ☎ *01458 831197.* ◯ *Easter–Oct: Tue–Sun; Nov–Easter: Tue–Sat & public hols.* ● *24–26 Dec, 1 Jan, Good Fri.* 📷 ♿ *limited.* 📷
🏛 **Lake Village Museum**
Tribunal, High St. ☎ *01749 832954.* ◯ *daily.* ● *25, 26 Dec.* 📷

Bishops' tombs circle the chancel. This sumptuous marble tomb, in the south aisle, is that of Bishop Lord Arthur Hervey, who was Bishop of Bath and Wells (1869–94).

The palace moat is home to swans which ring a bell by the gatehouse when they want to be fed. Feeding times are at 11am and 4pm.

The Bishop's Palace (1230–40)

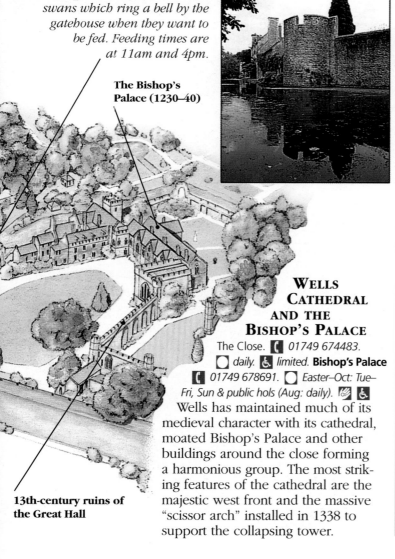

WELLS CATHEDRAL AND THE BISHOP'S PALACE
The Close. ☎ *01749 674483.* ◯ *daily.* ♿ *limited.* **Bishop's Palace** ☎ *01749 678691.* ◯ *Easter–Oct: Tue–Fri, Sun & public hols (Aug: daily).* 📷 ♿
Wells has maintained much of its medieval character with its cathedral, moated Bishop's Palace and other buildings around the close forming a harmonious group. The most striking features of the cathedral are the majestic west front and the massive "scissor arch" installed in 1338 to support the collapsing tower.

13th-century ruins of the Great Hall

Cheddar Gorge ⑤

DESCRIBED AS A "deep frightful chasm" by novelist Daniel Defoe in 1724, Cheddar Gorge is a spectacular ravine cut through the Mendip plateau by fast-flowing streams during the glacial phases of the last Ice Age. Cheddar has given its name to a rich cheese which originates from here and is now produced worldwide. The caves in the gorge once provided the perfect environment of constant temperature and high humidity for storing and maturing the cheese.

VISITORS' CHECKLIST

On B3135, Somerset. ℹ️
Cheddar Gorge (01934 744071).
🚌 from Wells. 📷 🔌 🍴 📺
Cheddar Showcaves, Jacob's Ladder & Museum 📞 01934 742343. ⭕ daily. ⬤ 24, 25 Dec. ♿ ⭐ limited. 🖥️ 🚻
Chewton Cheese Dairy, Chewton Mendip. 📞 01761 241666. ⭕ Mon–Wed, Fri, Sat. ⬤ 25, 26 Dec, 1 Jan. ♿ ⭐

The Chewton Cheese Dairy
(7 miles or 12 km east along the B3135) has demonstrations of traditional Cheddar cheeses being made by hand (except on Thursdays and Sundays).

The B3135 road winds round the base of the 3 mile (5 km) gorge.

"Cheddar Man", a 9,000-year-old skeleton, is on display in the museum.

A footpath follows the top of the gorge on its southern edge.

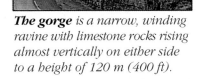

The gorge *is a narrow, winding ravine with limestone rocks rising almost vertically on either side to a height of 120 m (400 ft).*

Gough's Cave is noted for its cathedral-like proportions.

Tourist information

Cox's Cave contains unusually shaped stalactites and stalagmites.

Jacob's Ladder has 274 steps leading to the top of the gorge.

The rare Cheddar Pink *is among the astonishing range of plant and animal life harboured in the rocks.*

Prospect Tower has far-reaching views over the area to the south and west.

Bristol ⑥

See pp280–81.

Bath ⑦

See pp282–5.

Bradford-on-Avon ⑧

Wiltshire. 🏠 *9,500.* 🚉 **i** *Silver St (01225 865797).* 🛒 *Thu.*

THIS LOVELY COTSWOLD-STONE town with its steep flagged lanes is full of flamboyant houses built by wealthy wool and cloth merchants in the 17th and 18th centuries. One fine Georgian example is **Church House**, on Church Street. A little further along, **St Laurence Church** is a remarkably complete Saxon building founded in 705 *(see p51).* The church was converted to a

Typical Cotswold-stone architecture in Bradford-on-Avon

school and cottage in the 12th century and was rediscovered in the 19th century when a vicar recognized the characteristic cross-shaped roof.

In the middle of the medieval **Town Bridge** is a small stone cell, built as a chapel in the 13th century but later used as a lock-up for 17th-century drunks and vagrants. A short walk away, near converted mill buildings and a boat-filled stretch of the Kennet and Avon Canal, is the massive 14th-century **Tithe Barn** *(see pp32–3).*

🏛 **Tithe Barn**
Pound Lane. ◯ *daily.* ● *25, 26 Dec.* ♿

Corsham ⑨

Wiltshire. 🏠 *12,000.* **i** *High St (01249 714660).* 🛒 *Tue.*

THE STREETS of Corsham are lined with stately Georgian houses which make it a delight for connoisseurs of Cotswold-stone architecture. **St Bartholmew's Church** has an elegant spire and a lovely carved alabaster tomb (1960) to the late Lady Methuen, whose family founded Methuen publishers. The family acquired **Corsham Court** in 1745 with its picture gallery and a remarkable collection of Flemish, Italian and English paintings, including works by Van Dyck, Lippi and Reynolds. Peacocks wander through the grounds, adding their colour and elegance to the façade of the 18th-century mansion.

Peacock in grounds, Corsham Court

🏛 **Corsham Court**
off A4. **(** *01249 701610.* ◯ *Easter–Sep: Tue–Sun; Oct–Easter: Sat, Sun (pm).* 📷 ♿ *limited.*

Lacock ⑩

Wiltshire. 🏠 *1,000.*

MAINTAINED in its pristine state by the National Trust, with very few modern intrusions, Lacock is a picturesque and delightful village to explore. The meandering River Avon forms the boundary to the north side of the churchyard, while humorous stone figures look down from **St Cyriac Church**. Inside the 15th-century church is the splendid Renaissance-style tomb of Sir William Sharington (1495–1553). He acquired **Lacock Abbey** after the Dissolution of the Monasteries *(see pp54–5),* but it was a later owner, John Ivory Talbot, who had the buildings remodelled in the

Gothic revival style, in vogue in the early 18th century. The abbey is famous for the window (in the south gallery) from which his descendant William Henry Fox Talbot, an early pioneer of photography, took his first picture in 1835, and for the the sheets of snowdrops which cover the abbey grounds in spring. A 16th-century barn at the abbey gates has been converted to the **Fox Talbot Museum**, which has displays on Fox Talbot's experiments.

ENVIRONS: Designed by Robert Adam *(see pp28–9)* in 1769, **Bowood House** includes the laboratory where Joseph Priestley discovered oxygen in 1774, and a rich collection of sculpture, costumes and paintings. Italianate gardens surround the house while the lake-filled grounds, landscaped by Capability Brown *(see pp26–7),* contain a Doric temple, grotto, cascade and now a large adventure playground.

🏠 **Lacock Abbey**
(NT) High St. **(** *01249 730227.* ◯ *Apr–Oct: Wed–Mon (pm).* ● *Good Fri.* 📷 ♿ *limited in house.*
🏛 **Fox Talbot Museum**
(NT) High St. **(** *01249 730459.* ◯ *Mar–Oct: daily.* ● *Good Fri.* 📷 ♿
🏛 **Bowood House**
Derry Hill, nr Calne. **(** *01249 812102.* ◯ *Mar–Oct: daily.* 📷 ♿

William Henry Fox Talbot (1800–77)

Bristol ⑥

IT WAS IN 1497 that John Cabot sailed from Bristol on his historic voyage to North America. The city, at the mouth of the Avon, became the main British port for transatlantic trade, pioneering the era of the ocean-going steam liner with the construction of *s.s. Great Britain*. The city flourished as a major trading centre, growing rich on the distribution of wine, tobacco and, in the 17th century, slaves.

King Brennus, St John's Gate

Because of its docks and aero-engine factories, Bristol was heavily bombed during World War II and the city centre bears witness to the ideas of post-war planners. The docks have been shifted to deeper waters at Avonmouth and the old dock area is being transformed, taking on new life characterized by waterside cafés, shops and art galleries.

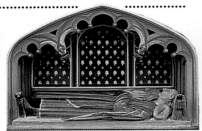

Memorial to William Canynge the Younger (1400–74)

Exploring Bristol

The most interesting part of the city lies around Broad Street, King Street and Corn Street. There is a lively covered market, part of which occupies the **Corn Exchange**, built by John Wood the Elder *(see p282)* in 1743. Outside are the famous Bristol Nails, four bronze 16th–17th-century pedestals which Bristol merchants used as tables when paying for goods – hence the expression "to pay on the nail". **St John's Gate**, at the head of Broad Street, has colourful medieval statues of Bristol's two mythical founders, King Brennus and King Benilus. Nearby between Lewins Mead and Colston Street, **Christmas Steps** is a steep lane lined with specialist shops. The **Chapel of the Three Kings** at the top was founded in 1504 and is now adjoined by the flamboyant Burgundian-style Foster's Almshouses of 1861–83.

A group of buildings around the cobbled King Street include the 17th-century timber-framed **Llandoger Trow** inn. It is

The Two Sisters **(c.1889) by Renoir, City Museum and Art Gallery**

here that Daniel Defoe is said to have met Alexander Selkirk, whose true-life island exile served as the inspiration for Defoe's novel *Robinson Crusoe* (1719). Just up from here is the **Theatre Royal**, a rare survival of a Georgian playhouse, built in 1766.

Not far away the renowned **Arnolfini Gallery** on Narrow Quay is a showcase for contemporary art, drama, dance and cinema. In front, a statue of John Cabot (1425– c.1500) looks wistfully across the old Floating Harbour which is now lined with cafés and pubs.

To the west of the city, the elegant suburbs of **Clifton** revel in ornate Regency crescents, many now used as lodgings or faculties of Bristol University. The impressive **Clifton Suspension Bridge** perfectly complements the drama of the steep Avon gorge. Completed in 1864, the bridge is testimony to Brunel's

engineering skill. **Bristol Zoo Gardens**, nearby, concentrates on breeding and conserving endangered species.

🛈 St Mary Redcliffe

Redcliffe Way. 📞 *0117 9291487.* ◻ *daily.* ♿ 🎫 *by arrangement.* ▣

There are few better places to discover the history of Bristol than this magnificent 14th-century church, claimed by Queen Elizabeth I to be "the fairest in England". The church owes much to the generosity of William Canynge the Elder and Younger, both famous mayors of Bristol. Inscriptions on the tombs of merchants and sailors tell of lives devoted to trade in Asia and the West Indies. Look out for the Bristol maze in the north aisle.

🏛 s.s. Great Britain

Gas Ferry Rd. 📞 *0117 9260680.* ◻ *daily.* ● *24, 25 Dec.* 🎫 ♿ *limited.* 🎫 *by arrangement.* ▣ ▢ 🅿

The *s.s. Great Britain*, designed by Isambard Kingdom Brunel, is the world's first large iron passenger ship and is a prototype of today's modern vessels. Launched in 1843, it travelled 32 times round the world before it was abandoned in the Falkland Islands in 1886. The wreckage was rescued in 1970 and now stands, being restored, in the dock where it was originally built. The ship is located next to the Maritime Heritage Centre and is an impressive reminder of the way in which Brunel revolutionized transport in the 19th century.

🏠 Georgian House

7 Great George St. 📞 *0117 9211362.* ◻ *Apr–Oct: Sat–Wed.*

Life in a wealthy Bristol merchant's house of the 1790s is illustrated by Adam-style furnishings in the elegant drawing room and by a miscellany of pots, pans, roasting spits and laundry in the servants' area below stairs.

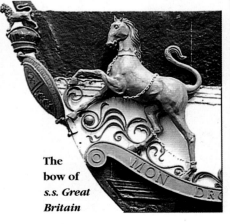

The bow of *s.s. Great Britain*

Warehouses overlooking the Floating Harbour

VISITORS' CHECKLIST

Avon. 👥 375,000. ✈ Lulsgate, 7 miles (11 km) SW Bristol. ⇄ Temple Gate (Temple Meads). 🚌 Marlborough St. ℹ St Nicholas St (0117 926 0767). 🔄 daily. 🎪 Harbour Regatta: Jul–Aug; International Balloon Fiesta: Aug; International Kite Festival: Sep.

🏛 Bristol Industrial Museum

Prince's Wharf. 📞 0117 9251470. ◯ Apr–Oct: Sat–Wed; Nov–Mar: Sat–Sun. ⬤ 25–27 Dec. ♿

The museum's diverse collection of vehicles and models illustrate the astonishing range of products made in Bristol over the last 300 years. Among them are luxurious Bristol cars, the once ubiquitous Bristol bus, the world's first touring caravan and Concorde, represented here by a full-scale model of the pilot's cockpit.

🏛 City Museum and Art Gallery

Queen's Rd. 📞 0117 9223571. ◯ daily. ⬤ 24–26 Dec, 1 Jan & public hols. ♿ limited. 🖥 📷

Varied collections include stuffed tigers, dinosaur fossils, Roman tableware, the largest collection of Chinese glass outside China and a fine collection of European paintings including works by Renoir and Bellini. Bristol artists include Sir Thomas Lawrence and Francis Danby.

⛪ Bristol Cathedral

College Green. 📞 0117 9264879. ◯ daily. **Donation.** ♿ limited.

Bristol's cathedral took an unusually long time to build. Rapid progress was made between 1298 and 1330, when the wonderfully inventive choir was built; the transepts and tower were finished in 1515, and another 350 years passed before the Victorian architect, GE Street, built the nave.

Humourous and eccentric medieval carving abounds – a small snail crawling across the stone foliage in the antechapel, musical monkeys in the 13th-century Elder Lady Chapel, and a famous set of wooden misericords in the choir.

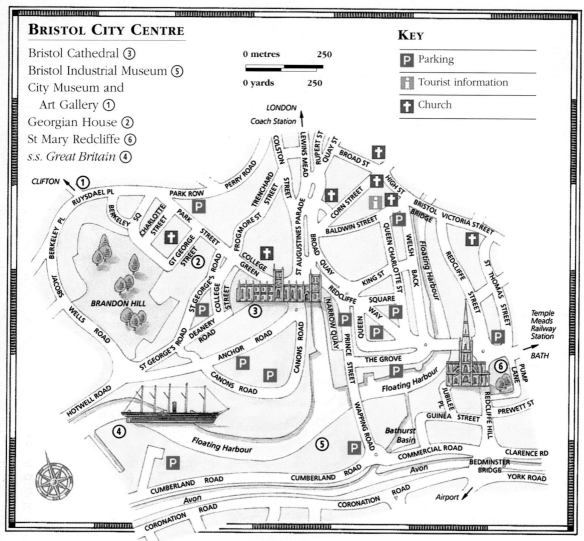

BRISTOL CITY CENTRE

Bristol Cathedral ③
Bristol Industrial Museum ⑤
City Museum and Art Gallery ①
Georgian House ②
St Mary Redcliffe ⑥
s.s. Great Britain ④

0 metres   250

0 yards   250

KEY

🅿 Parking

ℹ Tourist information

⛪ Church

Street-by-Street: Bath 7

BATH OWES ITS MAGNIFICENT Georgian townscape to the bubbling pool of water at the heart of the Roman Baths. The Romans transformed Bath into England's first spa resort and it regained fame as a spa town in the 18th century. At this time the two brilliant John Woods (Elder and Younger), both architects, designed the city's fine Palladian-style buildings. Many houses bear plaques recording the numerous famous people who have resided here.

The Circus
This is a daring departure from the typical Georgian square, by John Wood the Elder (1705–54).

No. 1 Royal Crescent

No. 17 is where the 18th-century painter Thomas Gainsborough lived *(see p157).*

Assembly Rooms and Museum of Costume

★ Royal Crescent
Hailed the most majestic street in Britain, this graceful arc of 30 houses (1767–74) is the masterpiece of John Wood the Younger. West of the Royal Crescent, Royal Victoria Park (1830) is the city's largest open space.

Jane Austen *(see p156),* the writer, stayed at No. 13 Queen's Square on one of many visits to Bath in her youth.

Milsom Street and New Bond Street contain some of Bath's most elegant shops.

KEY

- – – – Suggested route

0 metres   100

0 yards   100

Theatre Royal (1805)

STAR SIGHTS

- ★ **Royal Crescent**
- ★ **Roman Baths**
- ★ **Bath Abbey**

Pump Rooms
These tearooms once formed the social hub of the 18th-century spa community. They contain this decorative drinking fountain.

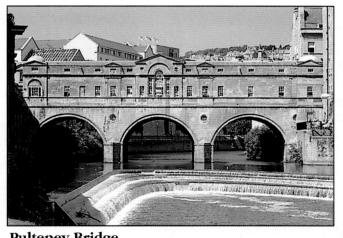

Pulteney Bridge

*This charming bridge (1769–74), designed by Robert
Adam, is lined with shops and links the centre with
the magnificent Great Pulteney Street. Look out
for a rare Victorian pillar box on the east bank.*

The Building of Bath Museum

VISITORS' CHECKLIST

Avon. 👥 *83,000.* ✈ *Lulsgate
Airport, 20 miles (32 km) W
Bath.* 🚆 *Dorchester St.*
🚌 *Manvers St.* ℹ *Abbey
Chambers, Abbey Church Yard
(01225 477101).* 🎭 *daily.* 🎪
International Festival: May–Jun.

★ **Bath Abbey**
*The splendid abbey stands at
the heart of the old city in the
Abbey Church Yard, a paved
piazza enlivened by buskers.
Its unique façade features
stone angels climbing Jacob's
Ladder to heaven.*

★ **Roman Baths**
*Built in the 1st century,
this bathing complex
is one of Britain's
greatest memorials
to the Roman era.*

**Holburne
Museum
and Crafts
Study
Centre**

Parade Grounds

*Courting couples came to this
pretty riverside park for secret
liaisons in the 18th century.*

**Rail
& coach stations**

Sally Lunn's House (1482)
is one of Bath's oldest houses.

Exploring Bath

Piazza cellist

THE BEAUTIFUL AND COMPACT CITY OF BATH is set among the rolling green hills of the Avon valley, and wherever you walk you will enjoy spendid views of the surrounding countryside. The traffic-free heart of this lively city is full of street musicians, museums, cafés and enticing shops, while the elegant honey-coloured Georgian houses, so characteristic of Bath, form an elegant backdrop to city life.

Bath Abbey, at the heart of the old city, begun in 1499

✝ Bath Abbey

Abbey Churchyard. 📞 01225 422462. ◯ daily. ● during services. **Donation.** ♿ ⬜

This splendid abbey was supposedly designed by divine agency. According to legend, God dictated the form of the church to Bishop Oliver King in a dream; this story has been immortalized in the wonderfully eccentric carvings on the west front. The bishop began work in 1499, rebuilding a church that had been founded in the 8th century. Memorials cover the walls and the varied Georgian inscriptions make fascinating reading. The spacious interior is remarkable for the delicate lace-like fan vaulting of the nave, an addition made by Sir George Gilbert Scott in 1874.

🏛 Assembly Rooms and Museum of Costume

Bennett St. 📞 01225 477789. ◯ daily. ● 25, 26 Dec. ♿ ⬜

The Assembly Rooms were built by Wood the Younger in 1769, as a meeting place for the fashionable elite and as an elegant backdrop for many glittering balls. Jane Austen's novel *Northanger Abbey* (1818) describes the atmosphere of gossip and flirtation here.

In the basements, kept dark to preserve the many precious textiles, is a collection of costumes in authentic period settings. The display illustrates changing fashions from the 16th century to the present day.

🏛 No. 1 Royal Crescent

Royal Crescent. 📞 01225 428 126. ◯ Tue–Sun & public hols. ● Dec, Jan, Good Fri. ♿ ⬜

This museum lets you look inside the first house of Bath's most beautiful terrace, giving a glimpse of what life was like for 18th-century aristocrats, such as the Duke of York, who lived here. The house is furnished down to such details as the dog-powered spit used to roast meat in front of the fire.

🏛 Holburne Museum and Crafts Study Centre

Great Pulteney St. 📞 01225 466669. ◯ daily (Nov–Easter: Tue–Sat, Sun pm). ● mid-Dec–mid-Feb. ♿ ♿

This historic building is named after Thomas Holburne of Menstrie (1793–1874), whose collections form the nucleus of the museum's impressive display of fine and decorative arts. Paintings by British artists such as Gainsborough and Stubbs can be seen together with 20th-century craftwork.

ROMAN BATHS MUSEUM

Stall St. 📞 01225 477784. ◯ daily. ● 25, 26 Dec. ♿ ♿ limited. 📷

According to legend, Bath owes its origin to the Celtic King Bladud who discovered the curative properties of its natural hot springs in 860 BC. Cast out from his kingdom as a leper, Bladud cured himself by imitating his swine and rolling in the hot mud at Bath.

In the first century, the Romans built baths around the spring, and a temple dedicated to the goddess Sulis Minerva, who combined the attributes of the water goddess Sulis, worshipped by the Celts, and the Roman goddess Minerva. Among the museum's Roman relics is a gilded bronze head of Sulis Minerva, discovered in 1727.

Medieval monks of Bath Abbey also exploited the springs' properties, but it was when Queen Anne visited in 1702–3 that Bath reached its zenith as a fashionable watering place.

Gilded bronze head of Sulis Minerva

🏛 Building of Bath Museum

The Paragon. 📞 01225 333895.
🕐 Tue–Sun & public hols.
⬤ end-Nov–mid-Feb. 🖼 ♿ limited.

This museum, housed in an old Methodist chapel, is an excellent starting point for exploring the city. It shows how, in the 18th century, Bath was transformed from a medieval wool town into one of Europe's most elegant spas. John Wood and his son designed the Classically inspired stone fronts of the Royal Crescent and the Circus, leaving individual property speculators to develop the houses behind. While the façades speak of harmony and order, the houses behind show the result of rampant individualism, with no two houses alike. The museum looks at every aspect of the buildings, from practical issues, such as heating, lighting and cooking, to fashionable whim.

🏛 American Museum

Claverton Manor, Claverton Down.
📞 01225 460503. 🕐 Aug: daily (pm); Mar–Oct, mid-Nov–mid-Dec: Tue– Sun (pm). 🖼 ♿ 💻 🏠

Founded in 1961 in an attempt to deepen mutual understanding between Britain and America, this was the first American museum to be established in this country. Rooms in the 1820 manor house are decorated in many styles, from the first rudimentary dwellings of settlers to opulent 19th-century homes. There are special sections on Shaker furniture, quilts and Native American art, and a replica of George Washington's Mount Vernon garden of 1785.

A 19th-century American Indian weathervane

RICHARD "BEAU" NASH (1674–1762)

Elected in 1704 as Master of Ceremonies, "Beau" Nash played a crucial role in transforming Bath into the fashionable centre of Georgian society. During his long career, he devised a never-ending round of games, balls and entertainment (including gambling) that kept the idle rich amused and ensured a constant flow of visitors.

The dome (1897) is based on St Stephen Walbrook church in London (see p119).

The Great Bath

The open-air Great Bath, which stands at the heart of the Roman spa complex, was not discovered until the 1870s. Leading off this magnificent pool were various bathing chambers which became increasingly sophisticated over the four centuries the Romans were here. The baths fell into ruin, but extensive excavations have revealed the remarkable skill of Roman engineering.

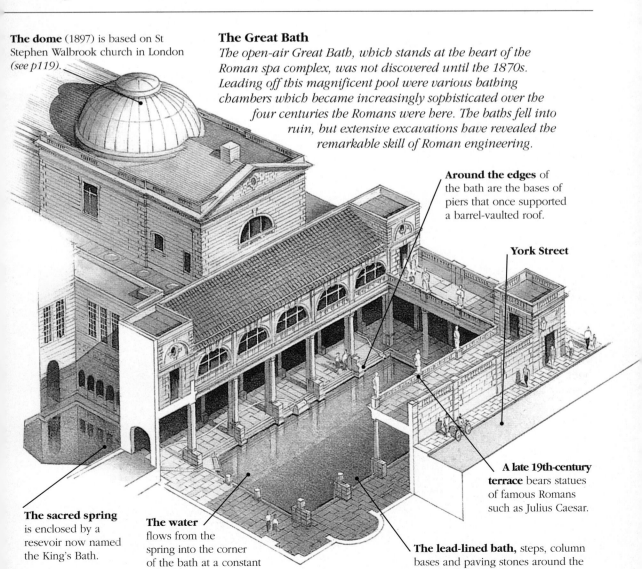

Around the edges of the bath are the bases of piers that once supported a barrel-vaulted roof.

York Street

A late 19th-century terrace bears statues of famous Romans such as Julius Caesar.

The sacred spring is enclosed by a resevoir now named the King's Bath.

The water flows from the spring into the corner of the bath at a constant temperature of 46° C (115° F).

The lead-lined bath, steps, column bases and paving stones around the edge all date from Roman times.

Stonehenge ⑪

Stonehenge as it is today

BUILT IN SEVERAL STAGES from about 3000 BC, Stonehenge is Europe's most famous prehistoric monument. We can only guess at the rituals that took place here, but the alignment of the stones leaves little doubt that the circle is connected with the sun and the passing of the seasons, and that its builders possessed a sophisticated understanding of both arithmetic and astronomy. Despite popular belief, the circle was not built by the Druids, an Iron Age priestly cult that flourished in Britain from around 250 BC – more than 1,000 years after Stonehenge was completed.

Finds from a burial mound near Stonehenge (Devizes Museum)

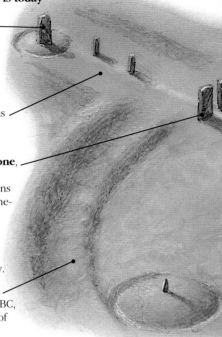

The Heal Stone casts a long shadow straight to the heart of the circle on Midsummer's day.

The Avenue forms a ceremonial approach to the site.

The Slaughter Stone, named by 17th-century antiquarians who believed Stonehenge to be a place of human sacrifice, was in fact one of a pair forming a doorway.

The Outer Bank, dug around 3000 BC, is the oldest part of Stonehenge.

BUILDING OF STONEHENGE

Stonehenge's monumental scale is all the more impressive given that the only tools available were made of stone, wood and bone. The labour involved in quarrying, transporting and erecting the huge stones at Stonehenge was such that its builders must have been able to command immense resources, and control vast numbers of people.

RECONSTRUCTION OF STONEHENGE

This illustration shows what Stonehenge probably looked like about 4,000 years ago.

A sarsen stone was moved on rollers and levered into a pit.

With levers supported by timber packing, it was gradually raised.

The stone was then pulled upright by about 200 men hauling on ropes.

The pit round the bas was packed tightly wit stones and chalk.

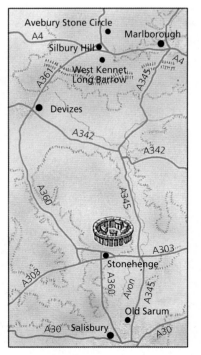

WILTSHIRE'S OTHER PREHISTORIC SITES

The open countryside of the Salisbury Plain made this area an important centre of prehistoric settlement, and today it is covered in many ancient remains. Ringing the horizon around Stonehenge are scores of circular barrows, or burial mounds, where members of the ruling class were honoured with burial close to the temple site. Ceremonial bronze weapons, jewellery and other finds excavated around Stonehenge and the other prehistoric sites in the area can be seen in the museums at Salisbury *(see pp290–91)* and Devizes.

Silbury Hill (NT) is Europe's largest prehistoric earthwork,

Silbury Hill

but despite extensive excavations its purpose remains a mystery. Built out of chalk blocks around 2750 BC, the hill covers 2 ha (5 acres) and rises to a height of 40 m (131 ft). Nearby **West Kennet Long Barrow** (NT) is the biggest

◁ **The natural limestone arch of Durdle Door, Dorset coast**

The Sarsen Circle was erected around 1500 BC and is capped by lintel stones held in place by mortice and tenon joints.

The Bluestone Circle was built around 2000 BC out of some 80 slabs quarried in south Wales. It was never completed.

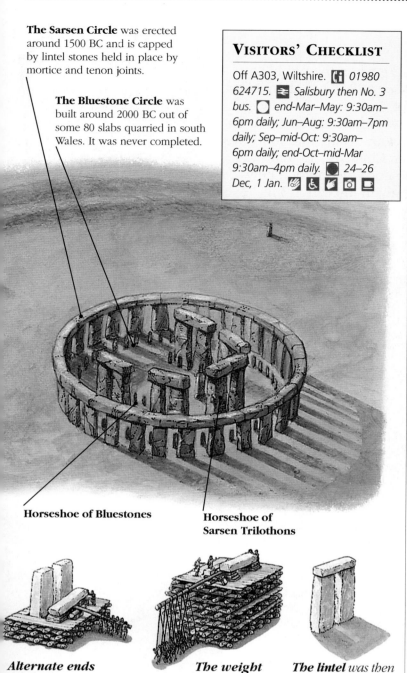

Horseshoe of Bluestones

Horseshoe of Sarsen Trilothons

VISITORS' CHECKLIST

Off A303, Wiltshire. 01980 624715. Salisbury then No. 3 bus. end-Mar–May: 9:30am–6pm daily; Jun–Aug: 9:30am–7pm daily; Sep–mid-Oct: 9:30am–6pm daily; end-Oct–mid-Mar 9:30am–4pm daily. 24–26 Dec, 1 Jan.

Alternate ends of the lintel were levered up.

The weight of the lintel was supported by a timber platform.

The lintel was then levered sideways on to the uprights.

chambered tomb in England, with numerous stone-lined "rooms" and a monumental entrance. Built as a communal cemetery around 3250 BC, it was in use for several centuries – old bodies were taken away to make room for newcomers.

Old Sarum is set within the massive ramparts of a 1st-century Romano-British hill fort. The Norman founders of Old Sarum built their own motte and bailey castle inside this ready-made fortification, and the remains of this survive along with the foundations of the huge cathedral of 1075. Above ground nothing remains of the town that once sat within the ramparts. The town's occupants moved to the fertile

river valley site that became Salisbury during the early 12th century (*see pp290–91*).

Old Sarum

Castle Rd. 01722 335398. daily. 24–26 Dec, 1 Jan. limited.

The chambered tomb of West Kennet Long Barrow (c.3250 BC)

Sarsen stone forming part of the Avebury Stone Circle

Avebury ⑫

Wiltshire. 600. Swindon then bus. The Great Barn Museum (01672 539425).

BUILT AROUND 2500 BC, the **Avebury Stone Circle** (NT) surrounds the village of Avebury and was probably once some form of religious centre. Superstitious villagers smashed many of the stones in the 18th century, believing the circle to have been a place of pagan sacrifice. The original form of the circle is best appreciated by a visit to the excellent **Alexander Keiller Museum** which illustrates the construction of the circle and its relation to the other monuments in the region. Housed in a splendid thatched barn nearby is the **Museum of Wiltshire Rural Life**, which covers everything from cheese-making to shepherding.

St James's Church has a Norman font carved with sea monsters, and a rare 15th-century choir screen.

ENVIRONS: A few minutes drive east, **Marlborough** is an attractive town with a long and broad High Street lined with colonnaded Georgian shops.

Alexander Keiller Museum

(NT) High St. 01672 539250. daily. 24–26 Dec, 1 Jan.

Museum of Wiltshire Rural Life

The Great Barn Museum. 01672 539425. daily (mid-Nov–mid-Mar: Sat, Sun). 25, 26 Dec.

Salisbury ⑬

SALISBURY WAS FOUNDED IN 1220, when the old hill-top settlement of Old Sarum *(see p289)* was abandoned, being too arid and windswept, in favour of a new site among the lush water meadows where the rivers Avon, Nadder and Bourne meet. Creamy white limestone was floated down the Nadder from Chilmark, 12 miles (20 km) west of Salisbury, for the construction of a new cathedral which was built mostly in the early 13th century, over the remarkably short space of 38 years. Its magnificent landmark spire – the tallest in England – was an inspired afterthought added in 1280–1310.

The 15th-century house of John A'Port, Queen's Street

network of alleys fans out from this point with a number of fine timber-framed houses. In the large bustling **Market Place** the **Guildhall** is an unusual grey-brick building from 1788–95, used for civic functions. More attractive are the brick and tile-hung houses on the north side of the square, many with Georgian façades concealing medieval houses.

Bishop's Walk and a sculpture by Elisabeth Frink (1930–93), Cathedral Close

The Cloisters are the largest in England. They were added between 1263 and 1284 in the Decorated style.

Exploring Salisbury

The spacious and tranquil **Close**, with its schools, hospitals, theological colleges and clergy housing, makes a fine setting for Salisbury's cathedral. Among the numerous elegant buildings here are the **Matrons' College**, built in 1682 as a home for clergy widows, and 13th-century **Malmesbury House** with its splendid Queen Anne façade (1719), fronted by lovely wrought-iron gates. Other buildings of interest include the 13th-century **Deanery**, the 15th-century **Wardrobe**, now a regimental museum, and the **Cathedral School**, housed in the 13th-century Bishop's Palace and famous for the quality of its choristers.

Beyond the walls of the Cathedral Close, Salisbury developed its chessboard layout, with areas devoted to different trades, perpetuated in street names such as Fish Row and Butcher Row. Leaving the close through **High Street Gate,** you reach the busy High Street leading to the 13th-century **Church of St Thomas**, which has a lovely carved timber roof (1450), and an early 16th-century Doom painting, showing Christ seated in judgement and demons seizing the damned. Nearby in Silver Street, **Poultry Cross** was built in the 15th century as a covered poultry market. An intricate

The Chapter House displays a copy of the *Magna Carta*. Its walls are decorated with scenes from the Old Testament.

The Trinity Chapel contains the grave of St Osmund who was bishop of Old Sarum from 1078–1099.

Choir stalls

Bishop Audley's Chantry, a magnificent 16th-century monument to the bishop, is one of several small chapels clustered round the altar.

Street signs reflecting trades of 13th-century Salisbury

Mompesson House

(NT) The Close. **(** 01722 335659.
○ Apr–Oct: Sat–Wed (pm).
限 限 limited. □

Built by a wealthy Wiltshire family in 1701, the handsomely furnished rooms of this house give an indication of life for the Close's inhabitants in the 18th century. The delightful garden, bounded by the north wall of the Close, has fine herbaceous borders.

Salisbury and South Wiltshire Museum

The Close. **(** 01722 332151.
○ Mon–Sat (Jul–Aug: daily).
● 24–26 Dec. 限 限 □ □

In the medieval King's House, this museum has displays on early man, Stonehenge and nearby Old Sarum (*see p289*).

ENVIRONS: The town of Wilton is renowned for its carpet industry, founded by the 8th Earl of Pembroke using French Huguenot refugee weavers. The town's ornate **church** (1844) is a brilliant example of Neo-Romanesque architecture, incorporating genuine Roman columns, Flemish Renaissance woodwork, German and Dutch stained glass and Italian mosaics.

Wilton House has been home to the Earls of Pembroke since it was converted from a nunnery after the Dissolution (*see pp54–5*). The house, largely rebuilt by Inigo Jones in the 17th century, includes one of the original Tudor towers, a fine collection of art and a landscaped park with a Palladian bridge (1737). The two glories of the house are the lavish Single and Double Cube State Rooms. Both have magnificently frescoed ceilings and gilded stucco work and were designed to hang a series of family portraits by Van Dyck.

The graceful spire
soars to a height of 123 m (404 ft).

The West Front *is decorated by rows of lavish symbolic figures and saints in niches.*

A roof tour takes you up to an external gallery at the base of the spire with views of the town and Old Sarum.

Wilton House

Wilton. **(** 01722 746729.
○ Easter–Oct: daily. 限 限 🍴 🛍

The clock dating from 1386 is the oldest working clock in Britain.

The nave is divided into ten bays by columns of polished Purbeck marble.

Northwest transept

SALISBURY CATHEDRAL

The Close. **(** 01722 555120. ○ daily. **Donation.** 限 □
The cathedral was mostly built between 1220 and 1258. It is a fine example of the Early English style of Gothic architecture, typified by tall, sharply pointed lancet windows, and it is rare in being almost uniform in style.

Numerous windows add to the airy and spacious atmosphere of the interior.

Double Cube room, designed by Inigo Jones in 1653

***The Longleat Tree* tapestry (1980) depicting a 400-year history**

Longleat House ⓮

Warminster, Wiltshire. *01985 844400.* *Warminster then taxi.* **House** *daily.* **Park** *mid-Mar–Oct.*

THE ARCHITECTURAL HISTORIAN John Summerson coined the term "prodigy house" to describe the exuberance and grandeur of Elizabethan architecture that is so well represented at Longleat. The house was started in 1540, when John Thynn bought the ruins of a priory on the site of Longleat for the sum of £53. The work he began here was continued by each generation, and over the centuries subsequent owners have added their own eccentric touches. These include the Breakfast Room and Lower Dining Room (dating from the 1870s), modelled on the Venetian Ducal Palace, and erotic murals painted by the present owner, the 7th Marquess of Bath. Today, the Great Hall is the only remaining room which belongs to Thynn's time.

In 1948, the 6th Marquess was the first landowner in Britain to open his stately home to the public, in order to fund the maintenance and preservation of the house and its vast estate. The grounds, landscaped by Capability Brown *(see p27)*, were turned into an expansive safari park in 1966, where lions, tigers and other wild animals roam freely. This, along with other commercial additions such as the world's largest maze, the Adventure Castle, and a range of special events, now draw even more visitors than the house.

Stourhead ⓯

STOURHEAD IS AMONG THE FINEST EXAMPLES of 18th-century landscape gardening in Britain *(see pp26–7)*. The garden was begun in the 1740s by Henry Hoare (1705–85), who inherited the estate and transformed it into a breathtaking work of art. Hoare created the lake, surrounding it with rare trees and plants, and Neo-Classical Italianate temples, grottoes and bridges. The Palladian-style house, built by Colen Campbell *(see p28)*, dates from 1724.

Pantheon
Hercules is among the statues of Roman gods housed in the elegant Pantheon (1753).

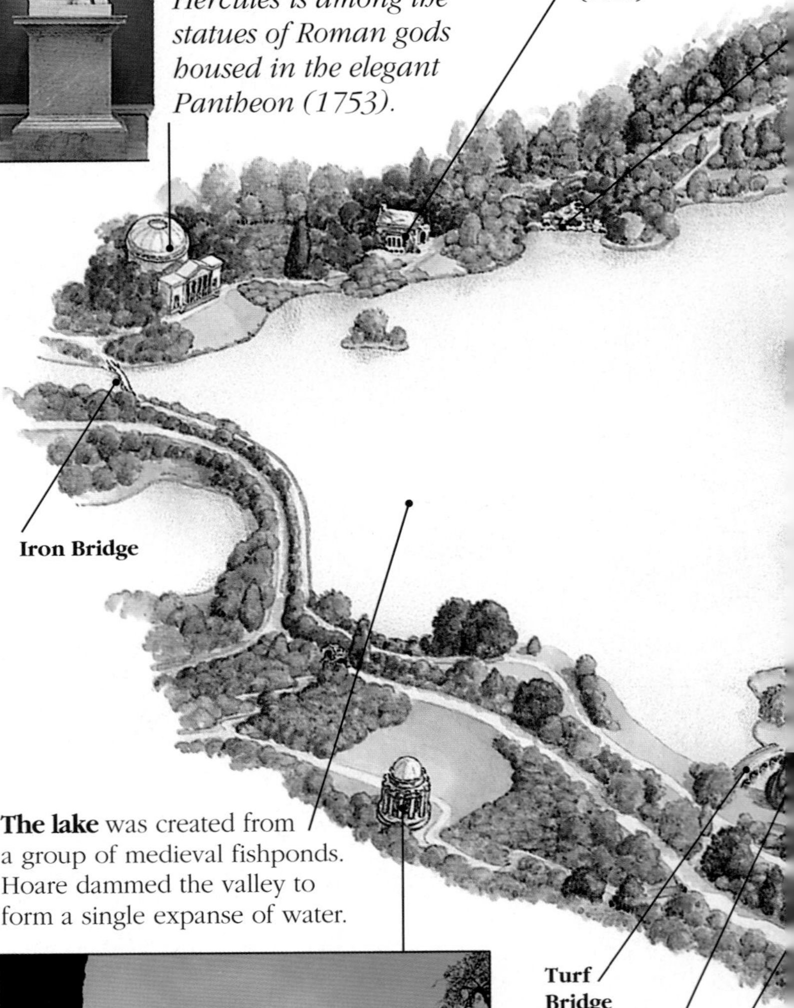
Gothic Cottage (1806)
Iron Bridge
The lake was created from a group of medieval fishponds. Hoare dammed the valley to form a single expanse of water.
Turf Bridge
Temple of Flora (1744)
A walk of 2 miles (3 km) round the lake provides a series of artistically contrived vistas.

★ Temple of Apollo
The Classical temples that dot the garden were all designed by architect Henry Flitcroft (1679–1769).

Grotto
Tunnels lead to an artificial cave with a pool and a life-size statue of the guardian of the River Stour, sculpted by John Cheere in 1748.

VISITORS' CHECKLIST

(NT) Stourton, Wiltshire.
☎ 01747 841152. 📠 0891 335205. 🚆 Gillingham then taxi.
House ◯ mid–Mar–Oct: noon–5:30pm Sat–Wed (last adm: 5pm).
Gardens ◯ 9am–7pm (or dusk if earlier) daily. 🌳 📷 except in house. ♿ limited. 🚻 🍴 ☕ 🛍

★ Stourhead House
Reconstructed after a fire in 1902, the house contains fine Chippendale furniture. The art collection reflects Henry Hoare's Classical tastes and includes The Choice of Hercules *(1637) by Nicolas Poussin.*

Colourful shrubs around the house include fragrant rhododendrons in spring.

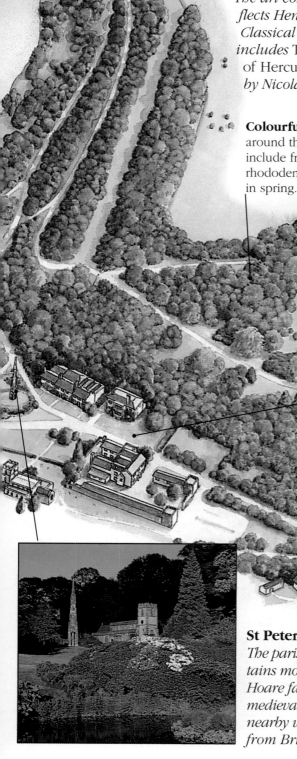

Stourton village was incorporated into Hoare's overall design. 🍴 💺

The reception contains exhibitions illustrating the story of Stourhead.

Entrance and car park

St Peter's Church
The parish church contains monuments to the Hoare family. The medieval monument nearby was brought from Bristol in 1765.

STAR SIGHTS
★ **Temple of Apollo**
★ **Stourhead House**

Shaftesbury ⑯

Dorset. 🏘 6,000. 🚌 ℹ️ 8 Bell St (01747 853514). 🚇 Thu.

HILLTOP SHAFTESBURY, with its cobbled streets and 18th-century cottages is often used as a setting for films and TV commercials to give a flavour of Old England. Picturesque **Gold Hill** is lined on one side by the wall of the demolished **abbey**, founded by King Alfred in 888. Only the excavated remains of the abbey church survive, and a few masonry fragments found in the local history museum.

The Almshouse (1437) adjoining the Abbey Church, Sherborne

Sherborne ⑰

Dorset. 🏘 9,500. 🚆 🚌 ℹ️ Digby Rd (01935 815341). 🚇 Thu, Sat.

FEW OTHER TOWNS in Britain have such a wealth of unspoilt medieval buildings. Edward VI (see p44) founded the famous Sherborne School in 1550, saving intact the splendid **Abbey Church**, the almshouse and other monastic buildings that might otherwise have been demolished after the Dissolution (see pp54–5). Remains of the first Saxon church can still be seen in the abbey's façade, but the most striking feature is the 15th-century fan-vaulted ceiling.

Sherborne Castle, built for Sir Walter Raleigh (see pp54–5) in 1594, is a wonderfully varied building that anticipates the flamboyant Jacobean style. Raleigh also lived briefly in the early 12th-century **Old Castle**, which now stands in ruins, demolished by Cromwell's supporters during the Civil War (see pp56–7).

ENVIRONS: West of Sherborne, past Yeovil, is the magnificent Elizabethan **Montacute House** (see pp262–3), set in 120 ha (300 acres) of grounds. It is noted for its collections of tapestries and 17th-century samplers, and for the Tudor and Jacobean portraits on display in the vast Long Gallery.

🏰 **Sherborne Castle**
Off A30. 📞 01935 813182.
🕐 Easter–Oct: Tue, Thu, Sat, Sun & public hols (pm). 📷

🏰 **Old Castle**
Off A30. 📞 01935 812730.
🕐 Easter–Oct: daily; Nov–Easter: Wed–Sun. ⬤ 25, 26 Dec, 1 Jan. 📷 ♿ 🚻

🏛 **Montacute House**
(NT) Montacute. 📞 01935 823289.
🕐 Apr–Oct: Wed–Mon (pm). 📷

Abbotsbury ⑱

Dorset. 🏘 400. ℹ️ West St (01305 871130).

THE NAME ABBOTSBURY recalls the town's 11th-century Benedictine abbey of which little but the huge tithe barn, built around 1400, remains.
    Nobody knows when the **Swannery** here was founded, but the earliest record dates to 1393. Mute swan come to nest in the breeding season, attracted by the reed beds which spread along the Fleet, a brackish lagoon protected from the sea by

The Swannery at Abbotsbury

a high ridge of pebbles called **Chesil Bank** (see p260). Its wild atmosphere makes an appealing contrast to the south coast resorts, although strong currents make swimming too dangerous. **Abbotsbury Sub-Tropical Gardens** are the frost-free home to many new plants, discovered by botanists travelling in South America and Asia in the last 30 years.

🦢 **Swannery**
New Barn Rd. 📞 01305 871684.
🕐 Apr–Oct: daily. 📷 ♿ 🖥 🚻

🍂 **Abbotsbury Sub-Tropical Gardens**
Off B3157 📞 01305 871387. 🕐 daily. ⬤ 25, 26 Dec, 1 Jan. 📷 ♿ 🖥

Weymouth ⑲

Dorset. 🏘 45,000. 🚆 🚌 ⛴
ℹ️ Pavilion Complex, The Esplanade (01305 785747). 🚇 Thu.

WEYMOUTH'S POPULARITY as one of Britain's earliest seaside resorts began in 1789 when George III paid the first of many summer visits here. The king's bathing machine can be seen in the **Timewalk**

Weymouth Quay, Dorset's south coast

museum, and his statue is a prominent feature on the seafront esplanade. Here gracious Georgian terraces and hotels look across to the beautiful expanse of Weymouth Bay. Different in character is the old town around Custom House Quay with its fishing boats and old timber-framed seamen's inns.

🏛 Timewalk
Hope Sq. 📞 01305 777622. ⚪ daily. ⚫ 25, 26 Dec, 2 wks in Jan. ♿

A 55 m (180 ft) giant carved on the chalk hillside, Cerne Abbas (NT)

Dorchester ㉓

Dorset. 🏘 15,000. 🚉 ℹ Antelope Walk (01305 267992). 🚍 Wed.

DORCHESTER, the county town of Dorset, is still recognizably the town that Thomas Hardy used as the background for his novel *The Mayor of Casterbridge* (1886). Here, among the many 17th-century and Georgian houses lining the High Street, is the **Dorset County Museum**, where the original manuscript of the novel is displayed, along with a reconstruction of Hardy's study. There are also finds from Iron Age and Roman sites on the outskirts of the town. **Maumbury Rings** (Weymouth Avenue), is a Roman amphitheatre, originally a Neolithic henge. To the west of the town,

many Roman graves have been found in a cemetery below the Iron Age hill fort, **Poundbury Camp**.

ENVIRONS: Just southwest of Dorchester, **Maiden Castle** *(see p47)* is a massive, awe-inspiring monument dating from around 100 BC. In AD 43 it was the scene for a battle as the Romans sought to conquer the Iron Age people of southern England.

To the north lies the charming village of **Cerne Abbas** with its magnificent medieval tithe barn and monastic buildings. The huge chalk-cut figure of a giant on the hillside here is a fertility figure thought to represent either the Roman hero-god Hercules or a 2,000-year-old Iron Age warrior.

East of Dorchester are the churches, thatched villages and rolling hills immortalized in Hardy's novels. Picturesque **Bere Regis** is the Kingsbere of *Tess of the D'Urbervilles*, where the tombs of the family whose name inspired the novel may still be seen sheltering beneath a fine roof in the Saxon **church**.

Hardy's Cottage is where the writer was born and **Max Gate** is the house he designed and lived in from 1885 until his death. Hardy's heart is buried alongside his family in the churchyard at **Stinsford** – his body was given a public funeral at Westminster Abbey in London *(see pp98–9)*.

Hardy's statue, Dorchester

There are beautiful gardens *(see p263)* designed in the 1890s and a magnificent medieval hall at 15th-century **Athelhampton House**.

🏛 Dorset County Museum
High West St. 📞 01305 262735. ⚪ Mon–Sat (Jul–Aug: daily). ⚫ 25, 26 Dec, Good Fri. 💷 ♿ ground floor.
🏚 Hardy's Cottage
(NT) Higher Bockhampton. 📞 01305 262366. ⚪ Apr–Oct: Sun–Thu. 💷 ♿ garden only.
🏚 Max Gate
(NT) Arlington Ave, Dorchester. 📞 01305 262538. ⚪ Apr–Sep: Sun, Mon & Wed (pm). 💷 ♿ limited.
🏚 Athelhampton House
Athelhampton. 📞 01305 848363. ⚪ Mar–Oct: Sun–Fri. 💷 ♿ gardens only. 🎫 🍴 🚻

THOMAS HARDY (1840–1928)

The vibrant, descriptive novels and poems of Thomas Hardy, one of England's best-loved writers, are set against the background of his native Dorset. The Wessex country-side provides a constant and familiar stage against which his characters enact their fate. Vivid accounts of rural life record a key moment in history, when mechanization was about to destroy ancient farming methods, just as the Industrial Revolution had done in the towns a century before *(see pp58–9)*. Hardy's power-fully visual style has made novels such as *Tess of the D'Urbervilles* (1891) popular with modern film-makers, and drawn literary pilgrims to the villages and landscapes that inspired his fiction.

Nastassja Kinski in Roman Polanski's film *Tess* (1979)

Corfe Castle ㉑

(NT) Corfe Castle, Dorset. ☎ 01929 481294. ⇄ Wareham then bus. ◯ daily. ● 25, 26 Dec. ♨ ♿ limited. ◨ ◻ ◻

The ruins of Corfe Castle, dating mainly from Norman times

T HE SPECTACULAR RUINS of Corfe Castle romantically crown a jagged pinnacle of rock above the charming un-spoilt village that shares its name. The castle has domi-nated the landscape since the 11th century, first as a royal fortification, then as the dra-matic ruins seen today. In 1635 the castle was purchased by Sir John Bankes, whose wife and her retainers – mostly women – courageously held out against 600 Parliamentary troops, in a six-week siege during the Civil War *(see pp56–7)*. The castle was eventually taken through trea-chery and in 1646 Parliament voted to have it "slighted" – deliberately blown up with dynamite to prevent it being used again. From the shattered ruins there are far-reaching views over the Isle of Purbeck and its wonderful coastline.

Isle of Purbeck ㉒

Dorset. ⇄ Wareham. ⛴ Shell Bay. ℹ Swanage (01929 422885).

T HE ISLE OF PURBECK, which is in fact a peninsula, is the source of the grey shelly limestone, known as Purbeck marble, from which the castle and surrounding houses were built. The geology changes to the southwest at **Kimmeridge**, where the muddy shale is rich in fossils and recently discovered oil reserves. The Isle is fringed with wonderful unspoilt beaches. **Studland Bay** (NT) – with its white sand spreading in a great arc, and its sand-dune nature reserve, rich in birdlife – has been rated one of Britain's best beaches. Sheltered **Lulworth Cove** is almost encircled by white cliffs and there is a fine clifftop walk to Durdle Door *(see pp260–61)*, a natural chalk arch eroded by the waves.

The main resort in the area is **Swanage**, the port where Purbeck marble was trans-ported by ship to London, to be used for everything from street paving to church build-ing. Unwanted masonry from demolished buildings was shipped back and this is how Swanage got its wonderfully ornate **Town Hall** façade, de-signed by Wren around 1668.

Poole ㉓

Dorset. 👥 135,000. ⇄ ◻ ⛴ ℹ The Quay (01202 253253).

S ITUATED ON ONE of the largest harbours in the world, Poole is an ancient, still thriv-ing, seaport. The quay is lined with old warehouses over-looking a safe sheltered bay, popular for water sports. The **Waterfront Museum**, partly housed in 15th-century cellars on the quay, tells the history of the port and town. A gallery in the museum is devoted to the history of the Boy Scout Movement – founded by Robert Baden-Powell after a trial camp was held on nearby **Brownsea Island** in 1907. Much of this island (reached

Beach adjoining Lulworth Cove, Isle of Purbeck

by boat from the quay) is given over to a woodland nature reserve with a waterfowl and heron sanctuary. Fine views of the Dorset coast add to the island's appeal.

🏛 Waterfront Museum
High St. 📞 01202 683138.
🔵 daily. ⚫ 25, 26 Dec, 1 Jan.
📷 ♿ 🛍

🐾 Brownsea Island
(NT) Poole. 📞 01202 707744.
🔵 Apr–Sep: daily. 📷 ♿ 📷 🖥

Boats in Poole harbour

Wimborne Minster ㉔

Dorset. 🏘 6,500. 🚇 ❓ 29 High St (01202 886116). 🛥 Fri–Sun.

THE FINE COLLEGIATE CHURCH of Wimborne's **Minster** was founded in 705 by Cuthburga, sister of King Ina of Wessex. It fell prey to marauding Danish raiders in the 10th century, and the imposing grey church we see today dates from the refounding by Edward the Confessor *(see pp52–3)* in 1043. Freemasons made use of the local Purbeck marble, carving beasts, biblical scenes, and a mass of zig-zag decoration.

The 16th-century **Priest's House Museum**, formerly the clergy's lodgings, has rooms furnished in the style of different periods.

ENVIRONS: Designed for the Bankes family after the destruction of Corfe Castle, **Kingston Lacy** was acquired by the National Trust in 1981. The estate has always been farmed by traditional methods and is astonishingly rich in

wildlife, rare flowers and butterflies. This quiet, forgotten corner of Dorset is grazed by rare Red Devon cattle and can be explored using paths and "green lanes" that date back to Roman and Saxon times. The fine 17th-century house at the centre of the estate contains an outstanding collection of paintings, including works by Rubens, Velazquez and Titian.

🏛 Priest's House Museum
High St. 📞 01202 882533.
🔵 Apr–Oct: Mon–Sat; Jun–Sep: daily
(Sun: pm only). 📷 ♿ limited. 🖥 🛍

🏛 Kingston Lacy
(NT) on B3082. 📞 01202 883402.
🔵 Apr–Oct: Sat–Wed.
📷 ♿ gardens only. 🍴 🛍

Bournemouth ㉕

Dorset. 🏘 155,000. ✈ 🚃 🚌
❓ Westover Rd (0906 80280234).

BOURNEMOUTH'S POPULARITY as one of England's favourite seaside resorts is due to an almost unbroken sweep of sandy beach, extending from the mouth of Poole Harbour to Hengistbury Head. Most of the seafront is built up, with many large seaside villas and exclusive hotels. To the west there are numerous clifftop parks and gardens, interrupted by beautiful wooded river ravines, known as "chines". The varied and colourful garden of **Compton Acres** was conceived as a museum of many different garden styles.

In central Bournemouth the amusement arcades, casinos, nightclubs and shops cater for the city's many visitors. During the summer, pop groups, TV comedians and the highly regarded Bournemouth

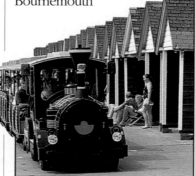

A toy train on the popular seafront at Bournemouth

Marchesa Maria Grimaldi **by Sir Peter Paul Rubens (1577–1640), Kingston Lacy**

Symphony Orchestra perform at the **Winter Gardens Theatre**, off Exeter Road. The **Russell-Cotes Art Gallery and Museum**, housed in a late Victorian villa, has an extensive collection with many fine Oriental and Victorian artefacts.

ENVIRONS: The magnificent **Christchurch Priory**, east of Bournemouth, is 95 m (310 ft) in length – the longest church in England. It was rebuilt between the 13th and 16th centuries and presents a sequence of different styles. The original nave, built around 1093, is an impressive example of Norman architecture, but the highlight is the intricate stone reredos which features a Tree of Jesse, tracing the lineage of Christ. Next to the Priory are the ruins of a Norman **castle**.

Between Bournemouth and Christchurch, **Hengistbury Head** is well worth climbing for grassland flowers, butterflies and far-reaching sea views, while **Stanpit March**, which lies to the west of Bournemouth, is an excellent spot for viewing herons and a variety of other wading birds.

🌸 Compton Acres
Canford Cliffs Rd. 📞 01202 700 778. 🔵 Mar–Oct: daily. 📷 ♿ 🍴

🏛 Russell-Cotes Art Gallery and Museum
Russell-Cotes Rd. 📞 01202 451800.
⚫ until spring 2000 for major refurbishment.

Ancient water tower at Trelissick, on the Cornish coast ▷

DEVON AND CORNWALL

DEVON AND CORNWALL

MILES OF MAGNIFICENTLY VARIED COASTLINE *dominate this magical corner of Britain. Popular seaside resorts alternate with secluded coves and unspoiled fishing villages rich in maritime history. In contrast there are lush gardens and the wild terrain of the moorland interior, dotted with tors and historic remains.*

Geographical neighbours, the counties of Devon and Cornwall are very different in character. Celtic Cornwall, with its numerous villages named after early Christian missionaries, is mostly stark and treeless at its centre. In many places it is still scarred by the remains of tin and copper mining that has played an important part in the economy for some 4,000 years. The Poldark Mine, just north of the town of Helston, is open to visitors. The area's mining past has an interesting link with the Cornish pastie, which was originally conceived as a sort of packed lunch containing a mixture of meat and vegetables.

The seas around Cornwall are a continuing source of awe, and surfers take advantage of the big waves at Newquay (which is also a popular family resort). The Cornish coastline, penetrated by deep tidal rivers and dotted with lighthouses and tiny coves, has provided inspiration for a panoply of stories. The best known of these are by Daphne du Maurier, who grew up in Cornwall. According to legend, King Arthur, one of the world's best-loved romantic figures, was born at Tintagel, a village on the dramatically contorted north coast. Here you can see the ruins of a 13th-century castle, which was built in Tintagel because of its supposed links with Arthur.

The Penwith peninsula, which includes England's westernmost point (Land's End), is a stretch of coastline characterized by breathtaking views and haunting prehistoric monuments, such as Merry Maidens, which was constructed in the Bronze Age. Lanyon Quoit, near Madron, is an excellent example of an ancient chambered tomb.

Beach huts on Torquay's popular seafront

◁ **Fishing boats in Port Isaac, on Cornwall's north coast**

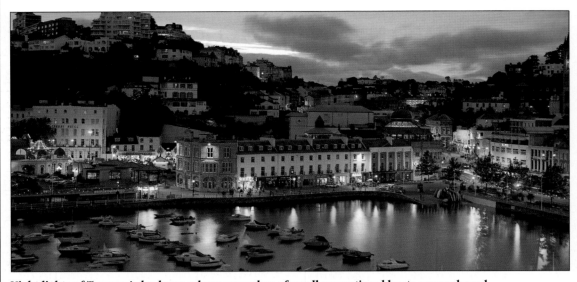

Night lights of Torquay's harbour, where a number of small recreational boats are anchored

The region also boasts a strong artistic tradition, inspired by the dramatic Penwith scenery. St Ives is home to the Barbara Hepworth Museum and the Tate Gallery, which displays works by artists such as Alfred Wallis. A widowed local fishermen "discovered" in 1928, Wallis painted primitive sea scenes on old pieces of cardboard to relieve his loneliness. Several independent galleries both in St Ives and in nearby Newlyn continue to show local work, and resident artists regularly open their studios to visitors.

In contrast to the rugged, sometimes ascetic beauty of Cornwall, Devon is the lush, primped counterpane of pastoral England: a patchwork of tiny fields threaded with narrow lanes and pathways.

Carn Brea Monument, near Redruth, Cornwall

Devon was once the home of a maritime tradition that produced the likes of adventurers Walter Raleigh and Francis Drake, but today only Plymouth continues to function as a major seaport (mainly for the Royal Navy). In this city you can explore the area's ocean-going history by visiting the Hoe, a park featuring naval memorials; and Mayflower Stone and Steps, from where the Pilgrim Fathers departed in 1620.

Today, Devon is essentially a land of small farmers, some of whom have given up struggling with European farming policies and turned their land into farm-based attractions. A number of small, largely agricultural communities have preserved some of Britain's more traditional annual fairs, including the tar barrel ceremony at Ottery St Mary, when the town's men run through the streets carrying blazing barrels; Widecombe's September fair, which has a traditional folk song associated with it that immortalized the names of several local villagers; and the obscure ceremony at Honiton, where heated pennies are thrown into a crowd.

About a third of all the people who visit Devon head straight for Torbay, which markets itself as the English Riviera and holds the British record for sunny days. Torbay consists of the seaside towns of Torquay, Paignton and Brixham. Top attractions include Paignton Zoo, which is one of the best in Britain; the 12th-century Torre Abbey; the prehistoric site of Kents Cavern Showcaves; Babbacombe Model Village; and, of course, some excellent beaches. Another popular tourist attraction is the Paignton and Dartmouth Steam Railway, which

Surfer riding a wave at Town Beach, Newquay

slowly chuffs its way through some of the best coastal scenery in Devon. Dartmouth, which has been an important port since Roman times, is home to the Royal Naval College and a 15th-century castle.

Dartmoor National Park covers some 370 square miles (950 sq km) and rises to 610 m (2,000 ft), which is the highest point in southern England. Dartmoor has two very different guises: the wooded

Maypool Viaduct on the Paignton and Dartmouth Railway

valleys and green flatlands punctuated with charming villages, such as Buckland-in-the-Moor; and the bleak, sometimes boggy moorland that is a training ground for the military, is home to one of Britain's highest security prisons, and was fitting inspiration for Conan Doyle's atmospheric novel, *The Hound of the Baskervilles.*

Less visited than the southern coast, the north Devon coast – from the tourist village of Clovelly to the clifftop Victorian settlement of Lynton – has some of Britain's finest cliff scenery. There are also some excellent beaches in the area, especially at Woolacombe

and Saunton. Victorian coastal resorts such as Ilfracombe and Bideford (which has some fine 17th-century merchants' houses) originally flourished with the arrival of the railways and have grown little since. This area of north Devon is also one of the most striking sections of the Southwest Coastal Path.

Overall, Devon and Cornwall are not known for their urban centres, but there are characterful places, such as Penzance, which has impressive gardens and an excellent view of St Michael's Mount; Truro, which is home to the informative Royal Cornwall Museum; and Exeter, with its magnificent 13th-century cathedral and medieval underground passages. Exeter in particular is remarkably intimate and friendly for a city: take tea in the cathedral close, and you could easily be fooled into thinking you were in a small country town.

Old Eddystone Lighthouse, Plymouth Hoe

Contrast between red cliffs and grey rocks on the Devon coast, near Peppercombe

Exploring Devon and Cornwall

ROMANTIC MOORLAND dominates the inland parts of Devon and Cornwall, ideal walking country with few roads and magnificent views stretching for miles. By contrast the extensive coastline is indented by hundreds of sheltered river valleys, each one seemingly isolated from the rest of the world – one reason why Devon and Cornwall can absorb so many visitors and yet still seem uncrowded. Wise tourists get to know one small part of Devon or Cornwall intimately, soaking up the atmosphere of the region, rather than rushing to see everything in the space of a week.

SIGHTS AT A GLANCE

Appledore **15**
Barnstaple **16**
Bideford **14**
Bodmin **10**
Buckfastleigh **22**
Buckland Abbey **25**
Bude **12**
Burgh Island **23**
Clovelly **13**
Cotehele **26**
Dartmoor pp328–9 **28**
Dartmouth **20**
Exeter **18**
Falmouth **6**
Fowey **9**
Helston and the
    Lizard Peninsula **5**
Lynton and Lynmouth **17**
Morwellham Quay **27**
Penzance **3**
Plymouth **24**
St Austell **8**
St Ives **2**
*St Michael's Mount
    pp310–11* **4**
Tintagel **11**
Torbay **19**
Totnes **21**
Truro **7**

Walks and Tours
Penwith Tour **1**

KEY

▬	Motorway
▬	Major road
▬	Minor road
▬	Scenic route
● –	Scenic path
～	River
☀	Viewpoint

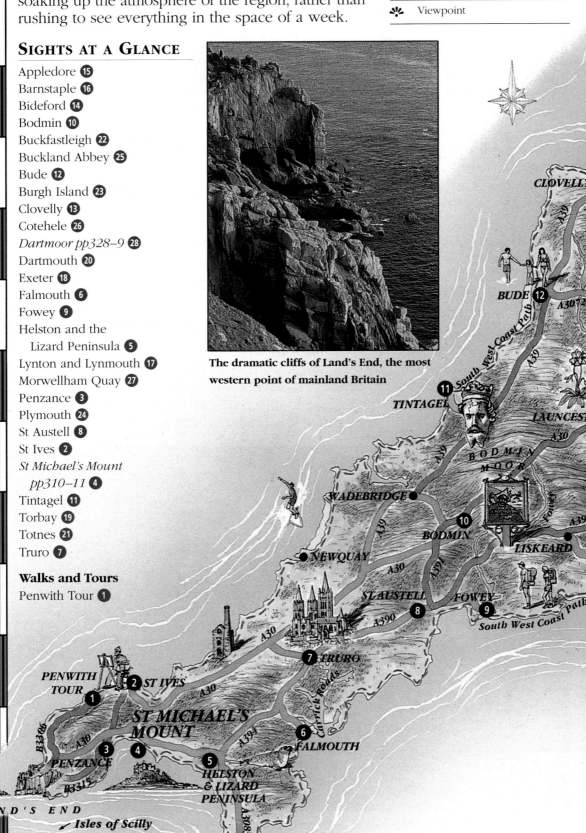

The dramatic cliffs of Land's End, the most western point of mainland Britain

Sub-tropical gardens at Torquay, the popular seaside resort

GETTING AROUND

Large numbers of drivers, many towing caravans, travel along the M5 motorway and A30 trunk road from mid-July to early September and travel can be slow, especially on Saturdays. Once in Devon and Cornwall, allow ample time if you are travelling by car along the region's narrow and high-banked lanes.

The excellent train services, running from Paddington to Penzance, along Brunel's historic Great Western Railway, stop at most major towns. Aside from this, you are dependent on taxis or infrequent local buses.

Typical thatched, stone cottages, Buckland-in-the-Moor, Dartmoor

0 kilometres 15

0 miles 10

The Art of Thatching

A ROW OF THATCHED COUNTRY COTTAGES is one of the quintessential images of rural England. In the past, thatch was used on all but the most important buildings, in both town and country, until well into the Tudor era. Gradually, its use was banned on new buildings in major towns because of the risk of fire. During the 18th and 19th centuries, tiled and slate roofs became fashionable and a thatched roof was, for the most part, limited to modest country dwellings. Thatching is no longer the economical form of roofing it once was, but a keen interest in the preservation of a traditional heritage has breathed life into what appeared to be a dying craft, not so long ago. Today, the number of master thatchers is growing.

Specially-grown reed *is bound into bundles. Most cutting is now done by machine.*

A thatcher *must strip off old thatch before replacing it with new. The pitch of the roof is steep so that rain and snow run off easily.*

COUNTRY COTTAGES

The style of thatched roofs may differ between regions of the country although the technique of thatching has changed little over the centuries. Within each local area the roofs may vary as each thatcher has his own personal style.

THATCHED COTTAGES

The two major areas of English thatch are the southern counties from West Sussex to Devon, including the Isle of Wight, and East Anglia. Thatch is not confined to houses, but is mainly seen on buildings with walls of cob, stone, flint or half-timbering.

Veryan, Cornwall, has several houses with a cone-shaped roof

The treatment of gables and dormers varies between thatchers

TOOLS OF THE TRADE

A thatcher's tools are not mechanized and each bundle of reeds must be placed and fixed. Working from the eaves up, a thatcher fixes each overlapping layer, or course, of yealms with hazel spars and sways, fixed with iron pins. Each course is shaped or "dressed" with a leggett and when the roof is finished, it is trimmed with a shearing hook.

Bunches of reeds, called yealms, are stacked up ready for use. The yealms are laid on the wooden framework of the roof and held in position with U-shaped twisted strips of hazel, called spars, and lengths of hazel called sways. Each yealm is laid in a course on the roof.

A thatcher trimming the roof

Pins hold the reeds in place

Decorative straw "dollies" are frequently made in the shape of birds. They are sometimes used as a thatcher's trademark, or added as a whim.

Rope is used to secure this heather thatch in Scotland. The rope, made from twined stems of heather, is held down with a row of stones at the eaves.

An unusual "catslide" roof on a cottage in Steyning, West Sussex

The double-thickness roof-coping often has a scalloped edge

Straw, wheat and water reed thatch can all be found in Oxfordshire

Penwith Tour ❶

THIS TOUR PASSES THROUGH a spectacular, remote Cornish landscape, dotted with relics of the tin mining industry, picturesque fishing villages and many prehistoric remains. The magnificent coastline varies between the gentle rolling moorland in the north and the rugged, windswept cliffs that characterize the dramatic south coast. The beauty of the area, combined with the clarity of light, has attracted artists since the late 19th century. Their work can be seen in Newlyn, St Ives and Penzance.

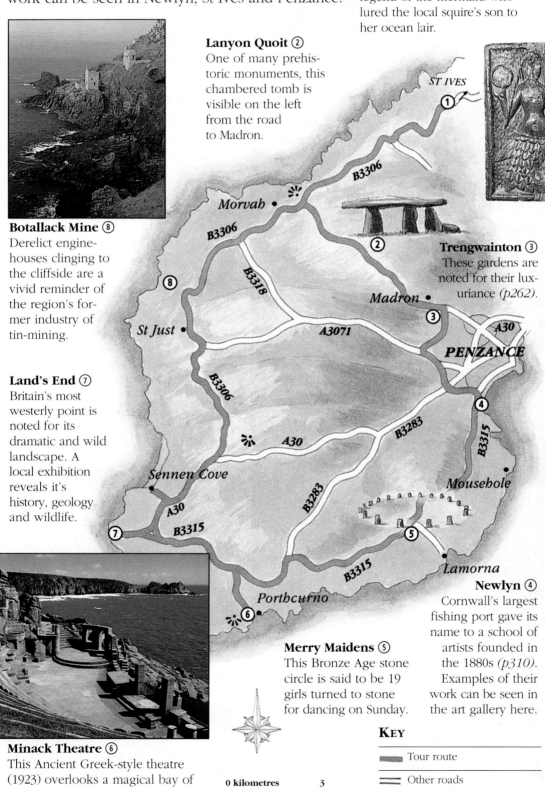

TIPS FOR DRIVERS

Tour length: 31 miles (50 km)
Stopping-off points: There are pubs and cafés in most villages. Sennen Cove makes a very pleasant mid-way stop.

Zennor ①
The carved mermaid in the church here recalls the legend of the mermaid who lured the local squire's son to her ocean lair.

Lanyon Quoit ②
One of many prehistoric monuments, this chambered tomb is visible on the left from the road to Madron.

Botallack Mine ⑧
Derelict enginehouses clinging to the cliffside are a vivid reminder of the region's former industry of tin-mining.

Land's End ⑦
Britain's most westerly point is noted for its dramatic and wild landscape. A local exhibition reveals it's history, geology and wildlife.

Trengwainton ③
These gardens are noted for their luxuriance (p262).

Merry Maidens ⑤
This Bronze Age stone circle is said to be 19 girls turned to stone for dancing on Sunday.

Newlyn ④
Cornwall's largest fishing port gave its name to a school of artists founded in the 1880s (p310). Examples of their work can be seen in the art gallery here.

Minack Theatre ⑥
This Ancient Greek-style theatre (1923) overlooks a magical bay of Porthcurno. It forms a magnificent backdrop for productions in summer.

0 kilometres   3

0 miles   2

KEY

Tour route

Other roads

Viewpoint

St Ives ②

Cornwall. 🏘 *11,000.* ⇄ 🚌
ℹ *Street-an-Pol (01736 796297).*

ST IVES is internationally renowned for the **Barbara Hepworth Museum** and the **Tate Gallery** which together celebrate the work of a group of young painters, potters and sculptors who set up a seaside art colony here in the 1920s. The Tate, designed to frame a panoramic view of Porthmeor Beach, reminds visitors of the natural surroundings that inspired the art on display within. The Barbara Hepworth Museum presents the sculptor's work in the house and garden where she lived and worked for many years. The studios are full of sculptors' paraphernalia, while the sub-tropical garden, is laid out as an art gallery.

The Lower Terrace, Tate Gallery

The town of St Ives remains a typical English seaside resort, surrounded by a crescent of golden sands. Popular taste rules in the town's many other art galleries tucked down winding alleys with names such as Teetotal Street, a legacy of the town's Methodist heritage. Many galleries are converted cellars and lofts where fish were once salted and packed. In between are whitewashed cottages with tiny gardens brimming with marigolds, geraniums, sunflowers and trailing lobelia, their vibrant colours made all the more intense by the unusually clear light that first attracted artists to St Ives.

🏛 Barbara Hepworth Museum
Barnoon Hill. 📞 *01736 796226.*
◯ *Jul–Aug: daily; Sep–Jun: Tue–Sun & public hols.* ● *25, 26 Dec.* 🎨
🏛 Tate Gallery
Porthmeor Beach. 📞 *01736 796226.*
◯ *Jul–Aug: daily; Sep–Jun: Tue–Sun & public hols.* ● *25, 26 Dec.*
🎨 ♿ 🍴 🏪

TWENTIETH-CENTURY ARTISTS OF ST IVES

Ben Nicholson and Barbara Hepworth formed the nucleus of a group of artists that made a major contribution to the development of abstract art in Europe. In the 1920s, St Ives together with Newlyn *(see p310)* became a place for aspiring artists. Among the prolific artists associated with the town are the potter Bernard Leach (1887–1979) and the painter Patrick Heron (1920–99) whose *Coloured Glass Window (see p258)* dominates the Tate Gallery entrance. Much of the art on display at the Tate is abstract and illustrates new responses to the rugged Cornish landscape, the human figure and the ever-changing patterns of sunlight on sea.

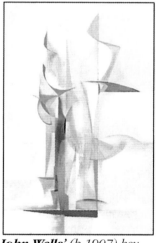

Barbara Hepworth *(1903–75) was one of the foremost abstract sculptors of her time.* Madonna and Child *(1953) can be seen in the church of St Ia.*

John Wells' *(b.1907) key interests are in light, curved forms and birds in flight, as revealed in* Aspiring Forms *(1950).*

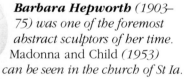

Ben Nicholson's *(1894–1982) work shows a change in style from simple scenes, such as the view from his window, to a preoccupation with shapes – as seen in this painting* St Ives, Cornwall *(1943–5). Later, his interest moved towards pure geometric blocks of colour.*

Penzance ❸

Cornwall. 🚶 *15,000.* 🚊 🚌 ⛴
ℹ *Station Rd (01736 362207).*

PENZANCE IS A BUSTLING resort
with a climate so mild that
palm trees and sub-tropical
plants grow happily in the lush
Morrab Gardens. The town
commands fine views of St
Michael's Mount and a great
sweep of clean sandy beach.

The main road through the
town is Market Jew Street, at
the top of which stands the
magnificent domed Market
House (1837), fronted by a
statue of Sir Humphrey Davy
(1778–1829). Davy, who came
from Penzance, invented the
miner's safety lamp which
detected lethal gases.

Chapel Street is lined with
curious buildings, none more
striking than the flamboyant

Egyptian House (1835), with
its richly painted façade and
lotus bud decoration. Just as
curious is **Admiral Benbow
Inn** (1696) on the same street,
which has a pirate perched on
the roof looking out to sea.
Opposite is a small **Maritime
Museum** displaying items
recovered from ancient wrecks.
The town's **Museum and Art
Gallery** has pictures by the
Newlyn School of artists.

ENVIRONS: A short distance
south of Penzance, **Newlyn** is
Cornwall's largest fishing port,
which has given its name to
the local school of artists *(see
p309)* founded by Stanhope
Forbes (1857–1947). They
painted outdoors, aiming to
capture the fleeting impres-
sions of wind, sun and sea.
Continuing south, the coastal
road ends at **Mousehole**

The Egyptian House (1835)

(pronounced Mowzall), a
pretty, popular village with a
tiny harbour, tiers of cottages
and a maze of narrow alleys.

North of Penzance, over-
looking the magical Cornish
coast, **Chysauster** is a fine
example of a Romano-British

St Michael's Mount ❹

(NT) Marazion, Cornwall. 📞 *01736
710507.* ⛴ *from Marazion (Apr–
Oct) or on foot at low tide.* ◯ *Apr–
Oct: Mon–Fri; Nov–Mar guided tours
only (phone to arrange).* 🎫 🍴 🛍

ST MICHAEL'S MOUNT emerges
dramatically from the waters
of Mount Bay, opposite the
small village of Marazion.

According to ancient Roman
historians, the mount was the
island of Ictis, an important
centre for the Cornish tin
trade during the Iron Age. It
is dedicated to the archangel
St Michael who, according to
legend, appeared here in 495.

When the Normans con-
quered England in 1066 *(see
pp50–51)*, they were struck
by the island's resemblance
to their own Mont-St-Michel,
whose Benedictine monks
were invited to build a small
abbey here. The abbey was
absorbed into a fortress at the
Dissolution of the Monasteries
(see pp54–5), when Henry
VIII set up a chain of coastal
defences to counter an expected attack from France.

In 1659 St Michael's Mount
was purchased by Sir John
St Aubyn whose descendants
subsequently turned the fortress into a magnificent house.

**View of St Michael's Mount
from Marazion**

**Harbourside
village**

Access to the island
is by boat from
Marazion or on foot
by a cobbled cause-
way at low tide.

The rocky slopes were
planted with sub-tropical
trees and shrubs by the
St Aubyn family.

**PLAN OF
MAIN FLOOR**

Priory Church · Choir · Blue Drawing Room · North Terrace · Hall · Map Room · Long Passage · South Terrace · Smoking Room · Exit · Entrance · Sir John's Room · Armoury · Library · Staircase to Museum and Exit · Chevy Chase Room

village. The site has remained almost undisturbed since it was abandoned in the 3rd century. The surrounding moorland is carpeted in rare wild flowers in spring.

From Penzance, regular boat and helicopter services depart for the **Isles of Scilly**, a beautiful archipelago forming part of the same granite mass as Land's End, Bodmin Moor and Dartmoor. Along with tourism, flower-growing forms the main source of income here.

🏛 **Maritime Museum**
19 Chapel St. 📞 01736 368890.
◯ Easter–Oct Mon–Sat. ♿

🏛 **Museum and Art Gallery**
Morrab Rd. 📞 01736 363625.
◯ Mon–Sat, (Jul–Aug Sun pm).
⬤ 25–26 Dec, 1 Jan. ♿ 🖥 📷

♘ **Chysauster**
Off B3311. 📞 01736 361889.
◯ Apr–Oct: daily. ♿

THE GROWTH OF METHODISM

The hard-working and independent mining and fishing communities of the West Country had little time for the established church, but they were won over by the new Methodist religion, with its emphasis on hymn singing, open-air preaching and regular or "methodical" Bible reading. When John Wesley, the founder of Methodism, made the first of many visits to the area in 1743, sceptical Cornish-

John Wesley (1703–91)

men pelted him with stones. His persistence, however, led to many conversions and by 1762 he was preaching to congregations of up to 30,000 people. Simple places of worship were built throughout the county; one favoured spot was the amphitheatre **Gwennap Pit**, at Busveal, south of Redruth. Methodist memorabilia can be seen in the Royal Cornwall Museum in Truro *(see p313)*.

Castle entrance

The South Terrace forms the roof of the large Victorian wing. Beneath it there are five floors of private quarters.

The Blue Drawing Room *was formed from the Lady Chapel in the mid-18th century and is decorated in charming Rococo Gothic style. It contains fine plaster work, furniture and paintings by Gainsborough and Thomas Hudson.*

The Armoury displays sporting weapons and military trophies brought back by the St Aubyn family from various wars.

The Priory Church, *rebuilt in the late 14th century, forms the summit of the island. Beautiful rose windows are found at both ends.*

The Chevy Chase Room *takes its name from a plaster frieze (1641) representing hunting scenes.*

Pinnacles of serpentine rock at Kynance Cove (NT), Lizard Peninsula

Helston and the Lizard Peninsula ⑤

Cornwall. 🚌 *from Penzance.* ⓘ *79 Meneage St (01326 565431).*

THE ATTRACTIVE TOWN of Helston makes a good base for exploring the windswept upland and unusual coastline of the Lizard Peninsula. The town is famous for its Furry Dance which welcomes spring with dancing through the streets *(see p66),* and the **Folk Museum** explains the history of this ancient custom. The elegant Georgian houses and inns of Coinagehall Street are a reminder that Helston was once a thriving stannary town where tin ingots were brought for weighing and

stamping before they could be sold. Locally mined tin was brought down river to a harbour at the bottom of this street until access to the sea was blocked in the 13th century by a sand and shingle bar which formed across the estuary. The bar created the freshwater lake, Loe Pool, and there is an attractive walk skirting its wooded shores. In 1880, Helston's trade was taken over by a new harbour created to the east on the River Helford, at Gweek. Today, Gweek is the home of the **National Seal Sanctuary**, where sick and injured seals are nursed back to health before being released again into the sea.

Cornwall's tin mining industry, from Roman times to the present day, is covered at

the **Poldark Mine** where underground tours reveal the working conditions of miners in the 18th century. Another major attraction is **Flambards Village Theme Park,** with its recreation of a Victorian village and of Britain during the Blitz.

Further south, huge receiver dishes rise spectacularly from the heathland. The **BT Satellite Station** visitors' centre here explores the world of satellite communications.

Local shops sell souvenirs carved from serpentine, a soft greenish stone which forms the unusual shaped rocks that rise from the sandy beach at picturesque **Kynance Cove**.

🏛 **Folk Museum**
Old Butter Market, Helston. ☏ *01326 564027.* ⭕ *Mon–Sat (Wed am only).* ⬤ *public hols.* ♿ 🚻
🦭 **National Seal Sanctuary**
Gweek. ☏ *01326 221361.* ⭕ *daily.* ⬤ *25 Dec.* 💷 ♿ 🎬 📷 🖥 🚻
🏛 **Poldark Mine**
Wendron. ☏ *01326 573173.* ⭕ *Easter–Oct: daily.* 💷
🏛 **Flambards Village Theme Park**
Culdrose Manor, Helston. ☏ *01326 573404.* ⭕ *Easter– Oct: daily (Apr, May, Sep, Oct phone first).* 💷 ♿ 🍴
🏛 **BT Satellite Station**
Goonhilly Downs, off B3293. ☏ *01326 221333.* ⭕ *Easter–Oct: daily.* 💷 ♿

Falmouth ⑥

Cornwall. 🏘 *18,000.* 🚆 🚌 ⛴ ⓘ *28 Killigrew St (01326 312300).*

FALMOUTH stands at the point where seven rivers flow into a long stretch of water called the **Carrick Roads**. The drowned river valley is so deep that huge ocean-going ships can sail up almost as far as Truro. Numerous creeks are ideal for boating excursions to view the varied scenery and birdlife. Falmouth's beautiful sheltered harbour forms the most interesting part of this popular seaside resort. Its many old houses include the striking **Customs House** and the chimney alongside, known as the "King's Pipe" because it was used for burning contraband tobacco seized from smugglers in the 19th century.

CORNISH SMUGGLERS

In the days before income tax was invented, the main form of government income came from tax on imported luxury goods, such as brandy and perfume. Huge profits were to be made by evading these taxes, which were at their height during the Napoleonic Wars (1780–1815). Remote Cornwall, with its coves and rivers penetrating deep into the mainland, was prime smuggling territory; estimates put the number of people involved, including women and children, at 100,000. Some notorious families resorted to deliberate wrecking, setting up deceptive lights to lure vessels onto the sharp rocks, in the hope of plundering the wreckage.

Pendennis Castle and St Mawes Castle, which stands opposite, were built by Henry VIII to protect the entrance of Carrick Roads.

ENVIRONS: To the south, **Glendurgan** (see p262) and **Trebah** gardens are both set in sheltered valleys leading down to delightful sandy coves on the River Helford.

Ship's figure-head, Falmouth

🏰 **Pendennis Castle**
The Headland. 📞 01326 316594. ⬭ daily. ⬤ 24–26 Dec. 📷 ♿ limited. 🗲 🖵 📷

🌿 **Glendurgan**
(NT) Mawnan Smith. 📞 01326 250906. ⬭ Mar–Oct: Tue–Sat & public hols. ⬤ Good Fri. 📷 📷

🌿 **Trebah**
Mawnan Smith. 📞 01326 250448. ⬭ daily. 📷 ♿ 🖵 📷

Truro ❼

Cornwall. 🏘 18,000. 🚆 🚌
ℹ Boscawen St (01872 274555). 🚩 Wed (cattle).

ONCE A market town and port, Truro is now the administrative capital of Cornwall. The town's many gracious Georgian buildings reflect Truro's prosperity during the tin mining boom of the 1800s. In 1876 the new diocese of Truro was created and the 16th-century parish church was rebuilt to create the first new **cathedral** to be built in England since Wren built St Paul's (see pp120–21) in the 17th century. With its noble central tower, tall lancet windows and numerous spires, the cathedral is an exuberant building that looks more French than English.

Truro's cobbled streets and numerous alleys lined with craft shops are a delight to explore. The **Royal Cornwall Museum** provides an excellent introduction to the county with displays on mining, Methodism (see p311), smuggling and archaeology. The art collection includes Impressionist-style pictures by artists of the Newlyn School (see p309).

ENVIRONS: On the outskirts of the city lie **Trewithen** and **Trelissick** gardens (see pp262–3). The former has a rich collection of Asiatic plants.

🏛 **Royal Cornwall Museum**
River St. 📞 01872 272205. ⬭ Mon–Sat. ⬤ public hols. 📷 ♿ 🖵 📷

🌿 **Trewithen**
Grampound Rd. 📞 01726 882763. ⬭ Mar–Sep: Mon–Sat (Apr, May: daily). 📷 ♿ 🗲 by arrangement.

🌿 **Trelissick**
(NT) Feock. 📞 01872 862090. ⬭ Mar–Oct: daily. 📷 ♿ 🍴 📷

The "Cornish Alps": china-clay spoil tips north of St Austell

St Austell ❽

Cornwall. 🏘 20,000. 🚆 🚌
ℹ BP Filling Station, Southbourne Rd (01726 76333). 🚩 Fri–Sun.

THE BUSY INDUSTRIAL town of St Austell is the capital of the local china-clay industry which rose to importance in the 18th century. Clay is still a vital factor in Cornwall's economy; China is the only other place in the world where such quality and quantity of clay can be found. Spoil tips are a prominent feature of the surrounding landscape. Viewed on a sunny day they look like snow-covered peaks, meriting the humorous local name, the "Cornish Alps".

ENVIRONS: The process of extracting and refining china clay is explained at the **Wheal Martyn Museum**. Trails weave through a clay pit and works that operated from 1878 until the 1920s. The waterwheels and pumps have been restored and the old tunnels and spoil tips have been colonized by a variety of wildlife.

🏛 **Wheal Martyn Museum**
Carthew. 📞 01726 850362. ⬭ Easter–Oct: daily. 📷 ♿ limited. 🖵

Truro Cathedral, designed by JL Pearson and completed in 1910

View of Polruan across the estuary from Fowey

Fowey ❾

Cornwall. 🏘 *2,000.* 🚢 ℹ *4 Custom House Hill (01726 833616).*

Fowey (pronounced Foy), has been immortalized under the name of Troy Town in the humorous novels of Sir Arthur Quiller-Couch (1863–1944), who lived here in a house called **The Haven**. A resort favoured by many wealthy Londoners with a taste for yachting and expensive

Daphne du Maurier

The period romances of Daphne du Maurier (1907–89) are inextricably linked with the wild Cornish land-scape where she grew up. *Jamaica Inn* established her reputation in 1936, and with the publication of *Rebecca* two years later she found herself one of the most popular authors of her day. *Rebecca* was made into a film directed by Alfred Hitchcock, star-ring Joan Fontaine and Lord Laurence Olivier.

seafood restaurants, Fowey is the most gentrified of the Cornish seaside towns. The picturesque charm of the flower-filled village is unde-niable, with its tangle of tiny steep streets and its views across the estuary to Polruan. The church of **St Fimbarrus** marks the end of the ancient Saint's Way footpath from Padstow – a reminder of the many Celtic mis-sionaries who arrived on the shores of Cornwall to convert people to Christian-ity. Its flower-lined path leads to a majestic porch and richly carved tower. Inside there are some fine 17th-century memorials to the Rashleigh family whose seat, Menabilly, became Daphne du Maurier's home and featured as Manderley in *Rebecca* (1938).

Environs: For a closer look at the town of **Polruan** and the ceaseless activity of the harbour there are a number of river trips up the little creeks. At the estuary mouth are the twin towers from which chains were once hung to demast invading ships – a simple but effective form of defence.

A fine stretch of coast leads further east to the picturesque fishing villages of **Polperro**, nestling in a narrow green ra-vine, and neighbouring **Looe**.

Upriver from Fowey is the tranquil town of **Lostwithiel**. Perched on a hill just to the north are the remains of the Norman **Restormel Castle**.

🏰 **Restormel Castle**
Lostwithiel. 📞 *01208 872687.* ⭕ *Apr–Oct: daily.* 🏷

Bodmin Moor ❿

Cornwall. 🚉 *Bodmin Parkway.* 🚌 *Bodmin.* ℹ *Mount Folly Sq, Bodmin (01208 76616).*

Bodmin, cornwall's capital, lies on the sheltered west-ern edge of the great expanse of moorland that shares its name. The history and archae-ology of the town and moor is covered by **Bodmin Town Museum**, while **Bodmin Jail**, where public executions took place until 1909, has been turned into a gruesome tour-ist attraction. The churchyard is watered by the ever-gushing waters of a holy spring, and it was here that St Guron estab-lished a Christian cell in the 6th century. The **church** itself is dedicated to St Petroc, an influential Welsh missionary who founded a monastery here in the same period, as well as many others in the region. The monastery has dis-appeared, but the bones of St Petroc remain, housed in a splendid 12th-century ivory casket in the church.

South of Bodmin is the **Lanhydrock** estate. Amid its extensive wooded acres and formal gardens *(see p263)* lies the massive house, rebuilt after a fire in 1881, but retain-ing some Jacobean features. The labyrinth of corridors and rooms illustrates life in a Victorian manor house and the fine 17th-century plaster ceiling in the Long Gallery depicts scenes from the Bible.

The lonely, desolate wilder-ness of Bodmin Moor is noted for its extensive network of prehistoric field boundaries. The main attraction, however, is the 18th-century **Jamaica Inn**, made famous by Daphne du Maurier's well-known tale of smuggling and romance. Today there is a restaurant and bar based on du Maurier's novel, and a small museum.

A 30-minute walk from the Inn is **Dozmary Pool**, reputed to be bottomless until it dried up in the drought of 1976. According to legend, the sword

Jamaica Inn, Bodmin Moor

The ruins of Tintagel Castle on the north coast of Cornwall

Excalibur was thrown into the pool after King Arthur's mortal wounding, when a hand rose from the lake to seize it.

To the east is the charming moorland village of **Altarnun**. Its spacious 15th-century church of **St Nonna** is known as the "Cathedral of the Moor".

🏛 Bodmin Town Museum
Mt Folly Sq, Bodmin. **📞** *01208 77067.* ◯ *Easter–Oct: Mon–Sat, Good Fri.* ● *public hols.* **⚐** *limited.*

🚭 Bodmin Jail
Berrycombe Rd, Bodmin. **📞** *01208 76292.* ◯ *daily.* ● *25 Dec.* 🖼 📷

🚭 Lanhydrock
(NT) Bodmin. **📞** *01208 73320.* **House** ◯ *Apr–Oct. Tue–Sun & public hols.* **Gardens** ◯ *daily.* 🖼 **⚐** *limited.*

Tintagel ⑪

Cornwall. 🏠 *1,700.* ⛴ *Thu (summer).*

THE ROMANTIC and mysterious ruins of **Tintagel Castle**, built around 1240 by Earl Richard of Cornwall, sit high on a hill-top surrounded by crumpled slate cliffs and yawning black caves. Access to the castle is by means of two steep staircases clinging to the cliffside where pink thrift and purple sea lavender abound.

The earl was persuaded to build in this isolated, windswept spot by the popular belief, derived from Geoffrey of Monmouth's fictitious *History of the Kings of Britain,* that this was the birthplace of the legendary King Arthur.

Large quantities of fine eastern Mediterranean pottery dating from around the 5th century have been discovered, indicating that the site was an important trading centre, long before the medieval castle was built. Whoever lived here, perhaps the ancient Kings of Cornwall, could evidently afford a luxurious lifestyle.

A clifftop path leads from the castle to Tintagel's **church** which has Norman and Saxon masonry. In Tintagel village the **Old Post Office** is a rare example of a 14th-century Cornish longhouse, beautifully restored and furnished with 17th-century oak furniture.

ENVIRONS: A short distance to the east, **Boscastle** is another pretty National Trust village. The River Valency runs down the middle of the main street to the fishing harbour, which is sheltered from the sea by high slate cliffs. Access from the harbour to the sea is via a channel cut through the rocks.

🏰 Tintagel Castle
Off High St. **📞** *01840 770328.* ◯ *daily.* ● *25, 26 Dec, 1 Jan.* 🖼

🚭 Old Post Office
(NT) Fore St. **📞** *01840 770024.* ◯ *Apr–Oct: daily.* 🖼

Bude ⑫

Cornwall. 🏠 *8,000.* ℹ *The Crescent car park (01288 354240).* ⛴ *Fri (summer).*

WONDERFUL beaches around this area make Bude a popular resort for families. The expanse of clean golden sand that attracts visitors today once made Bude a bustling port. Shelly, lime-rich sand was transported along a canal to inland farms where it was used to neutralize the acidic soil. The canal was abandoned in 1880 but a short stretch survives, providing a haven for birds such as kingfishers and herons.

King Arthur, from a 14th-century chronicle by Peter of Langtoft

KING ARTHUR

Historians think the legendary figure of King Arthur has some basis in historical fact. He was probably a Romano-British chieftain or warrior who led British resistance to the Saxon invasion of the 6th century *(see pp50–51).* Geoffrey of Monmouth's *History of the Kings of Britain* (1139) introduced Arthur to literature with an account of the many legends connected with him – how he became king by removing the sword Excalibur from a stone, his final battle with the treacherous Mordred, and the story of the Knights of the Round Table *(see p170).* Other writers, such as Alfred Lord Tennyson, took up these stories and elaborated on them.

Kingfisher

Clovelly ⑬

Devon. 🏛 *350.* 📞 *01237 431781.*
Town & Visitors' Centre ⬜ *daily.*
⬤ *25, 26 Dec.* 📷 ♿ *Visitors' Centre.*

CLOVELLY has been a noted
beauty spot since the novelist Charles Kingsley (1819–
75) wrote about it in his
stirring story of the Spanish
Armada, *Westward Ho!* (1855).
Today the whole village is
privately owned and has been
turned into a tourist attraction,
with little sign of the flourishing fishing industry to which
it owed its birth. It is a charming, picturesque village with
steep cobbled streets rising
up the cliff from the harbourside, gaily painted houses and
gardens brimming with brightly
coloured flowers. There are
superb views from the lookout
points and fine coastal paths
to explore from the tiny quay.
The Visitors' Centre offers an
introduction to the village.

The **Hobby Drive** toll road
(off the A39, near Bucks Cross)
is a scenic approach to the
village which runs through
woodland along the coast.
The road was constructed in

Bideford's medieval bridge, 203 m (666 ft) long with 24 arches

1811–29 to give employment to
local men who had been made
redundant at the end of the
Napoleonic Wars *(see pp58–9).*

Bideford ⑭

Devon. 🏛 *13,000.* 🚌 ℹ️ *Victoria
Park (01237 477676).* 🛒 *Tue, Sat.*

STRUNG OUT along the boat-
filled estuary of the River
Torridge, Bideford grew and
thrived from Elizabethan times
on the import of tobacco from
the New World *(see pp54–5).*
Some 17th-century merchants'
houses survive in Bridgeland
Street, including the splendid
bay-windowed house at No. 28

(1693). Beyond is Mill Street,
lined with many shops, leading to the parish church and
the splendid medieval bridge
which has carried traffic across
the Torridge since the 15th
century. The quay stretches
from here to a pleasant park
and a statue commemorating
Charles Kingsley, whose novels
helped revive the local economy by bringing visitors to
the area in the 19th century.

ENVIRONS: To the west of
Bideford, the village **Westward
Ho!** was built in the late 19th
century and named after one
of Kingsley's most popular
novels. The development was
unsuccessful and the Victorian
villas and hotels are now part
of a holiday resort that looks
out across the Taw estuary
onto Braunton Burrows nature
reserve. Rudyard Kipling *(see
p157)* was at school here and
the hill to the south, known as
Kipling Tors, was the background for *Stalky & Co* (1899),
stories based on his experiences of schoolboy life.

Henry Williamson's literary
classic, *Tarka the Otter* (1927)
describes the otters of the
Torridge Valley and naturalists are hoping to reintroduce
otters to this lovely valley.
Part of a Tarka Trail has been
laid out along the Torridge and
bicycles can be hired from
Bideford railway station. The
trail passes close to the Royal
Horticultural Society's magnificent **Rosemoor Garden**.

Day trips run from Bideford
to **Lundy** island, used in the
past as a pirate hideaway.
The island is abundant in
marine life, birds and wildlife.

🌸 **RHS Rosemoor Garden**
Great Torrington. 📞 *01805 624067.*
⬜ *daily.* ⬤ *25 Dec.* 📷 ♿ 🍴 🚻

Fishing boats in Clovelly's harbour

Fishermen's cottages, Appledore

Appledore ⑮

Devon. 👥 3,000.

Appledore's remote position at the tip of the Torridge Estuary has helped to preserve its charms intact. Busy boat-yards line the long riverside quay, which is also the departure point for fishing trips and ferries to the sandy beaches of Braunton Burrows on the opposite shore. Timeworn Regency houses line the main street which runs parallel to the quay, and behind is a network of narrow cobbled lanes with 18th-century fishermen's cottages. Several shops retain their original bow-windows and sell an assortment of crafts, antiques and souvenirs.

Uphill from the quay is the **North Devon Maritime Museum**, with an exhibition on the experiences of Devon emigrants in Australia and models and photographs explaining the work of local shipyards. The tiny **Victorian Schoolroom** which is affiliated to the museum, shows various documentary videos on local trades such as fishing and shipbuilding.

🏛 North Devon Maritime Museum
Odun Rd. 📞 01237 474852.
🕐 May–Sep: daily; April, Oct: pm only. 🎦 ♿ limited. 🚻

Barnstaple ⑯

Devon. 👥 33,000. 🚆 🚌 ℹ️ Tuly St (01271 375000). 🛒 Mon–Sat.

Although Barnstaple is an important distribution centre for the whole region, its town centre remains calm due to the exclusion of traffic. The massive glass-roofed **Pannier Market** (1855) has stalls of organic fruit and vegetables, honey and eggs, much of it produced by farmers' wives to supplement their income. Nearby is **St Peter's Church** with its twisted broach spire caused by a lightning strike which warped the timbers in 1810.

On the Strand is a wonderful arcade topped with a statue of Queen Anne. This was originally built as an exchange where merchants traded the contents of their cargo boats moored on the River Taw alongside. Nearby is the 15th-century bridge and the **Museum of North Devon**, where displays cover local history and the 700-year-old pottery industry, as well as local wildlife, such as the otters that are returning to rivers in the area. The 180 mile (290 km) Tarka Trail forms a figure of eight circuit centred around Barnstaple, much of which can be cycled.

Environs: Just to the west of Barnstaple, **Braunton "Great Field"** covers over 120 ha (300 acres) and is a well-preserved relic of medieval open-field cultivation.

Barnstaple's Pannier Market

Statue of Queen Anne (1708)

DEVONSHIRE CREAM TEAS

Devon people claim all other versions of a cream tea are inferior to their own. The essential ingredient is Devonshire clotted cream which comes from Jersey cattle fed on rich Devon pasture – anything else is second best, or so it is claimed. Spread thickly on freshly baked scones, with lashings of homemade strawberry jam, this makes a seductive, delicious, but fattening, tea-time treat.

A typical cream tea with scones, jam and clotted cream

Beyond lies **Braunton Burrows**, one of the most extensive wild-dune reserves in Britain. It is a must for plant enthusiasts who would like to spot sea kale, sea holly, sea lavender and horned poppies growing in their natural habitat. The sandy beaches and pounding waves at nearby Croyde and Woolacombe, are favourites among surfing enthusiasts, but there are also calmer areas of warm shallow water and rock pools.

Arlington Court, north of Barnstaple, has a collection of Napoleonic model ships, magnificent perennial borders and a lake. The stables are the biggest attraction, housing a collection of horse-drawn vehicles. Carriage rides are available and you can watch the mighty draught horses being fed at the end of the day.

🏛 Museum of North Devon
The Square. 📞 01271 346747. 🕐 Tue–Sat. 🔴 24 Dec–1 Jan. 🎦 ♿ 🚻
⛪ Arlington Court
(NT) Arlington. 📞 01271 850296. 🕐 Apr–Oct: Sun–Fri. 🎦 ♿ limited.

The village of Lynmouth

Lynton and Lynmouth ⑰

Devon. 🚶 *2,000.* 🚉 ℹ️ *Town Hall, Lee Rd (015987 52225). See pp274–5.*

SITUATED AT THE POINT where the East and West Lyn rivers meet the sea, Lynmouth is a picturesque, though rather commercialized, fishing village. The pedestrianized main street, lined with shops selling clotted cream and seaside souvenirs, runs parallel to the Lyn, now made into a canal with high embankments as a precaution against flash floods. One flood devastated the town at the height of the holiday season in 1952. The scars caused by the flood, which was fuelled by heavy rain on Exmoor, are now overgrown by trees in the pretty **Glen Lyn Gorge**, which leads north out of the village. Lynmouth's sister town, Lynton, is a mainly Victorian village perched on the clifftop 130 m (427 ft) above, giving lovely views across the Bristol Channel to the Welsh coast. It can be reached from the harbour front by a cliff railway or by a steep path alongside.

ENVIRONS: Lynmouth makes an excellent starting point for walks on Exmoor. There is a splendid 2 mile (3 km) trail that leads southeast to tranquil **Watersmeet** (see p275).
On the western edge of Exmoor, **Combe Martin** (see p274) lies in a lovely sheltered valley. On the main street, lined with Victorian villas, is the 18th-century Pack of Cards Inn, built by a gambler as a folly with 52 windows – one for each card in the pack.

Exeter ⑱

EXETER IS DEVON'S CAPITAL, a bustling and lively city with a great deal of character, despite the World War II bombing that destroyed much of its city centre. Built high on a plateau above the River Exe, the city is encircled by substantial sections of Roman and medieval wall, and the street plan has not changed much since the Romans first laid out what is now the High Street. Elsewhere the Cathedral Close forms a pleasant green, and there are cobbled streets and narrow alleys which invite leisurely exploration. For shoppers there is a wide selection of big stores and smaller speciality shops.

Exploring Exeter
The intimate green and the close surrounding Exeter's distinctive cathedral were the setting for Anthony Trollope's novel *He Knew He Was Right* (1869). Full of festive crowds listening to buskers in the summer, the close presents an array of architectural styles. One of the finest buildings here is the Elizabethan **Mol's Coffee House**. Among the other historic buildings that survived World War II are the magnificent **Guildhall** (1330) on the High Street (one of Britain's oldest civic buildings), the opulent **Custom House** (1681) by the quay, and the elegant 18th-century **Rougemont House** which stands near the remains of a Norman **castle** built by William the Conqueror (see pp50–51).
The port area has been transformed into a tourist attraction with its early 19th-century warehouses converted into craft shops, antique galleries and cafés. Boats can be hired for cruising down the short stretch of canal. The **Quay House Interpretation Centre**

The timber-framed Mol's Coffee House (1596), Cathedral Close

West front and south tower, Cathedral Church of St Peter

(open April–October) has audio-visual and other displays on the history of Exeter.

ℹ️ Cathedral Church of St Peter
Cathedral Close. 📞 *01392 255573.* 🕐 *daily.* ♿
Exeter's cathedral is one of the most gloriously ornamented in Britain. Except for the two Norman towers, the cathedral is mainly 13th-century and built in the style aptly known as Decorated because of the swirling geometric patterns of the window tracery. The façade, with its hundreds of stone statues, looks like a medieval parliament of knights and nobles, all seated in their stalls and leaning forward in anticipation of a rousing debate. Inside, the splendid Gothic vaulting sweeps from one end of the church to the other, impressive in its uniformity and punctuated by gaily painted ceiling bosses. Among the numerous tombs around the choir is that of Edward II's treasurer, Walter de Stapledon (1261–1326), who was murdered by a mob in London. Stapledon raised much of the money needed to fund the building of this cathedral

◁ **Rugged coastline near Hartland Point, Devon**

Collection of shells and other objects in the library of A La Ronde

VISITORS' CHECKLIST

Devon. 🐾 104,000. ✈ 5 miles
(8 km) east. 🚆 Exeter St David's,
Bonhay Rd; Exeter Central, Queen
St. 🚌 Paris St. ℹ Paris St
(01392 265700). 🚢 daily. 🎭
Exeter Festival: end Jun–mid-Jul.

and for Exeter College in
Oxford (see pp238–43).

🏛 Underground Passages

Roman Gate Passage. ℂ 01392
265887. ◯ Jul–Sep: daily;
Oct–Jun: Tue–Fri (pm), Sat.
● 25, 26 Dec, 1 Jan, Good
Fri & public hols. 🎫 📱

Beneath the city
centre lie the re-
mains of Exeter's
medieval water-
supply system. An
excellent video and
guided tour explain
how the stone-
lined tunnels were
built in the 14th
and 15th centuries
on a slight gradient
to bring in fresh
water from springs
outside the town.

**19th-century head
of an Oba, Royal
Albert Museum**

🏛 St Nicholas Priory

The Mint. ℂ 01392 265700.
◯ Easter–Oct.
Built in the 12th century, this
building has retained many
original features and rooms.
These trace its fascinating
history from austere monastic
beginnings, through its
secular use as a Tudor residence for wealthy merchants,
to its 20th-century incarnation
as five separate premises
occupied by various trades-
men including a bootmaker
and an upholsterer.

🏛 Royal Albert Memorial Museum and Art Gallery

Queen St. ℂ 01392 265858.
◯ Mon–Sat. ● 24–26 Dec, 1 Jan,
Good Fri. ♿ 📱 📷

This museum has a
wonderfully varied
collection, including
Roman remains, a zoo
of stuffed animals,
West Country art and
a particularly good
ethnographic display.
Highlights include
displays on silverware,
watches and clocks.

ENVIRONS: South of
Exeter on the A376,
the eccentric **A La
Ronde** is a 16-sided
house built in 1796
by two spinster sis-
ters, who decorated
the interior with shells, feathers and souvenirs gathered
while on tour in Europe.

Further east, the unspoilt
Regency town of **Sidmouth**
lies in a sheltered bay. There is
an eclectic array of architecture, the earliest buildings
dating from the 1820s when
Sidmouth became a popular
summer resort. Thatched cottages stand opposite huge
Edwardian villas, and elegant
terraces line the seafront. In
summer the town hosts the
famous International Festival
of Folk Arts (see p67).

North of Sidmouth lies the
magnificent church at **Ottery
St Mary**. Built in 1338–42 by
Bishop Grandisson, the church
is clearly a scaled-down version
of Exeter Cathedral, which he
also helped build. A memorial
in the churchyard wall recalls
the fact the poet Coleridge
was born in the town in 1772.

Nearby **Honiton** is famous
for its extraordinarily intricate
and delicate lace, made here
since Elizabethan times.

To the north of Exeter, just
off the M5, **Killerton** is home
to the National Trust's costume
collection. Here vivid tableaux
illustrate aristocratic fashions
from the 18th century to the
present day. Displays include
19th-century bustles, corsets
and crinolines, and the more
liberated bead skirts and
ostrich feathers of the 1920s.

Further north near Tiverton,
is **Knightshayes Court**, a
Victorian Gothic house with
fine gardens (see p262–3).

🏚 A La Ronde

(NT) Summer Lane, Exmouth.
ℂ 01395 265514. ◯ Apr–Oct:
Sun–Thu. 🎫 📱 📷

🏚 Killerton

(NT) Broadclyst. ℂ 01392 881345.
◯ Mar–Oct: Wed–Mon. 🎫 ♿ 🍴

♣ Knightshayes Court

(NT) Bolham. ℂ 01884 254665. ◯
Apr–Sep: Sat–Thu, Good Fri (gardens
daily Apr–Oct). 🎫 ♿ limited. 🍴 📷

**Mexican dancer at Sidmouth's
International Festival of Folk Arts**

Torbay ⑲

Devon. 🚊 🚌 *Torquay, Paignton.*
ℹ️ *Vaughan Parade, Torquay (01803 297428).*

THE THREE SEASIDE TOWNS of Torquay, Paignton and Brixham form an almost continuous resort around the great sweep of sandy beach and calm blue waters of Torbay. Because of its mild climate, extensive semi-tropical gardens and exuberant Victorian hotel architecture, this popular coastline has been dubbed the English Riviera. In its heyday, Torbay was patronized by the wealthy, especially during the Napoleonic Wars *(see p58)*, when touring the continent was neither safe nor patriotic. Today, mass entertainment is the theme and there are plenty of attractions, mostly in and around Torquay.

Torre Abbey includes the remains of a monastery founded in 1196 and now serves as an art gallery. There is a magnificent barn in the grounds where prisoners captured from the Spanish Armada of 1588 were once held. **Torquay Museum** nearby covers natural history and archaeology, including finds from **Kents Cavern Showcaves**, on the outskirts of the town. This is one of England's most important prehistoric sites and the spectacular caves serve as the background for displays on people and animals who lived here up to 350,000 years ago.

The charming miniature town of **Babbacombe Model Village** lies to the north of Torquay, while a mere mile (1.5 km) inland is the lovely little village of **Cockington**. Visitors travel by horse-drawn carriage to view the preserved Tudor manor house, church, thatched cottages and forge.

In Paignton, the celebrated **Paignton Zoo** teaches children about the planet's wildlife, and from here you can take the steam railway – an ideal way to visit Dartmouth.

Continuing south from Paignton, the pretty village of Brixham was once England's most prosperous fishing port.

Bayards Cove, Dartmouth

🏠 **Torre Abbey**
King's Drive, Torquay. 📞 *01803 293593.* ⭘ *Easter–Oct: daily.* 🖼️ 💻

🏛️ **Torquay Museum**
Babbacombe Rd, Torquay. 📞 *01803 293975.* ⭘ *daily (Nov–Easter: Mon–Fri).* ● *Christmas week, Good Fri.* 🖼️

🏛️ **Kents Cavern Showcaves**
Ilsham Rd, Torquay. 📞 *01803 294 059.* ⭘ *daily.* ● *25 Dec.* 🖼️ ♿ 🌿

🏛️ **Babbacombe Model Village**
Hampton Ave, Torquay. 📞 *01803 328 669.* ⭘ *daily.* ● *25 Dec.* 🖼️ ♿ 💻

🦒 **Paignton Zoo**
Totnes Rd, Paignton. 📞 *01803 557 479.* ⭘ *daily.* ● *25 Dec.* 🖼️ ♿

Dartmouth ⑳

Devon. 👥 *5,500.* 🚉 ℹ️ *Mayors Ave (01803 834224).* 🛥️ *Tue–Thu.*

SITTING HIGH ON THE CLIFFTOP above the River Dart is the **Royal Naval College**, where British naval officers have trained since 1905. Long before that, Dartmouth was an important port and it was from here that English fleets set sail to join the Second and Third Crusades.

Eighteenth-century houses adorn the cobbled quay of Bayards Cove, while carved timber buildings line the 17th-century Butterwalk; at No. 6 is the **Dartmouth Museum**. To the south is picturesque **Dartmouth Castle** (1481).

🏛️ **Dartmouth Museum**
6 Butterwalk. 📞 *01803 832923.* ⭘ *Mon–Sat.* ● *25 & 26 Dec, 1 Jan.* 🖼️ 🎫

🏰 **Dartmouth Castle**
Castle Rd. 📞 *01803 833588.* ⭘ *daily (Nov–Easter: Wed–Sun).* ● *24–26 Dec, 1 Jan.* 🖼️ 🎫

Torquay, on the "English Riviera"

Stained glass window in Blessed Sacrament Chapel, Buckfast Abbey

Totnes ㉑

Devon. 🏛 6,000. 🚆 🚌 🚢
ℹ The Plains (01803 863168).
🔺 Tue (summer), Fri.

TOTNES SITS at the highest navigable point on the River Dart with a Norman **castle** perched high on the hill above. Linking the two is the steep High Street, lined with bow-windowed Elizabethan houses. Bridging the street is the **Eastgate**, part of the medieval town wall. Life in the town's heyday is explored in the **Totnes Elizabethan Museum**, which also has a room devoted to the mathematician Charles Babbage (1791–1871) who is regarded as the pioneer of modern computers. There is a medieval **Guildhall**, and a **church** with a delicately carved and gilded rood screen. On Tuesdays in the summer, market stallholders dress in Elizabethan costume.

ENVIRONS: A short walk north of Totnes, **Dartington Hall** has 10 ha (25 acres) of lovely gardens and a world-famous music school where concerts are held in the heavily timbered 14th-century Great Hall.

♜ **Totnes Castle**
Castle St. 📞 01803 864406.
◯ Apr–Oct: daily; Nov–Mar: Wed–Sun. ● 24–26 Dec, 1 Jan. 🖼
🏛 **Totnes Elizabethan Museum**
Fore St. 📞 01803 863821. ◯ end Mar–Oct: Mon–Fri. 🖼 ♿ limited.
🏢 **Guildhall**
Rampart Walk. 📞 01803 862147.
◯ Apr–Oct: Mon–Fri. 🖼
🌿 **Dartington Hall Gardens**
Dartington Hall Estate. 📞 01803 862367. ◯ daily.

Buckfastleigh ㉒

Devon. 🏛 3,300. 🚆

THIS MARKET TOWN, situated on the edge of Dartmoor (see p328–9), is dominated by **Buckfast Abbey**. The original abbey, founded in Norman times, fell into ruin after the Dissolution of the Monasteries and it was not until 1882 that a small group of French Benedictine monks set up a new abbey here. Work on the present building was financed by donations and carried out by the monks themselves. The abbey was completed in 1938 and now lies at the heart of a thriving community.

Stallholders in Totnes market

The fine mosaics and modern stained glass window are also the work of the monks.

Nearby is the **Buckfast Butterfly Farm and Otter Sanctuary,** and the **South Devon Steam Railway** terminus where steam trains leave for Totnes, chugging down the scenic valley of the River Dart.

🏛 **Buckfast Abbey**
Buckfastleigh. 📞 01364 642519.
◯ daily. ● 25–27 Dec, Good Fri. ♿
🦋 **Buckfast Butterfly Farm and Otter Sanctuary**
Buckfastleigh. 📞 01364 642916.
◯ Easter–Nov: daily. 🖼 ♿

Burgh Island ㉓

Devon. 🚆 Plymouth, then taxi. ℹ The Barbican, Plymouth (01752 264849).

THE SHORT WALK across the sands at low tide from Bigbury-on-Sea to Burgh Island takes you back to the decadent era of the 1920s and '30s. It was here that the millionaire Archibald Nettlefold built the luxury **Burgh Island Hotel** in 1929. Created in Art Deco style with a natural rock sea-bathing pool, this was the exclusive retreat of famous figures, such as the Duke of Windsor and writers Agatha Christie and Noel Coward. The restored hotel is worth a visit for the photographs of its heyday and the Art Deco fittings. You can also explore the island village and **Pilchard Inn** (1336), reputed to be haunted by the ghost of a smuggler.

The Art Deco style bar in Burgh Island Hotel

Plymouth ㉔

Devon. 👥 250,000. ✈ ⇌ 🚌
🚢 ℹ️ *Island House, The Barbican.*
(01752 264849). 🅿️ *daily.*

THE TINY PORT from which
Drake, Raleigh, the Pilgrim
Fathers, Cook and Darwin all
set sail on pioneering voyages
has now grown to a substantial city, much of it boldly
rebuilt after wartime bombing.
Old Plymouth clus-
ters around the
Hoe, the famous
patch of turf on
which Sir Francis
Drake is said to
have calmly fin-
ished his game of
bowls as the in-
vading Spanish
Armada approached
the port in 1588 *(see pp54–5)*.
Today the Hoe is a pleasant
park and parade ground surrounded by memorials to
naval men, including Drake
himself. Alongside is Charles
II's massive **Royal Citadel**,
built to guard the harbour in

Drake's coat of arms

the 1660s, and the fascinating
Aquarium. A popular attraction is **Plymouth Dome**, a
visitor centre which uses high-
tech display techniques to
explain Plymouth's past and
present, including live satellite
weather pictures and radar
screens for monitoring ships
in the harbour. A short stroll
away, **Mayflower Stone and
Steps** is the spot where the
Pilgrim Fathers set sail for the
New World in
England's third
and successful
attempt at colon-
ization in 1620.

ENVIRONS: A boat
tour of the harbour
is the best way to
see Plymouth's
historic dockyard
complex where warships and
submarines have been built
and equipped since the
Napoleonic Wars *(see pp58–9)*.
There are also splendid views
of the numerous fine gardens,
such as **Mount Edgcumbe
Park** *(see pp262–3)*, that are

**Mid-18th-century carved wood
chimneypiece, Saltram House**

scattered around the coastline of the Plymouth Sound.
    East of the city, the mid-
18th-century **Saltram House**
has two opulent rooms by
Adam *(see pp28–9)*. There are
also portraits by Reynolds who
was born nearby in Plympton.

🏛 **Royal Citadel**
The Hoe. 📞 *01752 775841.* ◯
May–Sep: daily, 📷 *only.* ♿ *limited.*
🐟 **Aquarium**
Citadel Hill. 📞 *01752 600301.*
◯ *daily.* ⬤ *25 Dec, 1 Jan.* ♿
🏛 **Plymouth Dome**
The Hoe. 📞 *01752 603300.*
◯ *daily.* ⬤ *25 Dec.* 📷 ♿ 🖥 🏪
🌿 **Mount Edgcumbe Park**
Cremyll, Torpoint. 📞 *01752 822236.*
◯ *Apr–mid-Oct: Wed–Sun.* 📷 ♿
🏛 **Saltram House**
(NT) Plympton. 📞 *01752 336546.*
◯ *Apr–Oct: Sun–Thu, Good Fri.*
📷 ♿ 🍴 🏪

Buckland Abbey ㉕

(NT) Yelverton, Devon. 📞 *01822
853607.* 🚌 *from Yelverton.*
◯ *Fri–Wed (Nov–Mar: Sat & Sun
pm).* ⬤ *25,26 Dec; Jan.* 📷 ♿ 🍴

FOUNDED BY the Cistercian
monks in 1278, Buckland
Abbey was converted to a
house after the Dissolution of
the Monasteries and became
the home of Drake from 1581
until his death in 1596. Many
of the monastic buildings survive in a delightful garden
setting, the most impressive
being the huge 14th-century
tithe barn *(see pp32–3)*. Part
of the house explains Drake's
life and times through paintings, maps and memorabilia.

View of Plymouth Harbour from the Hoe

Cotehele 26

(NT) St Dominick, Cornwall.
📞 *01579 351346.* 🚃 *Calstock.*
House ○ *Apr–Oct: Sat–Thu & Good Fri.* **Grounds** ○ *daily.* 📷 🚻 *limited.*

MAGNIFICENT WOODLAND and lush river scenery make Cotehele (pronounced Coteal) one of the most delightful spots on the River Tamar and a rewarding day can be spent exploring the estate. Far from civilization, tucked into its wooded fold in the Cornwall countryside, Cotehele has slumbered for 500 years. The main attraction is the house and valley garden at its centre. Built mainly between 1489 and 1520, it is a rare example of a medieval house, set around three courtyards with a magnificent open hall, kitchen, chapel and a warren of private parlours and chambers. The romance of the house is enhanced by colourful terraced gardens to the east, leading via a tunnel into a richly planted valley garden. The path through this garden passes a large domed medieval dovecote and descends to a quay, from where lime and coal were once shipped. There are fine views up and down the winding reed-fringed Tamar and a gallery on the quayside specializes in local arts and crafts. The estate includes a village, riverside quay with a small maritime museum, working mill buildings, ancient lime kilns and a number of shops complete with 19th-century equipment.

Medieval dovecote in the gardens of Cotehele estate

Spanish Armada and British fleets in the English Channel, 1588

SIR FRANCIS DRAKE

Sir Francis Drake (c.1540–1596) was the first Englishman to circumnavigate the globe and he was knighted by Elizabeth I in 1580. Four years later he introduced tobacco and potatoes to England, after bringing home 190 colonists who had tried to establish a settlement in Virginia. To many, however, Drake was no more than an opportunistic rogue, renowned for his exploits as a "privateer", the polite name for a pirate. Catholic Spain was the bitter enemy and Drake further endeared himself to queen and people by his part in the victory over Philip II's Armada *(see pp54–5)*, defeated by bad weather and the buccaneering spirit of the English.

Morwellham Quay 27

Off A390, nr Gunnislake, Devon.
📞 *01822 832766.* 🚃 *Gunnislake.*
○ *daily.* ● *23 Dec–1 Jan.* 📷
🚻 *limited.* 🍴 🖥 🎁

MORWELLHAM QUAY was a neglected and overgrown industrial site until 1970, when members of a local trust began restoring the abandoned cottages, schoolhouse, farmyards, quay and copper mines to the condition they were in at the turn of the century.

Today, Morwellham Quay is a thriving and rewarding industrial museum, where you can easily spend a whole day partaking in the typical activities of a Victorian village, from preparing the shire horses for a day's work hauling carriages, to riding a tramway deep into a copper mine in the hillside behind the village. The museum is brought to life by characters in costumes who give demonstrations throughout the day. You can watch, or lend a hand to the cooper while he builds a barrel, attend a lesson in the schoolroom, take part in Victorian playground games or dress up in 19th-century hooped skirts, bonnets, top hats or jackets. The staff, who convincingly play the part of villagers, lead you through their lives and impart a huge amount of information about the history of this small copper-mining community.

Industrial relics at Morwellham Quay in the Tamar Valley

Dartmoor National Park 28

THE WILD AND MIST-SODDEN open moorland of Dartmoor's bleak and isolated heart provided the eerie background for Conan Doyle's thriller, *The Hound of the Baskervilles* (1902). Here at Princetown, surrounded by gaunt weathered outcrops of granite tors, is Britain's most secure prison. Also dotting the landscape are scores of prehistoric remains which have survived because of the durability of granite. Elsewhere the mood is very different. Streams tumble through wooded and boulder-strewn ravines forming pretty cascades and waterfalls, and cosy thatched cottages nestle in the sheltered valleys around the margins of the moor offering cream teas and warming fires to weary walkers.

Buzzard

Characteristic moorland near Drewsteignton

Okehampton has the Museum of Dartmoor Life and a ruined 14th-century castle.

LAUNCESTON

MELDON RESERVOIR

High Willhays

621 m
2,038 ft

Lydford

Lydford Gorge (open Apr–Oct) is a dramatic wooded ravine, leading to a waterfall.

MINISTRY OF DEFENCE FIRING RANGE

Brentor
This volcanic hill crowned by a tiny church (first built in 1130) is visible for miles.

The Ministry of Defence uses much of this area for training. Access is available on weekends.

Postbridge

Two Bridges

Tavistock

Merrivale

Blackbrook

Princetown

LISKEARD

KEY

ℹ️	Tourist information
▬	A road
═	B road
┄	Minor road
✺	Viewpoint

Main information centre

Yelverton

BURRATOR RESERVOIR

0 kilometres   5

0 miles   5

PLYMOUTH   Plym

PLYMOUTH

Ivybr

Postbridge
Dartmoor's northern fen is best explored from the village of Postbridge. The gently rolling moorland is crossed by many dry-stone walls.

◁ **Open expanse of central Dartmoor, grazed by wild ponies**

Dartmoor Ponies

These small, tough ponies have lived wild on the moor since at least the 10th century.

Grimspound is the impressive site of Bronze Age huts built nearly 4,000 years ago.

Castle Drogo is a magnificent mock-castle built by the architect Sir Edwin Lutyens *(see p29)* in 1910–30.

Becky Falls (open Easter–Nov) offers delightful woodland walks and a viewing platform over the 22 m (72 ft) waterfall.

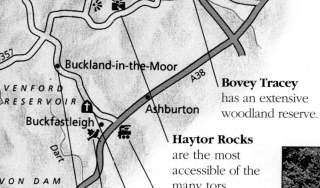

Hound Tor

This site includes the substantial remains of a deserted medieval settlement which was inhabited from Saxon times until around 1300.

Bovey Tracey has an extensive woodland reserve.

Haytor Rocks are the most accessible of the many tors.

South Devon Steam Railway

Buckfast Abbey was founded by King Canute *(see p171)* in 1018.

Dartmoor Butterfly and Otter Sanctuary

Dartmeet marks the lovely confluence point of the East and West Dart rivers.

Buckland-in-the-Moor

This is one of the most picturesque thatch-and-granite villages on Dartmoor.

THE MIDLANDS

Introducing the Midlands 332-339

The Heart of England 340-371

East Midlands 372-393

The Midlands at a Glance

THE MIDLANDS IS AN AREA that embraces wonderful landscapes and massive industrial cities. Visitors come to discover the wild beauty of the rugged Peaks, cruise slowly along the Midlands canals on gaily painted narrowboats and explore varied and enchanting gardens. The area encompasses the full range of English architecture from mighty cathedrals and humble churches to charming spa towns, stately homes and country cottages. There are fascinating industrial museums, many in picturesque settings.

Cheshire

Staffordshire

Shropshire

West Midlan

Tissington Trail (see p387) *combines a walk through scenic Peak District countryside with an entertaining insight into the ancient custom of well-dressing.*

Ironbridge Gorge (see pp354–5) *was the birthplace of the Industrial Revolution (see pp398–9). Now a World Heritage Centre, the site is a reminder of the lovely countryside in which the original factories were located.*

THE HEART OF ENGLAND
(see pp340–371)

Worcestershire

Herefordshire

Gloucestershire

The Cotswolds (see pp338–9) *are full of delightful houses built from local limestone, on the profits of the medieval wool trade. Snowshill Manor (left) is situated near the unspoilt village of Broadway.*

| 0 kilometres | 25 |
| 0 miles | 25 |

◁ **The front of the half-timbered Lord Leycester Hospital, Warwick**

Chatsworth House (see pp382–3), *a magnificent Baroque edifice, is famous for its gorgeous gardens. The "Conservative" Wall, a greenhouse for exotic plants, is pictured above.*

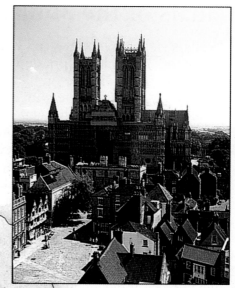

Lincoln Cathedral (see p391), *a vast, imposing building, dominates the ancient town. Inside are splendid misericords and the superb 13th-century Angel Choir, which has 30 carved angels.*

Nottinghamshire

Lincolnshire

Derbyshire

EAST MIDLANDS
(see pp372–393)

Leicestershire

Burghley House (see pp392–3) *is a dazzling landmark for miles around in the flat East Midlands landscape, with architectural motifs from the European Renaissance.*

Warwickshire

Warwick Castle (see pp364–5) *is an intriguing mixture of medieval power base and country house, complete with massive towers, battlements, a dungeon and state apartments, such as the Queen Anne Bedroom.*

Northamptonshire

Stratford-upon-Avon (see pp366–7) *has many picturesque houses connected with William Shakespeare's life, some of which are open to visitors. These black and white timber-framed buildings, which abound in the Midlands, are a typical example of Tudor architecture (see pp336–7).*

Canals of the Midlands

O NE OF ENGLAND'S FIRST CANALS was built by the 3rd Duke of Bridgewater in 1761 to link the coal mine on his Worsley estate with Manchester's textile factories. This heralded the start of a canal-building boom and by 1805, a 3,000 mile (4,800 km) network of waterways had been dug across the country, linking into the natural river system. Canals provided the cheapest, fastest way of transporting goods, until competition began to arrive from the railways in the 1840s. Cargo transport ended in 1963 but today nearly 2,000 miles (3,200 km) of canals are still navigable, for travellers who wish to take a leisurely cruise on a narrowboat.

The Grand Union Canal (pictured in 1931) is 300 miles (485 km) long and was dug in the 1790s to link London with the Midlands.

Lockside inns cater for narrowboats.

Lock-keepers were provided with canalside houses.

The Farmer's Bridge *is a flight of 13 locks in Birmingham. Locks are used to raise or lower boats from one level of the canal to another. The steeper the gradient, the more locks are needed.*

Heavy V-shaped timber gates close off the lock.

Water pressing against the gate keeps it shut.

The towpath is where horses pulled the canal boats before engines were invented. They were changed period- ically for fresh animals.

Narrowboats *have straight sides and flat bottoms and are pointed at both ends. Cargo space took up most of the boat, with a small cabin for the crew. Exteriors were brightly painted.*

Registered Nº 5089

NO 7

BILL O TOMS

NEW MARTON LOCK

RM&L

BUT

MIDLANDS CANAL NETWORK

The industrial Midlands was the birthplace of the English canal system and still has the biggest concentration of navigable waterways.

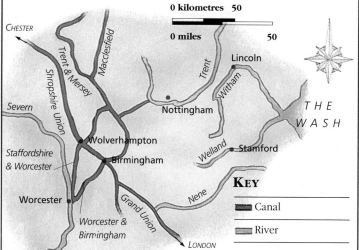

0 kilometres 50

0 miles 50

CHESTER

Macclesfield
Trent & Mersey
Shropshire Union
Severn
Trent
Lincoln
Witham
Nottingham
THE WASH
Staffordshire & Worcester
Wolverhampton
Birmingham
Welland
Stamford
Worcester
Grand Union
Nene
Worcester & Birmingham
LONDON

KEY

▬▬ Canal

▬▬ River

VISITORS' CHECKLIST

Companies specializing in canal boat holidays:
Blake's Holidays 🄲 01603 782911; Hoseasons 🄲 01502 501010; Canal Cruising Co 🄲 01785 813982; Black Prince Holidays 🄲 01527 575115; Alvechurch Boat Centres Ltd 🄲 0121 445 2909;

Canal museums:
Phone to check opening times: National Waterways Museum *(see p371)*; Canal Museum, Stoke Bruerne, Towcester 🄲 01604 862229; Boat Museum, South Pier Rd, Ellesmere Port. 🄲 0151 3555017.

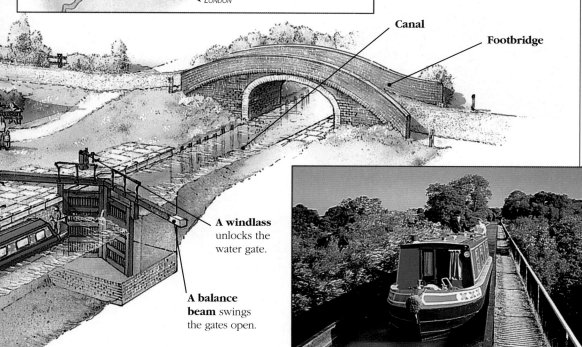

Canal

Footbridge

A windlass unlocks the water gate.

A balance beam swings the gates open.

CANAL LOCKS

Canals used tunnels, embankments and locks for the speedy transportation of goods across country. Locks were used to convey boats up or down hills.

***The Bearley Aqueduct**, just north of Stratford-upon-Avon, carries the canal in a cast iron trough. This is supported on brick piers for 180 m (495 ft), over roads and a busy railway line.*

CANAL ART

Canal boat cabins are very small and every inch of space is utilized to make a comfortable home for the occupants. Interiors were enlivened with colourful paintings and attractive decorations.

Furniture was designed to be functional and to brighten up the cramped cabin.

Narrowboats are often decorated with ornamental brass.

Water cans were also painted. The most common designs were roses and castles, with local variations in style.

Tudor Manor Houses

MANY STRIKING MANOR HOUSES were built in central England during the Tudor Age *(see pp54–5)*, a time of relative peace and prosperity. The abolition of the monasteries meant that vast estates were broken up and sold to secular landowners, who built houses to reflect their new status *(see p28)*. In the Midlands, **The Lucy family arms** wood was the main building material, and the gentry flaunted their wealth by using timber panelling for flamboyant decorative effect.

The decorative moulding on the south wing was carved during the late 16th century. Ancient motifs, such as vines and trefoils, are combined with the latest imported Italian Renaissance styles.

The rectangular moat was for decoration rather than defence. It surrounds a recreated knot garden (see p26) that was laid out in 1975 using plants known to have been available in Tudor times.

The Long Gallery, the last part of the Hall to be built (1580), was used for exercise. It has original murals portraying Destiny *(left)* and Fortune.

Brickwork chimney

Jetties (overhanging upper stories)

TUDOR MANSIONS AND TUDOR REVIVAL

There are many sumptuously decorated Tudor mansions in the Midlands. In the 19th century Tudor Revival architecture became a very popular "Old English" style, intended to invoke family pride and values rooted in the past.

Hardwick Hall in Derbyshire, whose huge kitchen is pictured, is one of the finest Tudor mansions in the country. These buildings are known as "prodigy" houses (see p392) due to their gigantic size.

Charlecote Park, Warwickshire, is a brick mansion built by Sir Thomas Lucy in 1551–59. It was heavily restored in Tudor style in the 19th century, but has a fine original gatehouse. According to legend, the young William Shakespeare (see pp366–7) was caught poaching deer in the park.

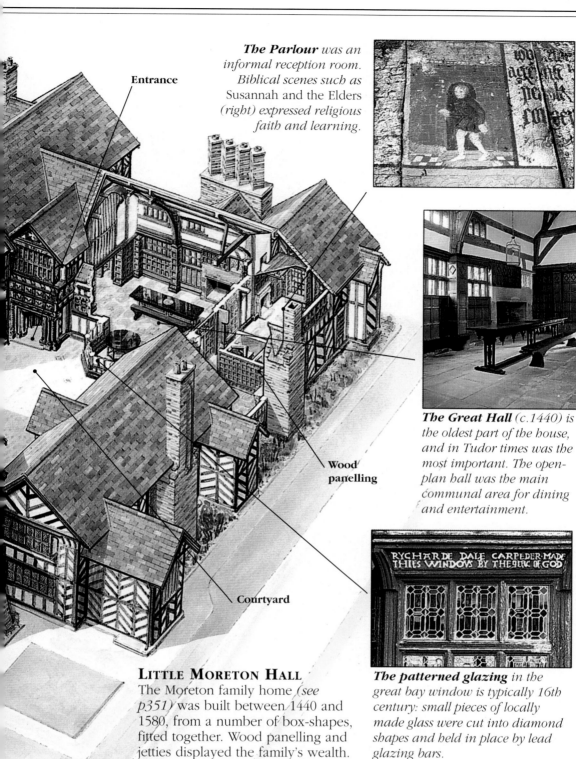

The Parlour *was an informal reception room. Biblical scenes such as Susannah and the Elders (right) expressed religious faith and learning.*

Entrance

Wood panelling

Courtyard

The Great Hall *(c.1440) is the oldest part of the house, and in Tudor times was the most important. The open-plan hall was the main communal area for dining and entertainment.*

RYCHARDE DALE CARPEDER MADE THIES WINDOW BY THE GRAC OF GOD

LITTLE MORETON HALL

The Moreton family home *(see p351)* was built between 1440 and 1580, from a number of box-shapes, fitted together. Wood panelling and jetties displayed the family's wealth.

The patterned glazing *in the great bay window is typically 16th century: small pieces of locally made glass were cut into diamond shapes and held in place by lead glazing bars.*

Packwood House *in Warwickshire is a timber-framed mid-Tudor house with extensive 17th-century additions. The unusual garden of clipped yew trees dates from the 17th century and is supposed to represent the Sermon on the Mount.*

Moseley Old Hall, *Staffordshire, has a red brick exterior concealing its early 17th-century timber frame. The King's Room is where Charles II hid after the Battle of Worcester (see pp56–7).*

Wightwick Manor, *West Midlands, was built in 1887–93. It is a fine example of Tudor Revival architecture and has superb late 19th-century furniture and decorations.*

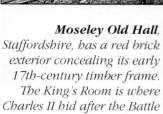

Building with Cotswold Stone

THE COTSWOLDS are a prominent range of limestone hills running over 50 miles (80 km) in a northeasterly direction from Bath *(see p282)*. The thin soils are difficult to plough but ideal for grazing sheep, and the wealth engendered by the medieval wool trade was poured into building majestic churches and opulent town houses. Stone quarried from these hills was used to build London's St Paul's Cathedral *(see pp120–21)*, as well as the villages, barns and manor houses that make the landscape so picturesque.

Dragon, Deerhurst Church

Arlington Row Cottages *in Bibury, a typical Cotswold village, were built in the 17th century for weavers whose looms were set up in the attics.*

Windows were taxed and glass expensive. Workers' cottages had only a few, not very large windows made of small panes of glass.

A drip mould keeps rain off the chimney.

The roof is steeply pitched to carry the weight of the tiles. These were made by master craftsmen who could split blocks of stone into sheets by using natural fault lines.

COTSWOLD STONE COTTAGE
The two-storey Arlington Row Cottages are asymmetrical and built of odd-shaped stones. Small windows and doorways make them quite dark inside.

Timber lintels and doors

Timber framing was cheaper than stone, and was used for the upper rooms in the roof.

VARIATIONS IN STONE
Cotswold stone is warmer-toned in the north, pearly in central areas and light grey in the south. The stone seems to glow with absorbed sunlight. It is a soft stone that is easily carved and can be used for many purposes, from buildings to bridges, headstones and gargoyles.

"Tiddles" is a cat's gravestone in Fairford churchyard.

Lower Slaughter *gets its name from the Anglo-Saxon word* slough, *or muddy place. It has a low stone bridge, over the River Eye.*

COTSWOLD STONE TOWNS AND VILLAGES

The villages and towns on this map are prime examples of places built almost entirely from stone. By the 12th century almost all of the villages in the area were established. Huge deposits of limestone resulted in a wealth of stone buildings. Masons worked from distinctive local designs that were handed down from generation to generation.

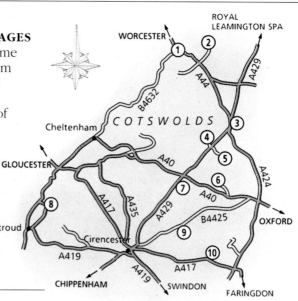

① Winchcombe
② Broadway
③ Stow-on-the-Wold
④ Upper and Lower Slaughter
⑤ Bourton-on-the-Water
⑥ Sherborne
⑦ Northleach
⑧ Painswick
⑨ Bibury
⑩ Fairford

Wool merchants' houses were built of fine ashlar (dressed stone) with ornamental cornerstones, doorframes and windows.

The eaves here have a dentil frieze, so-called because it resembles a row of teeth.

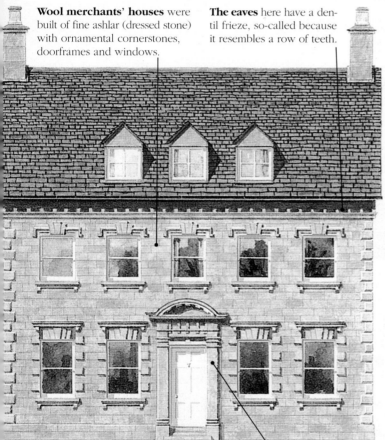

COTSWOLD STONE HOUSE

This early Georgian merchant's house in Painswick shows the fully developed Cotswold style, which borrows decorative elements from Classical architecture.

The door frame has a rounded pediment on simple pilasters.

STONE GARGOYLES

In Winchcombe's church, 15th-century gargoyles reflect a combination of pagan and Christian beliefs.

Pagan gods warded off pre-Christian evil spirits.

Fertility figures, always important in rural areas, were incorporated into Christian festivals.

Human faces often caricatured local church dignitaries.

Animal gods represented qualities such as strength in pagan times.

Dry-stone walling *is an ancient technique used in the Cotswolds. The stones are held in place without mortar.*

A stone cross (16th century) in Stanton village, near Broadway, is one of many found in the Cotswolds.

Table-top and "tea caddy", *fine 18th-century tombs, can be found in Painswick churchyard.*

Horses and jockeys lined up ready for the start of the Cheltenham Gold Cup steeplechase ▷

THE HEART OF
ENGLAND

The Cotswold Arms

Bar Snacks
Restaurant
Beer Garden
Morning Coffee

THE HEART OF ENGLAND

V ARIETY IS THE KEYNOTE *of England's central region. The gentle Cotswold hills, enfolding solid stone cottages and churches, give way to the flat, fertile plains of Warwickshire. Shakespeare country, with all its historical associations, borders on the industrial Midlands, once known as the workshop of the world.*

Many visitors to the Heart of England never penetrate further into this region than Stratford-upon-Avon, where they pay homage to the Bard (William Shakespeare), then head straight to London, perhaps pausing to make a quick detour to Warwick Castle. Yet a longer stay yields rich rewards.

Coventry, Birmingham and the Potteries (an area in northern Staffordshire) have been producing textiles, ceramics and heavy manufactured goods since the 18th century. In Victorian times, engines, bicycles and armaments were made here, so in the early 20th century it was natural for the blossoming car-manufacturing industry to base itself in the region. In the last 50 years, as these industries have declined, some of the old mills and factories have been converted into museums that commemorate the towns' industrial heyday and demonstrate forgotten techniques that were once part of everyday life. Among the most impressive of these museums are the five found at Ironbridge Gorge and the enormous Quarry Bank Mill at Styal. There are other interesting museums in Stoke-on-Trent, which has been the centre of British pottery and porcelain manufacturing since Josiah Wedgwood opened his Etruria earthenware firm here in 1769. Today the Etruria Industrial Museum is one of several factories open to the public where potters can be seen at work. The museum at Hanley is

Leisurely village pastimes, reminiscent of a more tranquil age

◁ **Cotswold stone: an extremely popular building material in the Heart of England** home to an exquisite collection of wares.

Another relic from the industrial age is the network of canals that were cut through the countryside in the 18th century. These waterways were the main means of transporting heavy goods until the railways were built. Today the canals have become

Rape field by Eastnor Castle, Herefordshire

leisure amenities: enthusiasts can buy or rent colourful narrow boats and glide through the shallow water at little more than walking pace, negotiating locks, penetrating dark tunnels that pierce the hills, and occasionally crossing dramatic aqueducts. The towpaths alongside the canals make superb footpaths.

Earlier history comes to mind on the Marches, which is located on the English side of the border with Wales. The massive walls of Chester, and the castles at Shrewsbury, Ludlow and Stokesay recall the times when the Welsh were locked in ferocious battle with the Norman barons and the harassed Marcher lords.

Today the Marches are a mosaic of rural communities served by the market towns of Leominster, Malvern and Ross-on-Wye, where charming buildings survive from the medieval, Tudor and Georgian periods. Shrewsbury and Ludlow are the two best-preserved

towns in the area. The cathedral at Hereford contains a rare treasure: the Mappa Mundi, a map depicting the world as it was envisaged in 1290. Other highlights include the majestic cathedrals at Worcester and Gloucester, the Norman abbey at Tewkesbury, and Coventry Cathedral. The original cathedral at Coventry was bombed during World War II, but after the war a new one was built using modern architectural styles.

Birmingham is one of England's most important cities. Being at the centre not only of the region but also of England, Birmingham is surrounded by motorways that have swamped many of the city's Victorian buildings. Birmingham's National Exhibition Centre is the largest such centre in the country; it brings in businesspeople from all over the world. The city's rich cultural life includes a world-class orchestra, a ballet company and a superb collection of pre-Raphaelite paintings in the City Museum and Art Gallery. Other popular attractions in Birmingham include the Museum of Science and Industry and the Botanical Gardens. The city also has a lively pub and club scene.

Picturesque village of Bourton-on-the-Water, Cotswolds, Gloucestershire

Parade ring at Cheltenham Festival, Cheltenham, Gloucestershire

Only a few miles from the metropolis of Birmingham, country pursuits thrive. Fox hunting has been a favourite sport in Midlands woods and

Section of Hidcote Manor Gardens known as The White Garden, Gloucestershire

fields for centuries, although today this practice is opposed by animal rights supporters. In spring, point-to-point race meetings, where amateur riders test the speed of their horses over purpose-built brush fences, are popular. Some of the horses and riders graduate from the point-to-point field to become professional steeplechasers. There are a number of picturesque small racecourses in the region, but the major racecourse is at Cheltenham. In March, this course hosts a three-day festival meeting that includes the Cheltenham Gold Cup, the blue-riband of steeplechasing and an important social occasion. For those who prefer flat racing, some of the country's finest thoroughbreds can be seen in the classic trials each May at Chester's delightful racecourse, which is set near the historic city centre.

The Royal Show is held at Stoneleigh, which is near Kenilworth, in the first week of July. It is the leading agricultural show of the year: farmers from all over Britain come to display their prize livestock and to monitor the latest developments in the industry. The prestigious annual spring and autumn flower shows at Malvern, under the auspices of the Royal Horticultural Society, are countrified versions of the glamorous Chelsea show, but with a marvellous open setting at the foot of the Malvern Hills. The organic garden at Ryton, near Coventry, is a mecca for gardeners who prefer to use natural, non-chemical methods. Apple-growing and cider-making are traditional pursuits in the area around Hereford, where numerous orchards can be seen from the roads. There is an intriguing cider museum and a museum of local history in Hereford itself.

A row of well-preserved shops, dating from the 16th century, in the main street of Chester, Cheshire

Exploring the Heart of England

THE HEART OF ENGLAND, more than any other region, takes its character from the landscape. Picturesque houses, pubs and churches, made from timber and Cotswold stone, create a harmonic appearance that delights visitors and adds greatly to the pleasures of exploration. The area around Birmingham and Stoke-on-Trent, however – once the industrial hub of England – contrasts sharply. The bleak concrete skyline may not appeal, but the area has a fascinating history that is reflected in the self-confident Victorian art and architecture, and a series of award-winning industrial heritage museums.

Arlington Row: stone cottages in the Cotswold village of Bibury

SIGHTS AT A GLANCE

Birmingham ⑬
Cheltenham ⑳
Chester ②
Chipping Campden ⑱
Cirencester ㉒
Coventry ⑭
Gloucester ㉑
Great Malvern ⑪
Hereford ⑧
Ironbridge pp354–5 ⑤
Ledbury ⑩
Leominster ⑦
Ludlow ⑥
Quarry Bank Mill, Styal ①
Ross-on-Wye ⑨
Shrewsbury ④
Stoke-on-Trent ③
Stratford-upon-Avon pp366–9 ⑰
Tewkesbury ⑲
Warwick pp362–5 ⑯
Worcester ⑫

GETTING AROUND

The Heart of England is easily reached by train, with InterCity rail services to Cheltenham, Worcester, Birmingham, and Coventry. The M5 and M6 motorways are the major road routes but are frequently congested. Coach companies provide regular shuttle services to Cheltenham and Birmingham. Travelling within the region is best done by car. Rural roads are delightfully empty, although major attractions, such as Stratford-upon-Avon, may be very crowded during the summer.

Walks and Tours

Midlands Garden Tour ⑮

0 kilometres   10

0 miles   10

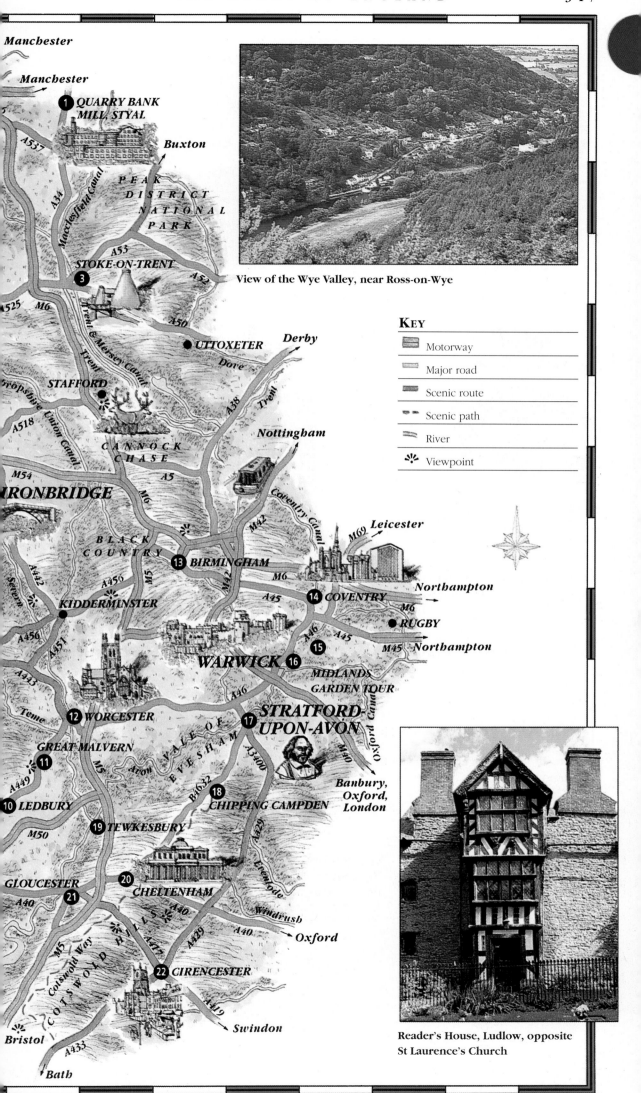

Manchester

Manchester

1 QUARRY BANK MILL, STYAL

Buxton

A537

A34

Macclesfield Canal

P E A K D I S T R I C T N A T I O N A L P A R K

A53

STOKE-ON-TRENT

A52

3

A525

M6

A50

Trent & Mersey Canal

Trent

● UTTOXETER

Derby

Dove

STAFFORD

A38

Trent

A518

Shropshire Union Canal

Nottingham

A54

C A N N O C K C H A S E

A5

IRONBRIDGE

M6

Coventry Canal

Leicester

M69

B L A C K C O U N T R Y

A442

A456

M5

13 BIRMINGHAM

M42

KIDDERMINSTER ●

A45

14 COVENTRY

M6

Northampton

A456

A451

● RUGBY

A46

A45

M45

Northampton

A443

15

WARWICK 16

Teme

12 WORCESTER

A46

MIDLANDS GARDEN TOUR

GREAT MALVERN

V A L E O F E V E S H A M

STRATFORD-UPON-AVON

Avon

A3400

A449

11

M5

Oxford Canal

M40

Banbury, Oxford, London

10 LEDBURY

B4632

18

B4029

CHIPPING CAMPDEN

M50

19 TEWKESBURY

A4₂₉

Evenlode

GLOUCESTER

20

A40

21

CHELTENHAM

Windrush

A40

A40

A429

Oxford

C O T S W O L D H I L L S

M5

A417

22 CIRENCESTER

Cotswold Way

A419

Swindon

Bristol

A433

Bath

View of the Wye Valley, near Ross-on-Wye

KEY

	Motorway
	Major road
	Scenic route
	Scenic path
	River
✹	Viewpoint

Reader's House, Ludlow, opposite St Laurence's Church

The Potteries

Josiah Wedgwood

THE SIX POTTERY TOWNS of Hanley, Tunstall, Burslem, Stoke, Fenton and Longston form Stoke-on-Trent, the heart of Britain's ceramics industry for hundreds of years. Many factors contributed to the establishment of the pottery industry in the area, including plentiful supplies of good clay and large stocks of coal to fire kilns. However, without gifted craftsmen, including Thomas Minton, Josiah Wedgwood, Thomas Spode and Sir Henry Doulton, the industry would not have flourished.

Coal-fired kilns, called potbanks, at the Gladstone Pottery Museum *(see p351)*

The Portland vase *(1790) is an example of jasperware, an unglazed, vitreous, fine stoneware, invented by Josiah Wedgwood. This is a first edition copy – the original Barberini, or Port-land, vase is made of cameo-glass and dates from 25 BC.*

SPODE PRINTING ROOM

Workers in the printing room at the Spode factory were responsible for the transferring of designs from a copper-plate engraving onto the unglazed earthenware. This method, perfected by Spode in 1784, was an improvement on the old method of hand-painting each design because it allowed the factory to produce its blue and white tableware in large quantities. Although this photo-graph was taken in 1930, the production process has changed little from the original method.

This Spode pot pourri vase *(1815) is deco-rated with gold and a hand-painted floral design. Each design that has ever been produced by Spode is recorded and kept in archived pattern books. This design, No. 2575, was one of their most popular.*

This vase *(1938) was des-igned by Susie Cooper, who was born in Tunstall and became a leading figure in ceramics design.*

These Minton tiles *display the artistry for which the company was famous. Decorated tiles were popular in the 19th century for walls, floors and washstands.*

THE STORY OF BONE CHINA

Bone china contains china clay, or kaolin (a white clay from Cornwall), china stone (white granite stone also from Cornwall) and fine, powdered bone ash or hydroxy-apatite. It is this final ingredient that gives bone china both its strength and its translucent quality. Originally made by hand, machines now ensure the clay "body" is as perfect as possible. The dry ingredients are combined with water in precise quantities in a huge mixing machine called a blunger until liquid clay, called slip, is formed. The slip is then sieved, treated to remove any iron particles and filtered to remove excess water. After a few days the clay passes through a pug mill, a machine that kneads the clay and removes the air bubbles. The pug mill creates a large continuous slab of perfect clay that is ready to be sliced off and used.

An engraving showing Josiah Spode's first piece of china

Royal Doulton's Top o' the Hill *figurine, first produced in 1937, is still sold today. The first range of figurines was produced in 1913 and about 4,000 designs have been added since then.*

Royal Doulton's Bunnykins *nurseryware range was designed by Barbara Vernon, a nun, in 1934. A highly popular range, it has been in production for more than 60 years and is still one of the company's best sellers*

Hand-painting *a piece of bone china is the final stage of a long process. Pieces are usually formed in a mould or cast, and spend at least 15 hours in a kiln before being hand-finished.*

Quarry Bank Mill, a working reminder of the Industrial Revolution

Quarry Bank Mill, Styal ❶

Cheshire. 📞 01625 527468.
🚆 Wilmslow then bus. ⭕ Apr–Sep:
daily; Oct–Mar: Tue–Sun. ⬛ 23-25
Dec. ♿ limited. 🍴 🏛

THE HISTORY of the Industrial Revolution (see pp58–9) is brought vividly to life at Quarry Bank Mill, an early factory now transformed into a museum. Here, mill master Samuel Greg first used the waters of the Bollin Valley in 1784 to power the water frame, a machine for spinning raw cotton fibres into thread. By the 1840s, the Greg cotton empire was one of the biggest in Britain, and the mill produced bolts of material to be exported all over the world.

Today the massive old mill buildings have been restored to house a living museum of the cotton industry. This dominated the Manchester area for nearly 200 years, but was finally destroyed by foreign competition.

The entire process, from the spinning and weaving to the bleaching, the printing and dyeing, is shown through a series of reconstructions, demonstrations and many exciting hands-on displays.

The weaving shed is full of clattering looms producing textiles. There are fascinating contraptions that demonstrate how water can be used to drive machinery, including an enormous wheel, 50 tons in weight and 7 m (24 ft) high, that is still used occasionally to provide power for the looms.

The Greg family realized the importance of having a healthy, loyal and stable work-force. A social history exhibition explains how the mill workers were housed in the purpose-built village of Styal, in spacious cottages which had vegetable gardens and toilets. Details of their wages, working conditions and medical facilities are displayed on information boards.

There are guided tours of the nearby **Apprentice House**. Local orphans lived here, and were sent to work up to 12 hours a day at the mill when they were just six or seven years old. Visitors can try the beds in the house and even sample the medicine they were given. Quarry Bank Mill is surrounded by over 115 ha (284 acres) of woodland.

Chester ❷

Cheshire. 🚶 120,000. 🚆 🚌
ℹ️ Town Hall, Northgate St (01244
402111). 🗓 daily.

FIRST SETTLED BY THE ROMANS (see pp48–9), who estab-lished a camp in AD 79 to defend fertile land near the River Dee, the main streets of Chester are now lined with timber buildings. These are the **Chester Rows**, which, with their two tiers of shops and continuous upper gallery, anticipate today's multi-storey shops by several centuries.

Although their oriel windows and decorative timber-work are mostly 19th century, the Rows were first built in the 13th and 14th centuries, and the original structures can be seen in many places. The façade of the 16th-century

Chester's 1897 clocktower

Bishop Lloyd's House in Watergate Street is the most richly carved in Chester. The Rows are at their most varied and attractive where Eastgate Street meets Bridge Street. Here, views of the cathedral and the town walls give the impres-sion of a perfectly preserved medieval city. This illusion is helped by the Town Crier, who calls the hour and announces news in summer from the Cross, which is a reconstruction of the 15th-century stone crucifix that was destroyed in the Civil War (see pp56–7).

A **Heritage Centre**, south of the Cross, explains the town's history. To the north is the **cathedral**. The choir stalls have splendid misericords (see p391), with scenes including a sow suckling her litter and

Examples of the intricate carving on Bishop Lloyd's House, a Tudor building in Watergate Street, Chester

The Chester Rows, where shops line the first-floor galleries

a quarrelling couple. In sharp contrast are the delicate spire-lets on the stall canopies. The cathedral is surrounded on two sides by the high **city walls**, originally Roman but rebuilt at intervals. The best stretch is from the cathedral to Eastgate, where a wrought-iron **clock** was erected in 1897. The route to Newgate leads to a **Roman amphi-theatre** built in AD 100.

🏛 **Heritage Centre**
Bridge St Row, Bridge St. 📞 *01244 317948.* ⬜ *daily.* ⬤ *25–26 Dec, 1 Jan, Good Fri.* 📷 ♿ *limited.*

🏛 **Roman Amphitheatre**
Little St John St. 📞 *01244 321616.* ⬜ *daily.* ⬤ *25, 26 Dec, 1 Jan, Good Fri.*

Stoke-on-Trent ❸

Staffordshire. 🏛 *250,000.* 🚆 🚌 ℹ️ *Quadrant Rd, Hanley (01782 236000).* 🛍 *Mon–Sat.*

FROM THE MID-18TH CENTURY, Staffordshire became a lead-ing centre for mass-produced ceramics. Its fame arose from the fine bone china and por-celain products of Wedgwood, Minton, Doulton and Spode,

but the Staffordshire potteries also make a wide range of utilitarian products such as baths, toilets and wall tiles.

In 1910 a group of six towns – Longton, Fenton, Hanley, Burslem, Tunstall and Stoke-upon-Trent – merged to form the conurbation of Stoke-on-Trent, also known as the Potteries. Fans of the writer Arnold Bennett (1867–1931) may recognise this area as the "Five Towns", a term he

used in a series of novels about the region (Fenton was excluded from the stories).

The **Gladstone Pottery Museum** is a Victorian com-plex of workshops, kilns, galleries and an engine house. There are demonstrations of traditional pottery techniques. The **Potteries Museum and Art Gallery** in Hanley has historic and modern ceramics.

Josiah Wedgwood began his earthenware firm in 1769 and built a workers' village, Etruria. The last surviving steam-powered pottery mill is on display at the **Etruria Industrial Museum**.

ENVIRONS: About 10 miles (16 km) north of Stoke-on-Trent is **Little Moreton Hall** (*see pp336–7*), a half-timbered early Tudor manor house.

🏛 **Gladstone Pottery Museum**
Uttoxeter Rd, Longton. 📞 *01782 319232.* ⬜ *daily.* ⬤ *24 Dec–2 Jan.* 📷 ♿ 🍴 🛍

🏛 **Potteries Museum and Art Gallery**
Bethesda St, Hanley. 📞 *01782 232323.* ⬜ *daily.* ⬤ *25 Dec–1 Jan.* ♿ 💻 🛍

🏛 **Etruria Industrial Museum**
Lower Bedford St, Etruria. 📞 *01782 233144.* ⬜ *Wed–Sun.* ⬤ *25 Dec–1 Jan.* 📷 📷 *by arrangement.* 💻

🚃 **Little Moreton Hall**
(**NT**) Congleton, off A34. 📞 *01260 272018.* ⬜ *Mar–Oct: Wed–Sat & public hols; Nov–19 Dec: Sat, Sun.*

STAFFORDSHIRE POTTERY

An abundance of water, marl, clay and easily mined coal to fire the kilns enabled Staffordshire to develop as a ceramics centre; and local supplies of iron, copper and lead were used for glazing. In the 18th century, pottery became widely accessible and affordable. English bone china, which used powdered animals' bones for strength and translucence, was shipped all over the world, and Josiah Wedgwood (1730–95) introduced simple, durable crockery – though his best known design is the blue jasperware decorated with white Classical themes. Coal-powered bottle kilns fired the clay until the 1950s Clean Air Acts put them out of business. They have been replaced by electric or gas-fired kilns.

Wedgwood candlesticks, 1785

Timber-framed, gabled mansions in Fish Street, Shrewsbury

Shrewsbury ④

Shropshire. 👥 96,000. 🚆 🚌
ℹ️ *The Square (01743 350761).*
🛒 *Tue, Fri, Sat.*

SHREWSBURY is almost an island, enclosed by a great loop of the River Severn. A gaunt **castle** of red sandstone, first built in 1083, guards the entrance to the town, standing on the only section of land not surrounded by the river. Such defences were necessary on the frontier between England and the wilder Marches of Wales, whose inhabitants fiercely defied Saxon and Norman invaders *(see pp50–51)*. The castle, rebuilt over the centuries, now houses the Shropshire Regimental Museum.

In AD 60 the Romans *(see pp48–9)* built the garrison town of *Viroconium*, modern Wroxeter, 5 miles (8 km) east of Shrewsbury. Finds from the excavations are displayed at **Rowley's House Museum**, including a decorated silver mirror from the 2nd century and other luxury goods imported by the Roman army.

The town's other main museum, the **Clive House Museum**, takes its name from Lord Clive *(see p548)*. Clive became the local Member of Parliament upon his return from India until his death,

Roman silver mirror in Rowley's House Museum

and was Mayor of Shrewsbury in 1762, while he lived in this house. The 18th-century brick building has a fine collection of local porcelain, displayed in period settings.

The town's medieval wealth as a centre of the wool trade is evident in the many timber-framed buildings found along the High Street, Butcher Row, and Wyle Cop. Two of the grandest High Street houses, **Ireland's Mansions** and **Owen's Mansions**, are named after Robert Ireland and Richard Owen, the wealthy wool merchants who built them in 1575 and 1570 respectively. Similarly attractive buildings in Fish Street frame a view of the **Prince Rupert Hotel**, which was briefly the headquarters of Charles I's nephew, Rupert, in the English Civil War *(see pp56–7)*.

Outside the loop of the river, the **Abbey Church** survives from the medieval monastery. It has a number of interesting memorials, including one to Lieutenant WES Owen MC, better known as the war poet Wilfred Owen (1893–1918), who taught at the local Wyle Cop school and was killed in the last days of World War I.

ENVIRONS: To the south of Shrewsbury, the road to Ludlow passes through the

landscapes celebrated in the 1896 poem by AE Housman (1859–1936), *A Shropshire Lad*. Highlights include the bleak moors of **Long Mynd,** with 15 pre-historic barrows, and **Wenlock Edge**, wonderful walking country with glorious, far-reaching views.

⚓ **Shrewsbury Castle**
Castle St. 📞 *01743 358516.*
🕐 *Easter–Oct: Tue–Sun; Oct–Mar: Thu–Sat; public hols.* ⬤ *22 Dec– mid-Feb.* ♿ 🅿️
🏛 **Rowley's House Museum**
Barker St. 📞 *01743 361196.*
🕐 *Tue–Sun (Oct–Easter: Tue–Sat); public hols.* ⬤ *22 Dec–8 Jan.*
♿ *limited.* 🅿️
🏛 **Clive House Museum**
College Hill. 📞 *01743 354811.*
🕐 *Tue–Sun (Oct–May: Tue–Sat); public hols.* ⬤ *2 wks over Christmas.*
♿ *limited.* 🅿️

Ironbridge Gorge ⑤

See pp354–5.

Ludlow ⑥

Shropshire. 👥 9,000. 🚆 ℹ️ *Castle St (01584 875053).*

LUDLOW ATTRACTS large numbers of visitors to its splendid castle, but there is much else to see in this town, with its small shops and its lovely half-timbered Tudor buildings. Ludlow is an important area of geological

The 13th-century south tower and hall of Stokesay Castle, near Ludlow

research and the **museum**, just off the town centre, has fossils of the oldest known land animals and plants.

The ruined **castle** is sited on cliffs high above the River Teme. Built in 1086, it was damaged in the Civil War *(see pp56–7)* and abandoned in 1689. *Comus,* a court masque using music and drama and a precursor of opera, by John Milton (1608–74) was first performed here in 1634 in the Great Hall. In early summer open-air performances of Shakespeare's plays are held within the castle walls.

Prince Arthur (1486–1502), elder brother of Henry VIII *(see pp54–5)*, died at Ludlow Castle. His heart is buried in **St Laurence Church** at the other end of Castle Square, as are the ashes of the poet AE Housman. The east end of the church backs onto the **Bull Ring**, with its ornate timber buildings. Two inns vie for attention across the street: **The Bull**, with its Tudor back yard, and **The Feathers**, with its flamboyant façade, whose name recalls the feathers used in arrow-making, once a local industry.

ENVIRONS: About 5 miles (8 km) north of Ludlow, in a lovely setting, is **Stokesay Castle**, a fortified manor house with a colourful moat garden.

Ludlow Castle
The Square. 01584 873355.
daily. *24 Dec–1 Feb.*
limited.

Ludlow Museum
Castle St. 01584 875384.
Easter–May, Sep–Oct: Mon–Sat; Jun–Aug: daily.

Stokesay Castle
Craven Arms, A49. 01588 672544.
Apr–Oct: daily; Nov–Mar: Tue–Sun.
24–26 Dec, 1 Jan.

Leominster 7

Herefordshire. *10,000.*
Corn Sq (01568 616460). *Fri.*

FARMERS COME TO LEOMINSTER (pronounced "Lemster") from all over this rural region of England to buy supplies. There are two buildings of note in the town, which has been a wool-manufacturing centre for 700 years. In the centre of the town stands the magnificent **Grange Court**, carved with bold and bizarre figures by the carpenter John Abel in 1633. Nearby is the **priory**, whose imposing Norman portal is carved with an equally strange mixture of mythical birds, beasts and serpents. The lions, at least, can be explained: medieval monks believed the name of Leominster was derived from *monasterium leonis*, "the monastery of the lions". In fact, *leonis* probably comes from medieval, rather than Classical Latin, and it means "of the marshes". The aptness of this description can readily be seen in the green lanes around the town, following the lush river valleys that come together at Leominster.

A view of Leominster, set on the River Lugg in rolling border country

A Tudor building in Leominster, built with the profits from wool

ENVIRONS: To the west of the town, along the River Arrow, are the showcase villages of **Eardisland** and **Pembridge**, with their well-kept gardens and timber-framed houses. To the northeast of Leominster is **Tenbury Wells**, which enjoyed a brief popularity as a spa in the 19th century. The River Teme flows through it, full of minnows and spawning salmon and beloved of the composer Sir Edward Elgar *(see p357)*, who came to seek inspiration on its banks. The river also feeds **Burford House Gardens**, on the western outskirts of Tenbury Wells, where the water is used to create winding streams, fountains and pools that are rich in a variety of unusual, moisture-loving plants.

Burford House Gardens
Tenbury Wells. 01584 810777.
daily. *25–26 Dec, 1 Jan.*

Ironbridge Gorge ❺

I RONBRIDGE GORGE was one of the most important centres of the Industrial Revolution *(see pp58–9)*. It was here, in 1709, Abraham Darby I (1678–1717) pioneered the use of inexpensive coke, rather than charcoal, to smelt iron ore. The use of iron in bridges, ships and buildings transformed Ironbridge Gorge into one of the world's great iron-making centres. Industrial decline in the 20th century led to the Gorge's decay, although today it has been restored as an exciting complex of industrial archaeology, with several museums strung along the wooded banks of the River Severn.

VISITORS' CHECKLIST

Shropshire. 🏛 2,900. ✈ *Telford then bus.* 📞 *01952 433522.* ◐ *Dec–Jun: 10am–5pm; Jul–Aug: 10am–5:30pm; Sep–Nov: 10am–5pm daily.* ● *24, 25 Dec. Some sites closed Nov–Apr, phone for information.* ♿ *most sites.* 🎨 🅿 🖥 🍴 🎭 *Midsummer Fair: Jun (craft workshops and demonstrations throughout the year). List of events available.*

Wrought-iron clock (1843) on the roof of the Museum of Iron

MUSEUM OF IRON

T HE HISTORY OF IRON and the men who made it is traced in this remarkable museum. Abraham Darby I's discovery of how to smelt iron ore with coke allowed the mass production of iron, paving the way for the rise of large-scale industry. His original blast furnace forms the museum's centrepiece.

One of the museum's themes is the history of the Darby dynasty, a Quaker family who had a great impact on the Coalbrookdale community. The social and working conditions faced by the labourers, who sometimes had to toil for 24 hours at a stretch, are also illustrated.

Ironbridge led the world in industrial innovation, producing the first iron wheels and cylinders for the first steam engine. A restored locomotive and cast-iron statues, many of them

commissioned for the 1851 Great Exhibition *(see pp60–61)*, are among the many Coalbrookdale Company products on display.

One of the Darby family's homes in the nearby village of Coalbrookdale, **Rosehill House**, has been furnished in mid-Victorian style.

MUSEUM OF THE RIVER

T HIS PARTLY CASTELLATED, Victorian building was a warehouse for storing products from the ironworks before they were shipped down the River Severn. The warehouse is now home to the Museum of the River, and has displays illustrating the history of the Severn and the development of the water industry.

Until the arrival of the railways in the mid-19th century, the Severn was the main form of transport and communication to and from the Gorge. Sometimes too shallow, at other times in flood, the river was not a particularly reliable means of transportation; by the 1890s river trading had stopped completely.

The highlight of the museum is a wonderful 12 m (40 ft) model of the Gorge as it would have appeared in 1796, complete with foundries, cargo boats and growing villages.

Europe **(1860), statue in the Museum of Iron**

JACKFIELD TILE MUSEUM

T HERE HAVE BEEN POTTERIES in this area since the 17th century, but it was not until the Victorian passion for decorative tiles that Jackfield became famous. There were two tile-making factories here – Maw and Craven Dunnill – that produced a tremendous variety of tiles from clay mined nearby.

Peacock Panel (1928), one of the tile museum's star attractions

Talented designers created an astonishing range of images. The Jackfield Tile Museum, in the old Craven Dunnill works, has a collection of the decorative floor and wall tiles that were produced here from the 1850s to the 1960s. Visitors can also watch small-scale demonstrations of traditional methods of tile-making in the old factory buildings, including the biscuit kilns and the decoration workshops.

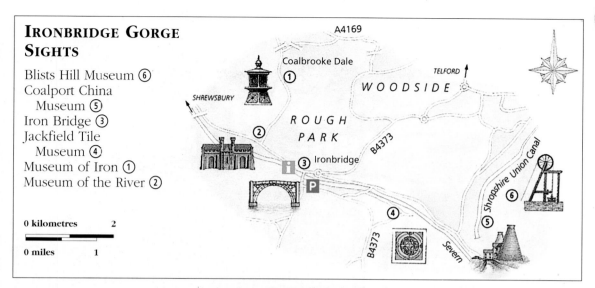

IRONBRIDGE GORGE SIGHTS

Blists Hill Museum ⑥
Coalport China
    Museum ⑤
Iron Bridge ③
Jackfield Tile
    Museum ④
Museum of Iron ①
Museum of the River ②

0 kilometres   2

0 miles   1

COALPORT CHINA MUSEUM

IN THE MID-19TH CENTURY the Coalport Works was one of the largest porcelain manufacturers in Britain, and its name was synonymous with fine china. The Coalport Company still makes porcelain but has long since moved its operations to Stoke-on-Trent *(see p351)*. Today the china workshops have been converted into a museum, where visitors can watch demonstrations of the various stages of making porcelain, including the skills of pot-throwing, painting and gilding. There is a superb collection of 19th-century china housed in one of the museum's distinctive bottle-shaped kilns.

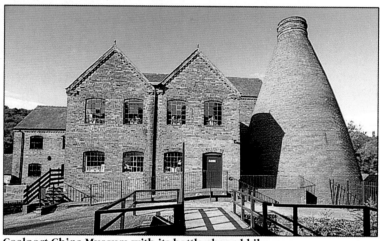
Coalport China Museum with its bottle-shaped kiln

Nearby is the **Tar Tunnel**, an important source of natural bitumen discovered 110 m (360 ft) underground in the 18th century. It once yielded 20,500 litres (4,500 gal) of tar every week; visitors can still explore part of the tunnel.

THE IRON BRIDGE

Abraham Darby III (grandson of the first man to smelt iron with coke) cast the world's first iron bridge in 1779, revolutionizing building methods in the process. Spanning the Severn, the bridge is a monument to the ironmasters' skills. The toll-house on the south bank charts its construction.

BLISTS HILL MUSEUM

THIS ENORMOUS OPEN-AIR museum recreates life in Ironbridge Gorge as it was 100 years ago. A group of 19th-century buildings has been reconstructed on the 20 ha (50 acre) site of Blists Hill, an old coal mine that used to supply the ironworks in the Gorge. Here, people in period costume enact roles and perform tasks such as iron forging.

The site has period housing, a church and even a Victorian school. Visitors can change money into old coinage to buy items from the baker or even pay for a drink in the local pub.

The centrepiece of Blists Hill is a complete foundry that still -produces wrought iron. One of the most spectacular sights is the Hay Inclined Plane, which was used to transport canal boats up and down a steep slope. Other attractions include steam engines, a saddlers, a doctors, a chemist, a candlemakers and a sweetshop.

Hereford ❽

Herefordshire. 👤 *50,000.* 🚆 🚌
ℹ️ *King St (01432 268430).*
🛒 *Wed (cattle), Sat (general).*

O NCE THE CAPITAL of the
Saxon kingdom of West
Mercia, Hereford is today an
attractive town which serves
the needs of a primarily rural
community. A cattle market is
held here every Wednesday,
and local produce is sold at
the covered market in the
town centre. Almost opposite,
the timber-framed **Old House**
of 1621 is now a museum of
local history, refurbished with
a mixture of reproduction and
original Jacobean furniture.

In the **cathedral**, only a
short stroll away, interesting
features include the Lady
Chapel, in richly ornamented
Early English style, and the
Chained Library, whose 1,500
books are tethered by iron
chains to bookcases as a
precaution against theft. The
best place for an
overall view of the
cathedral is at the
Bishop's Meadow,
south of the centre,
leading down to the
banks of the Wye,
scene of the annual
Hereford Regatta.

Hereford's many
rewarding museums
include the **City
Museum and Art
Gallery**, noted for its
Roman mosaics and
for watercolours by local
artists, and the **Churchill
House Museum** of 18th- and
19th-century furniture and
costume. Set outside the latter

Hereford's 17th-century Old House, furnished in period style

**Detail of figures on
Kilpeck Church**

is Roaring Meg, a cannon used
in the Civil War *(see pp56–7)*.
Visitors to the **Cider Museum
and King Offa Distillery** can
learn how local apples are
turned into 250 million litres
(55 million gal) of
cider a year, by a
range of old and
new methods.

ENVIRONS: During the
12th century, Oliver
de Merlemond made
a pilgrimage from
Hereford to Spain.
Impressed by several
churches he saw on
the way, he brought
French masons over
and introduced their
techniques to this area. One
result was **Kilpeck Church**,
6 miles (10 km) southwest,
covered in lustful figures
showing their genitals, and

tail-biting dragons – all seem-
ing more pagan than Christian.
At **Abbey Dore**, 4 miles (6
km) west, the Cistercian abbey
church is complemented by
the serene riverside gardens
of **Abbey Dore Court**.

🏛️ **Old House**
High Town. 📞 *01432 260694.*
⭕ *Apr–Sep: Tue–Sun; Oct–Mar: Tue–*
Sat; public hols. ⚫ *25, 26 Dec, 1 Jan,*
Good Fri . 📷 🚻

🏛️ **City Museum and Art
Gallery**
Broad St. 📞 *01432 260692.*
⭕ *Apr–Sep: Tue–Sun; Oct–Mar:*
Tue–Sat; public hols. ⚫ *25, 26 Dec, 1*
Jan, Good Fri. ♿ 🚻

🏛️ **Churchill House Museum**
Venns Lane. 📞 *01432 267409.*
⭕ *Apr–Oct: Tue–Sun (pm); Nov–Mar:*
Tue–Sat (pm) & public hols. ⚫ *25, 26*
Dec, 1 Jan, Good Fri. 📷 ♿ *limited.*

🏛️ **Cider Museum and King
Offa Distillery**
Ryelands St. 📞 *01432 354207.*
⭕ *Apr–Oct: daily; Nov–Mar: Mon–Sat*
& public hols. ⚫ *24–26 Dec, 1 Jan.*
📷 ♿ *limited.* 📋 *by arrangement.*

Ross-on-Wye ❾

Herefordshire. 👤 *10,000.* 🚌
ℹ️ *Eddie Cross St (01989 562768).*
🛒 *Thu, Sat.*

T HE FINE TOWN of Ross sits
on a cliff of red sandstone
above the water meadows of
the River Wye. There are wonderful views over the river
from the cliff-top gardens,

MEDIEVAL VIEW

Hereford Cathedral's most
celebrated treasure is the
Mappa Mundi, the Map of
the World, drawn in 1290
by a clergyman, Richard of
Haldingham. The world is
depicted here on Biblical
principles: Jerusalem is at
the centre, the Garden of
Eden figures prominently
and monsters inhabit the
margins of the world.

Central detail, *Mappa Mundi*

The wooded Wye Valley near Ross

given to the town by a local benefactor, John Kyrle (1637–1724). Kyrle was lauded by the poet Alexander Pope (1688–1744) in his *Moral Essays on the Uses of Riches* (1732) for using his wealth in a practical way, and he came to be known as "The Man of Ross". There is a memorial to Kyrle in **St Mary's Church**.

ENVIRONS: From Hereford to Ross, the **Wye Valley Walk** follows 16 miles (26 km) of gentle countryside. From Ross it continues south for 33 miles (54 km), over rocky ground in deep, wooded ravines.

Goodrich Castle, 5 miles (8 km) south of Ross, is a 12th-century red sandstone fort that sits on the summit of a rock high above the river.

🏰 **Goodrich Castle**
Goodrich. 📞 *01600 890538.*
◯ *daily.* ⬤ *24–26 Dec, 1 Jan.* 📷

Ledbury ⑩

Herefordshire. 🏃 *6,500.* ⇄ 🚌
ℹ️ *3 Homend (01531 636147).*

L EDBURY'S MAIN STREET is lined with timbered houses, including the **Market Hall** which dates from 1655. Church Lane, a cobbled alley running up from the High Street, has lovely 16th-century buildings: the **Heritage Centre** and **Butcher Row House** are both now museums. **St Michael and All Angels Church** has a massive detached bell tower, ornate Early English decoration and a collection of interesting monuments.

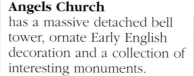

Medieval tile from the Priory at Great Malvern

🏛 **Heritage Centre**
The Homend. 📞 *01531 635680.*
◯ *Easter–Oct: daily.* ♿
🏛 **Butcher Row House**
Church Lane. ◯ *Easter–Oct: daily.*

Great Malvern and the Malverns ⑪

Worcestershire. 🏃 *40,000.* ⇄ 🚌
ℹ️ *21 Church St (01684 892289).*
🚼 *Fri.*

T HE ANCIENT GRANITE ROCK of the Malvern Hills rises from the plain of the River Severn, its 9 miles (15 km) of glorious scenery visible from afar. Composer Sir Edward Elgar (1857–1934) wrote many of his greatest works here, including the oratorio *The Dream of Gerontius* (1900), inspired by what the diarist John Evelyn (1620–1706) described as "one of the goodliest views in England". Elgar's home was in **Little Malvern**, whose truncated Priory Church of St Giles, set on a steep, wooded hill, lost its nave when the stone was stolen during the Dissolution of the Monasteries (*see pp54–5*). **Great Malvern**, capital of the hills, is graced with 19th-century buildings which look like Swiss sanitoria: patients would stay at institutions such as Doctor Gulley's Water Cure Establishment (now the Tudor Hotel). The water gushing from the hillside at St Ann's Well, above town, is bottled and sold throughout Britain.

Malvern's highlight is the **Priory**, with its 15th-century stained-glass windows and medieval misericords. The old monastic fishponds below the church form the lake of the **Winter Gardens**. Here the Festival Theatre hosts performances of Elgar's music and plays by George Bernard Shaw (*see p251*) during the Malvern Festival in late May.

A view of the Malverns range, formed of hard Pre-Cambrian rock

Worcester ⑫

Worcestershire. 🚶 *86,000.* 🚆 🚌
ℹ️ *High St (01905 722480).*
🔄 *Mon–Sat.*

WORCESTER is one of many English cities whose character has been transformed by modern development. The architectural highlight remains the **cathedral**, off College Yard, which suffered a collapsed tower in 1175 and a disastrous fire in 1203, before the present structure was started in the 13th century.

The nave and central tower were completed in the 1370s, after building was severely interrupted by the Black Death, which decimated the labour force *(see pp52–3)*. The most recent and ornate addition was made in 1874, when Sir George Gilbert Scott *(see p553)* designed the High Gothic choir, incorporating 14th-century carved misericords.

There are many interesting tombs, including King John's *(see pp52–3)*, a masterpiece

Charles I holding a symbol of the Church on Worcester's Guildhall

of medieval carving, in front of the altar. Prince Arthur, Henry VIII's brother *(see p353)*, who died at the age of 15, is buried in the chantry chapel south of the altar. Underneath, the huge Norman crypt survives from the first cathedral (1084).

From the cathedral cloister, a gate leads to College Green and the cathedral school, and out into Edgar Street and its

Georgian houses. Here the **Dyson Perrins Museum** displays Royal Worcester porcelain dating back to 1751. On the High Street, north of the cathedral, the **Guildhall** of 1723 is adorned with statues of Stuart monarchs, reflecting the city's Royalist allegiances. In Cornmarket you can see **Ye Olde King Charles House**, in which Prince Charles, later Charles II, hid after the Battle of Worcester in 1651 *(see pp56–7)*.

Some of Worcester's finest timber buildings are found in Friar Street: **Greyfriars**, built around 1480, has been newly decorated in period style. The **Commandery** was originally an 11th-century hospital. It was rebuilt in the 15th century and used by Prince Charles as a base during the Civil War. Now a Civil War museum, it has a fine hammerbeam roof and a painted chamber.

Elgar's Birthplace was the home of composer Sir Edward Elgar *(see p357)* and contains memorabilia of his life.

🏛 **Dyson Perrins Museum**
Severn St. 📞 *01905 23221.*
⭕ *daily.* ● *25, 26 Dec, 1 Jan, Easter Sun.* 🎫 ♿ 🎁 🍴 🛍

🏯 **Greyfriars**
(NT) Friar St. 📞 *01905 23571.* ⭕
Easter–Oct: Wed, Thu & public hols. 🎫

🏛 **Commandery**
Sidbury. 📞 *01905 361821.*
⭕ *daily (Sun: pm).* ● *25–26 Dec, 1 Jan.* 🎫 🛍 🛍

🏛 **Elgar's Birthplace**
Lower Broadheath. 📞 *01905 333224.*
⭕ *Thu–Tue.* ● *24–26 Dec; mid-Jan–mid-Feb.* 🎫 🛍

Birmingham ⑬

West Midlands. 🚶 *1,000,000.* ✈️
🚆 🚌 ℹ️ *City Arcade (0121 6432514).* 🔄 *Mon–Sat.*

BRUM, as it is affectionately known to its inhabitants, grew up as a major centre of the Industrial Revolution in the 19th century. A vast range of manufacturing trades was based in Birmingham and was responsible for the rapid development of grim factories and cramped housing. Since the clearance of several of these areas after World War II, Birmingham has raised its

Worcester Cathedral, overlooking the River Severn

◁ **Sweeping view of the Malvern Hills, north of Ledbury, Herefordshire**

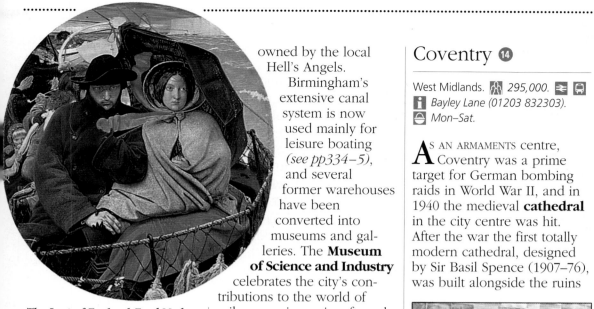

The Last of England, **Ford Madox Brown, Birmingham Art Gallery**

cultural profile. The city has succeeded in enticing Sir Simon Rattle to conduct the City of Birmingham Symphony Orchestra, and persuaded the former Royal Sadler's Wells Ballet (now the Birmingham Royal Ballet) to leave London for the more up-to-date facilities of Birmingham. The **National Exhibition Centre**, 8 miles (13 km) east of the centre, draws thousands of people to its conference, lecture and exhibition halls.

Set away from the massive Bullring shopping centre, Birmingham's 19th-century civic buildings are excellent examples of Neo-Classical architecture. Among them are the **City Museum and Art Gallery**, where the collection includes outstanding works by pre-Raphaelite artists such as Sir Edward Burne-Jones (1833–98), who was born here, and Ford Madox Brown (1821–93). The museum also organizes some interesting temporary exhibitions of art, ranging from Canaletto (1697–1768) to the gaudily decorated motorbikes

owned by the local Hell's Angels. Birmingham's extensive canal system is now used mainly for leisure boating *(see pp334–5)*, and several former warehouses have been converted into museums and galleries. The **Museum of Science and Industry** celebrates the city's contributions to the world of railway engines, aircraft, and the motor trade. The old jewellery quarter has practised its traditional crafts here since the 16th century.

Suburban Birmingham has many attractions, including the **Botanical Gardens** at Edgbaston, and the popular **Cadbury World** at Bournville, where there is a visitor centre dedicated to chocolate (booking advisable). Bournville village was built in 1890 by the Cadbury brothers, who were Quakers, for their workers and is a pioneering example of a garden suburb.

🏛 City Museum and Art Gallery
Chamberlain Sq. 📞 0121 303 2834. ◯ daily (Sun: pm). ● 24–27 Dec, 1, 2 Jan. ♿

🏛 Museum of Science and Industry
📞 0800 482000.
Being relocated to open mid-2000.

🌺 Botanical Gardens
Westbourne Rd, Edgbaston.
📞 0121 454 1860. ◯ daily. ●
25 Dec. 📷 ♿ 📷 by arrangement.

🏛 Cadbury World
Linden Rd, Bournville. 📞 0121 4514159. ◯ Apr–Oct: daily; Nov–Mar: selected days phone first.
● 23–25, 31 Dec. 📷 ♿

Coventry ⑭

West Midlands. 🚶 295,000. 🚊 🚌
ℹ Bayley Lane (01203 832303).
🛒 Mon–Sat.

AS AN ARMAMENTS centre, Coventry was a prime target for German bombing raids in World War II, and in 1940 the medieval **cathedral** in the city centre was hit. After the war the first totally modern cathedral, designed by Sir Basil Spence (1907–76), was built alongside the ruins

Epstein's *St Michael Subduing the Devil*, **on Coventry Cathedral**

of the bombed building. Sir Jacob Epstein (1880–1959) added dramatic sculptures, and Graham Sutherland (1903–80) the splendid tapestry, *Christ in Majesty*, on the east wall. Benjamin Britten *(see p211)* composed his *War Requiem* for the rededication ceremony, held on 30 May 1962.

The **Herbert Gallery and Museum** has displays on the 11th-century legend of Lady Godiva, who rode naked through the streets in protest when her husband, the Earl of Mercia, imposed taxes on the town. The city residents remained indoors, except for Peeping Tom, who was struck blind for his curiosity.

🏛 Herbert Gallery and Museum
Jordan Well. 📞 01203 832381. ◯ daily (Sun: pm) ● 24–26 Dec, 1 Jan.

Stately civic office buildings in Victoria Square, Birmingham

Midlands Garden Tour ⑮

T̲HE CHARMING COTSWOLD stone buildings perfectly complement the lush gardens for which the region is famous. This picturesque route from Warwick to Cheltenham is designed to show every type of garden, from tiny cottage plots, brimming with bell-shaped flowers and hollyhocks, to the deer-filled, landscaped parks of stately homes. The route follows the escarpment of the Cotswold Hills, taking in spectacular scenery and some of the prettiest Midlands villages on the way.

Plum tree in blossom

TIPS FOR DRIVERS

Tour length: *35 miles (50 km).*
Stopping-off points: *Hidcote Manor has excellent lunches and teas; there are refreshments at Kiftsgate Court and Sudeley Castle. Travellers will find a good choice in Broadway, from traditional pubs and tea shops to the de luxe Lygon Arms.*

Cheltenham Imperial Gardens ⑨
These colourful public gardens on the Promenade were laid out in 1817–18 to encourage people to walk from the town to the spa *(see p370).*

Sudeley Castle ⑧
The restored castle is complemented by box hedges, topiary and an Elizabethan knot garden *(see p26).* Catherine Parr, Henry VIII's widow, died here in 1548.

Broadway ⑤
Wisteria and cordoned fruit trees cover 17th-century cottages, fronted by immaculate gardens.

Stanway House ⑦
This Jacobean manor has many lovely trees in its grounds and a pyramid above a cascade of water.

Snowshill Manor ⑥
This Cotswold stone manor contains an extraordinary collection, from bicycles to Japanese armour. There are walled gardens and terraces full of *objets d'art* such as the clock (left). The colour blue is a recurrent theme.

Warwick Castle ①
The castle's gardens
(*see pp364–5*) include
the Mound, planted in
medieval style, with
grass, oaks, yew trees
and box hedges.

Anne Hathaway's Cottage ②
This has a pretty, informal 16th-
century-style garden (*see p369*).

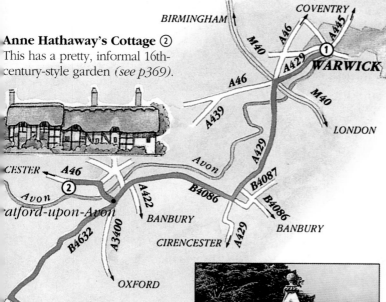

**Hidcote Manor
Gardens** ③
Started in the early
years of this century,
these beautiful gardens
pioneered the idea of a
garden as a series of
outdoor "rooms",
enclosed by high yew
hedges and planted
according to themes.

Kiftsgate Court Garden ④
This charmingly naturalistic garden
lies opposite Hidcote Manor. It has
many rare and unusual plants on a
series of hillside terraces, including
the enormous "Kiftsgate" Rose,
nearly 30 m (100 ft) high.

KEY

═══	Motorway
▬▬▬	Tour route
───	Other roads
✻	Viewpoint

0 kilometres   5

0 miles   5

Warwick ⑯

Warwickshire. 👥 28,000. 🚆 🚌
ℹ️ *The Courthouse, Jury St (01926
492212).* 🏛 *Sat.*

THOUGH WARWICK suffered a
major fire in 1694, some
spectacular medieval buildings survived. The **Warwick
Doll Museum** in Castle Street
(1573) displays rare toys and
dolls from all over the world.
At the west end of the High
Street, a row of medieval guild
buildings were transformed in
1571 by the Earl of Leicester
(1532–88), who founded the
Lord Leycester Hospital as
a refuge for his old retainers.
The arcaded **Market Hall**
(1670) is part of the Warwickshire Museum, renowned for
its unusual tapestry map of
the county, woven in 1558.
In Church Street, on the
south side of St Mary's Church,
the **Beauchamp Chapel**
(1443–64) survived the 1694
fire. It is a superb example of
Perpendicular architecture and
has fine tombs of the Earls of
Warwick. There is a bird's-eye
view of **Warwick Castle** (*see
pp364–5*) from St Mary's tower.

🏛 **Warwick Doll Museum**
Castle St. 📞 *01926 495546.*
🔵 *Easter–Oct: daily (Sun: pm);
(Nov–Easter: Sat).* 🈺 ♿ *limited.*
🏛 **Lord Leycester Hospital**
High St. 📞 *01926 491422.* 🔵 *Tue–
Sun & public hols.* ⚫ *25 Dec, Good
Fri.* **Gardens** 🔵 *same days as house
but Easter–Sep only.* 🈺 ♿ *limited.*
🏛 **Market Hall**
Market Place. 📞 *01926 412500.*
🔵 *Mon–Sat (May–Sep: daily).*
⚫ *24, 25 Dec,
1 Jan.* ♿ *limited.*

**The Lord Leycester Hospital,
now a home for ex-servicemen**

Warwick Castle

Neville family at prayer (c.1460)

WARWICK'S MAGNIFICENT CASTLE is a splendid medieval fortress which is also one of the country's finest stately homes. The original Norman castle was rebuilt in the 14th century, when huge outer walls and towers were added, mainly to display the power of the great feudal magnates, the Beauchamps and the Nevilles, the Earls of Warwick. The castle passed in 1604 to the Greville family who, in the 17th and 18th centuries, transformed it into a great country house. In 1978 the owners of Madame Tussaud's *(see p110)* bought the castle and set up tableaux of wax figures to illustrate its history.

Watergate Tower is where the ghost of Sir Fulke Greville, murdered by a servant in 1628, is said to walk.

The Mound has remains of the motte and bailey castle and the 13th-century keep.

Royal Weekend Exhibition
The waxwork valet is part of the award-winning exhibition of the Prince of Wales's visit in 1898.

★ Great Hall and State Rooms
Medieval apartments were transformed into the Great Hall and State Rooms, and rebuilt after a fire in 1871. The Great Hall is filled with arms, armour, furniture and curiosities.

Kingmaker Exhibition
Dramatic displays recreate medieval life as "Warwick the Kingmaker", Richard Neville, prepared for battle in the Wars of the Roses (see p53).

View of Warwick Castle, south front, by Antonio Canaletto (1697–1768)

VISITORS' CHECKLIST

Castle Lane, Warwick. 01926
495421. Apr–Oct: 10am–6pm
daily; Nov–Mar: 10am–5pm daily
(last adm: 30 mins before closing).
25 Dec. limited.

Ramparts and towers, of local grey sandstone, were added in the 14th century to fortify the castle.

Guy's Tower (1393) had lodgings for guests and members of the Earl of Warwick's retinue.

★ **Armoury**
The exhibits include Oliver Cromwell's helmet, a massive 14th-century two-handed sword and a fully armoured knight on horseback.

Entrance

STAR SIGHTS

★ **Great Hall and State Rooms**

★ **Armoury**

Caesar's Tower and dungeon contains a grisly collection of medieval torture instruments.

The Gatehouse is defended by portcullises and "murder holes" through which boiling pitch was dropped onto attackers beneath.

TIMELINE

Shield (1745), Great Hall

1000	1200	1400	1600	1800

1068 Norman motte and bailey castle built

1264 Simon de Montfort, champion of Parliament against Henry III, sacks Warwick Castle

Richard Neville

1356–1401 Present castle built by the Beauchamp family, Earls of Warwick

1449–1471 Richard Neville, Earl of Warwick, plays leading role in Wars of the Roses

1478 Castle reverts to Crown after murder of Richard Neville's son-in-law

1604 James I gives castle to Sir Fulke Greville

1600–1800 Interiors remodelled and gardens landscaped

1642 Royalists imprisoned in the castle

1893–1910 Visits from future Edward VII

1871 Anthony Salvin (1799–1881) restores Great Hall and State Rooms after fire

Street-by-Street: Stratford-upon-Avon ⑰

A 1930s jester

SITUATED ON THE WEST BANK of the River Avon, in the heart of the Midlands, is one of the most famous towns in England. Stratford-upon-Avon dates back to at least Roman times but its appearance today is that of a small Tudor market town, with mellow, half-timbered architecture and tranquil walks beside the tree-fringed Avon. This image belies its popularity as the most visited tourist attraction outside London, with eager hordes flocking to see buildings connected to William Shakespeare or his descendants.

Bancroft Gardens
There is an attractive boat-filled canal basin here and a 15th-century causeway.

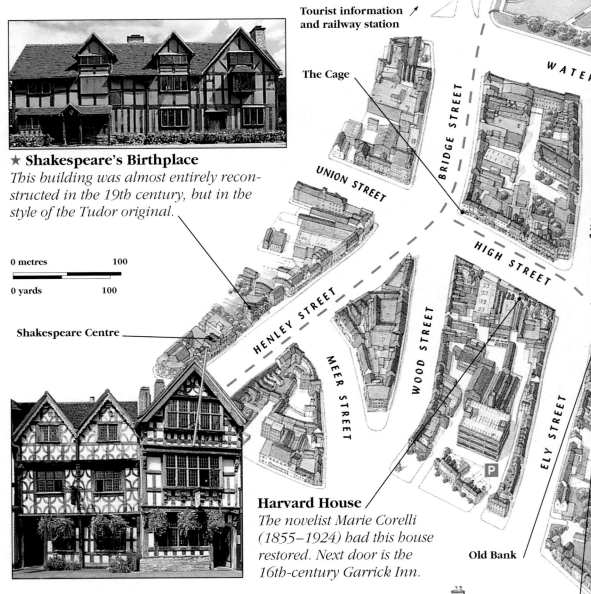

Tourist information and railway station

The Cage

★ **Shakespeare's Birthplace**
This building was almost entirely reconstructed in the 19th century, but in the style of the Tudor original.

```
0 metres          100
0 yards           100
```

Shakespeare Centre

UNION STREET
BRIDGE STREET
HIGH STREET
HENLEY STREET
MEER STREET
WOOD STREET
ELY STREET
SHEEP STREET
WATER S

Harvard House
The novelist Marie Corelli (1855–1924) had this house restored. Next door is the 16th-century Garrick Inn.

Old Bank

STAR SIGHTS

★ **Shakespeare's Birthplace**

★ **Hall's Croft**

★ **Holy Trinity Church**

Town Hall
Built in 1767, there are traces of 18th-century graffiti on the front of the building saying God Save the King.

Royal Shakespeare Theatre
The highly acclaimed resident theatre company, the RSC, has staged all of Shakespeare's plays since it began in 1961.

VISITORS' CHECKLIST

Warwickshire. 🏠 *22,000.*
✈ *20 miles (32 km) NW of Stratford-upon-Avon.* ➿ *Alcester Rd.* 🚌 *Bridge St.* ℹ *Bridge Foot (01789 293127); Shakespeare Centre, Henley St (01789 204016).*
🏛 *Fri.* 🎭 *Shakespeare's Birthday: Apr; Stratford Festival: Jul; Mop Fair: Oct.*

★ **Hall's Croft**
John Hall, Shakespeare's son-in-law, was a doctor. This delightful house has one room fitted out as a dispensary, with original Jacobean furniture.

★ **Holy Trinity Church**
Shakespeare's grave and copies of the parish register entries recording his birth and death are here.

Edward VI Grammar School

Guild Chapel

Nash's House
The foundations of New Place, where Shakespeare died, form the garden beside this house.

Anne Hathaway's Cottage

KEY

– – – – Suggested route

Swindon →

Exploring Stratford-upon-Avon

Mosaic of Shakespeare on the beautiful Old Bank (1810)

WILLIAM SHAKESPEARE was born in Stratford-upon-Avon on St George's Day, 23 April 1564. Admirers of his work have been coming to the town since his death in 1616. In 1847 a public appeal successfully raised the money to buy the house in which he was born. As a result Stratford has become a literary shrine to Britain's greatest dramatist. It also has a thriving cultural reputation as the provincial home of the prestigious Royal Shakespeare Company, whose dramas are usually performed in Stratford before playing a second season in London *(see p128).*

Anne Hathaway's Cottage, home of Shakespeare's wife

Around Stratford

The centre of Stratford-upon-Avon has many buildings that are connected with William Shakespeare and his descendants. On the High Street corner is the **Cage**, a 15th-century prison. It was converted into a house where Shakespeare's daughter Judith lived, and is now a shop. At the end of the High Street, the **Town Hall** has a statue of Shakespeare on the façade given by David Garrick (1717–79), the actor who in 1769 organized the first Shakespeare festival.

The High Street leads into Chapel Street where the half-timbered **Nash's House** is a museum of local history. It is also the site of **New Place**, where Shakespeare died in 1616, and which is now a herb and knot garden *(see p26).* In Church Street opposite, the **Guild Chapel** (1496) has a *Last Judgement* painting (c.1500) on the chancel wall. Shakespeare is thought to have attended the **Edward VI Grammar School** (above the former Guildhall) next door.

A left turn into Old Town leads to **Hall's Croft**, home of Shakespeare's daughter Susanna, which displays 16th- and 17th-century medical artefacts. An avenue of lime trees leads to **Holy Trinity Church**, where Shakespeare is buried. A walk along the river follows the Avon to **Bancroft Gardens**, which lies at the junction of the River Avon and the Stratford Canal.

🏛 Shakespeare's Birthplace

Henley St. 📞 *01789 204016.* ◯ *daily.* ⬛ *23–26 Dec.* 💷 ♿ *limited.* 🚪

Bought for the nation in 1847, when it was a public house, Shakespeare's Birthplace was converted back to Elizabethan style. Objects associated with Shakespeare's father, John, a glovemaker and wool merchant, are on display. The room in which Shakespeare was supposedly born (arbitrarily chosen by Garrick) has a window etched with visitors' autographs, including that of Sir Walter Scott *(see p622).*

Holy Trinity Church, seen across the River Avon

Harvard House

High St. **01789 204016.** *mid-May–Sep: Mon–Sat.* *limited.*

Built in 1596 and decorated with grotesque carved heads, this was the childhood home of Katherine Rogers. Her son, John Harvard, emigrated to America and in 1638 left his estate to a new college, later renamed Harvard University. The house displays material relating to the family.

ENVIRONS: No tour of Stratford would be complete without a visit to **Anne Hathaway's Cottage**. Before her marriage to William Shakespeare she lived at Shottery, 1 mile (1.5 km) west of Stratford. Despite fire damage in 1969, the cottage is still impressive, with some original 16th-century furniture. The Hathaway descendants lived here until the early 20th century and there is a fine garden *(see p363)*.

Anne Hathaway's Cottage

Cottage Lane. **01789 292100.** *daily.* *23–26 Dec, 1 Jan.*

Kenneth Branagh in *Hamlet*

THE ROYAL SHAKESPEARE COMPANY

The Royal Shakespeare Company is renowned for its new interpretations of Shakespeare's work. The company performs at the 1932 Royal Shakespeare Theatre, a windowless brick building adjacent to the Swan Theatre, built in 1986 to a design based on an Elizabethan playhouse. Next to it is a building displaying sets, props and costumes. The RSC also performs at the 150-seat theatre, known as the Other Place, and in London *(see p128)*.

Grevel House, the oldest house in Chipping Campden

Chipping Campden ⑱

Gloucestershire. **2,000.** *Hollis House, Stow-on-the-Wold (01451 831082).*

THIS PERFECT Cotswold town is kept in pristine condition by the Campden Trust. Set up in 1929, the Trust has kept alive the traditional skills of stonecarving and repair that make Chipping Campden such a unified picture of golden-coloured and lichen-patched stone. Visitors travelling from the northwest along the B4035 first see a group of ruins: the remains of **Campden Manor**, begun around 1613 by Sir Baptist Hicks, 1st Viscount Campden. The manor was burned by Royalist troops to stop it being sequestered by Parliament at the end of the Civil War *(see pp56–7)*, but the almshouses opposite the gateway were spared. They were designed in the form of the letter "I" (which is Latin for "J"), a symbol of the owner's loyalty to King James I.

The town's **Church of St James**, one of the finest in the Cotswolds, was built in the 15th century, financed by merchants who bought wool from Cotswold farmers and exported it at a high profit. Inside the church there are many elaborate tombs, and a magnificent brass dedicated to William Grevel, describing him as "the flower of the wool merchants of England". He built **Grevel House** (c.1380) in the High Street, the oldest in a fine row of buildings, which is distinguished by a double-storey bay window.

Viscount Campden donated the **Market Hall** in 1627. His contemporary, Robert Dover, founded in 1612 the "Cotswold Olimpicks", long before the modern Olympic Games had been established. The 1612 version included such painful events as the shin-kicking contest. It still takes place on the first Friday after each Spring Bank Holiday, followed by a torchlit procession into town ready for the Scuttlebrook Wake Fair on the next day. The setting for the games is a spectacular natural hollow on **Dover's Hill** above the town, worth climbing on a clear day for the marvellous views over the Vale of Evesham.

The 17th-century Market Hall in Chipping Campden

Tewkesbury's abbey church overlooks the town, crowded onto the bank of the River Severn

Tewkesbury ⑲

Gloucestershire. 👥 *11,000.*
ℹ️ *Barton St (01684 295027).*
🔄 *Wed, Sat.*

THIS LOVELY TOWN sits on the confluence of the rivers Severn and Avon. It has one of England's finest Norman abbey churches, **St Mary the Virgin**, which locals saved during the Dissolution of the Monasteries *(see p54)* by paying Henry VIII £453. Around the church, with its bulky tower and Norman façade, timbered buildings are crammed within the bend of the river. Warehouses and wharves are a reminder of past wealth, and the Borough Mill on Quay Street, the only mill left harnessed to the river's energy, still grinds corn to this day.

Pump Room detail, Cheltenham

ENVIRONS: Boat trips can be taken from the river marina to **Upton-on-Severn**'s riverside pubs, 6 miles (10 km) north.

Cheltenham ⑳

Gloucestershire. 👥 *107,000.* 🚆 🚌
ℹ️ *77 Promenade (01242 522878).*
🔄 *Sun.*

CHELTENHAM'S REPUTATION for elegance was first gained in the late 18th century, when high society flocked to the spa town to "take the waters", following the example set by George III *(see pp58–9)*. Many gracious terraced houses were built, in a Neo-Classical style, along broad avenues. These survive around the Queen's Hotel, near **Montpellier**, a lovely Regency arcade lined with craft and antique shops, and in the **Promenade**, with its smart department stores and couturiers. A more modern atmosphere prevails in the newly built Regency Arcade, where the star attraction is the 1987 **clock** by Kit Williams: visit on the hour to see fish blowing bubbles over the onlookers' heads. The **Museum and Art Gallery** is worth a visit to see its unusual collection of furniture and other crafts made by members of the influential Arts and Crafts Movement *(see p29)*, whose strict principles of utilitarian design were laid down by William Morris *(see p236)*.

Fashion from the Regency period to the 1960s is displayed in the domed **Pitville Pump Room** (1825–30), modelled on the Greek Temple of Ilissos in Athens and frequently used for performances during the town's renowned annual festivals of music (July) and literature (October).

The event that really attracts the crowds, though, is the Cheltenham Gold Cup – the premier event of the National Hunt season – held in March at Prestbury race course to the east of the town *(see p70)*.

🏛 **Museum and Art Gallery**
Clarence St. 📞 *01242 237431.*
⭕ *Mon–Sat.* ⚫ *25 Dec, 1 Jan & public hols.* ♿ 🎧 *by arrangement.*
♨️ **Pitville Pump Room**
Pitville Park. 📞 *01242 523852.*
⭕ *Wed–Mon.* ⚫ *25, 26 Dec, 1 Jan & for functions phone in advance.*

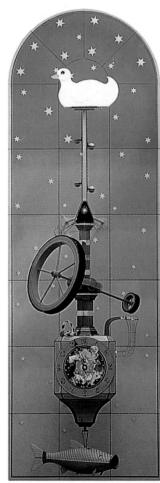

Fantasy clock, by Kit Williams, in Cheltenham's Regency Arcade

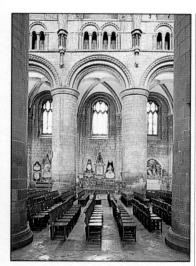
Gloucester Cathedral's nave

Gloucester ㉑

Gloucestershire. 🏛 *110,000.* ⇄ 🚌
ℹ *28 Southgate St (01452 421188).*
🏪 *Wed, Sat.*

GLOUCESTER has played a prominent role in the history of England. It was here that William the Conqueror ordered a vast survey of all the land in his kingdom, to be recorded in the Domesday Book of 1086 *(see p51)*.

The city was popular with the Norman monarchs and in 1216 Henry III was crowned in its magnificent **cathedral**. The solid, dignified nave was begun in 1089. Edward II *(see p513)*, who was murdered in 1327 at Berkeley Castle, 14 miles (22 km) to the southwest, is buried in a tomb near the high altar. Many pilgrims came to honour Edward's tomb, leaving behind generous donations, and Abbot Thoky was able to begin rebuilding in 1331. The result was the wonderful east window and the cloisters, where the fan vault was developed and then copied in other churches all over the country.

The impressive buildings around the cathedral include College Court, with its **Beatrix Potter Exhibition** in the house used by the children's author *(see p425)* for her illustrations of the story of the *Tailor of Gloucester*. A museum complex has been created in the **Gloucester Docks**, part of which is still a port, linked to the Bristol Channel by the Gloucester and Sharpness Canal (opened in 1827). In the old port, the

National Waterways Museum relates the history of canals, and the fascinating **Robert Opie Collection – Museum of Advertising and Packaging** looks at the promotion of household goods from 1870.

🏛 **Beatrix Potter Exhibition**
College Court. 📞 *01452 422856.*
⭕ *Mon–Sat.* ⬤ *public hols.* ♿ 🔲
🏛 **National Waterways Museum**
Llanthony Warehouse, Gloucester Docks. 📞 *01452 318054.* ⭕ *daily.*
⬤ *25 Dec.* ♿ ♿ 🔲 🔲
🏛 **Robert Opie Collection**
Albert Warehouse, Gloucester Docks.
📞 *01452 302309.* ⭕ *Mar–Sep: daily; Oct–Feb: Tue–Sun.* ⬤ *25, 26 Dec.*
♿ ♿ 🔲 🔲

Cirencester ㉒

Gloucestershire. 🏛 *18,000.* 🚌
ℹ *Market Place (01285 654180).*
🏪 *Mon, Tue (cattle) & Fri.*

KNOWN AS THE CAPITAL of the Cotswolds, Cirencester has as its focus a market place where cheeses, fish, flowers, and herbs are sold every Friday. Overlooking the market is the **Church of St John Baptist**, whose "wineglass" pulpit (1515) is one of the few pre-Reformation pulpits to survive in England. To the west, **Cirencester Park** was laid out by the 1st Earl of Bathurst from 1714, with help from the poet Alexander Pope *(see p357)*. The mansion is

surrounded by a massive yew hedge, claimed to be the tallest in the world. Clustering round the park entrance are the 17th- and 18th-century wool merchants' houses of Cecily Hill, built in grand Italianate style. Much humbler Cotswold houses are to be found in Coxwell Street, and underlying all this mellow stonework is a Roman town, evidence of which emerges whenever a spade is put in the ground.

The **Corinium Museum** (*Corinium* was the Latin name) features excavated objects in a series of tableaux illustrating life in a Roman household.

🌿 **Cirencester Park**
Cirencester Park. 📞 *01285 653135.*
⭕ *daily.* ♿
🏛 **Corinium Museum**
Park St. 📞 *01285 655611.*
⭕ *daily (Nov–Apr: Tue–Sun).*
⬤ *25 Dec, 1 Jan.* ♿ ♿ 🔲 🔲

Cirencester's fine parish church, one of the largest in England

ART AND NATURE IN THE ROMAN WORLD

Cirencester was an important centre of mosaic production in Roman days. Fine examples of the local style are shown in the Corinium Museum and mosaics range from Classical subjects, such as Orpheus taming lions and tigers with the music of his lyre, to the naturalistic depiction of a hare. At

Chedworth Roman Villa, 8 miles (13 km) north, mosaics are inspired by real life. In the *Four Seasons* mosaic, *Winter* shows a peasant, dressed in a woollen hood and a wind-blown cloak, clutching a recently caught hare in one hand and a branch for fuel in the other.

Hare mosaic, Corinium Museum

Sheep grazing by the still waters of Ladybower Reservoir, Derbyshire ▷

EAST MIDLANDS

EAST MIDLANDS

···

THREE CONTRASTING KINDS OF LANDSCAPE *converge on the East Midlands. In the west, wild moors rise to the heights of the Derbyshire Peak District. At the core of the region, these highlands give way to a low-lying plain and sprawling industrial towns. To the east, hills and limestone villages stretch to the long, flat seaboard.*

Nowhere in England are industrial and pastoral scenes interwoven so closely and so startlingly as in the East Midlands. The spa resorts, historical villages, stately homes and dramatic escarpments share a landscape shaped by industry over many centuries. The Romans mined lead and salt here and built a network of roads and fortresses. During the Middle Ages, profits from the wool trade led to the development of wealthy settlements such as Lincoln, which has a splendid cathedral. Long-standing manufacturing industries, such as lace production in Nottingham, made little impact on the landscape, but the Industrial Revolution in the late 18th century heralded major changes, as

deep coal mines and large factories scarred the once open countryside.

The East Midlands have been settled since prehistoric times. Anglo-Saxon and Viking influence can be detected in many place names, including that of the region's main magnet for visitors, the Peak District. This is not, as many suppose, named for the peaks on top of the hills – of which there are rather few – but after the Peak Cavern at Castleton, mentioned in the 11th-century Domesday Book as "Peak's Arse", or "Devil's Bottom". The hill above Peak Cavern came to be called Peak Hill, and on it a castle was built by the 11th-century Norman baron William Peveril, who is celebrated in Sir Walter Scott's "Peveril of the Peak". Over the years, the name Peak District has come to denote two distinct areas of

Well-dressing dance, an ancient custom at Stoney Middleton in the Peak District

◁ **West front of Chatsworth House, a superb Baroque stately home in the Peak District**

Shops and church spire in the town of Bakewell, Derbyshire

high moorland: the heather-covered Dark Peak in the north, and the limestone White Peak in the south. In 1951, the Peak District became Britain's first national park. Today, many visitors are drawn to the scenic beauty of the region, which includes the untamed splendour of the moors, picturesque wooded dales by the banks of the River Dove and traditional stone-walled meadows. The area is especially popular with hikers, rock climbers and potholers.

Red Leicester cheese

Many of the grand houses in the East Midlands have associations with one of the most formidable Englishwomen of the 16th century, Bess of Hardwick. Born in 1518, she was married four times and each new husband brought with him land and possessions to add to those she was to inherit from her rich father. It was her second husband, William Cavendish, who purchased the estate at Chatsworth for her. In 1552, a Tudor mansion was built, but this was replaced at the end of the 17th century by one of Britain's most magnificent and most visited stately homes, Chatsworth House. In 1568, Bess married her fourth husband, the sixth Earl of Shrewsbury, among whose houses were the former Rufford Abbey and Bolsover Castle, which are both near Sherwood Forest in Nottinghamshire. Today, the ruins of these buildings are open to visitors. Queen Elizabeth appointed Bess and the Earl as jailers to Mary Queen of Scots, who was held at Wingfield Manor, near Chesterfield, for some years. Wingfield Manor, which is also a ruin, is in the hands of English Heritage. In 1583, Bess inherited her birthplace, Hardwick Hall, and had a magnificent new hall built alongside it. Both the "new" hall and the remains of the old one are well worth visiting.

Gnarled tree roots in Sherwood Forest, Nottinghamshire

Althorp House, another stately home in the region, has a link with contemporary history. Diana, Princess of Wales, was born here in 1961. Diana's family, the Spencers, have lived on the estate, which is near Northampton, since the 16th century. (The present house dates mainly from the 1780s.) After Diana was killed in 1997, she was buried on an island in the middle of the lake at Althorp, which has become a place of pilgrimage for her admirers.

The East Midlands has had its share of turmoil: during the Wars of the Roses (15th century) and the Civil War (17th century), many ferocious battles were fought in the area. In the Jacobite rebellion of the 18th century, insurgents reached as far south as the town of Derby. The region was also badly affected by the plague.

In the 17th century the ancient custom of well-dressing on Ascension Day (May) was revived in the Peak District, probably to give thanks for the fact that the water was safe to drink after the disappearance of the plague. During this ritual the wells in several villages are lavishly decorated with seeds and flower petals. The completion of well-dressing is celebrated in a ceremony that may include a traditional folk dance. This part of the country is rich in such rites. Every 29 May there is a procession through Castleton – headed by a "garland king and queen" – thought to have originated at the time of the Restoration of Charles II in 1660. Every

Narrow boat traversing Foxton Locks, Leicestershire

July, Catholics make a pilgrimage from Hathersage to Grindleford in memory of the martyrs of Padley, three priests killed because they resisted the Reformation. In September is the Horn Dance at Abbots Bromley, where locals in medieval costume, some wearing antlers, dance around the village boundary. This ritual renews the right to hunt in nearby Needwood Forest. Among characters represented are Robin Hood and Maid Marian, the legendary heroes of this area.

Stepping stones over the River Dove, Peak District National Park, Derbyshire

Exploring the East Midlands

THE EAST MIDLANDS is a popular tourist destination, easily accessible by road, but best explored on foot. Numerous well-marked trails pass through the Peak District National Park. There are superb country houses at Chatsworth and Burghley and the impressive historic towns of Lincoln and Stamford to discover.

SIGHTS AT A GLANCE

Burghley pp392–3 **8**
Buxton **1**
Chatsworth pp382–3 **2**
Lincoln pp390–91 **7**
Matlock Bath **3**
Northampton **10**
Nottingham **6**
Stamford **9**

Walks and Tours

Peak District Tour **5**
Tissington Trail **4**

GETTING AROUND

The M6, M1 and A1 are the principal road routes to the East Midlands, but they are subject to frequent delays because of the volume of traffic they carry. It can be faster and more interesting to find cross-country routes to the region, for example through the attractive countryside and villages around Stamford and Northampton. Roads in the Peak District become very congested during the summer and an early start to the day is advisable. Lincoln and Stamford are well served by fast InterCity trains from London. Rail services in the Peak District are far more limited, but local lines run as far as Matlock and Buxton.

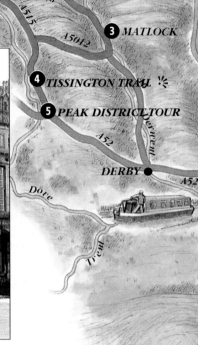

View of Burghley House from the north courtyard

KEY

Motorway
Major road
Scenic route
Scenic path
River
Viewpoint

Peak District countryside seen from the Tissington Trail

Lincoln Cathedral towering over half-timbered buildings

Dry-Stone Walling

STONE WALL FIELD BOUNDARIES are an integral feature of the traditional landscape of upland Britain. Some say that dry-stone walling, the building of walls without mortar, originated in medieval or even prehistoric times. However, it was a wave of stone-wall building between about 1750 and 1850 that totally transformed the face of the countryside. In this short period of time vast tracts of open agricultural land, common grazing land, heath and moorland as well as cleared forests, were all turned by parliamentary enclosure into a mosaic of fields bounded by dry-stone walls or hedges.

These moorland stone-wall field boundaries near Malham, West Yorkshire, were laid in the 1700s. Walls were built wider at the base than the top for stability.

The passage grave at Maes Howe in Orkney, Scotland, is an example of Neolithic dry-stone building. Dating from c3000 BC, it is quite a refined example.

Objects, such as this large millstone, are sometimes incorporated as decoration.

A squeeze stile allows people to pass through the walls, but not large animals, such as cattle or sheep.

STONE WALLS AROUND THE COUNTRY

Naturally, stone walls have always been built with whatever stone lies close to hand. As a result, they vary enormously in form, colour and construction from one region of Britain to another.

Oolitic limestone from the Cotswolds is easily worked and makes for neatly finished walls with small stones.

Slate is often laid in a herringbone pattern in Cornwall. The infill is earth, so flowers may seed themselves in the wall.

The name and position of coping stones vary from region to region. These stones are laid on as "cocks and hens".

The medieval village *of Hound Tor on Dartmoor, Devon, was deserted in the 14th century. Most buildings at that time were timber, but stone was used for foundations.*

PRESERVING A HERITAGE

Dry-stone walls are found where rocky outcrops are common and where the soil is too thin and the weather too harsh for hedges. Britain has an estimated 70,000 miles (112,000 km) of dry-stone walls, with the greatest density being in Derbyshire, North Yorkshire, Cumbria and Cornwall. Of these, the great majority are now in need of repair. Building or repairing dry-stone walls is slow and heavy work, starting with the careful preparation of the stone. However, once properly constructed, the walls will stand for 100–150 years.

A slate splitter preparing slate for a wall

CONSTRUCTING A WALL

A dry-stone wall is tightly packed so that rain cannot penetrate, and the core stays almost dry and frost-free. Most walls are two-sided and the space in the middle is filled with small stones or earth. "Throughs" are stones laid in the wall to bond the two faces, and "cope stones" are placed on top to prevent the two sides falling apart.

...hen often adds ...our to the roughly ...rried, grey-green ...e walls in Stone-...aite, Cumbria.

Walls from the Lake *District have stood for hundreds of years and have had to withstand the harshest elements.*

Plants *that are commonly found grow-ing on dry-stone walls include spleenwort, stonecrop and saxifrage.*

Millstone grit walls *are common in Derby-shire. It is difficult to acheive regular courses with this sandstone.*

Buxton Opera House, a late 19th-century building restored in 1979

Buxton ①

Derbyshire. 🏠 *20,000.* 🚆 🚌
ℹ️ *The Crescent (01298 25106).*
🛒 *Tue, Sat.*

BUXTON was developed as a spa town by the 5th Duke of Devonshire during the late 18th century. It has many fine Neo-Classical buildings, including the **Devonshire Royal Hospital** (1790), originally stables, at the entrance to the town. The **Crescent** was built (1780–90) to rival Bath's Royal Crescent *(see p282)*.

At its southwest end, the tourist information office is housed in the former town baths. Here, a spring where water surges from the ground at a rate of 7,000 litres (1,540 gallons) an hour can be seen. Buxton water is bottled and sold commercially but there is a public fountain at **St Ann's Well**, opposite.

Steep gardens known as the Slopes lead from the Crescent to the small, award-winning **Museum and Art Gallery**, with geological and archaeological displays. Behind the Crescent, overlooking the Pavilion Gardens, is the striking 19th-century iron and glass **Pavilion**, and the splendidly restored **Opera House**, where a Music and Arts Festival is held in summer.

🏛️ **Buxton Museum and Art Gallery**
Terrace Rd. 📞 *01298 24658.*
⬜ *Easter–Sep: Tue–Sun (Oct–Easter: Tue–Sat).* ⬛ *25 Dec–2 Jan.* 📷 ♿ 🏠
🎪 **Pavilion**
St John's Rd. 📞 *01298 23114.*
⬜ *daily.* ⬛ *25 Dec.* ♿

Chatsworth House and Gardens ②

CHATSWORTH IS ONE of Britain's most impressive stately homes. Between 1687 and 1707, the 4th Earl of Devonshire replaced the old Tudor mansion with this Baroque palace. The house has beautiful gardens, landscaped in the 1760s by Capability Brown *(see p27)* and developed by the head gardener, Joseph Paxton *(see pp60–61,* in the mid-19th century.

First house built in 1552 by Bess of Hardwick

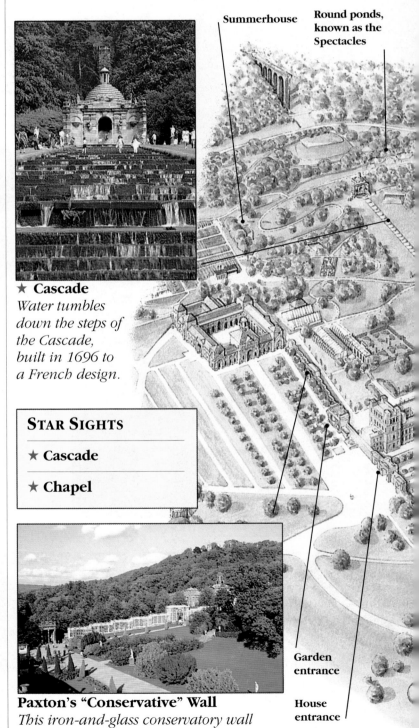

★ Cascade
Water tumbles down the steps of the Cascade, built in 1696 to a French design.

Summerhouse

Round ponds, known as the Spectacles

> ### STAR SIGHTS
> ★ **Cascade**
> ★ **Chapel**

Paxton's "Conservative" Wall
This iron-and-glass conservatory wall was designed in 1848 by Joseph Paxton, the creator of Chatsworth's Great Conservatory (now demolished).

Garden entrance

House entrance

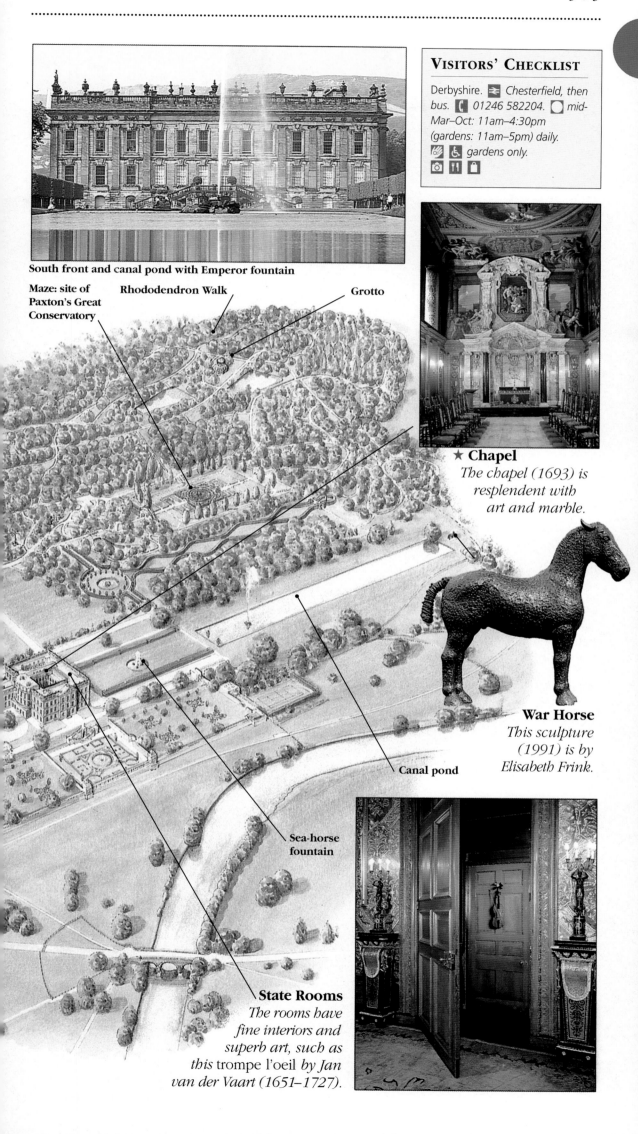

South front and canal pond with Emperor fountain

VISITORS' CHECKLIST

Derbyshire. 🚆 Chesterfield, then
bus. 📞 01246 582204. 🕐 mid-
Mar–Oct: 11am–4:30pm
(gardens: 11am–5pm) daily.
gardens only.

Maze: site of
Paxton's Great
Conservatory

Rhododendron Walk

Grotto

★ **Chapel**
*The chapel (1693) is
resplendent with
art and marble.*

War Horse
*This sculpture
(1991) is by
Elisabeth Frink.*

Canal pond

Sea-horse
fountain

State Rooms
*The rooms have
fine interiors and
superb art, such as
this* trompe l'oeil *by Jan
van der Vaart (1651–1727).*

Matlock ③

Derbyshire. 🏘 23,000. ⊷
ℹ *Crown Square (01629 583388).*

MATLOCK WAS DEVELOPED as a spa from the 1780s. Interesting buildings include the massive structure (1853) on the hill above the town, built as a hydrotherapy centre but now council offices. On the hill opposite is the excellent **Riber Castle Wildlife Park**, with a ruined mock-Gothic castle in its grounds.

From Matlock, the A6 winds through the outstandingly beautiful **Derwent Gorge** to **Matlock Bath**. Here, cable cars ascend to the **Heights of Abraham** pleasure park, with caves, nature trail and extensive views. Lead-mining is the subject of the **Peak District Mining Museum**, and visitors can inspect the old **Temple Mine** nearby. **Arkwright's Mill** (1771), the world's first water-powered cotton-spinning mill, is at the southern end of the gorge *(see p389)*.

🦌 **Riber Castle Wildlife Park**
Off A615, SE of Matlock. (*01629 582073.* ◯ *daily.* ● *25 Dec.* 🖼 ♿
🌲 **Heights of Abraham**
On A6. (*01629 582365.*
◯ *Easter–Oct: daily.* 🖼 ♿ *limited.*
🏛 **Peak District Mining Museum**
The Pavilion, off A6. (*01629 583834.*
◯ *daily.* ● *25 Dec.* 🖼 ♿ 🗂
⛏ **Temple Mine**
Temple Rd, off A6. (*01629 583834.*
◯ *daily (winter: pm).* ● *25 Dec.* 🖼
⛏ **Arkwright's Mill**
Mill Lane, Cromford. (*01629 824297.* ◯ *daily.* ● *25 Dec.* ♿ 🖼

Cable cars taking visitors to the Heights of Abraham

Tissington Trail ④

See p387.

Peak District Tour ⑤

See pp388–9.

Nottingham ⑥

Nottinghamshire. 🏘 270,000. ⊷
🚌 ℹ *Smithy Row (0115 9155330).*
🚏 *daily.*

THE NAME OF NOTTINGHAM often conjures up the image of the evil Sheriff, adversary of Robin Hood. The Sheriff may be fictional but **Nottingham Castle** is real enough, standing on a rock riddled with underground passages. The castle houses a museum, with displays on the city's history, and what was Britain's first municipal art gallery, featuring works by Sir Stanley Spencer (1891–1959)

and Dante Gabriel Rossetti (1828–82). At the foot of the castle, Britain's oldest tavern, the **Trip to Jerusalem** (1189), is still in business. Its name refers to the 12th- and 13th-century crusades, but much of the building dates from the 17th century.

There are several museums near the castle, ranging from the **Tales of Robin Hood**, which tells the story of the outlaw, to the **Museum of Costume and Textiles**. In the latter, Nottingham's role as a leading centre for embroidery, lace-making, tapestries and knitted textiles is explained.

ENVIRONS: Outstanding stately homes within a few miles' radius of Nottingham include the Neo-Classical **Kedleston Hall** *(see pp28–9)*. "Bess of Hardwick", the rapacious Countess of Shrewbury *(see p382)* built the spectacular **Hardwick Hall** *(see p336)*.

⛪ **Nottingham Castle and Museum**
Lenton Rd. (*0115 9153651.*
◯ *daily.* ● *Nov–Feb: Fri; 25, 26 Dec, 1 Jan.* 🖼 *Sat, Sun & public hols.* ♿
🏛 **Tales of Robin Hood**
30–38 Maid Marion Way. (*0115 9483284.* ◯ *daily.* ● *24–26 Dec.*
🖼 ♿ 🗂 🗂
🏛 **Museum of Costume and Textiles**
51 Castle Gate. (*0115 9153500.*
◯ *Wed–Sun.* ● *24 Dec–1 Jan.*
🏰 **Kedleston Hall**
(NT) off A38. (*01332 842191.*
◯ *Apr–Oct: Sat–Wed (pm).* 🖼 ♿
🏰 **Hardwick Hall**
(NT) off A617. (*01246 850430.*
◯ *Apr–Oct: Wed, Thu, Sat, Sun & public hols.* 🖼 ♿ *limited.* 🍴 🗂

ROBIN HOOD OF SHERWOOD FOREST

England's most colourful folk hero was a legendary swordsman, whose adventures are depicted in numerous films and stories. He lived in Sherwood Forest, near Nottingham, with a band of "merry men", robbing the rich to give to the poor. As part of an ancient oral tradition, Robin Hood figured mainly in ballads; the first written records of his exploits date from the 15th century. Today historians think that he was not one person, but a composite of many outlaws who refused to conform to medieval feudal constraints.

Victorian depiction of Friar Tuck and Robin Hood

◁ **Houses tucked away in the picturesque woodlands of Monsal Head, Derbyshire**

Tissington Trail ❹

THE FULL-LENGTH Tissington Trail runs for 12 miles (20 km), from the village of Ashbourne to Parsley Hay, where it meets the High Peak Trail. This is a short version, taking an easy route along a dismantled railway line around Tissington village and providing good views of the beautiful White Peak countryside. The Derbyshire custom of well-dressing is thought to have originated in pre-Christian times. It was revived in the early 17th century, when the Tissington village wells were decorated in thanksgiving for deliverance from the plague, in the belief that the fresh water had had a medicinal effect. Well-dressing is still an important event in the Peakland calendar, and can be seen in other villages where the water supplies are prone to dry up.

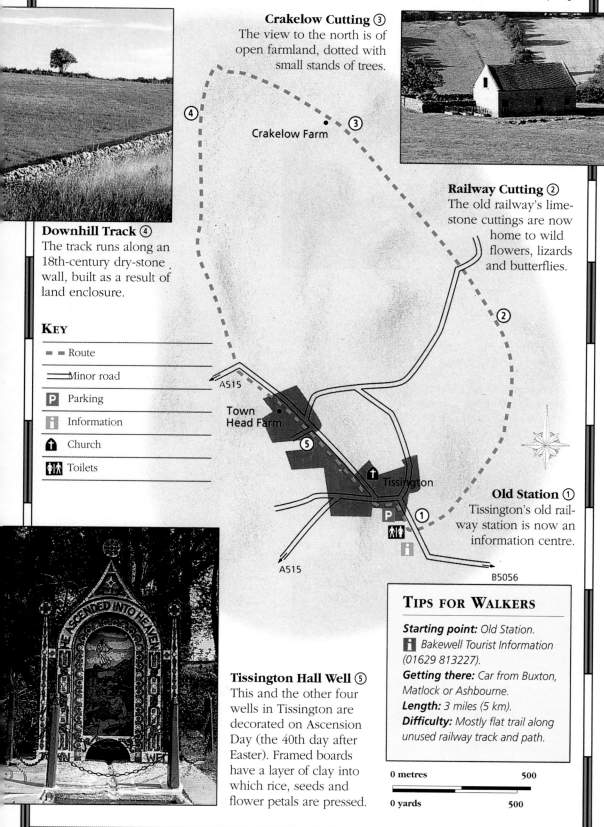

Crakelow Cutting ③
The view to the north is of open farmland, dotted with small stands of trees.

Crakelow Farm

Railway Cutting ②
The old railway's limestone cuttings are now home to wild flowers, lizards and butterflies.

Downhill Track ④
The track runs along an 18th-century dry-stone wall, built as a result of land enclosure.

KEY

- ▪ ▪ Route
- Minor road
- P Parking
- ℹ Information
- ✝ Church
- 🚻 Toilets

A515

Town Head Farm

Tissington

Old Station ①
Tissington's old railway station is now an information centre.

A515

B5056

Tissington Hall Well ⑤
This and the other four wells in Tissington are decorated on Ascension Day (the 40th day after Easter). Framed boards have a layer of clay into which rice, seeds and flower petals are pressed.

TIPS FOR WALKERS

Starting point: Old Station.
ℹ Bakewell Tourist Information (01629 813227).
Getting there: Car from Buxton, Matlock or Ashbourne.
Length: 3 miles (5 km).
Difficulty: Mostly flat trail along unused railway track and path.

0 metres	500
0 yards	500

Peak District Tour ⑤

Detail, Buxton Opera House

T HE PEAK DISTRICT's natural beauty and sheep-grazed crags contrast with the factories of nearby valley towns. Designated Britain's first National Park in 1951, the area has two distinct types of landscape. In the south are the gently rolling hills of the limestone White Peak. To the north, west and east are the wild, heather-clad moorlands of the Dark Peak peat bogs, superimposed on millstone grit.

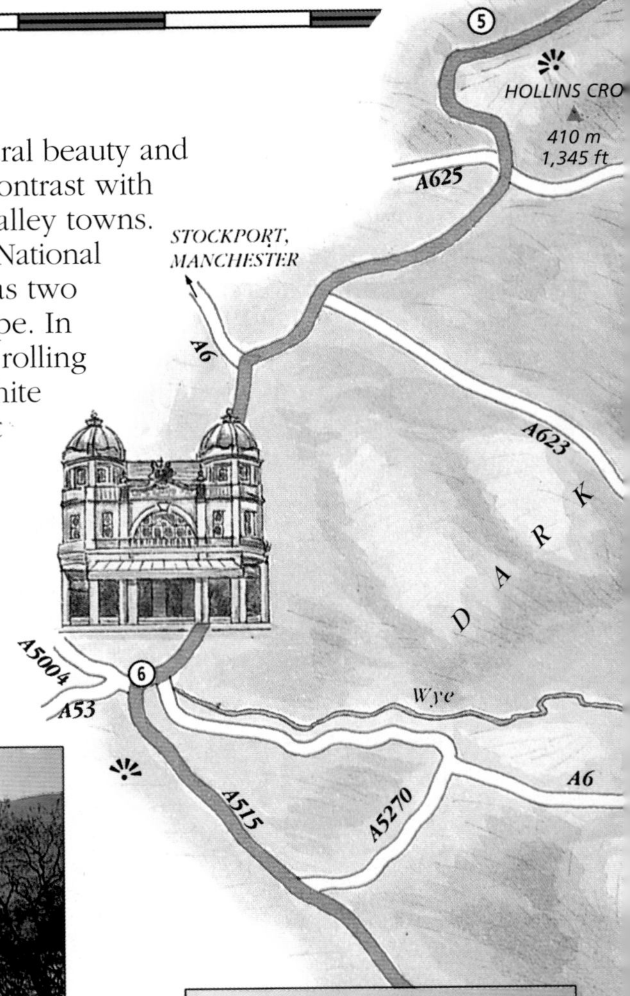

HOLLINS CRO
410 m
1,345 ft

A625

STOCKPORT, MANCHESTER

A6

A623

DARK

Edale ⑤
The high, dangerous peaks of scenic Edale mark the starting point of the 256 mile (412 km) Pennine Way footpath *(see p36)*.

A5004

A53

⑥

Wye

A515

A5270

A6

Buxton ⑥
This lovely spa town's opera house *(see p382)* is known as the "theatre in the hills" because of its magnificent setting.

TIPS FOR DRIVERS

Tour length: *40 miles (60 km).*
Stopping-off points: *There are refreshments at Crich National Tramway Museum and Arkwright's Mill in Cromford. Eyam has good old-fashioned tea shops. The Nag's Head in Edale is a charming Tudor inn. Buxton has many pubs and cafés.*

Arbor Low ⑦
This stone circle, known as the "Stonehenge of the North", dates from around 2000 BC and consists of 46 recumbent stones enclosed by a ditch.

KEY

 Tour route

Other roads

Viewpoint

Dovedale ⑧
Popular Dovedale is the prettiest of the Peak District's river valleys, with its stepping stones, thickly wooded slopes and wind-sculpted rocks. Izaac Walton (1593–1683), author of *The Compleat Angler,* used to fish here.

Dove

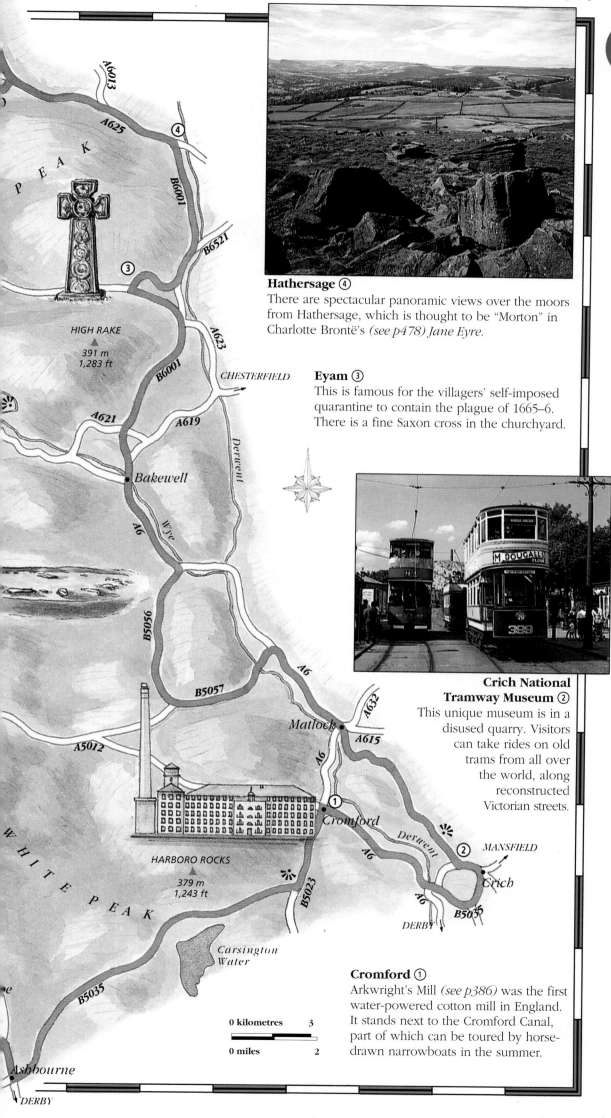

Hathersage ④
There are spectacular panoramic views over the moors from Hathersage, which is thought to be "Morton" in Charlotte Brontë's *(see p478) Jane Eyre*.

Eyam ③
This is famous for the villagers' self-imposed quarantine to contain the plague of 1665–6. There is a fine Saxon cross in the churchyard.

Crich National Tramway Museum ②
This unique museum is in a disused quarry. Visitors can take rides on old trams from all over the world, along reconstructed Victorian streets.

Cromford ①
Arkwright's Mill *(see p386)* was the first water-powered cotton mill in England. It stands next to the Cromford Canal, part of which can be toured by horse-drawn narrowboats in the summer.

HIGH RAKE
391 m
1,283 ft

HARBORO ROCKS
379 m
1,243 ft

0 kilometres   3

0 miles   2

Street-by-Street: Lincoln ⑦

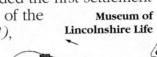

Carving in Angel Choir

Surrounded by the flat landscape of the Fens, Lincoln rises dramatically on a cliff above the River Witham, the three towers of its massive cathedral visible from afar. The Romans (*see pp48–9*) founded the first settlement here in AD 48. By the time of the Norman Conquest (*see p51*), Lincoln was the fourth most important city in England (after London, Winchester and York). The city's wealth was due to its strategic importance for the export of wool from the Lincolnshire Wolds to Europe. Lincoln has managed to retain much of its historic character. Many remarkable medieval buildings have survived, most of which are along the aptly named Steep Hill, leading to the cathedral.

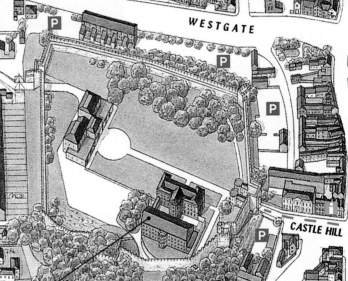

Humber Bridge ↑

2nd-century Newport Arch

Museum of Lincolnshire Life

WESTGATE

BAILGATE

CASTLE HILL

STEEP HILL

DRURY LANE

MICHAELGATE

House of Aaron the Jew

★ **Lincoln Castle**

The early Norman castle, rebuilt at intervals, acted as the city prison from 1787–1878. The chapel's coffin-like pews served to remind felons of their fate.

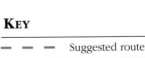

KEY

– – – Suggested route

Jew's House

Lincoln had a large medieval Jewish community. This fine early 12th-century stone house, one of the oldest of its kind in existence, was owned by a Jewish family.

15th-century Stonebow Gate and railway station

0 metres		100

0 yards		100

STAR SIGHTS

★ **Lincoln Castle**

★ **Lincoln Cathedral**

★ **Lincoln Cathedral**
*The west front is a harmonious mix of
Norman and Gothic styles. Inside, the
best features include the Angel Choir,
with the figure of the Lincoln Imp.*

**Alfred, Lord
Tennyson**
*A statue of the
Lincolnshire-born
poet (1809–92)
stands in the
grounds.*

TENNYSON

EASTGATE

POTTERGATE

MINSTER YARD

GREENSTONE PLACE

**The 14th-century
Potter Gate**

Arboretum

**Ruins of
Bishop's Palace**

DANESGATE

LINDUM ROAD

TERRACE

P

**Coach
station**

MISERICORDS

Misericords are ledges
that project from the
underside of the hinged
seat of a choir stall, which
provide support while standing.
Lincoln Cathedral's
misericords in the early
Perpendicular-style canopied
choir stalls are some of the best
in England. The wide variety of
subjects includes parables, fables,
myths, biblical scenes and irrev-
erent images from daily life.

**St Francis
of Assisi**

Usher Art Gallery
*This is packed with
clocks, ceramics,
and silver. There
are paintings
by Peter de
Wint (1784–
1849) and
JMW Turner*
(see p97).

One of a pair of lions

Burghley House ⑧

Portrait of Sir Isaac Newton, Billiard Room

WILLIAM CECIL, 1ST LORD BURGHLEY (1520–98) was Queen Elizabeth I's adviser and confidant for 40 years. He built the wonderfully dramatic Burghley House in 1560–87, probably designing it himself. The roof line bristles with stone pyramids, chimneys disguised as Classical columns and towers shaped like pepper pots. The busy skyline only resolves itself into a symmetrical pattern when viewed from the west, where a lime tree stands, one of many planted by Capability Brown *(see p27)* when the surrounding deer park was landscaped in 1760. Burghley's interior is lavishly decorated with Italian paintings of Greek gods enacting their dramas across the walls and ceiling.

★ **Old Kitchen**
Gleaming copper pans hang from the walls of the fan-vaulted kitchen, little altered since the Tudor period.

North Gate
Intricate examples of 19th-century wrought-iron work adorn the principal entrances.

The Billiard Room
has many fine portraits inset in oak panelling.

Cupolas were very fashionable details, inspired by European Renaissance architecture.

A chimney has been disguised as a Classical column.

Mullioned windows were added in 1683 when glass became less expensive.

The Gatehouse, with its side turrets, is a typical feature of the "prodigy" houses of the Tudor era *(see p336).*

West Front
Featuring the Burghley crest, the West Front was finished in 1577 and formed the original main entrance.

STAR SIGHTS
★ **Old Kitchen**
★ **Heaven Room**
★ **Hell Staircase**

VISITORS' CHECKLIST

Off A1 SE of Stamford, Lincolnshire.
☎ 01780 752451. ⇄ *Stamford.*
○ *1 Apr–3 Oct: 11am–5pm daily.*
● *one day early Sep (for horse
trials).* ⬛ ♿ *limited.* 🍴 ⬛ ⬛

★ Heaven Room

*Gods tumble from the sky,
and satyrs and nymphs play
on the walls and ceiling in
this masterpiece by Antonio
Verrio (1639–1707).*

**Obelisk and
clock (1585)**

The Great Hall has
a double hammer-
beam roof and was
a banqueting hall in
Elizabethan days.

The wine cooler
(1710) is thought
to be the largest
in existence.

**The Fourth George
Room**, one of a
suite, is panelled in
oak stained with ale.

★ Hell Staircase

*Verrio painted the
ceiling to show Hell
as the mouth of a
cat crammed with
tormented sinners.
The staircase, of
local stone, was
installed in 1786.*

Stamford ⑨

Lincolnshire. 🏛 *18,000.* ⇄ 🚌
ℹ *27 St Mary's St (01780 755611).*
⬛ *Fri.*

Stamford is a showpiece
town, famous for its many
churches and its Georgian
townhouses. Stamford retains
a medieval street plan, with a
warren of winding streets and
cobbled alleys.

The spires of the medieval
churches (five survive of the
original 11) give Stamford the
air of a miniature Oxford.

Barn Hill, leading up from
All Saints Church, is the best
place for a view of Stamford's
Georgian architecture in all its
variety. Below it is Broad
Street, where the **Stamford
Museum** covers the history
of the town. By far the most
popular exhibit is a waxwork
of Britain's fattest man, Daniel
Lambert, who was 336 kg (53
stone) and died while attending Stamford Races in 1809.

🏛 **Stamford Museum**
Broad St. ☎ *01780 766317.*
○ *Apr–Sep: daily. (Sun: pm);
Oct–Mar: Mon–Sat.* ● *25, 26 Dec.*
♿ *limited.* ⬛

Northampton ⑩

Northamptonshire. 🏛 *180,000.*
⇄ 🚌 ℹ *St Giles Square (01604
622677).* ⬛ *Tue–Sat (Thu: antiques).*

This market town was once
the centre of the shoe-
making industry, a heritage
reflected in the **Central
Museum and Art Gallery**
which holds the world's
largest collection of footwear.
Many fine old buildings still
stand, one of the gems being
the Victorian Gothic **Guildhall**.
Five miles west of the town is
stately **Althorp House**, the
family home of Diana Princess
of Wales. Visitors can tour the
house, grounds, and see her
island resting place.

🏛 **Central Museum and Art
Gallery**
Guildhall Rd. ☎ *01604 238548.*
○ *daily (Sun: pm).* ● *25, 26 Dec.* ♿
🏛 **Althorp House**
Great Brington (off A428). ☎ *01604
592020.* ○ *Jul–Aug daily.* ⬛ ♿

THE NORTH COUNTRY

INTRODUCING THE NORTH COUNTRY 396-403

LANCASHIRE AND THE LAKES 404-437

YORKSHIRE AND HUMBERSIDE 438-479

NORTHUMBRIA 480-503

The North Country at a Glance

Rugged coastlines, spectacular walks and climbs, magnificent stately homes and breathtaking cathedrals all have their place in the north of England, with its dramatic history of Roman rule, Saxon invasion, Viking attacks and border skirmishes. Reminders of the industrial revolution are found in cities such as Halifax, Liverpool and Manchester, and peace and inspiration in the dramatic scenery of the Lake District, with its awe-inspiring mountains and waters.

Hadrian's Wall (see pp496–7), *built around 120 to protect Roman Britain from the Picts to the north, cuts through rugged Northumberland National Park scenery.*

NORTHUMBRIA *(see pp480–503)*

Northumberland

The Lake District (see pp404–29) *is a combination of superb peaks, tumbling rivers and falls and shimmering lakes such as Wast Water.*

Durham

Cumbria

Yorkshire Dales National Park *(see pp448–50) creates a delightful environment for walking and touring the farming landscape, scattered with attractive villages such as Thwaite, in Swaledale.*

Lancashire

LANCASHIRE AND THE LAKES *(see pp404–437)*

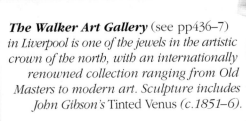

The Walker Art Gallery (see pp436–7) *in Liverpool is one of the jewels in the artistic crown of the north, with an internationally renowned collection ranging from Old Masters to modern art. Sculpture includes John Gibson's* Tinted Venus *(c.1851–6).*

Greater Manchester

Merseyside

◁ **The 11th-century Alnwick Castle, Alnwick, Northumberland, from across the River Aln**

Durham Cathedral (see pp502–3), *a striking Norman structure with an innovative southern choir aisle and fine stained glass, has towered over the city of Durham since 995.*

Fountains Abbey (see pp454–5), *one of the finest religious buildings in the north, was founded in the 12th century by monks who desired simplicity and austerity. Later the abbey became extremely wealthy.*

Castle Howard (see pp462–3), *a triumph of Baroque architecture, offers many magnificent settings, including this Museum Room (1805–10), designed by CH Tatham.*

Tyne and Wear

Cleveland

North Yorkshire

YORKSHIRE AND HUMBERSIDE (see pp438–479)

Humberside

West Yorkshire

South Yorkshire

York (see pp470–75) *is a city of historical treasures, ranging from the medieval to Georgian. Its magnificent minster has a large collection of stained glass and the medieval city walls are well preserved. Other sights include churches, narrow alleyways and notable museums.*

0 kilometres 25

0 miles 25

The Industrial Revolution in the North

THE FACE OF NORTHERN ENGLAND in the 19th century was dramatically altered by the development of the coal mining, textile and shipbuilding industries. Lancashire, Northumberland and the West Riding *(see p441)* of Yorkshire all experienced population growth and migration to cities. The hardships of urban life were partly relieved by the actions of several wealthy industrial philanthropists, but many people lived in extremely deprived conditions. Although most traditional industries have now declined sharply or disappeared as demand has moved elsewhere, a growing tourist industry has developed in many of the former industrial centres.

Back-to-backs *or colliers' rows, such as these houses at Easington, were provided by colliery owners from the 1800s onwards. They comprised two small rooms for cooking and sleeping, and an outside toilet.*

Coal mining *was a family industry in the North of England with women and children working alongside the men.*

1815 Sir Humphrey Davy invented a safety oil lamp for miners. Light shone through a cylindrical gauze sheet which prevented the heat of the flame igniting methane gas in the mine. Thousands of miners benefited from this device.

1750	1800
PRE-STEAM	STEAM AGE
1750	1800

1781 Leeds–Liverpool Canal opened. The building of canals facilitated the movement of raw materials and finished products, and aided the process of mechanization immeasurably.

1830 Liverpool a**Manchester** railw opened, connecting the tv biggest cities outsi London. Within a month t railway carried 1,2 passenge

Halifax's Piece Hall *(see pp478–9), restored in 1976, is the most impressive surviving example of industrial architecture in northern England. It is the only complete 18th-century cloth market building in Yorkshire. Merchants sold measures of cloth known as "pieces" from rooms lining the cloisters inside.*

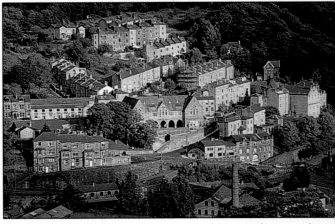

Hebden Bridge *(see p478), a typical West Riding textile mill town jammed into the narrow Calder Valley, typifies a pattern of workers' houses surrounding a central mill. The town benefited from its position when the Rochdale Canal (1804) and then the railway (1841) took advantage of this relatively low-level route over the Pennines.*

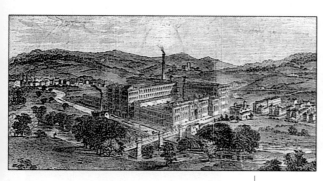

Saltaire (see p477) *was a model village built by the wealthy cloth merchant and mill-owner Sir Titus Salt (1803–76), for the benefit of his workers. Seen here in the 1870s, it included houses and facilities such as shops, gardens and sportsfields, with almshouses, a hospital, school and chapel. A disciplinarian, Salt banned alcohol and pubs from Saltaire.*

George Hudson *(1800–71) built the first railway station in York (see p474) in 1840–42. In the 1840s he owned more than a quarter of the railways in Britain and was known as the "railway king".*

1842 Coal Mines Act prevented women and children from working in harsh conditions in the mines.

Port Sunlight (see p437) *was founded by William Hesketh Lever (1851–1925) to provide housing for workers at his Sunlight soap factory. Between 1889 and 1914 he built 800 cottages. Amenities included a pool.*

Strikes to improve working conditions were common. Violence flared in July 1893 when colliery owners locked miners out of their pits and stopped their pay after the Miners' Federation resisted a 25 per cent wage cut. Over 300,000 men struggled without pay until November, when work resumed at the old rate.

1850		1900
FULL MECHANIZATION		
1850		1900

Power loom weaving *transformed the textile industry while creating unemployment among skilled hand loom weavers. By the 1850s, the West Riding had 30,000 power looms, used in cotton and woollen mills. Of 79,000 workers, over half were to be found in Bradford alone.*

Furness dry dock *was built in the 1890s when the shipbuilding industry moved north, in search of cheap labour and materials. Barrow-in-Furness, Glasgow (see pp644–59) and Tyne and Wear (see p498) were the new centres.*

Joseph Rowntree *(1836–1925) founded his chocolate factory in York in 1892, having formerly worked with George Cadbury. As Quakers, the Rowntrees believed in the social welfare of their workers (establishing a model village in 1904), and, with Terry's confectionary (1767), they made a vast contribution to York's prosperity. Today, Nestlé Rowntree is the world's largest chocolate factory and York is Britain's chocolate capital.*

North Country Abbeys

NORTHERN ENGLAND has some of the finest and best preserved religious houses in Europe. Centres of prayer, learning and power in the Middle Ages, the larger of these were designated abbeys and were governed by an abbot. Most were located in rural areas, considered appropriate for a spiritual and contemplative life. Viking raiders had destroyed many Anglo-Saxon religious houses in the 8th and 9th centuries *(see pp50–51)* and it was not until William the Conqueror founded the Benedictine Selby Abbey in 1069 that monastic life revived in the north. New orders, Augustinians in particular, arrived from the Continent and by 1500 Yorkshire had 83 monasteries.

Ruins of St Mary's Abbey today

Cistercian monk

The Liberty of St Mary was the name given to the land around the abbey, almost a city within a city. Here, the abbot had his own market, fair, prison and gallows – all exempt from the city authorities.

ST MARY'S ABBEY

Founded in York in 1086, this Benedictine abbey was one of the wealthiest in Britain. Its involvement in the wool trade in York and the granting of royal and papal privileges and land led to a relaxing of standards by the early 12th century. The abbot was even allowed to dress in the same style as a bishop, and was raised by the pope to the status of a "mitred abbot". As a result, 13 monks left in 1132, to found Fountains Abbey *(see pp454–5)*.

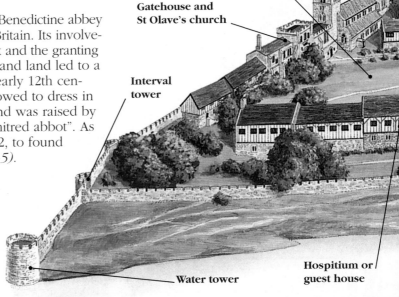

Gatehouse and St Olave's church

Interval tower

Water tower

Hospitium or guest house

MONASTERIES AND LOCAL LIFE

As one of the wealthiest landowning sections of society, the monasteries played a vital role in the local economy. They provided employment, particularly in agriculture, and dominated the wool trade, England's largest export during the Middle Ages. By 1387 two thirds of all wool exported from England passed through St Mary's Abbey, the largest wool trader in York.

Cistercian monks tilling their land

WHERE TO SEE ABBEYS TODAY

Fountains Abbey *(see pp454–5)*, founded by Benedictine monks and later taken over by Cistercians, is the most famous of the numerous abbeys in the region. Rievaulx *(see p457)*, Byland *(see p456)* and Furness *(see p428)* were all founded by the Cistercians, and Furness became the second wealthiest Cistercian house in England after Fountains. Whitby Abbey *(see p460)*, sacked by the Vikings, was later rebuilt by the Benedictine order. Northumberland is famous for its early Anglo-Saxon monasteries, such as Ripon, Lastingham and Lindisfarne *(see pp490–91)*.

Mount Grace Priory *(see p458), founded in 1398, is the best-preserved Carthusian house in England. The former individual gardens and cells of each monk are still clearly visible.*

THE DISSOLUTION OF THE MONASTERIES (1536–40)

By the early 16th century, the monasteries owned one-sixth of all English land and their annual income was four times that of the Crown. Henry VIII ordered the closure of all religious houses in 1536, acquiring their wealth in the process. His attempt at dissolution provoked a large uprising of Catholic northerners led by Robert Aske later that year. The rebellion failed and Aske and others were executed for conspiracy. The dissolution continued under Thomas Cromwell, who became known as "the hammer of the monks".

Thomas Cromwell (c.1485–1549)

The large Abbot's House testified to the grand lifestyle that late medieval abbots adopted.

The Chapter House, an assembly room, was the most important building after the church.

Lavatory

Kitchen

The Warming House was the only room in the monastery, apart from the kitchen, which had a fire.

Refectory

The Abbey Wall had battlements added in 1318 to protect it against raids by Scottish armies.

Common parlour

Cloister

Kirkham Priory, an Augustinian foundation of the 1120s, enjoys a tranquil setting on the banks of the River Derwent, near Malton. The finest feature of the ruined site is the 13th-century gatehouse which leads into the priory complex.

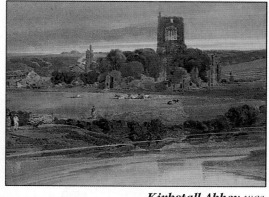

Kirkstall Abbey was founded in 1152 by monks from Fountains Abbey. The well-preserved ruins of this Cistercian house near Leeds include the church, the late Norman chapter house and the abbot's lodging. This evening view was painted by Thomas Girtin (1775–1802).

Easby Abbey lies beside the River Swale, outside the pretty market town of Richmond. Among the remains of this Premonstratensian house, founded in 1155, are the th-century refectory and sleeping arters and 14th-century gatehouse.

The Geology of the Lake District

Piece of Lake District slate

THE LAKE DISTRICT contains some of England's most spectacular scenery. Concentrated in just 900 sq miles (231 sq km) are the highest peaks, deepest valleys and longest lakes in the country. Today's landscape has changed little since the end of the Ice Age 10,000 years ago, the last major event in Britain's geological history. But the glaciated hills which were revealed by the retreating ice were once part of a vast mountain-chain whose remains can also be found in North America. The mountains were first raised by the gradual fusion of two ancient landmasses which, for millions of years, formed a single continent. Eventually the continent broke into two, forming Europe and America, separated by the widening Atlantic Ocean.

Honister Pass, with its distinctive U-shape, is an example of a glaciated valley, once completely filled with ice.

GEOLOGICAL HISTORY

The oldest rock formed as sediment under an ocean called Iapetus. Some 450 million years ago, Earth's internal movements made two continents collide, and the ocean disappear.

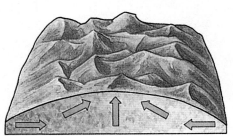

1 *The collision buckled the former sea bed into a mountain range. Magma rose from Earth's mantle, altered the sediments and cooled into volcanic rock.*

2 *In the Ice Age, glaciers slowly excavated huge rock basins in the mountainsides, dragging debris to the valley floor. Frost sculpted the summits.*

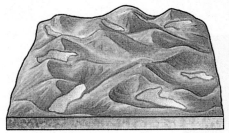

3 *The glaciers retreated 10,000 years ago, their meltwaters forming lakes in valleys dammed by debris. As the climate improved, plants colonized the fells.*

RADIATING LAKES

The diversity of lakeland scenery owes much to its geology: hard volcanic rocks in the central lakes give rise to rugged hills, while soft slates to the north produce a more rounded topography. The lakes form a radial pattern, spreading out from a central volcanic rock zone.

Scafell Pike is the highest peak in England. One of the three Scafell Pikes, its two neighbours are Broad Crag and Ill Crag.

Great Gable

Old Man of Coniston

Coniston Water

Wast Water is the deepest of the lakes. Its southeastern cliffs are streaked with granite scree – the debris formed each year as rock shattered by the winter frost tumbles down during the spring thaw.

MAN ON THE MOUNTAIN

The sheltered valley floors with their benign climate and fertile soils are ideal for settlement. Farmhouses, dry-stone walls, pasture and sheep pens are an integral part of the landscape. Higher up, the absence of trees and bracken are the result of wind and a cooler climate. Old mine workings and tracks are the relics of once-flourishing industries.

Plantations of coniferous trees are a recent feature of the landscape. Some see them as harming traditional views and disturbing the ecology.

Summer grazing

Copper and graphite mines

Tracks

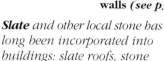

Dry-stone walls (*see p339*)

Slate and other local stone has long been incorporated into buildings: slate roofs, stone walls, lintels and bridges.

400–500 m (130–170 ft)

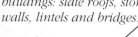

Hedges

300–400 m (100–130 ft)

Sheep pens for winter grazing

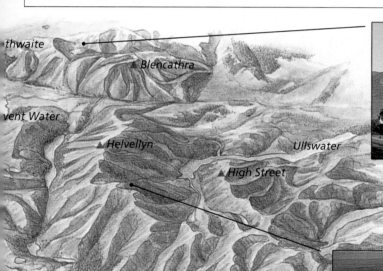

thwaite

Blencathra

vent Water

Helvellyn

Ullswater

High Street

Windermere

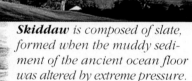

Skiddaw *is composed of slate, formed when the muddy sediment of the ancient ocean floor was altered by extreme pressure.*

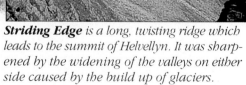

Striding Edge *is a long, twisting ridge which leads to the summit of Helvellyn. It was sharpened by the widening of the valleys on either side caused by the build up of glaciers.*

The Langdale Pikes *are remnants of the volcanic activity which once erupted in the area. They are made of hard igneous rocks, known as Borrowdale Volcanics. Unlike the Skiddaw Slates, they have not eroded smoothly, so they leave a craggy skyline.*

High Crag reflected in Buttermere, Lake District, Cumbria ▷

LANCASHIRE
AND THE
LAKES

MERSEYSIDE
MARITIME
MUSEUM

LANCASHIRE AND THE LAKES

LANDSCAPE PAINTER *John Constable (1776–1837) declared that the Lake District had "the finest scenery that ever was". The Normans built many religious houses here, and William II created estates for English barons. Today, the National Trust is its most important landowner, and it is visited by 18 million people annually.*

Within the 30-mile (45-km) radius of the Lake District lies an astonishing number of fells and lakes, radiating from a core of craggy mountains. Although dramatic and inspiring, this was not an easy place to farm in prehistoric times, and the early settlements were restricted to the broad lower valleys. The Romans built roads and forts (to subdue the local Celtic tribes), but it was left to later colonists, especially the Norse, to create more substantial clearings in the wilderness. The local dialect and many place names originated from these Scandinavian fishermen and farmers. Later, the Lakeland valleys were owned by the monks of Fountains and Furness, who were based at Furness Abbey (north of Barrow-in-Furness), which is now home to an exhibition that explores various aspects of monastic life. These monks introduced iron smelting and dairy farming to the area and established sheep walks across the fells.

Today hardy Herdwick sheep are scattered about the fells, surviving on even the leanest of pastures. According to tradition, this unique breed arrived in the region as a result of a shipwreck at the time of the invasion of the Spanish Armada in the 16th century.

Dotted throughout the Lake District are a diversity of historic sites, including stone circles, such as Castlerigg; Roman ruins, such as Hardknott Fort;

Jetty at Grasmere, one of the most popular regions of the Lake District

◁ **Restored Albert Dock, lining the River Mersey in Liverpool**

uplands features spectacular scenery and a variety of local wildlife, such as red deer, peregrine falcons and red squirrels. Two popular long-distance tracks that pass through the Lake District are the Cumbrian Way and the Coast-to-Coast Walk.

Many people who visit the Lake District are content to explore the quaint, compact settlements, such as Windermere and Buttermere, found along the lakes' shores. These towns offer an assortment of activities, including water sports, steamboat trips, and exhibitions of regional sports such as fell running and Cumberland wrestling. There is also the chance to follow in the footsteps of famous writers and artists. For many years the Romantic poet William Wordsworth lived in Dove Cottage, near Grasmere, which is now a museum. Devotees of children's writer Beatrix Potter can find exhibitions about her life and works in Keswick and Windermere. Paintings by the 19th-century critic John Ruskin can be viewed at his former house, Brantwood, near Hawkshead.

Royal Liver Building on the Pier Head, seen from Albert Dock, in the northern city of Liverpool

and stately homes, such as Dalemain, near Penrith. However, the most widespread monuments in the Lakelands are those associated with long-forgotten industries, and include green-slate quarries and silver mines. Even the beautiful local oak trees were once used as fuel: it is possible to find charcoal-burning platforms among the fell slopes.

Despite the huge volume of visitors to the Lake District, the area is still a picturesque amalgamation of indigo waters, open fields, thick woodlands, shimmering waterfalls and imposing hills and mountains. The network of walking paths that cover the

Blackpool Tower by night, Lancashire

Moving south, to the region around the border between Lancashire and Cumbria, verdant pastures begin to dominate. On the coast is Morecambe Bay, a tidal area home to thousands of wading birds. The Kent estuary, which feeds into the bay, is flanked by Grange and Arnside: two old-fashioned settlements at the foot of attractive wooded hills.

Rural homes nestled in the Troutbeck Valley, near Windermere, Cumbria

The heart of Wordsworth's Lake District: Lake Grasmere and surrounding hills, Cumbria

The county of Lancashire boasts a portfolio of tourist attractions that includes the county town of Lancaster, which has a Norman castle; lively Blackpool, with its bustling fairground and famous illuminated decorations; and the peaceful beaches to the south. On the stretch of coast between Southport and Great Crosby, it is possible to walk along a series of dune landscapes, where pools of brackish water are, in season, surrounded by a colourful display of flowering orchids. Inland, the most appealing regions are the Forest of Bowland, an expanse of heathery grouse moor, and the picturesque Ribble Valley, which is home to the ruins of a Roman fort and the remains of a Cistercian abbey.

Scafell Pike Trail, Cumbria

Further south are the industrial conurbations of Manchester and Merseyside. Manchester, which features many fine Victorian buildings, is a vibrant city with an air of confidence based partly on cup-winning football and best-selling rock music. Among its many attractions are the Museum of Science and Industry and the City Art Galleries. Liverpool, with its restored Albert Dock, is best known as the seaport city of the Beatles. The astonishing musical achievements of this ever-popular group can be explored at the Beatles Story exhibition. Liverpool's Walker Art Gallery has a renowned collection of fine paintings. The hinterland north of these cities is the heartland of rugby league, a sport that is more popular in the north of England than in the south of the country. Throughout this area there are several interesting mill towns, such as Bolton, which in the 19th century was an important centre for the coal mining and textiles industries.

Topiary garden at Levens Hall, Cumbria

Exploring Lancashire and the Lakes

THE LAKE DISTRICT'S natural scenery outweighs any of its man-made attractions. Its natural features are the result of geological upheavals over millennia *(see pp402–3)*, and four of its peaks are higher than 1,000 m (3,300 ft). Human influences have left their mark too: the main activities are quarrying, mining, farming and tourism.

The Lakes are most crowded in summer when activities include lake trips and hill-walking. The best bases are Keswick and Ambleside, while there are also good hotels on the shores of Windermere and Ullswater and in the Cartmel area.

Lancashire's Forest of Bowland is an attractive place to explore on foot, with picturesque villages. Further south, Manchester and Liverpool have excellent museums and galleries.

Canoeing, a popular sporting pastime, at Derwent Water in the Northern Fells and Lakes area

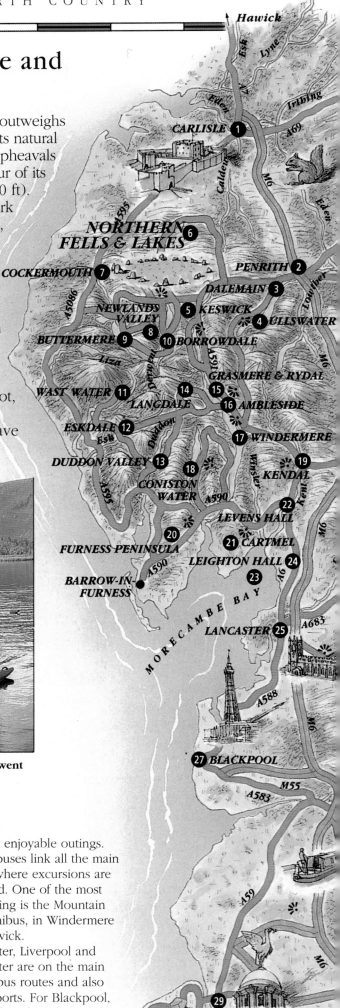

GETTING AROUND

For many, the first glimpse of the Lake District is from the M6 near Shap Fell, but the A6 is a more dramatic route. You can reach Windermere by train, but you need to change at Oxenholme, on the main InterCity route from Euston to Carlisle. Penrith also has rail services and bus links into the Lakes. L'al Ratty, the miniature railway up Eskdale, and the Lakeside & Haverthwaite railway, which connects with the steamers on Windermere,

make for enjoyable outings. Regular buses link all the main centres where excursions are organized. One of the most enterprising is the Mountain Goat minibus, in Windermere and Keswick.

Lancaster, Liverpool and Manchester are on the main rail and bus routes and also have airports. For Blackpool, you need to change trains in Preston. Wherever you go in the area, one of the best means of getting around is on foot.

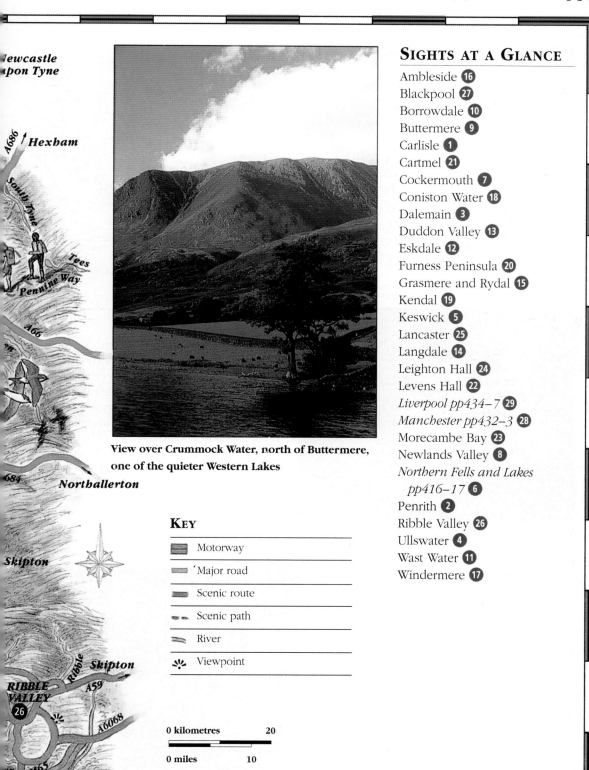

View over Crummock Water, north of Buttermere, one of the quieter Western Lakes

SIGHTS AT A GLANCE

Ambleside **16**
Blackpool **27**
Borrowdale **10**
Buttermere **9**
Carlisle **1**
Cartmel **21**
Cockermouth **7**
Coniston Water **18**
Dalemain **3**
Duddon Valley **13**
Eskdale **12**
Furness Peninsula **20**
Grasmere and Rydal **15**
Kendal **19**
Keswick **5**
Lancaster **25**
Langdale **14**
Leighton Hall **24**
Levens Hall **22**
Liverpool pp434–7 **29**
Manchester pp432–3 **28**
Morecambe Bay **23**
Newlands Valley **8**
Northern Fells and Lakes
  pp416–17 **6**
Penrith **2**
Ribble Valley **26**
Ullswater **4**
Wast Water **11**
Windermere **17**

KEY

▦	Motorway
▭	´Major road
▭	Scenic route
••	Scenic path
➤	River
☀	Viewpoint

0 kilometres   20

0 miles   10

Preserved docks and Liver Building, Liverpool

Writers and Artists of the Lakes

THE BEAUTY OF THE LAKE DISTRICT has been memorialized by countless writers and artists throughout the centuries. Possibly the most famous is William Wordsworth, who brought the Lake District to the public's attention through his work, along with contemporary poets such as Samuel Taylor Coleridge. There has always been a richness and diversity to the artistic talent in the area, and the artistic spark that the Lakes seems to set off has remained as strong in the 20th century. Even today, many writers and artists are drawn to the area for inspiration.

Beatrix Potter's Peter Rabbit

Dove Cottage, Grasmere

WILLIAM WORDSWORTH (1770–1850)

WORDSWORTH IS PROBABLY the writer who people most associate with the Lake District. This is not surprising, since the majority of his poems were inspired by the area and he made it his home throughout his life. His birthplace (Wordsworth House), Dove Cottage and Rydal Mount are all open to the public *(see p424),* and the latter two homes still contain some of the poet's personal belongings. The Fitz Park Museum and Art Gallery at Keswick preserves many of Wordsworth's original manuscripts as well as a small selection of his letters.

BEATRIX POTTER (1866–1943)

BEATRIX POTTER VISITED THE LAKES as a child and immediately fell in love with the area. Years later, with the royalties she made from her world-famous Peter Rabbit stories, she bought Hill Top, her home at Near Sawbry, Windermere. She had a great interest in conserving the natural beauty of the Lakes and donated land to the National Trust. Children will love the World of Beatrix Potter, Crag Brow – the gardens have a Squirrel Nutkin Trail that takes children through parkland and along the edge of Windermere *(see p423).*

Beatrix Potter outside her home, Hill Top

Brantwood House, Coniston

JOHN RUSKIN (1819–1900)

RUSKIN WAS AN INFLUENTIAL art critic, writer and draughtsman of his time. Although he was not born in the area, he was drawn to the Lakes and eventually made his home at Brantwood *(see p356).* This is a beautiful house in Coniston containing many of his personal articles. It is well worth a visit because it also houses paintings and drawings by both Ruskin and Turner *(see p97).* Ruskin is buried in St Andrew's Church, Coniston. At the back of the Coniston Mechanics Institute is the Ruskin Museum, which now sees as many visitors as Ruskin's home.

GEORGE ROMNEY AND THE LAKES

Born and buried in Dalton, Romney became one of the most famous portrait painters of his day. His work can be seen in the National Galley in London, but it is also displayed in many places around the Lake District. The Carlisle Museum and Art Gallery, Hutton-in-the-Forest at Penrith *(see p414)*, Belle Isle House on Belle Isle, and Sizergh Castle in Kendal *(see p428)* all house Romney's portraits. One of the best places to see his work, as well as examples of local artistic talent, is the Abbott Hall Art Gallery in Kendal *(see p428)*. It houses many paintings by George Romney, John Ruskin and also includes work by local modern artists.

The Four Friends (1796), by George Romney, Abbot Hall Gallery

Clear Evening, Wastwater by William Heaton Cooper

HEATON COOPER FAMILY

THE HEATON COOPERS ARE a family of artists that go back three generations. The Heaton Cooper Studio in Grasmere, founded by William Heaton Cooper (1903–1995), holds a permanent exhibition of work by William and his father Alfred Heaton Cooper (1863–1929); both leading watercolourists. The family tradition continues with William's son Julian, who paints, his daughter, Otalia, who makes pottery and his granddaughter Rebecca, who makes mixed media images. Examples of all their work are on display at the studio.

MELVYN BRAGG (1939–)

BORN IN WIGTON, Melvyn Bragg, novelist and broadcaster, now lives in London but sets most of his books within the Lakes area. His first novel, *The Maid of Buttermere*, is based on the story that began at the Old Fish Inn (now called the Fish Hotel) in Buttermere *(see p349)*. His other novels set in the area include *For Want of a Nail* (set in Cumberland), *Love and Glory* (based in New York and a Cumbrian market town) and *Josh Lawton* (based in Cumbria). His book, *The Land of the Lakes* is an entertaining description of the Lake District.

The Fish Hotel, Buttermere Village

Hunter Davies in the Lake District

HUNTER DAVIES (1936–)

BORN IN RENFREW, Hunter Davies, grew up in Carlisle. He now splits his time between London and the Lakes and is married to another Lakeland novelist, Margaret Forster. As well as working as a journalist, Davies has written over 30 books, including novels and children's books. His first novel *Here we Go Round the Mullberry Bush* (1965) was set in Carlisle and others that are more specific to the Lakes include *The Good Guide to the Lakes* and *A Walk Around the Lakes*. He has also written biographies of Beatrix Potter and William Wordsworth.

Carlisle ●

Cumbria. 🚶 *105,000.* ✈ ⇄ 🚌
ℹ *The Old Town Hall, Green Market
(01228 625600).*

DUE TO ITS proximity to the Scottish border, this city has long been a defensive site. Known as Luguvalium by the Romans, it was an outpost of Hadrian's Wall *(see pp496–7).* Carlisle was sacked and pillaged repeatedly by the Danes, the Normans and border raiders, and suffered damage as a Royalist stronghold under Cromwell *(see p56).*

Today, Carlisle is the capital of Cumbria. In its centre are the timber-framed Guildhall and market cross, and fortifications still exist around its West Walls, drum-towered gates and its Norman **castle**. The castle tower has a small museum devoted to the King's Own Border Regiment. The cathedral, originally an Augustinian priory, dates from 1133. One of its best features is a decorative east window. Carlisle's **Tullie House Museum** imaginatively recreates the city's past with sections on Roman history, border disputes

Saxon iron sword in the Tullie House Museum

Façade of Hutton-in-the-Forest with medieval tower on the right

and Cumbrian wildlife. Nearby lie the evocative sandstone ruins of **Lanercost Priory** (c.1166) surrounded by placid cattle meadows.

⚑ **Carlisle Castle**
Castle Way. 📞 *01228 591922.* ◯ *daily.* ● *25 Dec.* 🎫 ♿ *limited.* 📷
🏛 **Tullie House Museum**
Castle St. 📞 *01228 534781.* ◯ *daily (Sun: pm).* ● *25, 26 Dec.* 🎫 ♿
🏚 **Lanercost Priory**
Nr Brampton. 📞 *016977 3030.*
◯ *Apr–Oct: daily.* 🎫 ♿ *limited.* 📷

Penrith ●

Cumbria. 🚶 *13,000.* ℹ *Robinson's School, Middlegate (01768 867466).*
🚌 *Tue, Sat.*

TIMEWARP SHOPFRONTS on the market square and a 14th-century **castle** of sandstone are Penrith's main attractions. There are some strange hog-back stones in St Andrew's churchyard, allegedly a giant's

grave, and the 285 m (937 ft) Beacon provides stunning views of distant fells.

ENVIRONS: Just north of Penrith at Little Salkeld is one of the area's most notable ancient monuments, a Bronze Age circle (with about 70 tall stones) known as **Long Meg and her Daughters** *(see pp46–7).* Six miles (9 km) northwest of Penrith lies **Hutton-in-the-Forest**. The oldest part of this house is the 13th-century tower, built to withstand Scots raiders. Inside is a magnificent Italianate staircase, a sumptuously panelled 17th-century Long Gallery, a delicately stuccoed Cupid Room dating from the 1740s, and several Victorian rooms. Outside, you can walk around the walled garden and topiary terraces, or explore the woods.

⚑ **Penrith Castle**
Ullswater Rd. ◯ *daily.* ♿ *in grounds.*
🏰 **Hutton-in-the-Forest**
Off B5305. 📞 *017684 84449.*
House ◯ *May–Sep: Thu, Fri, Sun & public hols (pm); Aug: Wed, Sun & public hols (pm).* **Grounds** ◯ *Sun–Fri.* ● *25 Dec.* 🎫 ♿ *limited.*

Dalemain ●

Penrith, Cumbria. 📞 *017684 86450.*
⇄ 🚌 *Penrith then taxi.* ◯ *Apr–Sep: Sun–Thu.* 🎫 ♿ *limited.* 📷 🖵

ASEEMLY GEORGIAN façade gives this fine house near Ullswater the impression of architectural unity, but hides a greatly altered medieval and Elizabethan structure with a maze of rambling passages. Public rooms include a superb Chinese drawing room with hand-painted wallpaper, and

---

TRADITIONAL CUMBRIAN SPORTS

Cumberland wrestling is one of the most interesting sports to watch in the summer months. The combatants, clad in long-johns and embroidered velvet pants, clasp one another in an armlock and attempt to topple each other over. Technique and good balance outweigh physical force. Other traditional Lakeland sports include fell-racing, a gruelling test of speed and stamina up and down local peaks at ankle-breaking speed. Hound-trailing is also a popular sport in which specially bred hounds follow an aniseed trail over the hills. Sheep-dog trials, steam fairs, flower shows and gym-khanas take place in summer. The Egremont Crab Fair in September holds light-hearted events such as greasy-pole climbing.

Cumberland wrestlers

Sheep resting at Glenridding, on the southwest shore of Ullswater

a panelled 17th-century drawing room. Several small museums occupy various outbuildings, and the gardens contain a fine collection of fragrant shrub roses and a huge silver fir.

Sumptuous Chinese drawing room at Dalemain

Ullswater ④

Cumbria. ≋ *Penrith.* ℹ *Main car park, Glenridding, Penrith (017684 82414).*

OFTEN CONSIDERED the most beautiful of all Cumbria's lakes, Ullswater stretches from gentle farmland near Penrith to dramatic hills and crags at its southern end. The main western shore road can be very busy. In summer, two restored Victorian steamers ply regularly from Pooley Bridge to Glenridding. One of the best walks crosses the eastern shore from Glenridding to Hallin Fell and the moorland of Martindale. The western side passes Gowbarrow, where Wordsworth's immortalized "host of golden daffodils" bloom in spring *(see p424).*

Keswick ⑤

Cumbria. 🏘 *5,000.* ℹ *Moot Hall, Market Sq (017687 72645).*

POPULAR AS A tourist venue since the advent of the railway in Victorian times, Keswick now has guest houses, a summer repertory theatre, outdoor equipment shops and a serious parking problem in high season. Its most striking central building is the **Moot Hall**, dating from 1813, now used as the tourist office. The town prospered on wool and leather until, in Tudor times, deposits of graphite were discovered. Mining then took over as the main industry and Keswick became an important centre for pencil manufacture. In World War II, hollow pencils were made to hide espionage maps on thin paper. The old factory is now the **Pencil Museum** with interesting audiovisual shows. Among the many fine exhibits at the **Keswick Museum and Art Gallery** are the original manuscripts of Lakeland writers such as Robert Southey (1774–1843) and William Wordsworth *(see p424).*

To the east of the town lies the ancient stone circle of Castlerigg, thought to be older than Stonehenge.

🏛 **Pencil Museum**
Carding Mill Lane. ℹ *017687 73626.* ◯ *daily.* ● *25, 26 Dec, 1 Jan.*
📷 ♿ 🛍

🏛 **Keswick Museum and Art Gallery**
Fitz Park, Station Rd. ℹ *017687 73263.* ◯ *Easter–Oct: daily.* 📷 ♿

Outdoor equipment shop in Keswick

Northern Fells and Lakes ❻

The rare red squirrel, native to the area

Many visitors praise this northern area of the Lake District National Park for its scenery and geological interest (*see pp402–3*). It is ideal walking country, and nearby Derwent Water, Thirlmere and Bassenthwaite provide endless scenic views, rambles and opportunities for watersports. Large areas surrounding the regional centre of Keswick (*see p415*) are accessible only on foot, particularly the huge mass of hills known as Back of Skiddaw – located between Skiddaw and Caldbeck – or the Helvellyn range, east of Thirlmere.

The Whinlatter Pass is an easy route from Keswick to the forested Lorton Vale. It gives a good view of Bassenthwaite Lake and a glimpse of Grisedale Pike.

Bassenthwaite is best viewed from the east shore. The road passes through Dodd Wood at the foot of Skiddaw.

Lorton Vale

The lush, green farmland south of Cockermouth creates a marked contrast with the more rugged mountain landscapes of the central Lake District. In the village of Low Lorton is the private manor house of Lorton Hall, dating from the 15th century.

Derwent Water

Surrounded by woodland slopes and fells, this attractive oval lake is dotted with tiny islands. One of these was inhabited by St Herbert, a disciple of St Cuthbert (see p491), who lived there as a hermit until 687. A boat from Keswick provides a lake excursion.

CARLISLE

B5291

WORKINGTON

A66

BASSENTHWAITE LAKE

A591

High Lorton

LORTON VALE

WHINLATTER PASS

B5292

Derwent

Braithwaite

B5289

LOWESWATER

Newland Beck

DERWENT WATER

Grange

BUTTERMERE

THE MAJOR PEAKS

The Lake District hills are the highest in England. Although they seem small by Alpine or world standards, the scale of the surrounding terrain makes them look extremely grand. Some of the most important peaks are shown on the following pages. Each peak is regarded as having its own personality. This section shows the Skiddaw fells, which are north of Keswick.

① ②
③ ④ ⑤ ⑥

▲ Blencathra
▲ Skiddaw
▲ Grisedale Pike
▲ Grasmoor
▲ Knott Rigg
▲ Helvellyn
▲ Great Gable
▲ High Street
West Water ▲
Screes
▲ Scafell
▲ Hard Knott
▲ The Old Man of Coniston

KEY

━━ From ① Blencathra to ② Cockermouth (*see opposite*)

━━ From ③ Grisedale Pike to ④ the Old Man of Coniston (*see pp420–21*)

━━ From ⑤ the Old Man of Coniston to ⑥ Windermere and Tarn Crag (*see pp422–3*)

━━ National Park boundary

Skiddaw

At 931 m (3,054 ft) Skiddaw is Britain's fourth highest peak. Its rounded shape makes it a manageable two-hour walk for anyone reasonably fit.

Blencathra, also known as Saddleback because of its twin peaks (868 m; 2,847 ft), is a challenging climb, especially in winter.

St John's in the Vale

This valley contains Castle Rock for climbers, and its old legends were used by Sir Walter Scott (see p622) in The Bridal of Triermain. *Lakeland poet John Richardson is buried in the churchyard.*

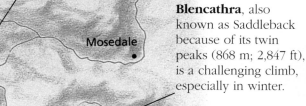

KEY

ℹ️ Information

▬▬ Major road

▬▬ Minor road

❋ Viewpoint

Thirlmere was created as a reservoir to serve Manchester in 1879.

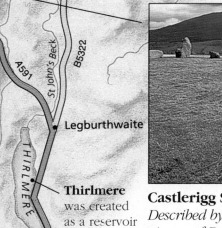

Castlerigg Stone Circle

Described by Keats (see p133) as "a dismal cirque of Druid stones upon a forlorn moor", these ancient stones overlook Skiddaw, Helvellyn and Crag Hill.

0 kilometres 5

0 miles 3

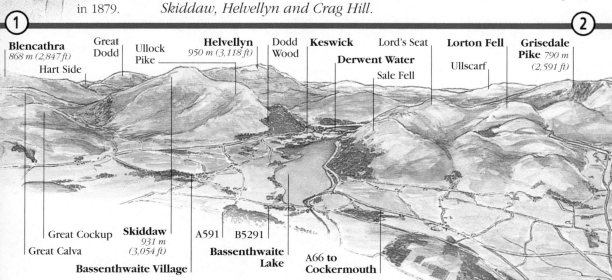

Crummock Water, one of the quieter "western lakes"

Cockermouth ⑦

Cumbria. 🏛 7,000. 🚆 Workington.
🚌 ℹ Town Hall, Market St (01900
822634). 🛒 Mon.

COLOURWASHED TERRACES and restored workers' cottages beside the river are especially attractive in the busy market town of Cockermouth, which dates from the 12th century. The place not to miss is the handsome **Wordsworth House**, in the High Street, where the poet was born *(see p424)*. This fine Georgian building still contains a few of the family's possessions, and is furnished in the style of the late 18th century. Wordsworth mentions the attractive terraced garden, which overlooks the River Derwent, in his *Prelude*. The local parish church contains a Wordsworth memorial window.

Cockermouth **castle** is partly ruined but still inhabited and not open to the public. The town also has small museums of printing, toys and a mineral collection, and an art gallery. The **Jennings Brewery**, founded in 1828, invites visitors for tours and tastings.

🏛 **Wordsworth House**
(NT) Main St. 📞 01900 824805.
◯ Apr–May, Sep, Oct: Mon–Fri, public hols; Jun–Aug: Mon–Sat.
🎨 ♿ gardens. 🖥 🎁
🍺 **Jennings Brewery**
Castle Brewery. 📞 01900 821011.
◯ Apr–Oct: daily. 🎫 🎁

Newlands Valley ⑧

Cumbria. 🚆 Workington then bus. 🚌
Cockermouth. ℹ Town Hall, Market St, Cockermouth (01900 822634).

FROM THE gently wooded shores of Derwent Water, the Newlands Valley runs through a scattering of farms towards rugged heights of 335 m (1,100 ft) at the top of the pass, where steps lead to the waterfall, Moss Force. Grisedale Pike, Grasmoor and Knott Rigg all provide excellent fell walks, passing through bracken-covered land grazed by hardy sheep. Local mineral deposits of copper, graphite, lead and even small amounts of gold and silver were extensively mined here from Elizabethan times onwards. **Little Town** was used as a setting by Beatrix Potter *(see p425)* in *The Tale of Mrs Tiggywinkle*.

Kitchen, with an old range and tiled floor, at Wordsworth House

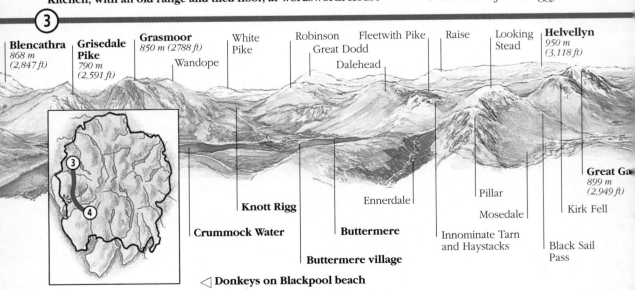

③

| Blencathra 868 m (2,847 ft) | Grisedale Pike 790 m (2,591 ft) | Grasmoor 850 m (2788 ft) Wandope | White Pike | Robinson Great Dodd Dalehead | Fleetwith Pike | Raise | Looking Stead | Helvellyn 950 m (3,118 ft) |

Great Ga 899 m (2,949 ft)

Knott Rigg

Crummock Water

Ennerdale

Buttermere

Buttermere village

Pillar

Mosedale

Innominate Tarn and Haystacks

Kirk Fell

Black Sail Pass

◁ **Donkeys on Blackpool beach**

Buttermere ⑨

Cumbria. 🚆 *Workington then bus.* 🚌 *Cockermouth.* ℹ *Town Hall, Market St, Cockermouth (01900 822634).*

INTERLINKING WITH Crummock Water and Loweswater, Buttermere and its surroundings contain some of the most appealing countryside in the region. Often known as the "western lakes", the three are remote enough not to become too crowded. Buttermere is a jewel amid grand fells: High Stile, Red Pike and Haystacks. Here the ashes of the celebrated hill-walker and author of fell-walking books, AW Wainwright, are scattered.

The village of Buttermere, with its handful of houses and a couple of inns, is a popular starting point for walks round all three lakes. Loweswater is hardest to reach and therefore the quietest, surrounded by woods and gentle hills. Nearby Scale Force is the highest waterfall in the Lake District, plunging 36 m (120 ft).

Verdant valley of Borrowdale, a favourite with artists

Borrowdale ⑩

Cumbria. 🚆 *Workington.* 🚌 *Cockermouth.* ℹ *Town Hall, Market St, Cockermouth (01900 822634).*

THIS ROMANTIC VALLEY, subject of a myriad sketches and watercolours before photography stole the scene, lies beside the densely wooded shores of Derwent Water under towering crags. It is a popular trip from Keswick and a great variety of walks are possible along the valley.

The tiny hamlet of **Grange** is one of the prettiest spots, where the valley narrows dramatically to form the "Jaws of Borrowdale". Nearby Castle Crag has superb views.

From Grange you can complete the circuit of Derwent Water along the western shore, or move southwards to the more open farmland around Seatoller. As you head south by road, look out for a National Trust sign *(see p29)* to the **Bowder Stone**, a delicately poised block weighing nearly 2,000 tonnes, which may have fallen from the crags above or been deposited by a glacier millions of years ago.

Two attractive hamlets in Borrowdale are **Rosthwaite** and **Stonethwaite**. Also worth a detour, preferably on foot, is Watendlath village, off a side road near the famous beauty spot of **Ashness Bridge**.

WALKING IN THE LAKE DISTRICT

Typical Lake District stile over dry-stone wall

Two long-distance footpaths pass through the Lake District's most spectacular scenery. The 70 mile (110 km) Cumbrian Way runs from Carlisle to Ulverston via Keswick and Coniston. The western section of the Coast-to-Coast Walk *(see p37)* passes through this area. There are hundreds of shorter walks along lake shores, nature trails or following more challenging uphill routes. Walkers should stick to paths to avoid erosion, and check weather conditions at National Park information centres.

---

④

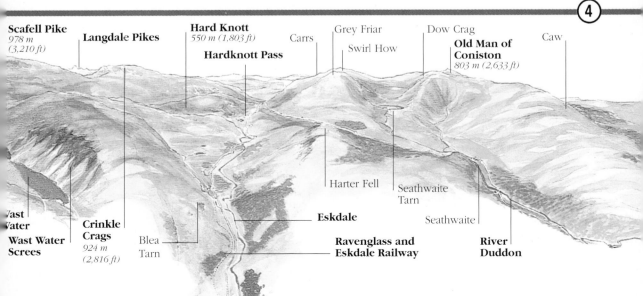

Scafell Pike
978 m
(3,210 ft)

Langdale Pikes

Hard Knott
550 m (1,803 ft)

Hardknott Pass

Carrs

Grey Friar

Swirl How

Dow Crag

Old Man of Coniston
803 m (2,633 ft)

Caw

Harter Fell

Seathwaite Tarn

Eskdale

Seathwaite

Wast Water

Wast Water Screes

Crinkle Crags
924 m
(2,816 ft)

Blea Tarn

Ravenglass and Eskdale Railway

River Duddon

Convivial Wasdale Head Inn at Wasdale Head

Wast Water ⑪

Cumbria. ⮐ *Whitehaven.* ℹ *12 Main St, Egremont (01946 820693).*

A SILENT REFLECTION of truly awesome surroundings, black, brooding **Wast Water** is a mysterious, evocative lake. The road from Nether Wasdale continues along its northwest side. Along its eastern flank loom walls of sheer scree over 600 m (2,000 ft) high. Beneath them the water looks inky black, whatever the weather, plunging an icy 80 m (260 ft) from the waterline to the bottom to form England's deepest lake. You can walk along the screes, but it is an uncomfortable and dangerous scramble. Boating on the lake is banned for conservation reasons, but fishing permits are available from the nearby National Trust camp site.

At **Wasdale Head** lies one of Britain's grandest views: the austere pyramid of **Great Gable**, centrepiece of a fine mountain composition, with the huge forms of Scafell and **Scafell Pike**. The scenery is utterly unspoilt, and the only buildings lie at the far end of the lake: an inn and a tiny church commemorating fallen climbers. Here the road ends, and you must turn back or take to your feet, following signs for Black Sail Pass and Ennerdale, or walk up the grand fells ahead. Wasdale's irresistible backdrop was the inspiration of the first serious British mountaineers, who flocked here during the 19th century, insouciantly clad in tweed jackets, carrying little more than a length of rope slung over their shoulders.

Eskdale ⑫

Cumbria. ⮐ *Ravenglass then narrow-gauge railway to Eskdale (Easter–Oct: daily; Dec–Feb: Sat, Sun).* ℹ *12 Main St, Egremont (01946 820693).*

THE PASTORAL DELIGHTS of Eskdale are best encountered over the gruelling **Hardknott Pass**, which is the most taxing drive in the Lake District, with steep gradients. You can pause at the summit (393 m; 1,291 ft) to explore the Roman **Hardknott Fort** or enjoy the lovely view. As you descend into Eskdale, rhododendrons and pines flourish in a landscape of small hamlets, narrow lanes and gentle farmland. The main settlements below are the attractive village of Boot and coastal Ravenglass, both with old **corn mills**.

Just south of Ravenglass is the impressive **Muncaster Castle**, the richly furnished home of the Pennington family. Another way to enjoy the spectacular scenery is to take a trip on the miniature railway (La'l Ratty) that runs from Ravenglass to Dalegarth.

🏚 **Eskdale Mill**
Boot. 📞 *019467 23335.* ☐ *Apr–Sep: Tue–Sun, public hols.* 🖼 🏞 🎁
🏚 **Muncaster Mill**
Ravenglass. 📞 *01229 717232.* ☐ *Apr–Oct: daily; Nov–Mar: Sat, Sun.* 🖼
⛺ **Muncaster Castle**
Ravenglass. 📞 *01229 717614.*
Castle ☐ *mid-Mar–mid-Nov: Sun–Fri (pm) & public hols.* **Garden** ☐ *daily.* 🖼 ♿ *ground floor only.* 🖥 🎁

Remains of the Roman Hardknott Fort, Eskdale

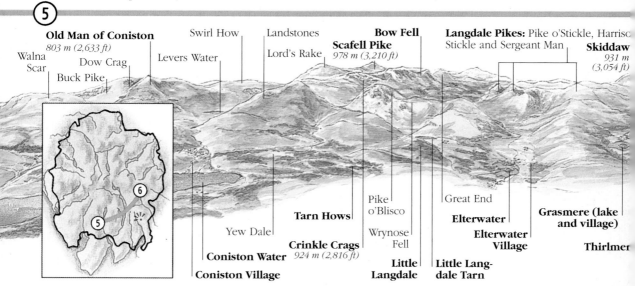

⑤

Old Man of Coniston 803 m (2,633 ft)

Walna Scar

Buck Pike

Dow Crag

Swirl How

Levers Water

Landstones

Lord's Rake

Scafell Pike 978 m (3,210 ft)

Bow Fell

Langdale Pikes: Pike o'Stickle, Harriso Stickle and Sergeant Man

Skiddaw 931 m (3,054 ft)

Great End

Yew Dale

Tarn Hows

Pike o'Blisco

Wrynose Fell

Elterwater

Elterwater Village

Grasmere (lake and village)

Thirlmer

Coniston Water 924 m (2,816 ft)

Coniston Village

Crinkle Crags

Little Langdale

Little Langdale Tarn

⑥

⑤

Autumnal view of Seathwaite, in the Duddon Valley, a popular centre for walkers and climbers

Duddon Valley ⓭

Cumbria. ⤢ *Ulverston.* ℹ *Ruskin Ave, Coniston (015394 41533).*

ALSO KNOWN as Dunnerdale, this picturesque tract of countryside inspired 35 of Wordsworth's sonnets *(see p424).* The prettiest stretch lies between Ulpha and Cockley Beck. In autumn the colours of heather moors and a light sprinkling of birch trees are particularly beautiful. Stepping stones and bridges span the river at intervals, the most charming being Birk's Bridge, near Seathwaite. At the southern end of the valley, where the River Duddon meets the sea at Duddon Sands, is

Broughton-in-Furness, a pretty village of 18th-century houses, with an 11th-century church. Note the old stocks, and the stone slabs used for fish on market day in the main square.

Langdale ⓮

Cumbria. ⤢ *Windermere.* ℹ *Central Buildings, Market Cross, Ambleside (015394 32582).*

STRETCHING FROM Skelwith Bridge, where the Brathay surges powerfully over waterfalls, to the summits of Great Langdale is the two-pronged Langdale Valley. Walkers and climbers throng here to take on **Pavey Ark, Pike o'Stickle,**

Crinkle Crags and **Bow Fell**. The local mountain rescue teams are the busiest in Britain.

Great Langdale is the more spectacular valley and it is often crowded, but quieter **Little Langdale** has many attractions too. It is worth completing the circuit back to Ambleside via the southern route, stopping at Blea Tarn. Reedy **Elterwater** is a picturesque spot, once a site of the gunpowder industry. Wrynose Pass, west of Little Langdale, climbs to 390 m (1,281 ft), a warm-up for Hardknott Pass further on. At its top is Three Shires Stone, marking the former boundary of the old counties of Cumberland, Westmorland and Lancashire.

Rydal Water, one of the major attractions of the Lake District

Ambleside 16

Cumbria. 🚶 3,400. 🚉 ℹ️ *Central Buildings, Market Cross (015394 32582).* ▣ *Wed.*

AMBLESIDE has good road connections to all parts of the Lakes and is an attractive base, especially for walkers and climbers. Mainly Victorian in character, it has dignified architecture and a good range of outdoor clothing, crafts and specialist food shops. An enterprising little cinema and a classical music festival, held in the summer months, give it additional life in the evenings. Sights in town are small-scale: the remnants of the Roman fort of Galava, AD 79, the Stock Ghyll Force waterfall and the **Bridge House** over Stock Beck, now a National Trust information centre.

ENVIRONS: Within easy reach are the wooded Rothay valley, the **Kirkstone Galleries** at Skelwith Bridge, with their unusual souvenirs, and the bleak Kirkstone Pass. At nearby Troutbeck you can visit

The tiny Bridge House over Stock Beck in Ambleside

Grasmere and Rydal 15

Cumbria. **Grasmere** 🚶 700. **Rydal** 🚶 100. 🚉 *Grasmere.* ℹ️ *Redbank Rd, Grasmere (015394 35245).*

THE POET William Wordsworth lived in both these pretty villages on the shores of two sparkling lakes. Fairfield, Hart Crag and Loughrigg Fell rise steeply above their reedy shores and offer good opportunities for walking. Grasmere is now a sizable settlement and the famous Grasmere sports *(see p414)* attract large crowds every August.

The Wordsworth family is buried in St Oswald's Church, and crowds flock to the annual ceremony of strewing the church's earth floor with fresh rushes. Most visitors head for **Dove Cottage**, where the poet spent his most creative years. The museum in the barn behind includes such artefacts as the great man's socks. The Wordsworths moved to a larger house, **Rydal Mount**, in

Rydal in 1813 and lived here until 1850. The grounds have waterfalls and a summerhouse where the poet often sat. Dora's Field nearby is a blaze of daffodils in spring and Fairfield Horseshoe offers an energetic, challenging walk.

🏛 **Dove Cottage and the Wordsworth Museum**
Off A591 nr Grasmere. 📞 *015394 35544.* ◻ *daily.* ● *24–26 Dec, mid-Jan–mid-Feb.* 🈺 ⛓ ⬜ 🅿
🏛 **Rydal Mount**
Rydal. 📞 *015394 33002.* ◻ *Wed–Mon.* ● *24, 25 Dec, three wks in Jan.* 🈺 ⛓ *limited.* 🅿

WILLIAM WORDSWORTH (1770-1850)

Best known of the Romantic poets, Wordsworth was born in the Lake District and spent most of his life there. After school in Hawkshead and a period at Cambridge, a legacy enabled him to pursue his literary career. He settled at Dove Cottage with his sister Dorothy and in 1802 married an old school friend, Mary Hutchinson. They lived simply, walking, bringing up their children and receiving visits from poets such as Coleridge and de Quincey. Wordsworth's prose works include one of the earliest guidebooks to the Lake District.

BEATRIX POTTER AND THE LAKE DISTRICT

Although best known for her children's stories with characters such as Peter Rabbit and Jemima Puddleduck, which she also illustrated, Beatrix Potter (1866–1943) became a champion of conservation in the Lake District after moving there in 1906. She married William Helis, devoted herself to farming, and was an expert on Herdwick sheep. To conserve her beloved countryside, she donated land to the National Trust.

Cover illustration of *Jemima Puddleduck* (1908)

the restored farmhouse of **Townend**, dating from 1626, whose interior gives an insight into Lakeland domestic life.

🏛 **Kirkstone Galleries**
Skelwith Bridge. 📞 015394 34002. ◯ daily. ● 24–26 Dec. ♿ limited.

🏛 **Townend**
(NT) Troutbeck. 📞 015394 32628. ◯ Apr–Oct: Tue–Fri, Sun & public hols. 📷

Windermere ⑰

Cumbria. 🚆 Station Rd. 🚌 Victoria St. 🛈 Victoria St (015394 46499) or Glebe Rd, Bowness-on-Windermere (015394 42895).

A T OVER 10 miles (16 km) long, this dramatic watery expanse is England's largest mere. Industrial magnates built mansions around its shores long before the railway arrived. Stately **Brockhole**, now a national park visitor centre, was one such grand estate. When the railway reached Windermere in 1847, it enabled crowds of workers to visit the area on day trips.

Today, a year-round car ferry service connects the lake's east and west shores (it runs between Ferry Nab and Ferry House), and summer steamers link Lakeside, Bowness and Ambleside on the north-south axis. Belle Isle, a wooded island on which a unique round house stands, is one of the lake's most attractive features, but landing is not permitted. The best place for swimming is **Fell Foot Park** at the south end of the lake, and there are good walks on the northwest shore. A quite stunning viewpoint is Orrest Head (238 m; 784 ft), northeast of Windermere town.

ENVIRONS: Bowness-on-Windermere, on the east shore, is a hugely popular centre. Many of its buildings display Victorian details, and St Martin's Church dates back to the 15th century. The **Windermere Steamboat Museum** recalls the Victorian age in a collection of superbly restored craft, and one of these vessels, *Osprey*, makes regular lake trips. The **World of Beatrix Potter** recreates her characters in an exhibition, and a film tells her life story.

Beatrix Potter wrote many of her books at **Hill Top**, the 17th-century farmhouse at Near Sawrey, northwest of Windermere. The house is so popular that it is advisable to avoid visits at peak times. Hill Top is furnished with many of Potter's possessions, and left as it was in her lifetime. The **Beatrix Potter Gallery** in Hawkshead has a permanent exhibition of her manuscripts.

🛈 **Brockhole Visitor Centre**
On A591. 📞 015394 46601. ◯ Apr–Oct: daily. ♿ 🖥 🚻

🍁 **Fell Foot Park**
(NT) Newby Bridge. 📞 015395 31273. ◯ daily. ♿ 🖥

🏛 **Windermere Steamboat Museum**
Rayrigg Rd, Windermere. 📞 015394 45565. ◯ 20 Mar–Oct: daily. 📷 ♿

🏛 **World of Beatrix Potter**
The Old Laundry, Crag Brow. 📞 015394 88444. ◯ daily. ● 25 Dec, three wks in Jan. 📷 ♿ 🖥

🚂 **Hill Top**
(NT) Near Sawrey, Ambleside. 📞 015394 36269. ◯ Apr–Oct: Sat–Wed.

🏛 **Beatrix Potter Gallery**
(NT) The Square, Hawkshead. 📞 015394 36355. ◯ Apr–Oct: Sun–Thu. 📷 🚻

Boats moored along the shore at Ambleside, the north end of Windermere

Peaceful Coniston Water, the setting of Arthur Ransome's novel, *Swallows and Amazons* (1930)

Coniston Water ⑱

Cumbria. 🚆 *Windermere then bus.* 🚌 *Ambleside then bus.* ℹ️ *Coniston car park, Ruskin Ave (015394 41533).*

For the finest view of this stretch of water just outside the Lake District, you need to climb. The 19th-century art critic, writer and philosopher John Ruskin, had a fine view from his house, **Brantwood**, where his paintings and memorabilia can be seen today. The Ruskin and Gandhi exhibition explores Ruskin's influence on India's legendary statesman, Mahatma Gandhi (1869–1948).

An enjoyable excursion is the summer lake trip from Coniston Pier on the National Trust steam yacht, *Gondola*, calling at Brantwood and Park-a-Moor. Coniston was also the scene of Donald Campbell's fatal attempt on the world water speed record in 1967. The green slate village of Coniston, once a centre for copper-mining, now caters for local walkers.

Also interesting is the traffic-free village of **Hawkshead** to the northwest, with its quaint alleyways and timber-framed houses. To the south is the vast Grizedale Forest, dotted with woodland sculptures.

Just north of Coniston Water is the man-made **Tarn Hows**, a landscaped pool surrounded by woods. There is a pleasant climb up the 803 m (2,635 ft) Old Man of Coniston.

🏛 **Brantwood**
Off B5285, nr Hawkshead. 📞 *015394 41396.* ○ *mid-Mar–mid-Nov: daily; mid-Nov–mid-Mar: Wed–Sun.* ● *25, 26 Dec.* ♿ *limited.* 🍴 💻 🎁

Kendal ⑲

Cumbria. 👥 *26,000.* 🚆 ℹ️ *Town Hall, Highgate (01539 725758).* 🚌 *Mon–Sat.*

A busy market town, Kendal is the administrative centre of the region and the southern gateway to the Lake District. Built in grey limestone, it has an arts centre, the **Brewery**, and a central area which is best enjoyed on foot. **Abbot Hall**,

Kendal mint cake, the famous lakeland energy-booster for walkers

built in 1759, has paintings by Turner and Romney as well as Gillows furniture *(see p430)*. In addition, the hall's stable block contains the **Museum of Lakeland Life and Industry**, with lively workshops demonstrating local crafts and trades. There are dioramas of geology and wildlife in the **Museum of Natural History and Archaeology**. About 3 miles (5 km) south of the town is

14th-century **Sizergh Castle**, with a fortified tower, carved fireplaces and a lovely garden.

🏛 **Abbot Hall Art Gallery and Museum of Lakeland Life and Industry**
Kirkland. 📞 *01539 722464.* ○ *mid-Feb–24 Dec: daily.* ♿ *gallery.* 🎥 *by arrangement.* 💻 🎁
🏛 **Kendal Museum of Natural History and Archaeology**
Station Rd. 📞 *01539 721374.* ○ *mid-Feb–24 Dec: Mon–Sat.* ♿ *limited.* 🎁
🏰 **Sizergh Castle**
(NT) off A591 & A590. 📞 *015395 60070.* ○ *Apr–Oct: Sun–Thu.* ♿ *grounds only.* 💻 🎁

Furness Peninsula ⑳

Cumbria. 🚆 🚌 *Barrow-in-Furness.* ℹ️ *28 Duke St, Barrow-in-Furness (01229 894784).*

Barrow-in-Furness *(see p399)* is the peninsula's main town. Its **Dock Museum**, cleverly built over a Victorian dock where ships were repaired, traces the history of Barrow using lively displays, including an old schooner, *Emily Barratt*.

Ruins of the red sandstone walls of **Furness Abbey** remain in the wooded Vale of Deadly Nightshade, with a small exhibition of monastic life. The historic town of Ulverston received its charter in 1280. **Ulverston Heritage**

◁ **The attractive woodland of Thirlmere, under the shadow of Helvellyn**

Centre charts its development from market town to port. Stan Laurel, the third comedian of Laurel and Hardy fame, was born here in 1890. His memorabilia **museum** has a cinema.

🏛 Dock Museum
North Rd, Barrow-in-Furness. 📞 01229 894444. ⬜ Apr–Oct: Wed–Sun; Nov–Mar: Wed–Sun (Sat, Sun: pm); public hols. ⬤ 25, 26 Dec, 1 Jan. ♿

🏠 Furness Abbey
Vale of Deadly Nightshade. 📞 01229 823420. ⬜ Easter–Sep: daily; Oct–Easter: Wed–Sun. ⬤ 24–26 Dec, 1 Jan. 📷 ♿ limited. 📷

🏛 Ulverston Heritage Centre
Lower Brook St. 📞 01229 580820. ⬜ Apr–Dec: Mon–Sat; Jan–Mar: Mon, Tue, Thu–Sat. ⬤ 25, 26 Dec, 1 Jan. 📷 ♿ limited.

🏛 Laurel and Hardy Museum
Upper Brook St, Ulverston. 📞 01229 582292. ⬜ daily. ⬤ 25 Dec; Jan. 📷 ♿

Staircase at Holker Hall

Cartmel ㉑

Cumbria. 👥 700. 🛈 Victoria Hall, Main St, Grange-over-Sands (015395 34026).

THE HIGHLIGHT of this pretty village is its 12th-century **priory**, one of the finest Lake District churches. Little remains of the original priory except the pretty gatehouse in the village centre, now leased as an art gallery. The restored church has an attractive east window, a stone-carved 14th-century tomb, and beautiful misericords.

Cartmel also boasts a small racecourse. The village has given its name to its surroundings, a hilly district of green farmland with variegated woods and limestone scars.

One of the main local attractions is **Holker Hall**, former residence of the Dukes of Devonshire. Inside are lavishly furnished rooms, with fine marble fireplaces, and a superb oak staircase. Outside are stunning gardens and a deer park.

🏛 Holker Hall
Cark-in-Cartmel. 📞 015395 58328. ⬜ Apr–Oct: Sun–Fri. 📷 ♿ limited. 📷 by arrangement. 💻 📷

Levens Hall ㉒

Nr Kendal, Cumbria. 📞 015395 60321. 🚌 from Kendal or Lancaster. ⬜ Apr–mid-Oct: Sun–Thu. 📷 ♿ gardens only. 💻 📷

THE OUTSTANDING attraction of this Elizabethan mansion is its famous topiary, but the house itself has much to offer. Built around a 13th-century fortified tower, it contains a fine collection of Jacobean furniture and watercolours by Peter de Wint (1784–1849). Also of note are the ornate plaster ceilings, carved Charles II dining chairs, the earliest example of English patchwork and the gilded hearts on the drainpipes.

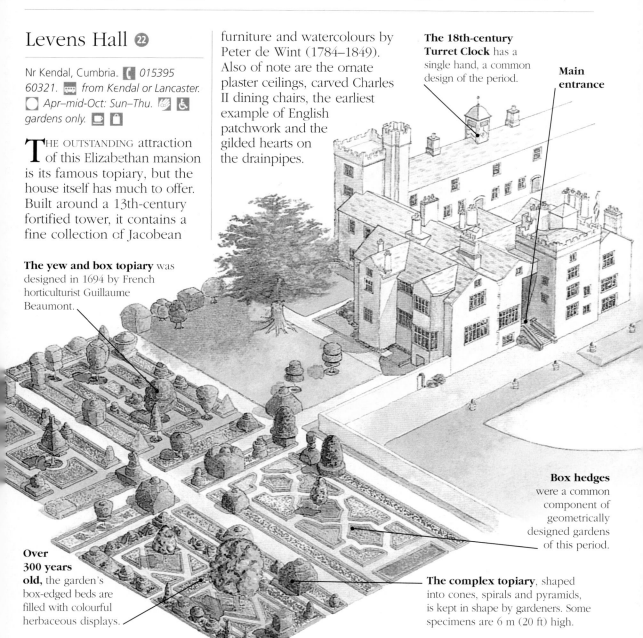

The yew and box topiary was designed in 1694 by French horticulturist Guillaume Beaumont.

Over 300 years old, the garden's box-edged beds are filled with colourful herbaceous displays.

The 18th-century Turret Clock has a single hand, a common design of the period.

Main entrance

Box hedges were a common component of geometrically designed gardens of this period.

The complex topiary, shaped into cones, spirals and pyramids, is kept in shape by gardeners. Some specimens are 6 m (20 ft) high.

Morecambe Bay, looking northwest towards Barrow-in-Furness

Morecambe Bay 🄫

Lancashire. 🚆 *Morecambe.*
⛴ *Heysham (to Isle of Man).* ℹ
Central Promenade (01524 582808).

THE BEST WAY to explore
Morecambe Bay is by train
from Ulverston to Arnside. The
track follows a series of low
viaducts across a huge expanse
of glistening tidal flats where
thousands of wading birds
feed and breed. The bay is
one of the most important
bird reserves in Britain. On
the Cumbrian side, retirement
homes have expanded the
sedate Victorian resort of
Grange-over-Sands, which
grew up after the arrival of
the railway in 1857. Its best
feature is its natural setting.
Nearby, **Hampsfield Fell**
and **Humphrey Head Point**
give fine views along the bay.

Leighton Hall 🄬

Carnforth, Lancashire. 📞 *01524
734474.* 🚌 *to Yealand Conyers
(from Lancaster).* ⭘ *May–Jul, Sep:
Tue–Fri & Sun (pm); Aug: Tue–Fri &
Sun; public hols.* ⬤ *special events.*
🖼 ♿ *ground floor only.* 📷 *only.* ▯

LEIGHTON HALL'S estate dates
back to the 13th century,
but most of the present building is 19th century, including
its pale Neo-Gothic façade. It
is owned by the Gillow family,
founders of the Lancastrian
furniture business, whose
exquisite products are now
highly prized antiques. Some
excellent pieces can be seen
here, including a ladies' work-

box inlaid with biblical scenes.
In the afternoon the hall's
large collection of birds of prey
display their aerial prowess.

Lancaster 🄭

Lancashire. 🏛 *45,000.*
🚆 🚌 ℹ *Castle Hill
(01524 32878).*
🛒 *Mon–Sat.*

THIS COUNTY TOWN
of Lancashire is
tiny compared to
Liverpool or
Manchester
(now counties
in their own
right), but it
has a long history. The Romans
named it after their camp over
the River Lune. Originally a
defensive site, it developed

into a prosperous port largely
on the proceeds of the slave
trade. Today, its university and
cultural life still thrive. The
Norman **Lancaster Castle** was
expanded in the 14th and 16th
centuries. It has been a crown
court and a prison since the
18th century. The Shire Hall is
decorated with 600 heraldic
shields. Some fragments from
Adrian's Tower (which has a
collection of torture instruments) are 2,000 years old.
The nearby priory church
of **St Mary** is on Castle Hill.
Its main features include a
Saxon doorway and carved
14th-century choir stalls. There
is an outstanding museum of
furniture in the 17th-century
Judge's Lodgings, while the
Maritime Museum, in the
Georgian custom house
on St George's Quay,
contains displays on the
port's history. The **City
Museum**, based in the
old town hall, concen-
trates on Lancaster's
shore-based aspects.
The splendid **Lune
Aqueduct** carries the
canal over the
River Lune on
five wide arches.
Other attractions
are found in
**Williamson
Park**, site of
the 1907 Ashton Memorial.
This folly was built by the
local linoleum magnate and
politician, Lord Ashton.

**Tawny eagle at
Leighton Hall**

CROSSING THE SANDS

Morecambe Bay sands are very dangerous. Travellers used to
cut across the bay at low tide to shorten the long trail around
the Kent estuary. Many perished as the rising water turned
the beach to quicksand, and sea fogs hid the paths. Locals
who knew the bay became guides, and today you can travel
with a guide from Kents Bank to Hest Bank near Arnside.

***The High Sheriff of Lancaster Crossing Morecambe Sands** (anon)*

There are fine views from the top of this 67 m (220 ft) domed structure. Opposite is the tropical butterfly house, and the pavilion café.

Façade of Lancaster's Judge's Lodgings, now a museum

♙ Lancaster Castle
Castle Parade. 🛈 *01524 64998.* ◯ *mid-Mar–mid-Dec: daily.* 🎟 *only but limited when court is in session.* 🔲 🔲

🏛 Judge's Lodgings
Church St. 🛈 *01524 32808.* ◯ *Good Fri–31 Oct: Mon–Sat (pm).* ⬤ *Nov–Maundy Thu.* 🔲 🔲

🏛 Maritime Museum
Custom House, St George's Quay. 🛈 *01524 64637.* ◯ *daily (Nov–Easter: pm).* ⬤ *24–26, 31 Dec, 1 Jan.* 🔲 🔲 🔲 🔲

🏛 City Museum
Market Sq. 🛈 *01524 64637.* ◯ *Mon–Sat.* ⬤ *24 Dec–2 Jan.* ♿ *limited.*

♣ Williamson Park
Wyresdale Rd. 🛈 *01524 33318.* ◯ *daily.* ⬤ *25–26 Dec, 1 Jan.* 🔲 ♿ *limited.* 🔲 🔲

Ribble Valley ㉖

Lancashire. 🚊 *Clitheroe.* ℹ️ *Market Place, Clitheroe (01200 425566).* 🛒 *Tue, Thu, Sat.*

CLITHEROE, A SMALL market town with a hilltop castle, is a good centre for exploring the Ribble Valley's rivers and old villages, such as Slaidburn. Ribchester has the remains of a **Roman fort**, and there is a ruined **Cistercian abbey** at Whalley. East is Pendle Hill (560 m; 1,830 ft) with a Bronze Age burial mound at its peak. West is the Forest of Bowland.

THE WITCHES OF PENDLE

In 1612, ten women were convicted of witchcraft at Lancaster Castle. The evidence against them was mostly based on the revelations of a small child who implicated them in satanic rituals. Many of the accused came from two peasant families, reduced to penury by a feud, who roamed the countryside begging, and cursing those who refused to oblige. Several of the women confessed to their crimes, but whether they were coerced, deranged or had indeed dabbled in the "black arts" is impossible to assess.

Mother Chattox, a Pendle "witch"

♙ Ribchester Roman fort
Ribchester. 🛈 *01254 878261.* ◯ *daily (Sat, Sun: pm).* ⬤ *24, 25 Dec, 1 Jan.* 🔲 ♿ 🎟 *by arrangement.*

⚐ Whalley Abbey
Whalley. 🛈 *01254 822268.* ◯ *daily.* ⬤ *24 Dec–2 Jan.* 🔲 ♿ 🔲 🔲

Blackpool ㉗

Lancashire. 👥 *150,000.* ✈️ 🚊 🚌 ℹ️ *Clifton St (01253 478222).*

BRITISH HOLIDAY patterns have changed in the past few decades, and Blackpool is no longer the apogee of seaside entertainment it once was. But it remains a unique experience. A seamless wall of amusement arcades, piers, bingo halls and fast-food stalls stretch behind the sands. Nostalgic trams run along the promenade. At night, entertainers strut their stuff under the bright lights. The town attracts thousands of visitors during September and October when the spectacular Illuminations trace the skeleton of the 158 m (518 ft) Blackpool Tower. Blackpool's resort life dates back to the 18th century, but it burst into prominence when the railway first arrived in 1840, bringing Lancastrian workers to their holiday resort.

Blackpool Tower, painted gold for its centenary in 1994

Manchester 28

Sign for the John Rylands Library

MANCHESTER'S HISTORY dates back to Roman times, when, in AD 79, Agricola's legions set up a base camp called Mancunium on the site of the present city. It rose to prominence in the late 18th century, when Richard Arkwright's steam-powered spinning machines introduced the brave new world of cotton processing. By 1830, the first railway linked Manchester and Liverpool, and in 1894 the Manchester Ship Canal opened, allowing cargo vessels 36 miles (55 km) inland. Confident civic buildings sprang up from the proceeds of cotton wealth, but these were in stark contrast to the overcrowded slums of the millworkers. Social discontent led writers, politicians and reformers to espouse liberal or radical causes. One result was the foundation in 1821 of the forthright local newspaper, the *Manchester Guardian*, now an important national daily. The city was the first to introduce massive slum clearance and smokeless zones during the 1950s.

Exploring Manchester

Manchester is a fine, compact city with much to see in its central areas. The imaginative restoration of the tram system has helped to ease the pressures of urban transport. The mills and docks have left a huge architectural heritage. Among the fine 19th-century buildings are the Neo-Gothic cathedral, the **John Rylands Library**, now part of the university, the **Town Hall**, the **Royal Exchange**, now a theatre and restaurant, and the **Free Trade Hall**, home of the famous Hallé concerts. Night-owls can enjoy the city's lively club scene, and its many ethnic restaurants.

The G-Mex Exhibition and Event Centre, once the central railway station

---

MANCHESTER CITY CENTRE

Air and Space Gallery ④
Castlefield ③
City Art Galleries ⑩
Free Trade Hall ⑥
G-Mex Centre ⑤
Granada Studios Tour ①
John Rylands Library ⑦
Museum of Science and
   Industry in Manchester ②
Royal Exchange ⑧
Town Hall ⑨

KEY

🚌 Bus station
🚍 Coach station
🚊 Tram
— Tramline

🚆 British Rail station
P Parking
ℹ️ Tourist information
✝ Church

0 metres   250
0 yards   250

Trafford Road Bridge on the Manchester Ship Canal

🏛 Museum of Science and Industry in Manchester

Liverpool Rd. ☎ 0161 832 2244. ◯ daily. ⬤ 24–26 Dec. 🎫 ♿ 🅿

Part of the Castlefield Urban Heritage Park, this museum captures the spirit of scientific enterprise and industrial might that characterized Manchester in its heyday. Among the best sections are the Power Hall, a collection of working steam engines, the Electricity Gallery, which traces the history of domestic power, and an exhibition on the Liverpool and Manchester Railway. There are hot air balloons and space suits in the Air and Space Gallery across the street.

🎬 Granada Studios Tour

Water St. ☎ 0161 832 9090. ◯ Jul–Aug: daily; Sep–Jun: Wed–Sun, public & school hols. ⬤ 20–25, 31 Dec. 🎫 ♿ 🍴 🅿

Here visitors can take a **tour** through the backlots of popular television shows. Most famous is the set of *Coronation Street*, Britain's longest-running soap opera.

Close by, in **Castlefield**, you can see the rebuilt "castle in the field" (the ruined Roman fort), and the restored wharves of the Bridgewater Canal.

🏛 City Art Galleries

Mosley St & Princess St. ☎ 0161 234 1456. ⬤ until summer 2001 for major refurbishment.

The porticoed building which Sir Charles Barry (1795–1860) designed in 1824, contains an excellent collection of British art, notably Pre-Raphaelites such as Holman Hunt and Dante Gabriel Rossetti. Early Italian, Flemish and French Schools are also represented. It has a fine collection of silver, ceramics and glass.

🏭 G-Mex Centre

Windmill St. ☎ 0161 834 2700. ◯ During exhibitions ring for details. ⬤ 25 Dec. ♿ 🍴

The former central railway station, closed in 1969, is now a huge exhibition centre. It has more than 9,290 sq m (100,000 sq ft) of pillarless floor space in which to host major concerts and shows, and looks particularly dramatic when lit up at night.

Jacob Epstein's *Genesis* (1930–1) in Whitworth Art Gallery

🏭 Manchester Ship Canal

This magnificent engineering feat was inaugurated by Queen Victoria in May 1894. It was designed to bring deep sea shipping from Eastham on the Mersey into the heart of the city, at Salford Quays, 36 miles (58 km) inland. Three thousand ships still use the canal every year, and the docks at the head of the canal are being restored.

🏛 Whitworth Art Gallery

University of Manchester, Oxford Rd. ☎ 0161 275 7450. ◯ daily (Sun: pm). ⬤ 23 Dec–10 Jan, Good Fri. ♿

This fine red-brick building, named after the Manchester machine tool manufacturer and engineer, Sir Joseph Whitworth, houses a superb collection of contemporary art, textiles and prints. Jacob Epstein's *Genesis* nude occupies the entrance, but the Turner (*see p97*) watercolours are more universally appreciated. Japanese woodcuts and some examples of one of Manchester's little-known industries, wallpaper-making, are an extra bonus.

THE PETERLOO MASSACRE

In 1819, the working conditions of Manchester's factory workers were so bad that social tensions reached breaking point. On 16 August, 50,000 people assembled in St Peter's Field to protest at the oppressive Corn Laws. Initially peaceful, the mood darkened and the poorly trained mounted troops panicked, charging the crowd with their sabres. Eleven were killed and many wounded. The incident was called Peterloo (the Battle of Waterloo had taken place in 1815). Reforms such as the Factory Act came in that year.

G Cruikshank's *Peterloo Massacre* cartoon

Liverpool ㉙

Traces of settlement on Merseyside date back to the 1st century. In 1207 "Livpul", a fishing village, was granted a charter by King John. The population was only 1,000 in Stuart times, but during the 17th and 18th centuries Liverpool's westerly seaboard gave it a leading edge in the lucrative Caribbean slave trade. The first docks opened in 1715 and eventually stretched 7 miles (11 km) along the Mersey. Liverpool's first ocean steamer set out from here in 1840, and would-be emigrants to the New World poured into the city from Europe, including a flood of Irish refugees from the potato famine. Many settled permanently in Liverpool and a large, mixed community developed. Today, the port still handles similar volumes of cargoes as in the 1950s and 1960s, but container ships use Bootle docks. Despite economic and social problems, the irrepressible "Scouse" or Liverpudlian spirit re-emerged in the Swinging Sixties, when four local lads stormed the pop scene. Many people still visit Liverpool to pay homage to the Beatles, but the city is also known for its orchestra, the Liverpool Philharmonic, its sport (football and the Grand National steeplechase) and its university.

Liver Bird on the Royal Liver Building

Victorian ironwork, restored and polished, at Albert Dock

Exploring Liverpool

Liverpool's waterfront by the Pier Head, guarded by the legendary Liver Birds (a pair of cormorants with seaweed in their beaks) on the Royal Liver Building, is one of the most easily recognized in Britain. Nearby are the famous ferry terminal across the River Mersey and the revitalized

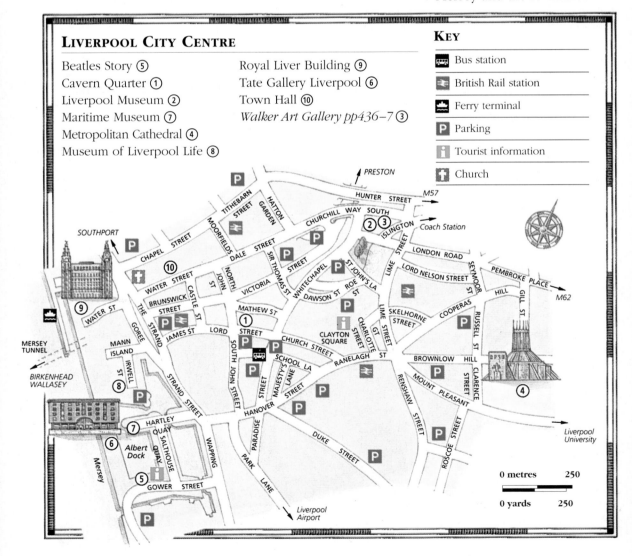

LIVERPOOL CITY CENTRE

Beatles Story ⑤
Cavern Quarter ①
Liverpool Museum ②
Maritime Museum ⑦
Metropolitan Cathedral ④
Museum of Liverpool Life ⑧
Royal Liver Building ⑨
Tate Gallery Liverpool ⑥
Town Hall ⑩
Walker Art Gallery pp436–7 ③

KEY

🚌 Bus station
🚆 British Rail station
⛴ Ferry terminal
🅿 Parking
ℹ Tourist information
✝ Church

0 metres   250
0 yards   250

docklands. Other attractions include top-class museums and fine galleries, such as the Walker Art Gallery (*see pp436–7*). Its wealth of interesting architecture includes some of Britain's finest Neo-Classical buildings in the city centre, and two cathedrals.

Albert Dock

Wapping. (0151 708 8854.) daily.) 25–26 Dec, 1 Jan.) some attractions.)

There are five warehouses surrounding Albert Dock, all designed

Ship's bell in the Maritime Museum

by Jesse Hartley in 1846. By the early 1900s the docks had become less important and had closed by 1972. After a decade of dereliction, these Grade I listed buildings were restored in a development that includes TV studios, museums, galleries, shops, restaurants and businesses.

Albert Dock quay beside the River Mersey

Maritime Museum

Albert Dock. (0151 478 4499.) daily.) 23–26 Dec, 1 Jan.) children free.) not Piermaster's House or basement.)

Devoted to the history of the Port of Liverpool, this large complex has good sections on shipbuilding and the Cunard and White Star liners as well as a new Transatlantic Slavery gallery. The area on the Battle of the Atlantic in World War II includes models and charts. Another gallery deals with emigration to the New World. The Customs and Excise section reveals the world of smuggling in all its modern forms, with sniffer dogs and swallowed heroin packages. Across the quayside is the rebuilt Piermaster's House and the Cooperage.

Museum of Liverpool Life

Mann Island. (0151 478 4080.) daily.) 24–26 Dec, 1 Jan.))

Many aspects of Liverpool culture converge here. Exhibits range from the oldest Trade Union banner in Britain to a recreated Co-op shop, and from the first Ford Anglia built at nearby Halewood, to a traditional print shop. There is a mock-up of Becher's Brook, the famous Grand National water jump at Aintree. One of the city's football teams, Everton, is also represented.

VISITORS' CHECKLIST

Merseyside.) 450,000.
) 7 miles (11 km) SE Liverpool.
) Lime St.) Norton St.
) from Pier Head to the Wirral, also sightseeing trips; to Isle of Man & N Ireland.
) Queens Sq (0151 709 3631).
) Sun (heritage market).
) Liverpool Show: May; River Festival: Jun; Beatles Festival: Aug.

Beatles Story

Britannia Pavilion. (0151 709 1963.) daily.) 25, 26 Dec.)))

This museum records the history of The Beatles' meteoric rise to fame, from their first record, *Love Me Do,* through Beatlemania to their last live appearance together in 1969, and their eventual break-up. The hits that mesmerized a generation can be heard.

Tate Gallery Liverpool

Albert Dock. (0151 709 3223.) Tue–Sun, public hols.) Mon; 24–26 Dec.) for some exhibitions.)) by arrangement.)

The northern Tate houses one of the best selections of contemporary art outside London. Marked by bright blue and orange panels, the gallery was converted from its warehouse setting by contemporary architect James Stirling. It opened in 1988 as the London Tate's first outstation. Three spacious floors provide an ideal setting for the changing exhibitions of painting and sculpture housed here.

THE BEATLES

Liverpool has produced many good bands and a host of singers, comedians and entertainers before and since the 1960s. But the Beatles – John Lennon, Paul McCartney, George Harrison and Ringo Starr – were the most sensational, and locations associated with the band, however tenuous, are revered as shrines in Liverpool. Bus and walking tours trace the hallowed ground of the Salvation Army home at *Strawberry Fields* and *Penny Lane* (both outside the city centre), as well as the boys' old homes. The most visited site is Mathew Street, near Central Station, where the Cavern Club first throbbed to the authentic Mersey Beat. The original site is now a shopping arcade, but the bricks have been used to create a replica. Nearby are statues of the Beatles and *Eleanor Rigby*.

Liverpool: Walker Art Gallery

Italian dish (c.1500)

FOUNDED IN 1873 by Sir Andrew Barclay Walker, a local brewer and Mayor of Liverpool, this gallery houses one of the finest art collections in the North. Paintings range from early Italian and Flemish works to Rubens, Rembrandt, Poussin, and French Impressionists such as Degas' *Woman Ironing* (c.1890). Among the strong collection of British artists from the 18th century onward are works by Millais and Turner and Gainsborough's *Countess of Sefton* (1769). There is 20th-century art by Hockney and Sickert, and the sculpture collection includes works by Henry Moore.

Seashells *(1870)*
Albert Moore (1841–93) painted female figures based on antique statues. Under the influence of Whistler (see p657), he adopted subtle shades.

Bowring gallery

Interior at Paddington
(1951) Lucian Freud's friend Harry Diamond posed for six months for this picture, intended by the artist to "make the human being uncomfortable".

1
2
5
6
7
8
9
4
12
11
10

First floor

Ground floor

Façade was designed by HH Vale and Cornelius Sherlock.

Main entrance

GALLERY GUIDE

All the picture galleries are on the first floor. The Cole and Bowring galleries house medieval and Renaissance paintings; the Wavertree and Audley have 17th-century Dutch, French, Italian and Spanish art. British 18th- and 19th-century works are in Rooms 1–9. Modern art is in Rooms 10 and 12, and Room 11 has Impressionists and Post-Impressionists.

Sleeping Shepherd *(1835)*
The greatest British Neo-Classical sculptor of the mid-19th century, John Gibson (1790–1866), used traditional colours to give his statuary a smooth appearance.

Cole gallery

Wavertree gallery

Audley gallery

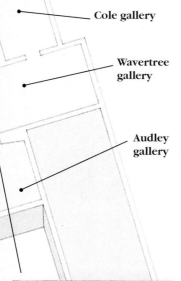

Christ Discovered in the Temple *(1342)*
Framed by a typically jewel-like Gothic setting, Simone Martini's Holy Family conveys emotional tension using graceful but highly expressive body language.

KEY TO FLOORPLAN

☐	13th–17th-century European
☐	18th–19th-century British, Pre-Raphaelites and Victorian
☐	19th-century British and temporary exhibitions
☐	Impressionist/Post-Impressionist
☐	20th-century British
☐	Sculpture gallery
☐	Non-exhibition space

The 7th-century Kingston Brooch in Liverpool Museum

🏛 Liverpool Museum

William Brown St. 📞 0151 478 4399.
🕐 daily (Sun: pm). 🔴 24–26 Dec, 1 Jan. ♿ 👶 💻 🎧
Five floors of exhibits in this excellent museum include a fine collection of Nigerian Benin bronzes, a section on Egyptian, Greek and Roman antiquities and some natural history galleries. It also has a fine ceramics collection, a planetarium, and a number of temporary exhibitions.

⛪ Anglican Cathedral

St James' Mount. 📞 0151 709 6271. 🕐 daily (Sun: pm). ♿ 💻 🎧
Although Gothic in style, this building was only completed in 1978. The largest Anglican cathedral in the world is a fine red sandstone edifice designed by Sir Giles Gilbert Scott. The foundation stone was laid in 1904 by Edward VII, but dogged by two world wars, building work dragged on to modified designs. The aisles are built as tunnels through the walls. Note the stained glass, high altar and sump-tuous embroidery collection.

⛪ Metropolitan Cathedral of Christ the King

Mount Pleasant. 📞 0151 709 9222.
🕐 daily. **Donation.** ♿ 💻 🎧
Liverpool's Roman Catholic cathedral rejected traditional forms in favour of a striking modern design. Early plans, drawn up by Pugin and later by Lutyens *(see p29)* in the 1930s, proved too expensive. The final version, brainchild of Sir Frederick Gibberd and built from 1962–7, is a circular building surmounted by a stylized crown of thorns 88 m (290 ft) high. It is irreverently known as "Paddy's Wigwam" by non-Catholics (a reference to Liverpool's large Irish population). Inside, the stained glass lantern, designed by John Piper and Patrick Reyntiens, floods the circular nave with diffused blueish light. A tour around the inner walls reveals many sculptures and a fine bronze of Christ by Elisabeth Frink (1930–94) on the altar.

ENVIRONS: A spectacular richly timbered building dating from 1490, **Speke Hall** lies 6 miles (10 km) east of Liverpool's centre, surrounded by lovely grounds. The oldest parts of the hall enclose a cobbled courtyard dominated by two yew trees, Adam and Eve. The 16th-century hiding places for persecuted priests still remain.

Birkenhead on the Wirral peninsula has been linked to Liverpool by ferry for over 800 years. Now, road and rail tunnels supplement access. The Norman Priory is still in use on Sundays, and stately Hamilton Square was designed from 1825–44 by J Gillespie Graham, one of the architects of Edinburgh's New Town.

On the Wirral side of the Mersey is the **Port Sunlight Village Trust** *(see p399)*, a Victorian garden village built by successful and enlightened soap manufacturer William Hesketh Lever for the benefit of his factory workers.

🏛 Speke Hall

(NT) The Walk, Speke. 📞 0151 427 7231. 🕐 Apr–Oct: Tue–Sun (pm); Nov–mid-Dec: Sat, Sun (pm); public hols. ♿ 👶 limited. 💻 🎧

🏛 Port Sunlight Village Trust

95 Greendale Rd, Port Sunlight, Wirral. 📞 0151 644 6466. 🕐 Apr–Oct: daily; Nov–Mar: Mon–Fri & public hols. 🔴 23 Dec–2 Jan. ♿ 👶 limited.

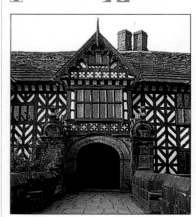

Entrance to the half-timbered manor house of Speke Hall

Farmland in north Yorkshire, with fields demarcated by stone walls ▷

YORKSHIRE
AND
HUMBERSIDE

YORKSHIRE AND HUMBERSIDE

WITH THE HISTORIC CITY *of York at its heart, this is an area of great scenic beauty, dramatic moorland, green valleys and picturesque villages. To the north lie the Yorkshire Dales and the North York Moors; eastwards, a coastline with beaches and birdlife; and southwards, a landscape of lush meadows.*

The Yorkshire countryside is as diverse as anywhere in Britain. It encompasses areas such as the spectacular limestone and gritstone hill country of the Yorkshire Dales National Park; the heather-clad plateaus of the North York Moors; the broad, arable expanses of the Vale of Pickering; the impressive cliffs of Flamborough and Bempton Head; and the constantly crumbling coastline of Holderness.

At the region's centre lies the historic city of York, which is one of the most complete medieval cities in England. It has been the capital of the northern provinces since the time of the Romans, who called the city Eboracum. York retains its medieval layout – with narrow, winding streets such as The Shambles – and its city walls. Walking around these walls is a good way to get an overview of the city. York's Viking past is spectacularly brought to life by the popular Jorvik Viking Centre, where visitors are transported back to the sights – and smells – of Eric Bloodaxe's Jorvik. But York's greatest glory is undoubtedly its superb Minster, a huge Gothic church with the largest collection of medieval stained glass in Britain. The influence of the Church permeates a large portion of Yorkshire's countryside: once-powerful monastic estates are scattered throughout the area. Today, what remains of these are evocative ruins, the most impressive of which is Fountains Abbey, in Skelldale, near the city of Ripon. This magnificent structure is widely regarded as the best-preserved example of a Cistercian abbey in England.

Lobster pots on the quayside at the picturesque fishing port of Whitby

◁ **The peaceful valley of Rosedale, North York Moors**

Other splendid remains can be found at Bolton Priory, in Wharfedale; Byland Abbey at the foot of the North York Moors; Rievaulx Abbey near Helmsley; and Whitby Abbey on the cliffs above the fishing town of Whitby – the home of the famous 18th-century explorer, Captain James Cook.

The present Yorkshire Dales National Park, founded in 1954, is a magnet for outdoor enthusiasts, who come in droves to enjoy the wonderfully varied landscapes. Some of the finest limestone scenery in Britain is found within the 680-sq-mile (1,750-sq-km) park, and features such as the impressive 90-m (300-ft) walls of Malham Cove are very popular with visitors. Furthermore, the challenge presented by the Yorkshire Three Peaks (Whernside, Ingleborough and Pen-y-Ghent) is irresistible to hill walkers. As well as enjoying magnificent views, visitors to Yorkshire Dales National Park can also experience some of the region's local history by visiting ancient fortifications such as Bolton castle, built in the 14th century, and Richmond castle, built in the 11th century. A completely different type of history is revealed by the ruins of lead mines, all that is left of an industry that once thrived in the area.

Almshouses in the village of Saltaire, Bradford

Rural petrol station, north Yorkshire

The other national park in Yorkshire is the North York Moors, which is spread across the mainly agricultural Vale of York. The great glory of this park is the beautiful uninterrupted expanse of heather moorland, punctuated occasionally by ancient boundary crosses. The Scottish-born writer and vet James Herriot used these moors as the setting for his popular stories about the life of a Yorkshire vet. The end of the moors is signalled by the highest cliffs on the east coast. These dramatic escarpments are at Boulby, which is near the pretty fishing villages of Robin Hood's Bay and Staithes.

Further south, beyond the seaside resort of Scarborough, the coastline meets the rolling Yorkshire Wolds.

The mill town of Hebden Bridge, west Yorkshire

View over the green pastures of north Yorkshire from Brimham Rocks

Here the local houses feature the distinctive red pantiles that are characteristic of village dwellings on the east coast. The Wolds come to a halt at the spectacular chalk sea cliffs of Flamborough and Bempton Head, which are home to thousands of seabirds. In the southeastern corner of the region is the mighty River Humber, which is about 40 miles (64 km) long. At the river's mouth – some 7 miles (11 km) wide – is the strange, other-worldly landscape of Holderness and Spurn Head, where the coastline is constantly being eaten away by erosion. The River Humber is lined by several major ports, such as Grimsby and Kingston upon Hull, which were both once thriving fishing settlements.

The southwestern corner of Yorkshire includes an industrial belt formed by cities such as Leeds, Bradford, Huddersfield and Sheffield – all important production centres during the Industrial Revolution. Today, these cities are proud of their industrial past but have largely become lively cultural centres. For a taste of how things were, a visit to the Victorian village of Saltaire (on the outskirts of Bradford) or the Armley Mills Museum in Leeds is recommended.

The bleak South Pennine moors, around the towns of Haworth and Hebden Bridge,

Ruins of Rievaulx Abbey, north Yorkshire

provided the inspiration for the novels of the Brontë sisters and, more recently, the late poet laureate, Ted Hughes. At Haworth, the Brontë Parsonage Museum contains a fine collection of Brontë manuscripts and personal effects. The South Pennine moors have their own brand of spartan wildness, and are now crossed by the 256-mile (412-km) Pennine Way national walking trail.

The people of Yorkshire are renowned for their independence and for the fierce pride they have in their homeland. Although Yorkshire folk are tough, and can be taciturn, they are unfailingly warm and hospitable to visitors. The residents of England's "Texas" rarely mince their words, but when friendships are made, loyalty is the watchword.

Malham Lings, a limestone pavement in the Malham area, north Yorkshire

Exploring Yorkshire and Humberside

Yorkshire covers a wide area, made up of three counties or "Ridings". Until the arrival of railways, mining and the wool industry in the 19th century, this was a farming area. Dry-stone walls dividing fields still pepper the northern part of the county, alongside 19th-century mill chimneys and country houses. Among the many abbeys are Rievaulx and the magnificent Fountains. The medieval city of York is a major attraction, as are Yorkshire's beaches. The region around the River Humber is characterized by the rolling countryside of the Wolds, and its nature reserves attract many birds.

Rosedale village in the North York Moors

Sights at a Glance

Bempton and Flamborough
  Head 26
Beverley 27
Bradford 35
Burton Agnes 25
Burton Constable 28
Byland Abbey 10
Castle Howard pp462–3 22
Coxwold 11
Eden Camp 23
Fountains Abbey pp454–5 7
Grimsby 31
Halifax 38
Harewood House 33
Harrogate 3
Haworth 36
Hebden Bridge 37
Helmsley 13
Holderness and Spurn
  Head 30
Hutton-le-Hole 16
Kingston upon Hull 29

Knaresborough 4
Leeds 34
Markenfield Hall 6
Mount Grace Priory 15
North York Moors Railway 18
Nunnington Hall 12
Rievaulx Abbey 14
Ripley 5
Ripon 8
Robin Hood's Bay 20
Scarborough 21
Sutton Bank 9
Whitby 19
Wharram Percy 24
York pp470–71 32
Yorkshire Dales National Park 1
Yorkshire Mining Museum 39
Yorkshire Sculpture Park 40

Walks and Tours
Malham Walk 2
North York Moors Tour 17

Section of Lendal Bridge (1863) crossing the Ouse in York

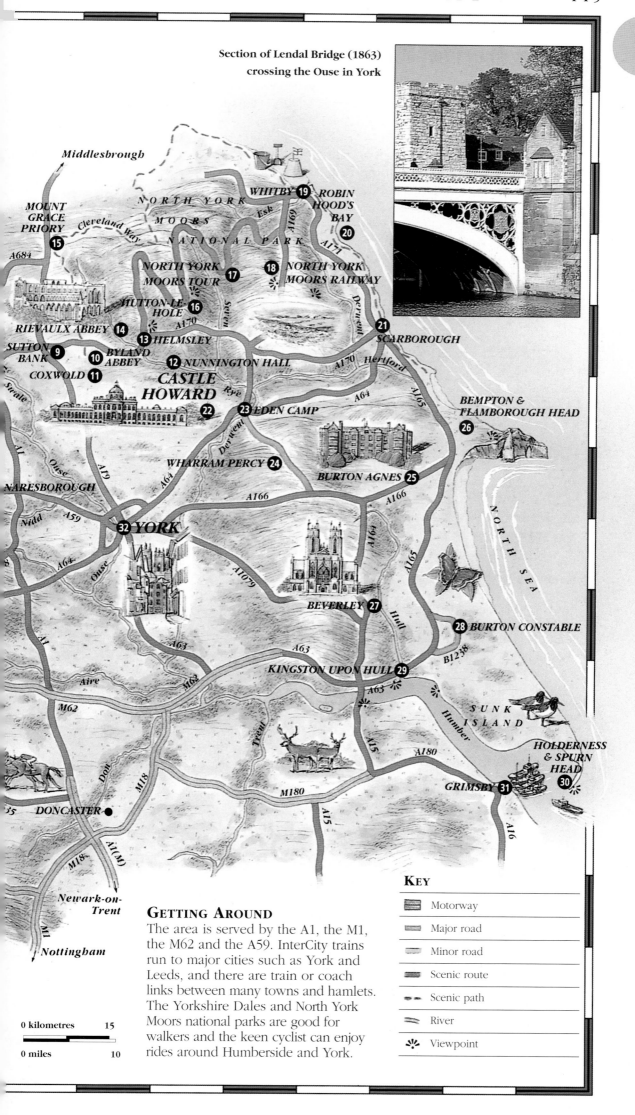

Middlesbrough

MOUNT
GRACE
PRIORY
15

A684

Cleveland Way

NORTH YORK

MOORS

NATIONAL PARK

WHITBY **19** ROBIN
HOOD'S
BAY
20

Esk

A169

A171

NORTH YORK
MOORS TOUR **17**

18 NORTH YORK
MOORS RAILWAY

Derwent

HUTTON-LE-
HOLE **16**

Seven

21
SCARBOROUGH

RIEVAULX ABBEY **14**

A170

HELMSLEY

SUTTON
BANK **9**

13

Rye

A170 Hertford

BEMPTON &
FLAMBOROUGH HEAD
26

10 BYLAND
ABBEY

12 NUNNINGTON HALL

A64

COXWOLD **11**

CASTLE
HOWARD

A165

Rye

22

23 EDEN CAMP

Derwent

WHARRAM PERCY **24**

BURTON AGNES **25**

NARESBOROUGH

Ouse

A19

A64

A166

A166

NORTH

Nidd

A59

Ouse

A1079

32 YORK

A64

SEA

BEVERLEY **27**

A165

Hull

28 BURTON CONSTABLE

B1238

A63

Aire

A63

KINGSTON UPON HULL **29**

A63

M62

A15

SUNK
ISLAND

Humber

M62

Trent

A180

HOLDERNESS
& SPURN
HEAD
30

M180

GRIMSBY **31**

A15

DONCASTER

A16

Don

M18

M18 A1(M)

Newark-on-
Trent

M1

Nottingham

GETTING AROUND

The area is served by the A1, the M1, the M62 and the A59. InterCity trains run to major cities such as York and Leeds, and there are train or coach links between many towns and hamlets. The Yorkshire Dales and North York Moors national parks are good for walkers and the keen cyclist can enjoy rides around Humberside and York.

0 kilometres 15

0 miles 10

KEY

	Motorway
	Major road
	Minor road
	Scenic route
	Scenic path
	River
	Viewpoint

James Herriot Country

THE NOVELS WRITTEN by the vet James Herriot were set in an area of Yorkshire of outstanding beauty. Herriot was based in the market town of Thirsk ("Darrowby") in the centre of the fertile farmlands of the Vale of York. To the west of Thirsk are the Yorkshire Dales with broad Wensleydale and the more rugged Swaledale, both typified by isolated stone barns and stone walls climbing the valley sides. To the east are the North York Moors with spectacular views, heather moorland, ancient abbeys and historic houses. The villages built in local stone add a charm of their own, too.

Alf Wight, who wrote under the pseudonym James Herriot

Market place, Thirsk

THIRSK

THE LARGE COBBLED MARKET PLACE in Thirsk is surrounded by numerous shops and fine houses and is typical of a number of North Yorkshire towns. Kirkgate leads off the Market Place to St Mary's Church, where Alf Wight ("Herriot") married Joan Danbury ("Helen") in 1941. The church itself dates back over 500 years and boasts a wagon roof. Kirkgate is also where you will find the World of James Herriot, housed in the author's former veterinary surgery. The surgery has been restored as it was in the 1930s, the period in which the books were set.

KILBURN

THE PICTURESQUE VILLAGE of Kilburn lies beneath the vast hill figure of Kilburn White Horse, a familiar sight to James Herriot when he visited the farms on his rounds. Robert Thompson of Kilburn, a customer of James Herriot, is noted world-wide for his hand-made oak furniture with its carved mouse trademark. The Mouse-man Visitor Centre in Kilburn displays some of his finest pieces and there is a chance to see one of the craftsmen demonstrating their skill, carving wood or finishing a piece with an adze, a traditional flat axe.

White Horse at Kilburn

Interior of Dale Countryside Museum, Hawes

HAWES

THE DALES COUNTRYSIDE MUSEUM at Hawes *(see p449)* in upper Wensleydale has a fascinating collection of agricultural artefacts that would have been used in James Herriot's day. Next to Gayle Beck is the Creamery where you can see Wensleydale cheese being made – and buy some to enjoy at home. Further down the valley is the picturesque village of Askrigg, with views over the full length of the dale. The village was used as the setting for Darrowby in the popular television series *All Creatures Great and Small*, which was adapted from Herriot's books.

THE MAN BEHIND JAMES HERRIOT

After veterinary college, Alf Wight, the writer of the Herriot stories, went to Thirsk to join Donald Sinclair in his practice. The rather insular local farmers believed in their own cures for animal ailments, often calling in the vet when all their own efforts had failed. It was these characters, his hard but rewarding working life and the spectacular scenery that Alf Wight combined into the stories that were to make fictional James Herriot the world's most famous vet. Alf Wight lived in and around Thirsk for 55 years until his death in 1995. He wrote about ten novels about his experiences as a vet, as well as books about the Yorkshire countryside.

VISITOR'S CHECKLIST

Thirsk Tourist Information Centre ℹ *14 Kirkgate, Thirsk (01845 522755).* ◯ *April to end of October.* **Northallerton Tourist Information Centre** ℹ *Applegarth, Northallerton (01609 776864).* ◯ *all year.* **World of James Herriot**, *famous surgery known as Skeldale House in Herriot books.* ◯ *daily, Mar to Oct: 10am–6pm; Nov to Feb: 10am–5pm.* ☎ *01845 524234,* FAX *01845 525333.*

FARNDALE

North York Moors around Farndale

THE RUGGED FARMS AND COUNTRYSIDE around Farndale *(see p459)* were used as the setting for the first film of Herriot's books, called *All Creatures Great and Small* (1974). Each spring, Farndale blooms with wild daffodils. The best displays of these flowers are all along the banks of the River Dove, where they grow wild. To see a spectacular view of some of the finest heather moorlands in England, follow the road between Pickering and Whitby and from Hutton le Hole to Castleton. The heather becomes a blaze of purple in August.

HELMSLEY

THE ATTRACTIVE SMALL TOWN of Helmsley was familiar to James Herriot – Helmsley Castle was popular with his children. To the southeast of the town is Nunnington Hall, which is owned by the National Trust and dates back to the 16th century. Helmsley is also the start of Cleveland Way Walk, one of the longest footpaths in the country, which links Helmsley and Filey. Only a short distance from Helmsley are the extensive ruins of Rievaulx Abbey set beside the River Rye and Byland Abbey lying under the Hambleton Hills, near Wass *(see p457).*

Helmsley Castle, Helmsley

SUTTON BANK

Footpath near Sutton Bank

THERE ARE EXTENSIVE VIEWS of the North York Moors from the top of the steep hill at Sutton Bank *(see p456)* and an indicator map pointing out the various places of interest. This was familiar walking country to James Herriot. The wooded hillside falls away to Lake Gormire sparkling like a jewel below. Beyond, the patchwork quilt of fields extend to the Pennines on the skyline. Near the large car-parking area is a North York Moors National Park Information Centre, which can supply information about places to visit in the surrounding area.

Yorkshire Dales National Park ●

THE YORKSHIRE DALES is a farming landscape, formed from three principle dales, Swaledale, Wharfedale and Wensleydale, and a number of small ones, such as Deepdale. Glaciation in the Ice Age helped carve out these steep-sided valleys, and this scenery contrasts with the high moorlands. However, 12 centuries of settlement have altered the landscape in the form of cottages, castles and villages which create a delightful environment for walking. A national park since 1954, the area provides recreation while serving local community needs.

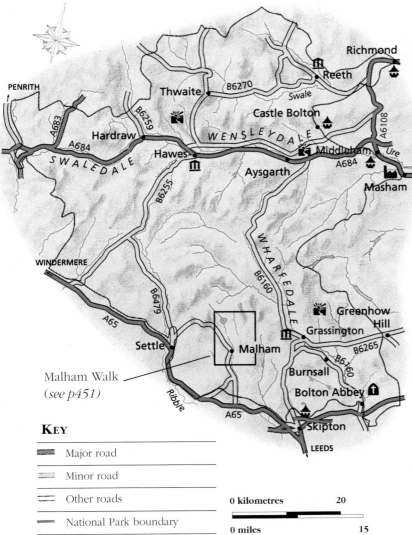

Malham Walk
(see p451)

KEY

▬▬	Major road
▭▭	Minor road
▬▬	Other roads
▬▬	National Park boundary

0 kilometres   20

0 miles   15

The green, rolling landscape of Deepdale, near Dent

Monk's Wynd – one of Richmond's narrow, winding streets

Exploring Swaledale

Swaledale's prosperity was founded largely on wool, and it is famous for its herd of sheep that graze on the wild higher slopes in the harshest weather. The fast-moving river Swale that gives the northernmost dale its name travels from bleak moorland down magnificent waterfalls into the richly wooded lower slopes, passing through the villages of Reeth, Thwaite and Richmond.

♠ Richmond Castle

Tower Street. ☎ *01748 822493.*
◻ *daily.* ● *25 Dec.* 🏷 ♿ *limited.*
Swaledale's main point of entry is the medieval market town of Richmond, which has the largest cobbled marketplace in England. Alan Rufus, the Norman 1st Earl of Richmond, began building the castle in 1071, and some of the masonry on the curtain walls probably dates from that time. It has a fine Norman keep, 30 m (100 ft) high with walls 3.3 m (11 ft) thick. An 11th-century arch leads into a courtyard containing Scolland's Hall (1080), one of England's oldest buildings.
   Richmond's marketplace was once the castle's outer bailey. Its quaint, narrow streets gave rise to the song, *The Lass of Richmond Hill* (1787), written by Leonard McNally for his wife, Frances L'Anson, who was brought up in Hill House, on Richmond Hill. Turner *(see*

p97) depicted the town many times. The Georgian Theatre (1788), which was restored in 1962, is the only one of its age still surviving.

⌂ Swaledale Folk Museum

Reeth Green. ☎ *01748 884059.* ◯ *Easter–Oct: daily.* ▨
Reeth, a town that became known as the centre of the lead-mining industry and helped bring prosperity to the region, houses this museum in a former Methodist Sunday school (1830). Included in it are mining and wool-making artefacts (wool from the hardy Swaledale sheep was another mainstay of the economy) and brass band memorabilia.

☆ Buttertubs

Near Thwaite, on the B6270 Hawes road, are a series of potholes that streams fall into. These became known as the Buttertubs when farmers going to market lowered their butter into the holes to keep it cool.

Buttertubs, near Thwaite

Exploring Wensleydale

The largest of the Yorkshire dales, Wensleydale is famous for its cheese and for James Herriot's books and television series, *All Creatures Great and Small (see pp446–7)*. It is easy walking country for anyone seeking an alternative to major moorland hikes.

⌂ Dales Countryside Museum

Station Yard, Hawes. ☎ *01969 667450.* ◯ *Easter–Oct daily.* ▨ ⚹
In a former railway goods warehouse in Hawes, capital of Upper Wensleydale, is a

Barrels at the Theakston Brewery

fascinating museum, filled with items from life and industry in the 18th- and 19th-century Upper Dales. This includes cheese- and butter-making equipment. Wensleydale cheese was created by monks at nearby Jervaulx Abbey. There is also a rope-making works a short walk away.

Hawes itself is the highest market town in England, at 259 m (850 ft) above sea level. It is a thriving centre where thousands of sheep and cattle are auctioned each summer.

☆ Hardraw Force

At the tiny village of Hardraw, nearby, is England's tallest single-drop waterfall, with no outcrops to interrupt its 29 m (96 ft) fall. It became famous in Victorian times when the daredevil Blondin walked across it on a tightrope. Today, you can walk right under this fine waterfall, against the rock face, and look through the stream without getting wet.

☆ Aysgarth Waterfalls

An old packhorse bridge gives a clear view of the point at which the previously placid River Ure suddenly begins to plunge in foaming torrents over wide limestone shelves. Turner painted the impressive lower falls in 1817.

⌂ Theakston Brewery

Masham. ☎ *01765 689057.* ◯ *Easter–Oct: daily; Nov: Wed, Sat, Sun.* ● *Dec–Mar.* ▨ ⚹ *limited.* ▨ ▯
The pretty village of Masham is the home of Theakston brewery, creator of the potent ale Old Peculier. The history of this local family brewery from its origin in 1827 is on

VISITORS' CHECKLIST

North Yorkshire. ⇄ *Skipton.*
ⓘ *Hebdon Road, Grassington (01756 752774).*

display in the visitors' centre. Masham village itself has an attractive square once used for sheep fairs, surrounded by 17th- and 18th-century houses. There is a medieval church.

⛫ Bolton Castle

Castle Bolton, nr Leyburn. ☎ *01969 623981.* ◯ *Mar–Nov: daily.* ▨ ▯
Situated in the village of Castle Bolton, this castle was built in 1379 by the 1st Lord Scrope, Chancellor of England, primarily for use as comfortable living quarters. It was used as a fortress from 1568 to 1569 when Mary, Queen of Scots *(see p55)* was held prisoner here by Elizabeth I *(see pp54–5)*, who feared rebellion. Three of the castle's four towers remain at their original height of 30 m (100 ft).

⛫ Middleham Castle

Middleham, nr Leyburn. ☎ *01969 623899.* ◯ *Apr–Oct: daily; Nov–Mar: Wed–Sun.* ● *24–26 Dec.* ▨ ⚹ ▯
Owned by Richard Neville, Earl of Warwick, it was built in 1170. The castle is better known as home to Richard III *(see p53)* when he was made Lord of the North. It was once one of the strongest fortresses in the north but became uninhabited during the 15th century, when many of its stones were used for nearby buildings. The keep provides a fine view of the landscape.

Remains of Middleham Castle, once residence of Richard III

Extensive ruins of Bolton Priory, dating from 1154

Exploring Wharfedale

This dale is characterized by gritstone moorland, contrasting with quiet market towns along meandering sections of river. Many consider Grassington a central point for exploring Wharfedale, but the showpiece villages of Burnsall, overlooked by a 506 m (1,661 ft) fell, and Buckden, near Buckden Pike (701 m; 2,302 ft), also make excellent bases.

The area contains the Three Peaks of Whernside (736 m; 2,416 ft), Ingleborough (724 m; 2,376 ft) and Pen-y-Ghent (694 m; 2,278 ft). They are known for their potholes and tough terrain, but this does not deter keen walkers from attempting to climb them all in one day. If you sign in at the Pen-y-Ghent café at Horton-in-Ribblesdale, and complete the 20 mile (32 km) course, reaching the summit of all three peaks in less than 12 hours, you can qualify for membership of the Three Peaks of Yorkshire Club.

🏛 Burnsall

St Wilfrid's, Burnsall. **(** 01756 720232. ◯ daily. &
Preserved in St Wilfrid's church graveyard are the original village stocks, gravestones from Viking times and a head-stone carved in memory of the Dawson family by sculptor Eric Gill (1882–1940). The village, centred around a century-old five-arched bridge, also hosts Britain's oldest fell race every August.

🏛 Upper Wharfedale Museum

The Square, Grassington.
◯ Apr–Sep: daily (pm); Oct–Mar: Sat & Sun (pm). 🖼 & limited.
This folk museum is set in two 18th-century lead miners' cottages. Its exhibits illustrate the domestic and working history of the area, including farming and lead mining.

🏛 Bolton Priory

Bolton Abbey, nr Skipton. **(** 01756 710238. ◯ daily. &
One of the most beautiful areas of Wharfedale is around the village of Bolton Abbey, set in an estate owned by the Dukes of Devonshire. While preserving its astounding beauty, its managers have incorporated over 30 miles (46 km) of foot-paths, many suitable for the disabled and young families.

The ruins of Bolton Priory, established by Augustinian canons in 1154 on the site of a Saxon manor, are extensive. They include a church, chapter house, cloister and prior's lodging. These all demonstrate the wealth accumulated by the canons from the sale of wool from their flocks of sheep. The priory nave is still used as a parish church. Another attraction of the estate is the "Strid", a point where the River Wharfe surges spectacularly through a gorge, foaming yellow and gouging holes out of the rocks.

🏚 Stump Cross Caverns

Greenhow, Pateley Bridge. **(** 01756 752780 or 01423 711042. ◯ daily (ring in winter as may be closed due to bad weather). ● 25 Dec. 🖼 🍴 🚻
These caves were formed over a period of half a million years: trickles of underground water formed intertwining passages and carved them into fantastic shapes and sizes. Sealed off in the last Ice Age, the caves were only discovered in the 1850s when lead miners sank a mine shaft into the caverns.

⚓ Skipton Castle

High St. **(** 01756 792442. ◯ daily (Sun: pm). ● 25 Dec. 🖼 🚻 🚻
Situated outside the national park boundary, the market town of Skipton is still one of the largest auctioning and stockraising centres in the north. Its 11th-century castle was almost entirely rebuilt by Robert de Clifford in the 14th century. Beautiful Conduit Court was added by Henry, Lord Clifford in Henry VIII's reign. Even more striking is the central yew tree, which Lady Anne Clifford planted in 1659 to mark restoration work to the castle after Civil War damage.

Conduit Court (1495) and yew tree at Skipton Castle

Malham Walk ②

THE MALHAM AREA, shaped by glacial erosion 10,000 years ago, has one of Great Britain's most dramatic limestone landscapes. The walk from Malham village can take over four hours if you pause to enjoy the viewpoints and take a detour to Gordale Scar. Those who are short of time tend to go only as far as Malham Cove. This vast natural amphitheatre, formed by a huge geological tear, is like a giant boot-heel mark in the landscape. Above lie the deep crevices of Malham Lings, where rare flora such as hart's-tongue flourishes. Unusual plants grow in the lime-rich Malham Tarn, said to have provided inspiration for Charles Kingsley's *The Water Babies* (1863). Coot and mallard visit the tarn in summer and tufted duck in winter.

Sandpiper at Malham Tarn

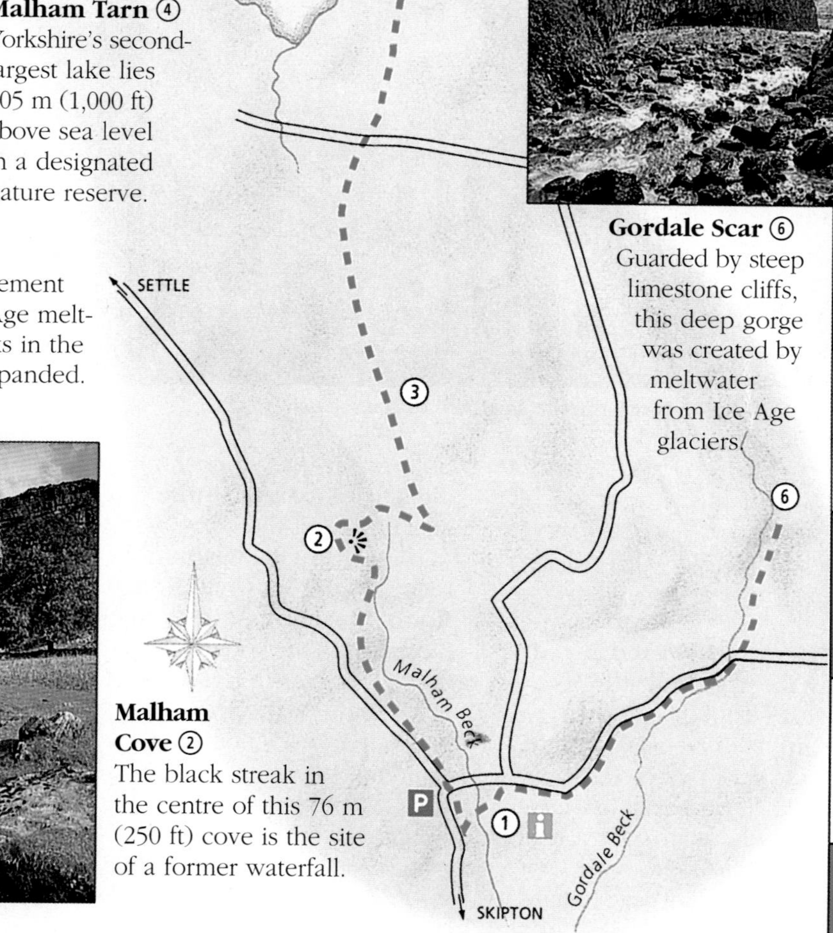

Where the path meets the road ⑤
From here, you can catch a bus back to Malham village.

Malham Tarn House

Malham Tarn ④
Yorkshire's second-largest lake lies 305 m (1,000 ft) above sea level in a designated nature reserve.

Malham Lings ③
This fine limestone pavement was formed when Ice Age meltwater seeped into cracks in the rock, then froze and expanded.

Gordale Scar ⑥
Guarded by steep limestone cliffs, this deep gorge was created by meltwater from Ice Age glaciers.

Malham Cove ②
The black streak in the centre of this 76 m (250 ft) cove is the site of a former waterfall.

SETTLE

SKIPTON

Malham Beck

Gordale Beck

Malham ①
An attractive riverside village, it has an information centre with details of drives and walks.

KEY

- – Walk route
- Minor road
- Viewpoint
- P Parking
- i Tourist information
- Toilets

0 kilometres 1

0 miles ½

TIPS FOR WALKERS

Starting point: *Malham.*
Getting there: *Leave M65 at Junction 14 and take A56 to Skipton, then follow signs to Malham which is off A65.*
Length: *7 miles (11 km).*
Difficulty: *Malham Cove is steep but the Tarn area is flatter.*

A 1920s poster advertising the spa town of Harrogate

Harrogate ❸

North Yorkshire. 👥 69,000. ⇄ 🚌
ℹ️ *Assembly Rooms, Crescent Rd
(01423 537300).* 🛒 *Mon–Sat.*

BETWEEN 1880 and World
War I, Harrogate was the
north's leading spa town, with
nearly 90 medicinal springs.
It was ideal for aristocrats who,
after a tiring London season,
were able to stop for a health
cure before journeying on to
grouse-shooting in Scotland.

Today, Harrogate's main
attractions are its spa town
atmosphere, fine architecture,
public gardens and its conven-
ience as a centre for visiting
North Yorkshire and the Dales.

The naturally welling spa
waters may not currently be
in use, but you can still go
for a Turkish bath in one of
the country's most attractive
steam rooms. The entrance at
the side of the Royal Assembly
Rooms (1897) is unassuming,
but once inside, the century-
old **Turkish Sauna Suite** is a
visual feast of tiled Victoriana.

The town's spa history is
recorded in the **Royal Pump
Room Museum**. At the turn of
the century, the waters were
thought to be rich in iron early
in the day. So, between 7am
and 9am the 1842 octagonal
building would have been
filled with rich and fashionable
people drinking glasses of
water as part of their rest cure.
Poorer people could take
water from the pump outside,
which still works. Today you
can sample the waters and
enjoy the museum's exhibits,
which include an 1874 Penny
Farthing bicycle.

Harrogate is also known for
the rainbow-coloured flower-
beds in **The Stray**, a common
space to the south of the town
centre, and for the ornamental
Harlow Car Gardens, owned
by the Northern Horticultural
Society. In spring and autumn,
(see p68) it holds two flower
festivals. Visitors can enjoy
the delicious cakes at **Betty's
Café Tea Rooms**.

🏛 **Turkish Sauna Suite**
Assembly Rooms, Crescent Rd. 📞
01423 556746. ◯ *Men: Mon, Wed
& Fri: (pm); Tue: (am); Sat. Women:
Mon (am); Tue & Thu: (pm); Fri (am);
Sun. Mixed (couples only in costume):
Fri (eve); Sun (eve).* ● *public hols.* 🖼

🏛 **Royal Pump Room
Museum**
Crown Pl. 📞 *01423 556188.* ◯ *daily.*
● *24–26 Dec, 1 Jan.* 🖼 ♿ 🏠

🏛 **Betty's Café Tea Rooms**
1 Parliament St. 📞 *01423 502746.*
◯ *daily.* ● *25–26 Dec, 1 Jan.*

🍁 **Harlow Car Gardens**
Crag Lane. 📞 *01423 565418.*
◯ *daily.* 🖼 ♿

Knaresborough ❹

North Yorkshire. 👥 *14,000.*
🚌 *from Harrogate.* ℹ️ *9 Castle
Courtyard, Market Place (01423
866886).* 🛒 *Wed.*

PERCHED PRECIPITOUSLY above
the River Nidd is one
of England's oldest towns,
mentioned in the Domesday
Book of 1086 *(see p52)*. Its
historic streets – which link the
church, John of Gaunt's ruined
castle, and the market place
with the river – are now lined
with fine 18th-century houses.

Nearby is **Mother Shipton's
Cave**, reputedly England's
oldest tourist attraction. It first
went on show in 1630 as the
birthplace of Ursula Sontheil,
a famous local prophetess.
Today, people can view the

**Mother Shipton's cave, with
objects encased in limestone**

Tudor gatehouse and moat at Markenfield Hall

effect the well near her cave has on objects hung below the dripping surface. Almost any item, from umbrellas to soft toys, will become encased in limestone within a few weeks.

🏛 Mother Shipton's Cave
Prophesy House, High Bridge.
📞 01423 864600. ☐ daily. ◯ 25 Dec. ♿ ♿ limited. 🖼 🖥 🏠

Ripley ❺

North Yorkshire. 👥 150. 🚌 from Harrogate or Ripon.

SINCE THE 1320s, when the first generation of the Ingilby family lived in an early incarnation of **Ripley Castle**, the village has been made up almost exclusively of castle employees. The influence of one 19th-century Ingilby had the most visual impact. In the 1820s, Sir William Amcotts Ingilby was so entranced by a village in Alsace Lorraine that he created a similar one in French Gothic style, complete with an *Hotel de Ville*. Present-day Ripley has a cobbled market square, and quaint cottages line the streets. The churchyard has a medieval cross with niches for kneeling at the base.

Ripley Castle, with its 15th-century gatehouse, was where Oliver Cromwell *(see p56)* stayed following the Battle of Marston Moor. The 28th generation of Ingilbys live here, and it is open for tours. The attractive grounds contain two lakes and a deer park, as well as more formal gardens.

⚓ Ripley Castle
Ripley. 📞 01423 770152. ☐ Apr–Jun, Sep, Oct: Thu–Sun; Jul–Aug: daily; Nov, Dec: Tue, Thu, Sat, Sun.
◯ 25 Dec. ♿ ♿ 🖼 🖥 🏠

Markenfield Hall ❻

Nr Markenfield, North Yorkshire.
ℹ 01765 604625. 🚌 from Harrogate or Ripon. ◯ until further notice.

A MOATED MANOR house dating from the 14th century, Markenfield Hall is not signposted and open only in the summer. To find it you need to drive 3 miles (5 km) south of Ripon, and turn up a farm track marked with a bridleway sign (Hell Wath Lane). On one side of the drawbridge, between the moat and the manor walls, is the farmer's vegetable patch. Once inside the L-shaped house, note the great banqueting hall, chapel and kitchen fireplace.

The Markenfields were one of the powerful northern families to oppose Henry VIII and the Dissolution of the Monasteries *(see p54)*. It was from their manor house that an army set off in 1569 in an unsuccessful attempt to remove Elizabeth I from the throne and replace her with the Catholic Mary, Queen of Scots.

Fountains Abbey ❼

See pp454–5.

Ripon ❽

North Yorkshire. 👥 14,000. 🚌 from Harrogate. ℹ Minster Rd (01765 604625). 🛒 Thu.

RIPON, A CHARMING small city, is best known for the cathedral and "the watch", which has been announced since the Middle Ages by the Wakeman. In return for protecting Ripon citizens, he would charge an annual toll of two pence per household. Today, a man still blows a horn in the Market Square each evening at 9pm, and every Thursday a handbell is rung to open the market.

The **Cathedral of St Peter and St Wilfrid** is built above a 7th-century Saxon crypt. At less than 3 m (10 ft) high and just over 2 m (7 ft) wide, it is held to be the oldest complete crypt in England. The cathedral is known for its collection of misericords *(see p391)*, which include both pagan and Old Testament examples. The architectural historian Sir Nikolaus Pevsner (1902–83) considered the cathedral's West Front the finest in England.

Ripon's **Prison and Police Museum**, housed in the 1686 "House of Correction", looks at the history of the police and, in its first floor cells, the conditions in Victorian prisons.

🏛 Prison and Police Museum
St Marygate. 📞 01765 690799.
☐ Apr–Jun, Sep, Oct: daily (pm); Jul, Aug: daily; public hols. ♿ ♿ limited.

Ripon's Wakeman, blowing his horn in the Market Square

Fountains Abbey ⓐ

Nestling in the wooded valley of the River Skell are the extensive sandstone ruins of Fountains Abbey and the outstanding water garden of Studley Royal. Fountains Abbey was founded by Benedictine monks in 1132 and taken over by Cistercians three years later. By the mid-12th century it had become the wealthiest abbey in Britain, though it fell into ruin during the Dissolution *(see p54)*. In 1720, John Aislabie, the MP for Ripon and Chancellor of the Exchequer, developed the land and forest of the abbey ruins. He began work, continued by his son William, on the famous water garden, the statuary and Classical temples in the grounds. This makes a dramatic contrast to the simplicity of the abbey.

Fountains Hall

Built by Sir Stephen Proctor around 1611, with stones from the abbey ruins, its design is attributed to architect Robert Smythson. It included a great hall with a minstrels' gallery and an entrance flanked by Classical columns.

The Abbey

The abbey buildings were designed to reflect the Cistercians' desire for simplicity and austerity. The abbey frequently dispensed charity to the poor and the sick, as well as travellers.

The Chapel of Nine Altars *at the east end of the church was built from 1203 to 1247. It is ornate, compared to the rest of the abbey, with an 18 m (60 ft) high window complemented by another at the western end of the nave.*

Chapter house

Cloister

Cellarium (storehouse)

Kitchen

Abbot's house

Monks' infirmary hall

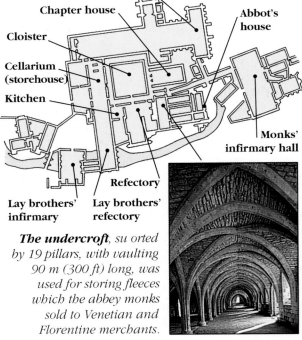

Lay brothers' infirmary

Lay brothers' refectory

Refectory

The undercroft, *su orted by 19 pillars, with vaulting 90 m (300 ft) long, was used for storing fleeces which the abbey monks sold to Venetian and Florentine merchants.*

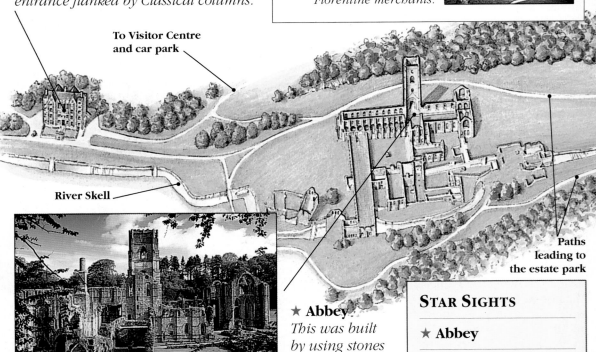

To Visitor Centre and car park

River Skell

Paths leading to the estate park

★ **Abbey**
This was built by using stones taken from the Skell valley.

Star Sights

★ **Abbey**

★ **Temple of Piety**

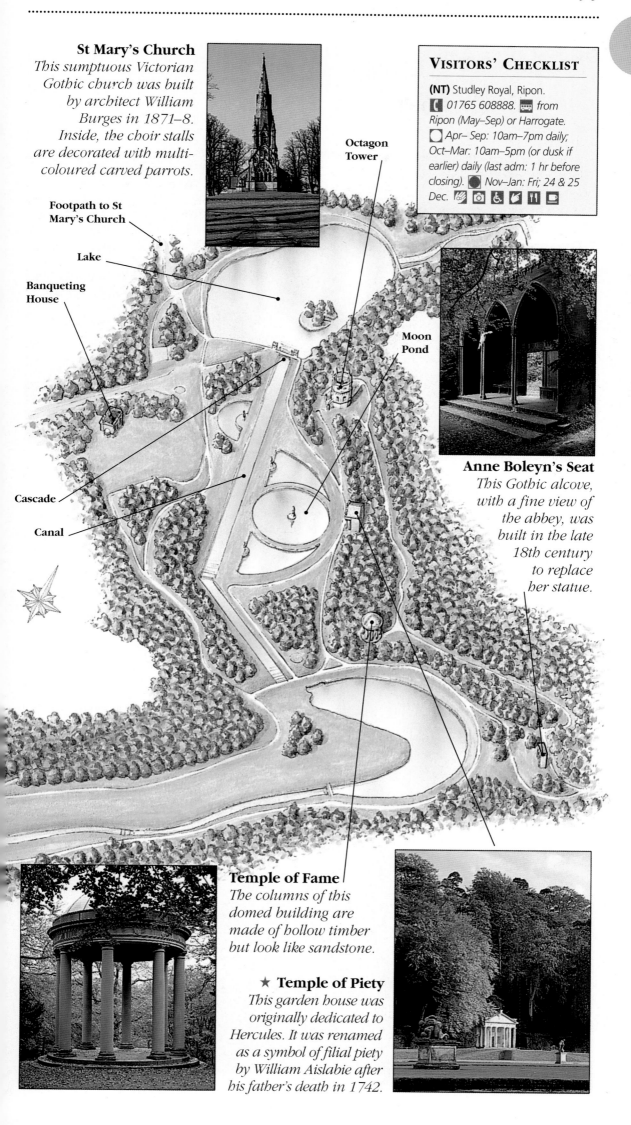

St Mary's Church

This sumptuous Victorian Gothic church was built by architect William Burges in 1871–8. Inside, the choir stalls are decorated with multi-coloured carved parrots.

Footpath to St Mary's Church

Lake

Banqueting House

Octagon Tower

Moon Pond

Cascade

Canal

VISITORS' CHECKLIST

(NT) Studley Royal, Ripon.
01765 608888. from Ripon (May–Sep) or Harrogate.
Apr– Sep: 10am–7pm daily; Oct–Mar: 10am–5pm (or dusk if earlier) daily (last adm: 1 hr before closing). Nov–Jan: Fri; 24 & 25 Dec.

Anne Boleyn's Seat

This Gothic alcove, with a fine view of the abbey, was built in the late 18th century to replace her statue.

Temple of Fame

The columns of this domed building are made of hollow timber but look like sandstone.

★ Temple of Piety

This garden house was originally dedicated to Hercules. It was renamed as a symbol of filial piety by William Aislabie after his father's death in 1742.

The 19th-century white horse, seen on one of the walks around Sutton Bank

Sutton Bank ❾

North Yorkshire. 🚆 *Thirsk.* ℹ️ *Sutton Bank (01845 597426).*

NOTORIOUS AMONG motorists for its 1 in 4 gradient, which climbs for about 107 m (350 ft), Sutton Bank itself is well known for its panoramic views. On a clear day you can see from the Vale of York to the Peak District *(see pp388–9).* William and his sister Dorothy Wordsworth stopped here to admire the vista in 1802, on their way to visit his future wife, Mary Hutchinson, at Brompton. Apart from Sutton Bank, where you can walk round the white horse, the area is less wild than the coastal side, and suitable for children.

Byland Abbey ❿

Coxwold, York. 📞 *01347 868614.* 🚌 *from York or Helmsley.* 🚆 *Thirsk.* ⭕ *Apr–Oct: daily.* ⚫ *Nov–Mar.* 📷 ♿ *limited.*

THIS CISTERCIAN monastery was founded in 1177 by monks from Furness Abbey in Cumbria. It featured what was then the largest church in Britain, 100 m (328 ft) long and 41 m (135 ft) wide across the transepts. The layout of the entire monastery, including extensive cloisters and the west front of the church, is still visible today, as is the green and yellow glazed tile floor. Fine workmanship is shown in carved stone details and in the carvings of the capitals, kept in the small museum.

In 1322 the Battle of Byland was fought nearby, and King Edward II *(see p44)* narrowly escaped capture when the invading Scottish army learned that he was dining with the Abbot. In his hurry to escape, the king had to leave many treasures behind, which were looted by the invading soldiers.

Coxwold ⓫

North Yorkshire. 👥 *160.* ℹ️ *23 Kirkgate, Thirsk (01845 522755).*

SITUATED JUST inside the bounds of the North York Moors National Park *(see p459),* this charming village nestles at the foot of the Howardian Hills. Its pretty houses are built from local stone, and the 15th-century church has some fine Georgian box pews and an impressive

Shandy Hall, home of author Laurence Sterne, now a museum

octagonal tower. But Coxwold is best known as the home of the author Laurence Sterne (1713–68), whose writings include *Tristram Shandy* and *A Sentimental Journey*.

Sterne moved here in 1760 as the church curate. He rented a rambling house that he named **Shandy Hall** after a Yorkshire expression meaning eccentric. Originally built as a timber-framed, open-halled house in the 15th century, it was modernized in the 17th century and Sterne later added a façade. His grave lies beside the porch at Coxwold's church.

The miniature Queen Anne drawing room at Nunnington Hall

⚜ Shandy Hall

Coxwold. 📞 *01347 868465.*
◯ *May–Sep: Wed & Sun (pm).* 🏷
🚻 *limited.* **Gardens** ◯ *May–Sep: Sun–Fri.* 📷

Nunnington Hall ⑫

(NT) Nunnington, York. 📞 *01439 748283.* ☞ *Malton, then bus or taxi.* ◯ *Apr–May, Sep–Oct: Wed–Sun (pm); Jun–Aug: Tue–Sun, public hols (pm).* 🏷 🚻 *ground floor* 📺 📷

SET IN ALLURING surroundings, this 17th-century manor house is a combination of architectural styles, including features from the Elizabethan and Stuart periods. Both inside and outside, a notable architectural feature is the use of the broken pediment (the upper arch is left unjoined).

Nunnington Hall was a family home until 1952, when Mrs Ronald Fife donated it to the National Trust. A striking feature is the panelling in the Oak Hall. Formerly painted, it extends over the three-arched screen to the Great Staircase. Nunnington's collection of 22 miniature furnished period rooms is popular with visitors.

A mid-16th-century tenant Dr Robert Huickes, physician to Henry VIII *(see p54–5)*, is best known for advising Elizabeth I that she should not, at the age of 32, consider having any children.

Helmsley ⑬

North Yorkshire. 🏘 *2,000.* 🚌 *from Malton.* ℹ *Town Hall, Market Place (01439 770173).* 🛒 *Fri.*

THIS PRETTY MARKET TOWN is noted for its **castle**, now an imposing ruin. Built from 1186 to 1227, its main function and supreme strength as a fortress is illustrated by the remaining keep, tower and curtain walls. The original D-shaped keep had one part blasted away in the Civil War *(see p56)*, but remains the dominant feature. The castle was so impregnable that there were few attempts to force entry. However, in 1644, after holding out for a three-month seige against Sir Thomas Fairfax, the Parliamentary general, the castle was finally taken and dismantled.

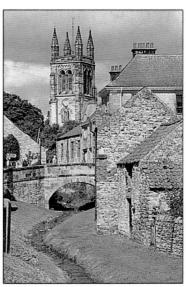
Helmsley church tower

Rievaulx Abbey ⑭

Nr Helmsley, North Yorkshire. 📞 *01439 798228.* ☞ *Thirsk, then bus or taxi.* ◯ *daily.* ⬤ *24–26 Dec.* 🏷 🚻 *limited.* 📺 📷

RIEVAULX IS PERHAPS the finest abbey in the area, partly due to its dramatic setting in the steep wooded valley of the River Rye and partly to its extensive remains. It is almost entirely surrounded by steep banks that form natural barriers from the outside world. Monks of the French Cistercian order from Clairvaux founded this, their first major monastery in Britain, in 1132. The main buildings, which include the Cistercian nave, were finished before 1200. The layout of the chapel, kitchens and infirmary give an idea of monastic life.

Rievaulx Abbey, painted by Thomas Girtin (1775–1802)

Mount Grace Priory ruins, with farm and mansion in foreground

Mount Grace Priory ⓯

(NT) Northallerton, North Yorkshire. 📞 01609 883494. 🚉 Northallerton then bus. ⭕ Apr–Oct: daily; Nov–Mar: Wed–Sun. ⬤ 24–26 Dec, 1 Jan. 🅿️ ♿ grounds & shop only. 🔳

FOUNDED BY Thomas Holland, Duke of Surrey, and in use from 1398 until 1539, this is the best-preserved Carthusian or charterhouse monastery *(see pp400–1)* in England. The monks, just 20 of them at the beginning, took a vow of silence and lived in solitary cells, each with his own garden and an angled hatch so that he would not even see the person serving his food. They only met at matins, vespers and feast-day services. Attempts at escape by those who could not endure the rigour of the rules were punished by imprisonment.

The ruins of the priory include the former prison, gatehouse and outer court, barns, guesthouses, cells and the church. The 14th-century church, the best-preserved section of the site, is particularly small, as it was only rarely used by the community. A cell has been reconstructed to give an impression of monastic life.

Hutton-le-Hole ⓰

North Yorkshire. 👥 400. 🚉 Malton then bus. ℹ️ Eastgate Car Park (01751 473791).

THIS PICTURESQUE VILLAGE is characterized by a spacious green, grazed by roaming sheep, and surrounded by houses, an inn and shops. Lengths of white wood, replacing stone bridges, span the moorland stream. Its cottages, some with date panels over the doors, are made from limestone, with red pantiled roofs. In the village centre is the excellent **Ryedale Folk Museum**,

Wheelwright's workshop at Ryedale Folk Museum

which records the lifestyle of an agricultural community by means of Romano-British artefacts and reconstructed buildings.

🏛 **Ryedale Folk Museum**
Hutton-le-Hole. 📞 01751 417367. ⭕ mid-Mar–mid-Nov: daily. 🅿️ ♿

North York Moors Tour ⓱

See p459.

North York Moors Railway ⓲

Pickering & Grosmont, North Yorkshire. 📞 01947 895359. ⭕ Apr–Oct: daily; some weekends in Nov & Dec. 🅿️ ♿

DESIGNED in 1831 by George Stephenson as a route along the Esk Valley linking Pickering and Whitby *(see p460)*, this railway was considered an engineering miracle. Due to budget constraints, Stephenson was not able to build a tunnel, so had to lay the route down the mile-long (1.5 km) incline between Beck Hole and Goathland. The area around Fen Bog had to be stabilized using timber, heather, brushwood and fleeces so that a causeway could be built over it. A horse was used to pull a coach along the track at 10 miles (16 km) per hour. After horse-power came steam, and for almost 130 years the railway linked Whitby to the rest of the country. In the early 1960s, the line was declared un-economic and closed. But in 1967, a group of locals began a campaign to relaunch the line, and in 1973 it was officially reopened by the Duchess of Kent. Today, the 18 mile (29 km) line runs from Pickering via Levisham, Newtondale Halt and Goathland before stopping at Grosmont, through the scenic heart of the North York Moors.

North York Moors Tour ⑰

THIS TOUR PASSES THROUGH part of the area between Cleveland, the Vale of York and the Vale of Pickering known as the North York Moors National Park. The landscape consists of bleakly beautiful moors interspersed with lush green valleys. Farming is the main source of income, and until the advent of coal, the communities' local source of fuel was turf. In the 19th century, the geology of the area created extractive industries which included ironstone, lime, coal and building stone.

Mallyan Spout ⑦
A footpath leads to this waterfall from Goathland.

Goathland ⑧
A centre for forest and moorland walks, it has 19th-century houses and good accommodation.

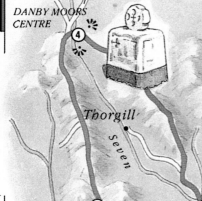

Farndale ③
During springtime, this area is famous for the beauty and profusion of its daffodils.

"Fat Betty" White Cross ④
In medieval times, coins would have been left under this cross for poor travellers.

Rosedale ⑤
This valley was a mining centre from 1856; remains of the iron kilns can still be seen.

Hutton-le-Hole ②
This lovely village has an excellent museum with displays on local crafts and customs.

Wade's Causeway ⑥
This road was built by the Roman army around AD 80, from sandstone slabs laid over a ridge of gravel and sand. It is said that a giant called Wade built the road as a footpath for his wife.

TIPS FOR DRIVERS

Tour length: 28 miles (45 km).
Stopping-off points: The Forge Tea Shop at Hutton-le-Hole is open daily from Mar–Oct and at weekends during Nov–Feb. The Mallyan Spout inn at Goathland is very popular with walkers.

0 kilometres 2

0 miles 2

Lastingham ①
Lastingham's church, dating from 1078, has a Norman crypt with ancient stone carving. Under the crypt lies St Cedd, founder of the original Saxon monastery in 654.

KEY

Tour route

Other roads

Viewpoint

Whitby ⑲

Jet comb (c.1870)

WHITBY'S KNOWN HISTORY dates back to the 7th century, when a Saxon monastery was founded on the site of today's famous 13th-century abbey ruins. In the 18th and early 19th centuries it became an industrial port and shipbuilding town, as well as a whaling centre. In the Victorian era, the red-roofed cottages at the foot of the east cliff were filled with workshops crafting jet into jewellery and ornaments. Today, the tourist shops that have replaced them sell antique-crafted examples of the distinctive black gem.

VISITORS' CHECKLIST

North Yorkshire. 🏘 13,500. ✈ Teeside, 50 miles (80 km) NW Whitby. ⇌ Station Sq. ℹ Langborne Rd (01947 602674). 🖴 Tue, Sat. 🎭 Whitby Festival: Jun; Angling Festival: Jul; Lifeboat Day: 29 Jul; Folk Week: 17–23 Aug; Whitby Regatta: Aug; Captain Cook Festival: Oct.

Exploring Whitby

Whitby is divided into two by the estuary of the River Esk. The Old Town, with its pretty cobbled streets and pastel-hued houses, huddles round the harbour. High above it is St Mary's Church with a wood interior reputedly fitted by ships' carpenters. The ruins of the 13th-century Whitby Abbey, nearby, are still used as a landmark by mariners. From them you get a fine view over the still-busy harbour, strewn with colourful nets. A pleasant place for a stroll, the harbour is overlooked by an imposing bronze clifftop statue of the explorer Captain James Cook (1728–79), who was apprenticed as a teenager to a Whitby shipping firm.

Lobster pots lining the quayside of Whitby's quaint harbour

Medieval arches above the nave of Whitby Abbey

🏛 Whitby Abbey

Abbey Lane. 📞 01947 603568. ☐ daily. ● 24–26 Dec. 🎫 🎁
The monastery that Abbess Hilda founded in 657 for men and women was sacked by Vikings in 870. At the end of the 11th century it was rebuilt as a Benedictine Abbey. The present ruins date mainly from 13th-century rebuilding.

⛪ St Mary's Parish Church

East Cliff. 📞 01947 603421. ☐ daily.
Stuart and Georgian alterations to this Norman church have left a mixture of twisted wood columns and maze-like 18th-century box pews. The 1778 triple-decker pulpit has rather avant-garde decor – ear-trumpets used by a Victorian rector's deaf wife.

🏛 Captain Cook Memorial Museum

Grape Lane. 📞 01947 601900. ☐ Mar: Sat & Sun; Apr–Oct: daily. 🎫
The young James Cook slept in the attic of this 17th-century harbourside house when he was apprenticed nearby. The museum has displays of period furniture in the style described in Cook's inventories and also watercolours by artists who travelled on his voyages.

🏛 Whitby Museum and Pannett Art Gallery

Pannett Park. 📞 01947 602908. ☐ May–Sep: daily; Oct– Apr: Tue–Sun. ● Sun: am; 24 Dec–2 Jan. 🎫 museum. 🚻 limited. 🎁
The Pannett park grounds, museum and gallery were a gift of Whitby solicitor, Robert Pannett (1834–1920), to house his art collection. Among the museum's treasures are fine collections of objects illustrating local history, such as jet jewellery, fossils, model ships and Captain Cook artefacts.

🏛 Museum of Victorian Whitby

Sandgate. 📞 01947 601221. ☐ daily. ● 25 Dec. 🎫 🎁
Among the exhibits on Victorian life in Whitby are the animated wheel-house of a whaling ship and a unique collection of miniature room settings.

⛪ Caedmon's Cross

East Cliff. 📞 01947 603421.
On the path side of the abbey's clifftop graveyard is the cross of Caedmon, an illiterate labourer who worked at the abbey in the 7th century. He had a vision that inspired him to compose cantos of Anglo-Saxon religious verse still sung today.

Cross of Caedmon (1898)

Robin Hood's Bay ⑳

North Yorkshire. 🏠 *1,400.* ≈ 🚌
Whitby. ℹ️ *Langbourne Rd, Whitby
(01947 602674).*

LEGEND HAS IT that Robin
Hood (*see p386*) kept his
boats here in case he needed
to make a quick getaway. The
village has a history as a smugglers' haven, and many houses
have ingenious hiding places
for contraband beneath the
floor and behind the walls. The
cobbled main street is so steep
that visitors need to leave
their vehicles in the car park.
In the village centre, attractive,
narrow streets full of colourwashed stone cottages huddle
around a quaint quay. There
is a rocky beach with rock
pools for children to play in.
At low tide, the pleasant walk
south to Boggle Hole takes
15 minutes, but you need to
keep an eye on the tides.

**Cobbled alley in the Bay Town
area of Robin Hood's Bay**

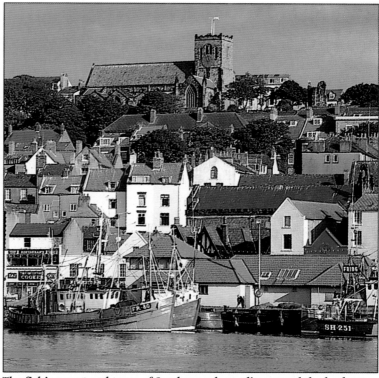

The fishing port and town of Scarborough nestling round the harbour

Scarborough ㉑

North Yorkshire. 🏠 *54,000.* ≈ 🚌
ℹ️ *Pavilion House, Valley Bridge Rd
(01723 373333).* 🛒 *Mon–Sat.*

THE HISTORY OF Scarborough
as a resort can be traced
back to 1626, when it became
known as a spa. In the Industrial Revolution (*see pp398–9*)
it was nicknamed "the Queen
of the Watering Places", but
the post-World War II trend
for holidays abroad has meant
fewer visitors. The town has
two separate beaches, and the
South Bay amusement arcades
contrast with the quieter atmosphere of North Bay. The

playwright Alan Ayckbourn
premiers his work at the
Joseph Rowntree theatre, and
Anne Brontë (*see p478*) is
buried in St Mary's Church.
   Bronze and Iron Age relics
have been found on the site
of **Scarborough Castle**, and
Wood End Museum exhibits
local geology and history. The
Rotunda (1828–9) was one of
Britain's first purpose-built
museums. Works by local
Victorian artist Atkinson
Grimshaw (1836–93) hang in
Scarborough Art Gallery.
The **Sea-Life Centre**, as well
as the more usual exhibits has
baby seahorses.

🏰 **Scarborough Castle**
Castle Rd. ☎️ *01723 372451.*
⭕ *Apr–Oct daily; Nov–Mar:
Wed–Sun.* ● *24–26 Dec.* 📷 ♿ 🏛
🏛 **Wood End Museum**
The Crescent. ☎️ *01723 367326.*
⭕ *May–mid-Oct: Tue–Sun; mid-
Oct–Apr: Wed, Sat, Sun & public hols.*
● *25, 26 Dec, 1 Jan.* 📷 🏛
🏛 **Rotunda Museum**
Vernon Rd. ☎️ *01723 374839.*
⭕ *May–mid-Oct: Tue–Sun; mid-
Oct–Apr: Tue, Sat, Sun & public hols.*
● *25, 26 Dec, 1 Jan.* 📷 🏛
🏛 **Scarborough Art Gallery**
The Crescent. ☎️ *01723 374753.*
⭕ *May–mid-Oct: Tue–Sun; mid-
Oct–Apr: Thu, Fri, Sat & public hols.*
● *25, 26 Dec, 1 Jan.* 📷 💻 🏛
🐠 **Sea-Life Centre**
Scalby Mills Rd. ☎️ *01723 376125.*
⭕ *daily.* ● *25 Dec, 1 Jan.* 📷 ♿ 💻

THE GROWING POPULARITY OF SWIMMING

During the 18th century, sea-bathing came to be regarded
as a healthy pastime, and from 1735 onwards men and
women, on separate stretches of the
coast, could be taken out into the
sea in bathing huts, or "machines".
In the 18th century, bathing was
segregated although nudity was
permitted. The Victorians brought
in fully clothed bathing, and
19th-century workers from
Britain's industrial heartlands
used the new steam trains to
visit the coast for their holidays. At this time, British
seaside resorts such as
Blackpool (*see p431*) and
Scarborough expanded to
meet the new demand.

A Victorian bathing hut on wheels

Castle Howard ㉒

Pillar detail in the Great Hall, carved by Samuel Carpenter

STILL OWNED and lived in by the Howard family, Castle Howard was created by Charles, 3rd Earl of Carlisle. When he came to his title in 1692, he commissioned Sir John Vanbrugh, a man of dramatic ideas but with no previous architectural experience, to design a palace for him. Vanbrugh's grand designs of 1699 were put into practice by architect Nicholas Hawksmoor *(see p28)* and the main body of the house was completed by 1712. The West Wing was built in 1753–9, using a design by Thomas Robinson, son-in-law of the 3rd Earl. Castle Howard was used as the location for the television version of Evelyn Waugh's novel *Brideshead Revisited* (1945).

Temple of the Four Winds
Vanbrugh's last work, designed in 1724, has a dome and four Ionic porticoes. Situated in the grounds at the end of the terrace, it is typical of an 18th-century "landscape building".

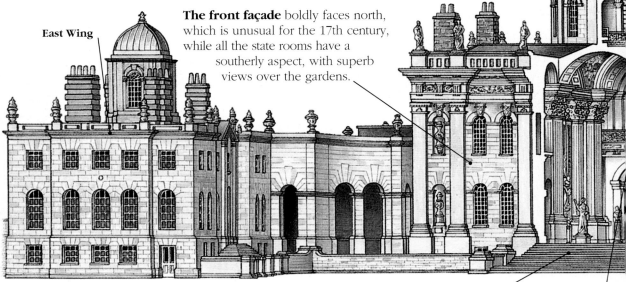

East Wing

The front façade boldly faces north, which is unusual for the 17th century, while all the state rooms have a southerly aspect, with superb views over the gardens.

North Front

★ Great Hall
Rising 20 m (66 ft), from its 515 sq m (5,500 sq ft) floor to the dome, the Great Hall has columns by Samuel Carpenter (1660–1713), wall paintings by Pellegrini and a circular gallery.

SIR JOHN VANBRUGH

Vanbrugh (1664–1726) trained as a soldier, but became better known as a playwright, architect and member of the Whig nobility. He collaborated with Hawksmoor over the design of Blenheim Palace, but his bold architectural vision, later greatly admired, was mocked by the establishment. He died while working on the garden buildings and grounds of Castle Howard.

Chapel Stained Glass

Admiral Edward Howard, Lord Lanerton, altered the chapel in 1870–75. The windows were designed by Edward Burne-Jones and William Morris.

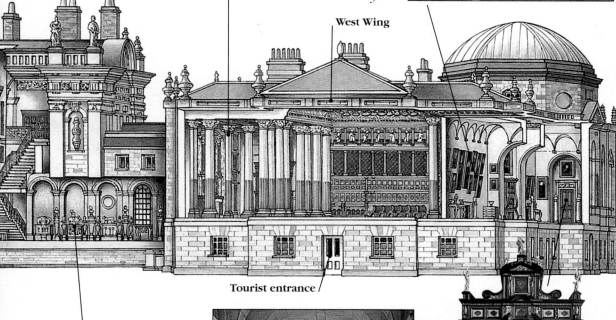

Bust of the 7th Earl

JH Foley sculpted this head and shoulders portrait, which stands at the top of the Grand Staircase in the West Wing, in 1870.

★ Long Gallery

The Howard lineage is illustrated here by a large number of portraits, including works by Lely and Van Dyck.

West Wing

Tourist entrance

Antique Passage

Antiquities collected in the 18th and 19th centuries by the various earls of Carlisle are on display here. The plethora of mythical figures and gods reflects contemporary interest in Classical civilizations.

Museum Room

Furniture here includes Regency chairs, Persian rugs and this 17th-century cabinet.

STAR SIGHTS

★ Great Hall

★ Long Gallery

Eden Camp 23

Malton, North Yorkshire. 📞 *01653 697777.* 🚉 *Malton then taxi.* ⭕ *mid-Jan–mid Feb: Mon–Fri; mid-Feb–Dec: daily.* ● *24 Dec–mid-Jan.* 📷 ♿ ▭

THIS IS AN UNUSUAL, award-winning theme museum which pays tribute to the British people during World War II. Italian and German prisoners of war were kept at Eden Camp between 1939 and 1948. Today, some original huts built by Italian prisoners in 1942 are used as a museum, with period tableaux and a soundtrack. Each hut adopts a theme to take the visitor through civilian life in war-time, from Churchill's radio announcement of the outbreak of hostilities to the coming of peace. Visitors, including schoolchildren and nostalgic veterans, can see the Doodle-bug V-1 bomb which crashed outside the Officers' Mess, take tea in the canteen or experi-ence a night in the Blitz. A tour can last for several hours.

British and American flags by the sign for Eden Camp

Wharram Percy 24

North Yorkshire. 📞 *0191 2611585 (English Heritage).* 🚉 *Malton, then taxi.* ⭕ *daily.*

THIS IS ONE of England's most important medieval village sites. Recent excavations have unearthed evidence of a 30-household community, with two manors, and the remains of a medieval church. There is also a millpond which has beautiful wild flowers in late spring. Wharram Percy is set in a pretty valley, sign-posted off the B1248 from Burdale, in the heart of the green, rolling Wolds. It is about 20 minutes' walk from the car park, and makes an ideal picnic stop.

Alabaster carving on the chimney-piece at Burton Agnes

Burton Agnes 25

Nr Driffield, East Yorkshire. 📞 *01262 490324.* 🚉 *Driffield, then bus.* ⭕ *Apr–Oct: daily.* 📷 ♿ *limited in house.*

OF ALL the grand houses in the triangle between Hull, York and Scarborough, Burton Agnes Hall is a firm favourite. This is partly because the attractive, red-brick Elizabethan mansion has such a homely atmosphere. One of the first portraits you see in the Small Hall is of Anne Griffith, whose father, Sir Henry, built the house. There is a monument to him in the local church.

Burton Agnes has remained in the hands of the original family and has changed little since it was built, between 1598 and 1610. You enter it by the turreted gatehouse, and the entrance hall has a fine Elizabethan alabaster chimney piece. The massive oak stair-case is an impressive example of Elizabethan woodcarving.

In the library is a collection of Impressionist and Post-Impressionist art, pleasantly out of character with the rest of the house, including works by André Derain, Renoir and Augustus John. The extensive grounds include a purpose-built play area for children.

Bempton and Flamborough Head 26

East Yorkshire. 👥 *4,300.* 🚉 *Bemp-ton.* 🚌 *Bridlington.* ℹ️ *25 Prince St, Bridlington (01262 673474).*

BEMPTON, which consists of 5 miles (8 km) of steep chalk cliffs between Speeton and Flamborough Head, is the largest seabird-breeding colony in England, and is famous for its puffins. The weathered ledges and fissures provide ideal nest-sites for more than 100,000 pairs of

Nesting gannet on the chalk cliffs at Bempton

◁ **Mist drifting through Hole of Horcum, North Yorkshire Moors** birds. Today, eight different species, including skinny black shags and kittiwakes, thrive on the Grade 1 listed Bempton cliffs. Bempton is the only mainland site for goose-sized gannets, well known for their dramatic fishing techniques. May, June and July are the best bird-watching months.

The spectacular cliffs are best seen from the north side of the Flamborough Head peninsula, which offers attractive walks.

Beverley ㉗

Humberside. 26,000.
34 Butcher Row (01482 867430).
Sat.

THE HISTORY of Beverley dates back to the 8th century, when Old Beverley served as a retreat for John, later Bishop of York, who was canonized for his healing powers. Over the centuries Beverley grew as a medieval sanctuary town. Like York, it is an attractive combination of both medieval and Georgian buildings.

The best way to enter Beverley is through the last of five town gates, the castellated North Bar that allowed the medieval inhabitants in and out of the town's surrounding walls. It was rebuilt in 1409–10.

Minstrel Pillar in St Mary's Church

The skyline is dominated by the twin towers of the magnificent **minster**. This was co-founded in 937 by Athelstan, King of Wessex, in place of the church that John of Beverley had chosen as his final resting place in 721. The decorated nave is the earliest surviving building work which dates back to the early 1300s. It is particularly famous for its 16th-century choir stalls and 68 misericords (see p391).

The minster contains many early detailed stone carvings, including a set of four from about 1308 that illustrate figures with ailments such as toothache and lumbago. On the north side of the altar is the richly carved 14th-century Gothic Percy tomb, thought to be that of Lady Idoine Percy, who died in 1365. Also on the north side is the Fridstol, or Peace Chair, said to date from 924–39, the time of Athelstan. Anyone who sat on it would then be granted 30 days' sanctuary. Within the North Bar, **St Mary's Church** has a 13th-century chancel and houses Britain's largest number of medieval

The inspiration for Lewis Carroll's White Rabbit, St Mary's Church

stone carvings of musical instruments. The brightly painted 16th-century Minstrel Pillar is particularly notable. Painted on the panelled chancel ceiling are portraits of monarchs after 1445. On the richly sculpted doorway of St Michael's Chapel is the grinning pilgrim rabbit said to have inspired Lewis Carroll's White Rabbit in *Alice in Wonderland*.

Southeast of the minster, the **Museum of Army Transport** contains over 100 exhibits of army vehicles. The Saturday market has existed here ever since the Middle Ages.

🏛 Museum of Army Transport
Flemingate. 01482 860445.
daily. 24–26 Dec.

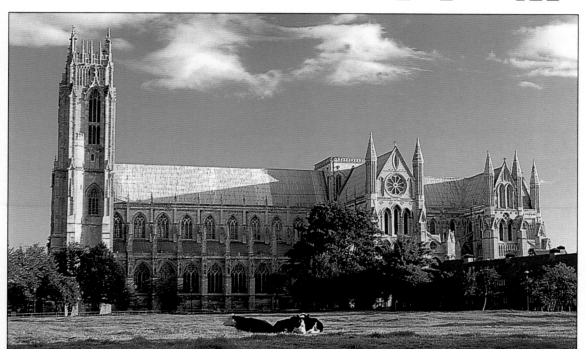
Beverley Minster, one of Europe's finest examples of Gothic architecture

Burton Constable ㉘

Nr Hull, Kingston upon Hull.
01964 562400. 🚢 Hull then taxi. ⭘
Easter– Oct: daily. 🖼 🚻 📷 ▭

T HE CONSTABLE FAMILY have been leading landowners since the 13th century, and have lived at Burton Constable since work began on it in 1570. It is an Elizabethan house, altered in the 18th century by Thomas Lightholer, Thomas Atkinson and James Wyatt. Today, its 30 rooms include Georgian and Victorian interiors. Burton Constable has a fine collection of Chippendale furniture and family portraits dating from the 16th century. Most of the collections of prints, textiles and drawings belong to Leeds City Art Galleries. The family still lives in the south wing.

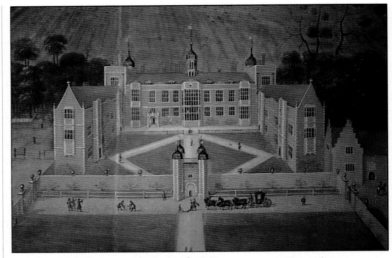
Painting of Burton Constable (c.1690) by an anonymous artist

Maritime Museum. Built in 1871 as the offices of the Hull Dock Company, it traces the city's maritime history. Among its exhibits are an ornate whalebone and vertebrae bench and a display of complicated rope knots such as the Eye Splice and the Midshipman's Hitch.

An imposing Elizabethan building, **Hands on History**, explores Hull's story through a collection of some of its families' artefacts.

In the heart of the Old Town, on a street that often reeks of salty sea air, is the **William Wilberforce House**, one of the surviving examples of the High Street's brick merchants' dwellings. Its first-floor oak-panelled rooms date from the 17th century, but most of the house is dedicated to the Wilberforce family, whose connection began in 1732 with the grandfather of the abolitionist. Among the more gruesome museum exhibits are iron ankle fetters for slaves. A fine Victorian doll collection strikes a lighter note.

Nearby is the **Streetlife Transport Museum**, Hull's newest and noisiest museum, popular with children. It includes a post-boy's boot from the 18th century, toughened to protect him against horses' hooves, and a recreation of a bicycle repair workshop.

🏛 **Maritime Museum**
Queen Victoria Sq. 🕿 01482 613903. ⭘ daily (Sun: pm).
● 23–27 Dec, 1 Jan, Good Fri, 🚻
🏛 **Hands on History**
South Churchside. 🕿 01482 613952.
⭘ weekends and school holidays. ●
23–27 Dec, 1 Jan, Good Fri. 🚻

The Princes' Dock in Kingston upon Hull's restored docks area

Kingston upon Hull ㉙

Kingston upon Hull. 🚶 270,000. 🚆
🚌 ⛴ ℹ Paragon St. (01482 223559). 🏪 Tue, Fri, Sat.

T HERE IS A LOT MORE to Hull than the heritage of a thriving fishing industry. The restored town centre docks are attractive, and Hull's Old Town, laid out in medieval times, is all cobbled, winding streets and quaintly askew red-brick houses. You can follow the Fish Trail, a path of inlaid metal fishes on the city's pavements that illustrates the many different varieties that have been landed in Hull, from anchovy to shark. In Victoria Square is the

---

WILLIAM WILBERFORCE (1758–1833)

William Wilberforce, born in Hull to a merchant family, was a natural orator. After studying Classics at Cambridge, he entered politics and in 1784 gave one of his first public addresses in York. The audience was captivated, and Wilberforce realized the potential of his powers of persuasion. From 1785 onwards, adopted by the Pitt government as spokesman for the abolition of slavery, he conducted a determined and conscientious campaign. But his speeches won him enemies, and in 1792, threats from a slave-importer meant that he needed a constant armed guard. In 1807 his bill to abolish the lucrative slave trade became law.

A 19th-century engraving of Wilberforce by J Jenkins

🏛 William Wilberforce House

South Churchside. 📞 *01482 613921.*
⭕ *daily (Sun: pm).* ⬤ *24–27 Dec,
1 Jan, Good Fri.* ♿ *limited.* 🏠

🏛 Streetlife Transport Museum

South Churchside. 📞 *01482 613956.*
⭕ *daily (Sun: pm).* ⬤ *25 Dec–
3 Jan, Good Fri.* ♿ 🖥 🏠

Holderness and Spurn Head ③⓪

East Riding. 🚉 *Hull (Paragon St)
then bus.* ℹ️ *120 Newbegin, Hornsea
(01964 536404).*

THIS CURIOUS FLAT AREA east
of Hull, with straight roads
and delicately waving fields of
oats and barley, in many ways
resembles Holland, except that
its mills are derelict. Beaches
stretch for 30 miles (46 km)
along the coastline. The main
resort towns are **Withernsea**
whose lighthouse is now a
museum and **Hornsea**, well
known for its pottery.

The Holderness landscape
only exists because of erosion
higher up the coast. The sea
continues to wash down tiny
bits of rock which accumulate.
Around 1560, this began to
form a sandbank, and by 1669
it had became large enough
to be colonized as Sonke
Sand. The last bits of silting
mud and debris joined the
island to the mainland as
recently as the 1830s. Today,
you can drive through the
eerie, lush wilderness of Sunk
Island on the way west to
Spurn Head. This is located at
the tip of the Spurn Peninsula,
a 3.5 mile (6 km) spit of land
that has also built up as the
result of coastal erosion elsewhere. Flora, fauna and birdlife have been protected here
by the Yorkshire Naturalists'
Trust since 1960. Walking here
gives the eerie feeling that the
land could be eroded from
under your feet at any time.
A surprise discovery at the end
of Spurn Head is a tiny community of pilots and lifeboat
crew, constantly on call to
guide ships into Hull harbour,
or help cope with disasters.

**Fishing boat at Grimsby's
National Fishing Heritage Centre**

Grimsby ③①

Northeast Lincolnshire. 👥 *92,000.*
🚉 🚌 ℹ️ *Heritage Sq (01472
323222).* 🛒 *Tue, Thu, Fri, Sat.*

PERCHED at the mouth of the
River Humber, Grimsby
was founded in the Middle
Ages by a Danish fisherman
by the name of Grim, and
rose to prominence in the 19th
century as one of the world's
largest fishing ports. Its first
dock was opened in 1800 and,
with the arrival of the railways,
the town secured the means
of transporting its catch all
over the country. Even though
the traditional fishing industry
had declined by the 1970s,
dock area redevelopment has
ensured that Grimsby's unique
heritage is retained.

This is best demonstrated by
the award-winning **National
Fishing Heritage Centre**, a
museum that recreates the
industry in its 1950s heyday,
capturing the atmosphere of
the period. Visitors sign on as
crew members on a trawler
and, by means of a variety
of vivid interactive displays,
travel from the back streets of
Grimsby to the Arctic fishing
grounds. On the way, they can
experience the roll of the ship,
the smell of the fish and the
heat of the engine. The tour
can be finished off with a
guided viewing of the restored
1950s trawler, the *Ross Tiger*.

Other attractions in Grimsby
include an International Jazz
Festival every July, a restored
Victorian shopping street
called Abbeygate, a market, a
wide selection of restaurants,
and the nearby seaside resorts
of Cleethorpes, Mablethorpe
and Skegness.

🏛 National Fishing Heritage Centre

Heritage Sq, Alexandra Dock.
📞 *01472 323345.* ⭕ *daily.*
⬤ *25, 26 Dec, 1 Jan.* 🖼 ♿ 🎞 🖥

Isolated lighthouse at Spurn Head, at the tip of Spurn Peninsula

Street-by-Street: York 32

Monk Bar coat of arms

THE CITY OF YORK has retained so much of its medieval structure that walking into its centre is like entering a living museum. Many of the ancient timbered houses, perched on narrow, winding streets, such as the Shambles, are protected by a conservation order. Cars are banned from the centre, so there are always student bikes bouncing over cobbled streets. Its strategic position led to its development as a railway centre in the 19th century.

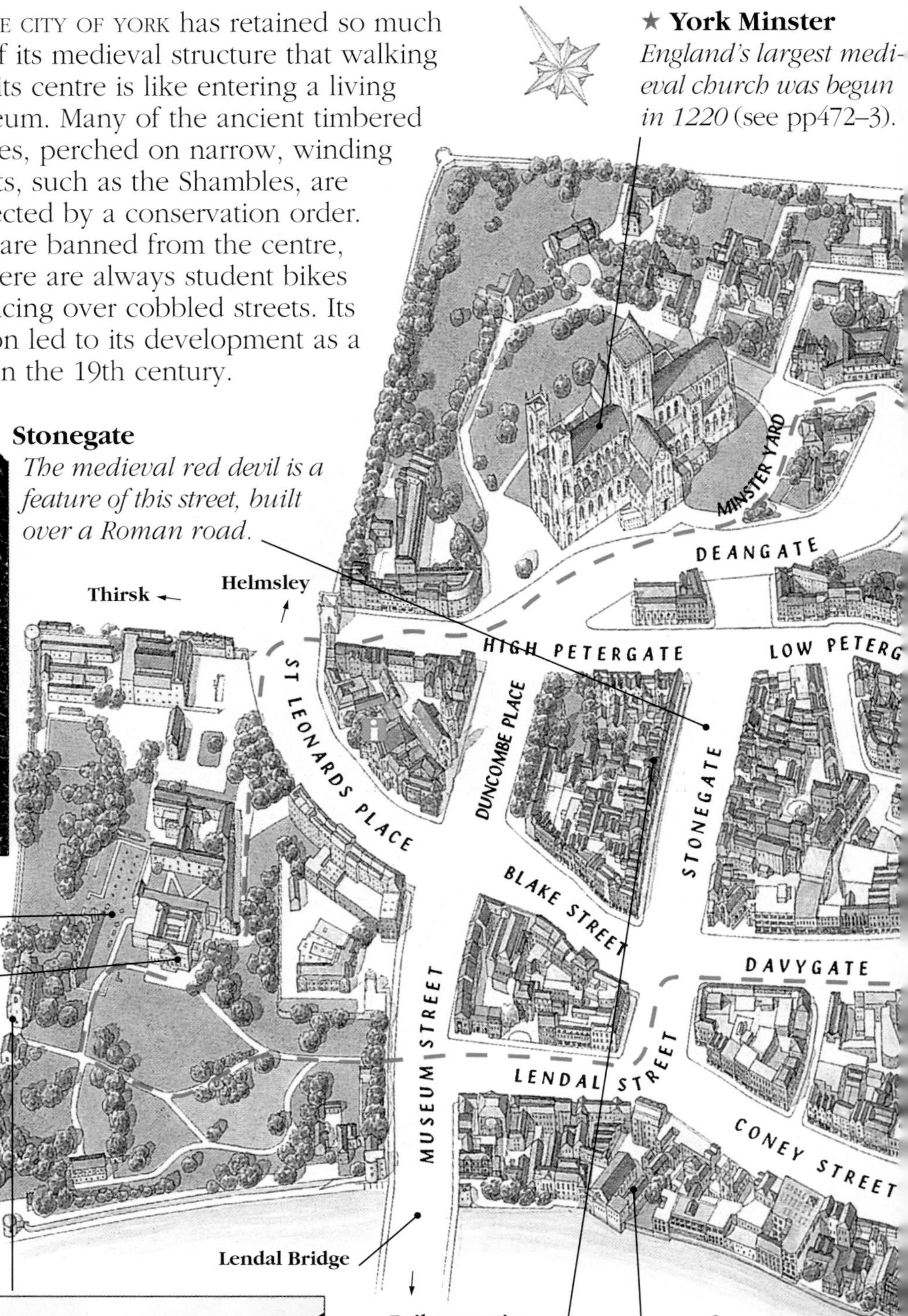

★ **York Minster**
England's largest medieval church was begun in 1220 (see pp472–3).

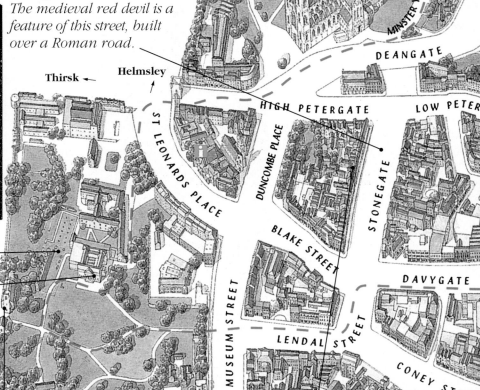

Stonegate
The medieval red devil is a feature of this street, built over a Roman road.

Thirsk ← Helmsley ↑

DEANGATE

HIGH PETERGATE

LOW PETERG

ST LEONARDS PLACE

DUNCOMBE PLACE

STONEGATE

St Mary's Abbey

BLAKE STREET

DAVYGATE

Yorkshire Museum
contains a fine collection of fossils, discovered at Whitby in the 19th century.

MUSEUM STREET

LENDAL STREET

CONEY STREET

Lendal Bridge

OUSE

Railway station, coach station, National Railway Museum, and Leeds

(see p400)

Ye Old Starre Inne is one of the oldest pubs in York.

St Olave's Church
The 11th-century church, next to the gatehouse of St Mary's Abbey (see p400), was founded by the Earl of Northumbria in memory of St Olaf, King of Norway. To the left is the Chapel of St Mary on the Walls.

Guildhall
This two-headed medieval roof boss is on the 15th-century Guildhall, situated beside the River Ouse and restored after bomb damage during World War II.

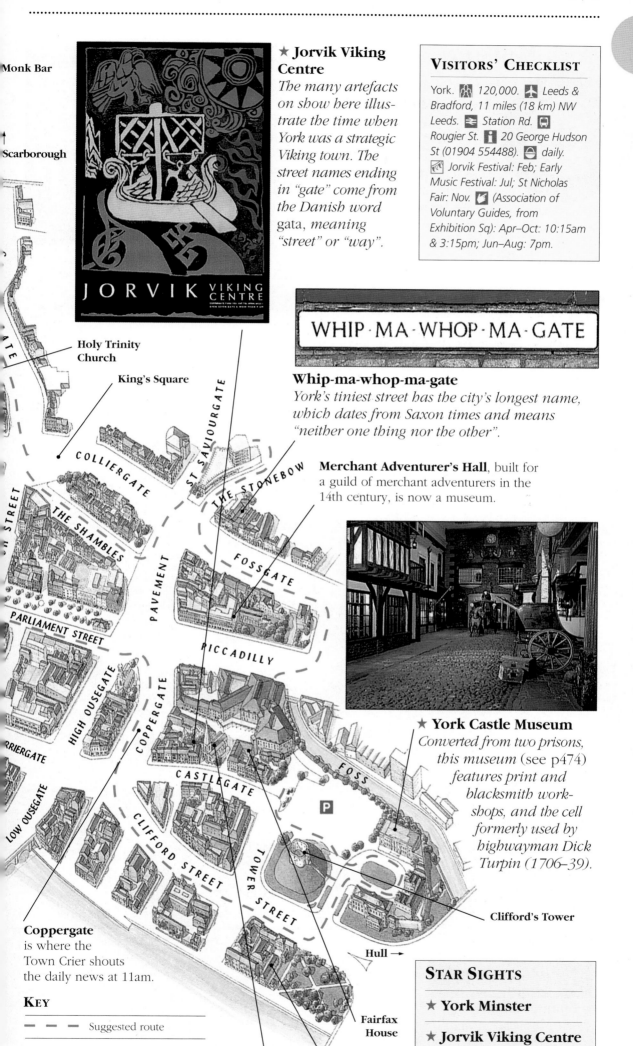

★ **Jorvik Viking Centre**
The many artefacts on show here illustrate the time when York was a strategic Viking town. The street names ending in "gate" come from the Danish word gata, meaning "street" or "way".

VISITORS' CHECKLIST

York. 120,000. Leeds & Bradford, 11 miles (18 km) NW Leeds. Station Rd. Rougier St. 20 George Hudson St (01904 554488). daily. Jorvik Festival: Feb; Early Music Festival: Jul; St Nicholas Fair: Nov. (Association of Voluntary Guides, from Exhibition Sq): Apr–Oct: 10:15am & 3:15pm; Jun–Aug: 7pm.

Monk Bar

Scarborough

Holy Trinity Church

King's Square

Whip-ma-whop-ma-gate
York's tiniest street has the city's longest name, which dates from Saxon times and means "neither one thing nor the other".

Merchant Adventurer's Hall, built for a guild of merchant adventurers in the 14th century, is now a museum.

COLLIERGATE

ST SAVIOURGATE

THE STONEBOW

THE SHAMBLES

FOSSGATE

PAVEMENT

PARLIAMENT STREET

PICCADILLY

HIGH OUSEGATE

COPPERGATE

★ **York Castle Museum**
Converted from two prisons, this museum (see p474) features print and blacksmith workshops, and the cell formerly used by highwayman Dick Turpin (1706–39).

RRIERGATE

CASTLEGATE

FOSS

LOW OUSEGATE

CLIFFORD STREET

TOWER STREET

Clifford's Tower

Coppergate
is where the Town Crier shouts the daily news at 11am.

Hull →

KEY

– – – Suggested route

0 metres   100

0 yards   100

Fairfax House

St Mary's Church

Museum of Automata

STAR SIGHTS

★ **York Minster**

★ **Jorvik Viking Centre**

★ **York Castle Museum**

York Minster

Central sunflower in rose window

THE LARGEST Gothic church north of the Alps, York Minster is 163 m (534 ft) long and 76 m (249 ft) wide across the transepts, and houses the largest collection of medieval stained glass in Britain *(see p475)*. The word "minster" usually means a church served by monks, but priests always served at York. The minster probably began as a wooden chapel used to baptize King Edwin of Northumbria in 627. There have been several cathedrals on the site, including an imposing 11th-century Norman structure. The present minster was begun in 1220 and completed 250 years later. In July 1984, the south transept roof was destroyed by fire. Restoration cost £2.25 million.

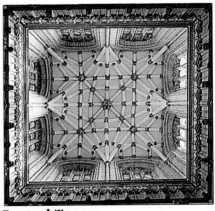

Central Tower
Reconstructed in 1420–65 (after partial collapse in 1407), from a design by the master stonemason William Colchester, its geometrical roof design has a central lantern.

Lady Chapel

The Choir has a vaulted entrance with a 12th-century boss of the Assumption of the Virgin.

Exit in south transept

The 16th-century rose window

★ **Choir Screen**
Sited between the choir and the nave, this 15th-century stone screen depicts kings of England from William I to Henry VI, and has a canopy of angels.

★ **Chapter House**
A Latin inscription near the entrance of the wooden-vaulted Chapter House (1260–85) reads: "As the rose is the flower of flowers, so this is the house of houses".

The Nave, built in 1291, was severely damaged by fire in 1840. Rebuilding costs were heavy, but it was re-opened with a new peal of bells in 1844.

Timbered interior of the Merchant Adventurers' Hall

The western towers, with their
15th-century decorative panelling
and elaborate pinnacles, contrast
with the simpler design of the
north transept. The southwest
tower is the minster belfry.

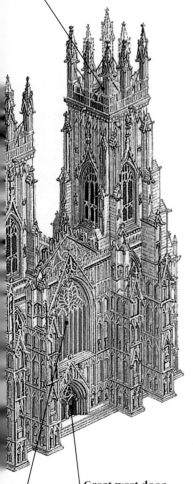

Great west door

Great west window
(see p475)

🚪 Monk Bar

This is one of York's finest original medieval gates, situated
at the end of Goodramgate. It
is vaulted on three floors, and
the portcullis still works. In
the Middle Ages, the rooms
above it were rented out, and
it was a prison in the 16th
century. Its decorative details
include men holding stones
ready to drop on intruders.

🏛 Museum of Automata

9 Tower St. ⬤ *until further notice.*
The history of mechanically
moving objects, from simple
articulated figurines of ancient
civilizations to more modern
20th-century artworks, is
charted in this museum.
Automata too fragile for
frequent operation, such as
the acrobats and clowns in
the French Gallery,
which date from the
1820s, are brought
to life using a
video wall.

**One of the mechanical toys on
show at the Museum of Automata**

🚪 Clifford's Tower

Clifford's St. 📞 01904 646940.
⬜ *daily.* ⬤ *24–26 Dec.* 📷 🔲
Sited on top of a mound that
William the Conqueror built
for his original wooden castle,
destroyed by fire during anti-
Jewish riots in 1190, Clifford's
Tower dates from the 13th
century. Built by Henry III,
it commemorates Roger de
Clifford who was hanged in
1322 after being captured at
the Battle of Boroughbridge.

🏛 ARC

St Saviourgate. 📞 01904 654324.
⬜ *Mon–Sat (Sat: pm).* ⬤ *mid-Dec–
5 Jan, Good Fri.* 📷 ♿ 🔲
Housed in a restored medieval
church off the Shambles, the
ARC is a centre for exploring
archaeology. Visitors are
allowed to handle ancient
finds and experiment with
traditional crafts and computers. Archaeologists show
how to identify exhibits such
as pottery by age and type.

🚪 Merchant Adventurers' Hall

Fossgate. 📞 01904 654818. ⬜ *mid-
Mar–mid-Nov: daily; mid-Nov–mid-Mar:
Mon– Sat.* ⬤ *24 Dec–3 Jan.* 📷 ♿
limited.
Built by the York Merchants'
Guild, which controlled the
northern cloth trade in the
15th–17th centuries, this build-
ing has fine timberwork. The
Great Hall is probably the best
example of its kind in Europe.
Among its paintings is an un-
attributed 17th-century copy of
Van Dyck's portrait of Charles
I's queen, Henrietta Maria.
Below the Great Hall is the
hospital, used by the guild un-
til 1900, and a private chapel.

Exploring York

THE APPEAL OF YORK is its many layers of history. A medieval city constructed on top of a Roman one, it was first built in AD 71, when it became capital of the northern province and was known as Eboracum. It was here that Constantine the Great was made emperor in 306, and reorganized Britain into four provinces. A hundred years later, the Roman army had withdrawn. Eboracum was renamed Eoforwic, under the Saxons, and then became a Christian stronghold. The Danish street names are the reminder that it was a Viking centre from 867, and one of Europe's chief trading bases. Between 1100 and 1500 it was England's second city. The glory of York is the minster *(see pp472–3)*. The city also boasts 18 medieval churches, 3 mile long (4.8 km) medieval city walls, elegant Jacobean and Georgian architecture and fine museums.

The Middleham Jewel, Yorkshire Museum

Grand staircase and fine plaster ceiling at Fairfax House

🏛 York Castle Museum

The Eye of York. **☎** *01904 653611.* ◯ *daily.* ● *25, 26 Dec, 1 Jan.* 🈸 **&** *ground floor only.* 🖵 🛈
Housed in two 18th-century prisons, the museum has a fine folk collection, started by Dr John Kirk of the market town of Pickering. Opened in 1938, its period displays include a Jacobean dining room, a moorland cottage, and a 1950s front room. It also contains a large collection of early 20th-century household gadgets.

The most famous exhibits include the reconstructed Victorian street of Kirkgate, complete with shopfronts and model carriage horse; and the Anglo Saxon York Helmet, the finest example of only three ever found, discovered in 1982.

🛈 York Minster

See pp472–3.

🏛 Jorvik Viking Centre

Coppergate. **☎** *01904 643211.* ◯ *daily.* ● *25 Dec.* 🈸 **&** *ring first.* 🖵
This popular centre is built on the site of the original Viking settlement which archaeologists uncovered at Coppergate. It is most famous for recreating the smells of Viking York. A "time car" travels through a model Viking street, and provides a commentary on its history. An exhibition illustrates how the best-preserved Viking village in Britain was discovered.

🏛 Yorkshire Museum and St Mary's Abbey

Museum Gardens. **☎** *01904 629745.* ◯ *daily.* ● *25, 26 Dec, 1 Jan.* 🈸 **&**
Yorkshire Museum was in the news when it purchased the 15th-century Middleham Jewel for £2.5 million, one of the finest pieces of English Gothic jewellery found this century. Other exhibits include 2nd-century Roman mosaics and an Anglo-Saxon silver gilt bowl.

St Mary's Abbey *(see p400)* in the riverside grounds is where the medieval York Mystery Plays are set every three years.

🏛 Fairfax House

Castlegate. **☎** *01904 655543.* ◯ *daily (Sun: pm, Fri: booked tour only).* ● *23–26 Dec, 1 Jan, 6 Jan–20 Feb.* 🈸 🎫 **&** *limited.* 🛈
From 1755 to 1762 Viscount Fairfax built this fine Georgian town house for his daughter, Anne. The house was designed by John Carr *(see p28)*, and restored in the 1980s. Between 1920 and 1965 it was a cinema and dancehall. Today, visitors can see the bedroom of Anne Fairfax (1725– 93), and a fine collection of 18th-century furniture, porcelain and clocks.

🏛 National Railway Museum

Leeman Rd. **☎** *01904 621261.* ◯ *daily.* ● *24–26 Dec.* 🈸 **&** 🖵 🛈
Set in a former steam engine maintenance shed, the world's largest railway museum covers nearly 200 years of history using paintings, photographs and visual aids. Visitors can try wheel-tapping and shunting in the interactive gallery, or find out what made Stephenson's *Rocket* so successful. Exhibits include uniforms, rolling stock from 1797 onward and Queen Victoria's Royal Train carriage, as well as the very latest rail innovations.

Reproduction of an engine and 1830s first-class carriage (left) in York's National Railway Museum

The Stained Glass of York Minster

YORK MINSTER houses the largest collection of medieval stained glass in Britain, some of it dating from the late 12th century. The glass was generally coloured during production, using metal oxides to produce the desired colour, then worked on by craftsmen on site. When a design had been produced, the glass was first cut, then trimmed to shape. Details

Window detail

were painted on, using iron oxide-based paint which was fused to the glass by firing in a kiln. Individual pieces were then leaded together to form the finished window.

Part of the fascination of the minster glass is its variety of subject matter. Some windows were paid for by lay donors who specified a particular subject, others reflect ecclesiastical patronage.

Miracle of St Nicholas *(late 12th century) was put in the nave over 100 years after it was made. It shows a Jew's conversion.*

The Five Sisters *in the north transept are the largest examples of* grisaille *glass in Britain. This popular 13th-century technique involved creating fine patterning on clear glass and decorating it with black enamel.*

St John the Evangelist, *in part of the Great West Window (c.1338), is holding an eagle, itself an example of stickwork, where paint is scraped off to reveal clear glass.*

Noah's Ark *with its distinct boat-like shape is easily identified in the Great East Window.*

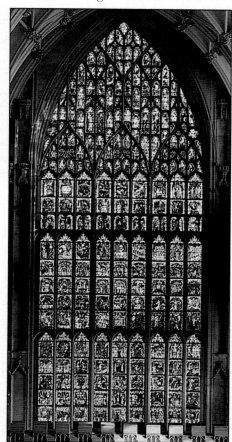

The Great East Window *(1405-8), the size of a tennis court, is the largest area of medieval painted glass in the world. The Dean and Chapter paid master glazier John Thornton four shillings a week for this celebration of the Creation.*

Edward III *is a fine example of the 14th-century "soft" style of painting, achieved by stippling the paint.*

Walter Skirlaw, *whose bishopric was revoked in favour of Richard Scrope, donated this window on its completion in 1408.*

Harewood House ❸❸

Harewood, Leeds. ☎ 0113 2886331.
🚆 Leeds then bus. ◯ Mar– Oct: daily.
📷 ♿ 📹 by arrangement.

Dᴇsɪɢɴᴇᴅ ʙʏ John Carr in 1759, Harewood House is the Yorkshire home of the Earl and Countess of Harewood.

The grand Palladian exterior is impressive, with interiors created by Robert Adam and an unrivalled collection of 18th-century furniture made specifically for Harewood by Yorkshire-born Thomas Chippendale (1711–79). Harewood has a fine collection of paintings by Italian and English artists, including Reynolds and Gainsborough, and two new watercolour rooms. The grounds, developed by Capability Brown (see p27) include the **Harewood Bird Garden**, which has exotic and native species on show and a breeding programme of certain endangered varieties.

Bali starling, one of Harewood's rare birds

Leeds ❸❹

Leeds. 👥 700,000. ✈ 🚆 🚌 🛈 Leeds City Station (0113 2425242). 🚐 Mon–Sat.

Tʜᴇ ᴛʜɪʀᴅ ʟᴀʀɢᴇsᴛ of Britain's provincial cities, Leeds was at its most prosperous during the Victorian period. The most impressive legacy from this era is a series of ornate, covered shopping arcades. Also of note is the **Town Hall**, designed by Cuthbert Brodrick and opened by Queen Victoria in 1858.

Today, although Leeds is primarily an industrial city, it also offers a thriving cultural scene. Productions at **The Grand** by Opera North, one of Britain's top operatic companies, are of a high quality.

The **City Art Gallery** has an impressive collection of British 20th-century art and fine examples of Victorian paintings including works by local artist Atkinson Grimshaw (1836–93). Among the late 19th-century French art are works by Signac, Courbet and Sisley. The Henry Moore Institute, added in 1993, is devoted to the research, study and display of sculpture of all periods. It comprises a reading room, study centre, library and video gallery, as well as galleries and an archive of material on and by Moore and other sculptural pioneers.

The **Armley Mills Museum**, in a 19th-century woollen mill, explores the industrial heritage of Leeds. Filled with original equipment, recorded sounds and models in 19th-century workers' clothes, it traces the history of the ready-to-wear industry.

A striking waterfront development by the River Aire has attracted two museums. The **Royal Armouries Museum**, from the Tower of London, tells the story of arms and armour around the world in battle, sport, self-defence and fashion, using live demonstrations, film, music and poetry. The attractions at **Tetley's Brewery Wharf** include a museum, brewery tours which run three times a day, and huge Shire horses, once used to deliver the beer around the city.

Leeds has two sights that are especially suitable for children. **Tropical World** features crystal pools, a rain-

The County Arcade, one of Leeds' restored shopping arcades

forest house, butterflies and tropical fish. There is also a farm and a Rare Breeds centre in the grounds of the Tudor-Jacobean **Temple Newsam House**, which has a collection of Chippendale furniture.

🏛 **City Art Gallery**
The Headrow. ☎ 0113 2478248.
◯ daily (Sun: pm). ● 25, 26 Dec, 1 Jan & public hols. ♿ 🖥 🛍

🏛 **Armley Mills Museum**
Canal Rd, Armley. ☎ 0113 2637861.
◯ Tue–Sun (Sun: pm), public hols.
● 24–26 Dec, 1 Jan. 📷 ♿ 🛍

🏛 **Royal Armouries**
Armouries Drive. ☎ 0113 2201999.
◯ daily. ● 24, 25 Dec. 📷 ♿ 🍴

🏛 **Tetley's Brewery Wharf**
The Waterfront. ☎ 0113 2420666.
◯ daily. ● 24–26 Dec, 1 Jan. 📷

🌿 **Tropical World**
Canal Gdns, Princes Ave. ☎ 0113 2661850. ◯ daily. ● 25, 26 Dec. ♿

🏚 **Temple Newsam House**
Off A63. ☎ 0113 2647321.
◯ Tue–Sun (Sun: pm), public hols.
● 25, 26 Dec, 1 Jan. 📷 ♿ limited in house. 🖥 🛍

Working loom at the Armley Mills Museum in Leeds

The Other Side (1990–93) by David Hockney at Bradford's 1853 Gallery in Saltaire

Bradford ③⑤

Bradford. 🏃 *475,000.* ✈
⇄ 🚍 🛈 *Bradford Central Library,
Prince's Way (01274 753678).*
🛒 *Mon–Sat.*

IN THE 16TH CENTURY, Bradford was a thriving market town, and the opening of its canal in 1774 boosted trade. By 1850, it was the world's capital for worsted (fabric made from closely twisted wool). Many of the city's well-preserved civic and industrial buildings date from this period, such as the Wool Exchange on Market Street. In the 1800s a number of German textile manufacturers settled in what is now called Little Germany. Their houses are characterized by decorative stone carvings that illustrated the wealth and standing of the occupants.

Daguerreotype camera by Giroux (1839)

The **National Museum of Photography, Film and Television**, founded in 1983, explores the technology and art of these media. There is a television section called TV Heaven, where visitors can ask to watch their favourite programme. They are also encouraged to see themselves read the news on TV. The giant IMAX screen uses the world's largest film format. Film subjects include journeys into space, Yellowstone Park in the USA and the original Rolling Stones band.

The **Colour Museum** traces dyeing and textile printing from ancient Egypt to the present day. Hands-on elements include taking charge of computerized technology to test the colour of a material.

Bradford Industrial Museum is housed in an original spinning mill. As well as seeing and hearing all the mill machinery, you can ride on a horse-drawn tram. Saltaire, a Victorian industrial village *(see p399)*, is on the outskirts of the city. Built by Sir Titus Salt for his Salts Mill workers, it was completed in 1873. The **1853 Gallery** in the main mill has works by David Hockney, born in Bradford in 1937.

🏛 **National Museum of Photography, Film and Television**
Pictureville. 🛈 *01274 727488.*
🕘 *daily (school hols); Tue–Sun (school term times); public holidays.* ⬤ *24–26 Dec.* ♿ 🍴 🖥 🛍

🏛 **Colour Museum**
82 Grattan Rd. 🛈 *01274 390955.* 🕘 *Tue–Sat.* ⬤ *19–30 Dec, 1 Jan.* ▨ ♿

🏛 **Bradford Industrial Museum**
Moorside Mills, Moorside Rd.
🛈 *01274 631756.* 🕘 *Tue–Sat, Sun (pm), public hols.* ⬤ *25, 26 Dec.* ▨ ♿ 🖥 🛍

🏛 **1853 Gallery**
Salts Mill, Victoria Rd. 🛈 *01274 531163.* 🕘 *daily.* ⬤ *25–26 Dec.* ♿

BRADFORD'S INDIAN COMMUNITY

Immigrants from the Indian subcontinent originally came to Bradford in the 1950s to work in the mills, but with the decline of the textile industry many began small businesses. By the mid-1970s there were 1,400 such enterprises in the area. Almost one fifth were in the food sector, born out of simple cafés catering for mill-workers whose families were far away. As Indian food became more popular, these restaurants thrived, and today there are over 200 serving the highly spiced dishes of the Indian subcontinent.

Balti in a Bradford restaurant

Haworth Parsonage, home to the Brontë family, now a museum

Haworth ㊱

West Yorkshire. 🚶 *5,000.*
🚉 *Keighley.* 🛈 *2–4 West Lane
(01535 642329).*

THE SETTING OF HAWORTH, in bleak Pennine moorland dotted with farmsteads, has changed little since it was home to the Brontë family. The town boomed in the 1840s, when there were more than 1,200 hand-looms in operation, but is more famous today for the Brontë connection.

You can visit the **Brontë Parsonage Museum**, home from 1820–61 to novelists Charlotte, Emily and Anne, their brother Branwell and their father, the Reverend Patrick Brontë. Built in 1778–9, the house remains decorated as it was during the 1850s. Eleven rooms, including the children's study and Charlotte's room, display letters, manuscripts, books, furniture and personal treasures.

Also evocative of the Brontë sisters' novels are the walks the family enjoyed, for which stout boots are advised, among them the **Brontë Falls** and **Brontë Bridge**. Nearby is the **Brontë Seat**, a chair-shaped stone.

In summer, the nostalgic Victorian **Keighley and Worth Valley Railway** runs through Haworth. It stops at Oakworth station, where parts of *The*

Railway Children were filmed. At the end of the line is the Railway Museum at Oxenhope.

🏛 **Brontë Parsonage Museum**

Church St. 📞 *01535 642323.*
⭘ *daily.* ⬤ *24–27 Dec, mid-Jan–early Feb.* ✍

Hebden Bridge ㊲

West Yorkshire. 🚶 *4,500.* 🚉 🛈 *1
Bridgegate (01422 843831).* 🛒 *Thu.*

HEBDEN BRIDGE is a delightful West Riding mill town, surrounded by steep hills and former 19th-century mills, and is home to Britain's last clog mill. The houses seem to defy gravity as they cling to the valley sides. Due to the gradient, one house is made from two bottom floors and the top two floors form another unit. To separate legal ownership of these "flying freeholds", an Act of Parliament was devised.

Charlotte Brontë's childhood story book, for her sister, Anne

There is a superb view of Hebden Bridge from nearby **Heptonstall**, where the cult poet Sylvia Plath (1932–63) is buried. The village contains a Wesleyan chapel (1764).

Halifax ㊳

West Yorkshire. 🚶 *88,000.* 🚉 🚌
🛈 *Piece Hall (01422 368725).*
🛒 *Thu–Sat.*

HALIFAX'S HISTORY has been influenced by textiles since the Middle Ages, but today's visual reminders date mainly from the 19th century. The town inspired William Blake's vision of "dark Satanic mills" in his poem *Jerusalem* (1820). The wool trade helped to make the Pennines into Britain's industrial backbone.

Until the mid-15th century cloth production was modest, but vital enough to inspire the 11th-century Gibbet Law, which stated that anyone caught stealing cloth could be hanged. There is a replica of the gibbet used for hanging at the bottom of Gibbet Street. Many of Halifax's 18th- and

CHARLOTTE BRONTË

During a harsh, motherless childhood, Charlotte (1816-55) and her sisters, Emily and Anne, retreated into fictional worlds of their own, writing poems and stories. As adults, they had to work as governesses or teachers, but still published a poetry collection in 1846. Only two copies were sold, but in the following year Charlotte had great success with *Jane Eyre*, which became a best seller. After the deaths of her siblings in 1848–9 Charlotte turned to the solitude of writing and published her last novel, *Villette*, in 1852. She married the Reverend Arthur Bell Nicholls, her father's curate, in 1854, but died shortly afterwards.

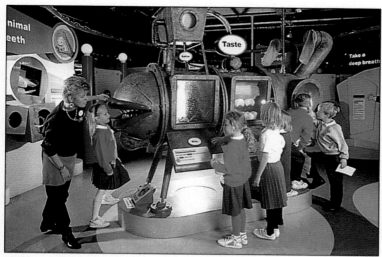

Children playing on the Giant Mouth at Halifax's Eureka! museum

19th-century buildings owe their existence to wealthy cloth traders. Sir Charles Barry (1795–1860), architect of the Houses of Parliament, was commissioned by the Crossley family to design the Town Hall. They also paid for the landscaping of the People's Park by the creator of the Crystal Palace, Sir Joseph Paxton (1801–65). Thomas Bradley's 18th-century **Piece Hall** is where wool merchants once sold their pieces of cloth, trading in one of the hall's 315 "Merchants' Rooms". It has a massive Italianate courtyard built by the town's wool merchants and now beautifully restored. Today, Halifax's market takes place here.

Adjoining Piece Hall is **Calderdale Industrial Museum**, which charts over 20 of the area's past industries from clock-making to sweet manufacturing. It has working displays of textile machinery. **Eureka!** is a museum designed for children, with "learning adventures" on exhibits such as the Giant Mouth Machine and the Wall of Water.

Shibden Hall Museum is a fine period house, parts of which date to the 15th century. It reflects the prosperous home life of a 17th–18th-century manufacturer. Its 17th-century Pennine barn is filled with horse-drawn vehicles. In the cobbled courtyard, 19th-century workshops include a saddler and a blacksmith.

▥ Calderdale Industrial Museum
Central Works, Square Rd.
📞 01422 358087. ● until 2000.
Phone for opening times.

▥ Eureka!
Discovery Rd. 📶 01426 983191.
📞 01422 330069 for group bookings & exhibition information.
◯ daily. ● 24–26 Dec. 📷 ♿

▥ Shibden Hall Museum
Listers Rd. 📞 01422 352246.
◯ daily (Sun: pm). ● 24 Dec– 2 Jan. 📷 ▯ 🛍

Yorkshire Mining Museum ㊴

Wakefield, West Yorkshire. 📞 01924 848806. ⇌ Wakefield then bus. ◯ daily. ● 24–26 Dec, 1 Jan. 📷 ♿ ✍

Housed in the old Caphouse Colliery, this museum gives visitors the chance to go into a real mine shaft: warm clothing is advised. An underground tour takes you 137 m (450 ft) down, equipped with a hat and a miner's lamp. You can enter some of the narrow seams and see exhibits such as life-size working models. Other displays depict mining methods and conditions from 1820 to the present day.

Yorkshire Sculpture Park ㊵

Wakefield, West Yorkshire. 📞 01924 830302. ⇌ Wakefield then bus. ◯ daily. ● 24–25, 29–31 Dec. ♿ ▯

This is one of Europe's leading open-air galleries situated in 45 ha (110 acres) of beautiful 18th-century parkland. Each year a programme of large temporary exhibitions of sculpture by international artists is organized alongside the existing collection, which includes work by Barbara Hepworth, Sol LeWitt and Mimmo Paladino. Henry Moore (1898-1986), the Park's first patron, believed that daylight and sun were necessary to appreciate sculpture. Bretton Country Park features his largest European collection.

Large Two Forms (1966–9) by Henry Moore in Bretton Country Park

Lindisfarne Castle, on the rocky coastline of the island of Lindisfarne, Northumberland ▷

Northumbria

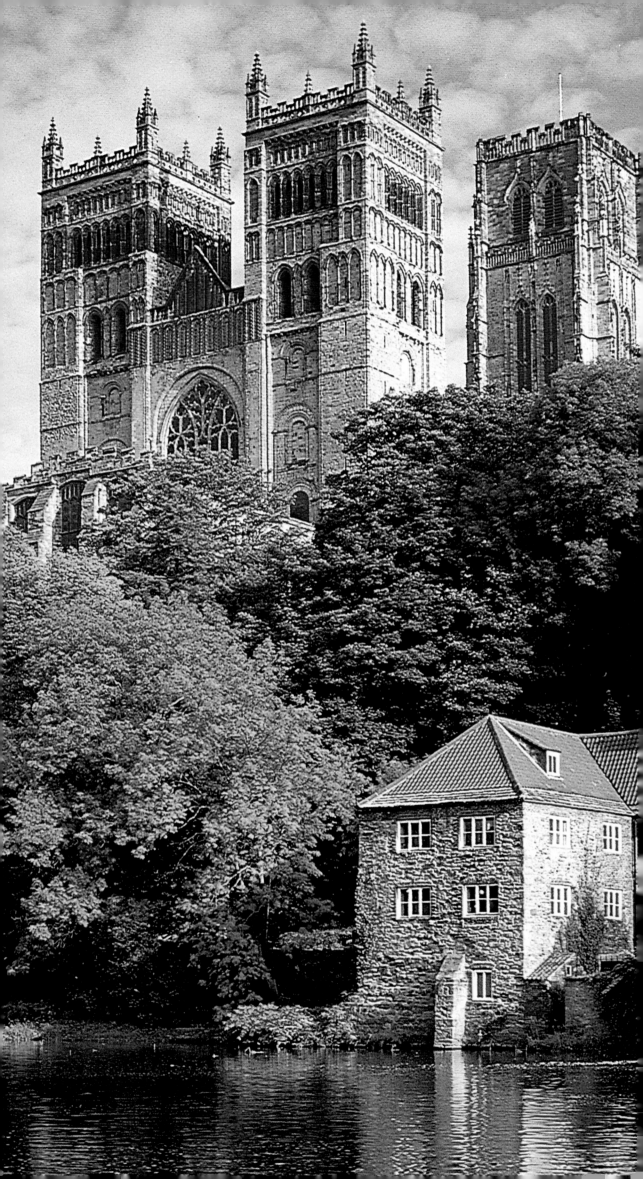

NORTHUMBRIA

ENGLAND'S NORTHEASTERN *extremity is a tapestry of moorland, ruins, castles, cathedrals and huddled villages. With Northumberland National Park and Kielder Water reservoir to the north, a rugged eastern coastline, and the cities of Newcastle and Durham to the south, the area combines a dramatic history with abundant natural beauty.*

The empty peaceful hills, elusive wildlife and panoramic vistas of Northumberland National Park belie the area's often violent history. Warring Scots and English, skirmishing tribes, cattle drovers and whisky smugglers have all left traces of ancient routes through the Cheviot Hills. Only recently has it been appreciated that these hills also form a perfectly preserved prehistoric landscape: Bronze Age field systems can still be traced along the sides of the hills, and Iron Age hillforts stand at the top of many of the grassy mounds.

The most prominent reminder of Northumbria's turbulent past is Hadrian's Wall, which slices through the southern edge of Northumberland National Park. This barrier, which marked the northern boundary of the Roman Empire, passes through some dramatic countryside, often following the crest of a precipitous ridge called the Whin Sill. Along the wall, the ruins of many forts and settlements once used to protect the border, such as Housesteads Fort, can be visited. As several of these sites are still being excavated or opened to view for the first time, there is a strong feeling of the past being brought to life with each new archaeological discovery.

The 350-year Roman occupation ended in 410, but by the middle of the 5th century, the Angles and Saxons from Germany started raiding the east coast of Britain. During the 6th century,

Section of Hadrian's Wall, built by the Romans in about 120, looking east from Cawfields

◁ **The towers of Durham Cathedral, rising above the River Wear**

View of rural Northumberland, from Cartington Hill

the Anglo-Saxons established the kingdom of Bernicia, and in the 7th century, Bernicia was permanently united with neighbouring Deira to form Northumbria. One of the major defensive fortifications of Bernicia was Bamburgh Castle, which was built by Ida the Flamebearer, Bernicia's first monarch. Today, Bamburgh Castle (which was rebuilt after the Norman Conquest of 1066) is a fascinating place to visit.

It was around the time that Bernicia and Deira merged that an Irish monk, St Aidan, arrived in the area and set about converting the local inhabitants to Christianity. Before long, Northumbria became the cradle of British Christianity. Echoes from this era resonate clearly on Holy Island (Lindisfarne), where you can visit Lindisfarne Castle and Lindisfarne Priory, built on the site of St Aidan's monastery. Other traces of this period can be found in towns such as Rothbury and Jarrow, which are home to crosses and tombs that feature intricate carved stonework. From 793 onwards, the dominance of Christianity was sharply countered by Viking

Medieval exterior of Alnwick Castle, Northumberland

raiders, who pillaged the Northumbria coast. Despite these attacks, a reverence for Northumbrian saints remains in the local psyche to this day. St Cuthbert, the area's favourite saint, and the Venerable Bede, who wrote *The Ecclesiastical History of the English People*, are both buried in Durham cathedral.

In 1018, the Scots enlarged their kingdom to its present extent, and thus began centuries of conflict with the English. Lasting peace proved elusive – even after the 1603 union between the two crowns – and one legacy of these clashes is the chain of massive, crenellated medieval castles found on or near the Northumbria coastline. Two very well-preserved examples of such fortifications are Warkworth Castle and Alnwick Castle. Other forts that once defended England's northern flank along the River Tweed lie mostly in ruins.

The 18th century Industrial Revolution made a strong impact on Northumbria. Perhaps most affected was Newcastle upon Tyne, which became the major shipbuilding centre in the region. Today, the city is known for its industrial heritage attractions, including the Museum of Science and Engineering, and for its urban regeneration schemes.

Another area of great importance during the Industrial Revolution was County Durham. By the 19th century, this region was one of the most significant areas of industrial growth in Britain. This was largely

Killhope Lead Mining Centre, County Durham

High Force waterfall, where the Tees river rushes across the rocky ridge of the Whin Sill

due to thriving coal and (to a lesser extent) lead mining industries. However, mining became less and less important as the 20th century progressed, and the region is now reinventing itself with a community forest and a host of cultural attractions. Not that the past is forgotten: one of County Durham's special qualities is the way it embraces and celebrates its history. Traditional music and activities remain popular, and it is easy to find folk clubs where smallpipes are played or pubs where long-sword dancing is performed. County Durham is also home to the Beamish Open Air Museum, which re-creates life in the region before World War I. To the south of this museum is the city of Durham, which features pretty cobbled streets and historic sites such as an 11th-century castle and a striking Norman cathedral.

One of the great attractions of Northumbria today is its many remote and beautiful areas. The moorlands of Northumberland and County Durham, which are among the most extensive in Britain, link together in such a way that it is sometimes possible to walk for two or three days without encountering a town or village. The sparse human population means that rare birds such as the merlin and the hen

Angel of the North sculpture, Tyne & Wear

harrier can flourish. Other treats in Northumbria for wildlife enthusiasts include the kittiwakes and fulmars that congregate around the coastal cliffs near Bamburgh, and the puffins and grey seals on the Farne Islands. The best-known walk in Northumberland is the Pennine Way, a challenging hike that starts in the Peak District 250 miles (400 km) to the south, but saves its most impressive and memorable moments for its last stage along the Border Ridge. To the west of the section of the Pennine Way that passes through the Northumberland National Park is Kielder Water, Europe's largest artificial lake. A wide variety of water sports are on offer here, including sailing and canoeing. Orienteering and mountain biking are very popular in the surrounding forest.

Escombe Church, a Saxon building near Bishop Auckland, County Durham

Eyemouth

BERWICK-UPON-TWEED

Kelso

Exploring Northumbria

Historic sites are plentiful along Northumbria's coast. South of Berwick-upon-Tweed, a causeway leads to the ruined priory and castle on Lindisfarne, and there are major castles at Bamburgh, Alnwick and Warkworth. The hinterland is a region of wide open spaces, with wilderness in the Northumberland National Park, and fascinating Roman remains of Hadrian's Wall at Housesteads and elsewhere. The glorious city of Durham is dominated by its castle and cathedral, and Newcastle upon Tyne has a lively nightlife.

SIGHTS AT A GLANCE

Alnwick Castle **5**
Bamburgh **4**
Barnard Castle **17**
Beamish Open Air Museum **13**
Berwick-upon-Tweed **1**
Cheviot Hills **8**
Corbridge **10**
Durham pp502–3 **14**
Farne Islands **3**
Hadrian's Wall pp496–7 **11**
Hexham **9**
Kielder Water **7**
Lindisfarne **2**
Middleton-in-Teesdale **16**
Newcastle upon Tyne **12**
Warkworth Castle **6**

Walks and Tours
North Pennines Tour **15**

OTTERBURN

KIELDER WATER **7**

CORBRIDGE

Carlisle

HEXHAM **9**

Tyne

15
NORTH
PENNINES
TOUR

Penrith

MIDDLETON-IN-TEESDALE **16**

Penrith

The wilderness of Upper Coquetdale in the sparsely populated Cheviot Hills

0 kilometres 10

0 miles 10

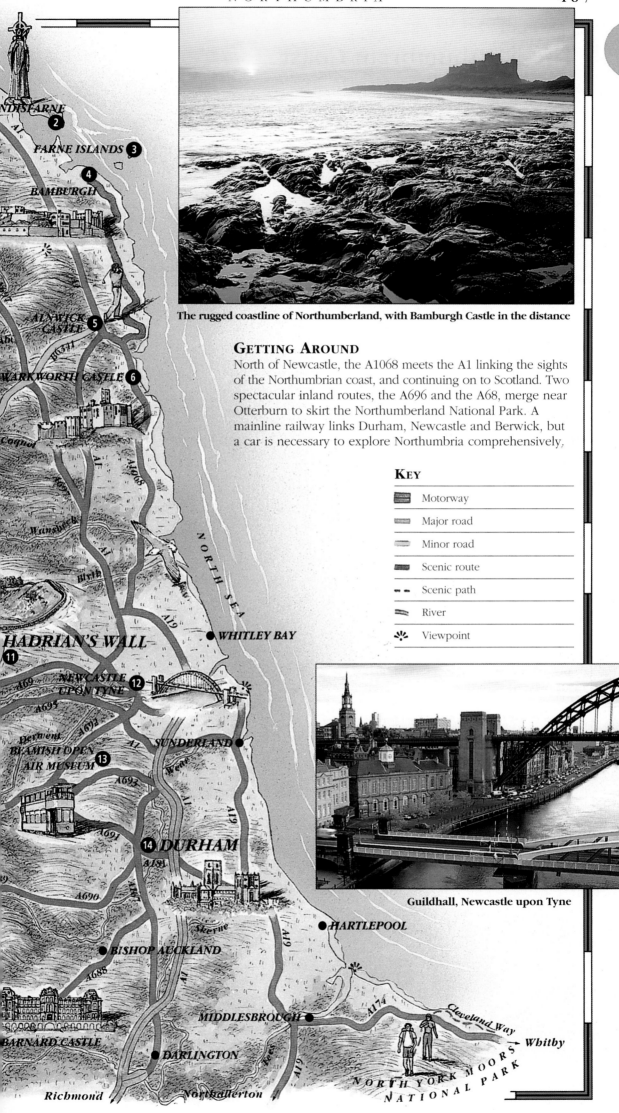

The rugged coastline of Northumberland, with Bamburgh Castle in the distance

GETTING AROUND

North of Newcastle, the A1068 meets the A1 linking the sights of the Northumbrian coast, and continuing on to Scotland. Two spectacular inland routes, the A696 and the A68, merge near Otterburn to skirt the Northumberland National Park. A mainline railway links Durham, Newcastle and Berwick, but a car is necessary to explore Northumbria comprehensively.

KEY

▬	Motorway
▬	Major road
▬	Minor road
▬	Scenic route
- -	Scenic path
⌇	River
☀	Viewpoint

Guildhall, Newcastle upon Tyne

Map labels:

LINDISFARNE ②
FARNE ISLANDS ③
④
BAMBURGH
ALNWICK CASTLE ⑤
WARKWORTH CASTLE ⑥
HADRIAN'S WALL
⑪
NEWCASTLE UPON TYNE ⑫
SUNDERLAND
BEAMISH OPEN AIR MUSEUM ⑬
⑭ DURHAM
WHITLEY BAY
HARTLEPOOL
BISHOP AUCKLAND
MIDDLESBROUGH
BARNARD CASTLE
DARLINGTON
Richmond
Northallerton
NORTH YORK MOORS NATIONAL PARK
Cleveland Way → Whitby
NORTH SEA
Coquet
Wansbeck
Blyth
Derwent
Wear
Skerne
Tees

The Northumbrian Coast

THE NORTHUMBRIAN COASTLINE, which is home for a wide variety of animals and plants, stretches some 70 miles (113 km) from Newcastle to Scotland. It is exposed to the ravages of the North Sea and to northerly Arctic gales, making it a fairly bleak area. However, it is directly opposite the southwest peninsula of Norway, which makes Northumberland a staging post for migrating birds to and from Scandinavia. The coastline is sheltered in places by precipitous cliffs and also littered with many islands, ranging from the Holy Island of Lindisfarne, some 2 miles (3.2 km) long, down to the smaller Farne Islands.

The mudflats of Budle Bay are an excellent place to watch migratory waders and wildfowl in autumn and spring.

The puffin, with its gaudy clown-like make-up and small, compact body, is always a pleasing bird to watch. Puffins live in clifftop colonies, where they build their nests in existing burrows or holes. Puffins can be observed with beaks full of sand eels, which they feed to their young.

THE FARNE ISLANDS

Just 4.5 miles (7 km) off the coast at Bamburgh are the Farne Islands. This group of islands consists of 28 small rocky outcrops. However, the number of islands does vary because some of them are so small they become completely submerged with the tides. The Farne Islands attract birdwatchers from all over Europe and can be visited by boat from Seahouses harbour *(see p490)*.

Arctic terns are very protective of their young. When visiting Arctic tern colonies, wear a hat – they peck the heads of visitors who get too close to their nests.

The kittiwake is a type of gull. It is strictly a coastal and seagoing bird, so look for its nests on rock ledges.

The eider duck has been valued for centuries for its warm, soft down. The down is collected from nests on the ground.

A STONE-AGE HERITAGE

The discovery of Neolithic artefacts preserved in the acidic waters of peat beds in Northumbria has provided evidence that people have lived in this part of Great Britain for thousands of years. Usually, organic materials perish with time, but items made from wood, bone and antler have all been preserved along with their stone components. These finds have provided archaeologists with a more rounded picture of the ways in which Neolithic people used the materials around them.

Neolithic weapon heads made from stone and flint

The northern marsh orchid has clusters of small flowers that range from reddish-purple to lilac.

The round-leaved wintergreen flourishes in the moist, acid soil conditions found along the Northumbrian coastline. The wintergreen is so-called because it is an evergreen plant, and its aromatic oil is used for medicinal purposes.

The butterwort is a carniverous plant. The leaves roll up to trap insects, which are then digested by the plant's enzymes.

Cliff ledges provide a safe place for birds to make their nests.

Grey seals can usually be seen on isolated rock ledges or beaches on many of the Farne Islands. The seals usually bask in the sunshine during the day.

Washington Wildlife Park, south of Newcastle, boasts an impressive number of bird species. The park is also home to 100 species of butterfly and moth.

St Cuthbert's Chapel is on Inner Farne Island. The saint lived here for eight years and returned to die on the island in 687.

View over Berwick-upon-Tweed's three bridges

Berwick-upon-Tweed ①

Northumberland. 🏠 13,000.
🚉 🛈 The Maltings, Eastern Lane
(01289 330733). 🔼 Wed, Sat.

BETWEEN THE 12th and 15th centuries Berwick-upon-Tweed changed hands 14 times in the wars between the Scots and English. Its position, at the mouth of the river which divides the two nations, made the town strategically vital.

The English finally gained permanent control in 1482 and maintained Berwick as a massively fortified garrison. Ramparts dating from 1555, 1.5 miles (2.5 km) long and 7 m (23 ft) thick, offer superb views over the Tweed. Within the same 18th-century barracks are the **King's Own Scottish Borderers Regimental Museum**, the town **museum**

and **art gallery**, and **By Beat of Drum**, which charts the history of British infantrymen.

🏛 King's Own Scottish Borderers Regimental Museum

The Barracks. 📞 01289 307427.
⬜ Mon–Sat. ⬤ 24 Dec–3 Jan, public hols. 🖳

Lindisfarne ②

Northumberland. 🚉 Berwick-upon-Tweed then bus. 🛈 The Maltings, Eastern Lane, Berwick-upon-Tweed (01289 330733).

TWICE DAILY a long, narrow neck of land sinks under the North Sea tide for five hours, separating Lindisfarne, or Holy Island, from the coast. At low tide, visitors stream over the causeway to the island made famous by St Aidan, St Cuthbert and the Lindisfarne

gospels. Nothing remains of the Celtic monks' monastery, finally abandoned in 875 after successive Viking attacks, but the magnificent arches of the 11th-century **Lindisfarne Priory** are still visible.

After 1540, stones from the priory were used to build **Lindisfarne Castle**, which was restored and made into a private home by Sir Edwin Lutyens (see p29) in 1903. It includes an attractive walled garden created by Gertrude Jekyll (see p27).

⚓ Lindisfarne Castle

(NT) Holy Island. 📞 01289 389244.
⬜ Apr–Oct: Sat–Thu & Good Fri (pm). 🖳

Farne Islands ③

(NT) Northumberland. 🚢 from Seahouses. 🛈 The Maltings, Eastern Lane, Berwick-upon-Tweed (01289 330733).

THERE ARE BETWEEN 15 and 28 Farne Islands off the coast from Bamburgh, some of them periodically covered by sea. The highest is around 31 m (100 ft) above sea level. Nature wardens and lighthouse keepers share them with seals, puffins and other seabirds.

Boat tours depart from **Seahouses** harbour and can only land on Staple and Inner Farne, site of St Cuthbert's 14th-century chapel.

Lindisfarne Castle (1540), the main landmark on the island of Lindisfarne

Celtic Christianity

St Cuthbert on a sea voyage

THE IRISH MONK St Aidan arrived in Northumbria in 635 from the island of Iona, off western Scotland, to evangelize the north of England. He founded the monastery on the island of Lindisfarne, and it became one of the most important centres for Christianity in England. This and other monastic communities thrived in Northumbria, becoming rich in scholarship, although the monks lived simply. It also emerged as a place of pilgrimage after miracles were reported at the shrine of St Cuthbert, Lindisfarne's most famous bishop. But the monks' pacifism made them defenceless against 9th-century Viking raids.

St Aidan's Monastery was added to over the centuries to become Lindisfarne Priory. This 8th-century relic with interlaced animal decorations is from a cross at the site.

The Venerable Bede (673–735), the most brilliant early medieval scholar, was a monk at the monastery of St Paul in Jarrow. He wrote The Ecclesiastical History of the English People in 731.

St Aidan (600–651), an Irish missionary, founded a monastery at Lindisfarne and became Bishop of Northumbria in 635. This 1960 sculpture of him, by Kathleen Parbury, is in Lindisfarne Priory grounds.

St Cuthbert (635–87) was the monk and miracle worker most revered of all. He lived as a hermit on Inner Farne (a chapel was built there in his memory) and later became Bishop of Lindisfarne.

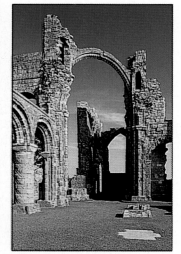
Lindisfarne Priory was built by Benedictines in the 11th century, on the site of St Aidan's earlier monastery.

THE LINDISFARNE GOSPELS

This book of richly illustrated portrayals of Gospel stories is one of the masterpieces of the "Northumbrian Renaissance" which left a permanent mark on Christian art and history-writing. The work was carried out by monks at Lindisfarne under the direction of Bishop Eadfrith, in around 700. Monks rescued the book and carried it with them when they fled from Lindisfarne in 875 after suffering repeated Viking raids. Other treasures were plundered.

Elaborately decorated initial to the *Gospel of St Matthew* (c.725)

Illustration of Grace Darling from the 1881 edition of *Sunday at Home*

Bamburgh ④

Northumberland. 🏛 *1,100.*
🚉 *Berwick.* ℹ *The Maltings,*
Eastern Lane, Berwick-upon-Tweed
(01289 330733).

DUE TO NORTHUMBRIA's history
of hostility against the
Scots, there are more strong-
holds and castles here than in
any other part of England.
Most were built from the 11th
to the 15th centuries by local
warlords, as was Bamburgh's
red sandstone **castle**. Its
coastal position had been
fortified since prehistoric times,
but the first major stronghold
was built in 550 by a Saxon
chieftain, Ida the Flamebearer.

In its heyday between 1095
and 1464, Bamburgh
was the royal castle
that was used by the
Northumbrian kings for
coronations. By the end
of the Middle Ages it had
fallen into obscurity, then
in 1894 it was bought by
Newcastle arms tycoon
Lord Armstrong, who re-
stored it. Works of art are
exhibited in the cavernous
Great Hall, and there are
suits of armour and
medieval artifacts in
the basement.

Bamburgh's other
main attraction is the
tiny **Grace Darling**
Museum which cele-
brates the bravery of
the 23-year-old, who,
in 1838, rowed through tem-
pestuous seas with her father,
the keeper of the Longstone
lighthouse, to rescue nine
people from the wrecked
Forfarshire steamboat.

Carrara marble
fireplace (1840) at
Alnwick Castle

⛪ Bamburgh Castle
Bamburgh. ☎ *01668 214515.*
◯ *mid-Mar–Oct: daily.* 🎫 ♿ 🖥
🏛 Grace Darling Museum
Radcliffe Rd. ☎ *01668 214465.*
◯ *Easter–Oct: daily.* ♿

Alnwick Castle ⑤

Alnwick, Northumberland. ☎ *01665*
510777. 🚉 🚌 *Alnmouth.*
◯ *Easter–Sep: daily.* 🎫 ♿ *limited.*

DOMINATING THE MARKET town
on the River Aln is another
great fortress, Alnwick Castle.
Described by the Victorians as
the "Windsor of the north", it is
the main seat of the Duke of
Northumberland, whose family,
the Percys, have lived here
since 1309. This
border stronghold
has survived many
battles, but now peace-
fully dominates the
pretty market town of
Alnwick, overlooking
landscape designed by
Capability Brown. The
stern medieval exterior
belies the fine treasure
house within, furnished
in palatial Renaissance
style with an exquisite
collection of Meissen
china and paintings by
Titian, Van Dyck and
Canaletto. The Postern
Tower contains a col-
lection of early British
and Roman relics. The
Regimental Museum
of Royal Northumberland
Fusiliers is in the Abbot's
Tower. Among other attractions
are the Percy State coach, the
dungeon, the gun terrace and
superb countryside views.

Warkworth Castle ⑥

Warkworth, nr Amble. ☎ *01665*
711423. ◯ *daily.* ⬤ *24–26 Dec,*
1 Jan. 🎫 ♿ *limited.*

WARKWORTH CASTLE sits on a
green hill overlooking
the River Coquet. It was the
Percy family home while
Alnwick Castle lay derelict.
Shakespeare's *Henry V* features the castle in scenes
between the Earl of Northumberland and his son, Harry
Hotspur. Much of the present-
day castle remains date from
the 14th century. The unusual
turreted, cross-shaped keep,
which was added in the 15th
century, is a central feature
of the castle tour.

Warkworth Castle reflected in the
River Coquet

Kielder Water ⑦

Yarrow Moor, Falstone, Hexham.
☎ *01434 240398.* ◯ *daily.* ⬤
24–26 Dec, 1, 2 Jan. ♿

ONE OF THE top attractions
of Northumberland,
Kielder Water lies close to the
Scottish border, surrounded
by spectacular scenery. With
a perimeter of 27 miles (44
km), it is Europe's largest
man-made lake, and offers
facilities for sailing, windsurfing, canoeing, water-skiing
and fishing. In summer, the
cruiser *Osprey* departs from
Leaplish on trips around the
lake. The Kielder Water
Exhibition, next to the Tower
Knowe Visitor Centre, depicts
the history of the valley from
the Ice Age to the present day.

Cheviot Hills 8

THESE BARE, LONELY MOORS, smoothed into rounded humps by Ice Age glaciers, form a natural border with Scotland. Walkers and outdoor enthusiasts find a near-wilderness unmatched anywhere else in England. This remotest extremity of the Northumberland National Park nevertheless has a long and vivid history. Roman legions, warring Scots and English border raiders, cattle drovers and whisky smugglers have all left traces along the ancient routes and tracks they carved out here.

VISITORS' CHECKLIST

Northumberland. ⚡ *Hexham.*
ℹ *Eastburn, South Park, Hexham.* ☎ *01434 605555.*

The Cheviots' isolated burns and streams are among the last habitats in England for the shy, elusive otter.

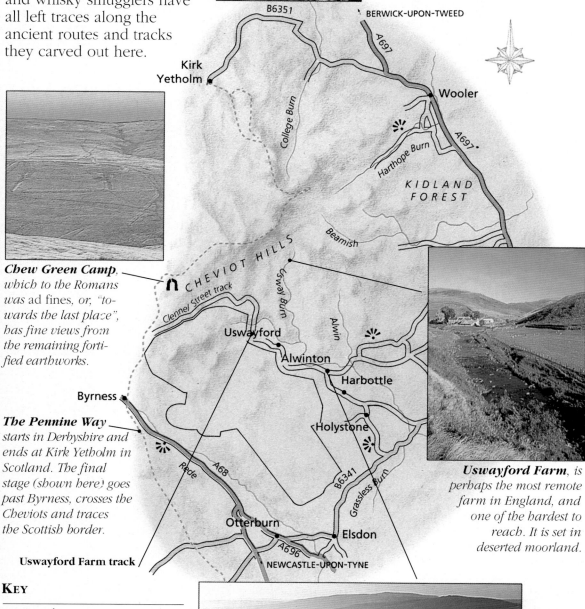

Chew Green Camp, which to the Romans was ad fines, or, "towards the last place", has fine views from the remaining fortified earthworks.

The Pennine Way starts in Derbyshire and ends at Kirk Yetholm in Scotland. The final stage (shown here) goes past Byrness, crosses the Cheviots and traces the Scottish border.

Uswayford Farm, is perhaps the most remote farm in England, and one of the hardest to reach. It is set in deserted moorland.

KEY

▬▬ A roads

▬▬ B roads

═══ Minor roads

--- Pennine Way

☀ Viewpoint

Alwinton, a tiny village built mainly from grey stone, is situated beside the River Coquet. It is an access point for many fine walks in the area, and the wild landscape is deserted except for sheep.

0 kilometres 5

0 miles 5

Hexham ⑨

Northumberland. 🏛 *10,000.* 🚆 🚌
ℹ *The Manor Office, Hallgate (01434 605225).* 🛒 *Tue.*

T HE BUSY MARKET TOWN of Hexham was established in the 7th century, growing up around the church and monastery built by St Wilfrid, but the Vikings sacked and looted it in 876. In 1114, Augustinians began work on a priory and abbey, building on the original church ruins to create

Hexham Abbey, which still towers over the market square today. The atmospheric Saxon crypt, built partly with stones from the former Roman fort at Corbridge, is all that remains

Ancient stone carvings at Hexham Abbey

of St Wilfrid's Church. The south transept of the abbey has a 12th-century night stair: stone steps leading from the dormitory. In the chancel is the Frith Stool, a Saxon throne in the centre of a circle which gave protection to fugitives. Narrow medieval streets and alleys, many with Georgian and Victorian shopfronts, spread out from the market square, The 15th-century Moot Hall was once a council chamber, and the old jail contains a **museum** charting border history.

Hadrian's Wall ⑪

O N THE ORDERS of Emperor Hadrian, work began in 120 on a 73 mile (117 km) wall to be erected across northern England, to mark and defend the northern limits of the British province and the northwest boundary of the Roman Empire. Troops were stationed at milecastles spaced along the wall, and large turrets, later forts, were built at 5 mile (8 km) intervals. The wall, now owned by the National Trust, was abandoned in 383 as the Roman Empire crumbled, but much of it remains.

Location of Hadrian's Wall

Vindolanda *is the site of several forts. The first timber fort dated from AD 90 and a stone fort was not built until the 2nd century. The museum has a collection of Roman writing tablets providing details of food, clothes and work.*

Great Chesters Fort was built facing east to guard Caw Gap, but there are few remains today. To the south and east of the fort are traces of a civil settlement and a bathhouse.

Carvoran Fort is probably pre-Hadrianic. Little of the fort survives, but the Roman Army museum nearby covers the wall's history.

Housesteads Settle ment includes the remains of terraced shops or taverns.

Emperor Hadrian *(76–138) came to Britain in 120 to order a stronger defence system. Coins were often cast to record emperors' visits, such as this bronze sestertius. Until 1971, the penny was abbreviated to d, short for* denarius, *a Roman coin.*

Cawfields, *2 mile (3 km) north of Haltwhistle, is the access point to on of the highest and most rugged sectio of the wall. To the east, the remains a milecastle sit on Whin Sill crag.*

◁ **Choir of Durham Cathedral, with its soaring ribbed vaults**

🔒 Hexham Abbey
Market Place. 📞 01434 602031.
⭕ daily. ♿

🏛 Border History Museum
Old Jail, nr Hallgate. 📞 01434
652349. ⭕ Apr–Oct: daily; Nov,
Feb, Mar: Sat, Mon, Tue. ▨

Corbridge 🔟

Northumberland. 👥 3,500. 🚃
ℹ Hill St (01434 632815).

THIS QUIET TOWN conceals a few historic buildings constructed with stones from the Roman garrison town of

The parson's 14th-century fortified tower house at Corbridge

nearby Corstopitum. Among these are the thickset Saxon tower of St Andrew's Church and the 14th-century fortified tower house built to protect the local clergyman. Excavations of Corstopitum, now known as **Corbridge Roman Site and Museum**, have exposed earlier forts, a well-preserved granary, temples, fountains and an aqueduct.

🏛 Corbridge Roman Site and Museum
📞 01434 632349. ⭕ Apr–Oct:
daily; Nov–Mar: Wed–Sun. ● 24–26
Dec, 1 Jan. ▨ ♿ limited. 📷

THE WALL COAST-TO-COAST

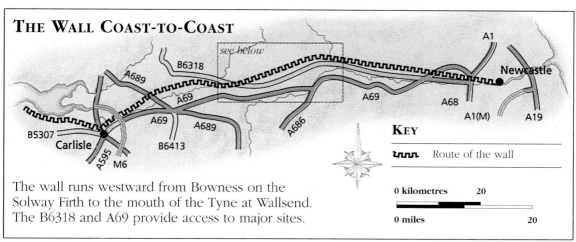

The wall runs westward from Bowness on the Solway Firth to the mouth of the Tyne at Wallsend. The B6318 and A69 provide access to major sites.

KEY

⌐⌐⌐ Route of the wall

0 kilometres 20

0 miles 20

Carrawburgh Fort, a 500-man garrison, guarded the Newbrough Burn and North Tyndale approaches.

Limestone Corner Milecastle is sited at the northernmost part of the wall and has magnificent views of the Cheviot Hills *(see p493)*.

Sewingshields Milecastle, with magnificent views west to Housesteads, is one of the best places for walking. This reconstruction shows the layout of a Roman milecastle on the wall.

Chesters Fort was a bridgehead over the North Tyne. In the museum are altars, sculptures and inscriptions.

Chesters Bridge crossed the Tyne. The original Hadrianic bridge was rebuilt in 207. The remains of this second bridge abutment can still be seen.

Housesteads Fort is the best-preserved site on the wall, with fine views over the countryside. The excavated remains include the commanding officer's house and a Roman hospital.

0 metres 500

0 yards 500

Newcastle upon Tyne ⑫

Tyne & Wear. 👥 273,000. ✈ ⇄
🚉 🛳 ℹ️ *City Library, Princess Sq*
(0191 2610610). 🚢 *Sun.*

NEWCASTLE OWES ITS NAME TO its Norman **castle** which was founded in 1080 by Robert Curthose, the eldest son of William the Conqueror *(see p51)*. The Romans had bridged the Tyne and built a fort on the site 1,000 years earlier. During the Middle Ages it was still a fortress town guarding the mouth of the river and was used as a base for English campaigns against the Scots. From the Middle Ages, the city flourished as a coal mining and exporting centre. It was known in the 19th century for engineering, steel production and later as the world's foremost shipyard. The city's industrial base has declined in recent years, but "Geordies", as inhabitants of the city are known, have refocused their civic pride on the ultra-modern Metro Centre shopping mall

Bridges crossing the Tyne at Newcastle

at Gateshead, some 4 miles (6 km) southwest of the city, and Newcastle United soccer team. The city's lively night scene includes clubs, pubs, theatres and ethnic restaurants. The visible trappings of its past are reflected in the magnificent Tyne Bridge and in Benjamin Green's monument commemorating Earl Grey. The grand façades of city centre thoroughfares, such as Grey Street, also reflect this former prosperity. Despite some derelict areas, many buildings on the quayside are being restored.

⛴ The Castle

St Nicholas St. 📞 *0191 2327938.* ⭕ *Tue–Sun & public hols.* ⭘ *24–26 Dec, 1 Jan, Good Fri.* 📷 🎟️ Curthose's original wooden "new castle" was rebuilt in stone in

Beamish Open Air Museum ⑬

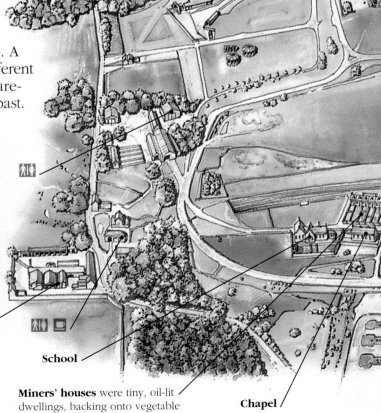

THIS GIANT OPEN AIR MUSEUM, spread over 120 ha (300 acres) of County Durham, re-creates an authentic picture of family, working and community life in the northeast before World War I. It has a typical High Street, a colliery village, a disused mine, a school, chapel and farm, all with guides in period costume. A restored tramline serves the different parts of the museum, which carefully avoids romanticizing the past.

Tram symbol

The station has locomotives, coaches, freight trucks, a platform, a signal box and a wrought-iron footbridge. Working locomotives are often found in station and colliery areas.

***Home Farm** recreates the atmosphere of an old-fashioned farmyard. Rare breeds of cattle and sheep, more common before the advent of mass breeding, can be seen.*

School

Miners' houses were tiny, oil-lit dwellings, backing onto vegetable plots and owned by the colliery.

Chapel

the 12th century. Only the thickset, crenellated keep remains intact with two suites of royal apartments. A series of staircases spiral up to the renovated battlements, from where there are fine views over the city and the Tyne. The castle also has a restored Norman chapel (c.1168–78), Great Hall and garrison room.

🛈 St Nicholas Cathedral

St Nicholas Sq. **℡** *0191 2321939.* ◯ *daily.* &

This is one of Britain's tiniest cathedrals. There are remnants inside of the original 11th-century Norman church on which the present 14th- and 15th-century structure was founded. Its most striking feature is its ornate "lantern tower" – half tower, half spire – of which there are only three others in Britain. First built in 1448, it was rebuilt in 1608, then repaired during the 18th and 19th centuries.

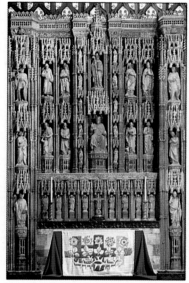

Reredos of the Northumbrian saints in St Nicholas Cathedral

🏛 Bessie Surtees' House

41–44 Sandhill. **℡** *0191 2611585.* ◯ *Mon–Fri.* ● *25 Dec–2 Jan, public hols.* 🖼

The story of beautiful, wealthy Bessie, who lived here before eloping with penniless John Scott, later Lord Chancellor of England, is the romantic tale behind these half-timbered 16th- and 17th-century houses. The window through which Bessie escaped now has a blue glass pane. These buildings also throw light on mercantile life in the quayside district.

🏛 Tyne Bridge

Newcastle–Gateshead. **℡** *0191 2328520.* ◯ *daily.* &

Opened by King George V in 1928, this two-pin steel arch was the longest of its type in Britain with a span of 162 m (531 ft). Designed by Mott, Hay and Anderson, it soon became the city's most potent symbol.

🏛 Earl Grey's Monument

Grey St. **℡** *0191 2328520.* ● *for restoration until mid-2000.*

Benjamin Green created this memorial to the 2nd Earl Grey, Liberal Prime Minister from 1830 to 1834 and responsible for the Great Reform Bill. The statue is by Edward H Baily.

The High Street *has a sweet shop, newspaper office, solicitor, dentist and music teacher. There is also a pub.*

The Co-op *stocked everything a family needed at the turn of the century. A full range of foods available in 1913 is displayed.*

Pockerley Manor farm

Steam Winding Engine

Entrance

P

Mahogany Drift mine, *a tunnel driven into coal seams near the surface, was here long before the museum and was worked from the 1850s to 1958. Visitors are given guided tours to underground pits.*

VISITORS' CHECKLIST

Beamish, County Durham. **℡** *01207 231811.* 🚃 🚌 *Durham, then bus.* ◯ *Mar–Oct: 10am– 5pm daily (last adm 3pm); Nov–Feb: High Street only 10am– 4pm Tue–Thu, Sat, Sun.* ● *18–25 Dec, 1 Jan, Good Fri.* 📷 🖥 🖼

Houses built by the London Lead Company in Middleton-in-Teesdale

Durham ⑭

See pp502–3.

North Pennines Tour ⑮

See p501.

**Cotherstone cheese, a speciality
of the Middleton-in-Teesdale area**

Middleton-in-Teesdale ⑯

County Durham. 🏠 *1,100.* 🚆
Darlington. ℹ️ *1C Chapel Row.*

CLINGING TO A HILLSIDE amid
wild Pennine scenery on
the River Tees is the old lead
mining town of Middleton-in-
Teesdale. Many of its rows of
grey stone cottages were built
by the London Lead Company,
a paternalistic, Quaker-run
organization whose influence
spread into every corner of its
employees' daily lives.

The company began mining
in 1753, and soon it virtually
owned the town. Workers
were expected to observe
strict temperance, send their
children to Sunday school
and conform to the many
company maxims. Today,
mining has all but ceased in
Teesdale, with Middleton
standing as a monument to
the 18th-century idea of the
"company town". The offices
of the London Lead Company
can still be seen, as well as
Nonconformist chapels from
the era and a memorial
fountain made of iron.

The crumbly Cotherstone
sheep's cheese, a speciality
of the surrounding dales, is
widely available in the shops.

Barnard Castle ⑰

County Durham. 🏠 *5,000.*
🚆 *Darlington.* ℹ️ *Woodleigh, Flatts
Rd (01833 690909).* 🔄 *Wed.*

BARNARD CASTLE, known in
the area as "Barney", is a
little town full of character,
with old shopfronts and a
cobbled market overlooked
by the ruins of the Norman
castle from which it takes its
name. The original Barnard
Castle was built around 1125–
40 by Bernard Balliol, ancestor
of the founder of Balliol
College, Oxford *(see p241)*, to
guard a river crossing point.
Later, the market town grew
up around the fortification.

Today, Barnard Castle is
known for the extraordinary
French-style château to the
east of the town, surrounded
by acres of formal gardens.
Started in 1860 by the local
aristocrat John Bowes and his
French wife Josephine, an artist
and actress, it was never a
private residence, but always
intended as a museum and
public monument. The château
finally opened in 1892, by
which time the couple were
both dead. Nevertheless, the
Bowes Museum stands as a
monument to his wealth and
her extravagance.

The museum houses a strong
collection of Spanish art which
includes El Greco's *The Tears
of St Peter*, dating from the
1580s, and Goya's *Don Juan
Meléndez Váldez*, painted in
1797. Clocks, porcelain, furniture, musical instruments, toys
and tapestries are among its
treasures, with a mechanical
silver swan as a showpiece.

🏛 **Bowes Museum**
Barnard Castle. ☎ *01833 690606.*
⭕ *daily.* ⬤ *25, 26 Dec,
1 Jan.* 🎫 ♿ 🖥 🛈

The Bowes Museum, a French-style château near Barnard Castle

North Pennines Tour ⑮

STARTING JUST TO THE SOUTH of Hadrian's Wall, this tour explores the South Tyne Valley, and Upper Weardale. It crosses one of England's wildest and most remote tracts of moorland, then heads north again. The high ground is mainly blanketed with heather, dotted with sheep or criss-crossed with dry-stone walls, a feature of this region. Harriers and other birds hover above, and streams tumble into valleys of tightly huddled villages.

Celts, Romans and other settlers have left imprints on the North Pennines. The wealth of the area was based on lead mining and stone quarrying which has long co-existed with farming.

Sheep grazing on the moors

Haltwhistle ①
In the Church of the Holy Cross is the tombstone of John Ridley, brother of Protestant martyr, Nicholas Ridley, burnt at the stake in 1555 (see p241).

Haydon Bridge ③
There are some delightful walks near this spa town where the painter John Martin was born in 1789. Nearby Langley Castle is worth a visit.

Hexham ④
A pretty old town (see p497), Hexham has a fine abbey.

Blanchland ⑤
Some houses in this 17th-century lead-mining village, are built on the site of a 12th-century abbey, using pieces of the original stone.

Bardon Mill ②
To the north is the Roman fort and civilian settlement of Vindolanda (see p496).

Allendale ⑦
With its capital at Allendale Town, this is an area of spectacular scenery, with many walking and trout fishing opportunities.

KEY

- ▬▬ Tour route
- ═══ Other roads
- ❋ Viewpoint

TIPS FOR DRIVERS

Length: 50 miles (80 km)
Stopping-off points: Several pubs in Stanhope serve bar meals, and the Durham Dales Centre provides teas all year round. Horsley Hall Hotel at Eastgate serves meals all day.

Stanhope ⑥
An 18th-century castle overlooks the market square. The giant stump of a fossilized tree, said to be 250 million years old, guards the graveyard.

0 kilometres 5

0 miles 5

Durham ⑭

Cathedral Sanctuary knocker

THE CITY OF DURHAM was built on Island Hill or "Dunholm" in 995. This rocky peninsula, which defies the course of the River Wear's route to the sea, was chosen as the last resting place for the remains of St Cuthbert. The relics of the Venerable Bede were brought to the site 27 years later, adding to its attraction for pilgrims. Durham Cathedral was treated by architects as an experiment for geometric patterning, while the Castle served as the Episcopal Palace until 1832, when Bishop William van Mildert gave it up and surrendered part of his income to found Britain's third university. The 23 ha (57 acre) peninsula has many footpaths, views and fine buildings.

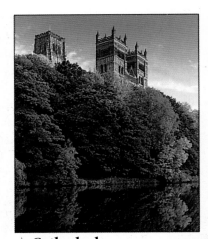

★ Cathedral
Built from 1093 to 1274, it is a striking Norman structure.

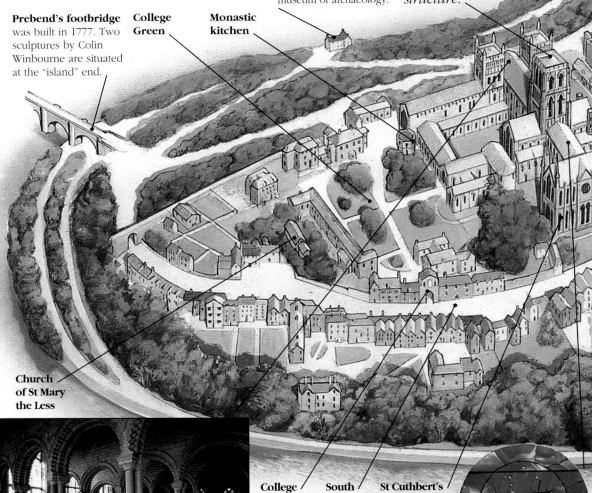

Old Fulling Mill, a largely 18th-century building, houses a museum of archaeology.

Prebend's footbridge was built in 1777. Two sculptures by Colin Winbourne are situated at the "island" end.

College Green

Monastic kitchen

Church of St Mary the Less

College gatehouse **South Bailey** **St Cuthbert's Tomb**

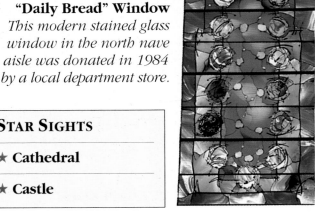

"Daily Bread" Window
This modern stained glass window in the north nave aisle was donated in 1984 by a local department store.

Galilee Chapel

Architects began work on the exotic Galilee Chapel in 1170, drawing inspiration from the Great Mosque of Cordoba in Andalusia. It was altered by Bishop Langley (d.1437) whose tomb is by the west door.

STAR SIGHTS

★ **Cathedral**

★ **Castle**

★ Castle

Begun in 1072, the castle is a fine Norman fortress. The keep, sited on a mound, is now part of the university.

Town Hall (1851)

St Nicholas' Church (1857)

Palace Green

VISITORS' CHECKLIST

County Durham. ⬌ Station Approach. 🚌 North Rd. ℹ Market Pl (0191 384 3720). 🔄 Sat. **Cathedral** ◯ May–Aug: 7:15am–8pm; Sep–Apr: 7:15am– 6pm. ✝ 11:15am, 3:30pm Sun. 📷 ♿ **Castle** ☎ 0191 374 3800. ◯ univ hols: daily; term: Mon, Wed, Sat (pm). 📷 🚻

Tunstal's Chapel

Situated at the end of the Tunstal's Gallery, the castle chapel was built c.1542. Its fine woodwork includes this unicorn misericord (see p391).

Castle Gatehouse

Traces of Norman stonework can be seen in the outer arch, while the sturdy walls and upper floors are 18th century, rebuilt in a style dubbed "gothick" by detractors.

University buildings were built by Bishop John Cosin in the 17th century.

Church of St Mary le Bow

Kingsgate Footbridge, built from 962–3, leads to North Bailey.

CATHEDRAL ARCHITECTURE

The vast dimensions of the 900-year-old columns, piers and vaults, and the inventive giant lozenge and chevron, trellis and dogtooth patterns carved into the stone columns, are the main innovative features of Durham Cathedral. It is believed that 11th- and 12th-century architects such as Bishop Ranulph Flambard tried to unify all parts of the structure. This can be seen in the south aisle of the nave below.

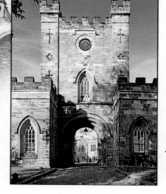

Ribbed vaults, criss-crossing above the nave, are now common in church ceilings. One of the major achievements of Gothic architecture, they were first built at Durham.

The lozenge shape is a pattern from prehistoric carving, but never before seen in a cathedral.

Chevron patterns on some of the piers in the nave are evidence of Moorish influence.

WALES

INTRODUCING WALES 506-513
NORTH WALES 514-537
SOUTH AND MID-WALES 538-565

Wales at a Glance

WALES IS A COUNTRY of outstanding natural beauty with varied landscapes. Visitors come to climb dramatic mountain peaks, go walking in the forests, fish in the broad rivers and enjoy the miles of unspoilt coastline. The country's many seaside resorts have long been popular with English holidaymakers. As well as outdoor pursuits there is the vibrancy of Welsh culture, with its strong Celtic roots, to be experienced. Finally there are many fine castles, ruined abbeys, mansions and cities full of magnificent architecture.

Beaumaris Castle *was intended to be a key part of Edward I's "iron ring" to contain the rebellious Welsh (see p510). Begun in 1295 but never completed, the castle (see p512) has a sophisticated defence structure that is unparalleled in Wales.*

Anglesey

Caernarfonshire & Merionethshire

Portmeirion (see pp536–7) *is a private village whose astonishing buildings seem rather incongruous in the Welsh landscape. The village was created by the architect Sir Clough Williams-Ellis to fulfill a personal ambition. Some of the buildings are assembled from pieces of architecture taken from sites around the country.*

Cardigan

Carmarthenshire

Pembrokeshire

St David's *is the smallest city in Britain. The cathedral (see pp552–3) is the largest in Wales, and its nave is noted for its carved oak roof and beautiful rood screen. Next to the cathedral is the medieval Bishop's Palace, now a ruin.*

◁ **Caernarfon's colourful quayside marina**

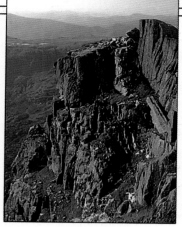

Llanberis and Snowdon

(see p531) *is an area famous for dangerous, high peaks, long popular with climbers. Mount Snowdon's summit is most easily reached from Llanberis. Its Welsh name,* Yr Wyddfa Fawr, *means "great tomb" and, it is the legendary burial place of a giant slain by King Arthur (see p315).*

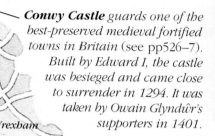

Flintshire

Aberconwy & Colwyn

Denbighshire

NORTH WALES
(see pp514–537)

Wrexham

Conwy Castle *guards one of the best-preserved medieval fortified towns in Britain (see pp526–7). Built by Edward I, the castle was besieged and came close to surrender in 1294. It was taken by Owain Glyndŵr's supporters in 1401.*

Powys

SOUTH AND MID-WALES
(see pp538–565)

The Brecon Beacons *(see pp556–7) is a national park, a lovely area of mountains, forest and moorland in South Wales, which is a favourite with walkers and naturalists. Pen-y-Fan is one of the principal summits.*

Cardiff Castle's

(see pp562–3) Clock Tower is just one of many 19th-century additions by the eccentric but gifted architect William Burges. His flamboyant style still delights and amazes visitors.

Monmouthshire

Cardiff, Swansea & Environs

0 kilometres   25

0 miles   25

A PORTRAIT OF WALES

LONG POPULAR WITH BRITISH HOLIDAYMAKERS, *the many charms of Wales are now becoming better known internationally. They include spectacular scenery and a vibrant culture specializing in male-voice choirs, poetry and a passionate love of team sports. Governed from Westminster since 1536, Wales has its own distinct Celtic identity and in 1999 finally gained partial devolution.*

Much of the Welsh landmass is covered by the Cambrian Mountain range, which effectively acts as a barrier from England. Wales is warmed by the Gulf Stream and has a mild climate, with more rain than most of Britain. The land is unsuitable for arable farming, but sheep and cattle thrive; the drove roads, along which sheep used to be driven across the hills to England, are now popular walking trails. It is partly because of the rugged terrain that the Welsh have managed to maintain their separate identity and their ancient language.

Welsh is an expansive, musical language, spoken by only one-fifth of the 2.7 million inhabitants, but in parts of North Wales it is still the main language of conversation. There is an official bilingual policy: road signs are in Welsh and English, even in areas where Welsh is little spoken. Welsh

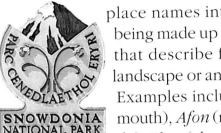

One of Wales's splendid National Parks

place names intrigue visitors, being made up of native words that describe features of the landscape or ancient buildings. Examples include *Aber* (river mouth), *Afon* (river), *Fach* (little), *Llan* (church) *Llyn* (lake) and *Nant* (valley).

Wales was conquered by the Romans, but not by the Saxons. The land and the people therefore retained Celtic patterns of settlement and husbandry for six centuries before the Norman Conquest in 1066. This allowed time for the development of a distinctive Welsh nation whose homogeneity continues to this day.

The early Norman kings subjugated the Welsh by appointing "Marcher Lords" to control areas bordering England. A string of massive castles provides evidence of the turbulent years when Welsh insurrection was a constant threat. It was not until 1535 that Wales formally became part of Britain, and today it is governed from Westminster, with a cabinet minister responsible for its affairs.

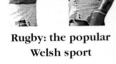

Rugby: the popular Welsh sport

Religious non-conformism and radical politics are deeply rooted in Welsh consciousness. Saint David converted the country to Christianity in the 6th century. Methodism, chapel and teetotalism became firmly entrenched in

Mountain sheep: a familiar sight in rural Wales

A *gorsedd* (assembly) of bards at the eisteddfod

of music derives from the ancient bards: minstrels and poets, who may have been associated with the Druids. Bardic tales of quasi-historical figures and magic were part of the oral tradition of the Dark Ages. They were first written down in the 14th century as the *Mabinogion,* which has inspired Welsh poets up to the 20th century's Dylan Thomas. The male-voice choirs found in many towns, villages and factories, particularly in the industrial south, express the Welsh musical heritage. Choirs compete in eisteddfods: festivals that celebrate Welsh culture.

the Welsh psyche during the 19th century. Even today some pubs stay closed on Sundays (alcohol is not sold at all in the Llŷn Peninsula). A long-standing oral tradition in Wales has produced many outstanding public speakers, politicians and actors. Welsh labour leaders have played important roles in the British trade union movement and the development of socialism.

Welsh heritage is steeped in song, music, poetry and legend rather than handicrafts, although one notable exception is the carved Welsh lovespoon – a craft recently revived. The well-known Welsh love

Welsh lovespoon

In the 19th century, the opening of the South Wales coalfield in Mid-Glamorgan – for a time the biggest in the world – led to an industrial boom, with mass migration from the countryside to the iron and steelworks. This prosperity was not to last: apart from a brief respite in World War II, the coal industry has been in terminal decline for decades, causing severe economic hardship. Today tourism is being promoted in the hope that the wealth generated, by outdoor activities in particular, will be able to take "King Coal's" place.

Conwy's picturesque, medieval walled town, fronted by a colourful harbour

The History of Wales

St David, patron saint of Wales

WALES HAS BEEN SETTLED since prehistoric times, its history shaped by many factors, from invasion to industrialization. The Romans set up bases in the mountainous terrain, but it was effectively a separate Celtic nation when Offa's Dyke was built as the border with England in 770. Centuries of cross-border raids and military campaigns followed before England and Wales were formally united by the Act of Union in 1535. The rugged northwest, the former stronghold of the Welsh princes, remains the heartland of Welsh language and culture.

Owain Glyndŵr, heroic leader of Welsh opposition to English rule

THE CELTIC NATION

Ornamental Iron Age bronze plaque from Anglesey

WALES WAS SETTLED by waves of migrants in prehistoric times. By the Iron Age *(see p46)*, Celtic farmers had established hillforts and their religion, Druidism. From the 1st century AD, until the legions withdrew around 400, the Romans built fortresses and roads, and mined lead, silver and gold. During the next 200 years, Wales was converted to Christianity by missionaries from Europe. St David *(see pp552–3)*, the Welsh patron saint, is said to have turned the leek into a national symbol. He persuaded soldiers to wear leeks in their hats to distinguish themselves from Saxons during a 6th-century skirmish.

The Saxons *(see pp50–51)* failed to conquer Wales, and in 770 the Saxon King Offa built a defensive earthwork along the unconquered territory *(see p549)*. Beyond Offa's Dyke the people called themselves *Y Cymry* (fellow countrymen) and the land *Cymru*. The Saxons called the land "Wales" from the Old English *wealas*, meaning foreigners. It was divided into kingdoms of which the main ones were Gwynedd in the north, Powys in the centre and Dyfed in the south. There were strong trade, cultural and linguistic links between each.

MARCHER LORDS

THE NORMAN INVASION of 1066 *(see p51)* did not reach Wales, but the border territory ("the Marches") was given by William the Conqueror to three powerful barons based at Shrewsbury, Hereford and Chester. These Marcher Lords made many incursions into Wales and controlled most of the lowlands. But the Welsh

Edward I designating his son Prince of Wales in 1301

princes held the mountainous northwest and exploited English weaknesses. Under Llywelyn the Great (d.1240), North Wales was almost completely independent; in 1267 his grandson, Llywelyn the Last, was acknowledged as Prince of Wales by Henry III.

In 1272 Edward I came to the English throne. He built fortresses and embarked on a military campaign to conquer Wales. In 1282 Llywelyn was killed in a skirmish, a shattering blow for the Welsh. Edward introduced English law and proclaimed his son Prince of Wales *(see p524)*.

OWAIN GLYNDŴR'S REBELLION

WELSH RESENTMENT against the Marcher Lords led to rebellion. In 1400 Owain Glyndŵr (c.1350–1416), a descendant of the Welsh princes, laid waste to English-dominated towns and castles. Declaring himself Prince of Wales, he found Celtic allies in Scotland, Ireland, France and Northumbria. In 1404 Glyndŵr captured Harlech and Cardiff, and formed a parliament in Machynlleth *(see p550)*. In 1408 the French made a truce with the English king, Henry IV. The rebellion then failed and Glyndŵr went into hiding until his death.

Union with England

WALES SUFFERED greatly during the Wars of the Roses *(see p53)* as Yorkists and Lancastrians tried to gain control of the strategically important Welsh castles. The wars ended in 1485, and the Welshman Henry Tudor, born in Pembroke, became Henry VII. The Act of Union in 1535 and other laws abolished the Marcher Lordships, giving Wales parliamentary representation in London instead. English practices replaced inheritance customs and English became the language of the courts and administration. The Welsh language survived, partly helped by the church and by Dr William Morgan's translation of the Bible in 1588.

Vernacular Bible, which helped to keep the Welsh language alive

Industry and Radical Politics

THE INDUSTRIALIZATION of south and east Wales began with the development of open-cast coal mining near Wrexham and Merthyr Tydfil in the 1760s. Convenient ports and the arrival of the railways helped the process. By the second half of the 19th century open-cast mines had been superseded by deep pits in the Rhondda Valley.

Living and working conditions were poor for industrial and agricultural workers. A series of "Rebecca Riots" in

Miners from South Wales pictured in 1910

South Wales between 1839 and 1843, involving tenant farmers (dressed as women) protesting about tithes and rents, was forcibly suppressed. The Chartists, trade unions and the Liberal Party had much Welsh support.

The rise of Methodism *(see p311)* roughly paralleled the growth of industry: 80 per cent of the population was Methodist by 1851. The Welsh language persisted, despite attempts by the British government to discourage its use, which included punishing children caught speaking it.

Wales Today

IN THE 20TH CENTURY the Welsh, for the first time, became a power in British politics. David Lloyd George, although not born in Wales, grew up there and was the first British Prime Minister to come from a Welsh family. Aneurin Bevan, a miner's son who became a Labour Cabinet Minister, helped create the National Health Service *(see p63)*.

Welsh nationalism continued to grow: in 1926 Plaid Cymru, the Welsh Nationalist Party, was formed. In 1955 Cardiff

was recognized as the capital of Wales *(see p560)* and four years later the ancient symbol of the red dragon became the emblem on Wales' new flag. Plaid Cymru won two parliamentary seats at Westminster in 1974, and in a 1998 referendum the Welsh espoused limited home rule.

The Welsh language has declined: whereas half the population could speak it in 1901, the figure was down to 21 per cent 70 years later. The 1967 Welsh Language Act gave it protection by making Welsh compulsory in schools and the television channel S4C (Sianel 4 Cymru), formed in 1982, broadcasts many programmes in Welsh.

From the 1960s the steel and coal industries declined, creating mass unemployment. This has been only partly alleviated by the emergence of new, high-tech industries, and by the recent growth in tourism and higher education.

The logo of S4C, Wales's own television station

Castles of Wales

A French 15th-century painting of Conwy Castle

WALES IS RICH in romantic medieval castles. Soon after the Battle of Hastings, in 1066 *(see p51)*, the Normans turned their attentions to Wales. They built earth and timber fortifications, later replaced by stone castles, initiating a building programme that was pursued by the Welsh princes and invading forces. Construction reached its peak during the reign of Edward I *(see p510)*. As the need for security lessened in the later Middle Ages, some castles became stately homes.

The north gatehouse was planned to be 18 m (60 ft) high, providing lavish royal accommodation, but its top storey was never built.

The inner ward was lined with a hall, granary, kitchens and stables.

Rounded towers, with fewer blind spots than square ones, gave better protection.

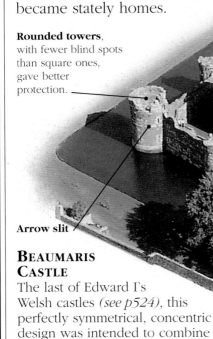

Arrow slit

BEAUMARIS CASTLE
The last of Edward I's Welsh castles *(see p524)*, this perfectly symmetrical, concentric design was intended to combine impregnable defence with comfort. Invaders would face many obstacles before reaching the inner ward.

Moat

Curtain wall

WHERE TO SEE WELSH CASTLES
In addition to Beaumaris, in North Wales there are medieval forts at Caernarfon *(see p524)*, Conwy *(see p526)* and Harlech *(see p536)*. Edward I also built Denbigh, Flint (near Chester) and Rhuddlan (near Rhyll). In South and mid-Wales, Caerphilly (near Cardiff), Kidwelly (near Carmarthen) and Pembroke were built between the 11th and 13th centuries. Spectacular sites are occupied by Cilgerran (near Cardigan), Criccieth (near Porthmadog) and Carreg Cennen *(see p556)*. Chirk Castle, near Llangollen, is a good example of a fortress that has since become a stately home.

Caerphilly, 6 miles (10 km) north of Cardiff, is a huge castle with concentric stone and water defences that cover 12 ha (30 acres).

Harlech Castle (see p536) is noted for its massive gatehouse, twin towers and the fortified stairway to the sea. It was the headquarters of the Welsh resistance leader Owain Glyndŵr (see p510) from 1404–8.

CASTELL-Ŷ-BERE

This native Welsh castle at the foot of Cader Idris *(see p536)* was founded by Llywelyn the Great in 1221 *(see p510)*, to secure internal borders rather than to resist the English.

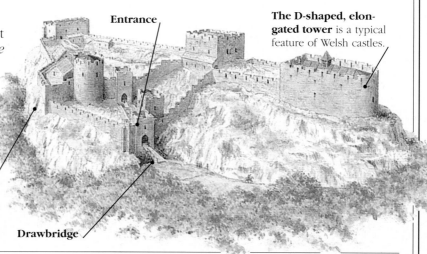

Entrance

The D-shaped, elongated tower is a typical feature of Welsh castles.

The castle's construction follows the shape of the rock. The curtain walls are too low and insubstantial to be of much practical use.

Drawbridge

The Chapel Tower has a beautiful medieval chapel.

The protected dock, on a channel that originally led to the sea, received supplies during sieges.

The inner wall, with an inner passage, was higher than the curtain wall to permit simultaneous firing.

Twin-towered gatehouse

EDWARD I AND MASTER JAMES OF ST GEORGE

In 1278 Edward I brought over from Savoy a master stonemason who became a great military architect, James of St George. Responsible for planning and building at least 12 of Edward's fine Welsh castles, James was paid well and liberally pensioned off, indicating the esteem in which he was held by the king.

Edward I (see p510) *was the warrior king whose castles played a key role in the subjugation of the Welsh people.*

A plan of Caernarfon Castle illustrates how its position, on a promontory surrounded by water, has determined the building's shape and defence.

Caernarfon Castle (see p524), *birthplace of the ill-fated Edward II (see p371), was intended to be the official royal residence in North Wales, and has palatial private apartments.*

Castell Coch was restored in Neo-Gothic style by Lord Bute and William Burges (see p562). Mock-castles were built by many Victorian industrialists.

Conwy Castle (see p527), *like many other castles, required forced labour on a massive scale for its construction.*

Brightly coloured heather adorning rolling hills near Llangollen, Denbighshire ▷

NORTH
WALES

NORTH WALES

THE NORTH WALES LANDSCAPE *has a dramatic quality reflected in its history. In prehistoric times, Anglesey was the stronghold of the Druids, an elite religious cult. Roman and Norman invasions concentrated on the coast, leaving the mountains to the Welsh. These wild areas are the centre of Welsh language and culture.*

Defence and conquest were the constant themes of Welsh history until the 15th century. North Wales saw ferocious battles between Welsh princes and Anglo-Norman monarchs, who were determined to establish English rule. The string of formidable castles that still stand in North Wales are as much a testament to Welsh resistance as to the wealth and strength of the invaders. Several massive fortresses, including Beaumaris, Caernarfon and Harlech, can be found just beyond the rugged high country of Snowdonia, a mountainous area that still possesses an untamed quality.

The remoteness of the region explains why it became the last stronghold of the Welsh language, which the English were seeking to discourage until well into the 20th century (even forbidding its use in schools). Of the 20 per cent of Welsh people who speak the language today, a large number live in the northern part of the country, particularly on the Llyn Peninsula and in more central communities such as Bala. This stubborn determination to preserve tradition is characteristic of the people of North Wales, who have always been keener advocates of self-rule than those in the south. In some cases their sense of separateness has manifested itself in hostility to outsiders, especially the English. In the 1980s scores of cottages used as weekend homes by their English owners were burned down by protesters. These actions were in part inspired by nationalism, but also by the fact that the houses were unoccupied for most of the week (which had a negative effect on the community), and that house prices had been forced to levels higher than the locals could

Caernarfon Castle, one of the forbidding fortresses built by Edward I

◁ **The River Dee at Llangollen, still an area of unspoilt natural beauty**

View of Mount Snowdon from Snowdonia National Park

afford. However, visitors to North Wales need not worry about any such anger being vented on them. The extremists are in a small minority and in any case have no quarrel with short-term tourists, on whom the modern Welsh economy partly depends.

Stone bridge over the River Conwy, Snowdonia

Sheep and cattle farming, which together form the traditional basis of the rural economy in North Wales, have been going through a difficult period, with lamb fetching low prices in the market and beef sales still affected by the bovine spongiform encephalopathy (BSE, or "mad cow disease") scare of the early 1990s.

Although no part of North Wales can truly be called industrial, in Snowdonia there are still remnants of the once-prosperous slate industry. In this area the stark, grey quarries provide a striking contrast to the natural beauty of the surrounding mountains, which are one of the region's principal attractions. At the foot of Snowdon, the highest mountain in Wales, the villages

of Beddgelert, Betws-y-Coed and Llanberis are popular bases for rock climbers and walkers, who come to enjoy the spectacular views and clean air Snowdonia has to offer.

The town of Llandudno, on the north coast, is a purpose-built Victorian resort that popularized the sandy beaches of the north coast in the 19th century. These beaches continue to attract visitors, though the major development is confined to the narrow coastal strip between Prestatyn and Llandudno. Watersports enthusiasts can enjoy some of Britain's best windsurfing, kayaking and rafting on the large lake at Bala (home of the National Whitewater Centre), on the River Dee at Llangollen or at Porth Neigwl (Hell's Mouth), a broad expanse of sea at the southern end of the lovely Llyn Peninsula. Those who prefer sailing tend to congregate around the new

Menai Bridge, viewed from the island of Anglesey

marina at Pwllheli, the principal town of Llyn.

On the northwest corner of Wales, across the Menai Straits, is the island of Anglesey. The modern road and rail bridge across the Straits is a few miles from Thomas Telford's magnificent construction, Menai Bridge. When this was built in 1826, it was the largest suspension bridge in the world, soaring 30 m (100 ft) above the water to allow tall ships to pass underneath. Holyhead, on the western tip of the island, is the terminal for the main ferry service between Britain and Ireland. Rhosneigr, a quaint seaside resort on the west coast of Anglesey, is a popular surfing centre. Off Anglesey's eastern extremity is Puffin Island, where lovers of wildlife may see – apart from the puffins – large colonies of razorbills, guillemots and choughs.

The coast of Wales is warmed by the Gulf Stream, which flows up from the south and makes for comparatively mild winters. This has encouraged the creation of some of Britain's most

The Pin Mill, Bodnant Gardens, near Conwy

splendid gardens. Chief among these is Bodnant, whose spectacular terraces run down to the River Conwy a few miles south of the town of Conwy. Since the garden has an enormous number of rhododendrons, azaleas and camellias, it is at its best in spring and early summer. However, the owner, Lord Aberconway, boasts that there is not a day in the year when at least one of his rhododendrons is not in flower, and the leaf colours in autumn are magnificent. Other interesting gardens in the area well worth visiting are at Penrhyn Castle, near Bangor, and at Plas Newydd, on the island of Anglesey (not to be confused with the other Plas Newydd, which is also in North Wales, near Llangollen). The 18th-century house at Plas Newydd on Anglesey, which was designed by James Wyatt and has a wall painting by Rex Whistler, is a fascinating building to explore.

Plaque on Offa's Dyke, Powys

Remains of Valle Crucis Abbey, which was established in 1200, near the town of Llangollen, Clwyd

Exploring North Wales

T HE DOMINANT FEATURE of North Wales is Snowdon, the highest mountain in Wales. Snowdonia National Park extends dramatically from the Snowdon massif south beyond Dolgellau, with thickly wooded valleys, mountain lakes, moors and estuaries. To the east are the softer Clwydian Hills, and unspoilt coastlines can be enjoyed on Anglesey and the beautiful Llŷn Peninsula.

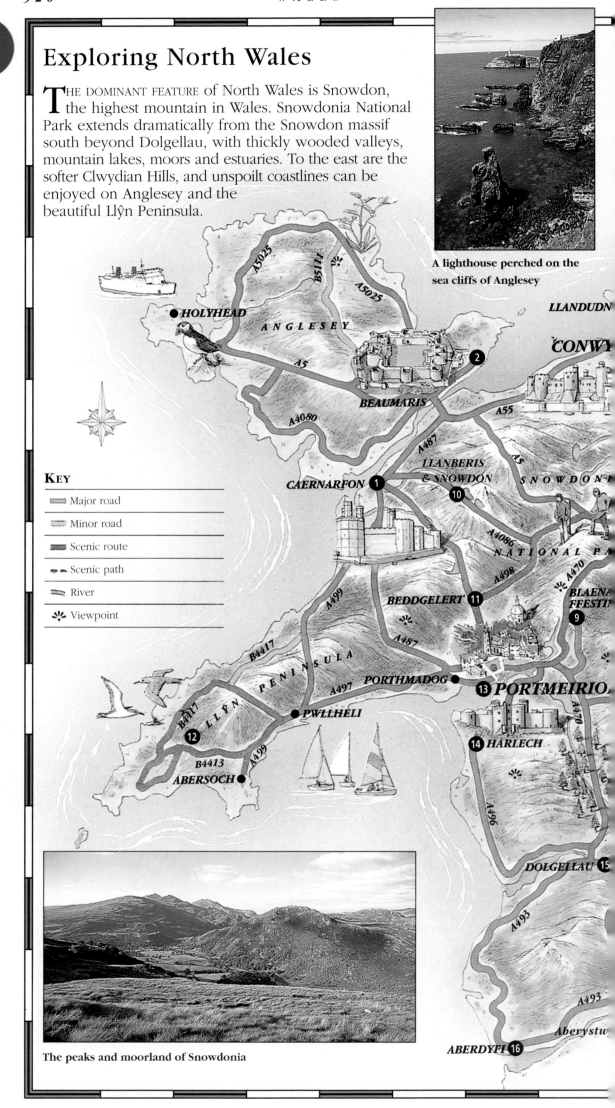

A lighthouse perched on the sea cliffs of Anglesey

LLANDUDN

HOLYHEAD

A N G L E S E Y

CONW

A5025

B5111

A5025

A5

A4080

BEAUMARIS

A55

A55

A487

LLANBERIS & SNOWDON

S N O W D O N

2

1 CAERNARFON

10

A4086

N A T I O N A L P A

A498

A470

BLAEN FFESTI

KEY

▭▭	Major road
▭▭	Minor road
▭▭	Scenic route
●━	Scenic path
⟿	River
☀	Viewpoint

11 BEDDGELERT

9

A487

B4417

L L Ŷ N   P E N I N S U L A

A499

A497

PORTHMADOG

13 PORTMEIRIO

B4417

L L Ŷ N

PWLLHELI

12

A499

B4413

ABERSOCH

14 HARLECH

A470

A496

DOLGELLAU 15

A493

A493

Aberystw

ABERDYFI 16

The peaks and moorland of Snowdonia

GETTING AROUND

The main route into North Wales from the northwest of England is the A55, a good dual carriageway which bypasses several places that used to be traffic bottlenecks, including Conwy. The other main route through the region is the A5 Shrewsbury to Holyhead road, which follows a trail through the mountains pioneered by the 19th-century engineer Thomas Telford (*see p527*). Rail services run along the coast to Holyhead, connecting with ferries across the Irish Sea to Dublin and Dun Laoghaire. Scenic branch lines travel from Llandudno Junction to Blaenau Ffestiniog (via Betws-y-Coed) and along the southern Llŷn Peninsula.

SIGHTS AT A GLANCE

Aberdyfi **16**
Bala **7**
Beaumaris **2**
Beddgelert **11**
Betws-y-Coed **8**
Blaenau Ffestiniog **9**
Caernarfon **1**
Conwy pp526–7 **3**
Dolgellau **15**
Harlech **14**
Llanberis and Snowdon **10**
LLandudno **4**
LLangollen **6**
Llŷn Peninsula **12**
Portmeirion pp536–7 **13**
Ruthin **5**

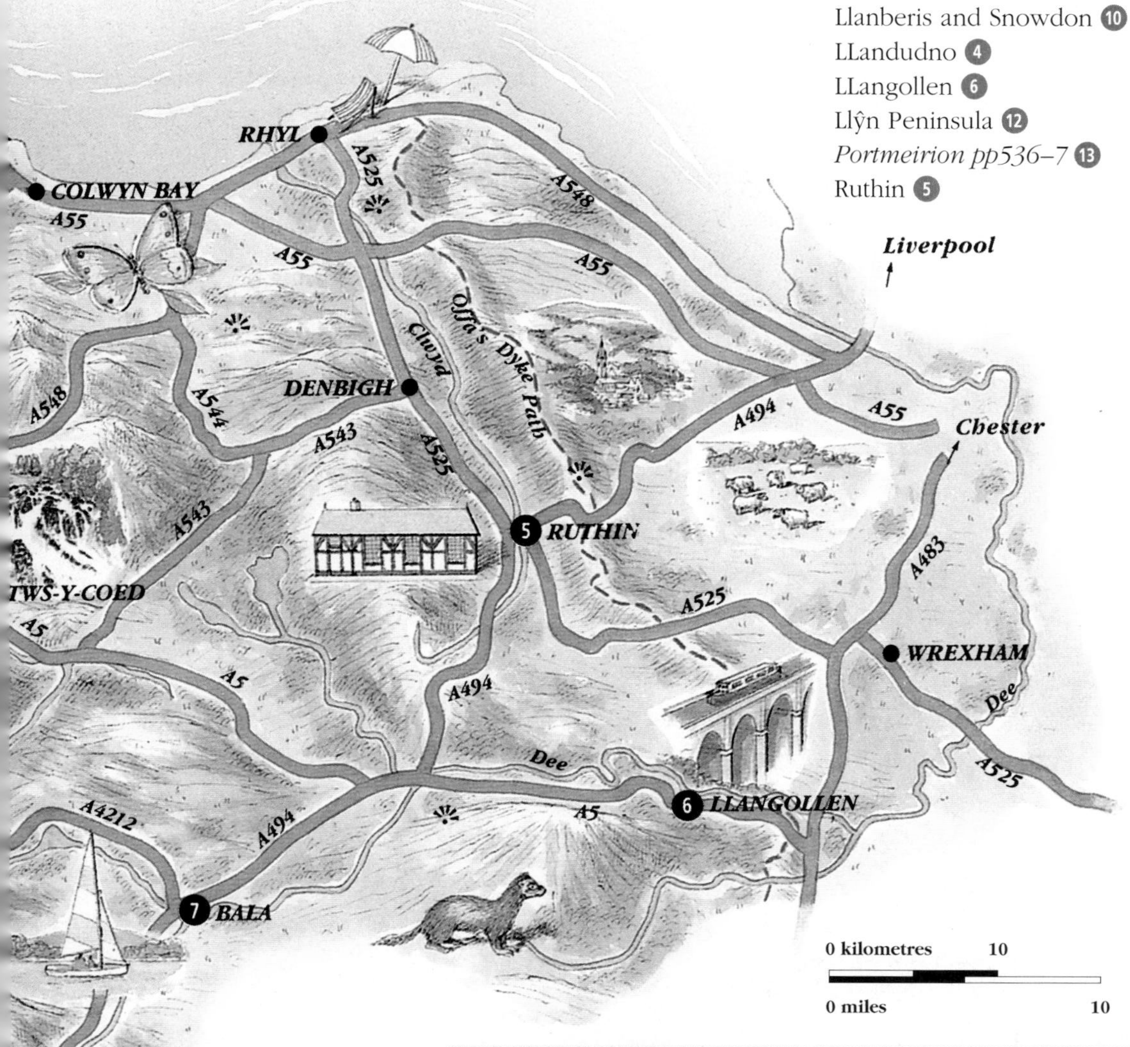

RHYL
COLWYN BAY
A55
A525
A548
A55
A548
A544
A543
DENBIGH
A55
Clwyd
Offa's Dyke Path
A494
A55
Liverpool
Chester
A543
A525
A483
TWS-Y-COED
A5
5 *RUTHIN*
A525
WREXHAM
A5
A494
Dee
A525
Dee
A4212
A494
A5
6 *LLANGOLLEN*
7 *BALA*

0 kilometres 10
0 miles 10

470
A458 → **Shrewsbury**

The imposing castle built at Conwy by Edward I in the 13th century

Sailing and Sea Sports

IF YOU CAN TAKE A CRAFT on the water, you can take it to North Wales. The region caters for everything from surfing and canoeing to learning to sail your first dinghy and offshore racing. The major marina is at Pwllheli, where a uniform depth and lack of strong tidal currents makes for the best sailing water in Britain. The highlight of the racing year is the Three Peaks Race. Starting at Barmouth, competitors sail to Caernarfon, Ravenglass and Fort William. Athletes leave their craft at each port and scale a mountain. The record stands at 2 days, 8 hours and 12 minutes.

Pwllheli Marina has 450 berths

CELTIC RACE WEEK, PWLLHELI

The largest regatta in the Tremadoc Bay area is Celtic Race Week, held in June every two years at Pwllheli. There are three different racing classes and more than 200 boats participate. On-shore social activities are also a feature of this regatta.

***Menai Strait regatta** takes place every August and is popular with amateurs and professionals alike. The course runs from Beaumaris to Caernarfon.*

Sometimes 100 boats or more may be racing in one event.

WATER SPORTS

The National Water Sports Centre at Plas Menai (Menai Strait) was a built in 1983 by the Sports Council for Wales. It is ideally located on sheltered coastline, so students can learn about the tides and other sea conditions, which is not possible on an inland lake. The Sports Centre offers tuition in most water sports, including windsurfing, canoeing, power boating, jet biking and sailing – from dinghies to yachts.

Windsurfing is one of the most popular sports in Wales

Surfing conditions are ideal at Anglesey, near Plas Menai

Lake Bala *is a long, deep, narrow lake that provides ideal water conditions on which to learn to sail. When the wind runs the length of the lake and crosswinds create interesting wind patterns, more experienced sailors come to hone their skills.*

The Pwllheli Regatta *takes place over a weekend. Anyone can enter the competition, but smaller regattas like this one usually attract only local competitors.*

Racing takes place every week *at picturesque Anglesey. The sailing club does not have a marina so smaller dayboats, such as keel boats, are the local favourites.*

tudents learn on land efore taking to the water

Canoeists can tackle the coast or the white water at Snowdonia

Some high-performance dinghies can travel very fast on the water

Caernarfon Castle, built by Edward I as a symbol of his power over the conquered Welsh

Caernarfon ❶

Caernarfonshire & Merionethshire (Gwynedd). 🏃 *10,000.* 🚌
ℹ️ *Castle St (01286 672232).* 🚢 *Sat.*

Oneof the most famous castles in Wales looms over this busy town. Both were created after Edward I's defeat of the last native Welsh prince, Llywelyn ap Gruffydd, in 1283 *(see p510)*. The town walls merge with shopping streets that spread beyond the medieval centre and open into a market square.

Overlooking the town and its harbour, **Caernarfon Castle** *(see p513)*, with its polygonal towers, was built as a seat of government for North Wales. Caernarfon was a thriving port in the 19th century, and during this period the castle ruins were restored by the architect Anthony Salvin. The castle now contains several interesting displays, including the Royal Welch Fusiliers Museum, and exhibitions tracing the history of the Princes of Wales and exploring the theme "Chieftains and Princes".

On the hill above the town are the ruins of **Segontium**, a Roman fort built in about AD 78. According to a rather unlikely local legend, the first Christian Emperor of Rome, Constantine the Great, was born here in 280.

♜ **Caernarfon Castle**
Y Maes. 📞 *01286 677617.* ◯ *daily.*
⬤ *24, 25 Dec, 1 Jan.* 🎫 🔲
⛰ **Segontium**
Beddgelert Rd. 📞 *01286 675625.*
◯ *daily (Sun: pm).* ⬤ *24, 25 Dec.*
🎫 ♿ *limited.*

The Investiture

In 1301 the future Edward II became the first English Prince of Wales *(see p510)*, a title since held by the British monarch's eldest son. In 1969 the investiture in Caernarfon Castle of Prince Charles *(above)* as Prince of Wales drew 500 million TV viewers.

Beaumaris ❷

Anglesey (Gwynedd). 🏃 *2,000.* 🚌
ℹ️ *Llanfair PG, Station Site, Holyhead Rd, Anglesey (01248 713177).*

Handsome georgian and Victorian architecture gives Beaumaris the air of a resort on England's southern coast. The buildings reflect this sailing centre's past role as Anglesey's chief port, before the island was linked to the mainland by the road and railway bridges built across the Menai Strait in the 19th century. This was the site of Edward I's last, and possibly greatest, **castle** *(see p512)*, which was built to command this important ferrying point to the mainland of Wales.

Ye Olde Bull's Head inn, on Castle Street, was built in 1617. Its celebrated literary patrons have included Dr Samuel Johnson (1709–84) and Victorian novelist Charles Dickens *(see p191)*.

The town's **Courthouse**, built in 1614, is still in use, and the restored 1829 **Gaol** preserves its soundproofed punishment room and a huge treadmill for prisoners. Two public hangings took place here. Richard Rowlands, the last victim, protested his innocence of murder and cursed the church clock as he was being led to the gallows, declaring that its four faces would never show the same times again. The clock failed to show consistent times until it had an overhaul in 1980.

Beaumaris's award-winning **Museum of Childhood** contains a nostalgic collection of toys and games from the 19th and 20th centuries.

♜ **Beaumaris Castle**
Castle St. 📞 *01248 810361.* ◯
daily. ⬤ *24–26 Dec, 1 Jan.* 🎫 ♿
🏛 **Courthouse**
High St. 📞 *01248 810921.* ◯ *Apr–Sep: daily.* 🎫 ♿ *limited.*
🏛 **Gaol**
Bunkers Hill. 📞 *01248 810921.*
◯ *Apr–Sep: daily.* 🎫
🏛 **Museum of Childhood**
Castle St. 📞 *01248 712498.* ◯ *25 Mar–Oct: daily (Sun: pm).* 🎫

ALICE IN WONDERLAND

The Gogarth Abbey Hotel, Llandudno, was the summer home of the Liddells. Their friend, Charles Dodgson (1832–98), would entertain young Alice Liddell with stories of characters such as the White Rabbit and the Mad Hatter. As Lewis Carroll, Dodgson wrote his magical tales in *Alice's Adventures in Wonderland* (1865) and *Through the Looking-Glass* (1871).

Arthur Rackham's illustration (1907) of *Alice in Wonderland*

Conwy ③

See pp526–7.

Llandudno ④

Aberconwy & Colwyn (Gwynedd).
🚶 *19,000.* 🚆 🚌 ℹ️ *1–2 Chapel St (01492 876413).* 🏛️ *Mon–Sat.*

Llandudno's crescent-shaped bay

LLANDUDNO retains much of the holiday spirit of the 19th century, when the new railways brought crowds to the coast. Its **pier**, more than 700 m (2,295 ft) long, and its canopied walkways recall the heyday of seaside holidays. The town is proud of its association with the author Lewis Carroll. **The Rabbit Hole** is a grotto decorated with life-sized scenes from his children's books.

Llandudno's cheerful and informal seaside atmosphere owes much to a strong sense of its Victorian roots – unlike many other British seaside towns, which have embraced the flashing lights and funfairs of the 20th century. To take full advantage of its wide,

sweeping beach, Llandudno was laid out between its two headlands, Great Orme's Head and Little Orme's Head.

Great Orme's Head, now a Country Park and Nature Reserve, rises to a height of 207 m (680 ft) and has a long history of human settlement. In the Bronze Age copper was mined here; the **copper mines** and their excavations are open to the public. The **church** on the headland was first built from timber in the 6th century by missionary St Tudno, rebuilt in stone in the 13th century, restored in 1855 and is still in use today. Great Orme's Head's history and wildlife can be traced in an information centre which is on the summit.

There are two effortless ways to reach the summit: on the **Great Orme Tramway**, one of only three cable-hauled street tramways in the world (the others are in San

Francisco and Lisbon), or by the **Llandudno Cable Car**. Both operate only in summer.

🏛️ The Rabbit Hole
Trinity Sq. 📞 *01492 860082.* ⭕ *Easter–Oct: daily; Nov–Easter: Mon–Sat.* ● *25–26 Dec, 1 Jan.* 🎫 ♿ 🛍️

⛰️ Great Orme Copper Mines
Off A55. 📞 *01492 870447.* ⭕ *Feb–Nov: daily.* 🎫 ♿ *limited.* 🎥 💻 🛍️

Ruthin ⑤

Denbighshire (Clwyd). 🚶 *5,000.* 🚌 ℹ️ *Craft Centre, Park Rd (01824 703992).* 🏛️ *1st Tue every month.*

RUTHIN'S LONG-STANDING prosperity as a market town is reflected in its fine half-timbered medieval buildings. These include the National Westminster and Barclays banks in St Peter's Square. The former was a 15th-century courthouse and prison, the latter the home of Thomas Exmewe, Lord Mayor of London in 1517–18. **Maen Huail** ("Huail's stone"), a boulder outside Barclays, is said to be where King Arthur *(see p315)* beheaded Huail, his rival in a love affair.

St Peter's Church, on the edge of St Peter's Square, was founded in 1310 and has a beautiful Tudor oak roof in the north aisle, with 500 carved panels. Next to the Castle Hotel is the 17th-century **Myddleton Arms** pub, whose seven unusual, Dutch-style, dormer windows are known locally as the "eyes of Ruthin".

The "eyes of Ruthin", an unusual feature in Welsh architecture

Street-by-Street: Conwy ③

Conwy is one of Britain's most underrated historic towns. Until the early 1990s it was famous as a traffic bottleneck, but thanks to a town bypass, its concentration of architectural riches – unparalleled in Wales – can now be appreciated. The castle dominates: a brooding, intimidating monument built by Edward I *(see p510)*. But Conwy is set apart from other medieval towns by its amazingly well-preserved town walls. Fortified with 21 towers and three gateways, the walls form an almost unbroken shield around the old town.

Smallest House
This fisherman's cottage on the quayside, just over 3 m (10 ft) high, is said to be the smallest house in Britain.

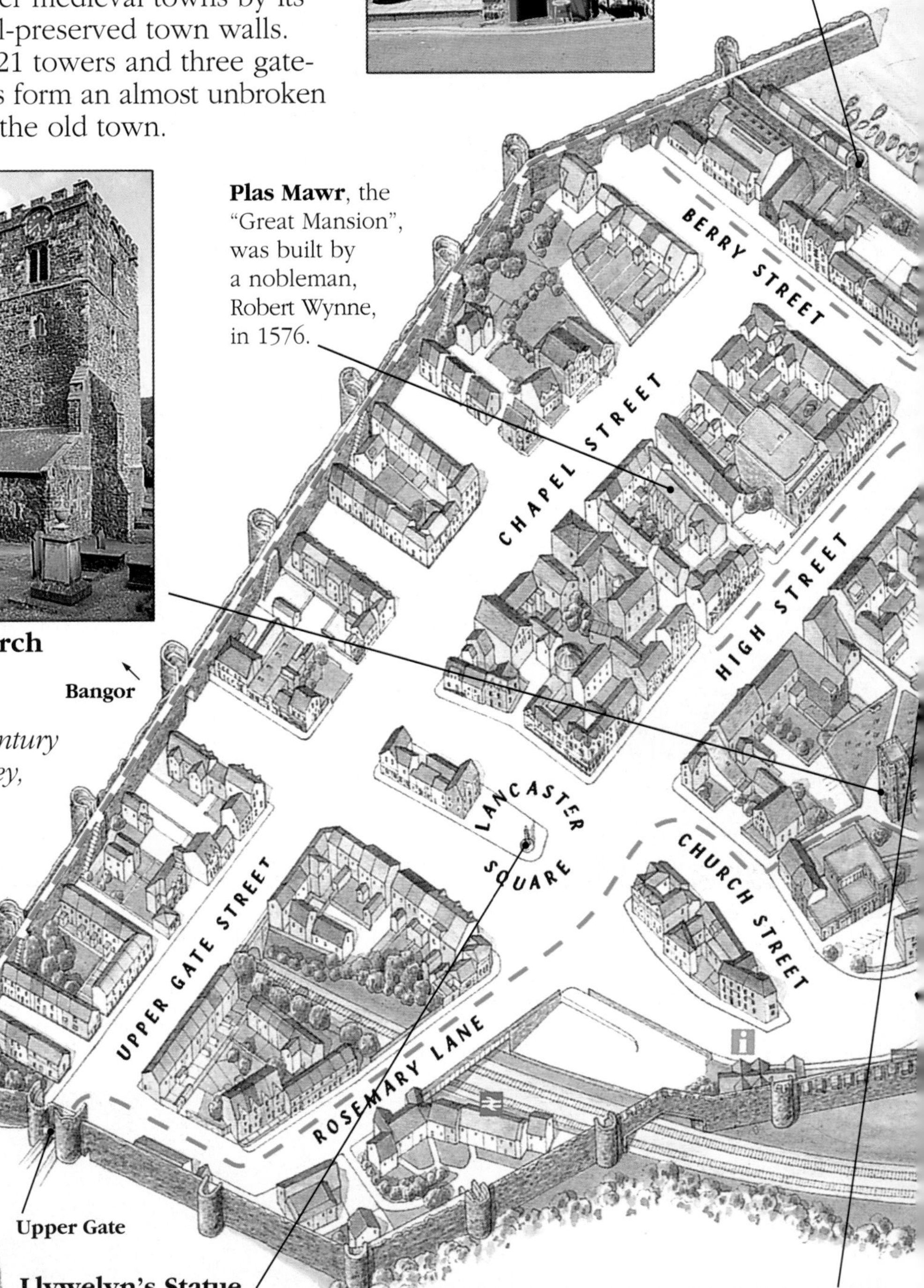

Plas Mawr, the "Great Mansion", was built by a nobleman, Robert Wynne, in 1576.

BERRY STREET

CHAPEL STREET

HIGH STREET

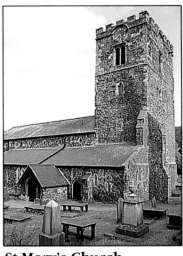

St Mary's Church
This medieval church, on the site of a 12th-century Cistercian abbey, is set in peaceful grounds.

Bangor

LANCASTER SQUARE

CHURCH STREET

UPPER GATE STREET

ROSEMARY LANE

Upper Gate

Llywelyn's Statue
Llywelyn the Great (see p510) was arguably Wales's most successful medieval leader.

Aberconwy House
This restored 14th-century house was once the home of a wealthy merchant.

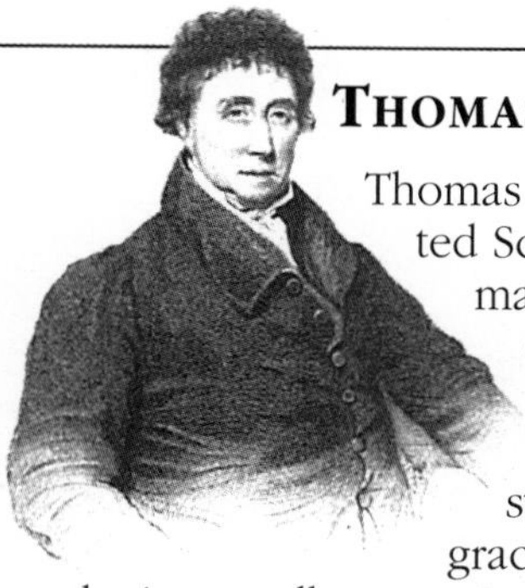

THOMAS TELFORD

Thomas Telford (1757–1834) was the gifted Scottish engineer responsible for many of Britain's roads, bridges and canals. The Menai Bridge, the Pontcysyllte Aqueduct *(see p530)* and Conwy Bridge are his outstanding works in Wales. Telford's graceful bridge at Conwy has aesthetic as well as practical qualities. Completed in 1826 across the mouth of the Conwy estuary, it was designed in a castellated style to blend with the castle. Before the bridge's construction the estuary could only be crossed by ferry.

VISITORS' CHECKLIST

Aberconwy & Colwyn (Gwynedd). *8,000.* *Conwy.* *01492 592248.* *Conwy Festival: Jul.*
Aberconwy House *01492 592246.* *Wed–Mon.* *Nov–Mar.* **Conwy Castle** *01492 592358.* *daily.* *25, 26 Dec, 1 Jan.* **Smallest House** *Apr–Oct: daily.*

Chester
NEW BRIDGE
CASTLE STREET
CASTLE SQUARE
L STREET
Telford's bridge
Railway bridge
0 metres 50
0 yards 50
Entrance to castle

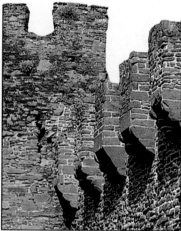

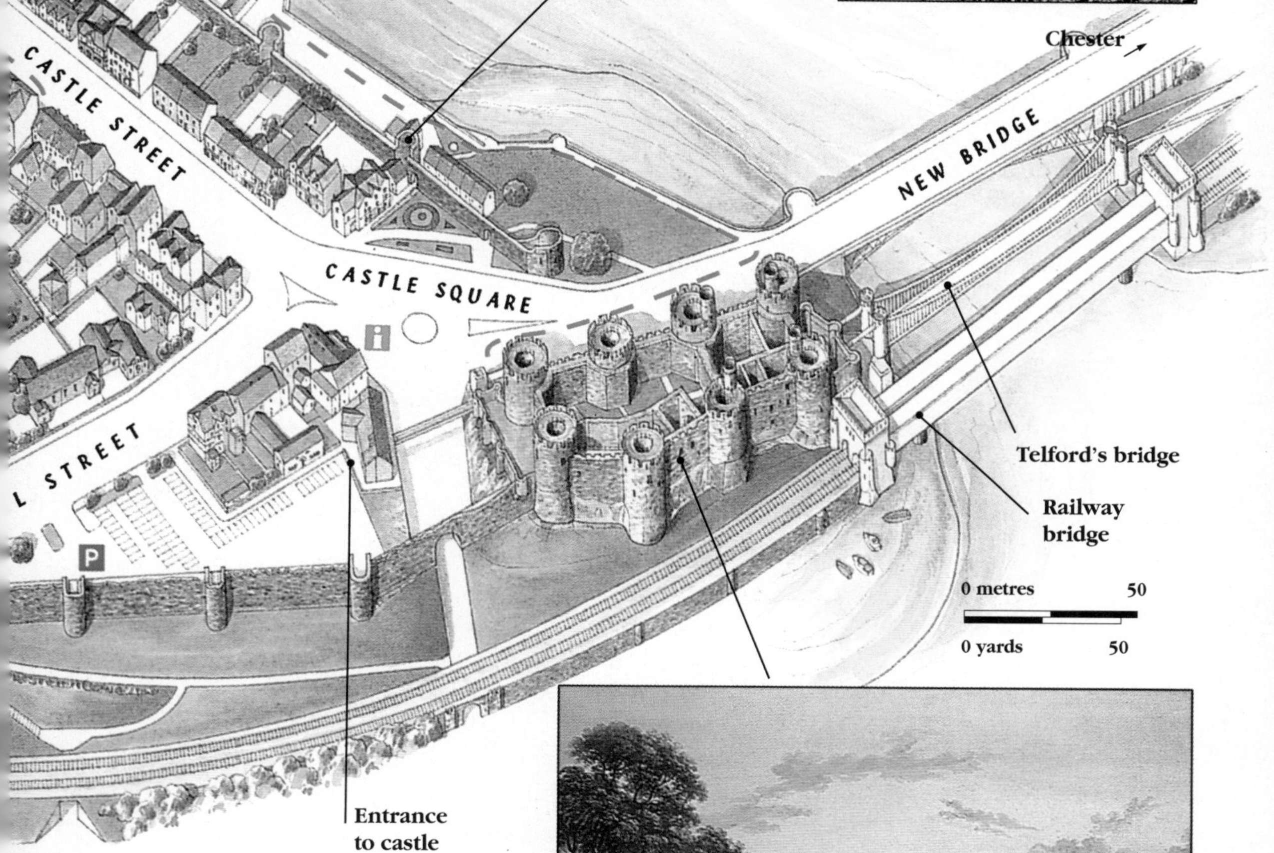

★ Town Walls
These remarkably well-preserved medieval walls are 1,280 m (4,200 ft) long and over 9 m (30 ft) high.

KEY

– – – Suggested route

STAR SIGHTS

★ Town Walls

★ Conwy Castle

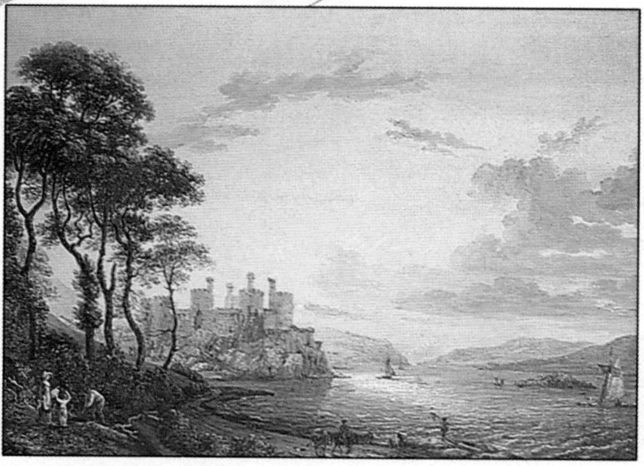

★ Conwy Castle
This atmospheric watercolour, Conwy Castle (c.1770), *is by the Nottingham artist Paul Sandby.*

Pontcysyllte Aqueduct, built in 1795–1805, carrying the Llangollen Canal

World Cultures in Llangollen

Llangollen's International Eisteddfod *(see p67)* in the first week of July draws musicians, singers and dancers from around the world. First held in 1947 as a gesture of post-war international unity, it now attracts over 12,000 performers from nearly 50 countries to the six-day-long competition-cum-fair.

Choristers at the eisteddfod, a popular Welsh festival

Llangollen ⑥

Denbighshire. 🏛 *5,000.* 🚃 ℹ️ *Town Hall, Castle St (01978 860828).* 🚜 *Tue.*

BEST KNOWN for its annual eisteddfod (festival), this pretty town sits on the River Dee, which is spanned by a 14th-century bridge. The town became notorious in the 18th century, when two eccentric Irishwomen, Lady Eleanor Butler and Sarah Ponsonby, the "Ladies of Llangollen", set up house together in the half-timbered **Plas Newydd**. Their unconventional dress and literary enthusiasms attracted such celebrities as the Duke of Wellington *(see p156)* and William Wordsworth *(see p424)*. The ruins of a 13th-century castle, **Castell Dinas Brân**, occupy the summit of a hill overlooking the house.

ENVIRONS: Boats on the **Llangollen Canal** sail from Wharf Hill in summer and cross the spectacular 300 m (1,000 ft) long Pontcysyllte Aqueduct, built by Thomas Telford *(see p527)*.

🏛 **Plas Newydd**
Hill St. 📞 *01978 861314.* ⭘ *Easter–Oct: daily.* 📷 ♿ *limited.*

Bala ⑦

Gwynedd. 🏛 *2,000.* 🚌 *from Llangollen.* ℹ️ *Penllyn, Pensarn Rd (01678 521021).*

BALA LAKE, Wales's largest natural lake, lies between the Aran and Arenig mountains at the fringes of Snowdonia

National Park. It is popular for water-sports and boasts a unique fish called a *gwyniad*, which is related to the salmon.

The little grey-stone town of Bala is a Welsh-speaking community, its houses strung out along a single street at the eastern end of the lake. Thomas Charles (1755–1814), a Methodist church leader, once lived here. A plaque on his former home recalls Mary Jones who, in 1800, walked 25 miles (40 km) barefoot from Abergynolwyn to buy a bible. This prompted Charles to establish the Bible Society, to provide cheap bibles to the working class.

The narrow-gauge **Bala Lake Railway** follows the lake shore from Llanuwchllyn, 4 miles (6 km) southwest.

Betws-y-Coed ⑧

Conwy. 🏛 *600.* 🚂 ℹ️ *Royal Oak Stables (01690 710426).*

THIS VILLAGE near the peaks of Snowdonia has been a hill-walking centre since the 19th century. To the west are

the **Swallow Falls**, where the River Llugwy flows through a wooded glen. The bizarre **Tŷ Hyll** ("Ugly House"), is a *tŷ unnos* ("one-night house"); traditionally, houses erected between dusk and dawn on common land were entitled to freehold rights, and the owner could enclose land as far as he could throw an axe from the door.

To the east is **Waterloo Bridge**, built by the talented engineer Thomas Telford to celebrate the famous victory against Napoleon.

🏛 **Tŷ Hyll**
Capel Curig. 📞 *01690 720287.* ⭘ *May–Oct: daily.* 📷 ♿ *limited.* 🅿️

The ornate Waterloo Bridge, built in 1815 after the famous battle

◁ **The picturesque village of Beddgelert in Snowdonia National Park**

A view of the Snowdonia countryside from Llanberis Pass, the most popular route to Snowdon's peak

Blaenau Ffestiniog ❾

Gwynedd. 🏠 5,500. ☎
ℹ️ Betws-y-Coed (01690 710426).
🚍 Tue (Jun–Sep).

BLAENAU FFESTINIOG, once the slate capital of North Wales, sits among mountains riddled with quarries. The **Llechwedd Slate Caverns**, overlooking Blaenau, opened to visitors in the early 1970s, marking a new role for the declining industrial town. The electric Miners' Tramway takes passengers on a tour into the original caverns.

On the Deep Mine tour, visitors descend on Britain's steepest passenger incline railway to the underground chambers, while sound effects recreate the atmosphere of a working quarry. The dangers included landfalls and floods, as well as the more gradual threat of slate dust breathed into the lungs.

There are slate-splitting demonstrations on the surface and a row of reconstructed quarrymen's cottages, each one furnished to illustrate the cramped and basic living conditions endured by workers between the 1880s and 1945.

The popular narrow-gauge **Ffestiniog Railway** (see pp532–3) runs from Blaenau to Porthmadog.

🏛 **Llechwedd Slate Caverns**
Crimea Pass. ☎ 01766 830306.
◯ daily. ⬤ 25, 26 Dec, 1 Jan. 💷
♿ except the Deep Mine. ▢ ◻

Llanberis and Snowdon ❿

Gwynedd. 🏠 2,100. ℹ️ High St, Llanberis (01286 870765).

SNOWDON, which at 1,085 m (3,560 ft) is the highest peak in Wales, is the main focus of the vast Snowdonia National Park, whose scenery ranges from this rugged mountain country to moors and sandy beaches.

The easiest route to Snowdon's summit begins in Llanberis: the 5 mile (8 km) **Llanberis Track**. From Llanberis Pass, the Miners' Track (once used by copper miners) and the Pyg Track are alternative paths. Walkers should beware of sudden weather changes and dress accordingly. The narrow-gauge **Snowdon Mountain Railway**, which opened in 1896, is an easier option.

Llanberis was a major 19th-century slate town, with grey terraces hewn into the hills. Other attractions are the 13th-century shell of **Dolbadarn Castle**, on a bluff between lakes Padarn and Peris, and, above Lake Peris, the **Electric Mountain**, which arranges tours of the biggest hydro-electric pumped storage station in Europe.

👜 **Dolbadarn Castle**
Off A4086 nr Llanberis.
☎ 01286 870765. ◯ daily. 💷
ℹ️ **Electric Mountain**
Llanberis. ☎ 01286 870636.
◯ Jan–Easter: Thu–Sun; Easter–23 Dec: daily, book in advance. 💷 ♿

BRITAIN'S CENTRE OF SLATE

Welsh slates provided roofing material for Britain's new towns in the 19th century. In 1898, the slate industry employed nearly 17,000 men, a quarter of whom worked at Blaenau Ffestiniog. Foreign competition and new materials later took their toll. Quarries such as Gloddfa Ganol and Llechwedd in Blaenau Ffestiniog now survive on the tourist trade.

The dying art of slate-splitting

The village of Beddgelert, set among the mountains of Snowdonia

Beddgelert ⑪

Caernarfonshire & Merionethshire
(Gwynedd). 🚶 *500.* ℹ *High St,
Porthmadog (01766 512981).*

BEDDGELERT enjoys a spec-
tacular location among
some of Snowdonia's most
dramatic landscapes. The village sits on the confluence of
the Glaslyn and Colwyn rivers
at the approach to two mountain passes: the beautiful Nant
Gwynant Pass, which leads to
Snowdonia's highest reaches,
and the Aberglaslyn Pass, a
narrow wooded gorge which
acts as a gateway to the sea.

Business was given a boost
by Dafydd Pritchard, the landlord of the Royal Goat Hotel,
who in the early 19th century
adapted an old Welsh legend
to associate it with Beddgelert.
Llywelyn the Great *(see p510)*
is said to have left his faithful
hound Gelert to guard his
infant son while he went hunting. He returned to find the
cradle overturned and Gelert
covered in blood. Thinking
the dog had savaged his son,
Llywellyn slaughtered Gelert,
but then discovered the boy,
unharmed, under the cradle.
Nearby was the corpse of a
wolf, which Gelert had killed
to protect the child. To support the tale, Pritchard created
Gelert's Grave (*bedd Gelert*
in Welsh) by the River Glaslyn,
a mound of stones a short
walk south of the village.

ENVIRONS: There are many fine
walks in the area: one leads
south to the Aberglaslyn Pass
and along a disused part of
the Welsh Highland Railway.
The **Sygun Copper Mine**,
1 mile (1.5 km) northeast of
Beddgelert, offers fascinating
guided tours of illuminated
caverns, recreating the life of
Victorian miners.

⛏ Sygun Copper Mine
On A498. 📞 *01766 890595.*
⭕ *Mar–Nov: daily; Dec–Feb: Sat, Sun.*
⭕ *24, 25 Dec.* 🅿 ♿ *limited.* 🅿

Ffestiniog Railway

**Engine
plaque**

THE FFESTINIOG narrow-gauge
railway takes a scenic 14
mile (22 km) route from
Porthmadog Harbour to the
mountains and the slate town
of Blaenau Ffestiniog *(see p531).*
Designed to carry slate from the
quarries to the quay, the railway
replaced a horse-drawn tramway
constructed in 1836, operating
on a 60 cm (2 ft) gauge. After closure in
1946, it was maintained by volunteers
and re-opened in sections after 1955.

Steam traction *trains were first used on
the Ffestiniog Railway in 1863. There are
some diesel engines but most trains on the
route are still steam-hauled.*

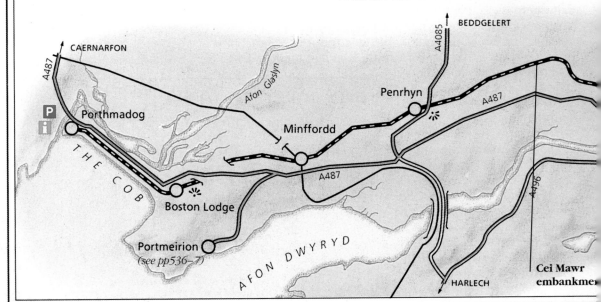

Llŷn Peninsula ⑫

Caernarfonshire & Merionethshire (Gwynedd). 🚃 🚌 Pwllheli.
⛴ from Pwllheli & Aberdaron to Bardsey Island. ℹ️ Min-y-don, Station Sq, Pwllheli (01758 613000).

THIS 24 MILE (38 km) finger of land points southwest from Snowdonia into the Irish Sea. Although it has popular beaches, notably at Pwllheli, Criccieth, Abersoch and Nefyn, the coast's overriding feature is its untamed beauty. Views are at their most dramatic in the far west and along the mountain-backed northern shores.

The windy headland of **Braich-y-Pwll**, to the west of Aberdaron, looks out towards Bardsey Island, the "Isle of 20,000 Saints". This became a place of pilgrimage in the 6th century, when a monastery was founded here. Some of the saints are said to be buried in the churchyard of the ruined 13th-century **St Mary's Abbey**. Close by is **Porth Oer**, a small bay also known as "Whistling Sands" (the sand is meant to squeak, or whistle, underfoot).

East of Aberdaron is the 4 mile (6.5 km) bay of **Porth Neigwl**, known in English as Hell's Mouth, the scene of many shipwrecks due to the bay's treacherous currents. Hidden in sheltered grounds above Porth Neigwl bay, 1 mile (1.5 km) northeast of Aberdaron, is **Plas-yn-Rhiw**, a small, medieval manor house with Tudor and Georgian additions and lovely gardens.

The former quarrying village and "ghost town" of **Llithfaen**, tucked away below the sheer cliffs of the mountainous north coast, is now a centre for Welsh language studies.

🏛 Plas-yn-Rhiw
(NT) off B4413. ☎ 01758 780219.
🕐 Apr–mid-May: Thu–Mon; mid-May–Sep: Wed–Mon. ♿ limited.

Llithfaen village, now a language centre, on the Llŷn Peninsula

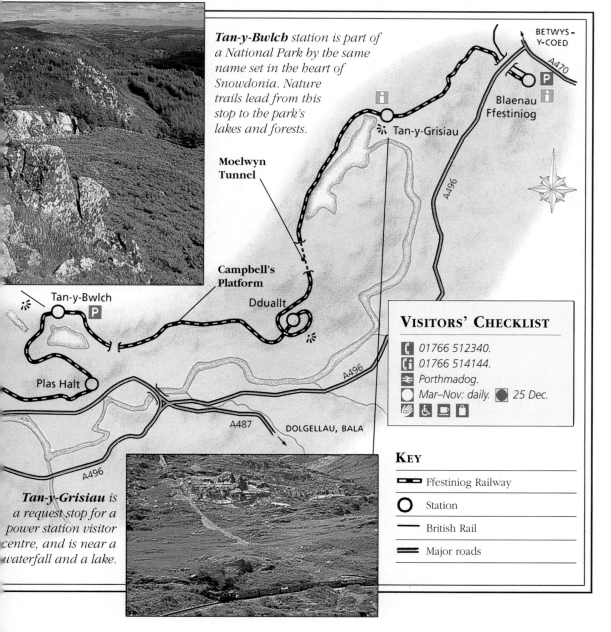

Tan-y-Bwlch station is part of a National Park by the same name set in the heart of Snowdonia. Nature trails lead from this stop to the park's lakes and forests.

Moelwyn Tunnel

Campbell's Platform

Dduallt

Tan-y-Bwlch

Plas Halt

Tan-y-Grisiau is a request stop for a power station visitor centre, and is near a waterfall and a lake.

Tan-y-Grisiau

Blaenau Ffestiniog

BETWYS-Y-COED

DOLGELLAU, BALA

VISITORS' CHECKLIST

☎ 01766 512340.
📠 01766 514144.
🚃 Porthmadog.
🕐 Mar–Nov: daily. ● 25 Dec.
♿ 💻 🏠

KEY

▭▬▭ Ffestiniog Railway

○ Station

— British Rail

═ Major roads

Portmeirion 13

Caernarfonshire & Merionethshire
(Gwynedd). 📞 01766 770228.
🚋 Minffordd. ○ daily. ● 25 Dec.
♿ limited. ▣ ⬛

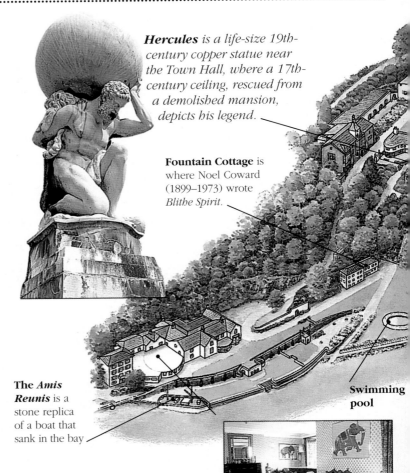

Hercules *is a life-size 19th-century copper statue near the Town Hall, where a 17th-century ceiling, rescued from a demolished mansion, depicts his legend.*

Fountain Cottage is where Noel Coward (1899–1973) wrote *Blithe Spirit.*

Swimming pool

The ***Amis Reunis*** is a stone replica of a boat that sank in the bay

The Portmeirion Hotel *has many exotic interiors: the furniture in the Jaipur Bar comes from Rajasthan, India.*

T HIS BIZARRE ITALIANATE village on a private peninsula at the top of Cardigan Bay was created by Welsh architect Sir Clough Williams-Ellis (1883–1978). He fulfilled a childhood dream by building a village "to my own fancy on my own chosen site". About 50 buildings surround a central piazza, in styles from Oriental to Gothic. Visitors can stay at the luxurious hotel or in one of the charming village cottages. Portmeirion has been an atmospheric location for many films and television programmes, including the popular 1960s television series *The Prisoner.*

Sir Clough Williams-Ellis at Portmeirion

Harlech 14

Caernarfonshire & Merionethshire
(Gwynedd). 🏘 1,300. 🚋 ℹ High St (01766 780658). 🏛 Sun (summer).

T HIS SMALL TOWN with fine beaches is dominated by **Harlech Castle**, a medieval fortress *(see p512)* built by Edward I between 1283 and 1289. The castle sits on a precipitous crag, with superb views of Tremadog Bay and the Llŷn Peninsula to the west, and Snowdonia to the north. When the castle was built, the sea reached a fortified stairway cut into the cliff, so that supplies could arrive by ship, but now the sea has receded. A towering gatehouse protects the inner ward, enclosed by walls and four round towers.

Despite its defences, Harlech Castle fell to Owain Glyndŵr *(see p510)* in 1404, and served as his court until its recapture four years later. The song *Men of Harlech* is thought to have been inspired by the castle's heroic resistance during an eight-year siege in the Wars of the Roses *(see p53).*

🏰 **Harlech Castle**
Castle Sq. 📞 01766 780552.
○ daily. ● 24–26 Dec, 1 Jan. ♿ ⬛

Dolgellau 15

Caernarfonshire & Merionethshire
(Gwynedd). 🏘 2,650. ℹ Eldon Sq (01341 422888). 🏛 Fri (livestock).

T HE DARK LOCAL STONE gives a stern, solid look to this market town, where the Welsh language and customs are still very strong. It lies in the long shadow of the 892 m (2,927 ft) mountain of Cader Idris where, according to legend, anyone who spends a night on its summit will awake a poet or a madman – or not at all.

Dolgellau was gripped by gold fever in the 19th century, when high-quality gold was

Harlech Castle's strategic site overlooking mountains and sea

◁ **Conwy Castle, overlooking the Conwy estuary**

The Triumphal Arch is the main entrance to Portmeirion village.

Central Piazza

Lodge

Campanile

Royal Dolphin Cottage

Bristol Colonnade

Viewing platform

The Ship Shop *sells Portmeirion's famous flowered pottery.*

The Pantheon *was built in 1958, but lack of funds meant that the dome was originally made from plywood instead of copper and painted green. The Pantheon's unusual façade is formed by the upper half of a music room fireplace by Norman Shaw (see p29).*

Dolgellau's grey-stone buildings, dwarfed by the mountain scenery

discovered in the Mawddach Valley nearby. The deposits were not large enough to sustain an intensive mining industry for long. Nevertheless, up until 1999, small amounts were mined and crafted locally into fine jewellery.

Dolgellau is a good centre for walking, whether you wish to take gentle strolls through beautiful leafy countryside or strenuous hikes across extreme terrain with dramatic mountain views. The lovely **Cregennen lakes** are set high in the hills above the thickly wooded **Mawddach Estuary** to the northwest; north are the harsh, bleak **Rhinog moors**, one of Wales's last true wildernesses.

Aberdyfi 🔟

Caernarfonshire & Merionethshire (Gwynedd). 🚶 *900.* 🚆 🛈 *Wharf Gardens (01654 767321).*

PERCHED ON THE MOUTH of the Dyfi Estuary, this little harbour resort and sailing centre makes the most of its splendid but rather confined location, its houses occupying every yard of a narrow strip of land between mountain and sea. In the 19th century, local slate was exported from here, and between the 1830s and the 1860s about 100 ships were built in the port. *The Bells of Aberdovey*, a song by Charles Dibdin for his opera *Liberty Hall* (1785), tells the legend of Cantref-y-Gwaelod, thought to have been located here, which was protected from the sea by dykes. One stormy night, the sluice gates were left open by Prince Seithenyn, when he was drunk, and the land was lost beneath the waves. The submerged church bells are said to peal under the water to this day.

Neat Georgian houses by the sea, Aberdyfi

SOUTH
AND
MID-WALES

SOUTH AND MID-WALES

THE LANDSCAPES OF SOUTH AND MID-WALES *are more varied than those of North Wales. There are remnants of a rich industrial past in Swansea, Cardiff and the southern valleys, which give way to the Brecon Beacons and to rural central Wales. Pembrokeshire, the westernmost part of the region, has the loveliest coastline in Wales.*

The coastal strip of South Wales has been settled for many centuries, and there are prehistoric sites in the Vale of Glamorgan and Pembrokeshire. The Romans established an important base at Caerleon and the Normans built castles all the way from Chepstow to Pembroke. In the 18th and 19th centuries, coal mines and iron works appeared in the valleys, blotting the landscape and attracting immigrants from all over Europe. This influx of people from outside of Wales diluted the area's strong Celtic identity and helps explain why nationalist sentiment is weaker here than in the northern part of the country. However, it is interesting to note that the number of Welsh speakers increases, and the sense of Welsh culture becomes stronger, the further you travel from the border with England.

The coal, iron and steel industries helped Swansea and Cardiff establish themselves as major ports. The docks at Cardiff (which was once a sleepy fishing village) for a time handled more coal than any other port in the world. The capital of Wales since 1955, Cardiff has today assumed new importance as the site of the first Welsh Assembly under the devolved constitution that gives Welsh people a greater say in running their own affairs.

The decline of the coal and steel industries in the late 20th century brought about tremendous change on the face of the area, perhaps most noticeably the transformation of slag heaps into green hills. However, the

The changing face of the coal industry: former miners take visitors down the Big Pit in Blaenafon

◁ **Magnificent coastal scenery near St David's, Pembrokeshire**

Site of the Welsh New Assembly, Cardiff Bay, Cardiff

downside is that the people of the valley towns, who are mostly from mining or steelworking families that go back for generations, are now struggling to find alternative forms of employment. Former coal mines, such as Blaenafon's Big Pit, are now tourist attractions. Many of the guides are former miners, who can give first-hand accounts of working conditions in the pits and of day-to-day life in the tight-knit town and village communities.

The southern boundary of the Brecon Beacons National Park also marks the beginning of rural Wales. To the north of this park is an area of small country towns, forestry plantations, hill sheep farms, spectacular artificial lakes and the beautiful valley of the Wye. The population here is sparser than anywhere in England. The Beacons themselves offer magnificent hill walks of varying difficulty, from leisurely to strenuous. Two long-distance footpaths begin in South Wales: the 186-mile (300-km) Pembrokeshire Coastal path, which follows the edge of the cliffs in the southwest corner of the country; and Offa's Dyke Path, which runs north from Chepstow close to the border with England. This path follows King Offa of Mercia's extraordinary defensive earthwork (built in the 8th century), parts of which are still clearly visible. Another favourite outdoor activity in this area is pony trekking. Many farms and stables in the vicinity of Rhayader, which is roughly in the centre of the region, rent out ponies and organize treks.

The sports that the locals enjoy range from fishing – the salmon in the Wye have a reputation for succulence – to rugby, which is more popular than football in South Wales (both as a participatory and a spectator sport). The rugged, lithe people of the valleys are good rugby players, and for some years the Welsh regularly beat the

Blaenant Mine, with grassed-over slag heaps behind

English, Scots, Irish and French in the annual Five Nations Championship (which will become the Six Nations from the year 2000, with the addition of Italy). However, in recent seasons, Welsh fortunes have been mixed.

The Welsh are famous for their strong, melodious singing voices and for the often all-male choirs that pro-liferate in the former mining valleys. These ensembles compete at a num-ber of eisteddfods (festivals), which culminate in the Royal National Eis-teddfod, which is held in the first week of August at a different Welsh venue each year. On a more intimate scale – and closer to the bardic tradition from which the national love of song is thought to have been derived – folk music thrives, often featuring the harp, the national musical instrument. There is an annual international folk fes-tival in late August at Pontardawe (West Glamorgan), and in May the Swansea Shanty Festival features music based on nautical themes.

For those who pre-fer words to music, the border town of Hay-on-Wye in the Black Mountains is famous for its second-hand bookshops. It also hosts an annual literary festival attended by many of Britain's most important and popular authors. Dylan Thomas, Wales's celebrated poet, was born in Swansea and lived for some years at

Outdoor book stalls, Hay-on-Wye, Powys

Laugharne, a village on the Taff estu-ary, near Carmarthen. This settlement gave Thomas inspiration for the town of Llareggub, which appears in the poet's "play for voices", *Under Milk Wood*. His former house is open to vis-itors, as is Brown's Hotel, where he was notorious for his heavy drinking.

Food in South and Mid-Wales ranges from simple roast lamb to traditional delicacies, such as laverbread, a Welsh speciality made from dark-coloured sea-weed. The sharp, white Caerphilly cheese is named after a town in the Rhymney Valley, and Glamorgan sausages, which are filled with cheese and spices, are popular with vegetarians. Trout from the rivers and cockles from the sea are delicious, while Welsh baked goods include tasty, distinctive cakes.

Selection of Welsh cheeses

Sandy beach and environs at Three Cliffs Bay, Gower Peninsula, near Swansea

Exploring South and Mid-Wales

MAGNIFICENT COASTAL SCENERY marks the Pembrokeshire Coast National Park and cliff-backed Gower Peninsula, while Cardigan Bay and Carmarthen Bay offer quieter beaches. Walkers can enjoy grassy uplands in the Brecon Beacons and gentler country in the leafy Wye Valley. Urban life is concentrated in the southeast of Wales, where old mining towns line the valleys north of Cardiff, the capital.

Cliffs of the Pembrokeshire Coast National Park

GETTING AROUND

The M4 motorway is the major route into Wales from the south of England, and there are good road links west of Swansea running to the coast. The A483 and A488 give access to mid-Wales from the Midlands. Frequent rail services connect London with Swansea, Cardiff and the ferry port of Fishguard.

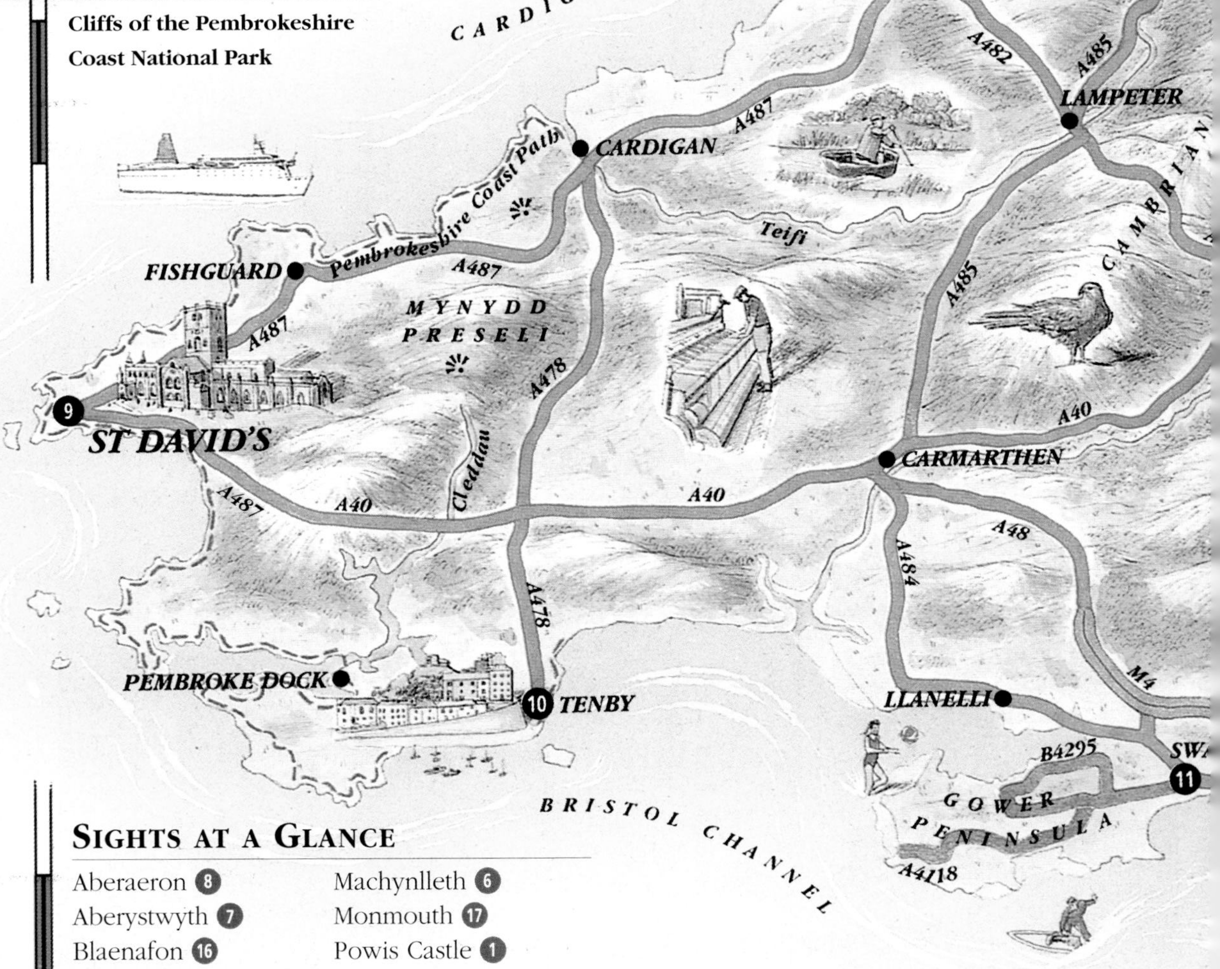

Map labels:
MACHYNLLETH
ABERYSTWYTH 7 · Rheidol
ABERAERON 8
LAMPETER
A482 · A485 · A487
CARDIGAN · Teifi
CARDIGAN BAY
Pembrokeshire Coast Path
FISHGUARD · A487
MYNYDD PRESELI
A478
ST DAVID'S 9
Cleddau
A40
CARMARTHEN
A48 · A484
PEMBROKE DOCK
TENBY 10
BRISTOL CHANNEL
LLANELLI · B4295 · SWA
GOWER PENINSULA · A4118
CAMBRIAN
M4

SIGHTS AT A GLANCE

Aberaeron **8**
Aberystwyth **7**
Blaenafon **16**
Brecon Beacons pp556–7 **13**
Caerleon **15**
Cardiff pp560–3 **14**
Elan Valley **5**
Hay-on-Wye **3**
Knighton **2**
Llandrindod Wells **4**
Machynlleth **6**
Monmouth **17**
Powis Castle **1**
St David's pp552–3 **9**
Swansea and the Gower Peninsula **11**
Tenby **10**
Tintern Abbey **18**

Walks and Tours
Wild Wales Tour **12**

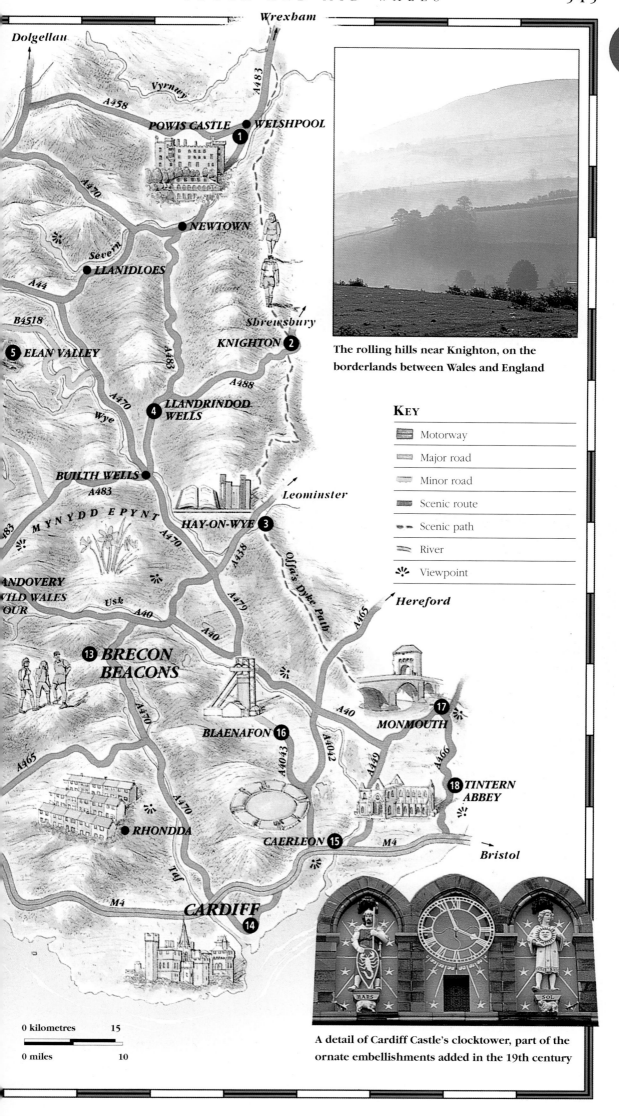

Dolgellau

Wrexham

Vyrnwy

A458

A483

POWIS CASTLE ● WELSHPOOL **1**

A470

● NEWTOWN

Severn

● LLANIDLOES

A44

Shrewsbury

B4518

5 ELAN VALLEY

A483

KNIGHTON **2**

A488

A470

4 LLANDRINDOD WELLS

Wye

BUILTH WELLS ●

A483

Leominster

M Y N Y D D E P Y N T

A470

HAY-ON-WYE **3**

A4518

A483

Offa's Dyke Path

ANDOVERY
WILD WALES
TOUR

Usk A40

A479

A40

A465

Hereford

13 BRECON BEACONS

A470

A40

A4043

A4042

MONMOUTH **17**

BLAENAFON **16**

A449

A466

18 TINTERN ABBEY

A465

A470

● RHONDDA

CAERLEON **15**

M4

Bristol

Taf

M4

CARDIFF **14**

The rolling hills near Knighton, on the
borderlands between Wales and England

KEY

▭	Motorway
▭	Major road
▭	Minor road
▭	Scenic route
●-●	Scenic path
≈	River
☀	Viewpoint

0 kilometres   15

0 miles   10

A detail of Cardiff Castle's clocktower, part of the
ornate embellishments added in the 19th century

Voices of Wales

WELSH MUSIC AND POETRY date back to pre-Christian times. The roar of a Welsh male voice choir in perfect harmony, the intimate, beguiling sound of a harp solo, and the lilt of a Welsh poet continue a popular tradition that began centuries ago, when bards sang of the deeds of pagan gods and heroes. The tradition is truly popular and every town and village has its choir and its poets, ordinary working people who see no distinction between art and life. The first recorded formal competition, or eisteddfod, for poets and musicians was held at Cardigan in 1176; today, the Royal National Eisteddfod, held each summer alternately in North or South Wales, includes awards for music, prose, drama and art, but its high point is still the "chairing" of the winning poet.

The first book printed in Welsh, 1546

THE BARDS

The Gorsedd (Assembly) of Bards of the Isle of Britain was formed in 1792 to promote and set standards for the arts in Wales. The writers, musicians and artists of the Gorsedd are called druids; an Archdruid is elected every three years. The Bards have close links with the National Eisteddfod: the Gorsedd crowns the best poet, presents a medal to the best author and awards a seat of honour for a long poem in strict metrical form.

The wine-filled Hirlas Horn (horn of plenty) is offered to the Archdruid by a young matron of the community

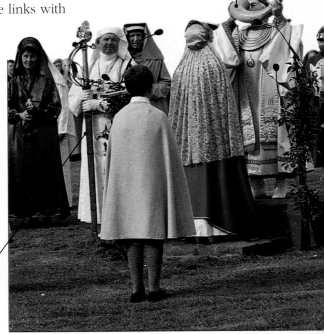

The modern Welsh harp is an important instrument in Welsh concert music. The original, simpler Celtic harp remains at the heart of Welsh folk music.

The Grand Sword, a symbol of peace, is never fully drawn from its sheath.

The BBC's Welsh Male Voice Choir shows the professional side of the traditon of choral singing that is maintained by amateurs in virtually every town and village in Wales.

Laugharne Boat House, Dylan Thomas's home from 1949

The Preselis Mountains, *according to legend, are the source of the Stonehenge blue-stones, flown from Wales to Wilt-shire by the wizard Merlin. They are mentioned in bardic epics.*

THE WELSH LANGUAGE

Welsh – Cymraeg to native speakers – is a Celtic language. It is part of a group of tongues that were spoken, hundreds of years ago, across Europe from present-day Spain to Poland. Despite centuries of English political domination, it was the only language

Welsh is now taught at school

for many Welsh people until early in the 20th century. After a long decline, a conscious effort to revive the language began in the 1970s. Today, many schools teach exclusively in Welsh, and the number of Welsh speakers is increasing annually. The tongue is also spoken in Patagonia, Argentina, where many Welsh people settled in the 1860s.

The three shafts of light on this banner symbolise truth, justice and love.

Senior bards are seated on traditional three-legged stools.

The Film, **How Green Was My Valley** *(1941), was adapted from Richard Llewellyn's best-selling novel of the same name. The story centres around the lives of a Welsh family in a mining community in South Wales.*

DYLAN THOMAS: A BARD FOR THE ENGLISH

Dylan Thomas (1914–53) was born in Swansea. He wrote exclusively in English, but brought a distinctive Welsh sensibility to English poetry. His early work reflected his inner wrestling on the great themes of sex and death, sin and redemption, and was drenched in Biblical imagery. His later work took on a bardic tone, and used complex technical effects to produce a visionary poetry quite unlike anything else being written in English at that time. Thomas's achievement was created against a constant struggle with poverty and alcohol. To help relieve these problems, the wife of historian A.J.P. Taylor bought him the Boat House at Laugharne, near Carmarthen, as a retreat where he could write in peace. The house is open to the public.

Dylan Thomas, one of Britain's leading writers

Italianate terraces and formal gardens at Powis Castle, adding a Mediterranean air to the Welsh borderlands

Powis Castle ①

(NT) Welshpool, Powys. ☐ 01938 554336. ☐ Welshpool then bus. ☐ Apr–Jun & Sep–Oct: Wed–Sun; Jul–Aug: Tue–Sun & public hols. ☐ ☐ limited. ☐

POWIS CASTLE – the spelling is an archaic version of "Powys" – has outgrown its military roots. Despite its sham battlements and dominant site, 1 mile (1.6 km) to the southwest of the town of Welshpool, this red-stone building has served as a country mansion for centuries. It began life in the 13th century as a fortress, built by the princes of Powys to control the border with England.

The castle is entered through one of few surviving medieval features: a gateway, built in 1283 by Owain de la Pole. The gate is flanked by two round towers with arrow slits and portcullis slots.

The castle's lavish interiors soon banish all thoughts of war. A **Dining Room**, decorated with fine 17th-century panelling and family portraits, was originally designed as the castle's Great

Hall. The **Great Staircase**, added in the late 17th century and elaborately decorated with carved fruit and flowers, leads to the main apartments: an early 19th-century library, the panelled **Oak Drawing Room** and the Elizabethan **Long Gallery**, where ornate plasterwork on the fireplace and ceiling date from the 1590s. In the **Blue Drawing Room** there are three 18th-century Brussels tapestries.

The Herbert family bought the property in 1587 and were proud of their Royalist connections; the panelling in

The richly carved 17th-century Great Staircase

the **State Bedroom** bears the royal monogram. Powis Castle was defended for Charles I in the Civil War *(see pp56–7)*, but fell to Parliament in 1644. The 3rd Baron Powis, a supporter of James II, had to flee the country when William and Mary took the throne in 1688 *(see pp56–7)*.

The castle's **Clive Museum** has an exhibition concerning "Clive of India" (1725–74), the general and statesman who helped strengthen British control in India in the mid-18th century. The family's link with Powis Castle was established by the 2nd Lord Clive, who married into the Herbert family and became the Earl of Powis in 1804.

The gardens at Powis are among the best-known in Britain, with their series of elegant Italianate terraces, adorned with statues, niches, balustrades and hanging gardens, all stepped into the steep hillside beneath the castle walls. Created between 1688 and 1722, these are the only formal gardens of this period in Britain that are still kept in their original form *(see pp26–7)*.

Knighton ②

Powys. 🏘 2,800. 🚉 🛈 West St
(01547 528753). 🛆 Thu.

KNIGHTON'S WELSH NAME, Tref y Clawdd ("The Town on the Dyke"), reflects its status as the only original settlement on **Offa's Dyke**. In the 8th century, King Offa of Mercia (central and southern England) constructed a ditch and bank to mark out his territory, and to enable the enforcement of a Saxon law: "Neither shall a Welshman cross into English land without the appointed man from the other side, who should meet him at the bank and bring him back again without any offence being committed." Some of the best-preserved sections of the 6 m (20 ft) high earthwork lie in the hills around Knighton. The Offa's Dyke Footpath runs for 177 miles (285 km) along the border between England and Wales.

Knighton is set on a steep hill, sloping upwards from **St Edward's Church** (1877) with its medieval tower, to the summit, where a castle once stood. The main street leads via the market square, marked by a 19th-century clock tower, along **The Narrows**, a Tudor street crowded with little shops. **The Old House**, on Broad Street, is a medieval "cruck" house (a style that uses pairs of curved timbers to form a frame to support the roof), and has a hole in the ceiling instead of a chimney.

Knighton's clock

Hay-on-Wye ③

Powys. 🏘 1,300. 🛈 Oxford Rd
(01497 820144). 🛆 Thu.

BOOK-LOVERS from all over the world come to this quiet border town in the Black Mountains. Hay-on-Wye has over 25 second-hand bookshops stocking millions of titles, and in early summer hosts a prestigious Festival of Literature. The town's love affair with books began when a bookshop was opened in the 1960s by Richard Booth, who claims the (fictitious) title of King of Independent Hay and lives in **Hay Castle**, a 17th-century mansion in the grounds of the original 13th-century castle. Hay's oldest inn, the 16th-century **Three Tuns** on Bridge Street, is still functioning as a pub and has an attractive half-timbered façade.

ENVIRONS: Hay sits on the approach to the Black Mountains, and is surrounded by lovely rolling hills. To the south are the heights of Hay Bluff and the Vale of Ewyas, where the 12th-century ruins of **Llanthony Priory** (see p557) retain fine stonework and pointed arches.

⛪ **Hay Castle**
Castle Sq. 📞 01497 820503. ⬤ daily. ● 25 Dec. ⬤ grounds only.

Llandrindod Wells ④

Powys. 🏘 5,000. 🚉 🛈 Memorial
Gardens (01597 822600). 🛆 Fri.

LLANDRINDOD is a perfect example of a Victorian town, with canopied streets, delicate wrought ironwork, gabled villas and ornamental parklands. This purpose-built spa town became Wales's premier inland resort of the

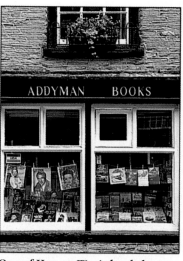

One of Hay-on-Wye's bookshops

19th century. Its sulphur and magnesium spring waters were taken to treat skin complaints, kidney diseases and a range of other ailments.

The town now makes every effort to preserve its Victorian character, with a boating lake and the well-tended **Rock Park Gardens**. The restored 19th-century **Pump Room** in the **Spa Centre** serves afternoon tea, and is the focus of the summer Victorian Festival, when residents don period costume and all cars are banned from the town centre.

The **Radnorshire Museum** traces the town's past as one of a string of 19th-century Welsh spas which included Builth (now a farming town), Llangammarch (a sleepy hamlet) and **Llanwrtyd** (now a pony trekking centre).

🏛 **Spa Centre**
Rock Park. 📞 01597 822997.
⬤ Mon–Fri. ● 20 Dec–2 Jan.
🚻 🍴
🏛 **Radnorshire Museum**
Memorial Gardens. 📞 01597 824513.
⬤ Tue–Sat & public hols.
● Christmas week. ⬤ 🚻 limited.

Victorian architecture on Spa Road, Llandrindod Wells

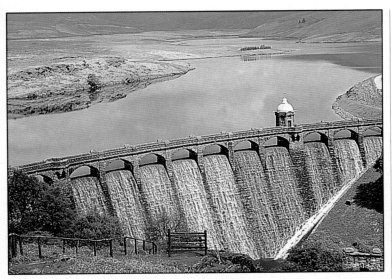

Craig Goch, one of the original chain of Elan Valley reservoirs

Elan Valley ⑤

Powys. ⊇ *Llandrindod.*
ℹ️ *Rhayader (01597 810898).*

A STRING OF SPECTACULAR reservoirs, the first of the country's man-made lakes, has made this one of Wales's most famous valleys. **Caban Coch**, **Garreg Ddu**, **Pen-y-Garreg** and **Craig Goch**, were created between 1892 and 1903 to supply water to Birmingham, 73 miles (117 km) away. They form a chain of lakes about 9 miles (14 km) long, holding 50 billion litres (13 billion gallons) of water. Victorian engineers selected these high moorlands on the Cambrian Mountains, for their high annual rainfall of 1,780 mm (70 inches). The choice created bitter controversy and resentment: more than a thousand people had to move from the valley that was flooded in order to create Caban Coch.

Unlike their more utilitarian modern counterparts, these dams were built during an era when decoration was seen as an integral part of any design. Finished in dressed stone, they have an air of grandeur which is lacking in the huge **Claerwen** reservoir, a stark addition built during the early 1950s to double the lakes' capacity. Contained by a 355 m (1,165 ft) dam, it lies 4 miles (6 km) along the B4518 that runs through Elan Valley and offers magnificent views.

The remote moorlands and woodlands surrounding the lakes are an important habitat for wildlife; the rare red kite can often be seen here. The **Elan Valley Visitors' Centre**, beside the Caban Coch dam, describes the construction of the lakes, as well as the valley's own natural history. **Elan Village**, set beside the centre, is an unusual example of a model workers' village, built during the 1900s to house the water-works staff. Outside the centre is a statue of the poet Percy Bysshe Shelley *(see p238)*, who stayed in the valley at the mansion of Nantgwyllt in 1810 with his wife, Harriet. The house now lies underneath the waters of Caban Coch, along with the rest of the old village. Among the buildings submerged were the village school and a church.

The trail from Machynlleth to Devil's Bridge, near Aberystwyth

Machynlleth ⑥

Powys. 👥 *2,200.* ⊇ ℹ️ *Canolfan Owain Glyndŵr (01654 702401).*
🛒 *Wed.*

HALF-TIMBERED BUILDINGS and Georgian façades appear among the grey-stone houses in Machynlleth. It was here that Owain Glyndŵr, Wales's last native leader *(see p510)*, held a parliament in 1404. The restored **Parliament House** has displays on his life and a brass-rubbing centre.

The ornate **Clock Tower**, in the middle of Maengwyn Street, was erected in 1874 by the Marquess of Londonderry to mark the coming of age of his heir, Lord Castlereagh. The Marquess lived in **Plas Machynlleth**, a 17th-century house in parkland off the main street, which is now a centre of Celtic heritage and culture.

Parliament House sign, Machynlleth

ENVIRONS: In an old slate quarry 2.5 miles (4 km) to the north, a "village of the future" is run by the **Centre for Alternative Technology**. A water-balanced cliff railway takes visitors to view low-energy houses and organic gardens, to see how to make the best of Earth's resources.

🏛 **Parliament House**
Maengwyn St. 📞 *01654 702827.*
🕐 *Easter–Sep: Mon–Sat.* ♿ 🅿
🏛 **Centre for Alternative Technology**
On A487. 📞 *01654 702400.* 🕐 *daily.* ⬤ *mid-Dec–early-Jan.* 🎫 🍴

Aberystwyth ⑦

Cardiganshire (Dyfed). 👥 *11,000.* ⊇ 🚌 ℹ️ *Terrace Rd (01970 612125).*

THIS SEASIDE AND UNIVERSITY town claims to be the capital of mid-Wales. By the standards of this rural area, "Aber" is a big place, its population increased for much of the year by students.

To Victorian travellers, Aberystwyth was the "Biarritz of Wales". There have been no great changes along the promenade, with its gabled hotels, since the 19th century. **Constitution Hill**, a steep outcrop at the northern end, can be scaled in summer on the electric **Cliff Railway**, built in 1896. At the top, in a *camera obscura*, a lens projects views of the town. The

Buskers on Aberystwyth's seafront

ruined **Aberystwyth Castle** (1277) is south of the promenade. In the town centre, the **Ceredigion Museum**, in an old music hall, traces the town's past. To the northeast of the town, **The National Library of Wales**, next to the university, has a valuable collection of ancient Welsh manuscripts.

ENVIRONS: During the summer the narrow-gauge Vale of Rheidol Railway runs 12 miles

---

SAVIN'S HOTEL

When the Cambrian Railway opened in 1864, businessman Thomas Savin put £80,000 into building a new hotel in Aberystwyth for package tourists. The scheme made him bankrupt, but the seafront building, complete with mock-Gothic tower, was bought by campaigners attempting to establish a Welsh university. The "college by the sea" opened in 1872, and is now the Theological College.

Mosaics on the college tower

(19 km) to **Devil's Bridge**, where a dramatic series of waterfalls plunges through a wooded ravine and a steep trail leads to the valley floor.

🏛 **Ceredigion Museum**
Terrace Rd. 📞 *01970 633088.*
⭘ *Mon–Sat.* ⬤ *25 Dec–3 Jan, Good Fri.* 🚻

Aberaeron ⑧

Cardiganshire (Dyfed). 🏠 *1,500.*
🚉 *Aberystwyth, then bus.* ℹ *The Quay (01545 570602).*

ABERAERON'S HARBOUR, lined with Georgian houses, became a trading port and

shipbuilding centre in the early 19th century. Its orderly streets were laid out in pre-railway days, when the ports along Cardigan Bay enjoyed considerable wealth. The last boat was built in 1994 and its harbour is now full of holiday sailors. It can be crossed in summer on the **Aeron Ferry**, a precarious-looking replica of the original 1885 hand-operated gondola. On the quayside, the **Honey Bee Exhibition** makes use of observation hives to show honey bees at work.

🏛 **Honey Bee Exhibition**
Cadwgan Pl. 📞 *01545 570445.*
⭘ *mid-May–mid-Sep: daily.* ♿

Rows of brightly painted Georgian houses lining the purpose-built harbour at Aberaeron

St David's ❾

S<small>T DAVID</small>, the patron saint of Wales, founded a monastic settlement in this remote corner of southwest Wales in about 550, which became one of the most important Christian shrines. The present cathedral, built in the 12th century, and the Bishop's Palace, added a century later, are set in a grassy hollow below St David's town, officially Britain's smallest city. The date of St David's death, 1 March, is commemorated throughout Wales.

Icon of Elijah, south transept

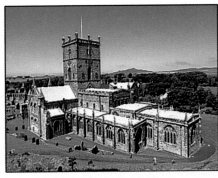

St David's Cathedral, the largest in Wales

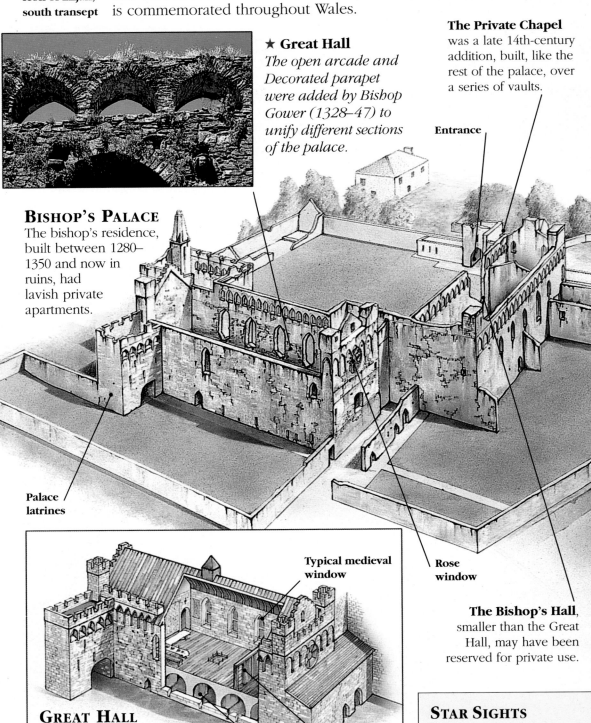

★ Great Hall
The open arcade and Decorated parapet were added by Bishop Gower (1328–47) to unify different sections of the palace.

The Private Chapel was a late 14th-century addition, built, like the rest of the palace, over a series of vaults.

Entrance

BISHOP'S PALACE
The bishop's residence, built between 1280–1350 and now in ruins, had lavish private apartments.

Palace latrines

Typical medieval window

Rose window

The Bishop's Hall, smaller than the Great Hall, may have been reserved for private use.

GREAT HALL
This reconstruction shows the hall before the lead was stripped from the roof. Bishop Barlow, St David's first Protestant bishop (1536–48), is thought to have been responsible for the lead's removal.

Wooden screen

Vault

STAR SIGHTS

★ **Great Hall**

★ **Nave Ceiling**

★ **St David's Shrine**

★ Nave Ceiling
The roof of the nave is lowered and hidden by an early 16th-century oak ceiling. A beautiful 14th-century rood screen divides the nave from the choir.

VISITORS' CHECKLIST

Cathedral Close, St David's. ☎ 01437 720202. ⊠ Haverfordwest then bus. ◯ 9am–6pm daily (Sat, Sun: pm). ✝ 7:30am, 8am, 6pm, Mon–Sat; 8am, 9:30am, 11:15am, 6pm Sun. ♿ ✓

CATHEDRAL
St David was one of the founders of the Celtic Christian church, so this became an important site of pilgrimage. Three visits here were equal to one to Jerusalem.

Stained Glass Window
In the nave's west end, eight panels, produced in the 1950s, radiate from a central window showing the dove of peace.

Bishop Vaughan's Chapel has a fine fan-tracery early Tudor roof.

St Mary's College Chapel

Entrance

Tower Lantern Ceiling
The medieval roof was decorated with episcopal insignia when restored in the 1870s by Sir George Gilbert Scott.

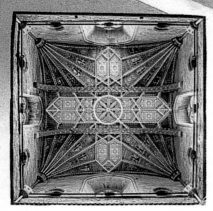

Sixteenth-Century Choir Stalls
The royal coat of arms on one of the carved choir stalls shows that the sovereign is a member of St David's Chapter. There are some interesting misericords (see p391) in these stalls.

★ St David's Shrine
The original was stolen in 1089 and this 1275 shrine was stripped of jewels in the Dissolution (see pp54–5). In 1866 relics of St David were found underneath the floor.

Tenby ⑩

Pembrokeshire (Dyfed). 5,000. ≷ ▢ ⬆ ℹ *The Croft (01834 842402).*

TENBY HAS SUCCESSFULLY trodden the fine line between over-commercialization and popularity, refusing to submit its historic character to the garish excesses of some seaside towns. Georgian houses overlook its handsome harbour, which is backed by a well-preserved medieval clifftop town of narrow streets and passages. The old town was defended by a headland fortress, now ruined, flanked by two wide beaches and a ring of 13th-century walls. These survive to their full height in places, along with a fortified gateway, the **Five Arches**.

The three-storeyed **Tudor Merchant's House** is a 15th-century relic of Tenby's highly prosperous seafaring days, with original fireplaces and chimneys. There are regular boat trips from the harbour to **Caldey Island**, 3 miles (5 km) offshore, home of a monastic community which makes perfume from local wild flowers.

⊞ Tudor Merchant's House (NT) Quay Hill. **☎** 01834 842279. ◯ Apr–Sep: Thu–Tue; Oct: Thur, Fri, Sun–Tue (Sun: pm).

A partly medieval restaurant next to the Tudor Merchant's House

Swansea and the Gower Peninsula ⑪

Swansea (West Glamorgan). 190,000. ≷ ▢ ⬆ ℹ *Plymouth St (01792 468321).* ◻ Mon–Sat.

SWANSEA, WALES'S SECOND CITY, is set along a wide, curving bay. The city centre was rebuilt after heavy bombing in World War II but, despite the modern buildings, a traditional Welsh atmosphere prevails. This is particularly noticeable in the excellent food market, full of Welsh delicacies such as laverbread (*see p40*) and locally caught cockles.

The award-winning **Maritime Quarter** redevelopment has transformed the old docklands. In an old warehouse on the waterfront, the **Maritime and Industrial Museum** has displays on the city's copper and tin-plate industries, and on the first passenger-carrying railway in the world, the horse-drawn Mumbles Railway, opened in 1807.

A statue of copper magnate John Henry Vivian (1779–1855) overlooks the marina. The Vivians, a leading Swansea family, founded the **Glynn Vivian Art Gallery**, which has exquisite Swansea pottery and porcelain. Archaeology and Welsh history feature at the **Swansea Museum**, established in 1838 and the oldest museum in Wales.

The poet Dylan Thomas (1914–53), whose statue overlooks the Maritime Quarter, spent his childhood in the hilly suburbs west of the city centre. **Cwmdonkin Park** was the scene of one of his early poems, *The Hunchback in the Park*, and its water garden has a memorial stone quoting from one of his most popular works, *Fern Hill*.

Swansea's austere **Guildhall** (1934) has a surprisingly rich interior. The huge panels, by

Swansea's most celebrated son, the poet Dylan Thomas

Picturesque fishermen's cottages at the Mumbles seaside resort

Sir Frank Brangwyn (1867–1956), on the theme of the British Empire, were originally painted for the House of Lords, but were considered too incongruous and colourful.

Swansea Bay leads to the **Mumbles**, a popular water-sports centre at the gateway to the 18 mile long (29 km) Gower Peninsula, which in 1956 was the first part of Britain to be declared an Area of Outstanding Natural Beauty. A string of sheltered, south-facing bays leads to Oxwich and Port-Eynon beaches, once the haunt of smugglers.

From Port-Eynon a curtain of limestone cliffs ends dramatically at Rhossili and the spectacular promontory of Worm's Head, accessible by a low-tide causeway. Rhossili's enormous beach leads to north Gower and a coastline of low-lying burrows, salt marshlands and cockle beds. The peninsula is littered with ancient sites such as **Parc Le Breose**, a prehistoric burial chamber.

🏛 Maritime and Industrial Museum
Museum Sq. **☎** 01792 650351. ◯ Tue–Sun & public hols. ● 25, 26 Dec, 1 Jan. ♿ ▢ ▯
🏛 Glynn Vivian Art Gallery
Alexandra Rd. **☎** 01792 655006. ◯ Tue–Sun & public hols. ● 23–26 Dec, 1 Jan. ♿ limited. ▯
🏛 Swansea Museum
Victoria Rd. **☎** 01792 653763. ◯ Tue–Sun & public hols. ● 25, 26 Dec, 1 Jan. ♿ limited. ▯
⊞ Guildhall
St Helen's Rd. **☎** 01792 636000. ◯ Mon–Fri. ● public hols. ♿ limited.

Wild Wales Tour ⑫

THIS TOUR WEAVES ACROSS the Cambrian Mountains' windswept moors, green hills and high, deserted plateaux. New roads have been laid to the massive Llyn Brianne Reservoir, north of Llandovery, and the old drover's road across to Tregaron has a tarmac surface. But the area is still essentially a "wild Wales" of hidden hamlets, isolated farmsteads, brooding highlands and traditional, quiet market towns.

Llanidloes ⑥
The town was a centre of religious and social unrest in the 17th and 18th centuries (see p511). There is a rare example of a free-standing Tudor market hall. The medieval church was restored in the late 19th century.

Devil's Bridge ④
This is a popular, romantic beauty spot with waterfalls, rocks, wooded glades and an ancient stone bridge – built by the Devil, according to legend.

Elan Valley ⑤
This is an area of lakes and important wildife habitats (see p550).

Strata Florida ③
This famous ruined abbey was an important political, religious and educational centre during the Middle Ages.

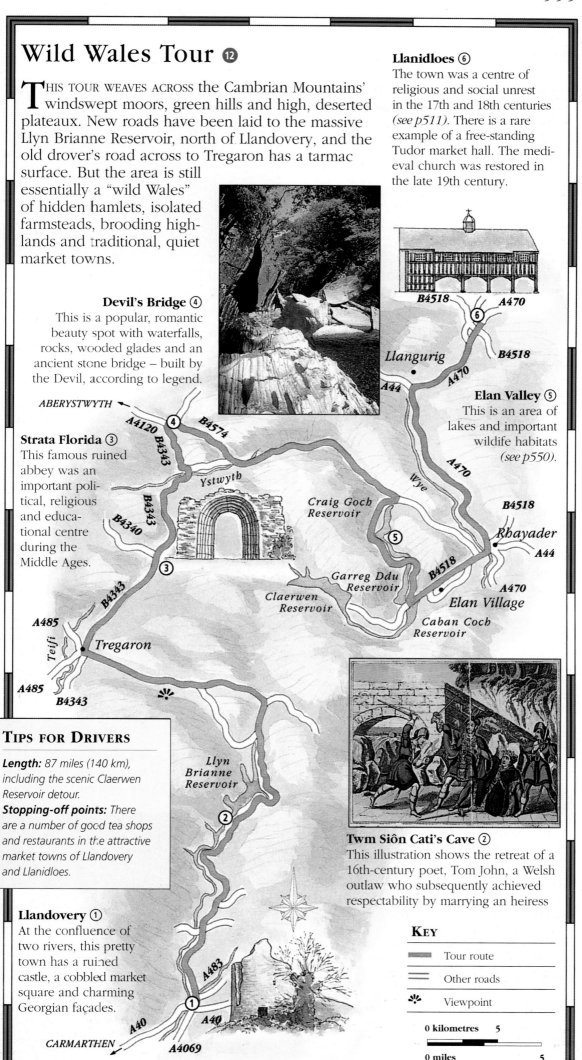

ABERYSTWYTH

A4120 ④ B4574
B4343
B4340
Ystwyth
Craig Goch Reservoir
⑤
Llangurig
A44
A470
Wye
A470
B4518
B4518
Rhayader
A44
Garreg Ddu Reservoir
Claerwen Reservoir
B4518
A470
Elan Village
Caban Coch Reservoir
A485
Teifi
A485
Tregaron
B4343
B4343
Llyn Brianne Reservoir
②

TIPS FOR DRIVERS

Length: *87 miles (140 km), including the scenic Claerwen Reservoir detour.*
Stopping-off points: *There are a number of good tea shops and restaurants in the attractive market towns of Llandovery and Llanidloes.*

Twm Siôn Cati's Cave ②
This illustration shows the retreat of a 16th-century poet, Tom John, a Welsh outlaw who subsequently achieved respectability by marrying an heiress

Llandovery ①
At the confluence of two rivers, this pretty town has a ruined castle, a cobbled market square and charming Georgian façades.

A483
①
A40
A40
CARMARTHEN
A4069

KEY

▬▬▬	Tour route
═══	Other roads
✹	Viewpoint

0 kilometres 5
0 miles 5

Brecon Beacons ⑬

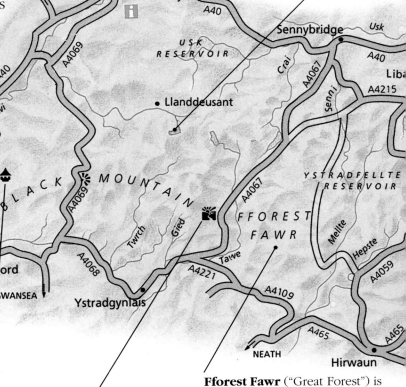

Trekking in the Beacons

THE BRECON BEACONS National Park covers 519 sq miles (1,345 sq km) from the Wales–England border almost all the way to Swansea. There are four mountain ranges within the park: the Black Mountain (to the west), Fforest Fawr, the Brecon Beacons and the Black Mountains (to the east). Much of the area consists of high, open country with smooth, grassy slopes on a bedrock of red sandstone. The park's southern rim has limestone crags, wooded gorges, waterfalls and caves. Visitors can enjoy many outdoor pursuits, from fishing in the numerous reservoirs to pony trekking, caving and walking.

Llyn y Fan Fach
This remote, myth-laden glacial lake is a 4 mile (6.5 km) walk from Llanddeusant.

The Black Mountain, a largely unexplored wilderness of knife-edged ridges and high, empty moorland, fills the western corner of the National Park.

0 kilometres 10

0 miles 5

Fforest Fawr ("Great Forest") is named after an area that was a medieval royal hunting ground.

Dan-yr-Ogof Caves
A labyrinth of caves runs through the Brecon Beacons. Guided tours of two large caves are offered here.

Carreg Cennen Castle
Spectacularly sited, the ruined medieval fortress of Carreg Cennen (see p512) stands on a sheer limestone cliff near the village of Trapp.

KEY

▦	A road
▤	B road
▦	Minor road
▪ ▪	Footpath
❀	Viewpoint

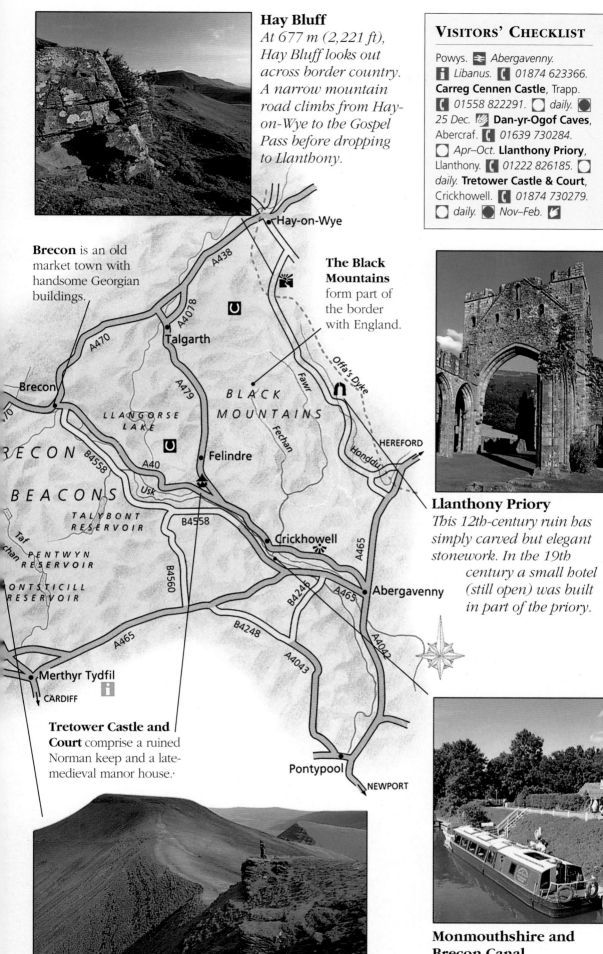

Hay Bluff
At 677 m (2,221 ft), Hay Bluff looks out across border country. A narrow mountain road climbs from Hay-on-Wye to the Gospel Pass before dropping to Llanthony.

Brecon is an old market town with handsome Georgian buildings.

The Black Mountains form part of the border with England.

Llanthony Priory
This 12th-century ruin has simply carved but elegant stonework. In the 19th century a small hotel (still open) was built in part of the priory.

Tretower Castle and Court comprise a ruined Norman keep and a late-medieval manor house.

Monmouthshire and Brecon Canal
This peaceful waterway, completed in 1812, was once used to transport raw materials between Brecon and Newport. It is now popular with leisure boats.

Pen y Fan
At 886 m (2,907 ft), Pen y Fan is the highest point in South Wales. Its distinctive, flat-topped summit, once a Bronze Age burial ground (see p46), can be reached by footpaths from Storey Arms on the A470.

Cardiff ⑭

CARDIFF WAS FIRST OCCUPIED by the Romans, who built a fort here in AD 75 *(see pp48–9)*. Little is known of its subsequent history until Robert FitzHamon *(see p562)*, a knight in the service of William the Conqueror, was given land here in 1093. By the 13th century, the settlement was substantial enough to be granted a royal charter, but it remained a quiet country town until the 1830s when the Bute family, who inherited land in the area, began to develop it as a port. By 1913 this was the world's busiest coal-exporting port, profiting from rail links with the South Wales mines. Its wealth paid for grandiose architecture, while the docklands became a raucous boom-town. Cardiff was confirmed as the first Welsh capital in 1955, by which time demand for coal was falling and the docks were in decline. The city is now dedicated to commerce and administration, and is being transformed by urban renewal programmes.

Fireplace detail in the Banqueting Hall, Cardiff Castle *(see pp562–3)*

near the Pier Head Building, has displays on the various building projects that are uniting the civic centre with the maritime district.

⛪ Cardiff Castle
See pp562–3.

🏛 City Hall and Civic Centre
Cathays Park. **[** *01222 871102.*
◯ *Mon–Fri.* ● *public hols.* ♿
Cardiff's civic centre of Neo-Classical buildings in white Portland stone is set among parks and avenues around Alexandra Gardens. The City Hall (1905), one of its first buildings, is dominated by its 60 m (200 ft) dome and clock tower. Members of the public can visit the first-floor Marble Hall, which is furnished with Siena marble columns and statues of Welsh heroes, among them St David, Wales's patron saint *(see pp552–3)*. The Crown Building, at the northern end of the complex,

City Hall's dome, adorned with a dragon, the emblem of Wales

Exploring Cardiff
Cardiff is a city with two focal points. The centre, laid out with Victorian and Edwardian streets and gardens, is the first of these. There is a Neo-Gothic castle and Neo-Classical civic buildings, as well as indoor shopping malls and a 19th-century **covered market**. Canopied arcades, lined with shops, lead off the main streets, the oldest being the **Royal Arcade** of 1856.

To the south of the centre, the docklands are now being transformed into the second focal point by the creation of a marina and waterfront. A new Cardiff is taking shape, especially around the Inner Harbour area. The **Pier Head Building**, constructed on Cardiff Bay in 1896 for the Cardiff Railway Company, is a reminder of the city's heyday. Its intricate decoration and terracotta detail was partly influenced by the red Mogul

buildings of India. Other attractions in the area are **National Techniquest**, a hands-on science museum, and the **Welsh Industrial Maritime Museum**, where exhibits such as a recreated ship's bridge illustrate the historical links between transport and industry in Wales.

The wooden **Norwegian Church** on Waterfront Park was first erected in 1868 for Norwegian sailors bringing wooden props for use in the coal pits of the South Wales valleys. Once surrounded by warehouses, it was taken apart and rebuilt during the dockland development. The **Cardiff Bay Visitor Centre**,

The Pier Head Building overlooking the redeveloped area of Cardiff Bay

◁ **Georgian houses overlooking boats moored in Tenby Harbour, Pembrokeshire**

now houses the Welsh Office, which is responsible for all Welsh government affairs.

🏛 National Museum of Wales

Cathays Park. 📞 01222 397951. ○ Tue–Sun & public hols. ● 24, 25 Dec. ⌨ 🚻 ♿ 💻 🏪

Opened in 1927, the museum occupies an impressive civic building with a colonnaded portico, guarded by a statue of David Lloyd George (see p511). Displays include a magnificent collection of Impressionist art by Renoir, Monet and Van Gogh, donated after World War II by two local sisters Gwendoline and Margaret Davies.

🏛 Crafts in the Bay

72 Bute St. 📞 01222 484611. ○ Tue–Sun. ♿

An extensive new crafts centre, organized by the Makers' Guild in Wales, opened here in March 1996. The building, which has been completely refurbished, now houses a wide variety of craft displays and demonstrations, including textile weaving and ceramic making.

As well as the permanent displays, there are frequently changing exhibitions on crafts-related themes. Visitors are free to browse around the centre or take part in any of the workshops which are regularly set up by the guild.

Statue of Welsh politician David Lloyd George

ENVIRONS: Established during the 1940s at St Fagans, on the western edge of the city, the open-air **Museum of Welsh Life** was one of the first of its kind. Buildings from all over Wales, including workers' terraced cottages, farmhouses, a tollhouse, a row of shops, a chapel and an old schoolhouse have been carefully reconstructed within the 40 ha (100 acre) parklands, along with a recreated Celtic village. There is also a Tudor mansion

which can be visited, boasting its own beautiful gardens in the grounds.

Llandaff Cathedral lies in a deep, grassy hollow beside the River Taf at Llandaff – a pretty "village suburb" which is 2 miles (3 km) northwest of the city centre. The cathedral was first a medieval building, occupying the site of a 6th-century monastic community.

Restored after suffering severe bomb damage during World War II, it was eventually reopened in 1957 with the addition of Sir Jacob Epstein's huge, stark statue, *Christus*, which is mounted on a concrete arch.

🏛 Museum of Welsh Life

St Fagans. 📞 01222 573500. ○ daily. ● 24, 25 Dec. ⌨ ♿ 🍴

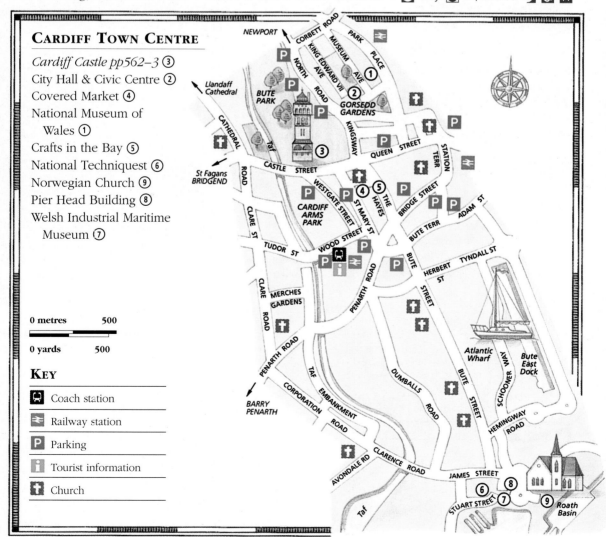

CARDIFF TOWN CENTRE

Cardiff Castle pp562–3 ③
City Hall & Civic Centre ②
Covered Market ④
National Museum of Wales ①
Crafts in the Bay ⑤
National Techniquest ⑥
Norwegian Church ⑨
Pier Head Building ⑧
Welsh Industrial Maritime Museum ⑦

0 metres   500
0 yards   500

KEY

🚌 Coach station

🚆 Railway station

🅿 Parking

ℹ Tourist information

✝ Church

Cardiff Castle

CARDIFF CASTLE BEGAN LIFE as a Roman fort, whose remains are separated from later work by a band of red stone. A keep was built within the Roman ruins in the 12th century. Over the following 700 years, the castle passed to several powerful families and eventually to John Stuart, the Earl of Bute, in 1766. His great-grandson, the 3rd Marquess of Bute, employed the "eccentric genius", architect William Burges, who created an ornate mansion between 1867 and 1881, rich in medieval images and romantic detail.

Arab Room
The gilded ceiling, with Islamic marble and lapis lazuli decorations, was produced by Arab craftsmen in 1881.

Herbert Tower

Animal Wall
A lion and other creatures guard the wall to the south of the castle. They were added between 1885 and 1930.

★ **Summer Smoking Room**
This was part of a complete bachelor suite in the Clock Tower, that also included a Winter Smoking Room.

Clock Tower

Main entrance to apartments

TIMELINE

AD 75 Roman fort constructed

1107 Castle inherited by Mabel Fitzhamon, whose husband is made Lord of Glamorgan

1183 Castle damaged during Welsh uprising

1423–49 Beauchamp family adds the Octagon Tower and Great Hall ceiling

1445–1776 Castle passes in turn to Nevilles, Tudors and Herberts

1867 3rd Marquess of Bute begins reconstruction

1000	1200	1400	1600	1800

1093 First Norman fort built by Robert Fitzhamon of Gloucester

1308–1414 Despenser family holds castle

Chaucer Room wall detail

1766 Bute family acquires the castle

1948 The castle is given in trust to the city of Cardiff

★ **Banqueting Hall**
*The design and decoration of
this room depicts the castle's
history, making impressively
ingenious use of the murals
and castellated fireplace.*

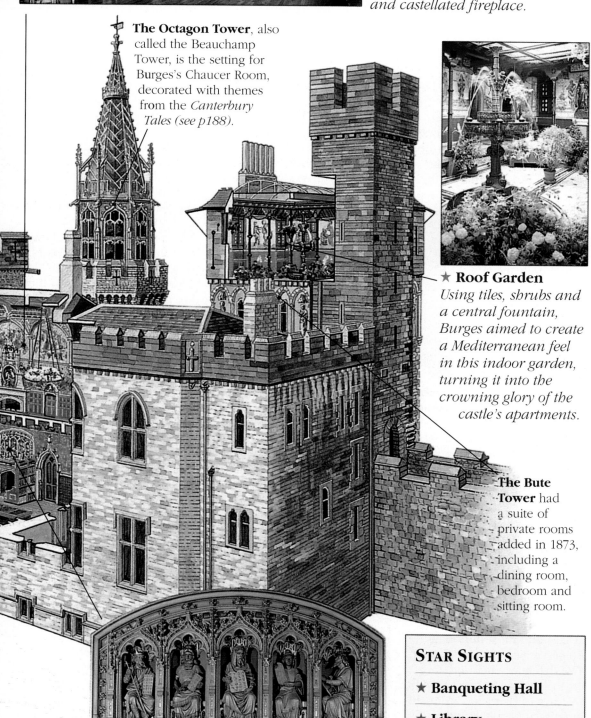

The Octagon Tower, also
called the Beauchamp
Tower, is the setting for
Burges's Chaucer Room,
decorated with themes
from the *Canterbury
Tales* (see p188).

★ **Roof Garden**
*Using tiles, shrubs and
a central fountain,
Burges aimed to create
a Mediterranean feel
in this indoor garden,
turning it into the
crowning glory of the
castle's apartments.*

**The Bute
Tower** had
a suite of
private rooms
added in 1873,
including a
dining room,
bedroom and
sitting room.

★ **Library**
*Carved figures representing ancient characters
of Greek, Assyrian, Hebrew and Egyptian
alphabets decorate the library's chimneypiece.*

STAR SIGHTS

★ **Banqueting Hall**

★ **Library**

★ **Summer Smoking
Room**

★ **Roof Garden**

Remains of Caerleon's amphitheatre, built in the 2nd century

Caerleon ⑮

Newport (Gwent). 🏃 *11,000.*
i *5 High St (01633 422656).*

TOGETHER WITH YORK *(see pp470–71)* and Chester *(see pp350–51)*, Caerleon was one of only three fortress settlements in Britain built for the Romans' elite legionary troops. From AD 74 Caerleon *(Isca* to the Romans, after the River Usk, which flows beside the town) was home to the 2nd Augustan Legion, which had been sent to Wales to crush the native Silures tribe. The remains of their base now lie between the modern town and the river.

The excavations at Caerleon are of great social and military significance. The Romans built not just a fortress for their crack 5,500-strong infantry division but a complete town to service their needs, including a stone amphitheatre. Judging by the results of the excavation work carried out since the archaeologist Sir Mortimer Wheeler unearthed the amphitheatre in 1926, Caerleon is one of the largest and most important Roman military sites in Europe. The defences enclosed an area of 20 ha (50 acres), with 64 rows of barracks, arranged in pairs, a hospital, and a bath-house complex.

Outside the settlement, the amphitheatre's large stone foundations have survived in an excellent state of preservation. Six thousand spectators

An altar at Caerleon's Legionary Museum

could sit here and enjoy the violence of blood sports and gladiators' combat.

More impressive still is the fortress baths complex, which opened to the public in the mid-1980s. The baths were designed on a lavish scale to bring all the home comforts to an army posted to barbaric Britain. The Roman troops could take a dip in the open-air swimming pool, play sports in the exercise yard or covered hall, or enjoy a series of hot, warm and cold baths.

Nearby are the foundations of the only Roman legionary barracks on view in Europe. The many excavated artefacts, including a collection of engraved gemstones, are now displayed at the **Legionary Museum.**

🏛 Legionary Museum
High St. **(** *01633 423134.* ◯
Mon–Sat, Sun (pm). ● *24–26 Dec, 1 Jan.* 📷 ♿ ▯

Big Pit Mining Museum, reminder of a vanished industrial society

Blaenafon ⑯

Torfaen (Gwent). 🏃 *9,500.*
i *Blaenafon Ironworks, North St.*
(*01495 792615.*

COMMERCIAL COAL-MINING has now all but ceased in the South Wales valleys – an area which only 100 years ago was gripped by the search for its "black gold". Though coal is no longer produced at **Big Pit** in Blaenafon, the **Mining Museum** provides a vivid reminder of this tough industry. The Big Pit closed as a working mine in 1980, and opened three years later as a museum. Visitors follow a marked-out route around the mine's surface workings to the miners' baths, the blacksmith's forge, the workshops and the engine house. There is also a replica of an underground gallery, where mining methods are explained. But the climax of any visit to Big Pit is beneath the ground. Kitted out with helmets, lamps and safety batteries, visitors descend by cage 90 m (300 ft) down the mineshaft and then are guided by ex-miners on a tour of the underground workings and pit ponies' stables.

Blaenafon also has remains of the iron-smelting industry. Across the valley from Big Pit stand the 18th-century smelting furnaces and workers' cottages that were once part of the **Blaenafon Ironworks**, and which are now a museum.

🏛 Big Pit Mining Museum
Blaenafon. **(** *01495 790311.*
◯ *Mar–Nov: daily.* 📷 ♿ *phone first.* 📷 ▯ ▯
🏛 Blaenafon Ironworks
North St. **(** *01495 792615.*
◯ *Apr–Oct: daily.* 📷

Monmouth ⑰

Monmouthshire (Gwent). 🏃 *8,500.*
🚌 **i** *Shire Hall (01600 713899).*
🚍 *Fri, Sat.*

THIS MARKET TOWN, which sits at the confluence of the Wye and Monnow rivers, has many historical associations. The 11th-century castle, behind Agincourt Square, is in ruins but the **Regimental Museum,**

Monnow Bridge in Monmouth, once a watchtower and jail

beside it, remains open to the public. The castle was the birthplace of Henry V *(see p53)* in 1387. A statue of Henry stands in the square, along with that of Charles Stewart Rolls (born at nearby Hendre), co-founder of the Rolls-Royce car manufacturers, who died in a flying accident in 1910.

Lord Horatio Nelson *(see p58)*, the famous admiral, visited Monmouth in 1802. An excellent collection of Nelson memorabilia, gathered by Lady Llangattock, mother of Charles Rolls, is displayed at the **Monmouth Museum**.

Monmouth was the county town of the old Monmouth-shire. The wealth of elegant Georgian buildings, including the elaborate **Shire Hall**,

which dominates Agincourt Square, reflect its former status. The most famous architectural feature in Monmouth is **Monnow Bridge**, a narrow 13th-century gateway on its western approach, thought to be the only surviving fortified bridge gate in Britain.

For a lovely view over the town, climb the Kymin, a 256 m (840 ft) hill crowned by a **Naval Temple** built in 1801.

Monmouth Castle and Regimental Museum
The Castle. **01600 772175.**
Apr–Oct: daily (pm); Nov–Mar: Sat & Sun (pm). 25 Dec.
Monmouth Museum
Priory St. **01600 713519.**
daily (Sun: pm). 24–26 Dec, 1 Jan.

Tintern Abbey ⑱

Monmouthshire (Gwent). **01291 689251.** Chepstow then bus. daily. 24–26 Dec, 1 Jan.

EVER SINCE THE 18th century, travellers have been enchanted by Tintern's setting in the steep and wooded Wye Valley and by the majestic ruins of its abbey. Poets were often inspired by the scene. Wordsworth's sonnet, *Lines composed a few miles above Tintern Abbey*, embodied his romantic view of landscape:

once again
Do I behold these steep and
* lofty cliffs,*
That on a wild, secluded
* scene impress*
Thoughts of more deep
* seclusion*

The abbey was founded in 1131 by Cistercian monks, who cultivated the surrounding lands (now forest), and developed it as an influential religious centre. By the 14th century this was the richest abbey in Wales, but along with other monasteries it was dissolved in 1536 by Henry VIII *(see p54)*. Its skeletal ruins are now roofless and exposed, the soaring arches and windows giving them a poignant grace and beauty.

Tintern Abbey in the Wye Valley, in the past a thriving centre of religion and learning, now a romantic ruin

SCOTLAND

INTRODUCING SCOTLAND 568-581

EDINBURGH 582-609

THE LOWLANDS 610-643

GLASGOW 644-659

THE HIGHLANDS AND ISLANDS 660-701

Scotland at a Glance

STRETCHING from the rich farmlands of the Borders to a chain of isles only a few degrees south of the Arctic Circle, the Scottish landscape has a diversity without parallel in Britain. As you travel northwest from Edinburgh, the land becomes more mountainous and its archaeological treasures more numerous. In the far northwest, Scotland's earliest relics stand upon the oldest rock on Earth.

Western Isles

Skye (see pp694–5), *renowned for its dramatic scenery, has one of Scotland's most striking coastlines. On the east coast, a stream plunges over Kilt Rock, a cliff of hexagonal basalt columns named after its likeness to an item of Scottish national dress.*

THE HIGHLANDS AND ISLANDS *(see pp660–701)*

Argyll and Bute

Clyde Valley

Ayrshire

The Trossachs (see pp634–5) *are a beautiful range of hills straddling the border between the Highlands and the Lowlands. At their heart, the forested slopes of Ben Venue rise above the still waters of Loch Achray.*

Culzean Castle (see pp628–31) *stands on a cliff's edge on the Firth of Clyde, amid an extensive country park. One of the jewels of the Lowlands, Culzean is a magnificent showcase of work by the Scottish-born architect, Robert Adam (see p28).*

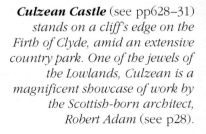

◁ **Loch Lomond, the Lowlands**

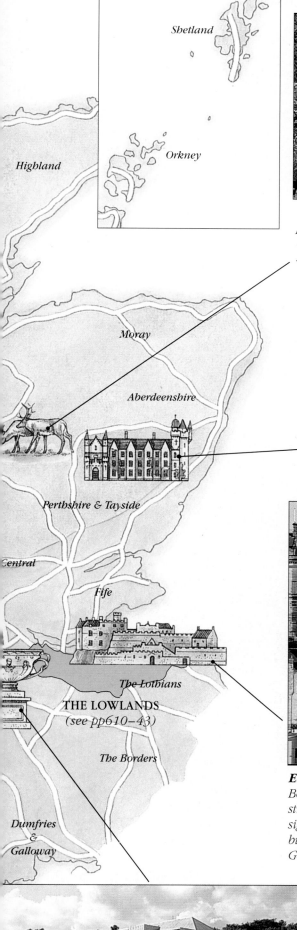

Shetland

Orkney

Highland

Moray

Aberdeenshire

Perthshire & Tayside

Central

Fife

The Lothians

THE LOWLANDS
(see pp610–43)

The Borders

Dumfries
&
Galloway

The Cairngorms (see pp682–3) *cover an area prized for its beauty and diversity of wildlife, though there are also many historical relics to be found, such as this early 18th-century arch at Carrbridge.*

Royal Deeside (see pp686–7) *in the Grampians has been associated with British royalty since Queen Victoria bought Balmoral Castle in 1852.*

Edinburgh (see pp582–609) *is Scotland's capital. Between its medieval castle and Holyrood Palace stretches the Royal Mile – a concentration of historic sights, ranging from the old Scottish Parliament buildings to the house of John Knox. By contrast, Georgian terraces predominate in the New Town.*

The Burrell Collection (see pp658–9), *on the southern outskirts of Glasgow, is a museum of some of the city's greatest art treasures. It is housed in a spacious, glass building opened in 1983.*

0 kilometres	50

| 0 miles | 50 |

A PORTRAIT OF SCOTLAND

WITH SUCH A DISTINCTIVE national dress, drink, bagpipe music, landscape and folklore, Scotland has shaped an identity recognizable the world over. It is a land of astonishing contrasts and possesses a magical quality, whether seen shrouded in mist or rising majestic above the mirror of a loch.

In a straight line from the far south to the far north, the Scottish mainland reaches about 440 km (275 miles), yet its coastline stretches nearly 10,000 km (6,200 miles). There are 787 major islands, almost all lying off the northern or western coasts. The topography is generally extremely mountainous with wild heather moorlands in the north and west, pine forests mixed with quality pasture in the middle, fertile farmland in the east and, in the south, the rounded, grass-covered hills of the Lowlands. Picturesque lochs and rivers are scattered throughout. Most of Scotland's five million people live in the country's Central Belt.

Red deer in the Highlands

The Scots cherish the differences that set them apart from the English, and cling tenaciously to the distinctions that differentiate them region by region – their customs, dialects and the Gaelic language. It is perhaps more by their differences than similarities that the Scots can be defined but, for all that, they are immensely proud of their nation and its separate institutions, such as education and law. The Scots can be dour but equally they can flash with inspiration. They delight in self-deprecating humour and continue to honour their tradition of hospitality.

A view from Edinburgh Castle over the rooftops of the capital to Calton Hill

◁ Isolated dwellings set among the lofty mountains on Skye, the largest island of the Inner Hebrides

POLITICS AND THE ECONOMY

Ever since the Treaty of Union in 1707, which combined the parliaments of Scotland and England into one governing body convening in Westminster (London), Scotland has felt estranged from the mechanisms of government, and short-changed by the small allocation of time given to Scottish affairs. Today, all the major political parties of the UK find support in Scotland. The Scottish National Party, which campaigns for complete independence, has gained in popularity. In 1997 the Scots voted for the re-establishment of a Scottish parliament, to begin in 1999. This parliament has a wide-ranging administrative role, though major financial controls and decisions of national interest are retained by Westminster.

A hammer-thrower at the Braemar Games

Scotland's economy has fluctuated in the last 100 years. It has had to fight back from the demise of its heavy industries – shipbuilding, coal mining and steel production. Today, the major contributors to the economy are North Sea oil, tourism and services, aided by a wide spectrum of light industries. Chief among these is the manufacture of electronic components and microchips, contributing to the sobriquet of a "Silicon Glen", but this industry, which employs many people, has become shaky in response to the global market.

Whisky production is a leading revenue earner for the Exchequer (treasury department), although it employs few people. Agriculture retains its importance but has become beleaguered by disastrous markets. Fishing also remains an important industry, yet there is increasing competition for dwindling stocks. Scotland's level of unemployment is on a par with the UK, though there are worse-off areas, such as the Western Isles where it reaches 15 per cent.

SOCIETY

The Scots are a gregarious people and enjoy company, whether this be in a small group at a Highland *ceilidh* (literally, a "visit"), a crowded bar, or as part of the colourful, and usually peaceful, Saturday armies of football (soccer) fans. Sometimes they have to travel far to find company; the Highland region has a population density of eight people per square kilometre (20 per sq mile), and the lack of public transport means a car is vital.

Church attendance is in decline in all but the Gaelic-speaking areas, where Sundays are observed as days of

Edinburgh bagpiper

rest. In most towns, and all cities, a full range of leisure activities and entertainment runs into the wee hours, but in rural areas opening hours are shorter, and restaurants may stop serving early.

Scotland is renowned as the home of golf, but football is without doubt the national passion, and England the favourite opponent. Other popular sports include hill-walking, skiing, rugby, shinty and curling. There are also annual Highland Games – great gatherings of whisky, music, craft stalls and tests of stamina and strength.

The Viking fire festival, *Up Helly Aa*, in Shetland

Small-scale farming in the Western Isles

festivals. The Scottish film industry is booming, following the success of *Trainspotting* (1993). The musical scene has also been enjoying a time of vibrancy, ranging from opera, Gaelic song, *pibroch* (the classical music of the bagpipes) to such varied international bands as Simple Minds, Runrig, Texas and Wet Wet Wet. Traditional music has experienced a renaissance over the last decade using rhythms and instruments from around the world. With an estimated four Scots living abroad for every one living in the homeland, this influence is not surprising. Bands like Macumba combine bagpipes and Brazilian percussion to wonderful effect. In dance, on offer are the varied delights of Scottish country, Highland and *ceilidh* dancing and step dancing, a tradition reintroduced from Cape Breton.

Yet for all their love of sports, the Scots are an unhealthy race. Their appetite for red meat and greasy fish and chips contributes to a high incidence of heart problems, and they have the highest consumption of alcohol and tobacco in the UK.

CULTURE AND THE ARTS

Scotland offers an excellent programme of the performing arts, subsidized generously by the Scottish Arts Council. The Edinburgh Festival and Fringe is the largest celebration of its kind in the world, and there are many smaller

Edinburgh's Festival Fringe Office detail

Although only about 50,000 people speak Gaelic, the language has been boosted by increased funding for Gaelic radio and television programmes. Literature has a strong following, too, with no shortage of respected Scottish authors and poets *(see pp580–81)*.

The blue waters of Loch Achray in the heart of the Trossachs, north of Glasgow

The History of Scotland

Bonnie Prince Charlie, by G Dupré

Sᴵɴᴄᴇ ᴛʜᴇ ʀᴏᴍᴀɴ ɪɴᴠᴀsɪᴏɴ of Britain, Scotland's history has been characterized by its resistance to foreign domination. The Romans never conquered the area, and when the Scots extended their kingdom to its present boundary in 1018, a long era of conflict began with England. After many wars, the Scots finally accepted union with the "auld enemy": first with the union of crowns, and then with the Union of Parliament in 1707. In 1999 the inauguration of the Scottish Parliament was a dramatic change.

An elaborately carved Pictish stone at Aberlemno, Angus

EARLY HISTORY

Tʜᴇʀᴇ ɪs ᴍᴜᴄʜ ᴇᴠɪᴅᴇɴᴄᴇ in Scotland of important prehistoric population centres, particularly in the Western Isles, which were peopled mostly by Picts who originally came from the Continent. By the time Roman Governor Julius Agricola invaded in AD 81, there were at least 17 independent tribes, including the Britons in the southwest, for him to contend with.

The Romans reached north to the Forth and Clyde valleys, but the Highlands deterred them from going further. By 120, they had retreated to the line where the Emperor Hadrian had built his wall to keep the Picts at bay (not far from today's border). By 163 the Romans had retreated south for the last time. The Celtic influence began when

"Scots" arrived from Ireland in the 6th century, bringing the Gaelic language with them.

The Picts and Scots united under Kenneth McAlpin in 843, but the Britons remained separate until 1018, when they became part of the Scottish kingdom.

THE ENGLISH CLAIM

Tʜᴇ ɴᴏʀᴍᴀɴ ᴋɪɴɢs regarded Scotland as part of their territory but seldom pursued the claim. William the Lion of Scotland recognized English sovereignty by the Treaty of Falaise (1174), though English control never spread to the northwest. In 1296 William Wallace, supported by the French (the start of the Auld Alliance, which lasted two centuries), began the long war of independence. During this bitter conflict, Edward I seized the sacred Stone of Destiny from Scone *(see p640)*, and took it to Westminister Abbey. The war lasted for more than 100 years. Its great hero was Robert the Bruce, who defeated the English in 1314 at Bannockburn. The English held the upper hand after that, even though the Scots would not accept their rule.

John Knox statue in Edinburgh

THE ROAD TO UNION

Tʜᴇ sᴇᴇᴅs ᴏꜰ ᴜɴɪᴏɴ between the crowns were sown in 1503 when James IV of Scotland married Margaret Tudor, daughter of Henry VII. When her brother, Henry VIII, came to the throne, James sought to assert independence but was defeated and killed at Flodden Field in 1513. His granddaughter, Mary, Queen of Scots *(see p55)*, married the French Dauphin in order to cement the Auld Alliance and gain assistance in her claim to

Bruce in Single Combat at Bannockburn (1906) by John Hassall

the throne of her English cousin, Elizabeth I. She had support from the Catholics wanting to see an end to Protestantism in England and Scotland. However, fiery preacher John Knox won support for the Protestants and established the Presbyterian Church in 1560. Mary's Catholicism led to the loss of her Scottish throne in 1568, and her subsequent flight to England, following defeat at Langside. Finally, after nearly 20 years of imprisonment she was executed for treason by Elizabeth in 1587.

The factories on Clydeside, once creators of the world's greatest ships

UNION AND REBELLION

O N ELIZABETH I's death in 1603, Mary's son, James VI of Scotland, succeeded to the English throne and became James I, king of both countries. Thus the crowns were united, though it was 100 years before the formal Union of Parliaments in 1707. During that time, religious differences within the country

Articles of Union between England and Scotland, 1707

reached boiling point. There were riots when the Catholic-influenced Charles I restored bishops to the Church of Scotland and authorized the printing of a new prayer book. This culminated in the signing, in Edinburgh in 1638, of the National Covenant, a document that condemned all Catholic doctrines. Though the Covenanters were suppressed, the Protestant William of Orange took over the English throne in 1688 and the crown passed out of Scottish hands

In 1745, Bonnie Prince Charlie (*see p695*), descended from the Stuart kings, tried to seize the throne from the Hanoverian George II. He marched far into England, but was driven back and defeated at Culloden field (*see p688*) in 1746.

INDUSTRIALIZATION AND SOCIAL CHANGE

I N THE LATE 18TH AND 19th centuries, technological progress transformed Scotland from a nation of crofters to an industrial powerhouse. In the notorious Highland Clearances (*see p692*), from the 1780s on, landowners ejected tenants from their smallholdings and gave the land over to sheep and other livestock. The first ironworks was established in 1760 and was soon followed by coal mining, steel production and shipbuilding on the Clyde. Canals were cut, railways and bridges built.

A strong socialist movement developed as workers sought to improve their conditions. Keir Hardie, an Ayrshire coal miner, in 1892 became the first socialist elected to parliament, and in 1893 founded the Independent Labour Party. The most enduring symbol of this time is the spectacular Forth rail bridge (*see p607*).

SCOTLAND TODAY

A LTHOUGH THE STATUS of the country appeared to have been settled in 1707, a strong nationalist sentiment remained and was heightened by the Depression of the 1920s and '30s which had severe effects on the heavily industrialized Clydeside. This was when the Scottish National Party formed, advocating self-rule. The Nationalists asserted themselves in 1950 by stealing the Stone of Scone from Westminister Abbey.

The discovery of North Sea oil in 1970 encouraged a nationalist revival and, in 1979, the Government promised to establish a separate assembly if 40 per cent of the Scottish electorate endorsed the plan in a referendum. This figure was finally surpassed in 1998, and the Scottish Parliament was duly inaugurated in 1999.

A North Sea oil rig, helping to provide prosperity in the 1970s

Scottish Gardens

SCOTLAND HAS A GREAT number of diverse and beautiful gardens. Some are renowned for their layout, such as Pitmedden, or for particular plants. Rhododendrons flourish in Scotland's acidic, peaty soil, and the Royal Botanic Garden in Edinburgh is famous for its spectacular, colourful display. Some gardens have a striking backdrop of lakes or mountains, while others form the grounds of a stately home. Gulf Stream gardens like Inverewe offer visitors a rare chance to view exotic, subtropical flora at a northern latitude. The gardens shown here are some of Scotland's finest.

Inverewe Gardens (see p698) *are renowned for their lush, exotic, subtropical flora. Ferns, lilies, giant forget-me-nots and rare palms are just some of the 2,500 species that thrive in the mild climate.*

Crarae Gardens (see p670) *are sited on a slope overlooking Loch Fyne, surrounded by mature woodland. There are many walks, all designed to cross a picturesque burn at the centre. The gardens are riotous with spectacular rhododendrons in spring and ablaze with golden and russet leaves during the autumn.*

The Botanic Gardens, Glasgow (see p657), *have a wonderful collection of orchids, begonias and cacti. Kibble Palace, a domed, iron conservatory, houses tropical tree ferns from around the world.*

Logan Botanic Garden is an outpost of the Royal Botanic Garden in Edinburgh. The garden is divided into two main areas – a walled garden with cabbage palms, and a woodland area. The Gulf Stream enables subtropical plants to grow here.

Inverewe
Gardens

Angus'
Garden

Crarae
Gardens

Arduaine
Garden

Bota
Garde
Glasg

Younger
Botanic
Garden

Logan
Botanic
Garden

THE RHODODENDRON

These examples illustrate three of the 900 rhododendron varieties. The first is tropical, grown under glass in Scotland; the second is evergreen; the third is an azalea, which used to be considered a separate species. Rhododendrons also fall into scaly-leaved and non-scaly groups.

Macgregoriae

Augustini

Medway

Drummond Castle Gardens *are laid out as a large boxwood parterre in the shape of a St Andrew's Cross. Yellow and red roses and antirrhinums provide the colour, and a sundial forms the centrepiece.*

THE GULF STREAM

The west coast of Scotland is the surprising location for a number of gardens where tropical and subtropical plants bloom. Although on the same latitude as Siberia, this area of Scotland lies in the path of a warm water current from the Atlantic. Inverewe is the most famous of the Gulf Stream gardens, with plants from South America, South Africa and the South Pacific. Other gardens include Achamore on the Isle of Gigha and Logan Botanic Garden near Stranraer.

Eucalyptus tree ferns warmed by the Gulf Stream, Logan Botanic Garden

Map labels:
Pitmedden Garden •
Crathes Gardens •
ummond stle rdens
• Royal Botanic Garden, Edinburgh
Kailzie Gardens •
• Dawyck Botanic Garden
• Priorwood Gardens

0 kilometres 50
0 miles 50

Pitmedden Garden *was created in 1675 and later restored to its full glory as a formal garden by the National Trust for Scotland. Split into two levels, it has four parterres, two gazebos, box hedges and a splendid fountain at its centre.*

Crathes Gardens' *topiary and scented borders are centred around the beautiful tower house, Crathes Castle (see p687). There are eight different themed gardens, such as the Golden Garden designed in the style of Gertrude Jeckyll.*

Dawyck Botanic Garden *is another branch of Edinburgh's Botanic Garden, and specializes in rare trees, such as the Dawyck Beech, flowering shrubs and blankets of narcissi. The garden's chapel was designed by William Burn.*

The Royal Botanic Garden, Edinburgh *(see p606), is internationally renowned as a base for scientific research, as well as having a marvellous range of plants. Enhanced by beautifully maintained lawns, it nurtures almost 17,000 species. Exotic plants are found in the many glasshouses.*

Clans and Tartans

Tʜᴇ ᴄʟᴀɴ sʏsᴛᴇᴍ, by which Highland society was divided into tribal groups led by autocratic chiefs, can be traced to the 12th century, when clans were already known to wear the chequered wool cloth later called tartan. All members of the clan bore the name of their chief, but not all were related by blood. Though they had noble codes of hospitality, the clansmen had to be warriors to protect their herds, as can be seen from their mottoes. After the Battle of Culloden *(see p688)*, all the clan lands were forfeited to the Crown, and the wearing of tartan was banned for nearly 100 years.

The Mackays, also known as the Clan Morgan, won lasting renown during the Thirty Years War.

The MacLeods are of Norse heritage. The clan chief still lives in Dunvegan Castle, Skye.

The Mackenzies received much of the lands of Kintail (see p693) *from David II in 1362.*

The MacDonalds were the most power-ful of all the clans, holding the title of Lords of the Isles.

CLAN CHIEF

The chief was the clan's patriarch, judge and leader in war, commanding absolute loyalty from his clansmen who gave mili-tary service in return for his protection. The chief sum-moned his clan to do battle by sending a run-ner across his land bearing a burning cross.

The Campbells were a widely feared clan who fought the Jacobites in 1746 (see p689).

Bonnet with eagle feathers, clan crest and plant badge.

Dirk

Sporran, or pouch, made of badger's skin.

Feileadh-mor, or "great plaid" (the early kilt), wrap-ped around waist and shoulder.

Basket-hilted sword

The Black Watch, raised in 1729 to keep peace in the Highlands, was one of the Highland regiments in which the wearing of tartan sur-vived. After 1746, civilians were punished by exile for up to seven years for wearing tartan.

The Sinclairs came from France in the 11th century and became Earls of Caithness in 1455.

The Frasers came over to Britain from France with William the Conqueror and his followers in 1066.

George IV, dressed as a Highlander, visited Edinburgh in 1822, the year of the tartan revival. Many tartan "setts" (patterns) date from this time, as the original ones were lost.

The Gordons were famously good soldiers; the clan motto was "by courage, not by craft".

The Stuarts were Scotland's royal dynasty. Their motto was "no one harms me with impunity".

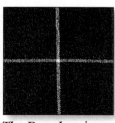

The Douglas clan was prominent in Scottish history, though its origin is unknown.

CLAN TERRITORIES

The territories of 10 major clans are marked here with their clan crests and tartan. The patterns shown are modern versions of original tartan designs.

PLANT BADGES

Each clan had a plant associated with its territory. It was worn on the bonnet, especially on the day of battle.

Scots pine was worn by the MacGregors of Argyll.

Rowan berries were worn by the Clan Malcolm.

Ivy was worn by the Clan Gordon of Aberdeenshire.

Spear thistle, now a national symbol, was a Stuart badge.

Cotton grass was worn by the Clan Henderson.

HIGHLAND CLANS TODAY

Once the daily dress of the clansmen, the kilt is now largely reserved for formal occasions. The one-piece *feileadh-mor* has been replaced by the *feileadh-beag*, or "small plaid", made from approximately 7 m (23 ft) of material with a double apron fastened at the front with a silver pin. Though they exist now only in name, the clans are still a strong source of pride for Scots, and many still live in areas traditionally belonging to their clans. Many visitors to Britain can trace their Scots ancestry back to the Highlands.

Modern Highland formal dress

Writers and Intellectuals

FROM MEDIEVAL POETS through Robert Burns to Irvine Welsh, writers in the three literary languages of Scotland – Scots, English and Gaelic – have created a body of literature expressing both their place in the European mainstream and the diversity within Scotland. Three centuries after the dissolution of its parliament, Scotland stands on the threshold of a new one. Political devolution follows three decades of ferment in which literature has reached new heights of success.

Robert Burns encircled by images of his literary creations

THE GOLDEN AGE BEFORE ENLIGHTENMENT

OFTEN REGARDED as the golden age of Scottish literature, the century leading up to the Reformation of 1560 showed strong links with the Continent and a rich tradition of poetry, culminating in the achievements of William Dunbar and Robert Henryson. John Barbour established the mythic heroism of the national hero in *The Bruce* (c.1375). Other early works were James I's *Kingis Quair* (c.1424) and Blind Harry's *Wallace* (c.1478).

Dunbar rose to pre-eminence for his polished art, from *Lament for the Makars* (1508), an elegy to poets, to his insult poetry known as "flyting". Henryson's work has insight, as in *The Testament of Cresseid* (c.1480), which tells the legend from the woman's point of view. Gavin Douglas translated Virgil's *Aeneid* into Scots in 1513. The golden age ended with Sir David Lindsay's much revived play, *A Satire of the Three Estates*, in 1540. The ballad tradition continues to influence Scottish literature.

ENLIGHTENMENT AND ROMANTICISM

THE INTELLECTUAL TRIUMPHS of the Enlightenment in Scotland were fuelled by the expanding educational system.

Philosopher David Hume

Among the great thinkers of the time were Adam Smith (1723–90), who theorized on political economy, and Adam Ferguson (1723–1816), who founded modern sociology. Other prominent figures were William Robertson (1721–93) and David Hume (1711–76), both of whom helped to define modern history. Hume's greatest legacy was in philosophy – his rigorous empiricism offended Christian orthodoxy and foretold crises of faith versus scientific knowledge. James Macpherson published the *Ossian Chronicles* in 1760, supposedly the documentation of his discovery of an old Celtic tradition in the Hebrides. This fictional work tapped a nostalgia for ancient civilizations and, allied to fears about progress, Romanticism was born. Allan Ramsay wrote poems in Scots, as did the tragic Robert Fergusson, who died in poverty aged 25.

The country's most fêted literary figure, Robert Burns (1759–96), was a man of his time. His "heaven-taught ploughman" persona fitted fashion but belied a sound education. His works ranged from love lyrics to savage satire (*Holy Willie's Prayer*), nationalism to radical ideals (*A Man's a Man for a' That*).

THE 19TH CENTURY

DESPITE THE importance of Edinburgh in British culture, it was the pattern of leaving Scotland to achieve fame in London, initiated in the mid-18th century by James Boswell and Tobias Smollett, that would predominate in the Victorian decades.

The poetry of Walter Scott (1771–1832) enjoyed phenomenal success. His novels, especially *Waverley* (1814), rose to greater glory. Francis Jeffrey's Whig-orientated *Edinburgh Review* led opinion, challenged by *Blackwood's* Tory alternative. James Hogg published by the latter work before writing his startling,

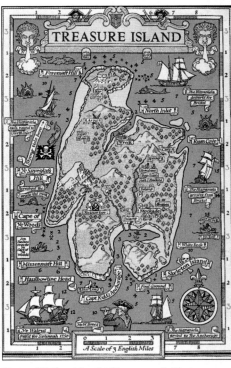

Map of Robert Louis Stevenson's Treasure Island, based on an island in the Firth of Forth

gothic *Private Memoirs and Confessions of a Justified Sinner* (1824). Following Susan Ferrier and John Galt, standards were modest, despite the prodigious career of Margaret Oliphant. Thomas Carlyle noted the provinciality of Edinburgh in the 1830s.

A later response to anxieties of the age came from Robert Louis Stevenson (1850–94) in *Dr Jekyll and Mr Hyde*. This contrasted with the sentimentality of home-spun or so-called kailyard (literally "cabbage patch") fiction, led by JM Barrie and SR Crockett. Barrie's dramas often catered for bourgeois tastes, as did the *Sherlock Holmes* stories of Arthur Conan Doyle (1859–1930), which endure today.

Arthur Conan Doyle's sleuth, Sherlock Holmes, in *The Graphic* (1901)

***Rob Roy* film poster (1995), from Walter Scott's novel of 1817**

EARLY 20TH-CENTURY RENAISSANCE

GEORGE DOUGLAS BROWN'S fierce anti-kailyard novel, *The House with the Green Shutters* (1901), opened the century and serious art was reborn. Hugh MacDiarmid's poetry in the 1920s carried literature into the stream of modernism. *A Drunk Man Looks at the Thistle* (1926) combines disparate Scottish dialects with political and social commentary in one of the century's great symbolist works. Edwin Muir also won international acclaim. Successors included Sidney Goodsir Smith and William Soutar. Fiction reached epic and innovative proportions with Neil Gunn (*Butcher's Broom*, 1933) and Lewis Grassic Gibbon (*A Scots Quair*, 1932–4). Others included Willa Muir, Nan Shepherd and Fionn MacColla. John Buchan attempted serious work and popular thrillers. Nationalist impetus was dissipated by the rise of fascism, and new directions were sought after World War II.

POST-1945

SORLEY MACLEAN wrote in his native Gaelic of the ancient Highland culture's plight. Norman MacCaig began a career characterized by metaphysical whimsy, and George Bruce and Robert Garioch evoked the strictures of nature and social class.

Edwin Morgan has celebrated art and modernity (*Sonnets from Scotland*, 1984), Liz Lochhead continues to produce fresh drama and poetry and, among the newest generation, Jackie Kay explores the experience of being a black Scottish citizen in prose and poetry. While James Bridie, Bill Bryden and John Byrne made an impact in the theatre, Muriel Spark rose to international acclaim for her blackly comic novels (*The Prime of Miss Jean Brodie*, 1961). Urban realism developed quietly before William MacIlvanney's breakthrough with *The Big Man* (1985).

Following Alasdair Gray's bizarre *Lanark* (1981), a powerful wave propelled fiction into the highly productive present, in which Iain Banks remains a bestseller (*The Crow Road*, 1992). Tom Leonard's poems initiated a tradition using urban demotic speech. James Kelman elevated this to new levels: the Booker Prize-winning *How Late it Was, How Late* (1994) affirms ordinary life within a Kafkaesque vision of sinister bureaucracy.

Irvine Welsh's portrayal of drug culture is now world famous, though the energy and profundity of *Trainspotting* (1993) is absent from its successors. The private dramas articulated in AL Kennedy's stories are poignant and mysterious (*So I am Glad*, 1995).

Poster for the film version of Irvine Welsh's novel

Houses in Edinburgh's Old Town, near Edinburgh Castle ▷

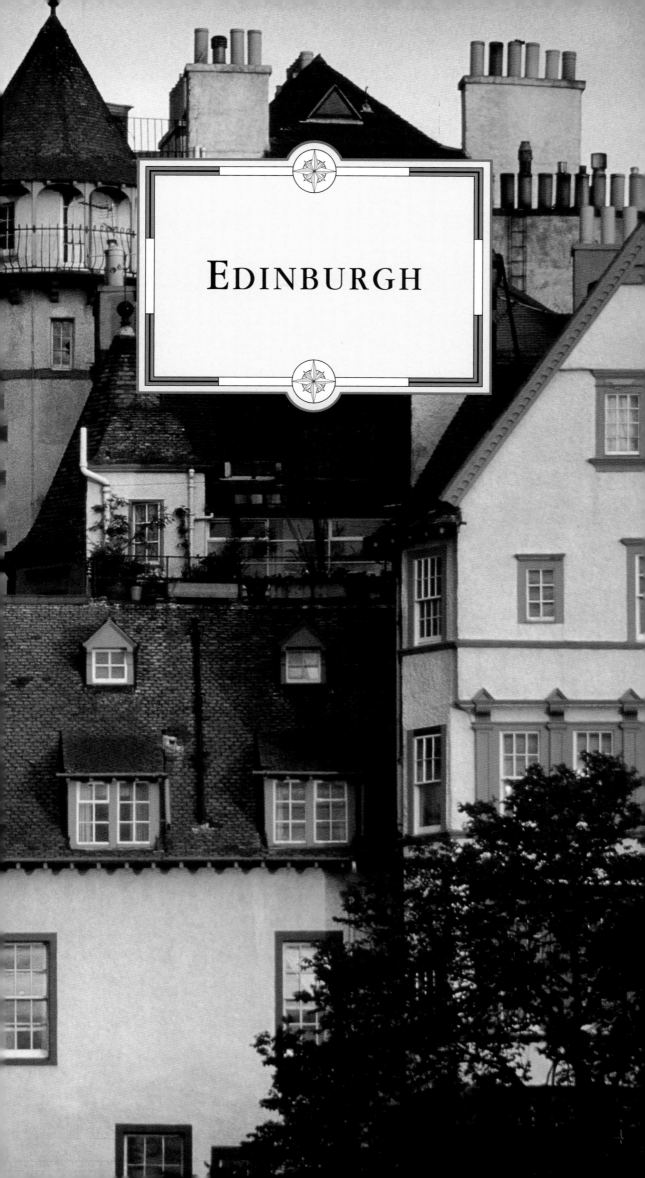

EDINBURGH

EDINBURGH

THE HISTORIC STATUS *of Edinburgh, the capital of Scotland, is beyond question, with ancient buildings scattered across the city, and the seat of Scotland's new parliament lying close to the royal residence of Holyrood Palace. The astonishing range of historical and artistic attractions draws visitors from all over the world.*

Edinburgh used to be known by the affectionate but unflattering epithet "Auld Reekie", a reference to the smoky, fog-ridden atmosphere of the Old Town before anti-pollution legislation cleared the air. Although winter fogs can still sometimes give the imposing granite buildings of the Old Town a grim and austere feel, Edinburgh today is a lively, vibrant city. It is one of the cultural centres of Europe and has been described as "The Athens of the North" because of its many notable ancient buildings.

Edinburgh's violent volcanic past can be seen everywhere in its landscape. The city's most prominent geological features – the extinct volcanic plug of Castle Rock and the hills of Salisbury Crags and Arthur's Seat – were all formed 350 million years ago when cataclysmic eruptions broke the calm of the Carboniferous seas and spewed ash and basaltic lava over the area in which Edinburgh now stands. Castle Rock in Edinburgh has been occupied since around 1000 BC in the Bronze Age, and recent research suggests that the name "Edinburgh" means "mountain stronghold". It is no surprise that Edinburgh was founded on Castle Rock, given its strategic views over the Firth of Forth, the great coastal gateway into Scotland from the east. Today, two great bridges straddle the Forth: the cantilevered Forth Rail Bridge, which was the first major steel-built bridge in the world and opened in 1890; and the graceful Forth Road Bridge, which

A juggler performing at the annual arts extravaganza, the Edinburgh Festival

◁ The Grassmarket area of the city, dominated by the imposing edifice of Edinburgh Castle

Looking down Princes Street, which connects Edinburgh's Old and New Towns

opened in 1964 and was once the longest suspension bridge outside the USA.

Edinburgh's most famous landmark, Edinburgh Castle, was built on the site of the first settlement in the city, Castle Rock. A favourite royal residence of Scottish kings before the Union of the Crowns in 1603, the Castle has

Waxwork, John Knox's House

witnessed several major events in Scottish history. Exploring the many buildings in the Castle complex gives a real insight into Edinburgh's, and in fact Scotland's, history. St Margaret's Chapel, for example, was built on the rocky summit of the crag early in the 12th century and features a fascinating stained-glass window. The castle is still very much a military stronghold, as shown by the famous Military Tattoo, held annually on the Esplanade in front of the Gatehouse. The Tattoo features

military bands from all over the world and never fails to attract huge crowds.

To the south and east of the Castle lies the Old Town, the site of the ancient city of Edinburgh. The Old Town developed along the route of the Royal Mile – which is one of the most interesting streets in Europe – and was the main thoroughfare of medieval Edinburgh. Because of the restrictions imposed by the city walls, houses in the Old Town had to grow upwards, and there are many tenements that climb up to 20 floors in height. A walk down the Royal Mile from Castlehill to Canongate is the best way to appreciate Edinburgh's impressive continuity of history, and when you reach the paved Heart of Midlothian in the square outside 15th-century St Giles Cathedral, you know you are in the heart of the city. Buskers and street entertainers give this part of Edinburgh a lively, colourful atmosphere; there is always something going on in this cobbled open space. At the eastern end of the Royal Mile, Holyrood Palace, which James IV made his royal residence in 1498, is still the official dwelling of the monarch in Scotland. Holyrood Palace includes many sumptuous royal apartments and is set in the 260 hectares (640 acres) of Holyrood Park. This park provides fine views across the city from the 250-m (820-ft) summit of Arthur's Seat.

Before the 19th century, overcrowding made the Old Town a

Fountain at the foot of Edinburgh Castle

dirty and difficult place to live. However, in the late 1700s, enlightened planners such as George Drummond, James Craig, Robert Adam and Robert Reid created what is still known as the New Town, to the north of the Castle. Based on a grid pattern and centred on sylvan squares such as Moray Place and Charlotte Square, the New Town is a monument to tasteful Georgian town planning. The area exudes an air of gracious living. The link between Old and New Town Edinburgh is Princes Street. This road is the focus for shopping and cultural activities – a bustling, cosmopolitan thoroughfare where shops, museums and art galleries comfortably coexist. At the time of the Festival in August, Princes Street is a vibrant, surging mass of humanity (the city's population doubles from around 400,000 to approximately 800,000 for the duration of the Festival)

Monument to philosopher Dugald Stewart, Calton Hill

who come not only to enjoy the extensive official programme of events, but also to sample the sometimes risqué and daring performances characteristic of the Festival Fringe.

However, it is not just in August that you can enjoy cultural events in Edinburgh. The King's Theatre hosts pantomimes and performances by touring companies, while the Edinburgh Playhouse often has runs of internationally successful musicals. The Edinburgh Festival Theatre hosts the Scottish Opera and the Royal Scottish National Orchestra. Jazz, folk and rock music venues are scattered around the city.

Watching over these diverse cultural attractions and contrasting architectural styles is the Gothic monument to Victorian novelist Sir Walter Scott, which stands in Princes Street Gardens. Scott was born in Edinburgh and spent a significant part of his life in the city. He remains one of Edinburgh's favourite sons.

Aerial view of the city: New Town in the foreground, the Castle to the right and Salisbury Crags beyond

Exploring Edinburgh

T HE CENTRE OF EDINBURGH is divided neatly in
half by Princes Street, the principal shopping
area. To the south lies the Old Town, site of the
ancient city, which grew along the route of the
Royal Mile, from the Castle Rock in the west to
Holyrood Palace in the east. At the end of the
18th century, building for the New Town started
to the north of Princes Street.
The area is still viewed today
as a world-class example of
Georgian urban architecture,
with its elegant façades and
broad streets. Princes Street
itself has lots to offer, including art galleries, the towering
Scott Monument and the landmark Balmoral Hotel clock
tower, as well as the city's
main train station, Waverley.

**Edinburgh Castle's
Royal Scots soldiers**

**North Bridge, opened in 1772 – the main
route connecting the Old and New Towns**

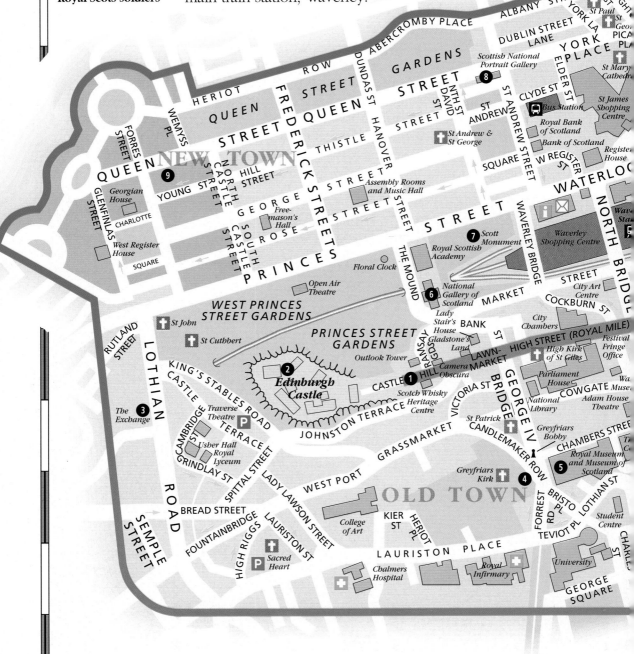

GETTING AROUND

Central Edinburgh is compact, so walking is an excellent way to explore the centre. Other options include a comprehensive bus service and a multitude of black taxis. Avoid exploring the centre by car, because the streets tend to be congested with traffic, and parking may be difficult. Car use has been actively discouraged by the local authority in recent years. On main routes special lanes are provided for buses, taxis and bicycles, and in the suburbs there is also a good network of bicycle paths.

SIGHTS AT A GLANCE

Historic Areas, Streets and Buildings

Edinburgh Castle pp596–7 ❷
The Exchange ❸
Greyfriars Kirk ❹
Holyrood Palace ⑪
New Scottish Parliament ⑬
New Town pp602–603 ❾
The Royal Mile pp592–5 ❶

Monuments

Scott Monument ❼

Landmarks

Calton Hill ❿
Holyrood Park and
  Arthur's Seat ⑭

Museums, Galleries and Exhibitions

Dynamic Earth ⑫
National Gallery of Scotland ❻
The Royal Museum and
  Museum of Scotland ❺
Scottish National Portrait
  Gallery ❽

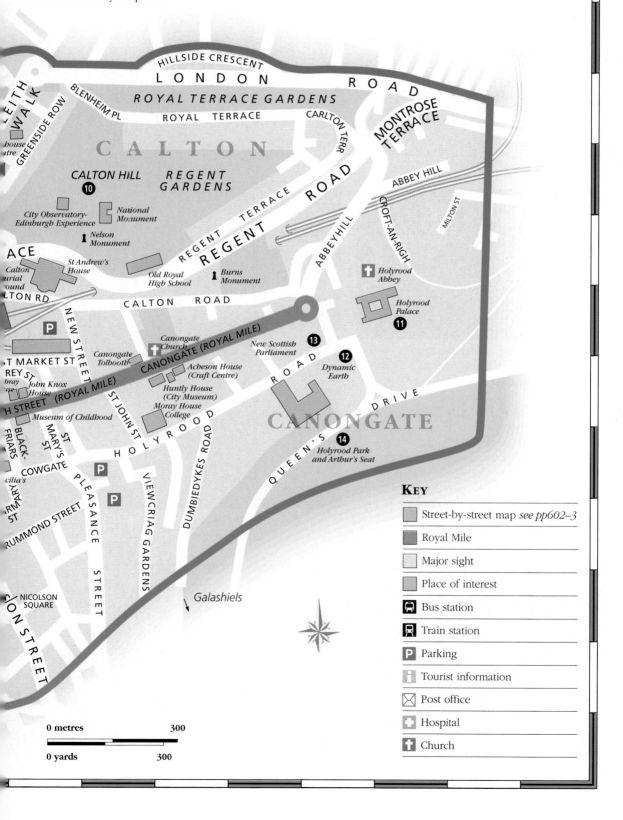

KEY

▨	Street-by-street map *see pp602–3*
▨	Royal Mile
□	Major sight
▨	Place of interest
🚌	Bus station
🚆	Train station
Ⓟ	Parking
ⓘ	Tourist information
✉	Post office
✚	Hospital
✝	Church

0 metres   300

0 yards   300

Edinburgh Festival

The Hub logo

For three weeks in August, Edinburgh's elegant city centre is transformed into a riot of colour, music and theatre as the world's top performers descend on the capital to take part in the Edinburgh International Festival. Founded in 1947 to raise spirits in the aftermath of the World War II, this annual extravaganza has grown dramatically to become one of the top events in the performing arts calendar. Running alongside the main festival are the Fringe Festival, Book Festival, Film Festival, Jazz and Blues Festival and the Military Tattoo, between them attracting some 500,000 visitors.

Fringe poster, 1998

Tickets can be bought directly from each festival. In 1999, the main Festival has a new home and festivals visitor centre called the Hub, which also has a club, café and shop.

The Jazz and Blues Festival *is one of the longest established festivals in Europe, and covers all styles – from trad to fusion.*

THE EDINBURGH TATTOO

Set against the stunning backdrop of Edinburgh Castle, the military tattoo is one of the most spectacular and popular events of the Festival. It was first performed in 1950 with pipes and army bands, but has since grown to include international performers, dancers, drill teams, cavalry and motorcyclists.

The Tattoo attracts around 200,000 spectators every year

Fringe performance groups often use the Festival to try out new shows.

Charlotte Square Gardens *hosts the Edinburgh Book Festival. For two weeks in August this elegant square is the focus of book-related events and talks.*

The Fringe Office provides tickets for almost 1,500 Fringe shows at 175 different venues.

Edinburgh Festival Theatre is one of the main venues for the International Festival, which attracts the world's top names in music, theatre, dance and opera.

Outdoor entertainment is very much a part of the Festival. With so much to see, many performers take their shows to the streets to encourage people to buy tickets.

Strange sights abound at the Fringe Festival, which was created in 1947 as an alternative to the official Festival. Everyone is allowed to perform – from amateur groups to well-established performers.

FESTIVAL INFORMATION AND TICKETS

Book Festival ①
Edinburgh
    Castle ②
Film Festival
    Office ⑥
Fringe Festival
    Office ⑦
The Hub ⑤
Jazz and Blues
    Festival Office ③
Military Tattoo
    Office ④

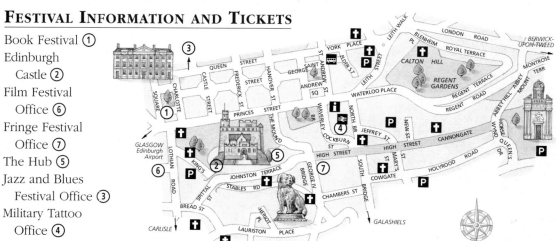

The Royal Mile ❶

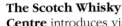

Eagle sign outside Gladstone's Land

T HE ROYAL MILE is a stretch of four ancient streets (from Castlehill to Canongate) which formed the main thoroughfare of medieval Edinburgh, linking the castle to Holyrood Palace. Confined by the city wall, the "Old Town" grew upwards, with some tenements climbing to 20 floors. It is still possible, among the 66 alleys and closes off the main street, to sense Edinburgh's medieval past.

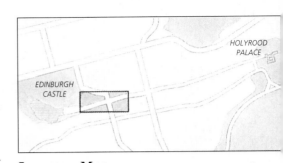

LOCATOR MAP

Gladstone's Land is a preserved 17th-century merchant's house.

The Scotch Whisky Centre introduces visitors to Scotland's national drink.

The Outlook Tower contains an observatory from which to view the city.

Edinburgh Castle

C A S T L E H I L L

L A W N M A R K E T

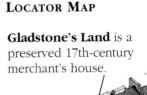

Lady Stair's House
This 17th-century house is now a museum of the lives and works of writers Burns, Scott and Stevenson.

The Tolbooth Kirk (c.1840) has the city's highest spire.

🏛 Outlook Tower

((0131) 226 3709. ⭘ *daily.* 📷 📺
The lower floors of this building date from the early 17th century and were once the home of the Laird of Cockpen. In 1852, Maria Short added the upper floor, the viewing terrace and the Camera Obscura – a large pinhole camera that pictures life in the city centre as it happens. A marvel at the time, it remains one of Edinburgh's most popular attractions.

🏛 Gladstone's Land

(NTS) 477B Lawnmarket.
((0131) 226 5856.
⭘ *Apr–Oct: daily.* 📷
This 17th-century merchant's house has been carefully restored. It provides a window on life in a typical Old Town house before overcrowding drove the rich inhabitants northwest to the ever-expanding Georgian New Town. "Lands", as they were then known, were tall,

narrow buildings erected on small plots of land. The six-floor house that is Gladstone's Land was named after Thomas Gledstanes, the merchant who built it in 1617. The house still has the original arcade booths on the street façade as well as a painted ceiling, with fine Scandinavian floral designs.

Although the house is extravagantly furnished, it also contains items, such as wooden overshoes that had to be worn in the dirty streets, which serve as a reminder of the less salubrious features that were part of the old city.

A chest in the beautiful Painted Chamber is said to have been given by a Dutch sea captain to a Scottish merchant who saved him from a shipwreck. A similar house, named Morocco's Land (*see p595*), can be found further to the east, on Canongate.

The bedroom of Gladstone's Land

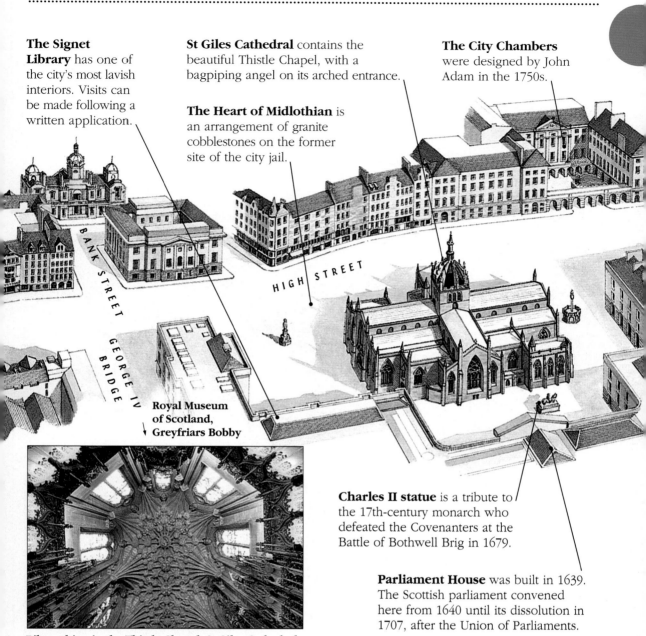

The Signet Library has one of the city's most lavish interiors. Visits can be made following a written application.

St Giles Cathedral contains the beautiful Thistle Chapel, with a bagpiping angel on its arched entrance.

The City Chambers were designed by John Adam in the 1750s.

The Heart of Midlothian is an arrangement of granite cobblestones on the former site of the city jail.

BANK STREET

HIGH STREET

GEORGE IV BRIDGE

Royal Museum of Scotland, Greyfriars Bobby

Charles II statue is a tribute to the 17th-century monarch who defeated the Covenanters at the Battle of Bothwell Brig in 1679.

Parliament House was built in 1639. The Scottish parliament convened here from 1640 until its dissolution in 1707, after the Union of Parliaments.

Rib-vaulting in the Thistle Chapel, St Giles Cathedral

🏛 **Writers' Museum**

Lady Stair's House, Lady Stair's Close. ☎ (0131) 529 4901. ◯ Mon–Sat.
This fine old town mansion was built in 1622. In the 1720s it was acquired by Elizabeth, Dowager Countess of Stair, and has since been called Lady Stair's House. Its official title reflects its role as a museum of memorabilia from Robert Burns, Sir Walter Scott and Robert Louis Stevenson.

🏛 **Parliament House**

Parliament Sq, High St. ☎ (0131) 225 2595. ◯ Mon–Fri. ♿ limited.
This majestic, Italianate building was constructed in the 1630s for the Scottish Parliament. Parliament House has been home to the Court of Session and the High Court since the Union of Parliaments in 1707. It is well worth seeing, as much for the spectacle of its many gowned and

wigged advocates as for the beautiful stained-glass window in the Great Hall, commemorating the inauguration of the Court of Session by King James V in 1532.

⛪ **St Giles Cathedral**

Royal Mile. ☎ (0131) 225 9442. ◯ daily. 📷
Properly known as the High Kirk (church) of Edinburgh, it is ironic that St Giles is popularly known as a cathedral. Though it was twice the seat of a bishop in the 17th century, it was from here that John Knox directed the Scottish Reformation, with its emphasis on individual worship freed from the authority of bishops. A tablet marks the place

where Jenny Geddes, a local market stallholder, scored a victory for the Covenanters in 1637 by hurling her stool at a preacher who was reading from an English prayer book.

The Gothic exterior of the cathedral is dominated by a 15th-century tower, the only part to escape heavy renovation in the 19th century. Inside, the impressive Thistle Chapel, with its rib-vaulted ceiling and carved heraldic canopies can be seen. The chapel honours the knights, past and present, of the Most Ancient and Most Noble Order of the Thistle. The carved royal pew in the Preston Aisle is used by Queen Elizabeth II when staying in Edinburgh.

Bagpiping angel from the entrance of the cathedral

Exploring Further Down the Royal Mile

THE SECTION of the Royal Mile from High Street to Canongate passes two monuments to the Reformation: John Knox's house and the Tron Kirk. The Canongate was once an independent district, owned by the canons of the Abbey of Holyrood, and sections of its south side have undergone excellent restoration. Beyond Morocco's Land, the road stretches for the final half-mile (800 m) to Holyrood Palace.

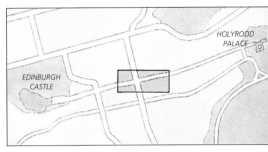

LOCATOR MAP

HIGH STREET

SOUTH BRIDGE STREET

The Mercat Cross marks the city centre. It was here that Bonnie Prince Charlie *(see p695)* was proclaimed king in 1745.

The Tron Kirk *was built in 1630 for the Presbyterians who left St Giles Cathedral when it came under the control of the Bishop of Edinburgh.*

John Knox's House

45 High St. (0131) 556 9579. Mon–Sat. limited. by appointment.

As a leader of the Protestant Reformation and minister at St Giles, John Knox (1513–72) was one of the most important figures in 16th-century Scotland. Ordained as a priest in 1536, Knox later became convinced of the need for religious change. He took part in the Protestant occupation of St Andrews Castle in 1547 and served two years as a galley slave in the French navy as punishment. On release, Knox went to London and Geneva to espouse the Protestant cause, returning to Edinburgh in 1559. The townhouse on the Royal Mile that bears his name dates from 1450 and it was here that he spent the last few months of his life. It is one of the few structures from this period that survive today. Displays tell the story of Knox's life in the context of the political and religious upheavals of his time.

Museum of Childhood

42 High St. (0131) 529 4142. Mon–Sat (Sun during Edinburgh Festival). limited. www.cec.org.uk

This museum is not merely a toy collection but a magical insight into childhood, with all its joys and trials. Founded in 1955 by a city councillor, Patrick Murray (who claimed to eat children for breakfast), it was the world's first museum of childhood. The collection includes medicines, school books and old-fashioned toys. With its nickelodeon, antique slot machines and enthusiastic visitors, this has been called the world's noisiest museum.

Canongate Tolbooth: The People's Story

163 Canongate. (0131) 529 4057. Mon–Sat (Sun during Edinburgh Festival).

Edinburgh's social history museum is housed in the Canongate Tolbooth, dating

An 1880 automaton of the Man on the Moon, Museum of Childhood

John Knox's House

Dating from 1450, the oldest house in the city was the home of the preacher John Knox during the 1560s. He is said to have died in an upstairs room. It contains relics of his life.

Morocco's Land is a reproduction of a 17th-century tenement house. It takes its name from the statue of a Moor which adorns the entrance.

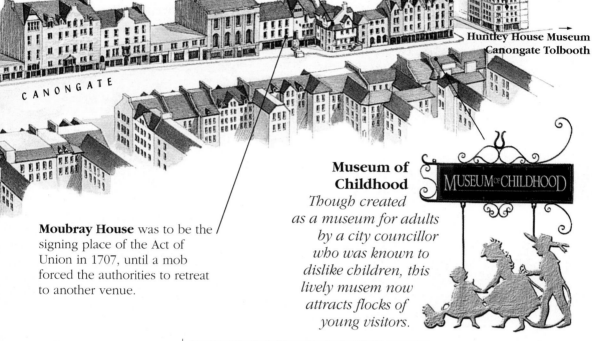

CANONGATE

Huntley House Museum
Canongate Tolbooth

Moubray House was to be the signing place of the Act of Union in 1707, until a mob forced the authorities to retreat to another venue.

Museum of Childhood

Though created as a museum for adults by a city councillor who was known to dislike children, this lively musem now attracts flocks of young visitors.

MUSEUM OF CHILDHOOD

---

from 1591. With its distinctive clock tower, this was the focal point for life in the Burgh of Canongate. Until the mid-19th century it contained law courts, a jail and the meeting place for the burgh council. It has been a museum since 1954.

Focusing on the lives of ordinary citizens from the late 18th century to the present, it covers subjects such as public health, recreation, trade unions and work. The riots, disease and poverty of the 19th century are also covered, and with subjects as diverse as wartime, football and punk rock, this collection gives a valuable insight into life in Edinburgh.

LIFE BELOW THE OLD TOWN

Until the 18th century most residents of Edinburgh lived along and beneath the Royal Mile and Cowgate. The old abandoned cellars and basements, which lacked any proper water supply, daylight or ventilation, were once centres of domestic life and industry. Under these conditions, cholera, typhus and smallpox were common. Mary King's Close, under the City Chambers, is one of the most famous of these areas – its inhabitants were all killed by the plague around 1645.

You can visit these areas with Robin's Ghost and History Tour – (0131) 661 0125 – or Mercat Walking Tours – (0131) 661 4541 www.mercat-tours.co.uk.

A prison cell in the Canongate Tolbooth: The People's Story

🏛 **Huntly House Museum**
142–146 Canongate. 🅒 *(0131) 529 4143.* ☐ *Mon–Sat (Sun during Edinburgh Festival).*
Huntly House was built in the early 16th century and damaged in the English raid on Edinburgh in 1544, although it was later substantially repaired. First used as a family townhouse, it was later divided into apartments but by the 19th

century it was little more than a slum. In 1924 the local authority bought the property and opened the museum in 1932. This local history collection includes exhibits such as Neolithic axe heads, Roman coins, military artifacts and glassware. A section is also dedicated to Field Marshal Earl Haig, Commander-in-Chief of the British Army during World War I.

Edinburgh Castle ❷

STANDING UPON the basalt core of an extinct volcano, Edinburgh Castle is an assemblage of buildings dating from the 12th to the 20th century, reflecting its changing role as fortress, royal palace, military garrison and state prison. Though there is evidence of Bronze Age occupation of the site, the original fortress was built by the 6th-century Northumbrian king, Edwin, from whom the city takes its name. The castle was a favourite royal residence until the Union of the Crowns *(see p45)* in 1603, after which the king resided in England. After the Union of Parliaments in 1707, the Scottish regalia were walled up in the Palace for over a hundred years. The Palace is now the zealous possessor of the so-called Stone of Destiny, a relic of ancient Scottish kings which was seized by the English and not returned to Scotland until 1996.

Beam support in the Great Hall

Scottish Crown
Now on display in the palace, the Crown was restyled by James V of Scotland in 1540.

Military Prison

Governor's House
Complete with Flemish-style crow-stepped gables, this building was constructed for the governor in 1742 and now serves as the Officers' Mess for the castle garrison.

Old Back Parade

Vaults
This French graffiti, dating from 1780, recalls the many prisoners who were held in the vaults during the wars with France in the 18th and 19th centuries.

MONS MEG

Now kept in the castle vaults, the siege gun (or *bombard*) Mons Meg was made in Belgium in 1449 for the Duke of Burgundy, who gave it to his nephew, James II of Scotland. It was used by James against the Douglas family in their stronghold of Threave Castle *(see p625)* on the Dee in 1455, and later by James IV against Norham Castle in England. After exploding during a salute to the Duke of York in 1682, it was kept in the Tower of London until it was returned to Edinburgh in 1829, at Sir Walter Scott's request.

STAR SIGHTS

★ **Great Hall**

★ **Palace**

Argyle Battery
This fortified wall commands a spectacular northern view of the city's New Town.

★ **Palace**
Mary, Queen of Scots, gave birth to James VI in this 15th-century palace, where the Stone of Destiny and Crown Jewels are displayed.

VISITORS' CHECKLIST

Castle Hill. 📞 (0131) 225 9846.
🕐 Apr–Oct: 9:30am–6pm daily; Nov–Mar: 9:30am–5pm daily (last admission: 45 mins before closing).
www.historic-scotland.gov.uk

Entrance

Royal Mile →

The Esplanade is the location of the Military Tattoo.

The Half Moon Battery was built in the 1570s as a platform for the artillery defending the eastern wing of the castle.

★ **Great Hall**
With its restored open-timber roof, the hall dates from the 15th century and was the meeting place of the Scottish Parliament until 1639.

St Margaret's Chapel
This stained glass window depicts Malcolm III's saintly queen, to whom the chapel is dedicated. Probably built by her son, David I, in the early 12th century, the chapel is the castle's oldest existing building.

The Standard Life Building, at the heart of the city's financial centre

The Exchange ❸

Lothian Rd, West Approach Rd and Morrison St.

LOCATED WEST of Lothian Road, The Exchange is the most important recent development in central Edinburgh. The once unsightly area was rejuvenated when Festival Square and the Sheraton Grand Hotel were built in 1985. Three years later the local authority published a plan to promote the area as a financial centre. In 1991 investment management firm Baillie Gifford opened Rutland Court on West Approach Road.

The ambitious **Edinburgh International Conference Centre**, on Morrison Street, was designed by Terry Farrell and opened in 1995. There has been a fever of construction work ever since. Standard Life opened a new headquarters on Lothian Road in 1997, which has some fine artistic features, and in 1998 Scottish Widows opened a bold new building.

🛈 **Edinburgh International Conference Centre**
📞 (0131) 300 3000. ♿

Greyfriars Kirk ❹

Greyfriars Place. 📞 (0131) 226 5429. ⬤ Easter–Oct: Mon–Sat; Nov–Easter: Thu. ♿ 🛈

GREYFRIARS KIRK occupies a key role in the history of Scotland, as this is where the National Covenant was signed in 1638, marking the Protestant stand against the imposition of an episcopal church by King Charles I. Greyfriars was then a relatively new structure, having been completed in 1620 on the site of a Franciscan friary.

Throughout the 17th century, during years of bloodshed and religious persecution, the kirkyard was used as a mass grave for executed Covenanters. The kirk also served as a prison for Covenanter forces captured after the 1679 Battle of Bothwell Brig. The Martyrs' Monument is a sobering reminder of those times. The original kirk building was severely damaged by fire in 1845 and substantially rebuilt.

But despite this turmoil, Greyfriars is best known for its association with a dog, Bobby, who lived by his master's grave from 1858 to 1872. Bobby's statue stands outside Greyfriars Kirk.

A tribute to Greyfriars Bobby

The Royal Museum and Museum of Scotland ❺

Chambers St. 📞 (0131) 225 7534. ⬤ daily (Sun: pm). 🖼 ♿ 🛈 www.nms.ac.uk

STANDING SIDE BY SIDE on Chambers Street, these two buildings could not be more different from one another. The older of the museums, **The Royal Museum of Scotland**, is a great Victorian palace of self improvement. Designed by Captain Francis Fowke of the Royal Engineers, the building was completed in 1888. Although it started life as an industrial museum, over time its collection was developed to include an eclectic assortment of exhibits, ranging from stuffed animals to ethnographic and technological items. These are all displayed in rooms leading off the large and impressive central hall.

There was, however, no room available to display Scotland's impressive array of antiquities. As a result, they were crammed into inadequate spaces in the National Portrait Gallery in Queen Street, or were hidden away altogether and put into storage.

As far back as the 1950s, recommendations were made that a new facility be built to house the nation's historical treasures. The government did not commit funding to the project until as recently as 1990. Work on a site next door to the Royal Museum of Scotland on Chambers Street started in 1993, and the building took five years to complete. The result was the **Museum of Scotland**, a contemporary flourish of confident design by architects Gordon Benson and Alan Forsyth, which opened to the public in December 1998.

Described as one of the most important buildings erected in Scotland in the second half of the 20th century, the museum tells the story of the country, starting with its geology and natural history. It then moves through to the early peoples of Scotland, the centuries when Scotland was a kingdom in its

The 9th-century Monymusk Reliquary on display at Edinburgh's Museum of Scotland

own right, and then on to later industrial developments. Some stunning items are on show, including St Fillan's Crozier, which was said to have been carried at the head of the Scottish army at Bannockburn in 1314. The Monymusk Reliquary is also on display. Dated to around AD 800, it was a receptacle for the remains of the Christian missionary, St Columba.

National Gallery of Scotland ⑥

The Mound. 📞 (0131) 556 8921. ⭕ daily. ♿ 📷 by appointment.

ONE OF SCOTLAND'S finest art galleries, the National Gallery of Scotland is worth visiting for its 15th- to 19th-century British and European paintings alone, though plenty more can be found to delight the enthusiastic art-lover.

Serried ranks of paintings hang on deep red walls behind a profusion of statues and other works of art. Some of the highlights among the Scottish works exhibited are the society portraits by Allan Ramsay and Henry Raeburn, including the latter's *Reverend Robert Walker Skating on Duddingston Loch*, thought to date from the beginning of the 19th century.

The collection of early German pieces contains Gerard David's almost comic-strip treatment of the *Three Legends of St Nicholas*, from around the beginning of the 16th century. Works by Raphael, Titian and Tintoretto accompany other southern European paintings, including Velazquez's *An Old Woman Cooking Eggs*, from 1620, and there is an entire room devoted to *The Seven Sacraments* by Nicholas Poussin, dating from around 1640. Flemish painters represented include Rembrandt, Van Dyck and Rubens, while among the British offerings are important works by Ramsay, Reynolds and Gainsborough.

Scott Monument ⑦

Princes Street Gardens East. ⭕ daily. 📷

SIR WALTER SCOTT (1771–1832) is one of the most important figures in the history of Scottish literature *(see p622)*. Born in Edinburgh, Scott initially pursued a legal career but he soon turned to writing full time as his ballads and historical novels began to bring him success. His works looked back to a time of adventure, honour and chivalry, and did much to promote this image of Scotland abroad.

In addition to being a celebrated novelist, Sir Walter was also a major public figure – he organized the visit of King George IV to Edinburgh in 1822. After Scott's death in 1832, the Monument was constructed on the south side of Princes Street as a tribute to his life and work. This great Gothic tower was designed by George Meikle Kemp and reaches a height of 61 m (200 ft). It was completed in 1840, and includes a statue of Sir Walter at its base, sculpted by Sir John Steell. Inside the huge structure, which has recently been renovated, are 287 steps up to the top-most platform. The rewards for those keen enough to climb up are excellent views around the city centre and across the Forth to Fife.

Rev Robert Walker Skating on Duddingston Loch

The imposing Gothic heights of the Scott Monument on Princes Street

Scottish National Portrait Gallery ⑧

1 Queen St. 📞 (0131) 556 8921. ⭕ daily. ♿ 📷 by appointment.

AN INFORMATIVE exhibition on the royal house of Stuart is just one of the attractions at the Scottish National Portrait Gallery. The displays detail the history of 12 generations of Stuarts, from the time of Robert the Bruce to Queen Anne. Memorabilia include Mary, Queen of Scots' jewellery and a silver travelling canteen left by Bonnie Prince Charlie *(see p695)* at the Battle of Culloden. The upper gallery has a number of portraits of famous Scots, including a picture of Robert Burns and works by Van Dyck and other artists.

Van Dyck's *Princess Elizabeth and Princess Anne*, National Portrait Gallery

Street-by-Street: New Town ❾

Albert Monument, Charlotte Square

T HE FIRST PHASE of Edinburgh's "New Town" was built in the 18th century, to relieve the congested and unsanitary conditions of the medieval old town. Charlotte Square at the western end formed the climax of this initial phase, and its new architectural concepts were to influence all subsequent phases. Of these, the most magnificent is the Moray Estate, where a linked series of very large houses forms a crescent, an oval and a twelve-sided circus. The walk shown here explores this area of monumental Georgian town planning.

Moray Place
The crowning glory of the Moray Estate, this circus consists of a series of immense houses and apartments, many still inhabited.

Dean Bridge
This was built in 1829 to the design of Thomas Telford. It gives views down to the Water of Leith and upstream to the weirs and old mill buildings of Dean Village.

The Water of Leith is a small river running through a delightful gorge below Dean Bridge. There is a riverside walkway to Stockbridge.

Ainslie Place, an oval pattern of town houses, forms the core of the Moray Estate, linking Randolph Crescent and Moray Place.

STAR SIGHTS

★ **Charlotte Square**

★ **The Georgian House**

NEW TOWN ARCHITECTS

The driving force behind the creation of the New Town was George Drummond (1687–1766), the city's Provost, or Mayor. James Craig (1744–95) won the overall design competition in 1766. Robert Adam (1728–92) introduced classical ornamentation to Charlotte Square. Robert Reid (1774–1856) designed Heriot Row and Great King Street, and William Playfair (1790–1857) designed Royal Circus. The monumental development of the Moray Estate was the work of James Gillespie Graham (1776–1855).

Robert Adam

No. 14 was the residence of judge and diarist Lord Cockburn from 1813 to 1843.

0 metres	100

0 yards	100

KEY

--- Suggested route

◁ **Sunset at the Forth Rail Bridge, with the Forth Road Bridge in the background**

★ **The Georgian House**
No. 7 is owned by the National Trust for Scotland and is open to the public. It has been repainted in its original colours and furnished with appropriate antiques, and is a testament to the lifestyle of the upper sector of 18th-century Edinburgh society.

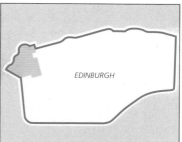

LOCATOR MAP
See Edinburgh Map pp588–9

Bute House is the official residence of the Secretary of State for Scotland, the minister of the UK government who represents Scotland.

★ **Charlotte Square**
The square was built between 1792 and 1811 to provide a series of lavish town houses for the most successful city merchants. Most of the buildings are now used as offices.

No. 39 Castle Street was the home of the writer Sir Walter Scott *(see p622)*.

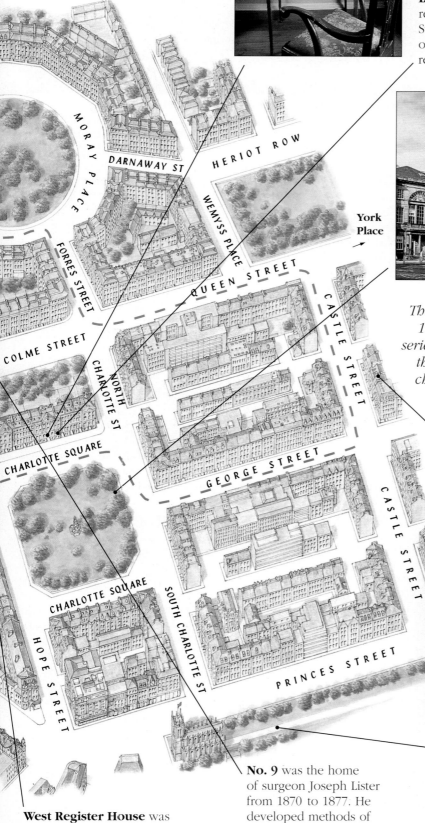

Princes Street Gardens
Princes Street was part of the initial building phase of the New Town. The north side is lined with shops; the gardens to the south lie below the castle.

No. 9 was the home of surgeon Joseph Lister from 1870 to 1877. He developed methods of preventing infection both during and after surgery.

West Register House was originally St George's Church, designed by Robert Adam.

A view from Edinburgh Castle across the towers and spires of the city to Calton Hill in the distance

Calton Hill ❿

City centre east, via Waterloo Pl.

CALTON HILL, at the east end of Princes Street, has one of Edinburgh's most memorable and baffling landmarks – a half-finished Parthenon. Conceived as the National Monument to the dead of the Napoleonic Wars, building began in 1822 but funds ran out and it was never finished. Public shame over its condition has given way to affection, as attitudes have softened over the last 170 years or so.

Fortunately, the nearby tower commemorating the British victory at Trafalgar was completed, in 1816. Named the **Nelson Monument**, the tower provides a fine vantage point over Edinburgh and the areas surrounding the city.

The Classical theme continues on top of Calton Hill with the old **City Observatory**, designed by William Playfair in 1818 and based on Athens' Temple of the Winds. One of the Observatory's domes has been converted into a theatre showing a slide show called the **Edinburgh Experience**.

Another Classical building, the old **Royal High School**, was created in the 1820s on the Regent Road side of Calton Hill. It was designed by Thomas Hamilton, with the Temple of Theseus at Athens in mind. Often cited as a possible home for a Scottish parliament, the building was the focus for the Vigil for Scottish Democracy, which campaigned from 1992 to 1997 for self government. A discreet cairn marking this effort stands a little way east of the National Monument on Calton Hill. It contains several "gift" stones, including one from Auschwitz in memory of a Scottish missionary who died there.

The final resting place of Thomas Hamilton is the **Old Calton Cemetery**, south of Waterloo Place, which he shares with philosopher David Hume and other celebrated Edinburgh residents.

City Observatory, Calton Hill, based on Classical Greek architecture

Nelson Monument
(0131) 556 2716. Mon–Sat (Apr–Sep: Mon pm only).

City Observatory
Calton Hill. (0131) 556 4365. by arrangement only.

Edinburgh Experience
City Observatory, Calton Hill. (0131) 337 8530. Apr–Oct: 10:30–5:30pm daily (last show 5pm). limited.

The grand façade of Holyrood Palace, renovated in the 17th century following an earlier fire

Holyrood Palace ⓫

East end of the Royal Mile. (0131) 556 1096. daily. check for seasonal closures. limited.

KNOWN TODAY AS Queen Elizabeth II's official Scottish residence, Holyrood Palace was built by James IV in the grounds of an abbey in 1498. It was later the home of James V and his wife, Mary of Guise, and was remodelled in the 1670s for Charles II. The Royal Apartments (including the Throne Room and Royal Dining Room) are used for investitures and for banquets whenever the Queen visits the palace. At other times these rooms are open to the public.

A chamber in the so-called James V tower is famously associated with the unhappy reign of Mary, Queen of Scots. It was probably in this room, in 1566, that Mary saw the murder of her trusted Italian secretary, David Rizzio, authorized by her jealous husband, Lord Darnley. She had married Darnley only a year earlier, in Holyrood chapel, and was six months pregnant when she witnessed the murder, during which Rizzio's body was pierced "with fifty-six wounds".

Last of the pretenders to the English throne, Charles Edward Stuart (Bonnie Prince Charlie) held court at Holyrood Palace in 1745. He dazzled Edinburgh society with his magnificent parties, even while in the early stages of the Jacobite uprising.

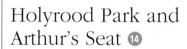

James V's arms, Holyrood Palace

Dynamic Earth 12

Holyrood Road. **[** (0131) 550 7800. Apr–Oct: daily; Nov–Mar: Wed–Sun. www.dynamicearth.co.uk

Dynamic Earth is a permanent exhibition about the planet, which opened in the spring of 1999. Visitors are taken on a journey from the earth's volcanic beginnings to the first appearance of life. Further displays concentrate on the world's climatic zones and dramatic natural phenomena such as tidal waves and earthquakes. State-of-the-art lighting and interactive techniques produce the special effects for 90 minutes of learning and entertainment.

The exhibition building is fronted by a 1,000-seat stone amphitheatre designed by Sir Michael Hopkins, and it incorporates a translucent tented roof. Situated beneath Salisbury Crags, the modern lines of Dynamic Earth contrast sharply with the natural landscape. The project was funded largely by the Millennium Commission, with funds raised by the UK's National Lottery.

New Scottish Parliament 13

Holyrood Rd. www.scottish-devolution.org.uk

Following decades of Scottish calls for more political self-determination, a referendum in 1997 on the issue of whether or not to have a Scottish parliament, with some powers devolving from the UK parliament in London, resulted in a majority "yes" vote. This site at Holyrood was chosen for the new parliament, and in early 1998 a worldwide competition was held to find a suitable designer for the building. The successful candidate was the innovative Enric Miralles, who gained prominence through his work on buildings at the 1992 Barcelona Olympics. This new parliament is scheduled to open for business in the autumn of 2001.

Holyrood Park and Arthur's Seat 14

Main access via Holyrood Park Rd, Holyrood Rd and Meadowbank Terrace.

Holyrood Park, adjacent to Holyrood Palace, covers over 260 hectares (640 acres) of varying terrain, topped by a rugged 250-m (820-ft) hill. Known as Arthur's Seat, the hill is actually a volcano that has been extinct for 350 million years. The area has been a royal hunting ground since at least the time of King David I, who died in 1153, and a royal park since the 16th century.

The name Holyrood, which means "holy cross", comes from an episode in the life of David I when, in 1128, he was knocked from his horse by a stag while out hunting. Legend has it that a cross appeared miraculously in his hands to ward off the animal and, in thanksgiving, the king founded the Abbey of the Holy Cross, Holyrood Abbey. The name Arthur's Seat is probably a corruption of Archer's Seat, a more prosaic explanation for the name than any link with the legendary King Arthur.

The park has three small lochs. St Margaret's near the Palace is the most romantic, with its resident swans and position under the ruins of St Anthony's Chapel. Dunsapie Loch is the highest and loneliest, sitting 112 m (367 ft) above sea level under the eastern side of Arthur's Seat. Duddingston Loch, on the south side of the park, is home to a large number of wildfowl.

The **Salisbury Crags** are among the park's most striking features. Their dramatic profile, along with that of Arthur's Seat, can be seen from many kilometres away. The Crags form a parabola of red cliffs that sweep round and up from Holyrood Palace, above a steep supporting hillside. A rough track, called the Radical Road, follows their base.

Arthur's Seat and the Salisbury Crags, looming above the city

Further Afield

ALTHOUGH INEXTRICABLY linked to the rest of Edinburgh, the inhabitants of Leith insist that they do not live in the city itself. More than just a docks area, Leith has plenty of attractions for the visitor. Close by is the magnificent Royal Botanic Garden. Dean Village offers riverside walks, galleries and antique shops. To the west of the city are the historic Hopetoun House and Linlithgow Palace, to the east is Haddington and a dramatic coastline.

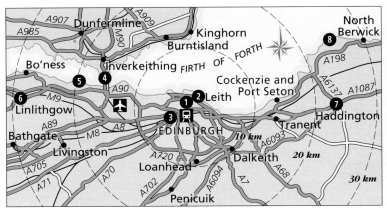

10km = 6miles

KEY

▢	Urban area
✈	Airport
▣	Train station
—	Intercity train line
▬	Motorway (highway)
▬	Major road
▬	Minor road

SIGHTS AT A GLANCE

Dean Village ③
East Lothian Coast ⑧
Forth Bridges ④
Haddington ⑦
Hopetoun House ⑤
Leith ②
Linlithgow Palace ⑥
Royal Botanic Garden ①

A specimen from the Palm House in the city's Royal Botanic Garden

Royal Botanic Garden ①

Inverleith Row. ☎ (0131) 552 7171.
▤ ◯ daily. ♿ ▨ www.rbge.org.uk

THIS MAGNIFICENT garden lies a short way to the north of the New Town, across the Water of Leith (a river that runs from the Pentland Hills down through Edinburgh and into the Firth of Forth at Leith).

The garden is a descendant of a Physic Garden near Holyrood House that was created by two doctors in 1670. It was moved to its present location in 1820, and since then has been progressively enlarged and developed. Public access is from the east (well served by buses) and from the west (offering better car parking). The garden benefits from a hill site, giving southerly views across the city.

There is a remarkable rock garden in the southeast corner and an indoor exhibition and interpretation display in the northeast corner. There are also extensive greenhouses in traditional and modern architectural styles, dedicated to different climatic conditions and offering fascinating hideaways on rainy days. Be sure not to miss the alpine display to the northwest of the greenhouses, or the beautiful and fragrant rhododendron walk.

Leith ②

Northeast of the city centre, linked by Leith Walk.

LEITH IS A HISTORIC port that has traded for centuries with Scandinavia, the Baltic and Holland, and has always been the port for Edinburgh. It was incorporated into the city in 1920, and now forms a northeastern suburb.

The medieval core of narrow streets and quays includes a number of historic warehouses and merchants' houses dating from the 13th and 14th centuries. There was a great expansion of the docks in the 19th century, and many port buildings date from this period.

Shipbuilding and port activities have diminished, but there has been a renaissance in recent years in the form of conversions of warehouse buildings to offices, residences and, most notably, restaurants. The Shore and Dock Place now has Edinburgh's most dense concentration of seafood bistros and varied restaurants.

The tourist attractions have been further boosted by the presence of the former British **Royal Yacht Britannia**, which is on display in Leith's western dock, before moving to a new "Ocean Terminal" in 2000.

▣ Royal Yacht Britannia

Western Harbour, Leith Docks.
☎ (0131) 555 8800. ◯ daily. ▨ ♿

The British Royal Yacht Britannia, berthed at Leith's western dock

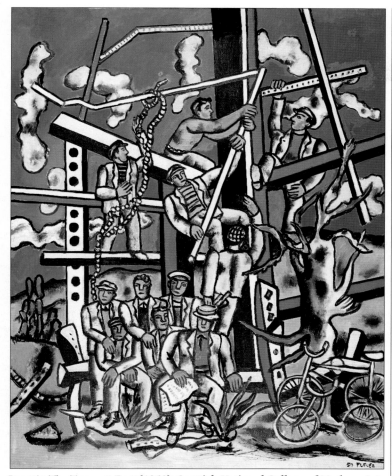

Leger's *The Team at Rest* (1950), Scottish National Gallery of Modern Art

Dean Village ❸

Northwest of the city centre.

THIS INTERESTING area lies in the valley of the Water of Leith, just a few minutes' walk northwest from Charlotte Square *(see map p588)*. A series of water mills along the river have been replaced by attractive buildings.

Access to Dean Village can be gained by walking down Bell's Brae from Randolph Crescent. A riverside walk threads its way between the historic buildings, crossing the river on a series of footbridges. Upstream from Dean Village the riverside walk leads in a few minutes to a footbridge and a flight of steps giving access to the **Scottish National Gallery of Modern Art**. This gallery offers an excellent collection of modern works of art. The main access for vehicles, as well as less energetic pedestrians, can be found on Belford Road.

Downstream from Dean Village, the riverside walkway passes under the magnificent high level bridge designed by Thomas Telford. It then passes

St Bernard's Well before arriving in the urban village of Stockbridge. Both antiques and curio shops can be found on the south side of the river in St Stephen Street. The riverside walk continues northeast, close to the Royal Botanic Garden. The city centre is a short walk away, via Royal Circus and Howe Street.

17th-century stone houses on the historic Bell's Brae

🏛 Scottish National Gallery of Modern Art
Belford Road. 📞 *(0131) 624 6200.*
⚪ *daily.* 🚫 *special exhibitions only.* ♿

Forth Bridges ❹

Lothian. 🚄 🚌 *Dalmeny, Inverkeithing.*

THE SMALL TOWN of South Queensferry is dominated by the two great bridges that span 1.5 km (1 mile) across the River Forth to the town of Inverkeithing. The spectacular rail bridge, the first major steel-built bridge in the world, was opened in 1890 and remains one of the greatest engineering achievements of the late Victorian era. Its massive cantilevered sections are held together by more than eight million rivets, and the painted area adds up to some 55 ha (135 acres). The saying "it's like painting the Forth Bridge" has become a byword for non-stop, repetitive endeavour. It was the rail bridge that inspired the book *The Bridge* (1986) by popular Scottish writer Iain Banks *(see p581)*.

The neighbouring road bridge was the largest suspension bridge outside the US when it was opened in 1964, a distinction now held by the Humber Bridge in England. The two bridges make an impressive contrast, best seen from the promenade at South Queensferry. The town received its name from Queen Margaret *(see p597)*, who reigned with King Malcolm III in the 11th century. She used the ferry here on her frequent journeys between Edinburgh and her home, the royal palace at Dunfermline in Fife *(see p642)*.

The huge, cantilevered Forth Rail Bridge, seen from South Queensferry

Hopetoun House ⑤

The Lothians. 📞 *(0131) 331 2451.*
🚆 *Dalmeny then taxi.* ◯ *mid-Apr–Sep: daily.* 🚫 ♿ *limited.* 🏷

A**N EXTENSIVE PARKLAND** by the Firth of Forth, designed in the style of Versailles, is the setting for one of Scotland's finest stately homes. The original house, of which only the central block remains, was completed in 1707 and later absorbed into William Adam's grand extension. The dignified, horseshoe-shaped plan and lavish interior represent Neo-Classical 18th-century architecture at its best. The red and yellow state drawing rooms, with their Rococo plasterwork and ornate mantelpieces, are particularly impressive. The present Marquess of Linlithgow is a descendant of the first Earl of Hopetoun, for whom the house was originally built.

A wooden panel above the main stairs depicting Hopetoun House

Linlithgow Palace ⑥

Kirk Gate, Linlithgow, Lothian.
📞 *(01506) 842896.* 🚆 🚌 ◯ *daily.* 🚫 ♿ *limited.*

S**TANDING ON THE** edge of Linlithgow Loch, the former royal palace of Linlithgow is now one of the country's most visited ruins. It dates back largely to the building commissioned by James V in 1425, following a fire the previous

Ornate fountain in the ruins of Linlithgow Palace

year, though some sections date from the 14th century. The vast scale of the building is demonstrated by the 28-m (94-ft) long Great Hall, with its huge fireplace and windows. The restored fountain in the courtyard was a wedding present in 1538 from James V to his wife, Mary of Guise. His daughter, Mary, Queen of Scots, was born at Linlithgow in 1542.

The adjacent Church of St Michael is Scotland's largest pre-Reformation church and a fine example of the Scottish Decorated style. Consecrated in the 13th century, the church was damaged by the fire of 1424. The building as it is today was completed in the 16th century.

Haddington ⑦

East Lothian. 🚆 *frequent services from Edinburgh and North Berwick.*

T**HIS ATTRACTIVE** county town is situated about 24 km (15 miles) east of Edinburgh. It was destroyed on various occasions during the Wars of Independence in the 13th–14th centuries, and again in the

16th century. The agricultural revolution brought great prosperity, giving Haddington many historic houses, churches, and other public buildings. A programme of restoration has helped the town to retain its character. The River Tyne encloses the town, and there are attractive riverside walks and parkland. ("A walk around Haddington" guide is available from newsagents.) The parish church of St Mary's, southeast of the centre, dates from 1462 and is one of the largest in the area. Parts of the church have been rebuilt in recent years, having been destroyed in the siege of 1548. A short way south of the town lies **Lennoxlove House**, with its ancient tower house.

🏛 Lennoxlove House
📞 *(01620) 823720.* ◯ *Easter–Oct: pm only Wed–Thu & Sat–Sun.* 🚫

East Lothian Coast ⑧

ℹ *North Berwick (01620) 892197.*

S**TRETCHING EAST** from Musselburgh for some 65 km (40 miles), the coast of East Lothian offers many opportunities for beach activities, windsurfing, golf, viewing seabirds and coastal walks. The coastline is a pleasant mixture of beaches, low cliffs, woodland, golf

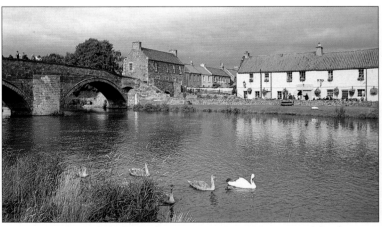

The historic and tranquil town of Haddington on the River Tyne

courses and some farmland. Although the A198 and A1 are adjacent to the coast for only short distances, they give easy access to a series of public car parks (a small charge is made in summer), from where it is a short walk to the shore. Among these visitor points are Longniddry Bents, a small west-facing bay favoured by windsurfers, and Gullane, perhaps the best beach for

Tantallon Castle, looking out to the North Sea

seaside activities. Yellowcraig, near Dirleton, is another lovely bay, lying about 400 m (440 yds) from the car park. Lime-tree Walk, near Tyninghame, has the long, east-facing beach of Ravensheugh Sands (a ten-minute walk along a woodland track). Belhaven Bay, just west of Dunbar, is a large beach providing walks along

the estuary of the River Tyne. Barns Ness, east of Dunbar, offers a geological nature trail and an impressive lighthouse. Skateraw Harbour is an attractive small bay, despite the presence of Torness nuclear power station to the east. Finally, there is another delightful beach to be found at Seacliff, reached by a private

toll road that leaves the A198 about 3 km (2 miles) east of North Berwick. This sheltered bay has spectacular views of the glistening white of the Bass Rock, home to one of the largest gannet (a type of marine bird) colonies in Britain.

The rock itself can be seen at close quarters by taking the boat trip from North Berwick harbour (summer only). Other features of interest along this coastline include **Dirleton Castle** and **Tantallon Castle**, perched on a cliff top near Seacliff beach. There is a small industrial museum at Prestonpans and bird watching in Aberlady Bay. North Berwick and Dunbar are towns worthy of a visit, and **Torness Power Station** has a visitors' centre.

🏯 **Dirleton Castle**
📞 (01620) 850330. ○ daily. 🖼

🏯 **Tantallon Castle**
📞 (01620) 892727. ○ Apr–Sep: daily; Oct–Mar: Sat–Thu am. 🖼

ℹ **Torness Power Station**
📞 (01368) 873000. ○ mid-Jan–mid-Dec: daily. ♿ 🖼

EAST LOTHIAN COASTAL WALK

For a very attractive longer coast walk, there is easy public access along the footpath from Gullane Bay to North Berwick. The path follows the coastline, crossing grassy heathland between the alternating sandy bays and low rocky headlands, with views of the coast of Fife to the north. There are small islands along the way. The last part of the walk into North Berwick has wonderful views east to the white slopes of the Bass Rock.

TIPS FOR WALKERS

Starting point: Gullane Bay.
Finishing point: North Berwick.
Length: 10 km (6 miles); 3 hours.
Getting there: by car; a bus service between Edinburgh and North Berwick gives access to both ends.
Level: easy (one steep section).

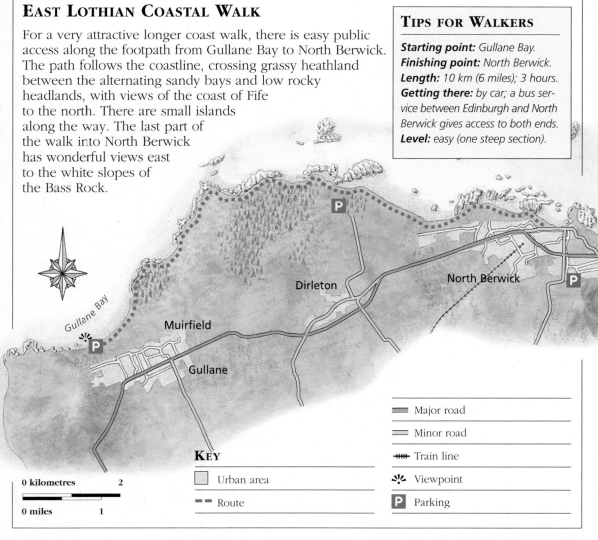

Dirleton

North Berwick

Gullane Bay

Muirfield

Gullane

KEY

	Urban area
▪▪	Route

▬	Major road
—	Minor road
╫╫	Train line
☀	Viewpoint
P	Parking

0 kilometres 2

0 miles 1

Wooded expanse of the Eildon Hills, with the River Tweed in the foreground ▷

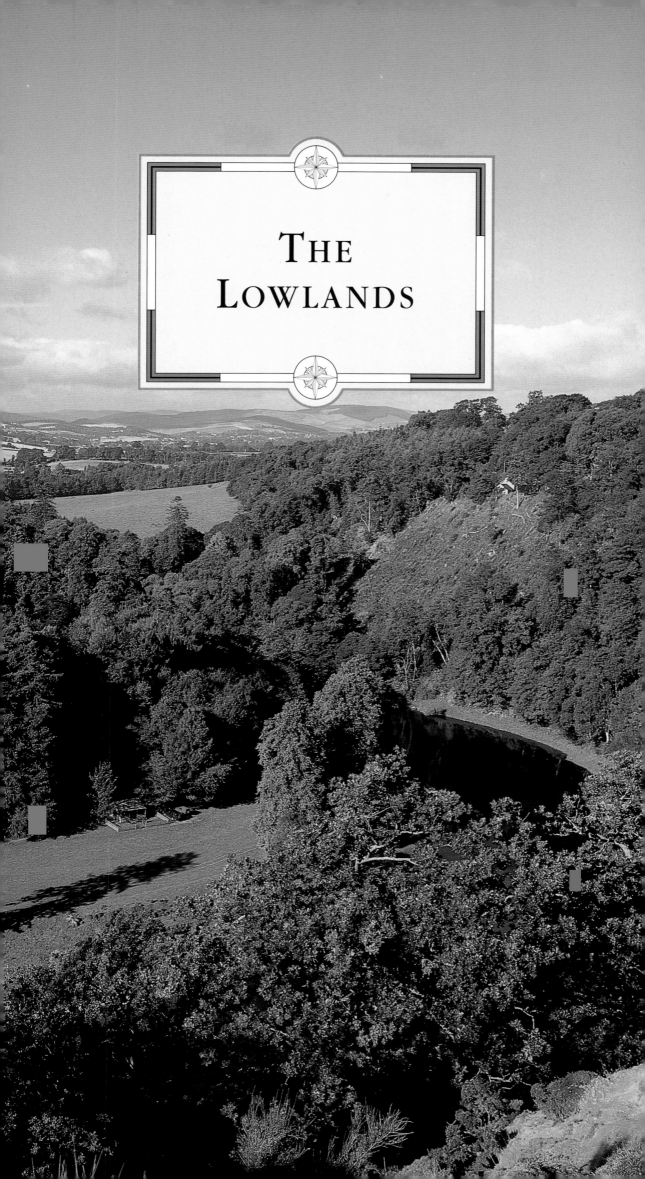

THE LOWLANDS

THE LOWLANDS

OUTHEAST *of the Highland boundary fault line lies a part of Scotland very different in character from its northern neighbour. If the Highlands embody the romance of Scotland, the Lowlands have traditionally been its powerhouse. Lowlanders have always prospered in agriculture and, more recently, in industry and commerce.*

Being the region of Scotland closest to the English border, the hotly-contested Lowlands inevitably became the crucible of Scottish history. For centuries after the Romans built the Antonine Wall across the Forth-Clyde isthmus (the neck of Scotland, with Glasgow on its west side and Edinburgh to the east), the area was engulfed in conflict. Parts of the Antonine Wall remain intact today, especially around Rough Castle, once the site of a Roman fort.

The Borders, a region of southeastern Scotland, is home to a number of fortified castles, evidence of a territory in uneasy proximity to rapacious neighbours. The ruins of medieval abbeys, such as Melrose Abbey, bear witness to the dangers of living on the invasion route from England. In a region of constant conflict, communities staked out their territories with shows of force, parading around the boundaries of their land on horseback. These so-called Common Ridings are now the focus of colourful summer festivals. Despite the unrest in the Borders, a flourishing woollen trade was founded in these parts by abbey monks. This industry is still active in Peebles and Hawick today. Peebles also features two museums and, nearby, Kailzie Gardens.

While many of the large land-owning estates of the more distant Highlands have fallen into foreign ownership, many of the Borders properties are still home to what remains of Scottish aristocracy. Abbotsford House, for example, built

A colourful display of flowers outside Deacon Brodie's Tavern on the Royal Mile in Edinburgh

◁ **Glamis Castle, 12 miles (19 km) north of Dundee, with its typically Scottish turreted exterior**

in the 19th-century by the writer Sir Walter Scott, is owned by his descendants, and is open to visitors. In the middle of the Borders are the picturesque Eildon Hills, to which Scott was a regular visitor. Scott's View, near Melrose, is now the best place to take in the full glory of these beautiful heights.

Dumfries and Galloway, a region in southwest Scotland, is frequently overlooked by visitors heading north. Yet this rural corner of the country holds many attractions, including the two highest villages in Scotland: Wanlockhead and Leadhills. This is also

Grey Mare's Tail waterfall, Borders

where some of Scotland's traditional summer games are held, including the "girding the cleek" (rolling a metal hoop with a wooden stick) world championships. Castles abound here, too. The magnificent ruins of Caerlaverock Castle, unusual because of its water-filled moat, makes a striking contrast to the sophisticated extravagance of Culzean Castle, which is near Ayr. Both castles are open to the public. Southwest Scotland was also home to Robert Burns, Scotland's most famous

son, who is justifiably revered as the "Bard of Humanity". The region is sprinkled with the poet's former residences and drinking places. His birthplace, Burns Cottage, can be found in Alloway, which is north of Culzean Castle. Next to this cottage is a museum that features a selection of Burns manuscripts and memorabilia.

The two major rivers of the Lowlands are the Tweed and the Clyde. The Tweed, which is full of salmon, surges past several noble estates, while the sluggish Clyde flows through a belt of industrialization before reaching Glasgow, which was once the supplier of ships and locomotives to the British Empire.

Topographically, Glasgow is hanging off the bottom lip of the Highlands, and boasts easy access to Loch Lomond – Britain's largest freshwater lake – and the Trossach mountains, a region famous for its scenery and association with Rob Roy (whose grave is in the area). Also close to Glasgow is the ruggedly beautiful west coast and islands, such as Arran and Bute. Arran is slightly unusual in that

One of the greens on Gleneagles golf course, Perthshire

At the battle of Sheriffmuir (1715) *the 12,000 Jacobites were defeated by the Duke of Argyll's force of just 3,000. Close to Dunblane, Sheriffmuir remains the unspoilt moor it was in the 18th century. A memorial stands as a reminder of the battle that took place there.*

At the Battle of Glenshiel (1719), *the Highland Jacobites joined forces with a group of Spanish mercenaries, but were defeated by the Hanoverians commanded by General Wightman.*

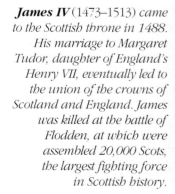

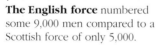

Kilsyth, near Glasgow, was the scene of a battle in 1645 between the Earl of Montrose, on behalf of Charles I, and the Scottish Covenanters.

Parts of the Highland army reached the English lines, but were overwhelmed by sheer numbers.

The English force numbered some 9,000 men compared to a Scottish force of only 5,000.

James IV (1473–1513) *came to the Scottish throne in 1488. His marriage to Margaret Tudor, daughter of England's Henry VII, eventually led to the union of the crowns of Scotland and England. James was killed at the battle of Flodden, at which were assembled 20,000 Scots, the largest fighting force in Scottish history.*

THE LONGBOW

The longbow was invented in 12th-century Wales. It was some 2 m (6 ft) long and strung with hemp or silk. The longbow requires great skill, practice and strength to master, but was as devastating as a modern assault rifle. It was first used to great effect in battle at Falkirk in 1298.

Longbow in use by a modern-day archer

The shattered crags and cliffs of St Abb's Head

St Abb's Head ❶

The Borders. 🚆 Berwick-upon-Tweed.
🚌 from Edinburgh. 📞 (01890)
771443. ◯ Easter–Oct: daily.

THE JAGGED CLIFFS of St Abb's Head, rising 91 m (300 ft) from the North Sea, offer a spectacular view of thousands of seabirds wheeling and diving below. This nature reserve is an important site for cliff-nesting sea birds and, during the May to June breeding season, it becomes the home of more than 50,000 birds, including fulmars, guillemots, kittiwakes and puffins.

St Abb's village has one of the few unspoiled working harbours on Scotland's east coast. A clifftop trail begins at the visitors' centre, where displays include identification boards and a touch table where young visitors can get to grips with wings and feathers.

Kelso ❷

The Borders. 🏘 6,035. 🚌 ℹ The
Square (01573) 223464, Easter–Oct.

KELSO HAS a charming centre, with a cobbled square surrounded by Georgian and Victorian buildings. Nearby **Kelso Race Course** holds regular horse races and is a popular attraction. The focus of the town, however, is the ruin of the 12th-century **abbey**. This was the oldest and wealthiest of the four Border Abbeys founded by David I, but it suffered from wars with England and was severely damaged in 1545. **Floors Castle** on the

northern edge of Kelso is more complete. Designed by William Adam in the 1720s, it was then substantially reworked by William Playfair after 1837.

ℹ **Kelso Race Course**
📞 (01573) 224767. ♿ ⌧
🏛 **Floors Castle**
📞 (01573) 223333. ◯ May–Oct: daily. ⌧ ♿ ⌧

Jedburgh ❸

The Borders. 🏘 4,250. 🚌
ℹ Murray's Green (01835) 863435.

THE TOWN IS home to the mock-medieval **Jedburgh Castle**. Built in 1820, the castle was once the local jail but now serves as a museum with some good displays on the area's history, and an exhibition on life in a 19th-century prison.

Built around 1500, **Mary, Queen of Scots' House** is so-called due to a visit by the queen in 1566. The house was converted into a general museum in the 1930s, and in 1987

Jedburgh's medieval Abbey church at the centre of the attractive town

(on the 400th anniversary of Mary's execution) it became a centre dedicated to telling her life story. Exhibits include a copy of her death mask.

Jedburgh Abbey is one of the great quartet of 12th-century Border Abbeys, along with Dryburgh, Kelso and Melrose. The Abbey church has some interesting features including a rose window, and there is an excellent visitors' centre.

🏛 **Jedburgh Castle**
📞 (01835) 863254. ◯ Easter–Oct: daily (Sun: pm). ⌧
🏛 **Mary, Queen of Scots' House**
📞 (01835) 863331. ◯ Mar–Nov: daily. ⌧
🏛 **Jedburgh Abbey**
📞 (01835) 863925. ◯ daily. ⌧

A picturesque view of the Eildon Hills in late summer sunshine

Eildon Hills ❹

The Borders. 🚌 ℹ Melrose (01896)
822555, Easter–Oct.

THE THREE PEAKS of the Eildon Hills dominate the central Borders landscape. Mid Hill is the tallest at 422 m (1,385 ft), while North Hill once had a Bronze Age hill fort dating from before 500 BC, and later a Roman fort. In this part of the country the most celebrated name is Sir Walter Scott *(see p622)*, who had a particular affection for these hills. A panorama of the Eildons called **Scott's View** lies just east of Melrose, near Dryburgh Abbey, and this is the best location to see the hills' position as they rise above the Tweed Valley.

Tour of the Border Abbeys ⑤

THE SCOTTISH BORDERS are scattered with the ruins of ancient buildings destroyed in conflicts between England and Scotland. Most poignant of all are the Border Abbeys, whose magnificent architecture bears witness to their former spiritual and political power. Founded during the 12th-century reign of David I, the abbeys were destroyed by Henry VIII in 1545. This tour takes in the abbeys and some other sights.

Kelso Abbey ②
The largest of the four Border Abbeys, Kelso was founded in 1128 and took 84 years to complete.

Melrose Abbey ⑥
Once one of the richest abbeys in Scotland, it is here that Robert the Bruce's heart is buried (*see p622*).

Floors Castle ①
Open in summer, the Duke of Roxburgh's 18th-century ancestral home is close to the Tweed.

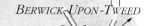

Scott's View ⑤
This was Sir Walter Scott's favourite view of the Borders. During his funeral, the hearse stopped here briefly as Scott had done so often in life.

Dryburgh Abbey ④
Also set on the bank of the Tweed, Dryburgh is considered the most evocative monastic ruin in Scotland. Sir Walter Scott is buried here.

KEY

▬▬	Tour route
═══	Other road
⚘	Viewpoint

TIPS FOR DRIVERS

Length: 50 km (32 miles).
Stopping-off points: Leave the car at Dryburgh Abbey and take a walk northwards to the footbridge over the River Tweed.

```
0 kilometres        5
0 miles             3
```

Jedburgh Abbey ③
The abbey was established in 1138, though fragments of 9th-century Celtic stonework survive from an earlier structure. The visitors' centre illustrates the lives of Augustinian monks.

The ruins of Melrose Abbey, viewed from the southwest

Melrose Abbey ⑥

Abbey St, Melrose, The Borders.
☎ (01896) 822562. ○ daily. ◢
♿ limited.

THE ROSE-PINK RUINS of this, one of the most beautiful of the Border Abbeys, bear testimony to the devastation of successive English invasions. Built by David I in 1136 for Cistercian monks from Yorkshire, and also to replace a 7th-century monastery, Melrose was repeatedly ransacked by English armies, most notably in 1322 and 1385. The final blow, from which none of the abbeys recovered, came in 1545 when Henry VIII of England implemented his destructive Scottish policy known as the "Rough Wooing". This resulted from the failure of the Scots to ratify a marriage treaty between Henry VIII's son and the infant Mary, Queen of Scots. What remains of the abbey are the outlines of cloisters, the kitchen, monastic buildings and the shell of the abbey church with its soaring east window and profusion of medieval carvings. The rich decorations of the south exterior wall include a gargoyle shaped like a pig playing the bagpipes and several animated figures, including a cook with his ladle.

An embalmed heart, found here in 1920, is probably that of Robert the Bruce, the abbey's chief benefactor, who had decreed that his heart be taken on a crusade to the Holy Land. It was returned to Melrose Abbey after its bearer, Sir James Douglas, was killed in Spain.

Abbotsford House ⑦

Galashiels, The Borders. ☎ (01896) 752043. ▦ from Galashiels. ○ mid-Mar–May & Oct: daily (Sun: pm); Jun–Sep: daily. ◢ ◪ ♿ limited.

FEW HOUSES BEAR the stamp of their creator so intimately as Abbotsford House, the home of Sir Walter Scott for the final 20 years of his life. He bought a farm here in 1811, known as Clarteyhole ("dirty hole" in Borders Scots), though he soon renamed it Abbotsford, in memory of the monks of Melrose Abbey who used to cross the River Tweed nearby. He later demolished the house to make way for the turreted building we see today, its construction funded by the sales of his popular novels.

Scott's library contains more than 9,000 rare books and his collections of historic relics reflect his passion for the heroic past. The walls bristle with an extensive collection of arms and armour, including Rob Roy's broadsword (see p635). Stuart mementoes include one of many crucifixes belonging to Mary, Queen of Scots and a lock of Bonnie Prince Charlie's hair. The surprisingly small study, in which Scott wrote his *Waverley* novels, is open to the public, as is the room overlooking the river, in which he died in 1832.

SIR WALTER SCOTT

Sir Walter Scott (1771–1832) was born in Edinburgh and trained as a lawyer. He is best remembered as a major literary figure and champion of Scotland, whose poems and novels (most famously his *Waverley* series) created enduring images of a heroic wilderness filled with the romance of the clans. His orchestration, in 1822, of the state visit of George IV to Edinburgh was an extravaganza of Highland culture that helped establish tartan as the national dress of Scotland. He served as Clerk of the Court in Edinburgh's Parliament House and for 30 years was Sheriff of Selkirk. He loved Central and Southern Scotland, putting the Trossachs *(see pp634–5)* firmly on the map with the publication of the *Lady of the Lake* (1810). His final years were spent writing to pay off a £114,000 debt following the failure of his publisher in 1827. He died with his debts paid, and was buried at Dryburgh Abbey in 1832.

The Great Hall at Abbotsford, adorned with arms and armour

Traquair House ⑧

Peebles, The Borders. ☎ *(01896) 830323.* 🚌 *from Peebles.* ⬜ *Apr–Sep: daily; Oct: Fri–Sun.* 🈚 ⟨♿⟩ *limited.*

A S SCOTLAND'S OLDEST continuously inhabited house, Traquair has deep roots in Scottish religious and political history stretching back over 900 years. Evolving from a fortified tower to a stout-walled 17th-century mansion, the house was a Catholic Stuart stronghold for 500 years. Mary, Queen of Scots was among the many monarchs to have stayed here. Her crucifix is kept in the house and her bed is covered by a counterpane that she made. Family letters and a collection of engraved Jacobite drinking glasses are among the relics recalling the period of the Highland rebellions.

Following a vow made by the fifth Earl, Traquair's Bear Gates (the "Steekit Yetts"), which closed after Bonnie Prince Charlie's visit in 1745, will not reopen until a Stuart reascends the throne. A secret stairway leads to the Priest's Room, which, with its clerical vestments that could be disguised as bedspreads, attests to the problems faced by Catholic families until Catholicism was legalized in 1829. Traquair House Ale is still produced in the adjacent 18th-century brewhouse.

Mary's crucifix, Traquair House

Peebles ⑨

The Borders. 🧍 *8,000.* 🚌 *from Galashiels.* ℹ️ *23 High St (01721) 720138.*

A CHARMING BORDERS town, Peebles has some fascinating sights, including the **Tweeddale Museum** which houses full-scale plaster casts of part of the Parthenon Frieze, and casts of an 1812 frieze depicting the entry of Alexander the Great into Babylon. Nearby, the **Scottish Museum of Ornamental Plasterwork** is housed in a quaint workshop full of ceiling decorations and cornices. The walled **Kailzie Gardens**, near Peebles, attract daytrippers from Edinburgh.

🏛 **Tweeddale Museum**
☎ *(01721) 724820.* ⬜ *Easter–Oct: Mon–Sat; Nov–Mar: Mon–Fri.* 🈚

🏛 **Scottish Museum of Ornamental Plasterwork**
☎ *(01721) 720212.* ⬜ *Mon–Fri.* ⬤ *First 2 weeks in Aug.* 🈚 ♿

🌿 **Kailzie Gardens**
☎ *(01721) 720007.* ⬜ *daily.* 🈚 🈚

Pentland Hills ⑩

The Lothians. 🚆 *Edinburgh, then bus.* ℹ️ *Regional Park Headquarters, Edinburgh (0131) 445 3383.*

T HE WILDS OF the Pentland Hills stretch for 26 km (16 miles) southwest of Edinburgh, and offer some of the best hill-walking country in Southern Scotland. Walkers can saunter along the many signposted footpaths, while the more adventurous can take the chairlift at the Hillend dry ski slope to reach the higher ground leading to the 493 m (1,617 ft) hill of Allermuir. Even more ambitious is the classic scenic route along the ridge from Caerketton to West Kip.

To the east of the A703, in the lee of the Pentlands, stands the exquisite and ornate 15th-century **Rosslyn Chapel**. It was originally intended as a church, but after the death of its founder, William Sinclair, it was used as a burial ground for his descendants. The delicately wreathed Apprentice Pillar recalls the legend of the apprentice carver who was killed by the master stonemason in a fit of jealousy at his pupil's superior skill.

🔒 **Rosslyn Chapel**
☎ *(0131) 440 2159.* ⬜ *daily.* 🈚 ♿ *www.rosslynchapel.org.uk*

Details of the highly ornate, decorative carved-stone vaulting in Rosslyn Chapel

The Classical 18th-century tenements of New Lanark on the banks of the Clyde

New Lanark ⑪

Clyde Valley. 👥 *150.* 🚃 🚌 *Lanark.*
ℹ️ *Horsemarket, Ladyacre Rd, Lanark
(01555) 661661.* 🅿️ *Mon.*

SITUATED BY THE beautiful
falls of the River Clyde,
with three separate waterfalls,
the village of New Lanark was
founded in 1785 by the industrial entrepreneur David Dale.

DAVID LIVINGSTONE

Scotland's great missionary
doctor and explorer was
born in Blantyre where he
began working life as a
mill boy at the age of ten.
Livingstone (1813–73)
made three epic journeys
across Africa, from 1840,
promoting "commerce and
Christianity". He became
the first European to see
Victoria Falls, and died in
1873 while searching for
the source of the Nile. His
body is buried in West-
minster Abbey in London.

Ideally located alongside the
river for the working of its
water-driven mills, the village
had become the largest producer of cotton in Britain by
1800. Dale and his successor,
and son-in-law, Robert Owen,
were philanthropists whose
reforms demonstrated that
commercial success need not
undermine the wellbeing of
the workforce. The manu-
facturing of cotton continued
here until the late 1960s.

Preserved as a museum,
New Lanark is a window on to
working life in the early 19th
century. The **Annie McLeod
Experience** provides a
special-effects ride into the
past, illustrating the life of a
10-year-old mill girl in 1820.

ENVIRONS: 24 km (15 miles)
north, the town of Blantyre
has a memorial to the Clyde
Valley's most famous son, the
explorer David Livingstone.

🏛 **Annie McLeod Experience**
New Lanark Visitor Centre.
📞 *(01555) 661345.* ⬜ *daily.*
♿ 🔖 *by appointment.*

Sanquhar ⑫

Dumfries & Galloway. 👥 *2,500.*
🚃 🚌 ℹ️ *The Post Office, High St
(01659) 50185.*

NOW OF CHIEFLY historic
interest, the town of
Sanquhar was famous in the
history of the Covenanters.

In the 1680s, two declarations
opposing the rule of bishops
were pinned to the Mercat
Cross, the site of which is
now marked by a granite
obelisk. The first protest was
led by a local teacher, Richard
Cameron, whose followers
became the Cameronian regiment. The Georgian **Tolbooth**
was designed by architect
William Adam in 1735 and
houses a local interest museum
and tourist centre. The Post
Office, opened in 1763, is the
oldest in Britain, predating
the mail coach service.

Drumlanrig Castle ⑬

Thornhill, Dumfries & Galloway.
ℹ️ *(01848) 330248.* 🚃 🚌 *Dumfries,
then bus.* ⬜ *May–Aug: Mon–Sun pm.*
♿ 🔖

RISING SQUARELY from a grassy
platform, the massive
fortress-palace of **Drumlanrig
Castle** was built from pink
sandstone between 1679 and
1691 on the site of a 15th-
century Douglas stronghold.
The castle's multi-turreted,

**The Baroque front steps and
doorway of Drumlanrig Castle**

formidable exterior conceals a priceless collection of art treasures as well as such Jacobite relics as Bonnie Prince Charlie's camp kettle, sash and money box. Hanging within oak-panelled rooms are paintings by Leonardo da Vinci, Holbein and Rembrandt. The emblem of a crowned and winged heart recalls Sir James, the "Black Douglas", who lived here. He bore Robert the Bruce's heart while on crusade to fulfil a vow made by the former king. After being mortally wounded he threw the heart at his enemies with the words "forward brave heart!"

The exterior of Burns Cottage, birthplace of Robert Burns

The sturdy island fortress of Threave Castle on the Dee

Threave Castle ⑭

(NTS) Castle Douglas, Dumfries & Galloway. ((01556) 502611. ⇄ Dumfries. ○ Apr–Sep: daily.

A MENACING GIANT of a tower, this 14th-century Black Douglas stronghold on an island in the Dee (accessed by rowing boat) commands the most complete medieval riverside harbour in Scotland. Douglas's struggles against the early Stewart kings culminated in his surrender here after a two-month siege in 1455 – but only after James II had brought the cannon Mons Meg to batter the castle. Threave was finally dismantled after an army of Protestant Covenanters defeated its Catholic defenders in 1640. Only the shell of the kitchen, great hall and domestic levels remains.

Burns Heritage Trail ⑮

South Ayrshire, Dumfries & Galloway. ℹ Dumfries (01387) 253862, Ayr (01292) 288688.

R OBERT BURNS (1759–91) left behind a remarkable body of work ranging from satirical poetry to tender love songs. His status as national bard is unchallenged and an official Burns Heritage Trail leads visitors around sights in southwest Scotland where he lived.

In Dumfries, the **Robert Burns Centre** focuses on his years in the town, while **Burns House**, where he lived from 1793 to 1796, contains memorabilia. His Greek-style mausoleum can be found in St Michael's Churchyard.

At **Ellisland Farm** on the River Nith there are further displays, with some of Burns' family possessions, along with the opportunity for riverside walks. Mauchline, some 18 km (11 miles) east of Ayr, has the **Burns House and Museum** in another former residence.

Alloway, just south of Ayr, is the real centre of the Burns Trail. The **Tam O'Shanter Experience** is a contemporary film and video centre based on his poem about witches. **Burns Cottage**, the poet's birthplace, houses memorabilia and a collection of manuscripts. The ruins of Alloway Kirk, where Burns' father is buried, and the 13th-century Brig o' Doon have the best period atmosphere.

🏛 **Robert Burns Centre**
Mill Rd, Dumfries. ((01387) 264808. ○ Apr–Sep: daily; Oct–Mar: Tue–Sat.
🏛 **Burns House**
Burns St, Dumfries. ((01387) 255297. ○ Apr–Sep: daily; Oct–Mar: Tue–Sat.
🏛 **Ellisland Farm**
Holywood Rd, Auldgirth. ((01387) 740426. ○ Apr–Sep: daily; Oct–Mar: Tue–Sat.
🏛 **Burns House and Museum**
Castle St, Mauchline. ((01290) 550045. ○ May–Oct: Tue–Sun. limited.
🏛 **Tam O'Shanter Experience**
Murdoch's Lane, Alloway. ((01292) 443700. ○ daily. by appointment.
🏛 **Burns Cottage**
Alloway. ((01292) 443700. ○ daily.

SCOTTISH TEXTILES

Weaving in the Scottish Borders goes back to the Middle Ages, when monks from Flanders established a thriving woollen trade with the Continent. Cotton became an important source of wealth in the Clyde Valley during the 19th century, when handloom weaving was overtaken by power-driven mills. The popular Paisley patterns were based on original Indian designs.

A colourful pattern from Paisley

The moated fairy-tale Caerlaverock Castle with red stone walls

Caerlaverock Castle ⑯

Near Dumfries, Dumfries & Galloway.
ⓘ *Historic Scotland, Edinburgh (0131) 668 8800.* ◯ *daily.* 🖼 ♿

T HIS IMPRESSIVE, three-sided, red stone structure, with its distinctive moat, is the finest example of a medieval castle in southwest Scotland. It stands 14 km (9 miles) south of Dumfries, and was built in around 1270 using masonry from an older castle situated close by.

Caerlaverock came to prominence in 1300, during the Wars of Independence, when it was besieged by Edward I, king of England, setting a precedent for more than three centuries of strife. Surviving chronicles of Edward's adventures describe the castle in much the same form as it stands today, despite being partially demolished and rebuilt on many occasions, due to the clashes between the English and Scottish forces during the 14th and 16th centuries. Throughout these troubled times, Caerlaverock Castle remained the stronghold of the Maxwell family, and the Maxwell crest and motto remain over the door. It was the struggle between Robert Maxwell, who was the first Earl of Nithsdale and a supporter of Charles I, and a Covenanter army that caused the castle's ruin in 1640.

Kirkcudbright ⑰

Dumfries & Galloway. 🚶 *3,600.* 🚌
ⓘ *Harbour Sq (01557) 330494.*
◯ *Easter–Oct: daily.*

B Y THE mouth of the River Dee, at the head of Kirkcudbright Bay, this attractive town has an artistic heritage. The Tolbooth, dating from the late 16th century, is now the **Tolbooth Art Centre**, which houses studios, and exhibits work by Kirkcudbright's 19th-century artists. The most celebrated of these artists was Edward Hornel (1864–1933), a friend of the Glasgow Boys, who painted striking images of Japanese women. Some of his work is displayed in his former home, Broughton House, on the High Street.

MacLellan's Castle in the town centre was built in 1582 by the then Provost of Kirkcudbright, while outside, the ruins of Dundrennan Abbey date from the 12th century. Mary, Queen of Scots spent her last night there before fleeing to England in May 1568.

🏛 **Tolbooth Art Centre**
High St. 📞 *(01557) 331556.* ◯ *May–Aug: daily; Oct–Apr: Mon–Sat.* 🖼 ♿
⛪ **MacLellan's Castle**
📞 *(0131) 668 8800.* ◯ *Apr–Sep: daily; Oct–Mar: Sat & Sun.* 🖼

Whithorn ⑱

Dumfries & Galloway. 🚶 *1,000.*
🚆 *Stranraer.* 🚌 ⓘ *Dashwood Sq, Newton Stewart (01671) 402431.*

T HE EARLIEST SITE of continuous Christian worship in Scotland, Whithorn (meaning white house) takes its name from the white chapel built by St Ninian in 397. Though nothing remains of the chapel, a guided tour of the archaeological dig reveals evidence of Northumbrian, Viking and Scottish settlements ranging from the 5th to the 19th centuries. **Whithorn: Cradle of Christianity** is a centre that provides audio-visual information on the excavations, and contains a fine collection of carved stones, one of which dates from 450 AD.

🏛 **Whithorn: Cradle of Christianity**
45–47 George St. 📞 *(01988) 500508.* ◯ *Apr–Oct: daily.* 🖼 📷 ♿

Galloway Forest Park ⑲

Dumfries & Galloway. 🚆 *Stranraer.* ⓘ *Clatteringshaws Forest Wildlife Centre, New Galloway (01644) 420285.* ◯ *Easter–Oct: daily.*

T HIS IS THE WILDEST stretch of country in Southern Scotland, with points of historical interest as well as great beauty. The park extends to 670 sq km

Traditional stone buildings on the shore at Kirkcudbright

Loch Trool, Galloway Forest Park, site of one of Robert the Bruce's victories

The Rhinns of Galloway ⓴

Dumfries & Galloway. 🚈 *Stranraer.* 🚌 *Stranraer, Portpatrick.* 🚢 *Stranraer.* 🅸 *28 Harbour St, Stranraer (01776) 702595.*

I N THE EXTREME southwest of Scotland, this peninsula is almost separated from the rest of the country by Loch Ryan and Luce Bay. It has a number of attractions, including the **Logan Botanic Garden**, near Port Logan. Established in 1900, subtropical species in the garden benefit from the area's mild climate.

Stranraer on Loch Ryan is the main centre and ferry port for Northern Ireland. The nearby **Portpatrick** is a prettier town, featuring a ruined church dating from 1629 and the remains of 16th-century Dunskey Castle.

🍁 **Logan Botanic Garden**
Near Port Logan, Stranraer. 🅲 *(01776) 860231.* ◯ *Mar–Oct: daily.* 🈳 ♿

(260 sq miles) just north of Newton Stewart. Clattering-shaws Loch, to the northeast, has a visitors' centre, but the principal focal point is Loch Trool. By Caldons Wood, to the west end of the loch, the Martyrs' Monument marks the spot where six Covenanters were killed at prayer in 1685. Bruce's Stone, above the north shore, commemorates an occasion in 1307 when Robert the Bruce routed English forces.

The hills to the north of Loch Trool are a considerable size, and worthy of note. Bennan stands at 562 m (1,844 ft), Benyellary at 719 m (2,359 ft), while Merrick, at 843 m (2,766 ft), is the tallest mountain in Southern Scotland. A round trip from Loch Trool to Merrick's summit and back, via the silver sands of Loch Enoch to the east, is a total of 15 km (9 miles) over rough but very rewarding ground.

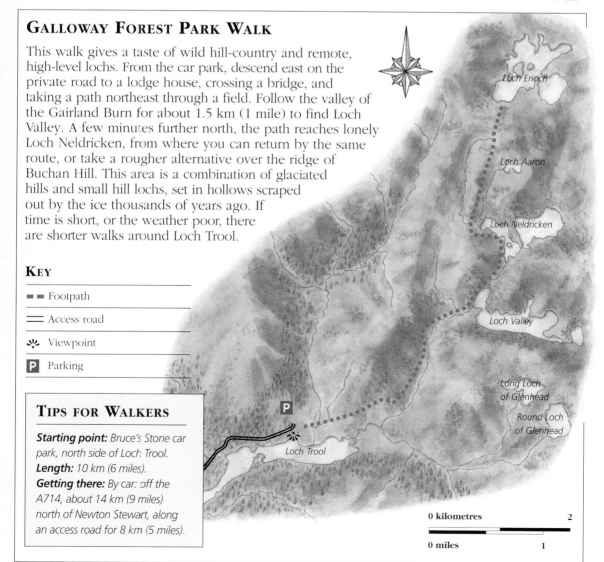

GALLOWAY FOREST PARK WALK

This walk gives a taste of wild hill-country and remote, high-level lochs. From the car park, descend east on the private road to a lodge house, crossing a bridge, and taking a path northeast through a field. Follow the valley of the Gairland Burn for about 1.5 km (1 mile) to find Loch Valley. A few minutes further north, the path reaches lonely Loch Neldricken, from where you can return by the same route, or take a rougher alternative over the ridge of Buchan Hill. This area is a combination of glaciated hills and small hill lochs, set in hollows scraped out by the ice thousands of years ago. If time is short, or the weather poor, there are shorter walks around Loch Trool.

KEY

▪▪ Footpath

═══ Access road

⚜ Viewpoint

🅿 Parking

TIPS FOR WALKERS

Starting point: *Bruce's Stone car park, north side of Loch Trool.*
Length: *10 km (6 miles).*
Getting there: *By car: off the A714, about 14 km (9 miles) north of Newton Stewart, along an access road for 8 km (5 miles).*

Loch Enoch

Loch Aaron

Loch Neldricken

Loch Valley

Long Loch of Glenhead

Round Loch of Glenhead

Loch Trool

0 kilometres   2

0 miles   1

Culzean Castle ㉑

Robert Adam by **George Willison**

S TANDING ON A CLIFF'S EDGE in an extensive parkland estate, the 16th-century keep of Culzean (pronounced Cullayn), home of the Earls of Cassillis, was remodelled between 1777 and 1792 by the Neo-Classical architect Robert Adam. Restored in the 1970s, it is now a major showcase of Adam's later style of work. The grounds became Scotland's first public country park in 1969 and, with farming flourishing alongside ornamental gardens, they reflect both the leisure and everyday activities of life on a great country estate.

View of Culzean Castle (c.1815), by Nasmyth

Lord Cassillis' Rooms contain typical mid-18th-century furnishings, including a gentleman's wardrobe of the 1740s.

The clock tower, fronted by the circular carriageway, was originally the family coach house and stables. The clock was added in the 19th century, and today the buildings are used for residential and educational purposes.

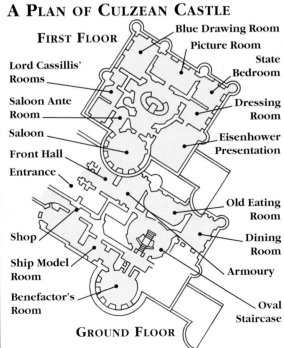

A PLAN OF CULZEAN CASTLE

FIRST FLOOR

- Blue Drawing Room
- Picture Room
- State Bedroom
- Lord Cassillis' Rooms
- Saloon Ante Room
- Saloon
- Front Hall
- Entrance
- Dressing Room
- Eisenhower Presentation
- Old Eating Room
- Shop
- Ship Model Room
- Benefactor's Room
- Dining Room
- Armoury
- Oval Staircase

GROUND FLOOR

Star Features

★ **Saloon**

★ **Oval Staircase**

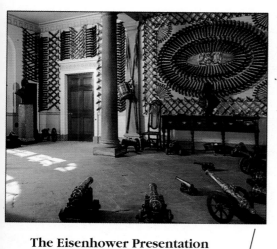

Armoury

On the walls are the bayonet blades and flintlock pistols issued to the West Lowland Fencible Regiment when Napoleon threatened to invade in the early 1800s.

VISITORS' CHECKLIST

(NTS) 6 km (4 miles) west of Maybole, Ayrshire. (01655) 760269. Ayr, then bus. **Castle** Apr–Oct: daily 10am– 5:30pm. **Grounds** dawn until dusk daily.

Fountain Court

This sunken garden is a good place to begin a tour of the grounds to the east.

The Eisenhower Presentation honours the general who was given the top floor of Culzean in gratitude for his role in World War II.

Carriageway

★ Saloon

With its restored 18th-century colour scheme and Louis XVI chairs, this elegant saloon perches on the cliff's edge 46 m (150 ft) above the Firth of Clyde. The carpet is a copy of one designed by Adam.

★ Oval Staircase

Illuminated by an overarching skylight, the staircase, with its Ionic and Corinthian pillars, is considered one of Adam's finest design achievements.

Firth of Clyde ㉒

Numerous counties west of Glasgow.
⬌ *Helensburgh and Dumbarton in the north; Troon and Ayr in the south.* ⛴ *from Largs to Great Cumbrae; from Gourock to Dunoon.* ℹ *Largs (01475) 673765; Dumbarton (01389) 742306.*

As MIGHT BE expected of a waterway that leads from Glasgow, a former economic powerhouse of the British Empire, to the Irish Sea and the Atlantic, the Firth of Clyde has many reminders of its industrial past. **Greenock**, some 40 km (25 miles) west of Glasgow, was once a ship-building centre. Few go there for the town's beauty, but the **McLean Museum and Art Gallery**, with its exhibits and information on the engineer James Watt *(see p58)*, a native of Greenock, is worth a visit. Princes Pier is a departure point for cruises along the Clyde. **Dumbarton**, 24 km (15 miles) from Glasgow on the northern bank, dates from the 5th century AD. Its ancient castle perches on a rock over-looking the rest of the town.

The Firth itself is L-shaped, heading northwest as it opens up beyond the Erskine Bridge. On reaching Gourock, just west of Greenock, the Firth branches south to more open water. Kip Marina at nearby **Inverkip** is a major yachting centre, while many towns on the Ayrshire coast have served as holiday resorts for Glasgow since Victorian times. **Largs**, site of the clash between Scots and Vikings in 1263, has a multimedia centre about the Vikings in Scotland, as well

The old harbour at Brodick, with Goat Fell Ridge in the distance

as a modern monument to the 1263 battle. A ferry service is offered to **Great Cumbrae Island**, which lies just off the coast. The main town on the island is Millport, which is built around a picturesque bay. The western side of the Firth of Clyde is much less developed, bor-dered by the Cowal Peninsula with its hills and lochs. The only town of note in this wild country is **Dunoon**. Again once a Victorian holiday resort, it still relies on tourism for its income. For many years there was a strong American influence in Dunoon due to the US nuclear submarine base at Holy Loch that is now closed.

🏛 **McLean Museum and Art Gallery**
Union St, Greenock. ☎ *(01475) 723741.* ◯ *Mon–Sat.*

Arran ㉓

North Ayrshire. 👥 *4,500.* ⛴ *from Ardrossan to Brodick; from Claonaig (Isle of Mull) to Lochranza (Apr–Oct only).* ℹ *Brodick (01770) 302140.*

ARRAN IS THOUGHT to have been populated as long ago as the end of the last Ice Age. The island's neolithic chambered burial tombs, such as the one at **Torrylinn** near Lagg in the south, indicate this. Bronze Age stone circles can also be seen around **Machrie** on the west coast. Vikings arrived from about AD 800 and exerted an influence for more than four centuries. After the Battle of Largs in 1263, when Alexander III defeated the Norsemen, Scotland bought Arran from the Vikings in 1266.

Today, visitors tend to come to Arran for outdoor pursuits. Golf is especially popular, with 18-hole courses at Brodick, Whiting Bay and Lamlash. Fishing is also popular.

Brodick is the island's only real town. The more mountainous parts offer some of the most spectacular hillwalking in Cen-tral Scotland.

The Goat Fell Ridge to the east of Glen Rosa and **Beinn Tarsuinn** to the west have a particular rugged beauty.

Golfer on the island of Arran

Robert the Bruce stayed on Arran on his return to Scotland in 1307. His followers had al-ready been harrassing the gar-rison at **Brodick Castle**, then occupied by supporters of the King of England. Legend states that it was from Arran that Bruce saw a signal fire on the Ayrshire coast that told him it was safe to return to the main-land and launch the campaign against the English. Parts of the Castle still date from the 13th century, though it has had many later additions.

⛫ **Brodick Castle (NTS)** Brodick. ☎ *(01770) 302202.* **Castle** ◯ *Apr–Oct: daily.* **Gardens** ◯ *daily.* 🎦 ♿

Largs seafront, the departure point for ferries to Great Cumbrae Island

◁ **Colourful gardens at Abbotsford House, near Galashiels**

The snowy peak of Ben Lomond rising majestically over Loch Lomond, part of the West Highland Way

Bute ㉔

Argyll & Bute. 🚹 7,000. 🚢 *from Wemyss Bay to Rothesay; from Colintraive to Rhubodach.* 🚌 *from Dunoon.* ℹ *Rothesay (01700) 502151.*

BUTE IS ALMOST an extension of the Cowal Peninsula, and the small ferry from Colintraive takes only five minutes to cross the Kyles of Bute to Rhubodach on the island. This route is a long drive from Glasgow, however, and most people choose to travel via Wemyss Bay on the Firth of Clyde across to the island's main town, Rothesay.

Just 25 km (16 miles) long by 8 km (5 miles) at its widest point, Bute has been occupied since at least the Bronze Age. The remains of the chapel at St Ninian's Point on the west coast date from around the 6th century, while **Rothesay Castle**, now ruined, is mostly

a 12th-century structure and was the site of struggles between islanders and Vikings in the 13th century. Over the last 120 years or so, Bute has played a more placid role as a popular holiday resort.

One of Bute's main attractions is **Mount Stuart House**, 5 km (3 miles) south of Rothesay. This great aristocratic house, built in 1877 by the third Marquess of Bute, is set in 18th-century gardens. The features of this wonderful Gothic edifice reflect the Marquess's interests in mythology, religion and astronomy.

⚓ **Rothesay Castle**
Castle Hill St, Rothesay. 📞 *(01700) 502691.* ⬜ *Apr–Sep: daily; Oct–Mar: Sat–Thu am (Sun: pm only).* 🏷
⚓ **Mount Stuart House**
Mount St. 📞 *(01700) 503877.* ⬜ *May–mid-Oct: Wed, Fri–Mon; mid-Oct–Apr: Mon–Fri by appointment.* 🏷 🎁 ♿

Loch Lomond ㉕

West Dunbartonshire, Argyll & Bute, Trossachs. 🚉 *Balloch, Tarbet.* 🚌 *Balloch, Balmaha.* ℹ *Dumbarton (01389) 742306.*

OF SCOTLAND'S many lochs, Lomond is perhaps the most popular and best loved. Lying just 30 km (19 miles) northwest of Glasgow, its accessibility has helped its rise to prominence. The loch is the largest body of fresh water in the British Isles, 35 km (22 miles) long and 8 km (5 miles) at its widest point in the south, where there are a scattering of over 30 islands, some with ancient ruins. The northern end is narrower and deeper.

Duncryne, a small hill some 5 km (3 miles) northeast of **Balloch** on the southern shore, gives an excellent view of the Loch. In general, the western shore is the more developed, with villages such as **Luss** and **Tarbet** attracting large numbers of visitors.

The contrast between the Loch and the surrounding mountains adds to the spectacle. **Ben Ime** in the Arrochar Alps, to the northwest of Lomond, stands at 1,011 m (3,317 ft) while **Ben Lomond** on the east side is 974 m (3,196 ft). Many walkers pass this way since Scotland's most popular long-distance footpath, the West Highland Way from Glasgow to Fort William, skirts the eastern shore. Boat trips around the loch operate regularly from Balloch Pier. The area is also good for water sports enthusiasts – speed boats, kayaks and jet skis can all be rented.

View of Bute with the 14th-century Kames Castle, at the head of Kames Bay

The Trossachs 26

Golden eagle

COMBINING THE RUGGEDNESS of the Grampians with the pastoral tranquillity of the Borders, this beautiful region of craggy hills and sparkling lochs is the colourful meeting place of the Lowlands and Highlands. Home to a wide variety of wildlife, including the golden eagle, peregrine falcon, red deer and the wildcat, the Trossachs have inspired numerous writers, including Sir Walter Scott *(see p622)* who made the area the setting for several of his novels. It was the home of Scotland's folk hero, Rob Roy, who was so well known that, in his own lifetime, he was fictionalized in *The Highland Rogue* (1723), a novel attributed to Daniel Defoe.

Loch Katrine
The setting of Sir Walter Scott's Lady of the Lake *(1810), this freshwater loch can be explored on the Victorian steamer* Sir Walter Scott, *which cruises from the Trossachs Pier.*

Loch Lomond
Britain's largest freshwater lake was immortalized in a ballad composed by a local Jacobite soldier, dying far from home. He laments that though he will return home before his companions who travel on "the high road", he will be doing so on "the low road" (of death).

The West Highland Way provides a good footpath through the area.

Luss
With its exceptionally picturesque cottages, Luss is one of the prettiest villages in Central Scotland. Surrounded by grassy hills, it occupies one of the most scenic parts of Loch Lomond's western shore.

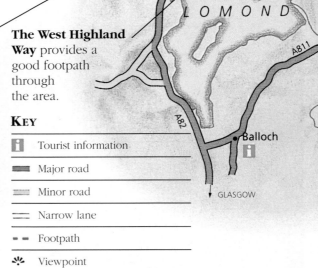

KEY

🈂	Tourist information
▬	Major road
▭	Minor road
═	Narrow lane
▪ ▪	Footpath
☀	Viewpoint

0 kilometres   5

0 miles   5

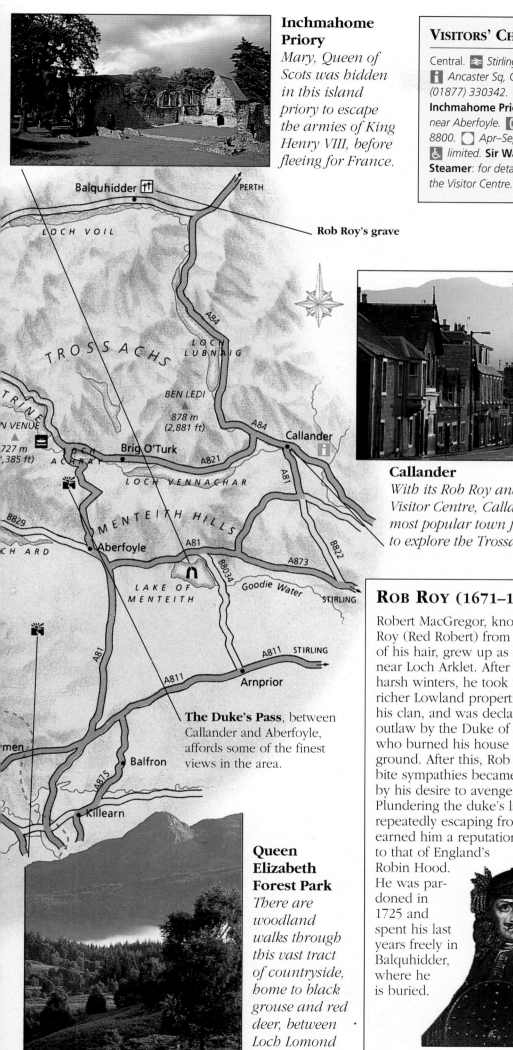

Inchmahome Priory

Mary, Queen of Scots was hidden in this island priory to escape the armies of King Henry VIII, before fleeing for France.

VISITORS' CHECKLIST

Central. 🚆 *Stirling.* 🚌 *Callander.*
ℹ️ *Ancaster Sq, Callander
(01877) 330342.* ◯ *Mar–Dec.*
Inchmahome Priory, *off A81,
near Aberfoyle.* 📞 *(0131) 668
8800.* ◯ *Apr–Sep: daily.*
♿ limited. **Sir Walter Scott
Steamer**: *for details, telephone
the Visitor Centre.*

Callander

With its Rob Roy and Trossachs Visitor Centre, Callander is the most popular town from which to explore the Trossachs.

The Duke's Pass, between Callander and Aberfoyle, affords some of the finest views in the area.

ROB ROY (1671–1734)

Robert MacGregor, known as Rob Roy (Red Robert) from the colour of his hair, grew up as a herdsman near Loch Arklet. After a series of harsh winters, he took to raiding richer Lowland properties to feed his clan, and was declared an outlaw by the Duke of Montrose who burned his house to the ground. After this, Rob Roy's Jacobite sympathies became inflamed by his desire to avenge the crime. Plundering the duke's lands and repeatedly escaping from prison earned him a reputation similar to that of England's Robin Hood. He was pardoned in 1725 and spent his last years freely in Balquhidder, where he is buried.

Queen Elizabeth Forest Park

There are woodland walks through this vast tract of countryside, home to black grouse and red deer, between Loch Lomond and Aberfoyle.

The 17th-century town house of the Dukes of Argyll

Stirling ㉗

Central. 🏘 *28,000.* ⚡ ▢
ℹ *41 Dunbarton Rd (01786) 475019.*

Sᴵᴛᴜᴀᴛᴇᴅ ʙᴇᴛᴡᴇᴇɴ the Ochil Hills and the Campsie Fells, the town of Stirling grew up around its castle, historically one of Scotland's most important fortresses. Below the castle the Old Town is still protected by the original walls, built in the 16th century to keep Mary, Queen of Scots safe from Henry VIII. The medieval **Church of the Holy Rude**, on Castle Wynd, where the infant James VI was crowned in 1567, has one of Scotland's few surviving hammerbeam oak roofs. In front of the church, the ornate façade of **Mar's Wark** is all that remains of a grand palace which, though never completed, was commissioned in 1570 by the first Earl of Mar. It was destroyed by the Jacobites in 1746. Opposite stands the beautiful 17th-century town house of the Dukes of Argyll.

Environs: Three kilometres (2 miles) south of Stirling, the **Bannockburn Heritage Centre** stands by the field where Robert the Bruce defeated the English in 1314 *(see p574)*. After the battle, he dismantled the castle so it would not fall back into English hands. A bronze equestrian statue commemorates the man who became an icon of Scottish independence.

ℹ **Bannockburn Heritage Centre**
(NTS) Glasgow Rd. ☎ *(01786) 812664.* ◯ *Mar–23 Dec: daily.* ● *24 Dec–Feb.* ♿ ♿

◁ **Loch Ard, near Stirling, in the Trossachs**

Stirling Castle

Gargoyle on castle wall

Rᴵꜱᴵɴɢ ʜᴵɢʜ on a rocky crag, this magnificent castle, which dominated Scottish history for centuries, now remains one of the finest examples of Renaissance architecture in Scotland. Legend says that King Arthur wrested the original castle from the Saxons, but there is no evidence of a castle before 1124. The present building dates from the 15th and 16th centuries and was last defended, against the Jacobites, in 1746. From 1881 to 1964 the castle was used as a depot for recruits into the Argyll and Sutherland Highlanders, though it now serves no military function.

Robert the Bruce
In the esplanade, this modern statue shows Robert the Bruce sheathing his sword after the Battle of Bannockburn in 1314.

Prince's Tower

Forework

Entrance

Stirling Castle in the Time of the Stuarts, **painted by Johannes Vorsterman (1643–99)**

★ Palace
The otherwise sparse interiors of the royal apartments contain the Stirling Heads. These Renaissance roundels depict 38 figures, thought to be members of the royal court at that time.

VISITORS' CHECKLIST

Castle Wynd, Stirling. ((01786) 450000. ◯ Apr–Sep: 9:30am–6pm daily; Oct–Mar: 9:30am–5pm daily (last admission: 45 mins before closing). 🅿 museum. ♿ limited.

The King's Old Building houses the Regimental Museum of the Argyll and Sutherland Highlanders.

★ Chapel Royal
Seventeenth-century frescoes by Valentine Jenkins adorn the chapel, reconstructed in 1594.

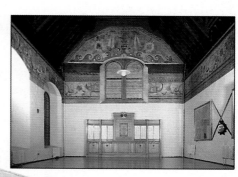

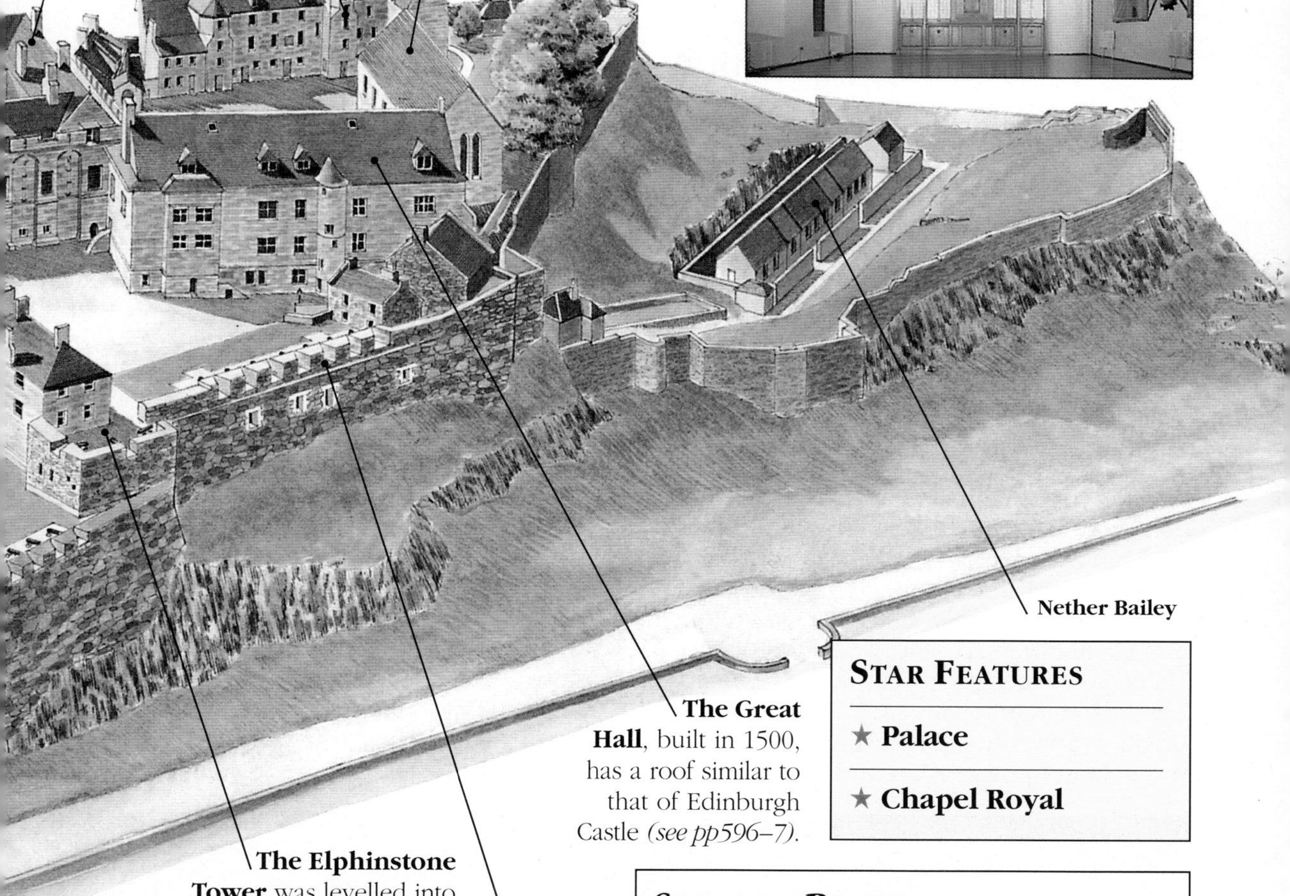

Nether Bailey

The Great Hall, built in 1500, has a roof similar to that of Edinburgh Castle (see pp596–7).

STAR FEATURES

★ Palace

★ Chapel Royal

The Elphinstone Tower was levelled into a gun platform in 1714.

Grand Battery
Following the unrest after the deposition of the Stuarts, this parapet was built in 1708, to strengthen the castle's defences.

STIRLING BATTLES

At the highest navigable point of the Forth and holding the pass to the Highlands, Stirling occupied a key position in Scotland's struggles for independence. Seven battlefields can be seen from the castle; the 67-m (220-ft) Wallace Monument at Abbey Craig recalls William Wallace's defeat of the English at Stirling Bridge in 1297, foreshadowing Bruce's victory in 1314.

The Victorian Wallace Monument

Perth seen from the east across the Tay

Doune Castle 28

Doune, Central. *(01786) 841742.*
Stirling then bus. *Apr–Oct:
daily; Nov–Mar: Sat–Thu.*
21 Dec–8 Jan. limited.

BUILT AS THE residence of
Robert, Duke of Albany,
in the late 14th century,
Doune Castle was a Stuart
stronghold until it fell into ruin
in the 18th century. Now fully
restored, it is one of the most
beautifully complete castles
of its time and offers a unique
view into the life of the medieval royal household.

The Gatehouse, once a self-
sufficient residence, leads
through to the central courtyard from which the Great
Hall can be entered. Complete
with its reconstructed open-
timber roof, minstrels' gallery
and central fireplace, the
Hall adjoins the Lord's Hall
and Private Room with its
original privy and well-hatch.
A number of private stairs and
narrow passages illustrate the
ingenious means by which the
royal family tried to protect
itself during times of danger.

Perth 29

Perthshire. *45,000.*
45 High St (01738) 638353.

ONCE THE CAPITAL of medieval Scotland, Perth's rich
heritage is reflected in many
of its buildings. It was in the
Church of St John, founded
in 1126, that the preacher
John Knox delivered the fiery
sermons which led to the destruction of many local monasteries. The Victorianized
Fair Maid's House (c.1600),
on North Port, is one of the
oldest houses in town and
was the fictional home of the
heroine of Sir Walter Scott's
The Fair Maid of Perth (1828).

In **Balhousie Castle**, the
Museum of the Black Watch
commemorates the first ever
Highland regiment, while the
Art Gallery and Museum has
displays on local industry and
exhibitions of Scottish painting.

ENVIRONS: Three km (2 miles)
north of Perth, the Gothic
Scone Palace stands on the
site of an abbey destroyed by
John Knox's followers in 1559.
Between the 9th and 13th
centuries, Scone guarded the
sacred Stone of Destiny, now
housed in Edinburgh Castle
(*see pp596–7*), on which the
Scottish kings were crowned.
The embroideries of Mary,
Queen of Scots are among the
many priceless artifacts on
display within the palace.

⚑ Balhousie Castle
RHQ Black Watch, Hay St.
(0131) 310 8530. *Apr–Sep:
Mon–Sat; Oct–Apr: Mon–Fri.*
23 Dec–6 Jan, last Sat in Jun.
🏛 Art Gallery and Museum
78 George St. *(01738) 632488.*
Mon–Sat. *24 Dec–4 Jan.*
⚑ Scone Palace
A93 to Braemar. *(01738) 552300.*
Good Fri–mid-Oct: daily.

Glamis Castle 30

Glamis, outside Forfar, Tayside.
(01307) 840242. *Dundee
then bus.* *Apr–Oct: daily.*
grounds.

WITH THE pinnacled out-
line of a Loire chateau,
the imposing medieval tower-
house of **Glamis Castle**
began as a royal hunting lodge

Glamis Castle with statues of James VI (left) and Charles I (right)

in the 11th century but underwent reconstruction in the 17th century. It was the childhood home of Queen Elizabeth the Queen Mother, and her former bedroom can be seen with a youthful portrait by Henri de Laszlo (1878–1956).

Behind the castle's greypink walls, many rooms are open to the public, including Duncan's Hall, the oldest in the castle and Shakespeare's setting for the king's murder in *Macbeth*. Together, the rooms present an array of china, paintings, tapestries and furniture spanning 500 years. In the grounds stand a pair of wrought-iron gates made for the Queen Mother on her 80th birthday in 1980.

View of St Andrews over the ruins of the cathedral

Dundee ③¹

Tayside. 🏃 *150,000.* ✈ ⇄ 🚌
ℹ *7–21 Castle St (01382) 527527.*
🛒 *Tue, Fri–Sun.*

Famous for its cake and marmalade, **Dundee** was also a major ship-building centre in the 18th and 19th centuries, a period which is recreated at the Victoria Docks.

HMS Unicorn, built in 1824, is the oldest British-built warship still afloat and is fitted as it was on its last voyage. Berthed at Craig Pier is the royal research ship **Discovery**. Built here in 1901 for the first of Captain Scott's voyages to the Antarctic, the *Discovery* was one of the last sailing ships to be made in Britain. Housed in a Victorian Gothic building, the **McManus Galleries** provide a

glimpse of Dundee's industrial heritage, with exhibitions of archaeology and Victorian art.

Environs: Along the coast, the pretty town of **Arbroath** is famed for its red stonework, ancient Abbey and "Arbroath Smokies" (smoked haddock). St Vigean's Museum displays a copy of *The Declaration of Arbroath*, attesting Scotland's independence.

🏛 **HMS Unicorn**
Victoria Docks.
☎ *(01382) 200900.*
🕐 *10am–5pm daily.*
⬤ *late Dec–early Jan.*
💰 ♿ *limited.*
www.frigateunicorn.org
🏛 **Discovery**
Discovery Point.
☎ *(01382) 201245.*
🕐 *daily.* 💰 ♿
📷 *by appointment.*
🏛 **McManus Galleries**
Albert Institute, Albert Square.
☎ *(01382) 432020.* 🕐 *Mon–Sun.*

**Insignia of St Mary's
College, St Andrews
University**

St Andrews ³²

Fife. 🏃 *14,000.* ⇄ *Leuchars.* 🚌
ℹ *70 Market St (01334) 472021.*

Scotland's oldest university town and one-time ecclesiastical capital, **St Andrews** is now a shrine to golfers from all over the world. Its main streets and cobbled alleys, full of crooked housefronts, dignified university buildings and medieval churches, converge on the venerable ruins of the 12th-century **cathedral**. Once the largest cathedral in Scotland, it was later pillaged for its stones, which were used to build the town. **St Andrew's Castle** was built for the town's bishops in the year 1200. The dungeon, in which many religious Reformers were held prisoner, can still be seen. St Andrews' golf courses occupy the land to the west of the city, and each is open for a modest fee. The **British Golf Museum**, which tells how the city's Royal and Ancient Golf Club became the ruling arbiter of the game, will delight golf enthusiasts.

⛴ **St Andrew's Castle**
The Scores. ☎ *(01334) 477196.*
🕐 *daily.* 💰 ♿ 📷
🏛 **British Golf Museum**
Bruce Embankment. ☎ *(01334) 478880.* 🕐 *Easter–mid-Oct: daily; mid-Oct–Easter: Thu–Mon.* 💰 ♿

THE BIRTHPLACE OF GOLF

Scotland's national game *(see p641)* was pioneered on the sandy links around St Andrews. The earliest record of the game being played dates from 1457, when golf was banned by James II because it was interfering with his subjects' archery practice. Mary, Queen of Scots was berated in 1568 for playing immediately after her husband, Darnley, had been murdered.

**Mary, Queen of Scots at
St Andrews in 1563**

The central courtyard of Falkland Palace, bordered by rose bushes

East Neuk ③

Fife. ⊠ *Leuchars.* ▦ *Glenrothes & Leuchars.* ⓘ *St Andrews (01334) 472021.*

A STRING of pretty fishing villages peppers the shoreline of the **East Neuk** (the eastern "corner") of Fife, stretching from Earlsferry to Fife Ness. Much of Scotland's medieval trade with Europe passed through these ports, a connection reflected in the Flemish-inspired crow-stepped gables of many of the cottages. Although the herring industry has declined and the area is now a peaceful holiday centre, the sea still dominates village life. The harbour is the heart of St Monans, a charming town of narrow twisting streets, while Pittenweem is the base for the East Neuk fishing fleet.

The town is also known for **St Fillan's Cave**, the retreat of a 9th-century hermit whose relic was used to bless the army of Robert the Bruce before the Battle of Bannockburn. A church stands among the cobbled lanes and colourful cottages of Crail; legend goes that the stone by the church gate was hurled across to the mainland from the Isle of May by the Devil.

A number of 16th- to 19th-century buildings in the village of Anstruther contain the **Scottish Fisheries Museum**, which tells the area's history with the aid of cottage interiors, boats and displays on whaling. From the village you can also embark for the nature reserve on the **Isle of May**, which teems with seabirds and a colony of grey seals. The statue of Alexander Selkirk in Lower Largo recalls the local boy whose seafaring adventures inspired Daniel Defoe's novel *Robinson Crusoe* (1719). After disagreeing with his captain, he was put ashore on an uninhabited island where he survived for four years.

🏛 Scottish Fisheries Museum
Harbour Head, St Ayles, Anstruther. 📞 *(01333) 310628.* ◯ *daily.* 📷 🚫 ♿

Falkland Palace ③④

(**NTS**) *Falkland, Fife.* 📞 *(01337) 857397.* ⊠ 🚌 *Ladybank, Kirkcaldy, then bus.* ◯ *Apr–Oct: daily (Sun: pm).* 📷

THIS STUNNING Renaissance palace was designed as a hunting lodge for the Stuart kings. Although its construction was begun by James IV in 1500, most of the work was carried out by his son, James V, in the 1530s. Under the influence of his two French wives, he employed French workmen to redecorate the façade of the East Range with dormers, buttresses and medallions, and to build the beautifully proportioned South Range. The palace fell into ruin during the years of the Commonwealth and was occupied briefly by Rob Roy *(see p635)* in 1715.

After buying the estates in 1887, the third Marquess of Bute became the Palace Keeper and subsequently restored the building. The richly panelled interiors are filled with superb furniture and contemporary portraits of the Stuart monarchs. The royal tennis court, built in 1539 for King James V, is the oldest in Britain.

Dunfermline ③⑤

Fife. 🚶 *45,000.* ⊠ 🚌 ⓘ *13–15 Maygate (01383) 720999.* ◯ *Apr–Oct.*

SCOTLAND'S CAPITAL until 1603, Dunfermline is dominated by the ruins of the 12th-century abbey and palace, which recall its royal past. The town first came to prominence in the 11th century as the seat of King Malcolm III, who founded a priory on the present site of the **Abbey Church**. With its Norman nave and 19th-century choir, the abbey church contains the tombs of 22 Scottish kings and queens, including that of the renowned Robert the Bruce.

The ruins of the **palace**, where Malcolm married his queen, Margaret, soar over the beautiful gardens of Pittencrieff Park. Dunfermline's most famous son, the philanthropist Andrew Carnegie (1835–1919),

---

THE PALACE KEEPER

Due to the size of the royal household and the necessity for the king to be itinerant, the office of Keeper was created by the medieval kings who required custodians to maintain and replenish the resources of their many palaces while they were away. Now redundant, it was a hereditary title and gave the custodian permanent and often luxurious lodgings.

James VI's bed in the Keeper's Bedroom at Falkland Palace

The 12th-century Norman nave of Dunfermline Abbey Church

had been forbidden entrance to the park as a boy. After making his fortune, however, he bought the entire Pitten-crieff estate and gave it to the people of Dunfermline. He was born in the town, but moved with his family to Pennsylvania in his teens. There, he made a vast fortune in the iron and steel industry, becoming one of the wealthiest men in the world, and donating some $350 million for the benefit of mankind. The **Carnegie Birthplace Museum** is still furnished as it was when he lived there, and tells the story of his meteoric career and many charitable donations.

🏛 **Carnegie Birthplace Museum**
Moodie St. 📞 (01383) 724302.
◯ daily. 🎫 ♿

Culross ㊱

Fife. 👥 450. 🚌 Dunfermline. 🚉 Dunfermline. ℹ National Trust, The Palace (01383) 880359. ◯ Apr–Sep: daily. 🎫 ♿ limited.

AN IMPORTANT religious centre in the 6th century, the town of Culross is reputed to have been the birthplace of St Mungo in 514. Now a beautifully preserved 17th- and 18th-century village, Culross prospered in the 16th century due to the growth of its coal and salt industries, most notably under the genius of Sir George Bruce. Descended from the family of Robert the Bruce, Sir George took charge of the Culross colliery in 1575 and created a drainage system called the "Egyptian Wheel" which cleared a mine 1.5 km (1 mile) long, running underneath the River Forth.

Throughout its subsequent decline of more than 150 years, Culross stood unchanged. The National Trust for Scotland began restoring the town in 1932 and now provides a guided tour. This starts at the **Visitors' Centre**, housed in the one-time village prison.

Built in 1577, Bruce's **palace** has the crow-stepped gables, decorated windows and red pantiles typical of the period. The interior retains its original early 17th-century painted ceilings, which are among the finest in Scotland. Crossing the square past the **Oldest**

House, dating from 1577, head for the **Town House** to the west. Behind it, a cobbled street known as the Back Causeway (with its raised section for nobility) leads to the turretted **Study**, built in 1610 as a house for the Bishop of Dunblane. The main room is open to visitors and should be seen for its original Norwegian ceiling. Continuing northwards to the ruined abbey, fine church and Abbey House, don't miss the Dutch-gabled **House with the Evil Eyes**.

The 17th-century study, with its decorated ceiling, at Culross

Antonine Wall ㊲

Falkirk. ℹ 2–4 Glebe St (01324) 620244. 🚉 Falkirk. ◯ Mon–Sat.

THE ROMANS were in Scotland from around AD 80; they withdrew south and built Hadrian's Wall between the Solway and the Tyne some 40 years later. They moved north once again around AD 140, in the reign of Emperor Antonius. His governor, Lollius Urbicus, supervised the building of a forward defence that ran from Old Kilpatrick on the Firth of Clyde through Central Scotland to east of Bo'ness on the Forth. The Antonine Wall is an earth rampart measuring 60 km (37 miles) with a ditch and forts at strategic points. There are a number of sites that give a good impression of its original condition, the best being Rough Castle, west of Falkirk, which not only has a very well-preserved section of wall and ditch but was also the location of a major Roman fortification.

The 16th-century palace of industrialist George Bruce, at Culross

Elevated view across Glasgow, revealing the city's many architectural styles ▷

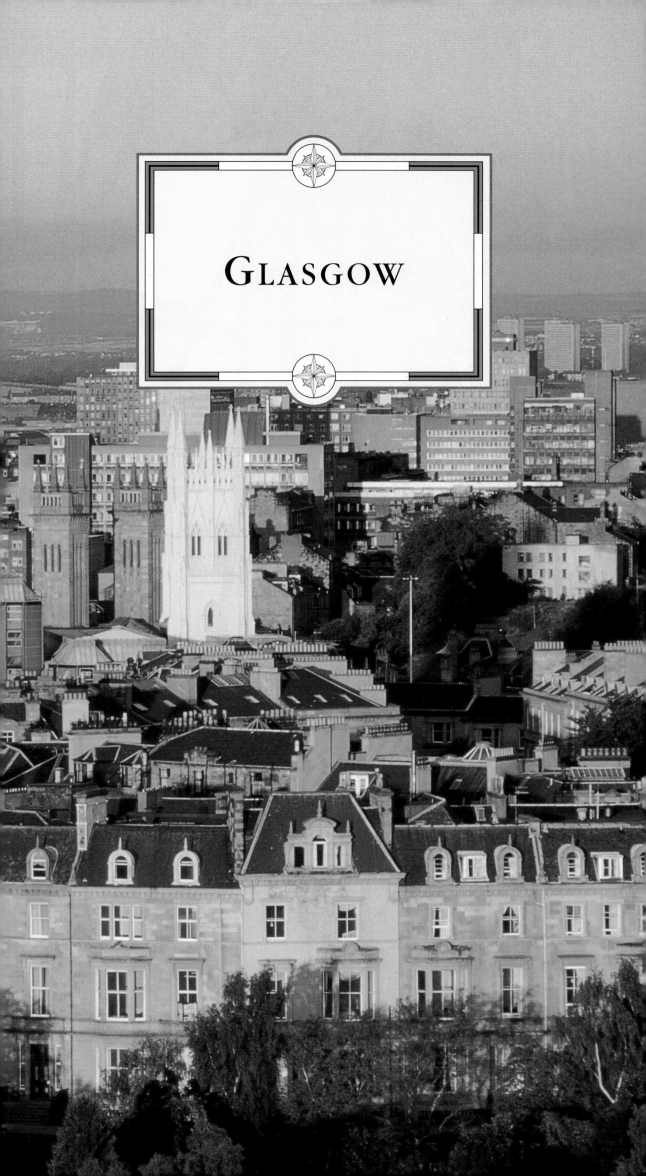

GLASGOW

GLASGOW

G LASGOW DISPLAYS *audacity in everything, from the profile of its new buildings, such as the Armadillo-like extension to the Scottish Exhibition and Conference Centre, to the wit of its people. As recently as the 1970s, this was a city with a fading industrial history and little sense of direction. Much has changed since then.*

Looking at the expansive Glasgow of today, it is hard to believe that Scotland's largest city – with a population of 611,000 people – was a town of relatively little significance as recently as 250 years ago. Although the Romans occupied the area 2,000 years ago, the city's history is officially measured from the 6th century, when a religious community was established by a priest called St Mungo. He chose a site – close to what is now St Mungo's Museum of Religious Life and Art – on the north bank of the River Clyde: a "dear green place" as he called it. The name "Glasgow" is thought to be a derivation of this description. St Mungo's community thrived, and by 1200, Glasgow had the commercial status of a burgh. The great cathedral was built around this time and is remarkably well preserved today.

The Union of Parliaments in 1707 ended England's monopoly on foreign trade, and Glasgow quickly cashed in on the lucrative import of tobacco and sugar from the American colonies. "Tobacco Lords" grew wealthy and built grandiose mansions to the west of what is now the city's commercial centre. The tobacco trade declined though, and in the middle of the 18th century the Industrial Revolution brought huge changes to the city. Glasgow became the cradle of Scotland's Industrial Revolution and was described as the "Workshop of the Empire". As a result, over the course

Fashionable brasseries in the rejuvenated Merchant City area of Glasgow

◁ Stained glass by architect and designer Charles Rennie Mackintosh, whose work can be seen all over the city

Statue by the sandstone building of Kelvingrove Art Gallery and Museum

of the 19th century, Glasgow was able to reinvent itself, first as a cotton manufacturing centre, and later as a site for shipbuilding and for heavy engineering. This flurry of activity created much employment and attracted incomers from poverty-stricken districts of the Scottish Highlands and islands, and of Ireland. Between the 1780s and the 1880s Glasgow's population exploded from around 40,000 to over 500,000. However, the social cost of this sudden influx of cheap labour was widespread poverty and sordid, cramped living conditions for many families. In an attempt to improve conditions, tenements – blocks of flats sharing a common toilet – were developed in the 1880s. Tenement life created a strong sense of community and wove the social fabric that endures to this day. "I belong tae Glasgow" are more than just words of a popular song.

Lavish marble interior of the City Chambers

The 20th century has been a bumpy ride for Glasgow. On the positive side, art has flourished, particularly with the distinctive styles of the "Glasgow Boys", led by Robert McGregor. In architecture, Charles Rennie Mackintosh

Celtic fans cheering on their football team

established a worldwide reputation with novel designs such as the one used for the Glasgow School of Art. However, the steady demise of shipbuilding resulted in huge unemployment and a significant population shift to satellite towns. The 1970s and 1980s saw a revitalization project, whereby the poorest housing blocks were replaced by high rises, the advantages of which are debatable.

Today, Glasgow is in an exciting period of transition, redeveloping its centre and rediscovering its architectural heritage. It is due to this rich architectural legacy that Glasgow is often referred to as the finest Victorian city in Britain. One outstanding 19th-century building is the City Chambers in George Square, which has doubled for both the Vatican and the Kremlin in films. Glasgow is also a city of contrasts: compare the raucous bustle of the Barras street market with, five minutes away, the sophistication of the Italian Centre, or the diversity of shops along Argyle Street, which is a favourite haunt of buskers.

"Glasgow's Alive and Kicking" runs a current city slogan, and indeed it is. The city boasts no less than 20 major museums and galleries, including the world-renowned Burrell Collection, Kelvingrove Art Gallery

Glass-roofed St Enoch's Shopping Centre

and Museum, the Mitchell Library and the Museum of Transport. With 72 parks (more per head of population than any other city in Europe), and its colourful Botanic Gardens, Glasgow was a natural choice to host the 1988 Garden Festival. In 1990, it was European City of Culture, and in 1999, it was United Kingdom City of Architecture. The city's annual events programme includes Celtic Connections, the largest celebration of folk music of its kind; an International Jazz Festival; and a selection of lesser-known spectacles

Stained glass window, Burrell Collection

such as pipe band championships and sheepdog trials.

Glasgow boasts a vibrant nightlife that includes everything from casinos to opera. Perhaps the best way to sample the Glasgow patter is to visit one of the many bars. Here it is impossible to avoid falling into conversation with Glaswegians, who are extraordinarily couthy (friendly), proud, down-to-earth and in possession of a dazzling wit. Glasgow is a cosmopolitan city – the rich variety of restaurants and cuisines reflects this – and there is an abundance of theatres, cinemas and night clubs. Not to be outdone by its great rival, Edinburgh, Glasgow's Hogmanay street festival is becoming one of the great places to be at New Year.

The city is also home to the Scotland's most successful football clubs, Celtic and Glasgow Rangers, and each has a large, impressive stadium. Hampden National Stadium hosts not only the finals of domestic cup competitions in November and May but also major international games.

Re-creation of a room inside an early 20th century Glaswegian tenement estate, Tenement House museum

Exploring Glasgow

GLASGOW CITY CENTRE is a neat grid of streets running east to west and north to south on the north bank of the River Clyde. This small area includes the main train stations, the principal shopping facilities and, at George Square, the tourist information office. Outside the centre, Byres Road to the west of Kelvingrove Park is the focus of the district known as "the West End", with its bars and restaurants near the University. Pollok Country Park, in the southwest, is home to the wonderful Burrell Collection.

Detail of St Mungo Museum's deceptively modern façade

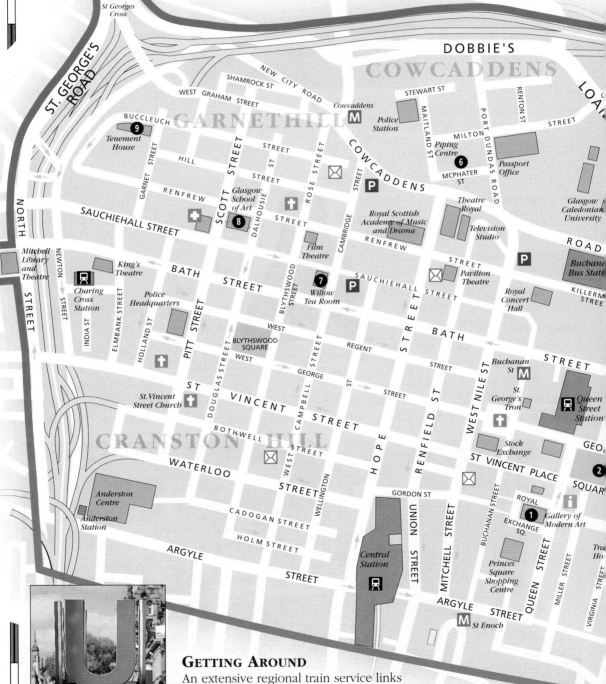

GETTING AROUND

An extensive regional train service links Glasgow with its suburbs. In the city itself there is an underground system that operates daily in a simple loop around the centre, both north and south of the River Clyde (limited hours on Sundays). The M8 motorway (highway) cuts through central Glasgow, linking Inverclyde and the airport in the west with Edinburgh in the east. Buses and black cabs are other options.

The distinctive "U" sign for the Glasgow Underground

SIGHTS AT A GLANCE

Historic Streets and Buildings
George Square ②
Glasgow Cathedral
    and Necropolis ⑤
Pollok House ⑰
Willow Tea Room ⑦

Museums and Galleries
Burrell Collection pp658–9 ⑱
Gallery of Modern Art ①
Hunterian Art Gallery ⑬
Kelvingrove Art Gallery
    and Museum ⑪
Museum of Transport ⑫

People's Palace ⑮
Provand's Lordship ③
St Mungo Museum of
    Religious Life and Art ④
Tenement House ⑨

Parks and Gardens
Botanic Gardens ⑭

Arts Centres
Glasgow School of Art ⑧
House for an Art Lover ⑯
Piping Centre ⑥
Scottish Exhibition Centre ⑩

Sauchiehall Street, the heart of the city's busy shopping district

KEY

Place of interest

Bus station

Train station

Underground station

Parking

Tourist information

Post office

Hospital

Church

0 metres   300

0 yards   300

OUTSIDE THE CENTRE

The imposing City Chambers in George Square, where a statue of Sir Walter Scott stands atop the central column

Gallery of Modern Art ❶

Queen Street. 📞 *(0141) 229 1996.*
⬜ *daily.* ♿ 📷
www.goma.glasgow.gov.uk

ONCE THE HOME of Glasgow's Royal Exchange (the city's centre for trade), this building dates from 1829 and also incorporates a late 18th-century mansion that formerly occupied the site. The local authority took over the Exchange just after World War II, and for many years it served as a library. It finally opened its doors as the Gallery of Modern Art in 1996. A controversial acquisitions policy and a somewhat limited budget has led

Ornate tower of the Gallery of Modern Art

the gallery to concentrate on the works of living artists, while a desire to attract a wide audience means the roly-poly figures of Beryl Cook hang alongside the stark photographic images of Jo Spence. Works of art by contemporary Scots, such as John Bellany, Elizabeth Blackadder and the new generation of Glasgow Boys, are displayed on the four themed floors that represent each of the elements – air, water, earth and fire.

George Square ❷

City centre. **City Chambers** 📞 *(0141) 287 2000.* ⬜ *Mon–Wed & Fri, 10:30am and 2:30pm for guided tours.* ♿ 📷 **Merchant House** 📞 *(0141) 221 8272.* 📷 *by appointment.*

GEORGE SQUARE was laid out in the late 18th century as a residental area, but redevelopment during Victorian times conferred its enduring status as the city's focal point. The only building not to be affected by the later 19th-century makeover is the Copthorne Hotel (1807) on the north side of the Square.

The 1870s saw a building boom, with the construction of the former Post Office (1876) at the southeast corner, and the **Merchant House** (1877) to the west side. The latter is home to Glasgow's Chamber of Commerce. Founded in 1781, it is the oldest organization of its kind in the UK. The most dominant structure in George Square, however, is the **City Chambers** on the east side. Designed by William Young, in an Italian Renaissance style, the imposing building was opened in 1888 by Queen Victoria. With the elegant proportions of the interior decorated with marble and mosaic, the opulence of this building makes it the most impressive of its kind in Scotland.

Provand's Lordship ❸

3 Castle St. 📞 *(0141) 287 2699.* ⬤ *for renovation until the year 2000.*

PROVAND'S LORDSHIP was originally built as a canon's house in 1471, and is now Glasgow's oldest surviving house, as well as a museum. Its low ceilings and austere wooden furnishings create a vivid impression of life in a wealthy 15th-century household. Mary, Queen of Scots *(see p55)* may have stayed here when she visited Glasgow in 1566 to see her cousin, and husband, Lord Darnley.

Provand's Lordship, Glasgow's only medieval house

St Mungo Museum of Religious Life and Art ④

2 Castle St. 📞 *(0141) 553 2557.*
⭘ *daily.* ♿ ✍ *by appointment.*

GLASGOW HAS strong religious roots, and the settlement that grew to become today's city started with a monastery founded in the 6th century AD by a priest called Mungo. He died in the early years of the 7th century, and his body lies buried underneath Glasgow Cathedral. The building itself dates from the 12th century, and stands on ground blessed by St Ninian as long ago as AD 397.

Detail from the St Mungo Museum

In recent years, the ever-growing numbers of visitors to the cathedral prompted plans for an interpretive centre. Despite the efforts of the Society of Friends of Glasgow Cathedral, however, sufficient funds could not be raised. The local authority decided to step in with money, and with the idea for a more extensive project – a museum of religious life and art. The site chosen was adjacent to the cathedral, where the 13th-century Castle of the Bishops of Glasgow once stood. The museum has the appearance of a centuries-old fortified house, despite the fact that it was completed as recently as 1993.

The top floor tells the story of the country's religion from a nondenominational perspective. Both Protestant and Catholic versions of Christianity are represented, as well as the other faiths of modern Scotland. The many, varied displays touch on the lives of communities as extensive as Glasgow's Muslims, who have had their own Mosque in the city since 1984, as well as local converts to the Baha'i faith.

The other floors are given over to works of art. The star of the show is Salvador Dalí's *Christ of St John of the Cross* (1951), which was brought to Glasgow in 1952 despite controversy over its subject matter. The painting was vandalized in 1961 but was subsequently restored. It now sits alongside religious artifacts and artworks, such as burial discs from Neolithic China (2000 BC), contemporary paintings by Aboriginal Australians, and some excellent Scottish stained glass from the early part of the 20th century.

Further displays in the museum examine issues of fundamental concern to people of all religions – war, persecution, death and the afterlife – and from cultures as far afield as West Africa and Mexico. In the grounds surrounding the building, there is a permanent Zen Garden, created by Yasutaro Tanaka. Such gardens have been a traditional aid to contemplation in Japanese Buddhist temples since the beginning of the 16th century.

Dalí's *Christ of St John of the Cross* at the St Mungo Museum of Religious Life and Art

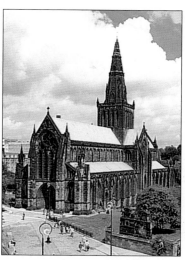

Glasgow's medieval cathedral viewed from the southwest

Glasgow Cathedral and Necropolis ⑤

Cathedral Square. **Cathedral**
📞 *(0141) 552 6891.* ⭘ *daily.* ♿
Necropolis ⭘ *daily.*

AS ONE OF THE FEW cathedrals to escape destruction during the Scottish Reformation *(see p593)* by adapting itself to Protestant worship, Glasgow Cathedral is a rare example of an almost complete original 13th-century church.

It was built on the site of a chapel founded by the city's patron saint, St Mungo, a 6th-century bishop of Strathclyde. According to legend, Mungo placed the body of a holy man, named Fergus, on a cart yoked to two wild bulls, telling them to take it to the place ordained by God. In the "dear green place" at which the bulls stopped, he built his church.

Because of its sloping site, the cathedral is built on two levels. The crypt contains the tomb of St Mungo, surrounded by an intricate forest of columns springing up to end in delicately carved rib-vaulting. The Blacader Aisle, which is reputed to have been built over a cemetery blessed by St Ninian, has a ceiling thick with decorative bosses.

Behind the cathedral, a likeness of Protestant reformer John Knox *(see p594)* surveys the city from his Doric pillar, overlooking a Victorian cemetery. The necropolis is filled with crumbling monuments to the dead of Glasgow's wealthy merchant families.

Piping Centre ⑥

30–34 McPhater St. ☏ *(0141) 353 0220.* ◯ *daily.* ♿♿

THE PIPING CENTRE, which opened its doors in a refurbished church in 1996, aims to promote the study and history of piping in Scotland. It offers tuition at all levels, and houses the **National Museum of Piping**, which traces the development of the instrument. Displays show that bagpipes were first introduced to Scotland as early as the 14th century, although the golden age of piping in the Highlands and islands was the 17th and 18th

Traditional bagpipes with brass drones

centuries. This was the era of the MacCrimmons of Skye (hereditary pipers to the chiefs of Clan MacLeod), when complex, extended tunes (*ceol mor*, or "the big music") were written for clan gatherings, battles and in the form of laments.

Willow Tea Room ⑦

217 Sauchiehall St. ☏ *(0141) 332 0521.* ◯ *Mon–Sat, Sun (pm).*

THIS IS THE SOLE survivor of a series of delightfully frivolous tea rooms created by the designer Charles Rennie Mackintosh *(see opposite page)* at the turn of the century for

The Mackintosh-designed interior of the Willow Tea Room

the celebrated restaurateur Miss Kate Cranston. Everything in the tearoom, from the high-backed chairs to the tables and cutlery, was of Mackintosh's own design. In particular, the 1904 **Room de Luxe** sparkles with eccentricity: striking mauve and silver furniture, coloured glass and a flamboyant leaded door create a remarkable venue in which to enjoy an afternoon tea of cakes and muffins.

The exterior of the Glasgow School of Art, Mackintosh's masterpiece

Glasgow School of Art ⑧

167 Renfrew St. ☏ *(0141) 353 4526.* ◯ *Mon–Sat (by appointment).* ● *26 Jun–2 Jul, 20 Dec–4 Jan.* ♿♿♿ *limited.* www.gsa.ac.uk

WIDELY CONSIDERED to be the greatest architectural work in the illustrious career of Charles Rennie Mackintosh, the Glasgow School of Art was built between 1897 and 1909 to a design he submitted in a competition. Due to financial constraints, it was built in two stages. The earlier eastern half displays a severity of style, likened by a contemporary critic to a prison. The later western half is characterized by a softer architectural style.

An art student will guide you through the building to the Furniture Gallery, Board Room and the Library, the latter being a masterpiece of spatial composition. Each room is an exercise in contrasts between

height, light and shade, with innovative details echoing the architectural themes of the structure. How much of the school can be viewed depends on curricular requirements at the time of visiting, as it still functions as an active and highly successful art college.

Tenement House ⑨

(NTS) 145 Buccleuch St. ☏ *(0141) 333 0183.* ◯ *Mar–Oct: daily (pm).* ♿♿ *by appointment.*

MORE A TIME CAPSULE than a museum, the Tenement House is an almost undisturbed record of life as it was in a modest Glasgow flat on a tenement estate in the early 20th century. Glasgow owed much of its vitality and neighbourliness to tenement life, though in later years many of these Victorian and Edwardian apartments were to earn a bad name for poverty and overcrowding, and many of them have been pulled down.

The Tenement House was first owned by Miss Agnes Toward, who lived here from 1911 until 1965. It remained largely unaltered during that time and, since Agnes threw very little away, the house has become a treasure-trove of social history. In the parlour, which would have been used only on formal occasions, afternoon tea is laid out on a white lace cloth. The kitchen, with its coal-fired range and box bed, is filled with the tools of a vanished era, such as a goffering-iron for crisping waffles, a washboard and a stone hot-water bottle.

Agnes's lavender water and medicines are still arranged in the bathroom, and it feels almost as though she stepped out of the house 70 years ago and simply forgot to return.

The preserved Edwardian kitchen of the Tenement House

Glasgow Artists

Detail from House for an Art Lover

THE LATE 19TH CENTURY was a time of great artistic activity in Glasgow, with influential painters such as Sir James Guthrie, Robert McGregor and others rising to prominence. But due to snobbery on the part of the Edinburgh-based arts establishment, these men often had to seek recognition outside Scotland. Only after a London exhibition in 1890 was the term "Glasgow School" coined, although the artists generally called themselves the "Glasgow Boys". Art Nouveau designer Charles Rennie Mackintosh was a contemporary, contributing his genius to the creative life of the city as well as to a new Glasgow School of Art, completed in two stages – 1899 and 1909. More recently, the term Glasgow Boys has been used to describe the generation of artists who attended the School of Art in the 1970s and '80s.

Stirling Station, *by* **William Kennedy** *(1859–1918), depicts the crowded platform with people waiting for a train. The rich colours, and steam from the trains, contribute to the atmosphere of this bustling station.*

A Star *(1891) by Sir John Lavery is indicative of the artist's dashing, fluid, style as a portraitist. Born in Belfast, Lavery studied at Glasgow and was part of the Whistler- and Impressionist-influenced Glasgow School.*

In **The Wayfarer**, *by Edward Arthur Walton (1860–1922), the winding path leads the viewer into the distance, in the direction of the wayfarer's gaze.*

Designed by Mackintosh in 1901*, the House for an Art Lover (see p657) was finally built in 1996. The design of the building and all of the furniture remains true to the original plans.*

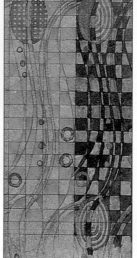

Mackintosh's stylized tulips *on a checkered background provide a striking example of Art Nouveau decoration, juxtaposing the organic with the geometric.*

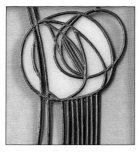

Mackintosh's unique fluidity of form *is seen in this detail from a stained-glass door in the House for an Art Lover.*

CHARLES RENNIE MACKINTOSH

Glasgow's most celebrated designer (1868–1928) entered Glasgow School of Art at the age of 16. After his success with the Willow Tea Room, he became a leading figure in the Art Nouveau movement. His characteristic straight lines and flowing detail are the hallmark of early 20th-century style.

Scottish Exhibition Centre ❿

Finnieston. 📞 *(0141) 248 3000.* ♿
📷 *by appointment.* www.secc.co.uk

WHEN THE SECC opened in 1985, it gave Glasgow a world-class facility for conferences, exhibitions and entertainment. The main auditorium holds up to 9,000 people and regularly hosts major rock concerts. The centre revitalized a derelict stretch of the Clyde, and, for the Glasgow Garden Festival in 1988 on the opposite bank, Bell's Bridge was built as a pedestrian link.

The exterior of the SECC has always left much to be desired, and has been described as an "ignominious shed", but an extension, completed in 1997, reclaimed a lot of design kudos. Named the Armadillo, the extension is a breathtaking building, reminiscent of a symmetrical, metallic Sydney Opera House, and contains a 3,000-seat auditorium. The nearby Clyde Navigation Trustees Crane No. 7 is a reminder of Glasgow's industrial past.

Kelvingrove Art Gallery and Museum ⓫

Argyle St, Kelvingrove. 📞 *(0141) 287 2699.* ⭕ *daily.* ♿ 📷

AN IMPOSING red sandstone building, Kelvingrove is Scotland's most popular gallery, housing a magnificent art collection. Best known for its

George Henry's *Japanese Lady with a Fan* (1894), at Kelvingrove

17th-century Dutch and 19th-century French paintings, the collection began as the gift of a Glasgow coachbuilder who died in 1854, leaving works by Botticelli, Giorgione and Rembrandt. Prominent among Continental artists are Degas, Millet and Monet, while in the Scottish Gallery, the famous work *Massacre of Glencoe* by James Hamilton (1853–94) is on display *(see p676),* alongside works by the Glasgow Boys *(see p655).* Other exhibitions in the museum cover an extraordinary number of subjects, including ceramics, silver, European arms and armour, and the geology of Scotland. The archaeological display includes a reconstruction of the Antonine Wall, which was built by the Romans to mark the boundary of their occupied area of Scotland.

Museum of Transport ⓬

1 Bunhouse Rd. 📞 *(0141) 287 2000.* ⭕ *daily.* ♿ 📷

HOUSED IN Kelvin Hall, this imaginative museum conveys much of the optimism and vigour of the city's industrial heyday. Model ships and ranks of gleaming Scottish-built steam engines, cars and motorcycles recall the 19th and early 20th centuries, when Glasgow's supremacy in shipbuilding, trade and manufacturing made her the "second city" of the British Empire. Old Glasgow can be seen through fascinating footage of the town in the cinema and through a reconstruction of a 1938 street, with Art Deco shop fronts, cinema and Underground station.

The Museum of Transport's 1938 street, with a reconstructed Underground station

Hunterian Art Gallery ⓭

82 Hillhead St. 📞 *(0141) 330 5431.* ⭕ *Mon–Sat.* ● *24 Dec–5 Jan.*

BUILT TO HOUSE a number of paintings bequeathed to Glasgow University by an ex-student and physician, Dr William Hunter (1718–83), the Hunterian Art Gallery contains Scotland's largest print collection. There are also works by many major European artists, dating from the 16th century. A collection of work by the designer Charles Rennie Mackintosh *(see p655)* is supplemented by a complete reconstruction of No. 6 Florentine Terrace, where he lived from 1906 to 1914. A major collection of 19th- and

Kelvingrove Art Gallery and the Glasgow University buildings, seen from the south

20th-century Scottish art includes work by William McTaggart (1835–1910), but by far the most famous collection is of work by the Paris-trained American painter, James McNeill Whistler (1834–1903), who influenced so many of the Glasgow School painters.

Whistler's *Sketch for Annabel Lee* (c.1869), Hunterian Art Gallery

Botanic Gardens ⑭

Great Western Rd. ☏ (0141) 334 2422. ◯ daily. ♿ 🍴 by appointment.

THESE GARDENS form a peaceful space in the heart of the city's West End, by the River Kelvin. Originally founded at another site in 1817, they were moved to the current location in 1839 and opened to the public three years later. Aside from the main range of greenhouses, with assorted displays including palm trees and an area given over to tropical crops,

one of the most interesting features is the **Kibble Palace**. Built at Loch Long in the Highlands by John Kibble, a Victorian engineer, the glass palace was moved to its present site in the early 1870s but its splendour is now much reduced.

People's Palace ⑮

Glasgow Green. ☏ (0141) 554 0223. ◯ daily. ♿

THIS VICTORIAN, sandstone structure was purpose-built in 1898 as a cultural museum for the people of Glasgow's East End. It houses everything from temperance tracts to trade-union banners, suffragette posters to the comedian Billy Connolly's banana-shaped boots, and thus provides a social history of the city from the 12th to the 20th century. A superb conservatory at the back of the building contains an exotic winter garden, with tropical plants and birds.

House for an Art Lover ⑯

Bellahouston Park, Dumbreck Rd. ☏ (0141) 353 4791. ◯ daily. ● during functions (telephone for details). 🍴 ♿

PLANS FOR THE House for an Art Lover were submitted by Charles Rennie Mackintosh and his partner Margaret Macdonald in response to a competition in a German magazine in the summer of 1900.

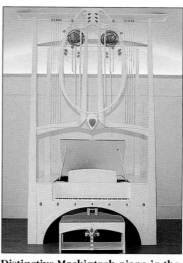

Distinctive Mackintosh piano in the Music Room, House for an Art Lover

The competition brief was to create a country retreat for someone of elegance and taste who loved the arts. As it was a theoretical exercise, the couple were unrestrained by logistics or budget and won a special prize for their efforts.

The plans lay unused for over 80 years until consulting engineer Graham Roxburgh, who had worked on the refurbishment of other Mackintosh interiors in Glasgow (including Craigie Hall), decided to try to build the House for an Art Lover. Work began in 1989 and was successfully completed in 1996. The House is host to a digital design studio and postgraduate study centre for students at the Glasgow School of Art, as well as a café.

It is the rooms on the main floor, however, that give a real insight into the vision of Mackintosh and the artistic talent of Macdonald. The Oval Room is a beautifully proportioned space in a single light colour, meant as a tranquil retreat for ladies, while the Music Room and its centre-piece piano that is played to add to the atmosphere is also bright and inspiring.

The Main Hall is darker than the other rooms and it leads into the Dining Room, with its long table, sideboard and relief stone fireplace. The great attention to detail shown throughout the House, in the panelling, light fixtures and other elements, is enormously impressive. The exterior of the building is no exception, as that too is an extraordinary achievement in art and design.

One of the greenhouses in Glasgow's peaceful Botanic Gardens

**The Georgian Pollok House,
viewed from the south**

Pollok House ⑰

(NTS) 2060 Pollokshaws Rd. █ (0141)
616 6410. ○ Apr–Oct: 10am–5pm
daily, Nov–Mar: 11am–4pm daily.

POLLOK HOUSE is Glasgow's
finest 18th-century domestic
building and contains one of
Britain's best collections of
Spanish paintings. The Neo-
Classical central block was
finished in 1750, the sobriety
of its exterior contrasting with
the exuberant plasterwork
within. The Maxwells have
lived at Pollok since the mid-
13th century, but the male line
ended with Sir John Maxwell,
who added the grand entrance
hall in the 1890s. A keen
plant collector, he also designed most of the terraced
gardens and parkland beyond.

Hanging above the family
silver, porcelain, hand-painted
Chinese wallpaper and Jacobean glass, the Stirling Pollok
paintings are strong on British
and Dutch schools, including
William Blake's *Sir Geoffrey
Chaucer and the Nine and
Twenty Pilgrims* (1745) as well
as William Hogarth's portrait
of James Thomson, who wrote
the words to *Rule Britannia*.

Spanish 16th- to 19th-
century art predominates: El
Greco's *Lady in a Fur Wrap*
(1541) hangs in the library,
while the drawing room contains works by Francisco de
Goya and Esteban Murillo. In
1966 Anne Maxwell Macdonald
gave the house and 146 ha
(361 acres) of parkland to the
City of Glasgow. The park
provides the site for the city's
fascinating Burrell Collection.

Burrell Collection ⑱

GIVEN TO THE CITY in 1944 by Sir
William Burrell (1861–1958), a
wealthy shipping owner, this internationally acclaimed collection is the
star of Glasgow's renaissance, with
objects of major importance in numerous fields of interest. The building
housing these pieces was purpose-
built in 1983. When the sun shines in,
the stained glass blazes with colour,
while the shaded tapestries seem a
part of the surrounding woodland.

Bull's Head
*Dating from the
7th century BC,
this bronze head
from Turkey was
once part of a
cauldron handle.*

Hutton Castle Dining Room
*This is a reconstruction of the Dining
Room at Burrell's own home – the
16th-century Hutton Castle, near
Berwick-upon-Tweed. The Hall
and Drawing Rooms can also
be seen nearby.*

**Hornby
Portal**
*This 14th-
century arch,
with its heraldic
display, comes
from Hornby
Castle in Yorkshire.*

Main entrance

STAR EXHIBITS

★ **Stained Glass**

★ **Tapestries**

Rembrandt van Rijn
This self-portrait, signed and dated 1632, has pride of place among the Dutch paintings hanging in the 17th- and 18th-century room.

VISITORS' CHECKLIST

2060 Pollokshaws Rd, Glasgow.
(0141) 649 7151. Pollok-shaws West. 45, 48, 50, 57 from Glasgow. 10am–5pm Mon–Sat, 11am–5pm Sun.

GALLERY GUIDE
Except for a mezzanine-floor display of Old Masters, the exhibitions are on the ground floor. Right of the entrance hall, rooms are devoted to tapestries, stained glass and sculpture, while ancient civilizations, Oriental art and the period galleries are ahead.

KEY TO FLOORPLAN

- Ancient civilizations
- Oriental art
- Medieval and post-medieval European art, stained glass and tapestries
- Period galleries
- Hutton Castle Rooms
- Paintings and drawings
- Temporary exhibition area

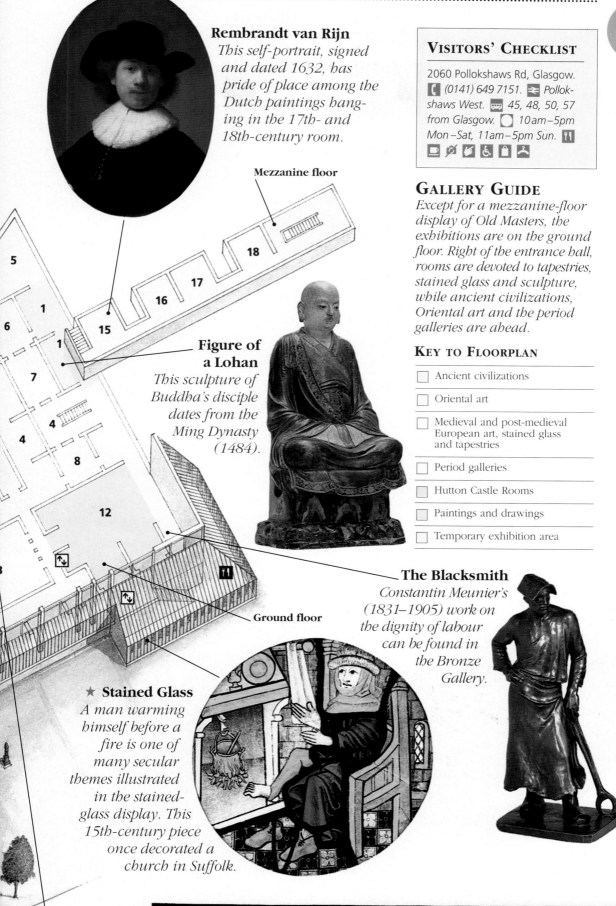

Mezzanine floor

Figure of a Lohan
This sculpture of Buddha's disciple dates from the Ming Dynasty (1484).

Ground floor

The Blacksmith
Constantin Meunier's (1831–1905) work on the dignity of labour can be found in the Bronze Gallery.

★ Stained Glass
A man warming himself before a fire is one of many secular themes illustrated in the stained-glass display. This 15th-century piece once decorated a church in Suffolk.

★ Tapestries
A detail from the Swiss work in wool, Scenes from the Life of Christ and of the Virgin (c.1450), is one of many tapestries on show.

Black Rock Cottage, Glencoe, Lochaber ▷

THE
HIGHLANDS
AND ISLANDS

THE HIGHLANDS AND ISLANDS

M OST OF THE STOCK IMAGES *of Scottishness – clans and tartans, whisky and porridge, bagpipes and heather – originate in the Highlands and enrich the popular picture of Scotland as a whole. But for many centuries the Gaelic-speaking, cattle-raising Highlanders had little in common with their southern neighbours.*

Clues to the non-Celtic ancestors of the Highlanders lie scattered across the Highlands and Islands in the form of stone circles, brochs and cairns. Many of the place-name endings (-ish for a peninsula, -vaig for a beach, and so on) are the legacy of early Viking invaders. Indeed, the people of the remote Shetland Islands, for example, feel as much kinship with Scandinavia as they do with Scotland.

The islands of Scotland, the last outposts of Britain, harbour many unique archaeological remains, including a 4,000-year-old neolithic village at Skara Brae in the Orkneys. This site was completely covered with sand until it was exposed during a violent storm in the 19th century.

At Callanish, on the Outer Hebridean island of Lewis, a ring of standing stones constitutes a Scottish Stonehenge. However, here – unlike at the famous Stonehenge in England – there are no perimeter fences to keep visitors at a distance.

By the end of the 6th century, Gaelic-speaking Celts had arrived from Ireland. Among them was St Columba, who is credited with introducing Christianity to Scotland. St Magnus Cathedral on Orkney is a product of the fusion of Christianity and Viking culture that occurred in the 8th and 9th centuries.

For over 1,000 years, Celtic Highland society was founded on a clan system, which is based on loyal family groups headed by a feudal chief. The fierce

A wintry dawn over the Cairngorms, the home of Britain's only herd of reindeer

◁ The picturesque harbour at Kallin on the island of Grimsay

Diving support platform, oil rig and standby vessel, North Sea

allegiance members felt to their clan often led to inter-clan rivalry and violent conflict. However, after 1746, following the failed Jacobite attempt on the British crown (led by Bonnie Prince Charlie), the clans were systematically torn apart by the English. For a while, wearing clan tartan was banned.

Islay malt whisky label

The more romantic vision of the Highlands presented to most modern visitors began early in the 19th century and was largely created by the writer Sir Walter Scott, who actually lived in the Lowlands. The novels and poetry Scott wrote celebrated the majesty and grandeur of a country previously considered, especially by English people, barbaric and poverty stricken. But behind this new sentimentality lay harsh economic realities. When absentee landowners decided that their land was better suited to sheep grazing than human habitation, many Scots were forced to seek a new life overseas.

Canada was the most popular New World destination, and today there are more Gaelic speakers in North America than there are in Scotland.

Another great champion of Highland life was Queen Victoria, whose passion for the royal castle at Balmoral helped establish the trend for acquiring sporting estates. Owners of such estates were usually enthusiasts of blood sports, such as grouse shooting, salmon fishing and deer stalking. Balmoral is still much loved by the present royal family: the Queen regularly spends a month at a time at the castle. While there, she usually attends the Highland Games at Braemar, where cabers are tossed and hammers are thrown. Such sporting gatherings are held all over the Highlands between June and September, and anyone is allowed to take part.

There are major topographical differences between the west and east coasts of the Highlands. On the west coast, mountains and cliffs appear to meet the sea and the stormy incoming weather in a head-on confrontation. The east coast, however, is drier

Old Man of Hoy rock pillar, Orkney

and gentler, with land and sea converging more harmoniously. A fault line, Great Glen, runs from one coast to the other. Along this line there are several lochs (lakes), including Loch Ness, made famous by the mythical monster. These lochs have been artificially linked to create the Caledonian Canal, which enables small craft to move between coasts without having to brave the wild seas around Cape Wrath and John O'Groats.

The principal centre on the east coast is the granite city of Aberdeen, which was given a new lease of life by the discovery of oil in the North Sea. Signs of prosperity in Aberdeen include new, well-patronized shopping centres and high house prices. On the west coast, Argyll is the region of elegant living and country-house hotels that serve excellent local seafood. In the southern part of Argyll is the friendly port of Oban, from which a busy traffic of ferries and yachts leaves for the Inner and Outer Hebrides. Further up the west coast, especially north of Ullapool, the land becomes increasingly inhospitable and the number of settlements gradually decreases. A combination of human endeavour and grazing animals has cleared much of the original forest in this northern area, but some native pines are being replanted.

Moored pleasure craft on Loch Lochy, wintertime

Red deer stag

Many of the more remote areas of the Highlands are worked by some 17,000 crofters, who combine farming and fishing with whatever part-time work might be available locally. However, for people such as crofters living in isolated areas, working from home via the Internet is now a possibility. Life remains hard for crofters, and some maintain the back-breaking tradition of manually cutting blocks of peat from the ground and stacking them to dry. Later these blocks are used as fuel for home fires. Crofters must also contend with an infamous midsummer pest: the biting midge, which rises from the heather in clouds whenever the wind drops.

Sheep grazing by Rubh'an Duin Lighthouse, island of Islay

Exploring the Highlands and Islands

To the north and west of Stirling, the historic gateway to the Highlands, lie the magnificent mountains and glens, fretted coastlines and lonely isles that are the epitome of Scottish scenery. Inverness, the Highland capital, makes a good starting point for exploring Loch Ness and the Cairngorms, while Fort William holds the key to Ben Nevis. Inland from Aberdeen lie Royal Deeside and the Spey Valley whisky heartland. The romantic Hebridean Islands are a ferry-ride from Oban, Mallaig or Ullapool.

A858   A857

LEWIS

HANDA ISLAND 40

B869

A837

A835

STORNOWAY

Loch Langava

A859

ULLAPOOL 39

A832

WESTERN ISLES 44

TARBERT

HARRIS

INVEREWE GARDENS 38

Loch Maree

A832

A865

NORTH UIST

LOCHMADDY

A855

A8..

WESTER ROSS 37

A832

BENBECULA

A850

ISLE OF SKYE 36

PORTREE

A890

A832

KYLE OF LOCHALSH

A863

SOUTH UIST

B8083

GLEN SHIEL 35

A851

0 kilometres 25

0 miles 25

BARRA

RUM, EIGG, MUCK AND CANNA 16

MALLAIG 17

COLL AND TIREE 10

ARDNAMURCHAN PENINSULA 15

ROAD TO THE ISLES TOUR 14

FORT WILLIAM 12 13

BEN NEVI

A849

11

GLENCOE

MULL 9

OBAN 8

IONA

A849

LOCH AWE 7

Firth of Lorne

A816

1 **INVERAR CASTLE**

AUCHINDRAIN MUSEUM 2

CRARAE GARDENS 3

Glasgo

JURA 4

A846

A83

A847

ISLAY 5

A846

A83

KINTYRE 6

CAMPBELTOWN

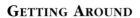

Highland cattle grazing on the Isle of Skye

Getting Around

There are no motorways in the region, though travel by car is made easy by a good system of A roads (major roads). Single-track roads predominate on the isles, which are served by a substantial ferry network and a bridge to Skye. The rail link ends to the west at Kyle of Lochalsh and to the north at Wick. There are regular flights from London to Inverness, Aberdeen and Wick.

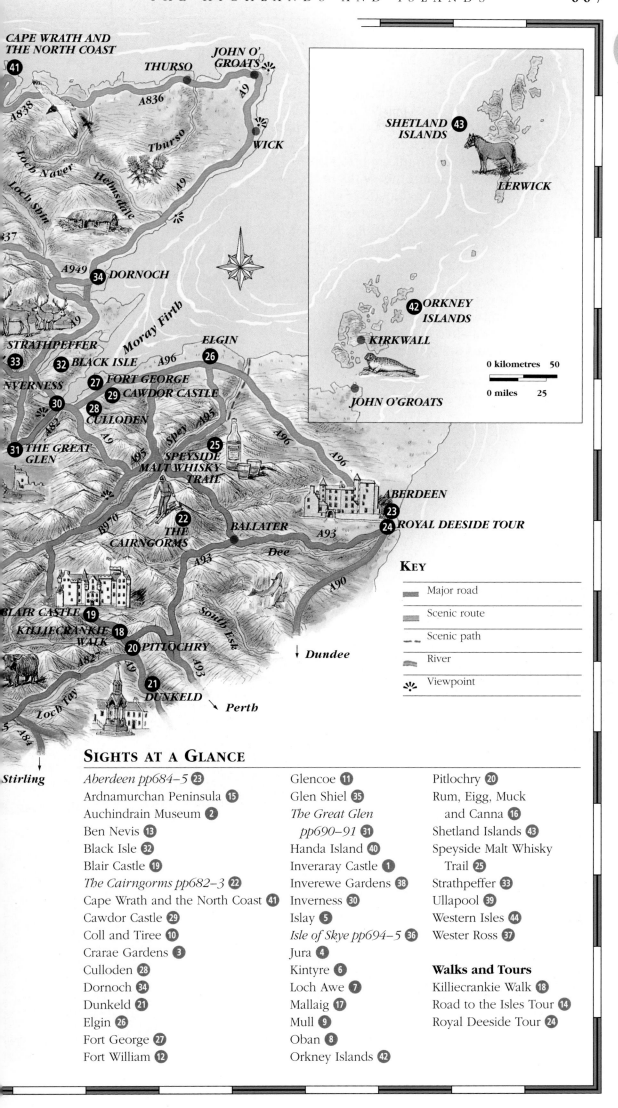

CAPE WRATH AND
THE NORTH COAST
41

THURSO

JOHN O'
GROATS

A836

A9

Thurso

WICK

Loch Naver

Helmsdale

Loch Shin

A838

37

A9

A949

34 DORNOCH

Moray Firth

ELGIN

STRATHPEFFER
33

BLACK ISLE
32

A96

26

INVERNESS

FORT GEORGE
27

CAWDOR CASTLE
29

30

28 CULLODEN

A82

A9

Spey

A95

31 THE GREAT
GLEN

A95

SPEYSIDE
MALT WHISKY
TRAIL
25

A96

A96

B970

22

THE
CAIRNGORMS

BALLATER

ABERDEEN

A93

23

24 ROYAL DEESIDE TOUR

Dee

A93

A90

BLAIR CASTLE
19

KILLIECRANKIE
WALK
18

South Esk

↓ *Dundee*

A82

20 PITLOCHRY

A9

A93

21
DUNKELD

↘ *Perth*

Loch Tay

5
A84

↓
Stirling

SHETLAND
ISLANDS
43

LERWICK

ORKNEY
42 ISLANDS

KIRKWALL

JOHN O'GROATS

0 kilometres 50

0 miles 25

KEY

▬▬▬	Major road
▬▬▬	Scenic route
– – –	Scenic path
∿	River
☀	Viewpoint

SIGHTS AT A GLANCE

Aberdeen pp684–5 **23**

Ardnamurchan Peninsula **15**

Auchindrain Museum **2**

Ben Nevis **13**

Black Isle **32**

Blair Castle **19**

The Cairngorms pp682–3 **22**

Cape Wrath and the North Coast **41**

Cawdor Castle **29**

Coll and Tiree **10**

Crarae Gardens **3**

Culloden **28**

Dornoch **34**

Dunkeld **21**

Elgin **26**

Fort George **27**

Fort William **12**

Glencoe **11**

Glen Shiel **35**

The Great Glen
pp690–91 **31**

Handa Island **40**

Inveraray Castle **1**

Inverewe Gardens **38**

Inverness **30**

Islay **5**

Isle of Skye pp694–5 **36**

Jura **4**

Kintyre **6**

Loch Awe **7**

Mallaig **17**

Mull **9**

Oban **8**

Orkney Islands **42**

Pitlochry **20**

Rum, Eigg, Muck
and Canna **16**

Shetland Islands **43**

Speyside Malt Whisky
Trail **25**

Strathpeffer **33**

Ullapool **39**

Western Isles **44**

Wester Ross **37**

Walks and Tours

Killiecrankie Walk **18**

Road to the Isles Tour **14**

Royal Deeside Tour **24**

The Munros

Scottish Mountaineering Club emblem

ABOUT 278 MOUNTAINS in Scotland rise above 915 m (3,000 ft). These are called Munros in honour of Sir Hugh Munro, a founder member of the Scottish Mountaineering Club. Munro listed the peaks in the Club's journal in 1891, and almost single-handedly started a new sport. Reverend AE Robertson was the first person to climb all the Munros, finishing in 1901. Thousands followed in his footsteps, and Munro bagging is now a major activity. One of the delights of climbing Munros is their variety – from the peaks of Skye to the mass of the Cairngorm plateau and the rounded Perthshire hills.

***Sir Hugh Munro**, in the kilt, is photographed at an early meet of the Scottish Mountaineering Club in 1891.*

Mountain peaks that are less than 915 m (3,000 ft) high are not Munros.

SISTERS OF KINTAIL

One of the finest mountain views in all of Scotland is the snow-capped peaks of the Five Sisters of Kintail *(see p693)*, three of which can be seen from the Mam Ratagan pass. The Sisters rise above Glen Shiel and their full traverse is one of the hardest hillwalks in Scotland. The smallest of the Sisters is not a Munro.

Loch Duich

***The face of Buachaille Etive Mor** (Great Herdsman of Etive) holds some severe climbs, but the long ridge south of the main summit, Stob Dearg, offers a superb day's walk.*

Ratagan is a small settlement on the south side of Loch Duich.

***Liathach**, (The Grey One) is seen over Loch Clair in Torridon. These hills contain some of the oldest rock in Scotland. Liatach is a tough climb, but the sea view from its summit ridge is worth the effort.*

***The River Cononish**, seen from Ben Lui (Peak of Calves), near Tyndrum, Perthshire. Ben Lui is one of a group of four Munros that are often climbed in one day.*

Walking in the Munros is a joy all year round, whether you stay in the glens or head for the heights. Apart from the Munros, there are many fine lower hills that are well worth exploring.

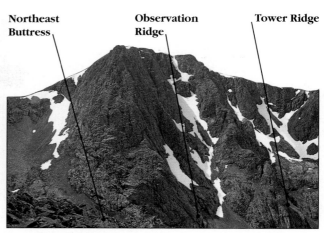

Northeast Buttress

Observation Ridge

Tower Ridge

Ben Nevis is Britain's highest peak at 1,344 m (4,406 ft). Its rugged north face holds a series of gullies and buttresses that provide classic climbing routes.

Sgurr nan Saighead 929 m (3,047 ft)

Sgurr Fhuaran 1,068 m (3,503 ft)

Sgurr na Carnach 1,002 m (3,286 ft)

The mighty rock buttresses of Slioch soar above Loch Maree. The loch, once a favourite of Queen Victoria, takes its name from the Celtic saint Maelrubha.

SAFETY

Waterproofs, warm clothes, a hat and gloves should be taken on any walk in the Munros. If you are walking in winter conditions you should also take an ice pick and crampons. Proper walking boots should always be worn. Plan your route in advance, and have an alternative ready in case conditions deteriorate – the weather can change rapidly at any time of year. Solo walkers should leave word with someone as to where they are going and a likely time of return.

Sgurr nan Gillean (Peak of the Young Men) is in the Cuillin range on Skye. The peaks in this area have been the training ground for some of the world's top mountaineers.

Climbers in Glencoe

Inveraray Castle ❶

Inveraray, Argyll & Bute. 🚉 *Arrochar, then bus.* 📞 *(01499) 302203.* 🅾 *Apr–Jun, Sep–Oct: Sat–Thu; Jul–Aug: daily.* 🅾 📷 ♿ *limited.*

The pinnacled Gothic exterior of Inveraray Castle

T HIS MULTI-TURRETED mock Gothic palace is the family home of the powerful Clan Campbell, who have been the Dukes of Argyll since 1701. It was built in 1745 by architects Roger Morris and William Adam on the site and ruins of a 15th-century castle. The conical towers were added later, after a fire in 1877.

The magnificent interiors, designed by Robert Mylne in the 1770s, form a backdrop to such treasures as Regency furniture, a huge collection of Oriental and European porcelain and portraits by Ramsay, Gainsborough and Raeburn. One of the most impressive displays is the Armoury Hall; the Campbells collected early weaponry to fight the Jacobite rebels. In the stables, the Combined Operations Museum commemorates the 250,000 allied troops who trained at Inveraray during World War II.

Auchindrain Museum ❷

Inveraray, Argyll & Bute. 📞 *(01499) 500235.* 🚌 *Inveraray, then bus.* 🅾 *Apr–Sep: daily.* 🅾 ♿ *limited.*

T HE FIRST OPEN-AIR museum in Scotland, Auchindrain illuminates the working lives of the kind of farming community typical of the Highlands until the late 19th century. Constituting a township of some 20 thatched cottages, the site was communally farmed by its tenants until the last one retired in 1962. Visitors can wander through the houses, most of which combine living space, kitchen and a cattle shed

all under one roof. They are furnished with box beds and rush lamps, and edged by herb gardens. These homes of Auchindrain are a truly fascinating memorial to a time before the Highland farmers made the transition from subsistence to commercial farming.

A traditional crofter's plough at the Auchindrain Museum

Crarae Gardens ❸

Crarae, Argyll & Bute. 📞 *Easter–Oct: (01546) 886614; Nov–Mar: (01546) 886388.* 🚌 *Inveraray, then bus.* 🅾 *daily.* 🅾 📷 *by appointment.* ♿ *limited.* www.crarae-gardens.ork

W IDELY CONSIDERED the most beguiling of the many gardens of the West Highlands, the Crarae Gardens *(see also pp576–7)* were created in the 1920s by Lady Grace Campbell. She was the aunt of explorer Reginald Farrer, whose specimens from Tibet were the beginnings of a collection of exotic plants. The gardens now

resemble a Himalayan ravine, nourished by the warmth of the Gulf Stream and the high rainfall of the region. Although many unusual Himalayan rhododendrons flourish here, the gardens are also home to exotic plants from Tasmania, New Zealand and the United States. Great plant collectors still contribute to the gardens, which are at their best in late spring.

Jura ❹

Argyll & Bute. 🏠 *250.* ⛴ *from Kennacraig to Islay, Islay to Jura.* ℹ *Bowmore (01496) 810254.*

B ARREN, MOUNTAINOUS and overrun by red deer, the Isle of Jura has only one road, which connects the single village of Craighouse to the Islay ferry. Though walking is restricted from August to October during the stalking (deer-hunting) season, Jura offers superb hill-walking, especially on the slopes of the three main peaks known as the Paps of Jura. The tallest of these is Beinn An Oir at 784 m (2,572 ft). Beyond the northern tip of the isle are the notorious whirlpools of Corryvreckan, virtually impossible to see. The author George Orwell, who came to the island to write his final novel, *1984*, nearly lost his life here in 1946 when he fell into the water. A legend tells of Prince

Lagavulin distillery, producer of one of Scotland's finest malts, on Islay

Mist crowning the Paps of Jura, seen at sunset across the Sound of Islay

Breackan who was drowned in his attempt to win the hand of a princess. He tried to keep his boat anchored in the whirlpool for three days, held by ropes made of hemp, wool and maidens' hair, until one rope, containing the hair of an unfaithful girl, finally broke.

Islay ⑤

Argyll & Bute. 🏚 *3,500.* ⚓ *from Kennacraig.* ℹ *Bowmore (01496) 810254.*

THE MOST SOUTHERLY of the Western Isles, Islay (pronounced 'Eyeluh') is the home of such respected Highland single malt whiskies as Lagavulin and Laphroaig. Most of the island's distilleries produce heavily-peated malts with a distinctive tang of the sea. The Georgian village of Bowmore has the island's oldest distillery and a circular church designed to minimize the Devil's possible lurking-places. The **Museum of Islay Life** in Port Charlotte contains a wealth of fascinating information concerning the island's social and natural history. Eleven kilometres (7 miles) east of Port Ellen stands the Kildalton Cross. A block of local green stone adorned with Old Testament scenes, it is one of the most impressive 8th-century

Celtic crosses in Britain. Worth a visit for its archaeological and historical interest is the medieval stronghold of the Lords of the Isles, **Finlaggan**, which is under excavation. Islay's superb beaches support a variety of bird life, some of which can be seen at the Royal Society for the Protection of Birds (RSPB) reserve at Gruinart.

🏛 Museum of Islay Life

Port Charlotte. 📞 *(01496) 850358.* ⭕ *Easter–Oct: daily.* 📷 ♿

Kintyre ⑥

Argyll & Bute. 🏚 *8,000.* 🚉 *Oban.* 🚌 *Campbeltown.* ℹ *Campbeltown (01586) 552056.*

A LONG, NARROW PENINSULA stretching far south of Glasgow, Kintyre has superb views across to the islands of Gigha, Islay and Jura. The 14 km (9 mile) Crinan Canal, which opened in 1801, is a

delightful inland waterway and its 15 locks bustle with pleasure craft in the summer. The town of Tarbert (meaning "isthmus" in Gaelic) takes its name from the neck on which it stands, which is narrow enough to drag a boat across, between the waters of Loch Fyne and West Loch Tarbert. This feat was first achieved by the Viking King Magnus Barfud who, in 1198, was granted by treaty as much land as he could sail around.

Travelling further south past Campbeltown, the B842 road ends at the headland known as the Mull of Kintyre, which was made famous when former Beatle Paul McCartney commercialized a traditional pipe tune of the same name. Westward from Kintyre lies the isle of Rathlin. It is here that Robert the Bruce learned patience in his constant struggles against the English by observing a spider weaving an elaborate web in a cave.

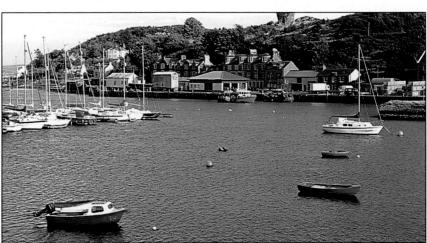

Sailing boats moored at Tarbert harbour, Kintyre

Loch Awe ⑦

Argyll. ⇄ ⊟ *Dalmally.* ⅰ *Inveraray (01499) 302063.*

ONE OF THE longest freshwater lochs in Scotland, Loch Awe stretches 40 km (25 miles) across a glen in the southwestern Highlands. A short drive east from the town of Lochawe are the remains of **Kilchurn Castle**, abandoned after being struck by lightning in the 18th century. Dwarfing the castle is Ben Cruachan. The huge summit of 1,125 m (3,695 ft) can be reached by the narrow Pass of Brander, where Robert the Bruce fought the Clan MacDougal in 1308. Near the village of Taynuilt, the preserved Lorn Furnace at Bonawe is a reminder of the iron-smelting industry that destroyed much of the area's woodland in the last centuries.

On the A816, to the south of the loch, is **Kilmartin House**. The museum here displays artifacts from local prehistoric sites, as well as reconstructions of boats, utensils and jewellery, providing a vivid glimpse of life in prehistoric Scotland.

Ⅲ Kilmartin House
Kilmartin. 【 *(01546) 510278.*
◯ *daily.* 🚫 ♿ www.kht.org.uk

McCaig's Tower looming over the houses and fishing boats of Oban

Oban ⑧

Argyll. 🏠 *8,500.* ⇄ ⊟ ⛴ ⅰ *Argyll Square (01631) 563122.*

KNOWN AS THE "Gateway to the Isles", this bustling port on the Firth of Lorne commands fine views of the Argyll coast. Shops crowd the seafront around the "little bay" which gives Oban its name, and fresh fish is always for sale on the busy pier. Regular ferries leave for Mull, Coll, Tiree, Barra, South Uist, Islay, Colonsay and Lismore, making Oban one of the most visited places on the west coast.

Built on a steep hill, the town is dominated by the immense **McCaig's Tower**, an eccentric Colosseum-like structure built in the 1800s. Other major landmarks are the pink granite cathedral and the 600-year-old ruined keep, **Dunollie Castle**, once the northern outpost of the Dalriadic Scots. Among Oban's other attractions are working centres for glass and pottery, and Oban Distillery, producers of fine malt whisky.

Early in August yachts converge on the town for West Highland Week, while at the end of the month, Oban's Highland Games take place. Nearby Kilmore, Taynuilt and Tobermory, on Mull, also host summer Highland Games.

ENVIRONS: A few miles north of Oban, off the A85, is the 13th-century **Dunstaffnage Castle** where Flora MacDonald was briefly imprisoned for helping Bonnie Prince Charlie escape in 1746. Further north at Barcaldine is **Oban Sealife Centre**, where panoramic aquariums allow you to view all manner of creatures swimming underwater. The **Rare Breeds Park**, situated 3 km (2 miles) south of Oban, has unusual breeds of farm animals such as Soay and Jacobs sheep, as well as shaggy Highland cattle. At Kilninver, **A World in Miniature** houses a collection of over 50 dolls' houses, some with interiors by Charles Rennie Mackintosh *(see p655)*.

Further south is **Arduaine Garden**, noted for its spectacular displays and for the diverse varieties of rhododendrons and azaleas that come into bloom in late spring.

♟ Dunstaffnage Castle
Connel. 【 *(01631) 562465.*
◯ *daily.* ⬤ *Oct–Mar: Thu pm & Fri.*
🚫 🔓

♙ Oban Sealife Centre
Barcaldine, near Connel. 【 *(01631) 720386.* ◯ *daily.* 🚫 ♿

♙ Rare Breeds Park
New Barren. 【 *(01631) 770608.*
◯ *Apr–Oct: daily.* 🚫 ♿

Ⅲ A World in Miniature
Kilninver. 【 *(01852) 316202.*
◯ *Easter–Sep: daily.* 🚫 ♿

♣ Arduaine Garden
(NTS) Kilmelford. 【 *(01852) 200366.*
◯ *daily.* 🚫 ♿ 🔓 *by appointment.*

The ruins of Kilchurn Castle on the shore of Loch Awe

The picturesque kaleidoscope of houses in Tobermory, one of Mull's most favoured tourist stops

Mull ⑨

Argyll. 🏘 2,800. ⛴ from Oban, Lochaline and Kilchoan; from Fionnphort, on Mull, to Iona. 🛈 Tobermory (01688) 302182; Craignure (01680) 812377.

THE LARGEST OF the Inner Hebridean islands, Mull features rough moorlands, the rocky peak of Ben More and a splendid beach at Calgary. Most roads follow the coastline, affording wonderful sea-views. From Craignure, the Mull and West Highland Railway offers a short trip to the baronial **Torosay Castle**. The gardens are lined with statues, and inside is a wealth of 19th-century paintings and furniture.

On a promontory to the east lies the 13th-century **Duart Castle**, home of the chief of Clan Maclean. You can visit the Banqueting Hall, State Rooms and the dungeons that once held prisoners from a Spanish Armada galleon, sunk in 1588 by one Donald Maclean. At the northern end of Mull is the town of **Tobermory**, with its brightly coloured buildings along the seafront. Built as a fishing village in 1788, it is now a popular harbour for yachts.

ENVIRONS: The small and very beautiful island of **Iona** is one of the biggest attractions on Scotland's west coast. A restored abbey stands on the site where Irish missionary St Columba began his crusade in 563 and made Iona "the Cradle of Christianity" in Europe. In the abbey grave-yard, 48 Scottish kings are said to be buried. During the summer months the abbey has a large influx of visitors.

If the weather is fine, make a trip to **Fingal's Cave** on the Isle of Staffa. One of Scotland's natural wonders, the cave is surrounded by "organ pipes" of basalt, the inspiration for Mendelssohn's *Hebrides Overture*. Boat trips run there from Fionnphort and Ulva, and to the seven **Treshnish Isles**. These uninhabited isles are a sanctuary for thousands of sea-birds, including puffins, razor-bills, kittiwakes and skuas. Dutchman's Cap is the most distinctive in shape, but Lunga is the main stop for tour boats.

🏰 Torosay Castle
Near Craignure. 📞 (01680) 812421. **Castle** ⬜ Easter–mid-Oct: daily. 🎫 **Gardens** ⬜ daily. 📷 ♿ gardens.
🏰 Duart Castle
Off A849, near Craignure. 📞 (01680) 812309. ⬜ May–mid-Oct: daily. 📷
🐦 Fingal's Cave and Treshnish Isles
⛴ Easter–Oct. 📞 (01688) 400242. Timetable varies, call for details. 📷

Coll and Tiree ⑩

Argyll. 🏘 950. ⛴ from Oban. ✈ from Glasgow to Tiree only. 🛈 Oban (01631) 563122.

THESE LOW, FERTILE islands are the most westerly in the Inner Hebrides and, despite frequent notices of winter gale warnings, record higher hours of sunshine than the rest of Britain. Predominantly crofting communities, they offer beautiful beaches and impressive surf. Tiree's soil is 60 per cent shell sand, so no trees can grow. In spring, both islands are ablaze with wild flowers.

Breacachadh Castle, the restored 15th-century home of Clan Maclean until 1750, overlooks a bay in south Coll but is not open to the public. Tiree has two free museums, the **Sandaig Thatched House Museum**, with items from life in the late 19th and early 20th centuries, and the **Skerryvore Lighthouse Museum** in Hynish – the lighthouse stands 20 km (12 miles) offshore.

A traditional croft building on the island of Coll

The Three Sisters, Glencoe, rising majestically in the late autumn sunshine

Glencoe ⑪

Lochaber. ⚞ *Fort William.*
🚌 *Glencoe.* ℹ️ *NTS Visitor Centre, Ballachulish (01855) 811296.*
◐ *Mar–Oct: daily.* 🈂️ ♿

R ENOWNED for its awesome scenery and savage history, Glencoe was compared by Dickens to "a burial ground of a race of giants". The precipitous cliffs of Buachaille Etive Mor and the knife-edged ridge of Aonach Eagach present a formidable challenge even to experienced mountaineers.

Against a backdrop of craggy peaks and the tumbling River Coe, the Glen offers superb hill-walking. Stout footwear, waterproofs and attention to safety warnings are essential. Details of routes, ranging from the easy half-hour between the NTS Visitor Centre and Signal Rock (from which the signal was given to commence the massacre) to a stiff 10-km (6-mile) haul up the Devil's Staircase can be had from the Visitor Centre. Guided walks are offered in summer by the NTS Ranger Service. East of

Glencoe lies Rannoch Moor, one of the emptiest areas in Britain. A dramatic way to view it is from the chairlift at the **Glencoe Ski Centre**.

To the southwest, a road leads through steep-sided Glen Etive to the coast near Oban. Winding round the many sea lochs, this road crosses the Appin Peninsula and gives a grand view of Castle Stalker (private).

At the Ballachulish Bridge a side road branches to Kinlochleven. This village, at the head of a long attractive loch, combines two contrasting images of dramatic mountains and an austere aluminium works.

⚡ **Glencoe Ski Centre**
Kingshouse, Glencoe. 📞 *(01855) 851226.* ◐ *daily.* 🈂️ ♿ *limited.*

Fort William ⑫

Lochaber. 👥 *11,000.* ⚞ 🚌
ℹ️ *Cameron Sq (01397) 703781.*

F ORT WILLIAM, one of the major towns on the west coast, is noted not for its looks but for its location at the foot of Ben Nevis. The **Jacobite Steam Train** runs the magical route from here to Mallaig (*see p679*), as do ordinary trains.

🚂 **Jacobite Steam Train**
⚞ *Fort William.* 📞 *(01397) 703791. Departs 10:20am late-Jun–Sep: Mon–Fri; also Sun late-Jul–early Sep.*

THE MASSACRE OF GLENCOE

In 1692, the chief of the Glencoe MacDonalds was five days late in registering an oath of submission to William III, giving the government an excuse to root out a nest of Jacobite supporters. For ten days 130 soldiers, captained by Robert Campbell, were hospitably entertained by the unsuspecting MacDonalds. At dawn on 13 February, in a terrible breach of trust, the soldiers fell on their hosts, killing some 38 MacDonalds. Many more died in their wintry mountain hideouts. The massacre, unsurprisingly, became a political scandal, though there were to be no official reprimands for three years.

Detail of *The Massacre of Glencoe* by James Hamilton

◁ **Sunset over Eilean Donan Castle (Five Sisters region), which is connected to the mainland by a causeway**

Ben Nevis ⑬

Lochaber. ⇄ *Fort William.* 🚌 *Glen Nevis.* ℹ️ *Ionad Nibheis Visitor Centre, Glen Nevis (01397) 705922.* ◐ *Easter–Oct: daily.* ♿

W ITH ITS SUMMIT in cloud for about nine days out of ten, and capable of developing blizzard conditions at any time of the year, Britain's highest mountain is a mishmash of metamorphic and volcanic rocks. The sheer northeastern face poses a technical challenge to experienced rock climbers. By contrast, thousands of visitors each year make their way to the peak via a relatively gentle, but long and stony, western path. Motorbikes, even cars, have ascended via this path, and runners pound up and down it during the annual Ben Nevis

Ben Nevis as seen from the northwest

Race. On one of the rare fine days, visitors who make their way to the summit will be rewarded with breathtaking views. On a cloudy day, a walk through the lush landscape of

Glen Nevis may be more rewarding than making an ascent, which will reveal little more at the summit than a ruined observatory and memorials testifying to the tragic deaths of walkers and climbers, either from exposure or from falls.

To the north of Ben Nevis, the **Nevis Range Gondola** provides access to a ski centre, restaurant and other tourist facilities, all situated at 650 m (2,130 ft).

🚠 **Nevis Range Gondola**
Off A82, Torlundy. 📞 *(01397) 705825.* ◐ *mid-Dec–mid-Oct: daily.*

CLIMBING BEN NEVIS

The main path up Ben Nevis, called the Old Bridle Path, starts in Glen Nevis. Numerous visitors each year are lulled into a false sense of security by mild weather conditions in the Glen, occasionally with fatal results. You must wear stout footwear (not trainers) and take hat and gloves and enough layers of clothing to allow for sub-zero temperatures at the top, even on a summer day. Also take plenty of food and drink, and an Ordnance Survey map and compass even if you think you won't need them. It is amazingly easy to lose the path in cloudy or snowy conditions, especially when starting the descent.

TIPS FOR WALKERS

Starting Point ①: *Visitor Centre.*
Starting Point ②: *Achintee.*
Starting Point ③: *400 m (440 yds) beyond campsite (very limited parking).*
Length: *16 km (10 miles); 6–8 hours average for round trip.*
Weather Information: *Metcall (0891) 500441.*
Level: *moderate difficulty on a dry day with broken cloud, but prone to rapid weather change; extremely difficult in snow.*

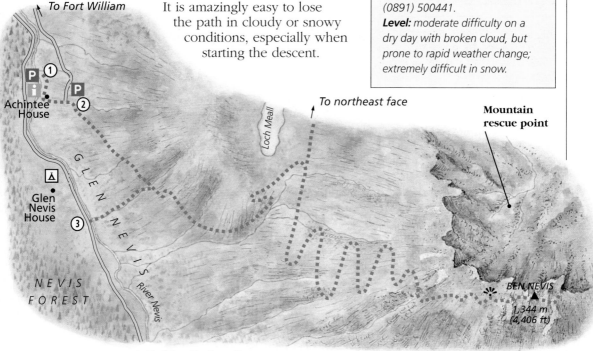

KEY

▪▪ Old Bridle Path
— Minor road
Ⓐ Camping
🔆 Viewpoint
Ⓟ Parking
ℹ️ Visitor centre

0 metres   1,000
0 yards   1,000

Road to the Isles Tour ⑭

T HIS SCENIC ROUTE goes past vast mountain corridors, breathtaking beaches of white sand and tiny villages to the town of Mallaig, one of the ferry ports for the isles of Skye, Rum, Eigg, Muck and Canna. In addition to stunning scenery, the area is steeped in Jacobite history *(see p689)*.

TIPS FOR DRIVERS

Tour length: 72 km (45 miles).
Stopping-off points: Glenfinnan NTS Visitors' Centre (01397 722-250) explains the Jacobite risings and serves refreshments; the Arisaig House Hotel in Beasdale serves excellent Scottish food.

Mallaig ⑦
The Road to the Isles ends at Mallaig, an active little fishing port with a very good harbour and one of the ferry links to the Isle of Skye *(see pp694–5)*.

Morar ⑥
The road continues through Morar, renowned for its white sands, and Loch Morar, rumoured to be the home of a 12-m (40-ft) monster known as Morag.

Prince's Cairn ⑤
The road crosses the Ardnish Peninsula to Loch Nan Uamh, where a cairn marks the spot from which Bonnie Prince Charlie left for France in 1746.

Ardnamurchan Peninsula ⑮

Argyll. 🚢 *from Fishnish, Tobermory (Mull) to Kilchoan.* ℹ️ *Kilchoan (01972) 510222; Fort William (01397) 703781.*

T HIS PENINSULA and the adjacent areas of Moidart and Morvern are some of the west coast's best-kept secrets. They are characterized by a sinuous coastline, rocky mountains and beaches. Some of the best beaches are found at the tip of the peninsula, the most westerly point of mainland Britain.
The **Ardnamurchan Point Visitor Centre** at Kilchoan explores the history of lighthouses and light-keeping, and at Glenmore you can visit the award-winning **Ardnamurchan Natural History Centre**. The centre has encouraged wildlife to inhabit its "living building", and wild red deer can even graze on its turf roof. An enchanting wooded road runs from Salen to Strontian, or you can go north to Acharacle.

A view from Roshven, near Arisaig, across to the islands of Eigg and Rum

The **Mingarry Museum** is dedicated to poaching and illicit whisky distilling.

ℹ️ **Ardnamurchan Point Visitor Centre**
Kilchoan. 📞 *(01972) 510210.* ⭕ *Apr–Oct: daily.* 🅿️ ♿
🏛️ **Ardnamurchan Natural History Centre**
Glenmore. 📞 *(01972) 500254.* ⭕ *Apr–Oct: daily.* 🅿️ *exhibition only.* ♿
🏛️ **Mingarry Museum**
Mingarry. 📞 *(01967) 431662.* ⭕ *Easter–Sep: Mon–Sat.* 🅿️ ♿ *limited.*

Rum, Eigg, Muck and Canna ⑯

Small Isles. 👥 *150.* 🚢 *from Mallaig or Arisaig.* ♿ *Canna only.* ℹ️ *Mallaig (01687) 462170.*

E ACH OF THE four "small isles" has an individual character and atmosphere, but shares a sense of tranquillity. Canna is a narrow island surrounded by cliffs and has a scattering of unworked archaeological sites.

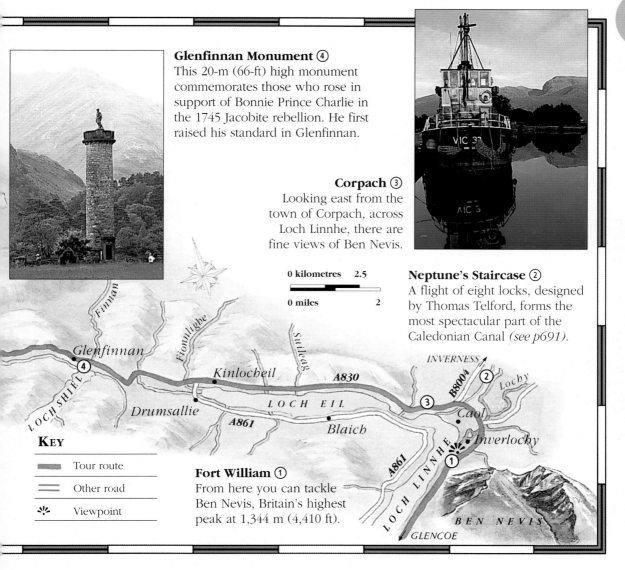

Glenfinnan Monument ④
This 20-m (66-ft) high monument commemorates those who rose in support of Bonnie Prince Charlie in the 1745 Jacobite rebellion. He first raised his standard in Glenfinnan.

Corpach ③
Looking east from the town of Corpach, across Loch Linnhe, there are fine views of Ben Nevis.

0 kilometres 2.5

0 miles 2

Neptune's Staircase ②
A flight of eight locks, designed by Thomas Telford, forms the most spectacular part of the Caledonian Canal *(see p691)*.

KEY
- Tour route
- Other road
- Viewpoint

Fort William ①
From here you can tackle Ben Nevis, Britain's highest peak at 1,344 m (4,410 ft).

Once owned by Gaelic scholar John Lorne Campbell, it now belongs to the National Trust for Scotland. It has few inhabitants and little accommodation.

Eigg is the most varied of the four islands. Dominated by the distinctive sugarloaf hill, the Sgurr of Eigg, it has a glorious beach with "singing sands" that make odd noises when moved by feet or by the wind. Here the islanders symbolize the spirit of community land ownership, having successfully led a high-profile campaign to buy their island from an unpopular landlord.

Muck takes its name from the Gaelic for "pig", which it is said to resemble in shape. The smallest of the islands, but no less charming, it is owned by a family who runs a farm and a hotel. Rum

is the largest and most magnificent island, with scabrous peaks that bear Norse names and are home to an unusual colony of Manx shearwater birds. The island's rough tracks make it best suited to the active visitor. Now owned by Scottish Natural Heritage and a centre for red deer research, it previously belonged to the wealthy Bullough family who built

Colourful fishing boats in Mallaig harbour

Kinloch Castle. Its design and furnishings were revolutionary at the time and it remains a fascinating piece of design history.

⚓ Kinloch Castle
(01687) 462037. ◯ Apr–Oct: daily; Nov–Mar: call for details.

Mallaig ⑰

Lochaber. 980. from Ardvasar (Skye). (01687) 462170.

THE HEART OF Mallaig is its harbour, which has an active fishing fleet and ferries that serve the "small isles" and Skye. The atmosphere is rather more commercial than leisurely, but it is set in an area of outstanding beauty. In the village itself is **Mallaig Marine World**, which incorporates aquariums and a permanent fishery exhibition.

Mallaig Marine World
(01687) 462292. ◯ Mar–Oct: daily; Nov–Feb: Mon–Sat. ● late Jan. by appointment.

Killiecrankie Walk ⑱

In an area famous for its scenery and historical connections, this circular walk offers views that are typical to the Highlands. The route is fairly flat, though ringed by mountains, and meanders through a wooded gorge, passing the Soldier's Leap and a Victorian viaduct.

There are ideal picnic spots along the way, and the shores of man-made Loch Faskally are lined with beautiful trees. Returning along the River Tummel, the route crosses one of Queen Victoria's favourite Highland areas before it doubles back to complete the circuit.

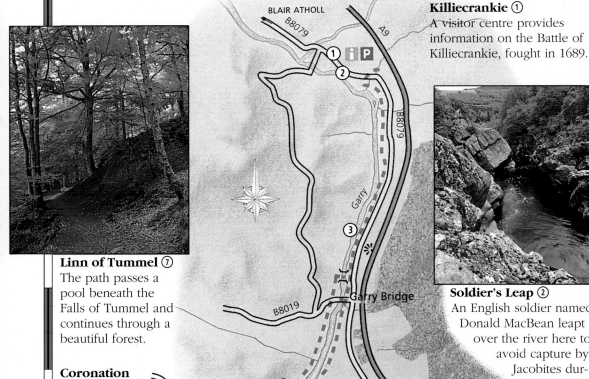

Killiecrankie ①
A visitor centre provides information on the Battle of Killiecrankie, fought in 1689.

Linn of Tummel ⑦
The path passes a pool beneath the Falls of Tummel and continues through a beautiful forest.

Coronation Bridge ⑥
Spanning the River Tummel, this footbridge was built in 1860 in honour of George IV.

Memorial Arch ⑤
Workers killed in the construction of the Clunie Dam are commemorated here.

Soldier's Leap ②
An English soldier named Donald MacBean leapt over the river here to avoid capture by Jacobites during the battle of 1689.

Killiecrankie Pass ③
This military road, built by General Wade in the 1600s, follows the gorge.

Clunie Foot Bridge ④
This bridge crosses the artificial Loch Faskally, created by the damming of the River Tummel for hydroelectric power in the 1950s.

Key

– –	Route
▤	Major road
▤	Minor road
▭	Narrow lane
✹	Viewpoint
P	Parking
i	Visitor centre

0 kilometres — 1
0 miles — 0.5

Tips for Walkers

Starting point: NTS Visitor Centre Killicrankie. ☎ (01796) 473233.
Getting there: Bus from Pitlochry or Aberfeldy.
Length: 10 km (6 miles).
Level: Very easy.

The distinctive white turrets and façade of the ducal Blair Castle

Blair Castle ⑲

Blair Atholl, Perthshire. ☎ *(01796) 481207.* ☒ *Blair Atholl.* ◯ *Apr–Oct: daily.* 🚫 🔋 ♿ *limited.*

THIS RAMBLING, turreted castle has been altered and extended so often in its 700-year history that it now provides a unique insight into the history and changing tastes of aristocratic life in the Highlands.

The elegant 18th-century wing, with its draughty passages hung with antlers, has a display that includes the gloves and pipe of Bonnie Prince Charlie *(see p695),* who spent two days here gathering support for a Jacobite uprising *(see p689).* Family portraits span 300 years, and include paintings by such masters as Johann Zoffany and Sir Peter Lely. Sir Edwin Landseer's *Death of a Hart in Glen Tilt* (1850) was painted nearby and hangs in the ballroom.

Queen Victoria visited the castle in 1844 and conferred on its owners, the Dukes of Atholl, the distinction of being allowed to maintain a private army. The Atholl Highlanders, as the men were christened, are still in existence today.

Pitlochry ⑳

Perthshire. 👥 *2,500.* ☒ 🚌 🛈 *22 Atholl Rd (01796) 472215.*

SURROUNDED BY the pine-forested hills of the central Highlands, Pitlochry became a famous town after Queen Victoria described it as one of the finest resorts in Europe.

In early summer, wild salmon leap up the ladder built into the Power Station Dam on their way to spawning grounds further up the river. The **Power Station Visitor Centre** outlines the hydro-electric scheme, which harnesses the waters of the River Tummel.

Blair Atholl Distillery is the home of Bell's whisky. Open for guided tours, the distillery gives visitors an insight into whisky making.

One of Scotland's most famous stages, the **Festival Theatre**, is located in Port-na-Craig. It operates a summer season, during which the programme of performances changes daily.

🏭 **Blair Atholl Distillery**
Perth Rd. ☎ *(01796) 472234.* ◯ *Easter–Sep: daily (Sun: pm); Oct–Easter: Mon–Fri.* 🚫 🔋 ♿ *limited.*

🎭 **Festival Theatre**
Port-na-Craig. ☎ *(01796) 472680.* ◯ *mid-May–Oct: daily.* 🚫 *for plays.* ♿ 🔋 www.pitlochry.org.uk

🛈 **Power Station Visitor Centre**
Port-na-Craig. ☎ *(01796) 473152.* ◯ *late Mar–Oct: daily.* 🚫 🔋

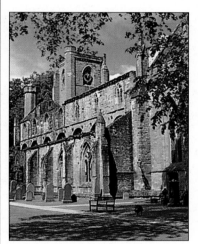

The ruins of Dunkeld Cathedral

Dunkeld ㉑

Tayside. 👥 *2,200.* ☒ *Birnam.* 🚌 🛈 *The Cross (01350) 727688.*

SITUATED BY the River Tay, this ancient and charming village was all but destroyed in the Battle of Dunkeld, a Jacobite defeat, in 1689. The **Little Houses** lining Cathedral Street were the first to be rebuilt, and remain fine examples of an imaginative restoration.

The sad ruins of the 14th-century **cathedral** enjoy an idyllic setting on shady lawns beside the Tay, against a backdrop of steep and wooded hills. The choir is used as the parish church, and its north wall contains a Leper's Squint (a little hole through which lepers could see the altar during mass). It was while on holiday in the countryside around Dunkeld that the children's author, Beatrix Potter, found the inspiration for her Peter Rabbit stories.

Salmon ladder at the Power Station Dam in Pitlochry

The Cairngorms ㉒

Wild goat

RISING TO A HEIGHT of 1,309 m (4,296 ft), the Cairngorm mountains form the highest landmass in Britain. Cairn Gorm itself is the site of one of Britain's first ski centres. A weather station at the mountain's summit provides regular reports, essential in an area known for sudden changes of weather. Walkers should be sure to follow the mountain code without fail. The chairlift that climbs Cairn Gorm affords superb views over the Spey Valley. Many estates in the valley have centres which introduce the visitor to Highland land use.

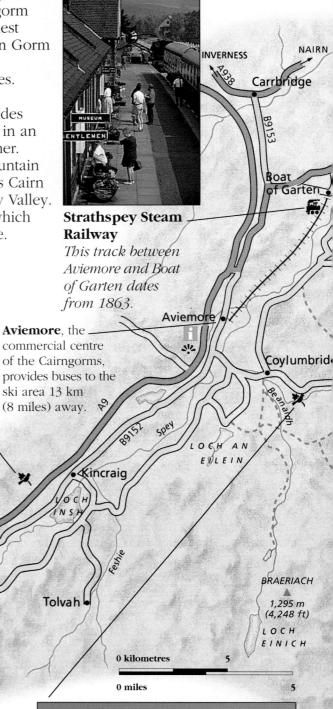

Strathspey Steam Railway
This track between Aviemore and Boat of Garten dates from 1863.

Aviemore, the commercial centre of the Cairngorms, provides buses to the ski area 13 km (8 miles) away.

Kincraig Highland Wildlife Park
Driving through this park, the visitor can see bison alongside bears, wolves and wild boar. All of these animals were once common in the Spey Valley.

The Cairngorms, viewed from Aviemore

Rothiemurchus Estate
Highland cattle can be seen among many other creatures at Rothiemurchus. A visitor centre provides guided walks and illustrates life on a Highland estate.

Loch Garten Nature Reserve

Ospreys now thrive in this reserve, which was established in 1959 to protect the first pair seen in Britain for 50 years.

GRANTOWN-ON-SPEY

A95

Nethy Bridge

B970

OCH ARTEN

The Cairngorm Reindeer Centre provides walks in the hills among Britain's only herd of reindeer.

Nethy

OCH ORLICH

P

CAIRN GORM

1,245 m
(4,084 ft)

LOCH AVON

BEN MACDHUI

1,309 m
(4,296 ft)

CAIRNGORM

MOUNTAINS

Ben MacDhui is Britain's second highest peak, after Ben Nevis.

Skiing

From the Coire na Ciste car park, a chairlift can be taken to the restaurant at the summit. There are 28 ski runs in all.

KEY

ℹ️	Tourist information
▬	Major road
▭	Minor road
▭	Narrow lane
- -	Footpath
☀️	Viewpoint

FLORA OF THE CAIRNGORMS

With mixed woodland at their base and the summits forming a sub-polar plateau, the Cairngorms present a huge variety of flora. Ancient Caledonian pines (once common in the area) survive in Abernethy Forest, while arctic flowers flourish in the heights.

The Cairngorm plateau holds little life except lichen (Britain's oldest plant), wood rush and cushions of moss campion, which is often completely covered with pink flowers.

Shady corries are important areas for alpine plants such as arctic mouse-ear, hare's foot sedge, mountain rock-cress and alpine speedwell.

Pinewoods occupy the higher slopes, revealing purple heather as they become sparser.

Mixed woodland covers the lower ground which is carpeted with heather and deergrass.

1,200 m
(3,950 ft)

1,000 m
(3,300 ft)

800 m
(2,650 ft)

600 m
(2,000 ft)

400 m
(1,300 ft)

200 m
(650 ft)

0 m
(0 ft)

An idealized section of the Cairngorm plateau

Aberdeen ㉓

Scotland's third largest city and Europe's offshore oil capital, Aberdeen has prospered since the discovery of oil in the North Sea in the early 1970s. The sea bed has now yielded 50 oilfields. Widely known as the Granite City, its forbidding and rugged outlines are softened by sumptuous year-round floral displays in the public parks and gardens, the Duthie Park Winter Gardens being the largest in Europe. The city harbour, one of Britain's most important fishing ports, is at its best early in the morning during the auctions at Scotland's largest fish market.

The spires of Aberdeen, rising behind the city harbour

Exploring Aberdeen

The city centre flanks the 1.5-km (1-mile) long Union Street, ending to the east at the Mercat Cross. The cross stands by Castlegate, the one-time site of the city castle, and now only a marketplace. From here, the cobbled Shiprow meanders southwest and passes Provost Ross's House on its way to the harbour. A bus can be taken 1.5 km (1 mile) north of the centre to Old Aberdeen, which, with its medieval streets and wynds (narrow, winding lanes), has the peaceful character of a separate village. Driving is restricted in some streets.

🏛 King's College

College Bounds, Old Aberdeen.
📞 *(01224) 273702.* ○ *daily.* ♿
Founded in 1495 as the city's first university, the college now has a visitor centre that provides details of its history. The interdenominational chapel, consecutively Catholic and Protestant in the past, has a distinctive lantern tower, rebuilt after a storm in 1633. Douglas Strachan's stained-glass windows add a modern touch to the interior, which contains a 1540 pulpit, later carved with heads of Stuart monarchs.

✝ St Andrew's Cathedral

King St. 📞 *(01224) 640119.* ○ *May–Sep: Mon–Sat.* ♿ 📷 *by arrangement.*
The Mother Church of the Episcopal Church in the United States, St Andrew's has a memorial to Samuel Seabury, the first Episcopalian bishop in the US, who was consecrated in Aberdeen in 1784. A series of coats of arms adorns the ceiling above the north and south aisles, contrasting colourfully with the white walls and pillars. They represent the American states and the Jacobite families of Aberdeenshire.

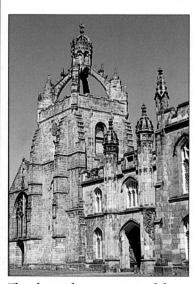

The elegant lantern tower of the chapel at King's College

🏛 Art Gallery

Schoolhill. 📞 *(01224) 646333*
○ *daily.* ♿ www.aberdeen.net.uk
Housed in a Neo-Classical building, the Art Gallery has a wide range of exhibitions, with an emphasis on modern works. A collection of Aberdonian silver is included among the decorative arts on the ground floor. A permanent collection of 18th- to 20th-century art features such names as Toulouse-Lautrec, Raeburn and Reynolds. Local granite merchant Alex Macdonald bequeathed a number of the works on display.

✝ Church of St Nicholas

George St. ○ *May–Sep: daily; Oct–Apr: Mon–Fri (am).* ♿
Founded in the 12th century, St Nicholas is Scotland's largest parish church. Though the present structure dates from 1752, many earlier relics can be seen inside. After damage during the Reformation, the interior was divided into two. A chapel in the East Church holds iron rings used to secure witches in the 17th century, while in the West Church there are embroidered panels attributed to Mary Jameson (1597–1644).

🏛 Maritime Museum

Shiprow. 📞 *(01224) 337700.*
○ *daily.* ♿
Overlooking the harbour is the Provost Ross's House, which dates back to 1593 and is one of the oldest residential buildings in town. The Maritime Museum housed here traces the history of Aberdeen's long seafaring tradition. The exhibitions cover numerous topics from shipwrecks, rescues and shipbuilding to models that illustrate the workings of the many oil installations situated off the east coast of Scotland.

✝ St Machar's Cathedral

The Chanonry. 📞 *(01224) 485988.*
○ *daily.* ♿ www.isb.net/stmachar
Dominating Old Aberdeen, the 15th-century St Machar's Cathedral is the oldest granite building in the city. The stonework of one arch dates back to the 14th century. The nave now serves as a parish church and its magnificent oak ceiling is adorned with the coats of arms of 48 popes, emperors and princes of Christendom.

PROVOST SKENE'S HOUSE

Guestrow. ☎ (01224) 641086. ☐ Mon–Sat. 🖼

Once the home of Sir George Skene, a 17th-century provost (mayor) of Aberdeen, the house was built in 1545 and remains one of the oldest houses in the city. Inside, period rooms span 200 years of design. The Duke of Cumberland stayed here during the weeks preceding the Battle of Culloden *(see p688)*.

VISITORS' CHECKLIST

Grampian. 👥 220,000.
✈ 13 km (8 miles) NW Aberdeen.
🚌 🚆 Guild St. ℹ Broad St (01224) 632727. ⚓ Thu, Fri, Sat.

The 18th-century Parlour, with its walnut harpsichord and covered fire-side chairs, was the informal room in which the family would have tea.

The Regency Room typifies early 19th-century elegance. A harp dating from 1820 stands by a Grecian-style sofa and a French writing table.

The Painted Gallery has one of Scotland's most important cycles of religious art. The panels are early 17th century, though the artist is unknown.

The 17th-century Great Hall contains heavy oak dining furniture. Provost Skene's wood-carved coat of arms hangs above the fireplace.

The Georgian Dining Room, with its Classical design, was the main formal room in the 16th century and still has its original flagstone floor.

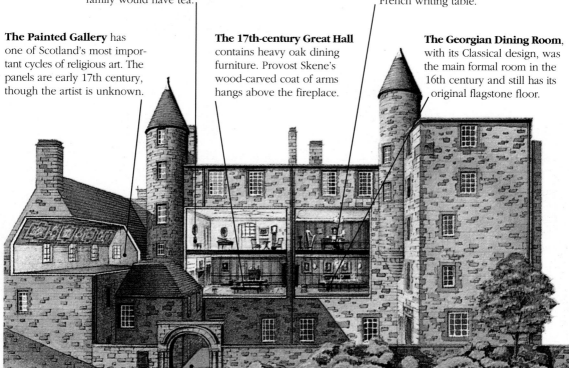

Entrance

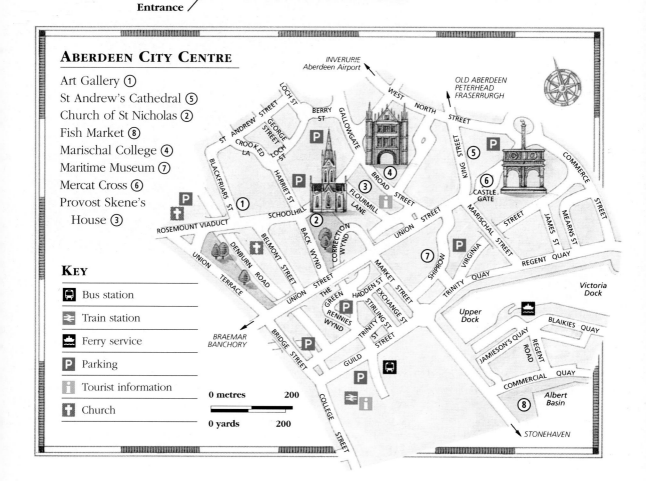

ABERDEEN CITY CENTRE

Art Gallery ①
St Andrew's Cathedral ⑤
Church of St Nicholas ②
Fish Market ⑧
Marischal College ④
Maritime Museum ⑦
Mercat Cross ⑥
Provost Skene's House ③

KEY

🚌 Bus station
🚆 Train station
⚓ Ferry service
🅿 Parking
ℹ Tourist information
✝ Church

0 metres   200
0 yards   200

Royal Deeside Tour ㉔

SINCE QUEEN VICTORIA's purchase of the Balmoral Estate in 1852, Deeside has been best known as the summer home of the British Royal Family, though it has been associated with royalty since the time of Robert the Bruce in the 1300s. This route follows the Dee, one of the world's most prolific salmon rivers, through some magnificent Grampian scenery.

Muir of Dinnet Nature Reserve ④
An information centre on the A97 provides an excellent place from which to explore this beautiful mixed woodland area, formed by the retreating glaciers of the last Ice Age.

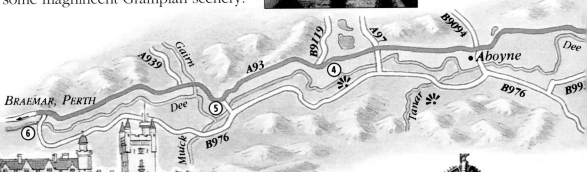

Balmoral ⑥
Bought by Queen Victoria for 30,000 guineas in 1852, after its owner choked to death on a fishbone, the castle was rebuilt in the Scottish Baronial style at Prince Albert's request.

Ballater ⑤
The old railway town of Ballater has royal warrants on many of its shop fronts. It grew as a 19th-century spa town, its waters reputedly providing a cure for tuberculosis.

Speyside Malt Whisky Trail ㉕

Grampian. ℹ *Elgin (01343) 542666.*

SUCH ARE THE climate and geology of the Grampian mountains and glens bordering the River Spey that half of Scotland's whisky distilleries are found on Speyside. They span a large area so a car is required. The signposted "Malt Whisky Trail" takes you to seven distilleries and one cooperage (a place where barrels are made), all with excellent visitor centres and tours of their premises.

There is no secret to whisky distilling: essentially barley is steeped in water and allowed to grow, a process called "malting"; the grains are then dried with peat smoke, milled, mixed with water and allowed to ferment; the frothy liquid goes through a double process of distillation. The final result is a raw, rough

Oak casks, in which the maturing whisky is stored at the distilleries

whisky that is then stored in old oak sherry casks for 3 to 16 years, during which time it mellows. Worldwide, an average of 30 bottles of Scotch whisky are sold every second.

The visitor centres at each Whisky Trail distillery provide similar, and equally good, guided tours of the workings and audio-visual displays of their individual histories. Their entry charges are usually redeemable against the purchase of a bottle of whisky. One visit to a single distillery can suffice, but a different slant on the process is given at the **Speyside Cooperage**. Here the visitor can learn about the making of the wooden casks that are eventually used to store the whisky.

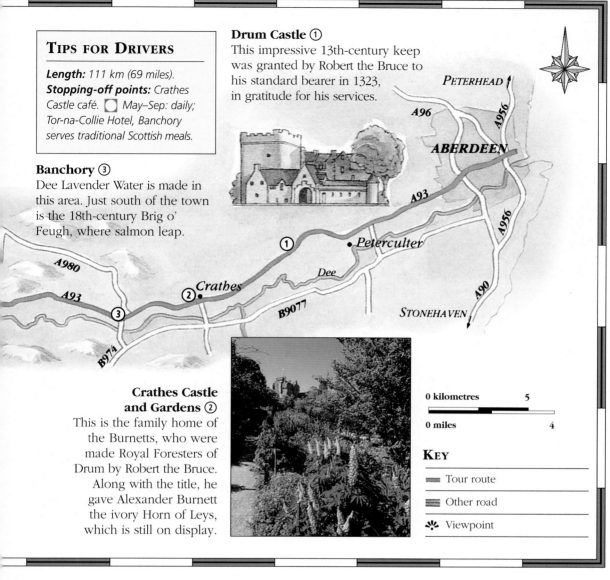

TIPS FOR DRIVERS

Length: *111 km (69 miles).*
Stopping-off points: *Crathes Castle café. ⃝ May–Sep: daily; Tor-na-Collie Hotel, Banchory serves traditional Scottish meals.*

Drum Castle ①
This impressive 13th-century keep was granted by Robert the Bruce to his standard bearer in 1323, in gratitude for his services.

Banchory ③
Dee Lavender Water is made in this area. Just south of the town is the 18th-century Brig o' Feugh, where salmon leap.

PETERHEAD
A96
ABERDEEN
A93
● Peterculter
Dee
Crathes
STONEHAVEN

Crathes Castle and Gardens ②
This is the family home of the Burnetts, who were made Royal Foresters of Drum by Robert the Bruce. Along with the title, he gave Alexander Burnett the ivory Horn of Leys, which is still on display.

0 kilometres   5
0 miles   4

KEY
━━ Tour route
━━ Other road
❋ Viewpoint

▲ Cardhu Distillery
Knockando. 📞 *(01340) 872550.*
⃝ *Jul–Sep: daily; Oct–Jun: Mon–Fri.*
▲ Dallas Dhu Distillery
Forres. 📞 *(01309) 676548.*
⃝ *Apr– Sep: daily; Oct–Mar: Sat–Thu.*
▲ Glenfarclas Distillery
Ballindalloch. 📞 *(01807) 500245.* ⃝
Mon–Fri (Jun–Sep: daily).
▲ Glenfiddich Distillery
Dufftown. 📞 *(01340) 820373.*
⃝ *Mon –Fri (Easter–mid-Oct: daily).*
▲ Glen Grant Distillery
Rothes. 📞 *(01542) 783303.* ⃝ *mid-Mar–Oct: daily.* limited.
▲ The Glenlivet Distillery
Glenlivet. 📞 *(01542) 783220.*
⃝ *mid-Mar–Oct: daily.*
limited.
▲ Speyside Cooperage
Craigellachie. 📞 *(01340) 871108.*
⃝ *Mon –Fri (Jun–Sep: Mon–Sat).*
limited.
▲ Strathisla Distillery
Keith. 📞 *(01542) 783044.*
⃝ *Feb–mid-Mar: Mon–Fri; mid-Mar–Nov: daily.* limited.

Elgin ㉖

Grampian. 👥 *25,000.* 🚆 🚌 ℹ
17 High St (01343) 542666. 🅿 *Sat.*

WITH ITS COBBLED market-place and crooked lanes, the popular town of Elgin still retains much of its medieval layout. The 13th-century **cathedral** ruins are all that remain of one of Scotland's architectural triumphs. Once known as the Lantern of the North, the cathedral was severely damaged in 1390 by the Wolf of Badenoch (the son of Robert II) in revenge for his excommunication by the Bishop of Moray. Further damage came in 1576 when the Regent Moray ordered the lead roofing to be stripped. Among the remains is a Pictish cross-slab in the nave and a basin where one of the town's benefactors, Andrew Anderson, was kept as a baby by his homeless mother. The **Elgin Museum** has anthropological

and geological displays, while the **Moray Motor Museum** has over 40 cars and motorbikes, dating back to 1904.

🏛 Elgin Museum
1 High St. 📞 *(01343) 543675.* ⃝
Easter–Oct: daily (Sun: pm).
🏛 Moray Motor Museum
Bridge St, Bishopmill. 📞 *(01343) 544933.* ⃝ *Easter–Oct: daily.*

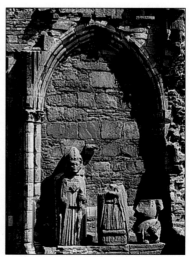

Details of the central tower of the 13th-century Elgin Cathedral

An aerial picture of Fort George, illustrating its imposing position

Fort George 27

Inverness. [📞] (01667) 462777. [🚆] [🚌] Inverness, Nairn. [◯] daily. [♻️] [🎫] [♿]

ONE OF THE FINEST examples of European military architecture, Fort George holds a commanding position on a windswept promontory jutting into the Moray Firth, ideally located to suppress the Highlands. Completed in 1769, the fort was built after the Jacobite risings to discourage further rebellion in the Highlanders, and has remained a military garrison ever since.

The **Regimental Museum** of the Queen's Own Highlanders is housed in the Fort. Some of the barrack rooms have been reconstructed to show the conditions of the common soldiers stationed here more than 200 years ago. The **Grand Magazine** contains an outstanding collection of arms and military equipment. Fort George's extensive battlements also make an excellent place from which to watch dolphins, which can be seen playing in the waters of the Moray Firth.

Culloden 28

(NTS) Inverness. [🚆] [🚌] Inverness.

A DESOLATE STRETCH of moorland, Culloden looks much as it did on 16 April 1746, the date of the last battle to be fought on British soil. Here the Jacobite cause, with the help of Bonnie Prince Charlie's

leadership (see p695), finally perished under the onslaught of nearly 9,000 Hanoverian troops, led by the Duke of Cumberland. All is explained, with audio-visual displays, in the excellent **NTS Visitor Centre** on the site.

ENVIRONS: Roughly 1.5 km (1 mile) east of Culloden are the outstanding Neolithic burial sites at **Clava Cairns**.

[ℹ️] **NTS Visitor Centre**
On the B9006 east of Inverness.
[📞] (01463) 790607. [◯] daily.
[●] Jan. [♻️] [♿]

Cawdor Castle 29

On B9090 (off A96). [📞] (01667) 404615. [🚆] Nairn, then bus or taxi. [🚌] from Inverness. [◯] May–mid-Oct: daily. [♻️] [♿] gardens and ground floor only.

WITH ITS TURRETED central tower, moat and drawbridge, Cawdor Castle is one of the most romantic stately homes in the Highlands. Though the castle is famed for being the 11th-century home of Shakespeare's tragic character Macbeth, and the scene of his murder of King Duncan, it is historically unproven that either figure came here.

An ancient holly tree preserved in the vaults is said to be the one under which, in 1372, Thane William's donkey, laden with gold, stopped for a rest during its master's search for a place to build a fortress. According to legend, this was how the site for the castle was chosen. Now, after 600 years of continuous occupation (it is still the home of

the Thanes of Cawdor) the house is a treasury of family history. It contains a number of rare tapestries and portraits by the 18th-century painters Joshua Reynolds (1723–92) and George Romney (1734–1802). Furniture in the Pink Bedroom and Woodcock Room includes work by the 18th-century designers Chippendale and Sheraton. In the Old Kitchen, the huge Victorian cooking range stands as a shrine to below-stairs drudgery. The castle's extensive grounds provide beautiful nature trails, as well as a nine-hole golf course.

The drawbridge on the eastern side of Cawdor Castle

Inverness 30

Highland. [🚶] 60,000. [🚆] [🚌] [ℹ️] Castle Wynd (01463) 234353.

IN THE HIGHLANDS, all roads lead to the region's "capital", Inverness, the centre of communication, commerce and administration for six million outlying acres and their scattered populations. Despite being the largest city in the

A contemporary picture, *The Battle of Culloden* (1746), by D Campbell

The red sandstone exterior of Inverness Castle high above the city centre, aglow in the light of the setting sun

north, it is more like a town in its atmosphere, with a compact and easily accessible centre. Although sadly defaced by modern architecture, Inverness earns a worthy reputation for its floral displays in summer, and for the River Ness, which flows through the centre and adds considerable charm. The river is frequented by salmon fishermen during the summer, even where it runs through the city centre. Holding the high ground above the city is **Inverness Castle**, a Victorian building of red sandstone, now used as the court house. Just below the castle, next to the tourist information office, is **Inverness Museum and Art Gallery,** which houses permanent and touring exhibitions and runs workshops for children. The main shopping area fans out in three directions from here and includes a lively pedestrian precinct where pipers and other musicians can be found busking.

Across the river is **Balnain House**, an innovative museum dedicated to Highland music. All aspects of the music are explained using recordings, and live sessions are held. Visitors can even have a shot at playing the bagpipes. Upstream from here, on the banks of the Ness, stands **Eden Court Theatre**, which has a varied programme of local and international performers.

Kilt maker with Royal Stuart tartan

Following the tree-lined banks of the river further upstream leads to the **Island Walks**, accessed by a pedestrian suspension bridge. This is an attractive and peaceful haven with a resident population of ducks. And beyond this, further upstream still, is **Inverness Sports Centre and Aquadome**, which offers swimming pools, spas and a variety of wild, spiralling flumes. Thomas Telford's Caledonian Canal (*see pp690–91*), constructed between 1804 and 1822, is still in constant use and can be viewed at Tomnahurich Bridge. From here, **Jacobite Cruises** runs regular summer cruises along the length of Loch Ness. These cruises are an excellent way to spend a

sunny afternoon. Inverness is an ideal base for touring the rest of the Highlands as it lies within easy reach of most of the region's best-known attractions, including the emotive battlesite of Culloden (*see pp618–19*), 8 km (5 miles) east.

🏛 **Inverness Museum and Art Gallery**
Castle Wynd. 📞 *(01463) 237114.*
🕐 *Mon–Sat.* ♿

🏛 **Balnain House**
40 Huntly St. 📞 *(01463) 715757.*
🕐 *May–Aug: daily; Sep–Apr: Mon–Sat.* 📷 ♿ *limited.*

🎭 **Eden Court Theatre**
Bishop's Rd. 📞 *(01463) 234234.* 📷 📷 ♿ www.edencourt.uk.com.

🏊 **Inverness Sports Centre and Aquadome**
Bught Park. 📞 *(01463) 667500.*
🕐 *daily.* 📷 ♿

🚢 **Jacobite Cruises**
Tomnahurich Bridge, Glenurquhart.
📞 *(01463) 233999.* 📷 ♿

THE JACOBITE MOVEMENT

The first Jacobites (mainly Catholic Highlanders) were the supporters of James VII of Scotland (James II of England) who was deposed by his Parliament in the "Glorious Revolution" of 1688. With the Protestant William of Orange on the throne, the Jacobites' desire to restore the Stuart monarchy led to the uprisings of 1715 and 1745. The first, in support of James VIII, the "Old Pretender", ended at the Battle of Sherrifmuir (1715). The failure of the second uprising, with the defeat at Culloden, saw the end of Jacobite hopes and led to the demise of the clan system and the suppression of Highland culture for more than a century.

James II, **by Samuel Cooper (1609–72)**

The Great Glen ③

FOLLOWING THE PATH of a geological fault, the Great Glen forms a scenic route from Inverness on the east coast to Fort William on the west. The glacial rift valley was created when the landmass split and moved 400 million years ago. A series of four lochs includes the famous Loch Ness, home of the elusive monster. The Caledonian Canal, built by Thomas Telford, provides a link between the lochs, and has been a shipping channel as well as a popular tourist route since 1822. Hiring a boat or taking a leisurely drive are ideal ways to view the Glen.

Common redpoll

THE GREAT GLEN

Spean Bridge is home to a Woollen Mill selling traditional knitwear and tweeds. Close to the village is the impressive Commando Memorial, a tribute to the local men who lost their lives in World War II.

Loch Lochy

Lochy is one of the four beautiful lochs of the Great Glen, formed by a fissure in the earth and erosion by glaciers. There are caves nearby where Bonnie Prince Charlie is said to have hidden after the Battle of Culloden.

STAR SIGHTS

★ **Loch Ness**

★ **Caledonian Canal**

Steall Waterfall

Located at the foot of the magnificent Ben Nevis, this impressive waterfall tumbles down into a valley of wild flowers. Found at the end of a walk through a dramatic gorge, this is the perfect place to picnic.

Loch Mullardoch

Kinlochourn

Loch Quoich

Loch Arkaig

Lochailort

A830

Loch Shiel

Invergar
South Lagg
Loch Loch
Spe Brid
FORT WILLIAM
Ben Nevis

A861
A82
Corran
Strontian
Ardgour
Onich
Glencoe
A861
A82
A884
Ballachulish
Loch Linnhe
Duror
A828
Port Appin

0 kilometres 10

0 miles 10

Ben Nevis (*see p677*) is Britain's highest mountain at 1,343 m (4,406 ft), but its broad, indefinable shape belies its immense size.

Fort Augustus is a pretty village situated at the southwestern end of Loch Ness. The base for boat cruises around the loch, it is also the site of a Benedictine Abbey.

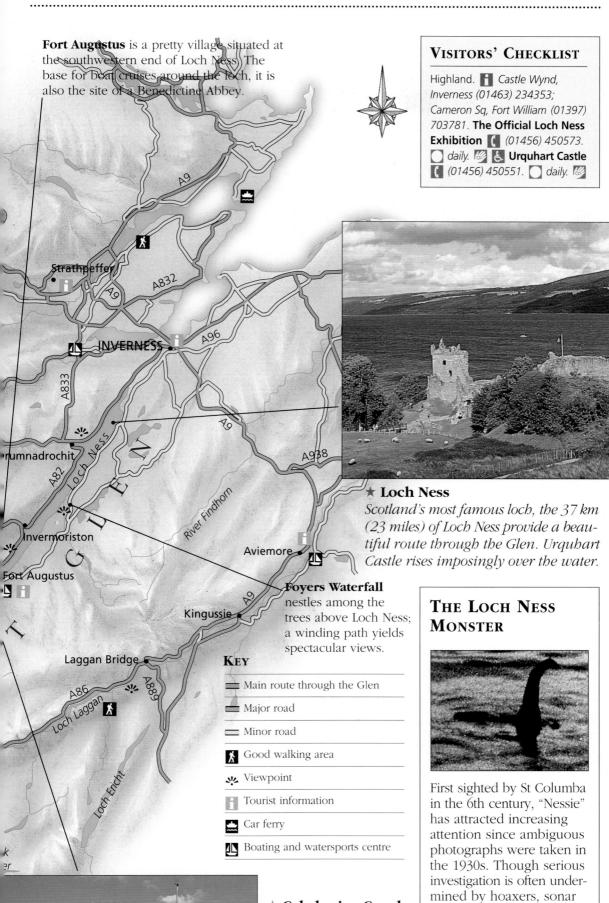

★ Loch Ness
Scotland's most famous loch, the 37 km (23 miles) of Loch Ness provide a beautiful route through the Glen. Urquhart Castle rises imposingly over the water.

Foyers Waterfall nestles among the trees above Loch Ness; a winding path yields spectacular views.

KEY

═══	Main route through the Glen
═══	Major road
───	Minor road
🚶	Good walking area
☀	Viewpoint
ℹ	Tourist information
⛴	Car ferry
⛵	Boating and watersports centre

★ Caledonian Canal
This splendid canal provides a base from which to view the Glen's beautiful surroundings. From Inverness, the canal travels via Fort Augustus to the eight locks at Neptune's Staircase – a feat of engineering.

THE LOCH NESS MONSTER

First sighted by St Columba in the 6th century, "Nessie" has attracted increasing attention since ambiguous photographs were taken in the 1930s. Though serious investigation is often undermined by hoaxers, sonar techniques continue to yield enigmatic results: plesiosaurs, giant eels and too much whisky are the most popular explanations. The Official Loch Ness Exhibition, at Drumnadrochit, presents the photographic evidence and wide variety of scientific explanations proffered over the years.

The shores of the Black Isle in the Moray Firth

Black Isle ③②

Ross & Cromarty. ⌂ *10,600.* ⊡
⊟ *Inverness.* ⓘ *North Kessock
(01463) 731505.*

THOUGH THE DRILLING plat-
forms in the Cromarty Firth
recall how oil has changed
the local economy, the broad
peninsula of the Black Isle is
still largely composed of farmland and fishing villages.
The town of **Cromarty** was
an important 18th-century port
with thriving rope and lace
industries. Many of its merchant houses still stand. The
award-winning museum in
the **Cromarty Courthouse**
provides heritage tours of
the town. The thatched **Hugh
Miller's Cottage** is a museum
to the theologian and geologist
Hugh Miller (1802–56), who
was born in Cromarty.

Fortrose boasts a ruined
14th-century cathedral, while
a stone on Chanonry Point
commemorates the Brahan
Seer, a 17th-century prophet.
He was burnt alive in a barrel
of tar by the Countess of
Seaforth after he foresaw her
husband's infidelity. For local
archaeology, the **Groam
House Museum** in the town
of Rosemarkie is worth a visit.

🏛 **Cromarty Courthouse**
Church St, Cromarty. ⓒ *(01381)
600418.* ◯ *Apr–Oct: daily; Nov–Mar:
daily (pm).* ● *23 Dec–Feb.* ⓐ
🏚 **Hugh Miller's Cottage**
(NTS) Church St, Cromarty.
ⓒ *(01381) 600245.* ◯ *May–Sep:
daily (Sun: pm).* ⓐ ⓔ *limited.*
🏛 **Groam House Museum**
High St, Rosemarkie. ⓒ *(01381)
620961.* ◯ *Easter week: pm only;
May–Sep: daily (Sun: pm); Oct–Apr: Sat
& Sun (pm).* ⓐ ⓔ *ground floor only.*

Strathpeffer ③③

Ross & Cromarty. ⌂ *1,400.*
⊟ *Dingwall.* ⊡ *Inverness.* ⓘ *North
Kessock (01463) 731505.*

STANDING 8 km (5 miles) east
of the Falls of Rogie, the
holiday centre of Strathpeffer
still retains the refined charm
that made it well-known as a
Victorian spa and health resort.
The town's huge hotels and
gracious layout recall the days
when European royalty and
lesser mortals flocked to the
chalybeate- and sulphur-laden
springs, believed to alleviate
tuberculosis. It is still possible
to sample the water at the
unmanned **Water Tasting
Pavilion** in the town centre.

🏛 **Water Tasting Pavilion**
The Square. ◯ *Easter–Oct: daily.*

Dornoch ③④

Sutherland. ⌂ *2,200.* ⊟ *Golspie,
Tain.* ⊡ *Inverness, Tain.* ⓘ *The
Square (01862) 810400.*

WITH ITS FIRST-CLASS golf
course and extensive
sandy beaches, Dornoch is a
popular holiday resort, but it
has retained a peaceful atmosphere. The medieval cathedral
(now the parish church) was
all but destroyed in a clan
dispute in 1570; it was finally
restored in the 1920s for its
700th anniversary. A stone at
the beach end of River Street
marks the place where Janet
Horne, the last woman to be
tried for witchcraft in Scotland,
was executed in 1722.

ENVIRONS: Nineteen kilometres
(12 miles) northeast of the
resort is the stately, Victorianized pile of **Dunrobin Castle**,
magnificently situated in a
great park with formal gardens
overlooking the sea. Since the
13th century this has been the
seat of the Earls of Sutherland.
Many of its rooms are open to
visitors, and a steam-powered
fire engine is among the miscellany of objects on display.
    To the south of Dornoch
stands the peaceful town of
Tain. Though once patronized
by medieval kings as a place
of pilgrimage, it became an

THE HIGHLAND CLEARANCES

During the heyday of the clan system *(see pp578–9)*, tenants
paid their land-holding chieftains rent in the form of military
service. However, with the destruction of the clan system
after the Battle of Culloden *(see p688)*, landowners began
to demand a financial rent, which their tenants were unable
to afford, and the land was gradually bought up by Lowland
and English farmers. In what became known as "the year
of the sheep" (1792), thousands of tenants were evicted,
sometimes forcibly,
to make way for live-
stock. Many emigrated
to Australia, America
and Canada. The ruins
of their crofts can still
be seen, especially in
Sutherland and the
Wester Ross.

The Last of the Clan
(1865) by Thomas Faed

administrative centre for the Highland Clearances, when the tolbooth was used as a jail. All is explained in the heritage centre, **Tain Through Time**.

⚜ **Dunrobin Castle**
Near Golspie. ☎ (01408) 633177.
◯ Apr–mid-Oct: daily. 🈺 ✦
🏛 **Tain Through Time**
Tower St. ☎ (01862) 894089.
◯ Apr–Oct: daily; Nov–Mar: by appointment. 🈺 ♿

The serene cathedral precinct in the town of Dornoch

Glen Shiel 35

Skye & Lochalsh. ⇄ Kyle of Lochalsh.
🚌 Glen Shiel. 🛈 Bayfield House, Bayfield Lane (01478) 612137.

DOMINATING one of Scotland's most haunting regions, the awesome summits of the Five Sisters of Kintail rear into view at the northern end of Loch Cluanie as the A87 enters Glen Shiel. The **visitor centre**

at Morvich offers ranger-led excursions in the summer. Further west, the road passes the romantic **Eilean Donan Castle**, connected to the land by a causeway. After becoming a Jacobite (see p689) stronghold, it was destroyed in 1719 by English warships. In the 19th century it was restored, and it now contains a number of relics of the Jacobite cause.

⚜ **Eilean Donan Castle**
Off A87, near Dornie. ☎ (01599) 555202. ◯ Apr–Oct: daily. 🈺

Isle of Skye 36

See pp694–5.

Wester Ross 37

Ross & Cromarty. ⇄ Achnasheen, Strathcarron. 🚌 Gairloch.
🛈 Gairloch (01445) 712130.

LEAVING LOCH CARRON to the south, the A890 suddenly enters the northern Highlands and the great wilderness of Wester Ross. The Torridon Estate, sprawling on either side of Glen Torridon, includes some of the oldest mountains on earth (Torridonian rock is over 600 million years old), and is home to red deer, wild cats and wild goats. Peregrine falcons and golden eagles nest in the towering sandstone mass of Beinn Eighe, above the village of Torridon, with its breathtaking views over Applecross towards Skye. The **Torridon**

Typical Torridonian mountain scenery in the Wester Ross

Countryside Centre offers guided walks in season, and essential information on the natural history of the region.
Further north, the A832 cuts through the **Beinn Eighe National Nature Reserve**, Britain's oldest wildlife sanctuary. Remnants of the ancient Caledonian pine forest still stand on the banks and isles of Loch Maree, providing shelter for pine martens and wildcats. Buzzards and golden eagles nest on the alpine slopes. **Beinn Eighe Visitor Centre** has information on the reserve.
Along the coast, a series of exotic gardens thrive in the warming influence of the Gulf Stream. The most impressive is Inverewe Gardens (see p698).

🏛 **Torridon Countryside Centre**
(NTS) Torridon. ☎ (01445) 791221.
◯ May–Sep: daily. 🈺 ✦ ♿
🍴 **Beinn Eighe Visitor Centre**
Near Kinlochewe, on A832. ☎ (01445) 760258. ◯ May–Sep: daily. ♿

The western side of the Five Sisters of Kintail, seen from a viewpoint above Ratagan

Isle of Skye 36

**Otter in the haven by
the coast at Kylerhea**

THE LARGEST of the Inner Hebrides, Skye can be reached by the bridge linking Kyle of Lochalsh and Kyleakin. A turbulent geological history has given the island some of Britain's most varied and dramatic scenery. From the rugged volcanic plateau of northern Skye to the ice-sculpted peaks of the Cuillins, the island is divided by numerous sea lochs, leaving the traveller never more than 8 km (5 miles) from the sea. Limestone grasslands predominate in the south, where the hillsides, now the home of sheep and cattle, are scattered with the ruins of crofts abandoned during the Clearances *(see p692)*. Historically, Skye is best known for its association with Bonnie Prince Charlie.

Skeabost has the ruins of a chapel which is associated with St Columba. Medieval tombstones can be found in the graveyard.

Grave of Flora MacDonald

Kilmuir

WESTERN ISLES

Uig

LOCH SNIZORT

Lusta

B886

Milovaig

A850

B884

Dunvegan

Skeabo

B885

A863

0 kilometres   10

0 miles   5

Portnalong

Talisker   B8009

CUI

SGU
ALASD

993
(3,258

Dunvegan Castle
The seat of the chiefs of the Clan MacLeod since the 11th century, Dunvegan contains the Fairy Flag, a fabled piece of magical silk treasured by the clan for its protection.

The Talisker distillery produces one of the best Highland malts, often described as "the lava of the Cuillins".

Cuillins
Britain's finest mountain range is within three hours' walk from Sligachan, and in summer a boat sails from Elgol to the desolate inner sanctuary of Loch Coruisk. As he fled across the surrounding moorland, Bonnie Prince Charlie is said to have claimed: "even the Devil shall not follow me here!"

KEY

ℹ	Tourist information
▬	Major road
▭	Minor road
▬	Narrow lane
✻	Viewpoint

Quiraing

A series of landslides has exposed the roots of this volcanic plateau, revealing a fantastic terrain of spikes and towers. They are easily explored off the Uig to Staffin road.

Loch Coruisk

Luib has a beautiful thatched cottage, preserved as it was 100 years ago.

The Storr

The erosion of this basalt plateau has created the Old Man of Storr, a monolith rising to 55 m (180 ft) by the Portree road.

Portree

With its colourful harbour, Portree (meaning "port of the king") is Skye's metropolis. It received its name after a visit by James V in 1540.

Bridge to mainland

KYLE OF LOCHALSH

Otters can be seen at the haven in Kylerhea.

Armadale Castle houses the Clan Donald visitor centre.

Kilchrist Church

This ruined pre-Reformation church once served Skye's most populated areas, though the surrounding moors are now deserted. Its last service was held in 1843, after a new church was built in Broadford.

BONNIE PRINCE CHARLIE

The last of the Stuart claimants to the Crown, Charles Edward Stuart (1720–88), came to Scotland from France in 1745 to win the throne. After marching as far as Derby, his army was driven back to Culloden where it was defeated. Hounded for five months through the Highlands, he escaped to Skye, disguised as the maidservant of a woman called Flora MacDonald, from Uist. From the mainland, he sailed to France in September 1746, and died in Rome. Flora was buried in 1790 at Kilmuir, on Skye, wrapped in a sheet taken from the bed of the "bonnie" (handsome) prince.

The prince, disguised as a maidservant

Dawn over the desolate tablelands of northern Skye, viewed from the Quiraing ▷

Inverewe Gardens ③⑧

On A832, near Poolewe, Highland.
☎ *(01445) 781200.* ○ *mid-Mar–Oct: daily.*

INVEREWE GARDENS attract over 130,000 visitors a year for the simple reason that they are considered a national treasure. The gardens contain an extraordinary variety of trees, shrubs and flowers from around the world, despite being at a latitude of 57.8° north.

Inverewe was started in 1862 by the 20-year-old Osgood Mackenzie after being given an estate of 4,860 ha (12,000 acres) of exposed, barren land next to his family's holding. At that time there was just one dwarf willow growing there. Mackenzie began by planting shelter trees and then went on to create a walled garden using imported soil. He found that the west coast's climate, warmed by the North Atlantic Drift from the Gulf Stream, encouraged the growth of exotic species *(see p577)*.

By 1922, the gardens had achieved international recognition as one of the great plant collections. In 1952 they were donated to the National Trust for Scotland. At Inverewe today you can find Blue Nile

Some of the many unusual plants cultivated at Inverewe Gardens

lilies, the tallest Australian gum trees growing in Britain and fragrant rhododendrons from China. Planting is designed to provide colour all year, but the gardens are at their best between spring and autumn.

Ullapool ③⑨

Highland. ♟ *1,800.* ➤ *Inverness.* 🚌 🚢 ℹ *Argyle St (01854) 612135.*

WITH ITS WIDE streets, white-washed houses, palm trees and street signs in Gaelic, Ullapool is one of the prettiest villages on the west coast. Planned and built as a fishing station in 1788, it occupies a peninsula jutting into Loch Broom. Fishing is no longer important, except when East European "klondyker" factory ships moor in the loch in the winter. The major activity is now the ferry to Stornoway on Lewis. The **Ullapool Museum** offers an insight into local history.

🏛 Ullapool Museum
7–8 Argyle St. ☎ *(01854) 612987.* ○ *Mon–Sat.*

ENVIRONS: The natural wonders of this area include the rugged Assynt Mountains, a short drive north, and, to the south, the deep and precipitous Corrieshalloch Gorge.

At **Achiltibuie**, it is worth visiting the **Hydroponicum**, a "Garden of the Future", where flowers grow without soil. The town also has a **Smokehouse** where the process of curing salmon can be viewed. Tour boats run from here, and from Ullapool, to the **Summer Isles** – a small, sparsely populated group, once the home of noted environmentalist, Fraser Darling. Achiltibuie is worth a visit for the scenic drive alone.

🌿 Hydroponicum
Achiltibuie. ☎ *(01854) 622202.* ○ *Easter–end Sep: daily.* ⚅ limited.
🐟 Smokehouse
Achiltibuie. ☎ *(01854) 622353.* ○ *Easter–end Sep: Mon–Sat.*

A tranquil, late-evening view of Ullapool and Loch Broom on the northwestern coast of Scotland

Majestic cliffs on Handa Island, a welcome refuge for seabirds

Handa Island ④⓪

Highland. 🚢 *from Tarbet, near Scourie, Apr–Aug.* ℹ️ *Scottish Wildlife Trust, Edinburgh (0131) 312 7765.*

LOCATED JUST offshore from Scourie on the west coast, this small island is an important breeding sanctuary for many species of seabirds.

In past centuries it was inhabited by a hardy people, who had their own queen and parliament. The last 60 inhabitants were evacuated in 1847 when their potato crop failed. The island was also used as a burial ground as it was safe from the wolves that inhabited the mainland.

The island is now managed by the Scottish Wildlife Trust. A walk takes visitors to the 100-m (328-ft) high northern cliffs. On the way you are liable to experience the intimidating antics of great and Arctic skuas (large migratory birds) swooping low over your head. Early in the year 11,000 pairs of razorbills can be found on Handa, and 66,000 pairs of guillemots, the largest breeding colony of this species in Britain.

ENVIRONS: The highest waterfall in Britain is **Eas Coul Aulin**, at 180 m (590 ft). It is best seen after rainfall, from a tour boat based at Kylesku, 24 km (15 miles) to the south of Handa.

Cape Wrath and the North Coast ④①

Highland. 🚌 🚢 *May–Sep (01971) 511376.* ℹ️ *John O'Groats (01955) 611373; Wick (01955) 602596.*

THE NORTHERN edge of mainland Scotland spans the full variety of Highland geography, from mountainous moorlands and dazzlingly white beaches to flat, green farmland.

Cape Wrath is alluring not only for its name but for its cliffs, constantly pounded by the Atlantic. There are many stacks rising out of the sea that swarm with seabirds. The lighthouse was among the last in Scotland to be automated in 1998. In summer, a minibus serves the 13-km (8-mile) road leading to Cape Wrath. In order to reach the bus, you must take the connecting passenger boat from the pier by the Cape Wrath Hotel, as the cape is cut off by the Kyle of Durness. At Durness is **Smoo Cave**, an awesome cavern hollowed out of limestone. **Smoo Innercave Tours** run trips there. Just outside Durness, a community of artists has established the **Balnakeil Craft Village**, displaying pottery, enamelwork, wood carving, printmaking and paintings. Astonishingly white beaches follow one after the other along the coast, and the road then loops round Loch Eriboll – the

A nesting kittiwake

deepest of the sea lochs and a base for Atlantic and Russian convoys during World War II.

The **Strathnaver Museum** in Bettyhill explains the notorious Sutherland "Clearances", the forced evictions of 15,000 people to make way for sheep. At Rossal, 16 km (10 miles) south of Bettyhill, is an archaeological walk around an excavated village, which provides important information on life in pre-Clearance days.

A gigantic white dome at **Dounreay** marks the nuclear reprocessing plant, where you can tour the works and visit the free exhibition centre in summer. The main town on the coast here is Thurso, a village of solid stone buildings. Once famous for its locally quarried stone slabs, Thurso's industry died with the advent of cement. Each September, Thurso hosts "Northlands", the Scottish Nordic Music Festival.

John O'Groats is probably the most famous name on the map here, said to be the very northerly tip of the mainland, although this is in fact nearby **Dunnet Head**. Apart from a quaint harbour where day trips leave for Orkney, John O'Groats is a tourist trap. More rewarding are the cliffs at **Duncansby Head**, where you can enjoy the natural ferocity of the Pentland Firth.

🚢 **Smoo Innercave Tours**
38 Sango Mor, Durness. ☎️ *(01971) 511259.* 🕐 *Apr–Sep: daily.* 🅿️
🏛️ **Strathnaver Museum**
Clachan, Bettyhill. ☎️ *(01641) 521418.* 🕐 *Apr–Oct: Mon–Sat.* 🅿️ ♿ *limited.*

Duncansby Head, Caithness, at the far northeast corner of Scotland

Orkney Islands ㊷

Orkney. 🏘 *19,800.* ✈ ⛴ *from Scrabster (Caithness), Aberdeen and Lewick on mainland Shetland, and from John O'Groats (May–Sept only).* ℹ *Kirkwall (01856 872856).* www.orkney.com

THE FERTILE ISLES of Orkney are remarkable for the wealth of prehistoric monuments which place them among Europe's most treasured archaeological sites. In the town of Kirkwall, **St Magnus Cathedral** – an 860-year-old masterpiece built using yellow and red stone – stands amid a charming core of narrow streets. Its many interesting tombs include that of its 12th-century patron saint. Nearby, the early 17th-century **Earl's Palace** is regarded as one of Scotland's finest Renaissance buildings. To the west of Kirkwall lies Britain's most impressive chambered tomb, the cairn of **Maes Howe**. Dating from 2000 BC, the tomb has runic graffiti on its walls believed to have been left by Norsemen returning from the crusades in 1150.

Nearby, the magnificent **Standing Stones of Stenness** may have been associated with Maes Howe rituals, though details of these remain a mystery. Further west, on a bleak heath, stands the Bronze Age **Ring of Brodgar**.

Another archaeological treasure can be found in the Bay of Skaill – the complete prehistoric village of **Skara Brae**. It was unearthed by a storm in 1850, after lying buried for some 4,500 years. Further south, the town of Stromness was a vital centre of Scotland's herring industry in the 18th century. Its story is told in the local museum, while the **Pier Arts Centre** displays work by British artists and holds regular exhibitions of international art.

🏛 **Earl's Palace**
Palace Rd, Kirkwall. 📞 *0131 668 8800.* ○ *Apr–Sep: daily (Sun: pm).* 📷 ♿ *limited.*
🏛 **Pier Arts Centre**
Victoria St, Stromness. 📞 *01856 850209.* ○ *Tue–Sat.* ● *24 Dec–10 Jan.* ♿ *limited.*

THE SHETLAND SEABIRD ISLES

As seabirds spend most of their time away from land, nesting is a vulnerable period in their lives. The security provided by the inaccessible cliffs at such sites as Noss and Herma Ness on Unst finds favour with thousands of migrant and local birds.

Puffin

Great Skua

Fulmar

Black Guillemot

Razorbills

Herring Gull

Shetland Islands ㊸

Shetland. 🏘 *23,000.* ✈ ⛴ *from Aberdeen and from Stromness on mainland Orkney.* ℹ *Lerwick (01595 693434).* www.shetland-tourism.co.uk

LYING SIX DEGREES SOUTH of the Arctic Circle, the rugged Shetland Islands are Britain's most northerly region and were, with the Orkney Islands, part of the kingdom of Norway until 1469. The Shetlanders' distinctive dialect is derived from this European connection. In the main town of Lerwick, the Islands' Norse heritage is remembered during the ancient midwinter festival Up Helly Aa *(see p572)*, in which costumed revellers set fire to a replica Viking longship. Also in the town, the **Shetland Museum** tells the story of a people

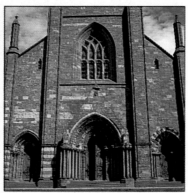

The Norman façade of the St Magnus Cathedral, Orkney

dependent on the sea, right up to modern times with the discovery of North Sea oil and gas in the 1970s. The museum contains artifacts from shipwrecks and the whaling era, and replicas of the St Ninian's Isle Treasure.

A boat from Lerwick sails to the isle of Noss where grey seals bask beneath sandstone cliffs crowded with Shetland seabirds – a spectacle best seen between May and June.

On the isle of Mousa stands one of Shetland's greatest treasures, an Iron Age tower known as **Mousa Broch**. It can be reached by boat from Sandwick. There is more ancient history at Jarlshof, where a museum explains the sprawling sea-front ruins which span 3,000 years, from the Neolithic to the Viking period. The nearby cliffs of Sumburgh Head are worth a visit, and on the west coast, the sand isthmus at St Ninian's Isle offers an interesting walk.

Fair Isle is famous for its abundance of seabirds and its patterned sweaters, and Foula (where Christmas Day is celebrated on 6 January) has dramatic 365-m (1,200-ft) cliffs.

🏛 **Shetland Museum**
The Hillhead, Lerwick. 📞 *01595 695057.* ○ *Mon–Sat.* ● *23–26 Dec, 1, 2 Jan.* ♿

Western Isles ㊹

WESTERN SCOTLAND ENDS with this remote chain of islands, made of some of the oldest rock on Earth. Almost treeless landscapes are divided by countless waterways, the western, windward coasts edged by miles of white sandy beaches. For centuries, the eastern shores, composed largely of peat bogs, have provided the islanders with fuel. Man has been here for 6,000 years, living off the sea and the thin turf, though such monuments as an abandoned Norwegian whaling station on Harris attest to the difficulties in commercializing the islanders' traditional skills. Gaelic, part of an enduring culture, is still widely spoken.

The Black House Museum, a traditional croft on Lewis

The monumental Standing Stones of Callanish in northern Lewis

Lewis and Harris

Western Isles. ✈ *Stornoway.* 🏠 *22,000.* ⛴ *Uig (Skye), Ullapool, Kyle of Lochalsh.* 🛈 *26 Cromwell St, Stornoway, Lewis (01851 703088).* **Black House Museum** ☎ *01851 710395.* ⬜ *Apr–Sep: Mon–Sat; Oct–Mar: Mon–Thu, Sat.* ⬤ *pub hols.*

Forming the largest landmass of the Western Isles, Lewis and Harris are a single island, though Gaelic dialects differ between the two areas. From the administrative centre of **Stornoway**, with its bustling harbour and colourful house fronts, the ancient **Standing Stones of Callanish** are only 16 miles (26 km) to the west. Just off the road on the way to Callanish are the ruins of **Carloway Broch**, a Pictish *(see p574)* tower over 2,000 years old. The more recent past can be explored at Arnol's **Black House Museum** – a showcase of crofting life as it was until only 50 years ago.

South of the rolling peat moors of Lewis, a range of mountains marks the border with Harris, which one enters as one passes Aline Lodge at the head of Loch Seaforth. Only a little less spectacular than the "Munros" (peaks over 914 m; 3,000 ft) of the

mainland and the Isle of Skye *(see pp694–5)*, the mountains of Harris are a paradise for the hillwalker and, from their summits on a clear day, the distant Isle of St Kilda can be seen 50 miles (80 km) to the west.

The ferry port of Tarbert stands on a slim isthmus separating North and South Harris. The tourist office provides addresses for local weavers of the tough Harris Tweed. Some still use indigenous plants to make their dyes.

From the port of Leverburgh, close to the southern tip of Harris, a ferry can be taken to the isles of Berneray and North Uist.

The Uists, Benbecula and Barra

Western Isles. 🏠 *7,200.* ✈ *Barra, Benbecula.* ⛴ *From Uig (Skye), Oban & Mallaig.* 🚌 ⛴ *Oban, Mallaig, Kyle of Lochalsh.* 🛈 *26 Cromwell St, Stornoway, Lewis (01851 703088).*

After the dramatic scenery of Harris, the lower-lying, largely waterlogged southern isles may seem an anticlimax, though they nurture secrets well worth discovering. Long, white, sandy beaches fringe the Atlantic coast, edged with one of Scotland's natural treasures: the lime-rich soil known as *machair*. During the summer months, the soil is covered with wild flowers, the unique fragrance of which can be smelled far out to sea.

From **Lochmaddy**, North Uist's main village, the A867 crosses 3 miles (5 km) of causeway to Benbecula, the isle from which the brave Flora MacDonald smuggled Bonnie Prince Charlie *(see p695)* to Skye. Another causeway leads to South Uist, with its golden beaches renowned as a National Scenic Area. From Lochboisdale, a ferry sails to the tiny isle of Barra. The ferry docks in Castlebay, affording an unforgettable view of **Kisimul Castle**, the ancestral stronghold of the clan MacNeil.

The remote and sandy shores of South Uist

General Index

Page numbers in bold type refer to main entries.

A

Abbeys and priories
Abbey Church (Shrewsbury) 352
Abbey Dore 356
Anglesey Abbey 218
Bath Abbey 270, 283, **284**
Battle Abbey 181
Beaulieu Abbey 168
Bolton Priory 450
Border Abbeys tour **620–21**
Buckfast Abbey **323**, 329
Buckland Abbey 324
Bury St Edmunds 216
Byland Abbey 400, 456
Cartmel Priory 429
Castle Acre Priory 203
Christchurch Priory 297
Dryburgh Abbey 621
Dunfermline Abbey 642
Easby Abbey 401
Fountains Abbey 397, 444, **454–5**
Furness Abbey 400, 407, **428–9**
Glastonbury Abbey 269, 277
Hexham Abbey 496, 497
Inchmahome Priory 635
Jedburgh Abbey 620, 621
Kelso Abbey 620
Kirkham Priory 401
Kirkstall Abbey 401
Lacock Abbey 279
Lanercost Priory 414
Leominster Priory 353
Lindisfarne Priory 484, 490, **491**
Llanthony Priory 549, 557
Malvern Priory 357
Melrose Abbey 612–13, 621, 622
Mount Grace Priory 400, **458**
North Country abbeys **400–401**
Rievaulx Abbey 443, 445, **457**
St Augustine's Abbey 188
St Mary's Abbey 400–401, 474
Sherborne Abbey Church 294
Strata Florida 555
Tewkesbury Abbey 344, 370
Tintern Abbey 545, **565**
Torre Abbey 302, 322
Whalley Abbey 431
Whitby Abbey 400, **460**
Abbotsbury 32, **294**
Abbotsbury Sub-Tropical Gardens 294
Abbotsford House 613–14, 622
Aberaeron 551
Aberdeen 665, **684–5**
Aberdyfi 537
Aberystwyth 544, **550–51**
Aberystwyth Castle 551
Aberystwyth Cliff Railway 551
Achiltibuie 698
Achray, Loch 573
Adam, Robert 28
Audley End 218–19
Culzean Castle 568, 628–9
The Adoration of Kings (Brueghel the Elder) 88
The Adoration of the Magi (Rubens) 223
Agincourt, Battle of (1415) 53
Agricultural shows 67
Royal Show 345
Agriculture 22–3, 34–5
Devon 302
East Anglia 196
Kent 162
Aislabe, John 454
Aislabe, William 455
Albert Dock (Liverpool) 406, **435**
Albert, Prince 61
Memorial 103
Memorial Chapel 254

Aldeburgh 210–211
Festival 24, 197, 211
Alfred, King **167**, 267
Alfriston 180
Alice in Wonderland (Rackham) 525
Allendale 501
Alnwick Castle 394, 487, **492**
Alresford Railway 166
Althorp House 376–7
Ambleside 424
Ancestry 31
Mr and Mrs Andrews (Gainsborough) 157
Angel of the North (Tyne and Wear) 485
Anglesey 519, 520
Anglesey Abbey 218
Anglo-Saxons 43, **50–51**
Animal parks *see* Zoos, animal and wildlife parks
Anne Hathaway's Cottage (Stratford-upon-Avon) 363, **369**
The Annunciation (Lippi) 88
Antonine Wall 613, **643**, 656
Appledore 317
Aquariums
Mallaig Marine World 679
Plymouth Aquarium 324
Sealife Centre (Oban) 672
Sea-Life Centre (Scarborough) 461
Arbor Low 388
Archaeology **46–7**
London 117
Wessex **272–3**
Architects 24
Edinburgh New Town 602
stately homes 28–9
Architecture
Durham Cathedral 503
medieval 222–3
rural 32–3
Ardnamurchan Peninsula 678
Arduaine Garden 672
Argyll 665
Aristocracy
coat of arms 30–31
hereditary peers 20
Arkwright, Richard 432
Arlington Court 317
Armada 43, 55
Plymouth 324
Arnolfini Marriage (van Eyck) 88
Arran 614–15, **632**
Art
fine arts 104–5
modern art 97
Art galleries *see* Museums and galleries
Art Nouveau style, Charles Rennie Mackintosh 655
Arthur, King 51, 267
Glastonbury 269, 277
Tintagel **315**, 301
Arthur's Seat (Edinburgh) 585, 586, 605
Artists 24
Glasgow 655
Lancashire and the Lakes 412–13
Newlyn 302, 308, 310
pre-Raphaelites 344, 361
St Ives 302, 309
Arts and Crafts movement, Kelmscott 236–7
Arundel Castle **172**
Ashmole, Elias 240
Ashmolean Museum (Oxford) 238, 240
Assembly Room (Stamford) 393
Astor, Nancy, Cliveden House 156
Astor, William Waldorf 191
Athelhampton House 295
Atlantic Ocean 10
Audley End **218–19**
Austen, Jane
Bath 282, 284
house 156, 172
Autumn events 68
Avebury Stone Circle 268, **289**

Aviemore 682
Awe, Loch 672

B

Babbacombe Model Village 302, 322
Back of the New Mills (Crome) 209
The Backs (Cambridge) 220, 224
Bakewell 376
Bala 517, 530
Bala Lake Railway 530
Balhousie Castle 640
Ballater 686
Balmoral Castle 664, **686**
Bamburgh 484, 492
Bamburgh Castle 484, 487, **492**
Banbury 232, **236**
Bancroft Gardens 366, 368
Bannockburn, Battle of (1314) 618–19, 638
Banqueting House (London) 95, 96
Barbican (London) 128, 130
Bards, Wales 509, 546
Barnard Castle 487, **500**
Barra 701
Barry, Charles, Houses of Parliament 78
Batemans (Burwash) 157
Bath 268–9, **282–5**
Roman baths 259, 285
Street-by-Street map 282–3
Bath Abbey 270, 283, **284**
Baths, Roman 49
Battersea Park 81
Battersea Shield 49
Battle Abbey 181
The Battle of Culloden (Campbell) 688
Battles of the Scottish Lowlands **618–19**
BBC *see* British Broadcasting Corporation
Beachcombing 260
Beaches
see Coasts
Norfolk 197
north Devon 303
Beachy Head 180
Beaker People 46
Beamish Open Air Museum 485, 487, **498–9**
Bearley Aqueduct 335
Beatles 64
Festival 67
Liverpool 409, **435**
Beaulieu **168**
Beaulieu Abbey 168
Beaumaris 520, **524**
Beaumaris Castle 506, **512–13**
Becket, Thomas à 161, 188
murder 52–3
shrine 189
Becky Falls 329
Beddgelert 518, **528–9**, **532**
Bede, Venerable 484
burial 502
Jarrow 491
Beefeaters (Tower of London) 5, 124
Beers 38
Beinn Eighe 668, 693
National Nature Reserve 693
Belfast, HMS (London) 79
Bell, Vanessa, Charleston 157
Bempton 466
Ben Lomond 633
Ben MacDhui 683
Ben Nevis 669, **677**, 690
Benbecula 701
Bere Regis 295
Berwick-upon-Tweed 486, **490**
Beth Chatto Garden 213
Betws-y-Coed 518, 530
Beverley 467
Beverley Minster 467
Bible Society 530
Bideford 303, 316
Big Ben (London) 82, 96
Birds *see* Wildlife

Birkenhead 437
Birmingham 344, **360–61**
Bishop's Palace (St David's) **552**
Bishop's Palace (Wells) 276, **277**
Black Death 52
Black Isle (Scotland) 692
Black Mountain (Wales) 556
Black Mountains (Wales) 557
Black Prince's Tomb 189
Black Watch 578
Blackmore, R D, *Lorna Doone* 275
Blackpool 408, 410, **431**
    Illuminations 68
Blaenafon 541–2, 564
Blaenau Ffestiniog 531, 532
Blair Castle 681
Blakeney Marshes 205
Blencathra 417
Blenheim Palace 152, 230
    architecture and estate **246–7**
    gardens 246–7
Blickling Hall **206**
Bloody Tower (Tower of London) 125
Bloomsbury Group (writers) 109, 157
Bloomsbury (London) **108–13**
    Sights at a Glance 109
    squares 113
Bluebell woods 160
Boadicea, Queen 195, **203**
Boating
    Cambridge 16
    canals 334
    Derwent Water 410
    Henley Royal Regatta 231, 234–5
    Kielder Water 485
    Loch Ness 689
    Norfolk Broads 195, 197, **206**
    River Thames operators 79, 253
    rowing and regattas **234–5**
    University Boat Race 70
    Wales 518–19
    North Wales **522–3**
Bodiam Castle 182
Bodleian Library (Oxford) 243
Bodmin Jail 314, 315
Bodmin Moor **314–15**
Bodnant Gardens 519
Boleyn, Anne 191
    Fountains Abbey 455
Bolton Castle 449
Bolton Priory 450
Bonnie Prince Charlie 681
    Culloden 575, 688
    monuments 678, 679
    Skye **695**
Bookshops 543, 549
Border Abbeys tour **620–21**
Borders (Scotland) 613–14
    conflicts 483
Borrowdale 421
Boscastle 315
Bossanyi, Erwin, stained glass 189
Botallack Mine 308
Botanic Garden (Cambridge) 225
Botanic Gardens (Oxford) 240
Botanic Gardens (Glasgow) 576, 649, **657**
Botanical Gardens (Birmingham) 344, 361
Bournemouth **297**
Bowder Stone (Lake District) 421
Bowood House 279
Box Hill 172
Bradford 477
Bradford-on-Avon 269, 279
Braemar, highland games 664
Bragg, Melvyn 413
Bramber 174
Bramber Castle 174
Brangwyn, Sir Frank, Swansea Guildhall 554
Braunton Burrows 317
Brecon 557
Brecon Beacons National Park 507, 542, 545

Brecon Beacons National Park (cont.)
    map and sights **556–7**
Brewing
    breweries 420, 428, 449
    hops 155
    museum 476
Bridge of Sighs (Cambridge) 220, **225**
Bridge of Sighs (Oxford) 239
Brighton
    Festival 66
    Palace Pier 163
    Royal Pavilion 175, **176–9**
    Street-By-Street map **174–5**
Brimham Rocks (north Yorkshire) 443
Bristol 268, **280–81**
    city centre map 281
Bristol Cathedral 281
Bristol Zoo Gardens 280
Britannia, Royal Yacht 606
British Broadcasting Corporation 24–5
British Library Reading Room (London) 113
British Museum (London) **112–13**
Britten, Benjamin, Aldeburgh 197, 211
Broadlands (Romsey) 156
The Broads (Norfolk) 195, 201, **206–7**
Broadway 362
Brodick Castle 632
Brompton Oratory (London) 103
Brontë sisters 443
    Charlotte Brontë **478**
    Haworth **478**
Brown, Capability 26
    Bowood House 279
    Chatsworth House 382
    Luton Hoo 249
    Stowe 248
Brownsea Island 296–7
Bruce, George 643
BT Satellite Station 312
Buckfast Abbey **323**, 329
Buckfast Butterfly Farm and Otter Sanctuary **323**
Buckfastleigh 323
Buckingham Palace 76, **92–3**
    Queen's Gallery 93
    Royal Mews 93
Buckland Abbey 324
Buckland-in-the-Moor 303, **329**
Buckler's Hard 168
Bude 315
Building materials
    Cotswold stone **338–9**, 342
    dry-stone walls **380–81**
    Georgian period 58–9
    Tudor manor houses 336–7
    villages 32–3
Bunker Hill, Battle of (1755) 58
Bunyan, John 249
Burford 229, 236
Burford House Gardens 353
Burgh Island 323
The Burghers of Calais (Rodin) 94
Burghley House 333, 378, **392–3**
Burlington Arcade (London) 90
Burns Heritage Trail 625
Burns, Robert 580, 614
Burnsall 450
Burrell Collection (Glasgow) 569, 649, **658–9**
Burton Agnes Hall 466
Burton Constable 468
Bury St Edmunds 216
Bury St Edmunds, churches 216
Bute 614, **633**
Bute House (Edinburgh) 603
Butterflies 166, 200, 260
    Common Blue 34
Buttermere 408, 420, 421
Buttertubs 449
Buxton 382, 388
Byland Abbey 400, 456

C

Cabinet War Rooms (London) 94, 95
Cable car, Llandudno 525
Cadbury Castle 273
Cadbury World (Birmingham) 361
Cader Idris 536
Caerlaverock Castle 614, 626
Caerleon 541, **564**
Caernarfon 520, **524**
    marina 504–5
Caernarfon Castle 512, **524**
Caerphilly Castle 512
Cairngorm Reindeer Centre 683
Cairngorms 569, **682–3**
Caldey Island 554
Caledonian Canal 665
    Inverness 689
    map **690–91**
Caley Mill (Norfolk) 204
Callander 635
Calton Hill 571, 604
Camber Castle 187
Camber Sands 187
Cambrian Mountains 508, 555
Cambridge
    boating 16, 198, 224
    Fitzwilliam Museum 222
    King's College 221, **222–3**
    Street-by-Street map **220–21**
Cambridge University 153, 196, **222–5**
    Boat Race 70
Camden (London) 134
Camera obscura (Aberystwyth) 551
Campbell clan 578
    Dukes of Argyll 670
Campbell, Colen 28
Canada Tower, Canary Wharf (London) 65, 135
Canals
    barges 59
    Caledonian Canal 689, **690–91**
    Llangollen Canal 530
    locks 335
    Manchester Ship Canal 432, 433
    Midlands 334–5, 344
    Monmouthshire and Brecon 557
    North Country 398
Canna 678–9
Canterbury 188
    pilgrimage 52, **166–7**
Canterbury Cathedral 161, 165
    history and layout **188–9**
    Pilgrims' Way 166–7
Canute, King 50
Cape Wrath 699
Car rally 68
Cardiff 541, 545, **560–63**
    see South and Mid-Wales
    City Hall and Civic Centre 560
    Llandaff Cathedral 561
    town centre map 561
Cardiff Castle 507, 545, **562–3**
Carfax Tower (Oxford) 229, 240
Carisbrooke Castle 168
Carlisle 414
Carlisle Castle 414
Carlisle, Earls of 462–3
Carr, John 28
Carreg Cennen Castle 556
Carrick Roads 312
Cartmel 429
Cartmel Priory 429
Castell Coch 513
Castell-ŷ-Bere 513
Castle Acre Priory (Swaffham) 203
Castle Drogo 329
Castle Howard 397, 445
    architecture and history **462–3**
Castlerigg Stone Circle 407, **417**
Castles
    Aberystwyth Castle 551

Castles (cont.)
Alnwick Castle 394, 487, **492**
Arundel Castle 172
Balhousie Castle 640
Balmoral Castle 664, **686**
Bamburgh Castle 484, 487, **492**
Beaumaris Castle 506, **512–13**
Blair Castle 681
Bodiam Castle 182
Bolton Castle 449
Bramber Castle 174
Brodick Castle 632
Caerlaverock Castle 614, 626
Caernarfon Castle 512
Caerphilly Castle 512
Camber Castle 187
Cardiff Castle 507, 545, **562–3**
Carisbrooke Castle 168
Carlisle Castle 414
Carreg Cennen Castle 556
Castell Coch 513
Castell-ŷ-Bere 513
Castle Drogo 329
Cawdor Castle 688
Clifford's Tower (York) 473
Cockermouth Castle 420
Conwy Castle 513, 521
Corfe Castle **296**
Crathes Castle 687
Culzean Castle 568, 614, **628–9**
Dartmouth Castle 322
Dirleton Castle 609
Dolbadarn Castle 531
Doune Castle 640
Dover Castle 161, 182, **183**
Drum Castle 687
Drumlanrig Castle 624–5
Duart Castle 673
Dunollie Castle 672
Dunrobin Castle 692
Dunstaffnage Castle 672
Dunster Castle 275
Dunvegan Castle 694
Durham Castle 503
Eastnor Castle 344
Edinburgh Castle **596–7**
Eilean Donan Castle 5, 662, 693
Floors Castle 620, 621
Framlingham Castle 211
Glamis Castle 640–41
Goodrich Castle 357
Harlech Castle 512, 536
Hay Castle 549
Hever Castle 191
Inveraray Castle 670
Inverness Castle 689
Jedburgh Castle 620
Kames Castle 633
Kilchurn Castle 672
Kinloch Castle 679
Kisimul Castle 701
Lancaster Castle 430
Leeds Castle 161, 167, 190
Lincoln Castle 390
Lindisfarne Castle 490
Ludlow Castle 344, 353
MacLellan's Castle 626
Middleham Castle 449
Muncaster Castle 422
Newcastle 498–9
Nottingham Castle 386
Okehampton Castle 328
Orford Castle 211
Pendennis Castle 313
Penrith Castle 414
Perth Castle 615
Portchester Castle 161, 169
Powis Castle 545, **548**
Restormel Castle 314
Richborough Castle 183
Richmond Castle 448
Ripley Castle 453

Castles (cont.)
Rochester Castle 190
Rothesay Castle 633
St Andrew's Castle 641
Scarborough Castle 461
Sherborne Castle 294
Shrewsbury Castle 344, 352
Sizergh Castle 428
Skipton Castle 450
Stirling Castle 615, **638–9**
Stokesay Castle 344, 352, 353
Sudeley Castle 362
Tantallon Castle 609
Threave Castle 625
Tintagel Castle 301, 315
Torosay Castle 673
Totnes Castle 323
Tretower Castle 557
Urquhart Castle 691
Wales **512–13**
Warkworth Castle 484, 492
Warwick Castle 333, 363, **364–5**
Windsor Castle 152, **254–5**
Wolvesey Castle 170
Castleton 375, 377
Cathedrals
Aberdeen (St Andrew's) 684
Aberdeen (St Machar's) 684
Beverley Minster 467
Bristol 281
Bury St Edmunds (St James's) 216
Canterbury 166–7, **188–9**
Chester 350–51
Chichester 171
Coventry 344, 361
Dunkeld 681
Durham 397, 482, **502–3**
Edinburgh (St Giles) 586, 593
Elgin 687
Ely 153, 196, 202–3
Exeter 303, 320–21
Glasgow (St Mungo's) 647, **653**
Gloucester 344, 371
Hereford 344, 356
Kirkwall 700
Lincoln 333, 379, 391
Liverpool (Anglican) 437
Liverpool (Roman Catholic) 437
Llandaff 561
Newcastle upon Tyne 499
Norwich 196, 208
Orkney (St Magnus's) 663
Peterborough 202
Ripon 453
Rochester 190
St Albans 251
St David's (Wales) **552–3**
St Paul's (London) 114, 118, **120–121**
Salisbury 259, **290–91**
Southwark 79, 123
Truro 313
Wells **276–7**
Westminster Abbey 77, 94, **98–9**
Winchester 19, 152, 161
Worcester 344, 360
York Minster 470, **472–3**, **475**
Catherine of Aragon, tomb 202
Caves
Cheddar Gorge 269, 278
Dan-yr-Ogof Caves 556
Fingal's Cave 673
Kents Cavern Showcaves 302, 322
Llechwedd Slate Caverns 531
Mother Shipton's Cave 452–3
Peak Cavern 375
Smoo Cave 699
Stump Cross Caverns 450
Twm Siôn Cati's Cave 555
Wookey Hole 276
Cawdor Castle 688
Cecil, William, 1st Lord Burghley 392

Celtic Britain
Christianity 484, **491**
St David 553
Scotland 663
Wales 508, 510
Cemeteries 81, 134
Cenotaph (London) 95
Central Region (Scotland) 615
see Lowlands (Scotland)
Centre for Alternative Technology
(Machynlleth) 550
Cerne Abbas 295
Chagall, window 171
Chalk hill figures
Cerne Abbas 295
Grimes Graves 47
Long Man of Wilmington 180
Sutton Bank White Horse 456
Uffington White Horse 237, 47
Westbury White Horse 268
Chanctonbury Ring 174
Changing of the Guard 76, **93**
Channel Tunnel 64, 163, 183
Chapel Royal (Hampton Court) 173
Chapel Royal (Stirling Castle) 639
Chapter House (Westminster Abbey) 99
Chapter House (York Minster) 472
Charlecote Park 336
Charles I, King, execution 56–7
Charles, Prince of Wales 65, 524
Charleston farmhouse (East Sussex) 157
Chartwell (Kent) 157, **191**
Chatham Dockyard 190
Chatsworth House 374, 376
gardens 382–3, 333
history and layout **382–3**
Chatto, Beth, Garden 213
Chaucer, Geoffrey 161, 188
Cheddar Gorge 269, **278**
caves 269, 278
"Cheddar Man" 278
Cheesemaking
Cheddar 269, 278
Wales 543
Wensleydale 449
Chelsea (London) **132**
Chelsea Flower Show 66
Chelsea Physic Garden 132
Cheltenham 345, 370
Cheltenham Imperial Gardens 362
Chesil Bank 260, 294
Chester 344, **350–51**
Bishop Lloyd's House 350
Chester Cathedral 350–51
Cheviot Hills 483, 486
map **493**
Chichester **171**
Chichester Cathedral 171
Children's museums
Bethnal Green Museum of Childhood 135
Cadbury World 361
Eureka! 479
Madame Tussaud's 110
Museum of Childhood (Beaumaris) 524
Museum of Childhood (Edinburgh) 594, 595
Natural History Museum (London) 102, **106**
Planetarium (London) 110
The Rabbit Hole 525
Science Museum (London) 102, **106**
Tales of Robin Hood 386
World of Beatrix Potter 425
A World in Miniature 672
Children's writers 412–13
China (bone china) **348–9**
China clay 313, 348
Chinatown (London) 86
Chinese New Year 86
Chippendale, Thomas 59
Chipping Campden 369
Chiswick House 140
Chiswick (London) 140

Christ Church College (Oxford) 228, 239, **242**
Christ Discovered in the Temple (Martini) 437
Christ of St John of the Cross (Dali) 653
Christchurch Priory (Dorset) 297
Churches, parish church 32–3
Churches in London
    All Souls, Langham Place 111
    Brompton Oratory 103
    Chapel of St John 125
    Queen's Chapel 91
    St Bartholomew-the-Great 116
    St Edward's Chapel 99
    St John's, Smith Square 130
    St Margaret's, Westminster 94
    St Mary-le-Bow 118
    St Paul's Cathedral 118, **120–121**
    St Paul's, Covent Garden 84
    St Stephen Walbrook 119
Churchill, Sir Winston
    Blenheim Palace 230, 246
    Chartwell 157
Chysauster 310–11
Cider making 345, 356
    Somerset 269, 276
Cinemas, London 129
Cinque Ports 181, **182**, 186
The Circus (Bath) 282
Cirencester 371
Cirencester Park 371
Cissbury Ring 174
City Chambers (Glasgow) 648, 652
City Hall and Civic Centre (Cardiff) 560
City of London **114–25**
    Sights at a Glance 115
    Street-by-Street map 118–19
City Observatory (Edinburgh) 604
A City on a River at Sunset (Turner) 97
Civil War 43, 56, 377
    Chipping Campden 369
    Oxford 230
Claerwen reservoir 550
Clandon Park 172
Clans and tartans 578–9, 692
    clan system 663–4
    Royal Stuart tartan 689
Mr and Mrs Clark and Percy (Hockney) 97
Class structure 20
Clear Evening, Wast Water (Heaton Cooper)
    413
Clergy House (Alfriston) 180
Cley Windmill (Norfolk) 205
Clifford's Tower (York) 473
Clifton Suspension Bridge 280
Climate **72–3**
Clitheroe 431
Clive, 2nd Lord, Powis Castle 548
Clive of India, Lord
    Clive House Museum 352
    Clive Museum (Powis Castle) 548
Cliveden House 156
Clovelly 316
Clyde, River 614, 647
Coal mining 398, 485, 499
    Wales 511, 541–2, 564
Coast **260–261**
    Northumbria **488–9**
Coast to Coast Walk (North Country) 37
Coastal paths 36–7
Coat of arms 30–31
Cobbett, William 154
Cockermouth 420
Cockermouth Castle 420
Coggeshall Grange Barn 213
Colchester 213
Coll 673
Colleges
    Cambridge 220–225
    Oxford 238–9, 242–3
Colman's mustard (Norwich) 209
Combe Martin 274, 320
Common Ridings (Borders) 613
Coniston Water 422, **428**

Conservative Party 21–2
Constable, John 196
    Constable Walk 199, 212
    Ipswich collection 211
    Lake District 407
Conwy 509, 520
    Street-by-Street map **526–7**
Conwy Castle 507, 521
    construction 513
    watercolour (Sandby) 527
Cookham 253
Copper mines 525, 532
Corbridge 497
Corfe Castle 269, **296**
Cornish Seal Sanctuary 312
Corn mill, Eskdale 422
Coronation 98
Corpach 679
Corsham 279
Corsham Court 279
Cotehele 325
    gardens 325
Cotswold stone **338–9**, 342
Cotswolds 332, 346, 362–3
Cotton mills *see* Textile industry; Industrial
    Revolution
Country houses *see* stately homes
Countryside **34–5**
Covent Garden (London) **84–7**
Coventry 361
Coventry Cathedral 344, 361
Coward, Noel 62
Coxwold 456–7
Crafts, Middle Ages 52
Cranmer, Thomas 190
Crarae Gardens 576, 670
Crathes Castle 687
Crathes Gardens 577, 687
Cricket 71, 131
Crofters (Scotland) 575, 665
Cromarty 692
Cromwell, Oliver 56, 195, 230
    Museum 218
Cromwell, Thomas, dissolution of
    monasteries **401**
Cross of Caedmon (Whitby) 460
Crown Jewels (England) **124**
Crown Jewels (Scotland) 596–7
Crummock Water 411
Crystal Palace (London) 60–1
Cuckmere, River 181
Cuillins **694–5**
Culloden 688
    Battle of (1746) 575, 688, 689
Culross 615, **643**
Culross Palace 643
Culture 23–5
    Scotland 573
Culzean Castle 568, 614
    history and layout **628–9**
Cwmdonkin Park (Swansea) 554
Cycling, Victorian period 61

D

Dalemain **414–15**
Dan-yr-Ogof Caves (Brecon Beacons) 556
Darby, Abraham I 354
Darby, Abraham III 355
Darling, Grace 492
Dartington Hall 323
    Gardens 323
Dartmeet 329
Dartmoor National Park 258, 303, 305
    map and sights **328–9**
Dartmouth 303, 322
Dartmouth Castle 322
Darwin, Charles, house 157
Davies, Hunter 413
Davy, Sir Humphrey 398
Dawyck Botanic Garden 577
Dean Village 607

Deeside 569, 686–7
The Depression (1920s) 62, 63
Derwent Water 410, 416
Design, gardens 26, 262–3
Devil's Bridge (Wales) 555
Devil's Den (Wessex) 273
Devil's Dyke (South Downs) 181
Devon and Cornwall **298–329**
    climate 72
    map 304–5
    portrait 300–303
Diana, Princess of Wales 21
    Althorp House 376–7
    death 21
    Kensington Palace 107
Dickens, Charles
    Bleak House 157
    Chatham **191**
    Museum (Portsmouth) 169
Dirleton Castle 609
Discovery 641
Disraeli, Benjamin 230, 251
Docklands (London) **135**
Dodgson, Charles,
    Llandudno 525
Dog show 66
Dolbadarn Castle 531
Dolgellau 536–7
Queen Mary's Dolls' House 255
The Dome (Brighton) 175
Dome (Millennium) **136–7**
Domestic service
    country house 29
    Georgian period 59
Dorchester 269, 295
Dornoch 692–3
Dorset Cursus 272
Douglas clan 579
Doune Castle 640
Dounreay 699
Dove Cottage (Grasmere) 424
Dovedale (Peak District) 388
Dover **183**
    White Cliffs 151, 163
Dover Castle 161, 182, **183**
Downing Street (London) 94, 95
Downs and Channel Coast 12, **158–91**
    climate 73
    map 164–5
    portrait 160–163
    Sights at a Glance 165
Dozmary Pool (Bodmin Moor) 314
Drake, Sir Francis **325**
    Buckland Abbey 324
    Plymouth, Armada 324
Drum Castle 687
Drumlanrig Castle 624–5
Drummond Castle Gardens 577
Dry-stone walling **380–81**
Dryburgh Abbey 621
du Maurier, Daphne 301, **314**
Duart Castle 673
Duddon Valley 421, 423
Dumbarton 632
Dumfries & Galloway 614
Dunbar, William 580
Duncansby Head 699
Dundee 641
Dunfermline 642–3
Dunfermline Abbey 642, 643
Dungeness 182
Dunkeld 681
Dunkeld Cathedral 681
Dunkery Beacon 275
Dunollie Castle 672
Dunoon 632
Dunrobin Castle 692
Dunstaffnage Castle 672
Dunster 275
Dunster Castle 275
Dunvegan Castle 694
Dunwich 210

Durdle Door 261, 269, 296
Durham (city) 485, 487
   map and sights **502–3**
Durham Castle 503
Durham Cathedral 397, 482, **502–3**

E

Earl Grey's Monument (Newcastle) 499
Earl's Palace (Kirkwall) 700
Eas Coul Aulin waterfall (Handa Island) 699
Easby Abbey 401
East Anglia 12, **192–225**
   climate 73
   map 198–9
   portrait 194–7
   Sights at a Glance 199
East End (London) 135
East Lambrook Manor, gardens 263
East Lothian coast 608–9
East Midlands **372–93**
   climate 73
   map 12
   Peak District Tour **388–9**
   portrait 374–7
   Sights at a Glance 378–9
East Neuk 615, **642**
Eastbourne **180**
Eastnor Castle 344
Economy, Scotland 572
Edale (Peak District) 388
Eden Camp 466
Edinburgh **582–609**
   architecture 59
   area map 588–9
   Calton Hill 571, 604
   Old Town 586–7
   outlying areas 606–9
   portrait 584–7
   Royal Botanic Garden 577, 606
   Sights at a Glance 589, 606
Edinburgh Castle 584, 585–6, **596–7**
   Argyle Battery 597
   Esplanade 597
   Governor's House 596
   Great Hall 597
   Half Moon Battery 597
   Mons Meg 596
   Palace 597
   St Margaret's Chapel 586
Edinburgh, Duke of 31
Edinburgh Festival 24, 67, 573
   events and venues **590–91**
Edinburgh, New Town 587, **602–3**
   Charlotte Square 603
   Georgian House 603
Edinburgh, Royal Mile 569, 586
   map and sights **592–5**
Edward the Confessor, King 51
Edward I, King
   Scotland 574, 626
   Wales 510, 513
Edward II, King
   birthplace 513
   Prince of Wales 510, 524
   Scotland 618
Edward III, King, coat of arms 30
Edward IV, King, sons 124, 125
Egyptian Mummies (British Museum) 112
Eigg 679
Eildon Hills 614, 620
Eilean Donan Castle 5, 662, 693
Eisteddfods 67, 543
   bards 509
   Llangollen 530
Elan Valley **550**, 555
Electricity 61
Elgar, Sir Edward
   Elgar's Birthplace 360
   Malvern Hills 357
Elgin 687
Elgin Cathedral 687

Elgin Marbles (British Museum) 112
Elizabeth I, Queen 54
Elizabeth II, Queen 92
   Balmoral 664
     wax figure 110
Ely 202–3
Ely Cathedral 153, 196, 202–3
Emmanuel College (Cambridge) 224
Engineering 648
English Channel 10
Entertainment, London **128–31**
Entrance to the Arsenal (Canaletto) 248
Epping Forest 197, 219
Eskdale 421, 422
Eton College (Berkshire) 253
European Community 64
Events, annual 66–71
Exchange (Edinburgh) 598
Exeter 303, **320–21**
Exeter Cathedral 303, 320
Exhibitions, annual 66–9
Exmoor National Park 258, 271, **274–5**
Eyam 389

F

Fairfax House 474
Fairs, Devon 302
Falkland Palace 615, 642
Falmouth 312–13
Farmer's Bridge (Birmingham) 334
Farming *see* Agriculture
Farndale 447
Farne Islands 485, 487, 490
Fashion 64–5
The Fens 195, 203
   portrait **200–201**, **204**
   windmills 200, 207
Ferguson, Adam 580
Festivals 66–9
   see Music festivals
Ffestiniog Railway 531, **532–3**
Fforest Fawr 556
Fife 615
Film industry 25
   museum 477
Fingal's Cave 673
Firth of Clyde 568, **632**
Firth of Forth 585
Fishbourne Palace 48–9, 161, 171
Fishing industry 196–7, 469
Fitzherbert, Maria 179
Fitzwilliam Museum (Cambridge) 222
Five Sisters of Kintail **668–9**, 693
Flag Fen 202
Flamborough and Bempton Head 443, 466–7
Flatford Mill (Suffolk) 196, 212
Flint mines 202–3
Flitcroft, Henry 292
Floors Castle 620, 621
Flora and fauna *see* Wildflowers; Wildlife
Flower shows
   Chelsea 66
   Malvern 345
Food
   regional 40–41
   typical 18
   Wales 543
Football 25
   FA Cup Final 70
   Glasgow 649
Footpaths *see* Long-distance footpaths
Forest parks 626–7, 635
Fort Amherst 190
Fort George 688
Fort William **676**, 679
Forth Bridges 585–6, **607**, 615
Fortnum and Mason (London) 90, 126
Fountains Abbey 441, 444
   history and layout **454–5**
Fountains Hall 454
Fowey 314

Fox Talbot, William Henry 279
Foyers Waterfall (Loch Ness) 691
Framlingham Castle 211
Fraser clan 579
Frink, Elisabeth, sculpture 290
Fruit growing 154–5, 162
Furness Abbey 400, 407, 428–9
Furness Peninsula 428–9
Furniture, Georgian 59

G

G-Mex Centre (Manchester) 432, 433
Gabriel's Wharf (London) 78
Gainsborough, Thomas
   house 157, 196
   museum 216
Galleries *see* Museums and galleries
Galloway Forest Park 626–7
Gaol (Beaumaris) 524
Garden cities 229
Garden of England (Kent) **154–5**
Gardens *see* Parks and gardens
Gardens of the Rose 231, 233, **251**
Gargoyles 339
Geology
   Edinburgh 585
   Lake District **402–3**
George I, King 186
George IV, King 579
   Royal Pavilion 179
George Square (Glasgow) 652
Georgian Britain 58–9
   townhouses 393
Gibbons, Grinling 121
   Hampton Court 173
Gladstone's Land 592
Glamis Castle 640–41
Glasgow 614, **644–59**
   Botanic Gardens 576, 649, 657
   Cathedral 647, 653
   portrait 646–9
   School of Art 654, 655
   Sights at a Glance 651
Glastonbury 269, **277**
   Tor 268, **273**
Glastonbury Abbey 269, 277
Glen Nevis 677
Glen Shiel 662, **693**
Glencoe 668–9, 676
Glendurgan (Falmouth), gardens 313
Gleneagles (Perthshire) 614
Glenfinnan Monument 679
Globe Theatre (London) **123**
Gloucester 371
Gloucester Cathedral 344, 371
Glynde Place 180
Glyndŵr, Owain 510, 550
Goat Fell Ridge 632
Goathland 459
Gold mining 537
Golf 71
   Scotland 614, 615, 641
Goodrich Castle 357
Goodwood House 171
Gordale Scar 451
Gordon clan 579
Government 20–22
   see also Parliament
Gower Peninsula 543, 544, **554**
Granada Studios Tour (Manchester) 433
Grand Prix 71
Grand Union Canal 334
Grasmere 407, 408, **424**
Great Britain
   portrait 16–25
   Through the Year 66–73
Great Britain, s.s. 268, 280
Great Cumbrae Island 632
Great Dixter (Northiam) 182
Great Exhibition (1851) 61
   Memorial 102

Great Fire of London 118, 120
Great Gable (Lake District) 422
Great Glen (Scotland) 665, **690–91**
Great Malvern 357
Great Orme copper mines 525
Great Orme Tramway 525
Great Orme's Head 525
Great Tew 236
Great Yarmouth 196, 207
Greater London see London
  map 13
Green Park (London) 81
Greenock 632
Greenwich (London) **135**
  The Dome **136–7**
Greenwich Park 81
Greville family, Warwick Castle 364
Greyfriars Bobby (Edinburgh) 593, 598
Greyfriars Kirk (Edinburgh) 598
Greyfriars (Worcester) 360
Grimes Graves (Norfolk) 202–3
Grimsby 443, 469
Grimspound 329
Guildford 166, **172**
Gulf Stream
  Scotland 577, 698
  Wales 508, 519
Gwennap Pit 311
Gwynfynydd Gold Centre and Mine 537

H
Habitats 34–5
Haddington 608
Hadrian, Roman Emperor 496, 574
Hadrian's Wall 48, 396, 483
  forts **496–7**
Halifax 398, **478**
  Piece Hall 398
Haltwhistle 501
Ham House 140
Hampstead (London) 133
Hampstead Heath (London) 81, **134**
Hampton Court Palace 26, 55
  clock 55
  plan **173**
Handa Island 699
Hanover, House of 45
Hardknott Pass 421, 422
Hardraw Force waterfall (Yorkshire) 449
Hardwick, Bess of 376
Hardwick Hall 336, 376, 386
Hardy, Thomas 269, **295**
Harewood Bird Garden 476
Harewood House 476
Harlech 536
Harlech Castle 512, 536
Harlow Car Gardens 452
Harold I, King 51, 181
Harris and Lewis **701**
Harrod's (London) 103, 126
Harrogate 452
Hastings 181
  Battle of 181
Hatfield House 57, 230, **249**
Hathersage 389
Hawick 613
Hawkshead 428
Hawksmoor, Nicholas
  Blenheim Palace 246, 28
  Castle Howard 462
Haworth 443, 478
Hay Bluff 557
Hay Castle 549
Hay-on-Wye 543, **549**
The Haywain (Constable) 89
Heart of England **340–71**
  climate 72
  map 12, 346–7
  Midlands Garden Tour 347
  portrait 342–5
  Sights at a Glance 346

Heart of Midlothian 586
Heaton Cooper family 413
Hebden Bridge 398, **478**
Heddon's Mouth 274
Heights of Abraham (Matlock) 386
Helmsley 447, 457
Helston 312
Helvellyn (Lake District) 420, 423, **426–7**
Hengistbury Head 297
Henley-on-Thames 231, 252
  Royal Regatta 70, **234–5**
Henry II, King 183
  coat of arms 30
Henry VI, King, statue 222–3
Henry VII, King
  Chapel 99
  coat of arms 30
Henry VIII, King
  Hampton Court 173
  portrait 42
  split from church of Rome 54
Henryson, Robert 580
Hepworth, Barbara 302, 309
Heraldry **30–31**
Hereford 344, **356**
Hereford Cathedral 344, 356
Hertford, Marquesses of 110
Hestercombe Garden 276
Hever Castle 191
Hexham 486, **496**, 501
Hexham Abbey 496, 497
Hidcote Manor Gardens 363
High Force waterfall (Durham) 485
Highgate (London) 81, **134**
Highgate Cemetery (London) 134
Highland Clearances 575, 692
Highland Games 66, 68, 71
  Braemar 664
Highland region (Scotland) see Highlands
  and Islands
Highlands and Islands **660–701**
  climate 73
  portrait 662–5
  Sights at a Glance (map) 667
  The Munros 668–9
History **43–65**
  Georgian Britain 58–9
  Great Britain 19
  Kings and Queens 44–5
  Middle Ages 52–3
  Prehistoric Britain 46–7
  Roman Britain 48–9
  Scotland 574–5
  Stuarts 56–7
  Tudor Renaissance 54–5
  20th century 62–5
  Victorian Britain 60–61
  Wales 510–11
Hoare, Henry 292
Hogarth, William 59
Holderness and Spurn Head 443, 469
Holker Hall 429
Holkham Hall 205
Holland, Henry 28, 178
Holland Park 80, 132–3
Holmes, Sherlock 110
Holy Trinity Church (Stratford-upon-Avon)
  367, 368
Holyhead 519
Holyrood, New Scottish Parliament 605
Holyrood Palace 586, 604–5
Holyrood Park 586, 605
Holywell Music Room (Oxford) 240–241
Honiton 321
Honours List 31
Hopetoun House 608
Hops 154–5, 167
Horse Guards (London) 95
Horse racing 70
  Cheltenham 345, 370
  museum 217
  Newmarket 196, 217

Horse of the Year Show 68, 71
Hound Tor 329
House of Windsor (monarchs) 45, 230,
  254
Houses
  see Stately homes
  country houses **28–9**
  Georgian town house 58–9
  tenements 648, 654
Houses of Parliament 78, 95
  Big Ben 82, 96
  House of Commons 96
  House of Lords 96
  plan **96**
Howard, Thomas, Earl of Suffolk 218
Hudson, George 399
Hughenden Manor 230, 251
Humber, River 443
Humberside see Yorkshire and Humberside
Hunstanton Cliffs 204
Huntingdon 218
Hutton-in-the-Forest 414
Hutton-le-Hole **458**, 459
Hyde Park (London) 81, 101, **107**
Hydroponicum (Achiltibuie) 698

I
Ickworth House 216
Ightham Mote 191
Immigrants 20
Inchmahome Priory 635
Indian community, Bradford 477
Industrial Revolution 19
  Beamish Open Air Museum 487,
    498–9
  Blaenafon Ironworks 564
  cotton mills 343, 350, 386
  Glasgow 647–8
  Ironbridge Gorge 343, 354–5
  Llechwedd Slate Caverns 531
  Midlands 343, 375
  museum 477, 479
  North Country 398–9, 484–5
  Scotland 575
  textile industry 398–9
  Wales 511
  Yorkshire 443
Industry
  engineering 575, 648
  shipbuilding 575, 648
Inns of Court (London) 78, **116**
Interior at Paddington (Freud) 436
Interiors
  Culzean Castle 628–9
  Georgian town house 58–9
  Little Hall 216
  Provost Skene's House 685
  Royal Pavilion **178–9**
  stately home 28–9
  Tudor manor houses 337
  Victorian pub 38–9
Inveraray Castle 670
Inverewe Gardens 576, 698
Inverkip 632
Inverness **688–9**
Inverness Castle 689
Iona 673
Ipswich 211
Ireland 20, 22
Iron Age 47
Iron Bridge (Shropshire) 355
Iron mining 459
Ironbridge Gorge 332, 343, **354–5**
Ironworking, Wales 541
Islay 665, 666, **671**
Isle of May, nature reserve 642
Isle of Purbeck 269, 296
Isle of Skye 666, **694–5**
  Kilt Rock 568
Isle of Wight 162, **168**
  Osborne House 156

Isles of Scilly 311
Islington (London) 134

J

Jacobite movement 676, **689**
  Culloden 688
Jacobite Steam Train 676
James Herriot Country 442, **446–7**
Richard James (Hogarth) 222
James I, King 56
James II (Cooper) 689
James IV, King of Scotland 618
James VI, King of Scotland 575
St James's Palace (London) 90
Japanese Lady with a Fan (Henry) 656
Jedburgh 620
Jedburgh Abbey 620, 621
Jedburgh Castle 620
Jekyll, Gertrude 27
Jesus College (Cambridge) 224
Jewel House (Tower of London) 125
John, King, *Magna Carta* 253
John O'Groats 667, 699
John Rylands Library (Manchester) 432
Jones, Inigo, Covent Garden 85
Jura 670–71

K

Kailzie Gardens 613, 623
Kames Castle 633
Katrine, Loch 634
Keats House 133
Kedleston Hall 29, 386
Keighley and Worth Valley Railway 478
Kelmscott 236–7
Kelmscott Manor 236–7
Kelso 620
Kelso Abbey 620, 621
Kemp, George Meikle 599
Kendal 428
Kensington (London) *see* South Kensington
Kensington Gardens (London) 80, 81, 101, **107**
Kensington Palace (London) **107**
Kent 154–5, 160, 162–3
Kent, William 28
Kents Cavern Showcaves (Torquay) 302
Kenwood House (London) 130, **134**
Keswick 415
Kew (London) 140
Kew Gardens (London) 80, 140
Kielder Water 485, 486, **492**
Kiftsgate Court Garden 363
Kilchurn Castle 672
Killiecrankie 680
  Battle of (1689) 680
  walk 680
Kilpeck Church 356
Kincraig Highland Wildlife Park 682
King's College (Aberdeen) 684
King's College (Cambridge) 221
  Chapel 221, **222–3**
King's Lynn 204–5
Kings and Queens **44–45**
Kingston Lacy 297
Kingston upon Hull 443, 468
Kinloch Castle 679
Kintail, Five Sisters of **668–9**, 693
Kintyre **671**
Kipling, Rudyard, Batemans 157
Kircudbright 626
Kirkham Priory 401
Kirkstall Abbey 401
Kirkwall Cathedral 700
Kisimul **701**
The Kiss (Rodin) 97
Knaresborough 452–3
Knebworth House 249
Knighton 545, **549**
Knights Templar 116
Knightshayes Court, gardens 263, 321

Knole 190–91
Knot Garden 27
Knox, John 575
  house 594, 595
Kynance Cove 312

L

Labour Party 20–22
Lacock 279
Lacock Abbey 279
A Lady and a Gentleman in a Carriage (Stubbs) 89
Laguerre, Louis, Blenheim Palace 247
Lake District 407–8, **414–28**
  geology **402–3**
  Northern Fells 416–17
  peaks 416–17, 420–21
  Sights at a Glance 410–11
Lamb House (Rye) 186
Lancashire and the Lakes **404–37**
  climate 72
  portrait 406–9
  Sights at a Glance 410–11
  writers and artists **412–13**
Lancaster 409, 410, **430–31**
  House of 44
Lancaster Castle 430
Land Gate (Rye) 187
Land use 34–5
Land's End 260, 304, 308
Landscape gardens 26–7
Landscapes 34–5
  Highlands and Islands 664–5
Lanercost Priory 414
The Lanes (Brighton) 175
Lanfranc, Bishop 188
Langdale 423
Lanhydrock 262, 314, 315
Lanyon Quoit 301, 308
Large Two Forms (Moore) 479
Largs 632
The Last of the Clan (Faed) 692
The Last of England (Brown) 361
Lastingham 459
Lavender fields (Norfolk) 195, 204
Lavenham 216
Layer Marney Tower (Colchester) 213
Lead mines (North Country) 442, 485, 501
Ledbury 357
Leeds **476**
Leeds Castle 161, 167, 190
Leighton Hall 430
Leighton House 133
Leith 606
Leith Hill (Surrey) 172
Lennoxlove House 608
Leominster 344, 353
Leominster Priory 353
The Leonardo Cartoon (Da Vinci) 88
Levens Hall **429**
Lever, William Hesketh 399
Lewes 180
Lewis 663, **701**
Libraries
  Bodleian Library 243
  British Library Reading Room 113
  John Rylands Library 432
  Mitchell Library 649
  National Library of Wales 551
  Old Library (Cardiff) 561
Lincoln 375
  Street-by-Street map **390–91**
Lincoln Castle 390
Lincoln Cathedral 333, 379, 391
Lincoln's Inn (London) 116
Lindisfarne 484, 487, 490
Lindisfarne Castle 490
Lindisfarne Gospels 113, **491**
Lindisfarne Priory 484, 490, **491**
Linley Sambourne House 133
Linlithgow Palace 608

Little Hall (Lavenham) 216
Little Moreton Hall (Cheshire) 337
Liverpool 409, 410, **434–7**
  Walker Art Gallery 436–7
Liverpool Cathedral (Anglican) 437
Liverpool Cathedral (Roman Catholic) 437
Lizard Peninsula 256, 312
Llanberis 507, 518, **531**
Llandaff Cathedral 561
Llandovery 555
Llandrindod Wells 549
Llandudno 518, **525**
Llangollen 516, 530
Llanidloes 555
Llanthony Priory 549, 557
Llechwedd Slate Caverns 531
Llithfaen 533
Lloyd George, David 511, 561
Lloyd's Building (London) 119
Llŷn Peninsula 517, 533
Llywelyn the Great 510, 526, 532
Loch Garten Nature Reserve 683
Loch Ness Monster 665, 691
Lochy, Loch 665, **690**
Logan Botanic Garden 576, 627
Lombard Street (London) 119
Lomond, Loch 614, 633, 634
London 12, 74–149
  see Greater London
  at a glance 76–7
  The City and Southwark **114–25**
  climate 73
  Covent Garden **84–7**
  Docklands 65
  entertainment **128–31**
  exhibitions 66–9
  Further Afield 132–40
  Millennium Dome **136–7**
  museums and galleries 86–9, 97, **102–6**
  parks and gardens **80–81**
  plague 57
  Regent's Park and Bloomsbury **108–13**
  River View **78–9**
  shops and markets **126–7**
  South Kensington and Hyde Park 80–1, **100–107**
  sports venues 131
  Street Finder maps **142–9**
  West End and Westminster **82–99**
London Coliseum 130
London Marathon 70
Long Man of Wilmington 180
Long Meg and her Daughters 414
Long Mynd 352
Long-distance footpaths **36–7**
  Coast to Coast Walk 37
  Offa's Dyke Footpath 36, 542
  Pembrokeshire Coastal path 36, 542
  Pennine Way 36, 388
  Pilgrims' Way 161, **166–7**
  Ridgeway 37, 231
  South Downs Way 37, 162
  Southwest Coastal Path 274, 303
  Thames Path 231
Longleat House **292**
Looe 314
Lord Leycester Hospital (Warwick) **330**, 363
Lord Mayor of London
  Show 68
  State Coach 117
Lord's Cricket Ground 131
Lostwithiel 314
Lowestoft 196, 207
Lowlands (Scotland) **610–59**
  climate 73
  battles **618–19**
  portrait 612–15
Ludlow 344, 347, **352–3**
Ludlow Castle 344, 353
Lugg, River 353
Lulworth Cove (Dorset) 269, 296
Lundy 316

Luss 633, 634
Luton Hoo 248–9
Lutyens, Sir Edwin 29
Lydford Gorge 328
Lynmouth 274
Lynton 303
Lytton, Lord 249

M

McCaig's Tower (Oban) 672
MacDiarmid, Hugh 581
MacDonald clan 578
    Glencoe massacre 676
MacDonald, Flora 695
Machynlleth 550
Mackay clan 578
Mackenzie clan 578
Mackintosh, Charles Rennie 648, **655**
    collection (Hunterian Art Gallery) 656
    Glasgow School of Art 654, 655
    stained glass 646
    Willow Tea Room 654, 655
MacLellan's Castle 626
MacLeod clan 578
Madame Tussaud's (London) **110**
Maen Huail (Ruthin) 525
Magdalen Bridge (Oxford) 242
Magdalen College (Oxford) 242
Magdalene Bridge (Cambridge) 220
Magdalene College (Cambridge) 225
Magna Carta (1215) 230, 253
Maiden Castle 47, 269, 295
Maldon 219
Malham Walk **451**
    Malham Cove 442, 451
    Malham Lings 443, 451
The Mall (London) **91**, 93
Mallaig 678, **679**
Malvern Hills 357
Malvern Priory 357
Manchester 409, 411, **432–3**
Manchester Ship Canal 432, 433
Manor houses, Tudor Age 336–7
Mansion House (London) 119
Mappa Mundi (Hereford) 344, 356
Maps
    Aberdeen 685
    Armada defeat 43
    Bath 282–3
    Brighton: Street-by-Street 174–5
    Bristol 281
    Cambridge: Street-by-Street 220–221
    Devon and Cornwall 304–5
    Downs and Channel Coast 164–5
    East Anglia 198–9
    East Midlands 378–9
    Edinburgh 588–9
    Edinburgh: New Town 602–3
    Edinburgh: Royal Mile 592–5
    Glasgow 650–51
    Great Britain 10–11
    Greater London 13
    Heart of England 346–7
    Ironbridge Gorge 354–5
    Lake District peaks 402, 416–7
    Lancashire and the Lakes 410–11
    Liverpool city centre 434
    London: at a glance 76–7
    London: City of London 118–9
    London: Covent Garden 84–5
    London: parks and gardens 80–81
    London: Piccadilly and St James's 90–91
    London: Regency London 111
    London: Regent's Park and Bloomsbury
        109
    London: River View 78–9
    London: South Kensington 102–3
    London: Street Finder **142–9**
    London: West End 83
    London: Whitehall and Westminster 94–9

Maps (cont.)
    Manchester: city centre 432
    Midlands: at a glance 332–3
    Midlands: canals 334–5
    North Country 15, 396–7
    North Norfolk Coastal Tour 204–5
    North Wales 520–21
    Northumbria 486–7
    Ordnance Survey 36
    Oxford: Street-by-Street 238–9
    Prehistoric Britain 46–7
    regions 12
    Scotland 14–15
    Scotland: at a glance 568–9
    Scotland: Ben Nevis 677
    Scotland: Cairngorms 682
    Scotland: Great Glen 690–91
    Scotland: Highlands and Islands 666–7
    Scotland: Isle of Skye 694–5
    Scotland: Trossachs 634–5
    Southeast England 152–3
    Stratford-upon-Avon 366–9
    Thames Valley 232–3
    Wales 506–7
    Wales: South and Mid-Wales 544–5
    Wessex 270–71
    West Country 258–9
    Yorkshire Dales 448
    Yorkshire and Humberside 444–5
Marble Hill House 140
Marcher Lords (Wales) 344, 508, 510
Margate 183
Markenfield Hall 453
Markets
    Barras (Glasgow) 649
    Camden 134
    Cardiff 560
    Covent Garden 84–5
    London **126–7**
    Pannier Market (Barnstaple) 317
    Petticoat Lane 19, 127
    Portobello Road 133
Marlborough 289
Marlborough, Dukes of 230, **246–7**
Marlow Bridge 233
Martello tower 182
Martyrs
    Catholic 377
    Memorial (Oxford) 238, **241**
    Protestant 55, 116
Mary, Queen of Scots 54–55
    claim to throne 574–5
    house 620
Mary Rose 169
Massacre of Glencoe (Hamilton) 656, 676
Mathematical Bridge (Cambridge) 221
Matlock 386
Maundy Thursday 66
Mayflower Stone and Steps (Plymouth) 302,
    324
Maze
    Chatsworth House 383
    Hampton Court 173
Media 24–5
    museum 477
Medicine, anatomy 57
Melrose Abbey 612–13, 621, 622
Menai Bridge (North Wales) 519
Mendip Hills 269
Mermaid Street (Rye) 186
Merry Maidens 301, 308
Mersey, River 434
Merton College (Oxford) 243
Methodism 311
    Wales 511
Middle Ages 52–3
Middleham Castle 449
Middleton-in-Teesdale 486, **500**
Midlands 12, **330–93**
    at a glance 332–3
    canals 334–5
    East Midlands **372–93**

Midlands (cont.)
    Heart of England **340–71**
    Midlands Garden Tour 347, **362–3**
Mildenhall Treasure (British Museum)
    113
Mileage chart 14
Military Tattoo (Edinburgh) 586
Mills *see* Water mills; Windmills; Textile
    industry
Milton, John 231, 249
Minack Theatre (Porthcurno) 308
Minehead 275
Mines and mining
    coal 19, 398, 499
    copper 525, 532
    Cornwall 301, 308, 312
    gold 537
    iron 459
    lead 442, 485, 501
    museum 479
    Poldark Mine 301, 312
    Temple Mine 386
    Wales 511, 541–2, 564
Minsmere Reserve 210
Minster Lovell Hall 236
The Mint (Rye) 186
Minton, Thomas 348
Misericord, Lincoln Cathedral 391
Mitchell Library (Glasgow) 649
Moat 336
Mompesson House 291
Monarchy 20–21, **44–5**
    coat of arms 30–31
    coronation 98
    England-Scotland union 575
    Restoration 57
Monasteries 54, 458
    dissolution 401, 454
    Fountains Abbey 454–5
    life in 400, 407
    ruins 442
    Wales 565
Monk Bar (York) 473
Monmouth **564–5**
Mons Meg 596
Montacute House 294
Moore, Henry, sculpture 479
Moot Hall (Keswick) 415
Morar 678
Morecambe Bay 408, 430
Morrab Gardens 310
Morris, William, Kelmscott Manor 236–7
Morwellham Quay 325
Mosaic, Roman 49
Moseley Old Hall 337
Mother Shipton's Cave (Knaresborough)
    452–3
Motoring, 1950s 63
Motorways, M25 13
Mount Edgecumbe Park 324
Mount Grace Priory (Northallerton) 400, **458**
Mount Stuart House 633
Mountains
    see Ben Nevis; Snowdon
    Cairngorms **682–3**
    Cuillins **694–5**
    Lake District **402–3**, 416–17, 420–21
    Scotland (Munros) **668–9**
    Wales 528–9, 555, 556–7
Mountbatten, Lord 31
    Broadlands 156
Mousa Broch 700
Muck 679
Muir of Dinnet Nature Reserve 686
Mull **673**
Mumbles 554
Muncaster Castle 422
Munro, Sir Hugh 668
The Munros (Scotland) **668–9**
Museums and galleries
    see also Children's museums
    A La Ronde 321

Museums and galleries (cont.)
  Abbott Hall Art Gallery and Museum 413, 428
  Aberconwy House 526
  Alexander Keiller Museum 289
  American Museum 285
  Anne of Cleves House 180
  Annie McLeod Experience 624
  ARC (York) 473
  Ardnamurchan Natural History Centre 678
  Arkwright's Mill 386, 389
  Armley Mills Museum 443, 476
  Arnolfini Gallery 280
  Art Gallery (Aberdeen) 684
  Ashmolean Museum 229, 238, **240**
  Auchindrain Museum 670
  Balnain House 689
  Bank of England Museum 119
  Bannockburn Heritage Centre 638
  Barbara Hepworth Museum 302, 309
  Beamish Open Air Museum 485, 487, **498–9**
  Beatles Story 435
  Beatrix Potter Gallery 425
  Beatrix Potter Museum 371
  Beatrix Potter's Lake District 415
  Bessie Surtees' House 499
  Big Pit Mining Museum 564
  Black House Museum 701
  Blaenafon Ironworks 564
  Blists Hill Museum 355
  Bodmin Town Museum 314, 315
  Border History Museum 496–7
  Bowes Museum 500
  Bradford Industrial Museum 477
  Brantwood 428
  Bridewell Museum 209
  Bristol Industrial Museum 281
  British Golf Museum 615, 641
  British Museum (London) 77, **112–13**
  Brontë Parsonage Museum 443, **478**
  Building of Bath Museum 285
  Burns Cottage 614, 625
  Burns House and Museum 625
  Burrell Collection 569, 649, **658–9**
  Butcher Row House 357
  Buxton Museum and Art Gallery 382
  Calderdale Industrial Museum 479
  Canongate Tolbooth 594–5
  Canterbury Heritage Museum 188
  Captain Cook Memorial Museum 460
  Carnegie Birthplace Museum 643
  Castle Museum (Colchester) 213
  Castle Museum (Norwich) 208
  Centre for Alternative Technology 550
  Ceredigion Museum 551
  Charles Dickens Museum 169
  Christchurch Mansion 211
  Churchill House Museum 356
  Cider Museum 356
  City Art Galleries (Manchester) 432, 433
  City Art Gallery (Leeds) 476
  City Museum and Art Gallery (Birmingham) 344, 361
  City Museum and Art Gallery (Bristol) 281
  City Museum and Art Gallery (Hereford) 356
  City Museum (Lancaster) 430, 431
  Clink Prison Museum 123
  Clive House Museum 352
  Clive Museum 548
  Coalport China Museum 355
  Cogges Manor Farm 236
  Coggeshall Grange Barn 213
  Colour Museum 477
  Commandery 360
  Corbridge Roman Site and Museum 497
  Corinium Museum 371
  Courtauld Institute Gallery 86
  Crich National Tramway Museum 389
  Cromarty Courthouse 692
  Cromwell Museum 218

Museums and galleries (cont.)
  Dales Countryside Museum 449
  Dartmouth Museum 322
  D-Day Museum 169
  Dennis Severs' House 135
  Design Museum 122
  Dickens House Museum 113
  Dock Museum 429
  Dorset County Museum 295
  Dove Cottage and the Wordsworth Museum 424
  Dynamic Earth 605
  Dyson Perrins Museum 360
  Eden Camp 466
  Edinburgh Experience 604
  Elgar's Birthplace 360
  Elgin Museum 687
  Elizabethan House Museum 207
  Ellisland Farm 625
  Eskdale Mill 422
  Etruria Industrial Museum 343
  Fairfax House 474
  Fitzwilliam Museum 222
  Folk Museum (Helston) 312
  Fox Talbot Museum 279
  Freud Museum 133
  Gainsborough's House 216
  Gallery, 1853 477
  Gallery of Modern Art (Glasgow) 652
  Georgian House (Bristol) 280
  Glynn Vivian Art Gallery 554
  Grace Darling Museum 492
  Groam House Museum 692
  Hall's Croft 367, 368
  Hardy's Cottage 295
  Harvard Museum 366, **369**
  Herbert Gallery and Museum 361
  Holburne Museum 284
  Honey Bee Exhibition 551
  House for an Art Lover 657
  Household Cavalry Museum 253
  Hugh Miller's Cottage 692
  Hunterian Art Gallery 656–7
  Huntly House Museum 595
  Inverness Museum and Art Gallery 689
  Ipswich Museum 211
  Jackfield Tile Museum 354
  James Herriot Museum 446
  Jennings Brewery 420
  Jorvik Viking Centre 441, 471, **474**
  Judge's Lodgings 430, 431
  Keats House 133
  Kelmscott Manor 236–7
  Kelvingrove Art Gallery and Museum 649, 656
  Kendal Museum of Natural History and Archaeology 428
  Keswick Museum and Art Gallery 415
  Killerton 321
  Kilmartin House 672
  Kirkstone Galleries 424–5
  Lake Village Museum 277
  Laurel and Hardy Museum 429
  Legionary Museum 564
  Liverpool Museum 437
  London Transport Museum 85, 86
  Lowestoft Museum 207
  Ludlow Museum 353
  McLean Museum and Art Gallery 632
  McManus Galleries 641
  Madame Tussaud's 110
  Mantegna Gallery (Hampton Court) 173
  Maritime and Industrial Museum (Swansea) 554
  Maritime Museum (Southampton) 169
  Maritime Museum (Aberdeen) 684
  Maritime Museum (Exeter) 321
  Maritime Museum (Lancaster) 430, 431
  Maritime Museum (Liverpool) 435
  Maritime Museum (Penzance) 310, 311
  Merchant Adventurer's Hall 471, **473**
  Mingarry Museum 678

Museums and galleries (cont.)
  Monmouth Castle and Regimental Museum 564–5
  Monmouth Museum 565
  Moot Hall 211
  Moray Motor Museum 687
  Morwellham Quay 325
  Moyse's Hall 216
  Museum of Army Transport 467
  Museum and Art Gallery (Cheltenham) 370
  Museum and Art Galley (Penzance) 310, 311
  Museum of Automata 473
  Museum of Costume 284
  Museum of Costume and Textiles 386
  Museum of Dartmoor Life 329
  Museum of the History of Science 238
  Museum of Iron 354
  Museum of Islay Life 671
  Museum of Lakeland Life and Industry 413, 428
  Museum of Liverpool Life 435
  Museum of London 117
  Museum of the Moving Image 129
  Museum of North Devon 317
  Museum of Oxford 241
  Museum of the River 354
  Museum of Science and Engineering (Newcastle) 484
  Museum of Science and Industry (Birmingham) 344, 361
  Museum of Science and Industry (Manchester) 432, 433
  Museum of Scotland 598–9
  Museum of Transport (Glasgow) 649, **656**
  Museum of Victorian Whitby 460
  Museum of Welsh Life 561
  Museum of Wiltshire Rural Life 289
  Nash's House 367, 368
  National Fishing Heritage Centre 469
  National Gallery (London) 75, 77, **88–9**
  National Gallery of Scotland 599
  National Horseracing Museum 217
  National Maritime Museum 135
  National Motor Museum 168
  National Museum of Photography, Film and Television 477
  National Museum of Piping 654
  National Museum of Wales 561
  National Portrait Gallery (London) 87
  National Railway Museum 474
  National Techniquest 560
  National Waterways Museum 371
  Natural History Centre (Malmsmead) 275
  Natural History Museum (London) 102, **106**
  North Devon Maritime Museum 317
  Old Grammar School 468
  Old House (Hereford) 356
  Old Royal Observatory 135
  Oxford Story 241
  Peak District Mining Museum 386
  Pencil Museum 415
  People's Palace 657
  Perth Art Gallery and Museum 640
  Pitt Rivers Museum 241
  Planetarium 110
  Plymouth Dome 324
  Poldark Mine 301, 312
  Pollok House 658
  Portsmouth Historic Ships 169
  Power of Wales Museum 531
  Priest's House Museum 297
  Prison and Police Museum 453
  Provand's Lordship 652
  Provost Skene's House 685
  Quarry Bank Mill 343, 350
  Queen Elizabeth's Hunting Lodge 197, 219
  Queen's Gallery 93
  Queen's House 135
  Quex House 183
  Radnorshire Museum 549

Museums and galleries (cont.)
Regimental Museum (Fort George) 688
Regimental Museum (King's Own Scottish Borderers) 490
Regimental Museum (Royal Northumberland Fusiliers) 492
River and Rowing Museum 234
Robert Burns Centre 625
Robert Opie Collection – Museum of Advertising and Packaging 371
Roman Baths Museum 284
Rotunda Museum 461
Rowley's House Museum 352
Royal Academy 87, 90
Royal Albert Memorial Museum and Art Gallery (Exeter) 321
Royal Armouries Museum 476
Royal Collection 255
Royal Cornwall Museum 303, 313
No.1 Royal Crescent 284
Royal Museum of Scotland 593, 598
Royal Pump Room Museum 452
Russell-Cotes Art Gallery and Museum 297
Ryedale Folk Museum 458
Sainsbury Centre for Visual Arts 209
St Mungo Museum of Religious Life and Art 653
Salisbury and South Wiltshire Museum 291
Sandaig Thatched House Museum 673
Scarborough Art Gallery 461
Science Museum (London) 102, **106**
Scottish Fisheries Museum 642
Scottish National Gallery of Modern Art 607
Scottish National Portrait Gallery 599
Sherlock Holmes Museum 110
Shetland Museum 700
Shibden Hall Museum 479
Sir John Soane's Museum 116
Skerryvore Lighthouse Museum 673
Somerset County Museum 269, 276
Somerset Rural Life Museum 277
Southwold Museum 210
Stamford Museum 393
Strathnaver Museum 699
Streetlife Transport Museum 468, 469
Swaledale Folk Museum 449
Swansea Museum 554
Tain Through Time 693
Tam O'Shanter Experience 625
Tate Gallery (Liverpool) 435
Tate Gallery (London) 77, **97**
Tate Gallery (St Ives) 302, 309
Temple Newson House 476
Tenement House 654
Tetley's Brewery Wharf 476
Theakston Brewery 449
Theatre Museum 86
Theatre Museum (London) 85
Timewalk (Weymouth) 294–5
Tolbooth Art Centre (Kirkcudbright) 626
Tolbooth (Sanquhar) 624
Tom Brown's School Museum 237
Torquay Museum 322
Totnes Elizabethan Museum 323
Town Docks Museum 468
Townend 425
Tudor House Museum 169
Tudor Merchant's House 554
Tullie House Museum 414
Tweeddale Museum 623
Ullapool Museum 698
Ulverston Heritage Centre 429
University Museum (Oxford) 241
Upper Wharfedale Museum 450
Usher Art Gallery 391
Verulamium Museum 231, 250
Victoria and Albert Museum 76, 102, **104–5**
Walker Art Gallery 396, **436–7**
Wallace Collection 110
Warwick Doll Museum 363

Museums and galleries (cont.)
Waterfront Museum 296, 297
Wells Museum 276
Welsh Industrial Maritime Museum 560
West Gate Museum 188
Westgate Museum 170
Westminster Abbey 99
Wheal Martyn Museum 313
Whitby Museum and Pannett Art Gallery 460
Whithorn: Cradle of Christianity 626
Whitworth Art Gallery 433
William Wilberforce House 468
Windermere Steamboat Museum 425
Wood End Museum 461
Wordsworth House 420
Writers' Museum (Edinburgh) 593, 593
York Castle Museum 471, **474**
Yorkshire Mining Museum 479
Yorkshire Museum 470, 474
Yorkshire Sculpture Park 479
Music
classical 130
clubs in London 131
popular 131
Wales 509, 543, **546–7**
Music festivals 24, 66–9
Aldeburgh Festival 211
Edinburgh Festival 587, **590–91**
eisteddfods 509, **530**, 543
Glasgow 649
Malvern Festival 357
Promenade Concerts 24, 67
Music Room (Royal Pavilion) 179

N

Narrowboats 334
Nash, John
Buckingham Palace 92, 93
Regency London **111**
Regent's Park 109
Royal Pavilion 178
Nash, Richard "Beau" **285**
National Exhibition Centre (Birmingham) 344, 361
National Gallery (London) 75, 77, **88–9**
National Library of Wales (Aberystwyth) 551
National Maritime Museum (London) 135
National Museum of Wales (Cardiff) 561
National Parks
Brecon Beacons 507, 545, **556–7**
Dartmoor 258, 303, 305, **328–9**
Exmoor 271, **274–5**
Lake District 402–3, 410–11, **414–28**
North York Moors 444, 459
Northumberland (Cheviot Hills) 493
Peak District 378, **388–9**
Pembrokeshire Coast 544
Snowdonia 520, **528–33**
Yorkshire Dales 396, **448–50**
National Portrait Gallery (London) 87
National Stud (Newmarket) 217
National Trust 29
Lake District 407
Nationalism 18
Scotland 18, 575
Wales 18, 511, 517–18, 541
Natural History Museum (London) 102, **106**
Nature reserves
Beinn Eighe National Nature Reserve 693
Cairngorm Reindeer Centre 683
Cornish Seal Sanctuary 312
Isle of May 642
Loch Garten 683
Minsmere Reserve 210
Muir of Dinnet 686
Handa Island 699
Navy, Tudor 54
Necropolis (Glasgow) 653
The Needles (Isle of Wight) 168

Nelson, Admiral Lord 58
coat of arms 31
Nelson Monument (Edinburgh) 604
Nelson's Column (London) 75
Neolithic Age 46
Neptune's Staircase (Caledonian Canal) 679
Ness, Loch 665, 691
Neville family, Earls of Warwick 364
Nevis Range Gondola 677
New Change (London) 118
New Forest 163, **168**, 169
New Lanark 624
New towns 62–3
Newcastle upon Tyne 484, 487, **498–9**
Cathedral 499
Newlands Valley 420
Newlyn 308, 310
Newman, John Henry 103
Newmarket 196, **217**
Newspapers 25
Newton, Sir Isaac 56
Nicholson, Ben 309
Nightingale, Florence 60
Claydon House 156
Norfolk Broads *see* The Broads
Norman invasion 161
Normans 43, 44
North Country **394–503**
abbeys and priories **400–401**
at a glance 396–7
geology (Lake District) 402–3
Industrial Revolution 398–9
Lancashire and the Lakes **404–37**
map 15
Northumbria **480–503**
Yorkshire and Humberside **438–79**
North Downs 162, 163, 166
North Pennines Tour 486, **501**
North Sea 10
oil 575, 664
North Wales **514–37**
climate 72
map 12, 520–21
portrait 516–19
sea sports **522–3**
Snowdonia National Park 520, 528–33
North York Moors 442, 446–7, **459**
North York Moors Railway **458**
Northumberland National Park 483, 493
Northumbria **480–503**
climate 73
coast **488–9**
portrait 482–5
Sights at a Glance 486–7
Norwegian Church (Cardiff) 560
Norwich **208–9**
Colman's mustard 209
museums 208–9
Norwich Cathedral 196, 208
Notting Hill (London) 133
Nottingham 375, 386
Nottingham Castle 386
Nunnington Hall 457

O

Oast house 155, 164
Oban 665, **672**
Offa's Dyke (Wales) 510, 549
Footpath 36, 542, 549
Oil
Aberdeen 665
North Sea 575, 664
Okehampton 328
Okehampton Castle 328
Old Library (Cardiff) 561
Old St Thomas's Operating Theatre 122
Old Post Office (Tintagel) 315
Old Sarum (Salisbury) 268, 289
Old Vic (London) 128
Olivier, Laurence, Brighton 174
Opera House (Buxton) 382

Ophelia (Millais) 60
Orford Castle 211
Orkney Islands 664, 667, **700**
 map 11, 15
Orwell, George, Jura 670
Osborne House 156, 168
The Other Side (Hockney) 477
Outlook Tower 592
Oval Cricket Ground 131
Overbecks (Salcombe), gardens 262
Oxburgh Hall 203
Oxford 229–30, **238–43**
 Street-by-Street 238–9
Oxford University 152, **242–3**
 Boat Race 70
 Bodleian Library 243
 colleges 228, 238–9, 242–3
 Radcliffe Camera 233, 239, 243
 Sheldonian Theatre 238, **241**, 242

P

Packwood House 337
Paignton and Dartmouth Steam Railway
 302–3
Paignton Zoo 302, 322
Palace Pier (Brighton) 164–5, 174
Palaces
 Blenheim Palace **246–7**
 Buckingham Palace 76, **92–3**
 Culross Palace 643
 in Edinburgh Castle 597
 Falkland Palace 615, 642
 Hampton Court Palace 26, 55, **173**
 Holyrood Palace 604–5
 St James's (London) 90
 Kensington Palace 107
 Linlithgow Palace 608
 Sandringham House 205
 Scone Palace 640
 in Stirling Castle 639
 Windsor Castle **254–5**
Pall Mall (London) 91
Pangbourne 231, 252
Pansy, development 27
Parc Le Breose 554
Parish church 32–3
Parks and gardens
 Abbotsbury Sub-Tropical Gardens 294
 Arduaine Garden 672
 Bancroft Gardens 366, 368
 Battersea Park 81
 Beth Chatto Garden 213
 Blenheim Palace 246–7
 Bodnant Gardens 519
 Botanic Garden (Cambridge) 225
 Botanic Gardens (Oxford) 240
 Botanic Gardens (Glasgow) 576, 649, **657**
 Botanical Gardens (Birmingham) 344, 361
 Burford House Gardens 353
 Chatsworth 382–3
 Chelsea Physic Garden 132
 Cheltenham Imperial Gardens 362
 Cirencester Park 371
 Compton Acres 297
 Cotehele 325
 Crarae Gardens 576, 670
 Crathes Castle 577, 687
 Cwmdonkin Park 554
 Dartington Hall Gardens 323
 Dawyck Botanic Garden 577
 design **262–3**
 Drummond Castle Gardens 577
 East Lambrook Manor 263
 Gardens of the Rose 231, 233, **251**
 Glendurgan 313
 Green Park 81
 Greenwich Park 81
 Hampstead Heath 81, **134**
 Hampton Court Palace 26
 Harlow Car Gardens 452
 Hestercombe Garden 276

Parks and gardens (cont.)
 Hidcote Manor Gardens 363
 Holland Park 80, 132–3
 Holyrood Park 605
 Hyde Park 76, 81, 101, **107**
 Hydroponicum 698
 Inverewe Gardens 576, 698
 Kailzie Gardens 613, 623
 Kensington Gardens 80, 81, 101, **107**
 Kew Gardens 80, 140
 Kiftsgate Court Gardens 363
 Knightshayes Court 263, 321
 Logan Botanic Garden 576, 627
 London **80–81**
 Midlands Garden Tour **362–3**
 Morrab Gardens 310
 Mount Edgecumbe Park 324
 Overbecks 262
 Parnham 263
 Penrhyn Castle 519
 Pitmedden 577
 Plas Newydd 519
 Powis Castle 548
 Princes Street Gardens 603
 Regent's Park 81, **109**
 Rosemoor Garden 316
 Richmond Park 80, 140
 Royal Botanic Garden (Edinburgh) 606
 St James's Park 81, 111
 Scotland **576–7**
 Stourhead 259, **292–3**
 Stowe 230, **248**
 Studley Royal **454–5**
 through the ages **26–7**
 Trebah 313
 Trelissick 313
 Trengwainton 262, 308
 Trewithen 262, 313
 West Country gardens **262–3**
 Williamson Park 431
 Windsor Great Park 253
 Winter Gardens (Malvern) 357
Parliament
 House of Lords 20
 Houses of Parliament 78, 95, **96**
 New Scottish Parliament 605
 Scottish Assembly 18
 State Opening 68
 Welsh Assembly 18, 541, 542
Parliament House (Edinburgh) 593
Parliament House (Machynlleth) 510, 550
Parnham (Beaminster), gardens 263
Parr, Catherine 362
Pavarotti, Luciano, wax model 110
Paxton, Joseph, Chatsworth House 382
Paycocke's 213
Peacock Panel (tile) 354
Peak Cavern (Castleton) 375
Peak District National Park **375–6**, 378
 Peak District Tour **388–9**
Peebles 613, 615, 623
Peers 31
Pembroke Dock 544
Pembrokeshire Coast National Park 540, 544
Pembrokeshire Coastal path 36, 542
Pen y Fan 557
Pencil manufacture 415
Pendennis Castle 313
Pendle, witches 431
Penn, William 229, 249
Pennine Way 36, 388, 443, 485, 493
Pennines
 moors 443
 North Pennines Tour 486, **501**
Penrhyn Castle, gardens 519
Penrith 414
Penrith Castle 414
Penshurst Place 191
Pentland Hills 623
Penwith Tour 308
Penzance 303, **310–11**
Perth 615, 640

Perth Castle 615
Peter Pan, statue 107
Peterborough 202
Peterborough Cathedral 202
Peterloo Massacre 433
Petticoat Lane market (London) 19, 127
Petworth House 172
Piazza (Covent Garden) 85
Piccadilly (London) **90–91**
Piccadilly Circus (London) 87, 91
Picts (Scotland) 574
Piece Hall (Halifax) 398, 479
Pier Head Building (Cardiff) 560
Pilgrim Fathers 57, 302, 324
Pilgrim's Way (Southeast) **166–7**
Piping Centre (Glasgow) 654
Pitlochry 681
Pitmedden (Scotland), gardens 577
Pitt Rivers Museum (Oxford) 241
Pitville Pump Room (Cheltenham) 370
Plague 57
Planetarium (London) **110**
Plantaganet kings 44
Plas Mawr (Conwy) 526
Plas Newydd (Anglesey) 519
 gardens 519
Plas Newydd (Llangollen) 530
Plas-yn-Rhiw 533
Plymouth 302, **324**
Poets' Corner (Westminster Abbey) 99
Poldark Mine 301, 312
Politics 20–2
Polo 71
Polperro 314
Polruan 314
Ponies, Dartmoor 329
Pony trekking, Wales 542
Poole 296–7
Porlock 275
Port Sunlight 399, 437
Portchester Castle 161, 169
Portmeirion 506, 520, **536–7**
Portobello Road (London) 133
Portree 695
Portsmouth **169**
 Historic Ships 169
Postbridge 328
Potter, Beatrix
 Lake District 408, **412**, **425**
 museum 425
The Potteries (Staffordshire) 343, **348–9**
Power stations 609
 Dounreay 699
 Pitlochry 681
Powis Castle 545, **548**
 gardens 548
Prehistoric Britain **46–7**
 Arbor Low 388
 Avebury Stone Circle 268, **289**
 Castlerigg Stone Circle 407, **417**
 "Cheddar Man" 278
 Flag Fen 202
 Grimes Graves 202–3
 Grimspound 329
 Long Meg and her Daughters 414
 Maiden Castle 47, 269, 295
 Merry Maidens 301, 308
 Mousa Broch 700
 Northumbria 483
 Old Sarum 268, 289
 Parc Le Breose 554
 Rollright Stones 236
 Silbury Hill 268, 288
 Skara Brae 663, **700**
 Standing Stones of Callanish 663, **701**
 Stonehenge 47, 259, **288–9**
 Uffington Castle 237
 Wayland's Smithy 237
 Wessex 267–8, **272–3**
 Windmill Hill **272**
Preselis Mountains 547
Prince Regent 109

Prince of Wales, investiture 510, 524
Princes Street (Edinburgh) 586, 587
Princes Street Gardens (Edinburgh) 603
Princes in the Tower 124, 125
Princess Elizabeth and Princess Anne (Van Dyck) 599
Protestant martyrs 55, 116
  memorial (Oxford) 238, **241**
Provand's Lordship (Glasgow) 652
Public holidays 69
Pubs **38–9**
  Falkland Arms 236
  food 41
  Jamaica Inn 314
  Lord Nelson 204
  Tetley's Brewery Wharf museum 476
  signs 39
  The Lamb and Flag 84
  Trip to Jerusalem 386
  Ye Olde Fighting Cocks 250
Pulteney Bridge (Bath) 268, 283
Pump Room (Cheltenham) 370
Pump Room (Llandrindod Wells) 549
Pump Rooms (Bath) 282
Puritan movement 249

Q

Quarry Bank Mill (Styal) 343, 350
Queen Elizabeth Forest Park 635
Queen Mary's Dolls' House 255
Queen's College (Cambridge) 221, 224–5, **242**
Quicksand 430
Quiraing 695

R

Radcliffe Camera (Oxford) 233, 239, 243
Radio 24
Railways
  see tramway
  Aberystwyth Cliff Railway 551
  Alresford 166
  Bala Lake Railway 530
  Ffestiniog 531, **532–3**
  George Hudson 399
  Jacobite Steam Train 676
  Keighley and Worth Valley 478
  National Museum 474
  North York Moors **458**
  Paignton and Dartmouth Steam Railway 302–3
  Ravenglass and Eskdale Railway 421
  Romney, Hythe and Dymchurch 183
  Snowdon Mountain Railway 531
  South Devon Steam Railway **323**
  Strathspey Steam Railway 682
Ransome, Arthur 413
Rare Breeds Park (Oban) 672
Ravenglass and Eskdale Railway 421
Reculver Fort 183
Red deer 571
Regattas **234–5**
Regent's Park (London) 81, **108–13**
  Sights at a Glance 109
Regions **12–13**
Religion 19
  museum 653
  Scotland 575
  Wales 508–9
Rembrandt, self-portrait 659
Renaissance
  Knot Garden 27
  Tudors **54–5**
Reservoirs, Elan Valley 550, 555
Restoration, monarchy 57
Restormel Castle 314
Rhinns of Galloway 627
Rhododendrons 519, 576
Ribble Valley 431
Riber Castle Wildlife Park 386

Richard III, King 53
Richborough Castle 183
Richmond Castle 448
Richmond (London) 140
Richmond Park 80, 140
Ridgeway (Thames Valley) 37, 231
Rievaulx Abbey 443, 445, **457**
Ripley Castle 453
Ripley (Yorkshire) 453
Ripon 453
Ripon Cathedral 453
Ritz Hotel (London) 87, 90
Rob Roy 614, 635
Robert the Bruce 627
  Bannockburn 638
Robin Hood (Nottingham) 377, 386
Robin Hood's Bay 442, 461
Rochester 190
Rochester Castle 190
Rochester Cathedral 190
Rokeby Venus (Velazquez) 89
Rollright Stones 236
Roman Britain **48–9**
  Antonine Wall 613, **643**, 656
  art and nature 371
  baths 282, **283**
  baths museum **284**
  Caerleon 541, **564**
  Chew Green Camp 493
  Chysauster 310–11
  Corbridge Museum 497
  Fishbourne Palace 161, 171
  Great Bath **285**
  Hadrian's Wall 396, 483, 487, **496–7**, 574
  Hardknott Fort 407, **422**
  Housesteads Fort 483, 497
  invasion 183
  Ribchester Roman fort 431
  Scotland 574
  Segontium 524
  theatre (St Albans) 250
  Verulamium 231, 250
  Vindolanda 496
  Viroconium 352
  Wade's Causeway 459
Romney, George **413**
Romney, Hythe and Dymchurch Railway 183
Romney Marsh 182–3
Rosemoor Garden (Great Torrington) 316
Ross-on-Wye 344, 356–7
Rosslyn Chapel 623
Rothesay Castle 633
Rothiemurchus Estate 682
Rotunda (Manchester) 61
Rowntree, Joseph 399
Royal Academy (London) 87, 90
Royal Albert Hall (London) 102, 130
Royal Ascot 70
Royal Botanic Garden (Edinburgh) 606
Royal Citadel (Plymouth) 324
Royal College of Music (London) 102
Royal Crescent (Bath) 268, **282**, 284
Royal Doulton china 348–9
Royal Exchange (Glasgow) 652
Royal Exchange (London) 119
Royal Exchange (Manchester) 432
Royal Festival Hall (London) 130
Royal High School (Edinburgh) 604
Royal Hospital (Chelsea) 132
Royal Liver Building (Liverpool) 408, 434
Royal Mile (Edinburgh) 592–5
Royal National Eisteddfod (Wales) 543, 546
Royal National Theatre (London) 128
Royal Naval College (Dartmouth) 303, 322
Royal Naval College (Greenwich) 135
Royal Opera House (London) 85, 130
Royal Pavilion (Brighton) 153, **175–7**
  history and interior **178–9**
Royal Shakespeare Company 128, 369

Royal Shakespeare Theatre (Stratford-upon-Avon) 367
Royal Tunbridge Wells 191
Rugby Union 70, 71
Rum 679
Runnymede 253
Rupert, Prince, Shrewsbury 352
Rural architecture **32–3**
Rural life 22–3
Ruskin, John 408, **412**, 428
Ruthin 525
Rydal 424
Rye 163
  Street-by-Street map **186–7**

S

Sackville, Thomas 190
Sackville-West, Vita 190
Sadler's Wells (London) 130
Sainsbury Centre for Visual Arts 209
St Abb's Head 620
St Aidan 484, 490, **491**
St Albans 232, **250–51**
St Albans Cathedral 251
St Andrew's Castle 641
St Andrew's Cathedral (Aberdeen) 684
St Andrews (Scotland) 615, **641**
St Augustine's Abbey (Canterbury) 188
St Austell (Cornwall) 313
St Columba 663
St Cuthbert 490, **491**, 502
St David 510, 552
  shrine 553
St David's (Wales) 506, 540, 544
St David's Cathedral (Wales) **552–3**
St George's Chapel (Windsor) 254
St Giles Cathdral (Edinburgh) 586, 593
St Ives 258, 302, **309**
St James's (London) **90–91**
  Palace 90
St James's Park (London) 81, 111
St Machar's Cathedral (Aberdeen) 684
St Magnus Cathedral (Orkney) 663
St Martin's Theatre (London) 84
St Mary Redcliffe Church (Bristol) 280
St Mary the Virgin Church (Oxford) 241
St Mary's Abbey (York) **400–401**, 474
St Mary's House (Bramber) 174
St Michael's Mount 303, **310–11**
St Mungo 647, 653
St Mungo's Cathedral (Glasgow) 647, **653**
St Ninian 653
St Paul's Cathedral (London) 77, 78, 114, 118, **120–21**
St Peter Mancroft Church (Norwich) 209
St Thomas's Hospital (London), Old Operating Theatre 122
Salisbury **290–91**
  Old Sarum 268, 289
Salisbury Cathedral 259, **290–91**
Salisbury Cathedral (Constable) 8
Salisbury Crags (Edinburgh) 585, 605
Salisbury Plain 268
Salmon 681, 698
Saltaire 399, 442, 443, 477
Saltram House 324
Sandringham 205
Sandringham House 205
Sanquhar 624
Savin's Hotel (Aberystwyth) 551
Saxe-Coburg, House of 45
Saxons 267
  Wales 510
Scafell Pike 402, 421, **422**
Scarborough 461
Scarborough Castle 461
Science Museum (London) 102, **106**
Scone Palace 640
Scotch Whisky Centre 592
Scotland **566–701**
  at a glance 568–9

Scotland (cont.)
Border Abbeys Tour 620–21
clans and tartans 578–9
culture and the arts 573
Edinburgh **582–609**
gardens 576–7
Glasgow **644–59**
Highlands and Islands **660–701**
history 574–5
Lowlands **610–59**
map 14–15
politics and economy 572
portrait 571–81
Road to the Isles Tour 678–9
Royal Deeside Tour 686–7
society 572–3
writers and intellectuals 580–81
Scott, Sir Giles Gilbert, Liverpool Anglican
Cathedral 437
Scott, Sir Walter 580, **622**, 664
Abbotsford House 613–14, 622
Monument 587, 599
Scott's View 614, 620, 621
Trossachs 634
Scottish Exhibition Centre (Glasgow) 656
Scottish textiles 625
Sea Life Centre (Brighton) 175
Seabirds 700
Seahouses 490
Seashells (Moore) 436
Seasons
events 66–9
fruit 154–5
Selworthy 275
Seven Sisters (Sussex) 180
Shaftesbury 267, 294
Shakespeare, William 54
birthplace 366, 368
Globe Theatre 23
Hamlet 369
Henry IV 123
Stratford-upon-Avon 366–9
Shandy Hall 456, 457
Shaw, George Bernard **251**
Shaw, Norman 29
Sheep 162, 196, 407, 518
Sheldon, Gilbert 241
Shelley, Percy Bysshe, memorial 238, 239
Shells 261
Sherborne 294
Sherborne Abbey Church 294
Sherborne Castle 294
Shetland Islands 11, 15, 667, **700**
Shipbuilding 399, 648
Dock Museum 428
Shops
Blackwell's bookshop 240
books 543, 549
chain stores 126, **127**
clothes 126, **127**
department stores 126, **127**
Fortnum and Mason 90, 126
Glasgow 649, 651
Harrod's 103, 126
Liberty 126
London **126–7**
St James's 90–91
shoes 126, **127**
Shrewsbury 344, **352**
Shrewsbury Castle 344, 352
Sidmouth 321
Silbury Hill 268, 288
"Silicon Glen" 572
Simonsbath 275
Sinclair clan 579
Sizergh Castle 428
Skara Brae (Orkneys) 663, **700**
Sketch for Annabel Lee (Whistler) 657
Skiddaw 403, 417
Skiing 676, 677, 683
Skinners' Hall (London) 118
Skipton Castle 450

Skye *see* Isle of Skye
Slate industry
Lake District 408
Wales 518, **531**, 532
Sleeping Shepherd (Gibson) 436
Slums 60
Small Isles (Scotland) 678–9
Smith, Adam 580
Smithfield 116–17
Smoo Cave (Durness) 699
Smuggling 161
Cornwall 312
Snowdon 507, **531**
Snowdon Mountain Railway 531
Snowdonia National Park 518, 520, **528–33**
Snowshill Manor 362
Soane, Sir John 116
Society and politics 20–22
Soho (London) 86
Somerleyton Hall 207
Somerset 268, 269
Somerset House (London) 86
Sonning Bridge 252
South Bank Centre (London) 128, 130
South Devon Steam Railway **323**
South Downs 163, **181**
South Downs Way (Sussex) 37, 162
South Kensington (London) 76, **100–107**
Sights at a Glance 101
Street-by-Street map 102–3
South and Mid-Wales **538–65**
climate 72
map 12
portrait 540–43
Sights at a Glance 544–5
Wild Wales Tour 555
South Queensferry 607
Southampton **168–9**
Southeast England 12, **150–255**
at a glance 152–3
Downs and Channel Coast **158–91**
East Anglia **192–225**
introduction 152–7
Thames Valley **226–55**
Southwark (London) **114–25**
Sights at a Glance 115
Southwark Cathedral (London) 79, 123
Southwest Coastal Path (Devon and
Cornwall) 274, 303
Southwold 197, 210
Spa Centre (Llandrindod Wells) 549
Spark, Muriel 581
Speaker's Corner (London) 107
Spean Bridge 690
Speke Hall 437
Spencer House (London) 90
Speyside Malt Whisky Trail 686
Spode, Josiah 348
Sporting Year **70–71**
Sports 25
see Boating
Aquadome (Inverness) 689
blood sports 664
cricket 71, 131
Cumbria 408, 414
football 25, 70, 649
golf 71, 614, 615
Grasmere sports 424
Highland Games 66, 68, 71
London venues 131
rowing and river sports **234–5**
Scotland 572, 615
sea sports **522–3**
sea-bathing and swimming 461
tennis 70, 131, 615
Wales **522–3**, 542–3
Spring events 66
Spurn Head 443, 469
Stained glass
Burrell Collection 659
Canterbury Cathedral 188–9
Chagall 171

Stained glass (cont.)
Charles Rennie Mackintosh 646
Durham Cathedral 502
St David's Cathedral 553
York Minster 475
Stamford 393
Standing Stones of Callanish 663, **701**
Stanton Drew (Wessex) 272
Stanway House 362
Stately homes **28–9**
Althorp House 376–7
Arlington Court 317
Athelhampton House 295
Audley End 218–19
Batemans 157
Blenheim Palace 230, **246–7**
Blickling Hall 206
Bowood House 279
Broadlands 156
Burghley House 333, 378, **392–3**
Burton Agnes Hall 466
Castle Howard 397, 445, **462–3**
Charlecote Park 336
Charleston farmhouse 157
Chartwell 157, **191**
Chatsworth House 333, **382–3**
Chiswick House 140
Clandon Park 172
Cliveden House 156
Corsham Court 279
Cotehele 325
Dalemain **414–15**
Fairfax House 474
Fountains Hall 454
Glynde Place 180
Goodwood House 171
Ham House 140
Hardwick Hall 336, 376, 386
Harewood House 476
Hatfield House 57, 230, **249**
Holker Hall 429
Holkham Hall 205
Hopetoun House 608
Hughenden Manor 230, 251
Hutton-in-the-Forest 414
Ickworth House 216
Ightham Mote 191
Kedleston Hall 386
Kingston Lacy 297
Knebworth House 249
Knole 190–191
Lanhydrock 262, 314, 315
Leighton Hall 430
Leighton House 133
Levens Hall **429**
Linley Sambourne House 133
Little Moreton Hall 337
Longleat House 292
Luton Hoo 248–9
Marble Hill House 140
Markenfield Hall 453
Minster Lovell Hall 236
Mompesson House 291
Montacute House 294
Moseley Old Hall 337
Mount Stuart House 633
Nunnington Hall 457
Osborne House 156, 168
Oxburgh Hall 203
Packwood House 337
Paycocke's 213
Penshurst Place 191
Petworth House 172
Plas-yn-Rhiw 533
Saltram House 324
Shandy Hall 456, 457
Snowshill Manor 362
Somerleyton Hall 207
Speke Hall 437
Stanway House 362
Stourhead House 293
Stratfield Saye 156

Stately homes (cont.)
  Syon House 140
  Temple Newsam House 476
  Thames Valley **230**
  Traquair House 623
  Tudor manor houses 336–7
  Uppark House 181
  Wightwick Manor 337
  Wilton House 291
  Woburn Abbey 230, 248
Steall Waterfall (Ben Nevis) 690
Steam age 398–9
Steam engine, Newcomen (1712) 106
Steel industry, Wales 541
Sterne, Laurence, Shandy Hall 456, 457
Stevenson, Robert Louis 580, 581
Steyning 174
Stirling **638**
Stirling Castle 615, **638–9**
Stirling Castle in the Time of the Stuarts
  (Vorsterman) 638
Stoke-on-Trent 343, **348**
Stokesay Castle 344, 352, 353
Stone, Cotswold 338–9
Stone circles 47, 272
Stone of Destiny 574, 640
  Edinburgh Castle 597
Stone walls **380–81**
Stonehenge (Wiltshire) 47, 268, 271
  construction 259, **288–9**
The Storr 695
Stour, River (Suffolk) 212
Stourhead, garden 259, **292–3**
Stourhead House 293
Stowe 230, **248**
  gardens 230, **248**
Strand Quay (Rye) 186
Strata Florida (Wales) 555
Stratfield Saye 156
Stratford-upon-Avon 333, **366–9**
  Anne Hathaway's Cottage 363
  Street-by-Street map **366–7**
  William Shakespeare 366–9
Strathpeffer 692
Strathspey Steam Railway 682
Striding Edge 403
Stuart clan 579
Stuarts 45, **56–7**
Studley Royal, gardens **454–5**
Stump Cross Caverns (Pateley Bridge) 450
Styal, Quarry Bank Mill 350
Sudeley Castle 362
Suffragettes 62
Summer events 67
Summer Isles (Scotland) 698
Sutton Bank 447, 456
Swaffham 203
Swaledale 448
Swallow Falls (Betws-y-Coed) 530
Swanage 296
Swannery (Abbotsbury) 294
Swansea 541, 554
  see South and Mid-Wales
Sygun Copper Mine 532
Syon House 140

T

Tain 692–3
Tamar Valley 325
Tan-y-Bwlch 533
Tan-y-Grisiau 533
Tantallon Castle 609
Tarbert 671
Tarbet 633
Tartans *see* Clans and tartans
Tate Gallery (Liverpool) 435
Tate Gallery (London) 77, **97**
Taunton 269, 276
Tea time
  Betty's Café Tea Rooms 452
  cream teas 317

Tea time (cont.)
  regional dishes 40
  Willow Tea Room 654
The Team at Rest (Leger) 607
Television 24–5
  Granada Studios Tour 433
  museum 477
Telford, Thomas
  Conwy Bridge 527
  Menai Bridge 519
  Neptune's Staircase 679
  Waterloo Bridge 530
Temple (London) 78, **116**
Temple of Mithras (London) 118
Temple Newsam House 476
Tenbury Wells 353
Tenby 554
Tennis
  London clubs 131
  Wimbledon 70
Tennyson, Alfred, Lord 391
Tewkesbury 370
Tewkesbury Abbey 344, 370
Textile industry
  Borders (wool) 613
  Bradford (wool) 477
  Glasgow (cotton) 648
  Halifax (wool) 479
  museum (wool) 476
  North Country 398–9
Thames Path (Thames Valley) 231
Thames, River 76–7
  river view of London **78–9**
  rowing and regattas **234–5**
Thames Valley **226–55**
  climate 72
  map 232–3
  portrait 228–31
  rowing and regattas **234–5**
  Sights at a Glance 232
  Touring the Thames 252–3
Thatcher, Margaret 22, 65
Thatching **306–7**
Theatre
  Restoration 56
  Tudor 54
Theatre Royal, Haymarket (London)
  111
Theatres
  Eden Court Theatre 689
  Edinburgh 587
  Globe **123**
  London **128–9**
  Pitlochry Festival Theatre 681
Theme parks, Flambards Village Theme Park
  312
Thetford 203
Thirlmere 426–7
Thirsk 446
Thomas, Dylan 543, **547**
Threave Castle 625
The Three Dancers (Picasso) 97
Three Peaks Race (North Wales)
  523
Tintagel 301, 315
Tintagel Castle 301, 315
Tintern Abbey 545, **565**
Tiree 673
Tissington Trail 332, 378, **387**
Titanic 169
Tithe barn 32
  Bradford-on-Avon 279
  Buckland Abbey 324
Titles 31
Tobermory 673
Torbay 302, 322
Torosay Castle 673
Torquay 302, 305, **322**
Torre Abbey 302, 322
Torridon 693
Totnes 323
Totnes Castle 323

Tours by Car
  Border Abbeys 621–2
  Midlands Garden Tour 347, **362–3**
  North Norfolk Coastal Tour 198, **204–5**
  North Pennines Tour 501
  North York Moors Tour **459**
  Peak District Tour **388–9**
  Penwith Tour 304, **308**
  Road to the Isles 678–9
  Royal Deeside 686–7
  Touring the Thames **252–3**
  Wild Wales Tour 555
Tower Bridge (London) 79, **122**
Tower of London 77, 79, **124–5**
Trade unions 60
Tradescant, John 240
Trafalgar Square (London) 75
Traitors' Gate (Tower of London) 125
Tramways
  Great Orme Tramway 525
  museum 389
Traquair House 623
Trebah (Falmouth), gardens 313
Trelissick (Truro), gardens 313
Trengwainton (Penzance), gardens 262, 308
Treshnish Isles (Scotland) 673
Tretower Castle 557
Trewithen (Truro), gardens 262, 313
Trinity College (Cambridge) 225
Tron Kirk 594
Trooping the Colour (London) 67
Tropical World (Leeds) 476
Trossachs 568, 614, **634–5**
Truro 303, 313
Truro Cathedral 313
Tudor manor houses 336–7
Tudor Revival 336, 337
Tudors 43, 44–5, **54–5**
Tummel, River 680
Tunbridge Wells *see* Royal Tunbridge Wells
Tunnels, Exeter 321
Turkish Sauna Suite (Harrogate) 452
Turner, J M W, bequest 97
Tweed, River 614, 615
Twentieth century **62–5**
  garden 27
Twm Siôn Cati's Cave (Wales) 555
The Two Sisters (Renoir) 280
Tŷ Hyll (Capel Curig) 530
Tyler, Wat 116
Tymperleys (Colchester) 213
Tyne Bridge 499
Tyne Valley 501

U

Uffington Castle 237
Uists 701
Ullapool 665, **698**
Ullswater 415
Umbrellas (Renoir) 89
Unemployment 63
Unicorn 641
Universities
  Cambridge 220–21, **222–5**
  Durham 502
  Oxford 238–9, **242–3**
University Boat Race 70
Uppark House 181
Urquhart Castle 691

V

Vale of the White Horse 232, **237**
Valley of the Rocks (Devon) 274
Vanbrugh, Sir John
  Blenheim Palace 246–7, 28
  Castle Howard 462
Vegetables 196
Verulamium (St Albans) 231, 250
Victoria and Albert Museum (London) 76,
  102, **104–5**

Victoria, Queen 60, 92
  Balmoral 664
  Osborne House 156
  statue 107
Victorian Britain **60–61**
  Glasgow 648
  pub 38
Victory, HMS 169
Vikings 50, 484, 663
Villages **32–3**
Vineyards 155
Vivien Leigh (McBean) 87

W

Wales **504–65**
  at a glance 506–7
  castles **512–13**
  history 510–11
  map 12
  North Wales **514–37**
  portrait 508–9
  Prince of Wales 510, 524
  South and Mid-Wales **538–65**
  Voices of Wales **546–7**
Walker Art Gallery (Liverpool) 396, **436–7**
Walker, William 171
Walkers' Britain **36–7**
Walking
  North Country 408, 485
  Snowdonia 518
Walks
  see Long-distance footpaths
  Ben Nevis 677
  Constable Walk 199, 212
  East Lothian Coast 609
  Galloway Forest Park 627
  Killiecrankie 680
  Lake District 421
  Malham Walk 451
  Tissington Trail 387
  West Highland Way 634
  Wye Valley 357
Wallace Collection (London) 110
Wallace, William 574
Walton, Izaac 170
Warkworth Castle 484, 492
Wars of the Roses 377
  Wales 511
Warwick 363
Warwick Castle 333, 363, **364–5**
View of Warwick Castle (Canaletto) 365
Warwick the Kingmaker 364
Wast Water 402, **422**
Water mills
  River Thames 252
Waterfalls
  Devon 329
  North Country 449, 485
  Scotland 690, 691
  Skye 568
  Wales 530, 551
Waterloo Chamber (Windsor Castle) 255
Watersmeet (Devon) 275, 320
Waterways
  see Canals
  Midlands canals 334–5
  museum 371
  Norfolk Broads 201, 206
Watt, James 58
Waugh, Evelyn, *Brideshead Revisited* 462
Wax figures, Warwick Castle 364
Wayland's Smithy 237
Wealden Hall House 32
Weardale 501
Webb, Philip 29
Webb, Sir Aston 104
Wedgwood, Josiah 343, 348
Well-dressing 375, **377**, 387
Wellington, Duke of, Stratfield Saye 156
Wells 258, **276–7**
Wells Cathedral **276–7**

Wells, John 309
Wells-next-the-Sea 199, 205
Welsh borders (Marches) 344
Welsh, Irvine 581
Welsh language 508, 511, **546–7**
Welwyn Garden City 62–3
Wembley Stadium and Arena 131
Wenlock Edge 352
Wensleydale 449
Wernher family 249
Wesley, John **311**
Wessex **264–97**
  map 12, 270–71
  portrait 266–9
  Prehistoric Britain 267–8, **272–3**
  Sights at a Glance 271
West Country 12, **256–329**
  at a glance 258–9
  climate 72
  Devon and Cornwall **298–329**
  gardens 262–3
  Wessex **264–97**
West End (London) 76, **82–99**
  Sights at a Glance 83
  theatres 128, **129**
Wester Ross 693
Western Isles 666, **701**
  see Highlands and Islands
Westminster (London) 76, **82–99**
  Sights at a Glance 83
  Street-by-Street map 94–5
Westminster Abbey (London) 77, 94, **98–9**
  Stone of Destiny 574
Westminster Bridge (London) 82
Westminster Pier (London) 95
Westward Ho! 316
Weymouth 269, **294–5**
Whalley Abbey (Clitheroe) 431
Wharfedale 450
Wharram Percy 466
Whin Sill 483, 485
Whipsnade Wild Animal Park 233, **248**
Whisky distilleries 681, 694
  Islay 670, 671
  Speyside 686–7
Whispering Gallery (London) 121
Whistler, James McNeill 657
Whitby **460**
Whitby Abbey 400, **460**
White Cliffs of Dover 151, 163
White Horse (Sutton Bank) 456
White Horse (Uffington) 47, 237
White Horse (Westbury) 268
White Tower (Tower of London) 125
Whitehall (London), Street-by-Street 94–5
Whithorn 626
Whitworth Art Gallery (Manchester) 433
Wicken Fen 201
Wight, Alf **446–7**
Wightwick Manor 337
Wigmore Hall (London) 130
Wilberforce, William, Hull **468**
Wild flowers **34–5**, 160, 260
Wildlife **34–5**
  see Nature reserves; Zoos, animal and
  wildlife parks
  Anglesey 519
  Cairngorms 683
  coast **260–61**
  Fens **200–201**
  Norfolk 197
  North Country 408, 485
  Northumbria coast **488–9**
William I (the Conqueror), King 44, 50, 51
  Battle of Hastings 181
  Tower of London 124
  Windsor Castle 254
Williams-Ellis, Sir Clough 536
Williamson Park (Lancaster) 431
Willow Tea Room (Glasgow) 654
Willy Lott's Cottage (Suffolk) 212
Wilton House 291

Wimbledon, tennis 70, 131
Wimborne Minster 297
Winchelsea 187
Winchester **170–71**
  Hospital of St Cross 171
Winchester Cathedral 19, 152, 161, **170–71**
Windermere 408, 423, **425**
Windmill Hill **272**
Windmills, Norfolk 194, 205, 207
Windsor 230, 253
  House of Windsor (monarchs) 45, 230, 254
Windsor Castle 152, 230, **254–5**
Windsor Great Park 253
Wine 154
Winter events 69
Winter Gardens (Malvern) 357
Wireless 62
Witches of Pendle 431
Woburn Abbey 230, 248
Wolsey, Cardinal 173
Wolvesey Castle 170
Woods, John, Bath 282
Wookey Hole 276
Wool trade 217
  Suffolk 196
Woollen mills *see* Textile industry
Worcester 360
Worcester Cathedral 344, 360
Wordsworth, William
  Grasmere 408, **412**, **424**
  museum 420, 424
World War I 62
World War II 63, 162
Wren, Sir Christopher **120**
  churches in London 118, 120
  Hampton Court Palace 173
  St Paul's Cathedral 120–21
Writers and poets 24
  Bloomsbury Group 109, 157
  children's writers 412–13
  Lancashire and the Lakes **412–13**
  Puritan movement 249
  Scotland 580–81
  Southeast England 156–7
Wycliffe, John 53
Wye Valley 357, 565

Y

Yeoman Warders (Tower of London) 5
York 397, 445, **470–75**
  history 441, 474
  House of York (monarchs) 44
  St Mary's Abbey **400–401**
  Street-by-Street (map) 470–71
York Minster 470, **472–3**, **475**
Yorkshire Dales National Park 442, **448–50**
  James Herriot Country **446–7**
  Three Peaks 442
Yorkshire and Humberside **438–79**
  climate 73
  portrait 440–43
  Sights at a Glance 444–5
Yorkshire Wolds 443
A Young Man Among Roses (Hilliard) 104
Ypres Tower (Rye) 187

Z

Zennor 308
Zoos; animal and wildlife parks
  see Aquariums
  Bristol Zoo Gardens 280
  Buckfast Butterfly Farm and Otter
  Sanctuary **323**
  Harewood Bird Garden 476
  Kincraig Highland Wildlife Park 682
  Paignton Zoo 302, 322
  Rare Breeds Park 672
  Riber Castle Wildlife Park 386
  Tropical World 476
  Whipsnade Wild Animal Park 233, **248**

Acknowledgments

DORLING KINDERSLEY would like to thank the following people whose contributions and assistance have made the preparation of this book possible.

MAIN CONTRIBUTOR
Michael Leapman was born in London in 1938 and has been a professional journalist since he was 20. He has worked for most British national newspapers and now writes about travel and other subjects for several publications, among them *The Independent, Independent on Sunday, The Economist* and *Country Life*. He has written 11 books, including the award-winning *Companion Guide to New York* (1983, revised 1995) and *Eyewitness Travel Guide to London*. In 1989 he edited the widely praised *Book of London*.

ADDITIONAL CONTRIBUTORS
Peter Brookesmith, Malcolm Boyes and Hazel Chester, Gerard Cheshire, Paul Cleves, Andrew Eames, Sue Gordon, James Henderson, Tony Hopkins, Lucy Juckes, John Lax, Sue Morony, Claire Musters, Michelle Pickering, Marcus Ramshaw, Alastair Scott, Roger Smith, Roly Smith, Sam Ward-Dutton.

ADDITIONAL ILLUSTRATIONS
Christian Hook, Gilly Newman, Paul Weston.

DESIGN AND EDITORIAL ASSISTANCE
Eliza Armstrong, Moerida Belton, Josie Barnard, Hilary Bird, Louise Boulton, Roger Bullen, Margaret Chang, Deborah Clapson, Elspeth Collier, Pauline Clarke, Gary Cross, Cooling Brown Partnership, Guy Dimond, Fay Franklin, Angela-Marie Graham, Danny Farnham, Joy Fitzsimmons, Ed Freeman, Andrew Heritage, Paul Hines, Annette Jacobs, Steve Knowlden, Charlie Hawkings, Martin Hendry, Nic Kynaston, Pippa Leahy, James Mills Hicks, Elaine Monaghan, Sean O'Connor, Mary Orchard, Marianne Petrou, Chez Picthall, Clare Pierotti, Mark Rawley, Jake Reimann, Carolyn Ryden, David Roberts, Alison Stace, Stewart Wild.

ADDITIONAL PHOTOGRAPHY
Max Alexander, Peter Anderson, K. Bayer, Steve Bere, June Buck, Joe Cornish, Geoff Dann, Michael Dent, Philip Dowell, Mike Dunning, Chris Dyer, Andrew Einsiedel, Philip Enticknap, Jane Ewart, Neil Fletcher, DK Studio/Steve Gorton, Frank Greenaway, Paul Harris, Stephen Hayward, John Heseltine, Ed Ironside, Dave King, Cyril Laubscher, Neil Mersh, Robert O'Dea, Stephen Oliver, Vincent Oliver, Roger Phillips, Rob Reichenfeld, Karl Shone, Chris Stevens, Jim Stevenson, Clive Streeter, Harry Taylor, Kim Taylor/Jane Burton, David Ward, Mathew Ward, Stephen W. Whitehorne, Stephen Wooster, Nick Wright, Colin Yeates.

PHOTOGRAPHIC AND ARTWORK REFERENCE
Christopher Woodward of the Building of Bath Museum, Franz Karl Freiherr von Linden, NRSC Air Photo Group, The Oxford Mail and Times and Mark and Jane Rees.

PHOTOGRAPHY PERMISSIONS
DORLING KINDERSLEY would like to thank the following for their assistance and kind permission to photograph at their establishments: Banqueting House (Crown copyright by kind permission of Historic Royal Palaces); Cabinet War Rooms; Paul Highnam at English Heritage; Dean and Chapter Exeter Cathedral; Gatwick Airport Ltd; Heathrow Airport Ltd; Thomas Woods at Historic Scotland; Provost and Scolars Kings College; Cambridge; London Transport Museum; Madame Tussaud's; National Museums and Galleries of Wales (Museum of Welsh Life); Diana Lanham and Gayle Mault at the National Trust; Peter Reekie and Isla Roberts at the National Trust for Scotland; Provost Skene House; Saint Bartholmew the Great; Saint James's Church; London St Paul's Cathdral; Masters and Wardens of the Worshiful Company of Skinners; Provost and Chapter of Southwark Cathdral; HM Tower of London; Dean and Chapter of Westminster; Dean and Chapter of Worcester Cathedral and all the other churches, museums, hotels, restaurants, shops, galleries and sights too numerous to thank individually.

PICTURE CREDITS
t = top; tl = top left; tlc = top left centre; tc = top centre; tr = top right; cla = centre left above; ca = centre above; cra = centre right above; cl = centre left; c = centre; cr = centre right; clb = centre left below; cb = centre below; crb = centre right below; bl = bottom left; b = bottom; bc = bottom centre; bcl = bottom centre left; br = bottom right; d = detail.

Works of art have been reproduced with the permission of the following copyright holders: Marc Chagall *Window N/E Corner, Chichester Cathedral, 1978* © ADAGP, Paris and DACS, London 1999 - 171t; Dame Barbara Hepworth *Two Figures* © Alan Bowness, Hepworth Estate 309bl; © David Hockney *Mr. and Mrs. Clark and Percy* 1970–1 - 97tr, *The Other Side* 1990–3 - 477t; Patrick Heron *Coloured Glass, 1953* © Estate of Patrick Heron 1999 all rights reserved DACS - 258cb; Fernand Leger *STUDY FOR LES CONSTRUCTEURS, THE TEAM AT REST, 1950* (c) ADAGP, Paris and DACS, London 1999 - 607t; Roy Lichtenstein *Whaam! 1963* © Estate of Roy Lichtenstein/DACS, 1999 - 77bl; Ben Nicholson *Cornwall, 1943-5* © Angela Verren-Taunt 1999 all rights reserved DACS 309br; Pablo Picasso *The Three Dancers, 1925* (c) Succession Picasso/DACS 1999 - 97c; Stanley Spencer *Swan Upping, 1914 - 19* © Estate of Sir Stanley Spencer 1999. All rights reserved DACS 253t.

The work of Henry Moore, *Large Two Forms*, 1966, illustrated on page 479b has been reproduced by permission of the Henry Moore Foundation.

The publisher would like to thank the following individuals, companies and picture libraries for permission to reproduce their photographs:

ABBOT HALL ART GALLERY AND MUSEUM, Kendal: 413t, 430b(d); ACTION PLUS: 572t; Steve Bardens 508c; MAX ALEXANDER: 25b; Printed by kind permission of MOHAMED AL FAYED: 103t; ALLSPORT: 71c; David Cannon 70tl; Mike Hewitt 345t; Gary M. Prior 70b; Ben Radford 70c; AMERICAN MUSEUM, Bath: 285tl; ANCIENT ART AND ARCHITECTURE COLLECTION: 46cb, 48ca, 48clb, 49ca, 49clb, 50bl, 50br, 52crb, 55ca, 250tl, 253br, 513t; T & R ANNAN & SON (D) 655br; ARCAID: Richard Bryant. Architect: Richard Rogers 136b; THE ARCHIVE & BUSINESS RECORDS CENTRE, University of Glasgow: 575t; ASHMOLEAN MUSEUM, OXFORD: 51t; MUSEUM OF AUTOMATA, YORK: 473b; AXIOM: Alberto Arzoz 22t, 24b.

BARNABY'S PICTURE LIBRARY: 64tr; BEAMISH OPEN AIR MUSEUM: 498c, 483b, 499ca, 499cb, 499b; JONATHAN BECKER/CUMBRIA LIFE MAGAZINE: 413b; BRIDGEMAN ART LIBRARY, LONDON & NEW YORK: 348bca, 349tl, 489tl/tc, 581t, 688b, 689b(d); Agnew and Sons, London 365t; Museum of Antiquities, Newcastle upon Tyne 48tl; Apsley House, The Wellington Museum, London 30tl; Bibliotheque Nationale, Paris *Neville Book of Hours* 364t(d); Birmingham City Museums and Gallery 361t; Bonham's, London, *Portrait of Lord Nelson with Santa Cruz Beyond*, Lemeul Francis Abbot 58cb(d); Bradford Art Galleries and Museums 53clb; City of Bristol Museums and Art Galleries 280c; British Library, London, *Pictures and Arms of English Kings and Knights* 4t(d), 43t(d), *The Kings of England from Brutus to Henry* 30bl(d), *Stowe manuscript* 44tl(d), *Liber Legum Antiquorum Regum* 50t(d), *Calendar Anglo -Saxon Miscellany* 50–1t(d), 50–1c(d), 50–1b(d), *Decrees of Kings of Anglo-Saxon and Norman England* 51clb, 53bl(d), *Portrait of Chaucer*, Thomas Occleve 53br(d), *Portrait of Shakespeare*, Droeshurt 55bl(d), *Historia Anglorum* 44bl(d), 254tl(d), *Chronicle of Peter of Langtoft* 315b(d), *Lives and Miracles of St Cuthbert* 491tl(d), 491cl(d), 491cr(d), *Lindisfarne Gospels* 491br(d), *Commendatio Lamentabilis intransitu Edward IV* 510b(d), *Histoire du Roy d'Angleterre Richard II* 512t(d), 688b;

Cheltenham Art Gallery and Museums, Glos 273tl; Christies, London 525t; Claydon House, Bucks, *Florence Knightingale*, Sir William Blake Richmond 156t; City of Edinburgh Museums & Galleries, *Chief of Scottish Clan*, Eugene Deveria 578bl, 618tr ; Department of Environment, London 52tr; Fine Art Society, London 655clb; Fitzwilliam Museum, University of Cambridge, *George IV as Prince Regent*, Richard Cosway 179cb, 222bl, *Flemish Book of Hours* 400tl(d); Giraudon/Musee de la Tapisserie, with special authorization of the city of Bayeux 51b,181b; Guildhall Library, Corporation of London, *The Great Fire*, Marcus Willemsz Doornik 57bl(d), *Bubbler's Melody* 58br(d), *Triumph of Steam and Electricity*, The Illustrated London News 61t(d), *Great Exhibition, The transept from Dickenson's Comprehensive Pictures* 60–1, *A Balloon View of London as seen from Hampstead* 111c(d); Harrogate Museum and Art Gallery, North Yorkshire 452t; Holburne Museum and Crafts Study Centre, Bath 57t; Imperial War Museum, *London Field Marshall Montgomery*, J Worsley 31cbr(d); Kedleston Hall, Derbyshire 28c, 28br; King Street Galleries, London, *Bonnie Prince Charlie*, G Dupré 574tl; Lambeth Palace Library, London, *St Alban's Chronicle* 53t; Lever Brothers Ltd, Cheshire 399cra; Lincolnshire County Council, Usher Gallery, Lincoln, *Portrait of Mrs Fitzherbert after Richard Cosway* 179b; London Library, *The Barge Tower from Ackermann's World in minature*, F Scoberl 59t; Manchester City Art Galleries 433b; Collection of Andrew McIntosh Patrick, UK 655cla; David Messum Gallery, London 527b; National Army Museum, London, *Bunker's Hill*, R Simkin 58ca; National Gallery, London, *Mrs Siddons the Actress*, Thomas Gainsborough 58t(d), 157ca; National Museet, Copenhagen 50ca; Phillips, the International Fine Art Auctioneers, *James I*, John the Elder Decritz 56b(d); Private Collections: 8–9, 30ca(d), 38tl, 52–3, 59cla, 59bl, 60clb, Vanity Fair 61br, 157t, *Ellesmere Manuscript* 190b(d), *Armada: map of the Spanish and British Fleets*, Robert Adam 325t, 460t, 496b; Royal Geographical Society, London 157cb(d); Royal Holloway & Bedford New College, the *Princes Edward and Richard in the Tower*, Sir John Everett Millais 125b; Scottish National Portrait Gallery, Edinburgh 618bl/br; Smith Art Gallery and Museum, Stirling 638b; Tate Gallery, London: 60crb, 255t; South African National Gallery, Cape Town 655cra; Thyssen-Bornemisza Collection, Lugo Casta, *King Henry VIII*, Hans Holbein the Younger 54b(d); By courtesy of the Board of Trustees of the Victoria and Albert Museum, London 28t(d), 60b, 103c, 212t, 348cl, 401cr, 457b; Walker Art Gallery, Liverpool 436c; Westminster Abbey, London, *Henry VII Tomb effigy*, Pietro Torrigiano 30br(d), 44bc(d); The Trustees of the Weston Park Foundation, *Portrait of Richard III*, Italian School 53cla(d); Christopher Wood Gallery, London, *High Life Below Stairs*, Charles Hunt 29c(d); reproduced with permission of the British Library Board: *Cotton Faustina BVII folio 85* 53cb, 113cl; © The British Museum: 46cr, 47cb, 77tl, 87c, 109, 112–3 all except 113t; © The Bronte Society: 478 all; Burton Constable Foundation: Dr David Connell 468t; Michael Busselle: 166, 244/5.

Cadogen Management: 90b; CADW – Welsh Historic Monuments (Crown Copyright), 564t; Laurie Campbell: 699t, 699c; Camera Press: Cecil Beaton 98bl; Cardiff City Council: 562tr, 563t, 563c; FKB Carlson: 39bcl; Castle Howard Estate Ltd: 463tl; Colin de Chaire: 205c; Trustees of the Chatsworth Settlement: 382b, 383b; Bruce Coleman Collection: 35br; Stephen Bond 328b; Jane Burton 35cra; Mark N. Boulton 35cl; Patrick Clement 34clb; Peter Evans 682tl; Paul van Gaalen 201cb, 274tl; Sir Jeremy Grayson 35bl; Dennis Green 166br; Gordon Langsbury 683t; Harald Lange 34bc; Werner Layer 200bl; George McCarthy 34t, 35bl, 260b, 315br; Paul Meitz 700clb; Dr Eckart Pott 34bl, 700t; Hans Reinhard 34cb, 35tc, 328t, 634tl; Dr Frieder Sauer 694t; N Schwiatz 35clb; Kim Taylor 35tl, 700cra; Konrad Wothe 700ca; Collections: David Bowie 167c, 201tr; David Davis 231t; Gena Davies 519c; Alain le Garsmeur 303t; Fay Godwin 273b; Robert Hallmann 231b;

McQuillan & Brown 348tl/tr; Michael Nicholson 488/9; Graeme Peacock (c) Antony Gormley, Tyne and Wear 485c, 484/5t, 485b, 488tr; Robert Pilgrim 230cl; Mike St. Maur Sheil 166c; Liz Stares 412cl, 534/5; Liba Taylor 234br; Paul Watts 302c; Robin Weaver 377b; Robin Williams 268b; George Wright 269b; Conran Restaurants: 31bc;
Corbis: Christopher Cormack 489br; Eric Crichton 307br; Bob Gibbons: Eye Ubiquitous 380cb; Chinch Gryniewicz; Ecoscene 542b; Dave G. Houser 381cr; Sandro Vannini 163t; Roger Wilmshurst; Frank Lane Picture Agency 307cl/crb; Adam Woolfitt 380ca, 619br; Michael S. Yamashita 306tr; Joe Cornish: 358, 408c, 469b, 615b; courtesy of the Corporation of London: 119b; Doug Corrance: 577br, 579b, 584, 586t, 590cb, 591tr/ca, 626t, 649b, 669bl, 673b, 681t, 686b, 688t, 689t; Eric Crichton Photos: 380bl/bc, 381bcr, 577cl, 577cr; John Crook: 171b; 1805 Club: 31t; 1853 Gallery, Bradford 477t; Edinburgh Festival Centre in Association with the Bank of Scotland: 590tl; Edinburgh Festival Fringe Society: Andy Manzie, Royal Blind School, Edinburgh 590tr; Empics: Andy Heading 234/5c; Steve Morton 234tr; Michael Steele 648c; English Heritage: 140b, 218c, 218b, 219b, 270–1b, 289b, 400br, 401b, 458t, 491tr, 491c; Avebury Museum 46ca; Devizes Museum 46br, drawing by Frank Gardiner 497br; Salisbury Museum 46t, 46bl; Skyscan Balloon Photography 47t, 288b; 458t; 497bl; English Life Publications Ltd, Derby: 392tl, 392tr, 393t, 393b; Et Archive: 45tc, 45cr, 56cb, 57clb, 62crb, 156b, 348bcb; Bodleian Library, Oxford 52crb; British Library, London 52tl, 52ca, 166/7c, 619t/ca; Devizes Museum 46cl, 47b, 272tl/tr/trb, 273tlb/tr, 288c; Garrick Club 510tl(d); Imperial War Museum, London 62clb(d), 63br; Labour Party Archives 64br; London Museum 47cla; Magdalene College 54ca; National Maritime Museum, London 43b; Stoke Museum Staffordshire Polytechnic 45bc, 56tl, 348bl/br; Victoria & Albert Museum, London 54t(d); Eureka!: 479t; Mary Evans Picture Library: 9 inset, 38tr, 44br, 45tl, 45cl, 45bl, 45br, 48bl, 48br, 50cb, 51cla, 55t, 55cb, 55br, 57crb, 58bl, 59br, 60tl, 62ca, 63ca, 63clb, 63crb, 85cb, 110t, 111t, 123br, 151 inset, 156cb, 157b, 167tr, 189c, 191c, 203b, 216c, 238bl, 246tl, 249c, 249bl, 249br, 252bl, 257 inset, 311t, 331 inset, 386b, 399t, 399cla, 431tr, 492t, 527tl, 574b, 580t, 580c, 580b, 618c, 619cb/bl, 622bl, 624c, 641b, 695br; Eye Ubiquitous: Dorothy Burrows 380tr; David Cumming 307bc; J. B. Pickering 381c; J. Shaw 307ca.

Chris Fairclough: 329b, 402b; Paul Felix: 252c; Ffotograff: Charles Aithie: 509t, 542t, 546bl, 546/7c; Fishbourne Roman Villa: 49t; Louis Flood: 578br; Foreign and British Bible Society: Cambridge University Library 511c; Fortean Picture Library: Janet & Colin Bord 272cr, 273cl, 547tl; Paul Broadhurst 273cr; Terence Meaden 272cl; Roger Vlitos 272b; Fotomas Index: 111cra.

Garden Picture Library: John Glover 27br; J. S. Sira 27ca, Steven Wooster 26t; Glasgow Museums: Art Gallery & Museum, Kelvingrove 676b, 692b; Museum of Transport 656c; John Glover: 66cr, 154cb, 213b, 576tr; The Gore Hotel, London. Ronald Grant Archive: Still from *'How Green was my Valley'* with John Loder and Donald Crisp 547cr, 581c; V. K. Guy Ltd: Mike Guy 23t, 25t, 230tr, 376t, 384/5, 543b, 558/9, 630/1, 673t; Paul Guy 163c/b, 226/7, 344t, 418/9, 600/1; Vic Guy 162c, 264/5, 302t, 306/7c, 615c.

Sonia Halliday and Laura Lushington Archive: 475t; Hambleton District Council: 446tr; Chris Barron 446cl/cr, 447b; Hampton Court Palace (Crown Copyright): 26b; Robert Harding Picture Library: 182t, 306br, 307tc/tr, 670t; Jan Baldwin 317b; M H Black 320t; L Bond 387b; Michael Botham 36br; C. Bowman 235tl; Lesley Burridge 338tr; Martyn F Chillman 339bc; Rob Cousins 268c; Philip Craven 107t, 208b, 367b, 412b; Nigel Francis 233b; Paul Freestone 242b; Lee Frost 197b; Brian Harrison 701b; Gavin Hellier 306bl; Michael Jenner 49b, 701c; Norma

Joseph 69b; Christopher Nicholson 277t; B O'Connor 37ca; Jenny Pate 155bc; Rainbird Collection 51crb; Roy Rainsford 37b, 168t, 332b, 388cr, 428t, 450t, 565b; Walter Rawling 21t; Hugh Routledge 2–3; Peter Scholey 333t; Michael Short 339br, 447cr; James Strachen 448b; Adina Tovy 65tl; Van der Hars 684t; Andy Williams 179t, 252br, 396c, 506t, 662; Ken Wilson 413cr; Adam Woolfitt 20t, 20c, 48tr, 49crb, 284b, 298, 300, 317ca, 339bl, 513bl, 556tl, 682tr; DENNIS HARDLEY: 345b, 408t, 518b, 610/11, 614t, 615t, 620c, 620b, 626b, 632t, 632b, 633b, 662, 665t/c, 678b, 679b, 698b; GORDON HENDERSON: 690c, 699b; HAREWOOD HOUSE: 476c; PAUL HARRIS: 36t, 66cl, 335bl(d), 381bcl/br, 388b, 425b; HARROGATE INTERNATIONAL CENTRE: 453b; HAYES DAVIDSON (computer-generated image): 123t; HEATON COOPER STUDIO, GRASMERE: William Heaton Cooper R. I. 413cl; Crown copyright is reproduced with the permission of the Controller of HMSO: 77br, 124bl, 124br, 125tl; CATHEDRAL CHURCH OF THE BLESSED VIRGIN MARY AND ST ETHELBERT IN HEREFORD: 356b; HERTFORDSHIRE COUNTY COUNCIL: Bob Norris 62–3; JOHN HESELTINE: 78t, 108, 113t, 114, 274tr, 274c, 557tl; HISTORIC ROYAL PALACES (Crown Copyright): 173 all; HISTORIC SCOTLAND (Crown Copyright): 596tr/c, 639c; PETER HOLLINGS: 399bl; BARRY J HOLMES: 67t; NEIL HOLMES: 282b(d), 284c, 316t, 431b, 503tl, 503tr, 531b; TONY HOPKINS: 484b, 485t; ANGELO HORNAK LIBRARY: 166tl, 167b, 472tl, 472bl, 472br, 475br, 494/5; Reproduced by permission of the CLERK OF RECORDS, HOUSE OF LORDS: 575c; DAVID MARTIN HUGHES: 150–1, 160; HULTON GETTY COLLECTION: 26c, 31cl, 31cr, 57cla, 58c, 60c, 61cb, 62tl 62tr, 62b, 63t, 64ca, 64bl, 156ca, 166bl, 169c, 200tr, 251b, 334t, 398c, 399crb, 400bl, 435b, 461b, 462br, 511t, 547b, 628tl, 635br, 691c; HUNTERIAN ART GALLERY, UNIVERSITY OF GLASGOW: 657tl; Mackintosh Collection 646, 655crb; HUTCHISON LIBRARY: Catherine Blacky 38cb; Bernard Gerad 573t; HUTTON IN THE FOREST: Lady Inglewood 414t.

THE IMAGE BANK, London: David Gould 411b; Romilly Lockyer 78bl; Colin Molyneux 557bl; Stockphotos/Steve Allen 432c, Trevor Wood 316b; Simon Wilkinson 180b; IMAGES COLOUR LIBRARY: 34cla, 47c, 237b, 252t, 271t, 162t, 192/3, 214/5, 274bl, 275b, 386t, 388cl, 389t, 403c; 480/1, 514/5, 614b, 660/1, Horizon/Robert Estall 512c; Landscape Only 37cb, 270, 423, 513br; IRONBRIDGE MUSEUM: 355b.

JARROLD PUBLISHERS: 222br, 247t(d), 338bl; MICHAEL JENNER: 23c, 25c, 303c, 338tl, 390b, 442t, 443c, 484c, 586c, 648b, 664b, 700b; B. K. JONES: 380br; JORVIK VIKING CENTRE, York: 471t.

KOS PICTURE SOURCE: 302B.

FRANK LANE PICTURE AGENCY: 466b(d); W Broadhurst 278b; Michael Callan 260crb; ANDREW LAWSON: 27bl, 262br, 263tl, 263tr, 263br, 576bl, 577tl, 577tr, 698t; LEEDS CASTLE ENTERPRISES: 161b; LEIGHTON HOUSE, Royal Borough of Kensington: 132br; published by kind permission DEAN AND CHAPTER OF LINCOLN 390t, 391cb, 391bl; LINCOLNSHIRE COUNTY COUNCIL: USHER GALLERY, Lincoln: c 1820 by William Ilbery 391bl; LLANGOLEN INTERNATIONAL MUSICAL EISTEDDFOD 530c; LONDON FILM FESTIVAL: 66t; LONDON TRANSPORT MUSEUM: 86t; LONGLEAT HOUSE: 292t.

TOM MACKIE: 158/9, 162b, 194, 196t, 196b, 197t, 200/1c, 268t, 298/9, 318/9, 344b, 345c, 372/3, 376b, 377t, 404/5, 409t/b, 438/9, 442b, 443t/b, 464/5, 519b, 586b; MADAME TUSSAUDS: 110b; MALDOM MILLENIUM TRUST: 219t; MANSELL COLLECTION, London: 31clb, 44tr, 56ca, 59cb, 285tr, 365bl, 399clb, 469b; NICK MEERS: 18t, 256–7; ARCHIE MILES: 258ca; SIMON MILES: 402tr; MINACK THEATRE: Murray King 308b; MIRROR SYNDICATION INTERNATIONAL: 80b, 93b, 116; BTA/Juilian Nieman 38ca; Philip Russell 426–7; MOLYNEUX PHOTOGRAPHY: Colin Molyneux 538/9; MUSEUM OF CHILDHOOD, Edinburgh: 594b, 595cr; MUSEUM OF LONDON: 48crb, 117t.

Edmund Naegele: 184/5, 196c, 587t, 665b, 674; NATIONAL FISHING HERITAGE CENTRE, Grimsby: 469t; NATIONAL GALLERY,

London: 77tr, 88–9 all; NATIONAL GALLERY OF SCOTLAND: *The Reverend Walker Skating on Duddington Loch*, Sir Henry Raeburn 599b; NATIONAL LIBRARY OF WALES: 510tr, 513c(d), 546tr, 555b; NATIONAL MUSEUM OF FILM AND TELEVISION, Bradford: 477c; Board of Trustees of the NATIONAL MUSEUMS AND GALLERIES ON MERSEYSIDE: Liverpool Museum 437t; Maritime Museum 435t; Walker Art Gallery 396b, 436tl, 436tr, 436b, 437c; NATIONAL MUSEUMS OF SCOTLAND: 598b; NATIONAL MUSEUM OF WALES: 510c; By courtesy of the NATIONAL PORTRAIT GALLERY, London: 602b; *First Earl of Essex*, Hans Peter Holbein 401t(d), Angus McBean 87b; NATIONAL TRAMWAY MUSEUM, Crich: 389c; NATIONAL TRUST FOR SCOTLAND: 592b, 628tr, 629tl, 629tr, 629br, 642b, 643c; Lindsey Robertson 629bl; Glyn Satterley 654br; NATIONAL TRUST PHOTOGRAPHIC LIBRARY: *Bess of Hardwick (Elizabeth, Countess of Shrewsbury)*, Anon 382tl(d); Mathew Antrobus 336br, 454cl, 455bl; Oliver Benn 29br, 310c, 325bl, 454b; John Bethell 311c, 311bl, 311br, 337t; Nick Carter 279b; Joe Cornish 303b, 409c, 540; Prudence Cumming 293c; Martin Dohrn 54crb; Andreas Von Einsiedel 29bl, 336cb, 337ca; Roy Fox 297; Geoffry Frosh 321t; Ray Hallett 201b; Jerry Harpur 262t, 262bl; Derek Harris 262clb, 293t; Nick Meers 292b, 293b, 362b, 381bl; John Miller 307bl; Rob Motheson 324t; Ian Shaw 548t; Richard Surman 337br, 420b; Rupert Truman 337br, 437b; Andy Tryner 336bl; Charlie Waite 455t; Jeremy Whitaker 337bc, 457t, 548b; Mike Williams 336ca, 455c; George Wright 262crb, 324c; NATIONAL TRUST FOR SCOTLAND: 568b; NATIONAL WATERWAYS MUSEUM at Gloucester: 335bc, 335br; NATURAL HISTORY PHOTOGRAPHIC AGENCY: Joe Blossom 200cb; Laurie Campbell 488bl, 571t; Bill Costner 489bl; Martin Garwood 459ca; Jane Gifford 22b; E. A. Janes 197c, 231c; Robert Thompson 200br; David Woodfall 23b, 380/1c, 489tr, 518c; NATURE PHOTOGRAPHERS: Andrew Cleave 260cla; E A James 35cla, 416t; Hugh Miles 493t; Owen Newman 35ca; William Paton 700crb; Paul Sterry 34crb, 34br, 35cb, 35crb, 252c, 279t, 451t, 700cla; Roger Tidman 205b; NETWORK PHOTOGRAPHERS: Laurie Sparham 572b; NEW MILLENNIUM EXPERIENCE COMPANY LTD.: Q. A. Photos 136t, 137t/b; NEW SHAKESPEARE THEATRE CO: 129t; NORFOLK MUSEUMS SERVICE: Norwich Castle Museum 209b.

'PA' NEWS PHOTO LIBRARY: EPA Photo AFP/Toru Yamanaka 71t; David Jones 71b; Martin Keene 66c; JOHN STILLWELL 65cr; PALACE THEATRE ARCHIVE: 128c; PHOTOLIBRARY WALES: Steve Benbow 543t, 547tr; Aled Hughes 546br; Rex Moreton 543c; David Williams 522tr/cl/bl, 522/3c, 523ca/cb/bl/br, 546cl; PHOTOS HORTICULTURAL: 155tlc, 155cra, 155cb, 155crb, 262ca, 263c; PLANET EARTH PICTURES: David Phillips 27cb; POPPERFOTO: 31br, 63bl, 64clb, 64crb, 65bl, 92tl, 154tr, 167tl, 211t, 314cl,412cr, 524b; AFP/Eric Feferber 65br; © 1996 POLYGRAM FILMED ENTERTAINMENT 581b; PORT MERION LTD: 536tl; PPL OXBOW: Alastair Black 522br, 523bc; Kevin Richardson 523t; PUBLIC RECORD OFFICE (Crown Copyright): 52b.

ROB REICHENFELD: 174t, 175c, 175b, 334b; REX FEATURES LTD: 30cb, 31ca, 45tr, 64tl, 65bc, 254c, 255br; Barry Beattie 283cl; Peter Brooke 31bc; Nils Jorgensen 30c; Hazel Murray 65tr; Tess, Renn-Burrill Productions 295b; Richard Young 64tl; Nick Rogers 65tc; Tim Rooke 68cr; Sipa/Chesnot 31bl; Today 21c; THE RITZ, London: 87t; ROYAL ACADEMY OF ARTS, London: 90ca; ROYAL BOTANIC GARDENS, KEW: 80ca; ROYAL COLLECTION © 1995 Her Majesty Queen Elizabeth II: *The Family of Henry VIII*, Anon 42(d), 91c, 92tr, 92bl, 93t, 254tr, 255tl(d), 255tr, 255bl; *George IV in full Highland Dress*, Sir David Wilkie 579tc; David Cripps 93c; John Freeman 92br; ROYAL BOTANIC GARDEN, Edinburgh 577bl; ROYAL COLLEGE OF MUSIC, London: 102c; ROYAL DOULTON: 349cr/br; ROYAL PAVILION, ART GALLERY AND MUSEUMS, Brighton: 178c, 178bl, 178br, 179cl, 179cr; ROYAL SHAKESPEARE THEATRE COMPANY: Donald Cooper 369c(d).

ST. ALBAN'S MUSEUMS: Verulamium Museum 250b; SARTAJ BALTI HOUSE: Clare Carnegie 477b; ALASTAIR SCOTT: 649c; SCOTTISH HIGHLAND PHOTO LIBRARY: 677t; SCOTTISH

MOUNTAINEERING CLUB: 668tr; Ken Crocket origination 668tl; SCOTTISH NATIONAL GALLERY OF MODERN ART: 607t; SCOTTISH NATIONAL PORTRAIT GALLERY: on loan from the collection of the Earl of Roseberry, *Execution of Charles I*, Unknown Artist 56–7; *Princess Elizabeth and Princess Anne*, van Dyck 599t; S4C (Channel 4 Wales): 511b; SIDMOUTH FOLK FESTIVAL: Derek Brooks 321b; SKYSCAN BALLOON PHOTOGRAPHY: 288t; JOHN SNOCKEN: 27cr/bc; SOUTHBANK PRESS OFFICE: 130t; SPODE: 348/9c, 349 tr/bl; SPORTING PICTURES: 414b; STILL MOVING PICTURES: Wade Cooper 575b; Doug Corrance 648t, 649t, 669tl, 670b; Distant Images 625t; ANGUS JOHNSTON: 668cl/bl; Derek Laird 574c; Robert Lees 69t; Paisley Museum 625b; Ken Paterson 590ca/bl/br, 603t; David Robertson 576cl, 691b; Scottish Tourist Board 682br, 683c; Paul Tomkins 669br, 701tr; Stephen J. Whitehorne 635t, 668br, 669cr; Harvey Wood 681b; TONY STONE IMAGES: 38–9, 518t, 519b; Rex A.Butcher 87c; Richard Elliott 68b; Glyn Kirk 340/1; John Lamb 408b; John Lawrence 286/7; Yann Layma 582/3; Mark A. Leman 664t; Ed Pritchard 587b; Alan Puzey 138/9; Rob Talbot 269t, 403ca; Trevor Wood 24t; David Woodfall 516.

TATE GALLERY, London: 77bl, 97 all except tl, 309c/bl/br; ROB TALBOT: 403cb; THAMES CARDS: Sue Milton 234bl/cl, 235tr/b; MARK THOMAS: 488ca/cb/br, 489bc; TUILLE HOUSE MUSEUM, Carlisle: 414c.

Courtesy of the Board of Trustees of the VICTORIA AND ALBERT MUSUEM, London: 76b, 104 –105 all except 104t.

CHARLIE WAITE: 671t; © WALES TOURIST BOARD: 507c, 508b, 512–3, 556br, 557tr, 557br; Roger Vitos 556tl, 556bl; THE WALLACE COLLECTION, London: 110cb; DAVID WARD: 663bt, 676t; Illustration from *The Tale of Peter Rabbit* by Beatrix Potter © FREDERICK WARNE & CO, 1902, 1987: 412t, Cover illustration of *Jemima Puddleduck* © FREDERICK WARNE & CO. 1908, 1987: 425t(d); Courtesy of the Trustees of THE WEDGWOOD MUSEUM,

Barlaston, Staffordshire, England: 351b; JEREMY WHITAKER: 246tr, 246c, 247b; WHITBREAD PLC: 38bl; STEPHEN J. WHITEHORNE: 590/1, 598tl, 599c, 604b, 633t, 669tr, 672t, 690b; WHITWORTH ART GALLERY, University of Manchester: courtesy of Granada Television Arts Foundation 433c; CHRISTOPHER WILSON: 470bl; WILTON HOUSE TRUST: 291b; WINCHESTER CATHEDRAL: 171t; WOBURN ABBEY – by kind permission of the Marquess of Tavistock and Trustees of the Bedford Estate: 54–5, 248t; TIMOTHY WOODCOCK PHOTOLIBRARY: 5b; WOODFALL WILD IMAGES: David Woodfall 447cl; Photo © WOODMANSTERNE, Watford, UK: Jeremy Marks 120t, 121t.

YORK CASTLE MUSEUM: 471cb; DEAN & CHAPTER YORK MINSTER: 475cla, 475ca, 475cl; Peter Gibson 475cra, 475cr, 475cl; Jim Korshaw 472tr; YORKSHIRE DALES NATIONAL PARK AUTHORITY: Dale Countryside Museum, Hawes 446b; Reproduced by couresty of the YORKSHIRE MUSEUM: 474c; YORKSHIRE SCULPTURE PARK: Jerry Hardman Jones 479b.

ZEFA: 68t, 130b, 289t, 295t; Bob Croxford 67cr; Weir 205t.

Cover: All special photography except THE BRIDGEMAN ART LIBRARY, LONDON & NEW YORK: front flap b; FFOTOGRAFF: Patricia Aithie front bl; V. K. GUY LTD.: Paul Guy front c; ROBERT HARDING PICTURE LIBRARY: Mark Mawson back ca; Andy Williams front flap c; NEW MILLENIUM EXPERIENCE COMPANY LTD: front tl and spine b.

Front Endpaper: All special photography except DOUG CORRANCE: tr, ROBERT HARDING PICTURE LIBRARY: Andy Williams tl, Adam Woolfitt bl; DAVID MARTIN HUGHES bc; NATIONAL TRUST PHOTOGRAPHIC LIBRARY: Joe Cornish ccl; TONY STONE IMAGES: David Woodfall cl, UNIVERSITY OF BRISTOL: Hunterian Art Gallery tcr.

Back Endpaper: All special photography except JOHN HESELTINE tl, br.

PROJECTS FOR THE MILLENNIUM

THE WORLD IS planning the biggest party in history to mark the turn of the Millennium. But long after the party-goers have gone home, Britain will benefit from an ambitious range of projects planned not only to mark the Millennium but also to create a lasting legacy in education and leisure. The following is a selection of projects from around the country.

LONDON

THE DOME, GREENWICH
0870 606 2000. 31 Dec 1999. www.dome2000.co.uk
The largest millennium project in Britain, this will be the focal point of the nation's new year celebrations. Designed by the Richard Rogers Partnership, and built on a former industrial site, the Dome is the largest structure of its kind in the world, and will house a performance arena and exhibition. *See pp136–7.*

THE BRITISH AIRWAYS MILLENNIUM WHEEL, LAMBETH
summer 1999.
At 150 m (492 ft), twice the height of the Statue of Liberty, this will be the world's largest ferris wheel. Sixty capsules, carrying up to 20 people each, will take 25 minutes to make the full circuit.

THE MILLENNIUM PEDESTRIAN BRIDGE, BANKSIDE
spring 2000.
The first new bridge in London since 1894, this will be the city's only pedestrian bridge, and will span the Thames between St Paul's Cathedral and the new Tate Bankside.

SOUTHEAST ENGLAND

HARBOUR MILLENNIUM SCHEME, PORTSMOUTH
01705 834576. 2000.
This scheme includes the 165-m (540-ft) Spinnaker Tower, 6 km (4 miles) of Millennium Promenades and the Gunwharf Quays leisure and visitor attraction. The Historic Naval Dockyards will be the location for the new Action Stations attraction, a National Museum of Armaments and a Maritime Research Centre.

THE WEST COUNTRY

AT-BRISTOL, BRISTOL
0117 909 2000. spring 2000. www.at-bristol.org.uk
At-Bristol includes two unique attractions: Wildscreen-at-Bristol, which recreates the extraordinary diversity of the natural world, and Explore-at-Bristol on exciting hands-on science centre. Also included are an IMAX® giant-screen cinema, plus new public squares and open spaces.

EDEN MILLENNIUM PROJECT, ST AUSTELL
01726 222 900. www.edenproject.com
In a former Cornish clay pit, the world's largest greenhouses are taking shape in a project to conserve a range of endangered plant species. The site will also support research into sustainable cultivation methods.

THE MIDLANDS

MILLENNIUM POINT, BIRMINGHAM
0121 303 2361. 2001. www.millenniumpoint.org.uk
The Hub is the centre of this £110 million project at Digbeth. Radiating walkways link the three major educational and leisure attractions: the Discovery Centre; the Technology Innovation Centre; and the University of the First Age.

NATIONAL SPACE SCIENCE CENTRE MILLENNIUM PROJECT, LEICESTER
0116 253 0811. 2001. www.nssc.co.uk
An awe-inspiring attraction where the whole family can enjoy the excitement of space in a way that is fun, educational and totally absorbing. The NSSC will house the first Challenger Learning Centre outside North America – a fascinating educational tool for groups of children or adults – and a 200-seat planetarium.

THE NORTH COUNTRY

THE EARTH CENTRE, DONCASTER
01709 322085/6. www.earthcentre.org.uk
A new kind of theme park providing an entertaining and thought-provoking day out. Set within a 160-ha (400-acre) Ecology Park, a variety of indoor and outdoor attractions, gardens, play areas, theatres and daily events, focus on sustainable development in a fun, interactive way.

THE LOWRY, SALFORD QUAYS
0161 955 2020. April 2000. www.thelowry.org.uk
The Lowry contains two theatres; two art galleries (one housing the works of LS Lowry, the other for visiting exhibitions); Artworks, a creative interactive experience for all the family; and spacious foyers, bars, shops and restaurants with waterside views overlooking the Salford Quays.

WALES

MILLENNIUM STADIUM, CARDIFF
01222 232 661. 31 Dec 1999. www.cardiff-stadium.co.uk
This £120 million re-development of Cardiff Arms Park, home of Welsh Rugby, is to open in time to play host to the Rugby World Cup in 1999. A new, retractable roof will allow all-weather play, and the new complex will include a rugby museum and hall of fame.

NATIONAL BOTANIC GARDEN OF WALES, LLANARTHNE
01558 668 768. Easter 2000. www.gardenofwales.org.uk
This huge environmental project will eventually provide Wales with one of the most important botanical gardens in the world. It will also include a number of fascinating educational exhibitions and research facilities.

SCOTLAND

GLASGOW SCIENCE CENTRE
0141 420 5000. Easter 2001. www.glasgowdevelopment.co.uk
This £71.5-million world-class science centre located at Pacific Quay will be made up of three interconnecting buildings: an Exhibits building, a Large Format Film Theatre and the 100-m (330-ft) Wing Tower. The overall theme of the centre will be human creativity, and its aim will be to excite and inspire visitors to learn more about science and technology.

THE MILLENNIUM LINK
Easter 2001.
Falkirk is to be the centre of this project to restore the Forth and Clyde and the Union canals. Scotland's own millennium wheel, sited at this point, will transfer people and boats between the two waterways.

Central London

**REGENT'S PARK
AND BLOOMSBURY**
*See pp108–113
Street Finder maps 3, 4*

REGENT'S PARK

GLOUCESTER PLACE
MARYLEBONE ROAD EUSTON ROAD
GOWER ST
TOTTENHAM COURT ROAD
BAKER STREET
HARLEY STREET
PORTLAND PLACE
GREAT PORTLAND STREET
CLEVELAND STREET
MORTIMER STREET
WIGMORE STREET
OXFORD STREET
OXFORD STREET
WARDOUR STREET
BROOK STREET
CONDUIT ST
REGENT STREET
MOUNT ST
BERKLEY ST
PICCADILLY
ST JAMES ST
PALL MALL

BAYSWATER ROAD
MARBLE ARCH

KENSINGTON PALACE GDNS

KENSINGTON
Round Pond
GARDENS

HYDE PARK
PARK LANE

SERPENTINE ROAD
Serpentine
ROTTEN ROW

GREEN PARK
THE MALL
ST JAMES PARK

KENSINGTON ROAD
KNIGHTSBRIDGE KNIGHTSBRIDGE

HYDE PARK CORNER

BUCKINGHAM PALACE GARDENS
Buckingham Palace

GROSVENOR PLACE

BUCKINGHAM GATE

EXHIBITION ROAD
Victoria and Albert Museum
BROMPTON ROAD

LOWER GROSVENOR PLACE
VICTORIA ST

ROCHESTER ROW
VAUXHALL BRIDGE

**SOUTH KENSINGTON
AND HYDE PARK**
*See pp100–113
Street Finder maps 2, 5*

**WEST END AND
WESTMINSTER**
*See pp82–99
Street Finder maps 4, 6*